D0459747

CALIFORNIA MIDDLE SCHOOL

Mathematics

Concepts and Skills

COURSE 1

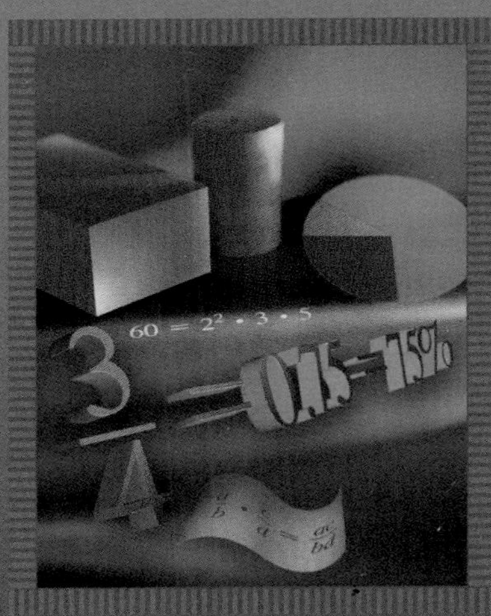

McDougal Littell

A HOUGHTON MIFFLIN COMPANY

Evanston, Illinois • Boston • Dallas

ISBN: 0-618-05045-0 3456789–DWO–04 03 02 01

Internet Web Site: http://www.mcdougallittell.com

About the Authors

RON LARSON is a professor of mathematics at Penn State University at Erie, where he has taught since receiving his Ph.D. in mathematics from the University of Colorado in 1970. He is the author of a broad range of instructional materials for middle school, high school, and college. Dr. Larson has been an innovative writer of multimedia approaches to mathematics, and his Calculus and Precalculus texts are both available in interactive form on the Internet.

LAURIE BOSWELL is a mathematics teacher at Profile Junior-Senior High School in Bethlehem, New Hampshire. A recipient of the 1986 Presidential Award for Excellence in Mathematics Teaching, she is also the 1992 Tandy Technology Scholar and the 1991 recipient of the Richard Balomenos Mathematics Education Service Award presented by the New Hampshire Association of Teachers of Mathematics.

TIMOTHY D. KANOLD is Director of Mathematics and a mathematics teacher at Adlai E. Stevenson High School in Lincolnshire, Illinois. In 1995 he received the Award of Excellence from the Illinois State Board of Education for outstanding contributions to education. A 1986 recipient of the Presidential Award for Excellence in Mathematics Teaching, he served as President of the Council of Presidential Awardees of Mathematics.

LEE STIFF is a professor of mathematics education in the College of Education and Psychology of North Carolina State University at Raleigh and has taught mathematics at the high school and middle school levels. He is the 1992 recipient of the W. W. Rankin Award for Excellence in Mathematics Education presented by the North Carolina Council of Teachers of Mathematics, and a 1995-96 Fulbright Scholar to the Department of Mathematics of the University of Ghana.

All authors contributed to planning the content, organization, and instructional design of the program, and to reviewing and writing the manuscript. Ron Larson played a major role in writing the textbook and in establishing the program philosophy.

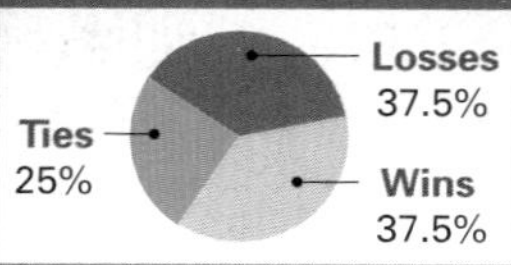

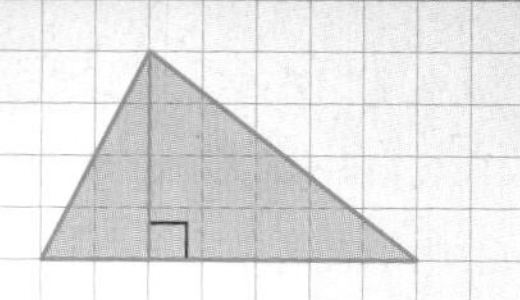

▶ California Reviewers

Kenneth Adiekweh
Mathematics Teacher
Bethune Middle School
Los Angeles, CA

Monica Azimiora
Mathematics Teacher
Hargitt Middle School
Norwalk, CA

Mary Beals
Mathematics Teacher
Robert Frost Junior High School
Granada Hills, CA

John Ghiozzi
Mathematics Teacher
Washington Middle School
Long Beach, CA

Tina Harvey
Mathematics Teacher
MacArthur Intermediate School
Santa Ana, CA

Mark Wirth
Mathematics Teacher
Smedberg Middle School
Elk Grove, CA

The California Reviewers read and commented on textbook chapters in pre-publication format. They also provided teaching suggestions for the Teacher's Edition.

California Consulting Mathematicians

Kurt Kreith
Professor of Mathematics
University of California, Davis

Don Chakerian
Professor of Mathematics
University of California, Davis

The California Consulting Mathematicians prepared the *Mathematical Background Notes* preceding each chapter in the Teacher's Edition of this textbook.

California Standards and Assessment

This book was written to help you learn the concepts and skills in the California Content Standards and in state assessment.

CALIFORNIA STANDARDS ▶

In each lesson, the key Standards taught in the lesson are listed in the margin. These lists provide a handy way of keeping track of your progress in learning the content in the Standards.

California Standards

In this lesson you'll:

- ▶ Solve problems involving multiplication of positive fractions. (NS 2.1)
- ▶ Explain the meaning of multiplication of fractions. (NS 2.2)

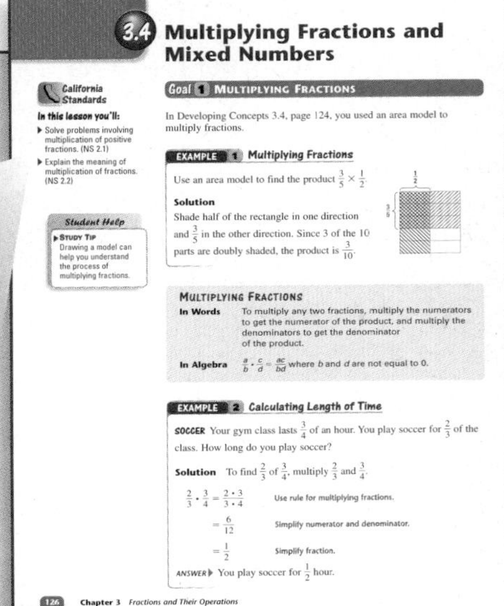

3.4 **Multiplying Fractions and Mixed Numbers**

California Standards

In this lesson you'll:

- ▶ Solve problems involving multiplication of positive fractions. (NS 2.1)
- ▶ Explain the meaning of multiplication of fractions. (NS 2.2)

Student Help

▶ STUDY TIP
Drawing a model can help you understand the process of multiplying fractions.

Goal 1 MULTIPLYING FRACTIONS

In Developing Concepts 3.4, page 124, you used an area model to multiply fractions.

EXAMPLE 1 *Multiplying Fractions*

Use an area model to find the product $\frac{3}{5} \times \frac{1}{2}$.

Solution

Shade half of the rectangle in one direction and $\frac{3}{5}$ in the other direction. Since 3 of the 10 parts are doubly shaded, the product is $\frac{3}{10}$.

MULTIPLYING FRACTIONS

In Words To multiply any two fractions, multiply the numerators to get the numerator of the product, and multiply the denominators to get the denominator of the product.

In Algebra $\frac{a}{b} \cdot \frac{c}{d} = \frac{ac}{bd}$ where b and d are not equal to 0.

EXAMPLE 2 *Calculating Length of Time*

SOCCER Your gym class lasts $\frac{3}{4}$ of an hour. You play soccer for $\frac{2}{3}$ of the class. How long do you play soccer?

Solution To find $\frac{2}{3}$ of $\frac{3}{4}$, multiply $\frac{2}{3}$ and $\frac{3}{4}$.

$\frac{2}{3} \cdot \frac{3}{4} = \frac{2 \cdot 3}{3 \cdot 4}$ Use rule for multiplying fractions.

$= \frac{6}{12}$ Simplify numerator and denominator.

$= \frac{1}{2}$ Simplify fraction.

ANSWER ▶ You play soccer for $\frac{1}{2}$ hour.

126 Chapter 3 *Fractions and Their Operations*

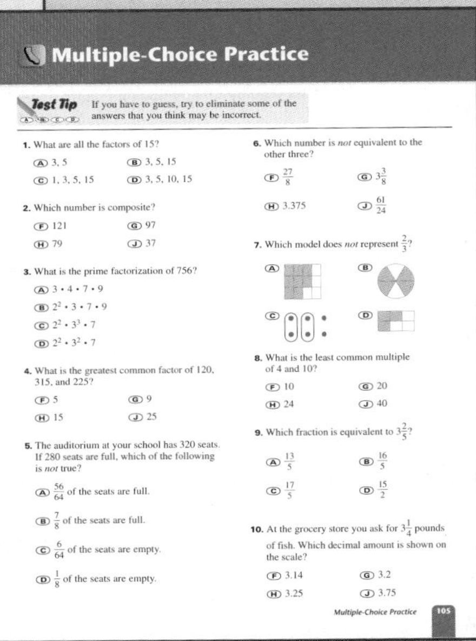

Multiple-Choice Practice

Test Tip If you have to guess, try to eliminate some of the answers that you think may be incorrect.

1. What are all the factors of 15?
   (A) 3, 5 (B) 3, 5, 15
   (C) 1, 3, 5, 15 (D) 3, 5, 10, 15
2. Which number is composite?
   (F) 121 (G) 97
   (H) 79 (J) 37
3. What is the prime factorization of 756?
   (A) $3 \cdot 4 \cdot 7 \cdot 9$
   (B) $2^2 \cdot 3 \cdot 7 \cdot 9$
   (C) $2^2 \cdot 3^3 \cdot 7$
   (D) $2^2 \cdot 3^2 \cdot 7$
4. What is the greatest common factor of 120, 315, and 225?
   (F) 5 (G) 9
   (H) 15 (J) 25
5. The auditorium at your school has 320 seats. If 280 seats are full, which of the following is *not* true?
   (A) $\frac{56}{64}$ of the seats are full.
   (B) $\frac{7}{8}$ of the seats are full.
   (C) $\frac{6}{64}$ of the seats are empty.
   (D) $\frac{1}{8}$ of the seats are empty.
6. Which number is *not* equivalent to the other three?
   (F) $\frac{27}{8}$ (G) $3\frac{3}{8}$
   (H) 3.375 (J) $\frac{61}{24}$
7. Which model does *not* represent $\frac{2}{3}$?
   (A) (B)
   (C) (D)
8. What is the least common multiple of 4 and 10?
   (F) 10 (G) 20
   (H) 24 (J) 40
9. Which fraction is equivalent to $3\frac{2}{5}$?
   (A) $\frac{13}{5}$ (B) $\frac{16}{5}$
   (C) $\frac{17}{5}$ (D) $\frac{15}{2}$
10. At the grocery store you ask for $3\frac{1}{4}$ pounds of fish. Which decimal amount is shown on the scale?
    (F) 3.14 (G) 3.2
    (H) 3.25 (J) 3.75

Multiple-Choice Practice 105

◀ MULTIPLE-CHOICE PRACTICE

At the end of every chapter there is a full page of Multiple-Choice Practice, with a Test Tip. Each lesson also includes Multiple-Choice Practice exercises. These exercises, based on the content of the lesson, help you become comfortable with multiple-choice format.

DEVELOPING CONCEPTS ▶

The Developing Concepts pages prepare you for upcoming lessons and help you strengthen your Mathematical Reasoning skills.

California Standards

- ▶ Explain the meaning of multiplication of positive fractions. (NS 2.2)
- ▶ Use diagrams to explain mathematical reasoning. (MR 2.4)

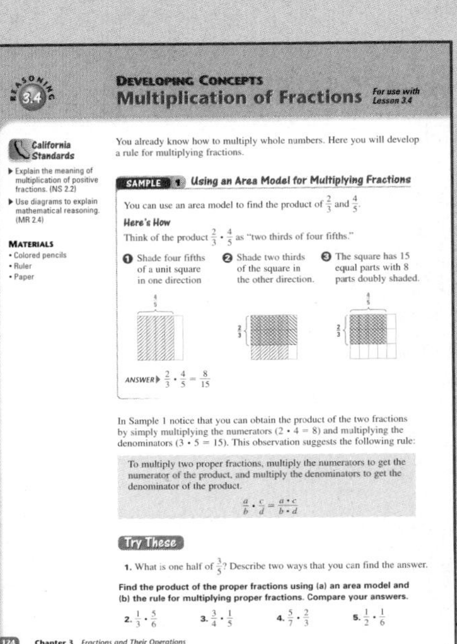

REASONING 3.4

DEVELOPING CONCEPTS
Multiplication of Fractions *For use with Lesson 3.4*

California Standards

- ▶ Explain the meaning of multiplication of positive fractions. (NS 2.2)
- ▶ Use diagrams to explain mathematical reasoning. (MR 2.4)

MATERIALS
- Colored pencils
- Ruler
- Paper

You already know how to multiply whole numbers. Here you will develop a rule for multiplying fractions.

SAMPLE 1 *Using an Area Model for Multiplying Fractions*

You can use an area model to find the product of $\frac{2}{3}$ and $\frac{4}{5}$.

Here's How

Think of the product $\frac{2}{3} \cdot \frac{4}{5}$ as "two thirds of four fifths."

1. Shade four fifths of a unit square in one direction
2. Shade two thirds of the square in the other direction.
3. The square has 15 equal parts with 8 parts doubly shaded.

ANSWER ▶ $\frac{2}{3} \cdot \frac{4}{5} = \frac{8}{15}$

In Sample 1 notice that you can obtain the product of the two fractions by simply multiplying the numerators ($2 \cdot 4 = 8$) and multiplying the denominators ($3 \cdot 5 = 15$). This observation suggests the following rule:

To multiply two proper fractions, multiply the numerators to get the numerator of the product, and multiply the denominators to get the denominator of the product.

$$\frac{a}{b} \cdot \frac{c}{d} = \frac{a \cdot c}{b \cdot d}$$

Try These

1. What is one half of $\frac{3}{5}$? Describe two ways that you can find the answer.

Find the product of the proper fractions using (a) an area model and (b) the rule for multiplying proper fractions. Compare your answers.

2. $\frac{1}{3} \cdot \frac{5}{6}$ 3. $\frac{3}{4} \cdot \frac{1}{5}$ 4. $\frac{5}{7} \cdot \frac{2}{3}$ 5. $\frac{1}{2} \cdot \frac{1}{6}$

124 Chapter 3 *Fractions and Their Operations*

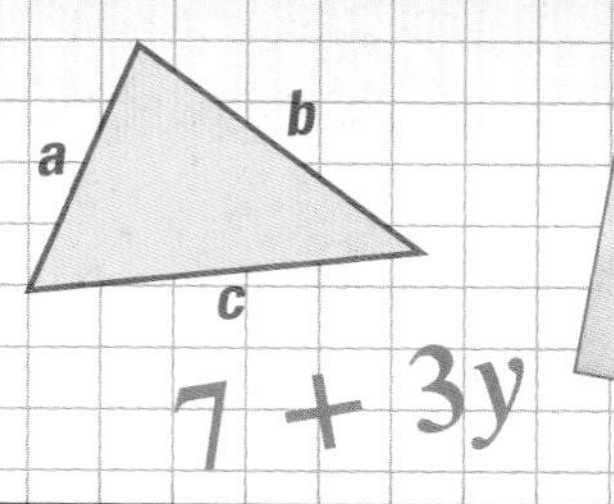

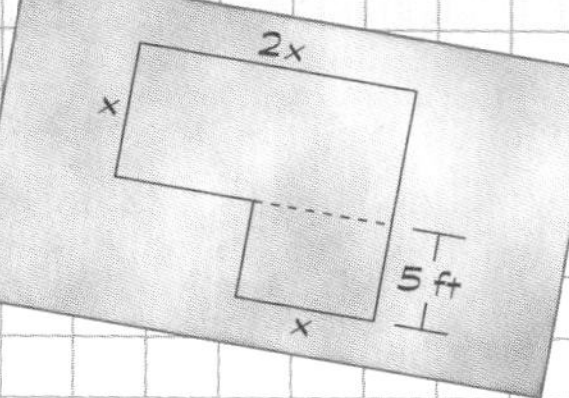

Algebra and Decimals

CALIFORNIA
Standards & Assessment

STUDENT HELP

APPLICATION HIGHLIGHTS

INTERNET

ASSESSMENT

Getting Ready

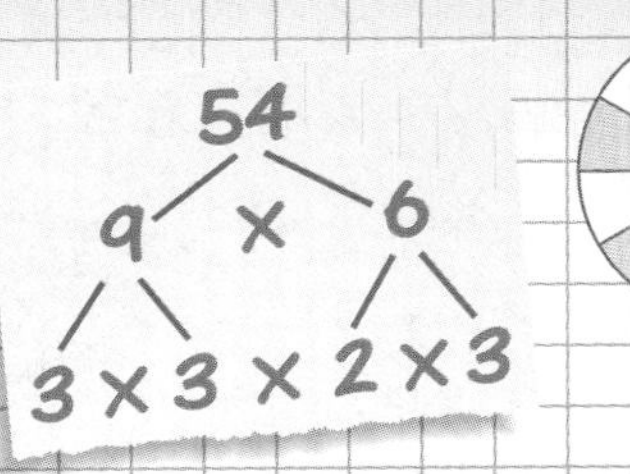

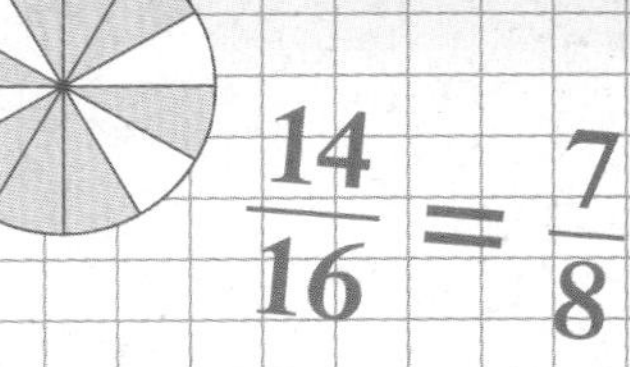

Number Relationships and Fractions

CALIFORNIA *Standards & Assessment*

STUDENT HELP

APPLICATION HIGHLIGHTS

INTERNET

ASSESSMENT

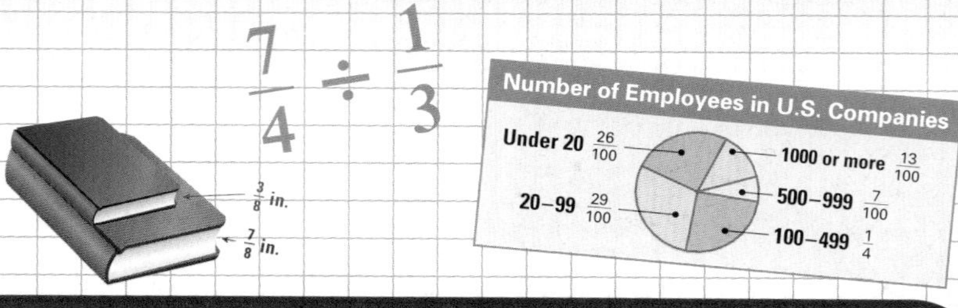

CHAPTER 3

Fractions and Their Operations

CALIFORNIA
Standards & Assessment

STUDENT HELP

APPLICATION HIGHLIGHTS

INTERNET

ASSESSMENT

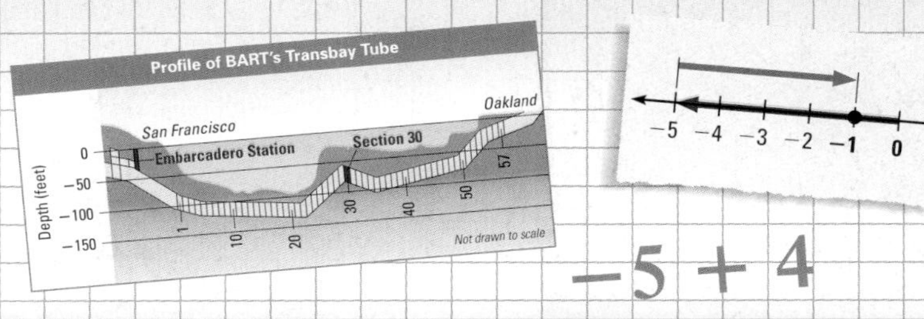

−5 + 4

Positive and Negative Numbers

CALIFORNIA
Standards & Assessment

Meeting the Standards *164, 167, 171, 176, 177, 181, 187, 188, 193, 198, 202, 212*
Multiple-Choice Practice *170, 175, 180, 185, 192, 197, 201, 205, 211*

STUDENT HELP

Study Tips *167, 178, 181, 187, 193, 198, 199*
Reading Tips *168, 172, 177, 213*
Vocabulary Tip *177*
Test Tips *185, 211*
Technology Tip *171*
Skills Review *167*
Look Back *202*

APPLICATION HIGHLIGHTS

Deep-Sea Fish *170*
Weightlifting *173*
Oil Wells *174*
Rapid Transit *185*
Tides *192*
Grand Canyon *196*
Stock Market Crash *201*
Oceanography *205*

INTERNET

168, 170, 172, 180, 182, 189, 190, 192, 196, 199, 201, 203, 205, 213

ASSESSMENT

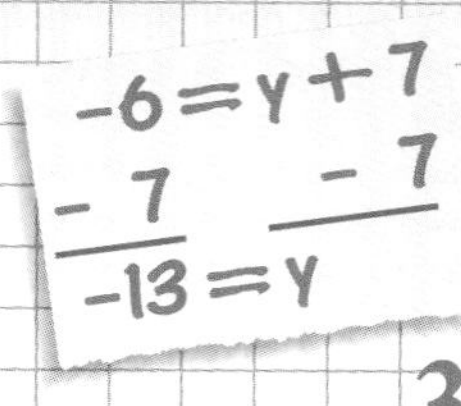

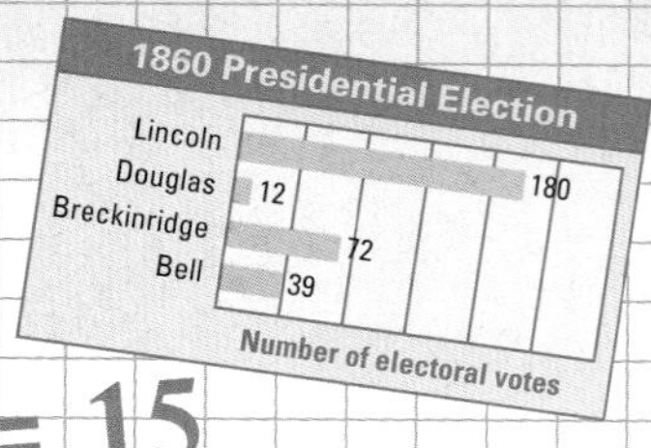

$3x = 15$

Solving Equations

ASSESSMENT

CALIFORNIA
Standards and Assessment

STUDENT HELP

APPLICATION HIGHLIGHTS

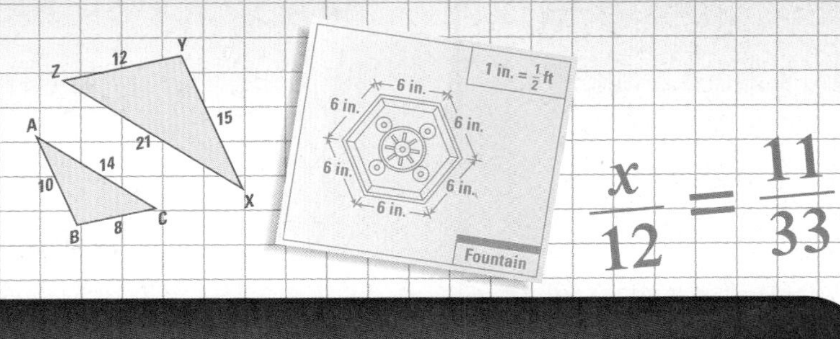

Ratios and Proportions

ASSESSMENT

CALIFORNIA *Standards & Assessment*

STUDENT HELP

APPLICATION HIGHLIGHTS

INTERNET

Rural Population in Selected States

State	Percent
Tennessee	39%
New Jersey	11%
Washington	24%
Kansas	31%

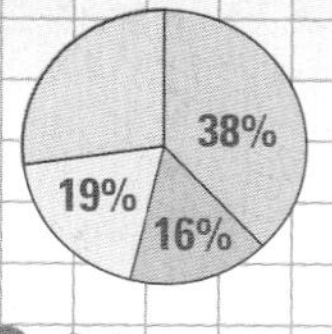

92% of 75

Percents

CALIFORNIA
Standards & Assessment

Meeting the Standards *308, 311, 316, 317, 322, 323, 328, 333, 338, 342, 352*
Multiple-Choice Practice *315, 321, 326, 332, 337, 341, 345, 351*

STUDENT HELP

Study Tips *318, 328, 333, 338, 339*
Reading Tip *318*
Test Tips *337, 341, 351*
Skills Review *336*
Look Back *317, 329*

APPLICATION HIGHLIGHTS

Vehicle Sales *312*
Mining *321*
Mach Numbers *326*
Heart Rate *331*
Energy Use *334*
Recycling *337*
Federal Debt *341*
Comparison Shopping *345*

INTERNET

312, 319, 324, 326, 331, 332, 334, 343, 345, 353

ASSESSMENT

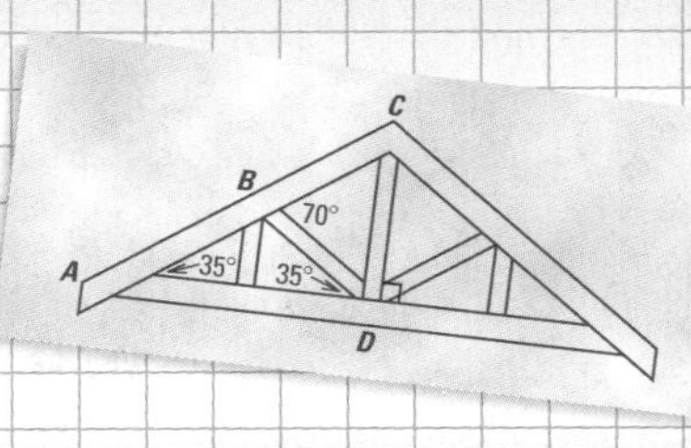

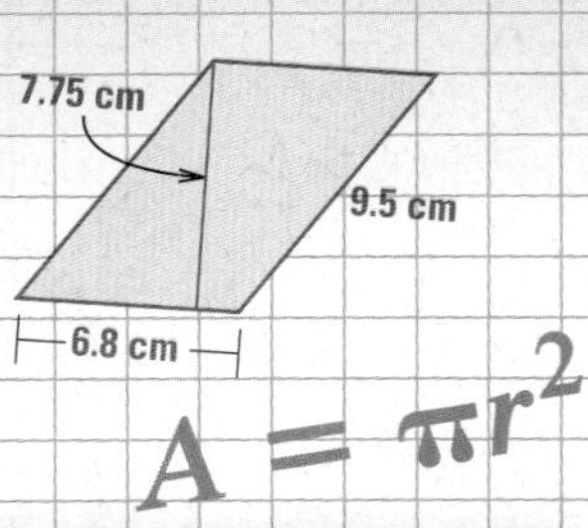

Geometry in the Plane

CALIFORNIA
Standards and Assessment

Meeting the Standards *354, 357, 362, 366, 371, 372, 376, 382, 386, 388, 392, 402*
Multiple-Choice Practice *361, 365, 370, 375, 380, 385, 391, 395, 401*

STUDENT HELP

Study Tips *362, 364, 366, 372, 373, 374, 376, 388*
Test Tips *375, 385, 401*
Skills Review *371*
Look Back *387*

APPLICATION HIGHLIGHTS

City Planning *361*
Orienteering *365*
Engineering *369*
Geography *375*
Museums *379*
Quilts *385*
Bicycle Tires *391*
Radar *395*

INTERNET

358, 361, 365, 373, 376, 383, 391, 403

ASSESSMENT

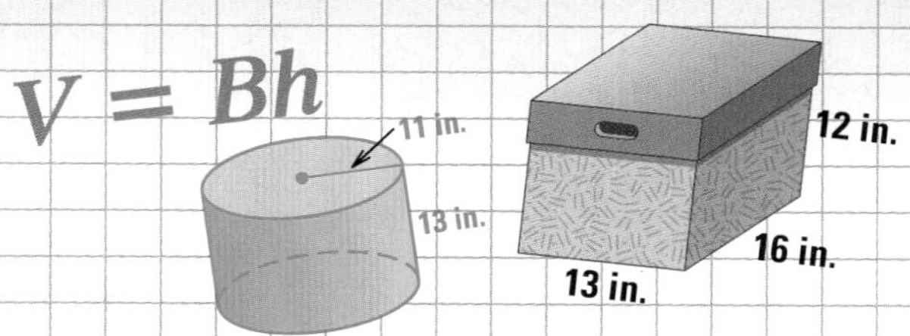

CHAPTER 9 Geometry in Space

CALIFORNIA *Standards & Assessment*

Meeting the Standards *404, 407, 411, 416, 418, 423, 428, 430, 434, 444, 448*
Multiple-Choice Practice *410, 415, 421, 427, 433, 437, 443*

STUDENT HELP

Study Tips *418, 423, 424, 434*
Reading Tips *408, 431*
Test Tips *415, 427, 437, 443*
Look Back *412, 418*

APPLICATION HIGHLIGHTS

Aviation *412*
Icebreakers *414*
Archeology *419*
Fountains *424*
Architecture *433*
Jellyfish *437*

INTERNET

408, 414, 424, 426, 430, 435, 436, 437, 445

ASSESSMENT

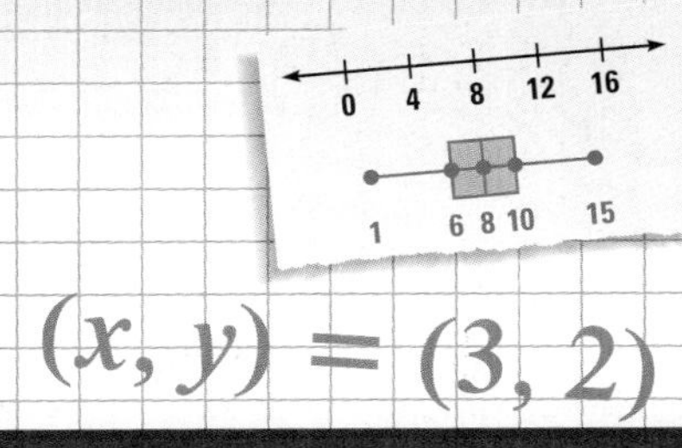

$(x, y) = (3, 2)$

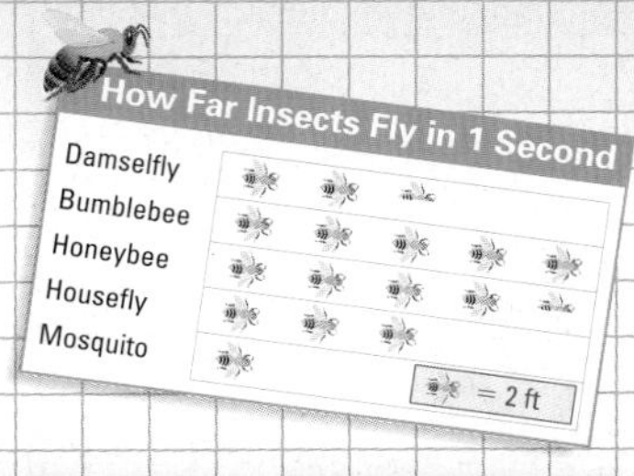

Data Analysis and Statistics

CALIFORNIA
Standards & Assessment

Meeting the Standards *450, 453, 457, 461, 466, 468, 474, 478, 483, 487, 498*
Multiple-Choice Practice *456, 460, 465, 472, 477, 482, 486, 491, 497*

STUDENT HELP

Study Tips *454, 457, 461, 466, 478, 487*
Reading Tip *468*
Test Tips *472, 497*
Skills Review *474*
Look Back *471*

APPLICATION HIGHLIGHTS

Law *454*
U.S. Congress *460*
Vehicle Prices *462*
Temperature Scales *469*
Insect Speeds *476*
Tornadoes *478*
Education *483*
TV Surveys *488*

INTERNET

453, 456, 458, 460, 462, 465, 469, 471, 475, 481, 486, 488, 490, 499

ASSESSMENT

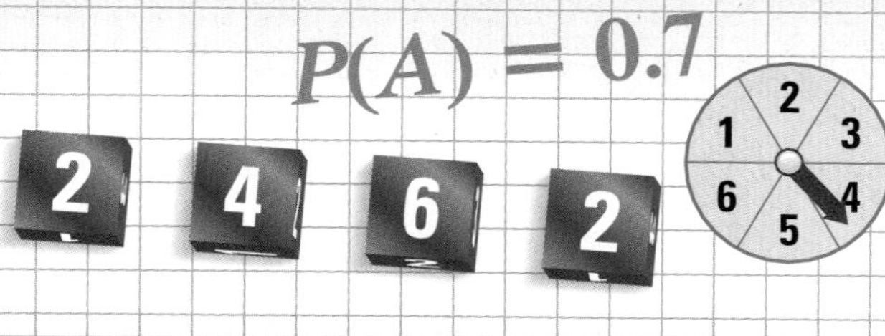

Probability and Discrete Mathematics

CALIFORNIA *Standards & Assessment*

STUDENT HELP

APPLICATION HIGHLIGHTS

INTERNET

ASSESSMENT

Contents of Student Resources

Pre-Course and Post-Course Assessment The Pre-Course Test on page xviii checks understanding of key skills from earlier courses, and the Pre-Course Practice on page xx provides additional practice on these skills. The End-of-Course Test checks mastery of the key concepts and skills in this course.

Getting Ready

Pre-Course Test

Number Sense

NUMBER SENSE

USING A NUMBER LINE (Skills Review pp. 554–555)

Use a number line to order the numbers from least to greatest.

1. 8, 2, 1, 5
2. 7, 12, 9, 14, 0
3. 19, 13, 17, 28, 24
4. 4, 0, 16, 6, 18, 3
5. 72, 29, 36, 99, 111, 53
6. 275, 400, 200, 350, 425, 250

Use a number line to determine which number is greater.

7. 4 or 0
8. 23 or 32
9. 180 or 210
10. 900 or 650

Use a number line to find the sum or difference.

11. $2 + 5$
12. $7 + 8$
13. $35 + 6$
14. $57 + 13$
15. $9 - 3$
16. $18 - 11$
17. $35 - 6$
18. $63 - 15$

OPERATIONS WITH WHOLE NUMBERS (Skills Review pp. 556–557)

Find the sum or difference.

19. $52 + 34$
20. $25 + 47$
21. $166 + 93$
22. $389 + 871$
23. $68 - 23$
24. $81 - 59$
25. $239 - 75$
26. $702 - 568$

Find the product or quotient.

27. 32×12
28. 59×68
29. 273×84
30. 905×782
31. $28 \div 7$
32. $54 \div 9$
33. $88 \div 11$
34. $300 \div 25$

LONG DIVISION (Skills Review p. 558)

Divide. Write the result as a quotient with a remainder.

35. $6\overline{)70}$
36. $8\overline{)53}$
37. $5\overline{)279}$
38. $9\overline{)3084}$
39. $13\overline{)482}$
40. $41\overline{)961}$
41. $76\overline{)5000}$
42. $180\overline{)7233}$

Measurement and Geometry 

MEASUREMENT AND GEOMETRY

CONVERTING UNITS OF MEASUREMENT (Skills Review p. 561)

Perform the conversion.

43. 4 feet to inches
44. 9 minutes to seconds
45. 20 quarts to gallons
46. 32 ounces to pounds
47. 3 meters to centimeters
48. 7000 milliliters to liters

SQUARES AND RECTANGLES (Skills Review p. 562)

Find the perimeter and the area of the square or rectangle.

49. 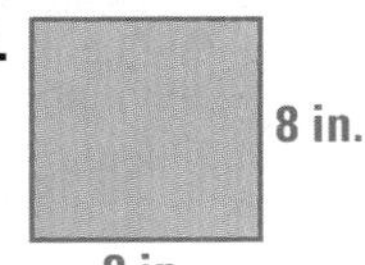

50. 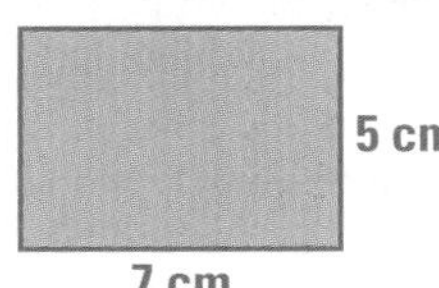

51. 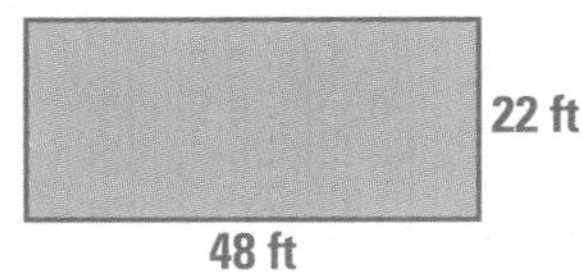

ANGLES AND THEIR MEASURES (Skills Review p. 563)

Use the protractor to find the measure of the angle.

52. 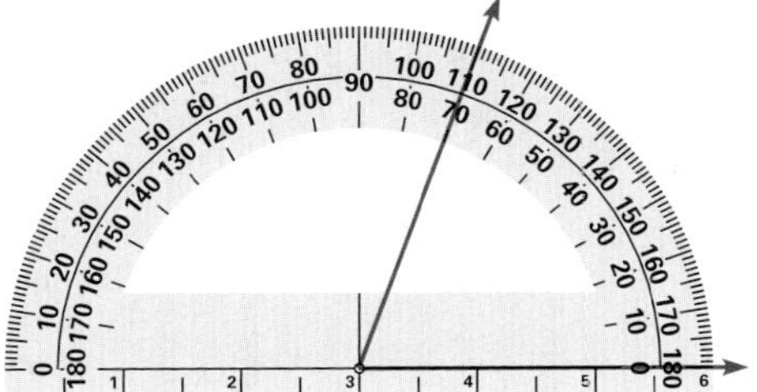

53. 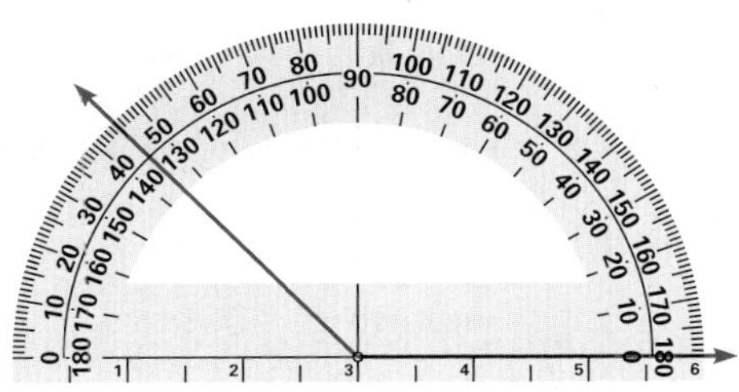

Statistics, Data Analysis, & Probability

STATISTICS, DATA ANALYSIS, & PROBABILITY

READING AND DRAWING A BAR GRAPH (Skills Review p. 564)

In Exercises 54–56, use the bar graph showing the revenue (in billions of dollars) from cable and pay TV in the United States for 1992–1997.

▶ Source: Statistical Abstract of the United States, 1999

54. What was the revenue from cable and pay TV in 1996?

55. During what years was the revenue from cable and pay TV less than $30 billion?

56. What was the *total* revenue from cable and pay TV during the years 1994–1997?

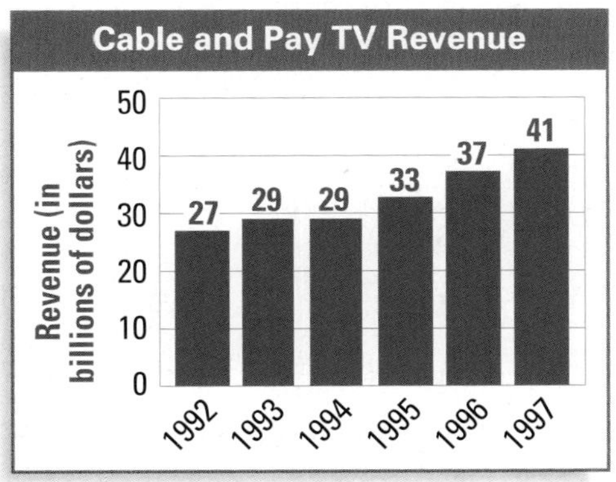

READING AND DRAWING A DOUBLE BAR GRAPH (Skills Review p. 565)

57. The table shows how the 6th and 7th graders at a middle school voted in an election for school mascot. Draw a double bar graph of the data.

Mascot	Badger	Bulldog	Cardinal	Hornet	Tiger	Wolf
6th grade votes	16	45	21	31	60	27
7th grade votes	23	32	37	18	48	42

Getting Ready

Pre-Course Practice

Number Sense 

NUMBER SENSE

USING A NUMBER LINE (Skills Review pp. 554–555)

Use a number line to order the numbers from least to greatest.

1. 4, 0, 9, 3 **2.** 17, 21, 13, 18 **3.** 101, 79, 92, 84

4. 7, 5, 10, 14, 2 **5.** 35, 25, 60, 50, 75 **6.** 47, 28, 19, 32, 41

7. 12, 30, 20, 6, 15, 1 **8.** 22, 28, 16, 33, 9, 11 **9.** 142, 124, 135, 149, 153, 130

10. 999, 1001, 990, 1010, 996 **11.** 72, 62, 52, 78, 68, 58, 48 **12.** 680, 710, 650, 820, 790, 770

Use a number line to determine which number is greater.

13. 6 or 8 **14.** 11 or 21 **15.** 1 or 0 **16.** 54 or 45

17. 91 or 89 **18.** 18 or 30 **19.** 77 or 66 **20.** 36 or 42

21. 222 or 219 **22.** 575 or 800 **23.** 1070 or 1110 **24.** 3400 or 3040

Use a number line to find the sum or the difference.

25. $6 + 3$ **26.** $7 + 5$ **27.** $2 + 9$ **28.** $0 + 4$

29. $5 + 9$ **30.** $8 + 10$ **31.** $16 + 1$ **32.** $14 + 7$

33. $12 + 13$ **34.** $9 + 9$ **35.** $17 + 11$ **36.** $28 + 8$

37. $32 + 15$ **38.** $16 + 22$ **39.** $44 + 19$ **40.** $78 + 12$

41. $8 - 2$ **42.** $7 - 5$ **43.** $9 - 6$ **44.** $10 - 4$

45. $11 - 3$ **46.** $14 - 7$ **47.** $19 - 8$ **48.** $16 - 12$

49. $23 - 9$ **50.** $37 - 10$ **51.** $28 - 13$ **52.** $20 - 17$

53. $46 - 5$ **54.** $33 - 11$ **55.** $55 - 19$ **56.** $82 - 24$

OPERATIONS WITH WHOLE NUMBERS (Skills Review pp. 556–557)

Find the sum.

57. $41 + 25$ **58.** $67 + 32$ **59.** $27 + 56$ **60.** $79 + 91$

61. $123 + 14$ **62.** $239 + 48$ **63.** $438 + 87$ **64.** $964 + 72$

65. $341 + 526$ **66.** $615 + 157$ **67.** $863 + 849$ **68.** $444 + 777$

69. $2582 + 214$ **70.** $9636 + 397$ **71.** $4165 + 5289$ **72.** $8768 + 6432$

Find the difference.

73. 57 − 20 **74.** 86 − 35 **75.** 61 − 49 **76.** 93 − 64

77. 888 − 53 **78.** 492 − 78 **79.** 759 − 92 **80.** 316 − 27

81. 581 − 351 **82.** 619 − 244 **83.** 943 − 826 **84.** 710 − 162

85. 4873 − 560 **86.** 1000 − 429 **87.** 2117 − 1247 **88.** 8069 − 3591

Find the product.

89. 42 × 9 **90.** 23 × 20 **91.** 61 × 61 **92.** 78 × 95

93. 533 × 11 **94.** 751 × 57 **95.** 198 × 35 **96.** 470 × 80

97. 221 × 100 **98.** 165 × 367 **99.** 419 × 639 **100.** 820 × 532

101. 3001 × 48 **102.** 1789 × 258 **103.** 4213 × 377 **104.** 2500 × 2500

Find the quotient.

105. 6 ÷ 2 **106.** 12 ÷ 3 **107.** 10 ÷ 5 **108.** 20 ÷ 4

109. 24 ÷ 3 **110.** 36 ÷ 18 **111.** 54 ÷ 6 **112.** 49 ÷ 7

113. 80 ÷ 20 **114.** 75 ÷ 25 **115.** 72 ÷ 12 **116.** 60 ÷ 5

117. 91 ÷ 13 **118.** 140 ÷ 10 **119.** 117 ÷ 9 **120.** 400 ÷ 50

LONG DIVISION (Skills Review p. 558)

Divide. Write the result as a quotient with a remainder.

121. $2\overline{)17}$ **122.** $5\overline{)62}$ **123.** $7\overline{)80}$ **124.** $4\overline{)75}$

125. $8\overline{)893}$ **126.** $6\overline{)124}$ **127.** $3\overline{)236}$ **128.** $9\overline{)500}$

129. $12\overline{)395}$ **130.** $24\overline{)210}$ **131.** $55\overline{)783}$ **132.** $40\overline{)904}$

133. $2\overline{)5741}$ **134.** $7\overline{)3517}$ **135.** $9\overline{)4423}$ **136.** $20\overline{)6398}$

137. $71\overline{)8890}$ **138.** $95\overline{)4000}$ **139.** $213\overline{)5909}$ **140.** $625\overline{)7742}$

Measurement and Geometry 

MEASUREMENT AND GEOMETRY

CONVERTING UNITS OF MEASUREMENT (Skills Review p. 561)

Perform the conversion.

141. 3 feet to inches **142.** 20 yards to feet **143.** 96 inches to feet

144. 7 minutes to seconds **145.** 14 days to hours **146.** 72 pints to gallons

continued on next page

Perform the conversion.

147. 4 cups to fluid ounces

148. 6 tons to pounds

149. 5 meters to centimeters

150. 4000 meters to kilometers

151. 9 liters to milliliters

152. 3000 grams to kilograms

153. 2 square feet to square inches

154. 81 cubic feet to cubic yards

155. 20 square kilometers to square meters

156. 8 cubic meters to cubic centimeters

SQUARES AND RECTANGLES (Skills Review p. 562)

Find the perimeter and the area of the square or rectangle.

157. 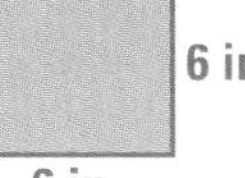

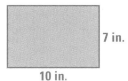

158. 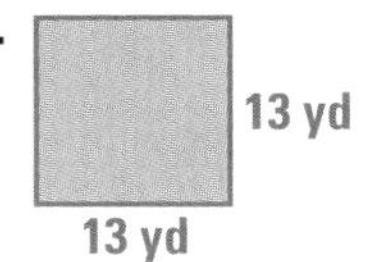

159. 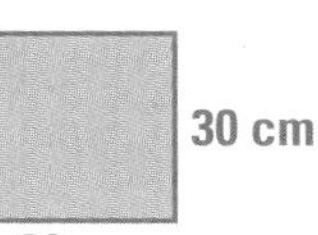

160. 

161. 

162. 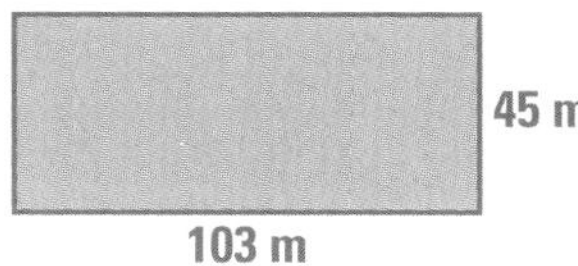

Find the perimeter and the area of the figure described.

163. A square with sides 3 in. long

164. A square with sides 7 ft long

165. A square with sides 9 cm long

166. A rectangle 6 in. long and 4 in. wide

167. A rectangle 42 m long and 37 m wide

168. A rectangle 55 mm long and 19 mm wide

ANGLES AND THEIR MEASURES (Skills Review p. 563)

Use the protractor to find the measure of the angle.

169. 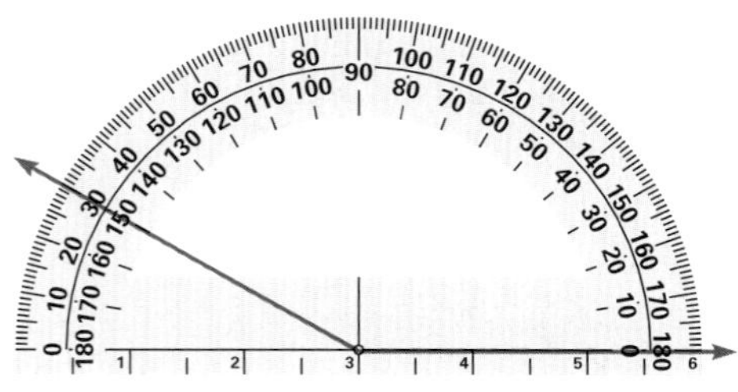

170. 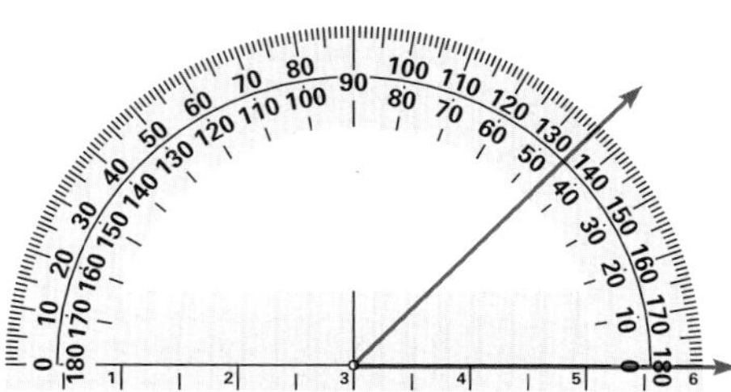

171. 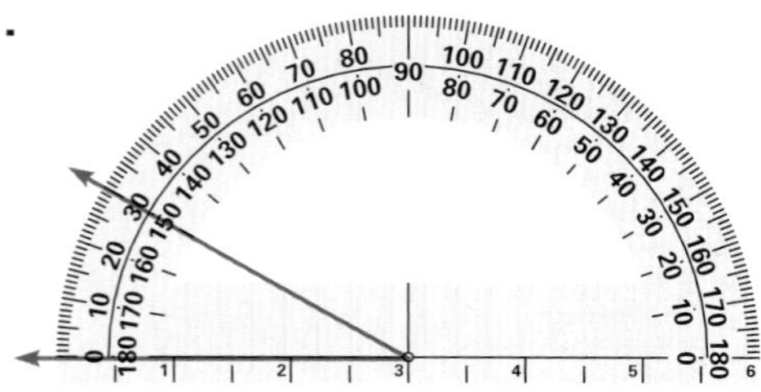

172. 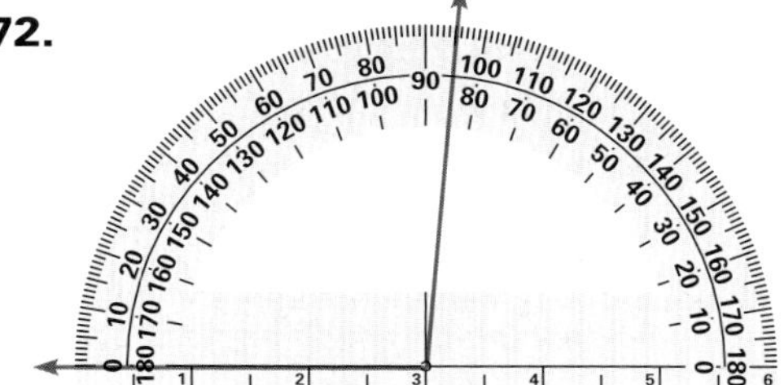

READING AND DRAWING A BAR GRAPH (Skills Review p. 564)

In Exercises 173–177, use the bar graph showing how many animal species of each type live in the forests of British Columbia, Canada.

▶ Source: British Columbia Ministry of Environment, Lands, and Parks

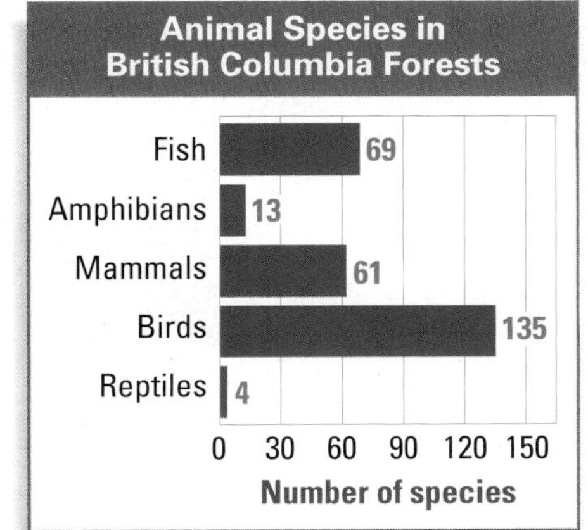

173. How many species of mammals live in the British Columbia forests?

174. Which animal category includes the greatest number of species? the least number of species?

175. How many more species of fish live in the British Columbia forests than species of reptiles?

176. How many animal species in the British Columbia forests are *not* birds?

177. Ticket sales for a new movie equal $11,000,000 during the first week it is shown. For the next 5 weeks, ticket sales equal $8,000,000, $5,000,000, $3,000,000, $2,000,000 and $1,000,000. Draw a bar graph of the ticket sales data.

READING AND DRAWING A DOUBLE BAR GRAPH (Skills Review p. 565)

In Exercises 178–180, use the double bar graph showing the average weekly sales of fiction at a bookstore.

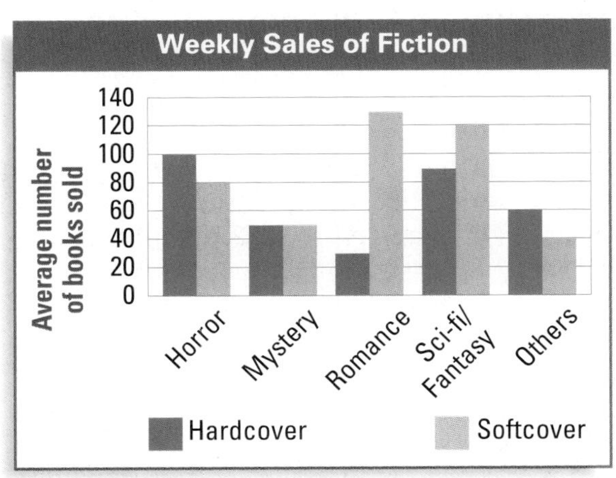

178. For what category of fiction are sales of hardcover and softcover books equal?

179. What category accounts for the greatest number of hardcover books sold? softcover books sold?

180. What category accounts for the greatest *total* sales of books?

181. The table below shows the amounts (in millions of tons) of municipal paper waste generated and recycled in the U.S. for various years. Draw a double bar graph of the data.

Year	1975	1980	1985	1990	1995
Paper waste generated	43	55	62	73	82
Paper waste recycled	8	12	13	20	33

Getting Ready

A Guide to Student Help

▸ Each chapter begins with Getting Ready

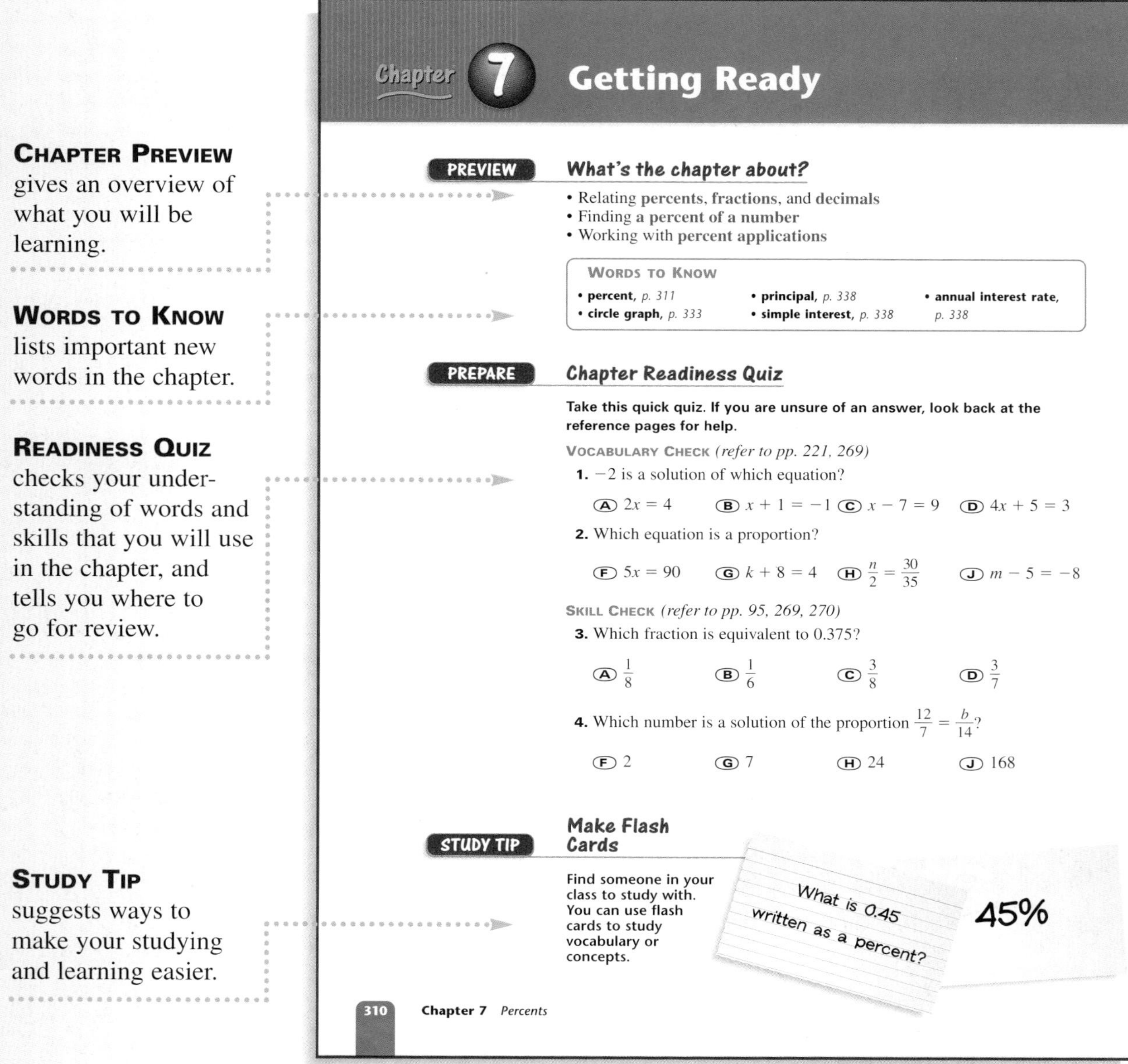

CHAPTER PREVIEW gives an overview of what you will be learning.

WORDS TO KNOW lists important new words in the chapter.

READINESS QUIZ checks your understanding of words and skills that you will use in the chapter, and tells you where to go for review.

STUDY TIP suggests ways to make your studying and learning easier.

Chapter 7 **Getting Ready**

PREVIEW **What's the chapter about?**

- Relating **percents, fractions,** and **decimals**
- **Finding a percent of a number**
- Working with **percent applications**

WORDS TO KNOW

- **percent,** *p. 311*
- **circle graph,** *p. 333*
- **principal,** *p. 338*
- **simple interest,** *p. 338*
- **annual interest rate,** *p. 338*

PREPARE **Chapter Readiness Quiz**

Take this quick quiz. If you are unsure of an answer, look back at the reference pages for help.

VOCABULARY CHECK *(refer to pp. 221, 269)*

1. -2 is a solution of which equation?

Ⓐ $2x = 4$ Ⓑ $x + 1 = -1$ Ⓒ $x - 7 = 9$ Ⓓ $4x + 5 = 3$

2. Which equation is a proportion?

Ⓕ $5x = 90$ Ⓖ $k + 8 = 4$ Ⓗ $\frac{n}{2} = \frac{30}{35}$ Ⓙ $m - 5 = -8$

SKILL CHECK *(refer to pp. 95, 269, 270)*

3. Which fraction is equivalent to 0.375?

Ⓐ $\frac{1}{8}$ Ⓑ $\frac{1}{6}$ Ⓒ $\frac{3}{8}$ Ⓓ $\frac{3}{7}$

4. Which number is a solution of the proportion $\frac{12}{7} = \frac{b}{14}$?

Ⓕ 2 Ⓖ 7 Ⓗ 24 Ⓙ 168

STUDY TIP **Make Flash Cards**

Find someone in your class to study with. You can use flash cards to study vocabulary or concepts.

What is 0.45 written as a percent?
45%

310 **Chapter 7** *Percents*

▸ *Student Help notes throughout the book*

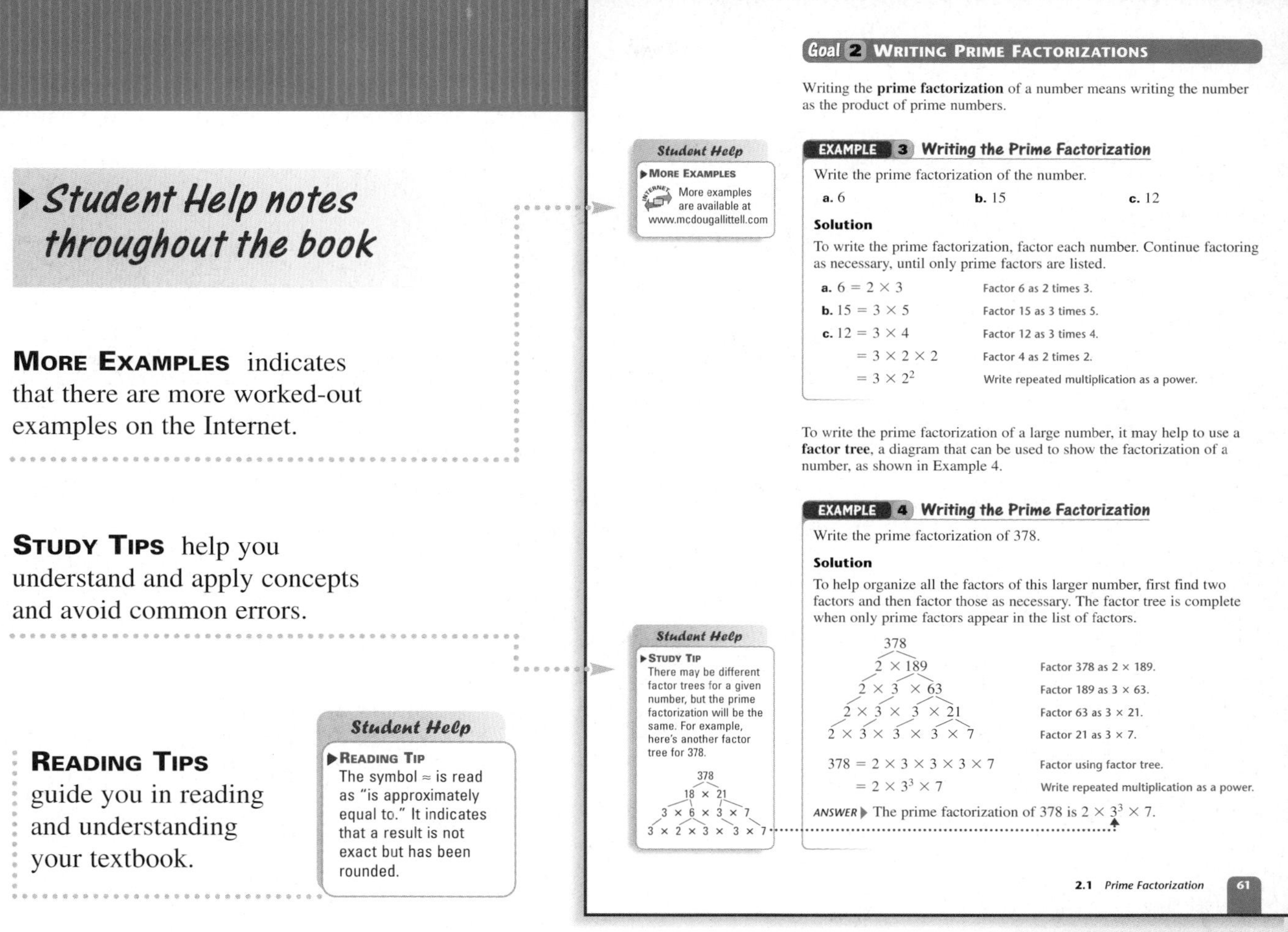

Goal 2 WRITING PRIME FACTORIZATIONS

Writing the **prime factorization** of a number means writing the number as the product of prime numbers.

Student Help
▸ MORE EXAMPLES
More examples are available at www.mcdougallittell.com

EXAMPLE 3 Writing the Prime Factorization

Write the prime factorization of the number.

a. 6 **b.** 15 **c.** 12

Solution

To write the prime factorization, factor each number. Continue factoring as necessary, until only prime factors are listed.

a. $6 = 2 \times 3$ Factor 6 as 2 times 3.
b. $15 = 3 \times 5$ Factor 15 as 3 times 5.
c. $12 = 3 \times 4$ Factor 12 as 3 times 4.
$= 3 \times 2 \times 2$ Factor 4 as 2 times 2.
$= 3 \times 2^2$ Write repeated multiplication as a power.

To write the prime factorization of a large number, it may help to use a **factor tree**, a diagram that can be used to show the factorization of a number, as shown in Example 4.

EXAMPLE 4 Writing the Prime Factorization

Write the prime factorization of 378.

Solution

To help organize all the factors of this larger number, first find two factors and then factor those as necessary. The factor tree is complete when only prime factors appear in the list of factors.

378
2×189 Factor 378 as 2 × 189.
$2 \times 3 \times 63$ Factor 189 as 3 × 63.
$2 \times 3 \times 3 \times 21$ Factor 63 as 3 × 21.
$2 \times 3 \times 3 \times 3 \times 7$ Factor 21 as 3 × 7.

$378 = 2 \times 3 \times 3 \times 3 \times 7$ Factor using factor tree.
$= 2 \times 3^3 \times 7$ Write repeated multiplication as a power.

ANSWER ▸ The prime factorization of 378 is $2 \times 3^3 \times 7$.

Student Help
▸ STUDY TIP
There may be different factor trees for a given number, but the prime factorization will be the same. For example, here's another factor tree for 378.

378
18×21
$3 \times 6 \times 3 \times 7$
$3 \times 2 \times 3 \times 3 \times 7$

2.1 *Prime Factorization* 61

MORE EXAMPLES indicates that there are more worked-out examples on the Internet.

STUDY TIPS help you understand and apply concepts and avoid common errors.

READING TIPS guide you in reading and understanding your textbook.

Student Help
▸ **READING TIP**
The symbol ≈ is read as "is approximately equal to." It indicates that a result is not exact but has been rounded.

SKILLS REVIEW refers you to the pages where you can go for review and practice of topics from earlier courses.

Student Help
▸ **SKILLS REVIEW**
For help with perimeter, see page 562.

HOMEWORK HELP lets you know when there are suggestions and strategies for solving homework exercises available on the Internet.

Student Help
▸ **HOMEWORK HELP**
Extra help with problem solving in Ex. 42 is available at www.mcdougallittell.com

VOCABULARY TIPS explain the meaning and origin of words.

Student Help
▸ **VOCABULARY TIP**
In English, to *distribute* means to give something to everyone in a group. In mathematics, the meaning of *distribute* is similar.

Other notes included are:

- **TECHNOLOGY TIP**
- **TEST TIP**
- **LOOK BACK**
- **MORE PRACTICE**

Algebra and Decimals

Why are algebra and decimals important?

Algebra is sometimes described as generalized arithmetic. It uses letters, called *variables*, to represent numbers. One important set of numbers in algebra is the set of *rational numbers*, which can be expressed as decimals.

Careers such as coaching (page 1) and computer programming (page 11) use algebra and decimals. For example, coaches can use an algebraic formula to help athletes in training.

Meeting the California Standards

The skills you'll develop in this chapter will help you meet state standards and prepare for standardized tests. In this chapter you'll:

- **Calculate and solve problems involving operations.** LESSONS 1.2, 1.7–1.9
- **Evaluate a variable expression having up to three variables.** LESSON 1.2
- **Apply order of operations and properties to expressions.** LESSONS 1.3, 1.4
- **Compare and order positive decimals and graph them.** LESSON 1.5
- **Give answers to a specified degree of accuracy.** LESSON 1.6
- **Use variables in expressions describing geometric quantities.** LESSON 1.7

Career Link **COACH** A coach uses algebra and decimals when:

- finding the *target heart rate* for an athlete in training.
- identifying the best batting average or the fastest racer.

EXERCISES

To remain in shape, an athlete exercises hard enough to get the heart beating quickly. How quickly the heart should beat during exercise depends on age. A coach might use the table below to estimate an athlete's target heart rate.

What is the target heart rate for each age?

1. 20 **2.** 23 **3.** 24

4. What pattern do you notice in the table?

In Lesson 1.2, you'll learn how to write and use a formula to find the target heart rate for an athlete older than 24.

Age (in years)	Target heart rate (in beats per minute)
20	160
21	159
22	158
23	157
24	156

Getting Ready

PREVIEW What's the chapter about?

- Evaluating **numerical and variable expressions**
- Using **order of operations**
- Performing operations with **decimals**

WORDS TO KNOW

- **numerical expression,** *p. 7*
- **variable,** *p. 8*
- **variable expression,** *p. 8*
- **power,** *p. 17*
- **exponent,** *p. 17*
- **base,** *p. 17*
- **decimal,** *p. 21*
- **number line,** *p. 21*
- **average, mean,** *p. 28*
- **polygon,** *p. 31*
- **perimeter,** *p. 31*

PREPARE Chapter Readiness Quiz

Take this quick quiz. If you are unsure of a Skill Check answer, look at the reference pages for help.

VOCABULARY CHECK

1. Which of the following represents a sum?

Ⓐ $12 - 4$ Ⓑ $12 + 4$ Ⓒ 12×4 Ⓓ $12 \div 4$

2. Which of the following represents a quotient?

Ⓕ $16 + 2$ Ⓖ $16 - 2$ Ⓗ 16×2 Ⓙ $16 \div 2$

3. Which of the following decimals is most likely to represent money?

Ⓐ 23.8 Ⓑ 2.38 Ⓒ 0.238 Ⓓ 0.0238

SKILL CHECK *(refer to pp. 556, 557)*

4. Which of the following has a sum of 100?

Ⓕ $43 + 47$ Ⓖ $23 + 32$ Ⓗ $67 + 33$ Ⓙ $12 + 98$

5. What is the product of 786 and 10?

Ⓐ 78,600 Ⓑ 7860 Ⓒ 786 Ⓓ 78.6

Student Help

▶STUDY TIP
"Student Help" boxes throughout the chapter give you study tips and tell you where to look for extra help in this book and on the Internet.

STUDY TIP Keep a Math Notebook

Keeping a notebook will help you organize all of the information you need to study math.

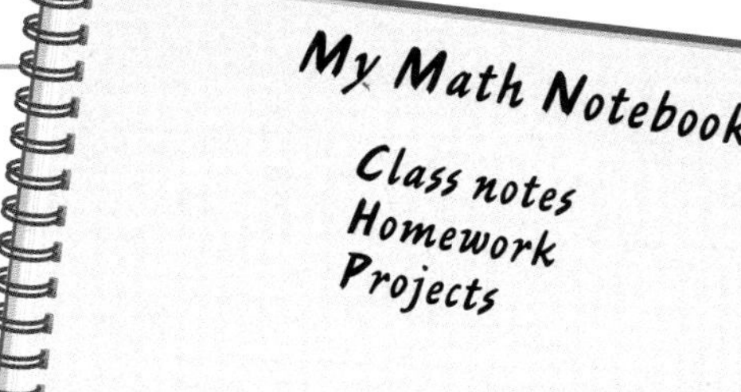

Problem Solving and Reasoning

California Standards

In this lesson you'll:

- Make decisions about how to approach problems. (MR 1.0)
- Distinguish between relevant and irrelevant information. (MR 1.1)

Goal 1 Using a Problem Solving Plan

You can use mathematics to solve problems. A problem solving plan can help you understand what you need to do.

Problem Solving Plan

1. **Understand the Problem** Read the problem carefully. Identify the question.
2. **Make a Plan** Decide on a problem solving strategy.
3. **Solve the Problem** Use the problem solving strategy to answer the question.
4. **Look Back** Check that your answer is reasonable.

Student Help

▶ **Skills Review**
For help with multiplication, see page 556.

Example 1 Using a Problem Solving Plan

Your class is working on a project. Each student needs 12 plastic straws. There are 24 students in your class. There are 50 plastic straws in a box. How many boxes of straws does your class need?

Solution

Understand the Problem You need to find the number of boxes of plastic straws (50 in a box) needed so each student in your class of 24 will have 12 straws.

Make a Plan Find the total number of straws needed. Use estimation to decide how many boxes you need.

Solve the Problem To find the total number of straws needed, multiply 24 by 12.

24	Number of students
$\times$ 12	Number of straws per student
288	Total number of straws

You need 288 straws. Round up to the nearest 50 to get 300. You need 6 boxes of straws, because $6 \cdot 50 = 300$.

Look Back You can use mental math and estimation to check your answer. Estimate $300 \div 24$ using $300 \div 25 = 12$. You have enough straws to give 12 straws to each of the 24 students with fewer than 50 left over.

Student Help

▶ **Study Tip**
When you look back to check your answer, it is helpful to use mental math. Notice in Example 1 that 25 was used instead of 24 because it makes the division easier.

Goal 2 IDENTIFYING IRRELEVANT INFORMATION

Student Help

▶ **VOCABULARY TIP**
Relevant information is **rel**ated to the problem. The prefix "ir" means "not," so **ir**relevant information is **not** related.

One thing that you have to do when you solve problems is to decide what information you need to use. Many real-life problems have information that you do not need in order to solve the problem.

Relevant information: Information you need to know to solve a problem

Irrelevant information: Information you do not need to know to solve a problem

When you read a problem, you should ask yourself whether the information given in the problem is relevant or irrelevant.

EXAMPLE 2 Using a Problem Solving Plan

SHOPPING Paul and Jeremy are shopping. Paul has $35 and Jeremy has $27. Paul wants to buy a T-shirt, a pair of jeans, and a pair of socks. Does he have enough money? If not, how much more money does he need?

SALE!
Jeans $24
T-Shirts $11
Sweaters $28
Socks $3

Solution

UNDERSTAND THE PROBLEM Paul wants to buy 3 items and has $35. You do not need to know how much money Jeremy has or the price of a sweater.

MAKE A PLAN Add the costs of the three items. Compare the total to the amount Paul has.

SOLVE THE PROBLEM

$24	Jeans
11	T-shirt
+ 3	Socks
$38	Total Cost

Paul needs $38, which is more than $35. He does not have enough money. He needs $3 more.

LOOK BACK You can use estimation to check that your result is reasonable. The clothes are about $25, $10, and $3.

$$25 + 10 + 3 = 38$$

So, it is reasonable that he needs about $3 more.

Student Help

▶ **SKILLS REVIEW**
For help with checking the reasonableness of a solution, see page 553.

1.1 Exercises

Guided Practice

1. Describe the four steps in the problem solving plan.

HIKING In Exercises 2 and 3, use the following problem. At 7:45 A.M. you begin a 12 mile hike. At 8:20 A.M. you have hiked one mile. At 9:10 A.M. you have hiked a total of two miles. How many minutes did it take you to hike the first mile?

2. For each solution step below, identify the corresponding step in the problem solving plan.

a. For the first mile, you hike 15 minutes from 7:45 A.M. to 8:00 A.M. and then 20 minutes from 8:00 A.M. to 8:20 A.M. So the first mile takes $15 + 20 = 35$ minutes.

b. Add the number of minutes before 8:00 A.M. and after 8:00 A.M.

c. You can use a clock face to check your answer.

d. The problem asks you to find the number of minutes it took to hike the first mile. The time when you completed the second mile and the length of the hike are irrelevant.

3. Did you hike the second mile at the same speed that you hiked the first mile? Explain.

Practice and Problem Solving

Student Help

▶MORE PRACTICE
Extra practice to help you master skills is on page 566.

In Exercises 4–7, use the problem solving plan to solve the problem. Identify any irrelevant information.

4. **SWIMMING** Each day at swim practice you must swim one mile. One-half mile is 36 lengths of the pool. How many lengths must you swim each day at practice?

5. **LANDSCAPING** Mary has a job mowing lawns. Jeff has a job walking dogs. Mary earns \$12 per lawn. She mows 3 lawns each day. How much money will she earn in 3 days?

6. **TESTING** A test has 6 parts, and you are given the same amount of time for each part. The total time for the test is 180 minutes. How much time are you given for each part of the test?

7. **GAMES** You are playing a card game. During the game, you pick up twice as many cards as you lay down. You lay down 7 cards. You now have 15 cards in your hand. How many cards did you start with?

Student Help

▶ **HOMEWORK HELP**
INTERNET Extra help with problem solving in Ex. 8 is available at www.mcdougallittell.com

8. VOLUNTEERING Robert, Rachel, and Kelly volunteer to work a total of 40 hours for a charity. Their teacher works 12 hours. Robert works 11 hours, Rachel works 21 hours, and Kelly works 9 hours.

a. Use the problem solving plan to find the total time the students work. Do the students fall short or go over the number of hours they volunteer to work? If so, by how much?

b. Does the problem contain irrelevant information? If so, identify it.

In Exercises 9–12, use the problem solving plan to solve the problem. Identify any irrelevant information.

9. MONEY How long is a row of dimes worth a total of $12?

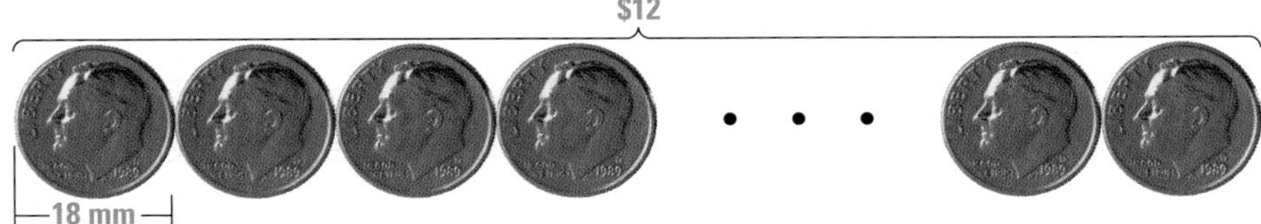

10. PETS Every day your cat eats 1 can of cat food and your 2 dogs each eat 2 cans of dog food. How many cans of dog food do you use in a week?

Student Help

▶ **STUDY TIP**
In Exercise 12, you may find it helpful to make a list of the possibilities.

11. MOVIE THEATER You want to buy tickets for yourself and some friends to see a movie. Tickets are $6 each, and a bag of popcorn is $4. You have $24 to spend for tickets. How many tickets can you buy?

12. CHALLENGE You have forgotten your friend's phone number. You remember that the first part of the phone number is 621 and the last four digits include 1, 3, 5, and 9. How many phone numbers would you have to try to guarantee you call the right one?

Multiple-Choice Practice

13. A company assembles six types of computers. The graph shows the number of each type of computer assembled each day. What is the total number of computers the company assembles each day?

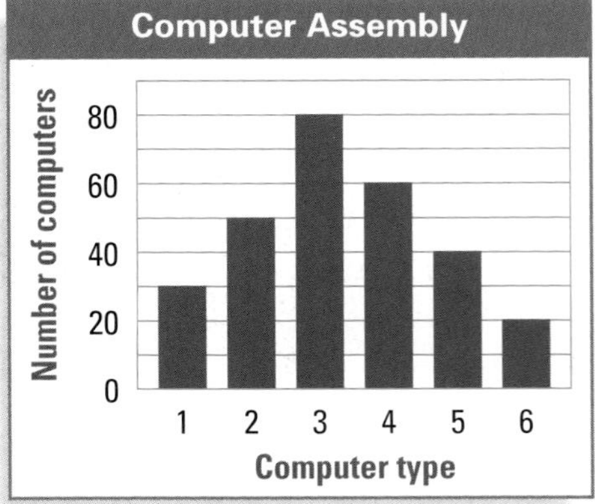

Ⓐ 200　　Ⓑ 280

Ⓒ 460　　Ⓓ 500

14. In 1998 you bought 1 CD. Each year after that, you bought 3 more CDs than you did the year before. Each CD costs $15. Which information is not needed to find how many CDs you will buy in 2010?

Ⓕ You bought 3 more CDs.　　Ⓖ Each CD costs $15.

Ⓗ In 1998, you bought 1 CD.　　Ⓙ All facts are necessary.

1.2 Expressions and Variables

California Standards

In this lesson you'll:

- Calculate and solve problems involving addition, subtraction, multiplication, and division. (NS 2.0)
- Evaluate a variable expression having up to three variables. (AF 1.2)

Goal 1 EVALUATING NUMERICAL EXPRESSIONS

There are four basic operations in mathematics: addition, subtraction, multiplication, and division.

Operation	Words and Symbols Used with the Operation
Addition	**plus** $3 + 4 = 7$ (3 and 4: **terms**; 7: **sum**)
Subtraction	**minus** $21 - 12 = 9$ (9: **difference**)
Multiplication	**times** $6 \times 7 = 42$ (6 and 7: **factors**; 42: **product**) **6×7 is also written as $6 \cdot 7$ and 6(7).**
Division	**divided by** $15 \div 5 = 3$ (15: **dividend**; 5: **divisor**; 3: **quotient**) **$15 \div 5$ is also written as $\frac{15}{5}$.**

An expression that represents a particular number is called a **numerical expression**. A numerical expression consists of numbers and the operations to be performed. For example, in the table above, $3 + 4$, $21 - 12$, 6×7 and $15 \div 5$, are all numerical expressions. Finding the value of the expression is called **evaluating the expression**.

EXAMPLE 1 Evaluating a Numerical Expression

Write the numerical expression given by the phrase. Then evaluate the expression.

a. The sum of 32 and 80

b. The difference of 140 and 9

c. The product of 5 and 13

d. The quotient of 72 and 8

Solution

a. $32 + 80 = 112$ — Add 32 and 80.

b. $140 - 9 = 131$ — Subtract 9 from 140.

c. $5 \cdot 13 = 65$ — Multiply 5 and 13.

d. $72 \div 8 = 9$ — Divide 72 by 8.

Student Help

STUDY TIP
In this book, the phrase *the difference of a and b* means you start with a and subtract b, so you write $a - b$. Similarly, the phrase the quotient of a and b means you start with a and divide by b, so you write $\frac{a}{b}$.

EXAMPLE 2 Evaluating a Numerical Expression

Evaluate the expression. Describe the result in words.

a. 3×8 **b.** $25 \cdot 6$ **c.** $\frac{20}{5}$

Solution

a. $3 \times 8 = 24$. The product of 3 and 8 is 24.

b. $25 \cdot 6 = 150$. The product of 25 and 6 is 150.

c. $\frac{20}{5} = 4$. The quotient when 20 is divided by 5 is 4.

Student Help

▶ **More Examples**

More examples are available at www.mcdougallittell.com

Goal 2 Evaluating Variable Expressions

A **variable** is a letter that is used to represent one or more numbers. The numbers are the **values** of the variable. A **variable expression** consists of numbers, variables, and the operations to be performed. To evaluate a variable expression, substitute a number for each variable and evaluate the resulting numerical expression.

Using variables and variable expressions to describe relationships between quantities is the focus of *algebra*.

EXAMPLE 3 Writing a Variable Expression

Write a variable expression given by the phrase.

a. The sum of x and y **b.** The product of j and k

Solution

a. $x + y$ **b.** $j \cdot k$

EXAMPLE 4 Evaluating a Variable Expression

Evaluate the variable expression for the given value of the variable.

a. $6m$ when $m = 3$ **b.** $x + 7$ when $x = 12$

Solution

a. $6m = 6(3)$ Substitute 3 for *m*.

$= 18$ Simplify.

b. $x + 7 = 12 + 7$ Substitute 12 for *x*.

$= 19$ Simplify.

Student Help

▶ **Study Tip**

When you multiply a variable by a number, you do not need to write a multiplication symbol. For example, you can write 6*m* which means 6 • *m*. Don't write 6 × *m* because it can be confused with 6*xm*.

EXAMPLE 5 Evaluating a Variable Expression

Evaluate $\frac{d}{t}$ when $d = 40$ and $t = 2$.

Solution

$\frac{d}{t} = \frac{40}{2}$ Substitute 40 for *d* and 2 for *t*.

$= 20$ Simplify.

EXAMPLE 6 Evaluating a Variable Expression

Evaluate $x + y + z$ when $x = 36$, $y = 58$, and $z = 43$.

Solution

$x + y + z = 36 + 58 + 43$ Substitute 36 for *x*, 58 for *y*, and 43 for *z*.

$= 137$ Simplify.

1.2 Exercises

Guided Practice

In Exercises 1–4, match the numerical expression with the operation.

A. Sum **B.** Difference **C.** Product **D.** Quotient

1. $90 \div 15$ **2.** $34 - 12$ **3.** $14 \cdot 7$ **4.** $22 + 72$

Evaluate the expression. Describe the result in words.

5. $35 + 62$ **6.** $170 + 28$ **7.** $125 - 8$ **8.** $215 - 103$

9. 4×13 **10.** 12×6 **11.** $\frac{56}{8}$ **12.** $125 \div 25$

Write the numerical expression given by the phrase. Then evaluate the expression.

13. The quotient of 15 and 3

14. The sum of 55 and 40

15. The product of 30 and 7

16. The difference of 23 and 9

17. The difference of 700 and 99

18. The quotient of 36 and 2

Evaluate the expression when $m = 4$, $n = 2$, and $p = 7$.

19. $n + 3$ **20.** $12 - m$ **21.** $m + n$ **22.** $63 \div p$

23. $10m$ **24.** np **25.** $m + p + n$ **26.** mnp

Practice and Problem Solving

Student Help

▶More Practice
Extra practice to help you master skills is on page 566.

27. Name the divisor and the dividend in the expression $72 \div 9$.

Evaluate the expression. Describe the result in words.

28. $5 + 26$ **29.** $73 + 19$ **30.** $56 - 22$ **31.** $980 - 198$

32. $35 \cdot 4$ **33.** 9×12 **34.** $120 \div 5$ **35.** $\frac{175}{25}$

In Exercises 36–43, write a numerical expression given by the phrase. Then evaluate the expression.

36. 56 plus 45
37. 54 divided by 3
38. 2 times 78
39. 67 minus 19
40. The quotient of 114 and 6
41. The sum of 14 and 16
42. The difference of 67 and 67
43. The product of 18 and 2

44. **ERROR ANALYSIS** Bob is using a calculator to find $45 \div 720$. He gets 16. What did Bob do wrong? What should the result be?

Write a variable expression given by the phrase.

45. The sum of a and b
46. The difference of x and y
47. m times n
48. y minus z
49. The product of x and y
50. The quotient of d and r

Evaluate the expression when $x = 5$, $y = 12$, and $z = 6$.

51. $5y$ **52.** $102 \div z$ **53.** $y - x$ **54.** $y + x + z$

CHALLENGE **Tell whether the product is *even* or *odd*. Give examples to support your answer.**

55. even $\times$ even **56.** even $\times$ odd **57.** odd $\times$ odd

In Exercises 58–63, evaluate the expression.

58. $k + 12$ when $k = 9$
59. $9j$ when $j = 11$
60. $x - 36$ when $x = 42$
61. $36 \div m$ when $m = 4$
62. $\frac{d}{r}$ when $d = 120$ and $r = 60$
63. xyz when $x = 5$, $y = 6$, and $z = 9$

Chapter Opener Link **In Exercises 64 and 65, look back at the target heart rate table on page 1.**

64. Use the pattern in the table to write an expression for the target heart rate of an athlete at age a.

65. Use your expression from Exercise 64 to find the target heart rate of an athlete who is 30 years old.

FOOD **In Exercises 66–68, use the table which shows the amounts of three fruits produced in the United States.** ▶ Source: U.S. Dept. of Agriculture

Fruit Production in the United States (in thousands of tons)			
Year	**Bananas**	**Strawberries**	**Grapefruit**
1996	7	813	2718
1997	7	814	2885
1998	11	844	2593

66. Did the production of strawberries *increase* or *decrease* from 1997 to 1998?

67. Did the production of grapefruit *increase* or *decrease* from 1996 to 1998?

68. Did the total combined production of these fruits *increase* or *decrease* from 1996 to 1998? Explain why your answer is reasonable.

COMPUTERS **In Exercises 69–71, use the bar graph. It shows the sales of software for 1996. Write and evaluate an expression to decide whether the statement is *true* or *false*.** ▶ Source: US Bureau of the Census

69. More money was spent on word processing and finance software than on entertainment, home education, and art software.

70. The difference between the amount spent on home education software and on finance software was $490 million.

71. More than $3000 million was spent on computer software in 1996.

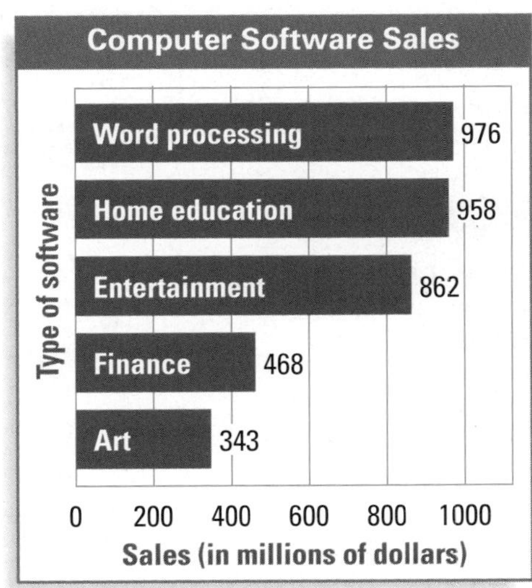

Link to Careers

COMPUTER PROGRAMMING
Programmers write, test, and maintain the programs, called software, that tell a computer what to do.

INTERNET More about computer programming available at www.mcdougallittell.com

Multiple-Choice Practice

72. Which phrase can be written as $12 - 4$?

Ⓐ The sum of 12 and 4 Ⓑ The quotient of 12 and 4

Ⓒ The product of 4 and 12 Ⓓ The difference of 12 and 4

73. Evaluate the expression $7c$ when $c = 6$.

Ⓕ 13 Ⓖ 42 Ⓗ 73 Ⓙ 76

1.3 Order of Operations

In this lesson you'll:

- Apply algebraic order of operations to evaluate expressions, and justify each step in the process. (AF 1.3)
- Apply the commutative and associative properties to evaluate expressions, and justify each step in the process. (AF 1.3)

Goal 1 USING ORDER OF OPERATIONS

An expression with more than one operation could be evaluated in different ways.

$2 + 3 \times 5$	$2 + 3 \times 5$
$(2 + 3) \times 5 = 25$	$2 + (3 \times 5) = 17$

To make sure everyone gets the same result when an expression is evaluated, mathematicians have established order of operations.

ORDER OF OPERATIONS (BASIC OPERATIONS)

1. Evaluate expressions inside grouping symbols.
2. Multiply and divide from left to right. *Left-to-right rule*
3. Add and subtract from left to right. *Left-to-right rule*

Grouping symbols, such as parentheses ( ) or brackets [ ], are used to indicate operations that are performed first.

EXAMPLE 1 *Using Order of Operations*

a. $20 - 4 \times 3 = 20 - 12$ First multiply 4 and 3.

$= 8$ Then subtract 12 from 20.

b. $(20 - 4) \times 3 = 16 \times 3$ First subtract inside parentheses.

$= 48$ Then multiply 16 and 3.

c. $18 \div 2 \times 3 = 9 \times 3$ First divide 18 by 2.

$= 27$ Then multiply 9 and 3.

d. $24 - 17 + 3 = 7 + 3$ First subtract 17 from 24.

$= 10$ Then add 7 and 3.

Student Help

STUDY TIP
As you can see in Example 1, using parentheses in an expression can change its value.

EXAMPLE 2 *Evaluating a Variable Expression*

Evaluate $2x + 3$ when $x = 4$.

Solution

$2x + 3 = 2 \cdot 4 + 3$ Substitute 4 for *x*.

$= 8 + 3$ First multiply 2 and 4.

$= 11$ Then add 8 and 3.

EXAMPLE 3 Evaluating a Variable Expression

Evaluate $s - 6 + t$ when $s = 13$ and $t = 5$.

Solution

$s - 6 + t = 13 - 6 + 5$ Substitute 13 for s and 5 for t.

$= 7 + 5 = 12$ Subtract and then add.

Goal 2 COMMUTATIVE AND ASSOCIATIVE PROPERTIES

The operations of addition and multiplication have special properties that do not apply to subtraction and division.

COMMUTATIVE PROPERTIES OF ADDITION AND MULTIPLICATION

In Words In a sum, you can add terms in any order.
In a product, you can multiply factors in any order.

In Algebra $a + b = b + a$ *Commutative property of addition*
$ab = ba$ *Commutative property of multiplication*

EXAMPLE 4 Using the Commutative Property

Explain why the orchards shown have the same number of trees.

Solution

To find the number of trees, multiply the number of rows by the number of trees in each row. Whichever order you use, 4×3 or 3×4, you get the same product because $4 \times 3 = 3 \times 4$.

ASSOCIATIVE PROPERTIES OF ADDITION AND MULTIPLICATION

In Words The value of a sum does not depend on how the terms are grouped.
The value of a product does not depend on how the factors are grouped.

In Algebra $(a + b) + c = a + (b + c)$ *Associative property of addition*
$(ab)c = a(bc)$ *Associative property of multiplication*

Student Help

▶ **More Examples**
More examples are available at www.mcdougallittell.com

EXAMPLE 5 Using the Associative Property

Use mental math to evaluate $(113 + 19) + 81$.

Solution

Notice that $19 + 81 = 100$. So, it is easier to group 19 and 81 before adding.

$(113 + 19) + 81 = 113 + (19 + 81)$	Associative property of addition
$= 113 + 100$	Add 19 and 81.
$= 213$	Add 113 and 100.

1.3 Exercises

Guided Practice

In Exercises 1–4, match the expression with its value.

A. 8 **B.** 6 **C.** 4 **D.** 53

1. $10 - 2 \times 3$

2. $12 \div 3 \times 2$

3. $6 - 3 + 10 \times 5$

4. $14 \div (5 + 2) \times 3$

In Exercises 5 and 6, evaluate the expression.

5. $5x - 6$ when $x = 2$

6. $x - 2 + y$ when $x = 3$ and $y = 4$

7. Use parentheses in the statement to make it true.

$7 - 2 + 3 = 2$

8. Use mental math to evaluate $45 + (30 + 55)$. Justify each step.

Practice and Problem Solving

Student Help

▶ **More Practice**
Extra practice to help you master skills is on page 566.

Evaluate the expression.

9. $11 + 5 \times 2$

10. $26 - 8 \times 3$

11. $20 - (4 + 8)$

12. $4 \times 7 \times 2$

13. $32 \div (4 \times 2)$

14. $54 \div 9 \div 2$

15. $8 + 5 \cdot (4 \div 2)$

16. $12 \times 3 - 6 \times 3$

17. $72 \div 9 + 56 \div 7$

Write the expression that is described. Then evaluate the expression.

18. Add 4 to the product of 8 and 4.

19. Subtract the product of 4 and 5 from 25.

20. Divide the sum of 2 and 10 by 3.

CALCULATOR In Exercises 21 and 22, use a calculator to evaluate the expression. Does your calculator use correct order of operations? Explain.

21. $56 + 128 \div 8 - 20$

22. $144 \div 2 - 54 \div 6$

23. **WRITING** You need to evaluate $168 \cdot (54 + 267) - 13 \cdot (7 \cdot 8)$. You want to use a calculator, but the one you have does not use order of operations. Describe the steps you need to use to evaluate the expression on your calculator.

Evaluate the expression.

24. $x \div 3 - 4$ when $x = 15$

25. $2a + 3b$ when $a = 3$ and $b = 9$

26. $7 + 3y$ when $y = 2$

27. $x - y - 2$ when $x = 15$ and $y = 1$

28. $5a + b - c$ when $a = 3$, $b = 7$, and $c = 5$

29. $w \div (x - 2) \cdot y$ when $w = 50$, $x = 7$, and $y = 9$

In Exercises 30–32, use mental math to evaluate the expression. Justify each step.

30. $2 \times (5 \times 23)$

31. $(43 + 29) + 57$

32. $5 \times (13 \times 20)$

33. Evaluate the expression. Does the associative property apply to subtraction? Explain your answer.

a. $(8 - 3) - 2$

b. $8 - (3 - 2)$

34. Evaluate the expression. Does the associative property apply to division? Explain your answer.

a. $(24 \div 6) \div 2$

b. $24 \div (6 \div 2)$

AMUSEMENT PARKS In 1998 there were about 750 amusement parks in the United States. About 300 million people visited the parks that year.

MATHEMATICAL REASONING Use the numbers 2, 4, 5, 7, or 9 to make the statement true.

35. $? \times ? \div ? = 18$

36. $? + ? \times ? = 25$

MATHEMATICAL REASONING Use the symbols +, −, ×, or ÷ to make the statement true.

37. $9 \; ? \; 7 \; ? \; 2 \; ? \; 6 = 17$

38. $3 \; ? \; 3 \; ? \; 3 \; ? \; 3 = 9$

AMUSEMENT PARK In Exercises 39–41, use the following information. At an amusement park, a 3-day pass costs $43 per person. The hotel costs $60 per night. A family of 4 plans to go to this park for 3 days and 2 nights.

39. Write an expression that represents how much the family will pay for 3-day passes and the hotel.

40. The family plans to spend $700 on the trip. Write an expression that represents the amount the family has left after paying for the 3-day passes and the hotel.

41. Evaluate the expressions from Exercises 39 and 40.

Student Help

▶ **HOMEWORK HELP**
Extra help with problem solving in Ex. 42 is available at www.mcdougallittell.com

42. SHOPPING Ceramic tile can be purchased by the square foot. Bill buys 70 square feet of tile priced at \$3 per square foot. Jamie buys 90 square feet of tile priced at \$2 per square foot. How much more does Bill spend than Jamie? Write and evaluate an expression to answer the question.

FUNDRAISING **In Exercises 43–45, use the following information.** Your class is selling cards and posters to raise \$600 for a class picnic. It costs \$115 for materials. Your class sells 112 posters for \$4 each and 220 cards for \$2 each.

43. How much money does your class raise?

44. Taking the cost of materials into account, does your class reach the \$600 goal?

45. By how much is the class below or above the \$600 goal?

Multiple-Choice Practice

46. Evaluate the expression $60 - 30 \div 5 \times 3$.

Ⓐ 2 Ⓑ 18 Ⓒ 42 Ⓓ 58

47. A cable television company charges \$24 for basic service and \$7 for each movie channel. You order the basic service and 2 movie channels. Which expression shows how much you will pay?

Ⓕ 2×7 Ⓖ $24 + 2 \times 7$ Ⓗ $(24 + 2) \times 7$ Ⓙ $7 + 24 \times 2$

Mixed Review

COMPUTERS **In Exercises 48 and 49, use the table. It shows the number of people employed in computer-related jobs in 1996 and the number expected to be employed in 2006.** ▶ Source: U.S. Bureau of Labor Statistics *(1.1)*

Year	Computer Engineer	Systems Analyst	Database Administrator
1996	216,000	506,000	212,000
2006	451,000	1,025,000	461,000

48. How many more systems analysts are expected in 2006 than in 1996?

49. Complete the statement: The number of people employed in computer-related jobs in 2006 will be about __?__ times the number in 1996.

Evaluate the expression. *(1.2)*

50. $r + t$ when $r = 3$ and $t = 7$

51. $w - v$ when $w = 43$ and $v = 16$

52. xy when $x = 7$ and $y = 4$

53. $\frac{k}{m}$ when $k = 42$ and $m = 6$

1.4 Powers and Exponents

California Standards

In this lesson you'll:

- Apply algebraic order of operations to evaluate expressions, and justify each step in the process. (AF 1.3)
- Solve problems manually by using the correct order of operations and by using a scientific calculator. (AF 1.4)

Goal 1 Using Exponents to Write Powers

The **power** a^m is a product of the form:

$$a^m = \underbrace{a \cdot a \cdot a \cdot \cdots \cdot a}_{m \text{ factors}}$$

The **exponent** m indicates the number of times the factor a, called the **base**, is repeated. For example, the power 10^3 means $10 \times 10 \times 10$ where the base 10 is repeated 3 times because the exponent is 3.

EXAMPLE 1 Evaluating a Power

Describe the power in words. Then evaluate the power.

a. 4^2 **b.** 2^3 **c.** 5^4

Solution

a. The power is read as "4 to the 2nd power," or "4 squared."

$4^2 = 4 \times 4 = 16$

b. The power is read as "2 to the 3rd power," or "2 cubed."

$2^3 = 2 \times 2 \times 2 = 8$

c. The power is read as "5 to the 4th power."

$5^4 = 5 \times 5 \times 5 \times 5 = 625$

EXAMPLE 2 Evaluating an Expression

Evaluate x^4 for the given value of x.

a. $x = 3$ **b.** $x = 17$

Solution

a. $x^4 = 3^4$ Substitute 3 for x.

$= 3 \times 3 \times 3 \times 3$ Write power as a product.

$= 81$ Multiply.

b. $x^4 = 17^4$ Substitute 17 for x.

KEYSTROKES	DISPLAY	
17 [y^x] 4 [=]	83521.	Use a calculator.

Student Help

TECHNOLOGY TIP
If your calculator has a [^] key, you can use the keystrokes 17 [^] 4 [=] to evaluate 17^4.

Goal 2 USING ORDER OF OPERATIONS WITH POWERS

You should evaluate powers before performing multiplication or division in an expression.

ORDER OF OPERATIONS (BASIC OPERATIONS AND POWERS)

1. Evaluate expressions inside grouping symbols.
2. Evaluate powers.
3. Multiply and divide from left to right. *Left-to-right rule*
4. Add and subtract from left to right. *Left-to-right rule*

EXAMPLE 3 Using Order of Operations with Powers

a. $(3 + 2)^2 \times 2 = 5^2 \times 2$ Add inside parentheses.

$= 25 \times 2$ Evaluate power.

$= 50$ Multiply.

b. $3 + 2^2 \times 2 = 3 + 4 \times 2$ Evaluate power.

$= 3 + 8$ Multiply.

$= 11$ Add.

Student Help

SKILLS REVIEW
For help with area, see page 562.

The area of a rectangle and the area of a square are given by the formulas at the right.

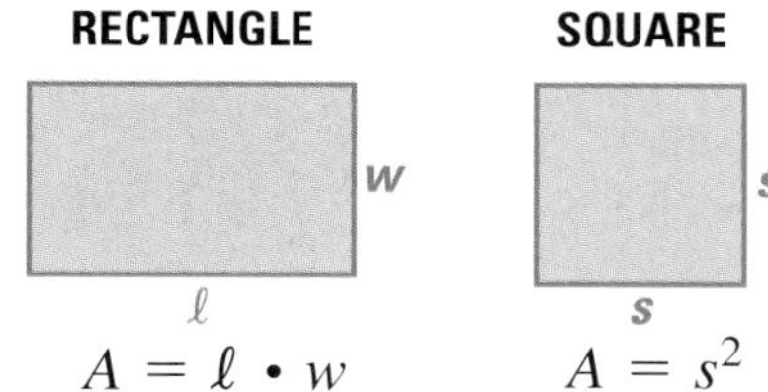

$A = \ell \cdot w$ $A = s^2$

EXAMPLE 4 Finding the Area of a Figure

TILE You plan to cover part of a wall with ceramic tile. You buy 30 square tiles and 10 rectangular border tiles. What is the area the tiles will cover?

6 in.

6 in.

Solution

Total area	$= 30 \cdot$	Area of a square tile	$+ 10 \cdot$	Area of a rectangular tile

$= 30 \cdot \mathbf{6^2} + 10(\mathbf{6 \cdot 1})$ Substitute areas of tiles.

$= 30 \cdot 36 + 10(6)$ Multiply inside parentheses, then evaluate power.

$= 1140 \text{ in.}^2$ Multiply and then add.

ANSWER ▶ The tiles will cover 1140 square inches.

1.4 Exercises

Guided Practice

In Exercises 1–3, identify the indicated part of 2^6.

1. Base **2.** Exponent **3.** Power

4. Describe the power 9^4 in words. Then write the power as a product.

ALGEBRA Evaluate the expression.

5. x^5 when $x = 2$ **6.** $2x^3$ when $x = 2$ **7.** 5^x when $x = 3$

CALCULATOR In Exercises 8–10, evaluate the power. You may wish to use a calculator.

8. 13^6 **9.** 8^7 **10.** 5^{10}

11. Is it true that $4^3 - 6 \times 10 + 5 = 585$? If not, what does it equal?

12. You are designing a walkway with the dimensions shown. The area of the walkway is given by $2x^2 + 5x$. Evaluate the area when $x = 7$ feet.

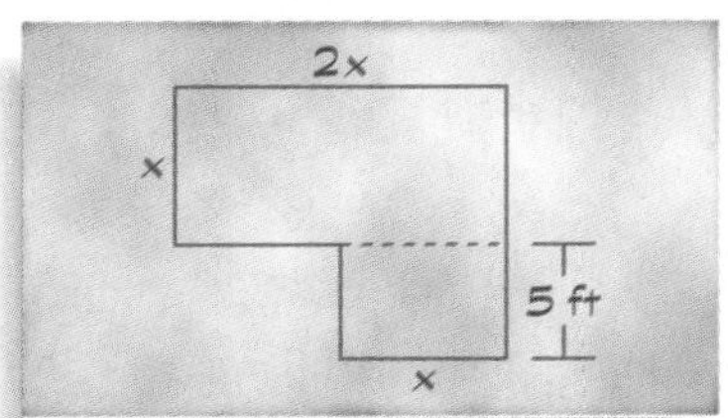

Practice and Problem Solving

Student Help

MORE PRACTICE Extra practice to help you master skills is on page 566.

Copy and complete the statement.

13. $36 = 6^{?}$ **14.** $16 = 2^{?}$ **15.** $27 = 3^{?}$ **16.** $32 = ?^5$

17. $81 = ?^2$ **18.** $64 = ?^3$ **19.** $\frac{1}{1,000} = \frac{1}{10^{?}}$ **20.** $\frac{1}{10,000} = \frac{1}{?^4}$

Describe the power in words. Then evaluate the power.

21. 4^4 **22.** 3^6 **23.** 9^3 **24.** 7^3

ALGEBRA Evaluate the expression.

25. x^5 when $x = 1$ **26.** 3^x when $x = 3$ **27.** $2x^4$ when $x = 3$

28. $4a^2$ when $a = 5$ **29.** $x^4 - 1$ when $x = 2$ **30.** $5y^3 - y$ when $y = 2$

31. $x^2 + x$ when $x = 6$ **32.** $2^x - x$ when $x = 5$ **33.** $8 - 2^x$ when $x = 3$

CALCULATOR Evaluate the power. You may wish to use a calculator.

34. 23^4 **35.** 125^3 **36.** 111^3 **37.** 50^4

38. 9^8 **39.** 16^5 **40.** 44^4 **41.** 6^8

Link to Science

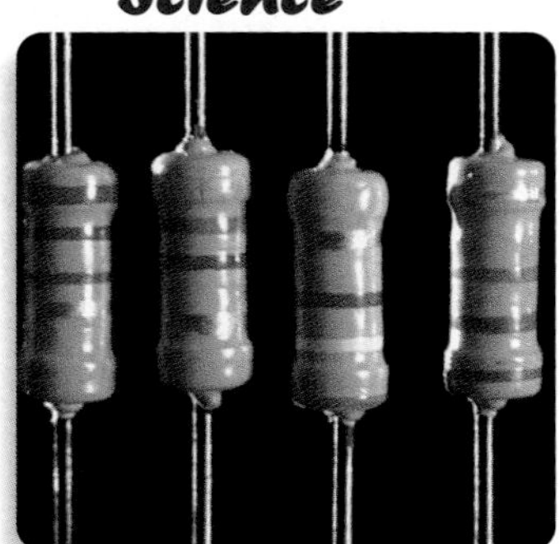

RESISTORS A resistor is part of an electric circuit that provides resistance to the flow of electric current.

INTERNET More about electric power at www.mcdougallittell.com

42. **Science Link** The electric power P (in watts) consumed by a resistor is given by $P = I^2R$ where I is the current (in amps) and R is the resistance (in ohms). How much electric power is used when $I = 4$ amps and $R = 58$ ohms?

In Exercises 43–51, evaluate the expression.

43. $(4 - 2)^5 - 5$ **44.** $8 + 2 \times 9^2$ **45.** $6 + 2^3 \div 8$

46. $30 + (11 - 1)^2$ **47.** $5^2 - (3^2 - 1^2)$ **48.** $2^5 - 5^2 - 2^2$

49. $10 + 3^2 \div 3$ **50.** $100 - 5^2 \times 4$ **51.** $6 \times 10^3 \div 10^2$

52. You evaluate $36 \div 6 \times 3^2$ using your calculator and get 54. Did your calculator use correct order of operations? Explain your reasoning.

CALCULATOR **In Exercises 53–58, evaluate the expression. You may wish to use a calculator.**

53. $8^4 \div 2^{11} \times 11$ **54.** $30 + 6^3 \div 12$ **55.** $(21^3 - 151) \div 10$

56. $1250 \div 5^4 + 2 \times 17$ **57.** $48 + 7^3 \div 49 - 39$ **58.** $(3^4 - 4^3)^2$

59. **MATHEMATICAL REASONING** Explain why the left-to-right rule means that you don't always do multiplication before division or addition before subtraction.

Write the powers in order from least to greatest.

60. $10^2, 2^7, 3^4$ **61.** $5^3, 1^8, 8^2$ **62.** $7^2, 2^6, 3^5$

GARDENING **In Exercises 63–65, use the figure which shows a rectangular flower bed surrounded by a stone border. The total area of the garden including the border can be modeled by $2x^2$.**

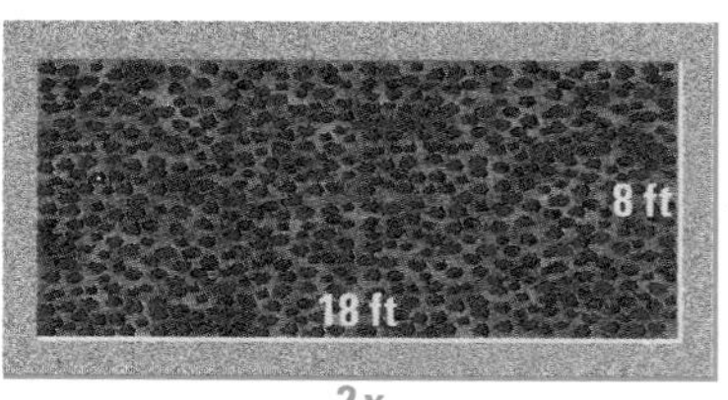

63. Calculate the total area of the garden when $x = 10$ feet.

64. Calculate the area of the flower bed.

65. Write and evaluate a numerical expression for the area of the border.

66. **CHALLENGE** Insert grouping symbols in the expression $3^2 \times 8 - 6 \div 2 + 19 - 2^3$ so that its value is 20.

Multiple-Choice Practice

67. What is the value of $2a^3$ when $a = 3$?

Ⓐ 18 Ⓑ 27 Ⓒ 54 Ⓓ 216

68. Evaluate $(6 + 1)^2 - 6$.

Ⓕ 1 Ⓖ 30 Ⓗ 43 Ⓙ 55

Comparing and Ordering Decimals

In this lesson you'll:

▶ Compare and order positive decimals and graph them on a number line. (NS 1.1)

Goal 1 GRAPHING DECIMALS

A **decimal** is a number that is written using the base-ten place-value system. For example, the decimal 2.58 has 2 ones, 5 tenths, and 8 hundredths, as shown below. The *decimal point* in 2.58 separates the number into two parts: the whole number part, 2, and the decimal part, 0.58.

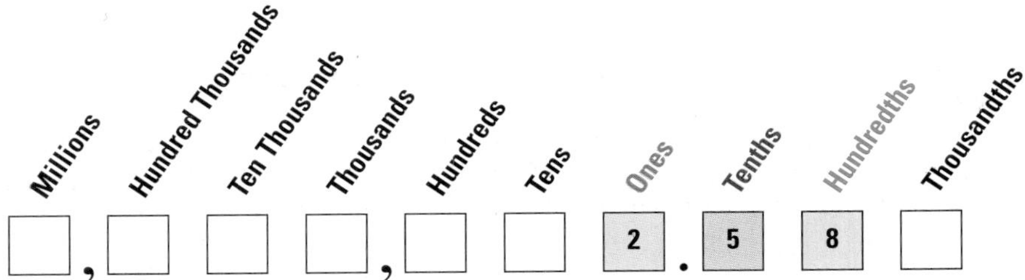

EXAMPLE 1 Reading a Decimal

a. 3.4 is read as "three and four tenths."

b. 3.04 is read as "three and four hundredths."

c. 30.40 is read as "thirty and forty hundredths."

A **number line** is a line on which every point is associated with a number. Points that correspond to whole numbers (0, 1, 2, 3, . . .) can be labeled with evenly spaced tick marks. Plotting the point that corresponds to a number is called **graphing** the number.

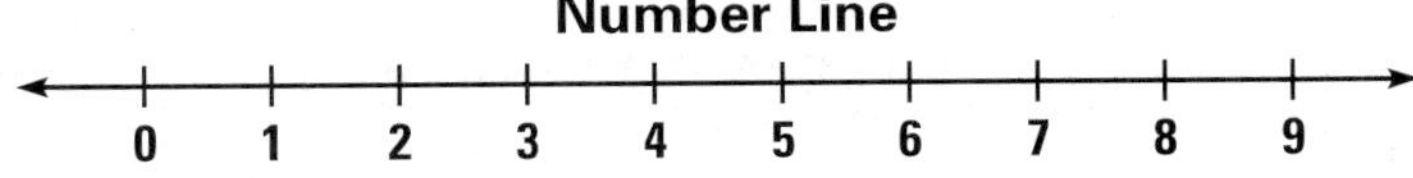

EXAMPLE 2 Graphing a Decimal

Graph 2.6 on a number line.

Solution

Begin by drawing a number line. Between 2 and 3, mark the tenths positions. Then plot the point that corresponds to 2.6.

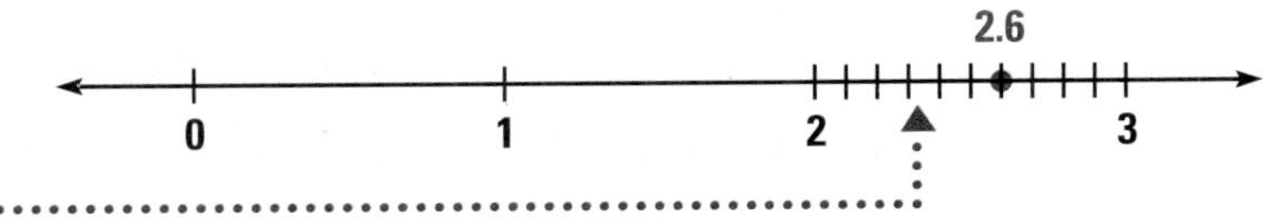

Student Help

▶ **STUDY TIP**
To show tenths between two consecutive whole numbers on a number line, you draw nine equally spaced tick marks.

Goal 2 COMPARING AND ORDERING DECIMALS

Student Help

▶ **READING TIP**
The inequality sign always points to the lesser number.

The symbol < is read "is less than," and the symbol > is read "is greater than." For example, $5 < 8$ means "5 is less than 8," and $8 > 5$ means "8 is greater than 5." On a number line, "a is less than b" means that a is to the left of b, and "a is greater than b" means that a is to the right of b.

EXAMPLE 3 Comparing Two Decimals with a Number Line

Use a number line to compare 1.7 and 1.6.

Solution

Begin by graphing 1.7 and 1.6 on the same number line.

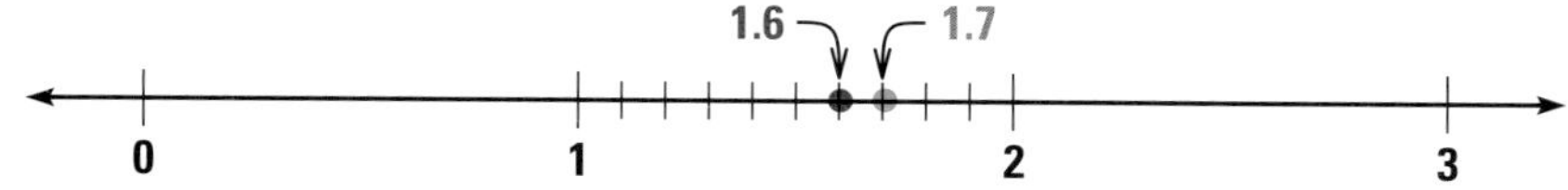

ANSWER ▶ Because 1.6 is to the left of 1.7, $1.6 < 1.7$, or $1.7 > 1.6$.

EXAMPLE 4 Ordering Decimals

Order 2.3, 2.09, 2.32, 2.27, and 2.37 from least to greatest.

Solution

Begin by graphing all five numbers on the same number line.

ANSWER ▶ In order, the numbers are 2.09, 2.27, 2.3, 2.32, and 2.37.

Student Help

▶ **SKILLS REVIEW**
For help with using a number line, see page 554.

EXAMPLE 5 Comparing Two Decimals by Place Value

SWIMMING Was the winner in the Olympic women's 100 meter freestyle faster in 1992 or 1980?

Solution

From left to right, the first digits in 54.64 and 54.79 that are different are in the tenths place. Because 7 is greater than 6, you know that 54.79 is greater than 54.64.

ANSWER ▶ The winner was faster in 1992.

Winning Times

Year	Time (seconds)	Country
1996	54.50	China
1992	54.64	China
1988	54.93	East Germany
1984	55.92	United States
1980	54.79	East Germany
1976	55.65	East Germany

1.5 Exercises

Guided Practice

In Exercises 1–4, match the number with the words.

1. 1.2 **A.** Twelve hundredths

2. 0.12 **B.** Twelve thousandths

3. 0.012 **C.** Twelve ten-thousandths

4. 0.0012 **D.** One and two tenths

5. Name the numbers represented by the letters on the number line.

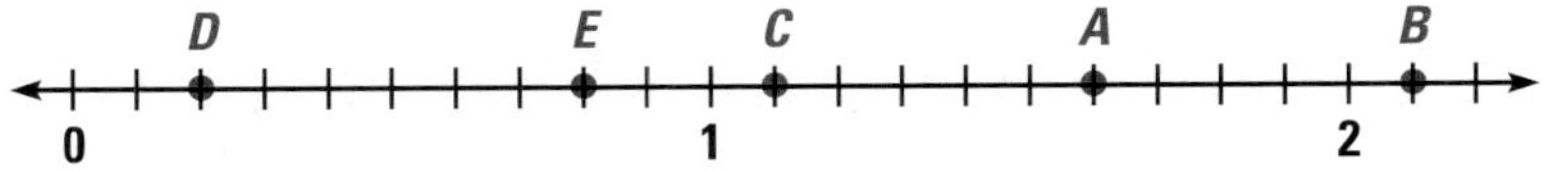

Student Help

▶ STUDY TIP
A zero added to the right side of a decimal does not change the value of the decimal. For example, 2.5 = 2.50.

Order the numbers from least to greatest.

6. 0.25, 0.5, 2.5, 0.2, 0.02

7. 0.10, 0.07, 0.17, 1.7, 0.7

Complete the statement using <, =, or >.

8. 0.05 **?** 0.3

9. 0.40 **?** 0.4

10. 3.109 **?** 3.011

Each bar of the bar graph represents a decimal between 0 and 1.

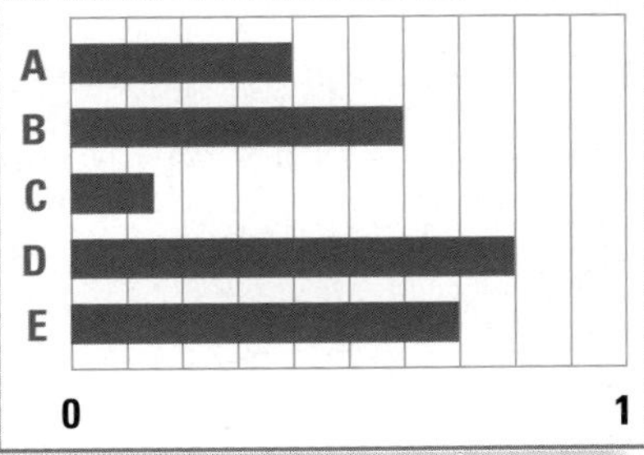

11. Write the length of each bar.

12. Order the lengths from least to greatest.

13. Which bars have lengths greater than 0.5?

14. Which bar has length less than 0.8 and greater than 0.6?

Practice and Problem Solving

Student Help

▶ MORE PRACTICE
Extra practice to help you master skills is on page 567.

Write the decimal.

15. One and three hundred five thousandths

16. One and thirty-five thousandths

17. One and thirty-five hundredths

18. One and three hundred five ten-thousandths

Graph the numbers on a number line.

19. 0.1, 1.2, 0.9

20. 0.6, 1.9, 1.3

21. 0.7, 1.7, 2.2

Link to Science

BAROMETER
Atmospheric pressure is measured with an instrument called a barometer. Storms are associated with areas of low pressure.

More about barometers at www.mcdougallittell.com

Order the numbers from least to greatest.

22. 3.4, 3.09, 3.9, 3.901, 3.1

23. 0.08, 0.8, 0.89, 0.09

24. 0.95, 0.954, 0.9054, 0.905

25. 12.608, 12.001, 12.8, 12.04, 12.5

26. 0.026, 0.26, 0.126, 0.06, 0.2

27. 5.143, 5.14, 5.13, 5.104, 5.1

28. 1.69, 1.107, 1.9, 1.709, 1.76

29. 4.281, 4.18, 4.118, 4.218, 4.081

In Exercises 30–41, complete the statement using <, =, or >.

30. 0.32 ? 0.3109

31. 0.006 ? 0.06

32. 2.38 ? 2.83

33. 0.98 ? 1.9

34. 0.5 ? 0.50

35. 0.18 ? 0.108

36. 1.075 ? 1.57

37. 1.09 ? 1.009

38. 1.04 ? 1.039

39. 3.60 ? 3.600

40. 10.92 ? 10.092

41. 255.07 ? 255.7

42. What is the largest whole number x for which $2x$ is less than 13.7?

Science Link **In Exercises 43–45, use the diagram which gives the barometer readings (in millibars) at locations in several states on the same day.**

43. In which state, Nebraska or Georgia, is the barometer reading greater?

44. In which state, Idaho or Pennsylvania, is the barometer reading lower?

45. Order the barometer readings from least to greatest.

ID 1014.8
CA 1013.3
NE 1016.7
NM 1015.4
LA 1017.7
IN 1023.7
PA 1014.2
GA 1016.6

OLYMPIC RUNNING **In Exercises 46–48, use the table which gives the winning times for the men's 100 meter run in the Olympics.**

Year	1980	1984	1988	1992	1996
Time (in seconds)	10.25	9.99	9.92	9.96	9.84

46. Compare the times for 1984 and 1992. Which winner was faster?

47. Order the times from least to greatest.

48. Graph the times on a number line.

49. **MATHEMATICAL REASONING** The numbers 923, 745, 306, and 114 are in order from greatest to least. Place a decimal point in each number so that the resulting decimals are in order from *least* to *greatest*. Do not rearrange the numbers.

50. **CHALLENGE** Bonnie has more money than Casey. Bonnie has less money than Maria. Larry has $.20 less than Nicole. Use the decimals below to find out how much money each person has.

$.56 $2.37 $2.05 $.76 $2.50

Multiple-Choice Practice

51. Which number is represented by the point on the number line?

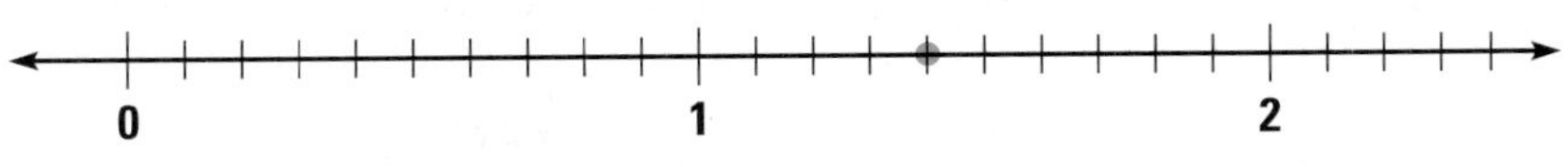

Ⓐ 0.4 Ⓑ 1.2 Ⓒ 1.4 Ⓓ 1.6

Test Tip

▶ **TEST TIP** In Exercise 52, try to eliminate choices by looking at the first two numbers in each choice.

52. Which numbers are ordered from least to greatest?

Ⓕ 0.4, 0.04, 0.54, 0.45 Ⓖ 0.04, 0.4, 0.45, 0.54

Ⓗ 0.45, 0.04, 0.54, 0.4 Ⓙ 0.54, 0.45, 0.4, 0.04

53. Which statement is true?

Ⓐ $27.65 > 28.64$ Ⓑ $27.50 < 27.5$

Ⓒ $28.92 < 27.93$ Ⓓ $28.79 > 28.64$

54. A surveyor determines the area of four properties. Which property has the greatest area?

Ⓕ Property A: 5.555 acres Ⓖ Property B: 5.500 acres

Ⓗ Property C: 5.550 acres Ⓙ Property D: 5.505 acres

Mixed Review

55. **RECYCLING** Recycling one pound of steel can save enough energy to keep a 60 watt light bulb burning for 26 hours. A company recycles 33 pounds of steel. The amount of energy saved is enough to keep a 60 watt light bulb burning for how many hours? *(1.1)*

56. Write a numerical expression for the product of 5 and 90. Then evaluate the expression. *(1.2)*

57. Evaluate the expression $p \div 6$ when $p = 420$. *(1.2)*

In Exercises 58–60, evaluate the expression. *(1.3)*

58. $24 - 6 \div 2$ **59.** $13 + (20 - 7)$ **60.** $4 + 8 \times 6 \div 2$

61. Use mental math to evaluate $(27 + 98) + 73$. Justify each step. *(1.3)*

62. Does $4 \div 2$ give the same result as $2 \div 4$? What does this tell you about the commutative property? *(1.3)*

Student Help

▶ **STUDY TIP** Draw a diagram to help see the phone tree in Exercise 63.

63. **SKI CLUB** The ski club sets up a telephone tree. The first person in the tree calls 4 people. Those 4 people each call 4 other people. They in turn each call 4 other people. How many people are called last? Write your answer as a power. *(1.4)*

Chapter 1 Mid-Chapter Test

Take this test as you would take a test in class. The answers to the exercises are given in the back of the book.

In Exercises 1–6, evaluate the expression.

1. $5 + 3 \times 4 + 2$
2. $90 - 18 \div 6 \times 10$
3. $12 + 8 \div 2 \times 3$
4. $42 - 21 \div 7 + 2^3$
5. $5 \times (4^2 + 3^2)$
6. $16 \div (2^2 \div 2)$

7. Explain how you can use mental math to evaluate $4 \times (17 \times 25)$. Justify each step.

8. AMUSEMENT PARK You ride a roller coaster that has a hill 150 feet high and lasts 3 minutes. You must wait in line 15 minutes each time you ride the roller coaster. Write a numerical expression for how many times you can ride the roller coaster in one hour and then evaluate the expression. Identify any irrelevant information.

Evaluate the power.

9. 8^2
10. 15^1
11. 5^3
12. 2^5

In Exercises 13–16, match the number with the words.

13. 23.6 **A.** Two hundred thirty-six thousandths

14. 2.36 **B.** Twenty-three and six tenths

15. 0.236 **C.** Two hundred thirty-six ten-thousandths

16. 0.0236 **D.** Two and thirty-six hundredths

NUTRITION **In Exercises 17–19, use the table which gives the protein (in grams) in different flavors of frozen fruit and yogurt drinks at a restaurant.**

Flavor	Protein (in grams)
Citrus	4.33
Cranberry	5.11
Peach	2.93
Banana	4.85
Strawberry	6.37
Kiwi	4.89

17. Which flavor has the most protein?

18. Which flavor, banana or kiwi, has more protein?

19. List the flavors in order from least protein to most protein.

20. Draw a number line from 0.6 to 0.7. Add 9 tick marks to divide the line into 10 equal parts. Label each tick mark. Graph and name three numbers on the line that are greater than 0.64.

21. TIC-TAC-TOE The tic-tac-toe game shown can be won only if the three numbers in a row, column, or diagonal are in order. The order can be from least to greatest or from greatest to least. Copy the game and draw lines through all possible ways to win.

0.9	**0.71**	**0.6**
0.04	**0.5**	**0.65**
0.05	**0.34**	**0.45**

Rounding Decimals

In this lesson you'll:

- Compute the mean of data sets. (SDP 1.1)
- Give answers to a specified degree of accuracy. (MR 2.6)

Goal 1 ROUNDING DECIMALS

In many real-life situations, decimals may have more digits than are needed. For example, if you buy 6 gallons of gasoline at $1.339 per gallon, then the exact total would be 6 × 1.339, or $8.034. You can't really pay this amount, so you round to the nearest cent.

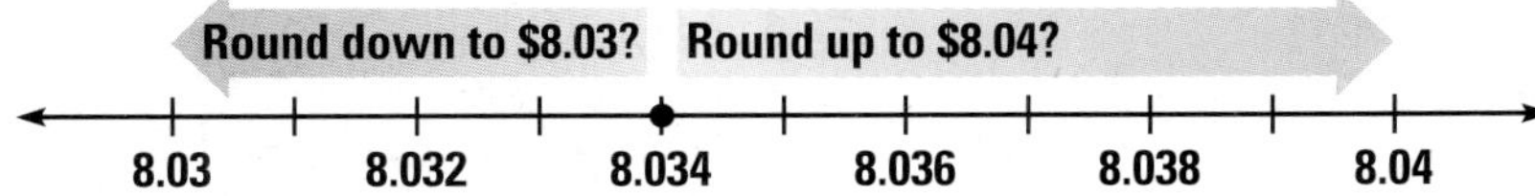

Round down to $8.03?
Round up to $8.04?

8.03 8.032 8.034 8.036 8.038 8.04

Because $8.034 is closer to $8.03 than to $8.04, you should round down to $8.03, as indicated by the following rules.

ROUNDING NUMBERS

To round to a given decimal place, look at the digit to its right.

- If the digit is 4 or less, round down.
- If the digit is 5 or greater, round up.

EXAMPLE 1 Rounding a Whole Number

	ROUND TO NEAREST	ORIGINAL NUMBER	ROUND UP OR DOWN?	ROUNDED NUMBER
a.	Ten	983	Round down.	980
b.	Ten	3146	Round up.	3150
c.	Hundred	6058	Round up.	6100
d.	Thousand	71,479	Round down.	71,000

EXAMPLE 2 Rounding a Decimal

	ROUND TO NEAREST	ORIGINAL NUMBER	ROUND UP OR DOWN?	ROUNDED NUMBER
a.	Thousandth	1.2852	Round down.	1.285
b.	Hundredth	3.157	Round up.	3.16
c.	Tenth	12.449	Round down.	12.4
d.	One	1359.5	Round up.	1360
e.	One	0.349	Round down.	0

Student Help

MORE EXAMPLES

INTERNET More examples are available at www.mcdougallittell.com

Goal 2 WRITING APPROXIMATE SOLUTIONS

Student Help

▶ **VOCABULARY TIP**
Data are numbers or facts that describe something.

Decimals often occur when you divide one whole number by another whole number, such as when finding an *average*.

To find the **average** of a set of numbers, or data, add the numbers and divide the sum by how many numbers are in the set. The average is also called the **mean**.

EXAMPLE 3 Dividing Whole Numbers

WEB SITE You manage an Internet Web site. You create a spreadsheet to show the number of visitors to the Web site each week for the last six weeks. Find the average number of weekly visitors.

	A	B	C
1	Week	Visitors	
2	1	112	
3	2	131	
4	3	120	
5	4	125	
6	5	114	
7	6	128	

Solution

To find the average number of weekly visitors, find the total number of visitors and divide by 6.

$112 + 131 + 120 + 125 + 114 + 128 = 730$

$730 \div 6 \approx 121.7$ Use long division or a calculator.

Student Help

▶ **READING TIP**
The symbol ≈ is read as "is approximately equal to." It indicates that a result is not exact but has been rounded.

ANSWER ▶ The average number of visitors is about 121.7. You can also write the division as a fraction.

$$\frac{730}{6} \approx 121.7$$

EXAMPLE 4 Using an Average to Estimate

WEB SITE In Example 3 you found the average number of weekly visitors to be 121.7. You wish to estimate the number of visitors to the Web site next week. What is a reasonable estimate?

Solution

The answer to Example 3 represents the average number of people who visited the Web site. It is not possible to have 0.7 of a person. Therefore, you should round your answer to a whole number. A reasonable estimate is 122.

1.6 Exercises

Guided Practice

1. What does the symbol ≈ mean?

2. Draw a number line model to round 0.24 to the nearest tenth.

In Exercises 3–8, round 453.0729 to the given place value.

3. Hundreds
4. Tens
5. Ones
6. Tenths
7. Hundredths
8. Thousandths

9. Complete: The average of a set of numbers is also called the __?__.

Find the average of the set of numbers.

10. 1, 5, 2, 3, 4, 4, 2
11. 10, 12, 14, 11, 13
12. 20, 40, 40, 20, 30, 30
13. 50, 25, 35, 40, 25, 45, 55, 35

Practice and Problem Solving

Student Help

▶ **MORE PRACTICE** Extra practice to help you master skills is on page 567.

Draw a number line model to round 6.263 to the given place value.

14. Hundredths
15. Tenths
16. Ones

Round the number to the given place value.

17. 269 (tens)
18. 34,475 (thousands)
19. 411,990 (hundreds)
20. 5.41 (tenths)
21. 20.3 (ones)
22. 8.5165 (thousandths)

Tell if the statement is *true* or *false*. If false, correct the red number.

23. 2.15 rounded to the nearest one is 2.

24. 13,099 rounded to the nearest thousand is **13,000**.

25. 5.445 rounded to the nearest tenth is **5.5**.

In Exercises 26 and 27, round the instrument reading to the given place value.

26. Odometer (hundreds)

27. Thermometer (ones)

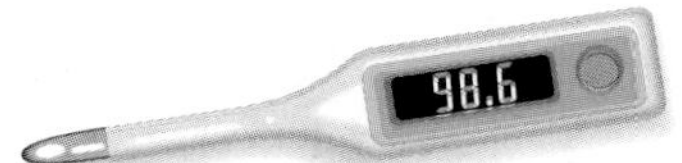

28. ERROR ANALYSIS Your friend is asked to round 6.3487 to the nearest tenth. Your friend first rounds to the nearest hundredth to get 6.35, and then rounds to the nearest tenth to get 6.4. Is your friend correct? Explain.

In Exercises 29–34, round to the nearest dollar.

29. \$32.25 **30.** \$25.49 **31.** \$611.50

32. \$1.79 **33.** \$89.19 **34.** \$95.11

35. **GASOLINE** You buy 12 gallons of gasoline at \$1.499 per gallon. How much do you owe? Round your answer to the nearest cent.

In Exercises 36–39, find the average of the set of numbers. Round the average to the nearest tenth.

36. 6, 6, 7, 8, 9, 9, 10 **37.** 1, 23, 24, 25, 26

38. 30, 35, 38, 32, 36, 34, 35 **39.** 80, 70, 50, 90, 60, 70, 90

40. **ALGEBRA** The expression for the average of x and 2 is $\frac{x + 2}{2}$. Evaluate this expression when $x = 0$, 1, 2, 3, and 4.

SCIENCE **In Exercises 41 and 42, use the following information.** For a class science project, students measure the height of a sunflower at the end of each week. Their data are shown.

Time (in weeks)	Height (in cm)
1	12.525
2	26.78
3	48.394
4	67.12

41. Round the data to the nearest tenth.

42. Round the data to the nearest one. How much does the plant grow between the second and third week?

Exercise 43

43. **POPULATION** The land area of Fremont, California, is approximately 77 square miles, and its population in 1990 was about 173,000. Find the average number of people per square mile in Fremont in 1990. Use mental math to check that your answer is reasonable.

▶ Source: US Bureau of the Census

44. **BUSINESS** Your brother has a job interview with a company that claims to have an average annual employee salary of \$35,000. He is disappointed to find out he would make only \$19,000 a year. Explain how the average annual salary could be so high.

45. **CHALLENGE** Find the mean of 8 numbers if the mean of the first five numbers is 23 and the mean of the last three numbers is 15.

Multiple-Choice Practice

46. What is 8.049 rounded to the nearest tenth?

Ⓐ 8.05 Ⓑ 8.0 Ⓒ 8.1 Ⓓ 10.0

47. You weigh packages and record their weights to the nearest pound. A package weighs 2.5 pounds. What weight should you record?

Ⓕ 2 pounds Ⓖ 2.5 pounds Ⓗ 3 pounds Ⓙ 10 pounds

1.7 Adding and Subtracting Decimals

California Standards

In this lesson you'll:

- Calculate and solve addition and subtraction problems, including those arising from concrete situations. (NS 2.0)
- Use variables in expressions describing geometric quantities. (AF 3.1)

Goal 1 Adding Decimals

When you add or subtract decimals, it helps to use a vertical format. The steps are similar to those used to add or subtract whole numbers. When using a vertical format, remember to line up the decimal places.

EXAMPLE 1 Using a Vertical Format to Add Decimals

Use a vertical format to add.

a. 4.72 + 2.5 **b.** 5.32 + 7 **c.** 0.247 + 1.9

Solution

a.
$$\begin{array}{r} 4.72 \\ +2.5 \\ \hline 7.22 \end{array}$$

Ones Tenths Hundredths

b.
$$\begin{array}{r} 5.32 \\ +7 \\ \hline 12.32 \end{array}$$

Ones Tenths Hundredths Thousandths

c.
$$\begin{array}{r} 0.247 \\ +1.9 \\ \hline 2.147 \end{array}$$

Student Help

SKILLS REVIEW
For help with operations with whole numbers, see pages 556 and 557.

A **polygon** is a closed geometric figure with 3 or more straight sides. The **perimeter** P of a polygon is the sum of the lengths of its sides. Examples of polygons are triangles and *pentagons* (5-sided figures).

TRIANGLE

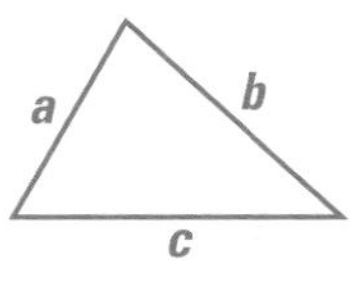

$P = a + b + c$

PENTAGON

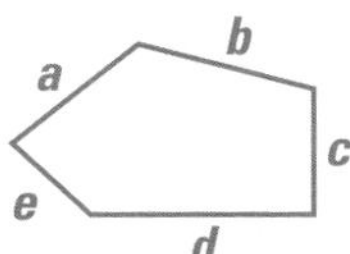

$P = a + b + c + d + e$

EXAMPLE 2 Finding the Perimeter of a Polygon

Find the perimeter of the triangle shown.

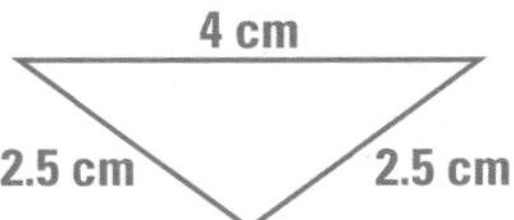

Solution

$P = a + b + c$ Write formula.

$= 2.5 + 4 + 2.5$ Substitute for *a*, *b*, and *c*.

$= 9$ Add.

ANSWER ▶ The perimeter is 9 centimeters.

Goal 2 SUBTRACTING DECIMALS

> **Student Help**
>
> ▶ **STUDY TIP**
> When you subtract a decimal from a whole number, as in part (c) of Example 3, it helps to write a decimal point and one or more zeros after the whole number.

EXAMPLE 3 Using a Vertical Format to Subtract Decimals

Use a vertical format to subtract.

a. $3.42 - 2.4$ **b.** $4.63 - 3$ **c.** $8 - 0.308$

Solution

	a.	b.	c.
Place values	Ones, Tenths, Hundredths	Ones, Tenths, Hundredths	Ones, Tenths, Hundredths, Thousandths
	3.42	4.63	8.000
	− 2.4	− 3	− 0.308
	1.02	1.63	7.692

EXAMPLE 4 Making Change

CONSUMER SPENDING You buy a shirt for \$12.69. You give the sales clerk \$20. How much change do you get back?

Solution

Method 1 Use a vertical format.

\$20.00	Amount you give clerk
−12.69	Cost of the shirt
\$ 7.31	Change

CHECK ✓ Add to check the result of a subtraction problem.

\$12.69	Cost of the shirt
+ 7.31	Change
\$20.00	Amount you give clerk

Method 2 Count the change.

Some sales clerks "count-up" to make change. Here is how a sales clerk might count your change.

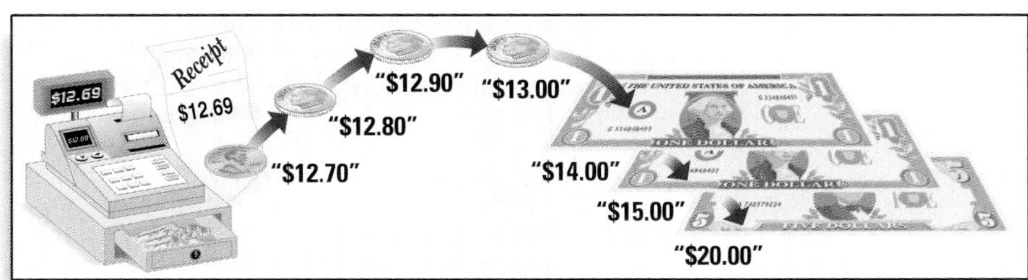

So, your change is

$$\$.01 + \$.10 + \$.10 + \$.10 + \$1.00 + \$1.00 + \$5.00 = \$7.31.$$

> **Student Help**
>
> ▶ **STUDY TIP**
> In Example 4 notice that you can use addition to check a subtraction problem. This works because addition and subtraction are *inverse operations.*

1.7 Exercises

Guided Practice

Use a vertical format to add.

1. 4.35 + 1.23 **2.** 2.36 + 0.4 **3.** 9.1 + 6.748

Find the perimeter.

4. 1.1 m, 0.5 m, 0.5 m, 1.1 m

5.

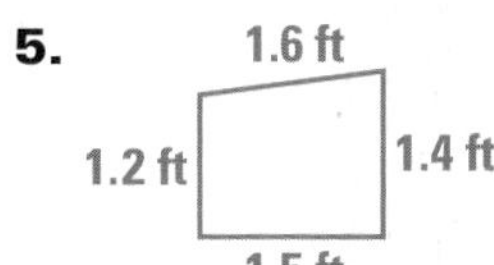

ERROR ANALYSIS **In Exercises 6–8, tell whether the vertical format is correct. If correct, subtract. If not correct, write the correct vertical format and subtract.**

6. $\begin{array}{r} 0.86 \\ -\ 0.2 \\ \hline \end{array}$ **7.** $\begin{array}{r} 3 \\ -\ 2.85 \\ \hline \end{array}$ **8.** $\begin{array}{r} 10.5 \\ -\ 0.82 \\ \hline \end{array}$

9. **CONSUMER SPENDING** You buy a poster for $9.85. You give the sales clerk $20. How much change do you get back?

Practice and Problem Solving

Student Help

▶MORE PRACTICE
Extra practice to help you master skills is on page 567.

Use a vertical format to add.

10. 6.87 + 7.24 **11.** 0.3 + 9.06

12. 0.08 + 8 **13.** 13.6 + 0.95 + 2.2

In Exercises 14–17, find the missing digits.

14. $\begin{array}{r} 3.8\,? \\ +\ 0.?\,5 \\ \hline ?.9\,5 \end{array}$ **15.** $\begin{array}{r} ?.0\,7 \\ +\ 3.?\,? \\ \hline 9.9\,1 \end{array}$ **16.** $\begin{array}{r} 4.?\,? \\ +\ 0.5 \\ \hline ?.3\,7 \end{array}$ **17.** $\begin{array}{r} ?.0\,2 \\ +\ 2.?\,? \\ \hline 6.3\,1 \end{array}$

18. Write three different addition problems whose sum is 10.45.

19. **ERROR ANALYSIS** Describe and correct the error at the right.

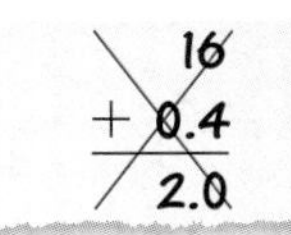

Find the perimeter.

20. 4.12 in., 6.3 in., 3.75 in., 3.4 in.

21. 0.82 cm, 1.8 cm, 1.06 cm, 2.14 cm

22.

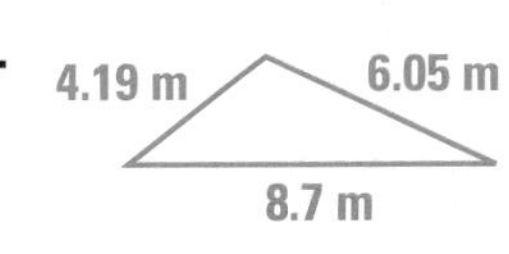

Link to Olympics

SKI JUMPING Jani Soininen of Finland won the gold medal for the 1998 Olympic 90 meter ski jump competition with a total score of 234.5.

SKI JUMPING In Exercises 23 and 24, use the following information. You participate in two jumps as an Olympic ski jumper. You score 115.5 on the first jump and 114.0 on the second jump. To win a medal, the total points from the two jumps must be at least the following: 233.5 for a gold medal, 231.0 for a silver medal, and 229.5 for a bronze medal.

23. Calculate your total score. Determine which medal you win.

24. Use mental math to find how many more points you needed to win a gold medal.

25. Copy and complete the pyramid. Each number is the sum of the two numbers below it.

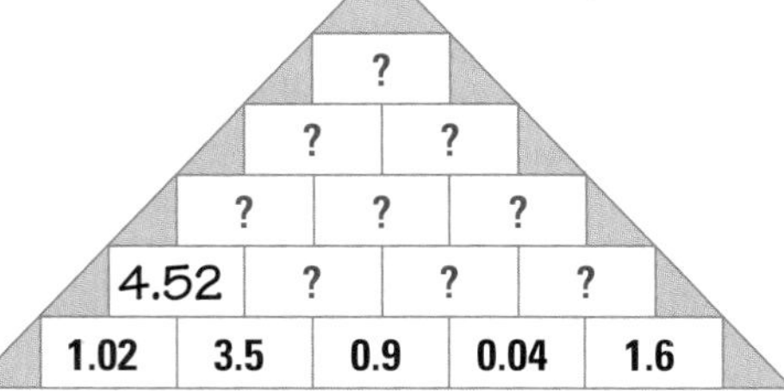

Use a vertical format to subtract.

26. 6.75 − 2.3 **27.** 4.33 − 3.9 **28.** 7.619 − 3.8

29. 5.452 − 2.91 **30.** 5 − 2.89 **31.** 12 − 7.652

32. 0.88 − 0.39 **33.** 1.25 − 0.056 **34.** 10 − 0.195

CONSUMER SPENDING In Exercises 35 and 36, tell whether the correct change was given. Explain.

35. You give the clerk a $20 bill and receive a $10 bill and 2 dimes in change for a purchase of $10.80.

36. You use $20 to buy a concert ticket for $18.74. The clerk counts your $1.26 change as "$18.75, $19.00, $20.00."

Science Link **In Exercises 37–39, use the table. It shows the percents of people 18–24 years old who are different heights.**

▶ Source: US Bureau of the Census

Height	Percent of Men	Percent of Women
5 ft 2 in.	0.16	8.62
5 ft 3 in.	0.27	11.31
5 ft 4 in.	1.76	12.75
5 ft 5 in.	1.48	16.28
5 ft 6 in.	4.39	16.67
5 ft 7 in.	7.94	10.61
5 ft 8 in.	10.50	6.93
5 ft 9 in.	12.21	3.93
5 ft 10 in.	14.77	2.11
5 ft 11 in.	14.59	1.04

37. Find the difference between the percents of men who are 5 ft 9 in. and 5 ft 8 in. tall.

38. Find the difference between the percents of women who are 5 ft 3 in. and 5 ft 2 in. tall.

39. **MATHEMATICAL REASONING** Find the sum of the percents in each percent column. What might account for the totals being less than 100?

Science Link **In Exercises 40–43, use the following information.** The Kelvin temperature scale begins at *absolute zero*, a temperature so cold that molecules have almost no energy of motion. There are no readings below zero in the Kelvin scale. To convert Kelvin temperature to Celsius, subtract 273.16. Find the Celsius temperature for the given Kelvin temperature.

40. Aluminum melts at 933.53 K.

41. Muffins bake at 478.16 K.

42. Body temperature is 310.16 K.

43. Gold melts at 1337.59 K.

NUTRITION **In Exercises 44 and 45, use the following information.** The map shows the average number of gallons of bottled water that people drank in 1998.

▶ Source: International Bottled Water Association

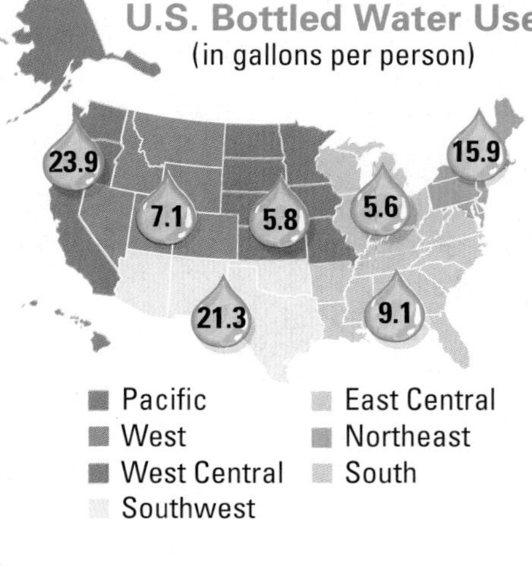

44. Where did people drink the most bottled water? Where did they drink the least? What is the difference between the amounts used in these two regions?

45. How many more gallons of bottled water did people in the Southwest drink than people in the Northeast?

46. **CHALLENGE** Find the missing digits.

$$\begin{array}{r} ?\,4\,?\,.\,6\,? \\ -\;6\,1\,3\,.\,?\,2 \\ \hline 2\,?\,7\,.\,8\,5 \end{array}$$

Multiple-Choice Practice

47. You want to buy shoes for \$31.99, shoe laces for \$1.09, a shirt for \$9.89, and socks for \$3.93. Which is the best estimate for the amount you need to make these purchases?

Ⓐ \$44 Ⓑ \$45 Ⓒ \$46 Ⓓ \$47

48. Evaluate 7.56 − 2.019 + 5.451.

Ⓕ 0.09 Ⓖ 10.992

Ⓗ 11.01 Ⓙ Not here

49. Your goal is to walk 10 miles every week. The data shown are the number of miles you have walked so far this week. How many more miles will you have to walk to complete your goal?

Ⓐ 0.6 miles Ⓑ 1.6 miles

Ⓒ 6.6 miles Ⓓ 9.4 miles

Day	Distance (in miles)
Sunday	1.3
Monday	1.8
Tuesday	2.1
Wednesday	1.6
Thursday	1.5
Friday	1.1

DEVELOPING CONCEPTS

Decimal Multiplication

For use with Lesson 1.8

- Calculate and solve problems involving multiplication. (NS 2.0)
- Use models to explain mathematical reasoning. (MR 2.4)

MATERIALS
- Grid paper
- Calculator

You can use a 10-by-10 square drawn on grid paper to model multiplication of whole numbers and decimals.

SAMPLE 1 Modeling Multiplication

You can use a model to find the product.

a. 6×7 **b.** 0.6×0.7

Here's How

First decide what the areas of the large square and each small square will represent. Then shade an appropriate number of rows and columns.

a. Let the area of the large square be 100, so the area of each small square is 1. Shade 6 rows of the large square red and 7 columns blue.

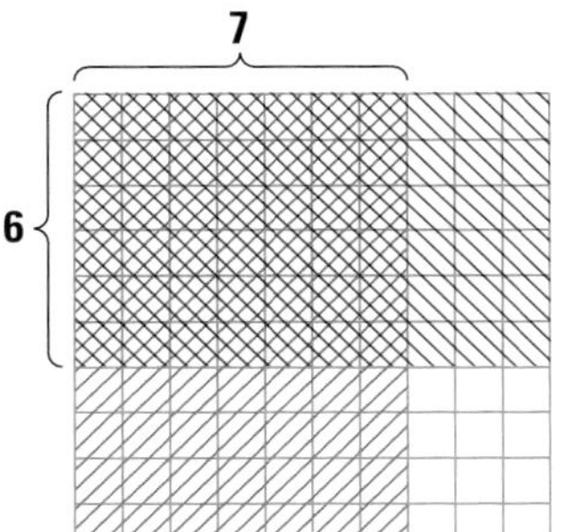

Since 42 small squares are doubly shaded, $6 \times 7 = 42$.

b. Let the area of the large square be 1, so the area of each small square is $\frac{1}{100}$, or 0.01. Shade 6 rows red and 7 columns blue.

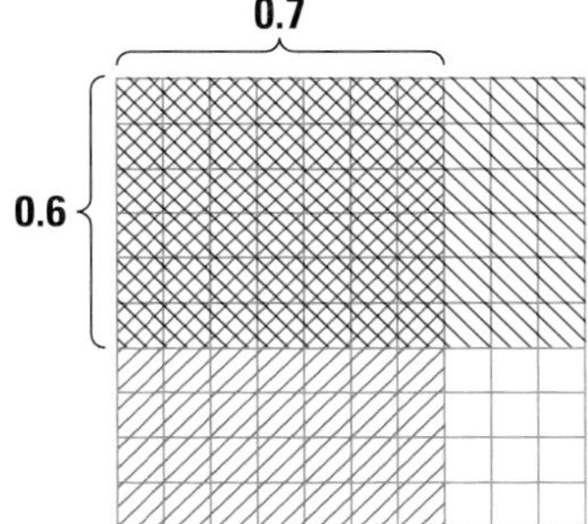

Since 42 small squares are doubly shaded, $0.6 \times 0.7 = \frac{42}{100} = 0.42$.

Try These

In Exercises 1–3, use a model to find the product.

1. 0.3×0.8 **2.** 0.5×0.9 **3.** 0.4×0.4

4. In Exercises 1–3, how do the numbers of decimal places in the factors relate to the number of decimal places in the product?

5. **ERROR ANALYSIS** Describe and correct the error.

~~0.4 × 0.2 = 0.8~~

6. **MATHEMATICAL REASONING** Predict what the product 0.06×0.07 is. Explain your reasoning, and use a model to illustrate.

SAMPLE 2 Modeling Multiplication

You can use a model to find the product 1.3 × 2.5.

Here's How

Use six 10-by-10 squares arranged in a rectangle, as shown. Let the area of each 10-by-10 square represent 1, so the area of a small square is $\frac{1}{100}$, or 0.01. Shade 13 rows of the rectangle red and 25 columns blue.

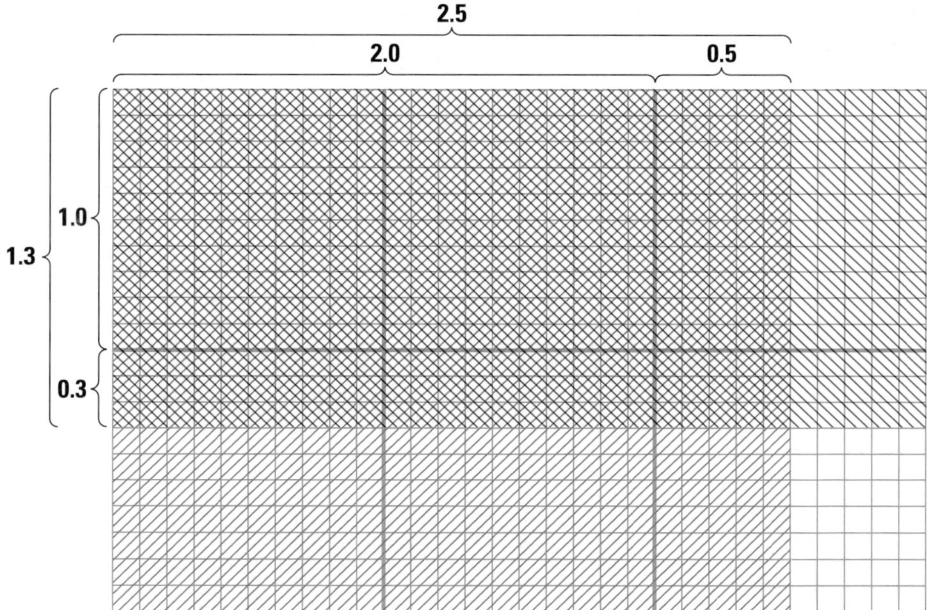

There are 100 + 30 + 100 + 30 + 50 + 15 = 325 small squares doubly shaded. Since 325 hundredths equals 3.25, 1.3 × 2.5 = 3.25.

Try These

7. Use a model to find the product 13 × 25. How does the product 13 × 25 compare with the product 1.3 × 2.5 from Sample 2?

8. How do the numbers of decimal places in the factors in Sample 2 relate to the number of decimal places in the product?

Predict the number of decimal places in the product. Then check your answer by using a calculator to find the product.

9. 0.2 × 1.98 **10.** 1.45 × 1.37 **11.** 2.981 × 1.43

1.8 Multiplying Decimals

In this lesson you'll:

- Calculate and solve multiplication problems, including those arising from concrete situations. (NS 2.0)
- Solve problems involving rates, average speed, distance, and time. (AF 2.3)

Goal 1 Multiplying Decimals

In Developing Concepts 1.8, page 36, you learned how to model decimal multiplication. Decimal multiplication is similar to multiplication with whole numbers. The number of decimal places in the product is equal to the sum of the number of decimal places in the factors.

EXAMPLE 1 Multiplying Decimals

Find the product 3.06×1.4. Use estimation to check that your answer is reasonable.

Solution

3.06	2 decimal places
× 1.4	1 decimal place
1224	
306	
4.284	2 + 1 = 3, so the product has 3 decimal places.

CHECK ✓ The answer seems reasonable because it is greater than $3 \times 1 = 3$ and less than $3 \times 2 = 6$.

EXAMPLE 2 Multiplying Decimals

1.46	2 decimal places
× 0.02	2 decimal places
0.0292	2 + 2 = 4, so the product has 4 decimal places.

Student Help

STUDY TIP
Write 0 in front of 292 to make 4 decimal places in the product.

EXAMPLE 3 Evaluating an Expression

Evaluate $x^2 + 3x$ when $x = 1.72$. Round your answer to the nearest hundredth.

Solution

$x^2 + 3x = (\mathbf{1.72})^2 + 3(\mathbf{1.72})$ Substitute 1.72 for *x*.

$= 2.9584 + 5.16$ Multiply decimals.

$= 8.1184$ Add decimals.

≈ 8.12 Round to nearest hundredth.

Student Help

▶ **SKILLS REVIEW**
For help with perimeter, see page 562.

You can use the formulas below to find the perimeter P of rectangles and squares.

RECTANGLE

$P = 2\ell + 2w$

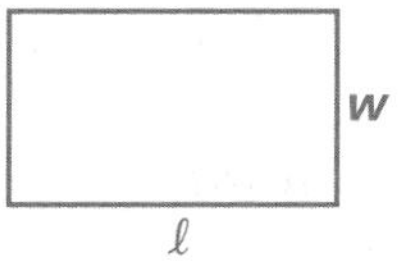

SQUARE

$P = 4s$

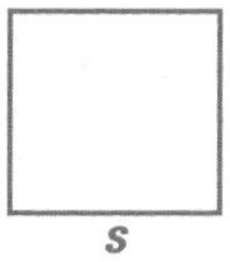

EXAMPLE 4 Finding the Perimeter of a Rectangle

Find the perimeter of the rectangle shown.

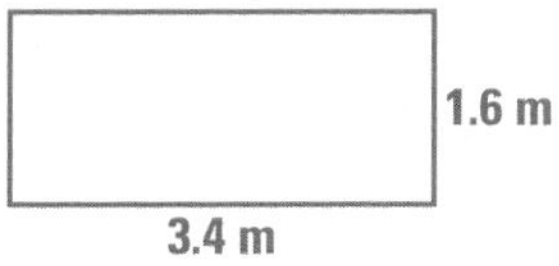

Solution

$P = 2\ell + 2w$	Perimeter of a rectangle
$= 2 \cdot \mathbf{3.4} + 2 \cdot \mathbf{1.6}$	Substitute 3.4 for ℓ and 1.6 for w.
$= 6.8 + 3.2$	First multiply from left to right.
$= 10$ m	Then add.

ANSWER ▶ The perimeter is 10 meters.

Student Help

▶ **STUDY TIP**
Speed is an example of a *rate*. That is why the variable r is used to represent speed. The formula $d = rt$ is often read as "distance equals rate times time."

Goal 2 SOLVING DISTANCE PROBLEMS

Speeds are measured in units such as miles per hour, feet per second, and kilometers per hour. When calculating with speeds, it helps to write them using fraction notation.

DISTANCE TRAVELED

In Words To find the distance traveled, multiply the speed by the time. That is, distance = (speed) × (time).

In Algebra $d = rt$

In Arithmetic Distance $= \frac{30\text{ mi}}{1\,\cancel{\text{h}}} \times 2\,\cancel{\text{h}} = 60$ mi

EXAMPLE 5 Finding the Distance Traveled

BIRDS A hummingbird flies at a rate of 28 miles per hour for half an hour. How far does the hummingbird fly?

Solution

$d = rt$	Write formula for distance.
$= \frac{28\text{ mi}}{1\,\cancel{\text{h}}} \times \mathbf{0.5}\,\cancel{\text{h}}$	Substitute 28 for r and 0.5 for t.
$= 14$ mi	Multiply.

ANSWER ▶ The hummingbird flies 14 miles.

Bee hummingbird (actual size)

1.8 Exercises

Guided Practice

Without multiplying, tell how many decimal places are in the product.

1. 0.08×5.2 **2.** 12.23×4.563 **3.** 44.358×3.001

Find the product. Use estimation to check that your answer is reasonable.

4. 0.63×31 **5.** 9.84×1.17 **6.** 8.55×3.26

ALGEBRA **In Exercises 7–9, evaluate the expression when $x = 2.61$. Round your answer to the nearest hundredth.**

7. $5x$ **8.** $4x + 5.269$ **9.** $6x - x^2$

10. You walk at a speed of 3.1 miles per hour for 1.25 hours. How far do you walk? Round your answer to one decimal place.

Practice and Problem Solving

Student Help

▶ MORE PRACTICE Extra practice to help you master skills is on page 567.

Use estimation to match the multiplication problem with its answer.

A. 12.22 **B.** 1.222 **C.** 122.2 **D.** 0.1222

11. 52×2.35 **12.** 0.52×0.235 **13.** 5.2×0.235 **14.** 5.2×2.35

Rewrite the product with the decimal point in the correct place.

15. $4.1 \times 2.5 = 1025$ **16.** $6.113 \times 31 = 189503$

17. $2.01 \times 8.01 = 161001$ **18.** $5.6 \times 2.115 = 118440$

19. MATHEMATICAL REASONING Multiply 2000 by 0.2, 0.5, 0.8, 0.9, 0.95, and 0.99. Explain what happens to the product as the second factor gets closer and closer to 1.

Find the product. Use estimation to check your answer.

20. 5.1×0.02 **21.** 0.985×2.5 **22.** 2.25×5.61

23. 7.72×0.08 **24.** 8.57×9.44 **25.** 5.89×1.125

26. 0.41×3.507 **27.** 0.034×8.802 **28.** 6.643×1.495

GEOMETRY **Find the perimeter and the area of the rectangle.**

29. 1.3 mm, 2.9 mm

30.

31.

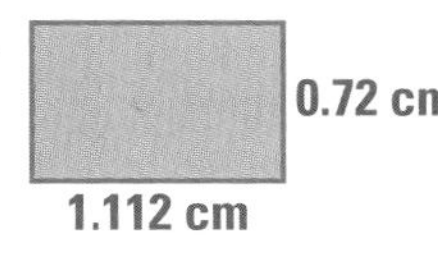

ALGEBRA In Exercises 32–37, evaluate the expression. Round your answer to the nearest hundredth.

32. y^2 when $y = 6.22$

33. x^3 when $x = 1.6$

34. $w^2 - 2w$ when $w = 4.27$

35. $5k + k^2$ when $k = 0.82$

36. $mn - n$ when $m = 2.2$ and $n = 1.23$

37. $x^2 + y$ when $x = 0.35$ and $y = 3.9$

38. The area of the rectangle is given by $x^2 + xy$. Find the area when $x = 6.7$ inches and $y = 11$ inches.

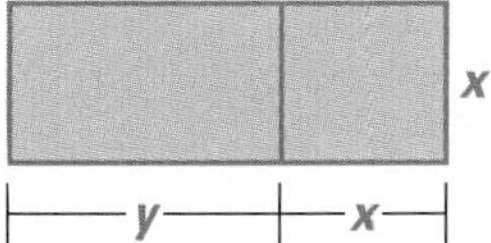

CAREERS In Exercises 39–42, use the table, which shows the average hourly pay for a college graduate just starting a career in 1997.

▶ Source: US Bureau of the Census

39. Find the weekly pay for an engineering graduate who works 40 hours per week.

40. Find the weekly pay for a social sciences graduate who works 40 hours per week.

41. Find the difference between the weekly pay for an engineering graduate and a social sciences graduate.

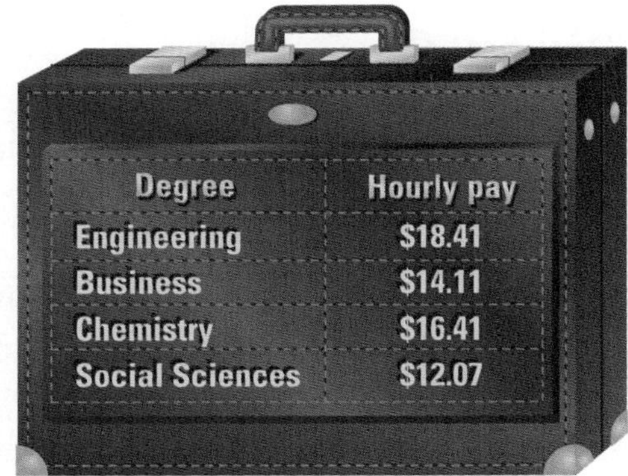

Degree	Hourly pay
Engineering	$18.41
Business	$14.11
Chemistry	$16.41
Social Sciences	$12.07

42. CHALLENGE Find the difference between the yearly salary for an engineering graduate and a social sciences graduate. Assume that both people work 40 hours per week for 52 weeks.

In Exercises 43–46, find the distance traveled. Round your answer to the nearest tenth.

43. $\frac{59.5 \text{ miles}}{1 \text{ hour}} \times 3.5$ hours

44. $\frac{5.75 \text{ kilometers}}{1 \text{ hour}} \times 2.2$ hours

45. $\frac{8.5 \text{ miles}}{1 \text{ minute}} \times 120.8$ minutes

46. $\frac{16.4 \text{ feet}}{1 \text{ second}} \times 7.25$ seconds

47. AIRPLANES On August 15–16, 1995, the Concorde, one of the world's first supersonic commercial planes, flew around the world. It completed the trip in 31.46 hours and traveled at a speed of 1114 miles per hour. How far did the Concorde travel? ▶ Source: *The World Almanac*

48. SILK You want to purchase 2.5 yards of silk fabric. The price of the silk fabric is $17.95 per yard. What will be your total cost?

49. RUNNING The perimeter of a soccer field is 356.62 meters. You run 12 laps around the field at a speed of 134.4 meters per minute. How far do you run?

SILK It is thought that silk was discovered in China about 2700 B.C.

INTERNET More about silk available at www.mcdougallittell.com

Multiple-Choice Practice

50. Find the product of 2.58 and 0.06.

Ⓐ 0.1548 Ⓑ 1.548 Ⓒ 15.48 Ⓓ 154.8

51. Find the area of the rectangle shown.

Ⓕ 6.24 cm^2 Ⓖ 36.48 cm^2

Ⓗ 364.8 cm^2 Ⓙ 62.4 cm^2

Test Tip Ⓐ Ⓑ Ⓒ Ⓓ

▶ **TEST TIP** In Exercise 52, use estimation to approximate the answer before doing any calculations.

52. Your family goes on a camping trip. At a speed of 65 miles per hour, it takes 4.25 hours to get to the campground. How far do you travel?

Ⓐ 2.7625 miles Ⓑ 27.625 miles

Ⓒ 276.25 miles Ⓓ 2762.5 miles

Mixed Review

53. Name the dividend and the divisor in the problem $40 \div 10 = 4$. *(1.2)*

54. Find numbers for x, y, and z so that $y \div z \cdot x = 64$. *(1.3)*

In Exercises 55–57, evaluate the expression. *(1.4)*

55. $6 + 7 \times 2^3$ **56.** $80 - (2^3 - 5)$ **57.** $(2^2 + 4^2) - 4 \div 2$

58. LIBRARY SCIENCE Many libraries use the Dewey decimal system to assign a decimal "call number" to a book according to its subject. Write the books in order from least to greatest by their call numbers. *(1.5)*

Book	Dewey decimal number
Mexico's Volcanoes	917.2
Yucatán Peninsula	917.26
Cancún Handbook	917.267
Bicycling Baja	917.22
Mexico	917.203

Find the average of the set of numbers. Round the average to the nearest tenth. *(1.6)*

59. 2, 4, 2, 6, 8, 7, 3, 4, 5, 7, 5 **60.** 18, 20, 16, 21, 19, 23, 19

61. 50, 65, 62, 58, 52, 59, 61, 55 **62.** 80, 60, 70, 60, 90, 100, 110

Use a vertical format to add or subtract. *(1.7)*

63. $2.7 + 3.1$ **64.** $3.05 + 8.4$ **65.** $0.25 + 10$

66. $4.7 - 1.8$ **67.** $9 - 6.5$ **68.** $0.7 - 0.02$

1.9 Dividing Decimals

California Standards

In this lesson you'll:

- Calculate and solve division problems, including those arising from concrete situations. (NS 2.0)
- Make precise calculations and check the validity of the results from the context of the problem. (MR 2.7)

Goal 1 DIVIDING A DECIMAL BY A WHOLE NUMBER

To divide a decimal by a whole number, use long division as you would with whole numbers. Line up the decimal places in the quotient with the decimal places in the dividend.

EXAMPLE 1 *Using Long Division*

Use long division to find $6.9 \div 3$.

Solution

$\begin{array}{r} 2.3 \\ 3\overline{)6.9} \end{array}$	Line up the decimal places.
$\underline{6}\downarrow$	$2 \times 3 = 6$
0 9	Subtract. Bring down the 9.
$\underline{9}$	$3 \times 3 = 9$
0	Subtract.

ANSWER ▶ $6.9 \div 3 = 2.3$

Student Help

▶**SKILLS REVIEW**
For help with long division, see page 558.

EXAMPLE 2 *Using Long Division in Real Life*

RESTAURANT A restaurant bill for 6 people is \$43.10. They decide to split the bill evenly. What is each person's share?

Solution

To find each person's share, divide \$43.10 by 6.

7.183	Line up the decimal places.
$6\overline{)43.100}$	Write 0 to make 3 places in the dividend.
$\underline{42}\downarrow$	$7 \times 6 = 42$
1 1	Subtract. Bring down the 1.
$\underline{6}\downarrow$	$1 \times 6 = 6$
50	Subtract. Bring down the 0.
$\underline{48}\downarrow$	$8 \times 6 = 48$
20	Subtract. Bring down the 0.
$\underline{18}$	$3 \times 6 = 18$
2	Subtract. Remainder is 2.

ANSWER ▶ Rounded to the nearest cent, each share is \$7.18. If each person pays this amount, however, the total is $6 \times \$7.18$, or \$43.08. So, two people must pay \$.01 more.

Student Help

▶**STUDY TIP**
When you divide with decimals, you can use estimation to check whether you have put the decimal point in the right position. In Example 2, since $42 \div 6 = 7$, you know that the answer is about 7, not 0.7 or 70.

Goal 2 Dividing a Decimal by a Decimal

Look at the division problems below. Notice that multiplying the divisor and the dividend by a multiple of 10 does not change the quotient. This is also the case when dividing by a decimal.

$$8 \div 4 = 2$$

$$80 \div 40 = 2$$

$$800 \div 400 = 2$$

To divide by a decimal, convert the division problem to a related one with a whole number divisor that has the same answer.

Dividing by a Decimal

In both divisor and dividend, move the decimal point the same number of places in the same direction. To do this, multiply both by the power of 10 that will make the divisor a whole number.

EXAMPLE 3 Dividing a Decimal

Divide using long division. Check your answer by multiplying.

a. 2.46 ÷ 0.3

b. 28 ÷ 0.02

Solution

a. Multiply the divisor and dividend by **10**.

$0.3\overline{)2.46}$ Move decimal points 1 place.

Solve the related division by a whole number.

$$\begin{array}{r} 8.2 \\ 3\overline{)24.6} \\ \underline{24} \\ 0\,6 \\ \underline{6} \\ 0 \end{array}$$

ANSWER ▶ Because 24.6 ÷ 3 = 8.2, 2.46 ÷ 0.3 = 8.2.

CHECK ✓ Multiply quotient by divisor.

$$\begin{array}{rl} 8.2 & \text{Quotient} \\ \times\ 0.3 & \text{Divisor} \\ \hline 2.46 & \text{Dividend} \end{array}$$

b. Multiply the divisor and dividend by **100**.

$0.02\overline{)28.00}$ Move decimal points 2 places.

Solve the related division by a whole number.

$$\begin{array}{r} 1400. \\ 2\overline{)2800.} \\ \underline{2} \\ 08 \\ \underline{8} \\ 0 \end{array}$$

Fill quotient with zeros up to the decimal point.

ANSWER ▶ Because 2800 ÷ 2 = 1400, 28 ÷ 0.02 = 1400.

CHECK ✓ Multiply quotient by divisor.

$$\begin{array}{rl} 1400 & \text{Quotient} \\ \times\ 0.02 & \text{Divisor} \\ \hline 28.00 & \text{Dividend} \end{array}$$

Student Help

▶ **More Examples**

More examples are available at www.mcdougallittell.com

1.9 Exercises

Guided Practice

1. **WRITING** Explain how to divide a decimal by a whole number using long division.

Divide using long division. Use estimation to decide whether your answer is reasonable.

2. 10.8 ÷ 4 3. 6.5 ÷ 2 4. 9.9 ÷ 3 5. 4.6 ÷ 4

Explain why the statement is false. Change exactly one word to make it true.

6. Before dividing decimals, you should change the quotient to a whole number.

7. Moving a decimal point two places to the right is the same as multiplying by 1000.

Divide using long division. Check your answer by multiplying.

8. 1.32 ÷ 6 9. 13.2 ÷ 0.6 10. 1.32 ÷ 0.6 11. 13.2 ÷ 0.06

Practice and Problem Solving

Student Help

▶ MORE PRACTICE
Extra practice to help you master skills is on page 567.

Divide using long division. Use estimation to decide whether your answer is reasonable.

12. 8.25 ÷ 5 13. 17.4 ÷ 3 14. 133.6 ÷ 8

15. 100.38 ÷ 21 16. 45.6 ÷ 12 17. 99.36 ÷ 4

18. 4.755 ÷ 3 19. 451.92 ÷ 8 20. 84.357 ÷ 7

ERROR ANALYSIS In Exercises 21–23, describe and correct the error in the problem. Explain how you know the answer is wrong.

21.
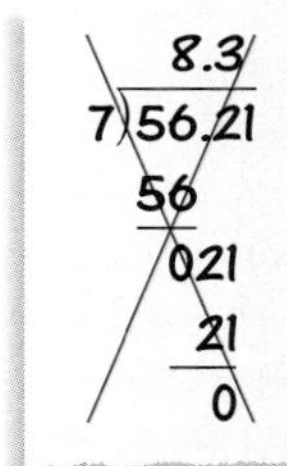

22.
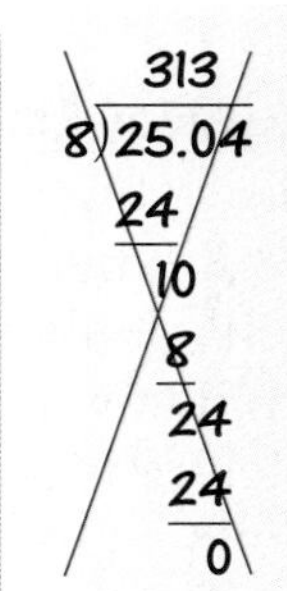

23.
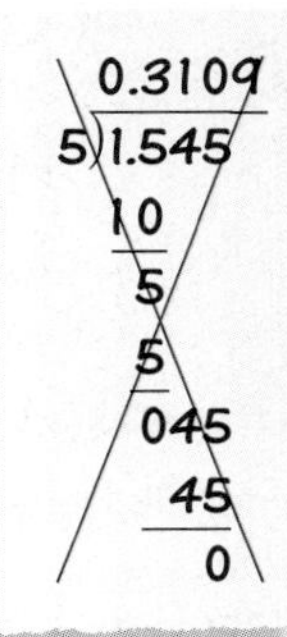

Student Help

▶ HOMEWORK HELP
Extra help with problem solving in Ex. 24 is available at www.mcdougallittell.com

24. **WOODWORKING** You are building a birdhouse from a piece of wood that is 56.25 inches long and 9.5 inches wide. You divide the wood into 5 pieces of the same length. Draw a diagram of this division. Find the dimensions of each piece.

25. **RESTAURANT** A restaurant bill for 12 people is \$118.32. The people split the bill evenly. Find each person's share.

26. **FRUIT** The cost for 3.5 pounds of apples is \$4.55. What is the cost per pound?

READING In Exercises 27–29, use the table. It shows the amount of money spent per year per person on reading material in the United States.

▶ Source: Veronis, Suhler & Associates

Year	1994	1995	1996
Newspapers	\$49.12	\$50.08	\$50.95
Magazines	\$36.36	\$36.10	\$36.63
Books	\$80.28	\$81.39	\$82.98

27. Find the average amount spent per person each week on books in 1994.

28. Find the average amount spent per person each month in each category in 1996.

29. Was the average amount spent per person each week on newspapers greater in 1994 or 1996?

MATHEMATICAL REASONING In Exercises 30 and 31, complete the statement using *sometimes*, *always*, or *never*. Give an example.

30. A decimal between 0 and 1 divided by a whole number other than 0 is __?__ greater than 1.

31. A whole number other than 0 divided by a decimal between 0 and 1 is __?__ greater than 1.

Divide using long division. Check your answer by multiplying.

32. $10.4 \div 0.8$
33. $0.36 \div 0.9$
34. $3.14 \div 0.2$
35. $33 \div 0.11$
36. $24.75 \div 2.2$
37. $0.816 \div 0.68$
38. $7.85 \div 0.005$
39. $204.02 \div 5.05$
40. $500 \div 0.25$

41. **Science Link** In the photo at the right, the onion cell is about 48 millimeters wide. The actual cell is only 0.04 millimeters wide. Find how many times larger the picture is than the actual cell by dividing 48 by 0.04.

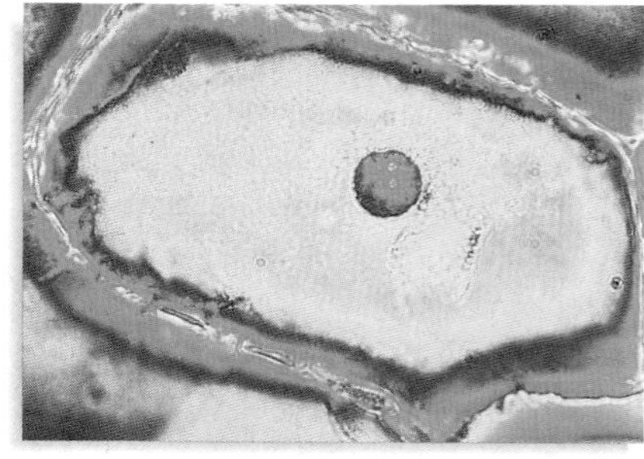

SPEED Find the animal's speed in miles per minute. (*Hint:* Divide by 60.)

42. Elk: 45 mi/h
43. Horse: 47.5 mi/h
44. Snail: 0.03 mi/h

ELK American elk, also known as wapiti, are members of the deer family. Male elk weigh 700 to 1100 pounds and grow antlers that can span more than 5 feet.

GEOMETRY Find the length of the side labeled *s* in the rectangle.

45. Area is 11.7 m^2.

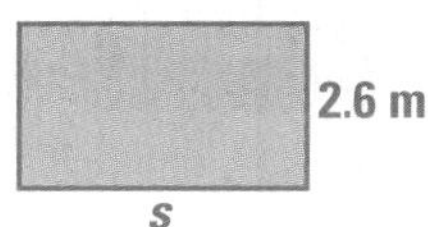

46. Area is 90.25 km^2.

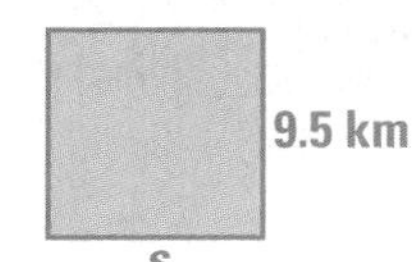

CALCULATOR Evaluate the expression. You may wish to use a calculator.

47. $3.34 + 6.4 \div 0.032$

48. $21.9 \div 0.073 - 40.5 \div 0.5$

WRITING In Exercises 49 and 50, write a word problem to match the description.

49. A problem solved by dividing a decimal by a whole number

50. A problem solved by dividing a decimal by a decimal

51. **WEATHER** The table below shows the monthly precipitation in inches for San Francisco in 1998. Find the average monthly precipitation.

▶ Source: U.S. National Oceanic and Atmospheric Administration

January	February	March	April	May	June
4.35	3.17	3.06	1.37	0.19	0.11
July	**August**	**September**	**October**	**November**	**December**
0.03	0.05	0.20	1.22	2.86	3.09

52. **CHALLENGE** Nancy wants to buy a car. She has saved \$700 so far and continues to save \$24.50 each week. The price of the car she wants to buy is \$1729. How many more weeks will she have to save?

Multiple-Choice Practice

53. Find the length of the side labeled *x* in the rectangle shown.

Ⓐ 10.1 centimeters　Ⓑ 2.5 centimeters

Ⓒ 5.5 centimeters　Ⓓ Not here

54. The perimeter of a square is 22.68 inches. How long is one side of the square?

Ⓕ 4.76 in.　Ⓖ 5.67 in.　Ⓗ 11.34 in.　Ⓙ 56.7 in.

55. Your uncle pays \$15.75 to fill up the gas tank in his car. If the tank holds 12.6 gallons, what is the cost per gallon?

Ⓐ \$.13　Ⓑ \$1.20　Ⓒ \$1.25　Ⓓ \$12.50

Chapter 1 Chapter Summary and Review

VOCABULARY

- **numerical expression,** *p. 7*
- **evaluating an expression,** *p. 7*
- **variable,** *p. 8*
- **value of a variable,** *p. 8*
- **variable expression,** *p. 8*
- **grouping symbols,** *p. 12*
- **commutative property** *p. 13*
- **associative property** *p. 13*
- **power, exponent, base** *p. 17*
- **decimal,** *p. 21*
- **number line,** *p. 21*
- **graphing a number,** *p. 21*
- **average, mean,** *p. 28*
- **polygon,** *p. 31*
- **perimeter,** *p. 31*

1.1 Problem Solving and Reasoning

Examples on pp. 3–4

EXAMPLE You ordered 10 boxes of pens to sell at your store. Each box contains 35 pens. You have four boxes left. How many pens did you sell?

Understand the Problem Use the number of boxes left to find the number of pens sold.

Make a Plan Find the number of boxes sold. Multiply the answer by the number of pens per box.

Solve the Problem To find the number of boxes sold, subtract 4 from 10. $10 - 4 = 6$.
To find the number of pens sold, multiply 6 by 35. $6 \times 35 = 210$.

Look Back Work backwards to check. You sold 210 pens, or 6 boxes. You are left with 4 boxes. So, you must have started with $6 + 4 = 10$ boxes of pens.

1. You buy 6 trees and some shrubs. The trees are \$12 each and the shrubs are \$7 each. You have \$100. How many shrubs can you buy?

1.2 Expressions and Variables

Examples on pp. 7–9

EXAMPLE **Evaluate $d \div r$ when $d = 30$ and $r = 6$.**

$d \div r = 30 \div 6$ Substitute 30 for *d* and 6 for *r*.

$= 5$ Simplify.

Evaluate the expression.

2. $8n$ when $n = 11$

3. $y - 25$ when $y = 75$

4. $g \div h$ when $g = 12$ and $h = 3$

1.3 ORDER OF OPERATIONS

Examples on pp. 12–14

EXAMPLE **Evaluate the expression 43 − 6 × (4 + 3).**

$43 - 6 \times (4 + 3) = 43 - 6 \times \mathbf{7}$ Simplify within grouping symbols.

$= 43 - 42$ Multiply from left to right.

$= 1$ Subtract from left to right.

In Exercises 5–7, evaluate the expression.

5. $50 - (6 \times 8) + 3$ **6.** $25 \div 5 \div 5$ **7.** $5 \times (3 + 7) - 8$

8. You wash seven cars. You earn $5 per car and receive $4 in tips. Write and evaluate a numerical expression to show the total amount you earn.

9. Use mental math to evaluate 125 + 67 + 875. Justify each step.

1.4 POWERS AND EXPONENTS

Examples on pp. 17–18

EXAMPLE **Evaluate the expression $(6 + 7) - 3 \times 2^2$.**

$(6 + 7) - 3 \times 2^2 = \mathbf{13} - 3 \times 2^2$ Simplify within grouping symbols.

$= 13 - 3 \times \mathbf{4}$ Evaluate power.

$= 13 - 12$ Multiply from left to right.

$= 1$ Subtract from left to right.

In Exercises 10–12, evaluate the expression.

10. $25 + 3^3 \times 2$ **11.** $(5 - 3)^4$ **12.** $4x^2$ when $x = 3$

13. The area of the rectangle is given by $2x^2 + 8x$. Evaluate the area when $x = 5$ feet.

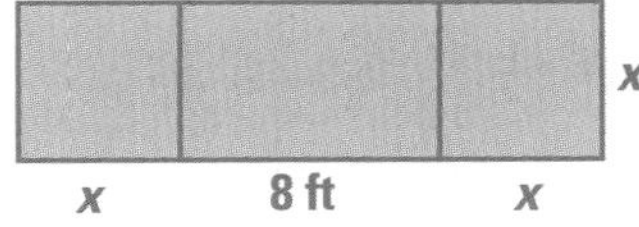

1.5 COMPARING AND ORDERING DECIMALS

Examples on pp. 21–22

You can order decimals by plotting them on a number line. To compare two decimals, compare their place values from left to right.

EXAMPLE **Use a number line to compare 1.45 and 1.54.**

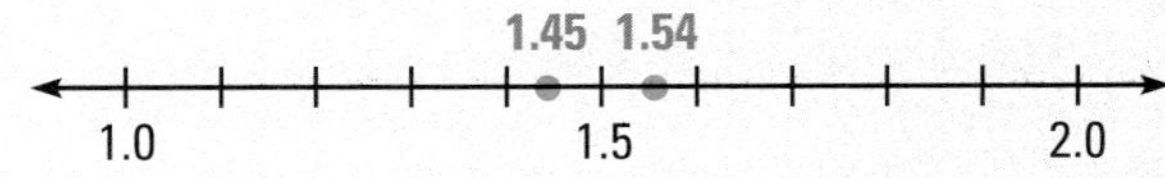

Because 1.45 is to the left of 1.54, 1.45 < 1.54 or 1.54 > 1.45.

The table gives the winning times (in seconds) for the women's 100 meter dash in the Olympics.

Year	1984	1988	1992	1996
Time	10.97	10.54	10.82	10.94

14. Compare the times of 1984 and 1996. Which time is faster?

15. Order the times from least to greatest.

1.6 ROUNDING DECIMALS

Examples on pp. 27–28

To round a number to a given place value, look at the digit to its right. Round down if the digit is 4 or less. Round up if the digit is 5 or more.

EXAMPLES 2.177, rounded to the nearest hundredth, rounds up to 2.18.

11.44, rounded to the nearest tenth, rounds down to 11.4.

In Exercises 16–18, round the number to the given place value.

16. 516,583 (hundreds) **17.** 2.9434 (thousandths) **18.** 10.4 (ones)

19. The prices (in U.S. dollars) of toothpaste in different cities around the world are shown below. Round each price to the nearest dollar.

City	Paris	Athens	London	Rome	Toronto
Price	$2.86	$3.19	$4.32	$3.57	$1.51

1.7 ADDING AND SUBTRACTING DECIMALS

Examples on pp. 31–32

EXAMPLES

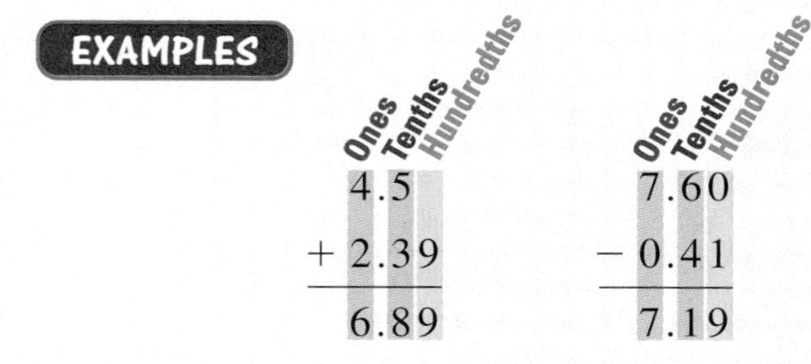

The table gives the prices at a school store.

Eraser	Pencil	Pen
$.33	$.22	$1.25

20. What is the total cost of a pen and an eraser?

21. Does an eraser cost more than a pencil? If so, how much more?

1.8 MULTIPLYING DECIMALS

Examples on pp. 38–39

When you multiply decimals, the number of decimal places in the product is equal to the sum of the number of decimal places in the factors.

EXAMPLE **Find the product of 0.25 × 1.3.**

0.25	2 decimal places
× 1.3	1 decimal place
075	
0 25	
0.325	2 + 1 = 3, so the product has 3 decimal places.

In Exercises 22–25, find the product. Use estimation to check your answer.

22. 4.52 × 12.35 **23.** 1300 × 0.06 **24.** 0.25 × 16.1 **25.** 0.47 × 3.8

26. A train travels for 8.5 hours at a speed of 50 miles per hour. Find the distance the train travels.

1.9 DIVIDING DECIMALS

Examples on pp. 43–44

To divide by a decimal, move the decimal point the same number of places in the divisor and the dividend.

$$0.45\overline{)1.395}\ \text{quotient } 3.1$$

Multiply divisor and dividend by **100**.
Move the decimal point **2** places to the right.

EXAMPLE **Use long division to find 1.395 ÷ 0.45.**

3.1 / 45)139.5	Line up the decimal places.
135↓	3 × 45 = 135
45	Subtract. Bring down the 5.
45	1 × 45 = 45
0	Subtract.

In Exercises 27–30, divide using long division. Check by multiplying.

27. 2.89 ÷ 17 **28.** 4.047 ÷ 0.095 **29.** 57.3 ÷ 0.003 **30.** 231.84 ÷ 12.6

31. The average person in the United States ate 2.1 pounds of frozen yogurt in 1997. How much is this per month? ▶ Source: U.S. Department of Agriculture

32. The area of the rectangle at the right is 3.75 square meters. Find the length of the side labeled x.

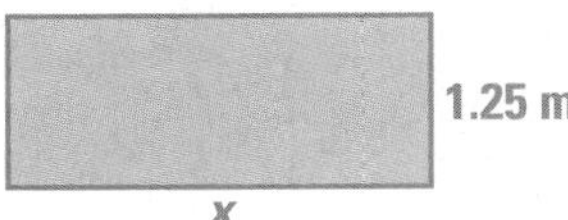

Chapter 1 Chapter Test

1. **HOCKEY** You take \$25 to a hockey game. Your friend takes \$15. You leave the game with \$9. How much have you spent?

2. **HIKING** At 7:45 A.M. you begin a 12 mile hike. At 8:20 A.M. you have hiked one mile. If you hike at the same speed the entire day, how many more hours will it take you to finish your hike?

Identify the property that the statement illustrates.

3. $4 \cdot 2 = 2 \cdot 4$
4. $8 + 5 = 5 + 8$
5. $(1 + 2) + 3 = 1 + (2 + 3)$

In Exercises 6–13, evaluate the expression.

6. $(10 + 5) \times 4$
7. $(27 - 3) \div 8$
8. $57 - 45 \div 3$
9. $2 \times 9 + 3$
10. 3^4
11. $1 + 5^2$
12. $(2 + 4)^2 \div 9$
13. $4^2 - 3^2$

14. Draw a number line from 3.2 to 3.3. Show nine tick marks to divide the line into 10 equal parts. Label each tick mark. Name three numbers on the line that are greater than 3.27.

Order the numbers from least to greatest.

15. 6.109, 6.2, 6.019, 6.19, 6.129

16. 32.89, 33.09, 32.94, 33.90, 32.08

POPULATION In Exercises 17 and 18, use the bar graph. It shows the average age of the U.S. population. ▶ Source: US Bureau of the Census

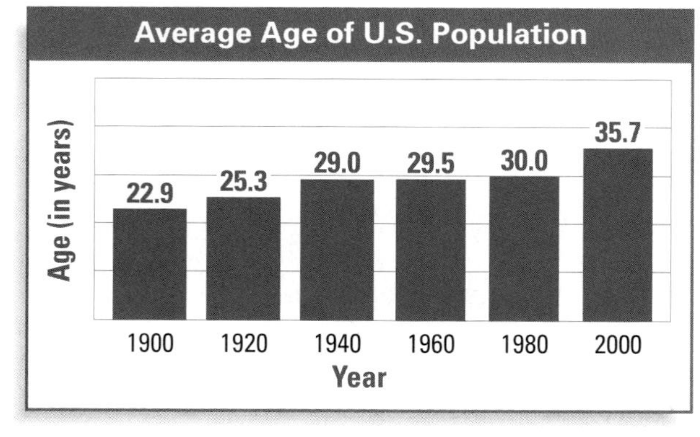

17. Round each number to nearest whole number.

18. Are the data still represented appropriately once you round the numbers? Explain.

Evaluate the expression. Round your answer to the nearest hundredth.

19. $5.6 - n$ when $n = 2.036$
20. $11y + 2y$ when $y = 0.78$
21. $3q^2 \div 4$ when $q = 1.02$

Find the indicated measurement.

22. Perimeter of polygon

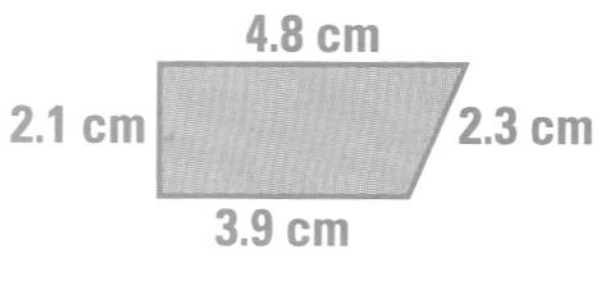

23. Area of rectangle

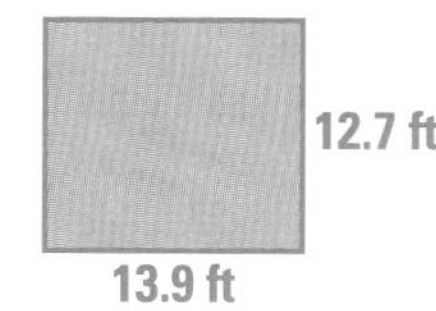

24. Side s of rectangle

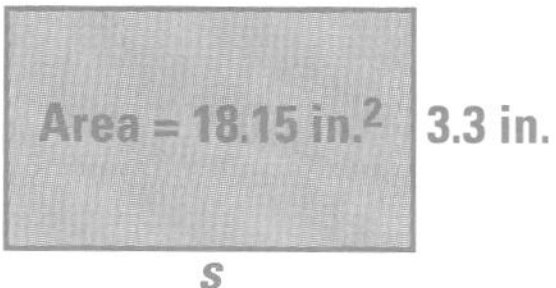

Multiple-Choice Practice

Test Tip Ⓐ Ⓑ Ⓒ Ⓓ Do the easy questions first. Then go back to the more difficult questions.

1. The Mayan calendar had 18 months. Each month had 20 days. At the end of each year, five extra days were added. Which expression represents the number of days in a Mayan year?

Ⓐ $(18 + 5) \times 20$

Ⓑ $(5 + 20) \times 18$

Ⓒ $18 \times 20 + 5$

Ⓓ $18 + 5 \times 20$

2. Evaluate $7 \times 3 + 4 - 2 \times 5$.

Ⓕ 135 Ⓖ 115

Ⓗ 39 Ⓙ 15

3. The area of a figure is given by $3x^2 + 5x$. What is the area when $x = 5$ centimeters?

Ⓐ 40 cm^2 Ⓑ 55 cm^2

Ⓒ 100 cm^2 Ⓓ 250 cm^2

4. You have 2^6 baseball cards. Ramona has 6^2 baseball cards. Richard has 6×2 baseball cards. Who has the most cards?

Ⓕ You

Ⓖ Ramona

Ⓗ Richard

Ⓙ You all have the same number.

5. Four tenths is less than which number?

Ⓐ 0.004 Ⓑ 0.04

Ⓒ 0.4 Ⓓ 4

6. What is 13.0285 rounded to the nearest hundredth?

Ⓕ 10 Ⓖ 13.0

Ⓗ 13.029 Ⓙ 13.03

7. You make $100 each week. What is the amount of your paycheck after the following deductions?

Federal Income Tax	$11.53
Social Security Tax	$6.27
Medicare Tax	$1.45
State Income Tax	$4.13

Ⓐ $77.62 Ⓑ $76.62

Ⓒ $23.38 Ⓓ $22.38

8. You buy 2 shirts that each cost $14.95 and a watch for $21.99. You pay $2.59 in sales tax. How much do you spend?

Ⓕ $39.53 Ⓖ $49.38

Ⓗ $54.48 Ⓙ $62.53

9. You run at a pace of 8.5 minutes per mile in a 26.2 mile marathon. How many minutes will it take to finish?

Ⓐ 2227 Ⓑ 222.7

Ⓒ 222 Ⓓ 22.7

10. Complete the statement: The quotient __?__ when the divisor is doubled.

Ⓕ is halved Ⓖ doubles

Ⓗ triples Ⓙ quadruples

Brain games

Decimal Shuffle

California Standards

- Calculate and solve problems involving multiplication and division. (NS 2.0)
- Develop generalizations of the results obtained and the strategies used and apply them in new problem situations. (MR 3.3)

Materials

- **30 cards, each labeled with a (decimal) × (multiple of 10)**
- **Calculators**

Directions

Object of the Game

Play in pairs or small groups. The player with the greatest product in each round keeps all the cards for that round. The student who collects all the cards, or the most cards if a time limit is placed, wins.

How to Play

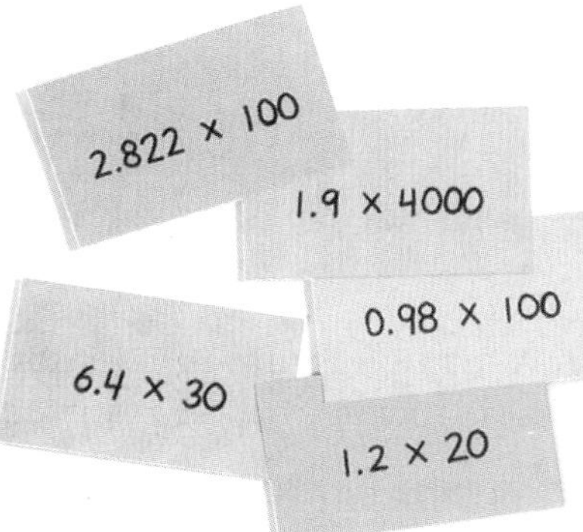

STEP 1 Players work together to make the game cards. One player shuffles all the cards and deals them out. Students turn over their top cards and mentally solve their own problem. Students take turns stating their solution. Opponents check solutions.

STEP 2 The student with the greatest product wins the round and collects all the cards. Play continues, with students shuffling and reusing cards as needed, until one player has all the cards or the game must end due to time restraints.

Another Way to Play

Player with the least product wins the round.

Brain Teaser

Targeting the solution

Use the numerals 2, 3, 5, and 8 to make multiplication or division problems with the following solutions:

26 66.5 28.4 4.16 2.75

The basic skills you'll review on this page will help prepare you for the next chapter.

Reviewing the Basics

EXAMPLE 1 Listing Multiples

A *multiple* of a number is the product of the number and any nonzero whole number.

Make an organized list to find the first 12 multiples of 8.

Solution

$1 \times 8 = 8$	$5 \times 8 = 40$	$9 \times 8 = 72$
$2 \times 8 = 16$	$6 \times 8 = 48$	$10 \times 8 = 80$
$3 \times 8 = 24$	$7 \times 8 = 56$	$11 \times 8 = 88$
$4 \times 8 = 32$	$8 \times 8 = 64$	$12 \times 8 = 96$

ANSWER ▶ The first 12 multiples of 8 are 8, 16, 24, 32, 40, 48, 56, 64, 72, 80, 88, and 96.

Try These

List the first 12 multiples of the given number.

1. 2 **2.** 4 **3.** 7 **4.** 9

5. 10 **6.** 12 **7.** 13 **8.** 20

9. 11 **10.** 15 **11.** 25 **12.** 100

EXAMPLE 2 Division with a Remainder

Find the quotient of $58 \div 4$.

Solution

$4\overline{)58}$ with quotient 14	Use long division.
4	$4 \times 1 = 4$
18	Subtract. Bring down the 8.
16	$4 \times 4 = 16$
2	Subtract. Remainder is 2.

ANSWER ▶ $58 \div 4 = 14$ R 2

Student Help

▶ **MORE EXAMPLES**

More examples and practice exercises available at www.mcdougallittell.com

Try These

Divide using long division.

13. $12 \div 5$ **14.** $20 \div 7$ **15.** $21 \div 8$

16. $25 \div 12$ **17.** $65 \div 15$ **18.** $53 \div 4$

19. $63 \div 8$ **20.** $123 \div 11$ **21.** $239 \div 9$

Number Relationships and Fractions

Why are number relationships and fractions important?

Fractions are used in many ways. For example, a fraction can describe a part of a whole, the division of two whole numbers, or a ratio. You will use fractions as you study proportions, percents, decimals, and probability.

Cryptographers (page 57) and agriculturists (page 76) use number relationships and fractions to do their jobs. For example, cryptographers use factors to create coded messages that can be read only by the person who has the key to decode them.

Meeting the California Standards

The skills you'll develop in this chapter will help you meet state standards and prepare for standardized tests. In this chapter you'll:

- **Write the prime factors of a number using exponents to show repeated factors.** LESSON 2.1
- **Determine the least common multiple and the greatest common divisor of whole numbers and use them to solve problems with fractions.** LESSONS 2.2, 2.4–2.6
- **Compare and order fractions, decimals, and mixed numbers and place them on a number line.** LESSONS 2.6–2.8

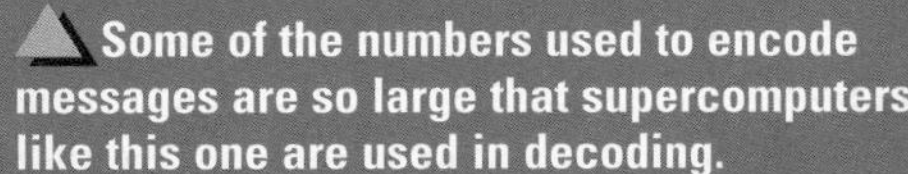
Some of the numbers used to encode messages are so large that supercomputers like this one are used in decoding.

Career Link **CRYPTOGRAPHER** A cryptographer uses number relationships when:

- creating a code for encrypting messages.
- predicting the difficulty of decoding an encrypted message.

EXERCISES

To keep e-mail and other electronic information private, cryptographers use large numbers that are difficult to factor. You can create a number that is difficult to factor by multiplying two large prime numbers together.

Multiply.

1. 11×19 **2.** 17×29 **3.** 13×31

In Lesson 2.1, you will use the encryption keys below to factor large numbers like the ones you just created.

Encryption Key A: A factor of the number is 29.

Encryption Key B: A factor of the number is 53.

Chapter 2 Getting Ready

PREVIEW What's the chapter about?

- Finding and applying **factors** and **multiples**
- Comparing and ordering **fractions** and **mixed numbers**
- Relating fractions and **decimals**

WORDS TO KNOW

- **prime number,** *p. 60*
- **composite number,** *p. 60*
- **prime factorization,** *p. 61*
- **factor tree,** *p. 61*
- **common factor,** *p. 65*
- **equivalent fractions,** *p. 73*
- **simplest form,** *p. 73*
- **multiple,** *p. 79*
- **least common multiple,** *p. 79*
- **least common denominator,** *p. 84*
- **improper fraction,** *p. 90*
- **mixed number,** *p. 90*

PREPARE Chapter Readiness Quiz

Take this quick quiz. If you are unsure of an answer, look back at the reference pages for help.

VOCABULARY CHECK *(refer to pp. 7, 21)*

$$4\overline{)232}\quad\text{quotient } 58$$

1. Which number is the divisor in the division problem shown?

Ⓐ 0 Ⓑ 4 Ⓒ 58 Ⓓ 232

2. The number 78.74 is which of the following?

Ⓕ Decimal Ⓖ Fraction Ⓗ Exponent Ⓙ Factor

SKILL CHECK *(refer to pp. 17, 22)*

3. Which of the following represents $3 \times 3 \times 3 \times 3 \times 3$?

Ⓐ 5×3 Ⓑ $5 + 3$ Ⓒ 3^5 Ⓓ 5^3

4. Which number is less than 5.062?

Ⓕ 5.06 Ⓖ 5.0620 Ⓗ 5.0634 Ⓙ 5.162

STUDY TIP Review Your Notes

Quickly review your notes from the current chapter each day. Doing this will help you spend less time studying for the chapter test.

Vocabulary

Prime number: A number greater than 1 whose only whole number factors are 1 and itself. Some examples are 2, 3, 5, 7, 11.

DEVELOPING CONCEPTS
Finding Factors

For use with Lesson 2.1

California Standards

▶ Use diagrams to explain mathematical reasoning. (MR 2.4)

MATERIALS

- Grid paper

A *factor* is a nonzero whole number that divides another nonzero whole number evenly. For example, 1, 2, 3, and 6 are all factors of 6.

SAMPLE 1 Writing Factors

You can find the factors of 12 by making rectangles out of 12 squares.

Here's How

1. Draw as many different rectangles as possible using 12 squares.
2. Label the length and width of each rectangle.
3. Use the lengths and widths to write 12 as a product.

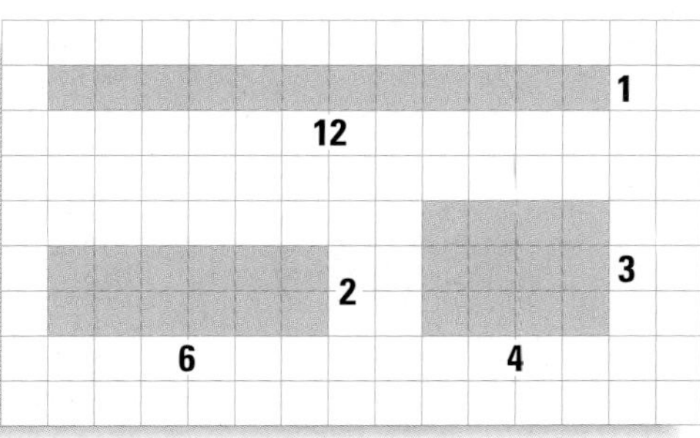

$12 \times 1, \quad 6 \times 2, \quad 4 \times 3$

ANSWER ▶ There are no other rectangles you can make with 12 squares, so 1, 2, 3, 4, 6, and 12 are all the factors of 12.

Student Help

▶ **STUDY TIP**
The products in Step 3 can also be written as 1×12, 2×6, and 3×4, but these products give you the same list of factors as in Sample 1.

Try These

Find all the factors of the number by making all of the possible rectangles using the given number of unit squares.

1. 14 **2.** 15 **3.** 8 **4.** 9 **5.** 13

6. In terms of its factors, how is the number 13 in Exercise 5 unlike all the other numbers in Exercises 1–5?

In Exercises 7–9, use the following information.
You can group the factors of a number by writing the factors in order from least to greatest and connecting pairs whose product is the number, as shown for the factors of 12.

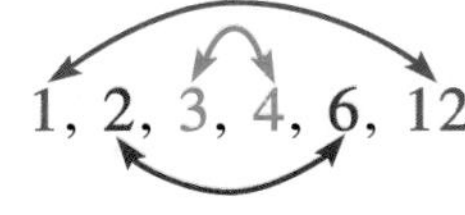

7. Write the factors of 24 from least to greatest. Group them in pairs.

8. **MATHEMATICAL REASONING** Is it possible for a number to have an odd number of factors? Explain and give an example.

9. **MATHEMATICAL REASONING** A student lists the factors of 20 as 1, 2, 5, 10, and 20. Explain how you can use pairing of factors to show that there is a factor missing.

2.1 Prime Factorization

In this lesson you'll:

- Write the prime factors of a number using exponents to show repeated factors. (Grade 5, NS 1.4)

Goal 1 CLASSIFYING PRIMES AND COMPOSITES

In Developing Concepts 2.1, page 59, whole numbers were written as the product of two whole number *factors*. When two nonzero whole numbers are multiplied together, each is a **factor** of the product. A nonzero whole number that is a factor of another nonzero whole number is also called a **divisor** of that number because it divides the number evenly.

$$7 \times 8 = 56$$

factors (7, 8) product (56)

Student Help

STUDY TIP
Noting that factors appear in pairs can help in checking that the list is complete.
1, 2, 3, 4, 6, 12

EXAMPLE 1 Finding Factors of a Number

To find all the factors of 12, make an organized list of products. Each product gives a pair of factors. Stop when the pairs of factors repeat.

WRITE 12 AS A PRODUCT.	FACTORS	
$12 = 1 \times 12$	1, 12	
$12 = 2 \times 6$	2, 6	
$12 = 3 \times 4$	3, 4	
$12 = 4 \times 3$	4, 3	Factors repeat.

ANSWER ▶ The factors of 12 are 1, 2, 3, 4, 6, and 12.

Whole numbers greater than 1 can be classified by the number of factors they have. A **prime number** is a number whose only whole number factors are 1 and itself. A **composite number** has factors other than 1 and itself. The number 1 is neither prime nor composite.

EXAMPLE 2 Classifying a Number as Prime or Composite

Tell whether 1, 2, 3, and 4 are *prime*, *composite*, or *neither*.

Solution

NUMBER	FACTORS	CONCLUSION
1	1	1 factor: neither prime nor composite
2	1, 2	2 factors: prime
3	1, 3	2 factors: prime
4	1, 2, 4	3 factors: composite

Goal 2 WRITING PRIME FACTORIZATIONS

Writing the **prime factorization** of a number means writing the number as the product of prime numbers.

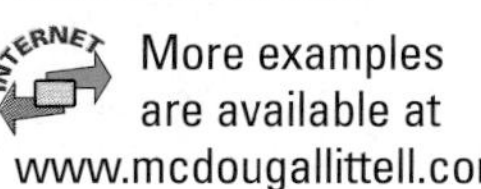

Student Help

▶MORE EXAMPLES

More examples are available at www.mcdougallittell.com

EXAMPLE 3 Writing the Prime Factorization

Write the prime factorization of the number.

a. 6 **b.** 15 **c.** 12

Solution

To write the prime factorization, factor each number. Continue factoring as necessary, until only prime factors are listed.

a. $6 = 2 \times 3$ Factor 6 as 2 times 3.

b. $15 = 3 \times 5$ Factor 15 as 3 times 5.

c. $12 = 3 \times 4$ Factor 12 as 3 times 4.

$= 3 \times 2 \times 2$ Factor 4 as 2 times 2.

$= 3 \times 2^2$ Write repeated multiplication as a power.

To write the prime factorization of a large number, it may help to use a **factor tree**, a diagram that can be used to show the factorization of a number, as shown in Example 4.

EXAMPLE 4 Writing the Prime Factorization

Write the prime factorization of 378.

Solution

To help organize all the factors of this larger number, first find two factors and then factor those as necessary. The factor tree is complete when only prime factors appear in the list of factors.

378

2×189 Factor 378 as 2 × 189.

$2 \times 3 \times 63$ Factor 189 as 3 × 63.

$2 \times 3 \times 3 \times 21$ Factor 63 as 3 × 21.

$2 \times 3 \times 3 \times 3 \times 7$ Factor 21 as 3 × 7.

$378 = 2 \times 3 \times 3 \times 3 \times 7$ Factor using factor tree.

$= 2 \times 3^3 \times 7$ Write repeated multiplication as a power.

ANSWER ▶ The prime factorization of 378 is $2 \times 3^3 \times 7$.

Student Help

▶STUDY TIP

There may be different factor trees for a given number, but the prime factorization will be the same. For example, here's another factor tree for 378.

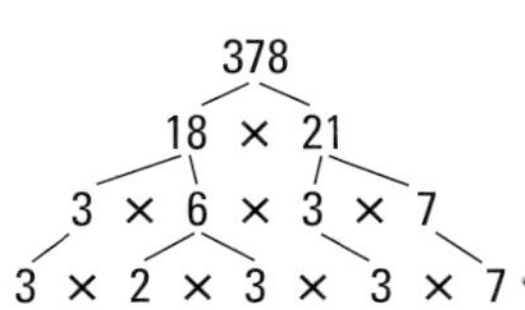

2.1 Exercises

Guided Practice

In Exercises 1 and 2, complete the statement.

1. A number with at least two whole number factors other than 1 is a(n) __?__ number.

2. Writing a number as the product of primes is called writing its __?__.

3. Name a nonzero whole number that is neither prime nor composite.

4. Name the only even prime number.

5. Find all the factors of 36.

Copy and complete the factor tree. Then write the prime factorization represented by the diagram.

6. 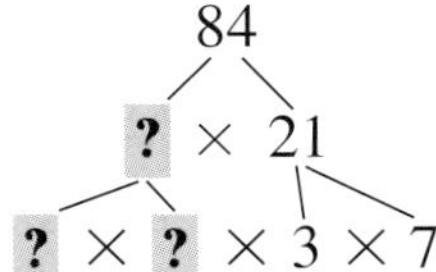

7. 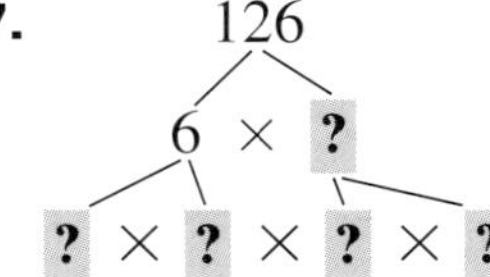

8. 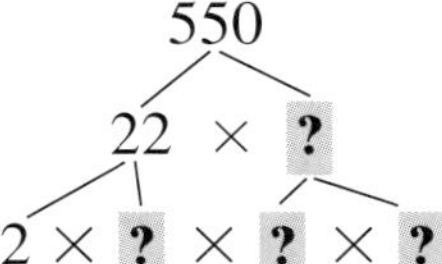

Practice and Problem Solving

> **Student Help**
>
> ▶ **MORE PRACTICE** Extra practice to help you master skills is on page 568.

In Exercises 9–16, find all the factors of the number.

9. 30	**10.** 42	**11.** 34	**12.** 99
13. 72	**14.** 87	**15.** 100	**16.** 88

17. Write the numbers from 5 to 25. For each number, tell whether it is *prime* or *composite*.

Tell whether the number is *prime* or *composite*.

18. 27	**19.** 31	**20.** 85	**21.** 47
22. 33	**23.** 81	**24.** 37	**25.** 794
26. 123	**27.** 197	**28.** 1000	**29.** 79
30. 53	**31.** 43	**32.** 69	**33.** 125

ALGEBRA Evaluate $3x + 5$ for the given value of x. Then tell whether the value of the expression is *prime* or *composite*.

34. $x = 8$	**35.** $x = 7$	**36.** $x = 9$	**37.** $x = 25$
38. $x = 21$	**39.** $x = 12$	**40.** $x = 10$	**41.** $x = 14$
42. $x = 18$	**43.** $x = 20$	**44.** $x = 100$	**45.** $x = 26$

Link to History

EUCLID Euclid was a Greek mathematician. He studied in Athens and then taught mathematics in Egypt.

More about Euclid is available at www.mcdougallittell.com

History Link Around 300 B.C. Euclid proved that no matter what number you choose, there is always a prime number larger than it. In Exercises 46–48, find a prime number that is larger than the given number.

46. 18 **47.** 75 **48.** 100

Copy and complete the factor tree. Then write the prime factorization represented by the diagram.

49.
32
2 × ?
2 × ? × 4
2 × ? × ? × ? × ?

50.
56
? × 8
? × ? × ?
? × ? × ? × ?

51.
120
12 × 10
? × ? × ? × ?
? × ? × ? × ? × ?

52.
?
? × ?
2 × 5 × 11

53.
?
? × ?
? × ? × ? × 4
2 × 2 × 3 × 2 × 2

54.
?
? × 6
4 × 5 × ? × 3
? × ? × ? × ? × 3

In Exercises 55–66, use a factor tree to write the prime factorization of the number.

55. 18 **56.** 33 **57.** 64 **58.** 75

59. 98 **60.** 140 **61.** 150 **62.** 144

63. 99 **64.** 135 **65.** 345 **66.** 222

67. Show two different factor trees for finding the prime factorization of 105. Show that the factor trees give the same prime factorization.

CALCULATOR **To encode information, computers use large numbers that have many prime factors. In Exercises 68–75, find the prime factorization of the number. You may wish to use a calculator.**

68. 5040 **69.** 672,000 **70.** 19,965 **71.** 16,170

72. 20,550 **73.** 90,000 **74.** 22,248 **75.** 30,336

Chapter Opener Link **Find the prime factorization of the number. If needed, use the suggested encryption key on page 57.**

76. 2958, (Key A) **77.** 3074, (Key B)

Student Help

▶ HOMEWORK HELP

Extra help with problem solving in Exs. 78–79 is available at www.mcdougallittell.com

MATHEMATICAL REASONING **Find the number described.**

78. A composite number is between 30 and 40. The sum of its prime factors is 12.

79. A composite number is between 31 and 50. It has an even number of factors. The sum of the prime factors is 16.

80. **MATHEMATICAL REASONING** Make a list of the odd numbers between 6 and 30. Can each number be written as the sum of three prime numbers? (You can use the same prime number more than once.) Explain why your list does not prove that this is always the case.

81. **CHALLENGE** Many clock faces show only 12 hours. For these, a 12 hour cycle is repeated twice to make a 24 hour day. What other clock faces could be used? Give the number of hours on each clock face and how many cycles would have to be repeated to make a 24 hour day.

Multiple-Choice Practice

▶ Eliminate choices that are obviously wrong. In Exercise 82, you can eliminate C because 81 = 9 • 9.

82. Which of the following is a prime number?

Ⓐ 75 Ⓑ 79 Ⓒ 81 Ⓓ Not here

83. Which number has the prime factorization $2^3 \times 3^3 \times 5$?

Ⓕ 30 Ⓖ 270 Ⓗ 1080 Ⓙ Not here

84. A store owner wants to display 72 boxes. Which of the following is *not* a way that the store owner could make the display?

Ⓐ 7 rows with 12 boxes in each row

Ⓑ 18 rows with 4 boxes in each row

Ⓒ 8 rows with 9 boxes in each row

Ⓓ 6 rows with 12 boxes in each row

Mixed Review

Evaluate the expression when $t = 3$ and when $t = 6$. *(1.2)*

85. $13t$ **86.** $28 - t$ **87.** $t + 98$ **88.** $144 \div t$

Find the average. Round your answer to the nearest tenth. *(1.6)*

89. 14, 45, 22 **90.** 109, 120, 99 **91.** 65, 80, 26, 94

92. Your friend multiplies 63.8 and 5.1 and gets 3253.8. Use estimation to check the answer. Is the answer reasonable? Explain. *(1.8)*

Find the perimeter and the area. *(1.4, 1.7, 1.8)*

93. Square

94. Rectangle

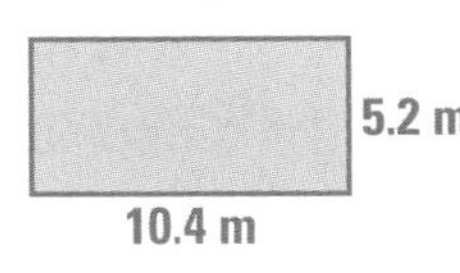

95. Rectangle

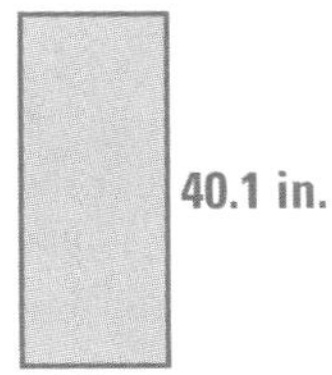

2.2 Greatest Common Factor

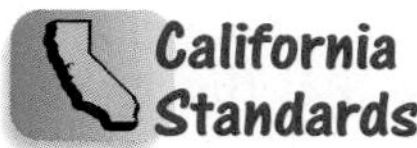

California Standards

In this lesson you'll:

- Determine the greatest common divisor of whole numbers. (NS 2.4)

Goal 1 FINDING THE GREATEST COMMON FACTOR

A whole number that is a factor of two or more nonzero whole numbers is a **common factor** of the two numbers.

EXAMPLE 1 Finding Common Factors

Find all common factors of 14 and 42.

Solution

List all the factors of each number. Then find the factors that are common to each number.

Factors of 14: **1**, **2**, **7**, **14**

Factors of 42: **1**, **2**, 3, 6, **7**, **14**, 21, 42

ANSWER ▶ The common factors are 1, 2, 7, and 14.

Any two numbers have 1 as a common factor. The largest number that is a factor of two or more nonzero whole numbers is their **greatest common factor (GCF),** or **greatest common divisor (GCD)**.

Student Help

▶ **STUDY TIP**
You can generalize the method in Example 2 to find the greatest common factor of *three* or more numbers. For example, the greatest common factor of 12, 18, and 30 is 6.

EXAMPLE 2 Finding the Greatest Common Factor

Find the greatest common factor of 28 and 36.

Solution

Factors of 28: 1, 2, **4**, 7, 14, 28

Factors of 36: 1, 2, 3, **4**, 6, 9, 12, 18, 36

ANSWER ▶ The greatest common factor of 28 and 36 is 4.

EXAMPLE 3 Finding the Greatest Common Factor

Find the greatest common factor of 16 and 37.

Solution

Factors of 16: **1**, 2, 4, 8, 16

Factors of 37: **1**, 37

ANSWER ▶ The greatest common factor of 16 and 37 is 1.

Goal 2 USING THE GREATEST COMMON FACTOR

EXAMPLE 4 Using the Greatest Common Factor

HISTORY LINK Ancient Egyptian calendars used 30 days as a lunar month and 365 days as a solar year.

a. Is it possible to choose a number of days in a week so that the month and the year are divided evenly into weeks?

b. Can the Egyptian year be divided evenly into 30-day months?

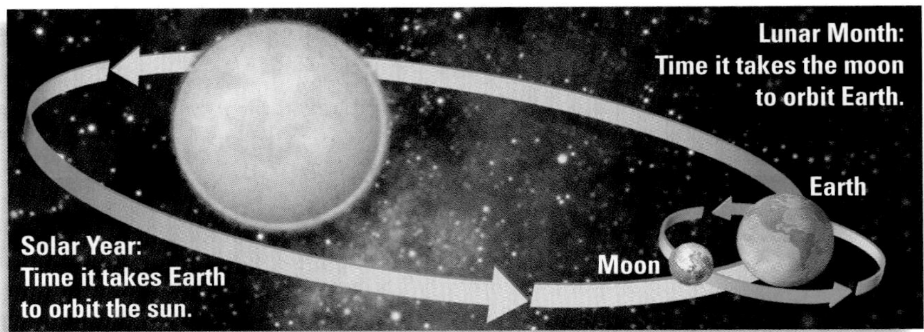

Solution

a. Common factors of 30 and 365 would be possible choices for the length of a week.

Factors of 30: 1, 2, 3, 5, 6, 10, 15, 30 **Factors of 365:** 1, 5, 73, 365

The greatest common factor of 30 and 365 is 5, so it would be possible to divide the 30-day lunar month into 6 five-day weeks and the 365-day solar year into 73 five-day weeks.

b. Because 365 is not evenly divisible by 30, the Egyptian year cannot be divided evenly into 30-day months.

Link to History

CALENDARS The columns of the temple at El-Karnak, Egypt, are oriented to admit the sunlight of the summer solstice. The 365-day calendar marked the earliest recorded year in history, 4236 B.C.

More about calendars available at www.mcdougallittell.com

EXAMPLE 5 Using Common Factors

Suppose that a lunar month had 28 days and a solar year had 364 days. To create a calendar, you want the number of days in a week to be a common factor of 28 and 364. What would be a reasonable choice for the number of days in a week?

Solution

Begin by listing the factors of 28 and 364.

Factors of 28: 1, 2, 4, 7, 14, 28

Factors of 364: 1, 2, 4, 7, 13, 14, 26, 28, 52, 91, 182, 364

The common factors are 1, 2, 4, 7, 14, and 28. These are all possible choices for the number of days in a week. Weeks that are one or two days long are probably too short, while weeks that are 14 or 28 days are probably too long. A reasonable choice would be 4 or 7.

Student Help

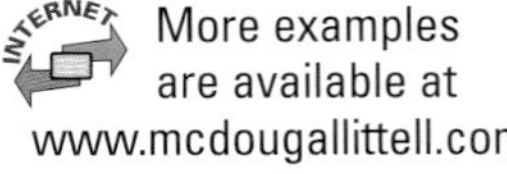

▶**MORE EXAMPLES**

More examples are available at www.mcdougallittell.com

2.2 Exercises

Guided Practice

1. Complete the statement: A __?__ is a whole number that is a factor of two or more nonzero whole numbers.

Find all common factors of the two numbers.

2. 8, 12 **3.** 17, 38 **4.** 25, 125 **5.** 18, 30

Match the numbers with their greatest common factor.

A. 7 **B.** 2 **C.** 6 **D.** 14

6. 12, 22 **7.** 42, 56 **8.** 24, 30 **9.** 63, 70

10. Which numbers have 1 as their greatest common factor?

A. 15, 35 **B.** 11, 13 **C.** 2, 8

11. **CONSTRUCTION** Three pieces of wood have lengths 12 feet, 42 feet, and 60 feet. A builder needs to cut the wood into pieces of the same length. Find the greatest possible length of the pieces.

Practice and Problem Solving

Student Help

▶**MORE PRACTICE**
Extra practice to help you master skills is on page 568.

Find all common factors of the two numbers.

12. 9, 21 **13.** 13, 42 **14.** 40, 80 **15.** 15, 36

16. 10, 55 **17.** 18, 72 **18.** 12, 30 **19.** 2, 24

20. 23, 41 **21.** 50, 100 **22.** 13, 17 **23.** 23, 69

In Exercises 24–32, find the greatest common factor by listing all the factors of the numbers.

24. 14, 21 **25.** 12, 35 **26.** 54, 63

27. 72, 84 **28.** 66, 96 **29.** 31, 35

30. 18, 27, 45 **31.** 16, 28, 44 **32.** 14, 28, 56

33. Two whole numbers whose greatest common factor is 1 are said to be *relatively prime*. Look back at the numbers in Exercises 24–29. Identify any numbers that are relatively prime.

34. The prime factorizations of 54 and 60 are shown. Describe how you can use the diagrams to find the greatest common factor.

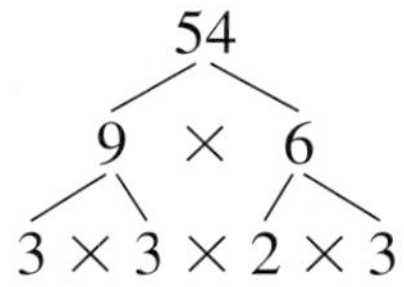

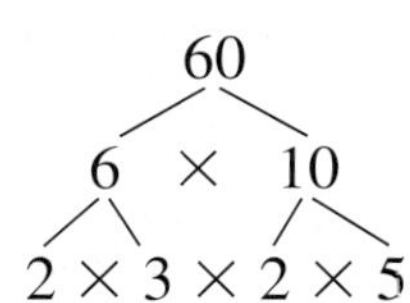

35. a. Find the greatest common factor of 32 and 48 by listing all the factors of each number.

b. Find the greatest common factor of 32 and 48 by writing the prime factorization of each number.

c. Which method do you prefer? Explain.

MATHEMATICAL REASONING In Exercises 36–38, complete the statement using *sometimes, always,* or *never*. Explain your answer.

36. The greatest common factor of two numbers is __?__ one of the two numbers.

37. The greatest common factor of two composite numbers is __?__ 1.

38. The greatest common factor of two different prime numbers is __?__ 1.

39. A teacher has two rolls of ribbon to make student awards of all the same size. One roll is 32 feet long. The other is 50 feet long. Find the longest possible length of each piece of ribbon.

Student Help

▶ HOMEWORK HELP

INTERNET Extra help with problem solving in Ex. 40 is available at www.mcdougallittell.com

History Link **In Exercises 40 and 41, use the following information.** The ancient Maya used two different calendars. The Haab calendar had 18 months of 20 days each, and a month of 5 days. The other calendar had 260 days.

Maya calendar, circa 590

40. What is the greatest common factor of the number of days of each calendar?

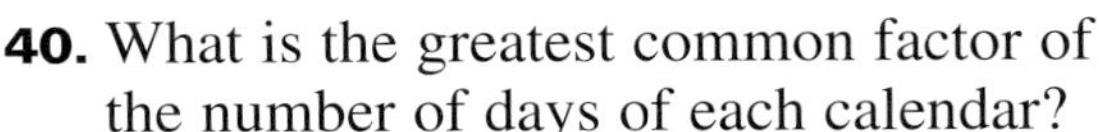

41. Why would your answer in Exercise 40 be a good choice for the number of days for a week in the Haab calendar?

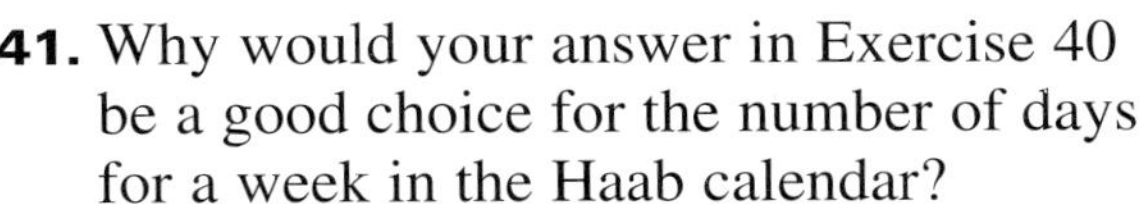

42. a. Find the greatest common factor of 66 and 88.

b. CHALLENGE Write the prime factorizations of 66 and 88. Then use your answer in part (a) to describe a procedure for finding the GCF of a pair of numbers using the prime factorizations of the numbers.

Multiple-Choice Practice

43. What is the greatest common factor of 88 and 64?

Ⓐ 2 Ⓑ 4 Ⓒ 6 Ⓓ 8

44. Which of the following is *not* a common factor of 24 and 60?

Ⓕ 3 Ⓖ 4 Ⓗ 5 Ⓙ 6

2.3 Fundamental Fraction Concepts

California Standards

In this lesson you'll:

- Interpret a fraction as a part of a whole or a part of a set. (Grade 4, NS 1.5)
- Use a model or diagram to explain mathematical reasoning. (MR 2.4)

Student Help

READING TIP
The symbol $\neq$ means "is not equal to."

Goal 1 A Fraction as Part of a Whole

A **fraction** is a number of the form $\frac{a}{b}$ ($b \neq 0$) where a is called the **numerator** and b is called the **denominator**. A fraction is used to describe one or more *parts of a whole*. Each part must have the same size. For example, the fraction $\frac{2}{5}$ represents 2 parts of a whole that has 5 equal parts. You can model the fraction $\frac{2}{5}$ by drawing a rectangle with five equal parts and shading two of them.

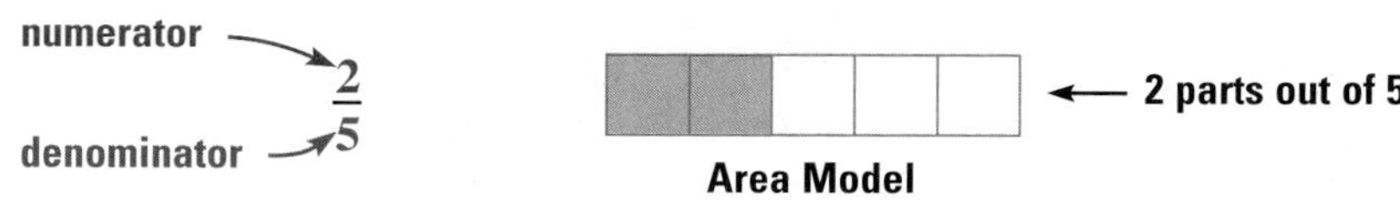

Area Model

EXAMPLE 1 Writing a Fraction

Write the fraction given by the verbal phrase. Identify the numerator and the denominator.

a. Two thirds **b.** Five eighths

Solution

a. $\frac{2}{3}$ ← numerator (2), denominator (3)

b. $\frac{5}{8}$ ← numerator (5), denominator (8)

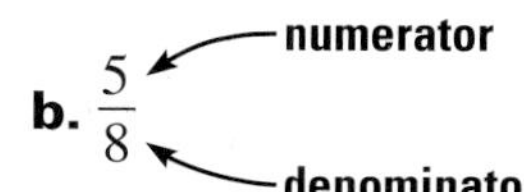

EXAMPLE 2 Interpreting a Fraction Model

The shaded part of each circle represents a fraction of the circle. Name each fraction using fourths. What do the denominators and the numerators represent?

a. **b.** **c.** **d.**

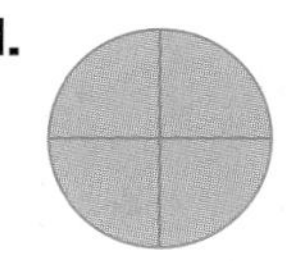

Solution

a. $\frac{1}{4}$ **b.** $\frac{2}{4}$ **c.** $\frac{3}{4}$ **d.** $\frac{4}{4}$

The denominators tell you that the circle is divided into 4 equal parts. The numerators tell you how many parts are shaded.

Goal 2 A Fraction as Part of a Set

Fractions can also be represented in terms of sets. To represent $\frac{3}{4}$ of a set with 20 elements, arrange the set into four equal groups. Then circle three of the four groups.

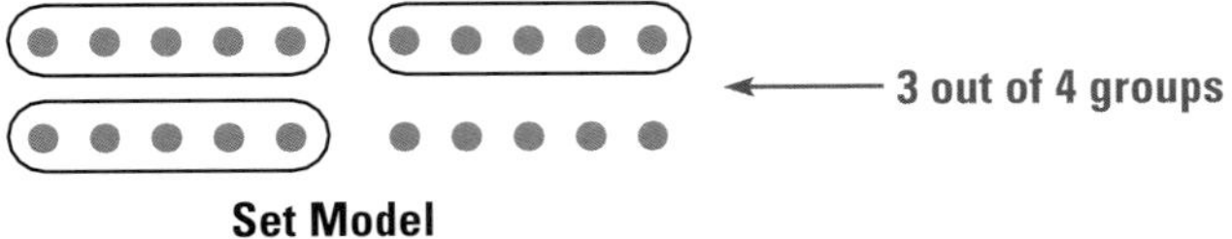

Set Model

EXAMPLE 3 Identifying a Fraction as Part of a Set

Identify the fraction shown by the set model.

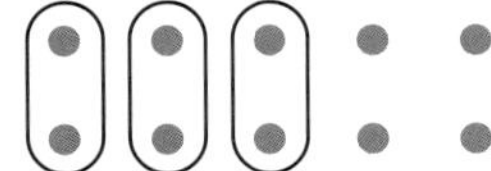

Solution

There are 5 groups of 2 dots in the model, and 3 of the 5 groups are circled. The fraction shown by the set model is $\frac{3}{5}$.

EXAMPLE 4 Using a Set Model

You are helping two spelling classes. Each class has 24 students.

a. In the first class, $\frac{5}{6}$ of the students spelled all the words correctly. Represent this fraction by a set model.

b. In the second class, $\frac{5}{8}$ of the students spelled all the words correctly. Represent this fraction by a set model.

c. Which class did better? Explain.

Solution

Draw 24 dots to represent the 24 students. Arrange the dots into six groups for the first class and into eight groups for the second class.

a. 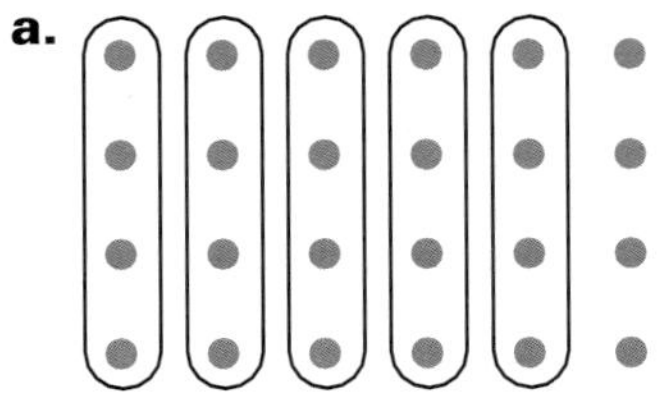
5 out of 6 groups

b. 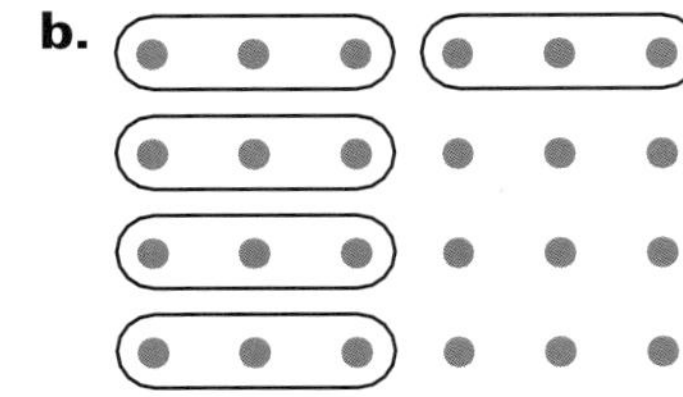
5 out of 8 groups

c. The first class did better, because 20 students spelled all the words correctly. Only 15 students in the second class did so.

2.3 Exercises

Guided Practice

In Exercises 1–3, write the fraction given by the verbal phrase. Then identify the numerator and the denominator.

1. One fourth

2. Six sevenths

3. Five twelfths

> **Student Help**
>
> ▶**STUDY TIP**
> A fraction bar represents division, so $\frac{1}{2}$ means $1 \div 2$.

4. Write $9 \div 10$ as a fraction.

5. Decide whether the shaded area is $\frac{4}{6}$ of the entire area of the figure. Explain your reasoning.

In Exercises 6–8, match the fraction with its model.

A. 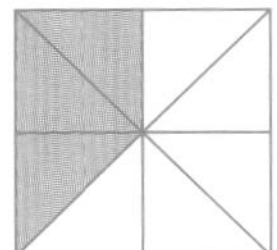

B. 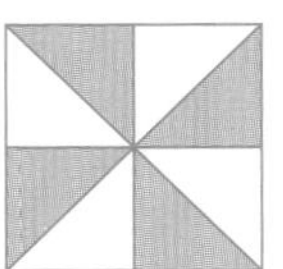

C. 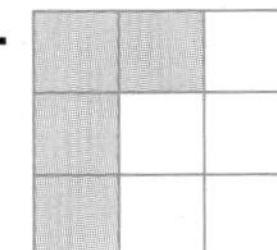

6. $\frac{3}{8}$

7. $\frac{4}{9}$

8. $\frac{4}{8}$

9. Show $\frac{5}{6}$ by copying the figure at the right, drawing lines to divide it into six equal parts, and shading.

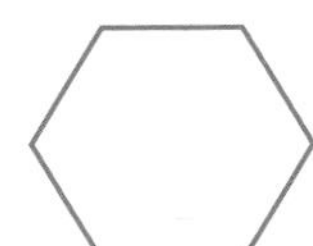

10. **WRITING** Describe three real-life situations in which you would use a fraction.

Practice and Problem Solving

> **Student Help**
>
> ▶**MORE PRACTICE**
> Extra practice to help you master skills is on page 568.

Write the fraction given by the verbal phrase. Then identify the numerator and the denominator.

11. One third

12. Four fifths

13. Seven eighths

14. Eleven twelfths

15. Five sevenths

16. Two halves

Decide whether the diagram is a good model to use for a fraction. If it is, write the fraction given by the model. If not, explain.

17.

18. 

19. 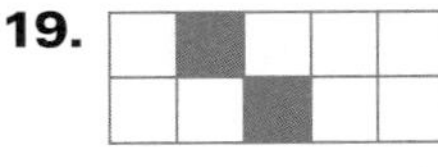

20. 

21. 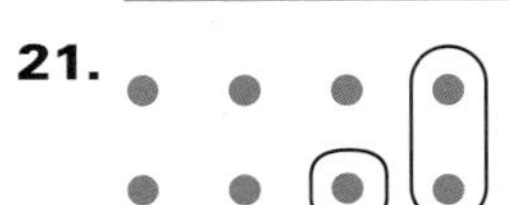

22. 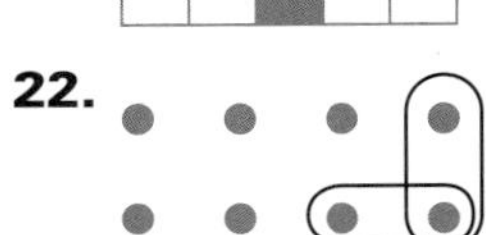

23. Draw a line segment 12 centimeters long. On the line, mark each centimeter. Shade $\frac{7}{12}$ of the line segment.

In Exercises 24–27, draw an area model and a set model for the fraction.

24. $\frac{4}{7}$ **25.** $\frac{3}{5}$ **26.** $\frac{7}{10}$ **27.** $\frac{8}{9}$

28. CAR SAFETY In 1987 the fraction of cars and vans with driver's side airbags was $\frac{1}{20}$. By 1994 the fraction was $\frac{18}{20}$. Draw a model to represent each fraction. ▶ Source: *USA Today*

29. Draw 20 small circles. Group them by 4s. Color three of the groups blue. Draw another 20 small circles. Group them by 5s. Color three of the groups blue. Use your drawings to explain which fraction is larger, $\frac{3}{4}$ or $\frac{3}{5}$.

30. SCHOOL Write a fraction for the number of days in a week that you normally attend school.

31. WALKING John walks 1760 feet in 5 minutes. What additional information is needed to find the fraction of a mile he walks?

32. SOLAR HEATERS Solar water heaters use the sun's energy to heat water. For a home with a 60 gallon hot water tank, one adult uses about $\frac{5}{12}$ of the capacity of the tank each day.

a. Draw an area model to show the portion used by an adult each day.

b. After this amount has been used, what portion remains?

CHALLENGE **Write three fractions that are close to the given number.**

33. 0 **34.** $\frac{1}{4}$ **35.** $\frac{1}{2}$ **36.** 1

Link to Technology

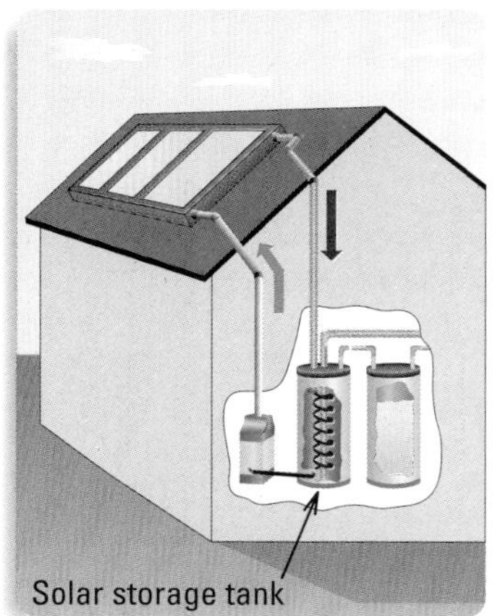

SOLAR HEATERS A small solar hot water tank holds 50–60 gallons. A small tank can heat enough water for a three-person home. Solar hot water tanks can hold as much as 120 gallons.

INTERNET More about solar energy available at www.mcdougallittell.com

Multiple-Choice Practice

37. Twenty seconds is what fraction of a minute?

Ⓐ $\frac{2}{3}$ Ⓑ $\frac{20}{30}$ Ⓒ $\frac{20}{60}$ Ⓓ $\frac{3}{20}$

38. Which fraction does the model below represent?

Ⓕ $\frac{4}{8}$ Ⓖ $\frac{4}{9}$

Ⓗ $\frac{1}{3}$ Ⓙ $\frac{2}{9}$

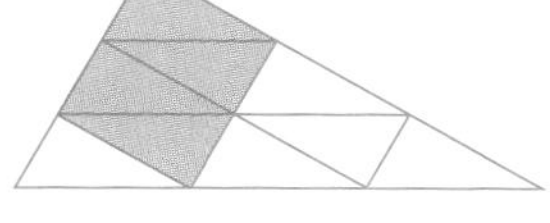

Test Tip 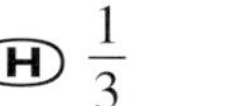

▶ In Exercise 38, you can eliminate F because the model is divided into ninths.

2.4 Fractions in Simplest Form

In this lesson you'll:

- Solve problems involving fractions and express answers in simplest form. (Grade 5, NS 2.3)
- Use the greatest common divisor of whole numbers to solve problems with fractions. (NS 2.4)

Goal 1 Writing Fractions in Simplest Form

Two fractions are **equivalent** if they represent the same number. You can use area models to show that fractions are equivalent.

EXAMPLE 1 Identifying Equivalent Fractions

To show that $\frac{3}{4}$ and $\frac{18}{24}$ are equivalent you can draw two rectangles that are the same size. Divide one into 4 equal parts and the other into 24 equal parts.

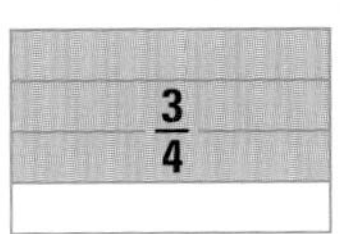

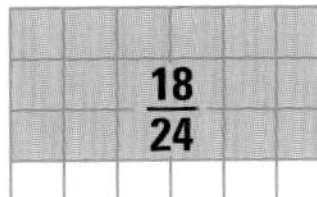

Notice that in the model for $\frac{18}{24}$, the number of shaded squares is 3×6 while the total number of squares is 4×6. This model shows that $\frac{3}{4}$ is equivalent to $\frac{3 \times 6}{4 \times 6}$. More generally, multiplying or dividing the numerator and denominator of a fraction by the same number results in an equivalent fraction.

Student Help

▶Study Tip
When you divide both the numerator and the denominator by a common factor, a common factor of 1 remains.

$$\frac{12}{18} = \frac{6 \cdot 2}{6 \cdot 3} = \frac{\overset{1}{\cancel{6}} \cdot 2}{\underset{1}{\cancel{6}} \cdot 3} = \frac{2}{3}$$

A fraction is in **simplest form** if its numerator and denominator have a greatest common factor of 1. Writing a fraction in simplest form is called *simplifying* the fraction. One way to simplify a fraction is to divide its numerator and denominator by their greatest common factor.

EXAMPLE 2 Writing a Fraction in Simplest Form

Write the fraction in simplest form. **a.** $\frac{12}{18}$ **b.** $\frac{28}{63}$

Solution

a. $\frac{12}{18} = \frac{\overset{1}{\cancel{6}} \cdot 2}{\underset{1}{\cancel{6}} \cdot 3}$ The greatest common factor of 12 and 18 is 6. Divide the numerator and denominator by 6.

$= \frac{2}{3}$ Simplify.

b. $\frac{28}{63} = \frac{\overset{1}{\cancel{7}} \cdot 4}{\underset{1}{\cancel{7}} \cdot 9}$ The greatest common factor of 28 and 63 is 7. Divide the numerator and denominator by 7.

$= \frac{4}{9}$ Simplify.

Goal 2 SOLVING PROBLEMS WITH FRACTIONS

Using a socket wrench to loosen a bolt

EXAMPLE 3 Using Fractions in Simplest Form

Different sized socket wrenches are used to loosen and tighten different sized bolts. You are using a socket set to loosen bolts on a bicycle.

The sockets in your set have the following measures (in inches).

$$\frac{5}{16}, \frac{3}{8}, \frac{7}{16}, \frac{1}{2}, \frac{9}{16}, \frac{5}{8}, \frac{11}{16}, \frac{3}{4}, \frac{13}{16}, \frac{7}{8}, \frac{15}{16}$$

You measure the head of a bolt as $\frac{14}{16}$ inch. Which socket should you use?

Solution

To find which socket to choose, rewrite $\frac{14}{16}$ in simplest form.

$$\frac{14}{16} = \frac{\overset{1}{\cancel{2}} \cdot 7}{\underset{1}{\cancel{2}} \cdot 8} = \frac{7}{8}$$

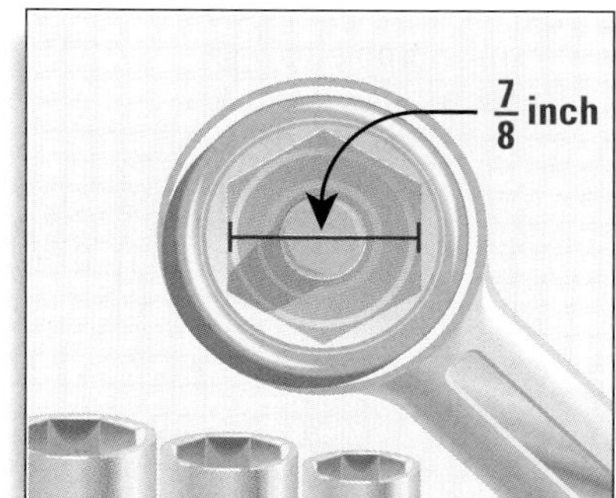

ANSWER ▶ You should choose the socket that is labeled $\frac{7}{8}$ inch.

When you simplify a fraction with large numbers in the numerator and denominator, writing the prime factorizations of the numbers may help.

EXAMPLE 4 Using Fractions in Simplest Form

TRAVEL There are 360 students in your school. Of these, 216 students have visited a foreign country. Is it true that three fifths of the students in your school have visited a foreign country?

Solution

You can write that $\frac{216}{360}$ of the students have visited a foreign country.

To find out if $\frac{216}{360}$ is equivalent to $\frac{3}{5}$, write the prime factorizations of 216 and 360.

216: $2 \times 2 \times 2 \times 3 \times 3 \times 3$ **360:** $2 \times 2 \times 2 \times 3 \times 3 \times 5$

Write $\frac{216}{360}$ in simplest form: $\frac{216}{360} = \frac{\overset{1}{\cancel{2}} \times \overset{1}{\cancel{2}} \times \overset{1}{\cancel{2}} \times \overset{1}{\cancel{3}} \times \overset{1}{\cancel{3}} \times 3}{\underset{1}{\cancel{2}} \times \underset{1}{\cancel{2}} \times \underset{1}{\cancel{2}} \times \underset{1}{\cancel{3}} \times \underset{1}{\cancel{3}} \times 5} = \frac{3}{5}$

ANSWER ▶ Yes, three fifths of the students have visited a foreign country.

2.4 Exercises

Guided Practice

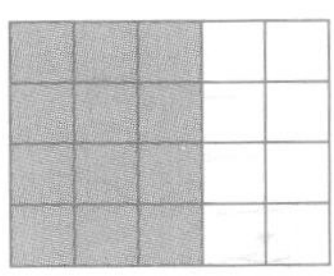

1. Write two equivalent fractions represented by the area model at the right.

2. Draw area models to show that $\frac{4}{5}$ and $\frac{8}{10}$ are equivalent.

Tell whether the fraction is in simplest form. Explain your reasoning.

3. $\frac{8}{9}$ 4. $\frac{12}{27}$ 5. $\frac{10}{55}$ 6. $\frac{9}{23}$

7. **SPORTS** In racquetball the first player to reach 15 points wins the game. Tell whether the fraction could be the fraction of points a player has out of 15.

a. $\frac{1}{5}$ b. $\frac{7}{15}$ c. $\frac{2}{3}$ d. $\frac{3}{10}$ e. $\frac{1}{3}$

Practice and Problem Solving

> **Student Help**
>
> ▶**MORE PRACTICE**
> Extra practice to help you master skills is on page 568.

In Exercises 8–10, match the fraction with its area model. Then write an equivalent fraction.

A. 

B. 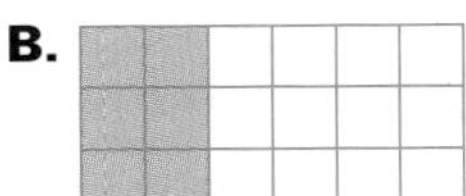

C. 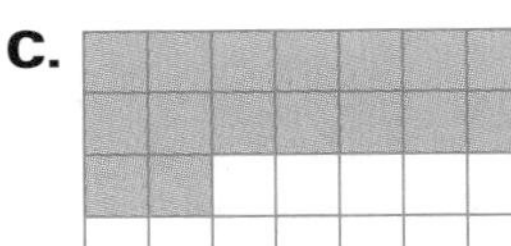

8. $\frac{1}{3}$ 9. $\frac{8}{14}$ 10. $\frac{3}{4}$

11. Draw area models to show that $\frac{2}{3}$ and $\frac{8}{12}$ are equivalent.

Identify the fraction that is *not* equivalent to the other three.

12. $\frac{4}{7}, \frac{14}{28}, \frac{28}{56}, \frac{7}{14}$ 13. $\frac{72}{81}, \frac{8}{9}, \frac{24}{27}, \frac{36}{42}$

Tell whether the fractions are equivalent. Explain why or why not.

14. $\frac{1}{6}, \frac{2}{12}$ 15. $\frac{1}{2}, \frac{4}{6}$ 16. $\frac{2}{5}, \frac{4}{9}$ 17. $\frac{5}{8}, \frac{15}{24}$

18. **ERROR ANALYSIS** Find and correct the error in simplifying $\frac{108}{120}$.

$\frac{108}{120} = \frac{4 \cdot 27}{4 \cdot 30} = \frac{27}{30}$

Write two different fractions that are equivalent to the given fraction. Include the simplest form of the fraction. Then show why the fractions are equivalent.

19. $\frac{25}{100}$ **20.** $\frac{18}{21}$ **21.** $\frac{32}{36}$ **22.** $\frac{16}{20}$

23. $\frac{2}{12}$ **24.** $\frac{33}{45}$ **25.** $\frac{11}{55}$ **26.** $\frac{48}{80}$

27. $\frac{284}{568}$ **28.** $\frac{136}{187}$ **29.** $\frac{4}{122}$ **30.** $\frac{98}{364}$

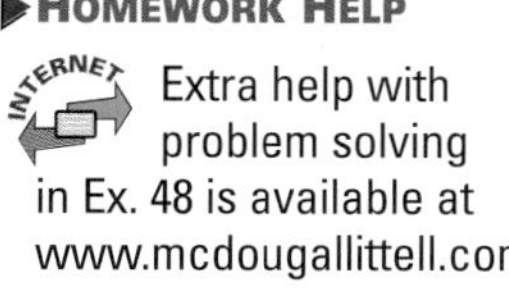

Student Help

HOMEWORK HELP

Extra help with problem solving in Ex. 48 is available at www.mcdougallittell.com

In Exercises 31–46, write the fraction in simplest form.

31. $\frac{30}{45}$ **32.** $\frac{9}{27}$ **33.** $\frac{12}{120}$ **34.** $\frac{27}{63}$

35. $\frac{13}{13}$ **36.** $\frac{10}{75}$ **37.** $\frac{26}{52}$ **38.** $\frac{6}{39}$

39. $\frac{48}{64}$ **40.** $\frac{72}{78}$ **41.** $\frac{35}{55}$ **42.** $\frac{66}{180}$

43. $\frac{15}{90}$ **44.** $\frac{44}{99}$ **45.** $\frac{770}{1260}$ **46.** $\frac{25,000}{85,000}$

47. **READING** You read 160 pages of a 240-page book. What fraction of the book have you read?

48. **BUDGET** You earn \$20 per week working at a supermarket. You spend \$9 on a cassette and \$5 for school supplies. What fraction of your weekly earnings do you spend?

Link to Careers

AGRICULTURIST
An agricultural technician records and analyzes data about seedlings. This can lead to new and superior plant varieties.

AGRICULTURE **In Exercises 49–52, use the diagram. The total amount of all fruits consumed per person in 1996 was 130 pounds. Write the amount of the type of fruit consumed as a fraction of the total in simplest form.**

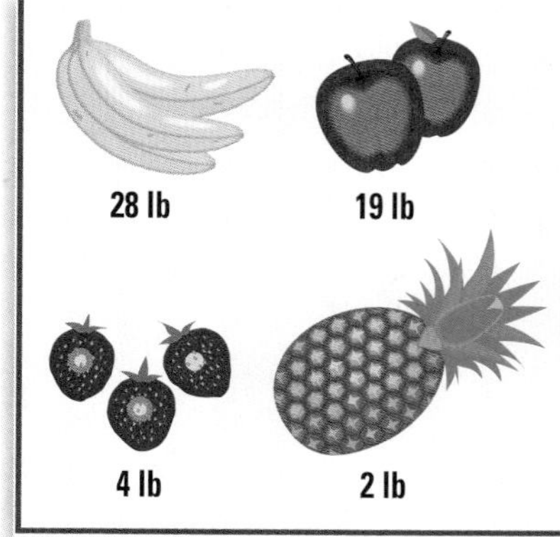

▶ Source: U.S. Dept. of Agriculture

49. Bananas

50. Pineapples

51. Apples

52. Strawberries

53. **CROP PRODUCTION** California led the nation in fresh vegetable and melon production in 1998, producing about $\frac{442}{1000}$ of all crops. Write the fraction in simplest form.

54. **EMPLOYMENT** In August of 1999, about $\frac{7,200,000}{135,200,000}$ of employed people held more than one job. Write the fraction in simplest form.

Student Help

▶ **LOOK BACK**

For help with set models, see page 70.

CHALLENGE In Exercises 55 and 56, use the following information. A survey asked 24 students to name their favorite subject. One fourth chose science, one third chose English, and one sixth chose computer science. The rest chose math.

55. Use a set model to find how many students chose each subject.

56. Write and simplify the fraction of students who chose math.

Multiple-Choice Practice

57. Which fraction is equivalent to $\frac{3}{24}$?

Ⓐ $\frac{1}{2}$ Ⓑ $\frac{1}{4}$ Ⓒ $\frac{1}{6}$ Ⓓ $\frac{1}{8}$

58. Which fraction is in simplest form?

Ⓕ $\frac{3}{12}$ Ⓖ $\frac{5}{19}$ Ⓗ $\frac{7}{49}$ Ⓙ $\frac{8}{30}$

Test Tip Ⓐ Ⓑ Ⓒ Ⓓ

▶ In Exercise 59, you can eliminate D because $\frac{365}{222}$ is greater than 1, which would be more than one school year.

59. The table shows the average number of school days for different countries. What fraction of a year (365 days) do students in Israel spend in school?

Ⓐ $\frac{43}{73}$ Ⓑ $\frac{178}{222}$ Ⓒ $\frac{9}{11}$ Ⓓ $\frac{365}{222}$

Country	Days in School per Year
France	174
United States	178
Israel	215
South Korea	222

▶ Source: *The Digest of Educational Statistics 1996*

Mixed Review

For Exercises 60 and 61, perform the following steps. Fold a piece of paper in half. Then unfold it to count the number of divisions in the paper. Next, fold the piece of paper in half twice before unfolding it to count the divisions. Repeat until you have folded the paper in half five times. *(1.4)*

60. Describe the pattern in the number of divisions after each fold.

61. Describe how the pattern relates to powers and exponents.

62. MATHEMATICAL REASONING Explain why all prime numbers other than 2 must be odd. *(2.1)*

Find the greatest common factor of the numbers. *(2.2)*

63. 15, 21 **64.** 20, 30 **65.** 36, 60 **66.** 35, 64, 81

Chapter 2 Mid-Chapter Test

Take this test as you would take a test in class. The answers to the exercises are given in the back of the book.

Find all the factors of the number.

1. 54 **2.** 83 **3.** 120 **4.** 210

In Exercises 5–8, tell whether the number is *prime* or *composite*.

5. 2 **6.** 63 **7.** 110 **8.** 67

9. SCIENCE FAIR You are making a display of shells for your science fair presentation. You have 24 shells in your collection. List and draw all of the possible rectangular formations for your display.

Use a factor tree to write the prime factorization of the number.

10. 360 **11.** 675 **12.** 1470 **13.** 1184

Find all common factors of the two numbers.

14. 19, 38 **15.** 36, 45 **16.** 15, 26 **17.** 8, 56

Find the greatest common factor of the numbers.

18. 9, 12 **19.** 25, 49 **20.** 72, 108 **21.** 8, 202

In Exercises 22–25, write the fraction represented by the shaded portion of the model.

22. 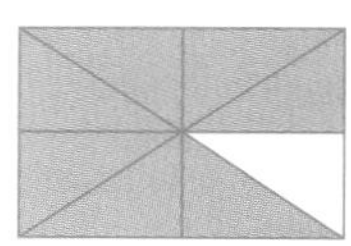

23. 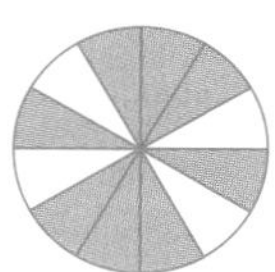

24. 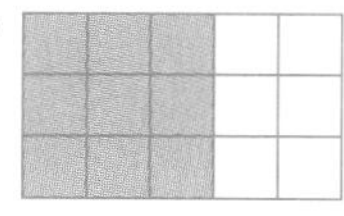

25. 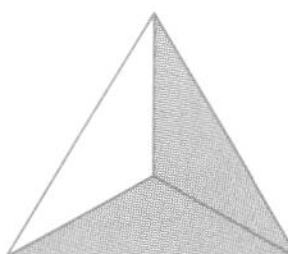

26. Explain why the model at the right is not a good model for $\frac{1}{2}$.

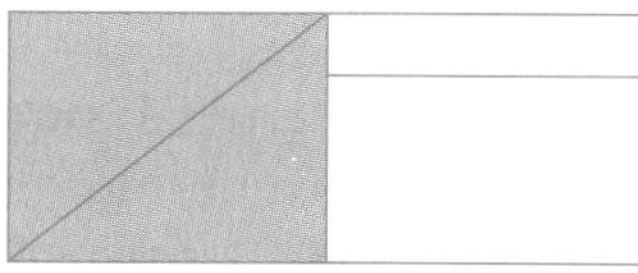

In Exercises 27–30, write the fraction in simplest form.

27. $\frac{3}{18}$ **28.** $\frac{12}{25}$ **29.** $\frac{40}{64}$ **30.** $\frac{45}{72}$

31. *Science Link* In five minutes, light from the sun travels $\frac{90,000,000}{150,000,000}$ of the way to Earth. Write this fraction in simplest form.

2.5 Least Common Multiple

California Standards

In this lesson you'll:

- Find the least common multiple of two whole numbers and use it to solve problems. (NS 2.4)

Goal 1 Finding LCM Using Lists of Multiples

A **multiple** of a number is the product of the number and any nonzero whole number. For example, the multiples of 5 are 1×5, 2×5, 3×5, and so on.

A **common multiple** of two numbers is a multiple shared by the numbers. For example, 20 is a common multiple of 2 and 5 because $20 = 2 \times 10$ and $20 = 5 \times 4$.

EXAMPLE 1 Finding Common Multiples

Write the common multiples of 2 and 3 that are less than 25.

Solution

List the multiples of 2 and the multiples of 3 that are less than 25.

Multiples of 2: 2, 4, **6**, 8, 10, **12**, 14, 16, **18**, 20, 22, **24**

Multiples of 3: 3, **6**, 9, **12**, 15, **18**, 21, **24**

ANSWER ▶ The common multiples of 2 and 3 that are less than 25 are 6, 12, 18, and 24.

Of all the common multiples of two or more numbers, the smallest is called the **least common multiple** (**LCM**). For example, the least common multiple of 4 and 6 is 12.

One way to find the least common multiple of two numbers is to list the first several multiples of each number. Then compare the lists and determine which common multiple is smallest.

EXAMPLE 2 Finding the Least Common Multiple

Find the least common multiple of 6 and 14.

Solution

Begin by listing several multiples of each number.

Multiples of 6: 6, 12, 18, 24, 30, 36, **42**, 48, . . .

Multiples of 14: 14, 28, **42**, 56, . . .

ANSWER ▶ The least common multiple of 6 and 14 is 42.

Student Help

▶ **Study Tip**
If two numbers have no common factor other than 1, their least common multiple is the product of the two numbers.

Goal 2 FINDING LCM USING PRIME FACTORIZATION

Another way to find the least common multiple of two numbers is to compare their prime factorizations.

Student Help

▶ **MORE EXAMPLES**

INTERNET More examples are available at www.mcdougallittell.com

EXAMPLE 3 Using Prime Factorization

Find the least common multiple of 24 and 60.

Solution

❶ Write the prime factorization of 24.	$24 = 2 \times 2 \times 2 \times 3$
❷ Write the prime factorization of 60.	$60 = 2 \times 2 \times 3 \times 5$
❸ Circle the factors that the two numbers share.	$24 = (2) \times (2) \times 2 \times (3)$ $60 = (2) \times (2) \times (3) \times 5$
❹ List the factors of both, writing any circled factors only once.	**2**, 2, 2, **3**, 5
❺ Multiply the factors in the list to get the least common multiple.	$2 \times 2 \times 2 \times 3 \times 5 = 120$

ANSWER ▶ The least common multiple of 24 and 60 is 120.

Sometimes it is useful to find the least common multiple in solving problems.

EXAMPLE 4 Using the Least Common Multiple

RUNNING Meg and Pam are running laps on a track. Meg circles the track in three minutes, and Pam circles the track in four minutes. They started running together at the same time. When will they be together again at the starting point?

Solution

The LCM of 3 and 4 is $3 \times 2 \times 2 = 12$. Meg and Pam will be together again after 12 minutes. To check that this answer is reasonable, think about the context of the problem.

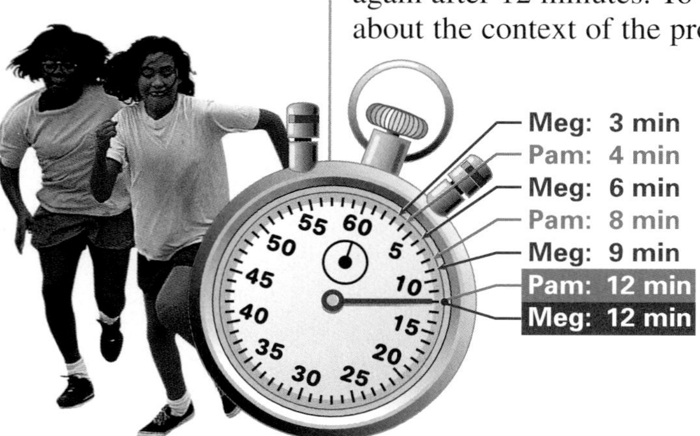

Meg crosses the starting point every 3 minutes, as her times shown next to the stopwatch indicate. Pam crosses the starting point every 4 minutes, also as shown.

You can see from the stopwatch that Meg and Pam will be together again at the starting point after 12 minutes.

2.5 Exercises

Guided Practice

For the given numbers, list the multiples less than 100. Then find the common multiples. What is the least common multiple?

1. 8, 10 **2.** 7, 11 **3.** 4, 6 **4.** 6, 8

5. 9, 11 **6.** 15, 25 **7.** 12, 16 **8.** 10, 14

9. 16, 20 **10.** 9, 33 **11.** 13, 39 **12.** 5, 9, 15

13. Use the method in Example 3 to find the least common multiple of 4 and 10 as follows.

a. Write the prime factorization of 4 and of 10.

b. Circle the factors that the two numbers share. Then list the factors, writing any circled factors only once.

c. Multiply the factors in the list to get the least common multiple.

Practice and Problem Solving

Student Help

▶ MORE PRACTICE
Extra practice to help you master skills is on page 569.

List the first eight multiples of the numbers. Then find the common multiples. What is the least common multiple?

14. 2, 7 **15.** 3, 7 **16.** 6, 9 **17.** 5, 10

18. 4, 20 **19.** 12, 14 **20.** 3, 4, 6 **21.** 4, 6, 8

Use prime factorization to find the least common multiple of the numbers.

22. 15, 75 **23.** 9, 24 **24.** 28, 32 **25.** 46, 115

26. 35, 40 **27.** 8, 25 **28.** 64, 72 **29.** 18, 20

xy ALGEBRA In Exercises 30–33, find the values of 2*n* and 3*n*. Then find the least common multiple of the two values.

30. $n = 4$ **31.** $n = 5$ **32.** $n = 6$ **33.** $n = 8$

34. **GARDENING** You are planting three different kinds of plants in rows that are 60 inches long. Every 6 inches you plant broccoli, every 15 inches you plant a tomato, and every 20 inches you plant a pepper. The three plants line up at the beginning of the rows. Will they ever line up again? If so, where?

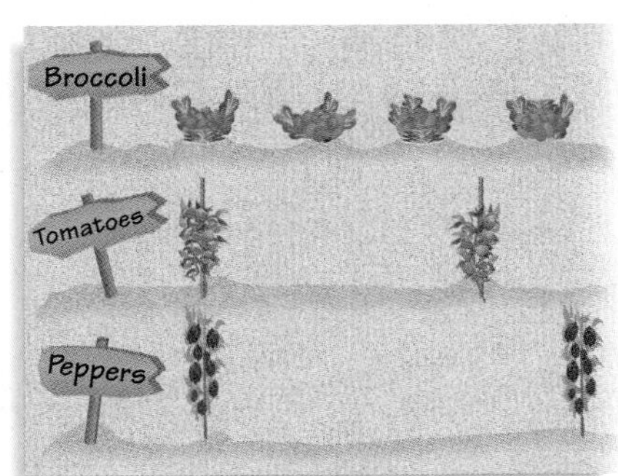

Student Help

▶ **LOOK BACK**
In Exercises 35 and 36, remember that 1 foot = 12 inches. For help with perimeter, see page 31.

DECORATING In Exercises 35 and 36, use the following information. You want to put a wallpaper border on the walls of some rooms. You would like the pattern on the border to match all the way around the room.

35. Will this pattern work out evenly, with no overlap, in a room that is 10 feet by 17 feet?

0 2 4 6 8 10 12 14 16 18 20 in.

one full pattern

36. Will this pattern work out evenly, with no overlap, in a room that is 18 feet by 20 feet?

0 2 4 6 8 10 12 14 16 18 20 in.

one full pattern

37. **CAR MAINTENANCE** The owner's manual for a new car suggests that the oil be changed every 3000 miles, the tires be rotated every 6000 miles, and the brakes be checked every 7500 miles. After how many miles will all three things need to be done at the same time?

38. **Science Link** Bamboo rarely produces flowers. One kind flowers every 30 years. Another kind flowers every 40 years, and another flowers every 60 years. If all three flower in the same year, how many years later will all three flower in the same year again?

Link to Science

BAMBOO Bamboo is a giant grass that is related to wheat, oats, and barley. It can grow as tall as 120 feet and have a diameter of 1 foot.

39. a. Find the GCF and the LCM of 6 and 12. How does the product (GCF)(LCM) compare to the product $6 \cdot 12$?

b. Choose two other nonzero whole numbers. Find their product and compare it with the product (GCF)(LCM).

c. Make a conjecture about how the product of two nonzero whole numbers relates to the product (GCF)(LCM).

40. **MATHEMATICAL REASONING** Give an example in which the least common multiple of two numbers is one of the numbers. Give an example in which the least common multiple is the product of the two numbers.

41. **CHALLENGE** To promote a new style of T-shirt, you put a gold sticker in every 15th package and a silver sticker in every 25th package. Customers who get both stickers in one package get a free T-shirt. When you sell 1000 packages, how many T-shirts will you give away?

Multiple-Choice Practice

42. What is the least common multiple of 14 and 21?

Ⓐ 14 Ⓑ 21 Ⓒ 42 Ⓓ 294

43. 231 is the least common multiple of which set of numbers?

Ⓕ 3, 7, 11 Ⓖ 3, 6, 11 Ⓗ 3, 6, 7 Ⓙ 6, 7, 21

2.6 Comparing and Ordering Fractions

California Standards

In this lesson you'll:

- Compare and order positive fractions. (NS 1.1)
- Solve problems involving fractions. (NS 2.4)

Goal 1 Comparing and Ordering Fractions

When you decide that one fraction is less than another fraction, you are *comparing* fractions. When you list fractions from least to greatest (or from greatest to least), you are *ordering* fractions. You can use the symbols > and < to replace words when you compare fractions.

Example 1 Comparing and Ordering Positive Fractions

a. Compare $\frac{2}{5}$ and $\frac{3}{5}$.

b. Write $\frac{2}{5}$, $\frac{2}{3}$, and $\frac{2}{4}$ in order.

Solution

a. For two positive fractions with the same denominator, the fraction with the lesser numerator is lesser.

ANSWER ▶ $\frac{2}{5}$ is less than $\frac{3}{5}$. You can write $\frac{2}{5} < \frac{3}{5}$.

b. For two positive fractions with the same numerator, the fraction with the lesser denominator is greater.

ANSWER ▶ $\frac{2}{5}$ is least, $\frac{2}{4}$ is next, and $\frac{2}{3}$ is greatest, or $\frac{2}{5} < \frac{2}{4} < \frac{2}{3}$.

Example 2 Comparing by Finding a Common Denominator

Compare $\frac{3}{4}$ and $\frac{5}{6}$.

Solution

To compare $\frac{3}{4}$ and $\frac{5}{6}$, rewrite both fractions with a common denominator. You might choose the product of the denominators for a common denominator.

$\frac{3}{4} = \frac{3 \cdot 6}{4 \cdot 6} = \frac{18}{24}$ Multiply the numerator and denominator by 6.

$\frac{5}{6} = \frac{5 \cdot 4}{6 \cdot 4} = \frac{20}{24}$ Multiply the numerator and denominator by 4.

ANSWER ▶ Because $\frac{18}{24} < \frac{20}{24}$, you know that $\frac{3}{4} < \frac{5}{6}$.

Student Help

▶ **Study Tip**
In Example 2, the product of the two denominators is a convenient choice for the common denominator, but any common multiple of 4 and 6 works.

Goal 2 FINDING A LEAST COMMON DENOMINATOR

The **least common denominator (LCD)** of two or more fractions is the least common multiple of their denominators. You can use the least common denominator to help you compare fractions.

EXAMPLE 3 Comparing Fractions by Finding the LCD

Compare $\frac{2}{9}$ and $\frac{1}{6}$.

Solution

The least common multiple of 9 and 6 is 18, so the least common denominator is 18.

$\frac{2}{9} = \frac{2 \cdot 2}{9 \cdot 2} = \frac{4}{18}$ Multiply the numerator and denominator by 2.

$\frac{1}{6} = \frac{1 \cdot 3}{6 \cdot 3} = \frac{3}{18}$ Multiply the numerator and denominator by 3.

Because $\frac{4}{18} > \frac{3}{18}$, you know that $\frac{2}{9} > \frac{1}{6}$.

CHECK ✓ Graph $\frac{2}{9}$ and $\frac{1}{6}$ on a number line that shows eighteenths.

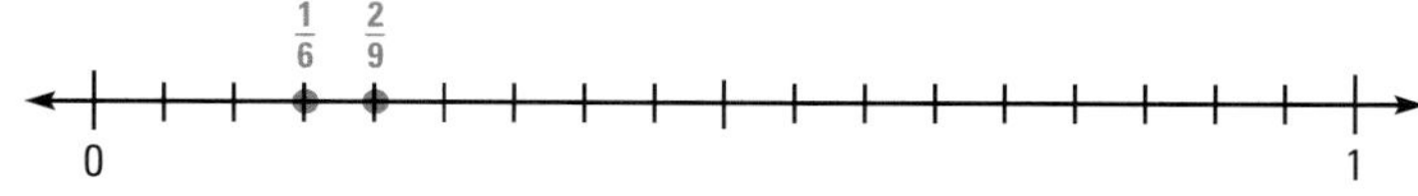

EXAMPLE 4 Using Fractions in Real Life

MARY'S TOY LAND
Remote Control Car
Regular Price $24
$\frac{2}{5}$ Off

SHOPPING Use the information at the left. You want to buy a remote control car. Which is the better buy?

Solution

Compare the fractions. The least common denominator is 15. Rewrite the fractions with the least common denominator.

$\frac{1}{3} = \frac{1 \cdot 5}{3 \cdot 5} = \frac{5}{15}$ Multiply the numerator and denominator by 5.

$\frac{2}{5} = \frac{2 \cdot 3}{5 \cdot 3} = \frac{6}{15}$ Multiply the numerator and denominator by 3.

Because $\frac{6}{15} > \frac{5}{15}$, you know that $\frac{2}{5} > \frac{1}{3}$.

ANSWER ▶ You get more money off the regular price at Mary's Toy Land, because $\frac{2}{5}$ of \$24 is greater than $\frac{1}{3}$ of \$24. Mary's Toy Land offers the better buy.

2.6 Exercises

Guided Practice

1. Name the fractions that are shown by the shaded portions of the models. Decide which fraction is greater. Write a statement using > to compare the fractions.

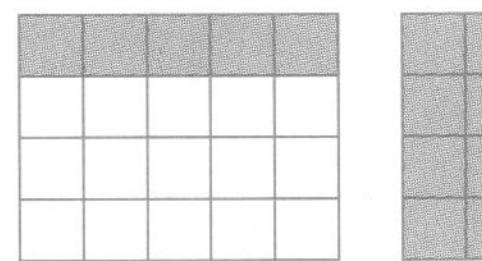

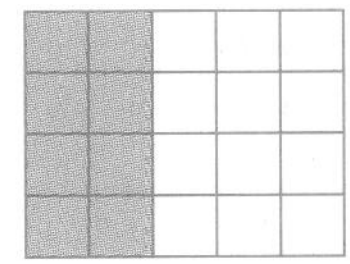

Compare the fractions.

2. $\frac{4}{9}, \frac{5}{9}$ **3.** $\frac{5}{7}, \frac{5}{6}$ **4.** $\frac{2}{13}, \frac{2}{15}$

Find the least common denominator of the fractions. Then compare the fractions.

5. $\frac{1}{3}, \frac{3}{4}$ **6.** $\frac{2}{3}, \frac{3}{7}$ **7.** $\frac{4}{5}, \frac{20}{25}$

8. $\frac{3}{5}, \frac{11}{20}$ **9.** $\frac{5}{6}, \frac{1}{4}$ **10.** $\frac{2}{3}, \frac{4}{5}$

In Exercises 11–13, write the fractions in order from least to greatest.

11. $\frac{6}{21}, \frac{6}{17}, \frac{6}{20}$ **12.** $\frac{13}{80}, \frac{17}{80}, \frac{11}{80}$ **13.** $\frac{13}{40}, \frac{3}{80}, \frac{19}{60}$

14. Randy finishes $\frac{3}{4}$ of an 80-question Spanish test. Gina finishes $\frac{4}{5}$ of the same test. Who finishes more of the test? Explain.

Practice and Problem Solving

Student Help

▸MORE PRACTICE
Extra practice to help you master skills is on page 569.

Name the fractions that are shown by the shaded portions of the models. Then decide which fraction is greater.

15.

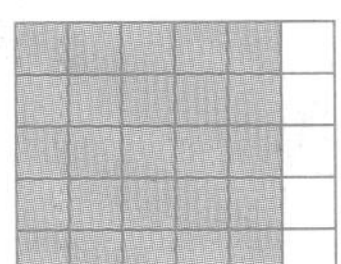

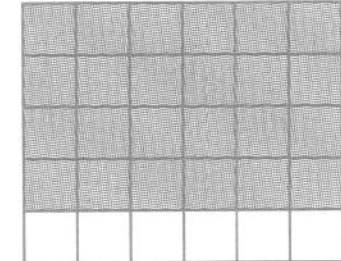

16.

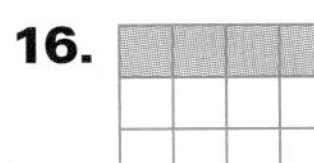

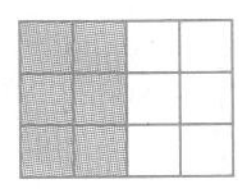

Compare the fractions.

17. $\frac{6}{7}, \frac{3}{7}$ **18.** $\frac{5}{12}, \frac{11}{12}$ **19.** $\frac{7}{10}, \frac{9}{10}$ **20.** $\frac{7}{8}, \frac{5}{8}$

21. $\frac{3}{5}, \frac{3}{8}$ **22.** $\frac{1}{8}, \frac{1}{5}$ **23.** $\frac{7}{10}, \frac{7}{9}$ **24.** $\frac{4}{7}, \frac{4}{11}$

25. $\frac{3}{5}, \frac{5}{6}$ **26.** $\frac{7}{9}, \frac{7}{12}$ **27.** $\frac{17}{20}, \frac{11}{15}$ **28.** $\frac{3}{10}, \frac{5}{24}$

Find the least common denominator of the fractions. Then compare the fractions.

29. $\frac{1}{3}, \frac{5}{12}$ **30.** $\frac{5}{6}, \frac{2}{3}$ **31.** $\frac{3}{8}, \frac{1}{2}$ **32.** $\frac{3}{4}, \frac{15}{16}$

33. $\frac{2}{3}, \frac{11}{16}$ **34.** $\frac{7}{10}, \frac{13}{15}$ **35.** $\frac{4}{9}, \frac{3}{8}$ **36.** $\frac{5}{18}, \frac{7}{30}$

Find a fraction that makes the statement true.

37. ? $< \frac{1}{2}$ **38.** ? $> \frac{7}{10}$ **39.** $\frac{13}{25} <$? **40.** $\frac{19}{45} >$?

In Exercises 41–43, copy the number line. Locate and label the four given fractions on the number line. Then write the fractions in order from least to greatest.

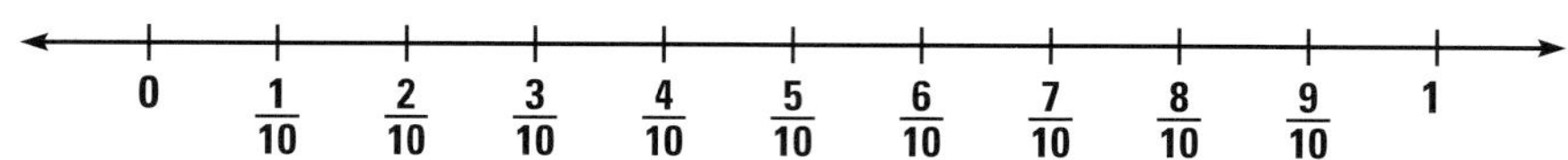

41. $\frac{2}{5}, \frac{5}{10}, \frac{4}{5}, \frac{3}{10}$ **42.** $\frac{3}{5}, \frac{1}{2}, \frac{4}{10}, \frac{1}{5}$ **43.** $\frac{6}{10}, \frac{1}{10}, \frac{4}{5}, \frac{1}{2}$

44. Write the fraction that is shown by the shaded portion of each model. Then write the fractions in order from least to greatest.

A. 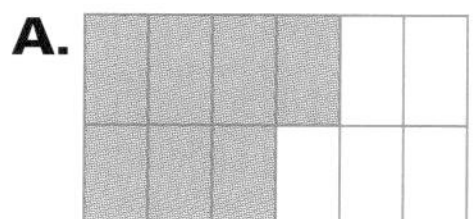 **B.** 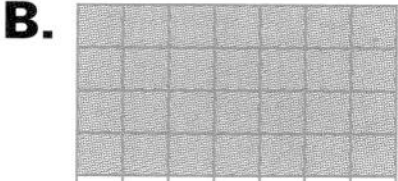 **C.** 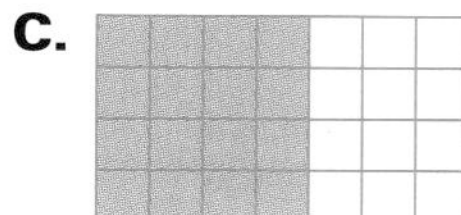

Link to History

ABRAHAM LINCOLN
Lincoln won the 1860 presidential election with 1,865,908 popular votes. He received 180 out of 303 electoral votes.

45. ***History Link*** Use the table at the right to put the candidates in order, beginning with the one who received the most votes.

1860 Popular Vote	
Candidate	**Portion of votes**
Stephen Douglas	$\frac{21}{70}$
Abraham Lincoln	$\frac{4}{10}$
John Bell	$\frac{12}{100}$
John Breckinridge	$\frac{8}{50}$

46. Of the fractions $\frac{7}{8}, \frac{7}{9}, \frac{7}{10}, \frac{7}{11}$, which is closest to 1? Explain.

47. Of the fractions $\frac{1}{4}, \frac{1}{5}, \frac{1}{6}, \frac{1}{7}$, which is closest to 0? Explain.

Compare each fraction to $\frac{1}{2}$. Then decide which fraction is greater.

48. $\frac{2}{4}, \frac{3}{4}$ **49.** $\frac{3}{5}, \frac{3}{6}$ **50.** $\frac{4}{6}, \frac{3}{8}$ **51.** $\frac{5}{9}, \frac{6}{13}$

Write a fraction that is greater than the first fraction and less than the second fraction.

52. $\frac{1}{6}, \frac{3}{6}$ **53.** $\frac{3}{8}, \frac{5}{8}$ **54.** $\frac{3}{10}, \frac{1}{2}$ **55.** $\frac{3}{8}, \frac{3}{4}$

56. **CHALLENGE** A mechanic needs a socket wrench to remove a bolt. A $\frac{1}{4}$ inch socket is too small. A $\frac{3}{8}$ inch socket is too large. Which of the remaining tools, a $\frac{3}{16}$ inch socket or a $\frac{5}{16}$ inch socket, should the mechanic choose? Explain.

Multiple-Choice Practice

57. Which fraction is greater than $\frac{3}{4}$?

Ⓐ $\frac{9}{16}$ Ⓑ $\frac{5}{8}$ Ⓒ $\frac{17}{24}$ Ⓓ $\frac{25}{32}$

58. Which fraction is less than $\frac{11}{26}$?

Ⓕ $\frac{31}{78}$ Ⓖ $\frac{22}{52}$ Ⓗ $\frac{47}{104}$ Ⓙ $\frac{12}{13}$

59. Which fractions are written in order from greatest to least?

Ⓐ $\frac{1}{12}, \frac{11}{24}, \frac{2}{3}, \frac{7}{8}$ Ⓑ $\frac{11}{24}, \frac{2}{3}, \frac{1}{12}, \frac{7}{8}$

Ⓒ $\frac{2}{3}, \frac{7}{8}, \frac{11}{24}, \frac{1}{12}$ Ⓓ $\frac{7}{8}, \frac{2}{3}, \frac{11}{24}, \frac{1}{12}$

Mixed Review

ALGEBRA Evaluate the expression. *(1.2)*

60. $x + 8$ when $x = 4$

61. $3k$ when $k = 30$

62. $m - 14$ when $m = 14$

63. $\frac{49}{c}$ when $c = 7$

64. $\frac{36}{w}$ when $w = 12$

65. $\frac{r}{s}$ when $r = 72$ and $s = 9$

In Exercises 66–69, order the numbers from least to greatest. *(1.5)*

66. 2.12, 2.2, 2.02, 2.3, 2.19

67. 8.32, 8.53, 8.45, 8.35, 8.3

68. 0.19, 0.09, 0.6, 0.05, 0.009

69. 2.15, 2.105, 2.05, 2.015, 2.01

70. **GEOGRAPHY** San Diego and Los Angeles are about 118 miles apart. On your map the cities are 1.75 inches apart. About how many actual miles does an inch represent on your map? Round your answer to the nearest mile. *(1.9)*

Use a factor tree to write the prime factorization of the number. *(2.1)*

71. 130 **72.** 424 **73.** 725 **74.** 1000

REASONING 2.7

DEVELOPING CONCEPTS

Using Fraction Models

For use with Lesson 2.7

California Standards

- Use words, numbers, and models to explain mathematical reasoning. (MR 2.4)
- Compare fractions and mixed numbers. (NS 1.1)

MATERIALS

- Paper
- Colored pencils

A *mixed number* is a sum of a whole number and a fraction. For example, $6\frac{3}{5}$, which represents $6 + \frac{3}{5}$, is a mixed number. An *improper fraction* is a fraction where the numerator is greater than or equal to the denominator. For example, $\frac{4}{3}$ and $\frac{8}{8}$ are improper fractions.

SAMPLE 1 Writing a Mixed Number as a Fraction

You can use an area model to write $2\frac{2}{5}$ as an improper fraction.

Here's How

1. Draw an area model for $2\frac{2}{5}$.

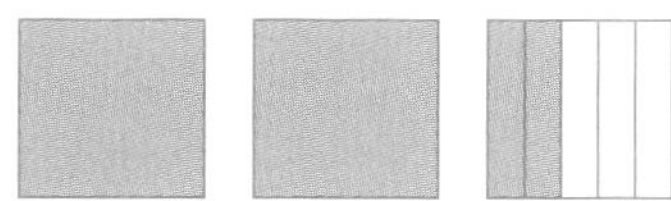

2. Think of each whole unit as $\frac{5}{5}$.

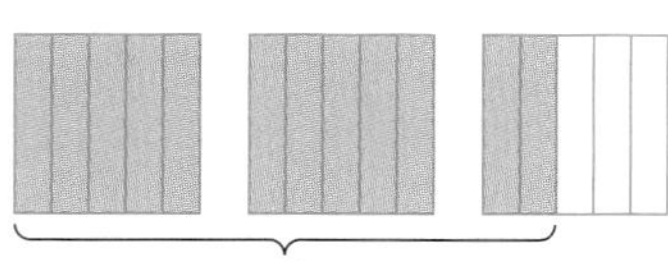

3. There are 12 fifths, or $\frac{12}{5}$, in $2\frac{2}{5}$.

ANSWER ▶ You can write $2\frac{2}{5}$ as $\frac{12}{5}$.

Try These

In Exercises 1 and 2, name the mixed number and the improper fraction that is shown.

1. 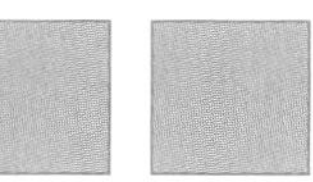 

2.   

In Exercises 3–6, use an area model to write the mixed number as an improper fraction.

3. $1\frac{3}{4}$ **4.** $2\frac{3}{5}$ **5.** $3\frac{1}{4}$ **6.** $2\frac{5}{6}$

7. **MATHEMATICAL REASONING** Describe a procedure for rewriting a mixed number as an improper fraction *without* using an area model. Give an example using your procedure.

You may want to write an improper fraction as a mixed number.

SAMPLE 2 Writing an Improper Fraction as a Mixed Number

You can use an area model to write $\frac{7}{3}$ as a mixed number.

Here's How

1. Draw unit squares divided into thirds. Draw as many squares as you think you'll need for $\frac{7}{3}$. Because 7 is more than two times 3, draw more than 2 squares.

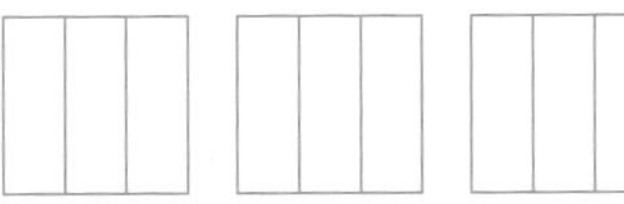

2. Shade 7 of the thirds.

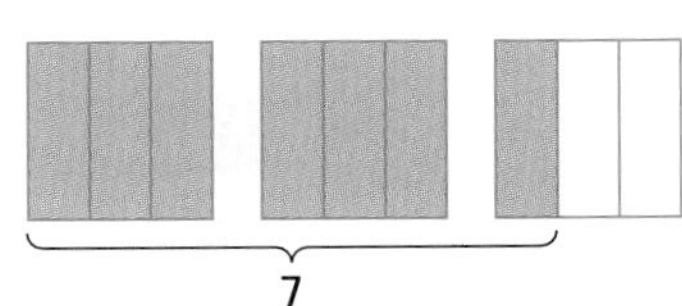

3. There are two whole units shaded plus $\frac{1}{3}$ unit, or $2\frac{1}{3}$ units, shaded.

ANSWER ▶ You can write $\frac{7}{3}$ as $2\frac{1}{3}$.

Try These

Name the improper fraction and the mixed number that is shown by the area model.

8. 

9. 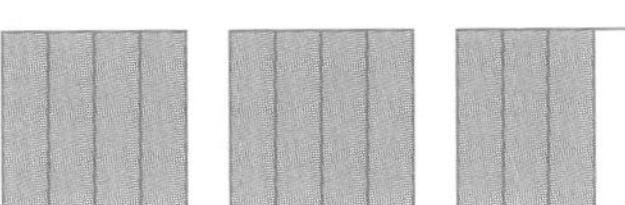

Use an area model to write the improper fraction as a mixed number.

10. $\frac{5}{4}$ **11.** $\frac{8}{3}$ **12.** $\frac{11}{6}$ **13.** $\frac{16}{5}$

14. MATHEMATICAL REASONING Describe a procedure for rewriting an improper fraction as a mixed number *without* using an area model. Give an example using your procedure.

2.7 Mixed Numbers and Improper Fractions

California Standards

In this lesson you'll:

- Compare and order fractions and mixed numbers and place them on a number line. (NS 1.1)

Goal 1 Mixed Numbers and Improper Fractions

A positive fraction is a **proper fraction** if it is between 0 and 1. A positive fraction is an **improper fraction** if it is greater than or equal to one. So, $\frac{7}{8}$ is a proper fraction and $\frac{7}{7}$ and $\frac{8}{7}$ are improper fractions. A **mixed number** has a whole number part and a fraction part.

$3\frac{2}{5}$	$=$	3	$+$	$\frac{2}{5}$
mixed number	**=**	**whole number**	**+**	**fraction**

As you saw in Developing Concepts 2.7, page 88, you can use an area model to help you write a mixed number as an improper fraction.

EXAMPLE 1 Writing Mixed Numbers as Improper Fractions

Write the mixed number as an improper fraction.

a. $4\frac{1}{3}$ **b.** $11\frac{1}{2}$

Solution

a. You want to find how many thirds are in $4\frac{1}{3}$.

An area model for $4\frac{1}{3}$ suggests the following numerical approach:

$4\frac{1}{3} = \mathbf{4} + \frac{1}{3}$ Rewrite as a sum.

$= \frac{\mathbf{12}}{\mathbf{3}} + \frac{1}{3}$ Rewrite 4 as $\frac{12}{3}$.

$= \frac{13}{3}$ Total number of thirds

b. You want to find how many halves are in $11\frac{1}{2}$.

$11\frac{1}{2} = \mathbf{11} + \frac{1}{2}$ Rewrite as a sum.

$= \frac{\mathbf{22}}{\mathbf{2}} + \frac{1}{2}$ Rewrite 11 as $\frac{22}{2}$.

$= \frac{23}{2}$ Total number of halves

Student Help

READING TIP
"$4\frac{1}{3}$" is read "four *and* one third" and means $4 + \frac{1}{3}$. It should not be confused with $4\left(\frac{1}{3}\right)$, which is 4 *times* $\frac{1}{3}$.

EXAMPLE 2 Writing Improper Fractions as Mixed Numbers

Write the improper fraction $\frac{22}{5}$ as a mixed number.

Solution

Start with a set model for 22. Make as many groups of 5 as you can.

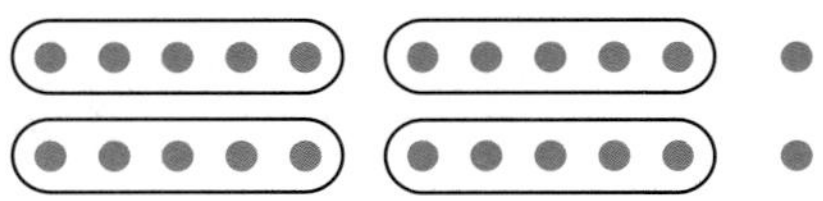

There are 4 groups of 5 with 2 left over, or 4 R2. So the whole number part is 4. To find the fraction part, write the remainder as part of a group of 5, or $\frac{2}{5}$.

ANSWER ▶ $\frac{22}{5} = 4\frac{2}{5}$. You can also treat $\frac{22}{5}$ as the division of 22 by 5.

$$\frac{22}{5} \longrightarrow \begin{array}{r} 4 \text{ R2, or } 4\frac{2}{5} \\ 5\overline{)22} \\ \underline{20} \\ 2 \end{array}$$

Student Help

▶ **LOOK BACK**
For help with rewriting a fraction as a division problem, refer back to the table on page 7.

Goal 2 ORDERING USING A NUMBER LINE

You can use a number line to compare and order fractions and mixed numbers.

Student Help

▶ **MORE EXAMPLES**
More examples are available at www.mcdougallittell.com

EXAMPLE 3 Graphing a Fraction on a Number Line

Graph the fraction $\frac{7}{5}$ on the number line.

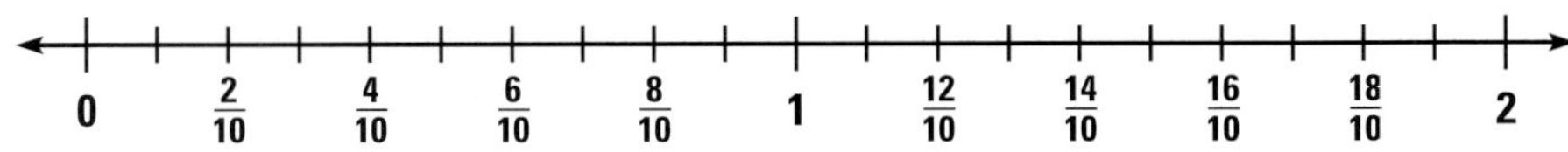

Solution

The fractions on the number line have 10 as a denominator. Begin by writing $\frac{7}{5}$ as an equivalent fraction with a denominator of 10.

$$\frac{7}{5} = \frac{7 \cdot 2}{5 \cdot 2} = \frac{14}{10}$$

Then graph the number on the number line.

EXAMPLE 4 Ordering Fractions and Mixed Numbers

Write the numbers in order from least to greatest.

$$\frac{4}{3}, \frac{5}{6}, 1, \frac{2}{3}, 1\frac{1}{6}$$

Solution

Begin by writing the numbers as fractions with the same denominator. The LCM of 1, 3, and 6 is 6, so you can use 6 as a common denominator.

$$\frac{4}{3} = \frac{4 \cdot 2}{3 \cdot 2} = \frac{8}{6} \qquad 1 = \frac{6}{6} \qquad \frac{2}{3} = \frac{2 \cdot 2}{3 \cdot 2} = \frac{4}{6} \qquad 1\frac{1}{6} = \frac{6}{6} + \frac{1}{6} = \frac{7}{6}$$

Then graph the numbers on a number line.

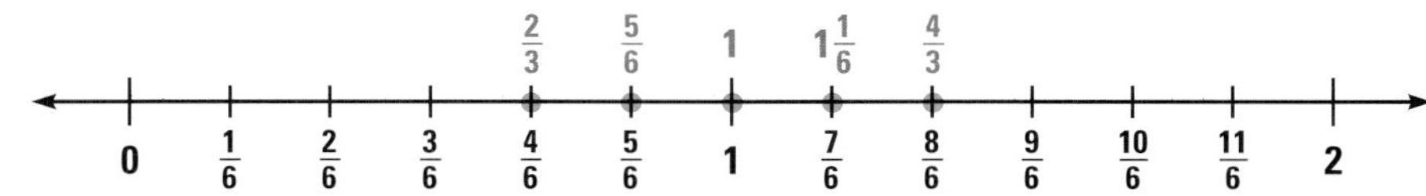

From the number line, you can see that the order is $\frac{2}{3}, \frac{5}{6}, 1, 1\frac{1}{6}, \frac{4}{3}$.

Student Help

▶ **STUDY TIP**
Remember that when comparing two positive fractions with the same denominator, the fraction with the greater numerator is greater.

2.7 Exercises

Guided Practice

Write the mixed number as an improper fraction.

1. $2\frac{1}{2}$ **2.** $4\frac{3}{4}$ **3.** $7\frac{3}{5}$ **4.** $10\frac{1}{3}$ **5.** $20\frac{3}{8}$

Write the improper fraction as a mixed number.

6. $\frac{9}{8}$ **7.** $\frac{17}{3}$ **8.** $\frac{27}{10}$ **9.** $\frac{22}{7}$ **10.** $\frac{23}{2}$

11. Copy the number line below. Graph $\frac{7}{4}$, 2, $\frac{1}{3}$, and $1\frac{1}{6}$. Then write the numbers in order from least to greatest.

ERROR ANALYSIS **Describe and correct the error.**

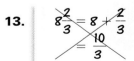

12. $\frac{16}{5} = 1\frac{3}{5}$ $\quad 5\overline{)16}$ with quotient 3, 15, 1

13. $8\frac{2}{3} = 8 + \frac{2}{3} = \frac{10}{3}$

Practice and Problem Solving

Student Help

▶ MORE PRACTICE
Extra practice to help you master skills is on page 569.

In Exercises 14–18, identify the number as a *proper fraction*, an *improper fraction*, or a *mixed number*.

14. $\frac{17}{4}$ **15.** $\frac{1}{6}$ **16.** $\frac{5}{5}$ **17.** $6\frac{7}{8}$ **18.** $\frac{8}{9}$

19. Write the mixed number and the equivalent improper fraction represented by the shaded portion of the model at the right.

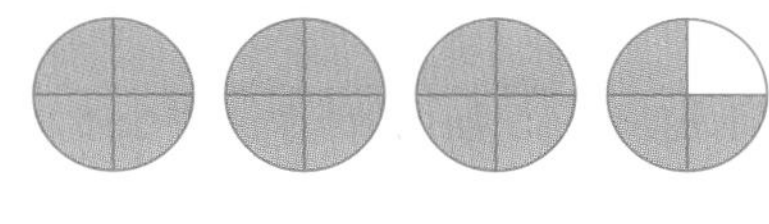

Complete the statement using *sometimes, always,* or *never.*

20. A mixed number is __?__ greater than 1.

21. A positive proper fraction is __?__ greater than 1.

22. A positive improper fraction is __?__ a whole number.

Write the mixed number as an improper fraction.

23. $5\frac{1}{2}$ **24.** $10\frac{1}{2}$ **25.** $8\frac{1}{3}$ **26.** $1\frac{3}{4}$

27. $2\frac{1}{6}$ **28.** $3\frac{3}{8}$ **29.** $4\frac{6}{7}$ **30.** $1\frac{5}{11}$

31. $12\frac{11}{12}$ **32.** $5\frac{4}{15}$ **33.** $18\frac{3}{4}$ **34.** $90\frac{5}{6}$

Write the improper fraction as a mixed number.

35. $\frac{7}{2}$ **36.** $\frac{7}{5}$ **37.** $\frac{11}{6}$ **38.** $\frac{16}{3}$

39. $\frac{27}{4}$ **40.** $\frac{23}{7}$ **41.** $\frac{28}{9}$ **42.** $\frac{35}{8}$

43. $\frac{47}{15}$ **44.** $\frac{112}{25}$ **45.** $\frac{173}{18}$ **46.** $\frac{219}{150}$

In Exercises 47–52, graph the numbers on a number line. Then write them in order from least to greatest.

47. $1\frac{3}{4}, \frac{5}{4}, \frac{9}{4}, \frac{1}{2}$ **48.** $\frac{1}{3}, 1\frac{2}{3}, 2\frac{5}{6}, \frac{7}{6}$ **49.** $\frac{19}{8}, \frac{1}{4}, \frac{16}{8}, 1\frac{3}{4}$

50. $\frac{17}{10}, \frac{5}{2}, \frac{3}{5}, 1\frac{4}{5}$ **51.** $\frac{5}{6}, 1\frac{1}{3}, \frac{1}{2}, \frac{2}{3}$ **52.** $1\frac{3}{10}, \frac{4}{5}, 1\frac{1}{2}, 1\frac{3}{5}$

53. **WINNING WEIGHTS** At a county fair prizes go to the three heaviest pumpkins. The pumpkin weights (in pounds) at this year's fair are $15\frac{15}{16}$, $16\frac{3}{16}$, $15\frac{7}{8}$, $16\frac{1}{4}$, and $16\frac{1}{8}$. Write the weights in order from heaviest to lightest, and state which pumpkins are prizewinners.

Chapter 2 Chapter Summary and Review

VOCABULARY

- **factor,** *p. 60*
- **divisor,** *p. 60*
- **prime number,** *p. 60*
- **composite number,** *p. 60*
- **prime factorization,** *p. 61*
- **factor tree,** *p. 61*
- **common factor,** *p. 65*
- **greatest common factor, greatest common divisor,** *p. 65*
- **fraction,** *p. 69*
- **numerator,** *p. 69*
- **denominator,** *p. 69*
- **equivalent fractions,** *p. 73*
- **simplest form,** *p. 73*
- **multiple,** *p. 79*
- **common multiple,** *p. 79*
- **least common multiple,** *p. 79*
- **least common denominator,** *p. 84*
- **proper fraction,** *p. 90*
- **improper fraction,** *p. 90*
- **mixed number,** *p. 90*
- **terminating decimal,** *p. 95*
- **repeating decimal,** *p. 95*

2.1 PRIME FACTORIZATION

Examples on pp. 60–61

EXAMPLE **Use a factor tree to write the prime factorization of 405.**

ANSWER ▶ The prime factorization of 405 is $3^4 \times 5$.

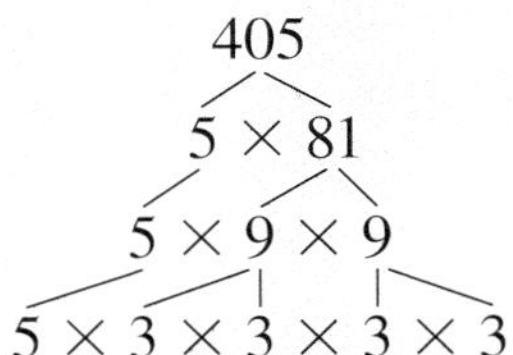

Use a factor tree to write the prime factorization of the number.

1. 47 **2.** 216 **3.** 750 **4.** 1815

2.2 GREATEST COMMON FACTOR

Examples on pp. 65–66

EXAMPLE **Find the greatest common factor of 18 and 30.**

List the factors for 18 and 30. Find the largest number common to both lists.

Factors of 18: 1, 2, 3, **6**, 9, 18

Factors of 30: 1, 2, 3, 5, **6**, 10, 15, 30

ANSWER ▶ The greatest common factor of 18 and 30 is **6**.

In Exercises 5–8, find the greatest common factor of the numbers.

5. 25, 36 **6.** 34, 68 **7.** 64, 96 **8.** 81, 108

2.3 FUNDAMENTAL FRACTION CONCEPTS

Examples on pp. 69–70

EXAMPLE **Draw an area model and a set model for $\frac{3}{12}$.**

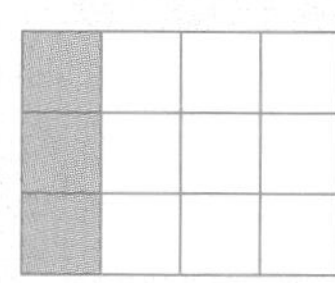
Area model

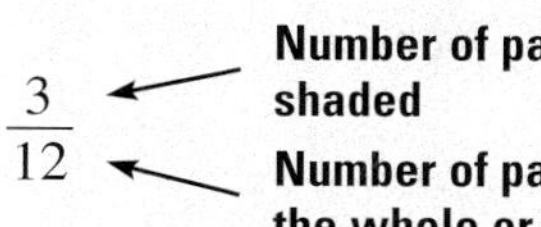

Set model

In Exercises 9–11, write the fraction given by the verbal phrase. Then identify the numerator and the denominator.

9. Three fourths **10.** Two sevenths **11.** Seven twelfths

In Exercises 12–14, write a fraction given by the shaded portion of the model.

12. 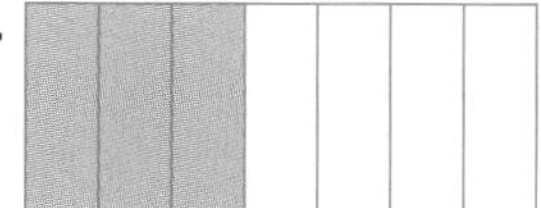 **13.** 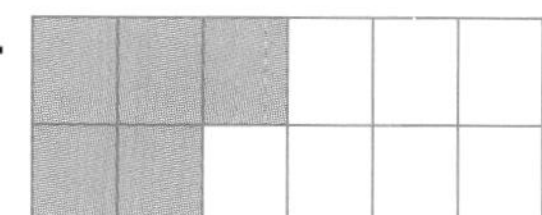 **14.** 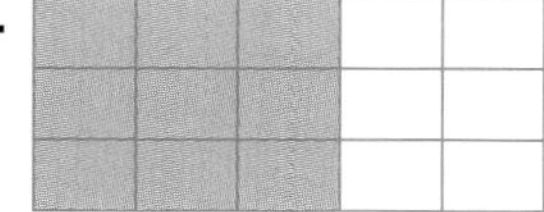

2.4 FRACTIONS IN SIMPLEST FORM

Examples on pp. 73–74

EXAMPLE **Write $\frac{28}{42}$ in simplest form.**

$$\frac{28}{42} = \frac{\overset{1}{\cancel{14}} \cdot 2}{\underset{1}{\cancel{14}} \cdot 3}$$ The greatest common factor is 14.

$$= \frac{2}{3}$$ Divide the numerator and denominator by 14.

15. Draw area models to show that $\frac{5}{6}$ and $\frac{10}{12}$ are equivalent.

Identify the fraction that is *not* equivalent to the other three.

16. $\frac{5}{8}, \frac{30}{48}, \frac{15}{16}, \frac{70}{112}$ **17.** $\frac{66}{88}, \frac{54}{72}, \frac{3}{4}, \frac{130}{140}$ **18.** $\frac{60}{135}, \frac{16}{81}, \frac{4}{9}, \frac{52}{117}$

Write the fraction in simplest form.

19. $\frac{36}{42}$ **20.** $\frac{25}{300}$ **21.** $\frac{18}{126}$ **22.** $\frac{39}{169}$

2.5 LEAST COMMON MULTIPLE

Examples on pp. 79–80

To find a least common multiple, you can use a list or prime factorization.

EXAMPLE **Find the least common multiple of 6 and 10.**

USING A LIST

Multiples of 6: 6, 12, 18, 24, **30**, 36, . . .

Multiples of 10: 10, 20, **30**, 40, 50, 60, . . .

The least common multiple of 6 and 10 is **30**.

USING PRIME FACTORIZATION

Prime factorization of 6: $\textcircled{2} \times 3$

Prime factorization of 10: $\textcircled{2} \times 5$

Write circled factors only once. The LCM of 6 and 10 is $2 \times 3 \times 5 = 30$.

List the first eight multiples of the numbers. Then find the common multiples. What is the least common multiple?

23. 4, 8 **24.** 5, 7 **25.** 3, 4 **26.** 10, 30

Use prime factorization to find the LCM of the numbers.

27. 5, 12 **28.** 6, 30 **29.** 16, 22 **30.** 72, 90

2.6 COMPARING AND ORDERING FRACTIONS

Examples on pp. 83–84

EXAMPLE **Compare $\frac{3}{8}$ and $\frac{5}{6}$.**

The least common multiple of 8 and 6 is 24, so the least common denominator is 24.

$\frac{3}{8} = \frac{3 \cdot 3}{8 \cdot 3} = \frac{9}{24}$ Multiply the numerator and denominator by 3.

$\frac{5}{6} = \frac{5 \cdot 4}{6 \cdot 4} = \frac{20}{24}$ Multiply the numerator and denominator by 4.

Because $\frac{9}{24} < \frac{20}{24}$, you know that $\frac{3}{8} < \frac{5}{6}$.

Find the least common denominator. Then compare the fractions using <, >, or =.

31. $\frac{2}{5}, \frac{1}{4}$ **32.** $\frac{5}{7}, \frac{3}{4}$ **33.** $\frac{1}{8}, \frac{3}{16}$ **34.** $\frac{11}{12}, \frac{1}{3}$

35. $\frac{13}{20}, \frac{7}{10}$ **36.** $\frac{3}{8}, \frac{5}{12}$ **37.** $\frac{1}{4}, \frac{1}{5}$ **38.** $\frac{7}{10}, \frac{3}{5}$

2.7 MIXED NUMBERS AND IMPROPER FRACTIONS

Examples on pp. 90–92

EXAMPLES

Write $5\frac{2}{3}$ as an improper fraction.

$5\frac{2}{3} = 5 + \frac{2}{3}$ Rewrite as a sum.

$= \frac{15}{3} + \frac{2}{3}$ Rewrite 5 as $\frac{15}{3}$.

$= \frac{17}{3}$ Add.

ANSWER ▶ You can write $5\frac{2}{3}$ as $\frac{17}{3}$.

Write $\frac{13}{4}$ as a mixed number.

$4\overline{)13}$ with quotient 3 — Divide 13 by 4.

12 — 3 × 4 = 12

1 — Subtract. The remainder is 1.

ANSWER ▶ After writing the remainder as a fraction, you have $\frac{13}{4} = 3\frac{1}{4}$.

Write the mixed number as an improper fraction.

39. $8\frac{1}{2}$ **40.** $2\frac{4}{9}$ **41.** $7\frac{2}{3}$ **42.** $4\frac{4}{7}$

In Exercises 43–46, write the improper fraction as a mixed number.

43. $\frac{34}{5}$ **44.** $\frac{53}{8}$ **45.** $\frac{17}{9}$ **46.** $\frac{23}{4}$

47. Plot $1\frac{1}{7}$, $\frac{18}{6}$, $\frac{7}{3}$, $\frac{7}{9}$, $3\frac{1}{2}$, and $\frac{13}{4}$ on a number line. Then order the numbers from least to greatest.

2.8 CONNECTING DECIMALS AND FRACTIONS

Examples on pp. 95–96

To write a fraction as a decimal, divide the numerator by the denominator.

EXAMPLES **a. Write $\frac{5}{8}$ as a decimal.**

a. Divide the numerator 5 by the denominator 8.

$8\overline{)5.000}$ = 0.625

ANSWER ▶ $\frac{5}{8} = 0.625$

b. Write 0.55 as a fraction.

b. $0.55 = \frac{0.55 \cdot 100}{100}$

$= \frac{55}{100}$

$= \frac{11}{20}$

Write the decimal as a fraction in simplest form.

48. 0.24 **49.** 0.08 **50.** 1.25 **51.** 3.8

Chapter 2 Chapter Test

Find all the factors of the number.

1. 32 **2.** 77 **3.** 80 **4.** 216

In Exercises 5–8, tell whether the number is *prime* or *composite*.

5. 3 **6.** 42 **7.** 59 **8.** 185

Use a factor tree to write the prime factorization of the number.

9. 78 **10.** 112 **11.** 135 **12.** 192

Find the greatest common factor of the numbers.

13. 16, 24 **14.** 20, 35 **15.** 44, 66 **16.** 50, 300

Write three equivalent fractions represented by the shaded portion of the model.

17.

18. 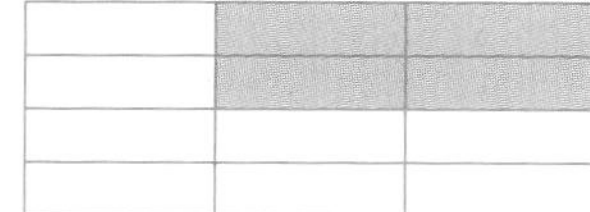

19. 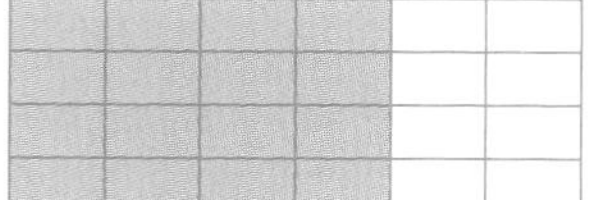

In Exercises 20–23, write the fraction in simplest form.

20. $\frac{8}{16}$ **21.** $\frac{12}{15}$ **22.** $\frac{14}{20}$ **23.** $\frac{6}{27}$

24. FAVORITE FOODS A survey asked 24 sixth graders to name their favorite type of food. One half chose Italian, one sixth chose Mexican, one twelfth chose Chinese, and one fourth chose American. Use a set model to find how many chose each type of food.

Find the least common multiple of the numbers.

25. 10, 18 **26.** 14, 15 **27.** 51, 68 **28.** 8, 9, 10

In Exercises 29–32, compare the fractions using <, >, or = .

29. $\frac{2}{4}$? $\frac{1}{4}$ **30.** $\frac{5}{8}$? $\frac{5}{7}$ **31.** $\frac{4}{7}$? $\frac{1}{2}$ **32.** $\frac{6}{12}$? $\frac{2}{3}$

33. Write each number graphed on the number line as a mixed number, an improper fraction, and a decimal.

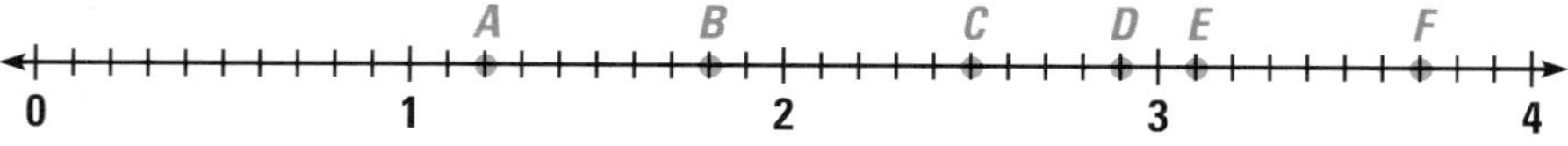

Multiple-Choice Practice

Test Tip If you have to guess, try to eliminate some of the answers that you think may be incorrect.

1. What are all the factors of 15?

(A) 3, 5 (B) 3, 5, 15

(C) 1, 3, 5, 15 (D) 3, 5, 10, 15

2. Which number is composite?

(F) 121 (G) 97

(H) 79 (J) 37

3. What is the prime factorization of 756?

(A) $3 \cdot 4 \cdot 7 \cdot 9$

(B) $2^2 \cdot 3 \cdot 7 \cdot 9$

(C) $2^2 \cdot 3^3 \cdot 7$

(D) $2^2 \cdot 3^2 \cdot 7$

4. What is the greatest common factor of 120, 315, and 225?

(F) 5 (G) 9

(H) 15 (J) 25

5. The auditorium at your school has 320 seats. If 280 seats are full, which of the following is *not* true?

(A) $\frac{56}{64}$ of the seats are full.

(B) $\frac{7}{8}$ of the seats are full.

(C) $\frac{6}{64}$ of the seats are empty.

(D) $\frac{1}{8}$ of the seats are empty.

6. Which number is *not* equivalent to the other three?

(F) $\frac{27}{8}$ (G) $3\frac{3}{8}$

(H) 3.375 (J) $\frac{61}{24}$

7. Which model does *not* represent $\frac{2}{3}$?

(A) 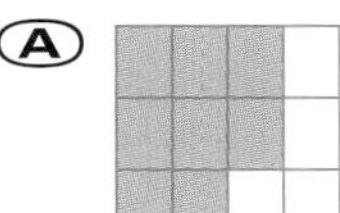 (B) 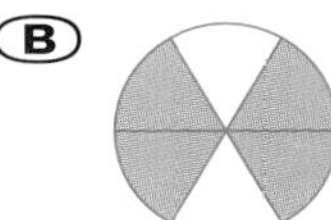

(C) 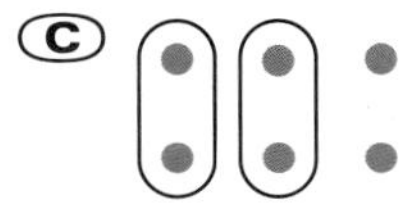 (D) 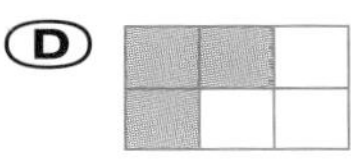

8. What is the least common multiple of 4 and 10?

(F) 10 (G) 20

(H) 24 (J) 40

9. Which fraction is equivalent to $3\frac{2}{5}$?

(A) $\frac{13}{5}$ (B) $\frac{16}{5}$

(C) $\frac{17}{5}$ (D) $\frac{15}{2}$

10. At the grocery store you ask for $3\frac{1}{4}$ pounds of fish. Which decimal amount is shown on the scale?

(F) 3.14 (G) 3.2

(H) 3.25 (J) 3.75

Brain games

California Standards

- Calculate and solve problems involving addition, subtraction, multiplication, and division. (NS 2.0)
- Make decisions about how to approach problems. (MR 1.0)

Factor-Finding Mission

Materials

- Colored pencils
- Game board

Directions

Object of the Game

Play this game in pairs. The object of the game is to have the most points when the entire game board is covered.

How to Play

STEP 1 Player A begins by circling any number on the game board with a colored pencil. The number picked is the number of points Player A scores for that round.

STEP 2 Player B uses a pencil of a different color to circle all of the factors of the number that Player A circled. The sum of those factors is Player B's score. For example, if Player A circles 20, Player B circles 1, 2, 4, 5, and 10, and scores 22 points. *Note:* Numbers may be circled only once.

STEP 3 Take turns being Player A. Repeat Steps 1 and 2 for all the remaining uncircled numbers. When all numbers have been circled, total your scores. The player with the highest score wins. Play several games and develop winning strategies.

Another Way to Play

- Play a variation in which the object of the game is to get the lowest score. Think about how your strategy will be different.
- Make a new game board that contains the numbers 1–50.

Brain Teaser

LOOK for a PATTERN

10, 15

1. Find the greatest common factor and the least common multiple for two nonzero whole numbers. Find the product of the GCF and LCM. Compare it to the product of the two numbers. What do you find?
2. Try other number pairs. What happens? How can you explain it?

6, 12

The basic skills you'll review on this page will help prepare you for the next chapter.

Reviewing the Basics

When you rewrite a measurement in another unit, you can use the relationships between the units.

12 inches = 1 foot	1 cup = 8 fluid ounces
3 feet = 1 yard	2 cups = 1 pint
5280 feet = 1 mile	2 pints = 1 quart
16 ounces = 1 pound	4 quarts = 1 gallon

Student Help

▶ SKILLS REVIEW
For help with converting units of measure, see page 561.

EXAMPLE 1 Converting Units of Measure

How many quarts are in two gallons?

Solution

Use the fact that 1 gallon = 4 quarts.

2×1 gallon = **?** quarts

2×4 quarts = 8 quarts   Substitute 4 quarts for 1 gallon.

There are 8 quarts in 2 gallons.

Try These

Complete the statement.

1. 3 yards = **?** feet

2. 3 miles = **?** feet

3. 24 ounces = **?** pounds

4. 5 pints = **?** cups

5. 60 inches = **?** feet

6. 4 cups = **?** fluid ounces

EXAMPLE 2 Adding and Subtracting Fractions

Add $\frac{1}{2} + \frac{3}{2}$.

Solution

Use area models to add.

$\frac{1}{2} + \frac{3}{2} = \frac{4}{2} = 2$

 + 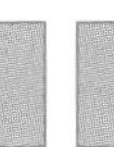 = 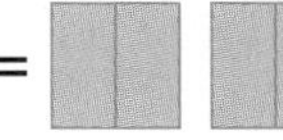

Try These

Add or subtract.

7. $\frac{3}{2} + \frac{3}{2}$

8. $\frac{5}{3} - \frac{2}{3}$

9. $\frac{1}{4} + \frac{5}{4}$

10. $\frac{6}{3} + \frac{6}{3}$

11. $\frac{7}{8} - \frac{5}{8}$

12. $\frac{4}{5} + \frac{6}{5}$

13. $\frac{9}{4} - \frac{6}{4}$

14. $\frac{11}{6} - \frac{3}{6}$

Student Help

▶ MORE EXAMPLES

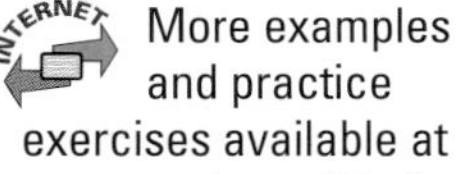

More examples and practice exercises available at www.mcdougallittell.com

Fractions and their Operations

Why are fraction operations important?

Operations with fractions are used in a variety of mathematical situations. For example, you can use the operation of multiplication to find $\frac{3}{4}$ of an amount. You will need to use operations with fractions as you study rates, ratios, and proportions.

Operations with fractions are used in many careers, including carpentry (page 109) and regional planning (page 137). For example, carpenters use fractions in order to find the cost, amount of materials, or time needed for a specific job.

Meeting the California Standards

The skills you'll develop in this chapter will help you meet state standards and prepare for standardized tests. In this chapter you'll:

- **Solve problems involving operations with fractions.** LESSONS 3.1–3.5
- **Explain and perform multiplication and division of fractions.** LESSONS 3.4, 3.5
- **Apply the distributive property to evaluate expressions.** LESSON 3.6
- **Convert one unit of measurement to another.** LESSON 3.7
- **Understand that rate is a measure of one quantity per unit value of another quantity.** LESSON 3.8

Career Link **CARPENTER** A carpenter uses fractions when:

- reading an architect's drawing.
- estimating how much wood to buy.
- selecting the right size of lumber.

Measurements of Cross-Section of Board (in inches)	
Before planing	After planing
1×2	$\frac{3}{4} \times 1\frac{1}{2}$
2×2	$1\frac{1}{2} \times 1\frac{1}{2}$
2×4	$1\frac{1}{2} \times 3\frac{1}{2}$
4×4	$3\frac{1}{2} \times 3\frac{1}{2}$

EXERCISES

Boards are named for their measurements when they are cut from logs. After a board is cut, its rough surfaces are *planed* off. The resulting board is smaller, as shown in the table. Find the height of each stack of boards before planing.

1. 2 × 4, 2 × 4, 2 × 4

2. 1×2, 1×2, 1×2, 2×2

3. 2 × 4, 2 × 4, 4 × 4

In Lesson 3.3, you will learn how to calculate the height of each stack after planing.

Chapter 3 Getting Ready

PREVIEW What's the chapter about?

- Performing operations with **fractions** and **mixed numbers**
- Using the **distributive property**
- Converting **units of measure**, and finding and comparing **rates**

WORDS TO KNOW

- **reciprocals,** *p. 134*
- **multiplicative inverses,** *p. 134*
- **rate of *a* per *b*,** *p. 148*
- **unit rate,** *p. 148*

PREPARE Chapter Readiness Quiz

Take this quick quiz. If you are unsure of an answer, look back at the reference pages for help.

VOCABULARY CHECK *(refer to pp. 60, 90)*

1. Which whole number is prime?

Ⓐ 1 Ⓑ 2 Ⓒ 9 Ⓓ 21

2. Which number is an example of an improper fraction?

Ⓕ $\frac{3}{5}$ Ⓖ $\frac{9}{12}$ Ⓗ $\frac{14}{5}$ Ⓙ $22\frac{5}{6}$

SKILL CHECK *(refer to pp. 69, 73)*

3. Which area model represents $\frac{5}{9}$?

 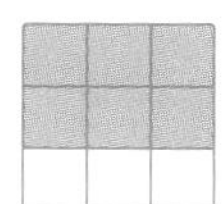 Ⓑ 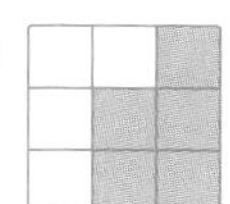 Ⓒ 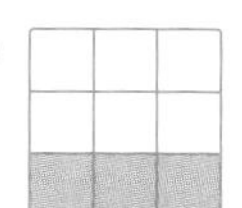 Ⓓ 

4. What is $\frac{12}{28}$ in simplest form?

Ⓕ $\frac{3}{7}$ Ⓖ $\frac{6}{14}$ Ⓗ $\frac{3}{8}$ Ⓙ $\frac{2}{3}$

STUDY TIP Make Example Cards

Example cards will help you remember how to solve problems.

Example Dividing Fractions

$\frac{3}{5} \div \frac{6}{7} = \frac{3}{5} \times \frac{7}{6}$

$= \frac{21}{30} = \frac{7}{10}$

3.1 Adding and Subtracting Fractions

California Standards

In this lesson you'll:

- Solve problems involving addition and subtraction of positive fractions. (NS 2.1)
- Use a common denominator to add or subtract two fractions. (NS 2.4)

Goal 1 USING COMMON DENOMINATORS

FRACTIONS WITH A COMMON DENOMINATOR

To add fractions with a common denominator, add their numerators and write the sum over the denominator.

To subtract fractions with a common denominator, subtract their numerators and write the difference over the denominator.

EXAMPLE 1 Adding and Subtracting Fractions

a. $\frac{1}{7} + \frac{3}{7} = \frac{1 + 3}{7}$ Add numerators.

$= \frac{4}{7}$ Simplify numerator.

b. $\frac{7}{10} - \frac{3}{10} = \frac{7 - 3}{10}$ Subtract numerators.

$= \frac{4}{10}$ Simplify numerator.

$= \frac{2}{5}$ Simplify fraction.

EXAMPLE 2 Adding Fractions

Find the height of the stack of books.

$\frac{3}{8}$ in.

$\frac{7}{8}$ in.

Solution

Add the fractions to find the height.

$\frac{3}{8} + \frac{7}{8} = \frac{3 + 7}{8}$

$= \frac{10}{8}$

$= \frac{\overset{1}{\cancel{2}} \cdot 5}{\underset{1}{\cancel{2}} \cdot 4} = \frac{5}{4}$

ANSWER ▶ The stack is $\frac{5}{4}$ inches, or $1\frac{1}{4}$ inches, high.

Goal 2 USING DIFFERENT DENOMINATORS

To add and subtract fractions with different denominators, first rewrite the fractions so they have the same denominator. You will then be able to add and subtract the fractions by adding and subtracting their numerators.

FRACTIONS WITH DIFFERENT DENOMINATORS

To add or subtract fractions with different denominators, you can rewrite the fractions using a common denominator, as follows.

Addition $\frac{a}{b} + \frac{c}{d} = \frac{ad}{bd} + \frac{bc}{bd} = \frac{ad + bc}{bd}$

Subtraction $\frac{a}{b} - \frac{c}{d} = \frac{ad}{bd} - \frac{bc}{bd} = \frac{ad - bc}{bd}$

Common denominator is *bd*.

When adding or subtracting fractions, you have many choices for a common denominator. One common denominator you can always use is *bd*.

Student Help

MORE EXAMPLES

INTERNET More examples are available at www.mcdougallittell.com

EXAMPLE 3 Adding Fractions

$\frac{1}{4} + \frac{2}{5} = \frac{1 \cdot 5}{4 \cdot 5} + \frac{4 \cdot 2}{4 \cdot 5}$	Choose a common denominator of 20.
$= \frac{5}{20} + \frac{8}{20}$	Simplify.
$= \frac{5 + 8}{20}$	Add numerators.
$= \frac{13}{20}$	Simplify numerator.

EXAMPLE 4 Subtracting Fractions

$\frac{3}{4} - \frac{1}{6} = \frac{3 \cdot 6}{4 \cdot 6} - \frac{4 \cdot 1}{4 \cdot 6}$	Choose a common denominator of 24.
$= \frac{18}{24} - \frac{4}{24}$	Simplify.
$= \frac{18 - 4}{24}$	Subtract numerators.
$= \frac{14}{24}$	Simplify numerator.
$= \frac{\overset{1}{\cancel{2}} \cdot 7}{\underset{1}{\cancel{2}} \cdot 12} = \frac{7}{12}$	Simplify fraction.

3.1 Exercises

Guided Practice

1. WRITING Explain how to add and subtract two fractions with different denominators. Give examples to support your explanation.

In Exercises 2–4, evaluate. Simplify if possible.

2. $\frac{3}{7} - \frac{2}{7}$ **3.** $\frac{5}{12} + \frac{5}{12}$ **4.** $\frac{1}{4} + \frac{5}{4}$

5. Two fractions have denominators of 6 and 8. What is a common denominator for the fractions? Explain your answer.

ERROR ANALYSIS **Describe and correct the error.**

6. $\frac{1}{3} + \frac{3}{5} = \frac{1}{15} + \frac{3}{15} = \frac{4}{15}$

7. 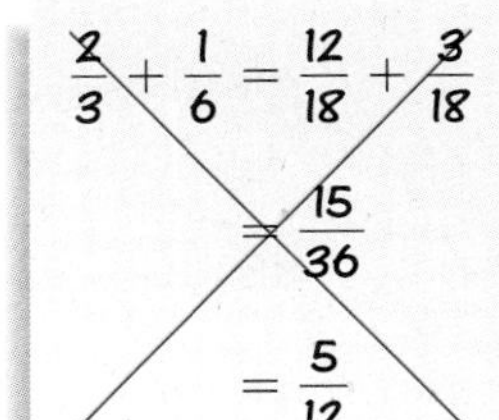

Practice and Problem Solving

Student Help

▶ MORE PRACTICE Extra practice to help you master skills is on page 570.

Evaluate. Simplify if possible.

8. $\frac{1}{6} + \frac{5}{6}$ **9.** $\frac{8}{9} - \frac{2}{9}$ **10.** $\frac{4}{7} + \frac{5}{7}$ **11.** $\frac{3}{10} - \frac{1}{10}$

12. $\frac{4}{9} - \frac{1}{9}$ **13.** $\frac{4}{16} + \frac{8}{16}$ **14.** $\frac{5}{12} - \frac{1}{12}$ **15.** $\frac{5}{20} + \frac{6}{20}$

16. $\frac{3}{4} - \frac{1}{2}$ **17.** $\frac{2}{3} + \frac{1}{5}$ **18.** $\frac{5}{6} - \frac{3}{4}$ **19.** $\frac{5}{9} - \frac{1}{6}$

20. $\frac{5}{7} + \frac{1}{3}$ **21.** $\frac{7}{11} + \frac{3}{4}$ **22.** $\frac{11}{5} - \frac{2}{3}$ **23.** $\frac{5}{6} - \frac{1}{3}$

Complete the statement with a fraction in simplest form.

24. $? + \frac{3}{4} = 1$ **25.** $\frac{9}{11} - ? = \frac{7}{11}$ **26.** $\frac{6}{13} - ? = \frac{2}{13}$

27. $\frac{1}{2} - ? = \frac{1}{6}$ **28.** $\frac{4}{7} + ? = \frac{17}{21}$ **29.** $? - \frac{4}{5} = \frac{3}{20}$

30. $? + \frac{1}{2} = \frac{15}{14}$ **31.** $? + \frac{3}{10} = \frac{4}{5}$ **32.** $\frac{21}{34} - ? = \frac{2}{17}$

Link to Business

SMALL BUSINESS The annual payroll for businesses with under 20 employees was 688 billion dollars in 1997. ▶ Source: US Bureau of the Census

MATHEMATICAL REASONING In Exercises 33–35, complete the statement with *sometimes, always,* or *never*. Give an example to support your answer.

33. The difference of two positive fractions that are each less than 1 is __?__ less than 1.

34. The sum of three positive fractions that are each less than 1 is __?__ greater than 1.

35. The product of the denominators of two fractions can __?__ be used as a common denominator.

BUSINESS In Exercises 36–38, use the circle graph below. It shows the fraction of employees that work in U.S. companies of various sizes. Find the fraction of employees who work in companies of the given size.

36. Fewer than 100 employees

37. Fewer than 500 employees

38. 100–999 employees

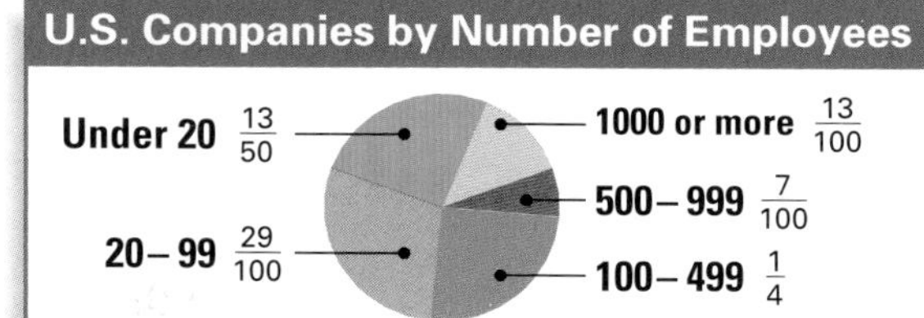

39. CHALLENGE You and a friend begin from the same place on a bike trail. You bike $\frac{1}{2}$ mile and stop. Your friend bikes $\frac{3}{5}$ mile, then turns around and bikes back $\frac{1}{8}$ mile in the direction from which he came. Who is farther ahead on the trail? How much farther? Use a diagram and words to explain your reasoning.

Multiple-Choice Practice

Test Tip Ⓐ Ⓑ Ⓒ Ⓓ

▶ Remember to find a common denominator before adding or subtracting fractions.

40. Evaluate $\frac{1}{3} + \frac{3}{5}$.

Ⓐ $\frac{4}{15}$ Ⓑ $\frac{4}{8}$ Ⓒ $\frac{4}{5}$ Ⓓ $\frac{14}{15}$

41. Evaluate $\frac{5}{6} - \frac{4}{7}$.

Ⓕ $\frac{1}{13}$ Ⓖ $\frac{11}{42}$ Ⓗ $\frac{9}{13}$ Ⓙ $1\frac{17}{42}$

42. You ride a go-cart for $\frac{2}{3}$ mile. Your friend rides for $\frac{8}{9}$ mile. How much farther does your friend ride than you do?

Ⓐ $\frac{1}{9}$ mi Ⓑ $\frac{2}{9}$ mi Ⓒ $\frac{1}{3}$ mi Ⓓ Not here

3.2 Using a Least Common Denominator

California Standards

In this lesson you'll:

- Solve problems involving addition and subtraction of positive fractions. (NS 2.1)
- Determine the least common multiple of whole numbers and use it to solve problems with fractions. (NS 2.4)

Goal 1 Using a Least Common Denominator

In Lesson 2.5 you learned to find the least common multiple of two or more whole numbers. When you add or subtract fractions with different denominators, a convenient common denominator is the least common multiple of their denominators. This number is called the least common denominator (LCD) of the fractions.

EXAMPLE 1 *Using a Least Common Denominator*

Add $\frac{3}{8}$ and $\frac{5}{12}$.

a. Use 8 • 12 as the common denominator.

b. Use the least common denominator.

c. Compare the two methods.

Solution

a. The denominators 8 and 12 can be multiplied together to find a common denominator.

$$\frac{3}{8} + \frac{5}{12} = \frac{3 \cdot 12}{8 \cdot 12} + \frac{8 \cdot 5}{8 \cdot 12}$$ Use 8 • 12 as the common denominator.

$$= \frac{36 + 40}{96}$$ Add fractions.

$$= \frac{76}{96}$$ Simplify numerator.

$$= \frac{\overset{1}{\cancel{4}} \cdot 19}{\underset{1}{\cancel{4}} \cdot 24} = \frac{19}{24}$$ Simplify fraction.

b. The least common multiple of the denominators 8 and 12 is 24. So, the least common denominator is 24.

$$\frac{3}{8} + \frac{5}{12} = \frac{3 \cdot 3}{8 \cdot 3} + \frac{5 \cdot 2}{12 \cdot 2}$$ Rewrite using LCM of 8 and 12 as the common denominator.

$$= \frac{9 + 10}{24}$$ Add fractions.

$$= \frac{19}{24}$$ Simplify numerator.

c. Using the least common denominator reduces the amount of simplifying you need to do.

Student Help

STUDY TIP
For help with finding the least common multiple, see page 79.

STAINED GLASS Artists who work with stained glass cut the glass to a precise size in order to create their designs.

EXAMPLE 2 Subtracting Measurements

ART Find the difference in the widths of the two pieces of stained glass shown.

$1\frac{3}{8}$ in.

$\frac{3}{10}$ in.

$\frac{3}{5}$ in.

$1\frac{3}{8}$ in.

Solution

$$\frac{3}{5} - \frac{3}{10} = \frac{3 \cdot 2}{5 \cdot 2} - \frac{3}{10} \quad \text{Rewrite using LCD.}$$

$$= \frac{6 - 3}{10} \quad \text{Subtract fractions.}$$

$$= \frac{3}{10} \quad \text{Simplify numerator.}$$

ANSWER ▶ One piece of stained glass is $\frac{3}{10}$ inch wider than the other.

Goal 2 USING THREE OR MORE FRACTIONS

EXAMPLE 3 Adding Three Fractions

Find the sum of $\frac{1}{3}$, $\frac{1}{4}$, and $\frac{3}{8}$.

Solution

$$\frac{1}{3} + \frac{1}{4} + \frac{3}{8} = \frac{1 \cdot 8}{3 \cdot 8} + \frac{1 \cdot 6}{4 \cdot 6} + \frac{3 \cdot 3}{8 \cdot 3} \quad \text{Rewrite using LCD.}$$

$$= \frac{8 + 6 + 9}{24} \quad \text{Add fractions.}$$

$$= \frac{23}{24} \quad \text{Simplify numerator.}$$

EXAMPLE 4 Evaluating a Variable Expression

Evaluate $x - y + z$ when $x = \frac{9}{10}$, $y = \frac{3}{4}$, and $z = \frac{1}{3}$.

Solution

$$x - y + z = \frac{9}{10} - \frac{3}{4} + \frac{1}{3} \quad \text{Substitute.}$$

$$= \frac{9 \cdot 6}{10 \cdot 6} - \frac{3 \cdot 15}{4 \cdot 15} + \frac{1 \cdot 20}{3 \cdot 20} \quad \text{Rewrite using LCD.}$$

$$= \frac{54 - 45 + 20}{60} \quad \text{Subtract and add fractions.}$$

$$= \frac{29}{60} \quad \text{Simplify numerator.}$$

3.2 Exercises

Guided Practice

1. **WRITING** Two fractions have denominators of 14 and 21. What is their least common denominator? Explain your reasoning in words and numbers.

Evaluate. Simplify if possible.

2. $\frac{1}{4} + \frac{3}{8}$

3. $\frac{9}{10} - \frac{2}{5}$

4. $\frac{4}{5} + \frac{1}{2}$

5. $\frac{5}{6} + \frac{1}{3} + \frac{3}{4}$

6. $\frac{3}{4} + \frac{1}{5} - \frac{1}{3}$

7. $\frac{3}{8} - \frac{1}{5} + \frac{5}{6}$

In Exercises 8 and 9, decide whether to add or subtract. Then solve.

8. **CRAFTS** You buy $\frac{3}{4}$ yard of fabric to make a craft project. You use only $\frac{2}{3}$ yard. How much material do you have left?

9. **COOKING** You are making a salad dressing mixture that calls for $\frac{1}{4}$ cup of vinegar, $\frac{1}{16}$ cup of lemon juice, and $\frac{1}{2}$ cup of oil. Find the total quantity of dressing produced by the recipe.

Practice and Problem Solving

Student Help

▶ **MORE PRACTICE** Extra practice to help you master skills is on page 570.

Find the least common denominator of the fractions.

10. $\frac{1}{3}, \frac{1}{9}$

11. $\frac{1}{6}, \frac{2}{7}$

12. $\frac{3}{4}, \frac{3}{10}$

13. $\frac{7}{12}, \frac{11}{18}$

Evaluate. Write the answer in simplest form.

14. $\frac{3}{4} + \frac{5}{8}$

15. $\frac{2}{3} - \frac{1}{9}$

16. $\frac{7}{9} + \frac{5}{6}$

17. $\frac{4}{5} - \frac{3}{4}$

18. $\frac{11}{12} - \frac{2}{9}$

19. $\frac{9}{10} + \frac{11}{15}$

20. $\frac{1}{7} + \frac{3}{7} + \frac{1}{14}$

21. $\frac{3}{5} + \frac{1}{10} + \frac{1}{4}$

22. $\frac{4}{5} + \frac{1}{2} - \frac{3}{10}$

23. $\frac{2}{9} - \frac{1}{12} + \frac{1}{2}$

24. $\frac{5}{8} - \frac{3}{16} + \frac{4}{3}$

25. $\frac{4}{5} + \frac{3}{11} - \frac{1}{10}$

26. **WRITING** Find the sum $\frac{4}{5} + \frac{1}{2} + \frac{1}{10}$ using two different methods. Explain which method you prefer.

ALGEBRA **Evaluate the expression $x + y - z$ for the given values.**

27. $x = \frac{4}{7}, y = \frac{1}{2}, z = \frac{1}{3}$

28. $x = \frac{8}{9}, y = \frac{2}{7}, z = \frac{4}{21}$

29. $x = \frac{3}{5}, y = \frac{1}{6}, z = \frac{2}{3}$

30. $x = \frac{4}{9}, y = \frac{5}{11}, z = \frac{1}{16}$

31. **MATHEMATICAL REASONING** Illustrate and verify the associative property of addition using fractions with different denominators.

MARKET RESEARCH **In Exercises 32–34, use the results of the survey on peanut butter preferences.**

32. How much greater is the fraction of people who prefer smooth than the fraction of people who prefer crunchy?

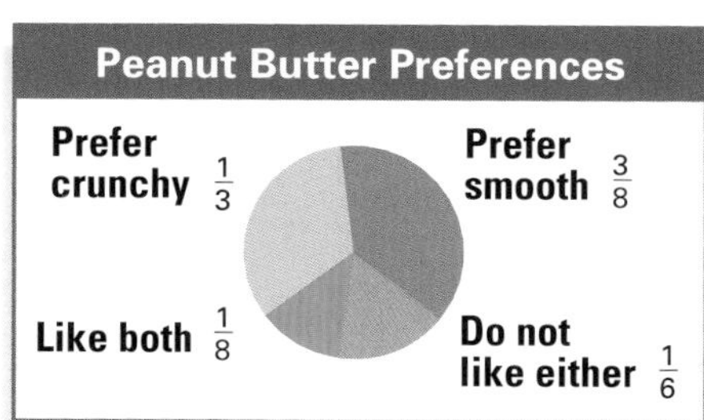

33. What fraction of people prefer either smooth or crunchy, but not both?

34. What fraction of people like some type of peanut butter?

Link to Music

MUSICAL NOTATION
The present system of musical notation, including time signature and tempo marks, began in the early 17th century.

MUSIC **In Exercises 35–38, use the values of the five musical notes shown at the right to find the sum of the notes in each measure.**

The sum of the values of the notes in the measure should be 1. Is it?

35.

36.

37.

38.

Multiple-Choice Practice

39. Which of the following does *not* have a sum of 1?

Ⓐ $\frac{5}{6} + \frac{2}{12}$ Ⓑ $\frac{1}{2} + \frac{4}{6}$ Ⓒ $\frac{1}{4} + \frac{6}{8}$ Ⓓ $\frac{4}{16} + \frac{3}{4}$

40. Evaluate $\frac{5}{6} + \frac{1}{12} - \frac{2}{3}$. Simplify if possible.

Ⓕ $\frac{1}{12}$ Ⓖ $\frac{1}{4}$ Ⓗ $\frac{1}{3}$ Ⓙ $1\frac{7}{12}$

3.3 Adding and Subtracting Mixed Numbers

In this lesson you'll:

- Solve problems involving addition and subtraction of mixed numbers. (NS 2.1)

Goal 1 ADDING AND SUBTRACTING MIXED NUMBERS

The associative and commutative properties allow you to add and subtract mixed numbers.

ADDING AND SUBTRACTING MIXED NUMBERS

1. Add or subtract the fractions.
2. Add or subtract the whole numbers.
3. Simplify if possible.

EXAMPLE 1 Adding With Common Denominators

$2\frac{2}{5} + 1\frac{4}{5} = \left(2 + \frac{2}{5}\right) + \left(1 + \frac{4}{5}\right)$ Write the mixed numbers as sums.

$= 3 + \frac{6}{5}$ Add whole numbers and add fractions.

$= 3 + 1 + \frac{1}{5}$ Rewrite the improper fraction.

$= 4\frac{1}{5}$ Write as mixed number.

EXAMPLE 2 Adding With Different Denominators

$8\frac{1}{3} + 4\frac{1}{6} = 8\frac{2}{6} + 4\frac{1}{6}$ Rewrite fractions with a common denominator.

$= 12\frac{3}{6}$ Add whole numbers and add fractions.

$= 12\frac{1}{2}$ Simplify.

EXAMPLE 3 Subtracting With Different Denominators

$9\frac{5}{7} - 3\frac{1}{2} = 9\frac{10}{14} - 3\frac{7}{14}$ Rewrite fractions with a common denominator.

$= 6\frac{3}{14}$ Subtract whole numbers and subtract fractions.

Goal 2 Regrouping to Subtract Mixed Numbers

When you subtract mixed numbers, the fractional part of the second number may be larger than the fractional part of the first number. You will need to rewrite the fractional part of the first number so that you can subtract. Here's an example using an area model.

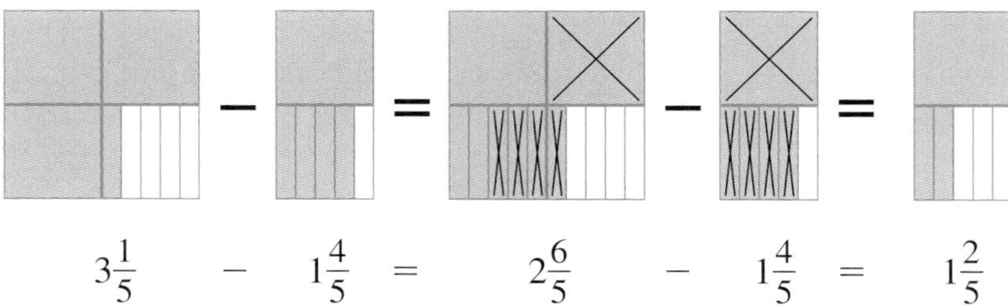

$$3\frac{1}{5} \quad - \quad 1\frac{4}{5} \quad = \quad 2\frac{6}{5} \quad - \quad 1\frac{4}{5} \quad = \quad 1\frac{2}{5}$$

Writing $3\frac{1}{5}$ as $2\frac{6}{5}$ is called *regrouping* because the 3 is regrouped as $2 + \frac{5}{5}$.

Student Help

▶ More Examples

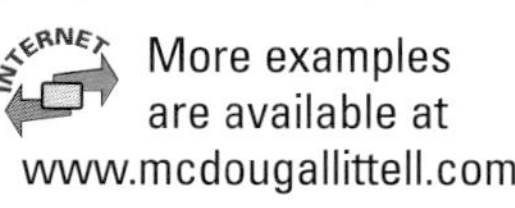

More examples are available at www.mcdougallittell.com

EXAMPLE 4 Regrouping to Subtract

$5\frac{1}{4} - 2\frac{3}{4} = 4\frac{5}{4} - 2\frac{3}{4}$	Regroup $5\frac{1}{4}$ as $4\frac{5}{4}$.
$= 2\frac{2}{4}$	Subtract.
$= 2\frac{1}{2}$	Simplify.

EXAMPLE 5 Regrouping to Subtract

COOKING You have $6\frac{1}{6}$ cups of cornmeal. You need $3\frac{1}{2}$ cups for a recipe. After you make the recipe, how much cornmeal will you have left?

Solution

You are using $3\frac{1}{2}$ cups from a total of $6\frac{1}{6}$ cups, so you subtract.

$6\frac{1}{6} - 3\frac{1}{2} = 6\frac{1}{6} - 3\frac{3}{6}$	Rewrite fractions with a common denominator.
$= 5\frac{7}{6} - 3\frac{3}{6}$	Regroup $6\frac{1}{6}$ as $5\frac{7}{6}$.
$= 2\frac{4}{6}$	Subtract.
$= 2\frac{2}{3}$	Simplify.

ANSWER ▶ You will have $2\frac{2}{3}$ cups of cornmeal left.

3.3 Exercises

Guided Practice

1. **WRITING** Describe the steps for adding and subtracting mixed numbers. Use examples.

2. In finding the sum of $1\frac{5}{6} + 2\frac{9}{10}$, in what order do the expressions below appear?

A. $= 3\frac{52}{30}$ **B.** $= 4\frac{11}{15}$ **C.** $= 1\frac{25}{30} + 2\frac{27}{30}$ **D.** $= 4\frac{22}{30}$

Evaluate. Simplify if possible.

3. $6\frac{5}{8} + 3\frac{1}{8}$ **4.** $2\frac{7}{20} - 1\frac{1}{20}$ **5.** $7\frac{7}{9} - 5\frac{5}{9}$ **6.** $5\frac{1}{12} + 8\frac{7}{12}$

7. $4\frac{5}{6} - 2\frac{1}{8}$ **8.** $4\frac{1}{2} + 3\frac{1}{4}$ **9.** $7\frac{1}{2} + 2\frac{2}{9}$ **10.** $3\frac{4}{5} - 3\frac{1}{3}$

Regroup to complete the statement.

11. $3\frac{5}{6} = 2\frac{?}{6}$ **12.** $5\frac{2}{5} = 4\frac{?}{5}$ **13.** $1\frac{1}{12} = \frac{?}{12}$ **14.** $12\frac{2}{7} = 11\frac{?}{7}$

Regroup and subtract. Simplify if possible.

15. $6\frac{1}{3} - 3\frac{2}{3}$ **16.** $4\frac{3}{5} - 1\frac{4}{5}$ **17.** $11\frac{2}{5} - \frac{4}{5}$ **18.** $5\frac{3}{8} - 1\frac{7}{8}$

19. $2\frac{1}{4} - 1\frac{1}{3}$ **20.** $4\frac{2}{13} - 3\frac{1}{2}$ **21.** $5\frac{1}{6} - 2\frac{3}{10}$ **22.** $11\frac{3}{7} - 4\frac{5}{9}$

Practice and Problem Solving

Student Help

MORE PRACTICE Extra practice to help you master skills is on page 570.

Simplify the mixed number.

23. $4\frac{9}{5}$ **24.** $6\frac{8}{6}$ **25.** $1\frac{26}{22}$ **26.** $2\frac{15}{10}$

27. $16\frac{15}{12}$ **28.** $12\frac{11}{9}$ **29.** $14\frac{24}{9}$ **30.** $17\frac{25}{20}$

Match the sum or difference with the numbers that can be used to make an estimate.

A. $9 - 1$ **B.** $4 + 2$ **C.** $7 + 1$ **D.** $5\frac{1}{2} - \frac{1}{2}$

31. $3\frac{9}{10} + 2\frac{1}{8}$ **32.** $6\frac{5}{6} + \frac{7}{8}$ **33.** $5\frac{4}{9} - \frac{4}{7}$ **34.** $9\frac{1}{6} - \frac{7}{8}$

Evaluate. Simplify if possible.

35. $7\frac{3}{5} + 5\frac{1}{5}$ **36.** $4\frac{5}{6} - 2\frac{1}{6}$ **37.** $6\frac{2}{3} - 2\frac{1}{3}$ **38.** $8\frac{5}{9} + 1\frac{2}{9}$

39. $3\frac{1}{8} + 5\frac{5}{6}$ **40.** $9\frac{1}{2} - 4\frac{1}{4}$ **41.** $5\frac{1}{2} - 2\frac{1}{3}$ **42.** $3\frac{2}{3} + 4\frac{3}{4}$

Chapter Opener Link **Look back at the exercises on page 109. Each board is labeled with its dimensions before planing. Use the information in the table.**

43. In Exercise 1 on page 109, what is the height of each board in the stack after planing? What is the total height of the stack after planing?

44. In Exercises 2 and 3 on page 109, what is the total height of each stack after planing?

In Exercises 45–48, tell whether the subtraction problem requires *finding a common denominator, regrouping,* or *both*. Do not subtract.

45. $5\frac{3}{4} - 1\frac{1}{3}$ **46.** $6 - 3\frac{3}{4}$ **47.** $9\frac{3}{8} - 4\frac{7}{12}$ **48.** $3\frac{1}{8} - 1\frac{5}{8}$

49. Summarize and explain the steps for the problem shown below.

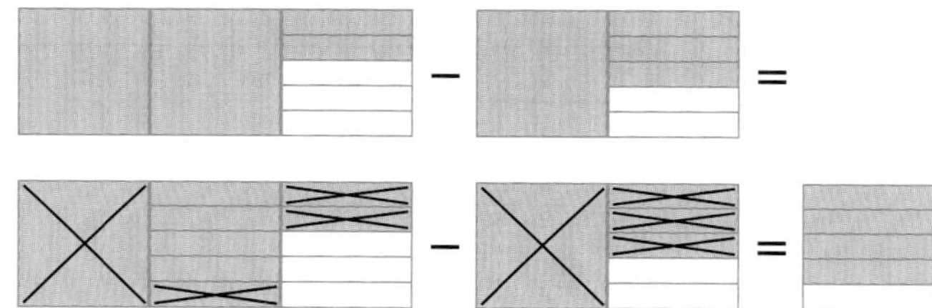

Regroup and subtract. Simplify if possible.

50. $3 - 1\frac{1}{8}$ **51.** $4 - 1\frac{7}{12}$ **52.** $2\frac{2}{5} - \frac{3}{5}$ **53.** $3\frac{1}{4} - \frac{3}{4}$

54. $6\frac{1}{6} - 3\frac{5}{6}$ **55.** $3\frac{4}{15} - 1\frac{7}{15}$ **56.** $6\frac{5}{16} - 1\frac{7}{16}$ **57.** $6\frac{1}{6} - 2\frac{11}{12}$

58. $3\frac{1}{5} - 2\frac{3}{10}$ **59.** $5\frac{1}{6} - 1\frac{2}{5}$ **60.** $5\frac{1}{10} - 3\frac{1}{3}$ **61.** $7\frac{1}{3} - 2\frac{5}{9}$

SEWING **Each quilt has an area of $4\frac{1}{8}$ square yards of fabric. Tell how many square yards of fabric in the quilt are *not* blue.**

62. $1\frac{3}{8}$ square yards are blue. **63.** $2\frac{5}{8}$ square yards are blue.

Student Help

HOMEWORK HELP

Extra help with problem solving in Exs. 62–63 is available at www.mcdougallittell.com

GYMNASTICS Gymnasts begin their routines with less than perfect scores. They must earn bonus points in order to be awarded a perfect score of 10 points.

▶ Source: USA Gymnastics Organization

64. GYMNASTICS In women's gymnastics competitions, the uneven bars can be adjusted to various heights above the floor, but they are never more than five feet from one another. Use any relevant information to find the height from the floor to the lower bar.

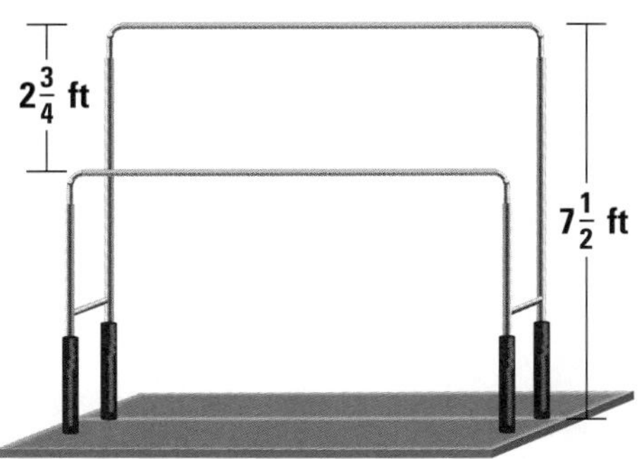

65. HIKING You are hiking on a $6\frac{3}{10}$ mile trail that is marked every $\frac{1}{10}$ mile. The marker you have just passed says $5\frac{1}{2}$ miles. How many miles must you hike until you reach the end of the trail? Explain why you used a particular operation to answer the question.

GEOMETRY **In Exercises 66–69, tell how much of the given fencing is left after the yard is fenced. Determine how to break the problem into simpler parts, and explain why you used a particular operation.**

66. Fencing: 60 ft

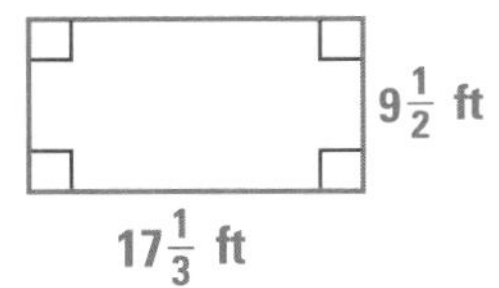

67. Fencing: 75 ft

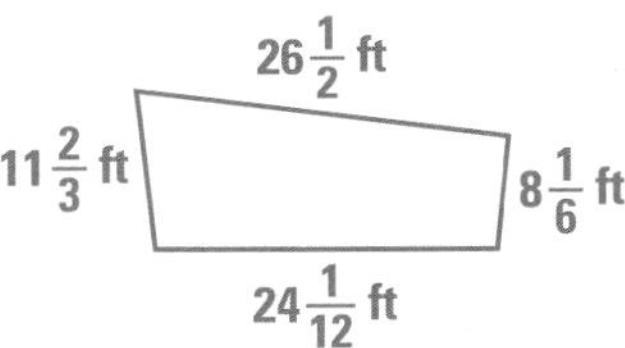

68. Fencing: 40 ft

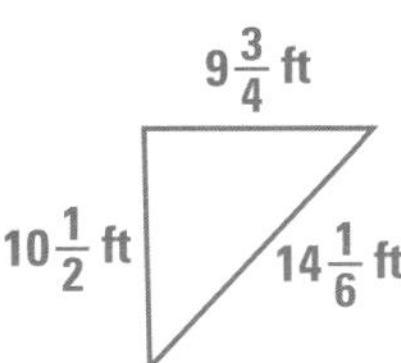

69. Fencing: 180 ft

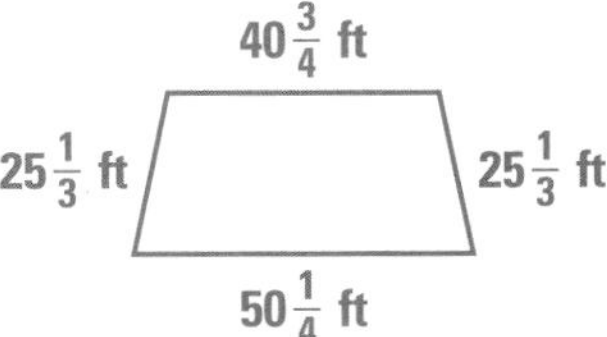

70. CHALLENGE A bowling lane is 62 feet $10\frac{3}{16}$ inches long and $3\frac{5}{12}$ feet wide. How much longer is the lane than it is wide?

▶ Source: American Bowling Congress

Multiple-Choice Practice

71. The best estimate for the sum $4\frac{11}{12} + 3\frac{1}{9} + 2\frac{7}{8}$ is __?__.

Ⓐ 9 Ⓑ 10 Ⓒ 11 Ⓓ 12

72. Evaluate $1\frac{1}{4} + 2\frac{5}{8}$.

Ⓕ $3\frac{3}{8}$ Ⓖ $3\frac{5}{8}$ Ⓗ $3\frac{7}{8}$ Ⓙ $4\frac{1}{8}$

DEVELOPING CONCEPTS

Multiplication of Fractions

For use with Lesson 3.4

California Standards

- Explain the meaning of multiplication of positive fractions. (NS 2.2)
- Use diagrams to explain mathematical reasoning. (MR 2.4)

MATERIALS

- Colored pencils
- Ruler
- Paper

You already know how to multiply whole numbers. Here you will develop a rule for multiplying fractions.

SAMPLE 1 Using an Area Model for Multiplying Fractions

You can use an area model to find the product of $\frac{2}{3}$ and $\frac{4}{5}$.

Here's How

Think of the product $\frac{2}{3} \cdot \frac{4}{5}$ as "two thirds of four fifths."

1. Shade four fifths of a unit square in one direction.
2. Shade two thirds of the square in the other direction.
3. The square has 15 equal parts with 8 parts doubly shaded.

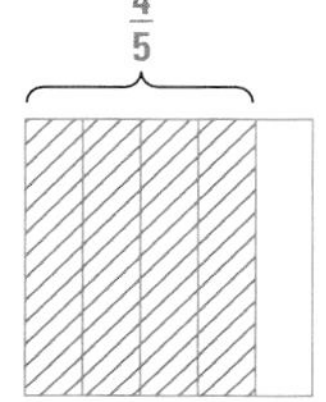

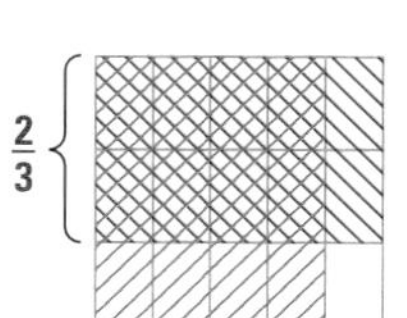

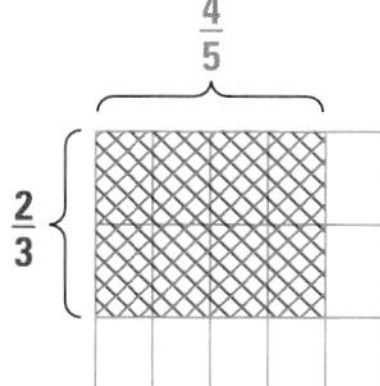

ANSWER ▶ $\frac{2}{3} \cdot \frac{4}{5} = \frac{8}{15}$

In Sample 1 notice that you can obtain the product of the two fractions by simply multiplying the numerators ($2 \cdot 4 = 8$) and multiplying the denominators ($3 \cdot 5 = 15$). This observation suggests the following rule:

To multiply two proper fractions, multiply the numerators to get the numerator of the product, and multiply the denominators to get the denominator of the product.

$$\frac{a}{b} \cdot \frac{c}{d} = \frac{a \cdot c}{b \cdot d}$$

Try These

1. What is one half of $\frac{3}{5}$? Describe two ways that you can find the answer.

Find the product of the proper fractions using (a) an area model and (b) the rule for multiplying proper fractions. Compare your answers.

2. $\frac{1}{3} \cdot \frac{5}{6}$ **3.** $\frac{3}{4} \cdot \frac{1}{5}$ **4.** $\frac{5}{7} \cdot \frac{2}{3}$ **5.** $\frac{1}{2} \cdot \frac{1}{6}$

You can also use an area model for multiplying improper fractions.

SAMPLE 2 Multiplying Improper Fractions

You can use an area model to find the product of $\frac{2}{3}$ and $\frac{7}{5}$.

Here's How

1. Divide 2 unit squares into fifths and shade seven fifths in one direction.

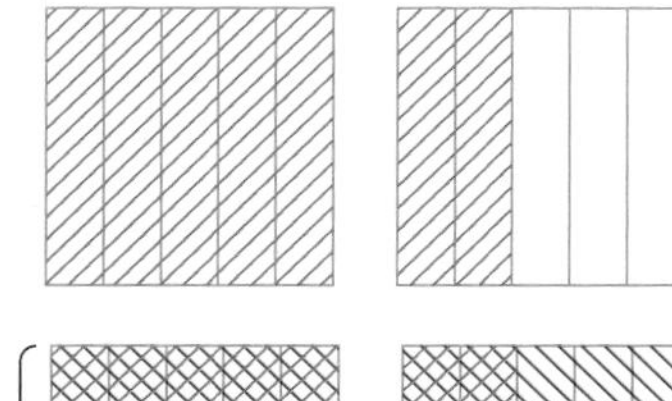

2. Shade two thirds of the unit squares in the other direction.

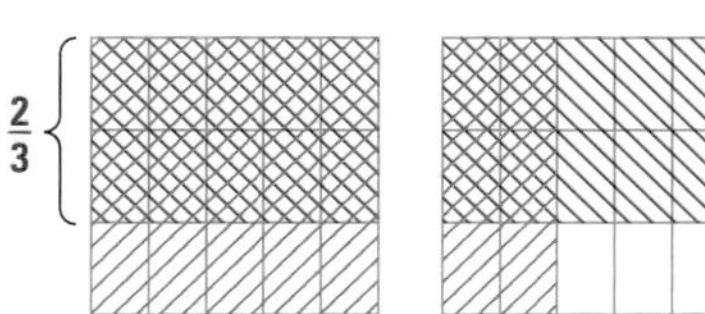

3. Each unit square is divided into 15 parts. Since 14 parts are doubly shaded, $\frac{2}{3} \cdot \frac{7}{5} = \frac{14}{15}$.

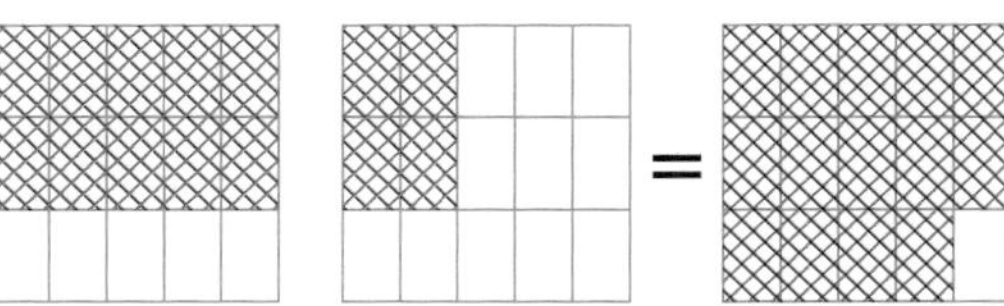

Try These

6. **MATHEMATICAL REASONING** Write a rule for multiplying improper fractions using $\frac{a}{b}$ and $\frac{c}{d}$.

Find the product using (a) an area model and (b) your rule from Exercise 6. Compare your answers.

7. $\frac{3}{2} \cdot \frac{3}{5}$ **8.** $\frac{9}{4} \cdot \frac{1}{4}$ **9.** $\frac{8}{7} \cdot \frac{2}{3}$ **10.** $\frac{7}{10} \cdot \frac{7}{5}$

11. Use an area model to find the product of $\frac{2}{3}$ and 4.

12. **MATHEMATICAL REASONING** Based on the result of Exercise 11, write a rule for multiplying a fraction $\frac{a}{b}$ and a whole number c.

Find the product using (a) an area model and (b) your rule from Exercise 12. Compare your answers.

13. $2 \cdot \frac{4}{5}$ **14.** $\frac{2}{3} \cdot 5$ **15.** $\frac{8}{5} \cdot 2$ **16.** $3 \cdot \frac{3}{4}$

3.4 Multiplying Fractions and Mixed Numbers

California Standards

In this lesson you'll:

- Solve problems involving multiplication of positive fractions. (NS 2.1)
- Explain the meaning of multiplication of fractions. (NS 2.2)

Student Help

STUDY TIP Drawing a model can help you understand the process of multiplying fractions.

Goal 1 MULTIPLYING FRACTIONS

In Developing Concepts 3.4, page 124, you used an area model to multiply fractions.

EXAMPLE 1 Multiplying Fractions

Use an area model to find the product $\frac{3}{5} \times \frac{1}{2}$.

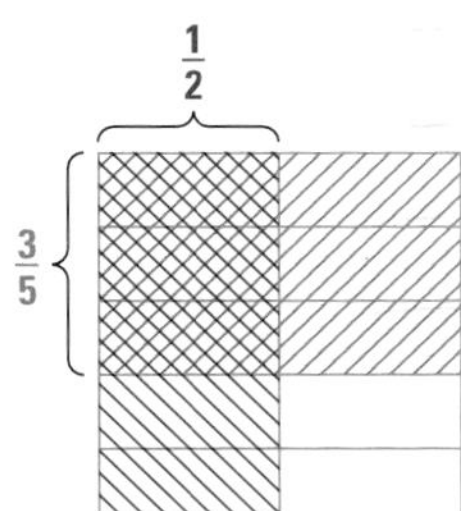

Solution

Shade half of the rectangle in one direction and $\frac{3}{5}$ in the other direction. Since 3 of the 10 parts are doubly shaded, the product is $\frac{3}{10}$.

MULTIPLYING FRACTIONS

In Words To multiply any two fractions, multiply the numerators to get the numerator of the product, and multiply the denominators to get the denominator of the product.

In Algebra $\frac{a}{b} \cdot \frac{c}{d} = \frac{ac}{bd}$ where b and d are not equal to 0.

EXAMPLE 2 Calculating Length of Time

SOCCER Your gym class lasts $\frac{3}{4}$ of an hour. You play soccer for $\frac{2}{3}$ of the class. How long do you play soccer?

Solution To find $\frac{2}{3}$ of $\frac{3}{4}$, multiply $\frac{2}{3}$ and $\frac{3}{4}$.

$\frac{2}{3} \cdot \frac{3}{4} = \frac{2 \cdot 3}{3 \cdot 4}$ Use rule for multiplying fractions.

$= \frac{6}{12}$ Simplify numerator and denominator.

$= \frac{1}{2}$ Simplify fraction.

ANSWER ▶ You play soccer for $\frac{1}{2}$ hour.

Goal 2 MULTIPLYING MIXED NUMBERS

MULTIPLYING MIXED NUMBERS

1. Rewrite the mixed numbers as improper fractions.
2. Multiply the numerators to get the numerator of the product, and multiply the denominators to get the denominator of the product.

Student Help

▶ STUDY TIP
Another way to do Example 3 is to divide out common factors before multiplying the numerators and denominators.

$$\frac{\overset{1}{\cancel{4}} \times \overset{5}{\cancel{15}}}{\underset{1}{\cancel{3}} \times \underset{1}{\cancel{4}}} = \frac{5}{1}$$
$$= 5$$

EXAMPLE 3 Multiplying Mixed Numbers

$1\frac{1}{3} \times 3\frac{3}{4} = \frac{4}{3} \times \frac{15}{4}$ Rewrite as improper fractions.

$= \frac{4 \times 15}{3 \times 4}$ Use rule for multiplying fractions.

$= \frac{60}{12}$ Simplify numerator and denominator.

$= 5$ Simplify fraction.

EXAMPLE 4 Multiplying a Mixed Number and a Fraction

$1\frac{1}{2} \cdot \frac{1}{4} = \frac{3}{2} \cdot \frac{1}{4}$ Rewrite $1\frac{1}{2}$ as improper fraction.

$= \frac{3 \cdot 1}{2 \cdot 4}$ Use rule for multiplying fractions.

$= \frac{3}{8}$ Simplify numerator and denominator.

EXAMPLE 5 Expanding a Recipe by a Fractional Amount

COOKING You decide to make $1\frac{1}{2}$ batches of salsa using the recipe at the left. How many tomatoes do you need?

Solution

Multiply $1\frac{1}{2}$ batches by 6 tomatoes per batch to find the new amount.

$1\frac{1}{2} \times 6 = \frac{3}{2} \times \frac{6}{1}$ Rewrite as improper fractions.

$= \frac{3 \times 6}{2 \times 1}$ Use rule for multiplying fractions.

$= \frac{18}{2}$ Simplify numerator and denominator.

$= 9$ Simplify fraction.

ANSWER ▶ You need 9 tomatoes.

Salsa Mexicana

Combine the following ingredients:
6 ripe tomatoes, chopped
1/2 cup chopped onion
4 fresh chiles, chopped
1/3 cup chopped cilantro
juice from 1/2 a lime
1 tsp. salt

3.4 Exercises

Guided Practice

Write the multiplication problem that is represented by the area model. Use the model to find the product.

1.

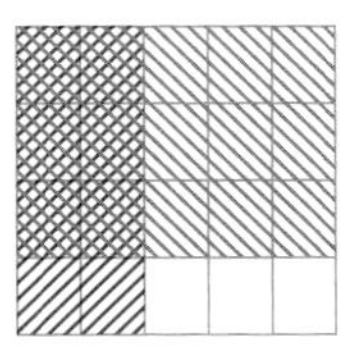

2.

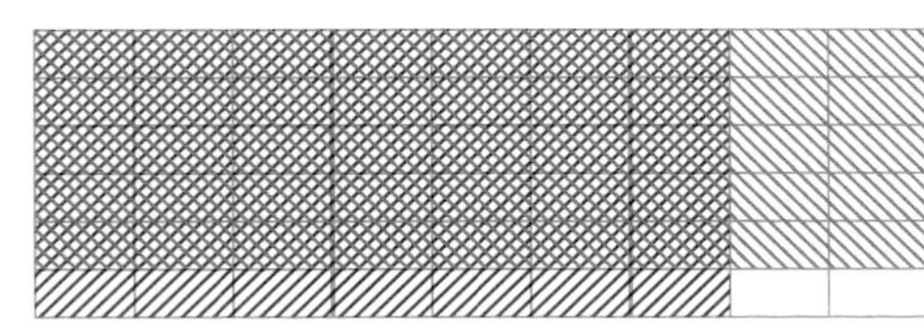

In Exercises 3–10, multiply. Simplify if possible.

3. $\frac{2}{3} \times \frac{1}{3}$ **4.** $\frac{1}{3} \times \frac{1}{4}$ **5.** $\frac{2}{7} \cdot \frac{2}{3}$ **6.** $\frac{1}{5} \cdot \frac{3}{4}$

7. $\frac{1}{2} \times 1\frac{1}{2}$ **8.** $1\frac{1}{3} \times \frac{1}{5}$ **9.** $1\frac{1}{2} \cdot 1\frac{1}{3}$ **10.** $2\frac{1}{4} \cdot 5\frac{2}{3}$

11. WRITING Write a rule for multiplying the fractions $\frac{c}{d}$ and $\frac{e}{f}$.

Practice and Problem Solving

Student Help

▶ MORE PRACTICE
Extra practice to help you master skills is on page 570.

In Exercises 12–23, multiply. Simplify if possible.

12. $\frac{1}{2} \times \frac{2}{5}$ **13.** $\frac{1}{5} \times \frac{2}{3}$ **14.** $\frac{3}{5} \times \frac{1}{4}$ **15.** $\frac{1}{7} \times \frac{1}{3}$

16. $\frac{2}{9} \times \frac{4}{15}$ **17.** $\frac{5}{8} \times \frac{2}{13}$ **18.** $\frac{2}{11} \times \frac{7}{8}$ **19.** $\frac{7}{12} \times \frac{6}{7}$

20. $\frac{2}{25} \times \frac{5}{6}$ **21.** $\frac{2}{17} \times \frac{9}{10}$ **22.** $\frac{6}{13} \times \frac{5}{8}$ **23.** $\frac{18}{19} \times \frac{5}{9}$

24. COOKING A recipe calls for 1 cup rice, $\frac{1}{2}$ teaspoon salt, and $2\frac{2}{3}$ cups water. What amounts do you need to make half of the recipe?

Multiply. Then simplify if possible.

25. $3\frac{1}{3} \cdot 1\frac{2}{5}$ **26.** $4\frac{1}{2} \cdot 2\frac{3}{4}$ **27.** $2\frac{4}{5} \cdot 1\frac{1}{4}$ **28.** $3\frac{1}{3} \cdot 4\frac{2}{5}$

29. $2\frac{4}{9} \cdot 3\frac{6}{11}$ **30.** $5\frac{3}{5} \cdot 5\frac{5}{7}$ **31.** $2\frac{6}{7} \cdot 5\frac{7}{9}$ **32.** $4\frac{8}{9} \cdot 3\frac{11}{13}$

GEOMETRY **Find the area of the rectangle.**

33. $1\frac{5}{6}$ ft, 4 ft

34.

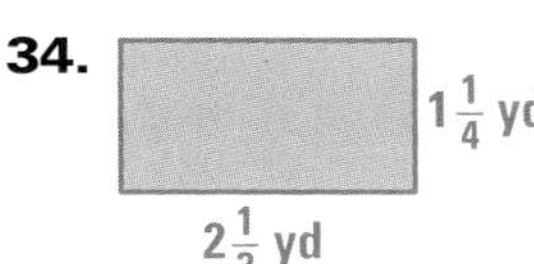

35. **SANTA MONICA PIER** The Pleasure Pier in Santa Monica, California, is $\frac{1}{20}$ mile wide and $\frac{1}{5}$ mile long. What is the area of the pier?

36. **ADVERTISING** You are making a rectangular banner to announce a school dance. How many square feet of material do you need to make a banner that is $6\frac{2}{3}$ feet long and $2\frac{1}{4}$ feet wide? Explain how you found the area in words and numbers.

37. **GARDENING** You are planning a rectangular vegetable garden that is $2\frac{1}{2}$ yards by $1\frac{3}{4}$ yards. Find the area of the vegetable garden.

Student Help

▶**HOMEWORK HELP**
Extra help with problem solving in Ex. 38 is available at www.mcdougallittell.com

38. **BEACH VOLLEYBALL** The dimensions of the playing area and free zone of a beach volleyball court are $78\frac{2}{3}$ feet by $49\frac{1}{6}$ feet. What is the area of a beach volleyball court?

▶ Source: California Beach Volleyball Association

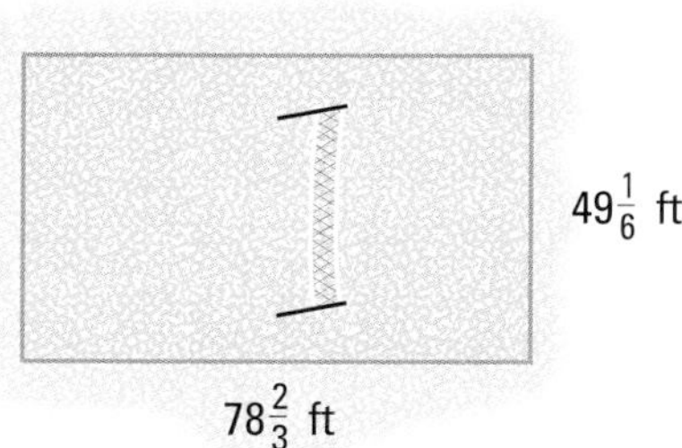

ALGEBRA **Evaluate the expression when $y = 2\frac{5}{6}$.**

39. $\left(\frac{2}{3}\right)y$ **40.** $\left(1\frac{1}{9}\right)y$ **41.** $\left(2\frac{5}{17}\right)y$

42. $\left(1\frac{1}{15}\right)y$ **43.** $\left(2\frac{9}{10}\right)y$ **44.** $(y)(y)$

History Link **The diagram shows the relative sizes of the pyramids of Khufu, Khafre, and Menkaure at Giza in Egypt. The smallest, the pyramid of Menkaure, is 218 feet high.**

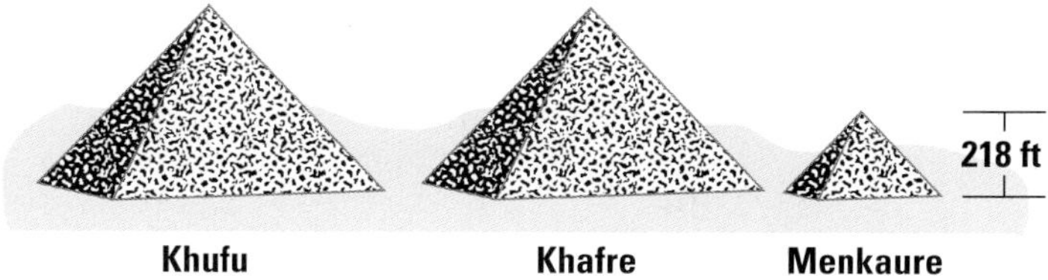

45. Estimate the height of the pyramid of Khafre if it is about $2\frac{1}{6}$ times the height of the pyramid of Menkaure.

46. Estimate the height of the pyramid of Khufu if it is about $2\frac{1}{5}$ times the height of the pyramid of Menkaure.

MATHEMATICAL REASONING **Complete the statement with *sometimes, always,* or *never*. (Assume all nonzero numbers are positive.)**

47. The product of two mixed numbers is __?__ greater than 1.

48. The product of a whole number and proper fraction is __?__ less than 1.

49. The product of a mixed number and zero is __?__ greater than 1.

Link to History

PYRAMID BUILDERS
About 4500 years ago, Egyptian kings built the pyramids at Giza. The pyramids at Giza are one of the Seven Wonders of the Ancient World.

More about pyramids available at www.mcdougallittell.com

Link to Science

GRAVITY The Apollo suit worn on the Moon weighed 41 pounds on the Moon and 246 pounds on Earth.

More about gravity available at www.mcdougallittell.com

Science Link **In Exercises 50–52, use the table below.**

The weight of a person depends on the force of gravity, which varies from planet to planet. An astronaut would weigh $2\frac{2}{5}$ times as much on Jupiter as on Earth, as shown in the table.

Relative Weight of One Pound on Various Planets

Mercury	Venus	Earth	Mars	Jupiter	Saturn	Uranus	Neptune	Pluto
$\frac{2}{5}$	$\frac{9}{10}$	1	$\frac{2}{5}$	$2\frac{2}{5}$	$\frac{9}{10}$	$\frac{9}{10}$	$1\frac{1}{10}$	$\frac{1}{10}$

Not drawn to scale

50. If an astronaut weighs 180 pounds on Earth, how much would the astronaut weigh on Jupiter?

51. If an astronaut weighs $160\frac{1}{2}$ pounds on Earth, how much would the astronaut weigh on Mars?

52. If an astronaut weighs $120\frac{2}{3}$ pounds on Earth, how much would the astronaut weigh on Venus?

53. **CHALLENGE** You run $3\frac{1}{3}$ times around a $1\frac{1}{8}$ mile track. How much farther must you run to reach your goal of $4\frac{1}{2}$ miles?

Multiple-Choice Practice

54. You have 6 pieces of string that are each $2\frac{3}{8}$ inches long. What is the total length of the string if you lay the pieces end to end?

Ⓐ $8\frac{3}{8}$ in. Ⓑ $12\frac{1}{6}$ in. Ⓒ $12\frac{3}{8}$ in. Ⓓ $14\frac{1}{4}$ in.

55. Evaluate $2\frac{1}{3} \times 3\frac{5}{12}$.

Ⓕ $6\frac{5}{36}$ Ⓖ $6\frac{5}{6}$ Ⓗ $7\frac{2}{3}$ Ⓙ $7\frac{35}{36}$

Mixed Review

In Exercises 56–59, evaluate the expression. *(1.3)*

56. $w - 6 \times 2$ when $w = 18$

57. $m + (7 - 4) \times 2$ when $m = 5$

58. $6 \cdot c + 12$ when $c = 4$

59. $a + 6 - b$ when $a = 2$ and $b = 3$

60. Your neighbor has 15 apples to sell. You buy 6 of them. What fraction of apples remains to be sold? *(2.3)*

Chapter 3 Mid-Chapter Test

Take this test as you would take a test in class. The answers to the exercises are given in the back of the book.

Evaluate. Simplify if possible.

1. $\frac{7}{6} - \frac{1}{6}$ **2.** $\frac{4}{9} + \frac{2}{9}$ **3.** $\frac{5}{4} + \frac{3}{4}$ **4.** $\frac{5}{7} - \frac{3}{7}$

Use the circle graph. It shows the types of flowers that are planted in a large garden.

5. Find the difference between the fraction of petunias and the fraction of marigolds.

6. Find the difference between the fraction of impatiens and the fraction of geraniums.

7. What fraction of flowers is in the "Other" category?

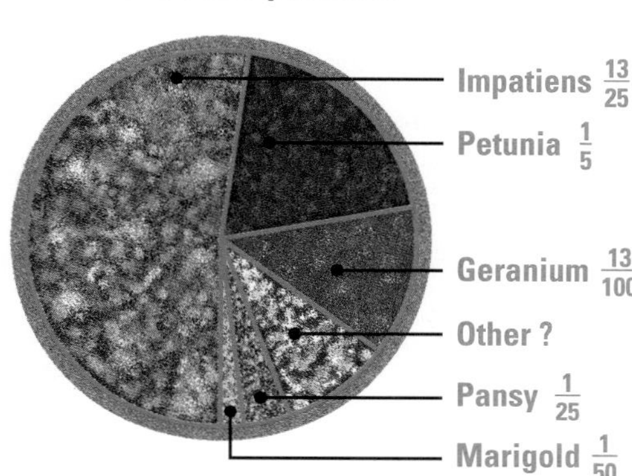

Evaluate. Simplify if possible.

8. $2\frac{7}{10} + 3\frac{9}{10}$ **9.** $5\frac{8}{9} - 1\frac{4}{9}$ **10.** $6\frac{3}{16} - 3\frac{1}{8}$ **11.** $3\frac{1}{3} + 6\frac{1}{8}$

Regroup and subtract. Simplify if possible.

12. $7\frac{3}{10} - 4\frac{2}{5}$ **13.** $3\frac{1}{8} - 2\frac{1}{3}$ **14.** $4\frac{3}{4} - 1\frac{5}{6}$ **15.** $8\frac{3}{7} - 2\frac{3}{5}$

Multiply. Simplify if possible.

16. $\frac{1}{4} \times \frac{2}{3}$ **17.** $\frac{3}{5} \times \frac{3}{8}$ **18.** $\frac{4}{9} \times \frac{5}{7}$ **19.** $\frac{2}{7} \times \frac{6}{11}$

20. $2\frac{1}{2} \times 1\frac{1}{4}$ **21.** $2\frac{1}{5} \times 3\frac{2}{5}$ **22.** $4\frac{1}{6} \times 2\frac{2}{3}$ **23.** $3\frac{1}{9} \times 4\frac{3}{5}$

GEOMETRY In Exercises 24–26, find the area of the rectangle.

24.

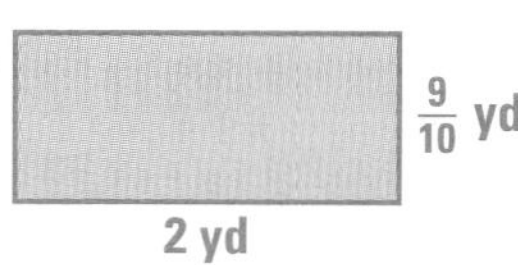

25.

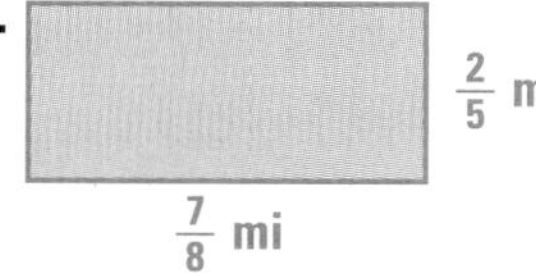

26.

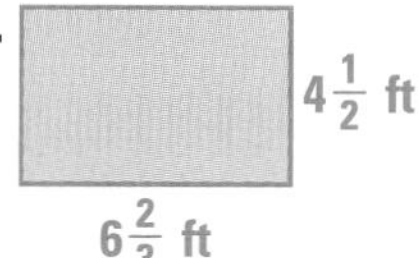

27. COOKING You plan to make 3 batches of pudding. One batch of pudding requires $4\frac{1}{3}$ cups of milk. How much milk do you need?

REASONING 3.5

DEVELOPING CONCEPTS
Division of Fractions

For use with Lesson 3.5

California Standards

- Explain the meaning of division of positive fractions (NS 2.2)
- Use diagrams to explain mathematical reasoning. (MR 2.4)

MATERIALS

- Paper and pencil

Multiplication and division are closely related operations. For example, dividing 6 by 2 gives the same result as multiplying 6 by $\frac{1}{2}$. This suggests the following approach to dividing a number by a fraction.

SAMPLE 1 Dividing by a Unit Fraction

You can use either division or multiplication to find the quotient $3 \div \frac{1}{2}$.

Here's How

Method 1 Use division.

Draw 3 unit squares. Divide each of the unit squares in half.

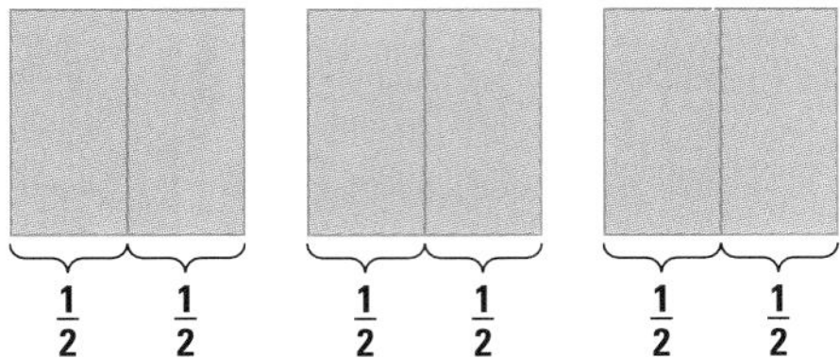

The 3 squares have a total of 6 halves. So, $3 \div \frac{1}{2} = 6$.

Method 2 Use multiplication.

You can multiply the total number of unit squares by the number of halves in one unit square. Since there are 2 halves in one unit square, there must be $3 \times 2 = 6$ halves in 3 unit squares.

In Sample 1, notice that dividing by $\frac{1}{2}$ gives the same result as multiplying by 2. This suggests that, in general, dividing a number by $\frac{1}{b}$ is the same as multiplying by b.

Try These

Find the quotient using both methods from Sample 1.

1. $2 \div \frac{1}{2}$ **2.** $4 \div \frac{1}{3}$ **3.** $2\frac{1}{2} \div \frac{1}{4}$ **4.** $3\frac{1}{3} \div \frac{1}{6}$

5. MATHEMATICAL REASONING You know that $10 \div 5 = 2$ because $2 \times 5 = 10$. Describe how you can use similar reasoning to check whether $3 \div \frac{1}{2} = 6$.

You can use the methods from Sample 1 to divide by any fraction.

SAMPLE 2 Dividing by any Fraction

You can use either division or multiplication to find the quotient $2\frac{1}{4} \div \frac{3}{4}$.

Here's How

Method 1 Use division.

Draw an area model for $2\frac{1}{4}$. Divide the model into groups of $\frac{3}{4}$.

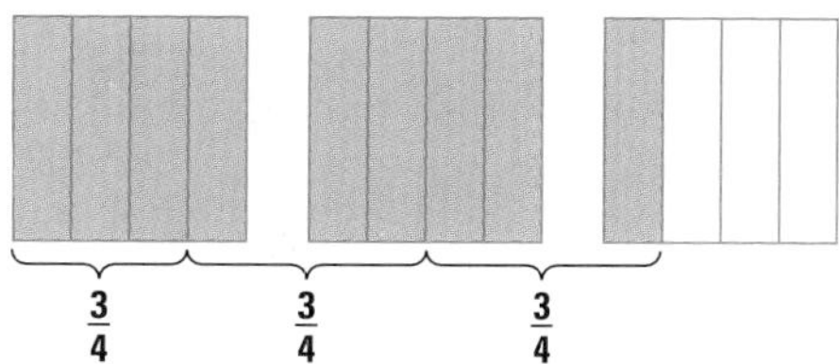

There are 3 groups of $\frac{3}{4}$. So, $2\frac{1}{4} \div \frac{3}{4} = 3$.

Method 2 Use multiplication.

In one unit square, there is 1 group of $\frac{3}{4}$ and $\frac{1}{3}$ of another group of $\frac{3}{4}$. So, one unit square contains $1\frac{1}{3}$, or $\frac{4}{3}$, groups of $\frac{3}{4}$. Since there are $\frac{4}{3}$ groups of $\frac{3}{4}$ in each whole, there must be $\frac{9}{4} \times \frac{4}{3} = 3$ groups of $\frac{3}{4}$ in $2\frac{1}{4}$.

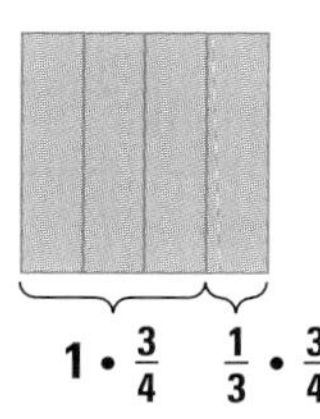

Dividing by $\frac{3}{4}$ gives the same result as multiplying by $\frac{4}{3}$. This suggests that, in general, dividing by $\frac{a}{b}$ is the same as multiplying by $\frac{b}{a}$.

Try These

Find the quotient using both methods from Sample 2.

6. $3 \div \frac{3}{4}$

7. $4 \div \frac{1}{6}$

8. $1\frac{1}{5} \div \frac{3}{5}$

9. $5\frac{1}{3} \div \frac{2}{3}$

10. MATHEMATICAL REASONING How would you rewrite $4\frac{3}{5} \div 1\frac{3}{5}$ as a multiplication problem? Explain your reasoning and find the quotient.

3.5 Dividing Fractions and Mixed Numbers

California Standards

In this lesson you'll:

- Solve problems involving division of positive fractions. (NS 2.1)
- Explain the meaning of division of fractions. (NS 2.2)

Goal 1 Dividing Fractions

Two numbers whose product is 1 are **reciprocals**, or **multiplicative inverses**. For $a \neq 0$ and $b \neq 0$, the reciprocal of $\frac{a}{b}$ is $\frac{b}{a}$ because $\frac{a}{b} \times \frac{b}{a} = 1$.

EXAMPLE 1 Writing Reciprocals

	ORIGINAL NUMBER	WRITE AS FRACTION	WRITE RECIPROCAL	CHECK BY MULTIPLYING
a.	$\frac{5}{12}$	$\frac{5}{12}$	$\frac{12}{5}$	$\frac{5}{12} \times \frac{12}{5} = 1$
b.	6	$\frac{6}{1}$	$\frac{1}{6}$	$6 \times \frac{1}{6} = \frac{6}{6} = 1$

As you saw in Developing Concepts 3.5, page 132, you can divide fractions as described below.

DIVIDING FRACTIONS

In Words To divide by a fraction, multiply by its reciprocal.

In Algebra $\frac{a}{b} \div \frac{c}{d} = \frac{a}{b} \cdot \frac{d}{c} = \frac{a \cdot d}{b \cdot c} = \frac{ad}{bc}$

In Arithmetic $\frac{2}{3} \div \frac{5}{4} = \frac{2}{3} \cdot \frac{4}{5} = \frac{2 \cdot 4}{3 \cdot 5} = \frac{8}{15}$

EXAMPLE 2 Dividing Fractions

a. $\frac{7}{4} \div \frac{1}{3} = \frac{7}{4} \times \frac{3}{1}$ Multiply by the reciprocal.

$= \frac{21}{4}$ Multiply fractions.

$= 5\frac{1}{4}$ Rewrite as a mixed number.

b. $\frac{3}{5} \div 4 = \frac{3}{5} \times \frac{1}{4}$ Multiply by the reciprocal.

$= \frac{3}{20}$ Multiply fractions.

Student Help

STUDY TIP
You can check your answer in part (b) of Example 2 by multiplying.

$\frac{3}{20} \times 4 = \frac{12}{20} = \frac{3}{5}$ ✓

Goal 2 Dividing Mixed Numbers

To divide mixed numbers, you can use what you know about rewriting mixed numbers and dividing fractions.

Dividing Mixed Numbers

In Words First rewrite the mixed numbers as improper fractions. Then use the rule for dividing fractions.

In Arithmetic $\frac{3}{4} \div 1\frac{1}{6} = \frac{3}{4} \div \frac{7}{6} = \frac{3}{4} \times \frac{6}{7} = \frac{18}{28} = \frac{9}{14}$

Student Help

▶More Examples

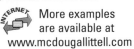

More examples are available at www.mcdougallittell.com

Example 3 Dividing Mixed Numbers

$3\frac{1}{5} \div 1\frac{1}{3} = \frac{16}{5} \div \frac{4}{3}$ Rewrite as improper fractions.

$= \frac{16}{5} \times \frac{3}{4}$ Multiply by the reciprocal.

$= \frac{48}{20}$ Multiply fractions.

$= \frac{12}{5}$ Simplify.

$= 2\frac{2}{5}$ Rewrite as a mixed number.

Example 4 Using Division in Real Life

NEWSPAPERS You work on a school newspaper. You need to know how many $1\frac{3}{4}$ inch columns of text you can fit into a space that measures 7 inches wide.

Solution

Divide the width of the space by the width of each column.

$7 \div 1\frac{3}{4} = \frac{7}{1} \div \frac{7}{4}$ Rewrite as improper fractions.

$= \frac{7}{1} \times \frac{4}{7}$ Multiply by the reciprocal.

$= \frac{28}{7}$ Multiply fractions.

$= 4$ Simplify.

ANSWER ▶ You can fit 4 columns of text in the space.

3.5 Exercises

Guided Practice

In Exercises 1 and 2, complete the statement.

1. The reciprocal of **?** is $\frac{7}{5}$.

2. The reciprocal of $1\frac{1}{9}$ is **?**.

ERROR ANALYSIS **Describe and correct the error.**

3. $\frac{3}{7} \div \frac{1}{5} = \frac{3}{7} \times \frac{1}{5} = \frac{3}{35}$

4. $3\frac{1}{2} \div 1\frac{2}{3} = \frac{7}{2} \div \frac{5}{3} = \frac{2}{7} \times \frac{5}{3} = \frac{10}{21}$

MATHEMATICAL REASONING **In Exercises 5 and 6, explain each step.**

5. $1\frac{3}{4} \div 2\frac{5}{8} = \frac{7}{4} \div \frac{21}{8}$
$= \frac{7}{4} \times \frac{8}{21}$
$= \frac{56}{84} = \frac{2}{3}$

6. $3\frac{1}{2} \div \frac{1}{10} = \frac{7}{2} \div \frac{1}{10}$
$= \frac{7}{2} \times \frac{10}{1}$
$= \frac{70}{2} = 35$

7. QUILTING A quilt design uses squares that are $7\frac{1}{2}$ inches on a side. Can the squares be divided into $\frac{3}{4}$ inch strips? If so, how many? Explain your reasoning in words and numbers.

Practice and Problem Solving

Student Help

▶ **More Practice**
Extra practice to help you master skills is on page 571.

Write the reciprocal of the number.

8. $\frac{4}{5}$ **9.** $\frac{7}{9}$ **10.** 8 **11.** $1\frac{5}{6}$

Match the expression with its value.

A. $\frac{8}{9}$ **B.** $1\frac{1}{8}$ **C.** $\frac{5}{18}$ **D.** 18

12. $4\frac{1}{2} \div 4$ **13.** $4\frac{1}{2} \div \frac{1}{4}$ **14.** $1\frac{1}{4} \div 4\frac{1}{2}$ **15.** $4 \div 4\frac{1}{2}$

Divide. Simplify if possible.

16. $\frac{5}{8} \div \frac{1}{6}$ **17.** $\frac{9}{10} \div \frac{2}{5}$ **18.** $\frac{7}{16} \div \frac{1}{4}$ **19.** $\frac{8}{9} \div \frac{2}{3}$

20. $\frac{14}{5} \div \frac{2}{3}$ **21.** $\frac{13}{10} \div \frac{3}{4}$ **22.** $\frac{22}{5} \div \frac{1}{3}$ **23.** $\frac{15}{4} \div \frac{5}{6}$

In Exercises 24–26, use division to answer the question.

24. How many $\frac{1}{4}$ yard pieces can you cut from $2\frac{3}{4}$ yard of ribbon?

25. How many $\frac{2}{3}$ cup servings are in a 12 cup box of cereal?

26. How many $\frac{1}{3}$ cup servings are there in $3\frac{1}{3}$ cups of dried black beans?

In Exercises 27–34, divide. Simplify if possible.

27. $1\frac{2}{5} \div 1\frac{2}{3}$ **28.** $6\frac{2}{3} \div 1\frac{1}{4}$ **29.** $7 \div 8\frac{2}{5}$ **30.** $2 \div 2\frac{3}{8}$

31. $4\frac{1}{6} \div 5$ **32.** $3\frac{4}{5} \div 4$ **33.** $10 \div 5\frac{5}{7}$ **34.** $9\frac{1}{4} \div \frac{3}{8}$

MATHEMATICAL REASONING **Complete the statement with *sometimes, always,* or *never*. Explain your reasoning.**

35. The reciprocal of a mixed number is __?__ less than 1.

36. A whole number divided by a mixed number is __?__ greater than 1.

37. A mixed number divided by a nonzero whole number is __?__ greater than 1.

AUTO RACING **In Exercises 38 and 39, refer to the table below.**

REGIONAL PLANNER
By consulting with community members and using computers to analyze data, regional planners develop short- and long-range plans for land use.

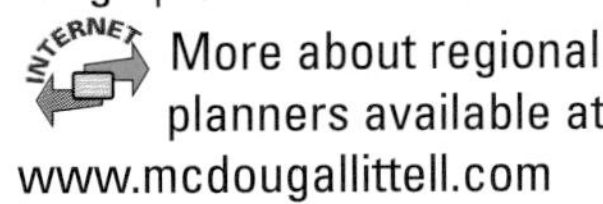

More about regional planners available at www.mcdougallittell.com

38. How *much longer* is the Indianapolis racetrack than the Fort Worth racetrack?

39. How *many times longer* is the Indianapolis racetrack than the Fort Worth racetrack?

Racetrack	Length
Indianapolis, Indiana	$\frac{5}{2}$ mi
Fort Worth, Texas	$\frac{3}{2}$ mi

40. SERVING SIZE You are making juice from a 12 ounce container of concentrate. You add the concentrate to 36 ounces of water. How many $7\frac{1}{2}$ ounce servings can you make?

41. REGIONAL PLANNER A regional planner reviews a proposal to build single-family homes. In the proposal, 6 acres of land would be divided into $\frac{3}{4}$ acre lots. How many homes could be built? Explain your reasoning using words, numbers, and a diagram.

42. GARDENING You are tying your tomato plants to stakes. You need $\frac{1}{2}$ foot of string for each plant. You have $8\frac{1}{4}$ feet of string to use. How many plants can you tie to stakes? Use estimation to verify the reasonableness of your answer.

Student Help

▶ **HOMEWORK HELP**

INTERNET Extra help with problem solving in Exs. 43–45 is available at www.mcdougallittell.com

BUTTERFLIES In Exercises 43–45, use the table at the right showing the wingspan of three kinds of butterflies.

Butterfly	Span
Great Purple Hairstreak	$1\frac{1}{8}$ in.
Tiger Swallowtail	$5\frac{3}{4}$ in.
Monarch	$3\frac{1}{2}$ in.

43. How many times wider is the Monarch than the Great Purple Hairstreak?

44. How many times wider is the Tiger Swallowtail than the Great Purple Hairstreak?

45. Find the average wingspan of the three kinds of butterflies.

FITNESS In Exercises 46–48, use the following information. Four friends go to exercise at the gym. The table shows the number of minutes each person used a stair climber and a stationary bicycle.

46. What is the average time spent on a stair climber?

47. What is the average time spent on a stationary bicycle?

48. How many times more is the average time on the bicycle than the average time on the stair climber?

Person	Stair climber	Stationary bicycle
You	$10\frac{1}{5}$ min	$19\frac{1}{4}$ min
Felicia	$11\frac{7}{10}$ min	$22\frac{1}{6}$ min
Enrico	$9\frac{1}{2}$ min	$22\frac{5}{12}$ min
Kali	$10\frac{3}{5}$ min	$20\frac{1}{6}$ min

49. **CHALLENGE** The rectangle shown has an area of $\frac{3}{8}$ square inches. Estimate the length of the rectangle using the figure. Then find the exact length using division.

$\frac{1}{4}$ in.

Multiple-Choice Practice

Test Tip A B C D

▶ In order to find the reciprocal of a mixed number, first write the mixed number as an improper fraction. Then find the reciprocal.

50. What is the reciprocal of $2\frac{3}{11}$?

Ⓐ $\frac{11}{25}$ Ⓑ $\frac{36}{11}$ Ⓒ $4\frac{1}{6}$ Ⓓ $5\frac{2}{3}$

51. Evaluate $\frac{7}{9} \div \frac{2}{3}$.

Ⓕ $\frac{14}{27}$ Ⓖ $\frac{6}{7}$ Ⓗ $1\frac{1}{6}$ Ⓙ $4\frac{1}{2}$

52. Evaluate $4\frac{1}{8} \div 2\frac{3}{4}$.

Ⓐ $1\frac{1}{32}$ Ⓑ $1\frac{1}{2}$ Ⓒ $2\frac{1}{6}$ Ⓓ $2\frac{1}{2}$

3.6 The Distributive Property

California Standards

In this lesson you'll:

- Apply the distributive property to evaluate expressions, and justify each step in the process. (AF 1.3)
- Evaluate an algebraic expression. (AF 1.2)

Goal 1 THE DISTRIBUTIVE PROPERTY

The area model below illustrates the *distributive property*. The area of the larger rectangle is the sum of the areas of the two smaller rectangles.

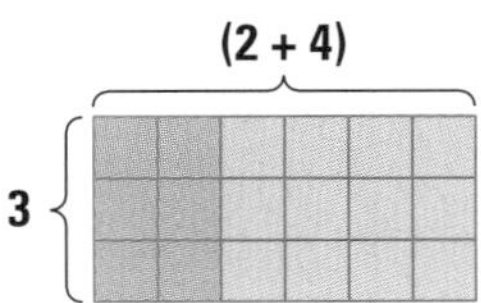

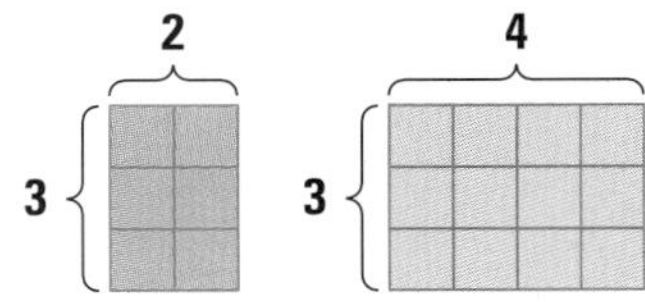

Area = Width × Length

$= 3(2 + 4)$

$= 3(6) = 18$

Area = Width × Length + Width × Length

$= 3(2) + 3(4)$

$= 6 + 12 = 18$

The areas of the models are equal. So, $3(2 + 4) = 3(2) + 3(4)$.

THE DISTRIBUTIVE PROPERTY

In Algebra For all numbers a, b, and c, $a(b + c) = ab + ac$.

In Arithmetic $5(11 + 2) = 5 \times 11 + 5 \times 2$

Student Help

▶ VOCABULARY TIP
In English, to *distribute* means to give something to everyone in a group. In mathematics, the meaning of *distribute* is similar.

EXAMPLE 1 Evaluating a Numerical Expression

Evaluate $3 \times \frac{2}{5} + 3 \times \frac{3}{5}$.

Solution

Method 1

$3 \times \frac{2}{5} + 3 \times \frac{3}{5} = \frac{6}{5} + \frac{9}{5}$	Use order of operations.
$= \frac{15}{5}$	Add.
$= 3$	Simplify.

Method 2

$3 \times \frac{2}{5} + 3 \times \frac{3}{5} = 3\left(\frac{2}{5} + \frac{3}{5}\right)$	Use distributive property.
$= 3\left(\frac{5}{5}\right)$	Add inside parentheses.
$= 3(1)$	Simplify.
$= 3$	Multiply.

Using the order of operations and using the distributive property give the same answer of 3.

Goal 2 USING THE DISTRIBUTIVE PROPERTY

ADMISSION PRICES

	Adult	Student
General Admission	\$7	\$5
Laser Show	\$3	\$2

EXAMPLE 2 Using the Distributive Property

FIELD TRIP Your class of 30 students is taking a field trip to a science museum. How much money will the class spend for the field trip if everyone goes to the museum and the laser show?

Solution

Use the admission information at the left to find the total cost.

Method 1 Total cost = Cost for museum + Cost for laser show

$= 30(5) + 30(2)$ Write the cost for admission and for the show.

$= 150 + 60$ Multiply.

$= 210$ Add.

ANSWER ▶ Your class will spend \$210 for the field trip.

Method 2 Total cost = Number of students × Cost per student

$= 30(5 + 2)$ Write the cost for the sum of admission and show.

$= 30(7)$ Add inside parentheses.

$= 210$ Multiply.

ANSWER ▶ Your class will spend \$210 for the field trip.

Both methods give the same solution because $30(5) + 30(2) = 30(5 + 2)$ by the distributive property.

EXAMPLE 3 Evaluating a Variable Expression

Evaluate the expression $3(x + 8)$ when $x = 4$.

Solution

$3(x + 8) = 3x + 3(8)$ Use distributive property.

$= 3(4) + 24$ Substitute 4 for *x*.

$= 36$ Use order of operations.

EXAMPLE 4 Rewriting a Variable Expression

Use the distributive property to rewrite the expression $2(9 + a)$.

Solution

$2(9 + a) = 2(9) + 2(a)$ Use distributive property.

$= 18 + 2a$ Simplify.

3.6 Exercises

Guided Practice

Complete the statement using + or ×.

1. $3 \; ? \; (6 + 8) = 3 \; ? \; 6 + 3 \; ? \; 8$ **2.** $(5 + 2) \; ? \; 3 = 5 \times 3 \; ? \; 2 \times 3$

ERROR ANALYSIS In Exercises 3 and 4, describe and correct the error.

3.

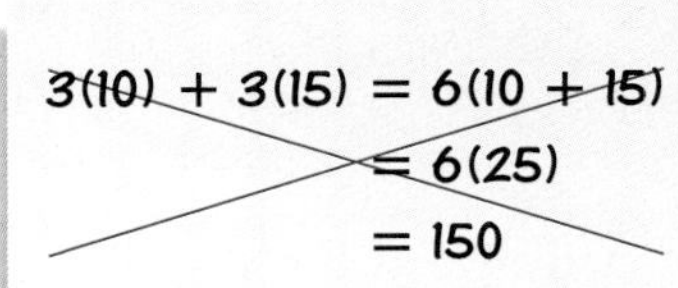

4.

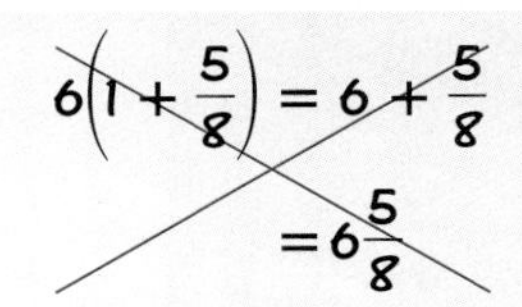

5. Which equation correctly illustrates the distributive property?

A. $4(12 + x) = 48 + 12x$ **B.** $3t + \frac{4}{5}t = \left(3 + \frac{4}{5}\right)t$

Practice and Problem Solving

Student Help

▶ **More Practice**
Extra practice to help you master skills is on page 571.

6. Write an equation that relates the distributive property to the area model.

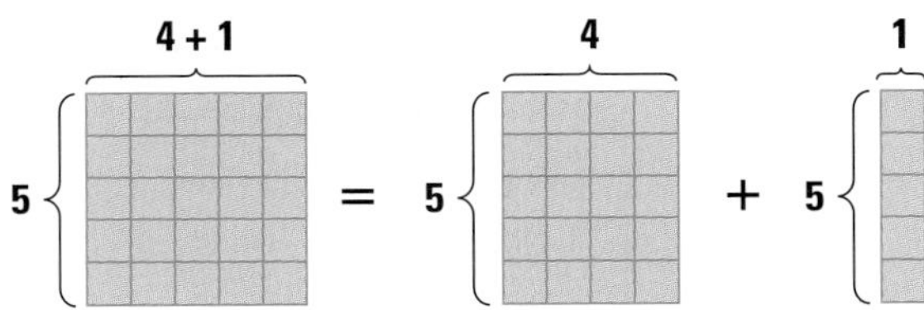

Evaluate the expression. Justify each step. Tell whether you used *order of operations* or the *distributive property.*

7. $5(3 + 8)$ **8.** $17(85 + 15)$ **9.** $10(5.9 + 1.2)$

10. $4\left(\frac{5}{6} + \frac{1}{4}\right)$ **11.** $6\left(\frac{1}{3} + \frac{1}{5}\right)$ **12.** $9\left(\frac{7}{9} + \frac{1}{3}\right)$

ALGEBRA Evaluate the two expressions when $x = 5$. What property accounts for the results?

13. $4\left(\frac{1}{2} + x\right)$ and $4\left(\frac{1}{2}\right) + 4x$ **14.** $3\left(x + \frac{2}{3}\right)$ and $3x + 3\left(\frac{2}{3}\right)$

Use the distributive property to rewrite the expression.

15. $3(t + 4)$ **16.** $12(5 + b)$ **17.** $6(4 + c)$

18. $3(15 + n)$ **19.** $1(x + 24)$ **20.** $5(p + q)$

21. $2(23 + c)$ **22.** $4(d + 13)$ **23.** $3(31 + y)$

Link to Careers

TRANSPORTATION ENGINEERS

Transportation systems, including highways and rural roads, are designed and monitored by transportation engineers.

More about transportation engineers available at www.mcdougallittell.com

ALGEBRA Match the expression with an equivalent expression. Evaluate both expressions when $n = 4$.

A. $6(5) + 6(n)$ **B.** $5(n) + 5(6)$ **C.** $3(8) + 3(n)$ **D.** $8(n) + 8(3)$

24. $3(8 + n)$ **25.** $5(n + 6)$ **26.** $8(n + 3)$ **27.** $6(5 + n)$

In Exercises 28–33, complete the calculation using the distributive property and mental math.

28. $3(11.2) = 3(11 + 0.2) = \underline{?}$ **29.** $5(20.1) = 5(20 + 0.1) = \underline{?}$

30. $10(2.5) = 10(2 + 0.5) = \underline{?}$ **31.** $11(2.3) = 11(2 + 0.3) = \underline{?}$

32. $20(5.5) = 20(5 + 0.5) = \underline{?}$ **33.** $2(12.4) = 2(12 + 0.4) = \underline{?}$

34. SHOPPING You buy 4 loaves of bread for $2.09 each. Use the distributive property and mental math to find the total cost.

35. CLOTHING You would like to buy 3 shirts. The cost of each shirt is $20.30. Use the distributive property and mental math to find the total cost.

36. TRANSPORTATION You are a transportation engineer evaluating traffic on Main Street. You determine that the average number of cars during peak traffic is 145 cars per hour. The average number of trucks during peak traffic is 55 trucks per hour. On average, how many cars and trucks travel on Main Street during peak traffic in a 2 hour period?

FIELD TRIP **In Exercises 37–39, use the following information. Your class of 75 students and 5 teachers takes a field trip to the aquarium.**

37. The admission prices are $7 for adults and $6 for students. How much does it cost for everyone to be admitted?

38. For lunch, each person gets a sandwich and juice for $5. How much does it cost for the entire group to eat lunch?

39. In which exercise, Exercise 37 or Exercise 38, can you use the distributive property? Explain your reasoning in words.

40. TALENT SHOW You have $100 to pay for a talent show. You allow each person 2 minutes to set up, $\frac{1}{2}$ minute for an introduction, and 5 minutes for the act. There are 20 people performing. How long will the talent show be? What information is relevant to answering the question? Explain your reasoning.

41. COMMUNITY SERVICE You are delivering Thanksgiving packages to the elderly. Each package contains a 12 pound turkey, 3 pounds of vegetables, and 4 pounds of potatoes. Assume that you can carry only 50 pounds. Estimate how many packages you can carry. Then use the distributive property to calculate if you can carry three packages.

42. CHALLENGE During the summer you mow lawns. You charge \$10.75 to mow a small lawn, \$15.50 to mow a large lawn, and \$11.25 to pull weeds from a garden. In one week, you mow six small lawns and six large lawns, and you pull weeds in four gardens. How much do you earn during the week?

Multiple-Choice Practice

Test Tip (A)(B)(C)(D)

▶ In order to figure out which expression is *not* equal, first rewrite the expression using the distributive property.

43. Which of the following is *not* equal to $6(x + 8)$?

(A) $48 + 6x$ (B) $6(x) + 6(8)$ (C) $6x + 8$ (D) $6x + 48$

44. Choose the equation that illustrates the distributive property.

(F) $5 \times 3 + 1 = 15 + 1$ (G) $\left(\frac{3}{4} + \frac{1}{2}\right) \times 8 = 6 + 4$

(H) $17 \times 23 = 23 \times 17$ (J) $3 + (9 + 7) = (3 + 9) + 7$

45. On Saturday, 4 friends go to the zoo. The admission is \$3.25 per person, and they buy 4 special exhibit tickets for \$1.35 each. Which expression could be used to find the total amount of money spent?

(A) $3.25 + 4 \times 1.35$ (B) $4 \times (3.25 + 1.35)$

(C) $3 \times (3.25 + 1.35)$ (D) $4 \times (3.25 \times 1.35)$

Mixed Review

Find the greatest common factor by listing all the factors of the numbers. *(2.2)*

46. 51, 68 **47.** 72, 98 **48.** 27, 64 **49.** 45, 72

50. 36, 57 **51.** 35, 210 **52.** 48, 100 **53.** 120, 64

In Exercises 54–61, write the fraction in simplest form. *(2.4)*

54. $\frac{39}{78}$ **55.** $\frac{28}{48}$ **56.** $\frac{99}{132}$ **57.** $\frac{44}{121}$

58. $\frac{7}{196}$ **59.** $\frac{6}{15}$ **60.** $\frac{36}{52}$ **61.** $\frac{24}{74}$

62. Samuel, Jessica, and Latasha ride the same bus home from school. Samuel rides the bus every other day. Jessica rides the bus every day. Latasha rides the bus every third day. They all ride the bus on Monday. If school meets five days a week, when will they ride together again? *(2.5)*

Graph the numbers on a number line. Then write them in order from least to greatest. *(2.6–2.8)*

63. $1.5, 1\frac{1}{4}, 3\frac{1}{2}, 4.3, \frac{10}{3}$ **64.** $2.2, \frac{7}{4}, 1\frac{1}{2}, \frac{4}{5}, 1.7$

3.7 Units of Measure

In this lesson you'll:

- Convert units of measure within a given system. (AF 2.1)
- Convert units of measure between the U.S. customary system and metric system. (AF 2.1)

Goal 1 Converting U.S. Customary Units

To convert from one unit of measure to another, use unit analysis to find the correct fraction, or conversion factor, by which to multiply. For example, to convert 3 feet to inches, use the conversion factor $\frac{12 \text{ in.}}{1 \text{ ft}}$.

$$3 \text{ ft} = 3 \cancel{\text{ft}} \times \frac{12 \text{ in.}}{1 \cancel{\text{ft}}} = \frac{3 \times 12}{1} \text{ in.} = 36 \text{ in.}$$

EXAMPLE 1 Converting Units of Length

A track has a perimeter of $\frac{2}{3}$ mile. What is the perimeter in feet?

Solution

The fact that 5280 feet = 1 mile means that (miles) $\times \frac{5280 \text{ ft}}{1 \text{ mi}}$ = (feet).

$\frac{2}{3} \text{ mi} = \frac{2}{3} \cancel{\text{mi}} \times \frac{5280 \text{ ft}}{1 \cancel{\text{mi}}}$ — Multiply by the conversion factor $\frac{5280 \text{ ft}}{1 \text{ mi}}$.

$= \frac{2 \times 5280}{3 \times 1} \text{ ft}$ — Multiply fractions.

$= \frac{10{,}560}{3} \text{ ft}$ — Simplify numerator and denominator.

$= 3520 \text{ ft}$ — Simplify fraction.

ANSWER ▶ The perimeter is 3520 feet.

Student Help

▶ **Skills Review**
For help with converting units, see page 561.

EXAMPLE 2 Converting Units of Time

BIOLOGY A healthy, adult, human heart rate at rest is 60 beats per minute. How many times would a person's heart beat in 24 hours?

Solution

$\frac{60 \text{ beats}}{1 \text{ min}} = \frac{60 \text{ beats}}{1 \cancel{\text{min}}} \times \frac{60 \cancel{\text{min}}}{1 \cancel{\text{h}}} \times \frac{24 \cancel{\text{h}}}{1 \text{ day}}$ — Multiply by two conversion factors.

$= \frac{60 \times 60 \times 24 \text{ beats}}{1 \times 1 \times 1 \text{ day}}$ — Multiply fractions.

$= \frac{86{,}400 \text{ beats}}{1 \text{ day}}$ — Simplify.

ANSWER ▶ A person's heart would beat 86,400 times in 24 hours.

Goal 2 CONVERTING METRIC UNITS

Student Help

▶**MORE EXAMPLES**

INTERNET More examples are available at www.mcdougallittell.com

EXAMPLE 3 Converting Units of Volume

PLANTS You buy a bottle of plant food that contains three fourths of a liter (L). The recommended dosage for your plant is 10 milliliters (mL). How many doses does the bottle contain?

Solution

$\frac{3}{4}\text{ L} = \frac{3}{4}\not{\text{L}} \times \frac{1000\text{ mL}}{1\not{\text{L}}}$ Multiply by the conversion factor $\frac{1000\text{ mL}}{1\text{ L}}$.

$= \frac{3 \times 1000}{4 \times 1}\text{ mL}$ Multiply fractions.

$= \frac{3000}{4}\text{ mL}$ Simplify.

$= 750\text{ mL}$ Simplify fraction.

To find the number of doses, divide 750, the number of milliliters in the bottle, by the dosage.

$\text{Doses} = \frac{750}{10}$ Divide by the recommended dosage.

$= 75$ Divide numerator by denominator.

ANSWER ▶ The bottle contains 75 doses.

Link to History

GOLD RUSH In 1848, the population of San Francisco was about 800 people. By 1850, after gold was found, the population was nearly 35,000 people.

INTERNET More about the gold rush available at www.mcdougallittell.com

Converting units between the U.S. customary system and the metric system is similar to converting units within a system. You multiply by the appropriate conversion factor. Most conversions between systems can only be approximate.

EXAMPLE 4 Converting Between Systems

HISTORY LINK Gold, being a precious metal, has influenced the course of history in the United States and throughout the world. All of the gold discovered in the world would fit into a cube 22 meters on a side. How many feet is one side of this cube? (1 meter ≈ 3.28 ft)

Solution

$22\text{ m} \approx 22\not{\text{m}} \times \frac{3.28\text{ ft}}{1\not{\text{m}}}$ Multiply by the conversion factor $\frac{3.28\text{ ft}}{1\text{ m}}$.

$= \frac{22 \times 3.28}{1}\text{ ft}$ Multiply fractions.

$= 72.16\text{ ft}$ Simplify.

ANSWER ▶ The length of one side of the cube is about 72 feet.

3.7 Exercises

Guided Practice

Choose the fraction that can be used in the conversion.

1. 4 yd = **?** in.; $\frac{1 \text{ yd}}{36 \text{ in.}}, \frac{36 \text{ in.}}{1 \text{ yd}}$

2. $\frac{5}{6}$ day = **?** h; $\frac{1 \text{ day}}{24 \text{ h}}, \frac{24 \text{ h}}{1 \text{ day}}$

3. 450 g = **?** kg; $\frac{1 \text{ kg}}{1000 \text{ g}}, \frac{1000 \text{ g}}{1 \text{ kg}}$

4. 46.5 cm = **?** in.; $\frac{1 \text{ in.}}{2.54 \text{ cm}}, \frac{2.54 \text{ cm}}{1 \text{ in.}}$

Convert. Round to the nearest hundredth if necessary.

5. 12 quarts to gallons
6. 108 inches to yards
7. $\frac{5}{8}$ mile to feet
8. 15 hours to seconds
9. 7 pounds to ounces
10. 5 days to hours
11. 8 liters to milliliters
12. 4 decades to years
13. 24 yards to inches

Find the price per meter. Use the fact that 1 foot ≈ 0.3048 meter.

14. Rope: $\frac{\$1.64}{1 \text{ ft}}$
15. Ribbon: $\frac{\$.05}{1 \text{ in.}}$
16. Pine board: $\frac{\$5}{1 \text{ yd}}$

Practice and Problem Solving

Student Help

▶ MORE PRACTICE Extra practice to help you master skills is on page 571.

ERROR ANALYSIS **Describe and correct the error.**

17. Milligrams to grams

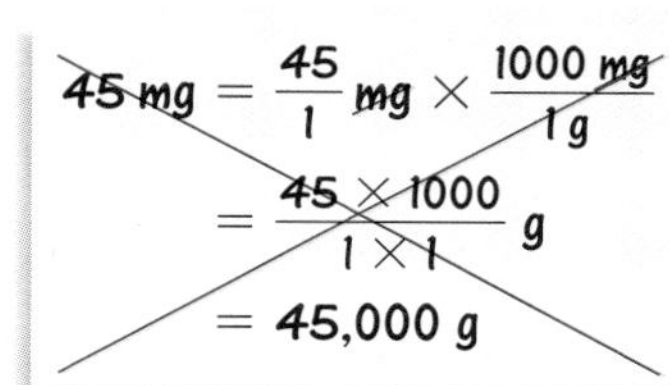

18. Tons to ounces

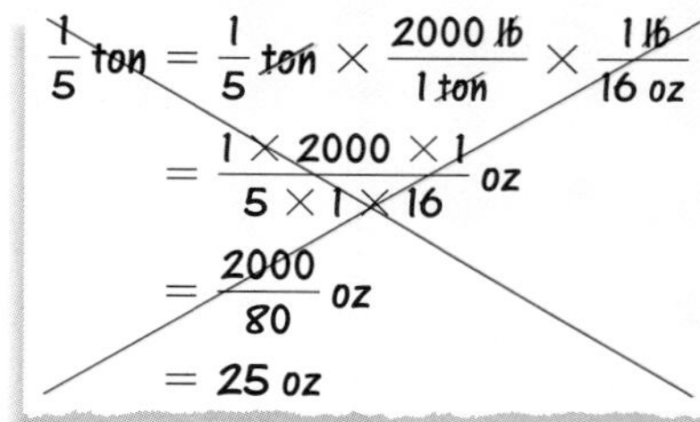

In Exercises 19–27, convert within the U.S. customary system.

19. 60 inches to feet
20. 12 gallons to quarts
21. 84 days to weeks
22. 5 tons to pounds
23. 3 pounds to ounces
24. 16 pints to quarts
25. $\frac{7}{8}$ mile to feet
26. 1 week to hours
27. 32 cups to gallons

28. **RACING** A swimmer completes a $1\frac{1}{2}$ mile race. How many yards did the swimmer swim?

29. **COOKING** A main dish cooks for $1\frac{3}{4}$ hours. For how many minutes does the main dish cook?

In Exercises 30–35, convert within the metric system.

30. $\frac{2}{5}$ kiloliter to liters

31. 34 grams to milligrams

32. 600 centimeters to meters

33. 10.5 kilograms to grams

34. 1 kilometer to centimeters

35. 875,000 milliliters to kiloliters

In Exercises 36–38, convert between systems.

36. A 100 meter swim to inches (1 meter ≈ 39.37 inches)

37. 10 kilograms of oranges to pounds (1 kilogram ≈ 2.21 pounds)

38. 2 gallons of milk to liters (1 gallon ≈ 3.79 liters)

39. **CRAFTS** You have 100 yards of lace. You need 72 inches of lace to trim one covered photo album. Describe and carry out the steps involved to find how many albums you can trim in lace.

40. **MATHEMATICAL REASONING** Put the list below in order from least to greatest. Explain your reasoning using words and numbers.

0.0005 km   4.3 cm   52.25 mm   0.53 m

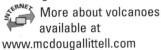

41. **Science Link** The heights (in meters) of six volcanic mountains on the western coast of the United States are listed in the table. Find the approximate height (in feet). Use the fact that 1 meter ≈ 3.28 feet.

Volcano	Height (in meters)	Volcano	Height (in meters)
Mount Shasta, CA	4318	Lassen Peak, CA	3188
Mount Hood, OR	3427	Mount Jefferson, OR	3200
Mount Rainier, WA	4393	Mount Saint Helens, WA	2549

▶Sources: *Volcanoes of North America* and U.S.G.S. Geographic Names Information Systems

42. **CHALLENGE** During the week from January 3, 2000, to January 10, 2000, the national debt increased $3,619,244,744. To the nearest dollar, how much did the national debt increase each second?

VOLCANOES Mount St. Helens is 2549 meters high and is only one of fifteen volcanoes in the Cascade Mountain range in Washington.

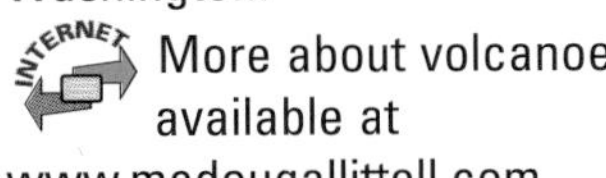

More about volcanoes available at www.mcdougallittell.com

Multiple-Choice Practice

43. Which measurement is equal to 8 inches?

Ⓐ $\frac{1}{9}$ yd   Ⓑ $\frac{2}{3}$ ft   Ⓒ $\frac{3}{4}$ ft   Ⓓ $\frac{1}{3}$ yd

44. While flying to Toronto, Canada, the pilot announces that you are 150 kilometers away. About how many miles are you from Toronto? (1 kilometer ≈ 0.62 mile)

Ⓕ 39 mi   Ⓖ 93 mi   Ⓗ 242 mi   Ⓙ 620 mi

3.8 Rates

California Standards

In this lesson you'll:

- Understand that rate is a measure of one quantity per unit value of another quantity. (AF 2.2)
- Use tables to solve problems involving rates. (AF 2.0)

Goal 1 Finding Rates

If two quantities a and b have different units of measure, then the **rate of a per b** is $\frac{a}{b}$. The units for a rate tell you which number goes in the numerator and which number goes in the denominator. For example,

$$\text{Miles per hour} = \frac{\text{Miles}}{\text{Hour}}.$$

When a rate is simplified so it has a denominator of 1, it is a **unit rate**.

Example 1 Finding a Unit Rate

TRAVELING You are traveling from San Jose, California, to Santa Rosa, California. You travel the distance of 101 miles in 2 hours. What is your average speed in miles per hour?

Solution

Speed is a type of unit rate. To find the average speed in miles per hour, divide the distance traveled by the time.

$$\text{Average speed} = \frac{\text{Distance}}{\text{Time}} = \frac{101 \text{ mi}}{2 \text{ h}} = \frac{50.5 \text{ mi}}{1 \text{ h}}$$

ANSWER ▶ Your average speed is 50.5 miles per hour.

You can use estimation to check that your result is reasonable.

$$\text{Average speed} = \frac{100 \text{ mi}}{2 \text{ h}} = \frac{50 \text{ mi}}{1 \text{ h}} \checkmark$$

Student Help

▶ **Vocabulary Tip**
In real life, rate has many different names such as speed, hourly wage, and unit price.

Example 2 Finding a Unit Price

SHOPPING In order to compare prices at the supermarket, you calculate unit prices. A 12 ounce box of cereal costs $3.72. What is the unit price of the cereal?

Solution

A unit price is a type of unit rate. Divide the cost by the weight.

$$\text{Unit price} = \frac{\text{Cost}}{\text{Weight}} = \frac{\$3.72}{12 \text{ oz}} = \frac{\$.31}{1 \text{ oz}}$$

ANSWER ▶ The unit price of the cereal is $.31 per ounce.

Goal 2 USING TABLES TO COMPARE RATES

Link to Sports

MARATHON RACING Jean Driscoll won the Boston Marathon in the women's wheelchair division seven years in a row.

EXAMPLE 3 Comparing Unit Rates

SPORTS Jean Driscoll completed the 26.2 mile Boston Marathon in about 102 minutes in 1999 and in about 113 minutes in 1996. Find Jean Driscoll's speed in minutes per mile for each year. Which was the faster unit rate?

Solution Use a table to organize the information.

Year	Time	Distance	Rate
1999	102 min	26.2 mi	? min/mi
1996	113 min	26.2 mi	? min/mi

1999: $\dfrac{\text{Time}}{\text{Distance}} = \dfrac{102 \text{ min}}{26.2 \text{ mi}} \approx 3.89$ minutes per mile

1996: $\dfrac{\text{Time}}{\text{Distance}} = \dfrac{113 \text{ min}}{26.2 \text{ mi}} \approx 4.31$ minutes per mile

ANSWER ▶ The *faster* rate is the *smaller* number. Her rate of 3.89 minutes per mile in 1999 was faster. Your solution is reasonable given that her overall time in 1999 was shorter.

EXAMPLE 4 Comparing Unit Rates

BABY-SITTING On Saturday you baby-sat for $2\frac{1}{2}$ hours and were paid \$10. On Sunday you baby-sat for 3 hours and were paid \$10.50. Find the hourly rate that you were paid on each day. Which is greater?

Solution Use a table to organize the information.

Day	Total	Time	Rate
Saturday	\$10	$2\frac{1}{2}$ h	? dollars/hour
Sunday	\$10.50	3 h	? dollars/hour

Saturday: $\dfrac{\text{Amount paid}}{\text{Time}} = \dfrac{\$10}{2\frac{1}{2}\text{ h}} = 10 \div \dfrac{5}{2} = 10 \times \dfrac{2}{5} = \dfrac{10 \times 2}{5} = \dfrac{\$4}{1 \text{ h}}$

Sunday: $\dfrac{\text{Amount paid}}{\text{Time}} = \dfrac{\$10.50}{3 \text{ h}} = \dfrac{\$3.50}{1 \text{ h}}$

ANSWER ▶ Your hourly rate was greater on Saturday. The answer is reasonable given that on Saturday you baby-sat $\frac{1}{2}$ hour less than on Sunday and received almost the same amount of money.

3.8 Exercises

Guided Practice

1. Two rates for answering questions on a test are given. Write each as a unit rate.

a. $\frac{60 \text{ minutes}}{75 \text{ questions}}$ **b.** $\frac{75 \text{ questions}}{60 \text{ minutes}}$

2. If you need to complete a 75 question test in 60 minutes, which unit rate from Exercise 1 would you prefer to use to complete the test on time? Explain.

3. **TRAVEL** You drive 1350 miles in 3 days. Each day you drive for 9 hours. What is your speed in miles per hour?

4. **SHOPPING** A 32 ounce bottle of window cleaner costs $2.69, and a 48 ounce bottle of window cleaner costs $4.29. Find the unit prices. Which is the better buy?

Practice and Problem Solving

Student Help

▶ MORE PRACTICE
Extra practice to help you master skills is on page 571.

Find the unit rate. Check the reasonableness of the unit rate in the given context.

5. It rains 28 inches in 8 hours.

6. You pay $2.73 for 100 sheets of paper.

7. A plane flies 2275 miles in 3.5 hours.

8. You are paid $90 for delivering newspapers for 6 days.

SHOPPING **In Exercises 9–11, tell which item is the better buy. Use estimation to verify the reasonableness of your answer.**

9. A. 16 oz of cereal for $3.49 **B.** 20 oz of cereal for $4.19

10. A. 2 lb bag of potatoes for $1.08 **B.** 5 lb bag of potatoes for $3.95

11. A. 0.5 L of juice for $1.25 **B.** 2 L of juice for $4

Student Help

▶ HOMEWORK HELP

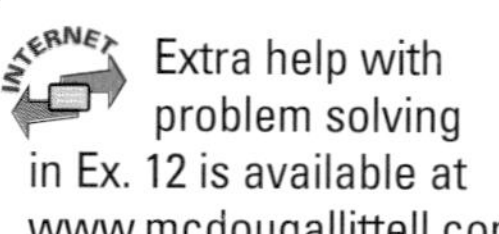

Extra help with problem solving in Ex. 12 is available at www.mcdougallittell.com

12. **TRIATHLON** You compete in a triathlon that consists of a $\frac{1}{4}$ mile swim, a 9 mile bike ride, and a 3 mile run. You complete the swim in 8 minutes, the bike ride in 24 minutes, and the run in 19 minutes. Which part did you finish with a faster average speed? Why can you estimate to answer the question?

13. **HOME VIDEOS** For the 5 year period from 1995 through 1999, the average American watched 256 hours of home videos. Find the average number of hours watched per year.

▶ Source: Veronis, Suhler, & Associates

14. **TYPING** Three students learn to type. Use the table below to find the unit rate for each student. Who types the fastest?

Student	Number of words	Time (in minutes)	Typing rate
Chung	126	3	? words/min
Shana	240	5	? words/min
Randy	180	4	? words/min

Link to Science

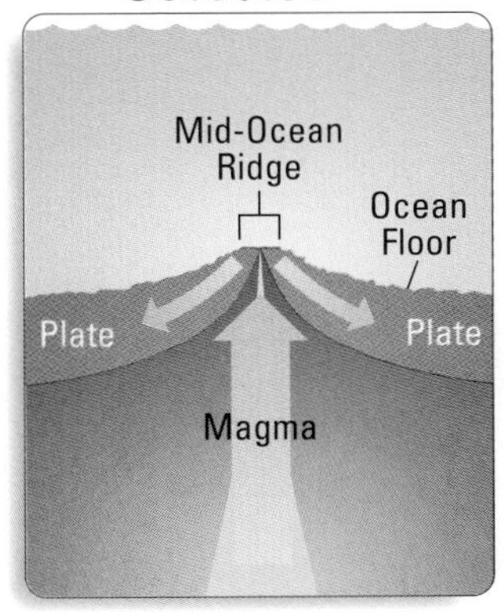

PLATE TECTONICS Earth's crust is made up of rigid, moving plates. Spreading of the ocean floor occurs when these plates move apart at mid-ocean ridges such as the Mid-Atlantic Ridge and the East Pacific Rise.

INTERNET More about plate tectonics available at www.mcdougallittell.com

In Exercises 15–18, make a table to help you answer the question.

15. **HIKING** Susan started hiking at 8:00 A.M. She hiked 6 miles to a waterfall in 2 hours. Ricardo began hiking another trail at 8:45 A.M. He hiked 5 miles to an overlook in 3 hours. Did they hike at the same rate? Explain. What information is important to solve the problem? What information is irrelevant?

16. **PET CARE** You take care of a neighbor's cats for seven days and are paid \$50. Your friend takes care of a neighbor's dogs for a three day holiday weekend and is paid \$30. Find your daily wage and your friend's daily wage. Who has a higher daily wage? Evaluate whether your answer is reasonable.

17. **Science Link** The Mid-Atlantic Ridge spreads 25 kilometers in one million years while the East Pacific Rise spreads more than 15 centimeters per year. Which has a faster unit rate of ocean floor spreading? Explain your reasoning using words and numbers.

18. **CHALLENGE** The accounting department recycles 396 pounds of paper in 30 days. The human resource department recycles 186 pounds of paper in two weeks. The computer resources department recycles 92 pounds of paper in a week. Which department recycles the most paper per day? Why do you need to use exact calculations? Explain your reasoning.

Multiple-Choice Practice

19. You are a sales representative. You make 30 sales calls and sell \$2400 of merchandise. Estimate the amount of sales that you make (in dollars per sales call).

(A) \$8 per sales call (B) \$80 per sales call

(C) \$125 per sales call (D) \$800 per sales call

20. Which is *not* a unit rate?

(F) 5 meters per second (G) 10 dollars per hour

(H) 12 seconds per 3 meters (J) 7 dollars per pound

Chapter 3 Chapter Summary and Review

VOCABULARY

- **reciprocals,** *p. 134*
- **multiplicative inverses,** *p. 134*
- **distributive property,** *p. 139*
- **rate of *a* per *b*,** *p. 148*
- **unit rate,** *p. 148*

3.1 ADDING AND SUBTRACTING FRACTIONS

Examples on pp. 111–112

To add or subtract two fractions, write the fractions with a common denominator if necessary. Then add or subtract their numerators and write the sum or difference over the denominator.

EXAMPLE **Evaluate $\frac{3}{4} - \frac{1}{8}$.**

$\frac{3}{4} - \frac{1}{8} = \frac{3 \cdot 8}{4 \cdot 8} - \frac{4 \cdot 1}{4 \cdot 8}$ Choose a common denominator of 32.

$= \frac{24}{32} - \frac{4}{32}$ Simplify.

$= \frac{20}{32} = \frac{5}{8}$ Subtract numerators and simplify fraction.

In Exercises 1–4, evaluate. Simplify if possible.

1. $\frac{6}{11} - \frac{3}{11}$ **2.** $\frac{5}{12} + \frac{3}{12}$ **3.** $\frac{3}{5} + \frac{1}{3}$ **4.** $\frac{7}{8} - \frac{5}{6}$

3.2 USING A LEAST COMMON DENOMINATOR

Examples on pp. 115–116

When you add or subtract fractions with different denominators, you can rewrite the fractions using their least common denominator.

EXAMPLE **Evaluate $\frac{5}{6} + \frac{1}{4} - \frac{5}{8}$.**

$\frac{5}{6} + \frac{1}{4} - \frac{5}{8} = \frac{5 \cdot 4}{6 \cdot 4} + \frac{1 \cdot 6}{4 \cdot 6} - \frac{5 \cdot 3}{8 \cdot 3}$ Rewrite using LCD of 24.

$= \frac{20 + 6 - 15}{24} = \frac{11}{24}$ Add and subtract fractions. Then simplify numerator.

In Exercises 5–8, evaluate. Simplify if possible.

5. $\frac{2}{7} + \frac{1}{2}$

6. $\frac{5}{6} - \frac{3}{4}$

7. $\frac{1}{3} + \frac{1}{2} + \frac{1}{6}$

8. $\frac{7}{8} - \frac{5}{6} + \frac{7}{12}$

3.3 ADDING AND SUBTRACTING MIXED NUMBERS

Examples on pp. 119–120

To add or subtract mixed numbers, first add or subtract the fractions. Then add or subtract the whole numbers. If you are subtracting, and the second fraction is larger than the first fraction, you will first need to regroup.

EXAMPLE **Evaluate $4\frac{1}{2} - 2\frac{2}{3}$.**

$4\frac{1}{2} - 2\frac{2}{3} = 4\frac{3}{6} - 2\frac{4}{6}$ Rewrite fractions with a common denominator.

$= 3\frac{9}{6} - 2\frac{4}{6}$ Regroup $4\frac{3}{6}$ as $3\frac{9}{6}$.

$= 1\frac{5}{6}$ Subtract fractions and whole numbers.

In Exercises 9–12, evaluate. Simplify if possible.

9. $4\frac{7}{8} + 2\frac{1}{6}$

10. $5\frac{6}{7} + \frac{3}{8}$

11. $9\frac{1}{4} - 3\frac{1}{2}$

12. $6\frac{2}{3} - 5\frac{4}{5}$

3.4 MULTIPLYING FRACTIONS AND MIXED NUMBERS

Examples on pp. 126–127

EXAMPLES

Evaluate $\frac{5}{6} \times \frac{3}{7}$.

$\frac{5}{6} \times \frac{3}{7} = \frac{5 \times 3}{6 \times 7}$ Multiply numerators and multiply denominators.

$= \frac{15}{42}$ Simplify numerator and denominator.

$= \frac{5}{14}$ Simplify fraction.

Evaluate $3\frac{1}{8} \times 1\frac{2}{3}$.

$3\frac{1}{8} \times 1\frac{2}{3} = \frac{25}{8} \times \frac{5}{3}$ Rewrite as improper fractions.

$= \frac{25 \times 5}{8 \times 3}$ Multiply numerators and multiply denominators.

$= \frac{125}{24} = 5\frac{5}{24}$ Simplify and rewrite as a mixed number.

In Exercises 13–16, multiply. Simplify if possible.

13. $\frac{3}{4} \times \frac{1}{6}$

14. $\frac{2}{3} \times \frac{4}{7}$

15. $1\frac{7}{8} \times 2\frac{2}{5}$

16. $3\frac{5}{6} \times 1\frac{2}{3}$

3.5 DIVIDING FRACTIONS AND MIXED NUMBERS

Examples on pp. 134–135

To divide two fractions, multiply the first fraction by the reciprocal of the second. If mixed numbers are involved, first write them as improper fractions.

EXAMPLE **Evaluate $3\frac{1}{3} \div 1\frac{5}{6}$.**

$3\frac{1}{3} \div 1\frac{5}{6} = \frac{10}{3} \div \frac{11}{6}$ Rewrite as improper fractions.

$= \frac{10}{3} \times \frac{6}{11}$ Multiply by the reciprocal.

$= \frac{60}{33}$ Multiply fractions.

$= \frac{20}{11} = 1\frac{9}{11}$ Simplify and rewrite as a mixed number.

In Exercises 17–20, divide. Simplify if possible.

17. $\frac{3}{8} \div \frac{2}{5}$ **18.** $\frac{15}{16} \div \frac{3}{8}$ **19.** $4\frac{2}{5} \div 2\frac{3}{4}$ **20.** $8 \div 2\frac{2}{3}$

3.6 THE DISTRIBUTIVE PROPERTY

Examples on pp. 139–140

EXAMPLES **Use the distributive property to evaluate the expression.**

a. $5(200 + 7) = 5 \times 200 + 5 \times 7$
$= 1000 + 35$
$= 1035$

b. $4 \times \frac{1}{6} + 4 \times \frac{1}{3} = 4\left(\frac{1}{6} + \frac{1}{3}\right)$
$= 4\left(\frac{1}{6} + \frac{2}{6}\right)$
$= 4\left(\frac{1}{2}\right) = 2$

In Exercises 21–24, use the distributive property to evaluate the expression.

21. $8 \cdot 23 + 8 \cdot 27$ **22.** $9(50 + 5)$ **23.** $12(2.2)$ **24.** $36 \cdot 87 + 36 \cdot 13$

25. Your 3 dogs eat $1\frac{1}{4}$ cups, 1 cup, and $1\frac{1}{3}$ cups of food each day. Use the distributive property to write and simplify an expression for the total amount of food the dogs eat for 5 days.

3.7 UNITS OF MEASURE

Examples on pp. 144–145

To convert from one unit to another, multiply by the appropriate conversion factor. Set up the fraction so that the units will divide out.

EXAMPLE **How many pints are in 10 gallons?**

$10 \text{ gallons} = \frac{10}{1} \cancel{\text{gallons}} \times \frac{4 \cancel{\text{quarts}}}{1 \cancel{\text{gallon}}} \times \frac{2 \text{ pints}}{1 \cancel{\text{quart}}}$ **Multiply by two conversion factors.**

$= \frac{10 \times 4 \times 2}{1 \times 1 \times 1} \text{ pints}$ **Multiply fractions.**

$= \frac{80}{1} = 80 \text{ pints}$ **Simplify.**

In Exercises 26–28, convert.

26. 8 pints to quarts **27.** 3 pounds to ounces **28.** 1510 milligrams to grams

29. A garden has a perimeter of 68 meters. You buy 200 feet of fencing. Is this enough to enclose the garden? Explain. (1 meter ≈ 39.37 inches)

3.8 RATES

Examples on pp. 148–149

EXAMPLE Mark types 6 pages in 36 minutes. Melissa types 5 pages in 30 minutes. To compare their typing speeds, use unit rates. Use a table to help organize the given information.

	Number of Pages	÷ Time	= Typing Rate
Mark	6	36 min	? pages/min
Melissa	5	30 min	? pages/min

Mark: $\frac{6 \text{ pages}}{36 \text{ min}} \approx \frac{0.17 \text{ page}}{1 \text{ min}}$ Melissa: $\frac{5 \text{ pages}}{30 \text{ min}} \approx \frac{0.17 \text{ page}}{1 \text{ min}}$

Their rates are the same, so Mark and Melissa type at the same rate.

In Exercises 30 and 31, find the unit rate.

30. A heart beats 252 times in 3 minutes. **31.** A car uses 3 gallons of gas to travel 78 miles.

In Exercises 32–34, tell which is the better buy.

32. A. 32 ounces of yams for \$2.09 **B.** 14 ounces of yams for \$.98

33. A. 10 pounds of oranges for \$6.75 **B.** 6 pounds of oranges for \$3.25

34. A. 2 liters of water for \$1.15 **B.** 5 liters of water for \$3.02

Chapter Test

Evaluate. Simplify if possible.

1. $\frac{2}{5} + \frac{4}{5}$ **2.** $\frac{11}{12} - \frac{7}{12}$ **3.** $\frac{4}{9} + \frac{1}{3}$ **4.** $\frac{7}{10} - \frac{1}{5}$

5. $5 - 3\frac{2}{9}$ **6.** $1\frac{5}{6} + \frac{7}{8}$ **7.** $6\frac{1}{4} - 3\frac{9}{10}$ **8.** $2\frac{1}{6} + 8\frac{11}{12}$

GEOMETRY **Find the perimeter of the figure.**

9.

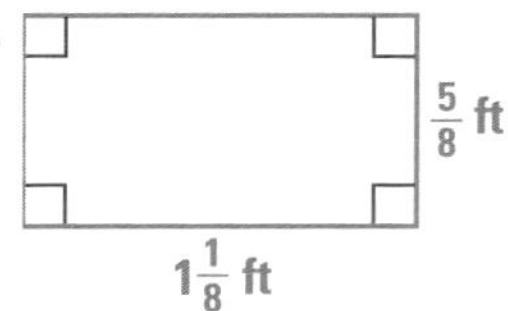

10.

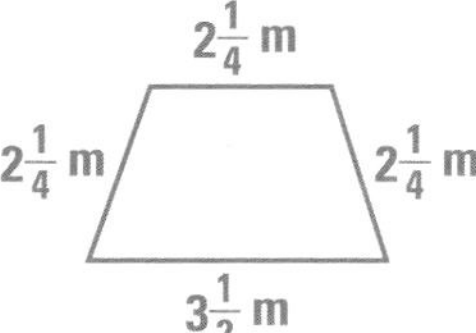

11.

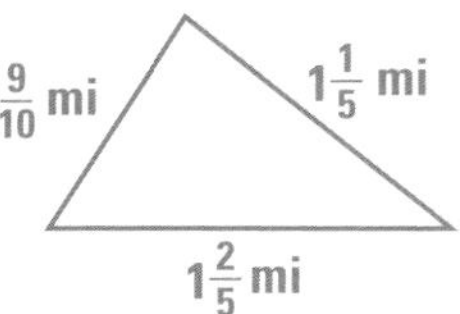

Evaluate. Simplify if possible.

12. $\frac{5}{8} \times \frac{1}{5}$ **13.** $4 \times \frac{3}{5}$ **14.** $3\frac{1}{6} \times \frac{2}{9}$ **15.** $2\frac{1}{3} \times 4\frac{3}{8}$

16. $\frac{11}{6} \div \frac{5}{6}$ **17.** $\frac{14}{5} \div \frac{3}{10}$ **18.** $2\frac{3}{4} \div \frac{3}{5}$ **19.** $5\frac{1}{2} \div 1\frac{5}{12}$

Use the distributive property to evaluate or rewrite the expression.

20. $4 \cdot \frac{11}{8} + 4 \cdot \frac{5}{8}$ **21.** $6(100 + 11)$ **22.** $p(12 + 23)$ **23.** $8(t + 5)$

Convert.

24. $\frac{7}{8}$ kilogram to grams **25.** 1.5 days to minutes **26.** 65 miles to kilometers (1 mile ≈ 1.61 kilometers)

In Exercises 27 and 28, tell which item is the better buy.

27. A. 3-pack of cassette tapes for \$6.45 **B.** 4-pack of cassette tapes for \$7.80

28. A. $\frac{1}{2}$ gallon of gasoline for \$0.56 **B.** 7 gallons of gasoline for \$9.03

MUSIC **In Exercises 29–31, use the figures shown.**

29. How much *longer* is the cello than the violin?

30. How much *wider* is the cello than the violin?

31. How *many times longer* is the violin than it is wide?

Violin

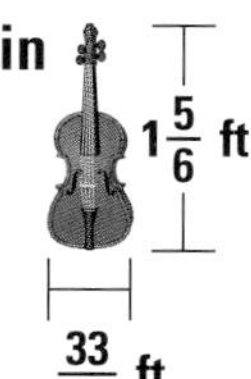

Cello

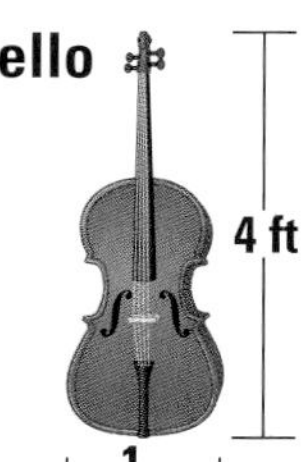

Multiple-Choice Practice

Test Tip Sometimes you can quickly eliminate wrong choices by rounding to estimate answers.

1. You practice piano for $\frac{3}{4}$ hour on Monday and $\frac{5}{6}$ hour on Wednesday. How many hours did you practice on the two days?

Ⓐ $\frac{5}{8}$ h Ⓑ $1\frac{1}{3}$ h

Ⓒ $1\frac{7}{13}$ h Ⓓ $1\frac{7}{12}$ h

2. Which statement about the rectangle is true?

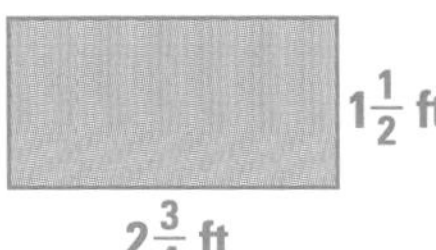

Ⓕ The perimeter is $4\frac{1}{8}$ ft.

Ⓖ The perimeter is $4\frac{1}{4}$ ft.

Ⓗ The area is $3\frac{3}{8}$ ft^2.

Ⓙ The area is $4\frac{1}{8}$ ft^2.

3. You have run $1\frac{5}{8}$ miles of a 3 mile run. How far is left to run?

Ⓐ $\frac{5}{8}$ mi Ⓑ $1\frac{3}{8}$ mi

Ⓒ $2\frac{3}{8}$ mi Ⓓ $2\frac{5}{8}$ mi

4. Rewrite $5(n + 6)$ using the distributive property.

Ⓕ $5n + 30$ Ⓖ $5n + 6$

Ⓗ $5n + 11$ Ⓙ $5 + n + 11$

5. A room is $12\frac{1}{2}$ feet by $10\frac{2}{3}$ feet. How much carpet will you need to cover the floor?

Ⓐ $46\frac{1}{3}$ ft^2 Ⓑ $120\frac{1}{3}$ ft^2

Ⓒ $121\frac{1}{6}$ ft^2 Ⓓ $133\frac{1}{3}$ ft^2

6. A bread recipe calls for 3 cups of flour. How many times do you have to fill a $\frac{3}{4}$ cup measuring cup with flour to measure the correct amount?

Ⓕ 3 times Ⓖ 4 times

Ⓗ 6 times Ⓙ Not here

7. Which expression is equal to $4(2 + 7)$?

Ⓐ $4 \times 2 + 7$

Ⓑ $4 \times 2 \times 7$

Ⓒ $4 \times 2 + 4 \times 7$

Ⓓ $4 + 2 + 7$

8. Three fourths of a gallon = **?** pints.

Ⓕ 3 pints Ⓖ 4 pints

Ⓗ 6 pints Ⓙ 12 pints

9. Which of the following is the best buy?

Ⓐ 2 lb bag of nails for \$1.79

Ⓑ 3 lb bag of nails for \$2.09

Ⓒ 5 lb bag of nails for \$2.79

Ⓓ 10 lb bag of nails for \$5.75

Brain games

▶ Solve problems involving positive fractions. (NS 2.1)

Fraction Shuffle

Materials

- **10 cards, each labeled with a number from 1 through 10**
- **A spinner with four equal sections labeled +, −, ×, and ÷**

Directions

Object of the Game

Play in pairs. Each round, you and your partner compare answers. The player with the greatest answer wins a point. The winner of the game is the player with the most points after a preset time or a preset number of rounds.

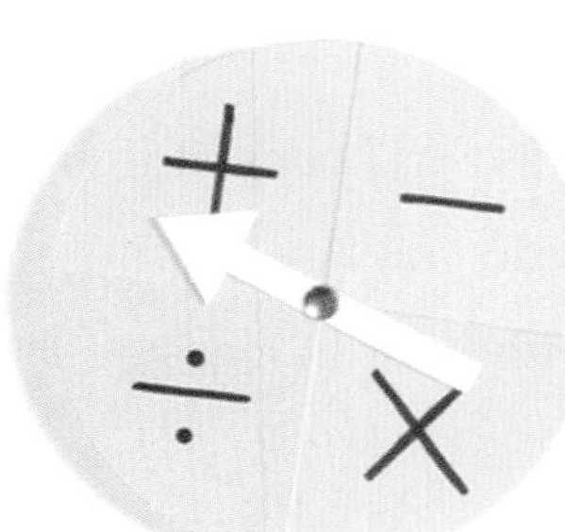

How to Play

STEP 1 One player shuffles the cards and places them face down. The other player spins the operation spinner. Players take turns drawing cards until both have four cards.

STEP 2 Each player chooses how to arrange his or her cards to form two fractions, then carries out the operation on the spinner. Players may try several arrangements to find the one that leads to the greatest answer. A time limit of one minute for each round may be helpful. Play continues with additional rounds, with players alternating card drawing and spinning.

Another Way to Play

Each player draws five cards and forms one fraction and one mixed number, using a fraction less than one in the mixed number.

Brain Teaser

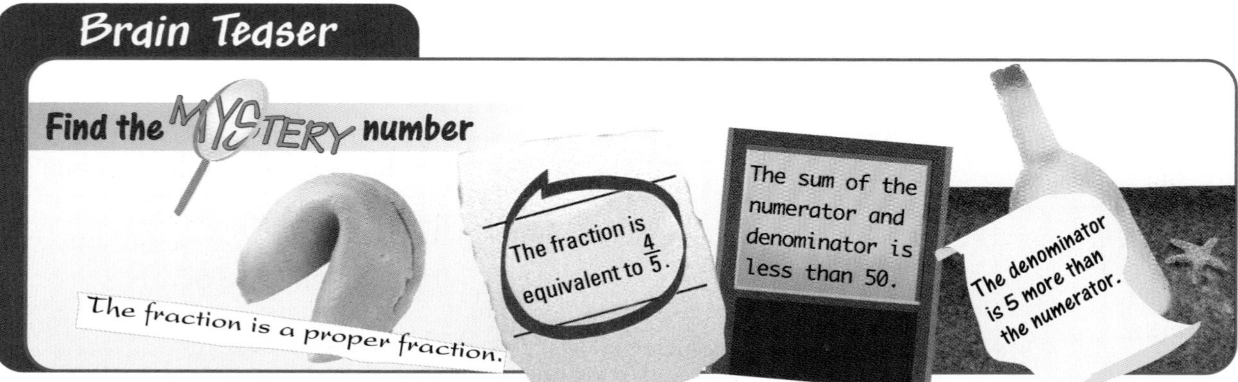

Find the MYSTERY number
The fraction is a proper fraction.
The fraction is equivalent to $\frac{4}{5}$.
The sum of the numerator and denominator is less than 50.
The denominator is 5 more than the numerator.

The basic skills you'll review on this page will help prepare you for the next chapter.

Reviewing the Basics

EXAMPLE 1 Graphing on a Number Line

Graph the numbers listed below on a number line.

$$2, \frac{1}{2}, 1.75, 0, 3\frac{1}{4}$$

Solution

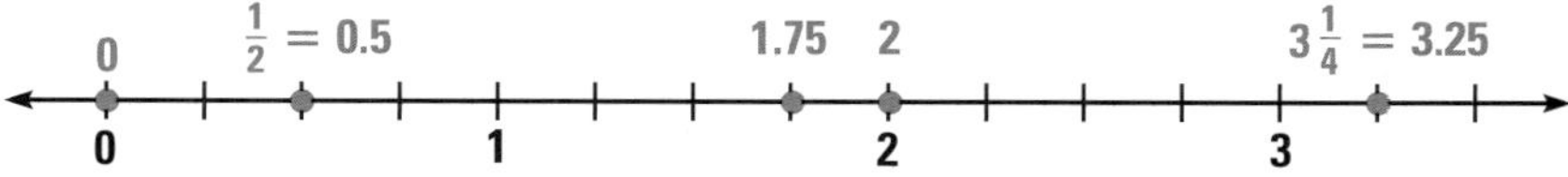

Try These

Graph the number on a number line.

1. 1　　**2.** 3　　**3.** 0.2　　**4.** 1.6

5. $2\frac{3}{4}$　　**6.** $\frac{3}{10}$　　**7.** $\frac{11}{5}$　　**8.** $1\frac{1}{5}$

EXAMPLE 2 Adding and Subtracting Using a Number Line

Model the description below on a number line. Then write the mathematical expression and evaluate it.

Start at 0, move 35 to the right, then move 15 to the left.

Solution

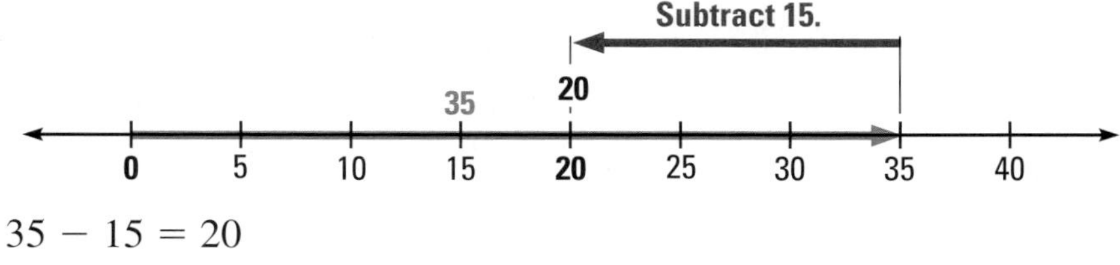

$35 - 15 = 20$

Try These

Model the description on a number line. Then write the mathematical expression and evaluate it.

9. Start at 0, move 9 to the right, then move 5 to the right.

10. Start at 0, move 15 to the right, then move 3 to the left.

11. Start at 0, move 30 to the right, then move 1 to the right.

12. Start at 0, move 7 to the right, move 3 to the right, then move 6 to the left.

Student Help

▶ **MORE EXAMPLES**

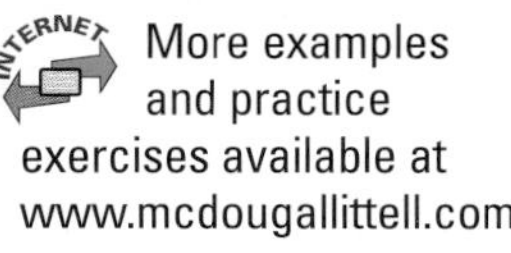

More examples and practice exercises available at www.mcdougallittell.com

Chapters 1-3 Cumulative Practice

Evaluate the expression. (1.3, 1.4)

1. $(2 \times 3^2) \div 6$ **2.** $4 + 24 \div 2 - 8$ **3.** $5 \times 10 - 2^5 - 2$

Order the numbers from least to greatest. (1.5, 2.6–2.8)

4. $\frac{1}{4}, \frac{3}{11}, \frac{2}{5}, \frac{2}{9}$ **5.** 4.04, 5.40, 4.45, 5.05 **6.** $\frac{7}{5}$, 1.04, $\frac{4}{9}$, 0.49

Round the number to the given place value. (1.6)

7. 14.8 (ones) **8.** 0.53 (tenths) **9.** 7.846 (hundredths)

Find the value of *x*. (1.4, 1.7–1.9)

10. Perimeter = 20.42 mi

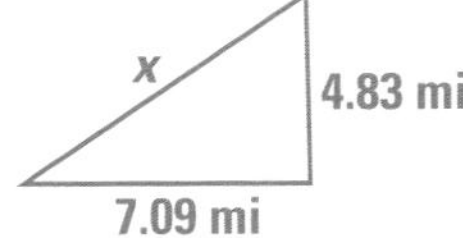

11. Area = 45.9 ft^2

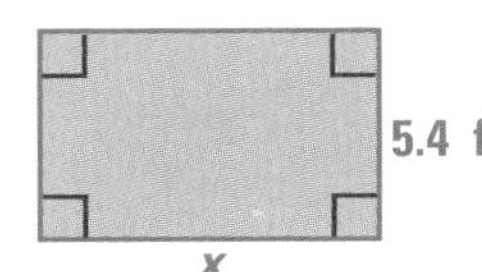

12. Area = x

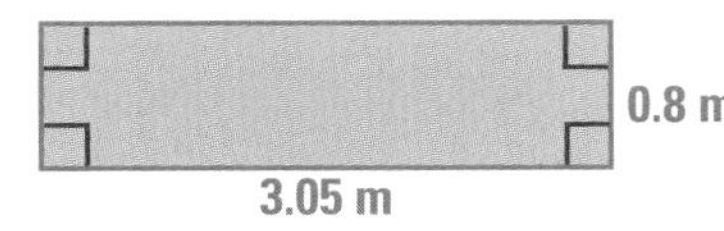

MATHEMATICAL REASONING **Decide whether the statement is *true* or *false*. If it is false, rewrite it as a true statement.** (2.1, 2.2)

13. 2, 3, 6, and 9 are all the factors of 18.

14. 1 is a prime number.

15. The prime factorization of 72 is $2^3 \times 3^2$.

16. The only whole number that is even and prime is 2.

17. The greatest common factor of 25 and 125 is 5.

18. The greatest common factor of two prime numbers is 1.

Decide whether the diagram is a good model to use for a fraction. If it is, write the fraction given by the model. If not, explain. (2.3)

19.

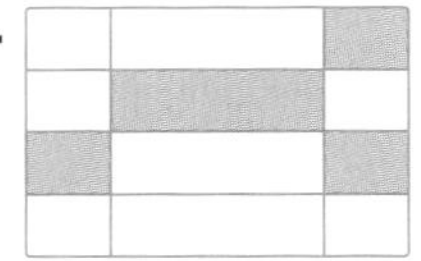

20.

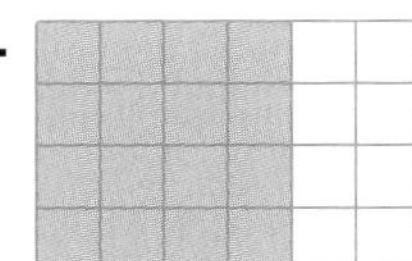

21.

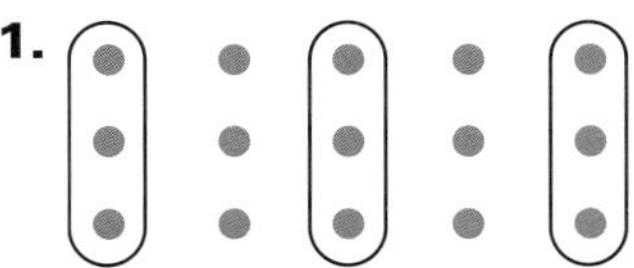

In Exercises 22–23, draw a set model to help you answer the question. (2.3)

22. You have 32 felt tip pens. Three fourths of them are worn out. How many of the pens are worn out?

23. You received 18 phone calls on Saturday and Sunday. One third were on Sunday. How many were on Saturday?

Write the fraction in simplest form. (2.4)

24. $\frac{14}{140}$ **25.** $\frac{35}{72}$ **26.** $\frac{35}{49}$ **27.** $\frac{44}{48}$ **28.** $\frac{25}{150}$

Find the least common multiple of the numbers. (2.5)

29. 12, 20 **30.** 24, 34 **31.** 5, 6, 8

Match the fraction with its equivalent fraction or mixed number. (2.4, 2.7)

A. $2\frac{1}{3}$ **B.** $\frac{3}{5}$ **C.** $4\frac{2}{3}$ **D.** $\frac{5}{3}$

32. $\frac{14}{3}$ **33.** $\frac{15}{25}$ **34.** $\frac{30}{18}$ **35.** $\frac{42}{18}$

Write the fraction as a decimal. Round to the nearest thousandth. (2.8)

36. $\frac{3}{8}$ **37.** $\frac{5}{12}$ **38.** $\frac{1}{6}$ **39.** $\frac{2}{9}$ **40.** $\frac{3}{15}$

Evaluate. Simplify if possible. (3.1–3.3)

41. $\frac{1}{3} + \frac{2}{3}$ **42.** $\frac{5}{6} - \frac{1}{6}$ **43.** $\frac{6}{7} + \frac{4}{5}$ **44.** $\frac{7}{10} - \frac{2}{5}$

45. $2\frac{3}{8} + 4\frac{1}{8}$ **46.** $4\frac{1}{5} - \frac{3}{5}$ **47.** $3\frac{2}{3} - 1\frac{1}{2}$ **48.** $6 - 1\frac{2}{7}$

Evaluate. Simplify if possible. (3.4, 3.5)

49. $\frac{1}{2} \times \frac{4}{5}$ **50.** $\frac{4}{7} \div \frac{3}{4}$ **51.** $\frac{3}{5} \div \frac{7}{8}$ **52.** $\frac{11}{12} \times \frac{5}{8}$

53. $4\frac{1}{4} \times 2\frac{1}{2}$ **54.** $6\frac{5}{9} \div 3\frac{1}{3}$ **55.** $8\frac{1}{8} \div 4\frac{3}{5}$ **56.** $3\frac{7}{8} \times 4\frac{9}{10}$

Use the distributive property to rewrite the expression. Then evaluate when $x = 7$. (3.6)

57. $6(x + 7)$ **58.** $5(8 + x)$ **59.** $12(x + 5)$ **60.** $4(x + 11)$

Convert. Round to the nearest hundredth if possible (3.7)

61. 48 ounces to pounds **62.** 4 quarts to pints **63.** 6 liters to milliliters

64. 80 centimeters to meters **65.** 50 meters to inches (1 meter ≈ 39.37 inches) **66.** 7 miles to yards

GAS CONSUMPTION **The table shows the miles driven and gallons used for two cars.** (3.8)

67. Find the unit rate for Robin's car.

68. Find the unit rate for Lorenzo's car.

69. Whose car has better gas mileage? Explain your reasoning in words and numbers.

	Gallons used	Miles driven
Robin	12	330
Lorenzo	10	300

Chapters 1-3 Project

- Compare and order positive fractions and mixed numbers. (NS 1.1)
- Solve problems involving division of positive fractions. (NS 2.1)

Materials

- Paper
- Pencil
- Ruler
- Books

Designing a Bookcase

OBJECTIVE Designing a bookcase that will hold 100 books.

INVESTIGATION

In Exercises 1–6, use a collection of books in a classroom library, in a school library, or at home.

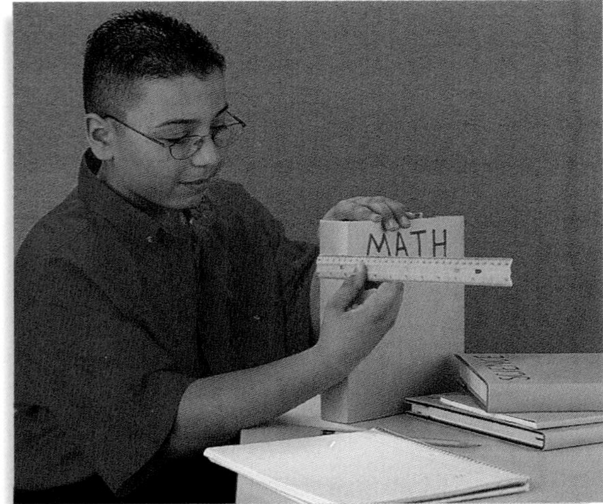

1. Measure and record the spine thicknesses of 20 books to the nearest $\frac{1}{4}$ inch.
2. Copy and complete the table to organize your results.

Book spine width (in inches)	$\frac{1}{4}$	$\frac{1}{2}$	$\frac{3}{4}$	1	$1\frac{1}{4}$	$1\frac{1}{2}$	$1\frac{3}{4}$	2
Number of books	?	?	?	?	?	?	?	?

3. Add a row labeled "Fraction of books" to your table. What fraction of the books you measured have a spine that is about $\frac{1}{4}$ inch wide? Record your answer in the table. Then complete the table.
4. Order your answers to Exercise 3 from least to greatest. What is the most common book spine width? the least common?
5. Choose the most common book width. How many books of that width will fit on a 3 foot long shelf? Write and solve a division problem. (*Note:* If there are two widths that are equally common, choose one.)
6. Calculate how many 3 foot long shelves you need to make a bookcase that holds 100 books.

PRESENT YOUR RESULTS

Write a report that includes the following information.

- Describe the purpose of the project.
- Present your data and calculations. Include your answers to Exercises 1–6.
- Sketch your bookcase. Label the lengths of the shelves.
- Explain why you believe that your bookcase will hold 100 books.
- Describe how you would predict the shelving needed for 80, 120, and 140 books.

EXTENSION

You have determined the length and number of shelves needed for your bookcase. How high and deep should the shelves be?

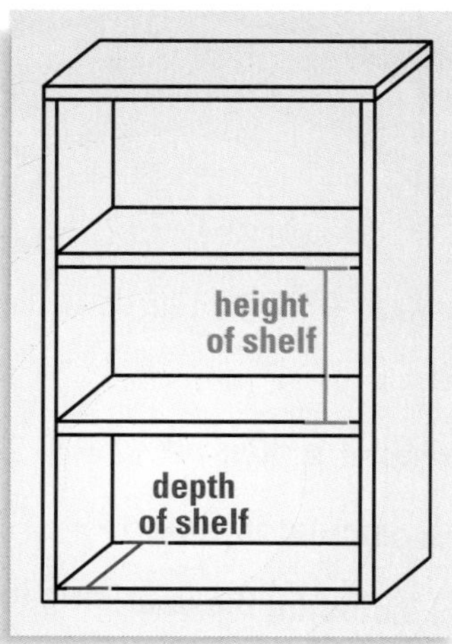

7. Decide how to find the best depth and height for the bookshelves. Which is more important, the average book height and depth or the range of book heights and depths? Do you want your shelves to be able to hold books of all possible sizes, or is it acceptable if some books don't fit? Describe how you will find the best depth and height for your bookshelves.

8. Use the method you described in Exercise 7 to find the best depth and height for your bookshelves.

9. On your sketch of your bookcase, label the depth and height of each shelf.

10. Calculate the measurements of the entire bookcase. What will be its total length? total height? total depth? Assume the bookcase is made of wood that is $\frac{3}{4}$ inch thick.

11. Write a paragraph convincing a furniture manufacturer that your bookcase will hold 100 books without wasting space or money.

Positive and Negative Numbers

Why are positive and negative numbers important?

Positive and negative numbers are used to describe signed quantities, such as temperatures above and below 0°, times before and after an event, and elevations above and below sea level. You will use positive and negative numbers later when you solve equations and draw graphs.

Archeologists (page 165), marine biologists (page 180), and electricians (page 190) use positive and negative numbers to do their jobs. For example, archeologists date objects found at a site, and order them from oldest to most recent.

Meeting the California Standards

The skills you'll develop in this chapter will help you meet state standards and prepare for standardized tests. In this chapter, you'll:

- **Order and graph positive and negative rational numbers.** LESSONS 4.1, 4.8
- **Solve problems manually or by using a scientific calculator.** LESSON 4.2
- **Use operations with integers to solve problems, including those arising in concrete situations.** LESSONS 4.2–4.6
- **Find the average of a data set.** LESSON 4.6
- **Apply order of operations and the distributive property to evaluate expressions.** LESSON 4.7

Career Link **ARCHEOLOGIST** An archeologist may use positive and negative numbers when:

- recording the locations at which artifacts were found.
- determining when an artifact was created.
- comparing the dates of artifacts to analyze how humans adapted to their environment over time.

EXERCISES

The dates of several artifacts are shown. Write each date as a positive or a negative number. For example, A.D. 400 is 400 and 23 B.C. is −23.

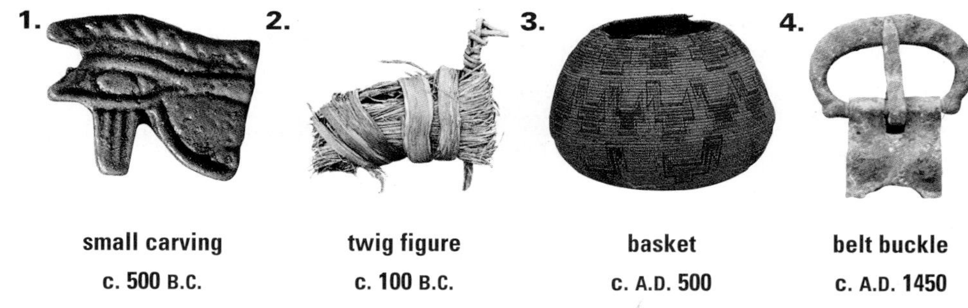

1. small carving c. 500 B.C.

2. twig figure c. 100 B.C.

3. basket c. A.D. 500

4. belt buckle c. A.D. 1450

In Lesson 4.1, you will learn how to order the artifacts on a time line.

Chapter 4 Getting Ready

PREVIEW

What's the chapter about?

- Adding, subtracting, multiplying, and dividing with **integers**
- Applying **order of operations** and the **distributive property**
- Graphing, comparing, and ordering **positive and negative numbers**

WORDS TO KNOW

- **integer,** *p. 167*
- **negative sign,** *p. 167*
- **opposites,** *p. 171*
- **absolute value,** *p. 177*

PREPARE

Chapter Readiness Quiz

Take this quick quiz. If you are unsure of an answer, look back at the reference pages for help.

VOCABULARY CHECK *(refer to pp. 7, 139)*

1. Performing which operation results in a quotient?

Ⓐ Addition Ⓑ Subtraction Ⓒ Division Ⓓ Multiplication

2. Which statement illustrates the distributive property?

Ⓕ $2 + 3 = 3 + 2$ Ⓖ $4 \cdot (5 \cdot 6) = (4 \cdot 5) \cdot 6$

Ⓗ $3(5 + 7) = 3(5) + 3(7)$ Ⓙ $8 \cdot (9 + 4) = 8 \cdot 13$

SKILL CHECK *(refer to pp. 18, 96)*

3. Evaluate $(3^3 - 7) \div (5 \times 2)$.

Ⓐ 0.2 Ⓑ 2 Ⓒ 8 Ⓓ 200

4. Which list is in order from least to greatest?

Ⓕ $\frac{1}{5}$, 0.5, 0.8, $\frac{11}{10}$, $\frac{7}{5}$ Ⓖ $\frac{4}{5}$, 0.75, $\frac{7}{8}$, 0.23, $\frac{2}{3}$

Ⓗ 5.2, $\frac{13}{4}$, $\frac{29}{7}$, 3.85, $\frac{9}{2}$, $\frac{10}{3}$ Ⓙ $\frac{7}{5}$, 1.04, $\frac{4}{9}$, 0.49, 1.4

STUDY TIP

Make Up a Test

Make up a test for yourself using homework exercises. Then take the test to find the areas you need to work on.

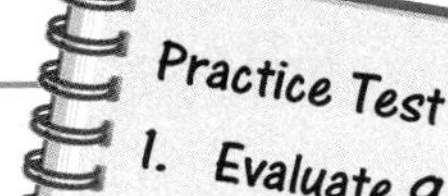

Practice Test

1. Evaluate $9 \cdot 28 + 9 \cdot 22$.
2. Write $\frac{15}{12}$ as a decimal.
3. Use a number line to compare 2.4 and 2.8.

Integers and the Number Line

California Standards

In this lesson you'll:

- Graph positive and negative integers on a number line. (NS 1.1)
- Compare and order positive and negative integers. (NS 1.1)

Goal 1 GRAPHING AND ORDERING INTEGERS

The numbers below are called **integers**, which can be divided into three categories: **negative integers**, zero, and **positive integers**. The symbol used to represent negative integers is a **negative sign**. You read -4 as "negative 4."

Zero

Negative integers | Positive integers

$\ldots, -4, -3, -2, -1, 0, 1, 2, 3, 4, \ldots$

On a number line, negative numbers are to the **left** of zero and positive numbers are to the **right** of zero.

Negative numbers | Positive numbers

$-5 \quad -4 \quad -3 \quad -2 \quad -1 \quad 0 \quad 1 \quad 2 \quad 3 \quad 4 \quad 5$

You can use a number line to compare and order integers.

Student Help

SKILLS REVIEW
For help with using a number line, see page 554.

EXAMPLE 1 Comparing Integers

Use a number line to compare -1 and -4.

Solution

Begin by graphing the integers on a number line.

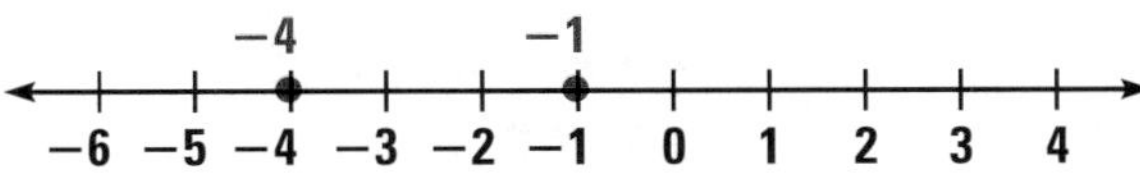

ANSWER ▶ -4 is to the left of -1, so $-4 < -1$ or $-1 > -4$.

EXAMPLE 2 Ordering Integers

Order the integers -2, 4, 0, 3, and -4 from least to greatest.

Solution

Begin by graphing the integers on a number line.

ANSWER ▶ From the number line, you can see that the order of the integers from least to greatest is -4, -2, 0, 3, and 4.

Student Help

STUDY TIP
Positive numbers are sometimes written with a positive sign: $+6 = 6$. When a number does not have a sign, it is understood to be positive.

Link to Science

IRON At −10°C, your skin will stick to an iron bar. As an iron bar is heated, it glows red, then orange, then yellow. At 1177°C, iron melts and becomes liquid.

More about this topic available at www.mcdougallittell.com

Goal 2 INTERPRETING INTEGERS IN REAL-LIFE

Negative numbers are used in real-life situations to represent sub-zero temperatures as well as losses, such as those that occur in business.

EXAMPLE 3 Estimating Integers

SCIENCE LINK A scientist measures the temperature of an iron bar under various conditions. Use the thermometer to estimate the given temperature of the iron bar in degrees Celsius. Describe the temperature in words.

a.

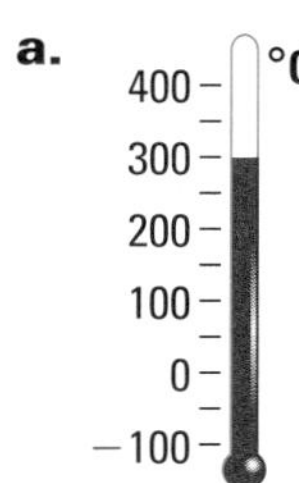

b.

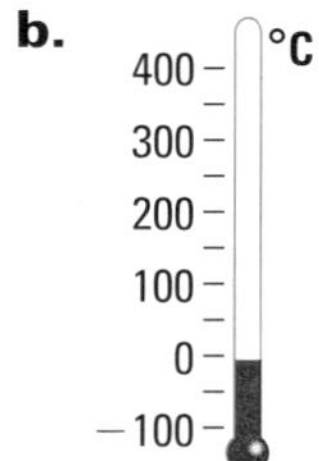

c.

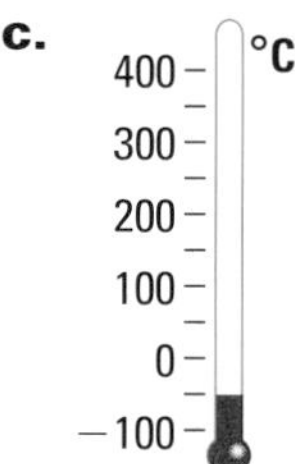

Solution

a. The temperature is about 300°C, or 300 degrees Celsius.

b. The temperature is about −10°C, or 10 degrees Celsius below zero.

c. The temperature is about −50°C, or 50 degrees Celsius below zero.

Businesses keep track of the money they spend (expenses) and the money they earn (income). They subtract expenses from income to find *profit*.

EXAMPLE 4 Ordering Integers

BUSINESS You are starting a part-time car washing business. Your profits for six months are shown below. Use a number line to order these profits from least to greatest. Which profit is least?

Month	April	May	June	July	Aug.	Sept.
Profit ($)	−50	−120	70	50	100	−10

Solution

Graph the integers from the table on a number line.

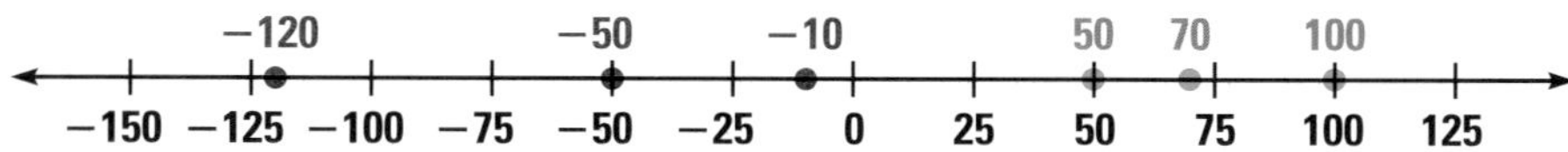

ANSWER ▶ You can see that the order of the profits from least to greatest is −120, −50, −10, 50, 70, 100, so −$120 is the least profit.

Student Help

▶ **READING TIP**
In business, profit can be positive, negative, or zero. A profit with a negative value is a *loss*. In Example 4, the *profit* of −$120 is the same as a *loss* of $120.

4.1 Exercises

Guided Practice

1. Complete the statement: On a horizontal number line, greater numbers are to the __?__ of lesser numbers.

2. Which of the following numbers are *not* integers?

$$9, 3.5, -\frac{1}{2}, 0, 2.75$$

3. What integer is neither positive nor negative?

Match the number with its location on the number line.

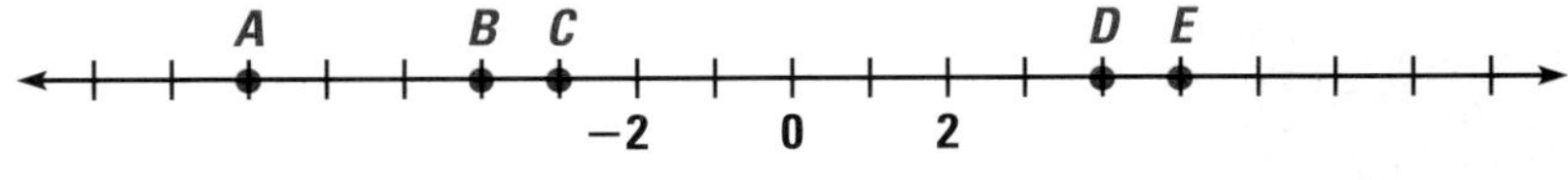

4. 4 **5.** −3 **6.** 5 **7.** −4 **8.** −7

Complete the statement using <, =, or >.

9. −6 ? 0 **10.** 7 ? 7 **11.** −4 ? −5 **12.** −2 ? 3

Order the integers from least to greatest.

13. 6, 1, −3, 3, −4 **14.** −2, 4, −9, −7, 0 **15.** −1, −6, −3, 0, −5

Practice and Problem Solving

Student Help

▶ **MORE PRACTICE** Extra practice to help you master skills is on page 572.

Graph the integers on a number line. Write the next two integers you expect to find in the pattern.

16. −9, −5, −1, 3, 7 **17.** −6, −4, −2, 0, 2

18. −5, 5, −4, 4, −3 **19.** −8, −7, −5, −2, 2

Complete the statement using <, =, or >.

20. 4 ? 0 **21.** 0 ? −1 **22.** −8 ? −6 **23.** −2 ? 2

24. 7 ? −1 **25.** 3 ? −3 **26.** −2 ? −1 **27.** −14 ? −4

In Exercises 28–31, order the integers from least to greatest.

28. −3, −8, 3, −9, 0 **29.** 8, −6, −10, 2, −2

30. −3, 9, −8, −12, 5, 1 **31.** 28, −36, −3, −15, −57

32. **MATHEMATICAL REASONING** Begin at 0 on a number line. Graph the integer that you end on if you move according to the expression *one step forward and two steps back*. Assume that a "step" is one unit and that "forward" means "to the right." If you continue these movements four more times, what integer will you end on? Explain.

MATHEMATICAL REASONING **Tell whether the statement is *true* or *false*. Support your answer using a number line.**

33. Four and negative four are the same distance from one.

34. Negative one is less than negative two.

In Exercises 35–38, write the integer corresponding to the real-life situation.

35. 12 degrees below zero

36. 5 bonus points

37. A debt of $45

38. 9 feet below sea level

39. **Chapter Opener Link** Copy the number line below. Then look back at the exercises on page 165. Using your answers to the exercises, graph each artifact on the number line as shown for the basket.

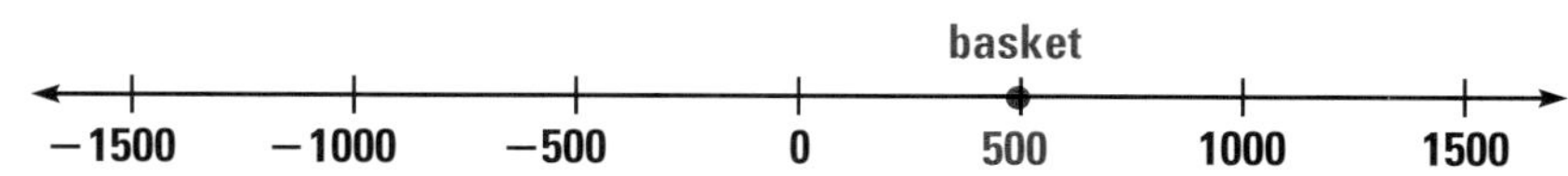

Link to Science

VIPERFISH When a viperfish closes its mouth, its large lower teeth remain outside its mouth.

Science Link **In Exercises 40 and 41, use the table showing the maximum depth at which each fish has been found.**

40. Which fish has been found at the greatest depth?

41. Order the depths from least to greatest.

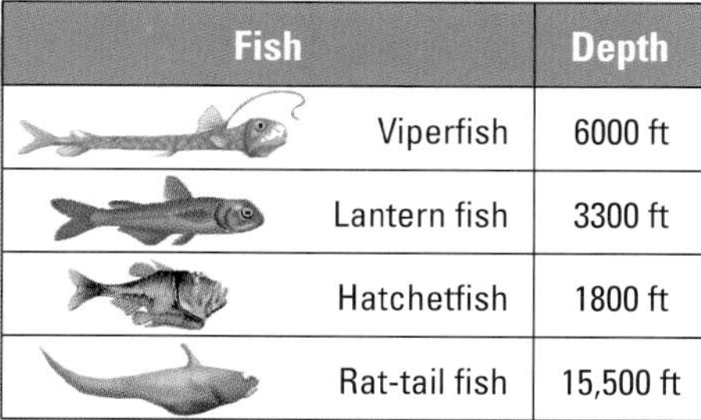

Fish	Depth
Viperfish	6000 ft
Lantern fish	3300 ft
Hatchetfish	1800 ft
Rat-tail fish	15,500 ft

▶ Source: Big Book of Animal Records

Student Help

▶ **HOMEWORK HELP**

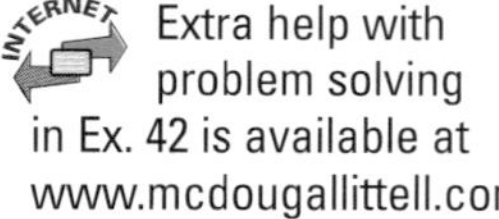

Extra help with problem solving in Ex. 42 is available at www.mcdougallittell.com

42. **CHALLENGE** Use the following clues to order the integers represented by the letters a, b, c, d, and e on a number line.

- c lies halfway between e and a.
- e lies halfway between d and c.
- a is a positive integer.
- c is a negative integer.
- b lies 6 units to the right of a.

Multiple-Choice Practice

43. Which pair of integers from the following list must switch positions for the integers to be in order from least to greatest?

$$-12, -6, -1, -3, 0, 5, 8$$

Ⓐ -6 and -1 Ⓑ -1 and -3 Ⓒ -3 and 0 Ⓓ 0 and 5

44. If the integers 20, 13, -3, 10, -11, 5, and -6 are put in order from least to greatest, which integer would come first in the list?

Ⓕ -6 Ⓖ 5 Ⓗ 10 Ⓙ -11

Adding Integers on a Number Line

California Standards

In this lesson you'll:

- Add positive and negative integers to solve problems, including those arising in concrete situations. (NS 2.3)
- Solve problems manually or by using a scientific calculator. (AF 1.4)

Goal 1 ADDING INTEGERS

You know from previous work in mathematics that you can use a number line to model adding two positive numbers. For example, to add 5 and 2, start at 0 on a number line. Move 5 units to the right, then move 2 more units to the right, which puts you at 7.

Use a similar approach when adding integers. A positive number indicates movement to the **right**. A negative number indicates movement to the **left**.

EXAMPLE 1 Adding Two Integers

Find the sum. **a.** $2 + (-5)$ **b.** $-6 + 8$

Solution

a. Start at 0. Move **2** units to the **right**. Then move **5** units to the **left**.

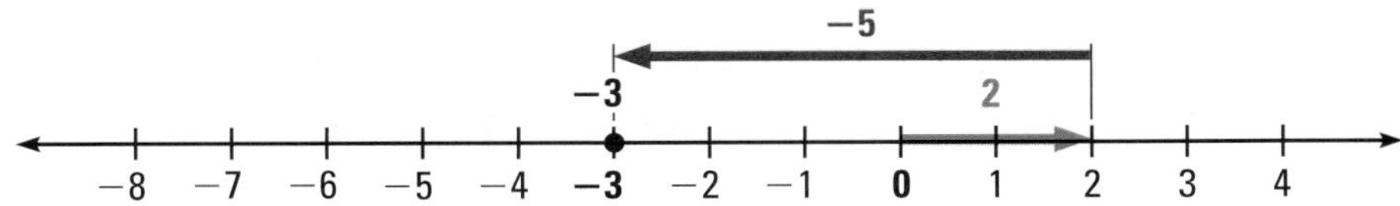

ANSWER ▶ Your final position is -3. So, $2 + (-5) = -3$.

b. Start at 0. Move **6** units to the **left**. Then move **8** units to the **right**.

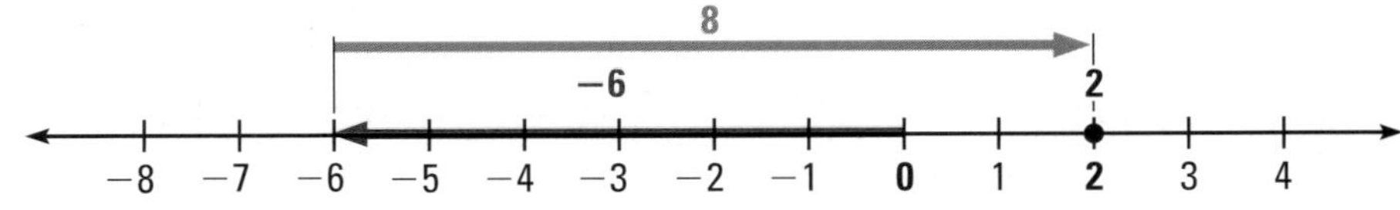

ANSWER ▶ Your final position is 2. So, $-6 + 8 = 2$.

Student Help

▶ **TECHNOLOGY TIP** You can check the results of part (b) of Example 1 with a calculator. If your calculator has a change sign key, [+/-], then you can use the keystrokes below.

6 [+/-] [+] 8 [=]

Two numbers are **opposites** if they are the same distance from 0 on the number line, but are on opposite sides of 0. For example, -3 and 3 are opposites, because they are both 3 units from zero, as shown below.

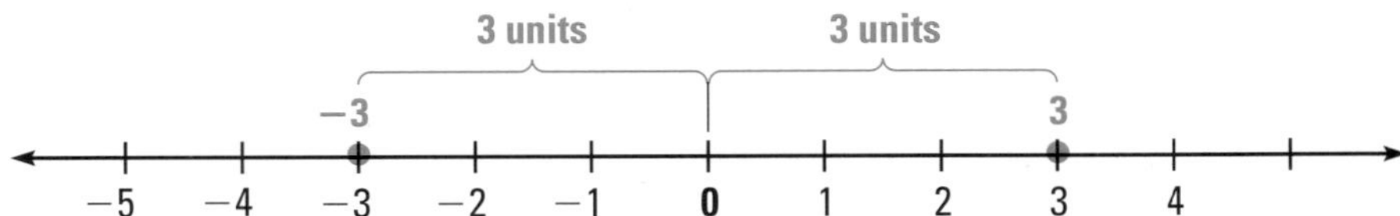

The expression -3 can be read as "the opposite of three" as well as "negative three." The expression $-(-3)$ can be read as "the opposite of negative three."

Student Help

▶ **MORE EXAMPLES**
More examples are available at www.mcdougallittell.com

EXAMPLE 2 Finding Opposites

Find the opposite of the number.

a. 1 **b.** -7 **c.** 0

Solution

a. The opposite of 1 is -1. Both 1 and -1 are 1 unit from zero.

b. The opposite of -7 is 7. Both -7 and 7 are 7 units from zero.

c. The opposite of 0 is 0.

EXAMPLE 3 Adding Opposites

To find the sum $-3 + 3$, start at 0. Move 3 units to the left. Then move 3 units to the right. Your final position is 0. So, $-3 + 3 = 0$.

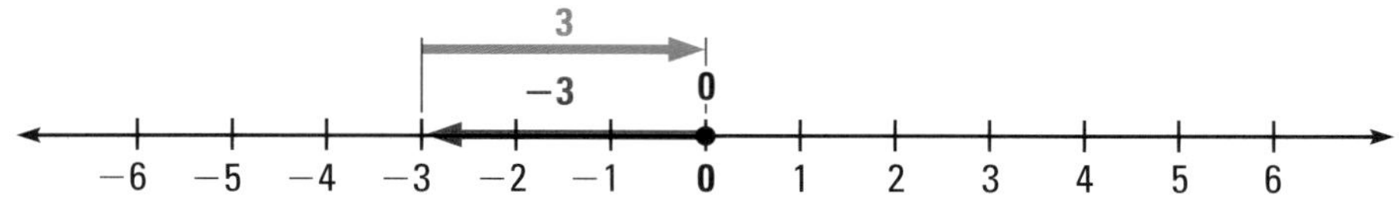

INVERSE PROPERTY OF ADDITION

In Words The sum of a number and its opposite is 0.

In Algebra $a + (-a) = 0$

Goal 2 ADDING INTEGERS TO SOLVE PROBLEMS

Student Help

▶ **READING TIP**
A *quarter* of a year is 3 months since there are a total of 12 months in a year and $\frac{1}{4} \cdot 12 = 3$.

EXAMPLE 4 Adding Three Integers

You run a small business. The table shows your monthly profits for the first quarter of the year. Find the total profit for the quarter.

Month	January	February	March
Profit	−$90	$150	−$40

Solution Use a number line to find the sum $-90 + 150 + (-40)$. Start at 0. Move 90 units to the left. Move 150 units to the right. Then move 40 units to the left.

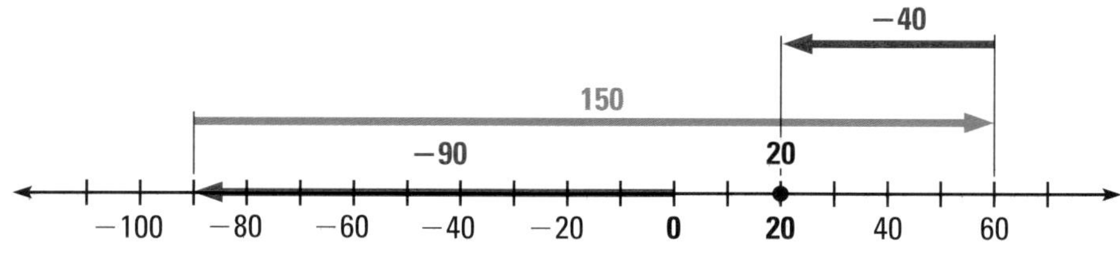

ANSWER ▶ Your final position is 20. Your total profit is $20.

Link to Weightlifting

WEIGHTS The standard sizes for plates used in Olympic weightlifting events are 1.25 kg, 2.5 kg, 5 kg, 10 kg, 20 kg, 25 kg, and 45 kg.

EXAMPLE 5 Using an Average

QUALITY CONTROL Your company makes weightlifting equipment. To check the quality of 45-kilogram weights, you test 5 weights to see how much each one varies from the 45-kilogram standard. From the sample, do the weights tend to be too heavy or too light?

	WEIGHT DEVIATION	NUMBER
WEIGHT 1:	57 grams too heavy	57
WEIGHT 2:	33 grams too light	−33
WEIGHT 3:	Correct weight	0
WEIGHT 4:	12 grams too light	−12
WEIGHT 5:	58 grams too heavy	58

Solution One way to answer the question is to find the average of the numbers. To find the average, you may want to use a calculator. Use the calculator's change sign key, [+/−], to enter negative numbers.

Find the sum: 57 [+] 33 [+/−] [+] 0 [+] 12 [+/−] [+] 58 [=] [70.]

Divide the sum by 5: 70 [÷] 5 [=] [14.]

ANSWER ▶ The average deviation is positive. In this sense, the weights tend to be too heavy.

4.2 Exercises

Guided Practice

1. Complete the statements: The opposite of −8 is _?_. The sum of −8 and its opposite equals _?_.

ERROR ANALYSIS **Describe and correct the error.**

2.

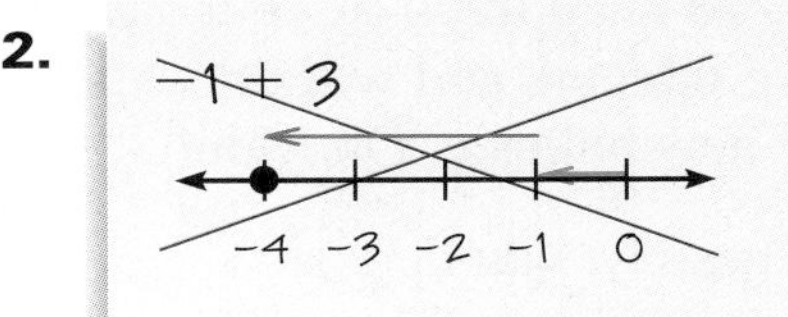

3.

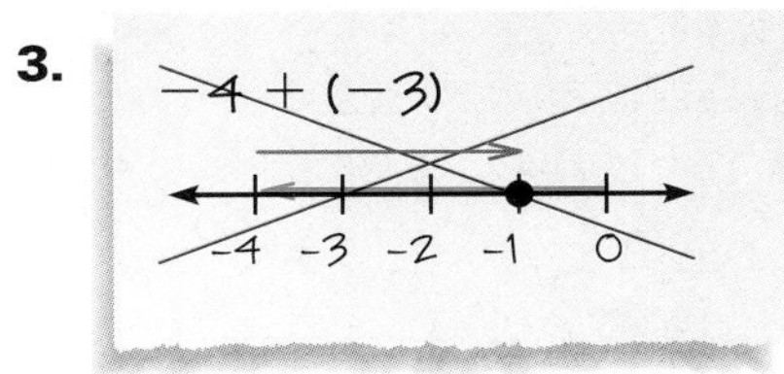

In Exercises 4–7, use a number line to find the sum.

4. 2 + 8 **5.** −4 + 3 **6.** −5 + 9 **7.** −1 + (−6)

8. **ARCHEOLOGY** A crew at an archeological site digs down 7 feet. Then they dig down another 4 feet. Express the position of the bottom of the hole relative to ground level as a negative integer.

Practice and Problem Solving

Student Help

▶ **MORE PRACTICE** Extra practice to help you master skills is on page 572.

Write the sum that is illustrated on the number line. Then find the sum.

9. 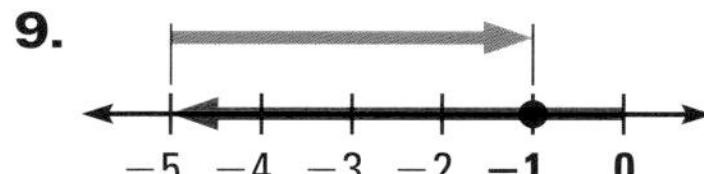

10. 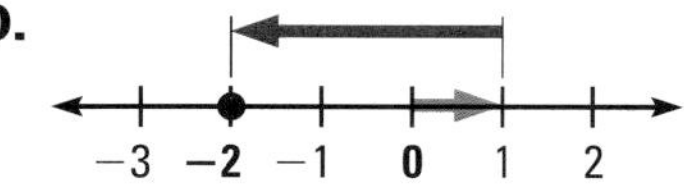

Match the expression with its sum.

A. 11 **B.** 5 **C.** -5 **D.** -11

11. $3 + 8$ **12.** $-6 + 1$ **13.** $-8 + (-3)$ **14.** $-3 + 8$

Use a number line to find the sum.

15. $7 + (-3)$ **16.** $-9 + 4$ **17.** $-2 + 1$ **18.** $-4 + 7$

19. $-9 + (-5)$ **20.** $-4 + (-11)$ **21.** $-6 + 13$ **22.** $-15 + 8$

Find the opposite of the number.

23. 5 **24.** -13 **25.** -100 **26.** 87

Find the sum.

27. $7 + (-7)$ **28.** $-5 + 5$

29. $11 + (-5) + (-8)$ **30.** $-3 + 5 + (-7)$

31. $50 + (-50) + 13$ **32.** $12 + (-13) + 12$

33. $2 + (-16) + (-2)$ **34.** $-120 + (-80) + 40$

ALGEBRA **In Exercises 35–38, evaluate the expression when $n = -1$.**

35. $-2 + n$ **36.** $5 + n$ **37.** $n + 1$ **38.** $n + (-7)$

OIL WELLS The depth of an oil well can range from several hundred feet to over 20,000 feet.

39. OIL WELLS A drilling crew drills a well 127 feet below Earth's surface. They then drill down another 146 feet. Express the position of the bottom of the well relative to ground level as a negative number.

40. BANKING To keep track of your savings account, you record deposits as positive integers and withdrawals as negative integers. You add to find your new balance. On Monday, you have \$15 in your account.

- On Tuesday, you deposit \$7.
- On Wednesday, you withdraw \$11.
- On Thursday, you deposit \$6, then withdraw \$13.

What is your balance at the end of Thursday?

41. MATHEMATICAL REASONING How can the sum of a positive integer and a negative integer be positive? negative? zero? Give examples to support your answers.

MINIATURE GOLF In Exercises 42 and 43, use the following information. In the game of miniature golf, your score for each hole is the number of strokes you take above or below par. (*Par* is the expected number of strokes you need to get the ball in the hole.) The "Score" column of the scorecard at the right shows the number of strokes above or below par.

Hole	Par	Score
1	3	+3
2	2	−1
3	4	+4
4	3	+3
5	3	−1
6	4	0
7	2	+3
8	3	−2
9	3	0

42. Find the player's total score above or below par.

43. On average, does the player tend to be above or below par? Explain.

44. **CHALLENGE** A football team needs to gain a total of 10 yards in four consecutive plays. On the first three plays, the team loses 4 yards, gains 2 yards, and then loses 10 yards. How many yards must the team gain on the fourth play?

Multiple-Choice Practice

45. Evaluate the expression $-10 + 10 + (-4)$.

Ⓐ -24 Ⓑ -10 Ⓒ -4 Ⓓ 4

46. Which expression has a value different from all the others?

Ⓕ $-3 + 4 + (-1)$ Ⓖ $3 + (-4) + 1$

Ⓗ $5 + 2 + (-7)$ Ⓙ $-5 + 7 + 2$

Mixed Review

47. The area of a square is given by s^2, where s is the length of a side. Find the area of the square when s is 9 inches. *(1.4)*

Copy the number line. Locate and label the four fractions on the number line. Then order the fractions from least to greatest. *(2.6)*

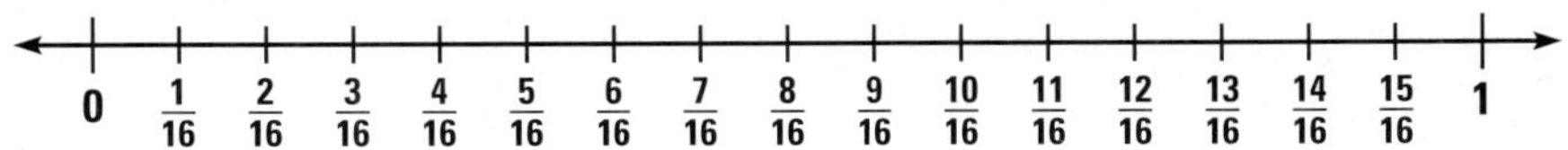

48. $\frac{5}{8}, \frac{11}{16}, \frac{3}{4}, \frac{1}{2}$ **49.** $\frac{9}{16}, \frac{7}{8}, \frac{1}{2}, \frac{3}{4}$ **50.** $\frac{3}{8}, \frac{1}{4}, \frac{3}{16}, \frac{1}{8}$

Evaluate. Simplify, if possible. *(3.4, 3.5)*

51. $\frac{3}{8} \times 2$ **52.** $5 \times \frac{4}{7}$ **53.** $\frac{5}{9} \times \frac{1}{2}$ **54.** $\frac{1}{6} \times \frac{3}{4}$

55. $1\frac{1}{7} \times 3\frac{2}{3}$ **56.** $\frac{3}{7} \times 2\frac{4}{5}$ **57.** $7\frac{1}{5} \div \frac{2}{5}$ **58.** $6\frac{1}{2} \div \frac{3}{4}$

DEVELOPING CONCEPTS
Integer Addition

For use with Lesson 4.3

California Standards

- Solve addition problems that use positive and negative integers. (NS 2.3)
- Analyze problems by observing patterns (MR 1.1)

MATERIALS

- Paper and pencil

By observing what happens to the arrows when two integers are added on a number line, you can develop rules for adding integers.

SAMPLE 1 Adding Integers with Different Signs

You can use a number line to develop a rule for adding integers with different signs.

Here's How

Consider the sums illustrated by the number lines below.

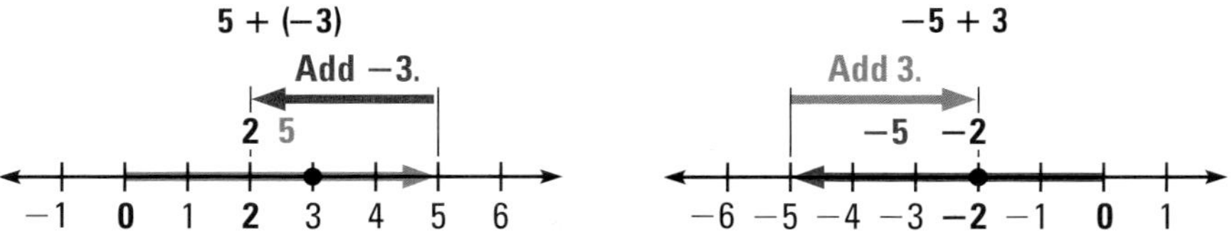

Notice that the arrows for 5 and -5 both have length 5, and the arrows for -3 and 3 both have length 3. Because the arrows point in *opposite* directions, you can see that the *difference* in the lengths of the arrows, 2, is related to each sum as follows.

- When the longer arrow represents a positive number, the sum is positive:

$$5 + (-3) = 2$$

- When the longer arrow represents a negative number, the sum is negative:

$$-5 + 3 = -2$$

This observation suggests the following rule:

> To add two integers with different signs using a number line, find the difference between the length of the longer arrow and the length of the shorter arrow. This difference is the sum when the longer arrow represents the positive number. The opposite of this difference is the sum when the longer arrow represents the negative number.

Try These

Confirm that the rule for adding integers with different signs, stated above, gives the correct result when you find the indicated sum.

1. $-4 + 6$ **2.** $2 + (-1)$ **3.** $-8 + 3$ **4.** $9 + (-2)$

5. **MATHEMATICAL REASONING** Using a number line, develop a rule for adding two negative integers. Give examples and explain your reasoning.

4.4 Subtracting Integers

In this lesson you'll:

- Subtract positive and negative integers. (NS 2.3)
- Subtract integers to solve problems arising in concrete situations. (NS 2.3)

Goal 1 SUBTRACTING USING A NUMBER LINE

In Lesson 4.2 you used a number line to add integers. You can also use a number line to subtract integers. The number lines below compare two simple problems involving positive integers: $8 + 5$ and $8 - 5$.

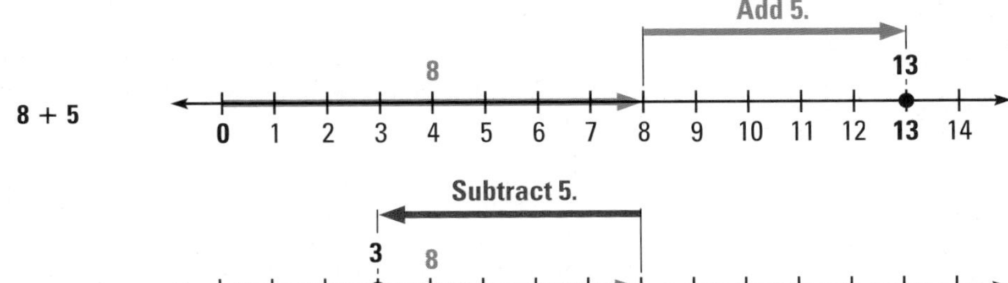

Notice that the direction you move to subtract 5 is the *opposite* of the direction you move to add 5. Generalizing this result to the difference of any two integers, you have the following:

- To subtract a positive integer, move in the negative direction.
- To subtract a negative integer, move in the positive direction.

Student Help

STUDY TIP
Check the result of a subtraction by using addition. For example, to check that $3 - 6 = -3$, note that $-3 + 6 = 3$.

EXAMPLE 1 *Subtracting a Positive Integer*

a. To find the difference $3 - 6$, begin at 0. Move 3 units to the right. Then move 6 units to the left.

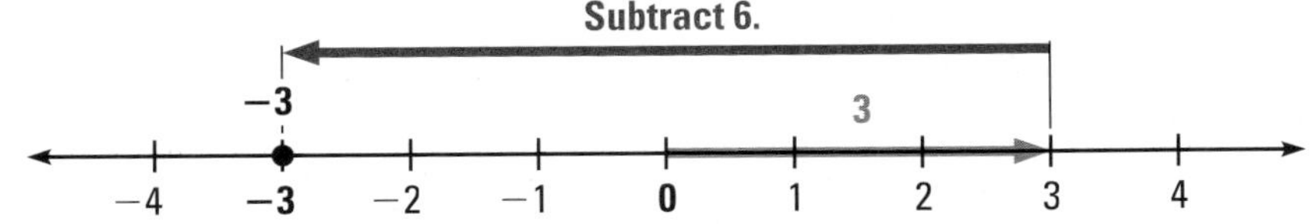

ANSWER ▶ Your final position is -3. So, $3 - 6 = -3$.

b. To find the difference $-2 - 7$, begin at 0. Move 2 units to the left. Then move 7 more units to the left.

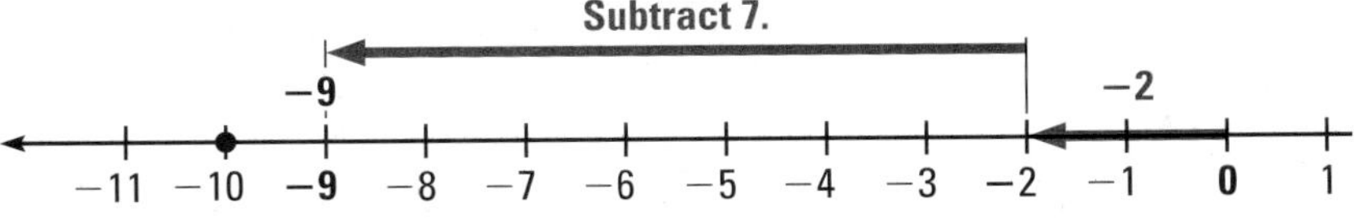

ANSWER ▶ Your final position is -9. So, $-2 - 7 = -9$.

Student Help

▶ **MORE EXAMPLES**

More examples are available at www.mcdougallittell.com

EXAMPLE 2 Subtracting a Negative Integer

To find the difference $6 - (-4)$ on a number line, begin at 0. Move 6 units to the right. Then move 4 units to the right.

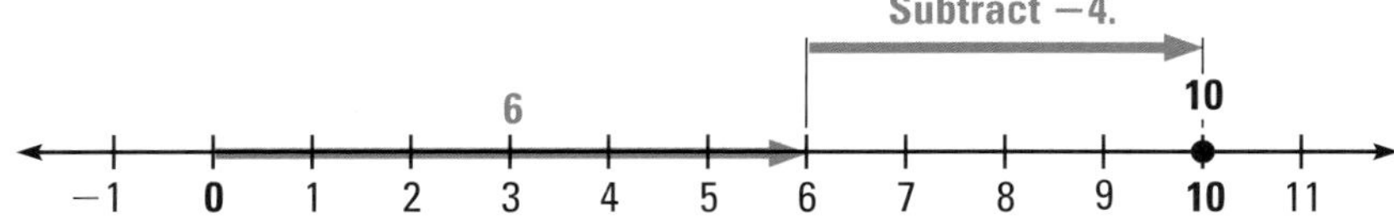

ANSWER ▶ Your final position is 10. So, $6 - (-4) = 10$.

Goal 2 SUBTRACTING USING THE SUBTRACTION RULE

In part (a) of Example 1, notice that you can get the same result by adding -6 to 3 as you get by subtracting 6 from 3. Similarly, in Example 2, you can get the same result by adding 4 to 6 as you get by subtracting -4 from 6. This suggests the following rule.

SUBTRACTING INTEGERS

In Words	To subtract an integer b from an integer a, add the opposite of b to a.
In Algebra	$a - b = a + (-b)$
In Arithmetic	$6 - 8 = 6 + (-8) = -2$

EXAMPLE 3 Subtracting a Positive Integer

Find the difference $5 - 7$.

Solution

$5 - 7 = 5 + (-7)$ To subtract 7, add its opposite.

$= -2$ Use rule for adding integers.

EXAMPLE 4 Subtracting Negative Integers

Find the difference.

a. $-9 - (-10)$ **b.** $54 - (-12)$

Solution

a. $-9 - (-10) = -9 + 10$ To subtract -10, add its opposite.

$= 1$ Use rule for adding integers.

b. $54 - (-12) = 54 + 12$ To subtract -12, add its opposite.

$= 66$ Use rule for adding integers.

Link to Geography

DEATH VALLEY At its lowest point, the floor of Death Valley is 282 feet below sea level. This is the lowest elevation in the United States.

EXAMPLE 5 Finding a Change in Elevation

DEATH VALLEY As shown in the diagram, suppose you start at 2600 feet above sea level. You then descend into Death Valley in California until you reach an elevation of 200 feet below sea level. Describe the change in your elevation.

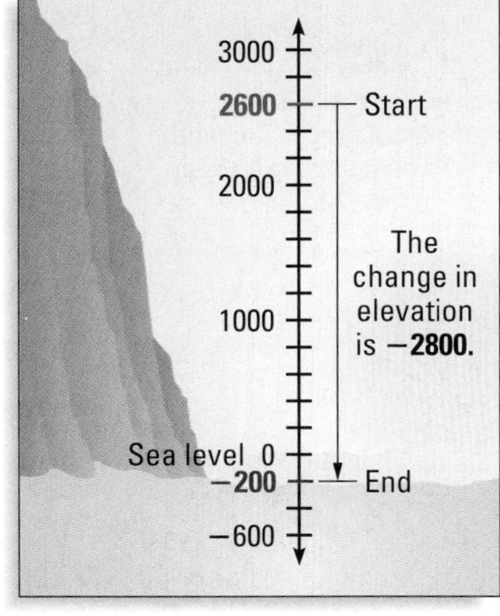

Solution

Find the difference of −200 and 2600.

Final elevation	−	Initial elevation	=	Change in elevation
−200	−	2600	=	−2800

ANSWER ▶ The change in elevation is negative, so your elevation decreased by 2800 feet.

4.4 Exercises

Guided Practice

Use a number line to find the difference.

1. $1 - 3$ **2.** $-4 - 1$ **3.** $-1 - (-7)$

Rewrite the expression as an addition expression. Then tell whether the value of the expression is *positive, negative,* or *zero*.

4. $12 - 13$ **5.** $-8 - 6$ **6.** $13 - (-14)$

7. $-6 - 6$ **8.** $-6 - (-6)$ **9.** $0 - (-5)$

10. **ERROR ANALYSIS** Describe and correct the error in the number line model for $-4 - 3$. Then find the difference.

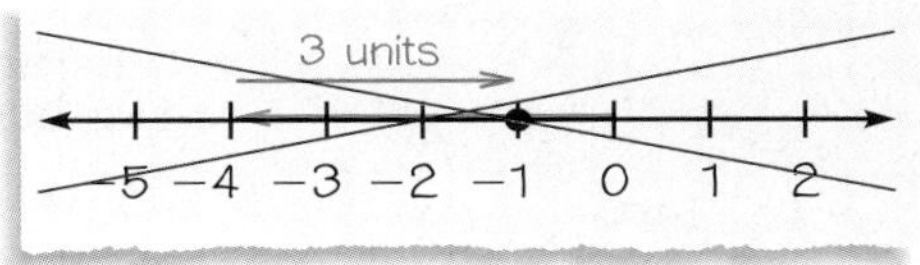

Find the difference without using a number line.

11. $-3 - (-3)$ **12.** $2 - 6$ **13.** $-11 - 7$

WEATHER **Two different temperature readings for the same day are given. Write an integer that represents the temperature change from 8 A.M. to 1 P.M.**

14. 8:00 A.M.: −2°F
1:00 P.M.: −7°F

15. 8:00 A.M.: −4°F
1:00 P.M.: 8°F

16. 8:00 A.M.: −10°F
1:00 P.M.: −3°F

Practice and Problem Solving

Student Help

▶ **MORE PRACTICE**
Extra practice to help you master skills is on page 572.

Use a number line to find the difference.

17. $5 - 11$ **18.** $-6 - 3$ **19.** $9 - (-2)$

20. $-8 - (-8)$ **21.** $4 - (-5)$ **22.** $-7 - 0$

23. $-20 - 60$ **24.** $-45 - 55$ **25.** $15 - (-10)$

Find the difference without using a number line.

26. $-4 - (-12)$ **27.** $-11 - 4$ **28.** $-10 - (-5)$

29. $0 - (-9)$ **30.** $7 - 14$ **31.** $-11 - (-13)$

32. $40 - (-90)$ **33.** $150 - 180$ **34.** $-100 - (-50)$

CALCULATOR **Match the expression with the calculator keystrokes. Then evaluate the expression.**

35. $-119 - 2127$ **A.** 119 [−] 2127 [+/−] [=] 

36. $119 - (-2127)$ **B.** 119 [−] 2127 [=]

37. $119 - 2127$ **C.** 119 [+/−] [−] 2127 [=]

ALGEBRA **Evaluate the expression when $x = 6$ and when $x = -1$.**

38. $x - 5$ **39.** $12 - x$ **40.** $-10 - x$ **41.** $x - (-3)$

42. $0 - x$ **43.** $-4 - x$ **44.** $x - (-2)$ **45.** $x - 10$

MATHEMATICAL REASONING **In Exercises 46 and 47, complete the statement with *positive* or *negative*. Explain your reasoning.**

46. If the value of the expression $0 - x$ is negative, then x is __?__.

47. If x is negative, then the value of the expression $0 - x$ is __?__.

48. MATHEMATICAL REASONING An integer is less than zero but greater than -13. When you subtract this integer from -11, the result is positive. Find the integer.

Science Link **In Exercises 49 and 50, use the following information.** The table shows the average air concentration level in parts per billion (ppb) of three air pollutants in 1987 and 1997 in the United States.

49. Subtract the 1987 level of each pollutant from its 1997 level to find the *change* in level from 1987 to 1997.

50. Explain why you do *not* subtract the 1997 level from the 1987 level to find the *change* in level.

Pollution Levels (ppb)

Year	1987	1997
Carbon monoxide	6710	3900
Ozone	124	105
Sulfur dioxide	9	5

▶ Source: U.S. Environmental Protection Agency

BART The Transbay Tube connecting Oakland and San Francisco is 3.6 miles in length.

BAY AREA RAPID TRANSIT (BART) **In Exercises 51 and 52, use the diagram. BART's Transbay Tube runs beneath the San Francisco Bay, connecting Oakland and San Francisco. The tube is made of 57 sections.**

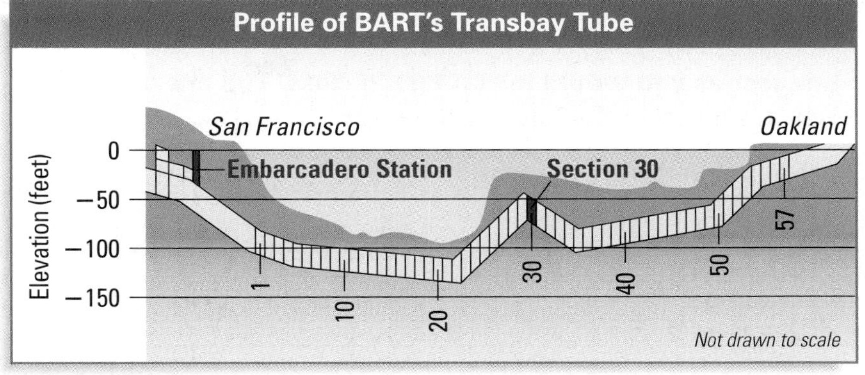

▶ Source: BART District

51. If Embarcadero Station has an elevation of -20 feet, by how much do you change your elevation to reach the deepest point in the tunnel at -135 feet?

52. Section 30 has an elevation of -50 feet. What is the difference between the elevation of Section 30 and -135 feet, the deepest point in the tunnel?

53. **CHALLENGE** You plant some seeds at the given positions below ground. How much deeper do you plant corn than carrots? How much deeper do you plant beets than carrots?

Beets	Carrots	Corn	Peas
$-\frac{1}{4}$ in.	$-\frac{1}{8}$ in.	-1 in.	$-\frac{1}{2}$ in.

Multiple-Choice Practice

Test Tip

▶ Read all the answer choices before deciding which is correct.

54. $4 - (-17) = \underline{\ ?\ }$

Ⓐ -21 Ⓑ -13 Ⓒ 13 Ⓓ 21

55. Which number do you expect next in the sequence 5, 2, -1, -4, . . .?

Ⓕ -6 Ⓖ -7 Ⓗ -8 Ⓙ -9

Mixed Review

Use a factor tree to write the prime factorization of the number. *(2.1)*

56. 81 **57.** 90 **58.** 112 **59.** 165

Evaluate the expression. *(3.1–3.3)*

60. $\frac{7}{8} - \frac{1}{16}$ **61.** $\frac{9}{10} + \frac{1}{15}$ **62.** $4\frac{1}{3} + 1\frac{1}{15}$ **63.** $5\frac{1}{3} - \frac{2}{3}$

Chapter 4 Mid-Chapter Test

Take this test as you would take a test in class. The answers to the exercises are given in the back of the book.

Match the number with its location on the number line.

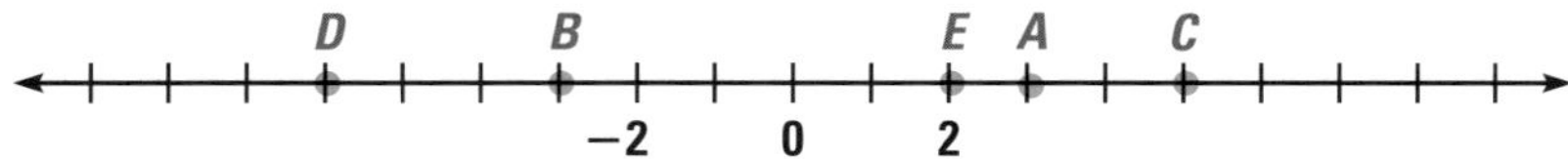

1. -3 **2.** 5 **3.** 2 **4.** -6 **5.** 3

Complete the statement using <, = , or >.

6. -9 ? -5 **7.** -2 ? -3 **8.** -4 ? 0 **9.** 1 ? -1

10. 6 ? -6 **11.** -10 ? -8 **12.** -8 ? 2 **13.** -4 ? -7

Order the numbers from least to greatest.

14. $-10, -1, 4, -5, 2$ **15.** $-13, -12, -11, -15, 10$

Find the sum or difference.

16. $-3 + 5$ **17.** $-6 + 2$ **18.** $-1 + (-9)$ **19.** $-8 + (-2)$

20. $11 - 13$ **21.** $2 + (-9)$ **22.** $-20 + 15$ **23.** $5 - (-5)$

24. $1 - (-4)$ **25.** $2 - 13$ **26.** $-13 - 6$ **27.** $-3 - (-4)$

In Exercises 28 and 29, use a number line to follow the steps, and write an addition or subtraction problem that matches the steps. Then find the sum or difference.

28. Start at 0. Move 7 units to the left. Move 4 units to the right. Then move 2 units to the left.

29. Start at 0. Move 3 units to the left. Move 5 units to the left. Then move 1 unit to the right.

30. **RUNNING** In a 4 mile race, a runner's time for each mile (in minutes and seconds) was compared to his best previous time as shown below. Write each comparison using an integer. How did the runner's total time compare with the total of his previous best times?

	1st mile	2nd mile	3rd mile	4th mile
Previous best	6:45	7:05	7:28	7:00
Current time	6:49	7:02	7:28	6:58
Comparison	4 seconds more	3 seconds less	Same time	2 seconds less

REASONING 4.5

DEVELOPING CONCEPTS
Integer Multiplication

For use with Lesson 4.5

California Standards

- Multiply positive and negative numbers. (NS 2.3)
- Solve problems using appropriate mathematical language. (MR 2.5)

MATERIALS

- Paper and pencil

Using properties you already know, you can show that -1 multiplied by any integer a equals the opposite of a. Consider the sum $(-1)a + a$:

$(-1)a + a = (-1)a + 1a$	A number multiplied by 1 is the number.
$= (-1 + 1)a$	Distributive property
$= 0 \cdot a$	Inverse property of addition
$= 0$	A number multiplied by 0 is 0.

So, $(-1)a + a = 0$. The inverse property of addition tells you that $(-1)a$ must be equal to the opposite of a for the sum of $(-1)a$ and a to be 0.

$$(-1)a = -a \text{ for any integer } a$$

SAMPLE 1 Multiplying with Negative Integers

You can use the rule $(-1)a = -a$ to find products of integers, such as $(-3)2$ and $(-4)(-5)$.

Here's How

a. $(-3)(2) = [(-1)(3)](2)$	$(-1)a = -a$
$= (-1)[(3)(2)]$	Associative property of multiplication
$= (-1)(6)$	Multiply positive integers.
$= -6$	$(-1)a = -a$

b. $(-4)(-5) = (-1)(4)(-1)(5)$	$(-1)a = -a$
$= (-1)(-1)(4)(5)$	Commutative property of mult.
$= (-1)[(-1)[(4)(5)]]$	Associative property of mult.
$= (-1)[(-1)(20)]$	Multiply positive integers.
$= (-1)(-20)$	$(-1)a = -a$
$= 20$	$(-1)a = -a$

Student Help

STUDY TIP
When you see multiple sets of grouping symbols (parentheses and brackets), do the operations inside the innermost grouping symbols first.

Try These

Use the rule $(-1)a = -a$ to find the product. Justify each step.

1. $(-6)(-9)$ **2.** $(-7)(8)$ **3.** $(-4)(-3)$ **4.** $(11)(-3)$

5. $(11)(-8)$ **6.** $(-3)(-13)$ **7.** $(12)(-6)$ **8.** $(-4)(-10)$

9. MATHEMATICAL REASONING Look at your results from Exercises 1–8. What is the sign of the product of two negative integers? of a negative integer and a positive integer? Explain your reasoning.

4.5 Multiplying Integers

In this lesson you'll:

- Multiply positive and negative integers to solve problems, including those arising in concrete situations. (NS 2.3)
- Evaluate an algebraic expression. (AF 1.2)

Goal 1 MULTIPLYING TWO INTEGERS

As you saw in Developing Concepts 4.5, page 187, any number multiplied by -1 is equal to the opposite of that number.

$$-1 \cdot a = -a$$

You can use this multiplicative property of -1 to develop general rules for multiplying integers. For example, $(-2) \cdot 3 = [(-1) \cdot (2)] \cdot 3 = (-1) \cdot [2 \cdot 3] = (-1) \cdot 6 = -6$, which suggests that the product of two integers with different signs is negative.

MULTIPLYING INTEGERS

Rule	Example
1. The product of two positive integers is positive.	3(7) = 21
2. The product of two negative integers is positive.	(−2)(−4) = 8
3. The product of two integers with different signs is negative.	(−3)(1) = −3 10(−6) = −60
4. The product of an integer and 0 is 0.	0(−5) = 0

EXAMPLE 1 Multiplying Integers with the Same Sign

Find the product.

a. $4(7)$ **b.** $(-11)(-4)$

Solution

a. $4(7) = 28$ The product of two positive integers is positive.

b. $(-11)(-4) = 44$ The product of two negative integers is positive.

EXAMPLE 2 Multiplying Integers with Different Signs

Find the product.

a. $5(-5)$ **b.** $(-8)(9)$

Solution

a. $5(-5) = -25$ The product of two integers with different signs is negative.

b. $(-8)(9) = -72$ The product of two integers with different signs is negative.

Student Help

▶ **MORE EXAMPLES**

INTERNET More examples are available at www.mcdougallittell.com

EXAMPLE 3 Evaluating Expressions

Evaluate the expression for the given values of the variables.

a. xy when $x = -15$ and $y = -6$

b. $(-a)(b)$ when $a = -4$ and $b = -8$

Solution

a. $xy = (-15)(-6)$ — Substitute -15 for x and -6 for y.

$= 90$ — The product of two negatives is positive.

b. $(-a)(b) = [-(-4)](-8)$ — Substitute -4 for a and -8 for b.

$= 4(-8)$ — The opposite of -4 is 4.

$= -32$ — The product of two integers with different signs is negative.

Goal 2 MULTIPLYING THREE OR MORE INTEGERS

To multiply three or more integers, work from left to right, multiplying two numbers at a time:

- Find the product of the first two numbers, then multiply that product by the next number to the right.
- Continue until all the numbers have been multiplied to find the final product.

EXAMPLE 4 Multiplying Three or More Integers

Find the product.

a. $2(-3)(4)$ **b.** $(-4)(5)(0)$ **c.** $(-1)(-2)(-3)(-4)$

Solution

a. $2(-3)(4) = (-6)(4)$ — Multiply $2(-3)$.

$= -24$ — Multiply $(-6)(4)$.

b. $(-4)(5)(0) = (-20)(0)$ — Multiply $(-4)(5)$.

$= 0$ — Multiply $(-20)(0)$.

c. $(-1)(-2)(-3)(-4) = 2(-3)(-4)$ — Multiply $(-1)(-2)$.

$= (-6)(-4)$ — Multiply $2(-3)$.

$= 24$ — Multiply $(-6)(-4)$.

The sign of a product depends on the number of factors (assuming all are nonzero) that are negative. An even number of negative factors produces a positive product, and an odd number produces a negative product.

Link to Careers

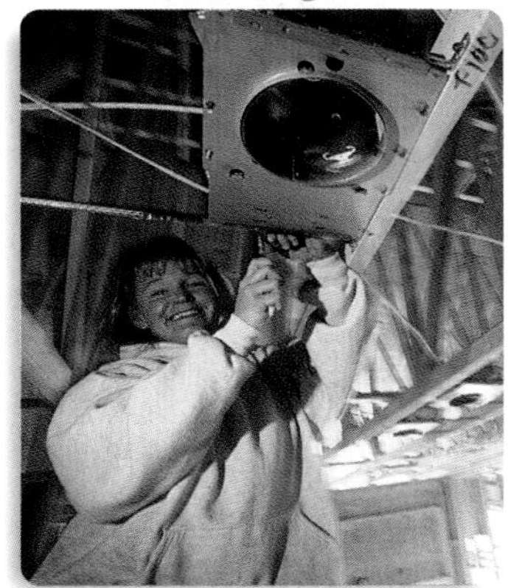

ELECTRICIANS use mathematics when working with electrical measurements involving units such as volts, amps, and watts. This helps them to ensure that electrical wiring is safely installed.

More about electricians is available at www.mcdougallittell.com

EXAMPLE 5 Modeling with Integer Multiplication

LIGHTS Rooms with two entrances often have a *3-way light switch* at each entrance. If the light is off, flipping either switch turns the light on. If the light is on, flipping either switch turns it off.

In the diagram at the right, both of the switches can turn the light on or off when flipped.

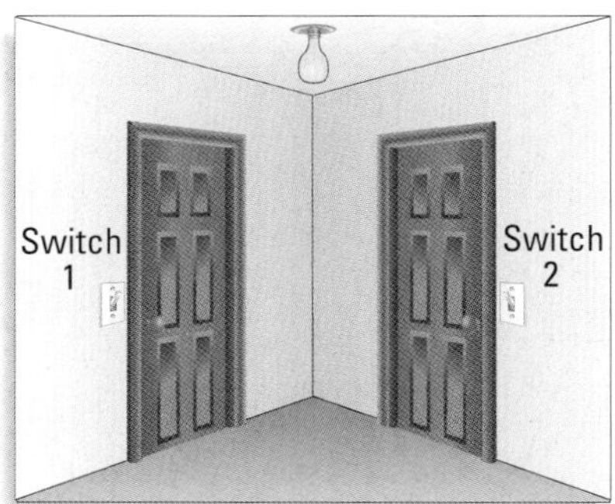

a. The light is off. Switch 1 is flipped twice and Switch 2 is flipped once. Is the light off or on?

b. The light is on. Switch 1 is flipped three times and Switch 2 is flipped twice. Is the light off or on?

Solution Use $-B$ to represent a light that is "off" and B to represent a light that is "on." Then model the action of flipping a switch using multiplication by -1. Multiplying by -1 changes on (B) to off ($-B$) and off ($-B$) to on (B).

a. $(-B) \times (-1)(-1) \times (-1) = B$ Light is on.

- $(-B)$: Light is off.
- $(-1)(-1)$: Flip Switch 1 twice.
- (-1): Flip Switch 2 once.

b. $B \times (-1)(-1)(-1) \times (-1)(-1) = -B$ Light is off.

- B: Light is on.
- $(-1)(-1)(-1)$: Flip Switch 1 three times.
- $(-1)(-1)$: Flip Switch 2 twice.

4.5 Exercises

Guided Practice

1. Complete: The product of two integers with the same sign is __?__.

2. Complete: The product of two integers with different signs is __?__.

Find the product.

3. $5(6)$ **4.** $(-2)(-8)$ **5.** $3(-12)$

6. $(-5)(7)$ **7.** $7(-3)(-1)$ **8.** $(-9)(-2)(-5)$

In Exercises 9–11, evaluate the expression when $m = -4$.

9. $m \cdot (-7)$ **10.** $9m$ **11.** $(-1)(-2)(-5)m$

12. **METEOROLOGY** A weather balloon descends 5 feet per second. Write an integer to represent the altitude change per second. What is the change in the altitude of the balloon in 11 seconds? in 17 seconds?

Practice and Problem Solving

Student Help

▶ **MORE PRACTICE** Extra practice to help you master skills is on page 573.

Without evaluating the expression, tell whether the product is *positive, negative,* or *zero.* Explain your reasoning.

13. $(3)(3)$ **14.** $4(-4)$ **15.** $3(14)$

16. $(-7)(0)$ **17.** $8(-2)$ **18.** $(-10)(-5)(8)$

Find the product.

19. $7(8)$ **20.** $(-5)(0)$ **21.** $9(-1)$

22. $(-2)(-13)$ **23.** $(-10)(25)$ **24.** $(-30)(-5)$

25. $17(-3)$ **26.** $(-8)(-12)$ **27.** $(-20)(-5)(-2)$

28. $(-1)(-16)(-1)$ **29.** $(2)(-4)(-9)$ **30.** $6(-5)(-1)(2)$

ALGEBRA **Evaluate the expression for the given values of the variables.**

31. xy when $x = 10$ and $y = -3$ **32.** ab when $a = -40$ and $b = -9$

33. $(2a)(b)$ when $a = 2$ and $b = -1$ **34.** $(x)(-y)$ when $x = 5$ and $y = -5$

35. $(-x)(2y)$ when $x = 3$ and $y = 6$ **36.** $-6ab$ when $a = -5$ and $b = 4$

Use the number line to decide whether the product is *positive, negative,* or *zero.* Explain your reasoning.

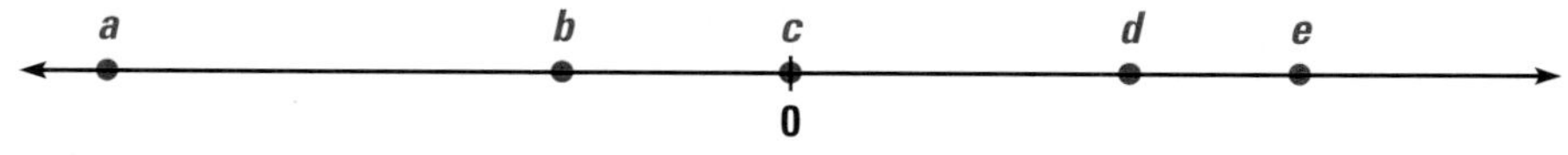

37. ab **38.** cd **39.** ad **40.** de

Write a numerical expression for the verbal phrase. Then find the product.

41. The product of negative one, negative seven, and nine

42. The product of five, negative six, and zero

43. The product of one, four, negative one, and negative eight

Write two different pairs of integers that have the given product.

44. 0 **45.** -12 **46.** -40 **47.** 35

48. -100 **49.** 32 **50.** 51 **51.** -84

LIGHTS **In Exercises 52 and 53, refer to Example 5 on page 190.**

52. The light is on. Switch 1 is flipped four times, and Switch 2 is flipped three times. Is the light off or on?

53. The light is off. Switch 1 is flipped twice, and Switch 2 is flipped three times. Is the light off or on?

Link to Science

TIDES are caused by the gravitational pull of the moon. Most beaches have high tides that are about half a day apart.

More about tides is available at www.mcdougallittell.com

Science Link **In Exercises 54 and 55, use the following information.** The water level of an ocean bay falls 3 feet per hour from high tide until low tide.

54. Write an integer to represent the hourly change in water level.

55. The bay reaches low tide in 6 hours. What is the change in the level of the water during this time?

PROGRAMMING **In Exercises 56 and 57, use the following information.** You are writing a computer program. For any nonzero whole number n, the program runs through the whole numbers 1 to n to see which of the numbers are factors of n. For each n, a *flag* is set equal to 1. Each time a factor of n is found, the flag is multiplied by -1.

56. Simulate the program by hand when $n = 1, 2, 3,$ and 4. For each value of n, what is the flag's value after all the factors are found?

57. Determine the purpose of the flag. In other words, tell what is special about the values of n for which the flag equals -1 when all the factors of n are found.

58. **CHALLENGE** The following steps demonstrate that $(-1)(-1) = 1$. Give a reason for each lettered step without using the rule $-1 \cdot a = -a$.

$(-1)(0) = 0$	**a.** ___?___
$(-1)[1 + (-1)] = 0$	**b.** ___?___
$[(-1)(1)] + [(-1)(-1)] = 0$	**c.** ___?___
$-1 + [(-1)(-1)] = 0$	**d.** ___?___
$1 + (-1) + [(-1)(-1)] = 1 + 0$	Add 1 to each side. (See page 233.)
$0 + [(-1)(-1)] = 1$	**e.** ___?___
$(-1)(-1) = 1$	**f.** ___?___

Multiple-Choice Practice

59. Which of the following statements is *false*?

Ⓐ $3(-4)(-7) = 84$ Ⓑ $-2(-5)(11) = 110$

Ⓒ $-8(-1)(-7) = 56$ Ⓓ $3(-6)(-5) = 90$

60. Which of the following statements about a and b is true if $0 < a < 1$ and $b < -1$?

Ⓕ The sum of a and b is a positive number.

Ⓖ If you subtract b from a, the result is a negative number.

Ⓗ The product of a and b is a positive number.

Ⓙ The product of a, b, and b is a positive number.

4.6 Dividing Integers

California Standards

In this lesson you'll:

- Divide positive and negative integers to solve problems, including those arising in concrete situations. (NS 2.3)
- Find the average of a data set. (SDP 1.1)

Goal 1 DIVIDING INTEGERS

A useful way to solve a division problem is to rewrite it as a multiplication problem.

DIVISION	MULTIPLICATION
$-15 \div 3 = ?$	$3 \times ? = -15$

You know that $3(-5) = -15$, so you can conclude that $-15 \div 3 = -5$. In other words, a negative number divided by a positive number is negative. You can use similar reasoning for other quotients of integers.

More generally, to divide two integers, divide their absolute values. Then use the following rules to find the sign of the quotient.

DIVIDING INTEGERS

Rule	Examples
1. The quotient of two positive integers is positive.	$\frac{10}{2} = 5$
2. The quotient of two negative integers is positive.	$(-8) \div (-4) = 2$
3. The quotient of two integers with different signs is negative.	$-12 \div 3 = -4$ $20 \div (-4) = -5$
4. The quotient of 0 and a nonzero integer is 0.	$\frac{0}{-3} = 0$

An expression with a 0 divisor, such as $12 \div 0$, is *undefined* because there is no number you can multiply by 0 to get the dividend. You cannot divide a number by 0.

Student Help

STUDY TIP
You can check the answer to a division problem by multiplying the quotient and the divisor. For example, you can check part (a) of Example 1 by writing $(-9) \times (-8) = 72$.

EXAMPLE 1 Dividing Integers

Find the quotient, if possible.

a. $72 \div (-8)$ **b.** $-42 \div 14$ **c.** $-49 \div (-7)$ **d.** $0 \div 3$

Solution

a. $72 \div (-8) = -9$ The quotient of two integers with different signs is negative.

b. $-42 \div 14 = -3$ The quotient of two integers with different signs is negative.

c. $-49 \div (-7) = 7$ The quotient of two negative integers is positive.

d. $0 \div 3 = 0$ The quotient of 0 and a nonzero integer is 0.

EXAMPLE 2 Evaluating an Expression

Evaluate the expression $\frac{-18}{x}$ for the given value of x.

a. $x = -3$

b. $x = 3$

Solution

a. $\frac{-18}{x} = \frac{-18}{-3}$ Substitute −3 for *x*.

$= 6$ The quotient of two negative integers is positive.

b. $\frac{-18}{x} = \frac{-18}{3}$ Substitute 3 for *x*.

$= -6$ The quotient of two integers with different signs is negative.

Goal 2 FINDING AN AVERAGE

LAKE MICHIGAN is the largest body of fresh water that lies entirely within the United States. It covers an area of 22,300 square miles and is 923 feet deep at its deepest point.

EXAMPLE 3 Finding an Average

GEOGRAPHY You are exploring the bottom of Lake Michigan. You take five measurements (in feet) of the lake bottom's elevation relative to the lake surface. What is the average of these elevations?

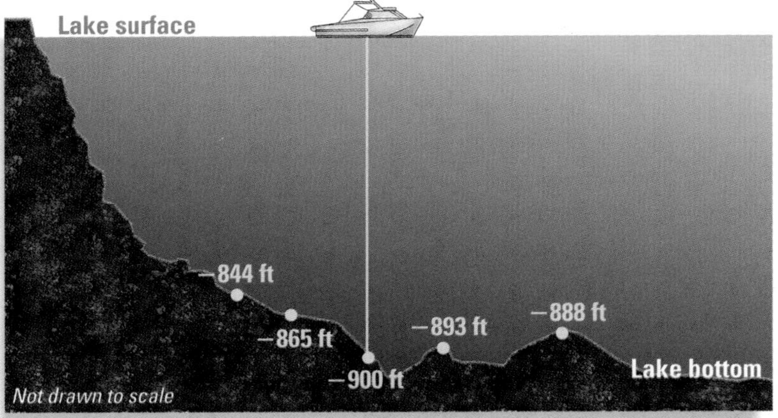

Solution

To find the average, first add the five measurements.

$$-844 + (-865) + (-900) + (-893) + (-888) = -4390$$

Then divide the sum by 5.

$$\text{Average} = \frac{-4390}{5} = -878$$

ANSWER ▶ The average of the elevation measurements is −878 feet, or 878 feet below the lake surface.

4.6 Exercises

Guided Practice

Tell whether the statement is *true* or *false*. Explain your reasoning.

1. A positive number divided by its opposite is equal to 1.

2. A negative number divided by its opposite is equal to -1.

Find the quotient, if possible.

3. $16 \div 2$ **4.** $0 \div (-4)$ **5.** $(-22) \div (-11)$

6. $\frac{81}{-9}$ **7.** $\frac{-30}{6}$ **8.** $\frac{-52}{-13}$

ERROR ANALYSIS **In Exercises 9 and 10, describe and correct the error.**

9. ~~$-12 \div 0 = -12$~~

10. ~~$0 \div (-8) = -8$~~

11. FINDING AN AVERAGE Changes in an icicle's length, in inches, for eight days are given. What is the average daily change in length?

$$-3, -2, -1, -2, 0, -1, -2, -1$$

Practice and Problem Solving

Student Help

▶**MORE PRACTICE** Extra practice to help you master skills is on page 573.

Tell whether the quotient is *positive* or *negative* without dividing.

12. $-81 \div 9$ **13.** $64 \div (-16)$ **14.** $45 \div 3$ **15.** $-70 \div (-10)$

Find the quotient, if possible.

16. $42 \div (-6)$ **17.** $-33 \div 11$ **18.** $0 \div 10$

19. $\frac{75}{-25}$ **20.** $\frac{52}{-4}$ **21.** $\frac{-125}{5}$

22. $0 \div (-18)$ **23.** $-88 \div (-2)$ **24.** $-28 \div 0$

25. $-76 \div (-4)$ **26.** $-45 \div (-9)$ **27.** $19 \div 0$

Write a numerical expression for the verbal phrase. Then find the quotient.

28. The quotient of forty-five and negative fifteen

29. The quotient of negative twenty-eight and negative fourteen

30. The quotient of zero and negative fifteen

31. The quotient of eighteen and negative nine

32. **MATHEMATICAL REASONING** Explain how to use division to solve this problem: *The product of an integer and* -4 *is* -244*. What is the integer?* Find the integer.

ALGEBRA Evaluate the expression when $x = 6$ and when $x = -6$.

33. $\frac{x}{3}$ 34. $\frac{6}{x}$ 35. $\frac{x}{2}$ 36. $\frac{-36}{x}$

AVERAGES In Exercises 37–40, find the average of the data.

37. Temperatures: $-10°$, $-6°$, $7°$, $-13°$, $5°$, $10°$, $-14°$

38. Golf scores: -2, $+1$, 0, -1, -2, $+1$

39. Stock price changes: $-\$2$, $-\$4$, $\$2$, $-\$1$, $-\$2$, $-\$3$, $\$2$, $\$0$, $-\$1$

40. Annual profit (in millions): $-\$21$, $-\$17$, $-\$6$, $\$4$, $\$10$, $\$18$

Link to Geography

GRAND CANYON Located in northwest Arizona, the Grand Canyon is 9165 feet above sea level at its highest point and 1200 feet above sea level at its lowest point.

GRAND CANYON In Exercises 41 and 42, use the following information. You are visiting the Grand Canyon in Arizona. You look at a tour map that tells you the change in elevation as you travel into the canyon on different trails.

Trail	Change in elevation (ft)
South Kaibab	−4620
Bright Angel	−4420
Tonto	−3000
North Kaibab	−5841

41. Find the average elevation change for the four trails to the nearest foot. Use a calculator if you wish.

42. Write each of the elevation changes in miles. Round to the nearest tenth. Use a calculator if you wish.

43. **GOLF** Your average score above or below par per hole for several holes of golf is -1. What additional information do you need to find your total score of points above or below par?

44. **CHALLENGE** Copy the maze shown. Your goal is to move from the *start* box to the *end* box. To move, divide the number in the *start* box by any integer. If the quotient is the integer in a neighboring box, you may move to that box. You may not move diagonally.

Now divide the number in the new box by any integer. If the quotient is in a neighboring box, you may move. Continue dividing and moving until you reach the *end* box. Keep a record of each division that results in a move. How many moves does it take you to reach the *end* box?

Integer Division Maze

480 START	−240	−85
100	240	75
135	−60	30
205	−55	−10
40	15	10 END

Student Help

▶ HOMEWORK HELP Extra help with problem solving in Ex. 44 is available at www.mcdougallittell.com

Multiple-Choice Practice

45. The price of a share of stock initially worth 34 cents changes −3 cents on Monday, −4 cents on Tuesday, 2 cents on Wednesday, −3 cents on Thursday, and −2 cents on Friday. Which number is *not* needed to find the average daily change in the stock price for the week?

(A) 34 (B) 2 (C) −3 (D) −4

In Exercises 46 and 47, use the graph, which shows a company's profits (in thousands of dollars) from January through June.

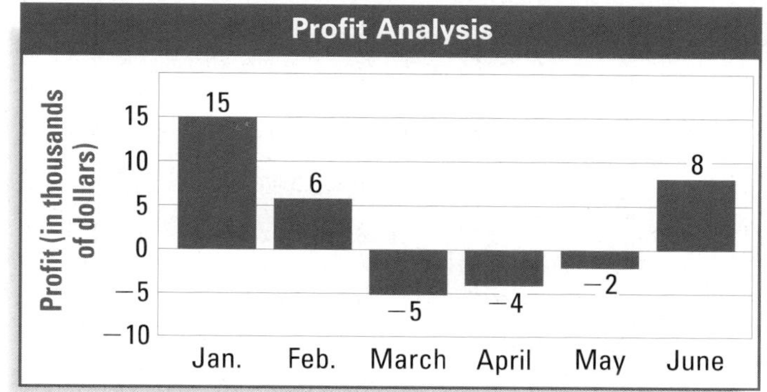

46. What is the company's average monthly profit?

(F) −$3000 (G) $3000 (H) $4500 (J) Not here

47. Which number describes the company's change in profit from February to March?

(A) −$11,000 (B) −$5000 (C) $1000 (D) $11,000

Mixed Review

In Exercises 48 and 49, evaluate the expression. *(1.3)*

48. $2 \times 165 - 121 \div 11$

49. $89 - 7 - 2 \times 17$

50. **PRINTING** You have used 225 of your 500 sheets of printer paper. What fraction of the paper have you used? *(2.4)*

51. **BAKE SALE** You have sold 120 of the 300 cookies made for a bake sale. What fraction of the cookies have *not* been sold? *(2.4)*

52. Write an equation that relates the distributive property to the area model. *(3.6)*

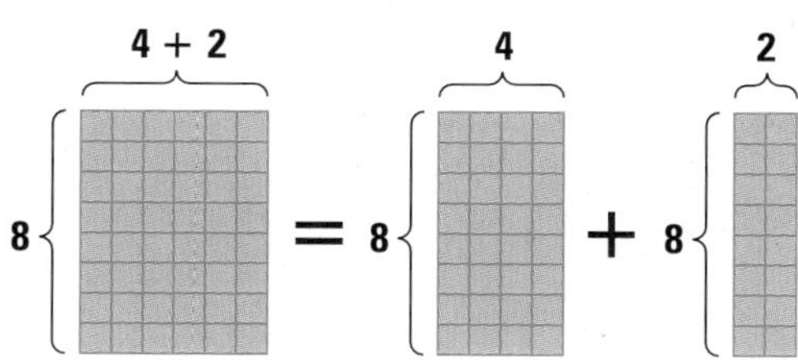

4.7 Integers and Order of Operations

California Standards

In this lesson you'll:

- Apply order of operations to evaluate expressions. (AF 1.3)
- Apply the distributive property to evaluate expressions. (AF 1.3)

Goal 1 USING THE ORDER OF OPERATIONS

In Lessons 1.3 and 1.4, you studied the order of operations for evaluating expressions that involve more than one operation. These rules also apply to operations with integers.

ORDER OF OPERATIONS

1. Evaluate expressions inside grouping symbols.
2. Evaluate powers.
3. Multiply and divide from left to right. — Left-to-right rule
4. Add and subtract from left to right. — Left-to-right rule

EXAMPLE 1 Using Order of Operations

Evaluate the expression.

a. $-17 + 4^2$ **b.** $(-17 + 4)^2$ **c.** $-15 \div 3 \times 5$

Solution

a. $-17 + 4^2 = -17 + 16$ — Evaluate power.

$= -1$ — Add.

b. $(-17 + 4)^2 = (-13)^2$ — Add inside parentheses.

$= (-13)(-13)$ — Write power as product.

$= 169$ — Multiply.

c. $-15 \div 3 \times 5 = -5 \times 5$ — Divide -15 by 3.

$= -25$ — Multiply -5 by 5.

EXAMPLE 2 Evaluating an Expression

Evaluate $-(a + b)$ when $a = -5$ and $b = 3$.

Solution

$-(a + b) = -(-5 + 3)$ — Substitute -5 for a and 3 for b.

$= -(-2)$ — Add inside parentheses.

$= 2$ — The opposite of -2 is 2.

Student Help

STUDY TIP
Taking the opposite is the same as multiplying by -1. So, when you use order of operations, treat taking the opposite as you would multiplication.

Goal 2 USING THE DISTRIBUTIVE PROPERTY

In Lesson 3.6, you studied the distributive property, $a(b + c) = ab + bc$. You can use the subtraction rule to justify a "subtraction version" of the distributive property.

$3(2 - 6) = 3(2 + (-6))$	Use rule for subtraction.
$= 3(2) + 3(-6)$	Use distributive property.
$= 3(2) + [-3(6)]$	Use rule for multiplication.
$= 3(2) - 3(6)$	Use rule for subtraction.

SUBTRACTION AND THE DISTRIBUTIVE PROPERTY

In Algebra $a(b - c) = ab - ac$

In Arithmetic $3(2 - 6) = 3(2) - 3(6)$

Student Help

▶ **MORE EXAMPLES**
INTERNET More examples are available at www.mcdougallittell.com

EXAMPLE 3 Using the Distributive Property

Evaluate the expression $-3(4 - 7)$ in two ways. Compare your results.

a. Subtract first, then multiply.

b. Use the distributive property.

Solution

a. $-3(4 - 7) = -3(-3)$	Subtract inside parentheses first.
$= 9$	Multiply.
b. $-3(4 - 7) = (-3)(4) - (-3)(7)$	Use the distributive property.
$= -12 - (-21)$	Multiply.
$= -12 + 21$	Use rule for subtraction.
$= 9$	Add.

ANSWER ▶ The result is the same for both methods. This is consistent with the subtraction version of the distributive property.

Student Help

▶ **STUDY TIP**
Another way to evaluate the expression in Example 4 is to use the distributive property.

$2(-16 + 4 + 10)$
$= 2(-16) + 2(4) + 2(10)$
$= -32 + 8 + 20$
$= -4$

EXAMPLE 4 Writing an Expression

Write an expression for the verbal phrase *twice the sum of −16, 4, and 10.* Then evaluate the expression.

Solution

$2(-16 + 4 + 10) = 2(-12 + 10)$	Left-to-right rule inside parentheses.
$= 2(-2)$	Add inside parentheses.
$= -4$	Multiply.

4.7 Exercises

Guided Practice

Tell which part of the expression should be evaluated first when you use order of operations.

1. $48 \div (-6) + 3$ **2.** $(-8 + 12) \div (-2)$ **3.** $(-8)(-5) \div 2$

Evaluate the expression.

4. $3^3 + (-5)$ **5.** $(-6 - 4) \div (-5)$ **6.** $9 + (-12) \div 2$

Evaluate the expression when $x = -4$ and $y = 2$.

7. $x^2 - (-6)$ **8.** $\frac{8}{xy}$ **9.** $\frac{x - y}{2}$

Write a numerical expression for the verbal phrase. Then evaluate the expression using the distributive property.

10. Twice the difference of -7 and 16

11. Three times the sum of 6, -4, and -7

Practice and Problem Solving

Student Help

▶**MORE PRACTICE** Extra practice to help you master skills is on page 573.

In Exercises 12 and 13, write the expression as a power. Then evaluate the expression.

12. $(-3)(-3)(-3)(-3)$ **13.** $(-2)(-2)(-2)(-2)(-2)$

14. MATHEMATICAL REASONING What do you know about the sign of a negative integer raised to an odd power? to an even power? Explain.

Evaluate the expression.

15. $54 + (-6) + 5$ **16.** $(-7)(-2) + 14$ **17.** $(20 + 10) + (-6)$

18. $12 - 4 \times 5$ **19.** $(2)(8) + 2^2$ **20.** $-14 + 2 - 2^3$

21. $(-2)^2 + (-8) \cdot 4$ **22.** $-5(-4 - 2)$ **23.** $(-3)^2 + 8 \cdot 0$

24. $\frac{(-7 + 10)^2}{3}$ **25.** $\frac{-84}{-3 \cdot 4}$ **26.** $\frac{-8 + 2}{-3 + 2}$

Evaluate the expression for the given value of the variable(s).

27. $4x + 3$ when $x = -4$ **28.** $\frac{5y}{-2}$ when $y = -6$

29. $-3(a - b)$ when $a = 8$ and $b = -3$ **30.** $\frac{q^2}{r}$ when $q = -10$ and $r = 5$

MARKET CRASHES
The stock market crash of 1929 happened near the beginning of a period of United States history known as the Great Depression. By 1932, the Dow Jones had lost 89% of its value, and 1 out of 4 workers was unemployed.

More about this topic is available at www.mcdougallittell.com

Evaluate the expression by first using order of operations and then by using the distributive property.

31. $2(5 - 8)$ **32.** $-6(-7 - (-2))$ **33.** $3(6 + (-1) - 4)$

In Exercises 34–36, write a numerical expression for the verbal phrase. Then evaluate the expression.

34. Twice the sum of -108, -36, and 84

35. Half the quotient of $(-12)^2$ and -8

36. The product of -2 and the sum of -24 and -14

37. **SUBMARINE** A submarine starts at sea level. It dives 700 feet, rises 100 feet, and then dives by an amount equal to 5 times the previous rise. Write an expression to represent these changes. Then find the final level of the submarine.

History Link **In Exercises 38 and 39, use the following information.** The stock market crash on October 19, 1987 was one of the largest single-day price drops in the history of the Dow Jones Industrial Average, a statistic used to monitor the general trend of stock prices. The Dow Jones declined 508 points on that day. In the two days after the crash, it rose 102 and 186 points.

38. The Dow Jones was at 2246 the day before the crash. What was the value of the Dow Jones after the changes described above?

39. Find the average change in the Dow Jones for the three days described above.

CHALLENGE **Use order of operations to evaluate the expression.**

40. $-4 + 7 \times 3 - (-5) + 12 \times (-6) \div (-3)$

41. $9 + (-8) - (-8) \times (-4) - (-18) \div 9 + 9 \div 3$

Multiple-Choice Practice

42. What is the value of $-4^2 - 3^2$?

Ⓐ 25 Ⓑ 7 Ⓒ -7 Ⓓ -25

43. Which expression makes the statement $5(-8 - 7) =$ **?** *true*?

Ⓕ $40 - 35$ Ⓖ $-40 - 35$ Ⓗ $-3 - 2$ Ⓙ $-3 + 2$

44. Which part of the expression $3 - (-9) + (-8) \times (-4) \div 2$ should be evaluated first?

Ⓐ $3 - (-9)$ Ⓑ $(-9) + (-8)$

Ⓒ $(-8) \times (-4)$ Ⓓ $(-4) \div 2$

4.8 Comparing Positive and Negative Numbers

In this lesson you'll:

- Graph positive and negative fractions, decimals, and mixed numbers. (NS 1.1)
- Compare and order positive and negative fractions, decimals, and mixed numbers. (NS 1.1)

Goal 1 Graphing Positive and Negative Numbers

So far in this chapter you have been studying negative integers. In this lesson you will study other types of negative numbers, such as negative fractions, negative decimals, and negative mixed numbers. One way to compare these numbers is to convert them to decimal form.

EXAMPLE 1 Graphing Negative Decimals

Graph -0.7 and -2.25 on a number line.

Solution

Begin by drawing a number line. To help you graph the numbers, mark the line with tick marks at each tenth.

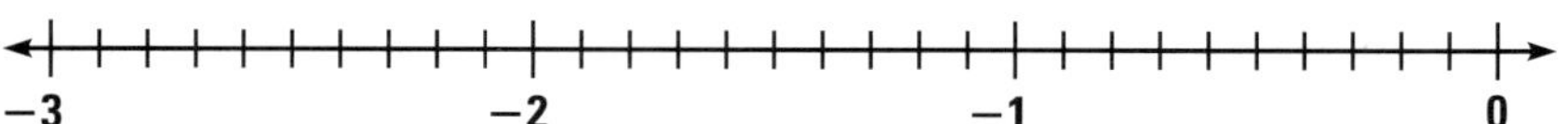

To graph -0.7, start at 0 and move seven tenths to the left.

To graph -2.25, locate the tick marks for $\mathbf{-2.2}$ and $\mathbf{-2.3}$. Then plot a point that is halfway between those two tick marks.

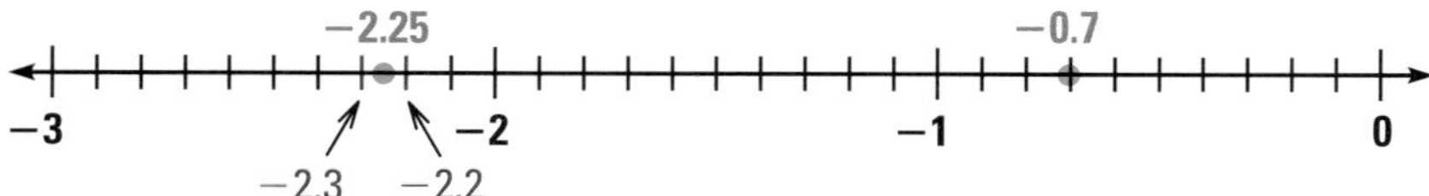

Student Help

▶ Look Back
Another way to compare fractions is to rewrite them with common denominators. For help with this, see Example 2 on page 83.

EXAMPLE 2 Graphing Negative Fractions

Graph $-\frac{1}{2}$, $-\frac{4}{3}$, and $-2\frac{3}{8}$ on a number line.

Solution

First rewrite each number as a decimal. If necessary, round to the nearest hundredth.

$$-\frac{1}{2} = -0.5 \qquad -\frac{4}{3} \approx -1.33 \qquad -2\frac{3}{8} = -2.375 \approx -2.38$$

Then use the decimal approximations to graph the numbers.

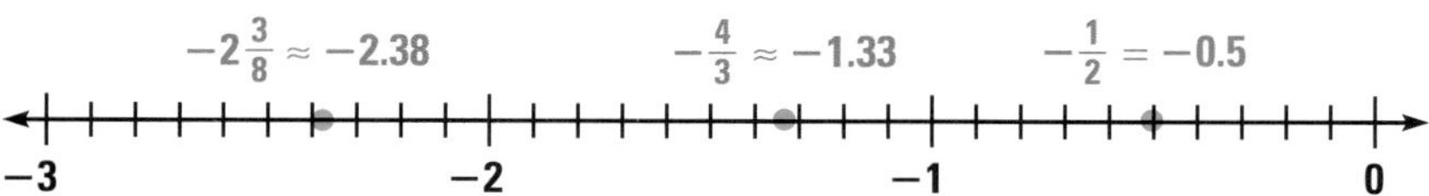

Goal 2 COMPARING POSITIVE AND NEGATIVE NUMBERS

Student Help

▶ **MORE EXAMPLES**

INTERNET More examples are available at www.mcdougallittell.com

EXAMPLE 3 Comparing Negative Numbers

Complete the statement using <, =, or >.

a. $-\frac{1}{6}$? -0.6 **b.** $-\frac{9}{8}$? -1.125 **c.** $-2\frac{1}{3}$? -2.1

Solution

Rewrite fractions and mixed numbers as decimals. Then graph the numbers on a number line.

a. 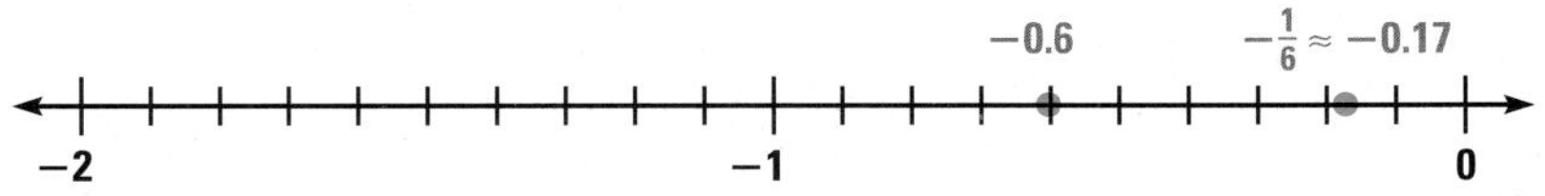

ANSWER ▶ $-\frac{1}{6}$ is to the right of -0.6, so $-\frac{1}{6} > -0.6$.

b. 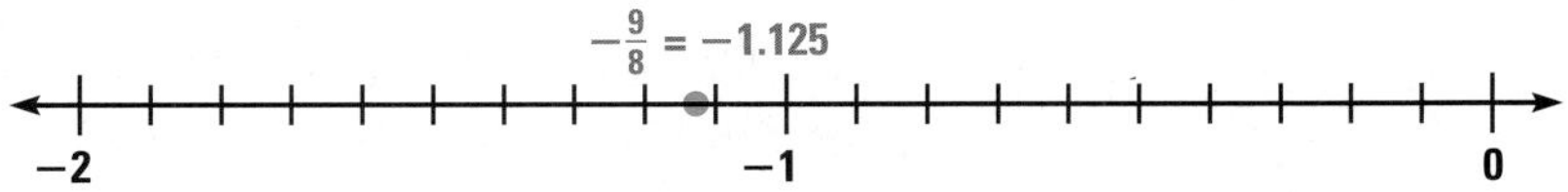

ANSWER ▶ $-\frac{9}{8}$ is the same point as -1.125, so $-\frac{9}{8} = -1.125$.

c. 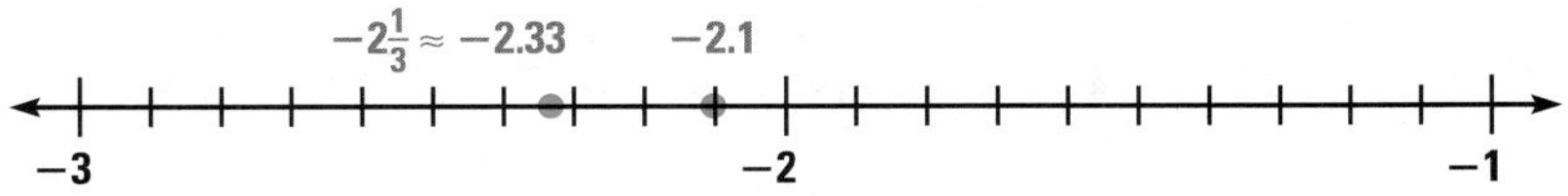

ANSWER ▶ $-2\frac{1}{3}$ is to the left of -2.1, so $-2\frac{1}{3} < -2.1$.

EXAMPLE 4 Ordering Positive and Negative Numbers

Write 1.3, $-2\frac{1}{2}$, -2.6, and $\frac{3}{8}$ in order from least to greatest.

Solution

First rewrite fractions and mixed numbers as decimals.

$$-2\frac{1}{2} = -2.5 \qquad \frac{3}{8} = 0.375$$

Then draw a number line. You can use estimation to plot the points.

ANSWER ▶ From least to greatest, the order is -2.6, $-2\frac{1}{2}$, $\frac{3}{8}$, 1.3.

4.8 Exercises

Guided Practice

In Exercises 1–4, match the fraction with the equivalent decimal.

A. -2.375 **B.** -1.2 **C.** -2.2 **D.** -2.05

1. $-\frac{6}{5}$ **2.** $-2\frac{1}{20}$ **3.** $-2\frac{3}{8}$ **4.** $-2\frac{1}{5}$

5. How does rewriting fractions as decimals help you to compare and order numbers?

Graph the numbers on a number line. Then write a statement using <, =, or > to compare the numbers.

6. $0.75, \frac{2}{3}$ **7.** $-\frac{27}{4}, -6$ **8.** $-1.5, -\frac{13}{9}$ **9.** $-\frac{5}{6}, -0.8$

Order the numbers from least to greatest.

10. $-3.8, \frac{35}{8}, -3$ **11.** $5.6, \frac{107}{18}, -5$ **12.** $1.3, -1.04, \frac{4}{3}$

Practice and Problem Solving

Student Help

▶ MORE PRACTICE
Extra practice to help you master skills is on page 573.

Rewrite the number as a decimal. If necessary, round to the nearest hundredth.

13. $\frac{7}{8}$ **14.** $-\frac{5}{4}$ **15.** $1\frac{1}{3}$ **16.** $-3\frac{3}{5}$

17. $-\frac{15}{7}$ **18.** $4\frac{1}{6}$ **19.** $-\frac{1}{9}$ **20.** $2\frac{5}{6}$

Graph the pair of numbers on a number line.

21. $4, -2$ **22.** $4.25, 4.52$ **23.** $-\frac{3}{4}, -\frac{3}{5}$ **24.** $-2.9, 1.7$

25. $-\frac{11}{3}, -4$ **26.** $2.33, 2\frac{1}{3}$ **27.** $-1\frac{3}{5}, \frac{2}{5}$ **28.** $-1.85, 2$

Complete the statement using <, =, or >.

29. -6 **?** -7.5 **30.** -0.5 **?** $-\frac{1}{2}$ **31.** $-\frac{2}{5}$ **?** -0.33

32. $-\frac{14}{5}$ **?** -3.2 **33.** $-2\frac{5}{6}$ **?** -2.9 **34.** -5.12 **?** $-5\frac{1}{9}$

35. $-6\frac{1}{3}$ **?** -6.3 **36.** $-6\frac{2}{5}$ **?** -6.45 **37.** -2.75 **?** $-\frac{11}{4}$

In Exercises 38–43, order the numbers from least to greatest.

38. $0, \frac{1}{2}, -3, -3.2, -\frac{16}{7}$

39. $5.5, -\frac{9}{4}, 2, -\frac{1}{2}, -2.5$

40. $-4.25, -7, -\frac{7}{2}, -1\frac{3}{4}, -5$

41. $-6.8, \frac{3}{8}, -2\frac{1}{5}, -2.3, \frac{7}{4}$

42. $1\frac{3}{8}, -\frac{5}{16}, 1.4, -1.3, -0.4$

43. $2.7, \frac{26}{9}, -2\frac{1}{11}, -0.1, -\frac{1}{8}$

44. MATHEMATICAL REASONING Explain why $\frac{-3}{4}$ and $\frac{3}{-4}$ are two other ways to write $-\frac{3}{4}$.

Link to Science

OCEANOGRAPHY
In 1960, United States Navy Lieutenant Don Walsh and Swiss scientist Jacques Picard rode the bathyscaphe *Trieste* to the bottom of the Marianas Trench.

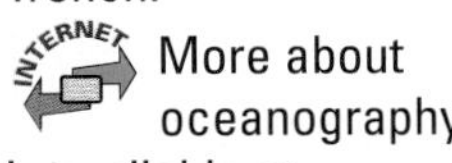

More about oceanography is available at www.mcdougallittell.com

45. STOCK MARKET A newspaper reports Monday's change in a company's stock price as -2.25. A television newscast reports Tuesday's change in the stock price as $-2\frac{5}{8}$. On which day did the price of the stock fall more? Explain.

Science Link **In Exercises 46–48, use the following information.**

The deepest areas of the ocean occur in long, narrow valleys called trenches. The table at the right shows the location (in miles) of three ocean trenches relative to sea level.

Trench	Location (miles)
Java	-4.4
Puerto Rico	$-5\frac{2}{5}$
Marianas	$-\frac{69}{10}$

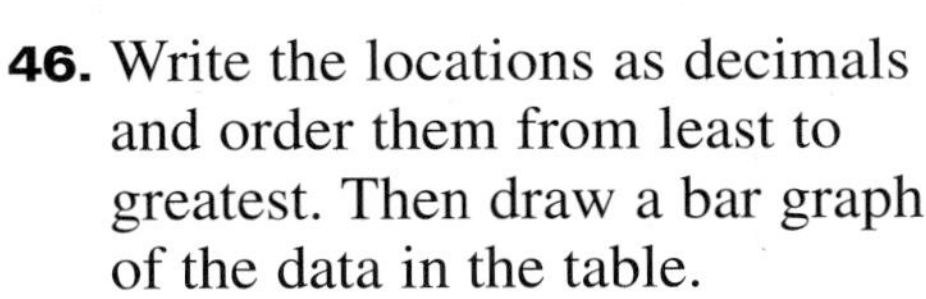

46. Write the locations as decimals and order them from least to greatest. Then draw a bar graph of the data in the table.

47. Which of the trenches is the farthest below sea level?

48. CHALLENGE Is the location of the trench that is farthest below sea level the greatest value or the least value in the table? Explain.

Multiple-Choice Practice

49. Which number is *not* a good estimate of the number graphed on the number line below?

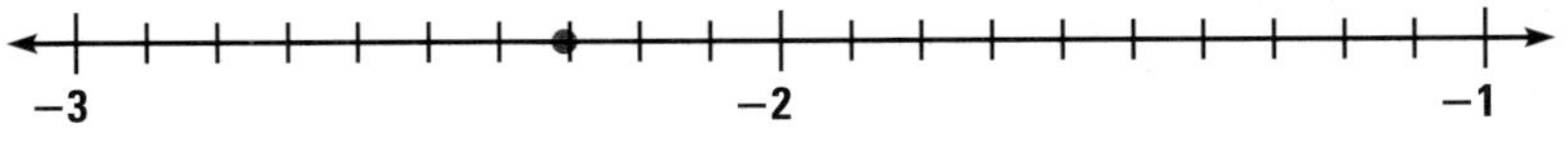

Ⓐ -2.3 Ⓑ $-\frac{7}{3}$ Ⓒ -2.33 Ⓓ $-2\frac{3}{4}$

50. Which number is greater than -8.25?

Ⓕ -10 Ⓖ -9.15 Ⓗ $-8\frac{3}{8}$ Ⓙ $-\frac{73}{9}$

Chapter 4 Chapter Summary and Review

VOCABULARY

- **integer,** *p. 167*
- **negative integer,** *p. 167*
- **positive integer,** *p. 167*
- **negative sign,** *p. 167*
- **opposites,** *p. 171*
- **absolute value,** *p. 177*

4.1 INTEGERS AND THE NUMBER LINE

Examples on pp. 167–168

EXAMPLE To order the integers −9, 3, 0, 4, and −8 from least to greatest, use a number line. Negative numbers are to the **left** of zero.

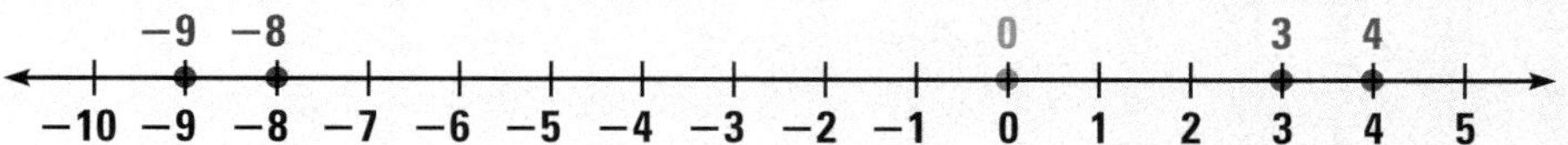

Use a number line to order the numbers from least to greatest.

1. 1, −6, −7, 6, −2

2. 3, 4, −6, −3, 1

RECORD LOWS **Use the table at the right that shows record low temperatures (in °F) for several states.**

3. Use a number line to order the temperatures from least to greatest.

4. Which state has the lowest record low temperature? Which state has the highest record low temperature?

State	Temp. (°F)
Maine	−48
New Jersey	−34
Oregon	−54
California	−45

▶ Source: National Climatic Data Center

4.2 ADDING INTEGERS ON A NUMBER LINE

Examples on pp. 171–173

EXAMPLE You can use a number line to find the sum 2 + 5 + (−3).

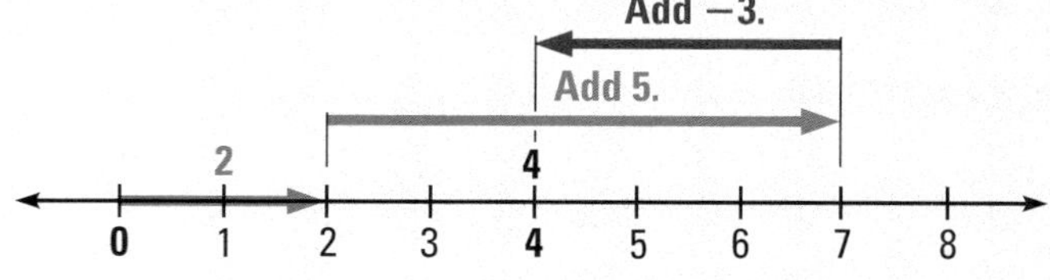

To add a positive integer on a number line, move to the **right**.

To add a negative integer on a number line, move to the **left**.

Your final position is 4. So, 2 + 5 + (−3) = 4.

In Exercises 5–8, use a number line to find the sum.

5. $-12 + (-5)$ **6.** $8 + (-12)$ **7.** $-9 + 9$ **8.** $0 + (-5)$

9. **BUSINESS** A small business has monthly profits of \$300, −\$125, −\$85, and \$210. What is the average monthly profit of the business?

4.3 ADDING INTEGERS USING ADDITION RULES

Examples on pp. 177–178

EXAMPLES

a. $-13 + (-9) = -22$ The signs are the same. Add absolute values. Write the common sign.

b. $-10 + 7 = -3$ The signs are different. Subtract the lesser absolute value from the greater absolute value. Write the sign of the integer with the greater absolute value.

Find the sum.

10. $15 + (-2)$ **11.** $-6 + (-8)$ **12.** $14 + (-14)$ **13.** $-2 + 3$

14. $8 + (-13)$ **15.** $-6 + 5$ **16.** $-9 + 12$ **17.** $-20 + (-30)$

4.4 SUBTRACTING INTEGERS

Examples on pp. 181–183

EXAMPLE You can use a number line to show that $-2 - 4 - (-8) = 2$.

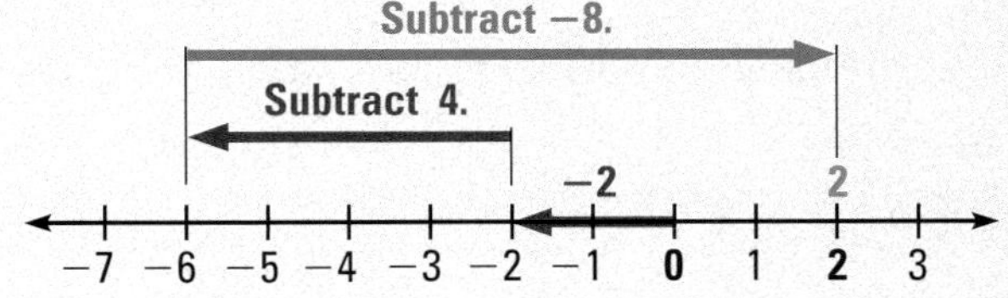

To subtract a positive integer on a number line, move to the **left**.

To subtract a negative number on a number line, move to the **right**.

Another way to subtract is to add the opposite: $7 - (-4) = 7 + 4 = 11$.

Find the difference.

18. $-5 - (-7)$ **19.** $8 - (-8)$ **20.** $9 - 13$

MODEL ROCKET Use the diagram of a model rocket's path.

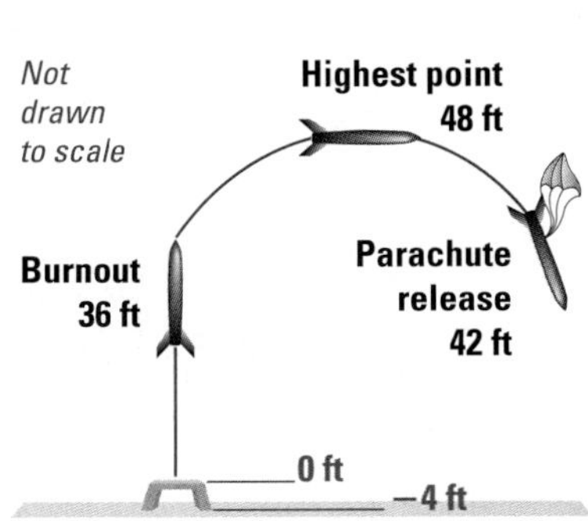

21. How much higher is the rocket at its highest point than at ground level?

22. The countdown to liftoff starts at −5 seconds. The rocket reaches its highest point 3 seconds after liftoff. How many seconds after the countdown starts is this?

4.5 MULTIPLYING INTEGERS

Examples on pp. 188–190

EXAMPLES

a. $-4 \times (-6) = 24$ The product of two integers with the same sign is positive.

b. $-3 \cdot 5 = -15$ The product of two integers with different signs is negative.

c. $-4 \cdot 0 = 0$ The product of an integer and 0 is 0.

In Exercises 23–30, find the product.

23. $-8 \times (-9)$ **24.** -7×5 **25.** $3 \cdot (-1)$ **26.** 11×7

27. $(-9)(-6)$ **28.** $-14 \times (-3)$ **29.** $-4 \cdot 11$ **30.** $12(-11)$

31. **STOCKS** On Monday, the change in value of a share of stock is -2 dollars. On Tuesday, the value changes three times as much. What is the change in the value of the stock on Tuesday?

4.6 DIVIDING INTEGERS

Examples on pp. 193–194

EXAMPLES

a. $\frac{-55}{-11} = 5$ The quotient of two integers with the same sign is positive.

b. $-14 \div 2 = -7$ The quotient of two integers with different signs is negative.

c. $0 \div (-1) = 0$ The quotient of 0 and a nonzero integer is 0.

In Exercises 32–37, find the quotient.

32. $-48 \div (-8)$ **33.** $\frac{-35}{7}$ **34.** $33 \div (-11)$

35. $\frac{40}{-5}$ **36.** $\frac{100}{-20}$ **37.** $-60 \div (-4)$

38. **GREAT LAKES** Use the table to find the average elevation relative to the lake surface of the five lake bottoms.

Lake	Lake Superior	Lake Michigan	Lake Huron	Lake Erie	Lake Ontario
Elevation (feet)	−1330	−923	−750	−210	−810

4.7 INTEGERS AND ORDER OF OPERATIONS

Examples on pp. 198–199

EXAMPLE

a. Evaluate $(-2 + (-16)) \div 3^2$.

$$\begin{aligned} (-2 + (-16)) \div 3^2 &= -18 \div 3^2 && \text{Add inside parentheses.} \\ &= -18 \div 9 && \text{Evaluate the power.} \\ &= -2 && \text{Divide.} \end{aligned}$$

b. Use the distributive property to evaluate $-6(3 - (-4))$.

$$\begin{aligned} -6(3 - (-4)) &= (-6)(3) - (-6)(-4) && \text{Use the distributive property.} \\ &= -18 - 24 && \text{Multiply.} \\ &= -18 + (-24) && \text{Use rule for subtraction.} \\ &= -42 && \text{Add.} \end{aligned}$$

Evaluate the expression.

39. $-45 - 10 \div (-2)$

40. $(5 - 8)^2 \times (-9)$

41. $-16 + 7 \cdot 0$

42. $9(7 - 12)$

43. $-2(-6 - (-10))$

44. $-4(-3 + 2 - 5)$

4.8 COMPARING POSITIVE AND NEGATIVE NUMBERS

Examples on pp. 202–203

EXAMPLE **Order -2.45, $\frac{11}{8}$, $-2\frac{3}{5}$, 1.25, and $-\frac{1}{2}$ from least to greatest.**

Begin by writing the fractions and mixed numbers as decimals.

$\frac{11}{8} = 1.375 \qquad -2\frac{3}{5} = -2.6 \qquad -\frac{1}{2} = -0.5$

Draw a number line. Use estimation to plot the points.

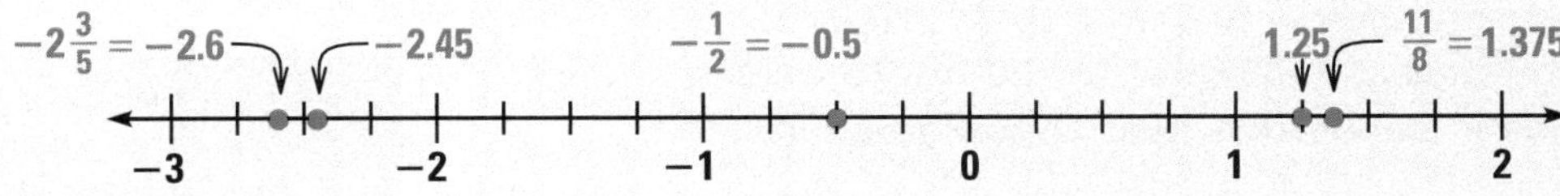

From least to greatest, the order is $-2\frac{3}{5}$, -2.45, $-\frac{1}{2}$, 1.25, $\frac{11}{8}$.

Graph the numbers on a number line. Then order them from least to greatest.

45. $-2.03, \frac{1}{6}, -2, -2\frac{1}{8}, 0.15$

46. $-\frac{5}{7}, -1, -1.18, \frac{1}{7}, -\frac{13}{8}$

47. $4.15, 3\frac{5}{8}, -\frac{13}{4}, -3, -4.2$

48. $-\frac{3}{4}, -0.9, \frac{5}{8}, -1, -\frac{8}{15}$

Chapter 4 Chapter Test

Complete the statement using <, =, or >.

1. 5 ? −2

2. −9 ? −8

3. 0 ? −1

Order the integers from least to greatest.

4. −11, 2, 0, −9, 7

5. −1, −2, −5, 2, 1

6. −6, 6, −4, −9, 3

Is the statement *true* or *false*? If it is false, explain why.

7. The absolute value of a negative number is negative.

8. Zero is its own opposite.

Evaluate the expression.

9. $4 + (-9)$

10. $-3 - 7$

11. $-17 - (-8)$

12. $-19 + 28$

13. $6 + (-6)$

14. $7 \cdot (-7)$

15. $(-3)(-12)$

16. $-72 \div (-8)$

17. $-84 \div 12$

Evaluate the expression for the given value(s).

18. $6x - 5^2$ when $x = -2$

19. $5(m - n)$ when $m = 7$ and $n = -3$

20. $\frac{y + 4}{-3}$ when $y = -22$

21. $\frac{v^3}{w}$ when $v = 2$ and $w = -4$

Evaluate the expression.

22. $-4(8 - 9)$

23. $7(-3 - (-5))$

24. $2(1 + (-3) + 6)$

Graph the numbers on a number line. Then order the numbers from least to greatest.

25. $-1.26, -1.269, 1, \frac{1}{3}$

26. $-4, 0, \frac{2}{3}, -4.25, -\frac{15}{4}$

GEOLOGY **For Exercises 27–29, refer to the photo, which shows house-sized holes in sandstone near Lake Powell in Utah.**

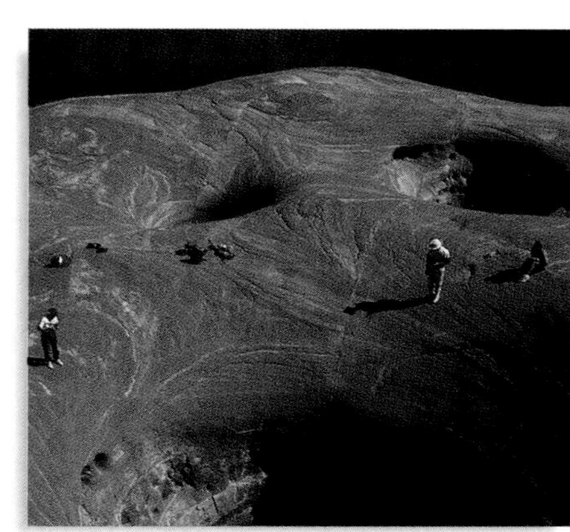

27. Geologists estimate that the holes were formed between 1,600,000 B.C. and 800,000 B.C. Which of these dates is more recent? Explain.

28. The first known residents of the area, the Anasazi people, lived there from about 10 B.C. to A.D. 1250. For about how many years did they live in the area?

29. Suppose the year 2000 is represented by 0 on a number line. What value would you use to represent the date A.D. 1250 in Exercise 28?

Multiple-Choice Practice

Test Tip Work as quickly as you can through easier sections.

1. Which list of integers is ordered from least to greatest?

Ⓐ 1, −4, 5, −7, −9

Ⓑ −4, −7, −9, 5, 1

Ⓒ −9, −7, −4, 1, 5

Ⓓ −9, −7, 5, −4, 1

2. Which statement is *false*?

Ⓕ The absolute value of 2 is 2.

Ⓖ The opposite of 0 is 0.

Ⓗ The absolute value of 7 is −7.

Ⓙ The opposite of −5 is 5.

3. Which expression has a value of −3?

Ⓐ $9 + (-6)$ Ⓑ $-9 + 6$

Ⓒ $-6 + 9$ Ⓓ $-6 + (-9)$

4. Your score in a golf tournament after 17 holes is −3 (3 under par). On the 18th (last) hole, you score 2 under par. What is your final score?

Ⓕ −6 Ⓖ −5

Ⓗ −1 Ⓙ +1

5. At 5 P.M. the temperature was −4°F. At 10 P.M. the temperature was −21°F. How many degrees did the temperature drop?

Ⓐ 15°F Ⓑ 17°F

Ⓒ 23°F Ⓓ 25°F

6. Evaluate the expression $-3 - y$ when $y = -4$.

Ⓕ −7 Ⓖ −1

Ⓗ 1 Ⓙ 7

7. $-5 \cdot (-8) =$ **?**

Ⓐ −40 Ⓑ −13

Ⓒ 40 Ⓓ Not here

8. Which statement is *true*?

Ⓕ $3 \cdot (-6) = -24$

Ⓖ $-2 \cdot (-9) = -18$

Ⓗ $6 \cdot (-4) = -24$

Ⓙ $-4 \cdot 8 = 32$

9. Which expression has a value of −6?

Ⓐ $48 \div (-6)$ Ⓑ $\frac{54}{-9}$

Ⓒ $\frac{56}{-8}$ Ⓓ $-36 \div (-6)$

10. What is the average of the numbers 9, −14, −10, 3, −2, and −16?

Ⓕ −9 Ⓖ −6

Ⓗ −5 Ⓙ 5

11. Which decimal is between $-2\frac{5}{8}$ and $-\frac{9}{4}$?

Ⓐ 2.375 Ⓑ −1.75

Ⓒ −2.125 Ⓓ −2.375

Brain games

▶ Solve problems that use positive and negative integers. (NS 2.3)

Integer Match-up

Materials

- **40 pennies**
- **1 "heads" spinner and 1 "tails" spinner, labeled 1–6**

Directions

Object of the Game

In this game, "heads" represent positive numbers, and "tails" represent negative numbers. The winner of the game is the player with the fewest pennies after five rounds of play.

How to Play

STEP 1 All pennies are placed between the players in the "bank." In the first round, you spin the heads spinner and take the number of pennies shown, displaying them as heads. Then spin the tails spinner and take the number of pennies shown, displaying them as tails. Then match pairs of heads (+1) and tails (−1), and return them to the bank.

Record your results in a table like the one below, which shows a turn where a player got 3 heads and 5 tails.

Round	Heads (+)	Tails (−)	Outcome
1	+3	−5	−2
2		−2*	

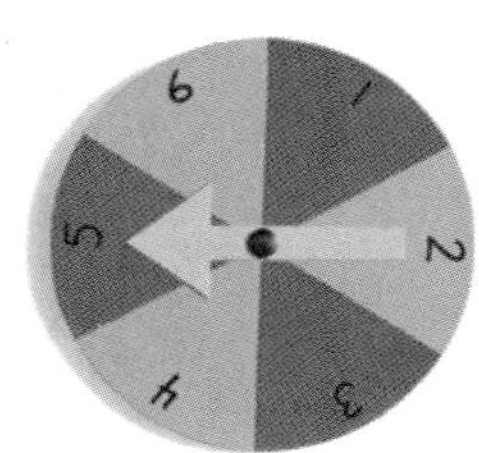

*Remaining from first round

STEP 2 Players take turns. In rounds 2–5, you may spin only one spinner of your choice, again matching heads and tails as in round 1. At the end of round 5, the player with the fewest pennies wins.

Brain Teaser

RIDDLE

After adding 2 to me,

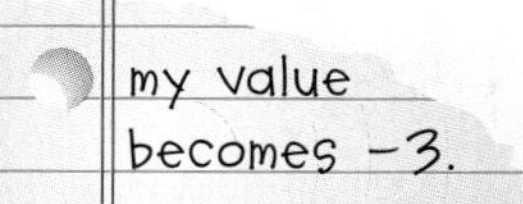

What number am I?

The basic skills you'll review on this page will help prepare you for the next chapter.

Reviewing the Basics

EXAMPLE 1 Translating Verbal Phrases

Write a numerical expression for the following verbal phrase.

Twice the sum of negative five and six

Solution

Because "twice" means to multiply by two and "sum" refers to addition, the numerical expression is $2(-5 + 6)$.

Student Help

▶ READING TIP
Translating verbal phrases is important for solving real-life problems. When you read a verbal phrase, be sure to identify and understand the key words that have mathematical meaning.

Try These

Write a numerical expression for the verbal phrase.

1. The quotient of fifty-five and eleven

2. The difference of ten and negative seven

3. The product of four and fourteen

4. Twice the quotient of twenty-five and five

5. Six minus the product of nine and four

6. Two times the sum of negative five and twelve

EXAMPLE 2 Evaluating a Variable Expression

Evaluate the expression $4a + 3$ when $a = -2$.

Solution

Substitute -2 for a, then evaluate.

$$\begin{aligned} 4a + 3 &= 4(\mathbf{-2}) + 3 \\ &= -8 + 3 \\ &= -5 \end{aligned}$$

Try These

Evaluate the expression for the given value of the variable.

7. $x + 4$ when $x = 5$

8. $8w$ when $w = -10$

9. $3d + 2$ when $d = -6$

10. $-4x - 4$ when $x = 9$

11. $-7 + 2k$ when $k = 2$

12. $x \div 9$ when $x = 27$

13. $\frac{24}{y}$ when $y = 5$

14. $8 - \frac{24}{p}$ when $p = -3$

Student Help

▶ MORE EXAMPLES

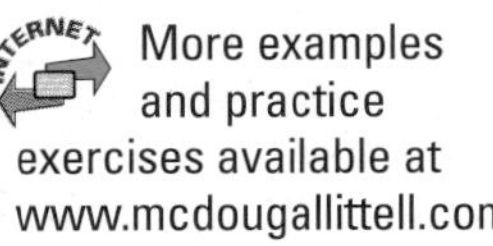

More examples and practice exercises available at www.mcdougallittell.com

Solving Equations

Why are equations important?

An equation states that two expressions are equal. You will write and solve equations to model problem situations and find unknown quantities, such as the cost of something or the time it takes something to happen. Solving equations will be useful later when you study proportions in geometry.

Equations are used to solve problems in many careers, including banking (page 215) and police work (page 232). For example, bankers use equations when calculating the interest earned by a savings account or when dealing with foreign money.

Meeting the California Standards

The skills you'll develop in this chapter will help you meet state standards and prepare for standardized tests. In this chapter you'll:

- **Write and evaluate an algebraic expression for a given situation.** LESSON 5.1
- **Solve problems involving addition, subtraction, multiplication, and division.** LESSONS 5.1, 5.2
- **Write and solve one-step linear equations in one variable.** LESSONS 5.2–5.6
- **Develop generalizations of strategies and apply them to new situations.** LESSON 5.7

Career Link **BANKER** A banker solves equations when:

- determining the interest due on a loan.
- calculating income from bank fees.
- dealing with foreign money.

EXERCISES

The table at the right shows the exchange rates for several international currencies. For example, you can get about 1.95 marks for 1 U.S. dollar ($1 U.S.)

EXCHANGE RATES

Country	Currency	Rate (per $1 U.S.)
Germany	Mark	1.9480
European Monetary Union	Euro	0.9952
Japan	Yen	102.4000

1. How many marks can you get for $100 U.S.?

2. How many euros can you get for $100 U.S.?

3. How many yen can you get for $100 U.S.?

In Lesson 5.6, you will write and solve an equation to find how many U.S. dollars you can get for 100 marks.

Chapter 5 Getting Ready

PREVIEW What's the chapter about?

- **Writing expressions** and **equations**
- **Solving** one-step and two-step **equations**

WORDS TO KNOW

- **equation,** *p. 221*
- **solution of an equation,** *p. 221*
- **solving an equation,** *p. 221*
- **inverse operations,** *p. 250*

PREPARE Chapter Readiness Quiz

Take this quick quiz. If you are unsure of an answer, look back at the reference pages for help.

VOCABULARY CHECK *(refer to pp. 8, 73)*

1. Which of the following is an example of a variable expression?

Ⓐ 8 Ⓑ $x + 4$ Ⓒ $x + 4 = 2$ Ⓓ $8 \div 4 \times 2$

2. Which fraction is in simplest form?

Ⓕ $\frac{2}{7}$ Ⓖ $\frac{6}{9}$ Ⓗ $\frac{21}{27}$ Ⓙ $1\frac{5}{15}$

SKILL CHECK *(refer to pp. 44, 126, 188)*

3. $4.995 \div 1.85 =$ __?__

Ⓐ 270 Ⓑ 2.7 Ⓒ 0.27 Ⓓ 0.027

4. $\frac{3}{10} \times \frac{12}{7} =$ __?__

Ⓕ 2 Ⓖ $\frac{15}{17}$ Ⓗ $\frac{18}{35}$ Ⓙ $\frac{1}{3}$

5. Which product is equal to 24?

Ⓐ $6(-4)$ Ⓑ $(-12)(2)$ Ⓒ $(-3)(-8)$ Ⓓ $(-1)(24)$

STUDY TIP Make a Plan

Writing a plan to solve an equation before you actually solve it will help you to organize your thoughts.

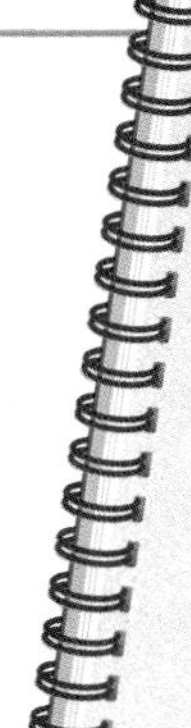

To solve the equation $x + 3 = 5$, I will:

1. *Subtract 3 from each side.*
2. *Simplify.*
3. *Check my solution.*

5.1 Writing Expressions

In this lesson you'll:

- Write an algebraic expression for a given situation. (AF 1.2)
- Solve problems involving addition, subtraction, multiplication, and division. (NS 2.0)

Goal 1 Translating Verbal Phrases

To use algebra in solving real-life problems, you need to translate words, phrases, and sentences into mathematical symbols. To do this, it helps to look for words that indicate operations.

EXAMPLE 1 Translating Addition Phrases

Verbal phrase	Variable expression
a. Ten more than a number	$x + 10$
b. The sum of -8 and a number	$-8 + y$
c. A number plus 3	$n + 3$

EXAMPLE 2 Translating Subtraction Phrases

Verbal phrase	Variable expression
a. Five minus a number	$5 - x$
b. The difference of 3 and a number	$3 - n$
c. Nine less than a number	$y - 9$

EXAMPLE 3 Translating Multiplication Phrases

Verbal phrase	Variable expression
a. Five times a number	$5y$
b. The product of 7 and a number	$7x$
c. A number multiplied by -2	$-2m$

Student Help

READING TIP Remember that subtraction and division are not commutative. The order in which you write the numbers and variables changes the meaning of the variable expression.

EXAMPLE 4 Translating Division Phrases

Verbal phrase	Variable expression
a. The quotient of a number and 6	$\frac{x}{6}$
b. Five divided by a number	$\frac{5}{n}$

Goal 2 TRANSLATING REAL-LIFE PHRASES

When you are modeling a real-life situation, use the following three steps.

Write a verbal model. → Assign labels to the model. → Write an algebraic model.

EXAMPLE 5 Writing an Expression

FITNESS You join a health club that has a membership fee and a court fee as shown at the right.

Write an expression for your total monthly cost.

HEALTH CLUB
JOIN TODAY!
Membership Fee
ONLY
$25.00 per month
Court Fee
$5.00 per use

Solution

VERBAL MODEL Membership fee + Court fee · Number of times you use a court

LABELS

Membership fee = **25** (dollars)

Court fee = **5** (dollars per court use)

Number of times you use a court = n (court uses)

ALGEBRAIC MODEL $25 + 5n$

Student Help

▶ **MORE EXAMPLES**

INTERNET More examples are available at www.mcdougallittell.com

EXAMPLE 6 Evaluating an Expression

Evaluate the expression in Example 5 when $n = 0, 1, 2, \ldots, 6$.

Solution

Substitute each value into the expression and simplify. For example, when $n = 0$, the value of the expression is $25 + 5n = 25 + 5(0) = 25$.

Organize your results in a table.

n	0	1	2	3	4	5	6
$25 + 5n$	25	30	35	40	45	50	55

Notice that your monthly cost begins at \$25. Each time n increases by 1, your monthly cost increases by \$5.

5.1 Exercises

Guided Practice

1. Complete the statement: The phrase *decreased by* represents the operation of __?__.

Write a variable expression for the verbal phrase.

2. Six more than y **3.** Five times a **4.** Two less than q

5. The sum of x and 1 **6.** d divided by 7 **7.** Nine minus n

In Exercises 8–13, write a verbal phrase for the variable expression.

8. $10t$ **9.** $n + 3.2$ **10.** $x - 6$

11. $\frac{8}{m}$ **12.** $-12 + b$ **13.** $\frac{y}{20}$

14. WRITING Explain how the expressions $6 - x$ and $x - 6$ are different.

15. TEMPERATURE The record high and low temperatures for Hawaii are 100°F and 12°F, respectively. If T represents today's temperature at Waikiki, write expressions for the number of degrees at Waikiki above Hawaii's record low and below Hawaii's record high.

Practice and Problem Solving

Student Help

▶ MORE PRACTICE Extra practice to help you master skills is on page 574.

Write a variable expression for the verbal phrase.

16. The product of six and a number **17.** A number increased by eight

18. The quotient of ten and a number **19.** A number divided by twelve

20. Twenty less than a number **21.** Negative four times a number

22. The difference of a number and negative two

23. Twice the sum of a number and negative seven

MATHEMATICAL REASONING Complete the statement with *add, subtract, multiply,* or *divide*. Explain your choice of operation.

24. A truck traveled 65 miles per hour for a number of hours. To find the number of miles traveled you __?__.

25. Your regular paycheck is increased by \$65 for working overtime. To find the total amount of your paycheck you __?__.

26. Sixty-five fewer people came than the number expected. To find the number of people who came you __?__.

27. Your grandmother is 5 years younger than her brother. To find your grandmother's age you __?__.

Link to Science

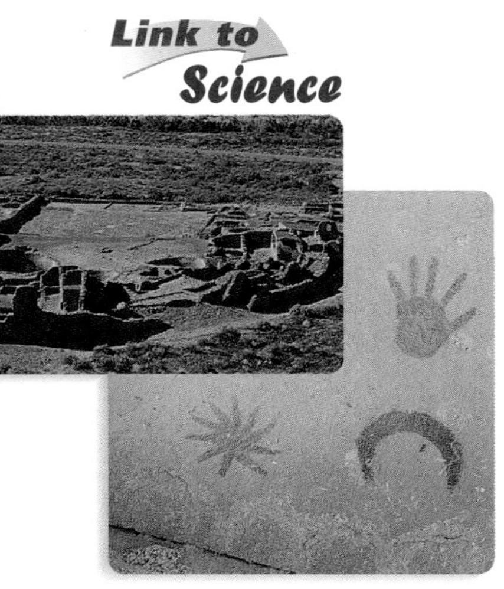

ANCIENT ASTRONOMERS
The symbols shown above were carved by the Anasazi Indians of Chaco Canyon (in present-day New Mexico). Scientists believe that the star symbol represents a supernova seen in A.D. 1054.

More about supernovas available at www.mcdougallittell.com

Write two different verbal phrases for the variable expression.

28. $v + 8$ **29.** $9k$ **30.** $p - 15$ **31.** $\frac{100}{x}$

In Exercises 32–37, evaluate the variable expression when $x = 1, 2, 3, 4, 5,$ and 6. Organize your results in a table.

32. $3x - 1$ **33.** $7 + 4x$ **34.** $4 + 5x$

35. $33 - 2x$ **36.** $\frac{x}{3}$ **37.** $\frac{3x}{4}$

38. ***Science Link*** A supernova is the explosion of a large star. Burning carbon at the star's center creates a shock wave that travels outward at about 30,000 kilometers per second. Write an expression that gives the distance traveled by the shock wave in t seconds. Then copy and complete the table for the given values of t.

Time t (in seconds)	1	2	3	4	5	6	7
Distance (in kilometers)	?	?	?	?	?	?	?

RECREATION In Exercises 39–42, use the following information. A community center charges a monthly fee of \$5, plus \$3 each time you use the swimming pool.

39. Write an expression for the total cost of swimming n times a month.

40. Evaluate the expression in Exercise 39 when $n = 0, 1, 2, \ldots, 8$. Organize your results in a table.

41. If you are willing to spend \$20 a month at the community center, up to how many times a month can you go swimming?

42. **MATHEMATICAL REASONING** Can you spend exactly \$40 a month at the community center? For \$40, up to how many times a month can you go swimming? Explain how you found your answer.

43. **CHALLENGE** Is the verbal phrase *9 times the sum of a number and 3* equivalent to *the sum of 27 and the product of a number and 9*? Use variable expressions to justify your answer.

Multiple-Choice Practice

44. Which variable expression represents the verbal phrase *the difference of a number and negative thirteen*?

(A) $b - (-13)$ (B) $-13 - b$ (C) $b - 13$ (D) $13 - b$

45. Which verbal phrase best describes the variable expression $6 - n$?

(F) The number of eggs in 6 cartons (G) n fewer eggs than 6

(H) n more eggs than 6 (J) 6 fewer than n eggs

5.2 Writing Equations

California Standards

In this lesson you'll:

- Write and solve one-step linear equations in one variable. (AF 1.1)
- Solve problems involving addition, subtraction, multiplication, and division. (NS 2.0)

Goal 1 Solving Equations Using Mental Math

An **equation** is a mathematical statement that uses an equal sign to separate two equal expressions.

Expression → $x + 5$; Equal sign → $=$; Expression → 7

$$x + 5 = 7$$

A **solution of an equation** involving one variable is a value of the variable that makes the equation true. For instance, 2 is a solution of $x + 5 = 7$ because

$$2 + 5 = 7$$

is a true statement. Finding all the solutions of an equation is called **solving the equation**.

Some equations are simple enough to solve using mental math. After you find a solution, you should check the solution by substituting it back into the original equation.

Student Help

Study Tip
An equation has two sides: a left side and a right side. The sides are separated by an equal sign.

Left side		Right side
$x + 5$	$=$	7

Example 1 Solving Equations Using Mental Math

Solve the equation using mental math.

a. $4 + y = 16$ **b.** $n - 3 = 6$ **c.** $3x = 15$ **d.** $\frac{n}{7} = 3$

Solution

It helps to think of the equation as a question.

Equation	Verbal question	Solution	Check
a. $4 + y = 16$	4 plus what number equals 16?	12	$4 + 12 = 16$
b. $n - 3 = 6$	Subtracting 3 from what number equals 6?	9	$9 - 3 = 6$
c. $3x = 15$	3 times what number equals 15?	5	$3 \cdot 5 = 15$
d. $\frac{n}{7} = 3$	What number divided by 7 equals 3?	21	$21 \div 7 = 3$

Goal 2 WRITING EQUATIONS

A phrase does not usually contain a verb, but a sentence must contain a verb. In Lesson 5.1 you learned that many phrases can be translated into variable expressions. You will now learn to translate sentences into algebraic equations. Here are examples of an expression and an equation.

Student Help

▶ **READING TIP**
You *evaluate* expressions, but you *solve* equations. For instance, the value of $5x$ when $x = 4$ is 20; the solution of $5x = 30$ is 6.

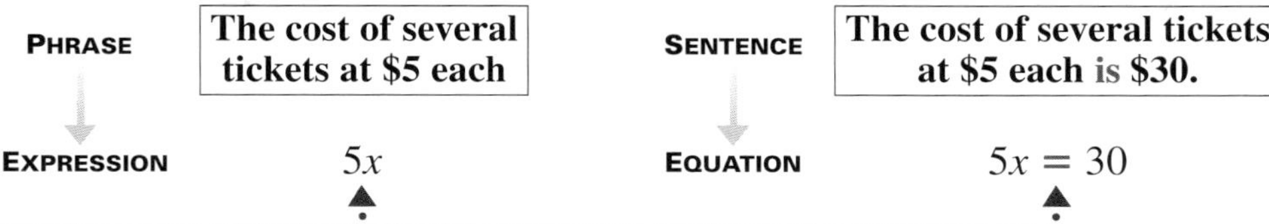

PHRASE
The cost of several tickets at $5 each
EXPRESSION
5x
SENTENCE
The cost of several tickets at $5 each is $30.
EQUATION
5x = 30

Note that the verb "is" in the sentence translates as "=" in the equation.

EXAMPLE 2 Translating Sentences

Verbal sentence	Algebraic equation
a. The sum of a number and 8 is 17.	$n + 8 = 17$
b. Five less than a number is 9.	$x - 5 = 9$
c. Fourteen equals 8 times a number.	$14 = 8m$
d. The quotient of 12 and a number is 4.	$\frac{12}{y} = 4$

EXAMPLE 3 Writing and Solving an Equation

YARD SALE You and three friends have a table at your family's yard sale. The total income is divided by 4, and each person gets $25. Write an equation to find the total income. Then solve the equation.

Solution

VERBAL MODEL
Total income ÷ **Number of people** = **Share for each person**

LABELS
Total income = T (dollars)
Number of people = **4** (people)
Share for each person = **25** (dollars per person)

ALGEBRAIC MODEL
$$\frac{T}{4} = 25$$

You need to find a number that can be divided by 4 to get 25. Using mental math, you determine that the solution is 100.

ANSWER ▶ The total income is $100.

CHECK ✓ $100 \div 4 = 25$ The solution is correct.

5.2 Exercises

Guided Practice

1. WRITING In your own words, describe what it means to solve an equation. Give an example.

Check whether the given number is a solution of the equation. If it is not, find the solution.

2. $-4y = -36; -9$ **3.** $x + 7 = -12; 5$ **4.** $\frac{16}{n} = 8; 2$

In Exercises 5–8, match the equation with its solution.

A. 14 **B.** 12 **C.** 24 **D.** 20

5. $21 - n = 1$ **6.** $n + 8 = 22$ **7.** $3n = 36$ **8.** $\frac{n}{4} = 6$

9. COMPACT DISCS You buy 4 equally priced CDs for a total of \$60. Use the verbal model below. Assign labels and write an equation to represent the problem. Then solve the equation to find the cost of each CD.

Number of CDs • Cost of a CD = Total cost

Practice and Problem Solving

Student Help

MORE PRACTICE
Extra practice to help you master skills is on page 574.

Check whether the given number is a solution of the equation. If it is not, find the solution.

10. $p + 11 = 14; 25$ **11.** $16 - x = 8; 12$

12. $7 + t = 40; 33$ **13.** $-9z = -54; 6$

14. $\frac{m}{2} = 13; 36$ **15.** $\frac{21}{y} = 7; 39$

16. $a - 5 = -10; 15$ **17.** $\frac{6}{x} = -6; -1$

18. $2.5 + n = 3.2; 0.7$ **19.** $-12 - b = -19; -7$

Use mental math to solve the equation. Then check your solution.

20. $18 + m = 25$ **21.** $x + 36 = 42$ **22.** $18 - s = 11$

23. $p - 11 = 12$ **24.** $9y = 54$ **25.** $\frac{40}{b} = 10$

26. $15n = 45$ **27.** $\frac{x}{5} = 7$ **28.** $\frac{r}{4} = 8$

29. $p - 17 = 18$ **30.** $n + 12 = 21$ **31.** $2m = 28$

Link to History

HOMESTEAD ACT The Homestead Act stated that any person over the age of 21 who was the head of a family could get 160 acres of free land by living on the land and improving it for 5 years.

Match the sentence with its equation.

A. $x - 44 = 4$ **B.** $4x = 44$ **C.** $44 - x = 4$ **D.** $x + 4 = 44$

32. The product of 4 and a number is 44.

33. A number subtracted from 44 equals 4.

34. 4 more than a number equals 44.

35. 44 less than a number is 4.

In Exercises 36–41, write an algebraic equation for the sentence. Then solve the equation.

36. A number added to 15 equals 30.

37. A number divided by 18 is 2.

38. The sum of 2 and a number equals 10.

39. A number decreased by 5 is 10.

40. The quotient of a number and 2 equals 7.

41. 35 equals 5 times a number.

42. **History Link** In the Homestead Act of 1862, each square mile of homestead land was divided equally among 4 settlers. The amount each settler received was called a *quarter* and it contained 160 acres. Use the verbal model below. Assign labels and write an equation. Then solve the equation to find the number of acres in a square mile.

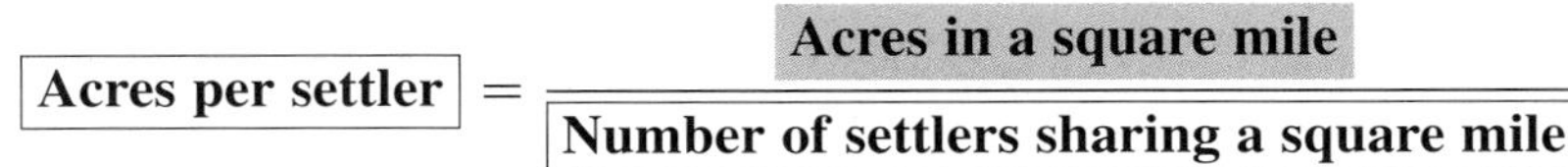

In Exercises 43–46, tell what operation you would use to write an equation for the problem. Explain your choice. Then write and solve an equation.

Student Help

▶ HOMEWORK HELP

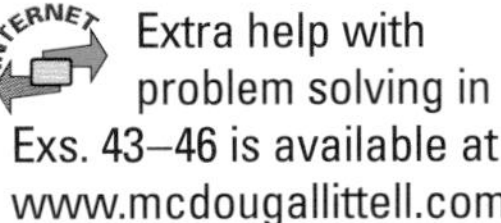

Extra help with problem solving in Exs. 43–46 is available at www.mcdougallittell.com

43. DRIVING RANGE You and three friends share the cost of hitting a bucket of golf balls at a driving range. You each pay \$1.50. What is the cost of hitting a bucket of golf balls?

44. ELEVATOR You enter an elevator and go up 17 floors to reach the 43rd floor of a building. On what floor did you enter the elevator?

45. MAKING A PURCHASE You give a cashier \$60 to pay for a pair of shoes. The cashier gives you \$8 in change. Find the cost of the shoes.

46. SPLITTING A BILL You and two of your friends go out for lunch. You share the cost of the meal evenly. The lunch (including tax and tip) costs \$19.50. Find each person's share.

47. MATHEMATICAL REASONING Explain why the equations $x + 3 = 5$ and $3 + x = 5$ have the same solution, but the equations $x - 3 = 5$ and $3 - x = 5$ do not.

48. **CHALLENGE** Use mental math to solve the equation $3x - 1 = 8$. Describe how you found a solution.

Multiple-Choice Practice

49. What is the solution of the equation $\frac{64}{t} = 4$?

Ⓐ 12 Ⓑ 14 Ⓒ 16 Ⓓ Not here

50. Which equation represents the following sentence?

7 added to a number is 30.

Ⓕ $m + 7 = 30$ Ⓖ $7 - d = 30$

Ⓗ $30 + p = 7$ Ⓙ $r - 7 = 30$

Test Tip ⒶⒷⒸⒹ

▶ Make sure you read directions carefully. Sometimes a test question will ask for the answer that is *not* correct, as in Exercise 51.

51. Which equation does *not* represent the perimeter of the figure shown?

Ⓐ $P = 21 + 10 + n$

Ⓑ $P = n + 31$

Ⓒ $P = n(7 + 10 + 14)$

Ⓓ $P = 7 + 10 + 14 + n$

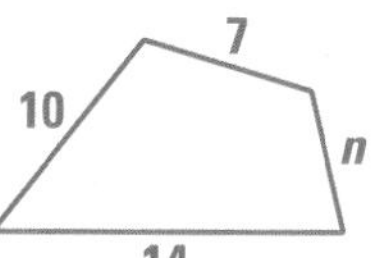

Mixed Review

BOY SCOUTS In Exercises 52 and 53, use the table showing the number of merit badges earned by boys in the Boy Scouts from 1911 to 1996. *(1.7)*

Type of badge	Badges earned (in millions)
First aid	5.32
Swimming	4.83
Cooking	3.70
Camping	3.49

▶ Source: Boy Scouts of America

52. Find the total number of cooking and camping badges earned from 1911 to 1996.

53. How many more first aid badges were earned than swimming badges?

Use a factor tree to write the prime factorization of the number. *(2.1)*

54. 60 55. 105 56. 321 57. 225

58. 96 59. 202 60. 88 61. 306

Evaluate. Simplify if possible. *(3.3)*

62. $4\frac{1}{4} + 3\frac{1}{2}$ 63. $2\frac{2}{3} + 3\frac{5}{6}$ 64. $7\frac{1}{5} - 5\frac{3}{5}$ 65. $1\frac{2}{7} - \frac{3}{4}$

Find the difference without using a number line. *(4.4)*

66. $30 - (-75)$ 67. $-25 - (-25)$ 68. $-80 - 80$ 69. $9 - (-9)$

DEVELOPING CONCEPTS
Addition Equations

For use with Lesson 5.3

California Standards

- Write and solve one-step addition equations in one variable. (AF 1.1)
- Use models to explain mathematical reasoning. (MR 2.4)

MATERIALS

- Algebra tiles

Algebra tiles can be used to solve equations. The square tile represents the number 1. The rectangular tile represents the variable x.

1 x

The 1-tiles above model the equation 5 = 5.

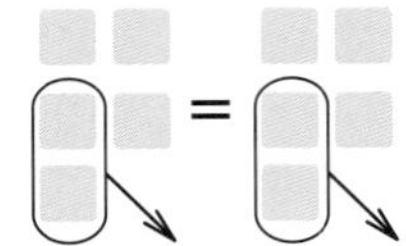

Removing two 1-tiles from each side of the equation produces a new equation.

The new equation is 3 = 3.

SAMPLE 1 Using Algebra Tiles to Solve an Equation

You can use algebra tiles to solve the equation $x + 2 = 8$.

Here's How

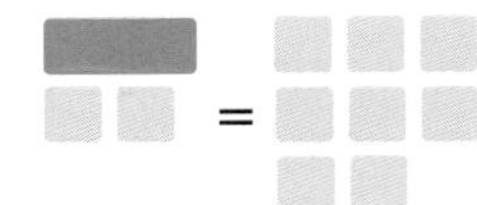

❶ Model the equation with algebra tiles.

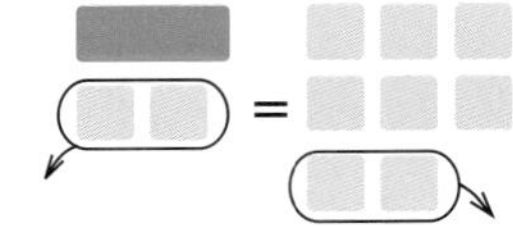

❷ Isolate the x-tile by removing two 1-tiles from each side of the equation.

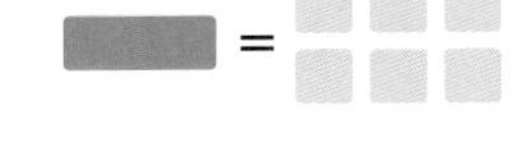

❸ The equation is now $x = 6$. The solution is 6.

Try These

Write the equation that is modeled with algebra tiles. Then use algebra tiles to solve the equation. Make a sketch of your steps.

1. 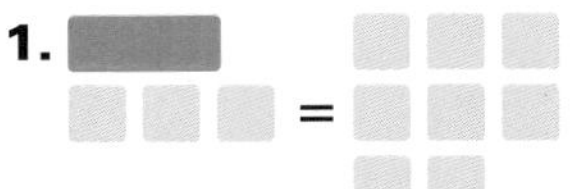

2. 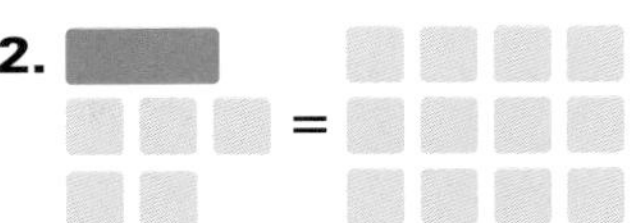

3. **MATHEMATICAL REASONING** In Exercises 1 and 2, how do you know how many 1-tiles to remove from each side of the equation?

Use algebra tiles to solve the equation. Make a sketch of your steps.

4. $x + 6 = 10$ **5.** $x + 7 = 9$ **6.** $x + 3 = 12$ **7.** $7 = x + 3$

Inverse operations are operations that "undo" each other, such as addition and subtraction. For example, if you start with the number 7 and add 3, you can get back to the number 7 by subtracting 3. The box model below illustrates this example.

7	7 $\xrightarrow{+3}$ 10	7 $\xleftarrow[-3]{}$ 10
Start with 7.	**Add 3 to 7 to get 10. The box model represents the equation 7 + 3 = 10.**	**To undo adding 3, subtract 3. The box model represents the equation 7 = 10 − 3.**

Box models can also be used to solve equations.

SAMPLE 2 Using a Box Model to Solve an Equation

You can use a box model to solve the equation $x + 5 = 8$.

Here's How

x $\xrightarrow{+5}$ 8	x $\xleftarrow[-5]{}$ 8	3 $\xleftarrow[-5]{}$ 8
❶ Draw a box model to represent the equation $x + 5 = 8$.	❷ Subtract 5 from 8 to undo adding 5. The box model now represents the equation $x = 8 - 5$.	❸ Because $8 - 5 = 3$, $x = 3$. The solution is 3.

Try These

8. MATHEMATICAL REASONING Does the box model at the right represent $x - 6 = 11$ or $x = 11 - 6$? Explain how the direction of the arrow gives you this information.

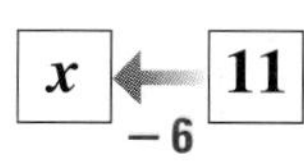

Write the equation represented by the box model.

9. 3 $\xrightarrow{+1}$ 4 **10.** a $\xrightarrow{+3}$ 12 **11.** y $\xleftarrow[-11]{}$ 15

Use a box model to solve the equation.

12. $x + 6 = 9$ **13.** $y + 7 = 13$ **14.** $t + 4 = 10$ **15.** $a + 2 = 14$

5.3 Solving Addition Equations

California Standards

In this lesson you'll:

- Write and solve one-step addition equations in one variable. (AF 1.1)

Goal 1 SOLVING ADDITION EQUATIONS

An addition equation is an equation involving the sum of a number and a variable. As you saw in Developing Concepts 5.3, page 226, you can solve an addition equation by subtracting the same number from each side of the equation so that the variable is isolated on one side of the equation.

Student Help

STUDY TIP
Although many of the equations in Lessons 5.3–5.6 can be solved using mental math, make sure you write out your steps. This will help you solve more difficult equations later. Mental math can be used as a check.

SUBTRACTION PROPERTY OF EQUALITY

In Words Subtracting the same number from each side of an equation produces a new equation having the same solution as the original.

In Algebra $x + a = b \longrightarrow x + a - a = b - a$

EXAMPLE 1 Solving Addition Equations

Solve the equation.

a. $n + 8 = -2$

b. $4 = x + 9$

Solution

a. Your goal is to isolate the variable n.

$n + 8 = -2$	Write original equation.
$\underline{-8} \quad \underline{-8}$	Subtraction property: subtract 8 from each side.
$n = -10$	Simplify. *n* is by itself.

ANSWER ▶ The solution is -10. Check this as follows.

CHECK ✓ Substitute for the variable in the original equation.

$n + 8 = -2$	Write original equation.
$-10 + 8 \stackrel{?}{=} -2$	Substitute −10 for *n*.
$-2 = -2$ ✓	Both sides are the same.

Student Help

READING TIP
The symbol $\stackrel{?}{=}$ in the check means "Is this statement true?"

b. Your goal is to isolate the variable x.

$4 = x + 9$	Write original equation.
$\underline{-9} \quad \underline{-9}$	Subtraction property: subtract 9 from each side.
$-5 = x$	Simplify. *x* is by itself.

ANSWER ▶ The solution is -5. Check this in the original equation.

Goal 2 WRITING ADDITION EQUATIONS

Student Help

▶ **MORE EXAMPLES**
INTERNET More examples are available at www.mcdougallittell.com

EXAMPLE 2 Writing and Solving an Addition Equation

FOOTBALL A friend keeps a record of your football team's gains and losses on each play of a game. The record is shown in the table below, but part of it is missing. Find the missing information by writing and solving an equation.

PLAY	PLAY GAIN or LOSS	OVERALL GAIN or LOSS
1st Down	Gain of 2 yards	Gain of 2 yards
2nd Down	Loss of 5 yards	Loss of 3 yards
3rd Down	Gain of 7 yards	Gain of 4 yards
4th Down	?	Loss of 7 yards

Solution

VERBAL MODEL

Yards on 4th down + **Overall yards after 3 downs** = **Overall yards after 4 downs**

LABELS

Yards on 4th down = x (yards)

Overall yards after 3 downs = **4** (yards)

Overall yards after 4 downs = **−7** (yards)

ALGEBRAIC MODEL

$x + 4 = -7$ Write equation.

$\quad -4 \quad -4$ Subtract 4 from each side.

$x = -11$ Simplify. x is by itself.

ANSWER ▶ The solution is −11. So, your team loses 11 yards on its 4th down.

Student Help

▶ **SKILLS REVIEW**
For help with checking whether a solution seems reasonable, see page 553.

EXAMPLE 3 Checking a Solution with a Diagram

You can use a number line to check the solution in Example 2. Start at 0. Move to the right for each gain and move left for each loss.

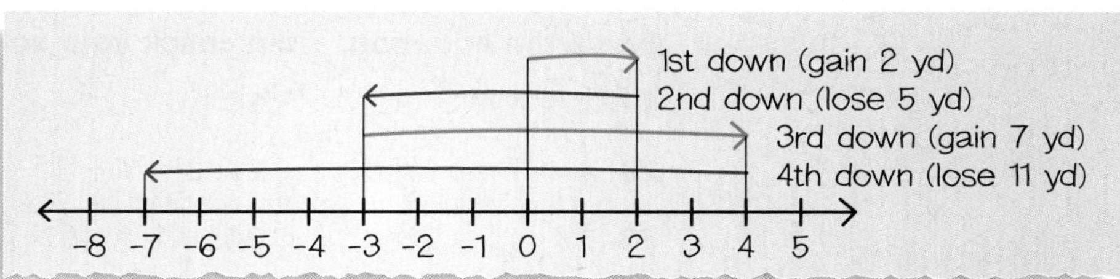

At the end of 4 downs, your team's overall loss is 7 yards. So, a loss of 11 yards on the 4th down is correct.

5.3 Exercises

Guided Practice

Describe each step used to solve the equation.

1.
$$\begin{array}{rcr} 12 + x & = & 8 \\ -12 & & -12 \\ \hline x & = & -4 \end{array}$$

2.
$$\begin{array}{rcr} -6 & = & y + 7 \\ -7 & & -7 \\ \hline -13 & = & y \end{array}$$

Tell which number is a solution of the equation.

3. $m + 1 = 1$ **A.** -2 **B.** 0 **C.** 2

4. $11 + t = 5$ **A.** -6 **B.** 16 **C.** 6

5. $-3 = p + 10$ **A.** 7 **B.** -7 **C.** -13

In Exercises 6–8, solve the equation. Then check your solution.

6. $5 + y = 4$ **7.** $3 + n = 6$ **8.** $a + 1 = 7$

9. Write an algebraic equation for the following sentence. Then solve the equation.

The sum of a number and 5 is -10.

10. **PERSONAL FINANCE** After you deposit a check for $65, the new balance of your account is $315. Write a verbal model, assign labels, and write an equation to represent the situation. Then solve the equation to find the amount that was in your account before you made the deposit.

Practice and Problem Solving

Student Help

▶ **MORE PRACTICE**
Extra practice to help you master skills is on page 574.

Check whether the given number is a solution of the equation. If it is not, find the solution.

11. $z + 2 = -7; -9$ **12.** $-9 + a = -23; 14$ **13.** $5 = m + 11; 6$

14. $p + 6 = -1; -7$ **15.** $-\frac{3}{8} + t = \frac{1}{4}; \frac{5}{8}$ **16.** $n + 7.5 = 11; 2.5$

Solve the equation. Then check your solution.

17. $x + 8 = 3$ **18.** $10 + a = 2$ **19.** $6 + y = 14$

20. $n + 7 = -7$ **21.** $2 = t + 15$ **22.** $-12 = 11 + p$

23. $37 + k = 28$ **24.** $-4 = 46 + b$ **25.** $z + 16 = -23$

26. $x + 15 = -13$ **27.** $-7 + y = -5$ **28.** $3.4 + t = 10.5$

29. $c + 1.7 = 2.6$ **30.** $\frac{5}{12} = m + \frac{1}{12}$ **31.** $\frac{3}{10} + x = \frac{4}{5}$

Link to Science

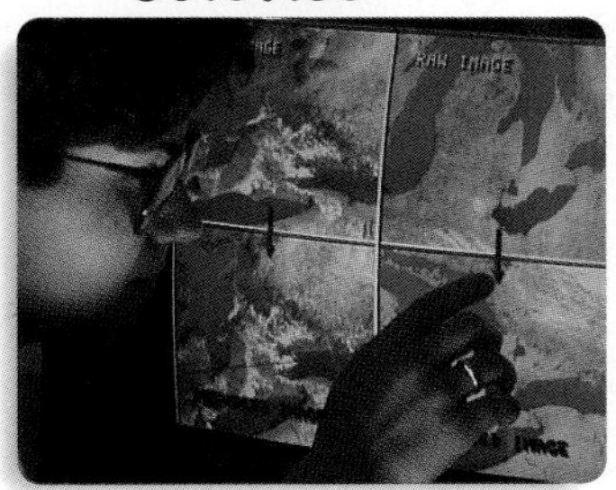

NATIONAL WEATHER SERVICE The National Weather Service gets temperature data from three kinds of sources: 123 forecast offices, 800 automated surface observing system stations, and 11,000 volunteer weather observers.

More about the National Weather Service available at www.mcdougallittell.com

Write an algebraic equation for the sentence. Then solve the equation.

32. The sum of a number and ten is ten.

33. The sum of fifteen and a number is negative fifteen.

34. Negative twenty is the sum of fourteen and a number.

35. Twenty-six is the sum of a number and seventeen.

36. A number added to four equals zero.

ERROR ANALYSIS **Describe and correct the error.**

37. 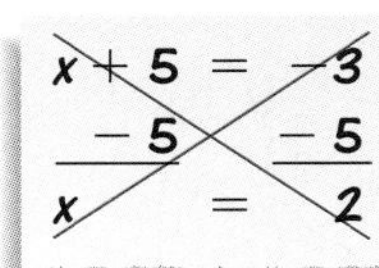

38. 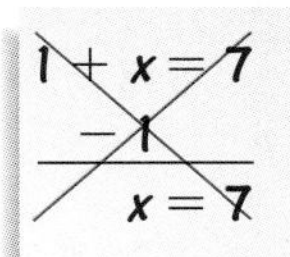

Write two different addition equations that have the given solution.

39. 4 **40.** -6 **41.** 9 **42.** $\frac{3}{4}$

Science Link **In Exercises 43 and 44, use the following information.** On January 22, 1943, in Spearfish, South Dakota, a strange temperature increase was recorded. At 7:30 A.M. the temperature was 24°F, and just two minutes later the temperature was 45°F.

43. Use the verbal model below. Assign labels and write an equation to represent the problem. Then solve the equation to find how many degrees the temperature rose.

Original temperature	+	Increase	=	New temperature

44. Use a number line to check your solution.

MUSIC **In Exercises 45 and 46, you want to buy a clarinet that costs \$224. You have saved \$172.**

45. Use the verbal model below. Assign labels and write an equation to represent the problem. Then solve the equation to find the amount you have left to save.

Amount saved	+	Amount left to save	=	Cost of clarinet

46. The clarinet goes on sale for \$199. Which of the addition equations below represents the amount the clarinet is discounted from the regular price? Explain your reasoning.

A. $x + 199 = 224$ **B.** $172 + x = 199$ **C.** $x + 224 = -199$

47. WRITING Describe a situation that can be modeled by the equation $x + 12 = 70$. Then solve the equation and relate the solution to the situation.

POLICE OFFICER Local police officers sometimes visit schools to educate students about safety. In 1996 there were about 583,000 local police officers employed in the United States.

More about police officers available at www.mcdougallittell.com

In Exercises 48–50, write a verbal model, assign labels, and write an equation to solve the problem. Check your answer.

48. FOOTBALL After a gain of 9 yards, you find that your team has gained 23 yards so far in the game. How many yards had your team gained before the 9 yard gain?

49. Science Link As temperature increases, ice melts to become water at its melting point of 32°F. Water then boils and becomes steam at its boiling point of 212°F. Find the minimum increase in temperature that it takes to turn ice to steam.

50. POLICE OFFICERS Police officers keep careful records of how their time is spent each day. During one 8 hour shift, an officer spent 1 hour directing traffic, $1\frac{1}{4}$ hours at an accident, and $3\frac{1}{2}$ hours writing tickets. Find the amount of time the officer spent on other duties.

EVENT PLANNING **In Exercises 51 and 52, use the following information.** You are buying supplies for your friend's surprise party. A package of balloons costs \$2.25, and a package of streamers costs \$5.60. You have a total of \$20 to spend, and you want to buy one package of streamers and as many packages of balloons as possible.

51. MATHEMATICAL REASONING What is the greatest number of packages of balloons that you can buy? Explain how you found your answer. Include any verbal or algebraic models you used.

52. Write and solve an equation to find the amount of money you will have left after buying the balloons and streamers.

CHALLENGE **Solve the equation.**

53. $\frac{3}{4} + x = -\frac{5}{6}$ **54.** $n + 9.86 = 2.99$ **55.** $-0.3 + y = -\frac{3}{5}$

Multiple-Choice Practice

56. What is the solution of the equation $-6 + c = 9$?

(A) -15 (B) -3 (C) 3 (D) Not here

57. Which equation does *not* have -2 as a solution?

(F) $x + 5 = 3$ (G) $x + (-2) = -4$

(H) $x + 5 = 7$ (J) $x + (-1) = -3$

58. Which equation *cannot* be used to find the missing side length of the triangle shown?

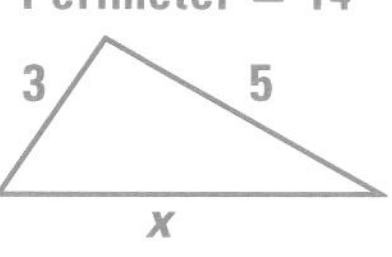

(A) $x + 3 + 5 = 14$ (B) $x + 14 = 8$

(C) $x + 8 = 14$ (D) $14 = 8 + x$

5.4 Solving Subtraction Equations

In this lesson you'll:

- Write and solve one-step subtraction equations in one variable. (AF 1.1)

Goal 1 SOLVING SUBTRACTION EQUATIONS

A subtraction equation is an equation involving a difference between a variable and a number. Just as you solved addition equations in Lesson 5.3 by subtracting, you can solve subtraction equations by adding. The goal is the same: to isolate the variable on one side of the equation.

ADDITION PROPERTY OF EQUALITY

In Words Adding the same number to each side of an equation produces a new equation having the same solution as the original.

In Algebra $x - a = b \longrightarrow x - a + a = b + a$

EXAMPLE 1 Solving Subtraction Equations

Solve the equation.

a. $n - 3 = -9$ **b.** $-5 = x - 8$

Solution

a. Your goal is to isolate the variable n.

$n - 3 = -9$	Write original equation.
$\underline{+3} \quad \underline{+3}$	Addition property: add 3 to each side.
$n = -6$	Simplify. n is by itself.

ANSWER ▸ The solution is -6. Check this as follows.

CHECK ✓ Substitute for the variable in the original equation.

$n - 3 = -9$	Write original equation.
$\mathbf{-6} - 3 \stackrel{?}{=} -9$	Substitute -6 for n.
$-9 = -9$ ✓	Both sides are the same.

b. Your goal is to isolate the variable x.

$-5 = x - 8$	Write original equation.
$\underline{+8} \quad \underline{+8}$	Addition property: add 8 to each side.
$3 = x$	Simplify. x is by itself.

ANSWER ▸ The solution is 3. Check this in the original equation.

Link to Science

BAY OF FUNDY TIDES
The Bay of Fundy in eastern Canada has the highest tides in the world. The photos above show the dramatic change in the bay's water level from low tide to high tide.

Goal 2 WRITING SUBTRACTION EQUATIONS

EXAMPLE 2 Writing a Subtraction Equation

BAY OF FUNDY At a pier in the Bay of Fundy, the difference between high tide and low tide is 53 feet 6 inches. The water level at the pier is 5 feet 9 inches high at low tide. Which equation can be used to find the water level at the pier at high tide?

A. $x - 5.75 = 53.5$ **B.** $5.75 - x = 53.5$ **C.** $53.5 - x = 5.75$

Solution

VERBAL MODEL: **Water level at high tide** − **Water level at low tide** = **Difference between tides**

LABELS:

Water level at high tide = x (feet)

Water level at low tide = **5.75** (feet)

Difference between tides = **53.5** (feet)

ALGEBRAIC MODEL: $x - 5.75 = 53.5$

ANSWER ▶ The equation in (**A**) models the situation.

Student Help

▶ **LOOK BACK**
For help with converting inches to feet in Example 2, see page 144.

EXAMPLE 3 Writing and Solving a Subtraction Equation

FUNDRAISING So far a school committee has raised \$317 for a dance performance. The chairperson announces that the committee has only \$243 left to raise. What is the total amount of money needed for the performance?

Solution

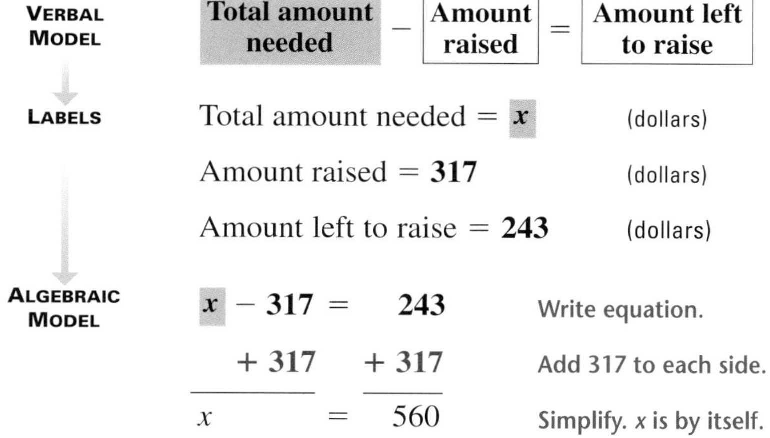

VERBAL MODEL: **Total amount needed** − **Amount raised** = **Amount left to raise**

LABELS:

Total amount needed = x (dollars)

Amount raised = **317** (dollars)

Amount left to raise = **243** (dollars)

ALGEBRAIC MODEL:

$x - 317 = 243$ Write equation.

$+317 \quad +317$ Add 317 to each side.

$x = 560$ Simplify. x is by itself.

ANSWER ▶ The total amount of money needed is \$560.

5.4 Exercises

Guided Practice

Tell whether you need to add or subtract to solve the equation. Explain your reasoning. Then solve the equation.

1. $t - 3 = 14$ **2.** $u + 5 = 33$ **3.** $-14 = s - 12$

In Exercises 4–7, match the equation with its solution.

A. 10 **B.** 2 **C.** -8 **D.** 8

4. $6 = n - 2$ **5.** $-10 = -2 + n$ **6.** $-5 + n = -3$ **7.** $n - 9 = 1$

8. Write an algebraic equation for the following sentence. Then solve the equation.

Fifteen less than a number is −12.

9. **TIDES** The water level fell $14\frac{3}{4}$ feet from high tide to low tide. The water level at a pier was $12\frac{1}{2}$ feet at low tide. Write a verbal model, assign labels, and write an equation to represent the situation. Then solve the equation to find the water level at the pier at high tide.

Practice and Problem Solving

Student Help

▶ **MORE PRACTICE** Extra practice to help you master skills is on page 575.

ERROR ANALYSIS **Describe and correct the error.**

10.

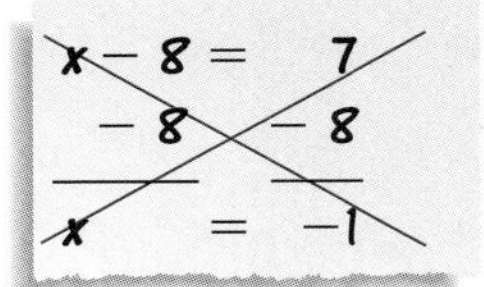

11.

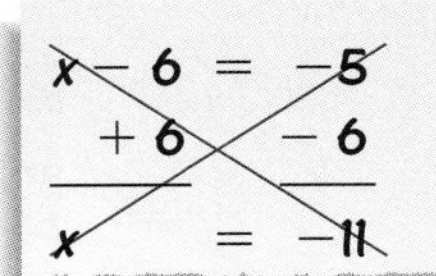

Solve the equation. Then check your solution.

12. $n - 5 = 16$ **13.** $t - 7 = 19$ **14.** $27 = p - 13$

15. $50 = x - 15$ **16.** $b - 14 = -2$ **17.** $s - 16 = -12$

18. $-3 = z - 18$ **19.** $-16 = y - 13$ **20.** $c - 6 = -20$

21. $z - 18.03 = -14$ **22.** $n - 9.32 = 16.2$ **23.** $2\frac{1}{6} = a - 1\frac{1}{3}$

Write an algebraic equation for the sentence. Then solve the equation.

24. The difference of a number and fifteen is negative fifteen.

25. Twenty-six is the sum of a number and forty.

26. Seven eighths is the difference of a number and one fourth.

Tell whether the equations have the same solution. Explain your reasoning.

27. $y - 13 = 10,\ 10 = y - 13$

28. $x - 7 = -4,\ 4 = x - 7$

29. $m - 4 = 5,\ m - 5 = 4$

30. $-17 + p = 12,\ 12 = p - 17$

31. $a - 8 = -8,\ a - 8 = 8$

32. $t - 15 = -5,\ -15 + t = -5$

In Exercises 33–36, write an addition equation and a subtraction equation that have the given solution.

33. -9 **34.** -16 **35.** 12 **36.** 0

37. **WEATHER** The greatest recorded temperature change within 24 hours occurred in Browning, Montana, on January 23–24, 1916. The temperature fell by 100°F to a final temperature of −56°F. Use the verbal model below. Assign labels and write an equation to represent the problem. Solve the equation to find the original temperature.

Original temperature	−	Amount the temperature dropped	=	Final temperature

Student Help

▶ VOCABULARY TIP
Earth's *axis* is an imaginary line through its center about which it rotates.

Science Link **In Exercises 38–41, use the following information.**
Earth's axis is tilted at an angle of 23.5°. As Earth revolves around the sun, the tilt of its axis stays the same, but Earth's distance from the sun changes. Earth is farthest from the sun in July. In January, when Earth is nearest the sun, it is about 3.1 million miles closer, at a distance of about 91.4 million miles.

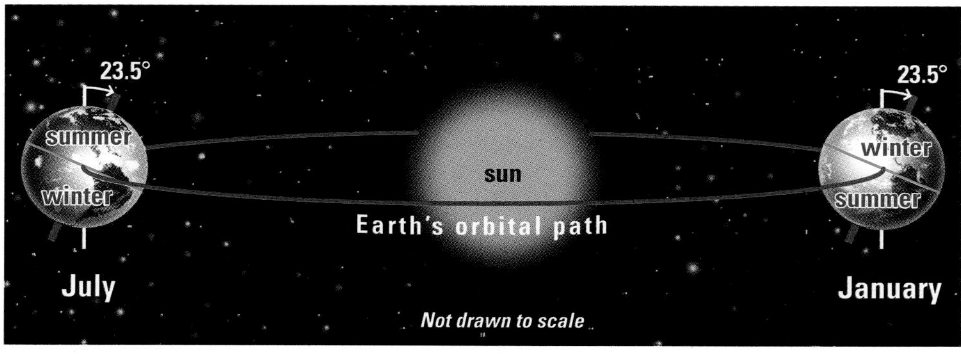

38. **MATHEMATICAL REASONING** To find Earth's maximum distance from the sun, what information given above do you need? What information is irrelevant?

39. Write a verbal model that can be used to find Earth's maximum distance from the sun.

40. Assign labels to your verbal model. Then write and solve an equation to find Earth's maximum distance from the sun.

41. **WRITING** Earth is farthest from the sun in July, yet this is when the Northern Hemisphere experiences summer. Why do you think this is so? Use the diagram to help explain your reasoning.

In Exercises 42 and 43, write a verbal model, assign labels, and write an equation to solve the problem.

42. **VIDEO GAMES** You purchase a video game that has a sale price of \$27. The sale price is \$9 off the original price. Find the original price.

43. **SALES TAX** You pay tax on the video game in Exercise 42. The total cost including tax is \$28.35. Find the amount of the tax.

CHALLENGE **Solve the equation.**

44. $x - \frac{5}{8} = -\frac{11}{12}$ **45.** $-8.3 = n - \frac{2}{5}$ **46.** $\frac{9}{10} = y - 3\frac{2}{7}$

Multiple-Choice Practice

Test Tip (A)(B)(C)(D)

▶ Try using mental math to estimate an answer in Exercise 47. If your estimate is one of the given choices, test that answer first.

47. What is the solution of the equation $p - (-3) = 7$?

(A) -10 (B) -4 (C) 4 (D) 10

48. Which equation has 6 as a solution?

(F) $12 - s = 18$ (G) $s - (-5) = 1$

(H) $s - 9 = -3$ (J) $-4 - s = 2$

49. On the radio you hear that the temperature has fallen 13°F in the last two hours. You look at a thermometer and see that it reads 25°F. Which equation could you use to find the temperature two hours ago?

(A) $T - 13 = 25$ (B) $T + 13 = 25$

(C) $T - (-13) = 25$ (D) $25 = 13 + T$

Mixed Review

Write the fraction in simplest form. *(2.4)*

50. $\frac{6}{54}$ **51.** $\frac{15}{30}$ **52.** $\frac{7}{35}$ **53.** $\frac{12}{60}$

Write the sum that is illustrated on the number line. Then find the sum. *(4.2)*

54.

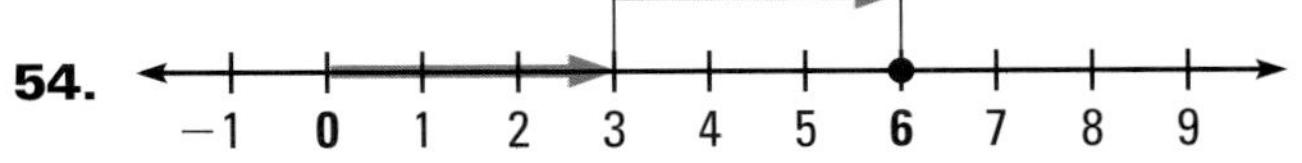

55.

−10 −9 −8 −7 −6 −5 −4 −3 −2 −1 0

56.

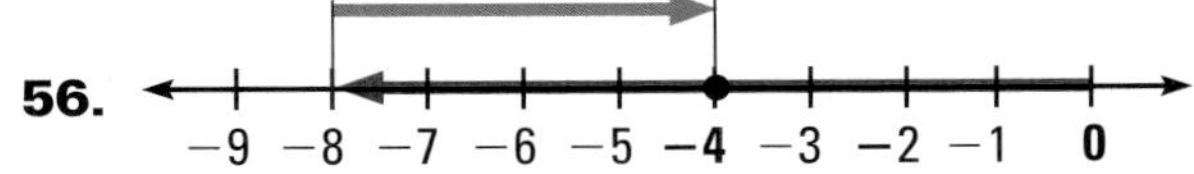

Chapter 5 Mid-Chapter Test

Take this test as you would take a test in class. The answers to the exercises are given in the back of the book.

Write a variable expression for the verbal phrase.

1. The sum of nine and a number

2. A number times eleven

3. The quotient of a number and three

4. Five less than a number

Evaluate the variable expression when $x = 1, 2, 3, 4, 5,$ and 6.

5. $3x + 8$

6. $100 - 5x$

7. $\frac{120}{x}$

8. $6x - 4$

Use mental math to solve the equation. Then check your solution.

9. $4 + b = 22$

10. $x - 15 = 34$

11. $3t = 39$

12. $8n = 88$

13. $\frac{54}{y} = 6$

14. $m + 6 = 15$

15. $y - 13 = 15$

16. $\frac{x}{2} = 48$

Write an algebraic equation for the sentence. Then solve the equation.

17. A number added to 44 equals 98.

18. The sum of a number and 12 is 180.

19. 125 minus a number is 65.

20. 54 divided by a number equals 3.

Solve the equation. Then check your solution.

21. $x + 14 = -3$

22. $19 + y = 87$

23. $-13 + b = 41$

24. $t + 5.6 = 9.1$

25. $12 + x = -12$

26. $-62 + z = -18$

27. $y - 34 = 27$

28. $12 = a - 44$

29. $p - 59 = -11$

30. $-4 = t - 3\frac{1}{3}$

31. $x - 4.33 = 2.17$

32. $\frac{4}{5} = y - \frac{7}{10}$

PRESIDENTIAL ELECTIONS **The bar graph shows how many of the 303 electoral votes each candidate received in the 1860 presidential election. Match the problem with the equation you would use. Then use the equation to solve the problem.**

A. $180 = x + 12$

B. $123 + x = 180$

C. $x + 180 = 303$

33. How many combined electoral votes did candidates other than Abraham Lincoln receive?

34. How many more electoral votes did Lincoln receive than the other candidates combined?

35. How many more electoral votes did Lincoln receive than Douglas?

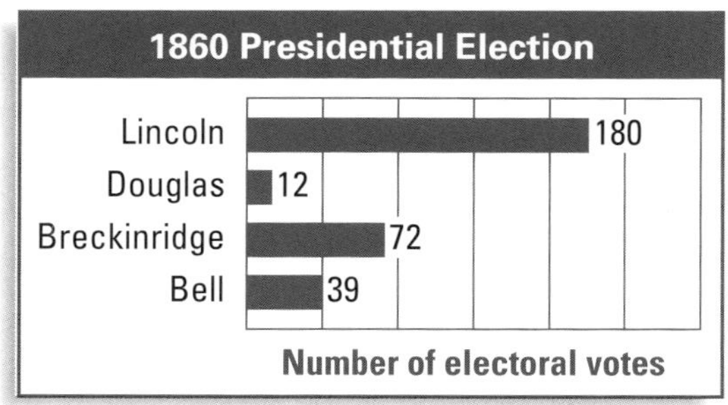

5.5 Solving Multiplication Equations

California Standards

In this lesson you'll:

- Write and solve one-step multiplication equations in one variable. (AF 1.1)

Goal 1 Solving Multiplication Equations

A multiplication equation is an equation involving a product of a variable and a number. Just as you solved subtraction equations in Lesson 5.4 by adding, you can solve multiplication equations by dividing. The goal is the same: to isolate the variable on one side of the equation.

Division Property of Equality

In Words Dividing each side of an equation by the same nonzero number produces a new equation having the same solution as the original.

In Algebra $ax = b \longrightarrow \frac{ax}{a} = \frac{b}{a}$ provided $a \neq 0$

Example 1 Solving Multiplication Equations

Solve the equation.

a. $5y = 42$ **b.** $-30 = 2.5n$

Solution

a. Your goal is to isolate the variable y.

$5y = 42$ Write original equation.

$\frac{5y}{5} = \frac{42}{5}$ Division property: divide each side by 5.

$y = 8.4$ Simplify. y is by itself.

ANSWER ▶ The solution is 8.4. Check this in the original equation.

CHECK ✓

$5y = 42$ Write original equation.

$5(\mathbf{8.4}) \stackrel{?}{=} 42$ Substitute 8.4 for y.

$42 = 42$ ✓ Both sides are the same.

b. Your goal is to isolate the variable n.

$-30 = 2.5n$ Write original equation.

$\frac{-30}{2.5} = \frac{2.5n}{2.5}$ Division property: divide each side by 2.5.

$-12 = n$ Simplify. n is by itself.

ANSWER ▶ The solution is -12. Check this in the original equation.

Student Help

▶ **Look Back** Make sure your solutions have the correct sign. For help with this, see page 193.

Student Help

▶ **MORE EXAMPLES**

INTERNET More examples are available at www.mcdougallittell.com

EXAMPLE 2 Writing and Solving a Multiplication Equation

STOCK MARKET In a social studies class, an 8 person team is studying the stock market. Each person on the team pretends to buy \$2000 worth of stocks and sells them at the end of a month. Team members agree to combine gains and losses and then split the team profit evenly. The individual gains and losses are as follows.

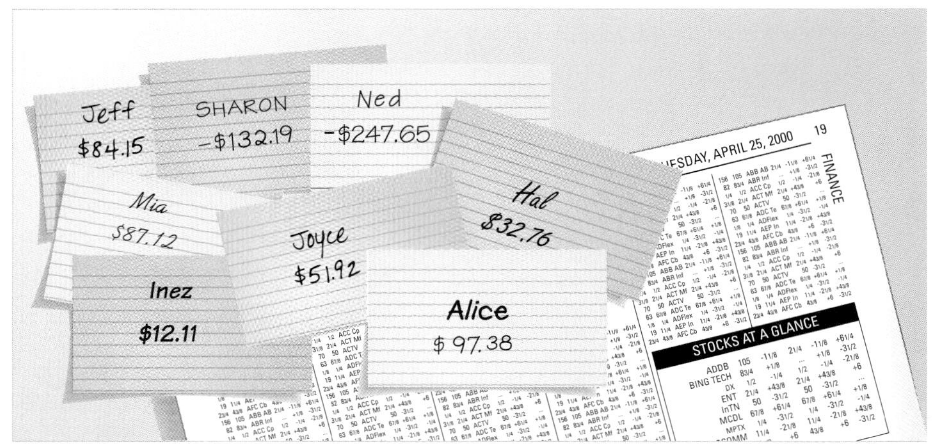

What is each person's share of the total profit?

Solution

Begin by adding all of the individual gains and losses to obtain a total of $-$14.40. Then use a verbal model to find each person's share of the total loss.

VERBAL MODEL

Number of people • Share of profit = Total profit

LABELS

Number of people = **8** (people)

Share of profit = x (dollars per person)

Total profit = **−14.40** (dollars)

ALGEBRAIC MODEL

$8x = -14.40$ Write equation.

$\frac{8x}{8} = \frac{-14.40}{8}$ Divide each side by 8.

$x = -1.8$ Simplify. x is by itself.

ANSWER ▶ Because the team agreed to share the profit equally, each person's share is, in theory, $-$1.80.

5.5 Exercises

Guided Practice

1. **ERROR ANALYSIS** Describe and correct the error made in solving the equation at the right.

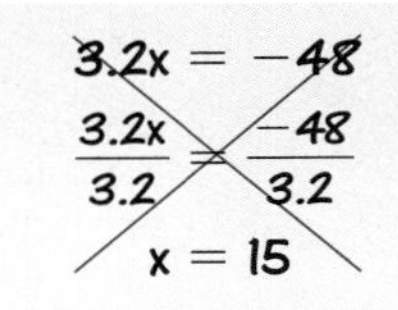

In Exercises 2–5, match the equation with its solution.

A. 0.8 **B.** -2 **C.** 1.25 **D.** 2

2. $4x = 5$ **3.** $4x = -8$ **4.** $-4x = -8$ **5.** $5x = 4$

6. **TEST SCORES** On five 100 point tests, a student received the following points for incorrect answers: -9, -3, -27, -6, -15. Use the verbal model below to find the mean of the five numbers. What does the mean represent?

Number of tests • **Mean** = Total points lost

Practice and Problem Solving

Student Help

▶**MORE PRACTICE** Extra practice to help you master skills is on page 575.

Without solving the equation, tell whether the solution is *positive* or *negative*.

7. $5n = -17$ **8.** $26 = 2x$ **9.** $-3t = -54$ **10.** $-4m = 38$

Check whether the given number is a solution of the equation. If it is not, find the solution.

11. $8n = -32$; 4 **12.** $2k = 101$; 50.5 **13.** $5x = 36.2$; 7

Solve the equation. Then check your solution.

14. $4y = 32$ **15.** $-2x = -4$ **16.** $-72 = 6m$

17. $5k = 0$ **18.** $3n = 7.2$ **19.** $12p = 9$

20. $-15a = -18$ **21.** $19t = -57$ **22.** $132 = -11z$

23. $-31 = -10b$ **24.** $9m = 94.5$ **25.** $\frac{1}{3} = 2x$

Write an algebraic equation for the sentence. Then solve the equation.

26. A number multiplied by -7 is 0.

27. -22 is -8 times a number.

28. -6 is the product of 9 and a number.

29. The product of 18 and a number equals 45.

Link to Science

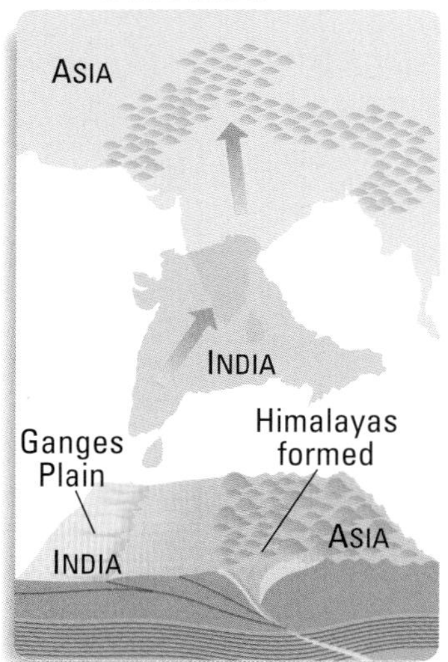

THE HIMALAYAS India was once an island. About 200 million years ago, plate movement began to drive India northward toward Asia. The collision created the Himalaya Mountains.

INTERNET More about the Himalayas available at www.mcdougallittell.com

30. **Science Link** The Himalaya Mountains are being pushed upward at a rate of about 0.34 inches per year. Use the verbal model below. Assign labels and write an equation to represent the problem. Solve the equation to find the number of years it takes for the Himalayas to rise 1 foot. ▶Source: United States Geological Survey

Inches of growth in 1 year • **Number of years** = **Number of inches in 1 foot**

GEOMETRY Write an equation using the given information about the rectangle. Then solve the equation to find *x*.

31. Area = 135 in.^{2}

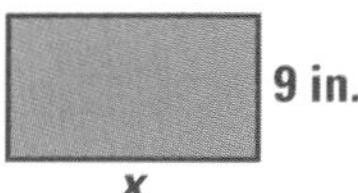

32. Area = 120 ft^2

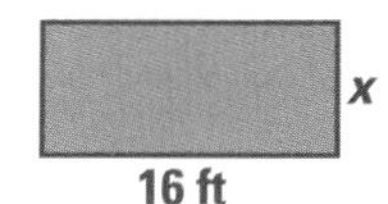

33. Area = $2\frac{2}{5}$ m^2

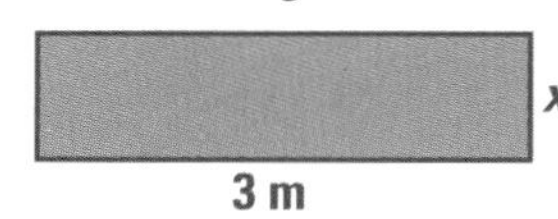

WATERFALLS In Exercises 34–36, use the graph at the right. Write and solve a multiplication equation for the given relationship. Use the graph to check whether your solution is reasonable.

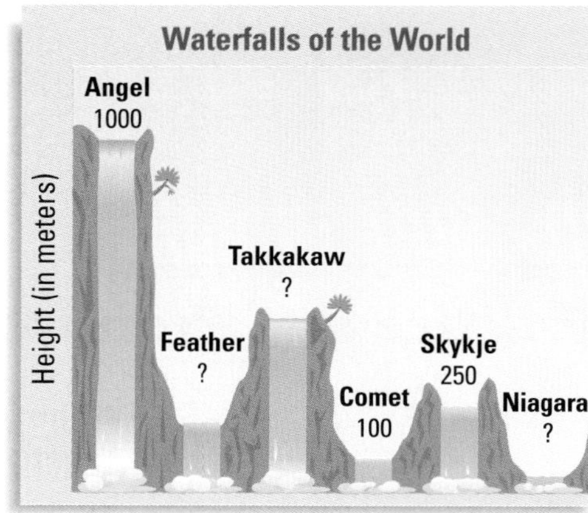

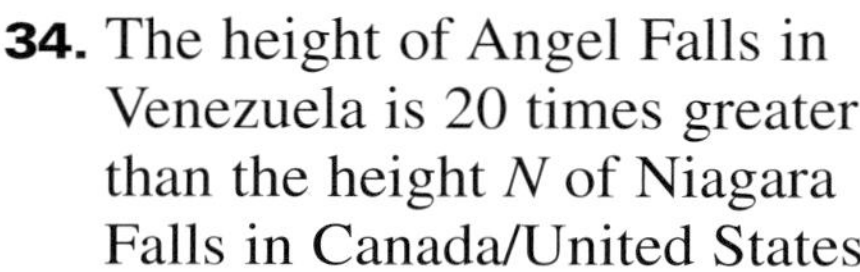

34. The height of Angel Falls in Venezuela is 20 times greater than the height N of Niagara Falls in Canada/United States.

35. The height of Comet Falls in Washington is $\frac{1}{5}$ the height T of Takkakaw Falls in British Columbia.

36. The height of Skykje Falls in Norway is 1.25 times greater than the height F of Feather Falls in California.

37. **MATHEMATICAL REASONING** Four friends want to pay equal shares of a $22.10 bill. Write and solve an equation to find each person's share. Can they split the bill evenly? Explain why or why not.

38. **CHALLENGE** Solve each equation below. Write and solve two more equations that appear to follow the pattern you observe.

$$1.5x = -3,\ 1.5x = -6,\ 1.5x = -9$$

Multiple-Choice Practice

39. Which equation does *not* have −3 as a solution?

(A) $4y = -12$ (B) $-15y = 45$ (C) $-y = -3$ (D) $5y = -15$

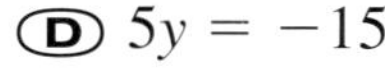

40. What is the solution of the equation $24t = 4$?

(F) $\frac{1}{6}$ (G) $\frac{1}{3}$ (H) 6 (J) Not here

5.6 Solving Division Equations

In this lesson you'll:

- Write and solve one-step division equations in one variable. (AF 1.1)

Goal 1 Solving Division Equations

A division equation is an equation involving a quotient of a variable and a nonzero number. Just as you solved multiplication equations in Lesson 5.5 by dividing, you can solve division equations by multiplying. The goal is the same: to isolate the variable on one side of the equation.

Multiplication Property of Equality

In Words Multiplying each side of an equation by the same nonzero number produces a new equation having the same solution as the original.

In Algebra $\frac{x}{a} = b \longrightarrow a \cdot \frac{x}{a} = a \cdot b$ provided $a \neq 0$

Example 1 Solving Division Equations

Solve the equation.

a. $\frac{x}{-3} = 79$

b. $20 = \frac{n}{3.1}$

Solution

a. Your goal is to isolate the variable x.

$\frac{x}{-3} = 79$	Write original equation.
$\mathbf{-3}\left(\frac{x}{-3}\right) = \mathbf{-3}(79)$	Multiplication property: multiply each side by −3.
$x = -237$	Simplify. x is by itself.

ANSWER ▶ The solution is −237. Check this in the original equation.

b. Your goal is to isolate the variable n.

$20 = \frac{n}{3.1}$	Write original equation.
$\mathbf{3.1}(20) = \mathbf{3.1}\left(\frac{n}{3.1}\right)$	Multiplication property: multiply each side by 3.1.
$62 = n$	Simplify. n is by itself.

ANSWER ▶ The solution is 62. Check this in the original equation.

EXAMPLE 2 Solving a Division Equation

Solve $\frac{y}{5} = \frac{1}{6}$.

Solution

$\frac{y}{5} = \frac{1}{6}$ Write original equation.

$5 \cdot \frac{y}{5} = 5 \cdot \frac{1}{6}$ Multiplication property: multiply each side by 5.

$y = \frac{5}{6}$ Simplify. y is by itself.

ANSWER ▶ The solution is $\frac{5}{6}$. Check this as follows.

CHECK ✓ $\frac{y}{5} = \frac{1}{6}$ Write original equation.

$\frac{1}{5} \cdot \frac{5}{6} \stackrel{?}{=} \frac{1}{6}$ Substitute $\frac{5}{6}$ for y.

$\frac{5}{30} = \frac{1}{6}$ ✓ The fractions are equivalent.

Student Help

▶ **STUDY TIP**
Dividing by a number is the same as multiplying by its reciprocal. In the check of Example 2, $\frac{y}{5}$ is equivalent to $\frac{1}{5}y$.

Goal 2 WRITING DIVISION EQUATIONS

EXAMPLE 3 Writing and Solving a Division Equation

BUSINESS Your business had an average monthly profit of $-\$135$ for the first quarter of the year. Find the total profit for the quarter.

Solution

VERBAL MODEL

$$\boxed{\text{Average profit per month}} = \frac{\text{Total profit for quarter}}{\text{Number of months in quarter}}$$

LABELS

Average profit per month = $\mathbf{-135}$ (dollars per month)

Total profit for quarter = $\boldsymbol{x}$ (dollars)

Number of months in quarter = $\mathbf{3}$ (months)

ALGEBRAIC MODEL

$\mathbf{-135} = \frac{\boldsymbol{x}}{\mathbf{3}}$ Write equation.

$3(-135) = 3\left(\frac{x}{3}\right)$ Multiply each side by 3.

$-405 = x$ Simplify. x is by itself.

ANSWER ▶ Because $x = -405$, the total profit for the quarter was $-\$405$.

Link to History

SEWARD'S FOLLY
Secretary of State William Henry Seward pushed for the purchase of Alaska. Seen as an icy wasteland, Alaska was dubbed "Seward's Folly." Alaska not only proved to be rich in resources, but also played an important role in World War II.

EXAMPLE 4 Writing and Solving a Division Equation

HISTORY LINK Alaska covers 375 million acres. In 1867 the United States purchased Alaska from Russia for about \$.02 per acre. What was the approximate total amount paid for Alaska?

Solution

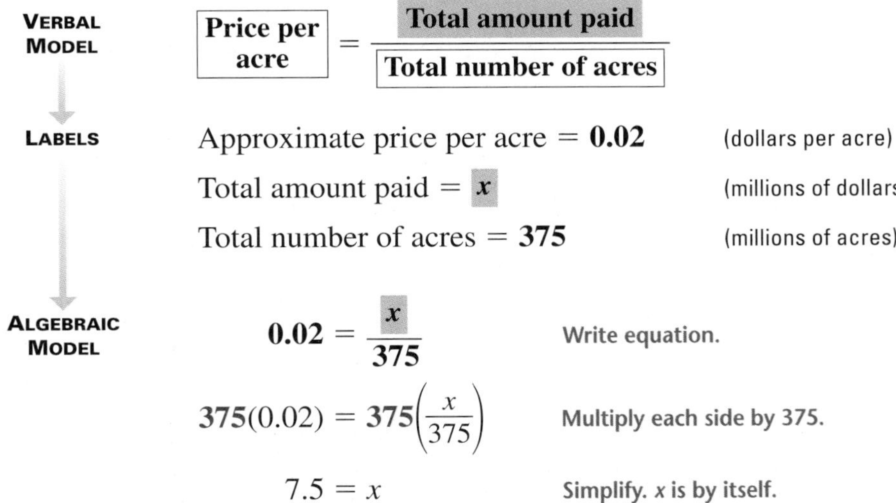

VERBAL MODEL

Price per acre = Total amount paid / Total number of acres

LABELS

Approximate price per acre = **0.02** (dollars per acre)

Total amount paid = x (millions of dollars)

Total number of acres = **375** (millions of acres)

ALGEBRAIC MODEL

$$0.02 = \frac{x}{375}$$ Write equation.

$$375(0.02) = 375\left(\frac{x}{375}\right)$$ Multiply each side by 375.

$$7.5 = x$$ Simplify. x is by itself.

ANSWER ▶ The solution is 7.5. So, the total amount paid for Alaska was about \$7.5 million.

5.6 Exercises

Guided Practice

Complete the statement using the words *multiply* or *divide*.

1. To solve $\frac{n}{12} = -60$, __?__ both sides of the equation by 12.

2. To solve $12n = -60$, __?__ both sides of the equation by 12.

In Exercises 3–6, solve the equation. Then check your solution.

3. $\frac{m}{5} = 15$ **4.** $-6 = \frac{s}{-42}$ **5.** $\frac{z}{-11} = 4$ **6.** $-3 = \frac{y}{17}$

7. TRAVEL You drove from Los Angeles to New York City and averaged 45 miles per hour. The driving time totaled 62 hours. Use the verbal model below. Assign labels to represent the situation. Write and solve an equation to find the distance you traveled.

Average speed = Distance traveled / Time you traveled

Practice and Problem Solving

Student Help

▶ MORE PRACTICE
Extra practice to help you master skills is on page 575.

Without solving the equation, tell whether the solution is *positive* or *negative.*

8. $\frac{g}{3} = 6$ **9.** $-2 = \frac{x}{-2}$ **10.** $\frac{a}{3.1} = 7.75$ **11.** $\frac{n}{4} = -9$

Check whether the given number is a solution of the equation. If it is not, find the solution.

12. $\frac{t}{5} = 25;\ 5$ **13.** $6 = \frac{y}{-12};\ -72$ **14.** $\frac{b}{3} = 7.5;\ 225$

Solve the equation. Then check your solution.

15. $\frac{d}{10} = 12$ **16.** $-5 = \frac{n}{4}$ **17.** $-15 = \frac{x}{-8}$ **18.** $\frac{t}{28} = 9$

19. $\frac{x}{-6} = 13$ **20.** $-12 = \frac{a}{-3}$ **21.** $\frac{b}{3} = 8.2$ **22.** $\frac{x}{5.3} = 0.7$

23. $\frac{p}{2.3} = 4$ **24.** $\frac{y}{50} = -21$ **25.** $\frac{1}{2} = \frac{d}{4}$ **26.** $\frac{3}{4} = \frac{a}{8}$

Write an algebraic equation for the sentence. Then solve.

27. A number divided by nine equals two thirds.

28. Negative eleven equals the quotient of a number and five.

Write a multiplication equation and a division equation that have the given solution.

29. 5 **30.** -3 **31.** 2.5 **32.** 1

Student Help

▶ HOMEWORK HELP
Extra help with problem solving in Exs. 33–36 is available at www.mcdougallittell.com

PAINTING **In Exercises 33–35, use the following information to match the problem with one of the equations. Then solve the problem.** It took 700 hours and 295 gallons of paint for a crew of painters to repaint the "Hollywood" sign on Mount Lee in California in 1995.

A. $\frac{x}{9} = 700$ **B.** $700x = 295$ **C.** $295 = 9x$

33. About how many gallons of paint did it take to paint a letter?

34. Suppose it cost \$9 per hour for the labor to paint the sign. What was the total cost of labor?

35. About how many gallons of paint were used per hour?

36. MATHEMATICAL REASONING What additional information would you need to find the total cost of repainting the "Hollywood" sign?

Link to Science

SPACE SHUTTLE The combined personal items of a space shuttle astronaut must weigh no more than 1.5 lb and must fit in a 5 in. by 8 in. by 2 in. space. Shown above, astronaut Richard Richards took a stuffed tiger, his college mascot.

37. ***Science Link*** Space shuttle missions require 3.8 pounds of food per person per day. Suppose a 6 person crew is going on an 8 day mission. Use the verbal model below. Assign labels to represent the problem. Write and solve an equation to find the total weight of the food.

▶ Source: NASA

$$\boxed{\text{Weight of food per person per day}} \cdot \boxed{\text{Crew size}} = \frac{\boxed{\text{Total weight of food}}}{\boxed{\text{Number of days}}}$$

In Exercises 38 and 39, write a verbal model, assign labels, and write an equation to solve the problem.

38. **FUNDRAISING** The booster club runs a concession stand at home basketball games. The average monthly profit for the 4 month season is \$450. What is the total profit for the season?

39. ***Chapter Opener Link*** Look back at the table on page 215. When you return from Germany, you still have 100 marks left. How many U.S. dollars will you get when you exchange your marks at the bank?

40. **CHALLENGE** Show how you could use multiplication to solve $\frac{2}{3}x = 8$. Then show how you could use division to solve the same problem.

Multiple-Choice Practice

41. What is the solution of the equation $\frac{x}{3.2} = 6$?

Ⓐ 192 Ⓑ 19.2 Ⓒ 18.75 Ⓓ 1.875

42. Which equation has a solution of -5?

Ⓕ $\frac{m}{-20} = 0.2$ Ⓖ $\frac{m}{2} = 2.5$ Ⓗ $\frac{m}{-10} = 0.5$ Ⓙ $\frac{m}{-5} = -1$

Mixed Review

Find the least common multiple of the numbers. *(2.5)*

43. 20, 50 **44.** 15, 18 **45.** 64, 80 **46.** 4, 6, 8

In Exercises 47–50, multiply or divide. Simplify if possible. *(3.4, 3.5)*

47. $\frac{7}{8} \times \frac{4}{5}$ **48.** $1\frac{1}{9} \times 1\frac{5}{6}$ **49.** $\frac{3}{10} \div 1\frac{4}{5}$ **50.** $1\frac{2}{3} \div 2\frac{1}{6}$

51. **BASKETBALL** The Valley Middle School basketball team scored 96 points to win last night's game. They beat their opponents by 19 points. Write a verbal model, assign labels, and write an equation to represent the situation. Then solve the equation to find the number of points scored by Valley's opponents. *(5.3)*

DEVELOPING CONCEPTS
Two-Step Equations

For use with Lesson 5.7

California Standards

- Determine when and how to break a problem into simpler parts. (MR 1.3)
- Develop generalizations of strategies and apply them to new situations. (MR 3.3)

MATERIALS

- Algebra tiles

Some equations, such as $x + 3 = 7$, contain a single operation. This type of equation is called a *one-step equation* because it can be solved by using just one inverse operation. Other equations, such as $3x + 4 = 10$, contain two operations. This type of equation is called a *two-step equation*.

SAMPLE 1 Using Algebra Tiles to Solve an Equation

You can use algebra tiles to solve the equation $3x + 4 = 10$.

Here's How

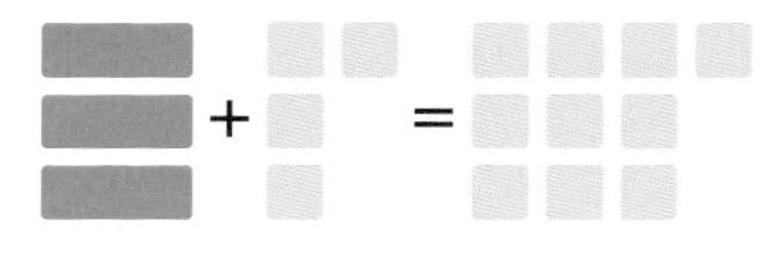

Original equation: $3x + 4 = 10$

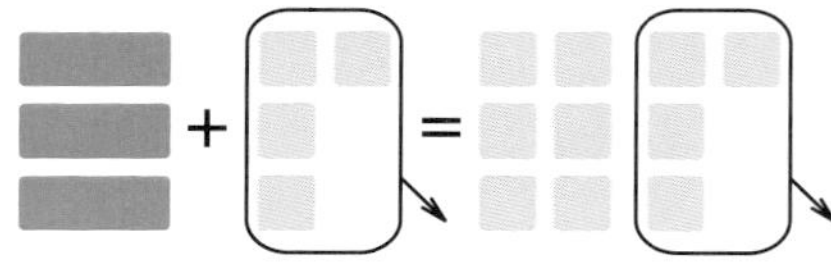

As a first step, subtract four yellow tiles from each side of the equation.

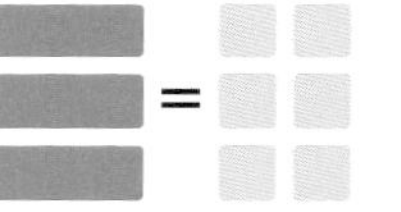

Simplify the equation.

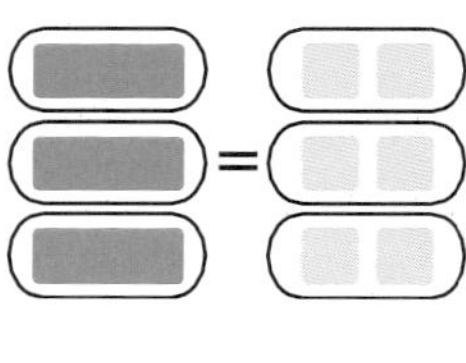

As a second step, divide each side into 3 groups. Then take one third of each side.

The solution is 2.

Try These

Write the equation that is modeled with algebra tiles. Then use algebra tiles to solve the equation. Make a sketch of your steps.

1.

2.

Use algebra tiles to solve the equation. Make a sketch of your steps.

3. $2x + 3 = 7$ **4.** $3x + 5 = 14$ **5.** $4x + 1 = 13$

The types of equations that can be solved with algebra tiles are limited. For more flexibility, you can model two-step equations using box models.

SAMPLE 2 Using a Box Model to Solve an Equation

Use a box model to solve the equation $4x - 7 = 13$.

Here's How

Begin by drawing a box model to represent the equation. Then use inverse operations to solve the equation.

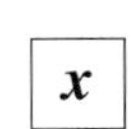

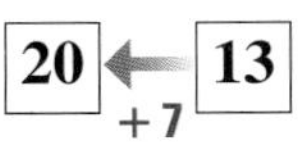

The solution is 5.

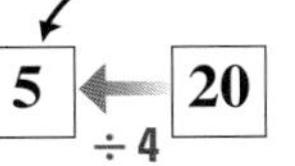

13

1. Multiply x by 4. Then subtract 7 to get 13.
2. Add 7 to 13 to undo subtracting 7.
3. Divide 20 by 4 to undo multiplying by 4.

Notice that a box model for a two-step equation lists operations in the order that they are performed on the variable. In the sample above, x is first multiplied by 4, and then 7 is subtracted from the result. When you solve an equation using a box model, you perform inverse operations in the reverse order that the operations are performed on the variable.

Try These

Write the equation represented by the box model. Then use the box model to solve the equation.

6. x →(×5)→ ? →(+7)→ -13

7. b →(×2)→ ? →(−2)→ 11

8. y →(÷4)→ ? →(+5)→ -21

Use a box model to solve the equation.

9. $5x + 2 = -8$

10. $2y - 7 = 5$

11. $\frac{t}{3} + 4 = -2$

12. $\frac{b}{4} - 5 = 1$

13. $6z + 5 = 23$

14. $-3x - 9 = -21$

15. **MATHEMATICAL REASONING** Name the operations, in the order you would use them, to solve the equation $2(x - 1) = 6$. Explain your reasoning.

5.7 Solving Two-Step Equations

California Standards

In this lesson you'll:

- Write and solve linear equations in one variable. (AF 1.1)
- Develop generalizations of strategies and apply them to new situations. (MR 3.3)

Goal 1 SOLVING TWO-STEP EQUATIONS

In Lessons 5.3–5.6 you solved one-step equations by using a single *inverse operation.* **Inverse operations** are operations that "undo" each other. Addition and subtraction are inverse operations. Multiplication and division are also inverse operations.

In Developing Concepts 5.7, page 248, you used models to help you solve *two-step equations.* Two-step equations involve two operations and require using two inverse operations, in succession, to solve.

EXAMPLE 1 Solving Two-Step Equations

Solve the equation.

a. $6x - 3 = -33$

b. $\frac{y}{2} + 4 = -12$

Solution

To solve a two-step equation, first use an inverse operation that will transform the two-step equation into a one-step equation.

a. Your goal is to isolate the variable x.

$6x - 3 = -33$	Write original equation.
$\quad + 3 \quad + 3$	Addition property: add 3 to each side.
$6x = -30$	Simplify.
$\frac{6x}{6} = \frac{-30}{6}$	Division property: divide each side by 6.
$x = -5$	Simplify. x is by itself.

ANSWER ▶ The solution is -5. Check this in the original equation.

b. Your goal is to isolate the variable y.

$\frac{y}{2} + 4 = -12$	Write original equation.
$\quad - 4 \quad - 4$	Subtraction property: subtract 4 from each side.
$\frac{y}{2} = -16$	Simplify.
$2\left(\frac{y}{2}\right) = 2(-16)$	Multiplication property: multiply each side by 2.
$y = -32$	Simplify. y is by itself.

ANSWER ▶ The solution is -32. Check this in the original equation.

Student Help

▶ **STUDY TIP**
When you solve an equation, perform inverse operations in the reverse order that the operations are performed on the variable.

Goal 2 WRITING TWO-STEP EQUATIONS

Student Help

▶ **MORE EXAMPLES**

INTERNET More examples are available at www.mcdougallittell.com

EXAMPLE 2 Writing and Solving a Two-Step Equation

Write an algebraic equation for the following sentence. Then solve the equation.

Fourteen subtracted from the product of 3 and a number equals 25.

Solution

Let x represent the number.

$3x - 14 = 25$	Write equation.
$+14 \quad +14$	Add 14 to each side.
$3x = 39$	Simplify.
$\frac{3x}{3} = \frac{39}{3}$	Divide each side by 3.
$x = 13$	Simplify. x is by itself.

ANSWER ▶ The solution is 13. Check this in the original equation.

EXAMPLE 3 Writing and Solving a Two-Step Equation

PRINTING Your math club is printing a booklet of math puzzles. The printer charges \$2 per booklet, plus a setup fee of \$90. How many booklets can you have printed for \$500?

Solution

VERBAL MODEL

Cost per booklet • Number of booklets + Setup fee = Total cost

LABELS

Cost per booklet = **2**	(dollars per booklet)
Number of booklets = x	(booklets)
Setup fee = **90**	(dollars)
Total cost = **500**	(dollars)

ALGEBRAIC MODEL

$2x + 90 = 500$	Write equation.
$-90 \quad -90$	Subtract 90 from each side.
$2x = 410$	Simplify.
$\frac{2x}{2} = \frac{410}{2}$	Divide each side by 2.
$x = 205$	Simplify. x is by itself.

ANSWER ▶ You can have 205 booklets printed.

5.7 Exercises

Guided Practice

Describe each step of the solution.

1.
$$\begin{aligned} \frac{n}{2} + 6 &= 3 \\ -6 \quad & \quad -6 \\ \hline \frac{n}{2} &= -3 \\ 2\left(\frac{n}{2}\right) &= 2(-3) \\ n &= -6 \end{aligned}$$

2.
$$\begin{aligned} 9y - 13 &= -4 \\ +13 \quad & \quad +13 \\ \hline 9y &= 9 \\ \frac{9y}{9} &= \frac{9}{9} \\ y &= 1 \end{aligned}$$

Check whether the given number is a solution of the equation. If it is not, find the solution.

3. $3a - 2 = -8; -2$ **4.** $-5y + 6 = 1; -1$ **5.** $\frac{b}{4} - 12 = -8; 8$

6. $2x + 5 = -11; 3$ **7.** $-4x - 4 = 8; -3$ **8.** $\frac{w}{-2} + 5 = 13; 9$

9. **BOWLING** At a bowling alley, shoes cost \$.75 to rent, and each game costs \$2.25. Use the verbal model below. Assign labels to represent the problem. Write and solve an equation to find the number of games you can bowl with \$12.

Cost of shoes	+	Cost per game	•	Number of games	=	Total cost of bowling

Practice and Problem Solving

Student Help

▶**MORE PRACTICE** Extra practice to help you master skills is on page 575.

Describe the first step you would take toward solving the equation.

10. $3x + 10 = 4$ **11.** $-16 + 4m = 12$ **12.** $-2 = \frac{z}{4} - 5$

Solve the equation. Then check your solution.

13. $3y + 5 = 23$ **14.** $8b - 16 = 12$ **15.** $\frac{x}{-4} + 6 = 22$

16. $15 + 4m = -1$ **17.** $-6x - 12 = 6$ **18.** $\frac{a}{3} - 2 = 5$

19. $\frac{n}{8} - 3 = -3$ **20.** $2t - 8 = 10$ **21.** $7 = \frac{b}{5} + 9$

22. $-11 + 2y = 0$ **23.** $5.7 + 3z = 9.3$ **24.** $\frac{k}{12} + \frac{1}{3} = \frac{1}{2}$

Link to Science

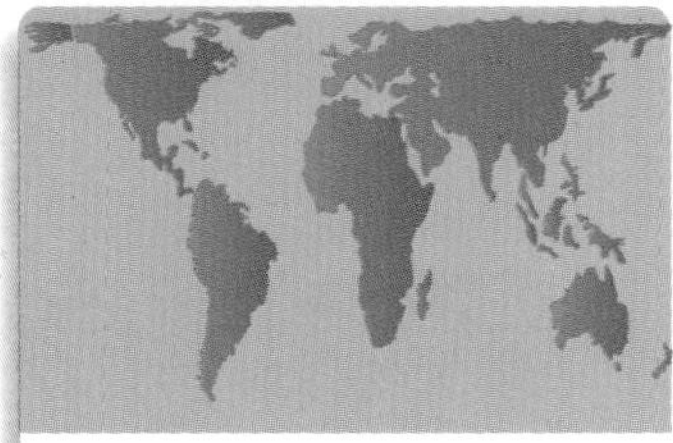

SURFACE AREA If Earth's landmasses are rearranged, it is easier to see that about $\frac{3}{4}$ of Earth's surface area is covered by water. This means that about $\frac{3}{4}$ of the space material that rains down on Earth rains over water.

In Exercise 25–28, write an algebraic equation for the sentence. Then solve the equation.

25. The sum of five and negative two times a number is negative seven.

26. Eight plus the quotient of a number and four is two.

27. Nine more than the product of five and a number is negative six.

28. Twelve less than twice a number equals twenty.

29. **MATHEMATICAL REASONING** Use the clues given below to find the values of a, b, c, and d. Explain how you approached the problem and why you approached it that way.

$$\frac{d}{8} - b = c \qquad \frac{a}{3} + b = 0 \qquad 4c - b = a \qquad b = 2$$

Science Link **In Exercises 30 and 31, use the following information.** Each day dust-like material from space rains down on Earth, and about 250 tons of this material rains over land. This is about 500 tons less than the amount of material that rains over water. About $\frac{3}{4}$ of Earth's surface area is covered by water.

30. Use the verbal model below. Assign labels to represent the problem. Write and solve an equation to find the total amount of space material that rains down on Earth each day.

Part of Earth covered by water • **Total material raining on Earth** − 500 tons = **Material raining over land**

31. **WRITING** Earth's surface area is covered by about 49.3 million square miles of land. If 250 tons of space material rain over land each day, why aren't people more affected by it? Explain your reasoning.

32. **PUMPING GAS** You just filled your tank with gas for \$1.34 per gallon (including tax). You gave the clerk a \$20 bill and received \$5.93 in change. Write a verbal model, assign labels, and write an equation to find the number of gallons of gas you pumped.

33. **CHALLENGE** Show how the equation $5x - 10 = 25$ can be solved by adding first then dividing, and also by dividing first and then adding.

Multiple-Choice Practice

34. What is the solution of the equation $6m + 11 = 23$?

Ⓐ −21 Ⓑ −2 Ⓒ 2 Ⓓ 21

35. The total cost for 35 people to go on a trip to a museum is \$212. This includes transportation and admission tickets. The transportation costs are \$86. What is the cost per person for admission tickets?

Ⓕ \$2.48 Ⓖ \$3.60 Ⓗ \$6.06 Ⓙ \$8.51

Chapter 5 Chapter Summary and Review

VOCABULARY

- **equation,** *p. 221*
- **solving an equation,** *p. 221*
- **inverse operations,** *p. 250*
- **solution of an equation,** *p. 221*

5.1 WRITING EXPRESSIONS

Examples on pp. 217–218

EXAMPLE **Write a variable expression for the verbal phrase.**

Verbal phrase	Variable expression
a. The sum of a number and 20	$x + 20$
b. Six less than a number	$y - 6$
c. The product of 14 and a number	$14n$
d. The quotient of a number and -2	$\frac{m}{-2}$

EXAMPLE **Evaluate the expression $2m + 7$ when $m = 0, 1, 2,$ and 3. Organize your results in a table.**

Substitute values of m in $2m + 7$:

$2(\mathbf{0}) + 7 = 0 + 7 = 7$

$2(\mathbf{1}) + 7 = 2 + 7 = 9$

$2(\mathbf{2}) + 7 = 4 + 7 = 11$

$2(\mathbf{3}) + 7 = 6 + 7 = 13$

m	0	1	2	3
$2m + 7$	7	9	11	13

Write a variable expression for the verbal phrase.

1. Negative thirteen multiplied by a number

2. The difference of 16 and a number

3. The quotient of 18 and a number

4. Four times the sum of a number and 4

BUSINESS **A company charges $15 for a soccer trophy plus $.50 for each letter engraved on the trophy's plate.**

5. Write an expression for the total cost of a trophy with x letters engraved on it.

6. Evaluate the expression in Exercise 5 when $x = 10, 15, 20, 25,$ and 30. Organize your results in a table.

5.2 WRITING EQUATIONS

Examples on pp. 221–222

EXAMPLE Together, you and a friend caught 26 fish. Of these, you caught 15. How many fish did your friend catch?

VERBAL MODEL **Fish your friend caught** + **Fish you caught** = **Total number of fish**

LABELS Fish your friend caught = ***F***

Fish you caught = **15**

Total number of fish = **26**

ALGEBRAIC MODEL $F + 15 = 26$

You need to find a number that you can add to 15 to get 26. Using mental math, you determine that the solution is 11.

ANSWER ▶ Your friend caught 11 fish.

CHECK ✓ $11 + 15 = 26$ The solution is correct.

In Exercises 7–10, use mental math to solve the equation. Then check your solution.

7. $x + 5 = 13$ **8.** $\frac{m}{6} = 9$ **9.** $p - 4 = 49$ **10.** $3y = 18$

11. Write and solve an equation for this problem: You take \$25 to a hockey game. You leave the game with \$9. How much money did you spend?

5.3-5.4 SOLVING ADDITION AND SUBTRACTION EQUATIONS

Examples on pp. 228–229 and pp. 233–234

Subtracting the same number from each side of an equation produces a new equation having the same solution as the original.

EXAMPLE **Solve the equation $m + 6 = -10$.**

Your goal is to isolate the variable m.

$m + 6 = -10$ Write original equation.

$\underline{\quad -6 \quad\;\; -6}$ Subtraction property: subtract 6 from each side.

$m \quad = -16$ Simplify. m is by itself.

ANSWER ▶ The solution is -16. Check the solution by substituting -16 for m in the original equation.

Adding the same number to each side of an equation produces a new equation having the same solution as the original.

EXAMPLE **Solve the equation $b - 5 = -8$.**

Your goal is to isolate the variable b.

$b - 5 = -8$	Write original equation.
$+5 \quad +5$	Addition property: add 5 to each side.
$b = -3$	Simplify. b is by itself.

ANSWER ▶ The solution is -3. Check the solution by substituting -3 for b in the original equation.

In Exercises 12–19, solve the equation. Then check your solution.

12. $13 + x = 6$ **13.** $-13 = n + 13$ **14.** $7 + d = 15$ **15.** $\frac{7}{8} + n = 2\frac{1}{8}$

16. $x - 13 = 6$ **17.** $m - 7 = -7$ **18.** $-11 = y - 6$ **19.** $n - 2.5 = 3.1$

20. **ELEVATION** A sign at the base of a building says that the elevation is -5 feet. The building is 22 feet tall. Use the verbal model below. Assign labels and write an equation to represent the problem. Solve the equation to find the elevation at the roof of the building.

Elevation at roof	$-$	Height of building	$=$	Elevation at base

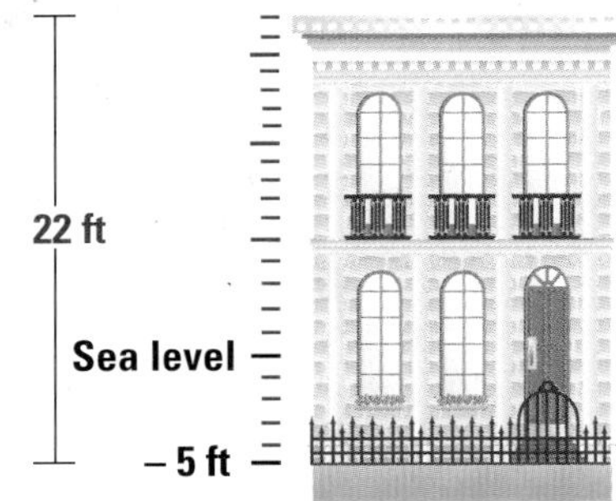

5.5-5.6 SOLVING MULTIPLICATION AND DIVISION EQUATIONS

Examples on pp. 239–240 and pp. 243–244

Dividing each side of an equation by the same nonzero number produces a new equation having the same solution as the original.

EXAMPLE **Solve the equation $6c = 45$.**

Your goal is to isolate the variable c.

$6c = 45$	Write original equation.
$\frac{6c}{6} = \frac{45}{6}$	Division property: divide each side by 6.
$c = 7.5$	Simplify. c is by itself.

ANSWER ▶ The solution is 7.5. Check this in the original equation.

Multiplying each side of an equation by the same nonzero number produces a new equation having the same solution as the original.

EXAMPLE **Solve the equation $\frac{m}{4} = 7$.**

Your goal is to isolate the variable m.

$\frac{m}{4} = 7$	Write original equation.
$4 \cdot \frac{m}{4} = 4 \cdot 7$	Multiplication property: multiply each side by 4.
$m = 28$	Simplify. m is by itself.

ANSWER ▶ The solution is 28. Check this in the original equation.

In Exercises 21–28, solve the equation. Then check your solution.

21. $-124 = -8c$ **22.** $2.3x = 11.5$ **23.** $0.44x = 22$ **24.** $\frac{3}{4} = -5w$

25. $\frac{m}{5} = 12.5$ **26.** $\frac{a}{6} = -33$ **27.** $13 = \frac{w}{3.5}$ **28.** $\frac{a}{9} = \frac{1}{2}$

29. **ENVIRONMENT** Geologists calculate that a section of beach erodes at a rate of 18 centimeters per year. How many years will it take for the beach to erode 72 centimeters? Write a verbal model, assign labels, and write an equation to represent the problem. Then solve the equation.

5.7 SOLVING TWO-STEP EQUATIONS

Examples on pp. 250–251

To solve a two-step equation, use two inverse operations in succession.

EXAMPLE **Solve the equation $4x - 6 = 10$.**

Your goal is to isolate the variable x.

$4x - 6 = 10$	Write original equation.
$ + 6 \quad + 6$	Addition property: add 6 to each side.
$4x = 16$	Simplify.
$\frac{4x}{4} = \frac{16}{4}$	Division property: divide each side by 4.
$x = 4$	Simplify. x is by itself.

ANSWER ▶ The solution is 4. Check this in the original equation.

Solve the equation. Then check your solution.

30. $-3 + 5d = 1$ **31.** $\frac{c}{4} + 8 = 11$ **32.** $3.5s + 13 = 23.5$ **33.** $\frac{m}{6} - 3 = 2$

Chapter 5 Chapter Test

Write two different verbal phrases for the variable expression.

1. $y - 11$ **2.** $\frac{15}{x}$ **3.** $6m - 2$ **4.** $7(g + 1)$

In Exercises 5–8, evaluate the variable expression when $t = 0, 1, 2, 3, 4,$ 5, and 6. Organize your results in a table.

5. $t - 3$ **6.** $2t + 6$ **7.** $\frac{t}{4}$ **8.** $15 - 3t$

9. Use mental math to solve the equation $17 + n = 32$. Then check your solution.

10. PHYSICAL EDUCATION There are 30 students in your physical education class. You want to make teams of 5 to play basketball. Use the verbal model below. Assign labels and write an equation to represent the situation. Then solve the equation to find how many teams of 5 you can form.

Number of teams	•	Number of people on each team	=	Number of students in your class

Solve the equation. Then check your solution.

11. $m + 16 = 7$ **12.** $-14 = y + 22$ **13.** $11.8 = 7.25 + z$ **14.** $-11 = t - 11$

15. $x - \frac{1}{6} = \frac{3}{4}$ **16.** $-6w = 96$ **17.** $9.62 = 4.81k$ **18.** $-4y = -68$

19. $\frac{a}{6.5} = -4$ **20.** $6 + \frac{n}{6} = -90$ **21.** $7h - 1 = -36$ **22.** $3 = \frac{n}{10} + 6$

GEOMETRY **In Exercises 23 and 24, write an equation to find x. Then solve the equation.**

23. Area = 117 square centimeters

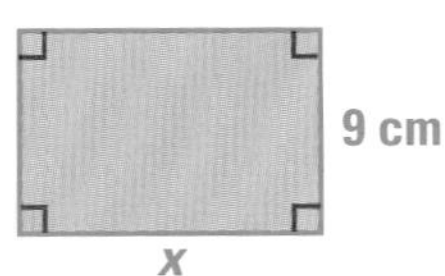

24. Perimeter = 22 feet

25. SPORTS RETAIL You buy a badminton set on sale for \$63.75. The original price for the set was \$85. Write a verbal model, assign labels, and write an equation to represent the situation. Then solve the equation to find the amount of money you saved by buying the badminton set on sale.

Multiple-Choice Practice

Test Tip Do the easy questions first. Then go back to the harder questions.

1. A sweatshirt costs $35. You can have your name sewn on for $1 per letter. Which expression can be used to represent the cost of a sweatshirt with n letters sewn on?

   Ⓐ $35n + 1$ Ⓑ $35 + n$

   Ⓒ $1 - 35n$ Ⓓ $35n - 1$

2. Which equation represents the following sentence?
   The difference of a number and −4 is 4.

   Ⓕ $y + (-4) = 4$ Ⓖ $n - 4 = 4$

   Ⓗ $b - (-4) = 4$ Ⓙ $z - 4 = -4$

3. You want to buy a CD player that costs $146. You have already saved $74. Which equation could you use to find the amount of money you still need?

   Ⓐ $x + 146 = 74$ Ⓑ $146 + 74 = x$

   Ⓒ $74 + x = 146$ Ⓓ $x - 146 = 74$

4. Which step should you take to solve the equation $x - 22 = 43$?

   Ⓕ Add 22 to each side.

   Ⓖ Add 43 to each side.

   Ⓗ Subtract 22 from each side.

   Ⓙ Subtract 43 from each side.

5. What is the solution of the equation $24.5 + x = 115.37$?

   Ⓐ 139.87 Ⓑ 90.87

   Ⓒ 4.71 Ⓓ 91.32

6. You buy 4 copies of the same book for $12.50 per book. Which equation could be used to find the total cost?

   Ⓕ $12.50t = 4$ Ⓖ $4t = 12.50$

   Ⓗ $t - 4 = 12.50$ Ⓙ $\frac{t}{4} = 12.50$

7. Which situation could be modeled by the equation $4x = 7$?

   Ⓐ You buy 7 pencils for $4.

   Ⓑ You earn $4 each day for 7 days.

   Ⓒ The temperature fell 4° in 7 hours.

   Ⓓ It costs $7 to bowl 4 games.

8. What is the solution of the equation $\frac{y}{4} = 14.2$?

   Ⓕ 56.8 Ⓖ 18.2

   Ⓗ 10.2 Ⓙ 3.55

9. A waitress makes $76 in tips during her 7 hour shift. If her wages and tips total $104 that day, which equation can be used to find her hourly wage?

   Ⓐ $7h = 180$ Ⓑ $7h + 76 = 104$

   Ⓒ $7h = 104$ Ⓓ $104 + 7h = 76$

10. What is the solution of the equation $0.18x + 1 = 10$?

    Ⓕ 8.5 Ⓖ 50

    Ⓗ 51 Ⓙ 61.1

Brain games

California Standards

- Students analyze problems by identifying relationships. (MR 1.1)
- Develop generalizations of the results obtained and the strategies used and apply them in new problem situations. (MR 3.3)

Think Tank

Materials

- **Paper and pencil**

Directions

Object of the Game

Play in pairs. Each round one player secretly writes down a variable expression and the other player tries to guess what it is. A correct guess earns you 2 points. An incorrect guess earns your opponent 1 point. Players alternate roles each round. The winner of the game is the first to earn 7 points.

How to Play

STEP 1 Player A secretly chooses two integers between (and including) -10 and 10 for the values of the variables a and b. Player A records these values on a piece of paper.

STEP 2 Player B gives a value for x in the expression $ax + b$. Player A evaluates the expression and tells Player B the result. Player B records the result on a piece of paper.

STEP 3 Repeat Step 2. Player B must then guess the values of a and b in the expression.

Another Way to Play

Use an expression of the form $ax - b$, $\frac{x}{a} + b$, or $\frac{x}{a} - b$.

Brain Teaser

Guess My Age

When I was 9 years old, my father was 35 years old.

Now my father is twice my age.

How old am I?

Make up a brain teaser like this for your friends to solve.

The basic skills you'll review on this page will help prepare you for the next chapter.

Reviewing the Basics

EXAMPLE 1 Writing Fractions in Simplest Form

Write the fraction in simplest form.

a. $\frac{15}{20}$ **b.** $\frac{25}{10}$

Solution

Divide the numerator and denominator by their greatest common factor.

a. $\frac{15}{20} = \frac{\cancel{5}^{1} \cdot 3}{\cancel{5}_{1} \cdot 4} = \frac{3}{4}$

b. $\frac{25}{10} = \frac{\cancel{5}^{1} \cdot 5}{\cancel{5}_{1} \cdot 2} = \frac{5}{2}$, or $2\frac{1}{2}$

Try These

Write the fraction in simplest form.

1. $\frac{7}{14}$ **2.** $\frac{10}{5}$ **3.** $\frac{9}{36}$ **4.** $\frac{5}{25}$

5. $\frac{12}{18}$ **6.** $\frac{21}{27}$ **7.** $\frac{10}{4}$ **8.** $\frac{81}{27}$

EXAMPLE 2 Comparing Fractions

Complete the statement using < or >.

a. $\frac{3}{7}$? $\frac{4}{7}$ **b.** $\frac{5}{8}$? $\frac{7}{12}$

Solution

a. The denominators are the same. Compare the numerators.
Because $3 < 4$, $\frac{3}{7} < \frac{4}{7}$.

b. The denominators are different. Rewrite the fractions with a common denominator. Then compare the numerators.

$\frac{5}{8} = \frac{5 \cdot 3}{8 \cdot 3} = \frac{15}{24}$ $\frac{7}{12} = \frac{7 \cdot 2}{12 \cdot 2} = \frac{14}{24}$

Because $15 > 14$, $\frac{5}{8} > \frac{7}{12}$.

Try These

Complete the statement using < or >.

9. $\frac{5}{13}$? $\frac{7}{13}$ **10.** $\frac{9}{17}$? $\frac{2}{17}$ **11.** $\frac{1}{6}$? $\frac{1}{8}$

12. $\frac{3}{5}$? $\frac{7}{8}$ **13.** $\frac{5}{16}$? $\frac{3}{4}$ **14.** $\frac{13}{20}$? $\frac{9}{30}$

Student Help

MORE EXAMPLES

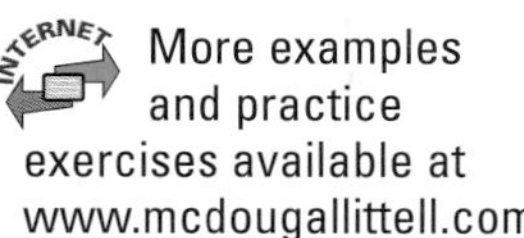

More examples and practice exercises available at www.mcdougallittell.com

Ratios and Proportions

Why are ratios and proportions important?

A ratio is a comparison of two quantities, such as length and width. In proportional relationships, the ratio of two quantities is constant. You will use ratios and proportions when you study topics such as similarity and probability.

Ratios and proportions are used by many people, including photographers (pages 263 and 273) and warden pilots (page 295). Photographers represent shutter speeds as ratios, and they use proportions when planning enlargements of photographs.

Meeting the California Standards

The skills you'll develop in this chapter will help you meet state standards and prepare for standardized tests. In this chapter you'll:

- **Interpret and use ratios in different contexts.** LESSONS 6.1, 6.5
- **Use proportions to solve problems. Use and understand cross-multiplication.** LESSONS 6.2–6.5
- **Solve problems involving rates.** LESSON 6.3
- **Express simple geometric relationships in symbolic form.** LESSON 6.4
- **Represent probabilities as ratios, proportions, and decimals.** LESSON 6.6

Career Link **PHOTOGRAPHER** A photographer uses ratios and proportions when:

- determining the shutter speed for a shot.
- resizing photographs.

EXERCISES

A photographer uses fast shutter speeds for action shots so the picture won't be blurry. The shutter speed tells how long the shutter of the camera is open when the picture is taken.

1. Which is faster, a shutter that opens for $\frac{1}{60}$ second or a shutter that opens for $\frac{1}{120}$ second? Explain your reasoning.

On cameras, shutter speeds are marked as whole numbers like 2, 15, 60, and 120. In Lesson 6.1, you will learn what a shutter speed of 120 means and whether it is faster or slower than a shutter speed of 60.

fast shutter speed

slow shutter speed

Chapter 6 Getting Ready

PREVIEW What's the chapter about?

- Finding **ratios**, and writing and solving **proportions**
- Working with **similar polygons** and **scale drawings**
- Finding and using **probabilities**

WORDS TO KNOW

- **ratio,** *p. 265*
- **proportion,** *p. 269*
- **cross products,** *p. 269*
- **similar polygons,** *p. 280*
- **corresponding angles,** *p. 280*
- **corresponding sides,** *p. 280*
- **scale drawing,** *p. 285*
- **scale factor,** *p. 285*
- **event,** *p. 292*
- **probability of an event,** *p. 292*

PREPARE Chapter Readiness Quiz

Take this quick quiz. If you are unsure of an answer, look back at the reference pages for help.

VOCABULARY CHECK *(refer to p. 148)*

1. Which fraction represents a rate?

Ⓐ $\frac{90 \text{ miles}}{2 \text{ hours}}$ Ⓑ $\frac{3 \text{ hours}}{7 \text{ hours}}$ Ⓒ $\frac{250 \text{ miles}}{100 \text{ miles}}$ Ⓓ $\frac{6 \text{ people}}{36 \text{ people}}$

SKILL CHECK *(refer to pp. 73, 239)*

2. What is the simplest form of the fraction $\frac{24}{60}$?

Ⓕ $\frac{1}{3}$ Ⓖ $\frac{8}{20}$ Ⓗ $\frac{3}{10}$ Ⓙ $\frac{2}{5}$

3. What is the solution of the equation $6x = 78$?

Ⓐ 11   Ⓑ 12   Ⓒ 13   Ⓓ 14

STUDY TIP Don't Erase Mistakes

Instead of erasing mistakes you make on your homework, try making corrections next to the mistakes in a different color.

$\frac{x}{5} = \frac{9}{15}$

$x \cdot 15 = 5 \cdot 9$

$15x = 14$ ← $15x = 45$

$x = \frac{14}{15}$ ⟵ $x = 3$

6.1 Ratios

California Standards

In this lesson you'll:

- Use appropriate notations for ratios. (NS 1.2)
- Interpret and use ratios in different contexts to show the relative sizes of two quantities. (NS 1.2)

Goal 1 Finding Ratios

The **ratio** of a number a to a nonzero number b is the quotient you get when a is divided by b. You can write the ratio of a to b as the fraction $\frac{a}{b}$ (or an equivalent decimal), as $a : b$, or as "a to b."

EXAMPLE 1 Finding a Ratio

BATTING AVERAGES A baseball player's batting average is the ratio of the number of hits to the number of official times at bat. During the 1999 professional baseball season, Nomar Garciaparra got 190 hits in his 532 at bats. Find Garciaparra's batting average.

Solution

$$\text{Batting average} = \frac{190 \text{ hits}}{532 \text{ at bats}} = \frac{\cancel{38} \cdot 5}{\cancel{38} \cdot 14} = \frac{5}{14} \approx 0.357 \text{ (hits per at bat)}$$

Garciaparra's batting average was $\frac{5}{14}$, or about 0.357. (Batting averages are usually reported as decimals rounded to the nearest thousandth.) You can also write this ratio as 5 : 14 or as "5 to 14."

EXAMPLE 2 Comparing Two Ratios

FISH Find the ratio of the number of fish in Tank A to the number in Tank B. Then find the ratio of the volume of water in Tank A to the volume in Tank B. What can you conclude about the two ratios?

A.

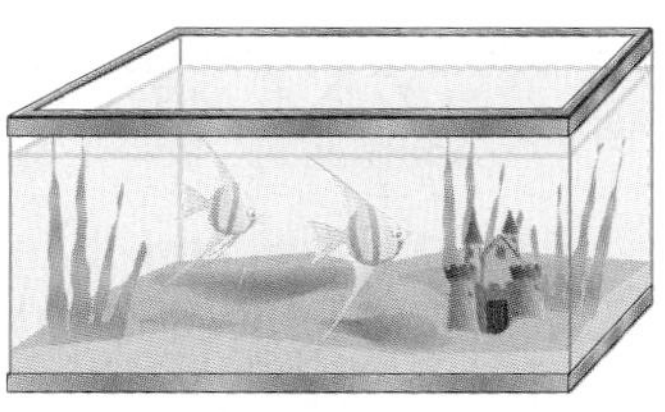

40 quarts

B.

15 gallons

Solution

$$\frac{\text{Fish in Tank A}}{\text{Fish in Tank B}} = \frac{2 \cancel{\text{fish}}}{3 \cancel{\text{fish}}} = \frac{2}{3}$$

$$\frac{\text{Volume of Tank A}}{\text{Volume of Tank B}} = \frac{40 \text{ quarts}}{15 \text{ gallons}} = \frac{10 \cancel{\text{gallons}}}{15 \cancel{\text{gallons}}} = \frac{\cancel{5} \cdot 2}{\cancel{5} \cdot 3} = \frac{2}{3}$$

ANSWER ▶ The two ratios are equal.

Student Help

▶ **STUDY TIP**
When a and b are like quantities (such as volumes) given in different units (such as quarts and gallons), it is desirable to express them in terms of a *common* unit. When a common unit is used, the ratio $a : b$ does not have units.

Goal 2 Comparing Three or More Ratios

> **Student Help**
>
> ▶ **Study Tip**
> When comparing ratios, make sure the ratios have the same units (or no units). For instance, the ratios in Method 1 of Example 3 are all expressed in wins per loss. The ratios in Example 2 on page 265 both have no units.

EXAMPLE 3 Comparing Three Ratios

SOCCER Use ratios to compare the records of the soccer teams at the three given schools. Which team has the best record?

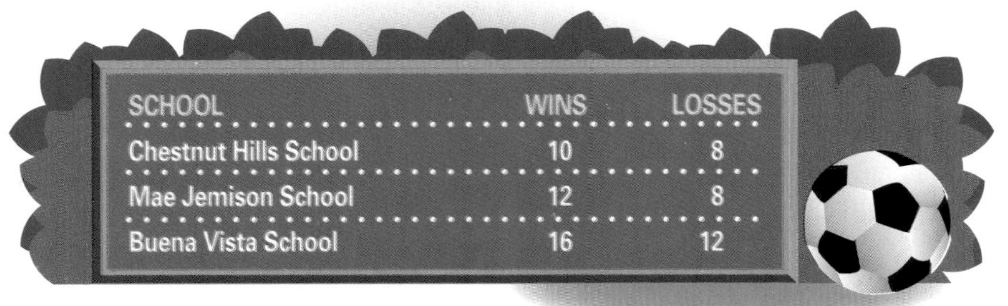

SCHOOL	WINS	LOSSES
Chestnut Hills School	10	8
Mae Jemison School	12	8
Buena Vista School	16	12

Solution

Method 1 Find the team with the greatest ratio of wins to losses.

Chestnut Hills: $\frac{\text{Wins}}{\text{Losses}} = \frac{10}{8} = \frac{\cancel{2} \cdot 5}{\cancel{2} \cdot 4} = \frac{5}{4} = 1.25$ (wins per loss)

Mae Jemison: $\frac{\text{Wins}}{\text{Losses}} = \frac{12}{8} = \frac{\cancel{4} \cdot 3}{\cancel{4} \cdot 2} = \frac{3}{2} = 1.5$ (wins per loss)

Buena Vista: $\frac{\text{Wins}}{\text{Losses}} = \frac{16}{12} = \frac{\cancel{4} \cdot 4}{\cancel{4} \cdot 3} = \frac{4}{3} \approx 1.33$ (wins per loss)

ANSWER ▶ Because 1.5 is greater than 1.25 and 1.33, the team from Mae Jemison School has the best record.

Method 2 Find the team with the greatest ratio of wins to total games.

Chestnut Hills: $\frac{\text{Wins}}{\text{Games}} = \frac{10}{18} = \frac{\cancel{2} \cdot 5}{\cancel{2} \cdot 9} = \frac{5}{9} \approx 0.556$ (wins per game)

Mae Jemison: $\frac{\text{Wins}}{\text{Games}} = \frac{12}{20} = \frac{\cancel{4} \cdot 3}{\cancel{4} \cdot 5} = \frac{3}{5} = 0.6$ (wins per game)

Buena Vista: $\frac{\text{Wins}}{\text{Games}} = \frac{16}{28} = \frac{\cancel{4} \cdot 4}{\cancel{4} \cdot 7} = \frac{4}{7} \approx 0.571$ (wins per game)

ANSWER ▶ Because 0.6 is greater than 0.556 and 0.571, the team from Mae Jemison School has the best record.

> **Student Help**
>
> ▶ **Study Tip**
> The ratios found in Examples 1 and 3 are rates, which you studied in Lesson 3.8. A rate is a ratio of two quantities with *different* units of measure.

In Example 3 notice that expressing the ratios as decimals makes it easy to compare them. You can also compare ratios by writing them as fractions with a common denominator. For example, you can write the ratios of wins to losses for Chestnut Hills, Mae Jemison, and Buena Vista as $\frac{15}{12}$, $\frac{18}{12}$, and $\frac{16}{12}$, respectively, to see that the team from Mae Jemison School has the best record.

6.1 Exercises

Guided Practice

In Exercises 1 and 2, write the ratio in the forms $\frac{a}{b}$, $a:b$, and "a to b."

1. One out of 3 households in the United States owns a dog. Find the ratio of the number of households that own a dog to the number of households that do not.

2. In a survey of 100 dentists, 75 of the dentists prefer Toothpaste A to Toothpaste B. Find the ratio of the number of dentists who prefer Toothpaste A to the number of dentists surveyed.

3. **ERROR ANALYSIS** One student writes the ratio of 9 feet to 5 yards as $\frac{9}{5}$. Explain the student's mistake. Then write the correct ratio.

Tell which ratio is *not* equal to the other two.

4. $\frac{\text{3 balloons}}{\text{5 people}}, \frac{\text{3 people}}{\text{5 balloons}}, \frac{\text{6 balloons}}{\text{10 people}}$

5. $\frac{\text{3 inches}}{\text{1 foot}}, \frac{\text{15 feet}}{\text{60 feet}}, \frac{\text{4 inches}}{\text{20 inches}}$

Practice and Problem Solving

> **Student Help**
>
> ▶ **MORE PRACTICE**
> Extra practice to help you master skills is on page 576.

Rewrite the given ratio in two other ways.

6. 4 to 5 **7.** $\frac{9}{10}$ **8.** 7 : 13

Write the ratio as a fraction in lowest terms. Include units (if any) in your answer.

9. $\frac{\text{9 pounds}}{\text{6 pounds}}$ **10.** 14 feet : 8 sec **11.** $\frac{\text{16 quarts}}{\text{12 gallons}}$

12. 6 acres to 20 acres **13.** 8 wins to 32 games **14.** 1 hour : 15 sec

Tell which of the two ratios is greater.

15. $\frac{\text{4 trees}}{\text{3 trees}}, \frac{\text{21 trees}}{\text{18 trees}}$ **16.** $\frac{\text{220 mi}}{\text{4 hours}}, \frac{\text{300 mi}}{\text{6 hours}}$ **17.** $\frac{\text{10 inches}}{\text{5 feet}}, \frac{\text{6 feet}}{\text{3 yards}}$

GEOMETRY **Find the ratio of the perimeter of the shaded region to the perimeter of the entire region.**

> **Student Help**
>
> ▶ **HOMEWORK HELP**
> INTERNET Extra help with problem solving in Exs. 18–20 is available at www.mcdougallittell.com

18.

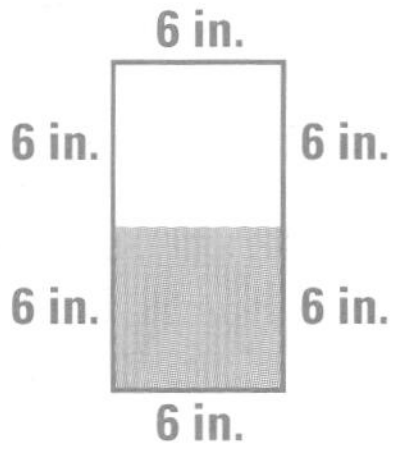

6 in.
6 in. 6 in.
6 in. 6 in.
6 in.

19.

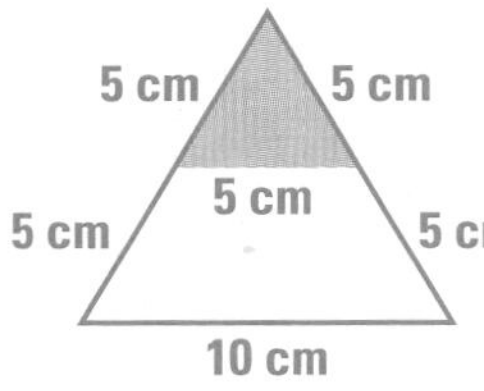

5 cm 5 cm
5 cm
5 cm 5 cm
10 cm

20.

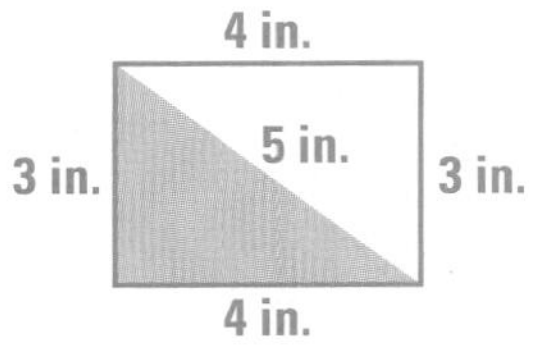

4 in.
3 in. 5 in. 3 in.
4 in.

21. Find the ratio of the number of hands to the number of fingers in a group of people.

22. Find the ratio of the number of legs to the number of eyes in a group of cats.

MARBLES **In Exercises 23–25, use the diagram of the marbles below.**

23. What is the ratio of purple marbles to total marbles?

24. What is the ratio of red marbles to yellow marbles?

25. What is the ratio of blue marbles to red marbles?

Student Help

LOOK BACK
For help with finding batting averages, see Example 1 on page 265.

26. BATTING AVERAGES Which of the following professional baseball players had the best batting average during the 1999 season?

Garret Anderson:	188 hits in 620 official at bats
Jason Giambi:	181 hits in 575 official at bats
Raul Mondesi:	152 hits in 601 official at bats

Chapter Opener Link **In Exercises 27 and 28, use the following information.** A camera's shutter speed is the ratio of the number of pictures taken to the time the shutter is open. To take 1 picture, the shutters on Camera A and Camera B open for $\frac{1}{60}$ sec and $\frac{1}{120}$ sec, respectively.

27. Find each camera's shutter speed. Include units in your answers.

28. MATHEMATICAL REASONING Which is faster, the shutter speed for Camera A or the shutter speed for Camera B? Explain.

29. CHALLENGE In 1948 a typical car had 55 wires and 150 feet of wiring. In 1994 a typical car had 1500 wires and 1 mile of wiring. Which had a greater relative increase from 1948 to 1994, the number of wires or the length of wiring? Explain using ratios. ▶Source: *USA Today*

Multiple-Choice Practice

30. In an Olympic triathlon, competitors swim 1.5 km, bicycle 40 km, and run 10 km. What is the ratio of running to swimming distance?

(A) 20 : 103 (B) 2 : 3 (C) 20 : 3 (D) 80 : 3

31. A shopper buys a 1 gallon jug of milk and an 8 fluid ounce can of juice. What is the ratio of the volume of milk to the volume of juice?

(F) 1 : 16 (G) 1 : 8 (H) 8 : 1 (J) 16 : 1

6.2 Solving Proportions

California Standards

In this lesson you'll:

- Understand cross multiplication as the multiplication of both sides of an equation by multiplicative inverses. (NS 1.3)
- Use cross multiplication as a method for solving proportions. (NS 1.3)

Goal 1 Using the Cross Products of a Proportion

An equation that equates two ratios is a **proportion**. The proportion $\frac{a}{b} = \frac{c}{d}$ is read as "a is to b as c is to d." A proportion has two **cross products**, $a \cdot d$ and $b \cdot c$, as shown below. The process of forming cross products is called *cross multiplying*.

$$\frac{a}{b} \times \frac{c}{d} \quad \begin{matrix} \longrightarrow b \cdot c \\ \longrightarrow a \cdot d \end{matrix}$$

Cross products

Cross Products Property

In Words In a proportion, the cross products are equal.

In Algebra If $\frac{a}{b} = \frac{c}{d}$, then $a \cdot d = b \cdot c$.

In Arithmetic Because $\frac{3}{4} = \frac{6}{8}$, you know that $3 \cdot 8 = 4 \cdot 6$.

EXAMPLE 1 Using Mathematical Reasoning

Show that the cross products property is true.

Solution

$\frac{a}{b} = \frac{c}{d}$	Write general proportion.
$\frac{1}{b} \cdot a = \frac{1}{d} \cdot c$	Change division to multiplication.
$b \cdot \frac{1}{b} \cdot a = b \cdot \frac{1}{d} \cdot c$	Multiply each side by b, the multiplicative inverse of $\frac{1}{b}$.
$a = \frac{1}{d} \cdot b \cdot c$	$b \cdot \frac{1}{b} = 1$ and $1 \cdot a = a$.
$d \cdot a = d \cdot \frac{1}{d} \cdot b \cdot c$	Multiply each side by d, the multiplicative inverse of $\frac{1}{d}$.
$a \cdot d = b \cdot c$	$d \cdot a = a \cdot d$, $d \cdot \frac{1}{d} = 1$, and $1 \cdot b \cdot c = b \cdot c$.

The steps above show that if $\frac{a}{b} = \frac{c}{d}$, then $a \cdot d = b \cdot c$. So, the cross products property is true.

Student Help

Look Back
For help with multiplicative inverses, see page 134.

Student Help

▶ STUDY TIP
An if-then statement has the form "If *p*, then *q*." The contrapositive of this statement is "If not *q*, then not *p*," and the converse is "If *q*, then *p*." The truth of an if-then statement implies the truth of its contrapositive but not *necessarily* the truth of its converse.

The fact that the cross products property is true implies that its *contrapositive* is also true: If the cross products formed from two ratios are *not* equal, then the ratios themselves are not equal. The *converse* of the cross products property is true as well: If the cross products formed from two ratios *are* equal, then the ratios are equal (see Exercise 18). You can use these results to determine whether any two ratios are equal.

EXAMPLE 2 Telling Whether Ratios Are Equal

Use cross products to tell whether the two ratios are equal.

a. $\frac{2}{3}$ and $\frac{12}{16}$ **b.** $\frac{4}{14}$ and $\frac{6}{21}$

Solution

a. The cross products for $\frac{2}{3}$ and $\frac{12}{16}$ are $\mathbf{2} \cdot \mathbf{16} = 32$ and $\mathbf{3} \cdot \mathbf{12} = 36$.
Because the cross products are not equal, the ratios are not equal.

b. The cross products for $\frac{4}{14}$ and $\frac{6}{21}$ are $\mathbf{4} \cdot \mathbf{21} = 84$ and $\mathbf{14} \cdot \mathbf{6} = 84$.
Because the cross products are equal, the ratios are equal.

Goal 2 SOLVING PROPORTIONS

In many problems involving a proportion, one of the numerators or one of the denominators is a variable. Here is an example:

$$\frac{8}{x} = \frac{2}{3}$$

To *solve* this proportion, you find the value of x that makes the equation true. You can use the cross products property to solve proportions.

EXAMPLE 3 Solving a Proportion

Solve the proportion $\frac{8}{x} = \frac{2}{3}$.

Solution

$\frac{8}{x} = \frac{2}{3}$	Write original proportion.
$8 \cdot 3 = x \cdot 2$	Use cross products property.
$\frac{8 \cdot 3}{2} = \frac{x \cdot 2}{2}$	Divide each side by 2.
$12 = x$	Simplify. x is by itself.

ANSWER ▶ The solution is 12.

Student Help

▶ STUDY TIP
To check the solution in Example 3, substitute 12 for x in the original proportion:

$$\frac{8}{x} = \frac{2}{3}$$

$$\frac{8}{12} \stackrel{?}{=} \frac{2}{3}$$

$$\frac{2}{3} = \frac{2}{3} \checkmark$$

EXAMPLE 4 Solving a Proportion in Real Life

WORLD WIDE WEB In 1998, a survey asked a sample of 3290 World Wide Web users in the United States how often they bought items on-line. The graph shows the results. Using the proportion below, estimate how many of the 57 million Web users in the U.S. made on-line purchases monthly in 1998.

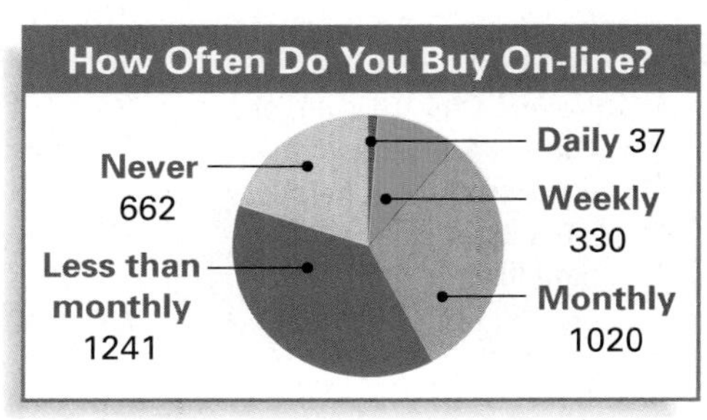

▶ Source: GVU's Tenth WWW User Survey

$$\frac{\text{Monthly purchasers in sample}}{\text{Total Web users in sample}} = \frac{\text{Monthly purchasers in U.S.}}{\text{Total Web users in U.S.}}$$

Solution

Let x be the number (in millions) of monthly on-line purchasers in the United States. Substitute x and the known quantities into the given proportion. Then solve the proportion to find the value of x.

$\frac{1020}{3290} = \frac{x}{57}$ Substitute into proportion.

$1020 \cdot 57 = 3290 \cdot x$ Use cross products property.

$\frac{1020 \cdot 57}{\mathbf{3290}} = \frac{3290 \cdot x}{\mathbf{3290}}$ Divide each side by 3290.

$17.7 \approx x$ Simplify. x is by itself.

ANSWER ▶ In 1998 about 17.7 million Web users in the United States made on-line purchases monthly.

6.2 Exercises

Guided Practice

Write the verbal description as a proportion.

1. 5 is to x as 2 is to 3.

2. 3 is to 5 as 2 is to x.

3. 5 is to 2 as x is to 3.

4. x is to 5 as 2 is to 3.

Use cross products to tell whether the two ratios are equal.

5. $\frac{3}{4}$ and $\frac{9}{12}$

6. $\frac{21}{15}$ and $\frac{3}{2}$

7. $\frac{7}{5}$ and $\frac{56}{35}$

8. $\frac{24}{44}$ and $\frac{6}{11}$

Solve the proportion.

9. $\frac{x}{6} = \frac{1}{2}$

10. $\frac{15}{x} = \frac{5}{4}$

11. $\frac{16}{40} = \frac{14}{n}$

12. $\frac{11}{5} = \frac{k}{3}$

Practice and Problem Solving

Student Help

▶**MORE PRACTICE** Extra practice to help you master skills is on page 576.

In Exercises 13–16, write the verbal description as a proportion.

13. 7 is to x as 14 is to 20.

14. n is to 9 as 10 is to 18.

15. 35 is to 25 as p is to 5.

16. 53 is to 2 as 6 is to y.

17. ERROR ANALYSIS One student solves the proportion $\frac{4}{3} = \frac{12}{x}$ as shown. Explain the student's mistake. Then find the correct solution.

$$\frac{4}{3} = \frac{12}{x}$$
$$4 \cdot 12 = 3 \cdot x$$
$$\frac{4 \cdot 12}{3} = \frac{3 \cdot x}{3}$$
$$16 = x$$

18. MATHEMATICAL REASONING Show that the converse of the cross products property is true: If $a \cdot d = b \cdot c$ for two ratios $\frac{a}{b}$ and $\frac{c}{d}$, then the ratios are equal.

Use cross products to tell whether the two ratios are equal.

19. $\frac{4}{5}$ and $\frac{15}{20}$

20. $\frac{20}{36}$ and $\frac{5}{9}$

21. $\frac{10}{4}$ and $\frac{25}{10}$

22. $\frac{32}{6}$ and $\frac{17}{3}$

23. $\frac{7}{8}$ and $\frac{49}{64}$

24. $\frac{9}{10}$ and $\frac{99}{100}$

25. $\frac{121}{77}$ and $\frac{33}{21}$

26. $\frac{123}{287}$ and $\frac{93}{217}$

In Exercises 27–38, solve the proportion.

27. $\frac{x}{12} = \frac{1}{4}$

28. $\frac{x}{6} = \frac{9}{54}$

29. $\frac{8}{x} = \frac{16}{10}$

30. $\frac{3}{8} = \frac{x}{32}$

31. $\frac{6}{20} = \frac{9}{a}$

32. $\frac{k}{22} = \frac{21}{14}$

33. $\frac{3}{16} = \frac{r}{2}$

34. $\frac{27}{8} = \frac{18}{s}$

35. $\frac{49}{91} = \frac{v}{52}$

36. $\frac{39}{u} = \frac{63}{2}$

37. $\frac{3.6}{w} = \frac{9}{10}$

38. $\frac{5}{1.25} = \frac{18}{y}$

Student Help

▶**HOMEWORK HELP** INTERNET Extra help with problem solving in Exs. 39–40 is available at www.mcdougallittell.com

39. SUMMER CAMP You are hiring counselors for a summer camp. You need 2 counselors for every 15 campers. You expect to have 180 campers. Use the proportion below to find the number of counselors you should hire.

$$\frac{\text{Number of counselors}}{\text{Number of campers}} = \frac{2}{15}$$

40. TRAVEL You are driving from Dubuque, Iowa, to Cleveland, Ohio. On your way you pass through Chicago, Illinois. It takes you 3.5 hours to drive the 180 miles from Dubuque to Chicago. Use the proportion below to estimate how long it will take to drive the remaining 350 miles from Chicago to Cleveland.

$$\frac{\text{Dubuque-to-Chicago distance}}{\text{Dubuque-to-Chicago time}} = \frac{\text{Chicago-to-Cleveland distance}}{\text{Chicago-to-Cleveland time}}$$

Link to Careers

AERIAL PHOTOGRAPHERS use mathematics to find flying altitudes that produce the best pictures. The greater the altitude, the smaller objects in an aerial photograph appear.

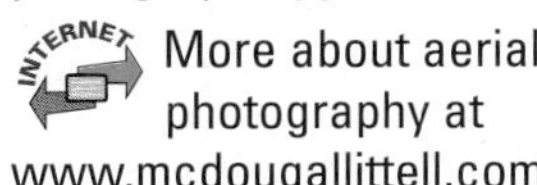
More about aerial photography at www.mcdougallittell.com

41. AERIAL PHOTOGRAPHY You are photographing a river 300 meters wide from a hot air balloon. You want the river's image on the 35 millimeter film to be 17.5 millimeters wide so that the river occupies half the width of the photographs. The *focal length* of the camera lens (the distance from the lens to the film) is 50 millimeters. Use the proportion below to find the altitude at which you should fly.

$$\frac{\text{Width of river's image}}{\text{Actual width of river}} = \frac{\text{Focal length}}{\text{Altitude of balloon}}$$

In Exercises 42–47, solve the proportion.

EXAMPLE ***Solving Proportions with Variable Expressions***

Solve the proportion $\frac{x-4}{6} = \frac{5}{2}$.

Solution

$\frac{x-4}{6} = \frac{5}{2}$ Write original proportion.

$(x-4) \cdot 2 = 6 \cdot 5$ Use cross products property.

$2x - 8 = 30$ Use distributive property and simplify.

$2x = 38$ Add 8 to each side.

$x = 19$ Divide each side by 2.

ANSWER ▶ The solution is 19. Check this in the original proportion.

42. $\frac{2x}{25} = \frac{4}{5}$ **43.** $\frac{9}{4x} = \frac{3}{8}$ **44.** $\frac{5}{6} = \frac{y+10}{30}$

45. $\frac{21}{2n+1} = \frac{7}{3}$ **46.** $\frac{2}{3} = \frac{7}{5w-2}$ **47.** $\frac{x-6}{8} = \frac{3}{2}$

CHALLENGE **Decide whether the statement is *true* or *false*. If the statement is true, give an algebraic argument for why it is true. If the statement is false, give an example that shows it is false.**

48. If $\frac{a}{b} = \frac{c}{d}$, then $\frac{d}{b} = \frac{c}{a}$. **49.** If $\frac{a}{b} = \frac{c}{d}$, then $\frac{a}{d} = \frac{b}{c}$.

Multiple-Choice Practice

50. If $\frac{12}{m} = \frac{n}{3}$, what is the value of $m \cdot n$?

Ⓐ 4 Ⓑ 9 Ⓒ 15 Ⓓ 36

51. What is the solution of $\frac{28}{x} = \frac{7}{4}$?

Ⓕ 12 Ⓖ 14 Ⓗ 16 Ⓙ 20

6.3 Writing Proportions

California Standards

In this lesson you'll:

- Use proportions to solve problems. (NS 1.3)
- Solve problems involving rates. (AF 2.3)

Goal 1 WRITING PROPORTIONS TO SOLVE PROBLEMS

In Lesson 5.2 you learned a problem solving strategy for writing sentences as equations. You can also use this strategy to write proportions.

EXAMPLE 1 Writing a Proportion

HISTORY LINK A monument in Abu Simbel, Egypt, is shown at the right. The statues are of the pharaoh Ramses II. You are drawing the monument. You make the flat wall behind the statues 8 inches tall in your drawing. How tall should you make each statue?

Solution

The height of a statue compared with the height of the wall—that is, the ratio of statue height to wall height—should be the same in your drawing as it is in the actual monument. Write and solve a proportion.

VERBAL MODEL

$$\frac{\text{Statue height in drawing}}{\text{Wall height in drawing}} = \frac{\text{Actual statue height}}{\text{Actual wall height}}$$

LABELS

Statue height in drawing = x (inches)

Wall height in drawing = **8** (inches)

Actual statue height = **67** (feet)

Actual wall height = **100** (feet)

ALGEBRAIC MODEL

$$\frac{x \text{ inches}}{8 \text{ inches}} = \frac{67 \text{ feet}}{100 \text{ feet}}$$ Write algebraic model.

$$x \cdot 100 = 8 \cdot 67$$ Cross products property

$$\frac{x \cdot 100}{100} = \frac{8 \cdot 67}{100}$$ Divide each side by 100.

$$x = 5.36$$ Simplify. x is by itself.

ANSWER ▶ You should draw each statue about 5.4 inches tall.

Student Help

▶ **STUDY TIP**
When you write a proportion, be sure each side compares quantities in the same order. For instance, each side of the proportion in Example 1 compares statue height to wall height.

Goal 2 SOLVING RATE PROBLEMS

You can use proportions to solve many real-life problems involving rates, as the next example illustrates.

Link to Science

LOIHI SEAMOUNT is fueled by the same underground lava source that fuels Hawaii's two other active volcanoes, Kilauea (shown above) and Mauna Loa.

More about volcanoes is available at www.mcdougallittell.com

EXAMPLE 2 Solving a Rate Problem

SCIENCE LINK Loihi Seamount is an underwater volcano off the coast of Hawaii. Loihi's peak is about 3180 feet below the surface of the Pacific Ocean. Scientists estimate that Loihi has grown about 300 feet during the last 1000 years. Assuming this rate of growth continues, predict when Loihi will reach the ocean surface.

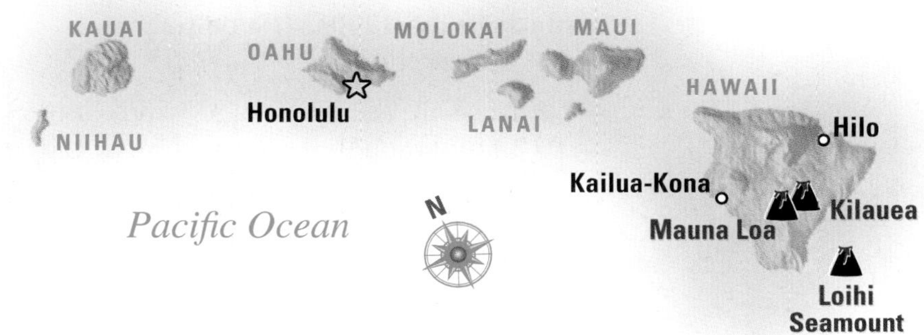

Solution

Loihi's rate of growth is its increase in height divided by the elapsed time. Write a proportion equating the future and past rates of growth.

VERBAL MODEL

$$\frac{\text{Additional height needed}}{\text{Additional time needed}} = \frac{\text{Past increase in height}}{\text{Past time}}$$

LABELS

Additional height needed = **3180** (feet)

Additional time needed = x (years)

Past increase in height = **300** (feet)

Past time = **1000** (years)

ALGEBRAIC MODEL

$$\frac{3180 \text{ feet}}{x \text{ years}} = \frac{300 \text{ feet}}{1000 \text{ years}}$$ Write algebraic model.

$$3180 \cdot 1000 = x \cdot 300$$ Cross products property

$$\frac{3180 \cdot 1000}{300} = \frac{x \cdot 300}{300}$$ Divide each side by 300.

$$10{,}600 = x$$ Simplify. x is by itself.

ANSWER ▶ You can predict that Loihi will reach the ocean surface in about 10,600 years.

Student Help

▶ **MORE EXAMPLES**

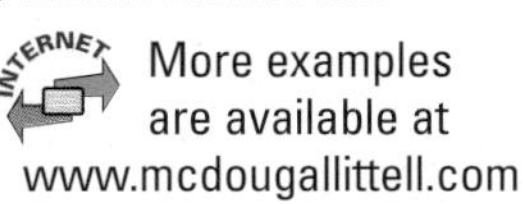

More examples are available at www.mcdougallittell.com

6.3 Exercises

Guided Practice

1. **READING A BOOK** You are reading a 220 page book. It takes you 15 minutes to read the first 10 pages. Use the proportion below to estimate the time it will take you to read the entire book.

$$\frac{10 \text{ pages}}{15 \text{ minutes}} = \frac{220 \text{ pages}}{x \text{ minutes}}$$

History Link **In Exercises 2 and 3, use the photograph showing a Chinese rug made in the 1700s. The actual rug is 154 inches long.**

2. Measure the length and width of the photograph to the nearest inch. Using the verbal model below, write and solve a proportion to find the width of the actual rug.

$$\frac{\text{Length of photo}}{\text{Width of photo}} = \frac{\text{Length of rug}}{\text{Width of rug}}$$

3. Suppose you have a different photograph of the rug. In your photograph the rug is 16 centimeters wide. How long is the rug in your photograph?

Practice and Problem Solving

Student Help

▶ **MORE PRACTICE** Extra practice to help you master skills is on page 576.

In Exercises 4 and 5, tell which of the proportions you could *not* use to solve the problem. Explain your answer.

4. **STAMPS** You are an artist designing a new postage stamp. The stamp must be 3 centimeters tall by 2 centimeters wide. You make a sketch of the stamp that is 6 inches tall. How wide should the sketch be?

A. $\frac{3 \text{ cm}}{2 \text{ cm}} = \frac{6 \text{ in.}}{x \text{ in.}}$ **B.** $\frac{3 \text{ cm}}{6 \text{ in.}} = \frac{2 \text{ cm}}{x \text{ in.}}$ **C.** $\frac{3 \text{ cm}}{x \text{ in.}} = \frac{2 \text{ cm}}{6 \text{ in.}}$

5. **PAINTING** One gallon of paint covers 900 square feet. What area does one quart of the same paint cover?

A. $\frac{4 \text{ qt}}{900 \text{ ft}^2} = \frac{1 \text{ qt}}{x \text{ ft}^2}$ **B.** $\frac{1 \text{ qt}}{4 \text{ qt}} = \frac{900 \text{ ft}^2}{x \text{ ft}^2}$ **C.** $\frac{4 \text{ qt}}{1 \text{ qt}} = \frac{900 \text{ ft}^2}{x \text{ ft}^2}$

6. **WRITING** Describe a real-life situation that can be modeled by a proportion. Write a verbal model for the proportion. Then use the verbal model to write an algebraic equation, and solve it.

BUSINESS In Exercises 7 and 8, use the following information. A company pays all employees the same hourly wage for overtime. The graph shows how many overtime hours employees worked in the first six months of the year. In January the company paid \$2160 for overtime.

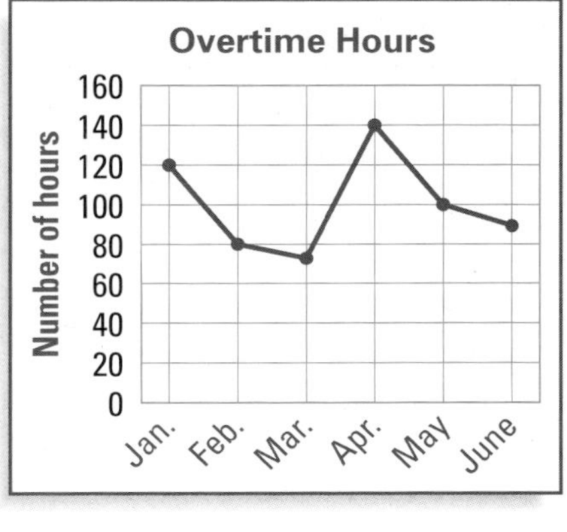

7. Use the verbal model below to estimate how much the company paid for overtime in May.

$$\frac{\text{Overtime paid in January}}{\text{Overtime hours in January}} = \frac{\text{Overtime paid in May}}{\text{Overtime hours in May}}$$

8. The company can afford to pay only \$1300 for overtime in July. At most how many overtime hours can employees work in July?

In Exercises 9–13, use proportions to solve the problems.

9. EXCHANGE RATE The unit of money in Kenya is the shilling. In September, 1999, \$1.00 from the United States was worth about 76 Kenyan shillings. Suppose a traveler returning to the United States from Kenya wants to exchange 9500 shillings for dollars. At the given exchange rate, how many dollars will the traveler receive?

10. REAL ESTATE You can rent an office with 350 square feet of floor space for \$1400 per month. You can rent a larger office in the same building for \$2500 per month. The cost per square foot is the same for both offices. Find the amount of floor space in the larger office.

11. *Science Link* For a science fair, you are creating a mobile of the nine planets in the solar system. In your mobile the diameter of Jupiter is 18 inches. The actual diameter of Jupiter is about 88,700 miles. Given that the actual diameter of Earth is about 7930 miles, what should the diameter of Earth be in your mobile?

12. ELECTRICITY A 100 watt light bulb left on for one 30-day month uses 72 kilowatt-hours of electricity. Suppose the cost of this electricity is \$5.76. How much electricity does a 100 watt light bulb use in one week? How much money does this electricity cost?

13. *History Link* The first census of the United States population was taken in 1790. At that time the U.S. population was about 3,929,000, and the population of Maryland was about 320,000.

a. In 1998 the U.S. population was about 270,299,000. If Maryland's share of the U.S. population was the same in 1998 as it was in 1790, what would the population of Maryland have been in 1998?

b. MATHEMATICAL REASONING Maryland's actual population in 1998 was about 5,135,000. Compare this population with your answer from part (a). Why are the numbers so different?

Link to History

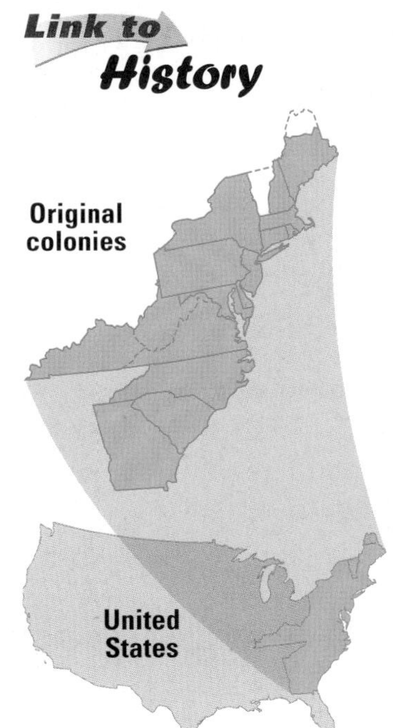

EARLY U.S. HISTORY The map shows the United States in 1790, when there were only 13 states. These had been the original 13 colonies of Great Britain before the U.S. gained its independence.

14. CHALLENGE You plant a rectangular tomato garden that is 6 feet by 10 feet. The garden produces 192 pounds of tomatoes. The next year, you increase the garden's size to 8 feet by 15 feet. Estimate how many pounds of tomatoes the larger garden will produce. Explain your approach to the problem and show any proportions you used.

Multiple-Choice Practice

15. A college advertises that it has a student-to-faculty ratio of 16 to 1 and an enrollment of 2400 students. Which proportion can you use to find the number of faculty at the college?

Ⓐ $\frac{1}{16} = \frac{x}{2400}$ Ⓑ $\frac{1}{2400} = \frac{16}{x}$ Ⓒ $\frac{x}{16} = \frac{1}{2400}$ Ⓓ $\frac{16}{1} = \frac{x}{2400}$

16. A person who weighs 90 pounds on Earth would weigh only 15 pounds on the moon. How much would a person who weighs 120 pounds on Earth weigh on the moon?

Ⓕ 17 lb Ⓖ 20 lb Ⓗ 45 lb Ⓙ 720 lb

17. A 10.5 ounce can of clam chowder contains 220 Cal. About how many calories are in an 18.5 ounce can of the same clam chowder?

Ⓐ 125 Cal Ⓑ 304 Cal Ⓒ 388 Cal Ⓓ 440 Cal

Mixed Review

Perform the indicated conversion. *(3.7)*

18. 7 feet to inches

19. 450 milliliters to liters

20. 80 ounces to pounds

21. 24 hours to minutes

22. 20 gallons to pints

23. 3000 cm^2 to square meters

Perform the indicated operation. *(4.3–4.6)*

24. $4 - (-8)$

25. $-27 \div 3$

26. $21 + (-4)$

27. $-15 \cdot 3$

28. $-16 - (-12)$

29. $-72 \div (-9)$

In Exercises 30–35, solve the equation and check your solution. *(5.3–5.6)*

30. $x + 8 = -2$

31. $y - 5 = 6$

32. $-4c = -24$

33. $\frac{k}{3} = -7$

34. $6.8 = m + 1.6$

35. $9.9 = 4.5x$

MAKO SHARKS can grow up to 12 feet long and weigh over 1000 pounds. Makos have been known to leap out of the water and onto passing boats.

36. Science Link The short-finned mako shark is thought to be the world's fastest fish. The mako's top speed is about 50 feet per second. Write and solve an equation to find the time it takes a mako shark to swim 300 feet. Compare your answer with the time it takes the fastest humans to run the same distance (about 10 seconds). *(5.2)*

Chapter 6 Mid-Chapter Test

Take this test as you would take a test in class. The answers to the exercises are given in the back of the book.

Rewrite the given ratio in two other ways.

1. $\frac{3}{5}$ **2.** 17 to 2 **3.** 2 to 17 **4.** 1 : 9

Write the ratio as a fraction in lowest terms. Include units (if any) in your answer.

5. $\frac{25 \text{ meters}}{35 \text{ meters}}$ **6.** 4 miles to 6 hours **7.** $\frac{76 \text{ people}}{16 \text{ pies}}$ **8.** 12 ounces : 3 pounds

Tell which of the two ratios is greater.

9. $\frac{20 \text{ movies}}{6 \text{ movies}}, \frac{30 \text{ books}}{8 \text{ books}}$ **10.** $\frac{\$5}{2 \text{ gallons}}, \frac{\$9}{4 \text{ gallons}}$ **11.** $\frac{1 \text{ week}}{1 \text{ day}}, \frac{1 \text{ day}}{1 \text{ hour}}$

CARS In Exercises 12–14, use the diagram at the right to find the indicated ratio.

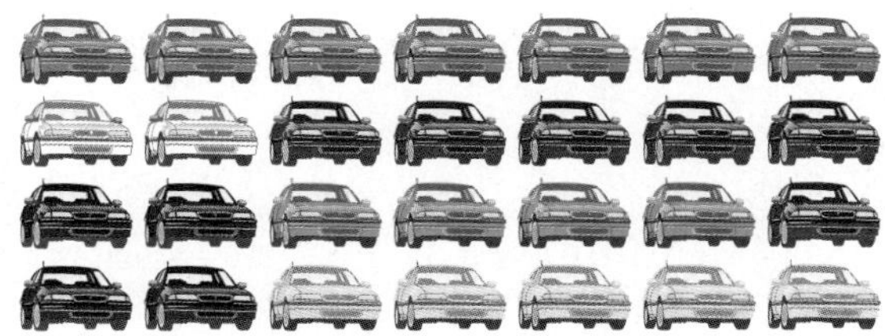

12. Yellow cars to total cars

13. Yellow cars to blue cars

14. White cars to red cars

Write the verbal description as a proportion.

15. x is to 3 as 6 is to 18. **16.** 11 is to t as 1 is to 5.

17. 28 is to 42 as 10 is to p. **18.** a is to u as b is to v.

Use cross products to tell whether the two ratios are equal.

19. $\frac{5}{2}$ and $\frac{15}{6}$ **20.** $\frac{3}{4}$ and $\frac{14}{18}$ **21.** $\frac{8}{30}$ and $\frac{12}{40}$ **22.** $\frac{135}{54}$ and $\frac{65}{26}$

In Exercises 23–26, solve the proportion.

23. $\frac{x}{36} = \frac{4}{9}$ **24.** $\frac{12}{y} = \frac{28}{21}$ **25.** $\frac{6}{7} = \frac{4}{k}$ **26.** $\frac{6.6}{11} = \frac{a}{21.5}$

27. **STAIR CLIMBING** On February 16, 1993, Geoff Case climbed the 1575 steps of the Empire State Building in 618 seconds. Find the approximate number of steps he climbed in 1 minute.

28. **Science Link** About 3 tons of rock must be mined to produce 0.007 ounce (1 carat) of diamonds. How much rock must be mined to produce 1 ounce of diamonds? How many ounces of diamonds would you expect 10 tons of rock to produce?

6.4 Similar Polygons

California Standards

In this lesson you'll:

- Use a proportion to find the length of a side of a polygon similar to a known polygon. (NS 1.3)
- Express in symbolic form simple relationships arising from geometry. (AF 3.2)

Goal 1 Using Similar Polygons

From Lesson 1.7 you know that a polygon is a closed geometric figure with straight sides. Polygons are classified based on their number of sides.

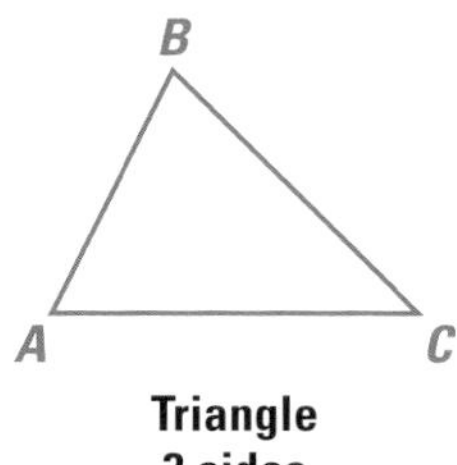

Triangle
3 sides

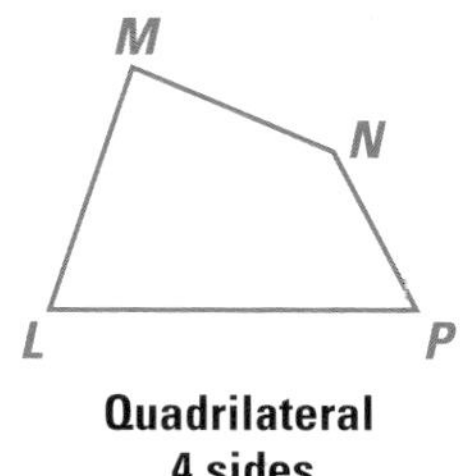

Quadrilateral
4 sides

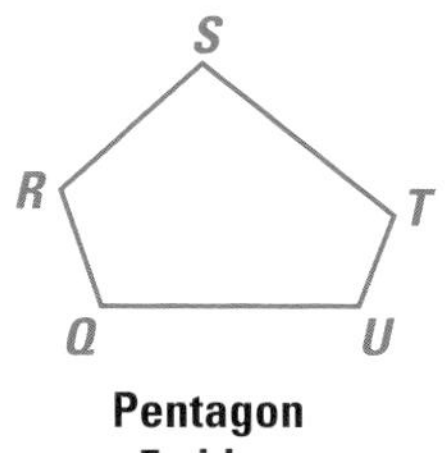

Pentagon
5 sides

You can name a polygon using the letters at the polygon's corners. For example, the triangle above can be named "triangle *ABC*." Here is some notation you can use to name parts of triangle *ABC*.

$\overline{AB}$: the side joining points *A* and *B*

AB: the length of side $\overline{AB}$

$\angle A$: the angle at point *A*

$m\angle A$: the measure of $\angle A$

EXAMPLE 1 Identifying Parts of a Polygon

Tell what type of polygon figure *WXYZ* is. Use the mathematical notation described above to identify the polygon's sides, the lengths of the sides, and the angle measures.

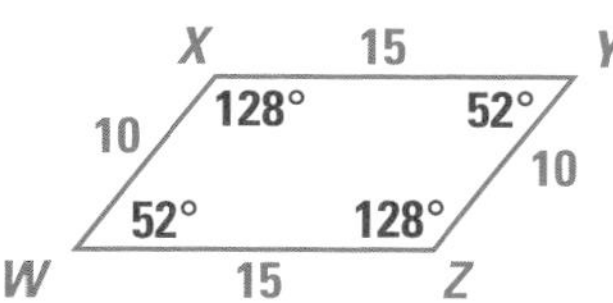

Solution

Because polygon *WXYZ* has 4 sides, it is a quadrilateral. The sides of the polygon are $\overline{WX}$, $\overline{XY}$, $\overline{YZ}$, and $\overline{WZ}$. The lengths of the sides are $WX = 10$, $XY = 15$, $YZ = 10$, and $WZ = 15$. The angle measures are $m\angle W = 52°$, $m\angle X = 128°$, $m\angle Y = 52°$, and $m\angle Z = 128°$.

Student Help

▶ Skills Review
For help with angles and their measures, see page 563.

Two polygons are **similar** if you can pair up their angles and their sides so that these conditions are met:

- Paired angles, called **corresponding angles**, have equal measure.
- The ratios of the lengths of paired sides, called **corresponding sides**, are equal. The sides of the polygons are then said to be **proportional**.

EXAMPLE 2 Finding Ratios of Corresponding Side Lengths

Triangle ABC and triangle PQR are similar. What is the ratio of the length of a side of triangle ABC to the length of the corresponding side of triangle PQR?

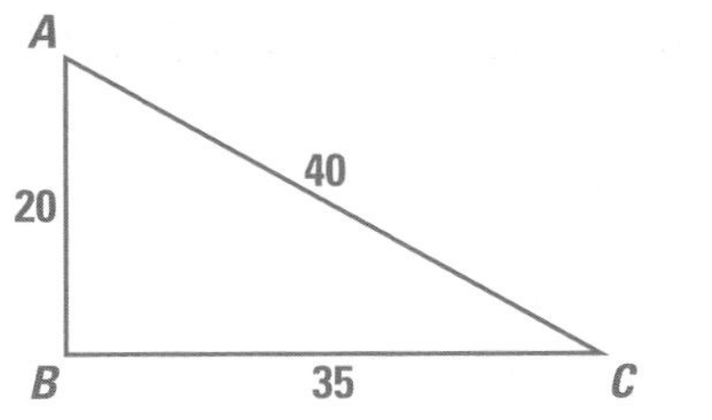

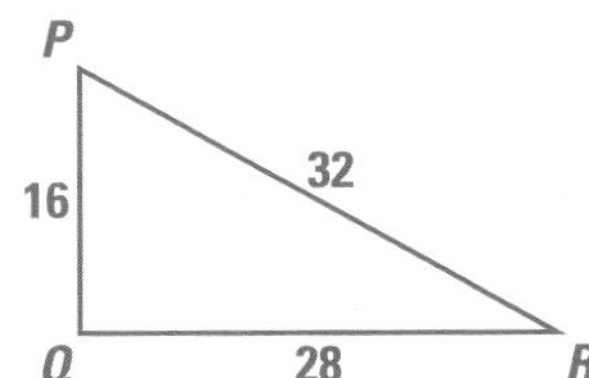

Solution

Here are the pairs of corresponding sides: $\overline{AB}$ and $\overline{PQ}$, $\overline{BC}$ and $\overline{QR}$, and $\overline{AC}$ and $\overline{PR}$. The ratios of the side lengths of triangle ABC to the corresponding side lengths of triangle PQR are as follows:

$$\frac{AB}{PQ} = \frac{20}{16} = \frac{5}{4} \qquad \frac{BC}{QR} = \frac{35}{28} = \frac{5}{4} \qquad \frac{AC}{PR} = \frac{40}{32} = \frac{5}{4}$$

ANSWER ▶ The ratio of the lengths of corresponding sides is $\frac{5}{4}$.

Student Help

▶ **STUDY TIP**
When naming similar polygons, list letters for corresponding angles in the same order. In Example 2, for instance, you could not write "triangle ABC and triangle RQP are similar" because $\angle A$ and $\angle R$ are not corresponding angles.

EXAMPLE 3 Finding Missing Measures in a Polygon

Quadrilaterals $ABCD$ and $EFGH$ are similar.

a. Find the measure of $\angle G$.

b. Find the length of side $\overline{FG}$.

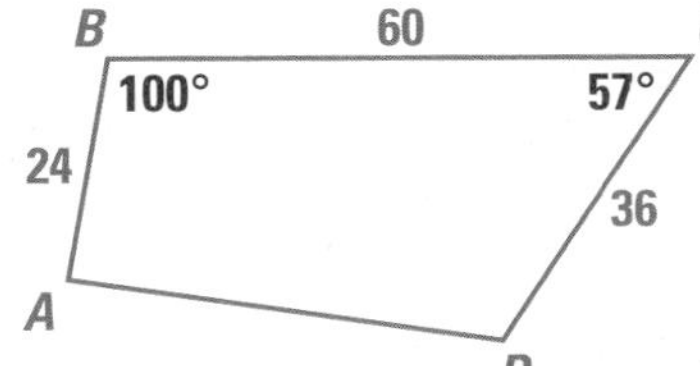

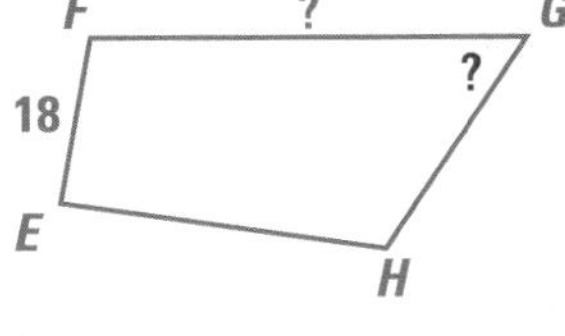

Solution

a. $\angle G$ and $\angle C$ are corresponding angles, so $m\angle G = m\angle C = 57°$.

b. Use the fact that ratios of corresponding side lengths are equal.

$\frac{AB}{EF} = \frac{BC}{FG}$ — Write a proportion involving FG.

$\frac{24}{18} = \frac{60}{FG}$ — Substitute known values.

$24 \cdot FG = 18 \cdot 60$ — Cross products property

$\frac{24 \cdot FG}{24} = \frac{18 \cdot 60}{24}$ — Divide each side by 24.

$FG = 45$ — Simplify. FG is by itself.

Goal 2 USING SIMILAR TRIANGLES IN REAL LIFE

You can show that two polygons are similar by checking that corresponding angles have equal measure and corresponding sides are proportional. For triangles, you can also use the simpler similarity test given below. (In geometry this test is called a *postulate*, which is a statement that is accepted as true without proof.)

ANGLE-ANGLE SIMILARITY TEST FOR TRIANGLES

If two angles of one triangle have the same measures as two angles of another triangle, then the triangles are similar.

EXAMPLE 4 Measuring a Height Indirectly

FLAGPOLES Lisa is in Dorris, California, home of the tallest flagpole in the United States. To estimate the flagpole's height, she stands so that the end of her shadow meets the end of the pole's shadow, as shown below. Find the height of the flagpole.

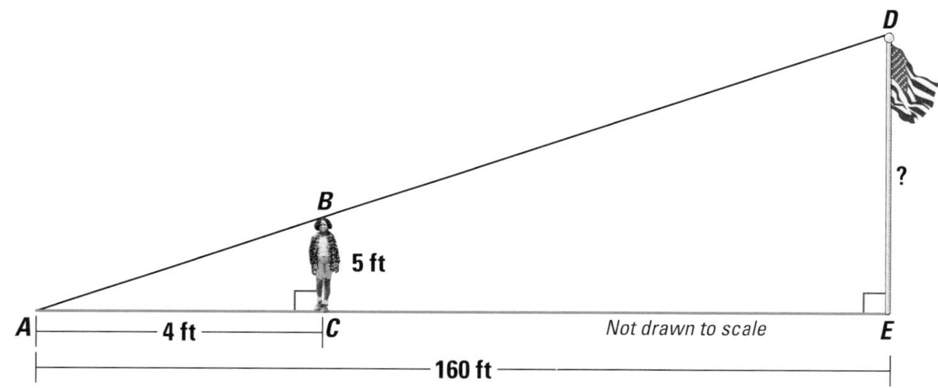

Solution

Notice that triangle ABC and triangle ADE share $\angle A$ and that $m\angle C = m\angle E = 90°$. Because two angles of triangle ABC have the same measures as two angles of triangle ADE, the triangles are similar. Therefore, ratios of corresponding side lengths are equal.

$\frac{BC}{DE} = \frac{AC}{AE}$ Write a proportion involving DE, the height of the flagpole.

$\frac{5}{DE} = \frac{4}{160}$ Substitute known values.

$5 \cdot 160 = DE \cdot 4$ Cross products property

$\frac{5 \cdot 160}{4} = \frac{DE \cdot 4}{4}$ Divide each side by 4.

$200 = DE$ Simplify. DE is by itself.

ANSWER ▶ The flagpole is 200 feet tall.

Student Help

▶ **READING TIP**
The symbol ⌐ at $\angle C$ and at $\angle E$ represents a right angle, which has a measure of 90°.

Student Help

▶ **MORE EXAMPLES**

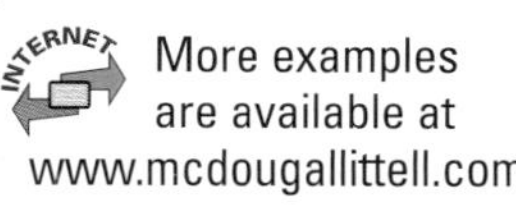

More examples are available at www.mcdougallittell.com

6.4 Exercises

Guided Practice

1. MATHEMATICAL REASONING Draw a quadrilateral $PQRS$. Draw a second quadrilateral $WXYZ$ that is similar to $PQRS$. Is there only one quadrilateral similar to $PQRS$? Use diagrams to explain your answer.

In Exercises 2–5, use the similar triangles *DEF* and *LMN* shown.

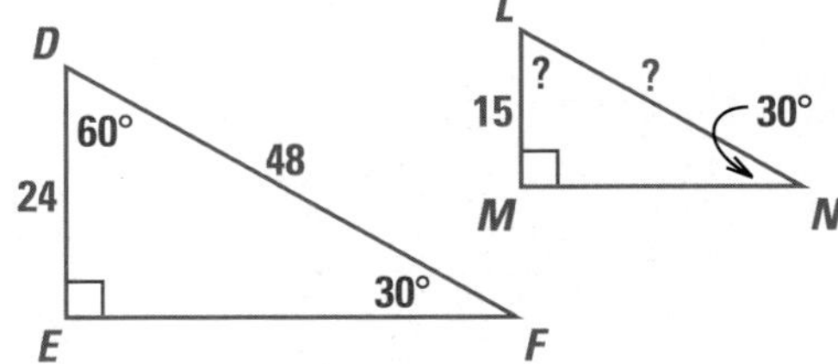

2. Match the angles and sides of triangle DEF with the corresponding angles and sides of triangle LMN.

3. What is the measure of $\angle L$?

4. What is LN?

5. What is the ratio of EF to MN?

Practice and Problem Solving

Student Help

▶ **MORE PRACTICE**
Extra practice to help you master skills is on page 577.

Tell what type of polygon the figure is. Use mathematical notation to identify the polygon's sides, the side lengths, and the angle measures.

6.

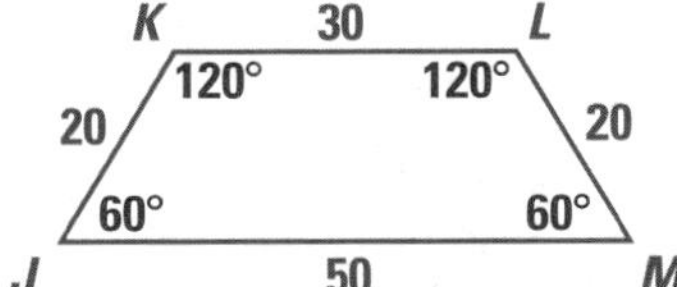

7.

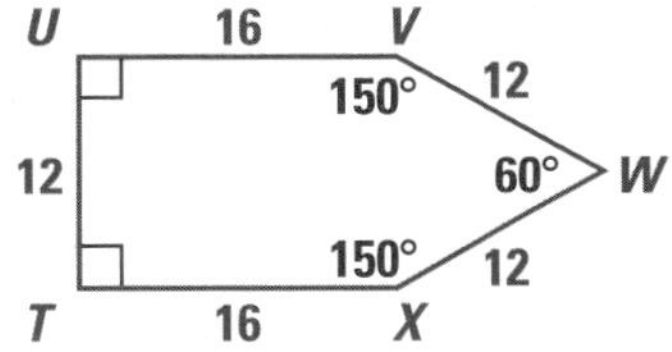

In Exercises 8 and 9, the two polygons are similar. Find the ratio of the length of a side of the smaller polygon to the length of the corresponding side of the larger polygon.

8.

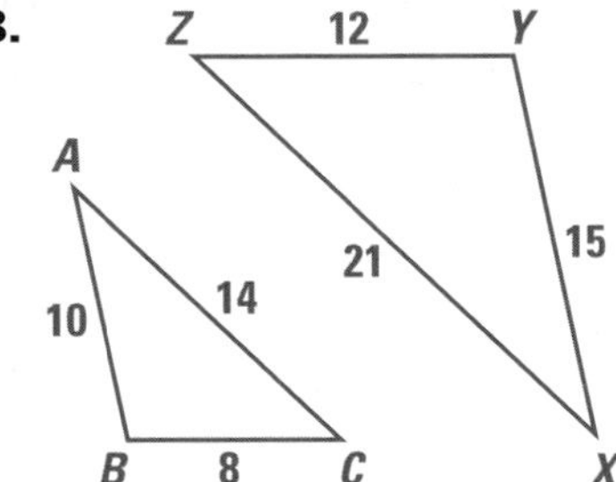

9.

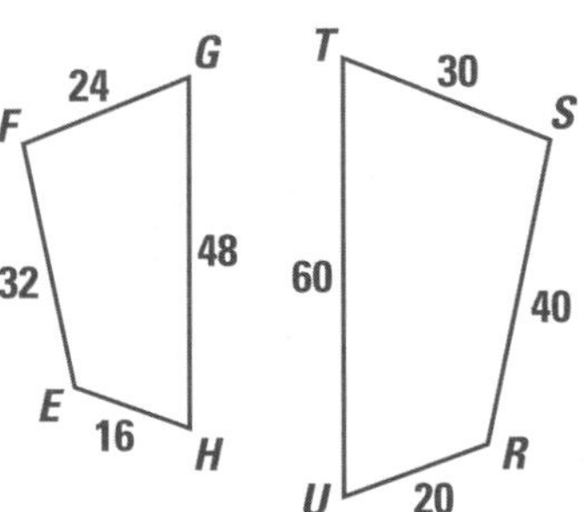

MATHEMATICAL REASONING **Tell whether all polygons of the given type are similar. Explain your answer.**

10. Triangles

11. Quadrilaterals

12. Squares

13. Rectangles

Find the indicated missing measures in the similar figures.

14. 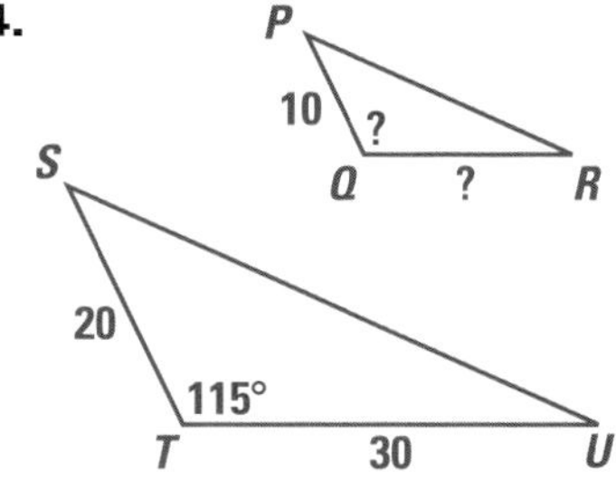

15. 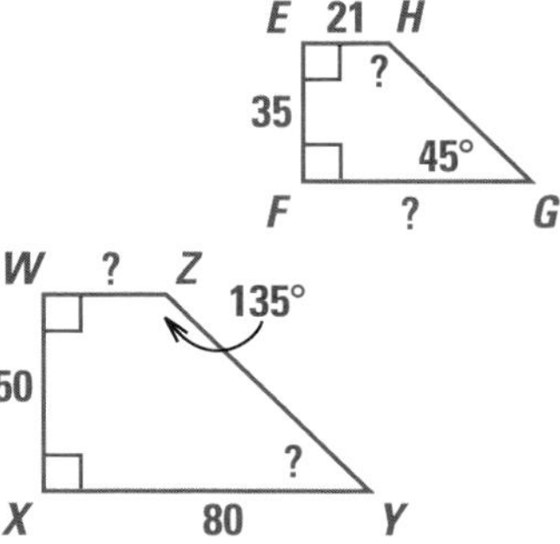

OBELISKS are tall, four-sided columns of stone that usually rise to a point. The photo shows the Axum obelisks from Exercise 17.

More about obelisks is available at www.mcdougallittell.com

16. CHALLENGE The dimensions of Rectangle A are 2 cm by 3 cm. Rectangle B is similar to Rectangle A. The ratio of the side lengths of Rectangle B to the corresponding side lengths of Rectangle A is $r : 1$. (*Note:* This means that Rectangle B is $2r$ cm by $3r$ cm.)

a. Show that the ratio of the perimeter of Rectangle B to the perimeter of Rectangle A is also $r : 1$.

b. Show that the ratio of the area of Rectangle B to the area of Rectangle A is $r^2 : 1$.

17. *History Link* The city of Axum, Ethiopia, is the site of several obelisks built around 1050 B.C. by King Ethiopius. The largest obelisk still standing is 79 feet tall. Suppose a person 5 feet tall casts a 7 foot shadow whose end meets the end of this obelisk's shadow. Draw a diagram of the situation. How long is the obelisk's shadow?

18. FERRIS WHEELS Mark is in Yokohama, Japan, where the world's largest Ferris wheel, the Cosmoclock 21, is located. Mark is 6 feet tall. He stands so that the end of his 5 foot shadow meets the end of the Ferris wheel's 287 foot shadow. Find the height of the Cosmoclock 21.

Multiple-Choice Practice

In Exercises 19 and 20, Rectangle A and Rectangle B are similar.

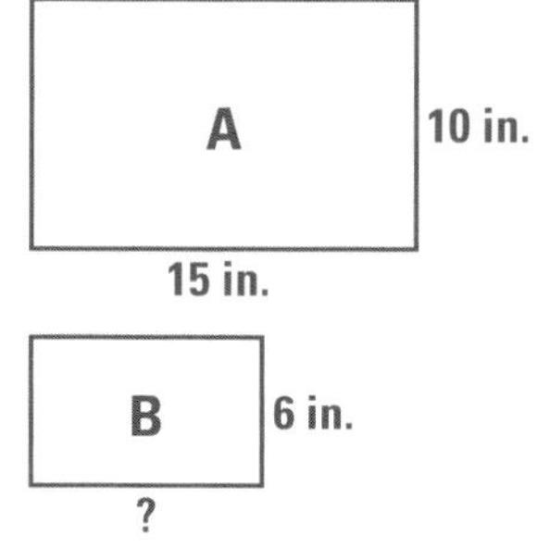

19. What is the perimeter of Rectangle B?

Ⓐ 15 in. Ⓑ 25 in.

Ⓒ 30 in. Ⓓ 50 in.

20. What is the area of Rectangle B?

Ⓕ 54 in.^{2} Ⓖ 60 in.^{2}

Ⓗ 90 in.^{2} Ⓙ 150 in.^{2}

6.5 Scale Drawings

In this lesson you'll:

- Interpret and use ratios in different contexts. (NS 1.2)
- Use a proportion to find the length of a side of a polygon similar to a known polygon. (NS 1.3)

Goal 1 Using Scale Drawings

In a **scale drawing** of an object, the dimensions in the drawing are proportional to the actual dimensions of the object. The **scale** for the drawing gives the relationship between the drawing's dimensions and the actual dimensions, such as "1 in. = 2 ft." This scale means that 1 inch in the drawing represents an actual distance of 2 feet.

The **scale factor** for a scale drawing is the ratio of the dimensions in the drawing to the corresponding actual dimensions.

EXAMPLE 1 Reading a Scale Drawing

BLUEPRINTS The house blueprint below has a scale of 1 in. = 8 ft. On the blueprint the bedroom is 2.25 inches wide. Find (**a**) the actual width of the bedroom and (**b**) the blueprint's scale factor.

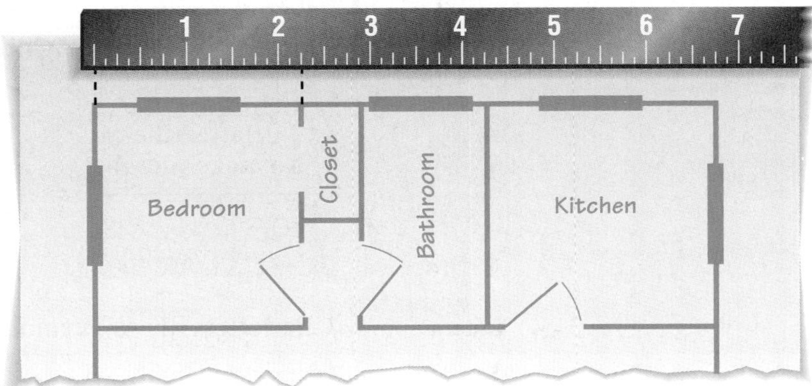

Solution

a. Let x be the actual width (in feet) of the bedroom.

$$\frac{\text{Bedroom's width in blueprint}}{\text{Bedroom's actual width}} = \frac{1 \text{ inch}}{8 \text{ feet}}$$ Write a proportion.

$$\frac{2.25 \text{ inches}}{x \text{ feet}} = \frac{1 \text{ inch}}{8 \text{ feet}}$$ Substitute.

$$2.25 \cdot 8 = x \cdot 1$$ Cross products property

$$18 = x$$ Simplify. x is by itself.

ANSWER ▶ The actual width of the bedroom is 18 feet.

b. The scale factor is $\frac{1 \text{ in.}}{8 \text{ ft}} = \frac{1 \text{ in.}}{96 \text{ in.}} = \frac{1}{96}$. So, distances in the actual house are 96 times as great as they appear in the blueprint.

Goal 2 USING MAPS

The distance on a map between two locations is proportional to the actual distance between them. Therefore, a map is a type of scale drawing.

EXAMPLE 2 Reading a Map

VIRGINIA A place mat shows a map of Virginia with no scale. You use a ruler to measure distances on the map as shown. You know that the actual distance from Charlottesville to Richmond is about 70 miles. Approximate the actual distance from Charlottesville to Roanoke.

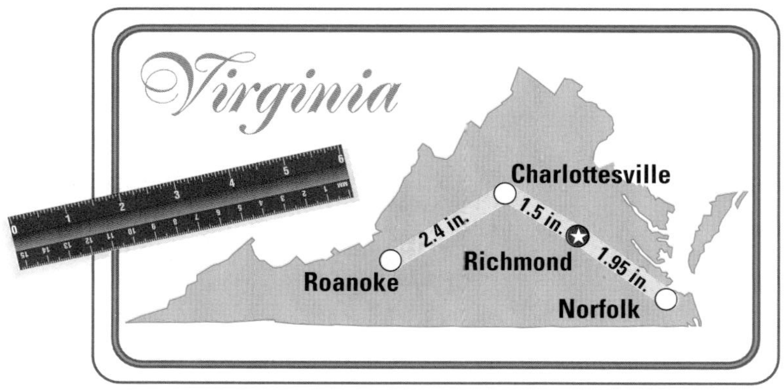

Solution

VERBAL MODEL

$$\frac{\text{Charlottesville to Roanoke (map)}}{\text{Charlottesville to Roanoke (actual)}} = \frac{\text{Charlottesville to Richmond (map)}}{\text{Charlottesville to Richmond (actual)}}$$

LABELS

Charlottesville to Roanoke (map) = **2.4** (inches)

Charlottesville to Roanoke (actual) = x (miles)

Charlottesville to Richmond (map) = **1.5** (inches)

Charlottesville to Richmond (actual) = **70** (miles)

ALGEBRAIC MODEL

$$\frac{\textbf{2.4 inches}}{x \textbf{ miles}} = \frac{\textbf{1.5 inches}}{\textbf{70 miles}}$$ Write algebraic model.

$$2.4 \cdot 70 = x \cdot 1.5$$ Cross products property

$$\frac{2.4 \cdot 70}{\mathbf{1.5}} = \frac{x \cdot 1.5}{\mathbf{1.5}}$$ Divide each side by 1.5.

$$112 = x$$ Simplify. x is by itself.

ANSWER ▶ The actual distance from Charlottesville to Roanoke is about 112 miles.

Student Help

▶ **STUDY TIP**
In Example 2, the map shows that the distance from Charlottesville to Roanoke is between 1 and 2 times the distance from Charlottesville to Richmond. So the solution, 112 miles, is reasonable because $112 > 70$ and $112 < 2 \cdot 70 = 140$.

6.5 Exercises

Guided Practice

In Exercises 1–3, a length in a scale drawing and the corresponding actual length are given. Match the lengths with the correct scale factor.

A. $\frac{1}{220{,}000}$ **B.** $\frac{1}{40}$ **C.** $\frac{1}{84}$

1. Drawing: 4 in.
Actual: 28 ft

2. Drawing: 1.5 ft
Actual: 20 yd

3. Drawing: 5 cm
Actual: 11 km

4. **BLUEPRINTS** Look back at the blueprint in Example 1 on page 285. Use the given scale to estimate the width of the bathroom.

5. **MAPS** Look back at the map of Virginia in Example 2 on page 286. Approximate the actual distance from Richmond to Norfolk.

6. **MOUNTAINS** You are making a scale model of Mount Everest, the tallest mountain in the world. You measure the height of your model to be 18 inches. To find the model's scale factor, what additional information do you need?

Practice and Problem Solving

Student Help

▶ **MORE PRACTICE**
Extra practice to help you master skills is on page 577.

Find the scale factor for the given scale.

7. 1 in. = 9 ft **8.** 1 in. = 200 yd **9.** 1 cm = 17 m

10. 1 cm = 10 km **11.** 1 ft = 0.5 mi **12.** 1 yd = 0.25 in.

In Exercises 13 and 14, find the scale factor for the situation described.

13. **AIRPLANES** A model airplane has a wingspan of 13 inches. The actual airplane has a wingspan of 130 feet.

14. **COMPUTERS** A scale drawing of a square computer chip shows the sides to be 8 inches long. The actual chip's sides are 0.5 inch long.

Use the scale on the blueprint to find the perimeter of the actual object.

15.

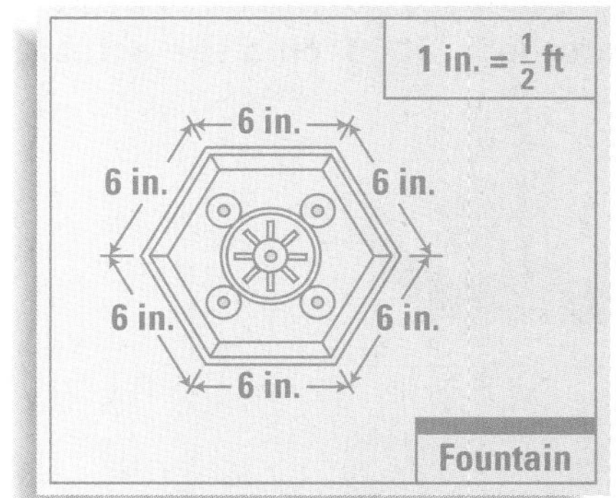

16.

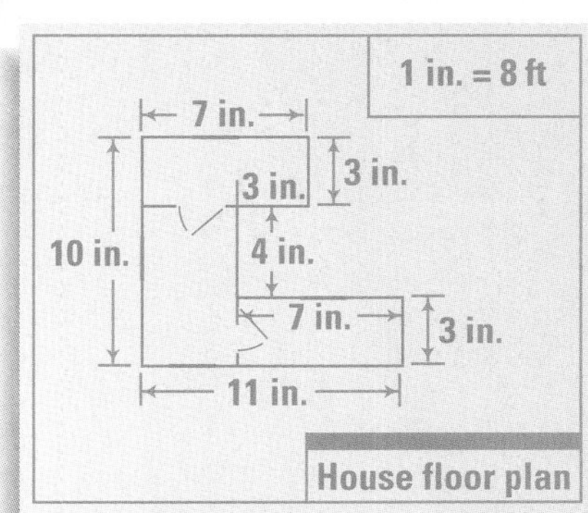

Student Help

▶ **HOMEWORK HELP**

INTERNET Extra help with problem solving in Exs. 17–18 is available at www.mcdougallittell.com

17. **Science Link** Diatoms are microscopic, single-celled organisms. You want to draw a diatom whose actual width is 0.025 mm. You plan to use a scale of 1 cm = 0.005 mm.

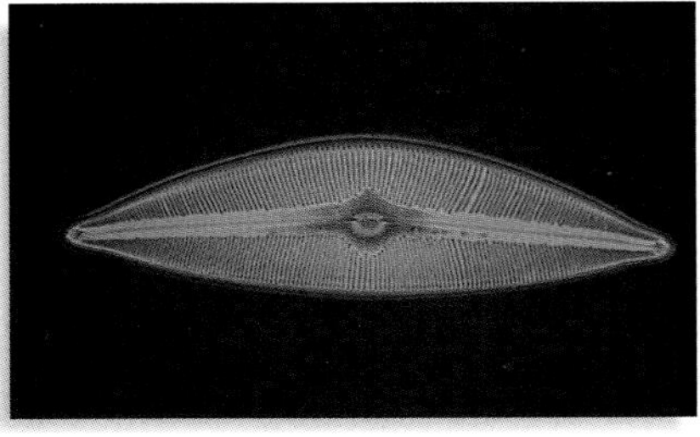

Diatom

a. What will the width of the diatom be in your drawing?

b. What is the scale factor for your drawing?

18. DINOSAURS On a museum tour you see a 15-foot-long model of a Brachiosaurus, a giant plant-eating dinosaur that lived about 150 million years ago. Your tour guide says that the model was built using a scale factor of 1 : 5. How long was an actual Brachiosaurus?

MAPS **In Exercises 19–22, use the map of Texas. Measure the distance on the map between the given cities to the nearest millimeter. Use your measurement to estimate the actual distance between the cities.**

19. Lubbock and Dallas

20. Dallas and San Antonio

21. Houston and Austin

22. Austin and El Paso

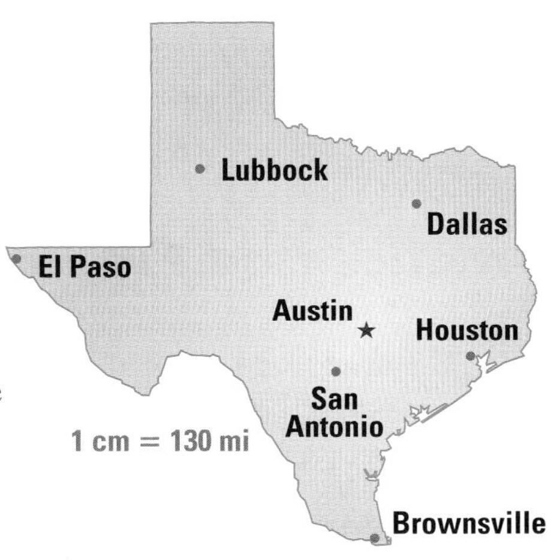

23. MATHEMATICAL REASONING If the map distances you measured in Exercises 19–22 are accurate to the nearest millimeter, by at most how many miles can your estimated actual distances between cities differ from the true distances?

24. CHALLENGE You are designing a new kitchen for a home. You make a drawing of the kitchen using a scale of 1 in. = 2 ft. In your drawing one of the two kitchen countertops is 1 in. by 1.5 in., and the other countertop is 1 in. by 2.5 in. How many square feet of counter space will the actual kitchen have?

SHIPS **In Exercises 25 and 26, a scale drawing of a ship is shown. The scale factor is 1 : 1000. Find the actual length of the ship in meters.**

25.

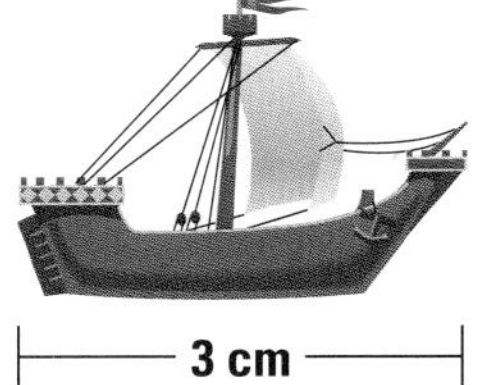

26.

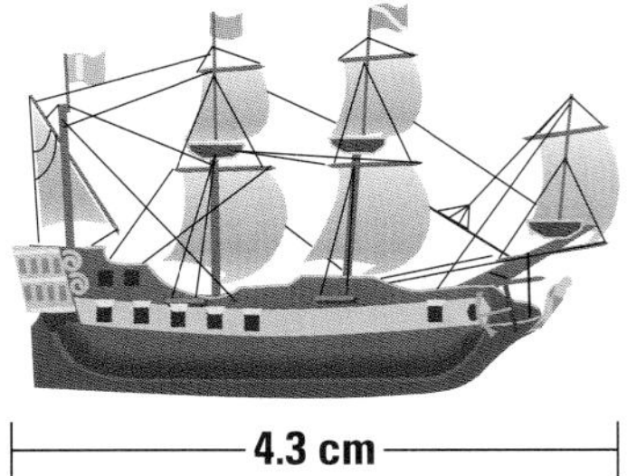

Multiple-Choice Practice

27. A set designer for a play is making a scale model of one of the sets. The width of the stage in the model is 30 inches, and the stage's actual width is 60 feet. A table used in the set has an actual width of 8 feet. How long should the table in the model be?

Ⓐ 3 in. Ⓑ 4 in. Ⓒ 10 in. Ⓓ 16 in.

28. An architecture student is asked to make a scale drawing of the Golden Gate Bridge in San Francisco, California. The bridge is 10 inches long in the student's drawing. The actual length of the bridge is about 9000 feet. What scale factor is the student using?

Ⓕ $\frac{1}{75}$ Ⓖ $\frac{1}{900}$ Ⓗ $\frac{1}{9000}$ Ⓙ $\frac{1}{10{,}800}$

Test Tip Ⓐ Ⓑ Ⓒ Ⓓ

▶For Exercise 29, write a problem about a scale drawing that is larger than the object drawn. Find the drawing's scale factor and use it to eliminate one or more answer choices.

29. If a scale drawing of an object is larger than the actual object, what is true about the scale factor f?

Ⓐ $f > 1$ Ⓑ $f < 1$

Ⓒ $f = 1$ Ⓓ Not enough information

Mixed Review

Insert parentheses to make the statement true. *(1.3)*

30. $22 - 10 \times 16 \div 8 = 24$ **31.** $7 + 5 \times 9 - 3 = 72$

Evaluate the expression. *(1.4)*

32. 13^2 **33.** 5 cubed **34.** x^6 when $x = 2$

Write a fraction that represents the shaded portion of the figure. *(2.3)*

35. 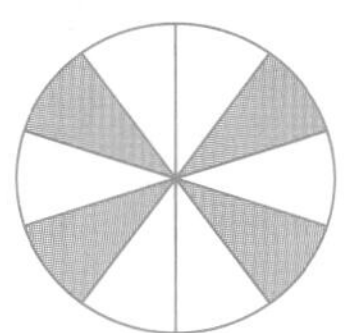 **36.** 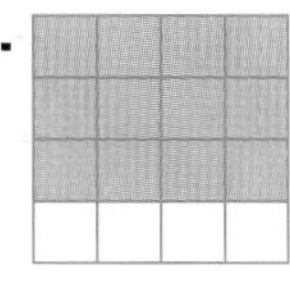 **37.** 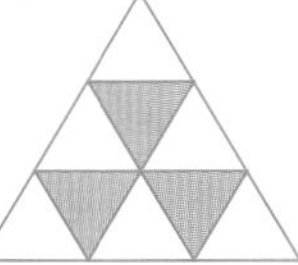

Use the distributive property to evaluate the expression. *(3.6)*

38. $5(8 + 4)$ **39.** $10(5 + 9)$ **40.** $8(11 + 3)$

Use the distributive property to rewrite the expression. *(3.6)*

41. $2(x + 7)$ **42.** $9(6 + m)$ **43.** $3(u + v)$

44. **COOKING** You are making a loaf of bread and a batch of muffins. You need $3\frac{1}{8}$ cups of flour for the bread and $2\frac{1}{2}$ cups of flour for the muffins. How much flour do you need for both foods? Write your answer as a mixed number. *(3.3)*

DEVELOPING CONCEPTS

Finding Probabilities

For use with Lesson 6.6

California Standards

- Determine theoretical and experimental probabilities. (SDP 3.0)
- Represent probabilities as ratios and decimals between 0 and 1. (SDP 3.3)

MATERIALS

- Number cube

The *probability* of an event is a measure of the likelihood that the event will occur. Probabilities can be expressed as fractions or decimals from 0 to 1. One way to estimate a probability is by performing an experiment.

SAMPLE 1 Estimating a Probability from an Experiment

You can perform an experiment to estimate the probability of rolling a number greater than 4 on a number cube.

Here's How

Roll a number cube repeatedly. Record the number of rolls greater than 4 and the total number of rolls. The results of 18 rolls are shown.

A number greater than 4 occurs on **7** of the **18** rolls, so an estimate for the desired probability is as follows:

$$\text{Probability of number greater than 4} = \frac{\text{Number of rolls greater than 4}}{\text{Total number of rolls}}$$

$$= \frac{\mathbf{7}}{\mathbf{18}}$$

$$\approx 0.389$$

The probability in Sample 1 is called an *experimental probability* because it is based on the results of an experiment.

Suppose an experiment consists of a certain number of *trials* (such as rolls of a number cube). For a given event (such as rolling a number greater than 4), each trial where the event occurs is called a *success*. You can find the event's experimental probability using this formula:

$$\text{Experimental probability of event} = \frac{\text{Number of successes}}{\text{Number of trials}}$$

When you find a probability by reasoning mathematically rather than by performing an experiment, the result is called a *theoretical probability*.

SAMPLE 2 Finding a Theoretical Probability

You can use mathematical reasoning to find the theoretical probability of rolling a number greater than 4 on a number cube.

Here's How

When you roll the cube, there are six possible outcomes: 1, 2, 3, 4, 5, and 6. Two of the outcomes, 5 and 6, correspond to rolling a number greater than 4. Because all outcomes are equally likely, on average **2** of every **6** rolls will produce a number greater than 4. Therefore:

$$\text{Probability of number greater than 4} = \frac{\mathbf{2}}{\mathbf{6}} = \frac{1}{3} \approx 0.333$$

In general, the outcomes corresponding to the event you are interested in are called *favorable outcomes*. In Sample 2 the favorable outcomes for the event "rolling a number greater than 4" are 5 and 6.

When all the outcomes of a procedure are equally likely, then:

$$\text{Theoretical probability of an event} = \frac{\text{Number of favorable outcomes}}{\text{Total number of outcomes}}$$

Try These

In Exercises 1–4, (a) find the experimental probability of the event by rolling a number cube 30 times, and (b) find the theoretical probability of the event.

1. Rolling a 5

2. Rolling a number less than 5

3. Rolling an even number

4. Rolling a multiple of 3

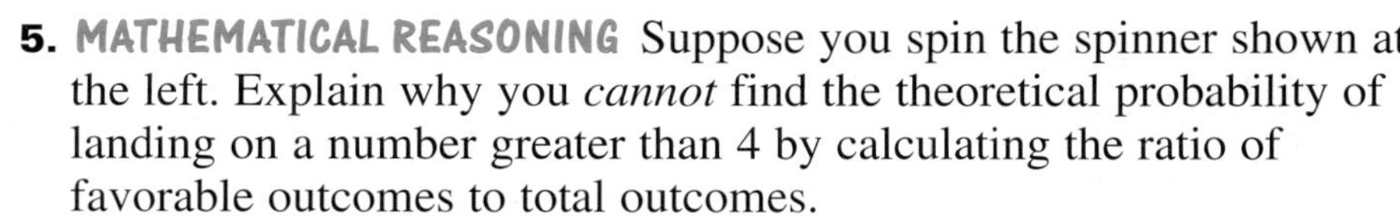

5. **MATHEMATICAL REASONING** Suppose you spin the spinner shown at the left. Explain why you *cannot* find the theoretical probability of landing on a number greater than 4 by calculating the ratio of favorable outcomes to total outcomes.

6. Use the formulas for experimental and theoretical probability to explain why a probability must be a number from 0 to 1.

6.6 Probability

In this lesson you'll:

- Determine theoretical and experimental probabilities. (SDP 3.0)
- Represent probabilities as ratios, proportions, and decimals between 0 and 1, and verify that the probabilities computed are reasonable. (SDP 3.3)

Goal 1 Finding the Probability of an Event

When you perform an experiment, the possible results are called **outcomes**. An **event** is a collection of outcomes. Once you specify an event, the outcomes for that event are called **favorable outcomes**.

The **probability** P of an event is a measure of the likelihood that the event will occur. Probability is measured on a scale from 0 to 1.

$P = 0$	$P = 0.25$	$P = 0.5$	$P = 0.75$	$P = 1$
Impossible	Not likely	Likely to occur half the time	Quite likely	Certain

As you saw in Developing Concepts 6.6, page 290, the probability of an event when all outcomes of an experiment are equally likely is:

$$\text{Probability of event} = \frac{\text{Number of favorable outcomes}}{\text{Total number of outcomes}}$$

Student Help

Study Tip
In Example 1 the number of red marbles, 6, is less than half the total number of marbles, 15. So it makes sense that the probability of choosing a red marble is less than 0.5.

Example 1 Finding a Probability

A jar contains 15 marbles: 3 blue, 5 green, 6 red, and 1 yellow. You choose one marble at random. Find the probability that it is red.

Solution

The number of favorable outcomes equals **6**, which is the number of red marbles. The total number of outcomes is **15**.

$$\text{Probability of choosing red} = \frac{6}{15} = \frac{\cancel{3} \cdot 2}{\cancel{3} \cdot 5} = \frac{2}{5} = 0.4$$

Example 2 Finding a Probability

A number octahedron has 8 sides numbered 1 through 8. If you roll the octahedron, what is the probability of getting an even number?

Solution

There are **4** favorable outcomes: getting a 2, 4, 6, or 8. The total number of outcomes is **8**.

$$\text{Probability of even number} = \frac{4}{8} = \frac{\cancel{4} \cdot 1}{\cancel{4} \cdot 2} = \frac{1}{2} = 0.5$$

Because half of the sides on the octahedron show an even number, it makes sense that the probability of rolling an even number is 0.5.

Goal 2 TYPES OF PROBABILITY

The probabilities in Examples 1 and 2 are **theoretical probabilities** because they were found by mathematical reasoning alone. A probability based on repeated *trials* of an experiment (such as repeated rolls of a number octahedron) is called an **experimental probability**. For a particular event, each trial where the event occurs is called a *success.*

As you saw in Developing Concepts 6.6, page 290, the experimental probability of an event is given by this formula:

$$\text{Experimental probability of event} = \frac{\text{Number of successes}}{\text{Number of trials}}$$

Student Help

▶ STUDY TIP
In probability, an "experiment" does not have to be a scientific procedure performed in a laboratory. Experimental probabilities can also be based on surveys, historical data, or simple activities like tossing a thumbtack.

EXAMPLE 3 Finding an Experimental Probability

A thumbtack is tossed 120 times and lands "point up" 75 times. Find the experimental probability of landing "point up."

Solution

There are **120** trials (tosses) and **75** successes ("point up" landings).

$$\begin{array}{c}\text{Experimental probability}\\ \text{of landing "point up"}\end{array} = \frac{\mathbf{75}}{\mathbf{120}} = \frac{\cancel{15} \cdot 5}{\cancel{15} \cdot 8} = \frac{5}{8} = 0.625$$

EXAMPLE 4 Connecting Probability and Proportions

The residents of a town are voting on whether to build a new middle school. A poll finds that 56 of the 80 registered voters surveyed support the new school. The town has 6300 registered voters. Find **(a)** the experimental probability that a voter supports the new school and **(b)** about how many voters in the town are school supporters.

Solution

a. The **80** voters surveyed represent trials, and the **56** of these who support the new school represent successes. So the experimental probability that a voter supports the new school is $\frac{\mathbf{56}}{\mathbf{80}} = \frac{7}{10}$.

b. Let x be the number of voters in the town who support the new school. The ratio of school supporters to all voters should be roughly the same for the entire town as for the group surveyed.

$\frac{x}{6300} = \frac{7}{10}$ Write a proportion.

$x \cdot 10 = 6300 \cdot 7$ Use the cross products property.

$x = 4410$ Divide each side by 10 and simplify.

ANSWER ▶ About 4410 of the town's voters support the school.

Student Help

▶ MORE EXAMPLES
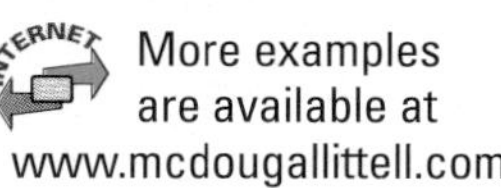
More examples are available at www.mcdougallittell.com

6.6 Exercises

Guided Practice

In Exercises 1–5, match the event with the letter on the number line that indicates the event's probability.

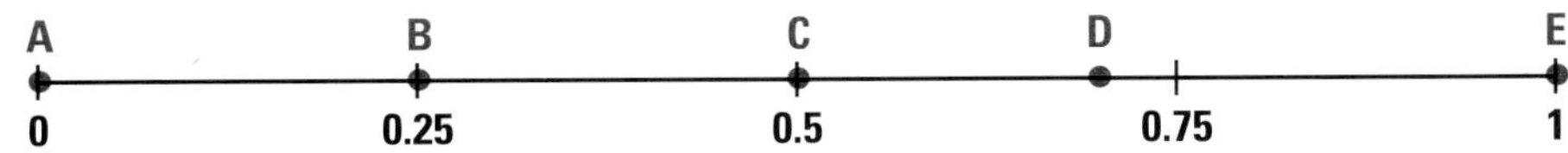

1. A tossed coin lands heads up.

2. A telephone number ends with a digit less than 7.

3. You guess the correct answer to a multiple choice question with 4 answer choices.

4. You roll a number octahedron and get a positive number.

5. You select a white marble from the jar in Example 1 on page 292.

6. LEFT-HANDEDNESS In a high school class of 32 students, 4 students are left-handed. Find the experimental probability that a student is left-handed. Then estimate how many of the school's 1600 students are left-handed.

Practice and Problem Solving

Student Help

▶MORE PRACTICE Extra practice to help you master skills is on page 577.

Match the spinner with the probability that the pointer lands on blue. Assume that the spinner is divided into equal parts.

A. 0.4 **B.** 0.7 **C.** 0.3

7.

8.

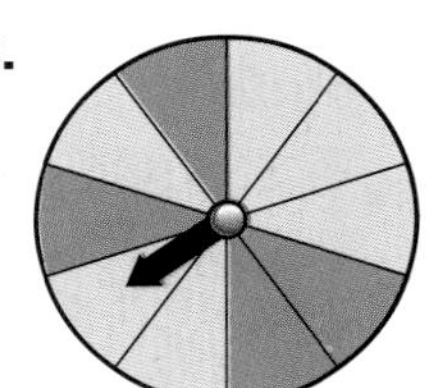

9.

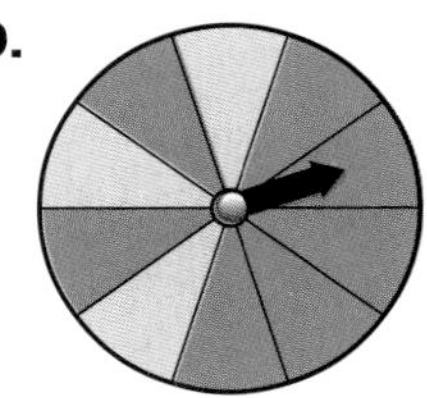

POETRY **In Exercises 10–12, you randomly choose a word from the first two verses of *Paul Revere's Ride*. Find the probability of the event.**

10. The word is *of*.

11. The word begins with *t*.

12. The word is an article (either *a*, *an*, or *the*).

Listen, my children, and you shall hear
Of the midnight ride of Paul Revere,
On the eighteenth of April, in Seventy-five;
Hardly a man is now alive
Who remembers that famous day and year.

He said to his friend, "If the British march
By land or sea from the town tonight,
Hang a lantern aloft in the belfry arch
Of the North Church tower as a signal light—
One, if by land, and two, if by sea; ..."

13. **MUSIC** A piano has 52 white keys. Eight of these keys produce C notes. What is the probability that you play a C note if you randomly hit a white key? Explain why your answer is reasonable.

DINING In Exercises 14 and 15, use the bar graph. The graph is based on a survey of 500 people and shows their main reasons for dining out at restaurants. ▶ Source: Thomas Food Industry Register

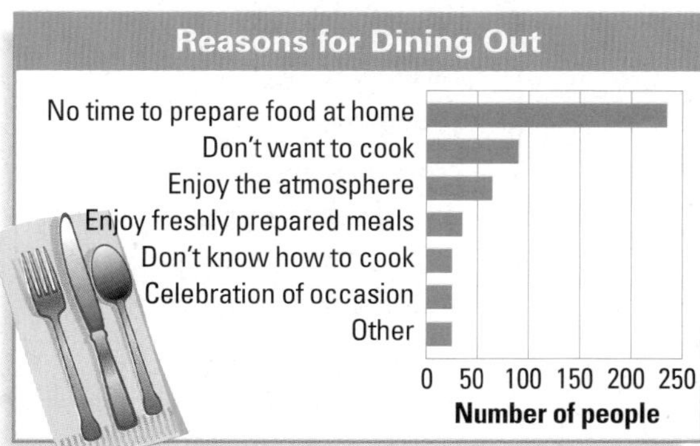

14. Estimate the experimental probability that a person dines out mainly for the given reason.
    a. No time to prepare food at home
    b. Enjoy the atmosphere
    c. A reason other than celebrating an occasion

15. At a restaurant there are 75 customers. Estimate how many of them are dining out mainly because they don't want to cook.

16. **BASKETBALL** During the 1999 season of a women's professional basketball league, Yolanda Griffith made 145 of the 235 free throws she attempted. Find the experimental probability that Griffith makes an attempted free throw. Explain why your answer is reasonable.

WARDEN PILOTS may restock remote lakes with fish by dropping the fish from airplanes.

INTERNET More about warden pilots is available at www.mcdougallittell.com

FISH In Exercises 17 and 18, use the following information. In a certain lake, a wildlife biologist catches 250 trout and finds that 90 are at least 12 inches long. (Trout smaller than this must be released if caught.)

17. Find the experimental probability that a trout can be kept if caught.

18. If the lake has 15,000 trout, about how many can be kept if caught?

19. **CHALLENGE** You roll two number cubes. What is the probability that the sum of the numbers showing on the cubes is at least 9?

Multiple-Choice Practice

20. The probability that it will rain is 0.15. Which statement is the best interpretation of this probability?

    (A) It will certainly rain. (B) It is likely to rain.

    (C) It is unlikely to rain. (D) It will certainly not rain.

21. A jar contains 15 blue, 10 yellow, 20 orange, and 5 black beads. If you choose a bead at random, what is the probability that it is yellow?

    (F) 0.1 (G) 0.2 (H) 0.3 (J) 0.4

Chapter 6 Chapter Summary and Review

VOCABULARY

- **ratio,** *p. 265*
- **proportion,** *p. 269*
- **cross products,** *p. 269*
- **cross products property,** *p. 269*
- **similar polygons,** *p. 280*
- **corresponding angles,** *p. 280*
- **corresponding sides,** *p. 280*
- **proportional,** *p. 280*
- **scale drawing,** *p. 285*
- **scale,** *p. 285*
- **scale factor,** *p. 285*
- **outcome,** *p. 292*
- **event,** *p. 292*
- **favorable outcome,** *p. 292*
- **probability of an event,** *p. 292*
- **theoretical probability,** *p. 293*
- **experimental probability,** *p. 293*

6.1 RATIOS

Examples on pp. 265–266

The ratio of a to b (where b is not 0) is the quotient you get when a is divided by b. You can write the ratio of a to b as the fraction $\frac{a}{b}$ (or an equivalent decimal), as $a : b$, or as "a to b."

EXAMPLES

a. A car travels 350 miles and uses 15 gallons of gasoline. The ratio of the distance traveled to the gasoline used is:

$$\frac{\text{Distance}}{\text{Gasoline}} = \frac{350 \text{ miles}}{15 \text{ gallons}} = \frac{\cancel{5} \cdot 70}{\cancel{5} \cdot 3} = \frac{70}{3} \approx 23.3 \text{ (miles per gallon)}$$

You can also write the ratio above as 70 : 3 or as "70 to 3."

b. One night after school, you spend 30 minutes watching TV and 2 hours doing homework. The ratio of the time spent watching TV to the time spent doing homework is:

$$\frac{\text{Time watching TV}}{\text{Time doing homework}} = \frac{30 \text{ min}}{2 \text{ hours}} = \frac{30 \cancel{\text{min}}}{120 \cancel{\text{min}}} = \frac{\cancel{30} \cdot 1}{\cancel{30} \cdot 4} = \frac{1}{4} = 0.25$$

You can also write the ratio above as 1 : 4 or as "1 to 4."

In Exercises 1–4, write the ratio as a fraction in lowest terms. Include units (if any) in your answer.

1. $\frac{10 \text{ grams}}{18 \text{ grams}}$ **2.** 42 trees : 9 acres **3.** 75 feet to 5 seconds **4.** $\frac{12 \text{ hours}}{2 \text{ days}}$

5. FOOTBALL A professional football team scores 312 points in 16 regular-season games. Write the ratio of points scored to games in three different ways.

6.2 SOLVING PROPORTIONS

Examples on pp. 269–271

You can solve a proportion using the cross products property:

If $\frac{a}{b} = \frac{c}{d}$, then $a \cdot d = b \cdot c$.

EXAMPLE **Solve the proportion $\frac{n}{15} = \frac{7}{21}$.**

$\frac{n}{15} = \frac{7}{21}$ Write original proportion.

$n \cdot 21 = 15 \cdot 7$ Use cross products property.

$\frac{n \cdot 21}{\mathbf{21}} = \frac{15 \cdot 7}{\mathbf{21}}$ Divide each side by 21.

$n = 5$ Simplify. *n* is by itself.

Solve the proportion.

6. $\frac{3}{5} = \frac{x}{30}$ **7.** $\frac{y}{7} = \frac{12}{28}$ **8.** $\frac{20}{m} = \frac{4}{13}$ **9.** $\frac{6}{16} = \frac{45}{r}$

6.3 WRITING PROPORTIONS

Examples on pp. 274–275

EXAMPLE In January you spend \$12.75 for 85 min of long-distance calls. What is the cost of 120 min of long-distance calls made in February?

VERBAL MODEL $\frac{\text{January cost}}{\text{January time}} = \frac{\text{February cost}}{\text{February time}}$

LABELS

January cost = **12.75** (dollars)

January time = **85** (minutes)

February cost = ***x*** (dollars)

February time = **120** (minutes)

ALGEBRAIC MODEL

$\frac{\textbf{12.75 dollars}}{\textbf{85 minutes}} = \frac{\boldsymbol{x} \textbf{ dollars}}{\textbf{120 minutes}}$ Write algebraic model.

$12.75 \cdot 120 = 85 \cdot x$ Use cross products property.

$\frac{12.75 \cdot 120}{\mathbf{85}} = \frac{85 \cdot x}{\mathbf{85}}$ Divide each side by 85.

$18 = x$ Simplify. *x* is by itself.

ANSWER ▶ Your cost for long-distance calls in February is \$18.

In Exercises 10 and 11, use a proportion to solve the problem.

10. BUSINESS A company spends $5850 to buy electronic organizers for its 13 salespeople. How much would it cost the company to buy organizers for the 7 employees in its human resources department?

11. *Science Link* About 37 million gallons of water flow over Niagara Falls every minute. Suppose you videotape Niagara Falls for 35 seconds while on vacation. During that time, how many gallons of water flow over the falls?

6.4 SIMILAR POLYGONS

Examples on pp. 280–282

Two polygons are similar if you can pair up their angles and their sides so that corresponding angles have equal measure and corresponding sides are proportional.

EXAMPLE **Triangles *ABC* and *DEF* are similar. Find (a) the measure of $\angle E$ and (b) the length of side $\overline{BC}$.**

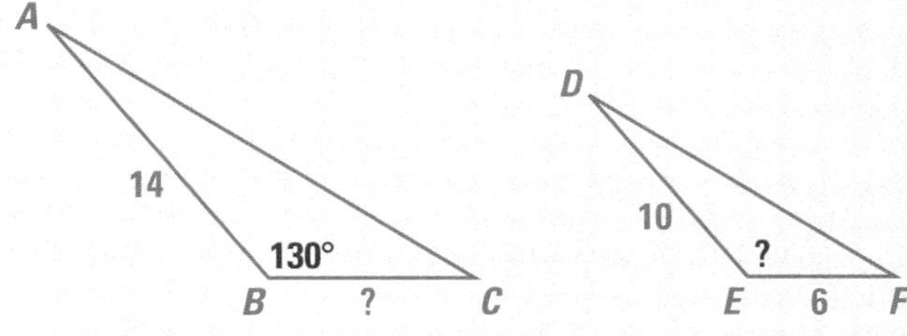

a. $\angle E$ and $\angle B$ are corresponding angles, so $m\angle E = m\angle B = 130°$.

b. Use the fact that ratios of corresponding side lengths are equal.

$\frac{AB}{DE} = \frac{BC}{EF}$ Write a proportion involving *BC*.

$\frac{14}{10} = \frac{BC}{6}$ Substitute known values.

$14 \cdot 6 = 10 \cdot BC$ Use cross products property.

$8.4 = BC$ Divide each side by 10 and simplify.

In Exercises 12–14, use the similar quadrilaterals *PQRS* and *TUVW*.

12. What is the measure of $\angle U$?

13. What is the length of side $\overline{VW}$?

14. What is the ratio of *PS* to *TW*? Explain.

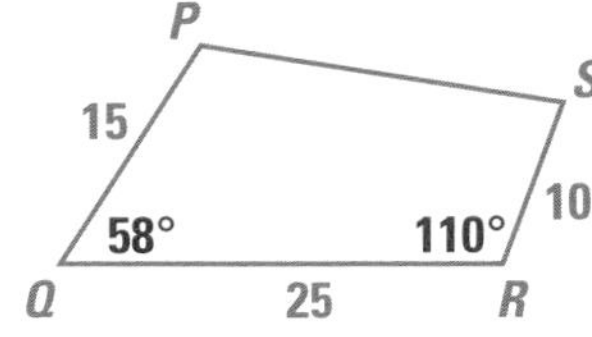

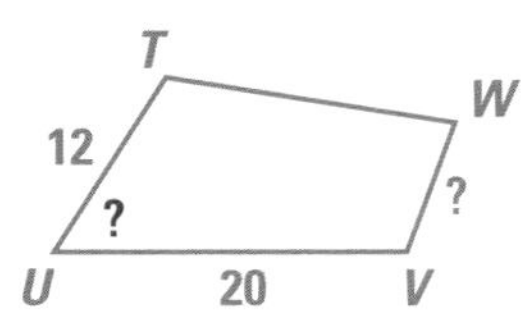

6.5 SCALE DRAWINGS

Examples on pp. 285–286

EXAMPLE A pool on a blueprint is 4 inches wide. The blueprint has a scale of 1 in. = 5 ft. Find **(a)** the actual width of the pool and **(b)** the blueprint's scale factor.

a. Let x be the actual width (in feet) of the pool.

$$\frac{\text{Pool's width in blueprint}}{\text{Pool's actual width}} = \frac{1 \text{ inch}}{5 \text{ feet}}$$ Write a proportion.

$$\frac{4 \text{ inches}}{x \text{ feet}} = \frac{1 \text{ inch}}{5 \text{ feet}}$$ Substitute.

$$4 \cdot 5 = x \cdot 1$$ Use cross products property.

$$20 = x$$ Simplify. x is by itself.

ANSWER ▶ The actual width of the pool is 20 feet.

b. The scale factor is $\frac{1 \text{ in.}}{5 \text{ ft}} = \frac{1 \not{\text{in.}}}{60 \not{\text{in.}}} = \frac{1}{60}$. So, the dimensions of the actual pool are 60 times as great as they appear in the blueprint.

15. **CITY PLANNING** An architect wants to make a scale drawing of a new city park to be built. The architect plans to use a scale of 1 in. = 30 ft. The actual park will be a rectangle 840 feet wide by 1200 feet long. What should the dimensions of the park be in the drawing?

16. What is the scale factor for the drawing from Exercise 15?

6.6 PROBABILITY

Examples on pp. 292–293

When all outcomes of an experiment are equally likely, the probability of an event is given by this ratio:

$$\text{Probability} = \frac{\text{Number of favorable outcomes}}{\text{Total number of outcomes}}$$

EXAMPLE A desk drawer contains 20 writing utensils: 8 pens, 6 pencils, 5 markers, and 1 crayon. If you randomly choose one utensil, the probability of getting a pen is as follows:

$$\begin{array}{l}\text{Probability of}\\ \text{choosing pen}\end{array} = \frac{\text{Number of pens}}{\text{Total number of utensils}} = \frac{8}{20} = \frac{2}{5} = 0.4$$

Find the probability of randomly choosing the given utensil from the drawer in the example above.

17. Pencil **18.** Marker **19.** Crayon **20.** Pen or pencil

Chapter 6 Chapter Test

In Exercises 1–4, write the ratio as a fraction in lowest terms. Include units (if any) in your answer.

1. $\frac{14 \text{ pounds}}{42 \text{ pounds}}$ **2.** $\frac{50 \text{ questions}}{45 \text{ minutes}}$ **3.** 16 meters : 52 sec **4.** 5 gallons to 10 quarts

5. MUSIC A music store sells a pack of 3 blank cassette tapes for $6.45 and a pack of 4 blank cassette tapes for $8.20. Use ratios to determine which pack is a better deal.

In Exercises 6–9, solve the proportion.

6. $\frac{2}{5} = \frac{x}{35}$ **7.** $\frac{10}{n} = \frac{40}{12}$ **8.** $\frac{y}{126} = \frac{21}{54}$ **9.** $\frac{15}{7} = \frac{12}{k}$

10. FLAGS The length-to-width ratio of the United States flag is 19 to 10. What is the width of a U.S. flag that is 4 feet long?

11. **Science Link** When flying, a hummingbird may breathe at a rate of 600 breaths per minute. If a hummingbird hovers beside a flower for 80 seconds, about how many breaths does it take during that time?

Find the indicated missing measures in the similar figures.

12.

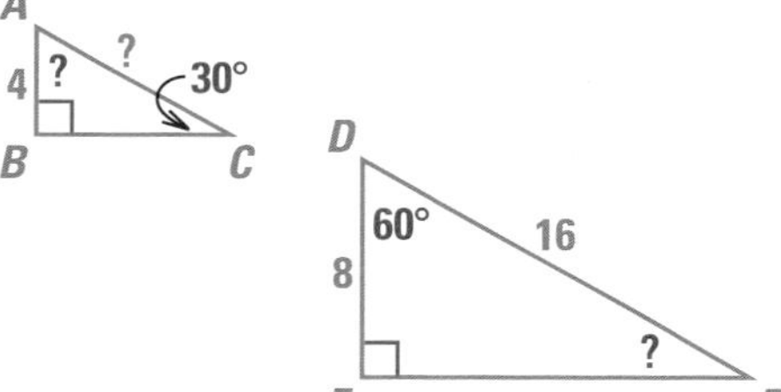

13.

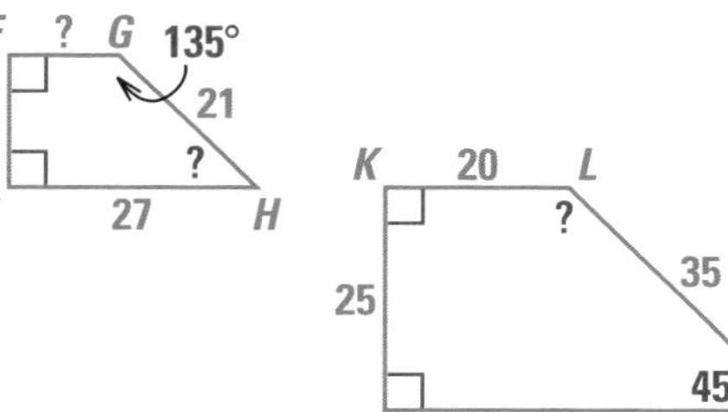

TRAINS **In Exercises 14 and 15, use the following information.**
An artist illustrating a book about trains is making a scale drawing of an early steam-powered locomotive. The artist uses a scale of 1 in. = 12 ft. The length of the locomotive's engine in the drawing is 6 inches.

14. What is the actual length of the engine?

15. What is the scale factor for the drawing?

History Link **Abraham Lincoln's *Gettysburg Address* begins with the phrase "Four score and seven years ago . . . ." Find the probability of the given event if you randomly choose a letter from this phrase.**

16. The letter is an *s*. **17.** The letter is an *m*.

18. The letter is a vowel (*a*, *e*, *i*, *o*, or *u*). **19.** The letter is capitalized.

Multiple-Choice Practice

Test Tip Don't look for the answer until you are sure you understand the question.

1. What is the ratio of the shaded region's perimeter to the entire region's perimeter?

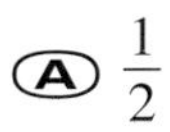
(A) $\frac{1}{2}$

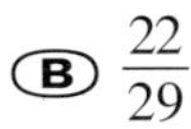
(B) $\frac{22}{29}$

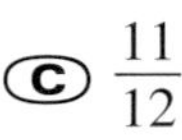
(C) $\frac{11}{12}$

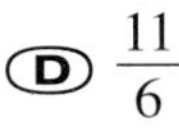
(D) $\frac{11}{6}$

2. Which ratio is not equal to the other three?

(F) $\frac{1 \text{ yd}}{6 \text{ yd}}$ (G) $\frac{3 \text{ ft}}{18 \text{ ft}}$

(H) 3 ft : 6 yd (J) 6 ft to 24 ft

3. What is the solution of $\frac{8}{12} = \frac{12}{n}$?

(A) 3 (B) 8 (C) 16 (D) 18

4. You are taking a 700 mile trip by car. You drive the first 140 miles in 3 hours. Which proportion can you use to estimate the time x (in hours) that it will take to drive the remaining distance?

(F) $\frac{140}{3} = \frac{700}{x}$ (G) $\frac{140}{3} = \frac{560}{x}$

(H) $\frac{140}{700} = \frac{3}{x}$ (J) $\frac{140}{560} = \frac{x}{3}$

5. You buy 8 place settings of dinnerware for $192. Later you decide to buy 3 more identical place settings. How much will the additional place settings cost?

(A) $8 (B) $64 (C) $72 (D) $96

In Exercises 6 and 7, use the similar figures below.

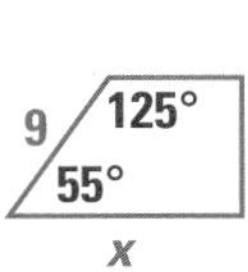

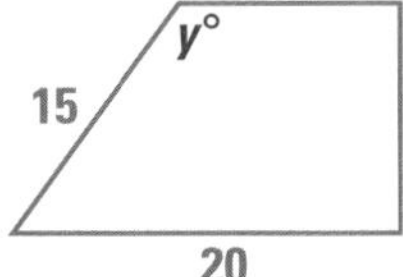

6. What is the value of x?

(F) 6.75 (G) 12 (H) 15 (J) 20

7. What is the value of y?

(A) 55 (B) 92 (C) 125 (D) 208

8. Greg, who is 6 feet tall, wants to estimate the height of a lighthouse. He stands so that the end of his 9 foot shadow meets the end of the lighthouse's 75 foot shadow. How tall is the lighthouse?

(F) 50 feet (G) 54 feet

(H) 112.5 feet (J) 450 feet

9. The scale on a map is 1 in. = 20 mi. The distance on the map from Town A to Town B is 5.75 inches. What is the actual distance between the towns?

(A) 115 miles (B) 120 miles

(C) 125 miles (D) 130 miles

10. A number octahedron has eight sides numbered 1 through 8. If you roll the octahedron, what is the probability of getting a multiple of 3?

(F) 0 (G) $\frac{1}{8}$ (H) $\frac{1}{4}$ (J) $\frac{3}{8}$

Brain games

California Standards

- Use cross multiplication as a method for solving proportions. (NS 1.3)

Patching Together Proportions

Materials

- **24 index cards**
- **Calculator (optional)**

Directions

Object of the Game

Play in pairs. For each turn, one player solves a proportion. If the solution is correct, the player gets 1 point. The winner is the player with the most points after each player has 6 turns. (A tie occurs if the players have the same number of points.)

Set 1

Set 2

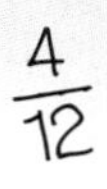

How to Play

STEP 1 Each player makes a set of 12 cards. Each card in Set 1 shows a ratio containing a number and a variable. Each card in Set 2 shows a ratio of two numbers.

STEP 2 Set 1 and Set 2 are placed face down in separate piles. One player turns over the top card in each pile and solves the proportion formed by equating the ratios. The other player checks the solution, using a calculator if desired. The players switch roles and keep playing until each player has 6 turns.

Another Way to Play

One player turns over the top cards in Set 1 and Set 2 and predicts whether the proportion's solution is a whole number. The other player checks the prediction. A correct prediction earns one point.

Brain Teaser

Find the Proportion

When you use the cross products property, you get $3 \cdot 8 = 4 \cdot n$.

The ratios in the proportion equal 0.75.

The variable is on the right side of the proportion.

The basic skills you'll review on this page will help prepare you for the next chapter.

Reviewing the Basics

EXAMPLE 1 Writing Fractions as Decimals

Write the fraction as a decimal.

a. $\frac{2}{5}$

b. $\frac{10}{3}$

Solution Divide the numerator by the denominator.

a. $5\overline{)2.0}$ with quotient 0.4. So, $\frac{2}{5} = 0.4$.

b. $3\overline{)10.00}$ with quotient $3.33...$ So, $\frac{10}{3} = 3.\overline{3}$.

Try These

Write the fraction as a decimal. Use bar notation if necessary.

1. $\frac{1}{2}$ **2.** $\frac{5}{4}$ **3.** $\frac{7}{8}$ **4.** $\frac{5}{6}$

5. $\frac{7}{12}$ **6.** $\frac{9}{5}$ **7.** $\frac{10}{9}$ **8.** $\frac{1}{11}$

9. $\frac{17}{9}$ **10.** $\frac{35}{8}$ **11.** $\frac{15}{4}$ **12.** $\frac{2}{27}$

EXAMPLE 2 Multiplying Decimals

Find the product.

a. 0.25×200

b. 4.59×0.06

Solution

Multiply as with whole numbers. The number of decimal places in the product is the sum of the numbers of decimal places in the factors.

a.

0.25	2 decimal places
× 200	0 decimal places
50.00	2 decimal places

b.

4.59	2 decimal places
× 0.06	2 decimal places
0.2754	4 decimal places

Try These

Find the product.

13. 0.2×25 **14.** 0.5×32 **15.** 45×0.09

16. 120×0.33 **17.** 0.66×180 **18.** 239×0.375

19. 0.15×10.2 **20.** 0.2×54.96 **21.** 0.4×36.98

22. 0.06×0.08 **23.** 2.25×5.41 **24.** 42.72×0.69

Student Help

▶More Examples

INTERNET More examples and practice exercises available at www.mcdougallittell.com

Chapters 1-6 Cumulative Practice

Evaluate the expression. (1.3, 1.4)

1. $15 - 6 \div 3 + 4$ **2.** $3 \times 9 + 12 \div 6$ **3.** $(25 - 3) \div (5 + 6)$

4. 6 cubed **5.** $4x^5$ when $x = 2$ **6.** $27 + 3^4 \div 9$

Order the numbers from least to greatest. (1.5, 2.6, 2.8)

7. 3.12, 3.2, 3.02, 3.22, 3.19 **8.** 0.02, 0.11, 0.011, 0.01, 0.1

9. $\frac{3}{8}, \frac{3}{5}, \frac{3}{4}, \frac{4}{9}$ **10.** $\frac{4}{7}, \frac{4}{5}, \frac{1}{2}, \frac{2}{3}$

11. $1.75, \frac{9}{5}, \frac{8}{3}, \frac{7}{2}, \frac{5}{9}, 2.65$ **12.** $\frac{9}{8}, 1.25, 1.05, \frac{3}{2}, \frac{6}{5}, 1.1$

Round the number to the given place value. (1.6)

13. 6.93 (tenths) **14.** 24.8 (ones) **15.** 7.5117 (thousandths)

Write the prime factorization of the number. (2.1)

16. 72 **17.** 75 **18.** 112 **19.** 189

Find the greatest common factor and the least common multiple of the numbers. (2.2, 2.5)

20. 6 and 14 **21.** 24 and 56 **22.** 25 and 30 **23.** 42 and 72

SURVEYS In Exercises 24–26, use the circle graph showing the results of a survey of a class of 30 students. The graph gives the fraction of the students who prefer each of several types of quiz questions.

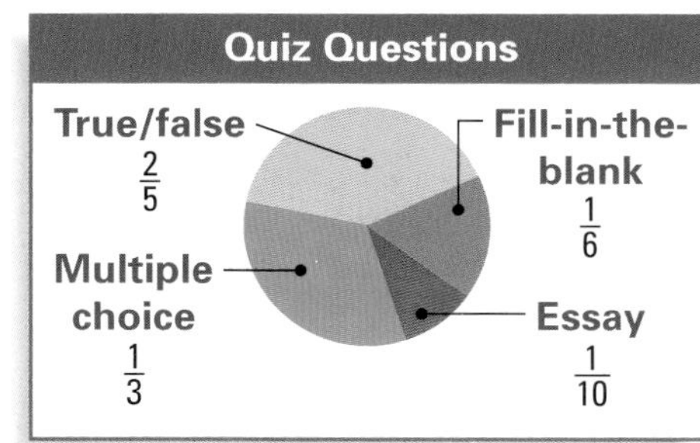

24. Use a set model to find how many students prefer multiple choice questions. (2.3)

25. What fraction of the students prefer either fill-in-the-blank questions or essay questions? (3.1)

26. What fraction of the students do *not* prefer true/false questions? (3.1)

Evaluate. Simplify if possible. (3.1–3.5)

27. $\frac{2}{3} + \frac{1}{6}$ **28.** $\frac{3}{4} - \frac{3}{5}$ **29.** $6\frac{1}{4} - 4\frac{3}{8}$ **30.** $2\frac{5}{8} + 7\frac{5}{12}$

31. $\frac{1}{4} \times \frac{6}{7}$ **32.** $2\frac{1}{2} \times 3\frac{2}{5}$ **33.** $\frac{14}{9} \div \frac{7}{8}$ **34.** $4\frac{1}{6} \div 4$

Evaluate the expression in two ways. (3.6)

35. $4(9 + 6)$ **36.** $3(12 + 10)$ **37.** $7(8 + 2)$ **38.** $3(13 + 2)$

In Exercises 39–46, perform the indicated operation. (4.3–4.6)

39. $14 - 27$ **40.** $3 + (-6)$ **41.** $-7 + 12$ **42.** $18 - (-10)$

43. $4 \cdot (-8)$ **44.** $-3 \cdot (-7)$ **45.** $-45 \div 3$ **46.** $-20 \div (-4)$

47. AVIATION An airplane flying at an altitude of 35,000 feet begins descending at a rate of 1200 feet per minute. Write an expression for the altitude of the airplane after t minutes. (5.1)

Solve the equation. Then check your solution. (5.3–5.7)

48. $b + 7 = 5$ **49.** $15 + c = -4$ **50.** $-7 + t = -1$

51. $3g = 27$ **52.** $-2f = 30$ **53.** $\frac{r}{16} = -4$

54. $2m + 3 = 33$ **55.** $6 - 3j = 27$ **56.** $-7k + 4 = -24$

Write and solve an equation to find the value of *x*. (5.2, 5.3, 5.5)

57. Perimeter $= 11$ cm

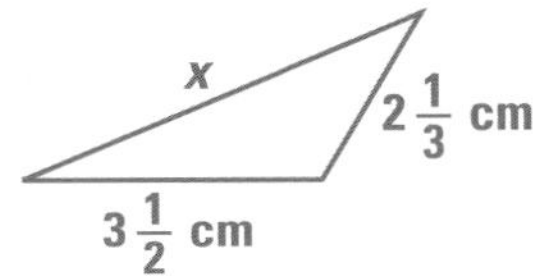

58. Area $= 3\frac{3}{5}$ ft^2

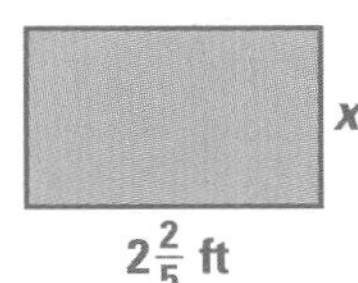

In Exercises 59–62, solve the proportion. (6.2)

59. $\frac{x}{45} = \frac{3}{27}$ **60.** $\frac{8}{5} = \frac{m}{45}$ **61.** $\frac{24}{n} = \frac{2}{7}$ **62.** $\frac{33}{36} = \frac{22}{w}$

63. ENERGY USE Over a 7 day period, a certain house uses 350 kilowatt-hours of electricity. Write and solve a proportion to predict how many kilowatt-hours of electricity the house will use in a 30 day month. (6.3)

64. MATHEMATICAL REASONING Rectangle A is 9.6 meters long and 5.6 meters wide. Rectangle B is 13.2 meters long and is similar to Rectangle A. What is the width of Rectangle B? (6.4)

Science Link **In Exercises 65–67, use the following information.** A book on ocean ecology shows an illustration of a blue whale. The illustration is 5 inches long and includes the caption "1 in. = 16 ft." (6.5)

65. How long is an actual blue whale?

66. What is the scale factor for the illustration?

67. Suppose you make a scale drawing of a blue whale that is 4 inches long. What is the scale for your drawing?

Find the probability of randomly drawing the given type of marble from a jar containing 8 blue marbles, 10 green marbles, 15 red marbles, and 7 yellow marbles. (6.6)

68. Blue **69.** Green **70.** Red **71.** Red or yellow

Chapters 4-6 Project

California Standards

- Solve problems, including those arising in concrete situations, that use positive and negative integers. (NS 2.3)
- Convert one unit of measurement to another. (AF 2.1)
- Use proportions to solve problems. (NS 1.3)

Materials

- Newspaper or internet
- Paper
- Ruler
- Colored pencils or markers

Making a Weather Map

OBJECTIVE Create a weather map that shows low temperatures.

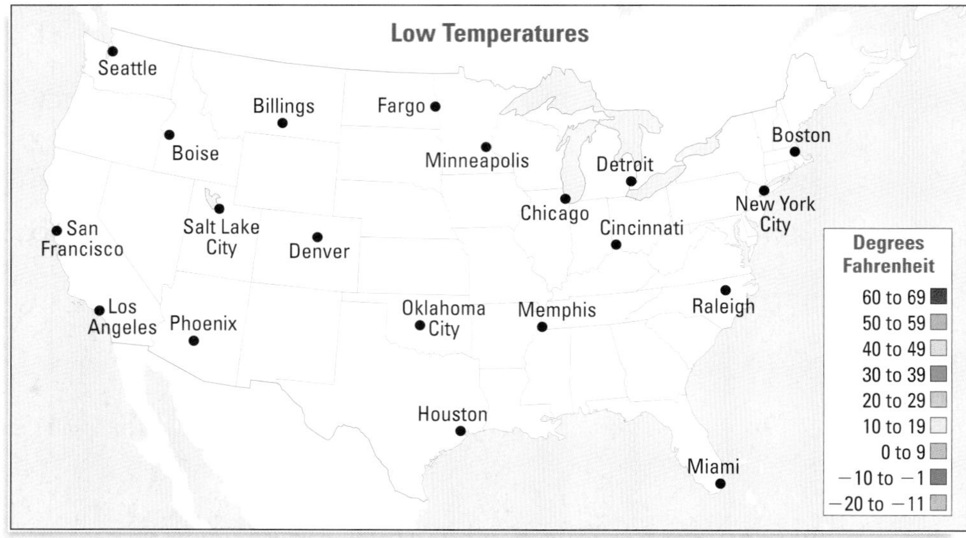

Investigation

1. Use a newspaper, the Internet, or a television news report to obtain the low temperatures in degrees Fahrenheit for 20 cities across the 48 contiguous states. Use cities from both the North and the South.

2. Use the formula $C = \frac{5}{9}(F - 32)$ to convert the low temperatures from degrees Fahrenheit F to degrees Celsius C. Round your answers to the nearest degree.

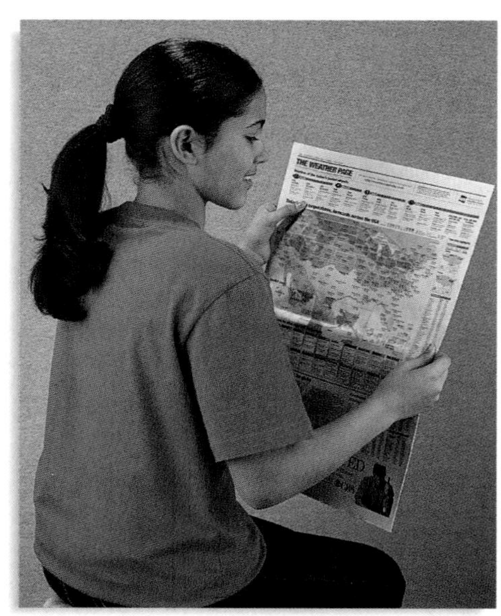

3. Draw a United States map that is about 10 inches wide from west to east. Label the 20 cities from Exercise 1.

4. The distance from San Francisco to Boston is about 2700 miles. Using your map, complete the scale below.

   Scale: 1 inch = **?** miles

   Add the scale to your map.

5. On your map, write the low temperature for each city in degrees Fahrenheit and in degrees Celsius (for example, 34°F/1°C).

6. Make a color legend like the one on the map on page 306. Use the legend to color the dot locating each city based on the city's temperature.

Present Your Results

Create a poster to present your results. Your poster should include all of the following:

- Your map with the 20 cities labeled. The dot marking each city should be colored to indicate the low temperature for the city.
- A color legend that explains the colors of the cities' dots.
- The low temperature for each city written in degrees Fahrenheit and in degrees Celsius.
- The map's scale factor.
- A concluding paragraph. What patterns do you notice on the map? Which regions are the coldest? Which are the warmest? Are there any patterns as you look at the temperatures from south to north? from west to east?

Extension

If you know a temperature in degrees Fahrenheit F, you can use the formula $F = 2C + 30$ to estimate the temperature in degrees Celsius C.

7. Choose a city from Exercise 1. In the formula above, substitute the city's temperature in degrees Fahrenheit for F. Then solve the equation to find C.

8. Compare your estimate from Exercise 7 to the actual temperature that you calculated in Exercise 2. How good is the estimate?

Percents

Why are percents important?

A percent shows a relationship between two quantities in terms of "per 100." Percents are often used to describe data, to make comparisons, and to represent part-whole relationships. You will use percents as you study future topics, such as probability and statistics.

Many people use percents in their careers, including ecologists (page 309) and personal trainers (page 331). For example, ecologists use percents to describe animal populations and soil composition.

Meeting the California Standards

The skills you'll learn in this chapter will help you meet state standards and prepare for standardized tests. In this chapter you'll:

- **Interpret and use ratios in different contexts.** LESSON 7.1
- **Calculate given percentages of quantities and solve problems involving discounts at sales, interest earned, and tips.** LESSONS 7.1–7.4, 7.6, 7.7
- **Solve problems involving percentages.** LESSON 7.4
- **Compute statistical measurements for data sets.** LESSON 7.5
- **Analyze data displays.** LESSON 7.5

Career Link **ECOLOGY** An ecologist uses percents when:

- comparing animal populations.
- recording changes to ecosystems.

EXERCISES

An ecologist is planning a zoo's desert and arctic habitats, as shown in the table.

Planned Vertebrate Species

	Desert habitat	Arctic habitat
Mammals	21	9
Birds	6	14
Reptiles	73	0

1. What fraction of all the vertebrate species in the desert habitat will be mammals? birds? reptiles?

2. What fraction of all the vertebrate species in the arctic habitat will be mammals? birds? reptiles?

3. Which habitat will have a greater fraction of mammal species? Explain.

In Lesson 7.4, you will learn how to use percents to describe the number of reptile species in the habitats. In Lesson 7.5, you will learn how to make a circle graph of the data.

Chapter 7 Getting Ready

PREVIEW What's the chapter about?

- Relating **percents, fractions,** and **decimals**
- Finding **a percent of a number**
- Working with **percent applications**

WORDS TO KNOW

- **percent,** *p. 311*
- **circle graph,** *p. 333*
- **principal,** *p. 338*
- **simple interest,** *p. 338*
- **annual interest rate,** *p. 338*

PREPARE Chapter Readiness Quiz

Take this quick quiz. If you are unsure of an answer, look back at the reference pages for help.

VOCABULARY CHECK *(refer to pp. 221, 269)*

1. -2 is a solution of which equation?

(A) $2x = 4$ (B) $x + 1 = -1$ (C) $x - 7 = 9$ (D) $4x + 5 = 3$

2. Which equation is a proportion?

(F) $5x = 90$ (G) $k + 8 = 4$ (H) $\frac{n}{2} = \frac{30}{35}$ (J) $m - 5 = -8$

SKILL CHECK *(refer to pp. 95, 269, 270)*

3. Which fraction is equivalent to 0.375?

(A) $\frac{1}{8}$ (B) $\frac{1}{6}$ (C) $\frac{3}{8}$ (D) $\frac{3}{7}$

4. Which number is a solution of the proportion $\frac{12}{7} = \frac{b}{14}$?

(F) 2 (G) 7 (H) 24 (J) 168

STUDY TIP Make Flash Cards

Find someone in your class to study with. You can use flash cards to study vocabulary or concepts.

What is 0.45 written as a percent?
45%

7.1 Percents, Fractions, and Decimals

In this lesson you'll:

- Calculate percents. (NS 1.4)
- Interpret and use ratios in different contexts. (NS 1.2)

Goal 1 Writing Percents in Different Forms

The word *percent* means "per hundred." The symbol for percent is %. A **percent** is a ratio whose denominator is 100. For example, in the square at the right, 25 of the 100 squares are blue. So, you can say that 25% of the squares are blue. This can be written three ways.

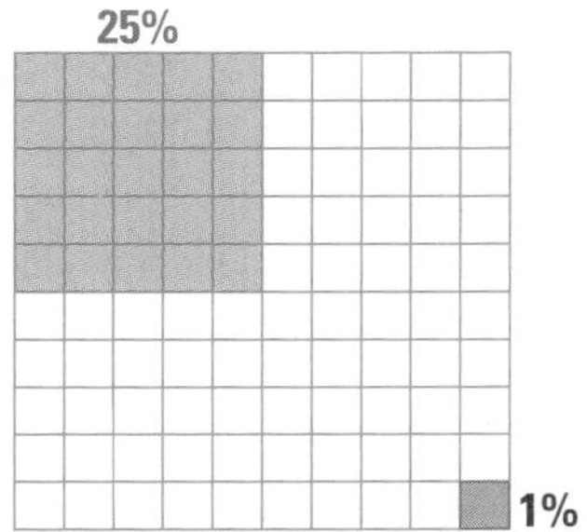

PERCENT FORM	FRACTION FORM	DECIMAL FORM
25%	$\frac{25}{100}$	0.25

Writing Different Forms

To write a fraction or a decimal as a percent or to write a percent as a fraction or a decimal, the first step is to rewrite the given form as a fraction with a denominator of 100.

EXAMPLE 1 Writing Fractions as Percents

a. $\frac{1}{4} = \frac{1 \times 25}{4 \times 25} = \frac{25}{100} = 25\%$

b. $\frac{2}{5} = \frac{2 \times 20}{5 \times 20} = \frac{40}{100} = 40\%$

EXAMPLE 2 Writing Decimals as Percents

a. $0.75 = \frac{75}{100} = 75\%$

b. $0.8 = \frac{8}{10} = \frac{8 \times 10}{10 \times 10} = \frac{80}{100} = 80\%$

c. $0.104 = \frac{104}{1000} = \frac{104 \div 10}{1000 \div 10} = \frac{10.4}{100} = 10.4\%$

EXAMPLE 3 Writing Percents as Fractions or Decimals

a. $86\% = \frac{86}{100} = 0.86$

b. $15\% = \frac{15}{100} = 0.15$

Goal 2 ROUNDING PERCENTS

In order to write some fractions as percents, you may want to round the percent to a specified decimal place.

EXAMPLE 4 Rounding Percents

a. Write $\frac{1}{8}$ as a percent, rounded to the nearest whole percent.

$$\frac{1}{8} = 0.125 = \frac{125}{1000} = \frac{125 \div 10}{1000 \div 10} = \frac{12.5}{100} = 12.5\% \approx 13\%$$

b. Write $\frac{1}{3}$ as a percent, rounded to the nearest tenth of a percent.

$$\frac{1}{3} \approx 0.333 = \frac{333}{1000} = \frac{333 \div 10}{1000 \div 10} = \frac{33.3}{100} = 33.3\%$$

Link to Transportation

VEHICLE SALES In 1990 about 5.9 million households owned sport utility vehicles (SUVs). By 1995 over 12 million households owned SUVs, an increase of about 107%.

More about vehicle sales available at www.mcdougallittell.com

EXAMPLE 5 Interpreting a Survey

VEHICLE SALES In 1998 about 15.5 million cars and other light vehicles were sold in the United States. The graph shows the number of vehicles sold in each category. Write the numbers as percents of the total number of vehicles sold. Round to the nearest percent. What is the sum of the three percents? ▶ Source: *Ward's Automotive Yearbook 1999*

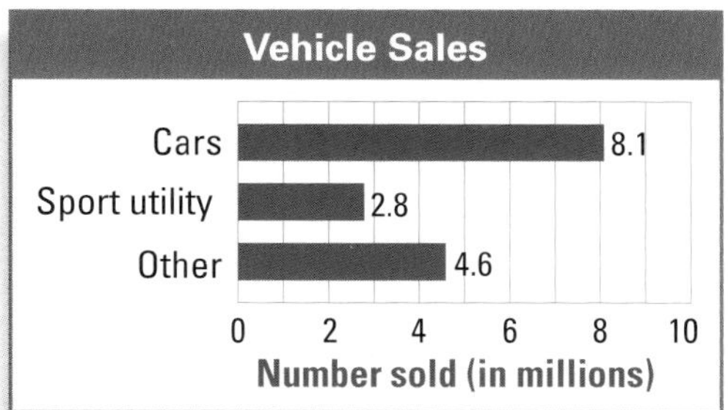

Solution

First write the number for each category as a fraction of the total sales. Then rewrite the fraction as a percent of the total.

Car: $\frac{8.1}{15.5} \approx 0.5226 = \frac{5226}{10{,}000} = \frac{52.26}{100} = 52.26\% \approx 52\%$

Sport utility: $\frac{2.8}{15.5} \approx 0.1806 = \frac{1806}{10{,}000} = \frac{18.06}{100} = 18.06\% \approx 18\%$

Other: $\frac{4.6}{15.5} \approx 0.2968 = \frac{2968}{10{,}000} = \frac{29.68}{100} = 29.68\% \approx 30\%$

ANSWER ▶ After rounding, the sum of the three percents is 100%. This means that all 15.5 million vehicles are accounted for.

7.1 Exercises

Guided Practice

Write the decimal, fraction, and percent shown by the shaded portion of the figure.

1. 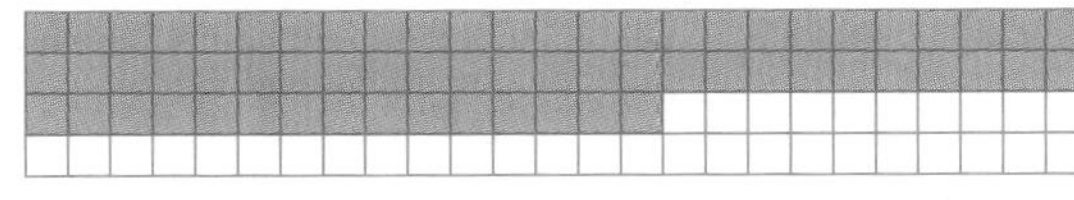

2. 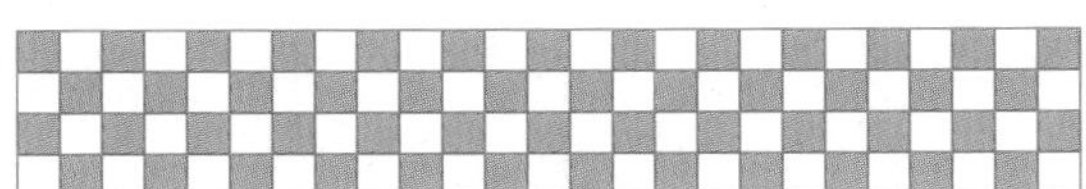

Explain each step in the conversion.

3. $0.62 = \frac{62}{100} = 62\%$

4. $36\% = \frac{36}{100} = 0.36$

In Exercises 5–8, write the number in two other forms.

5. $\frac{15}{100}$

6. 0.45

7. 67%

8. $\frac{1}{16}$

9. **TEST GRADE** You earned a score of 42 points out of 50 points on a test. As a fraction, you answered $\frac{42}{50}$ of the test correctly. As a percent, how much of the test did you get correct?

10. **MATHEMATICAL REASONING** Thirty percent of the students in your class bring their lunch to school. What percent of the students in your class do *not* bring their lunch to school? Explain.

Practice and Problem Solving

Student Help

▶MORE PRACTICE
Extra practice to help you master skills is on page 578.

Write the fraction and the percent shown by the shaded portion of the figure.

11. 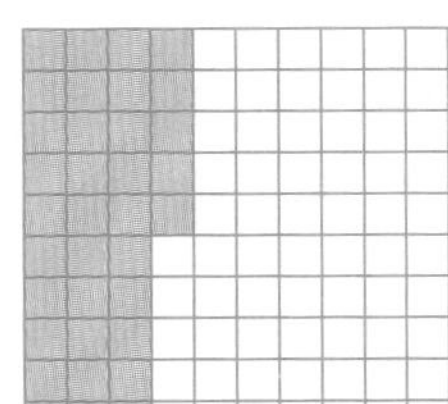

12. 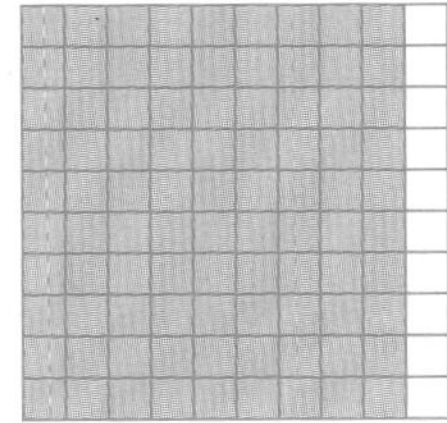

13. 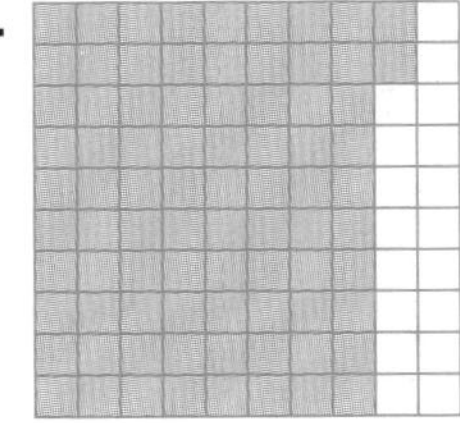

MATHEMATICAL REASONING **Tell whether the statement is *true* or *false*. If false, change the right-hand side to make a true statement.**

14. $\frac{53}{100} = 53\%$

15. $\frac{2}{100} = 20\%$

16. $99\% = \frac{999}{1000}$

17. $0.25 = 25\%$

18. $80\% = 0.8$

19. $0.01 = 10\%$

Write the fraction as a percent, rounded to the nearest tenth of a percent.

20. $\frac{33}{100}$ **21.** $\frac{1}{10}$ **22.** $\frac{3}{4}$ **23.** $\frac{1}{6}$

24. $\frac{1}{9}$ **25.** $\frac{2}{3}$ **26.** $\frac{3}{50}$ **27.** $\frac{7}{8}$

28. $\frac{4}{5}$ **29.** $\frac{2}{15}$ **30.** $\frac{10}{23}$ **31.** $\frac{14}{25}$

Write the decimal as a percent.

32. 0.85 **33.** 0.24 **34.** 0.12 **35.** 0.49

36. 0.9 **37.** 0.6 **38.** 0.4 **39.** 0.02

40. 0.05 **41.** 0.095 **42.** 0.026 **43.** 0.088

Write the percent as a decimal and as a fraction in simplest form.

44. 9% **45.** 43% **46.** 50% **47.** 5%

48. 90% **49.** 18% **50.** 22% **51.** 45%

52. 1.9% **53.** 4.3% **54.** 1.8% **55.** 4.5%

Write the percent shown by the shaded portion of the figure.

56.

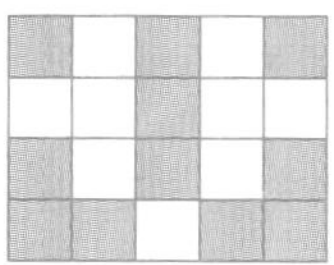

57.

58.

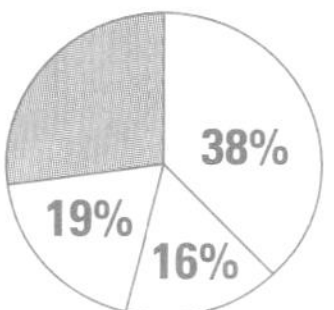

In Exercises 59–62, use the diagram below.

59. What percent of the dots are yellow?

60. What percent of the dots are green or yellow?

61. What percent of the dots are not blue?

62. What percent of the dots are neither orange nor green?

MATHEMATICAL REASONING **Determine which number does not belong in the list. Explain your reasoning.**

63. 0.68, $\frac{34}{50}$, 68%, $\frac{14}{25}$, $\frac{68}{100}$

64. $\frac{19}{200}$, 9.5%, 0.095, $\frac{95}{100}$, $\frac{9.5}{100}$

65. 24%, $\frac{6}{25}$, $\frac{24}{100}$, 2.4, $\frac{12}{50}$

66. 0.04, $\frac{40}{100}$, 0.4, $\frac{2}{5}$, 40%

AIR Most air pollutants are the result of human activities. Sulfur dioxide is a poisonous gas that enters the air when coal and fuel oil are burned.

In Exercises 67–70, estimate the time (in hours) you spend doing the activity during a typical weekday. Write your answer as a fraction with a denominator of 24. Then write or approximate it as a percent.

67. Attend school

68. Watch television

69. Sleep

70. Do homework

Science Link **In Exercises 71 and 72, use the table. It shows the components of the atmosphere.**

Components of the Atmosphere	
Component	**Percent**
Nitrogen	78.1
Oxygen	20.9
Other	1

71. Write the percents as decimals and as fractions in simplest form.

72. What is the sum of the three percents?

MUSIC **In Exercises 73–75, use the following information.** In 1998 music sales were about $13.8 million. The table shows the total sales from different outlets used to buy music recordings.

▶ Source: Recording Industry Association of America, Inc.

Sales Outlet	Sales (in millions)
Record store	7
Other store	5
Music club	1.2
Mail order	0.4
Internet	0.2

73. Write the sales at each outlet as a percent, rounded to the nearest tenth of a percent, of the total sales in 1998.

74. What is the sum of the five percents?

75. What could be responsible for the percents not adding up to 100?

CHALLENGE **Write the percent as a decimal, rounded to the nearest tenth, and as a fraction in simplest form.**

76. $37\frac{1}{2}\%$

77. $10\frac{3}{4}\%$

78. $5\frac{1}{3}\%$

79. $15\frac{2}{3}\%$

Multiple-Choice Practice

80. The fraction $\frac{15}{120}$ is the same as which percent?

Ⓐ 8.13% Ⓑ 12.5% Ⓒ 15% Ⓓ 20%

81. Which fraction is the same as 28%?

Ⓕ $\frac{7}{50}$ Ⓖ $\frac{14}{100}$ Ⓗ $\frac{7}{25}$ Ⓙ $\frac{28}{50}$

DEVELOPING CONCEPTS
Working with Percents

For use with Lesson 7.2

California Standards

- Calculate a given percent of a quantity. (NS 1.4)
- Use models to explain mathematical reasoning. (MR 2.4)

MATERIALS

- Grid paper

Since *percent* means "per hundred," you can find the percent of a number by dividing the number into 100 equal parts or by using a fraction with a denominator of 100.

SAMPLE 1 Finding a Percent of a Number

Find 35% of 200.

Here's How

Method 1 Use a diagram.

Use 200 dots to represent the number 200, and use a 10-by-10 grid (with 100 small squares) to organize the dots into equal groups of 2 dots.

Since you want 35% of 200, shade 35 of the small squares. These squares contain a total of 70 dots.

Method 2 Use a fraction.

Since 35% is $\frac{35}{100}$ in fraction form, you can find 35% of 200 by multiplying $\frac{35}{100}$ and 200.

$35\% \text{ of } 200 = \frac{35}{100} \cdot \frac{200}{1}$ Rewrite 35% and 200 as fractions.

$= \frac{7000}{100}$ Multiply.

$= 70$ Simplify.

ANSWER ▶ 35% of 200 is 70.

Try These

In Exercises 1–6, use either of the methods shown in Sample 1 to find the percent of the number.

1. 20% of 200 **2.** 32% of 300 **3.** 45% of 400

4. 68% of 500 **5.** 3% of 700 **6.** 95% of 600

7. **MATHEMATICAL REASONING** Why should you expect the two methods shown in Sample 1 to produce the same result? Explain.

7.2 Finding a Percent of a Number

California Standards

In this lesson you'll:

- Calculate a given percent of a quantity. (NS 1.4)

Goal 1 FINDING A PERCENT OF A NUMBER

In Developing Concepts 7.2, page 316, you learned two methods for finding the percent of a number, such as 30% of 400. These methods are based on the proportion

$$\frac{\text{Percent}}{100} = \frac{\text{Percent of a number}}{\text{Number}}$$

EXAMPLE 1 *Using a Proportion*

Find 30% of 400.

Solution

$\frac{30}{100} = \frac{x}{400}$ Set up a proportion.

$30 \cdot 400 = 100x$ Cross products property

$\frac{30 \cdot 400}{100} = \frac{100x}{100}$ Divide each side by 100.

$120 = x$ Simplify.

ANSWER ▶ So, 120 is 30% of 400.

CHECK ✓ $\frac{30}{100} \stackrel{?}{=} \frac{120}{400}$ Substitute 120 for x in the proportion.

$\frac{3}{10} = \frac{3}{10}$ ✓ Simplify both sides.

Student Help

▶ LOOK BACK
For help with solving proportions, see page 269.

EXAMPLE 2 *Finding a Percent of a Number*

TRAVEL You drive 300 miles. The first 20% of the road is under construction. How many miles of the road are under construction?

Solution

$\frac{20}{100} = \frac{x}{300}$ Set up a proportion.

$20 \cdot 300 = 100x$ Cross products property

$\frac{20 \cdot 300}{100} = \frac{100x}{100}$ Divide each side by 100.

$60 = x$ Simplify.

ANSWER ▶ So, 60 miles of the road are under construction.

As you learned in Developing Concepts 7.2, page 316, one way to find the percent of a number is to write the percent as a fraction and multiply by the number.

EXAMPLE 3 Multiplying by a Fraction

Find the percent of the number.

a. 50% of 46

b. 75% of 120

Solution

a. 50% of 46 $= \frac{1}{2} \cdot 46$ — As a fraction in simplest form, $50\% = \frac{1}{2}$.

$= 23$ — Multiply.

b. 75% of 120 $= \frac{3}{4} \cdot 120$ — As a fraction in simplest form, $75\% = \frac{3}{4}$.

$= 90$ — Multiply.

Student Help

▶ READING TIP The word "of" in a mathematical sentence means to multiply.

Goal 2 USING DECIMAL FORM

As you saw in Example 3, you can multiply a given percent written as a fraction by a given number to find the percent of the number. You can also write the given percent as a decimal and then multiply by the given number to find the percent of the number.

EXAMPLE 4 Multiplying by a Decimal

Find the percent of the number. Check that the answer is reasonable.

a. 35% of 150

b. 92% of 75

Solution

a. 35% of 150 $= 0.35 \cdot 150$ — Write percent in decimal form.

$= 52.5$ — Multiply.

The answer seems reasonable because 35% is about one third, and one third of 150 is 50.

b. 92% of 75 $= 0.92 \cdot 75$ — Write percent in decimal form.

$= 69$ — Multiply.

The answer seems reasonable because 92% is about 90%. Because 100% of 75 is 75 and 10% of 75 is 7.5, 92% is about $75 - 7.5 = 67.5$.

Student Help

▶ STUDY TIP Estimation is often a good way to check that your answer is reasonable. For example, you know that 10% of 200 is 20. So, you can estimate that 11% of 200 is a little more than 20.

Link to Transportation

COMMUTING In 1990 5.3% of workers in the United States used public transportation to get to work.

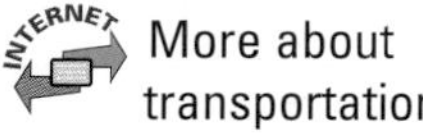

More about transportation available at www.mcdougallittell.com

EXAMPLE 5 Finding a Percent of a Number

COMMUTING In the 1990 census, 8 million workers in New York reported how they got to work. Their responses are shown in the graph. How many people are in each category?

▶ Source: US Bureau of the Census

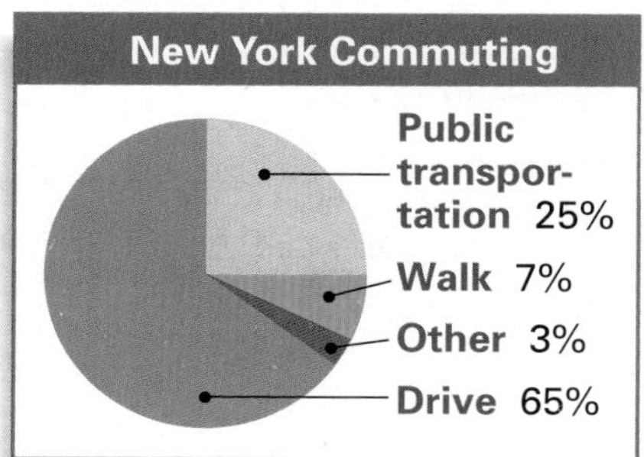

Solution

Drive: 65% of 8 million = 0.65 • 8 million = 5.2 million

Public transportation: 25% of 8 million = 0.25 • 8 million = 2 million

Walk: 7% of 8 million = 0.07 • 8 million = 0.56 million

Other: 3% of 8 million = 0.03 • 8 million = 0.24 million

CHECK ✓ The answers seem reasonable because 5.2 + 2 + 0.56 + 0.24 = 8.

7.2 Exercises

Guided Practice

Write the percent as a fraction in simplest form.

1. 25% **2.** 30% **3.** 15% **4.** 80%

5. 45% **6.** 90% **7.** 10% **8.** 60%

Find the percent of the number by multiplying by a fraction.

9. 10% of 250 **10.** 25% of 84 **11.** 50% of 320

12. 60% of 200 **13.** 20% of 48 **14.** 45% of 110

In Exercises 15–20, find the percent of the number by multiplying by a decimal. Check that the answer is reasonable.

15. 32% of 90 **16.** 26% of 115 **17.** 18% of 210

18. 29% of 120 **19.** 44% of 180 **20.** 91% of 360

21. **BAKING** You bake 96 of the 150 snacks needed for a bake sale. You estimate that 65% of the baking is done. Is your estimate reasonable? Explain.

22. **WRITING** Describe a real-life problem that can be solved using the equation 0.30 • 150 = 45.

Practice and Problem Solving

Student Help

▶ More Practice Extra practice to help you master skills is on page 578.

In Exercises 23–31, find the percent of the number by multiplying by a fraction.

23. 50% of 64 **24.** 25% of 160 **25.** 80% of 50

26. 70% of 20 **27.** 15% of 80 **28.** 60% of 45

29. 75% of 325 **30.** 90% of 45 **31.** 20% of 490

In Exercises 32–40, find the percent of the number by multiplying by a decimal. Check that the answer is reasonable.

32. 6% of 4 **33.** 16% of 425 **34.** 52% of 300

35. 8% of 150 **36.** 96% of 125 **37.** 48% of 50

38. 18% of 250 **39.** 4% of 60 **40.** 72% of 72

41. **ERROR ANALYSIS** Describe and correct the error below.

7% of 160
= 0.7 • 160
= 112

The answer seems reasonable because 7% is more than 5% = 0.5, and half of 160 is 80.

42. **EDUCATION** A group of 50 students took a test. The portion of students who received each letter grade is shown in the table. Find the number of students who received each grade.

Letter grade	A	B	C	D
Percent of students	40%	30%	20%	10%

43. ***Science Link*** There are about 326 million cubic miles of water on Earth. About 97% of this amount is salt water. How many million cubic miles of salt water does Earth have?

44. **RECYCLING** Your class collects used telephone books to recycle. The class goal is to collect 300 telephone books. So far your class has reached 73% of its goal. How many telephone books has your class already collected?

45. ***History Link*** The United States census is a *tally*, or counting, of the population every ten years. The first census to include Texas was in 1850, when its population was about 1% of the entire population of the United States. In 1990 the population of Texas was about 7% of the entire population of the United States. Use the table to find the population of Texas in 1850 and in 1990.

Population of the United States	
1850	23,191,876
1990	248,709,873

▶ Source: US Bureau of the Census

Link to History

CENSUS Tallies are used to help people plan for the future. The tally above dates back to 2800 B.C. and gives information about fields and crops.

46. MINING In 1998 there were about 2400 metric tons of gold mined in the world. The bar graph at the right shows the percent of the 2400 metric tons that was mined in South Africa, the United States, and Canada. How much gold was mined in each of these three countries?

▶Source: U.S. Geological Survey

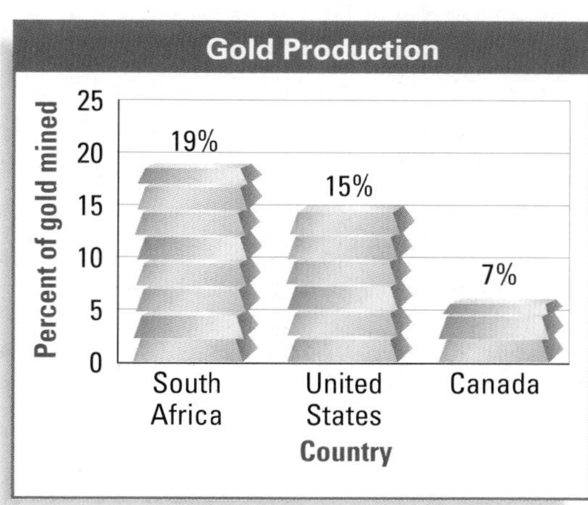

47. CHALLENGE Of the 528 people who respond to a survey, 62.5% answer *yes* to a certain question and 25% answer *no*. How many people are undecided?

Multiple-Choice Practice

48. What is 35% of 320?

Ⓐ 9 Ⓑ 100 Ⓒ 112 Ⓓ 224

49. In a reading contest, your class read a total of 40 books. You read 20% of the class total. How many books did you read?

Ⓕ 2 Ⓖ 4 Ⓗ 5 Ⓙ 8

Mixed Review

Evaluate the expression. *(4.7)*

50. $16 + (-44) \div 4$ **51.** $-4 - (-2)^3 \div 2$ **52.** $(9 + (-6)) \times (-4)$

Complete the statement with <, =, or >. *(4.8)*

53. -8 **?** -9.2 **54.** -1.5 **?** $-\frac{3}{2}$ **55.** $-4\frac{1}{5}$ **?** $-\frac{9}{2}$

In Exercises 56 and 57, write an algebraic equation for the sentence. Then solve the equation. *(5.2)*

56. The difference of six and a number is one.

57. A number divided by negative four equals five.

58. CAR REPAIR The total cost (parts and labor) of a car repair bill is \$456. The parts cost \$240. If a mechanic worked on the car for 6 hours, how much did the labor cost per hour? *(5.7)*

Solve the proportion. *(6.2)*

59. $\frac{7}{12} = \frac{x}{60}$ **60.** $\frac{54}{15} = \frac{n}{5}$ **61.** $\frac{m}{3} = \frac{36}{4}$

DEVELOPING CONCEPTS

Percents Greater Than 100%

For use with Lesson 7.3

California Standards

- Calculate a given percent of a quantity. (NS 1.4)
- Use models to explain mathematical reasoning. (MR 2.4)

MATERIALS

- Grid paper

In Lesson 7.2 you worked with percents less than 100%, but percents can also be equal to or greater than 100%.

SAMPLE 1 Working with a Percent Greater than 100%

a. Use a model to represent 120%.

b. Find 120% of 80.

Here's How

a. Think of 120% as 100% + 20%. Use a 10-by-10 grid to represent 100%. You need a second 10-by-10 grid to represent 20%. Shade all 100 of the small squares on the first grid and 20 of the small squares on the second grid, as shown.

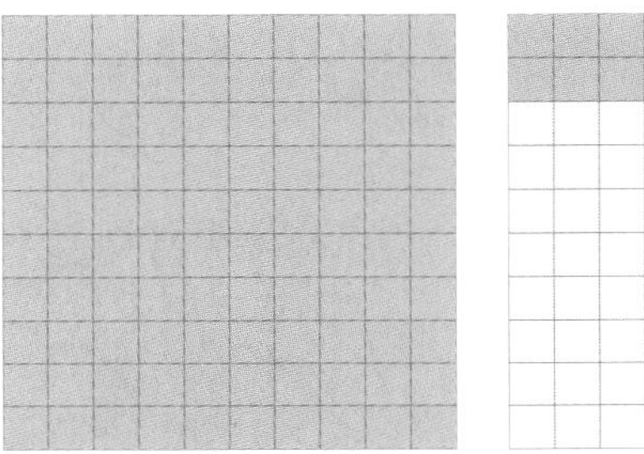

b. As part (a) suggests, you can think of 120% of 80 as 100% of 80 plus 20% of 80.

120% of 80	= (100% of 80) + (20% of 80)	Rewrite as a sum.
	= (1 • 80) + (0.2 • 80)	Use decimal form.
	= 80 + 16	Multiply.
	= 96	Add.

Notice that 96 > 80, which is reasonable because 120% > 100%.

Try These

Use a model to represent the given percent. Then find the given percent of 80.

1. 110% **2.** 140% **3.** 175% **4.** 200%

5. **MATHEMATICAL REASONING** In Sample 1, what decimal does 120% represent? Show how you can use the decimal form of 120% to find 120% of 80. Do you get the same result as in part (b) of Sample 1?

7.3 Large and Small Percents

In this lesson you'll:

- Calculate a given percent of a quantity and solve problems involving tips. (NS 1.4)

Goal 1 Using Large and Small Percents

In Developing Concepts 7.3, page 322, you worked with percents greater than 100%, but percents can also be less than 1%. The methods you learned in Lesson 7.2 can be used with these percents.

EXAMPLE 1 Rewriting Numbers

a. Rewrite 1.4 as a percent.

b. Rewrite $\frac{1}{2}\%$ as a decimal.

Solution

a. $1.4 = 1\frac{4}{10} = \frac{14}{10} = \frac{14 \times 10}{10 \times 10} = \frac{140}{100} = 140\%$

b. $\frac{1}{2}\% = 0.5\% = \frac{0.5}{100} = \frac{0.5 \times 10}{100 \times 10} = \frac{5}{1000} = 0.005$

EXAMPLE 2 Finding a Large Percent of a Number

You can use either of two methods to find 130% of 250.

Method 1 Set up a proportion.

$$\frac{130}{100} = \frac{x}{250}$$

$$32{,}500 = 100x$$

$$325 = x$$

Method 2 Rewrite 130% as a decimal.

$$\mathbf{130\%} \text{ of } 250 = \mathbf{1.3} \cdot 250 = 325$$

EXAMPLE 3 Finding a Small Percent of a Number

You can use either of two methods to find 0.5% of 40.

Method 1 Set up a proportion.

$$\frac{5}{1000} = \frac{x}{40}$$

$$200 = 1000x$$

$$0.2 = x$$

Method 2 Rewrite 0.5% as a decimal.

$$\mathbf{0.5\%} \text{ of } 40 = \mathbf{0.005} \cdot 40 = 0.2$$

Goal 2 ESTIMATING THE PERCENT OF A NUMBER

In many real-life situations, such as figuring the amount for a tip, it is helpful to use mental math to estimate the percent of a number.

Student Help

▶ **MORE EXAMPLES**

INTERNET More examples are available at www.mcdougallittell.com

EXAMPLE 4 Estimating a Large Percent of a Number

Use mental math to estimate 123% of 84.

Solution

123% is about 125%.	Relate given percent to an easy-to-use percent.
100% of $84 = 84$	$125\% = 100\% + 25\%$
$+\ 25\%$ of $84 = 21$	Use mental math with easy-to-use percent.
125% of $84 = 105$	Add.

ANSWER ▶ Since 123% is a little less than 125%, 123% of 84 is a little less than 105.

EXAMPLE 5 Finding a Small Percent of a Number

Use mental math to find $\frac{1}{2}\%$ of 140.

Solution

$\frac{1}{2}\%$ is half of 1%.	Relate given percent to an easy-to-use percent.
1% of $140 = 1.4$	Use mental math with easy-to-use percent.
Half of 1.4 is 0.7.	Find desired percent of 140 using previous result.

ANSWER ▶ So, $\frac{1}{2}\%$ of 140 is 0.7.

Thank you	
Orange juice	\$ 2.15
Mineral water	\$ 2.15
Lemon chicken	\$ 14.99
Shrimp stir-fry	\$ 15.99
Frozen yogurt	\$ 4.49
Fruit salad	\$ 3.99
Total	\$ 43.76

EXAMPLE 6 Estimating a Tip

Estimate a 15% tip for a restaurant bill of \$43.76.

Solution

\$43.76 is about \$45.	Round bill to nearest \$5.
10% of \$45 = \$4.50	Use mental math with easy-to-use percent.
+ 5% of \$45 = \$2.25	5% is half of 10%.
15% of \$45 = \$6.75	Add.

ANSWER ▶ So, 15% of \$43.76 is about \$6.75.

7.3 Exercises

Guided Practice

Match the percent with an equivalent decimal.

A. 0.018 **B.** 1.8 **C.** 0.18 **D.** 0.0018

1. 180% **2.** 0.18% **3.** 1.8% **4.** 18%

In Exercises 5–7, use mental math to estimate the percent of the number. Explain your reasoning.

5. 325% of 120 **6.** $\frac{1}{4}$% of 400 **7.** 124% of 150

8. HEIGHTS The average height in your class is 60 inches. John's height is 120% of the class average. How tall is John?

9. WRITING Write a real-life problem that uses a percent greater than 100%.

Practice and Problem Solving

Student Help

▶ **MORE PRACTICE** Extra practice to help you master skills is on page 578.

Write the percent as a decimal and as a fraction in simplest form.

10. 170% **11.** $\frac{3}{8}$% **12.** $\frac{5}{9}$% **13.** 135%

14. 0.3% **15.** 450% **16.** $\frac{4}{5}$% **17.** $\frac{16}{21}$%

Write the fraction or decimal as a percent.

18. 1.95 **19.** $\frac{4}{3}$ **20.** 0.005 **21.** $\frac{13}{2}$

22. $\frac{1}{125}$ **23.** 2.5 **24.** 0.00875 **25.** $\frac{3}{400}$

Complete the statement using <, = , or >.

26. 280% **?** 0.28 **27.** 0.0125 **?** $\frac{1}{8}$% **28.** $\frac{2}{5}$% **?** $\frac{1}{25}$

Find the percent of the number.

29. 110% of 50 **30.** $\frac{1}{4}$% of 200 **31.** 0.06% of 12

32. $\frac{4}{5}$% of 25 **33.** $\frac{7}{20}$% of 120 **34.** 160% of 450

35. 0.2% of 28 **36.** 255% of 390 **37.** 0.035% of 10

Use mental math to estimate the percent of the number. Explain your reasoning.

38. 48% of 80 **39.** 152% of 16 **40.** 198% of 150

41. 119% of 75 **42.** 277% of 92 **43.** 405% of 124

44. $\frac{3}{4}$% of 160 **45.** $\frac{1}{2}$% of 42 **46.** $\frac{1}{4}$% of 124

Use mental math to estimate a 15% tip and a 20% tip for the bill.

47. \$18.75 **48.** \$26.10 **49.** \$59.50

In Exercises 50 and 51, find the percent of each number. Assuming the percents continue to increase by the same amount, list the next two numbers in the sequence.

50. $\frac{1}{5}$% of 125, $\frac{2}{5}$% of 125, $\frac{3}{5}$% of 125, $\frac{4}{5}$% of 125

51. 110% of 150, 120% of 200, 130% of 250, 140% of 300

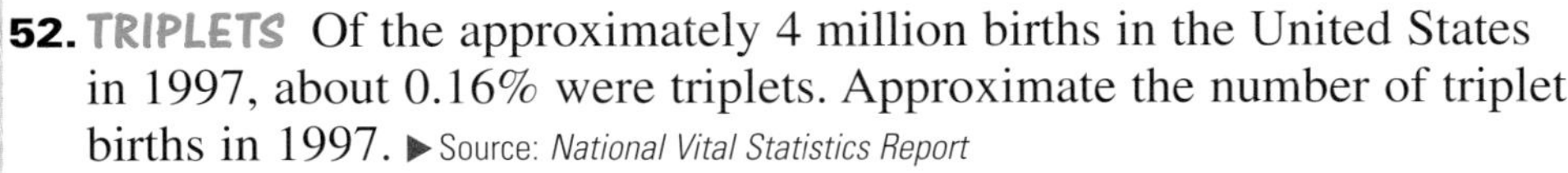

52. **TRIPLETS** Of the approximately 4 million births in the United States in 1997, about 0.16% were triplets. Approximate the number of triplet births in 1997. ▶ Source: *National Vital Statistics Report*

53. **QUADRUPLETS** The number of quadruplet births in the United States in 1990 was 185. By 1997 it had increased about 276%. Approximate the number of quadruplet births in 1997. ▶ Source: *National Vital Statistics Report*

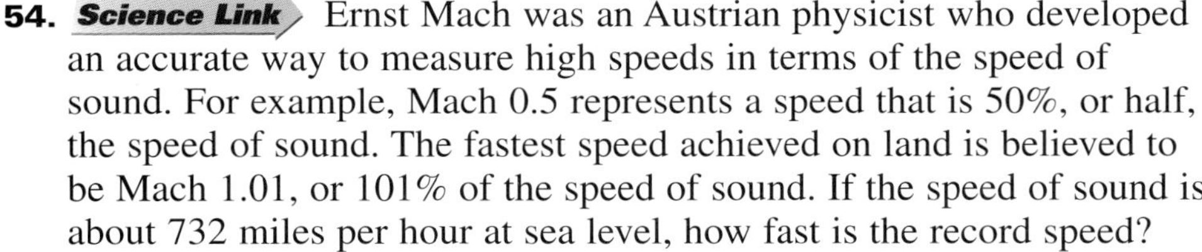

54. **Science Link** Ernst Mach was an Austrian physicist who developed an accurate way to measure high speeds in terms of the speed of sound. For example, Mach 0.5 represents a speed that is 50%, or half, the speed of sound. The fastest speed achieved on land is believed to be Mach 1.01, or 101% of the speed of sound. If the speed of sound is about 732 miles per hour at sea level, how fast is the record speed?

55. **CHALLENGE** A store advertises that for a sale, sweaters are marked 40% off the ticket prices that have already been discounted 35%. You have a coupon for an additional 25% off any item. Because 35% + 40% + 25% = 100%, can you get a sweater for free? Explain.

CONCORDE The Concorde is a supersonic airplane that began passenger service in 1976. It can travel at Mach 2.

More about Mach numbers available at www.mcdougallittell.com

Multiple-Choice Practice

56. Which of the following is *not* the same as $\frac{4}{25}$%?

(A) 0.0016 (B) 0.16% (C) $\frac{32}{200}$% (D) $\frac{16}{100}$

57. It costs you \$12 to build a birdhouse. You sell the birdhouse for 175% of your cost. What is the price of a birdhouse?

(F) \$9 (G) \$15 (H) \$21 (J) \$2100

Chapter 7 Mid-Chapter Test

Take this test as you would take a test in class. The answers to the exercises are given in the back of the book.

Write the fraction and percent shown by the shaded portion of the figure.

1. 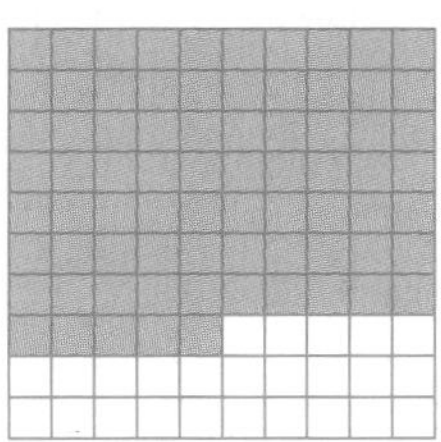

2. 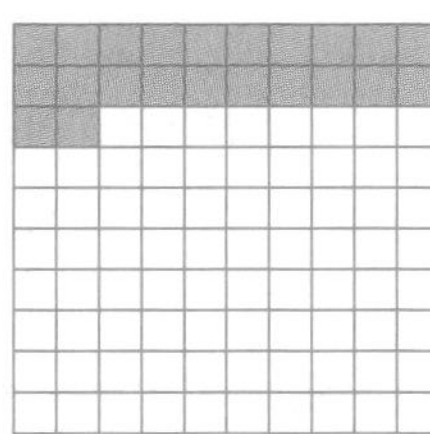

3. 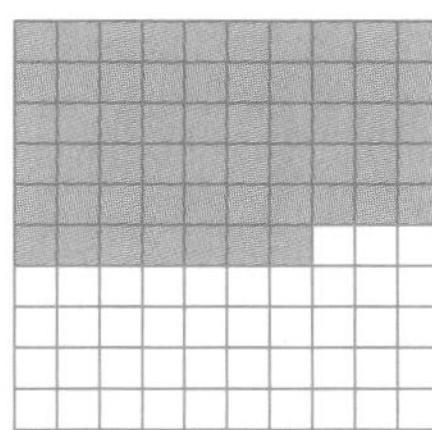

Write the number as a percent, rounded to the nearest tenth of a percent.

4. 0.124 **5.** 0.037 **6.** 0.067 **7.** 0.289

8. $\frac{3}{5}$ **9.** $\frac{13}{180}$ **10.** $\frac{7}{20}$ **11.** $\frac{16}{65}$

RURAL LIVING In Exercises 12–15, use the table which shows the percent of the population that lived in rural areas of various states in 1990. In each exercise, you are given the population for an entire state. Find the number of people who lived in the state's rural areas.

12. Tennessee 4,877,000

13. New Jersey 7,730,000

14. Washington 4,867,000

15. Kansas 2,478,000

Rural Population in Selected States	
State	Percent
Tennessee	39%
New Jersey	11%
Washington	24%
Kansas	31%

Find the percent of the number.

16. 10% of 8 **17.** 44% of 300

Write the fraction or decimal as a percent.

18. 2.61 **19.** $\frac{15}{2}$ **20.** $\frac{1}{250}$ **21.** 0.007

In Exercises 22–25, complete the statement using <, =, or >.

22. 0.625% **?** $\frac{1}{16}$ **23.** 1.2% **?** $\frac{3}{250}$ **24.** 137% **?** $\frac{11}{8}$ **25.** 6.5% **?** $\frac{13}{200}$

26. **CRAFTS** It costs you $8.25 to make a pottery bowl. You sell the bowls for 300% of your cost. What is the price of a bowl?

7.4 Solving Percent Problems

California Standards

In this lesson you'll:

- Solve problems involving percents. (NS 1.0)
- Calculate percents and solve problems involving discounts at sales. (NS 1.4)

Goal 1 Finding Percents

You can use a proportion to find what percent one number is of another number. The statement "a is p percent of b" is expressed by the proportion below, where a is part of the base, b is the base, and p is the percent.

$$\frac{a}{b} = \frac{p}{100} \qquad \frac{\text{Part of base}}{\text{Base}} = \frac{\text{Percent}}{100}$$

EXAMPLE 1 Finding a Percent

What percent of 40 is 15?

Solution

$\frac{a}{b} = \frac{p}{100}$ Write proportion.

$\frac{15}{40} = \frac{p}{100}$ Substitute 15 for a and 40 for b.

$15 \cdot 100 = 40 \cdot p$ Cross products property

$1500 = 40p$ Simplify.

$37.5 = p$ Divide each side by 40.

ANSWER ▶ 15 is 37.5% of 40.

EXAMPLE 2 Finding a Percent

SOFTBALL Your team won 19 of its 25 softball games. What percent of its games did it win?

Solution

$\frac{\text{Games won}}{\text{Games played}} = \frac{\text{Percent}}{100}$ Write verbal model.

$\frac{19}{25} = \frac{p}{100}$ Substitute known values.

$19 \cdot 100 = 25 \cdot p$ Cross products property

$1900 = 25p$ Simplify.

$76 = p$ Divide each side by 25.

ANSWER ▶ Your team won 76% of its games.

Student Help

▶ **STUDY TIP**
Use mental math to check that your answer is reasonable. In Example 2, 19 is a little less than four fifths of 25, so the percent should be a little less than 80%.

Goal 2 USING PROPORTIONS

You can use proportions to find a base or a part of a base.

EXAMPLE 3 Finding a Part of a Base

SALE PRICE You buy a pair of pants on sale. The price is 80% of the regular price of \$24.50. What is the sale price?

Solution

$$\frac{\text{Sale price}}{\text{Regular price}} = \frac{\text{Percent}}{100}$$ Write verbal model.

$$\frac{a}{24.50} = \frac{80}{100}$$ Substitute known values.

$$100 \cdot a = 24.50 \cdot 80$$ Cross products property

$$100a = 1960$$ Simplify.

$$a = 19.6$$ Divide each side by 100.

ANSWER ▶ The sale price for the pants is \$19.60.

In Example 3 you could also have solved the problem by writing the percent in decimal form and multiplying by the base:

$$80\% \text{ of } 24.50 = 0.8 \times 24.50 = 19.6$$

EXAMPLE 4 Finding a Base

8 is 32% of what number?

Solution

Method 1 Write and solve a proportion.

$$\frac{8}{b} = \frac{32}{100}$$ Write proportion.

$$8 \cdot 100 = 32 \cdot b$$ Cross products property

$$800 = 32b$$ Multiply.

$$25 = b$$ Divide each side by 32.

Method 2 Write and solve an equation.

$$8 = 0.32b$$ Write equation.

$$\frac{8}{0.32} = \frac{0.32b}{0.32}$$ Divide each side by 0.32.

$$25 = b$$ Simplify.

ANSWER ▶ 8 is 32% of 25.

Student Help

▶ LOOK BACK
For help with solving equations, see page 239.

EXAMPLE 5 Finding a Base

EMPLOYMENT In 1997 about 12%, or 17 million, of the workers in the United States were over 55 years of age. How many people were in the work force in 1997?

Solution

$\frac{17}{b} = \frac{12}{100}$	Write proportion.
$17 \cdot 100 = 12 \cdot b$	Cross products property
$1700 = 12b$	Simplify.
$142 \approx b$	Divide each side by 12.

ANSWER ▶ There were about 142 million people in the work force.

SOLVING PERCENT PROBLEMS

$\frac{a}{b} = \frac{p}{100}$ a is p percent of b.

UNKNOWN	QUESTION	WHERE TO LOOK
p (percent)	a is what percent of b?	See Examples 1 and 2.
a (part of base)	What is p percent of b?	See Example 3.
b (base)	a is p percent of what?	See Examples 4 and 5.

7.4 Exercises

Guided Practice

Complete the proportion. Then solve the proportion and answer the question.

1. What percent of 20 is 17?

$$\frac{?}{?} = \frac{p}{100}$$

2. 25 is 20% of what number?

$$\frac{?}{b} = \frac{?}{100}$$

ERROR ANALYSIS **Describe and correct the error.**

3. 36 is what percent of 150?

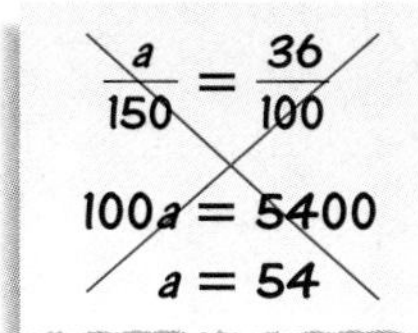

4. 4 is 8% of what number?

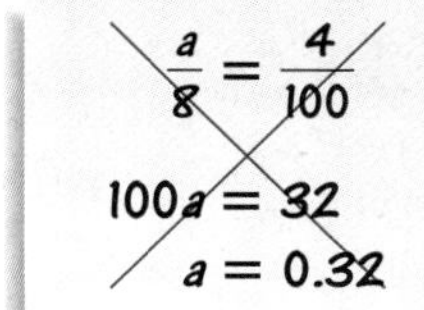

Practice and Problem Solving

Student Help

▶**MORE PRACTICE** Extra practice to help you master skills is on page 578.

In Exercises 5–12, use a proportion to answer the question.

5. What is 24% of 75?

6. What percent of 145 is 29?

7. 99 is what percent of 396?

8. 12% of what number is 42?

9. 30 is 250% of what number?

10. $33\frac{1}{3}\%$ of what number is 3?

11. What is 200% of 150?

12. 14 is what percent of 280?

13. **SCHOOL** You spend about 30% of a 24 hour day at school. How many hours are you at school?

14. **SURVEY** In a survey 15%, or 30 people, said that pretzels were their favorite snack food. How many people were surveyed?

15. **WEATHER** In Bishop, California, the weather is clear about 55% of the time. About how many days of the year is it clear?

16. **Chapter Opener Link** Look back at the table on page 309. What percent of the vertebrates in each habitat will be reptiles?

17. **PETS** The table gives the numbers and percents, by type, of the 128,600,000 companion animals in the United States. Copy and complete the table. Then use the table to find the total number and the total percent. Explain why these totals do or do not match the actual total number and 100%. ▶Source: American Veterinary Medical Association

Animal	Dogs	Cats	Birds	Horses
Number	?	59,100,000	?	4,000,000
Percent	41.1%	?	9.8%	?

18. **WORLD POPULATION** The population of the world in 1998 was about 5,900,000,000 people. Use the graph to estimate the percent of the world population in 1998 in each of the listed countries.

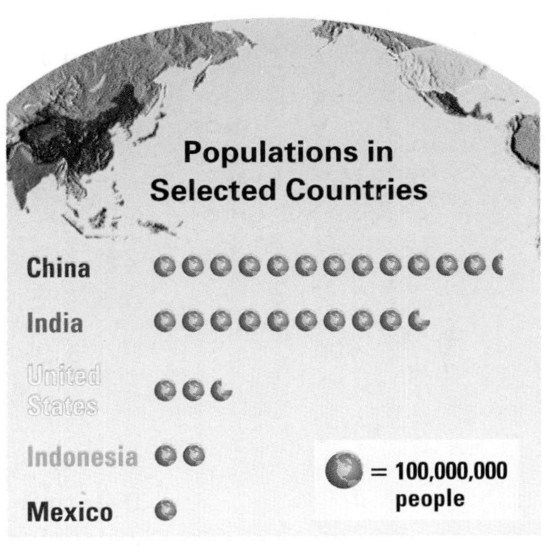

19. **HEALTH** Your gym teacher says that your heart rate will be about 110 beats per minute when you are exercising. This is 175% of your heart rate at rest. What is your resting heart rate?

Link to Careers

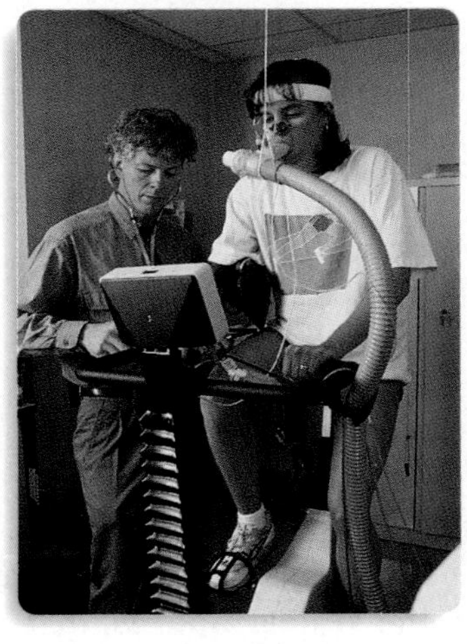

PERSONAL TRAINERS advise people about exercise and dietary principles. They are educated in the area of muscle structure and function, as well as proper diet and exercise.

More about exercise available at www.mcdougallittell.com

Student Help

▶ HOMEWORK HELP

Extra help with problem solving in Ex. 20 is available at www.mcdougallittell.com

20. PARKS In 1996 about 747,812,000 people visited state parks and recreation areas in the United States. The table shows the number of visitors (in thousands) to parks in several states. For each state, find the percent, rounded to the nearest tenth of a percent, of the total number of visitors to state parks and recreation areas in 1996.

State	California	Georgia	New York	Tennessee
Visitors	70,952,000	13,945,000	65,358,000	30,101,000

21. CHALLENGE Out of 80 students taking algebra, 95% passed the final exam. About 80% of those who passed the exam got a grade better than a C. How many students got an A or a B?

Multiple-Choice Practice

22. You run for treasurer of the Student Council. Of the 500 students who vote in the election, 325 vote for you. What percent of the votes do you get?

Ⓐ 35%   Ⓑ 65%   Ⓒ 154%   Ⓓ 175%

23. You buy a stereo on sale. The sale price is \$195, which is 75% of the original price. What is the original price?

Ⓕ \$146.25   Ⓖ \$260   Ⓗ \$270   Ⓙ Not here

Mixed Review

24. RUNNING Kelsey runs 100 meters in 13 seconds, Julian runs 200 meters in 27 seconds, and Melinda runs 400 meters in 50 seconds. Who runs with the greatest average speed? *(3.8)*

Solve the equation. Then check your solution. *(5.5, 5.6)*

25. $8x = 92$ **26.** $\frac{k}{4} = 5$ **27.** $\frac{m}{2.23} = 6$ **28.** $12x = 15$

GEOMETRY **Find the indicated missing lengths in the similar figures.** *(6.4)*

29.

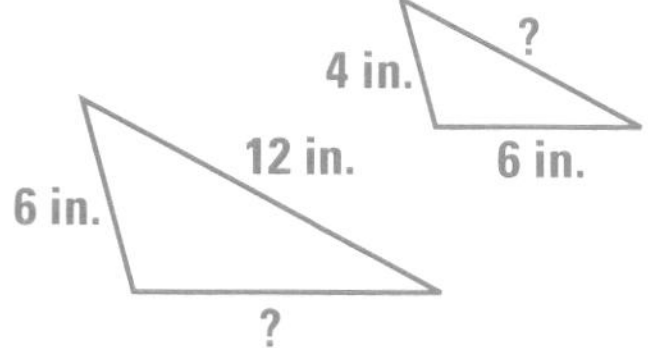

30.

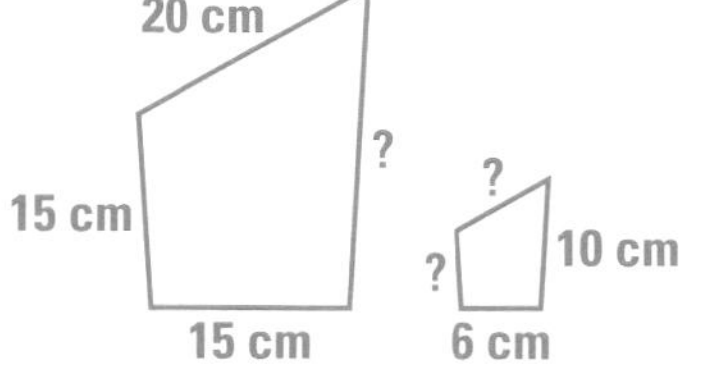

Determine which number does not belong in the list. Explain your reasoning. *(7.1)*

31. $45\%, \frac{9}{20}, 0.45, \frac{4}{5}, \frac{45}{100}$

32. $\frac{25}{40}, 625\%, \frac{5}{8}, 0.625, 62.5\%$

7.5 Circle Graphs

In this lesson you'll:

- Compute statistical measurements of data sets. (SDP 1.0)
- Analyze data displays. (SDP 2.3)

Goal 1 Angle Measures of a Circle Graph

A **circle graph** represents data as parts of a circle. Each wedge represents a percent of the area of the whole circle, and the percents assigned to the wedges add up to 100%. The percent of a circle's area that a wedge represents is determined by its angle. The angle of a wedge can be found by solving a proportion using the fact that there are 360° in a circle. For example, if $x°$ is the measure of the angle of a wedge that represents 30% of a circle's area, you solve the proportion $\frac{x}{360} = \frac{30}{100}$, which gives

$x = \frac{30}{100} \cdot 360 = 30\%$ of 360.

EXAMPLE 1 Finding the Angle Measures of a Circle Graph

You are planning to plant an orchard with 24 apple trees, 20 peach trees, 16 cherry trees, 12 apricot trees, and 8 plum trees. A circle graph can be used to organize the data. What are the angle measures in the circle graph?

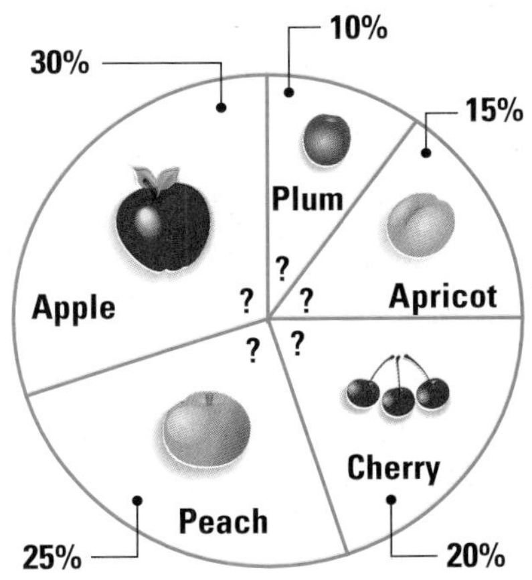

Solution

First find the total number of trees.

$$24 + 20 + 16 + 12 + 8 = 80$$

Then find the percent (using 80 as the base) and the angle measure for each type of tree.

TREE	NUMBER	PERCENT	ANGLE MEASURE
Apple	24	$\frac{24}{80} = 30\%$	$0.30 \times 360° = 108°$
Peach	20	$\frac{20}{80} = 25\%$	$0.25 \times 360° = 90°$
Cherry	16	$\frac{16}{80} = 20\%$	$0.20 \times 360° = 72°$
Apricot	12	$\frac{12}{80} = 15\%$	$0.15 \times 360° = 54°$
Plum	8	$\frac{8}{80} = 10\%$	$0.10 \times 360° = 36°$

Student Help

STUDY TIP
Use addition to check your answers. The sum of the percents should be 100% and the sum of the angle measures should be 360°.

Goal 2 MAKING A CIRCLE GRAPH

To make a circle graph, you can use a protractor to measure and draw each angle in the graph, or you can use *circle graph paper*, as shown. Each section on the graph paper represents 5°.

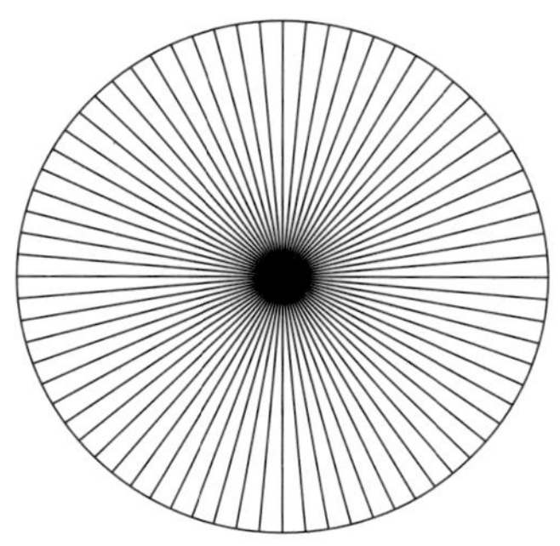

EXAMPLE 2 Making a Circle Graph

Student Help

▶MORE EXAMPLES

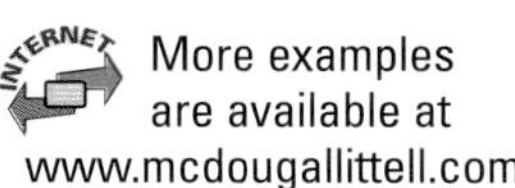

More examples are available at www.mcdougallittell.com

ENERGY The table at the right gives total energy use by category in United States households in 1997. Represent the data in the table with a circle graph.

▶Source: Energy Information Administration

Energy Use	Percent
Space heating	50%
Air conditioning	6%
Water heating	18%
Refrigerators	4%
Appliances	22%

Solution

When finding the angle for each category in the table, you can round the angle measure to the nearest degree.

ENERGY USE	PERCENT AS DECIMAL	ANGLE MEASURE
Space heating	$50\% = 0.50$	$0.50 \times 360° = 180°$
Air conditioning	$6\% = 0.06$	$0.06 \times 360° \approx 22°$
Water heating	$18\% = 0.18$	$0.18 \times 360° \approx 65°$
Refrigerators	$4\% = 0.04$	$0.04 \times 360° \approx 14°$
Appliances	$22\% = 0.22$	$0.22 \times 360° \approx 79°$

To make the circle graph, you can use circle graph paper, as shown.

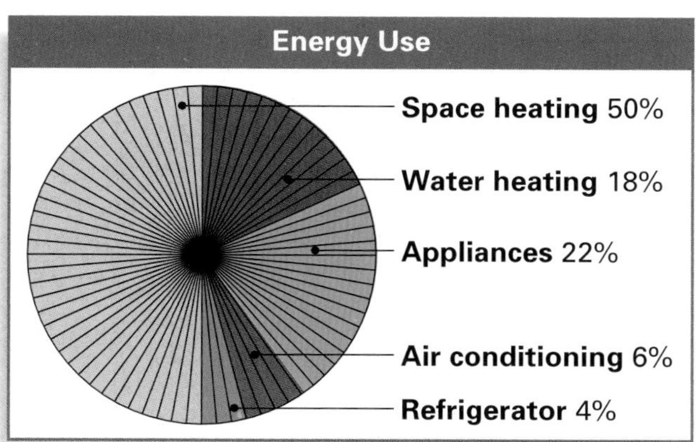

7.5 Exercises

Guided Practice

1. The list below shows the unordered steps to make a circle graph given the parts of some whole. Put the steps in order.

A. Use circle graph paper to draw each angle.

B. Find the measure of each part's angle.

C. Add up the percents and angle measures as a check.

D. Find the percent of the whole that each part represents.

Find the missing angle measure of a circle graph with the given parts.

2. 12°, 48°, 125°, **?** **3.** 220°, 75°, 15°, **?** **4.** 86°, 51°, 98°, **?**

Find the measure of the angle corresponding to the percent of a circle.

5. 40% **6.** 35% **7.** 52% **8.** 9%

ERROR ANALYSIS **Describe and correct the error.**

9.

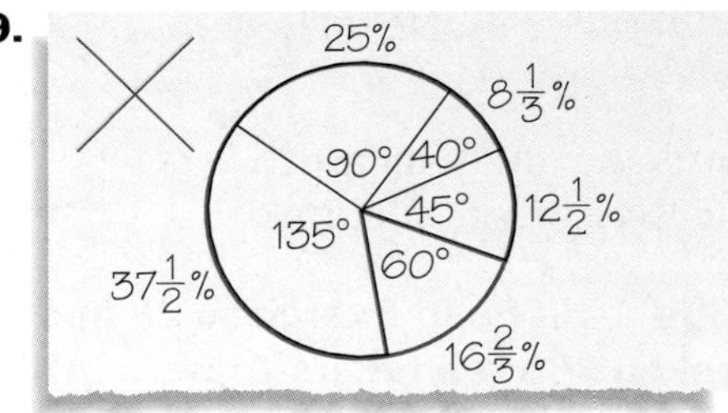

10.

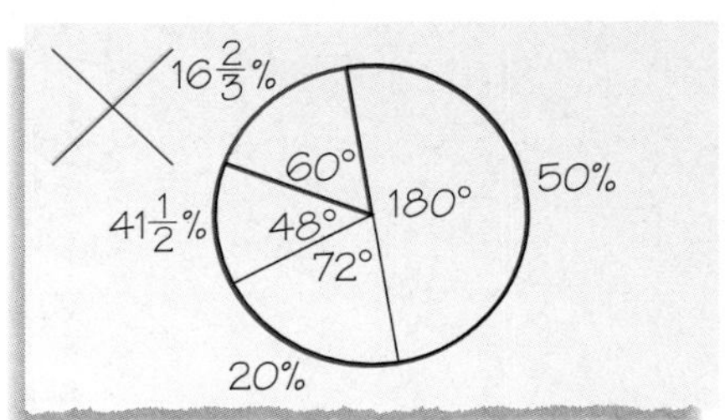

Practice and Problem Solving

Student Help

▶ **MORE PRACTICE** Extra practice to help you master skills is on page 579.

Find the measure of the angle corresponding to the percent of a circle.

11. 50% **12.** 65% **13.** 90% **14.** 19%

15. 12% **16.** 83% **17.** 36% **18.** 95%

Find the missing measures.

19.

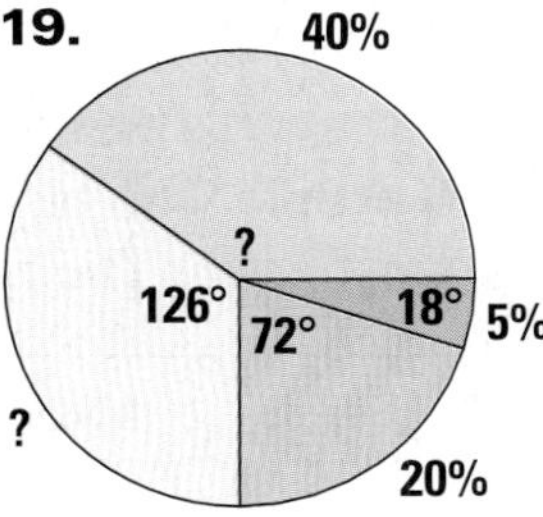

20.

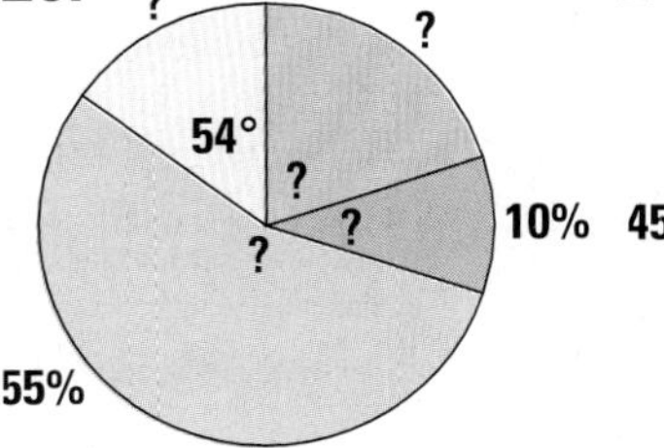

21.

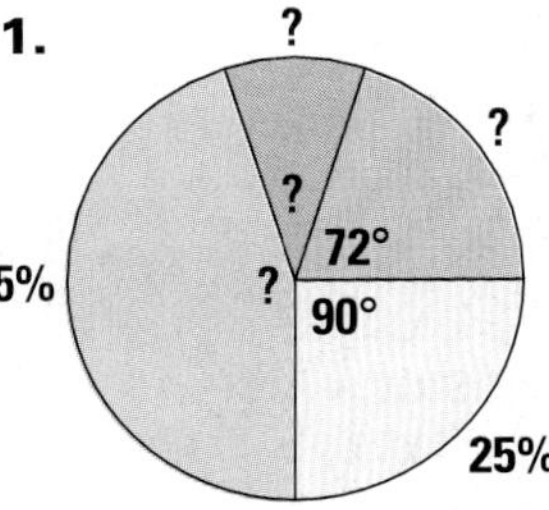

ENERGY In Exercises 22 and 23, use the circle graph which shows how electricity is generated in the United States.

▶ Source: Energy Information Administration

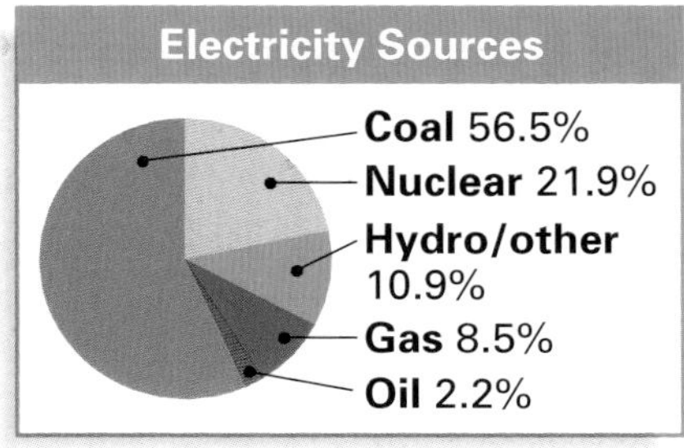

22. Find the angle measure of each part.

23. Show that the sum of the parts equals 100%. Show that the sum of the angles equals 360°.

BUSINESS In Exercises 24–27, use the circle graph. A survey asked 150 executives to name the most valuable second language for business in the United States. ▶ Source: Accountemps

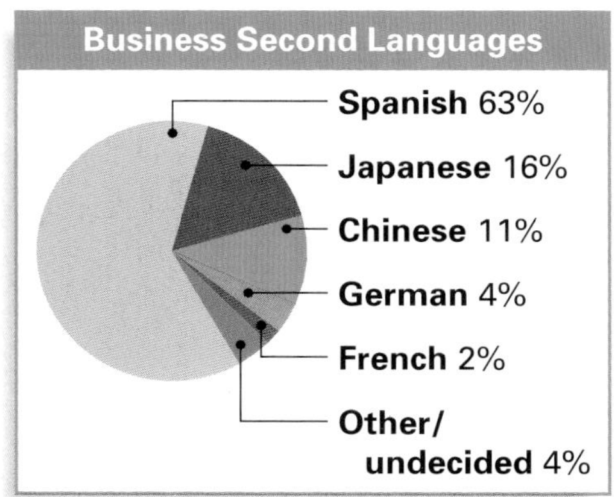

24. About how many executives chose Spanish?

25. About how many more executives chose Spanish than Chinese?

26. About how many times more executives chose Spanish as Japanese?

27. What is the angle measure of the "Japanese" section?

TELEVISION SHOWS In Exercises 28 and 29, use the table below. A survey asked 150 teenagers to name their favorite type of show.

Comedies	Drama	Cartoons	News Shows	Other
60	42	27	18	3

28. Make a circle graph of the data.

29. Show how to check the accuracy of your circle graph.

In Exercises 30 and 31, make a circle graph of the data.

30. ELECTRICITY The percents of electricity used in the United States in 1996 were: residential, 34.9%; commercial, 28.6%; industrial, 33.3%; and other uses, 3.1%. ▶ Source: Energy Information Administration

31. SURVEY A survey of 36 people who buy books regularly asked which type of book they buy most often. The results are shown in the table.

Fiction	Biography	Horror	Mystery	Romance	Other
12	6	6	3	3	6

Student Help

▶ **SKILLS REVIEW** For help with angles, see page 563.

Link to Recycling

RECYCLING In 1996 about 12.3 million tons of newspapers were produced. About 54% of these newspapers were recovered through recycling.

32. **Chapter Opener Link** Look back at the table on page 309. Make a circle graph of the data.

MATHEMATICAL REASONING **In Exercises 33 and 34, decide whether the data can be displayed using a circle graph. Explain your reasoning. If possible, make a circle graph of the data.**

33. A survey of 200 people asked which sporting event they most like to attend. The results are shown in the table.

Baseball	Basketball	Football	Hockey	Soccer	Other
70	50	40	20	12	8

34. **RECYCLING** A survey asked 200 people to name ways they help the environment. The results are shown in the table.

Recycle at home.	Buy biodegradable products.	Recycle at work.	Support environmental groups.
180	142	124	74

35. **CHALLENGE** The circle graph represents an annual family budget. If $9500 is spent on food, how much is the total budget?

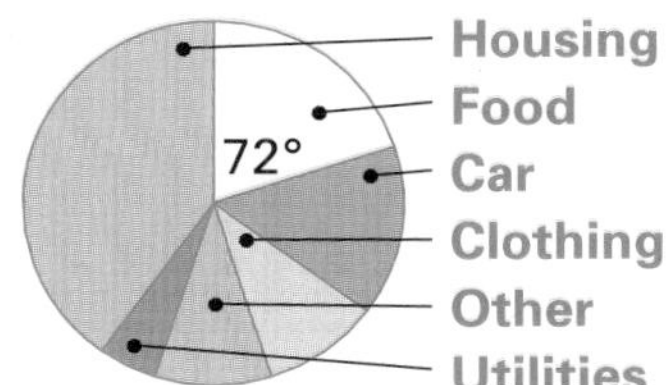

Multiple-Choice Practice

36. One part of a circle graph represents 60%. What is the measure of the angle of this part?

(A) 60° (B) 108° (C) 120° (D) 216°

37. In a survey of 300 people, 120 said that they walk for exercise. What angle of a circle graph should represent these 120 people?

(F) 40° (G) 120° (H) 144° (J) 162°

In Exercises 38 and 39, use the circle graph which shows the results of a survey of 600 people.

38. Which part of the circle corresponds to the response of 90 people?

(A) Part A (B) Part B

(C) Part C (D) Part D

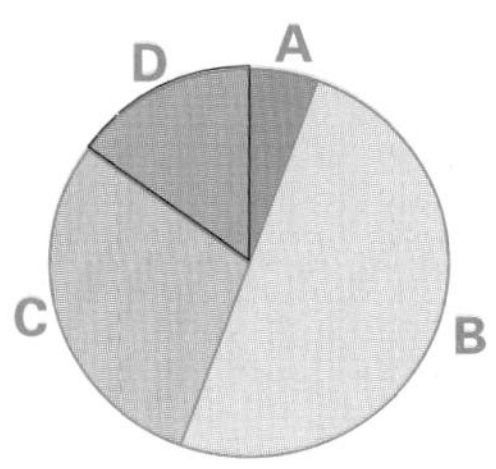

39. Part B represents approximately how many people?

(F) 90 (G) 180

(H) 200 (J) 300

Test Tip (A)(B)(C)(D)

▶In Ex. 39 think about how many people represent 50%, and use mathematical reasoning to find the answer.

7.6 Simple Interest

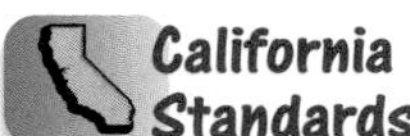
California Standards

In this lesson you'll:

- Write and evaluate an algebraic expression for a given situation, using up to three variables. (AF 1.2)
- Calculate percents and solve problems involving interest earned. (NS 1.4)

Goal 1 FINDING SIMPLE INTEREST

When you put money in a savings account at a bank, the bank pays you interest. When you borrow money from a bank, you must pay interest to the bank (in addition to paying back the amount you borrowed).

A **principal** is an amount borrowed, loaned, or saved. An **annual interest rate** is the percent of the principal you earn or pay as interest for one year. **Simple interest** is the product of the principal, the annual interest rate, and the time in years.

$$\text{Interest} = \text{Principal} \times \text{Rate} \times \text{Time}$$
$$I = Prt$$

EXAMPLE 1 Finding Simple Interest

You borrow \$1500 from a friend for the down payment on a car. Your friend charges you an annual interest rate of 8%. Find the simple interest you will pay in 1 year.

Solution

$I = Prt$	Formula for simple interest
$= \mathbf{1500(0.08)}(1)$	Substitute. Write 8% as 0.08.
$= 120$	Multiply.

ANSWER ▶ The simple interest you will pay in 1 year is \$120.

Student Help

▶ **STUDY TIP**
When you compute simple interest for a time that is less than 1 year, you should write the time as a fraction of a year.

EXAMPLE 2 Finding Simple Interest

You deposit \$300 in a savings account. The annual interest rate is 3%. Find the simple interest you will earn in 1 month.

Solution

Because time must be in years, express 1 month as $\frac{1}{12}$ year.

$I = Prt$	Formula for simple interest
$= \mathbf{300(0.03)}\left(\frac{1}{12}\right)$	Substitute. Write 3% as 0.03.
$= 0.75$	Multiply.

ANSWER ▶ The simple interest you will earn in 1 month is \$.75.

Goal 2 SOLVING SIMPLE INTEREST PROBLEMS

When you know the values of any three of the variables in the formula $I = Prt$, you can use algebra to find the value of the fourth variable.

Student Help

▸ **STUDY TIP**
Another type of interest is called *compound interest* in which interest is figured more than once per year on the principal plus the interest earned from the previous time period.

EXAMPLE 3 Comparing Two Annual Interest Rates

You have two savings accounts that earn simple interest. Which account pays the greater annual interest rate?

Account A: You deposit \$450 and earn \$6.75 in 3 months.

Account B: You deposit \$510 and earn \$8.50 in 4 months.

Solution

Account A: Use $I = \$6.75$, $P = \$450$, and $t = \frac{1}{4}$ year.

$I = Prt$	Formula for simple interest
$6.75 = 450(r)\left(\frac{1}{4}\right)$	Substitute for *I*, *P*, and *t*.
$6.75 = 112.5r$	Simplify.
$0.06 = r$	Divide each side by 112.5.

Account B: Use $I = \$8.50$, $P = \$510$, and $t = \frac{1}{3}$ year.

$I = Prt$	Formula for simple interest
$8.50 = 510(r)\left(\frac{1}{3}\right)$	Substitute for *I*, *P*, and *t*.
$8.50 = 170r$	Simplify.
$0.05 = r$	Divide each side by 170.

ANSWER ▸ The annual interest rate is 6% for Account A and 5% for Account B. So, Account A pays the greater rate.

EXAMPLE 4 Finding a Principal

Your savings account earns \$68 in simple interest in 1 year. The annual interest rate is 8%. What is the principal?

Solution

$I = Prt$	Formula for simple interest
$68 = P(0.08)(1)$	Substitute for *I*, *r*, and *t*.
$68 = 0.08P$	Simplify.
$850 = P$	Divide each side by 0.08.

ANSWER ▸ The principal is \$850.

7.6 Exercises

Guided Practice

Match the word with the description.

1. Principal
2. Interest rate
3. Interest

A. A percent of the principal

B. Amount paid to lender or saver for use of money

C. Amount of money borrowed, loaned, or saved

Solve for the unknown quantity.

4. $I = ?$, $P = \$4500$, $r = 10\%$, $t = 5$ years

5. $I = \$6.75$, $P = \$90$, $r = ?$, $t = 3$ years

6. $I = \$13.75$, $P = ?$, $r = 8\%$, $t = 6$ months

In Exercises 7–10, write the time period as a fraction of a year.

7. 2 months
8. 4 months
9. 7 months
10. 5 months

11. **SAVINGS ACCOUNT** You deposit \$250 in a savings account. The annual interest rate is 5%. How much simple interest will you earn in 3 months? How much simple interest will you earn in 1 year?

Practice and Problem Solving

Student Help

▶ **MORE PRACTICE** Extra practice to help you master skills is on page 579.

Write the time period as a fraction of a year.

12. 3 months
13. 6 months
14. 8 months
15. 9 months

Find the interest you earn for depositing the given principal in an account earning simple interest.

16. $P = \$600$, $r = 5\%$, $t = 2$ years

17. $P = \$1250$, $r = 3\%$, $t = 4$ months

18. $P = \$7000$, $r = 5.5\%$, $t = 18$ months

Find the simple interest you pay for borrowing the given principal.

19. $P = \$12{,}000$, $r = 15\%$, $t = 5$ years

20. $P = \$4500$, $r = 9\%$, $t = 5$ months

21. $P = \$900$, $r = 12\%$, $t = 15$ months

22. **CHOOSING A BANK** You want to open an account with \$100. At Bank A you will earn \$.65 in 3 months. At Bank B you will earn \$2.25 in one year. At which bank will you open your account? Explain.

23. **SAVINGS ACCOUNT** Your friend tells you that he opened a savings account that pays 2.5% annual interest. In one year, he earned \$20 in simple interest. How much did he originally deposit?

Link to Government

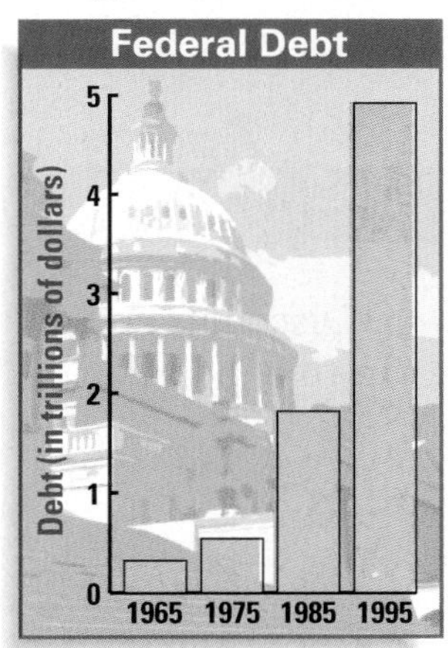

FEDERAL DEBT When the government does not take in as much money as it spends, it has to borrow money. The accumulation of this borrowing is the federal debt.

24. FEDERAL DEBT The United States' federal debt in September of 1999 was about 5600 billion dollars. If simple interest was paid on this amount at an annual rate of 8%, how much interest would be paid in 1 month?

25. CHALLENGE You deposit $1200 in an account at a bank that pays 5.25% annual simple interest. After 4 months the interest rate on your account increases to 5.65% annual simple interest. After 1 year from the original deposit, how much have you gained from the increase in the interest rate?

CREDIT CARDS **In Exercises 26–29, use the table below. It shows the average annual interest rate for credit cards from 1993 to 1997. Find the interest owed in one month using the given year and amount of debt. Round your answer to the nearest cent.**

Year	1993	1994	1995	1996	1997
Rate	16.8%	15.7%	16%	15.6%	15.8%

26. A debt of $250 in 1993

27. A debt of $900 in 1995

28. A debt of $1000 in 1996

29. A debt of $1050 in 1997

MATHEMATICAL REASONING **In Exercises 30 and 31, decide whether your answer is reasonable. Explain why or why not.**

30. A friend borrows $50 from you for 6 months. You charge an annual interest rate of 10%. You calculate that your friend has to pay you $30 in simple interest after 6 months.

31. You deposit $250 in a savings account that pays 2% annual interest. You calculate that you will earn $8.75 in simple interest in 21 months.

Multiple-Choice Practice

32. In which of the following situations do you earn the most simple interest during one year?

(A) Invest $100 at 12% interest. (B) Invest $150 at 4% interest.

(C) Invest $50 at 8% interest. (D) Invest $200 at 4% interest.

33. What is the simple interest owed on $300 borrowed for 4 months at an annual interest rate of 5%?

(F) $4 (G) $5 (H) $60 (J) $75

34. You borrow $525 and are charged 15% annual simple interest. How much do you owe after 10 months if you make no payments?

(A) $531.56 (B) $590.63 (C) $603.75 (D) $787.50

Test Tip (A)(B)(C)(D)

▶ In Ex. 33 you may find it easier to multiply the principal and the time before multiplying by the rate.

7.7 Discounts and Sales Tax

California Standards

In this lesson you'll:

- Solve problems involving percents. (NS 1.0)
- Calculate percents and solve problems involving discounts at sales. (NS 1.4)

Goal 1 FINDING A DISCOUNT

A reduction in the price of an item is called a *discount*. Discounts are often calculated using a percent of the original price. To find the sale price of an item that is discounted:

1. Find the amount of the discount.
2. Subtract the discount from the original price.

EXAMPLE 1 Finding a Sale Price

You buy a pair of walking shoes. The original price of \$65 is discounted by 35%. What is the sale price?

Solution

1. Find the amount of the discount.

   Discount = 35% of \$65

   = 0.35 • 65 — Write percent in decimal form.

   = 22.75 — Multiply.

2. Subtract the discount from the original price.

   Sale price = **Original price** − **Discount**

   = **65.00** − **22.75** = 42.25

ANSWER ▶ The sale price is \$42.25.

EXAMPLE 2 Comparing Two Prices

Which television's sale price is less expensive?

Television A: Discount of 25% off the original price of \$575

Television B: Discount of 30% off the original price of \$585

Solution

Television A	**Television B**
Sale price = 575 − (0.25 • 575)	Sale price = 585 − (0.30 • 585)
= 575 − 143.75	= 585 − 175.5
= 431.25	= 409.5

ANSWER ▶ Television B's sale price of \$409.50 is less expensive.

Goal 2 FINDING A SALES TAX

A *sales tax* is an amount added to the price of a purchased item. Sales tax is often calculated using a percent of the price. To find the total price of an item including sales tax:

1. Find the amount of the sales tax.
2. Add the sales tax to the price.

EXAMPLE 3 Finding a Total Price

You buy a CD. The price is \$15.95 and the sales tax is 8.25%. What is the total price?

Solution

1. Find the amount of the sales tax.

   Sales tax = 8.25% of \$15.95

   $= 0.0825 \cdot 15.95$ — Write percent in decimal form.

   ≈ 1.32 — Multiply and round to 2 decimal places.

2. Add the sales tax to the price.

   Total price = **Price** + **Sales tax**

   $=$ **15.95** + **1.32** $= 17.27$

ANSWER ▶ The total price is \$17.27.

EXAMPLE 4 Finding a Total Price

Shirts in a store are on sale for 30% off. The sales tax is 7.25%. What is the total price of a shirt that has an original price of \$29.95?

Solution

First find the discount and the sale price. Then find the sales tax and the total price.

Discount = 30% of \$29.95

$= 0.30 \cdot 29.95 \approx 8.99$

Sale price = Original price − Discount

$= 29.95 - 8.99 = 20.96$

Sales tax = 7.25% of \$20.96

$= 0.0725 \cdot 20.96 \approx 1.52$

Total price = Sale price + Sales tax

$= 20.96 + 1.52 = 22.48$

ANSWER ▶ The total price is \$22.48.

Student Help

▶ **MORE EXAMPLES**

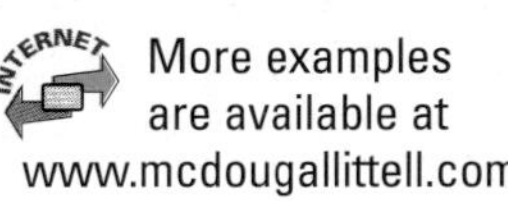

More examples are available at www.mcdougallittell.com

7.7 Exercises

Guided Practice

Based on the calculations, identify the dollar value or percent that matches the description.

1. Original price

2. Discount percent

3. Sale price

4. Amount of the discount

$0.25 \cdot 80 = 20$
$80 - 20 = 60$

Find the discount or sales tax to the nearest cent.

5. \$28 shirt; 5% off

6. \$18.59 book; 30% off

7. \$49.50 watch; 7% sales tax

8. \$8.99 poster; 7.25% sales tax

Find the sale price or total price to the nearest cent.

9. \$175 stereo; 40% off

10. \$29.99 jeans; 25% off

11. \$16.95 CD; 8.25% sales tax

12. \$12.79 shoes; 8.5% sales tax

Practice and Problem Solving

Student Help

▶More Practice
Extra practice to help you master skills is on page 579.

ERROR ANALYSIS **Describe and correct the error.**

13. \$15.75 toy; 45% off

~~$15.75 × 0.45 ≈ $7.09~~
~~Sale Price = $7.09~~

14. \$32.97 skates; 8% sales tax

~~$32.97 × 0.08 ≈ $2.64~~
~~$32.97 − $2.64 = $30.33~~
~~Total Price = $30.33~~

Find the discount and sale price.

15. Original price: \$60.50
Discount percent: 20%

16. Original price: \$75.25
Discount percent: 60%

17. Original price: \$357.59
Discount percent: 15%

18. Original price: \$27.90
Discount percent: 55%

19. Original price: \$235.49
Discount percent: 25%

20. Original price: \$105.99
Discount percent: 35%

Find the sales tax and total price.

21. Price: \$17.65
Sales tax rate: 8%

22. Price: \$426.42
Sales tax rate: 7.75%

23. Price: \$48.71
Sales tax rate: 7.25%

24. Price: \$215.68
Sales tax rate: 8.25%

25. Price: \$119.37
Sales tax rate: 6.75%

26. Price: \$218.45
Sales tax rate: 6.5%

27. **COMPARISON SHOPPING** Your family plans to buy a tent. After comparison shopping, you find the same tent on sale at two different stores. Store A is selling it for 15% off of \$289.98, and Store B is selling it for 20% off of \$309.99. Which tent is less expensive?

28. **BASEBALL OUTING** While attending a baseball game, you buy a souvenir T-shirt for \$20, a hat for \$12, and a poster for \$7.95. The sales tax on all three items is 7.75%. Find the total price.

29. **DINING OUT** You go out to dinner with some friends. The bill is \$23.80 before tax and tip are added.

a. What is the total including 8% sales tax?

b. If a 15% tip is left on the bill including tax, how much is the tip?

> *Student Help*
>
> ▶**HOMEWORK HELP**
>
> INTERNET Extra help with problem solving in Ex. 30 is available at www.mcdougallittell.com

30. **SPORTING GOODS** A volleyball that has an original price of \$37.50 is on sale for 10% off. The sales tax is 7.25%. Find the total price.

31. **CHALLENGE** The original price of a pair of sneakers is \$65.89. The sneakers are discounted 30%. You have a coupon for an additional 10% off the sale price. Find the total price you will pay for the sneakers.

Shoe Sale
SNEAKERS
30% OFF
SANDALS
15% OFF
CASUAL SHOES
25% OFF
DRESS SHOES
20% OFF
BONUS COUPON
Take 10% off the sale price of any 1 item.

32. Take 80% of the original price in Exercise 15. How does it compare with the sale price?

33. Take 40% of the original price in Exercise 16. How does it compare with the sale price?

34. **MATHEMATICAL REASONING** Describe the pattern you see in Exercises 32 and 33. How can this pattern help you find sale prices using only one step? Write a general formula to support your answer and explain why the formula works.

Multiple-Choice Practice

35. It costs \$8 per hour to rent skates at a park. Students get a 20% discount. How much do students pay per hour for skates?

Ⓐ \$9.60 Ⓑ \$8.80 Ⓒ \$6.40 Ⓓ \$5

36. You buy a car for \$14,500. What is the total price if the sales tax is 7.25%?

Ⓕ \$15,551.25 Ⓖ \$13,448.75 Ⓗ \$1450 Ⓙ \$1051.25

37. You go out to dinner, and the bill, including tax, is \$25.98. How much is the tip if you want to leave a 20% tip?

Ⓐ \$31.18 Ⓑ \$20.78 Ⓒ \$5.20 Ⓓ \$5

Chapter 7 Chapter Summary and Review

VOCABULARY

- **percent,** *p. 311*
- **circle graph,** *p. 333*
- **principal,** *p. 338*
- **simple interest,** *p. 338*
- **annual interest rate,** *p. 338*

7.1 PERCENTS, FRACTIONS, AND DECIMALS

Examples on pp. 311–312

EXAMPLES

a. Write $\frac{5}{8}$ as a percent.

$$\frac{5}{8} = 0.625 = \frac{625}{1000} = \frac{625 \div 10}{1000 \div 10} = \frac{62.5}{100} = 62.5\%$$

b. Write 20% as a decimal.

$$20\% = \frac{20}{100} = 0.2$$

Write the fraction or decimal as a percent, rounded to the nearest tenth of a percent.

1. $\frac{17}{40}$ **2.** 0.5625 **3.** 0.0442 **4.** $\frac{3}{11}$

Write the percent as a decimal and as a fraction in simplest form.

5. 40% **6.** 15% **7.** 72% **8.** 37%

7.2 FINDING A PERCENT OF A NUMBER

Examples on pp. 317–319

To find a percent of a number, use a proportion. Or, write the percent as a fraction or decimal and then multiply by the number.

EXAMPLE **Find 25% of 60.**

Method 1

$\frac{25}{100} = \frac{x}{60}$ Set up a proportion.

$25 \cdot 60 = 100x$ Cross products property

$\frac{25 \cdot 60}{100} = \frac{100x}{100}$ Divide each side by 100.

$15 = x$ Simplify.

Method 2

$25\% \text{ of } 60 = 0.25 \cdot 60$ Write percent in decimal form.

$= 15$ Multiply.

In Exercises 9–16, find the percent of the number.

9. 25% of 32 **10.** 75% of 280 **11.** 16% of 85 **12.** 35% of 210

13. 9% of 80 **14.** 90% of 200 **15.** 4% of 3 **16.** 52% of 340

17. HEALTH In a school of 1050 students, 22% of the students missed school because of the flu. How many students missed school?

18. INVESTING An investment firm charges a 1.5% fee on an investment of $25,000. How much is the fee?

7.3 LARGE AND SMALL PERCENTS

Examples on pp. 323–324

EXAMPLE **Use mental math to estimate 178% of 60.**

178% is about 175%, or 100% + 75%.

100% of 60 = 60 75%, or $\frac{3}{4}$, of 60 = 45

Because 175% of 60 = 60 + 45 = 105, 178% of 60 is a little more than 105.

In Exercises 19–22, find the percent of the number.

19. 120% of 250 **20.** 0.25% of 10 **21.** $\frac{1}{10}$% of 400 **22.** 250% of 30

23. Use mental math to estimate 152% of 80. Explain your process.

7.4 SOLVING PERCENT PROBLEMS

Examples on pp. 328–330

To find what percent a number is of another number, you can use the proportion $\frac{a}{b} = \frac{p}{100}$, where a is part of the base, b is the base, and p is the percent.

EXAMPLES

a. What percent of 120 is 48?

$\frac{48}{120} = \frac{p}{100}$ Write proportion.

$4800 = 120p$ Cross products property

$40 = p$ Simplify.

b. 13.5 is 27% of what number?

$\frac{13.5}{b} = \frac{27}{100}$ Write proportion.

$1350 = 27b$ Cross products property

$50 = b$ Simplify.

In Exercises 24–27, use a proportion to answer the question.

24. What is 18% of 120? **25.** What percent of 160 is 96?

26. 9% of what number is 54? **27.** 6 is 75% of what number?

In Exercises 28–30, use a proportion to solve the problem.

28. SURVEY In a survey, 45%, or 81 people, said that their favorite color was blue. How many people were surveyed?

29. RETAIL You buy a tennis racket for 60% of the original price. You pay $60. What was the original price of the racket?

30. HEALTH A typical healthy blood pressure is 120/80, or "120 over 80." The first number is your *systolic* pressure, and the second number is your *diastolic* pressure. If a systolic pressure measures 105, what percent of the typical healthy reading is this?

7.5 CIRCLE GRAPHS

Examples on pp. 333–334

EXAMPLE Of 48 games played, the Springfield Stars had 18 wins, 18 losses, and 12 ties. Represent the data with a circle graph.

CATEGORY	NUMBER	PERCENT	ANGLE MEASURE
Ties	12	$\frac{12}{48} = 25\%$	$0.25 \times 360° = 90°$
Wins or Losses	18	$\frac{18}{48} = 37.5\%$	$0.375 \times 360° = 135°$

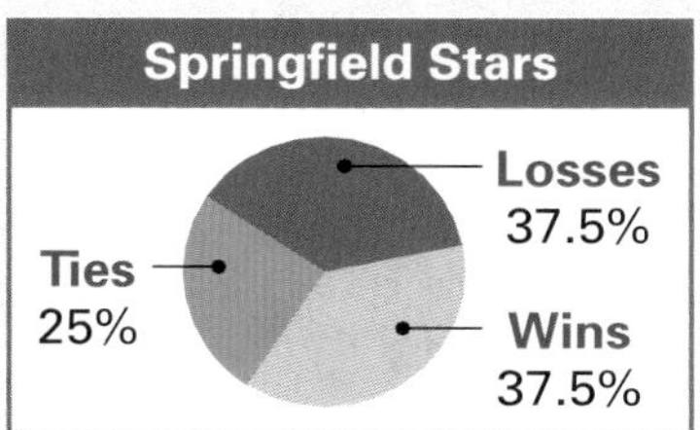

In Exercises 31 and 32, find the missing measures.

31.

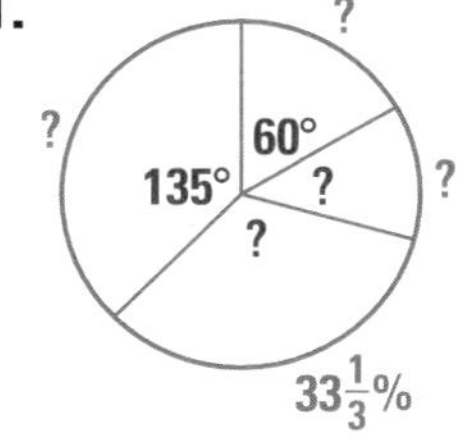

32.

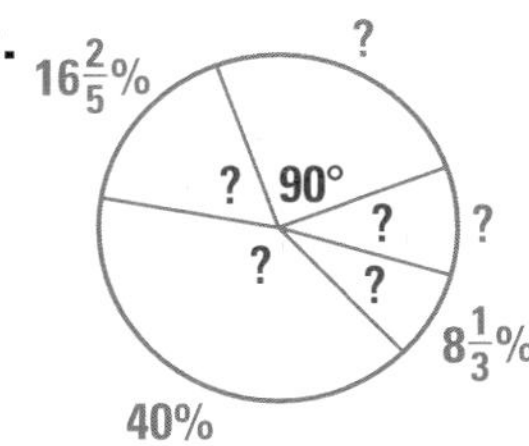

SURVEY **In Exercises 33 and 34, use the circle graph which shows the results of a survey in which 30 students on a bus were asked which grade they are in.**

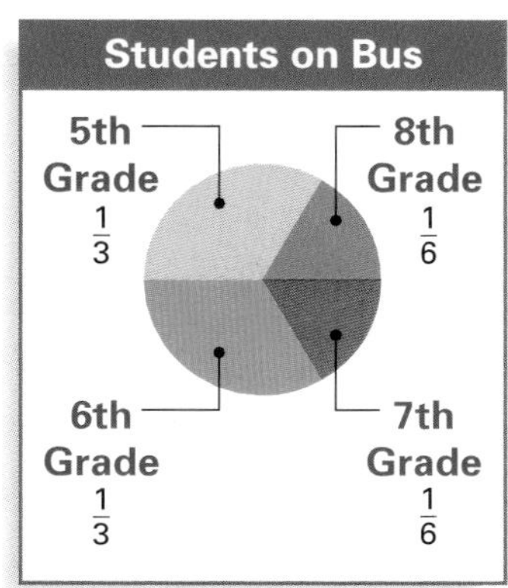

33. How many students are in each grade?

34. What is the angle measure for each part of the circle graph?

35. MEDICINE A survey asked 200 people to name their blood type. Represent the results in the table with a circle graph.

O+	A+	B+	O−	A−	AB+	B−	AB−
76	68	18	14	12	6	4	2

7.6 SIMPLE INTEREST

Examples on pp. 338–339

To find simple interest use the formula $I = Prt$, where I is the interest, P is the principal, r is the annual interest rate, and t is the time in years.

EXAMPLE You deposit $150 in an account that pays 5% annual interest. How much simple interest will you earn in 4 months?

$I = Prt$ Formula for simple interest

$= 150(0.05)\left(\frac{4}{12}\right)$ Substitute. Write 5% as 0.05.

$= 2.5$ Use a calculator.

The simple interest you will earn in 4 months is $2.50.

36. LOAN You borrow $150 and are charged an annual interest rate of 18%. How much simple interest will you pay in one month?

37. BANKING One bank advertises that a deposit of $150 will earn $2.75 in 6 months. A second bank advertises that a deposit of $175 will earn $2 in 4 months. Which bank pays the higher simple interest rate?

38. SAVINGS On the day that Ann is born, her grandparents deposit $3000 in a trust fund. The annual interest rate on the fund is 4%. How much simple interest will the trust fund earn by Ann's first birthday?

7.7 DISCOUNTS AND SALES TAX

Examples on pp. 342–343

To find the sale price of a discounted item, find the amount of the discount and subtract the discount from the original price. Finding sales tax is similar, except you add the amount of the sales tax to the price of the item.

EXAMPLES

Regular price: $25.80

Discount: 20% of $25.80

$0.20 \times \$25.80 = \$5.16$

Sale price: $\$25.80 - \$5.16 = \$20.64$

Regular price: $23.75

Sales tax: 8% of $23.75

$0.08 \times \$23.75 = \$1.90$

Total price: $\$23.75 + \$1.90 = \$25.65$

39. BOARD GAMES A board game that regularly sells for $16.50 is on sale for 40% off. How much is the discount?

40. FURNITURE Find the total price of a $780 sofa if the sales tax is 6.4%.

41. COMPUTERS A computer is on sale for 30% off its original price of $1200. The sales tax is 7.75%. What is the total price?

Chapter 7 Chapter Test

Write the percent as a decimal and as a fraction in simplest form.

1. 74% **2.** 5% **3.** 60% **4.** 216%

Write the fraction or decimal as a percent.

5. 0.88 **6.** $\frac{7}{10}$ **7.** 0.047 **8.** $\frac{3}{75}$

9. $\frac{22}{5}$ **10.** 0.00625 **11.** $\frac{11}{4000}$ **12.** 3.03

Find the percent of the number.

13. 75% of 24 **14.** 5% of 145 **15.** 38% of 11

16. 220% of 5 **17.** $\frac{1}{5}$% of 500 **18.** 0.08% of 150

In Exercises 19–22, use a proportion to answer the question.

19. 60% of what number is 63? **20.** 22 is 4% of what number?

21. 84 is what percent of 25? **22.** What percent of 400 is 2?

23. **SURVEY** A survey asked 200 people to name their favorite marine mammal. The results are shown in the table at the right. Make a circle graph of the data.

Dolphin	Seal	Whale	Other
76	68	32	24

24. **CONSUMER SPENDING** You borrow $1650 to buy a computer. The annual interest rate is 16%. How much simple interest will you pay for 2 months?

25. **SAVINGS** After 8 months, your friend earns $30 in interest from a savings certificate that pays 6% annual simple interest. How much did your friend originally deposit?

26. **SCHOOL RESOURCES** Your school wants to order sets of calculators for use in math classes. The table shows the discount the school will receive for ordering sets of 10, 25, or 100. What is the sale price for a set of each size?

Number in set	10	25	100
Regular price	$62.50	$156.25	$625
Discount	8%	18%	27%

27. **SHOPPING** You have a coupon for 25% off the price of a mystery book that regularly sells for $7. You also have a coupon for 20% off the price of a science fiction book that regularly sells for $6.25. The sales tax is 7.25%. Which book can you buy if you have only $5.50? Explain.

Multiple-Choice Practice

When checking your work, try to use a method other than the one you originally used to get your answer. If you use the same method, you may make the same mistake twice.

1. Which number does not belong in the list? **A**

$$3.6\%, 0.36, \frac{9}{25}, \frac{27}{75}$$

Ⓐ 3.6% Ⓑ 0.36

Ⓒ $\frac{9}{25}$ Ⓓ $\frac{27}{75}$

2. A store charges 138% of its cost for sneakers. The store's cost is \$28. How much does the store charge? **H**

Ⓕ \$17.36 Ⓖ \$29.06

Ⓗ \$38.64 Ⓙ \$39.20

3. A store sells jeans at 60% off the original price of \$32. For final clearance, the store takes \$5 off the sale price. What is the final clearance price? **A**

Ⓐ \$7.80 Ⓑ \$12.80

Ⓒ \$14.20 Ⓓ \$19.20

4. In a survey, 28 sixth graders said that their favorite lunch was spaghetti. This was 16% of the class. How many students are in the class? **H**

Ⓕ 32 Ⓖ 57

Ⓗ 175 Ⓙ 188

5. You deposit \$750 in an account that pays 5% annual interest. How much simple interest will you earn in 6 months? **D**

Ⓐ \$375 Ⓑ \$185.50

Ⓒ \$37.50 Ⓓ \$18.75

6. Complete: The decimal number 0.00068 is not the same as __?__. **J**

Ⓕ 0.068% Ⓖ $\frac{68}{100,000}$

Ⓗ $\frac{17}{25,000}$ Ⓙ $\frac{6.8}{1000}$

7. A survey finds that 20% of students like peas. Out of 200 students, how many like peas? **D**

Ⓐ 4 Ⓑ 10

Ⓒ 20 Ⓓ 40

8. This year, 592 students said they recycle. This is 320% of the number who recycled 8 years ago. How many students recycled 8 years ago? **G**

Ⓕ 54 Ⓖ 185

Ⓗ 189 Ⓙ 1894

9. Find the missing angle measure. **B**

Ⓐ 135°

Ⓑ 144°

Ⓒ 154°

Ⓓ Not here

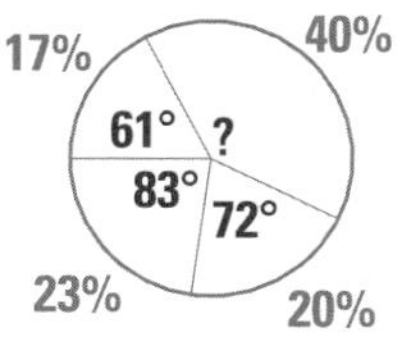

10. Which equation can be used to answer the question? **H**

14 is 25% of what number?

Ⓕ $\frac{25}{x} = \frac{14}{100}$ Ⓖ $\frac{x}{14} = \frac{25}{100}$

Ⓗ $\frac{14}{x} = \frac{25}{100}$ Ⓙ $\frac{x}{25} = \frac{100}{14}$

Brain games

- Calculate percents and solve problems involving discounts at sales. (NS 1.4)
- Apply strategies and results from simpler problems to more complex problems. (MR 2.2)

100% Winner

Materials

- Index cards

Directions

Object of the Game

Play in pairs. Take turns drawing cards. When you think the sum of your cards is as close as you can get to 100%, stop drawing cards. The player closest to 100% without going over wins the game.

How to Play

STEP 1 Make an index card for each value listed.

$\frac{1}{2}$	$\frac{1}{3}$	$\frac{2}{3}$	$\frac{1}{4}$	$\frac{3}{4}$	$\frac{1}{5}$	$\frac{2}{5}$	$\frac{3}{5}$	$\frac{4}{5}$	$\frac{1}{10}$
0.01	0.02	0.05	0.15	0.2	0.25	0.3	0.35	0.4	0.45
0.5%	1%	2%	3%	4%	5%	6%	7%	8%	9%

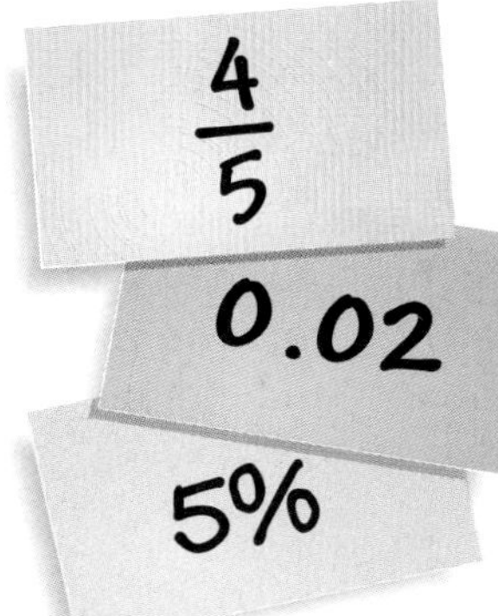

STEP 2 Shuffle the cards and then place them face down in a stack. Take turns drawing cards. If the value is a fraction or decimal, rewrite it as a percent. Continue drawing cards until you think you are as close as you can get to 100%. Announce that you are finished, and stop drawing cards. Let your opponent continue drawing cards until he or she is ready to stop. The player closest to 100% without going over wins the game.

Another Way to Play

End the game when one player stops. As in the original version, the player closest to 100% wins the game.

Brain Teaser

BUYER BEWARE!

The tickets show the original prices. Which coat is the better deal?

The basic skills you'll review on this page will help prepare you for the next chapter.

Reviewing the Basics

EXAMPLE 1 Evaluating an Expression

Evaluate the expression when $x = 3$ and $y = 5$.

a. $8xy$

b. $2xy + 6$

Solution Substitute 3 for x and 5 for y. Then simplify.

a. $8(3)(5) = 120$

b. $2(3)(5) + 6 = 36$

Try These

Evaluate the expression.

1. $p + 4$ when $p = 7$

2. $9x$ when $x = 6$

3. lw when $l = 2$ and $w = 8$

4. $\frac{m}{n}$ when $m = 35$ and $n = 7$

5. $\frac{1}{2}bh$ when $b = 12$ and $h = 3$

6. $2x + 2y$ when $x = 4$ and $y = 1$

EXAMPLE 2 Finding Perimeter and Area

Find the perimeter and the area of the figure made from a square and a rectangle.

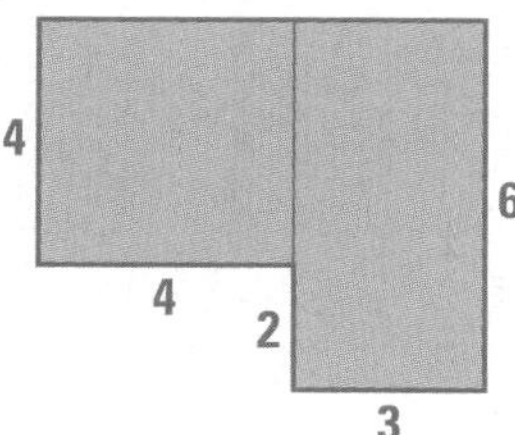

Solution To find the perimeter, add up the side lengths. To find the area of the entire figure, calculate the areas of the square and rectangle and add the areas.

Perimeter (P):

Top edge: $4 + 3 = 7$

$P = 7 + 6 + 3 + 2 + 4 + 4$

$= 26$ units

Area (A):

Square: $4 \times 4 = 16$

Rectangle: $3 \times 6 = 18$

$A = 16 + 18 = 34$ square units

Try These

Find the perimeter and the area of the figure made from rectangles.

7.

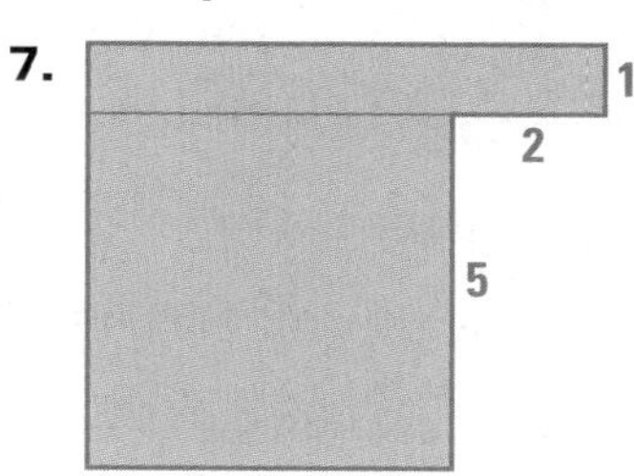

8.

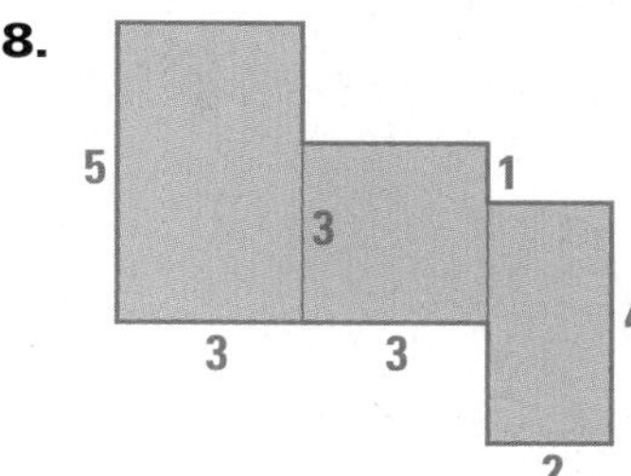

Student Help

▶ MORE EXAMPLES

INTERNET More examples and practice exercises available at www.mcdougallittell.com

Geometry in the Plane

Why is plane geometry important?

Plane geometry deals with flat, or two-dimensional, shapes. Knowing the properties of these shapes allows you to find unknown angle measures or side lengths. You will use plane geometry as you study the surfaces of three-dimensional objects in Chapter 9.

Many careers, including interior design (page 355) and surveying (page 361), require an understanding of geometry. For example, interior designers use angle measures to position mirrors that enhance a room's appearance, and they calculate areas of various shapes to plan for rugs and wall coverings.

Meeting the California Standards

The skills you'll learn in this chapter will help you meet state standards and prepare for standardized tests. In this chapter you'll:

- **Identify angle relationships.** LESSON 8.1
- **Use the properties of complementary and supplementary angles and the sum of the angles of a triangle to solve problems.** LESSONS 8.1, 8.2
- **Describe the properties of two-dimensional figures.** LESSONS 8.3, 8.5
- **Draw figures from given information.** LESSONS 8.3, 8.5, 8.6
- **Use expressions describing geometric quantities.** LESSONS 8.4, 8.6, 8.7
- **Know formulas for the circumference and area of a circle.** LESSONS 8.7, 8.8

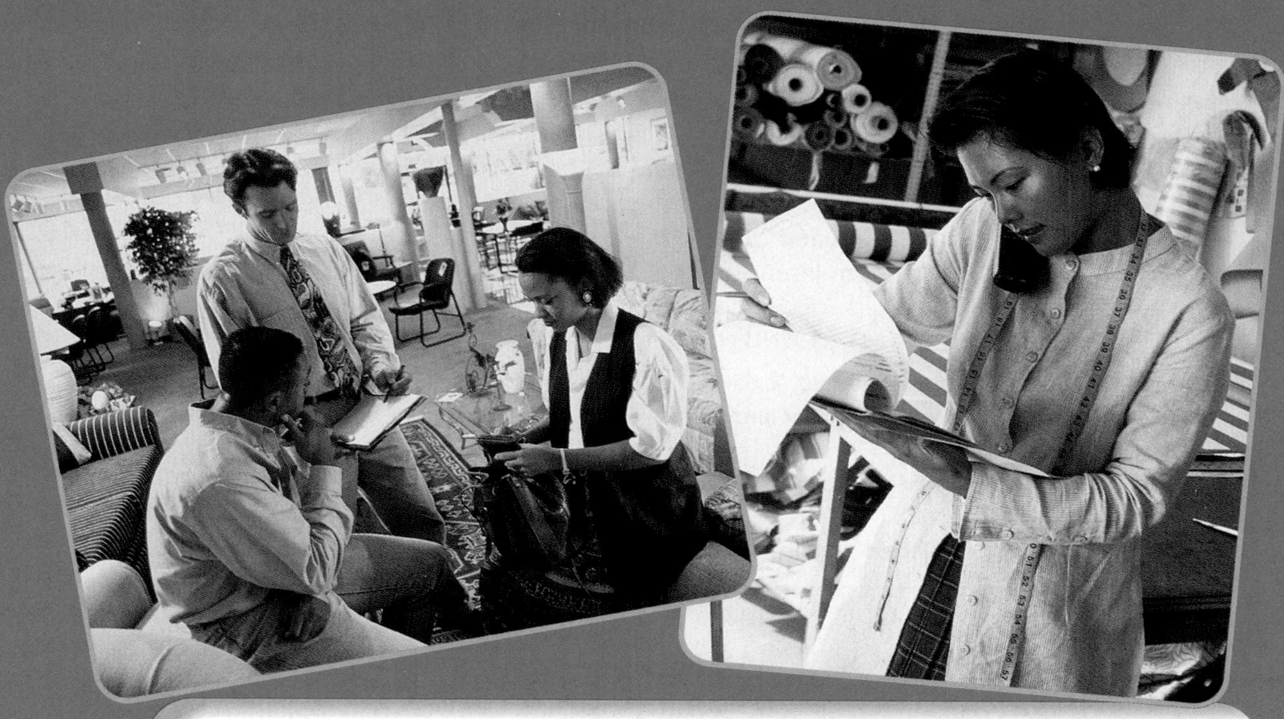

Career Link **INTERIOR DESIGN** An interior designer uses plane geometry when:

- calculating areas for wall and floor coverings.
- positioning mirrors on walls.

EXERCISES

An interior designer is planning to cover the wall at the right with fabric. To estimate how much fabric to buy, the designer finds the area of the wall. To make a rough estimate of the area, the designer ignores the door and the window.

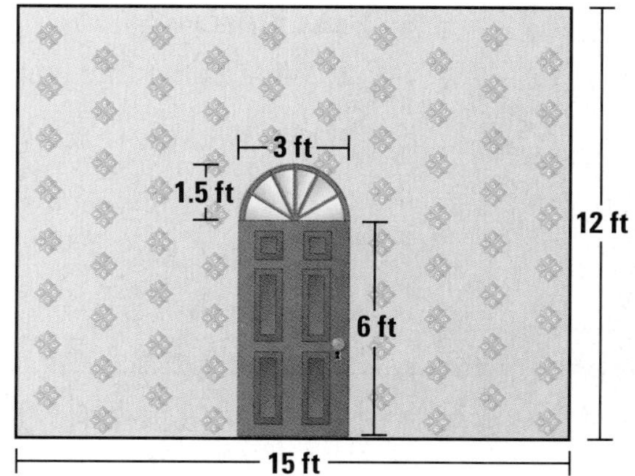

1. What is the area of the 15 ft by 12 ft rectangle?

2. Each roll of fabric covers 30 square feet. About how much fabric should the designer buy?

In Lesson 8.8, you will learn how to find the area of the wall by subtracting the areas of the door and the window. The window is half of a circle.

Chapter 8 Getting Ready

PREVIEW

What's the chapter about?

- Relating the **angles** formed by **intersecting lines**
- Classifying and finding the areas of **triangles**
- Classifying and finding the areas of **parallelograms**
- Finding the circumferences and the areas of **circles**

WORDS TO KNOW

- **vertical angles,** *p. 357*
- **complementary angles,** *p. 358*
- **supplementary angles,** *p. 358*
- **adjacent angles,** *p. 358*
- **equilateral, isosceles, and scalene triangles,** *p. 366*
- **right, acute, and obtuse triangles,** *p. 367*
- **quadrilateral,** *p. 376*
- **parallelogram,** *p. 376*
- **rectangle,** *p. 377*
- **circle,** *p. 388*
- **radius,** *p. 388*
- **diameter,** *p. 388*
- **circumference,** *p. 388*

PREPARE

Chapter Readiness Quiz

Take this quick quiz. If you are unsure of an answer, look back at the reference pages for help.

VOCABULARY CHECK *(refer to p. 31)*

1. The __?__ of the rectangle is 20 ft.

(A) Area (B) Length

(C) Width (D) Perimeter

SKILL CHECK *(refer to p. 239)*

2. What is the first step in solving the equation $6x = 72$?

(F) Add 6 to each side. (G) Subtract 6 from each side.

(H) Multiply each side by 6. (J) Divide each side by 6.

STUDY TIP

Attend Class Every Day

Try to attend every class. If you are absent, find a reliable friend to call for assignments and help.

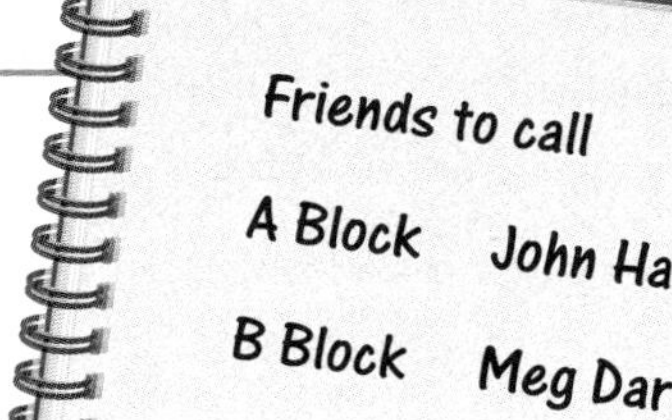

Intersecting Lines and Angle Measures

California Standards

In this lesson you'll:

- Identify angles as vertical, adjacent, complementary, or supplementary. (MG 2.1)
- Use the properties of complementary and supplementary angles to find angle measures. (MG 2.2)

Goal 1 PARALLEL AND INTERSECTING LINES

A **plane** is a flat surface that extends indefinitely in all directions. Two lines that lie in the same plane *intersect* if they meet at a point.

If two lines in the same plane do not intersect, they are **parallel**. Parallel lines are indicated using arrowheads on the lines as shown in the diagram.

In a plane, two different lines are either parallel or they intersect. In the diagram above, line a and line b are parallel, while line a and line c intersect.

Consider the four angles formed by the intersecting lines shown in the diagram at the right. The angles opposite each other are called **vertical angles**. Two angles are **congruent** if they have the same measure. The symbol $\cong$ means "is congruent to."

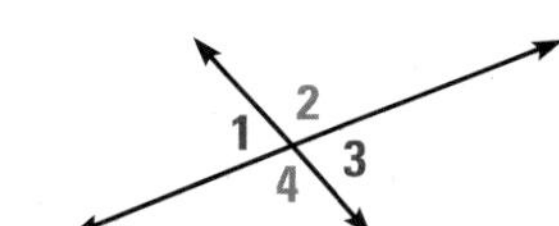

$\angle 1$ and $\angle 3$ are vertical angles.
$\angle 2$ and $\angle 4$ are vertical angles.

As you will see in Exercise 32, the following theorem is true.

VERTICAL ANGLES THEOREM

Vertical angles are congruent to each other. In the diagram above,

$\angle 1 \cong \angle 3$ and $\angle 2 \cong \angle 4$.

EXAMPLE 1 Using the Vertical Angles Theorem

The measure of $\angle 1$ is 72°, and the measure of $\angle 2$ is 108°. Find the measures of $\angle 3$ and $\angle 4$.

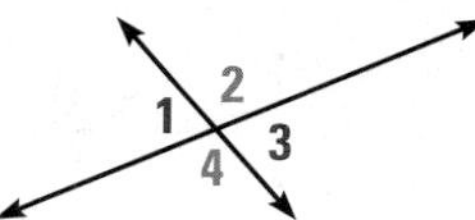

Solution

Because $\angle 1 \cong \angle 3$ by the vertical angles theorem, the measure of $\angle 3$ equals the measure of $\angle 1$. The measure of $\angle 3$ is 72°.

Because $\angle 2 \cong \angle 4$ by the vertical angles theorem, the measure of $\angle 4$ equals the measure of $\angle 2$. The measure of $\angle 4$ is 108°.

Goal 2 Special Pairs of Angles

Two angles are **complementary** if the sum of their measures is 90°. Two angles are **supplementary** if the sum of their measures is 180°.

Student Help

▶ **More Examples**

More examples are available at www.mcdougallittell.com

EXAMPLE 2 Complementary and Supplementary Angles

State whether the angles are *complementary*, *supplementary*, or *neither*.

a.

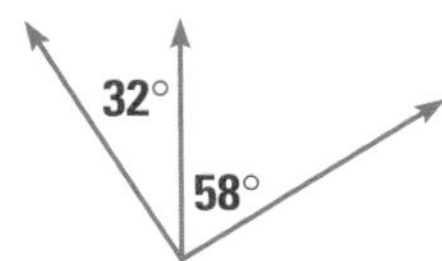

b.

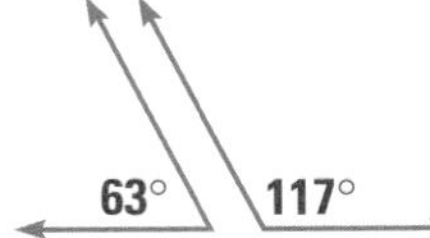

c.

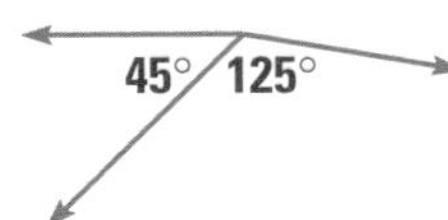

Solution

a. $32° + 58° = 90°$

The angles are complementary.

b. $63° + 117° = 180°$

The angles are supplementary.

c. $45° + 125° = 170°$

The angles are neither complementary nor supplementary.

A **vertex** is a point where the sides of an angle meet. Two angles in the same plane that share a vertex and a common side but do not overlap are called **adjacent angles**. Complementary angles and supplementary angles do not have to be adjacent.

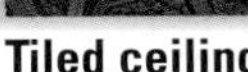

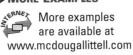

Tiled ceiling

EXAMPLE 3 Identifying Adjacent Angles

Tell whether ∠1 and ∠2 are adjacent.

a.

b.

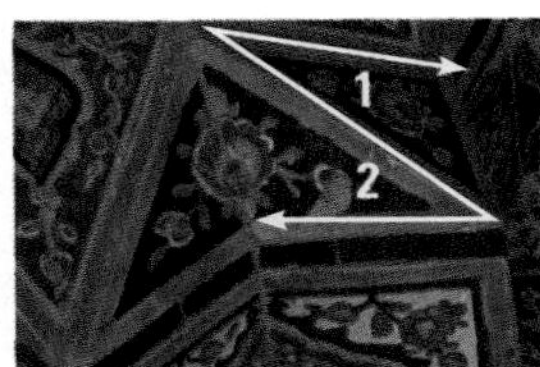

c.

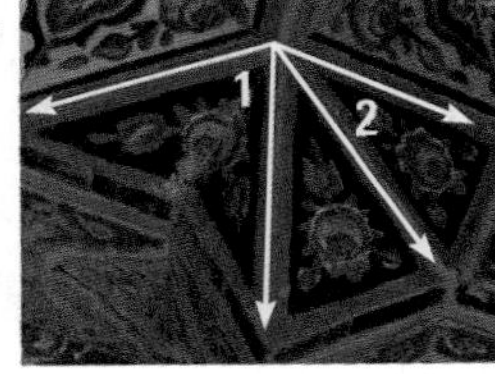

Solution

a. Yes, they are adjacent. They share a side and a vertex.

b. No, they are not adjacent. They share a side but not a vertex.

c. No, they are not adjacent. They share a vertex but not a side.

When two lines intersect, each pair of adjacent angles is supplementary, a fact that is used in the next example.

EXAMPLE 4 Finding Angle Measures

Find the value of x.

a.

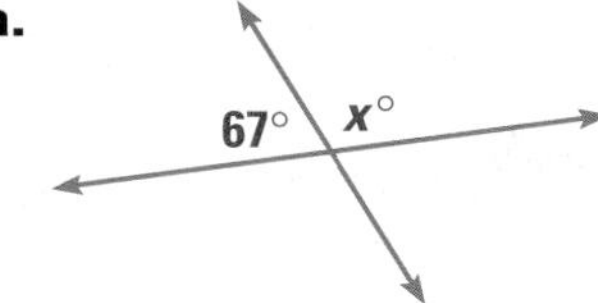

b.

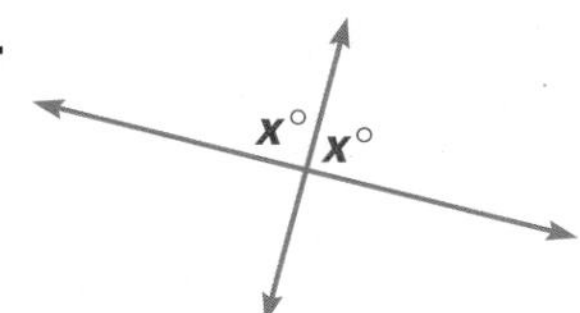

Solution

a.

$$\begin{aligned} x + 67 &= 180 \\ -67 &= -67 \\ \hline x &= 113 \end{aligned}$$

b.

$$\begin{aligned} x + x &= 180 \\ 2x &= 180 \\ \frac{2x}{2} &= \frac{180}{2} \\ x &= 90 \end{aligned}$$

> **Student Help**
>
> ▶ **STUDY TIP**
> In part (b) of Example 4, $x + x$ can be thought of as $1 \cdot x + 1 \cdot x$. Using the distributive property, you can write this as $(1 + 1)x$, which equals $2x$.

In part (b) of Example 4, notice that each of the angles formed by the intersecting lines has a measure of 90°. An angle with a measure of 90° is a **right angle**. When an angle formed by two intersecting lines is a right angle, the lines are **perpendicular**. All of the angles formed by perpendicular lines are right angles.

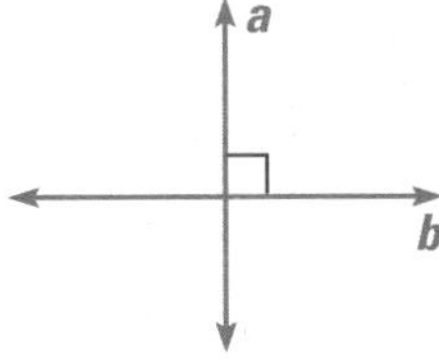

8.1 Exercises

Guided Practice

In Exercises 1–4, use the diagram.

1. Name four pairs of vertical angles.

2. Name four pairs of adjacent angles.

3. Tell whether the statement is *true* or *false*.

a. $\angle 1$ and $\angle 4$ are complementary angles.

b. $\angle 1$ and $\angle 3$ are adjacent angles.

c. $\angle 5$ and $\angle 6$ are supplementary angles.

d. $\angle 6$ and $\angle 8$ are vertical angles.

4. Find the measure of each angle. The measure of $\angle 1$ is 130° and the measure of $\angle 6$ is 50°.

a. $\angle 3$ **b.** $\angle 2$ **c.** $\angle 5$ **d.** $\angle 8$

Practice and Problem Solving

Student Help

▶ MORE PRACTICE Extra practice to help you master skills is on page 580.

In Exercises 5–8, use the figure at the right. Find the measure of the angle.

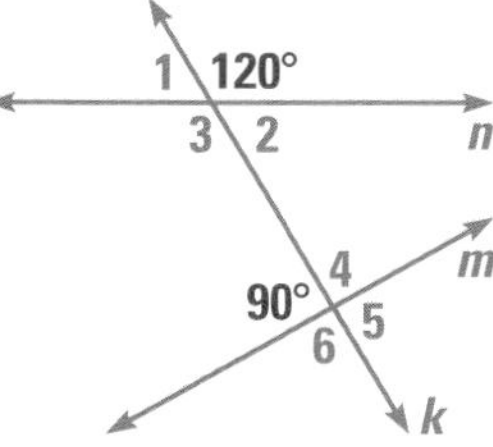

5. $\angle 1$

6. $\angle 4$

7. $\angle 5$

8. $\angle 2$

MATHEMATICAL REASONING **Complete the statement using *sometimes, always,* or *never*.**

9. Parallel lines __?__ meet.

10. Vertical angles are __?__ congruent.

11. Complementary angles are __?__ congruent.

12. Supplementary angles are __?__ adjacent.

13. The sum of the measures of supplementary angles is __?__ 90°.

In Exercises 14–16, find the measures of $\angle 1$ and $\angle 2$.

14.

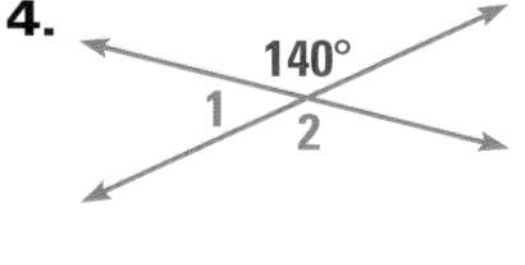

15.

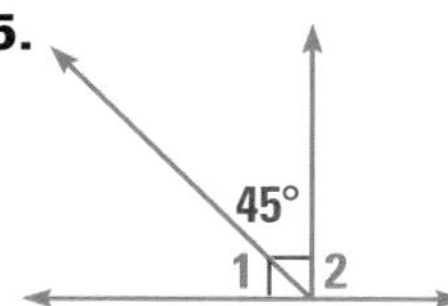

16.

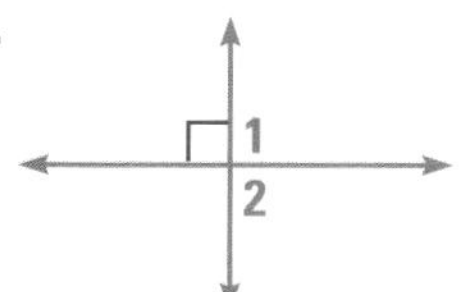

17. An angle has a measure of 40°. What is the measure of a complement of the angle?

18. An angle has a measure of 10°. What is the measure of a supplement of the angle?

19. Draw two intersecting lines and label the four angles formed. Name a pair of vertical angles, a pair of adjacent angles, and a pair of supplementary angles.

20. An angle has a measure of 35°. Find the measures of a complementary angle and a supplementary angle.

21. **MATHEMATICAL REASONING** What must be true about the measure of an angle if it has a supplement but no complement? What must be true if it has both a supplement and a complement?

Find the value of *x*.

22.

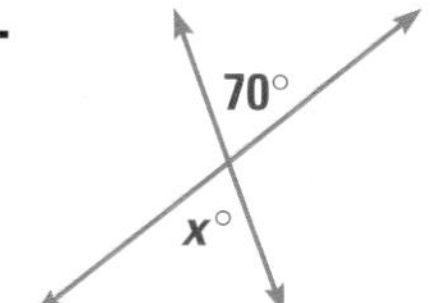

23.

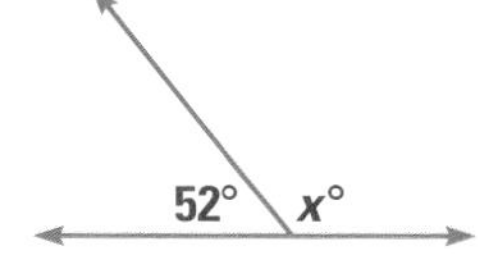

24.

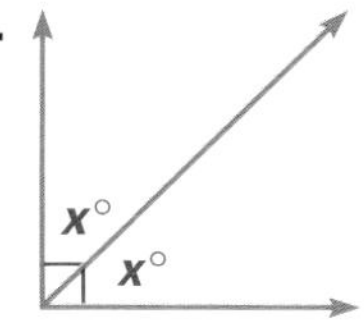

Link to Careers

SURVEYOR Surveyors measure distances and angles between points. Their work is important for establishing property lines and preparing construction sites.

More about surveyors available at www.mcdougallittell.com

CITY PLANNING In Exercises 25–28, use the diagram below. It shows a street map for the downtown portion of a city.

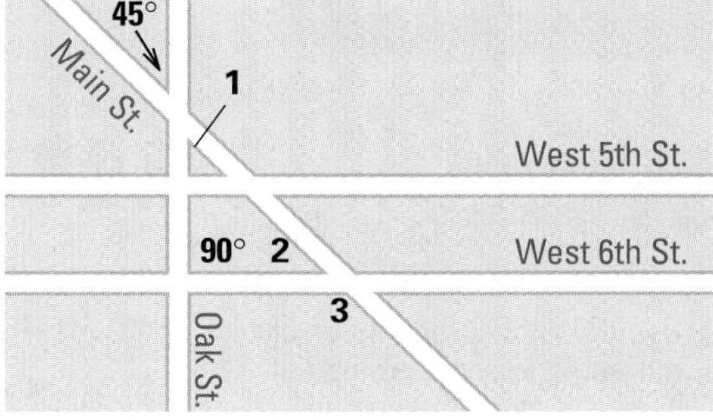

25. Which street is parallel to West 5th Street?

26. Which streets intersect West 6th Street?

27. Find the measure of $\angle 1$.

28. What do you know about $\angle 2$ and $\angle 3$?

In Exercises 29–31, use the following information. The measure of $\angle 4$ in the diagram at the right is $55°$.

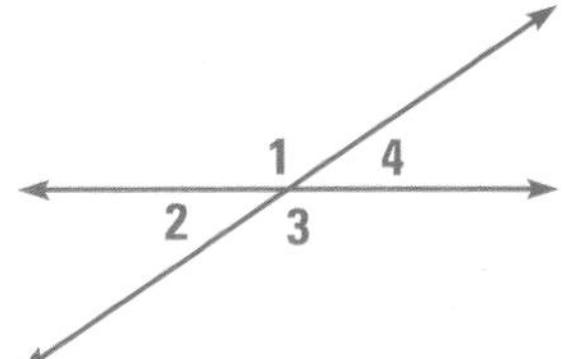

29. What is the measure of $\angle 3$? How do you know?

30. What is the measure of $\angle 1$? How do you know?

31. Can you show that the measure of $\angle 1$ is equal to the measure of $\angle 3$ without relying on the vertical angles theorem? Explain.

32. **CHALLENGE** Use the following steps to prove the vertical angles theorem.

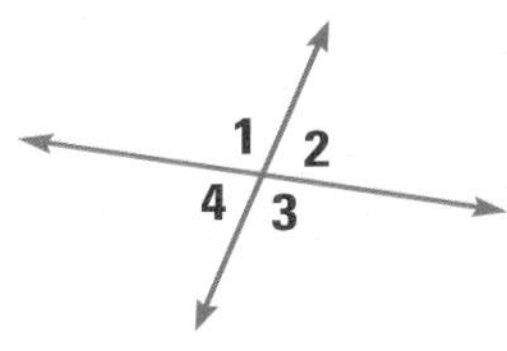

a. Begin with intersecting lines and label the angles 1, 2, 3, and 4 as shown. You need to prove that $\angle 1 \cong$ **?**.

b. $\angle 1$ and $\angle 2$ are supplementary, so the sum $m\angle 1 + m\angle 2 =$ **?**.
$\angle 2$ and $\angle 3$ are supplementary, so the sum $m\angle 2 + m\angle 3 =$ **?**.

c. Tell which property you can use to justify the fact that $m\angle 1$ and $m\angle 3$ are equal to the same quantity, and thus the angles are equal in measure to each other.

Multiple-Choice Practice

In Exercises 33 and 34, use the diagram.

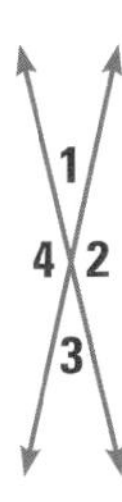

33. Which angle is congruent to $\angle 1$?

(A) $\angle 2$ (B) $\angle 3$

(C) $\angle 4$ (D) Not here

34. $\angle 3$ and $\angle 4$ are __?__.

(F) Vertical angles (G) Complementary angles

(H) Adjacent angles (J) Right angles

8.2 Angles of a Triangle

In this lesson you'll:

- Use the sum of the angles of a triangle to solve problems involving an unknown angle measure. (MG 2.2)
- Use the properties of complementary angles to solve problems involving an unknown angle measure. (MG 2.2)

Goal 1 MEASURING A TRIANGLE'S ANGLES

Draw any triangle and cut it out. Tear off the three angles and arrange them so that they are adjacent to each other. What do you observe?

Cut out a triangle. **Tear off the angles.** **Arrange them as adjacent angles.**

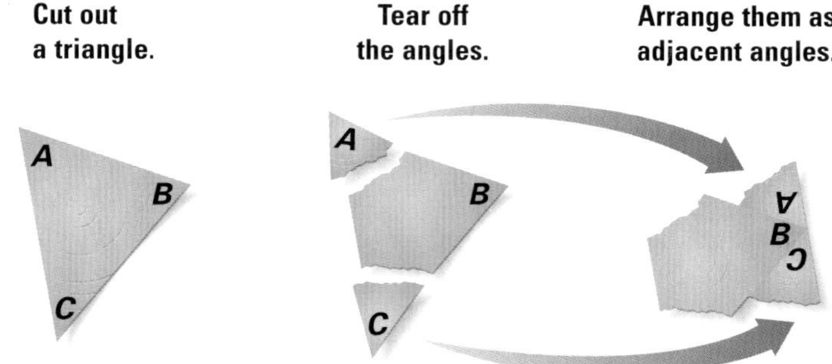

From the arrangement on the far right, it appears that the sum of the three angle measures is 180°. Try this with other triangles. You should always get the same result. Using inductive reasoning, you can conjecture that the sum of the measures of any triangle is 180°.

Student Help

▶ STUDY TIP
In a later geometry course, you will learn how to use deductive reasoning to prove that the sum of the measures of the angles of a triangle is 180°.

ANGLES OF A TRIANGLE

The sum of the measures of the angles of a triangle is 180°.

In Lesson 8.1 you used numbers to label angles. In some situations you can name them by vertex letters. In Example 1 below, $\angle 1$ can also be called $\angle RPQ$, $\angle QPR$, or just $\angle P$. Remember from Lesson 6.4 that you can write "the measure of $\angle P$" as "$m\angle P$."

EXAMPLE 1 Finding the Measure of an Angle

In the triangle at the right, what is $m\angle P$?

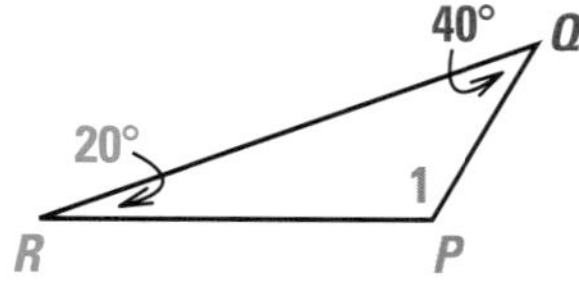

Solution

The sum of the measures of the angles must be 180°. To find the measure of $\angle P$, subtract the measures of $\angle Q$ and $\angle R$ from 180°.

$m\angle P = 180° - m\angle Q - m\angle R$ Subtract $m\angle Q$ and $m\angle R$ from 180°.

$= 180° - 40° - 20°$ Substitute for $m\angle Q$ and $m\angle R$.

$= 120°$ Simplify.

ANSWER ▶ The measure of $\angle P$ is 120°.

Goal 2 FINDING ANGLE MEASURES

Notice that the triangle in Example 1 has two angles with measures less than 90° and one angle with a measure greater than 90°. An angle whose measure is between 0° and 90° is called an **acute angle**. An angle whose measure is between 90° and 180° is called an **obtuse angle**.

EXAMPLE 2 Finding the Measure of an Angle

The measure of $\angle A$ is 43°.
What is the measure of $\angle B$?

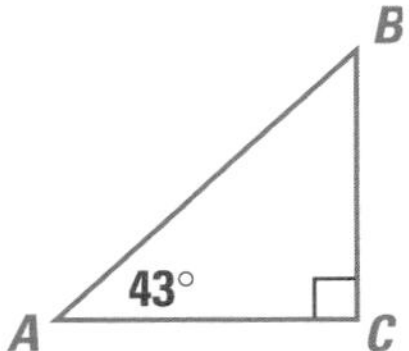

Solution

To find the measure of $\angle B$, subtract the measures of $\angle A$ and $\angle C$ from 180°. Because $\angle C$ is a right angle, you know that its measure is 90°.

$m\angle B = 180° - m\angle A - m\angle C$ Subtract $m\angle A$ and $m\angle C$ from 180°.

$= 180° - 43° - 90°$ Substitute for $m\angle A$ and $m\angle C$.

$= 47°$ Simplify.

ANSWER ▶ The measure of $\angle B$ is 47°.

In Example 2 notice that because the triangle has a right angle, the two acute angles, $\angle A$ and $\angle B$, must be complementary.

EXAMPLE 3 Using Deductive Reasoning

Show that the acute angles of a triangle with a right angle are complementary angles.

Solution

Draw a triangle ABC with the right angle at C. To show that $\angle A$ and $\angle B$ are complementary angles, show that the sum of their measures is 90°.

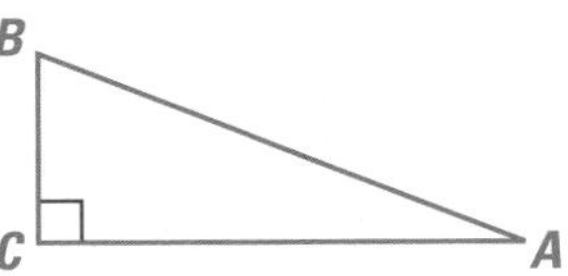

$m\angle A + m\angle B + m\angle C = 180°$ Sum of the angle measures is 180°.

$m\angle A + m\angle B = 180° - m\angle C$ Subtract $m\angle C$ from each side.

$m\angle A + m\angle B = 180° - 90°$ Substitute 90° for $m\angle C$.

$m\angle A + m\angle B = 90°$ Simplify.

ANSWER ▶ $\angle A$ and $\angle B$ are complementary angles.

8.2 Exercises

Guided Practice

In Exercises 1 and 2, complete the statement.

1. The sum of the measures of the angles of a triangle is __?__.

2. In a triangle with a right angle, the sum of the measures of the acute angles is __?__.

In Exercises 3–8, you are given two angles of a triangle. Find the measure of the third angle.

3. 90°, 45° **4.** 28°, 39° **5.** 33°, 17°

6. 34°, 52° **7.** 115°, 30° **8.** 127°, 18°

9. In the figure at the right, find the measures of ∠1, ∠2, and ∠3. (*Hint:* You can use supplementary and vertical angles.)

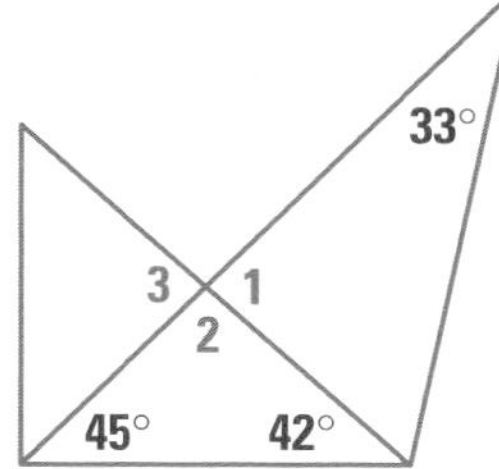

10. PYRAMIDS Each triangular face of the Great Pyramid Khufu at Giza in Egypt has two 52° angles. What is the measure of the other angle?

Practice and Problem Solving

Student Help

MORE PRACTICE Extra practice to help you master skills is on page 580.

Find the value of *x*.

11.

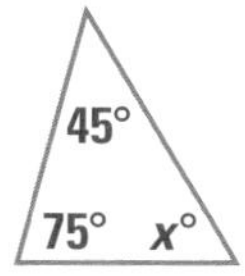

12.

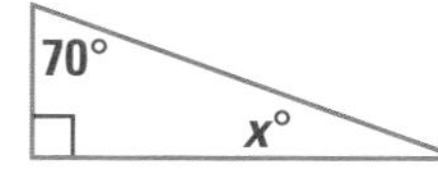

13.

Student Help

STUDY TIP In Exercises 14–17, look for complementary and supplementary angles.

In Exercises 14–17, use the figure below to match the angle with its measure. Explain your reasoning.

14. ∠1 **A.** 120°

15. ∠2 **B.** 60°

16. ∠3 **C.** 30°

17. ∠4 **D.** 90°

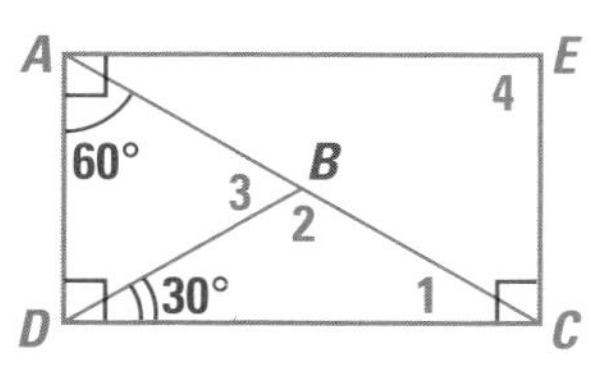

MATHEMATICAL REASONING **Decide whether a triangle can have the given angle measures. Explain your reasoning.**

18. 115°, 35°, 30° **19.** 55°, 90°, 45° **20.** 45°, 45°, 45°

21. 61°, 55°, 64° **22.** 60°, 50°, 70° **23.** 100°, 30°, 30°

24. 100°, 45°, 35° **25.** 120°, 30°, 30° **26.** 60°, 60°, 65°

Student Help

▶ HOMEWORK HELP
Extra help with problem solving in Ex. 27 is available at www.mcdougallittell.com

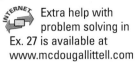

27. Use the figure at the right to find the measures of $\angle 1$, $\angle 2$, and $\angle 3$.

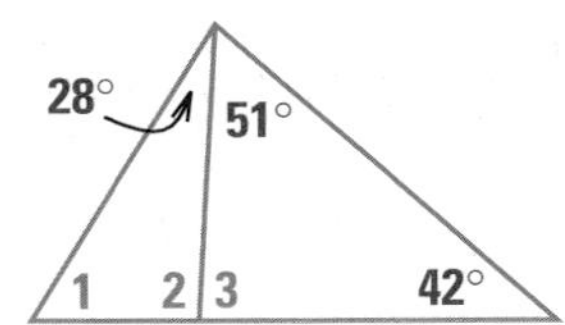

MATHEMATICAL REASONING Complete the statement using *sometimes, always,* or *never*. Explain your reasoning.

28. A triangle __?__ has two right angles.

29. The sum of the measures of the angles of a triangle is __?__ 180°.

30. A triangle __?__ has three acute angles.

31. A triangle __?__ has three obtuse angles.

Link to Sports

ORIENTEERING
Participants use a map and compass to find their way through the woods on a set course, going from checkpoint to checkpoint to complete the course.

ORIENTEERING In Exercises 32 and 33, use the following information.
You are hiking on the trail in the diagram at the right. You begin at point *A* and hike southwest. When you get to point *B*, you turn 135° and hike directly east.

32. When you get to point *C*, you turn to face point *D*. How many degrees do you turn?

33. What is the measure of $\angle CDA$?

34. **CHALLENGE** Figure *ABCD* at the right has been divided into two triangles. You know that the sum of the angle measures of each triangle is 180°. Explain how you can use this information to find the sum of the angle measures of the figure.

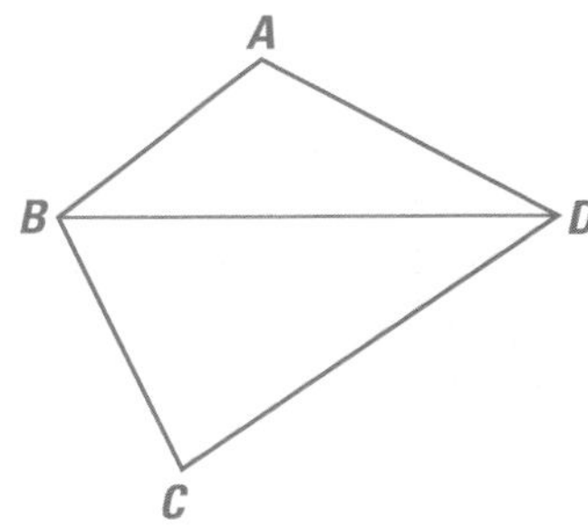

Multiple-Choice Practice

35. What is the measure of $\angle A$ in triangle *ABC*?

Ⓐ 115° Ⓑ 55°

Ⓒ 30° Ⓓ Not here

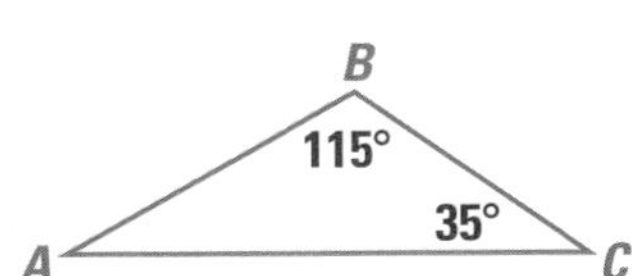

36. What is the measure of $\angle D$ in triangle *DEF*?

Ⓕ 115° Ⓖ 55°

Ⓗ 30° Ⓙ Not here

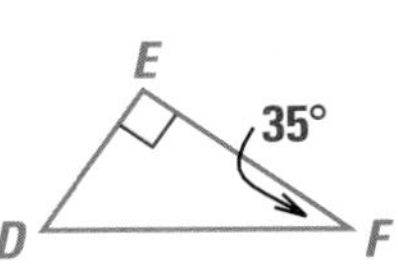

8.3 Classifying Triangles

In this lesson you'll:

- Identify and describe the properties of triangles. (MG 2.0)
- Draw triangles from information given about them. (MG 2.3)

Goal 1 Classifying Triangles by Their Sides

You can classify triangles according to the lengths of their sides.

- An **equilateral triangle** has three sides of the same length.
- An **isosceles triangle** has at least two sides of the same length.
- A **scalene triangle** has three sides of different lengths.

The Venn diagram at the right illustrates how these three types of triangles are related. Notice that every equilateral triangle is also isosceles, but when you classify triangles by their side lengths, you should use the most specific name.

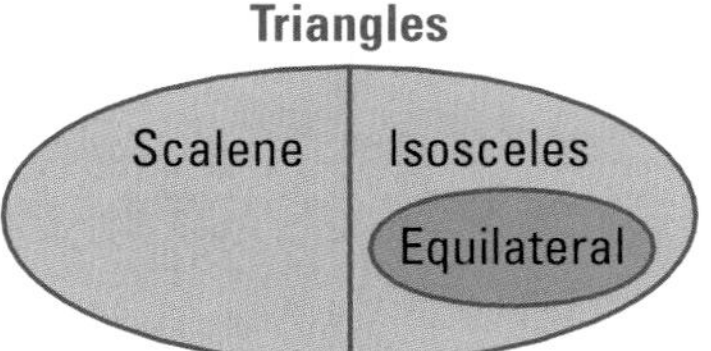

EXAMPLE 1 Classifying Triangles by Their Sides

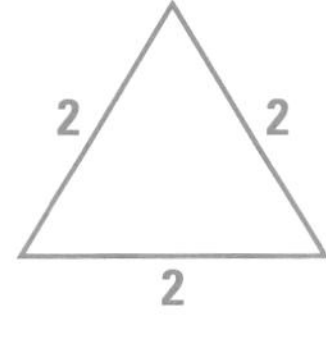

EQUILATERAL

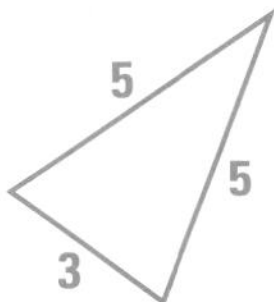

ISOSCELES

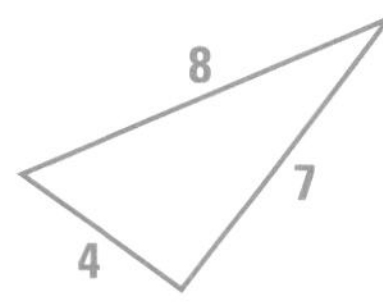

SCALENE

Student Help

▶ Study Tip
You can name triangles by their vertex letters. The order of the letters does not matter.

EXAMPLE 2 Classifying Triangles by Their Sides

Classify the triangles in the diagram at the right as *equilateral*, *isosceles*, or *scalene*.

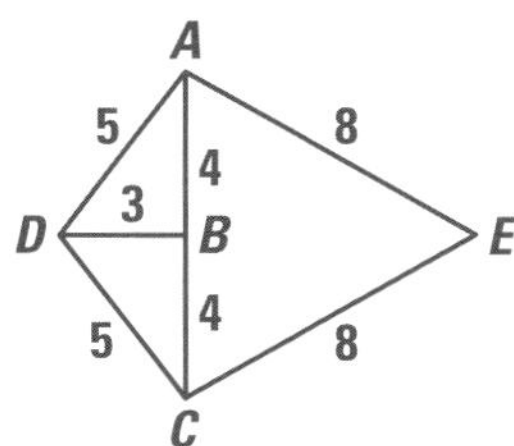

Solution

You can use a table to organize the information about the triangles.

Triangle	Side Lengths	Type
ABD	3, 4, 5	Scalene
BCD	3, 4, 5	Scalene
ADC	5, 5, 8	Isosceles
ACE	8, 8, 8	Equilateral

Goal 2 CLASSIFYING TRIANGLES BY THEIR ANGLES

You can also classify triangles according to the measures of their angles.

- An **acute triangle** has three acute angles.
- A **right triangle** has one right angle.
- An **obtuse triangle** has one obtuse angle.

EXAMPLE 3 Classifying Triangles by Their Angles

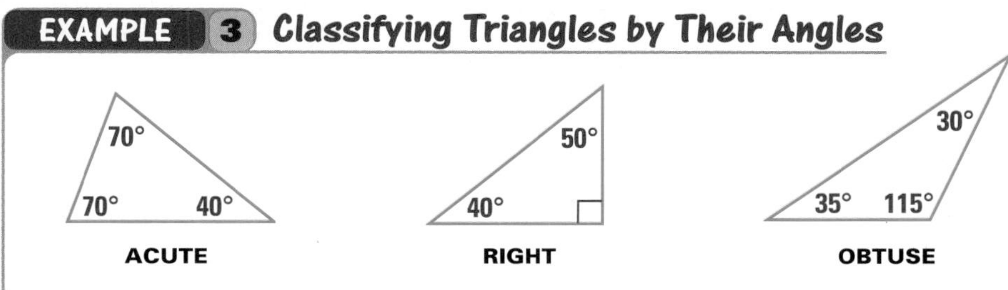

Link to Engineering

TRUSSES Engineers use triangles to design trusses for roofs, bridges, and cranes. Triangles are used because they can bear heavy loads.

EXAMPLE 4 Identifying Triangles

In the diagram of the roof truss, identify an acute triangle, a right triangle, and an obtuse triangle.

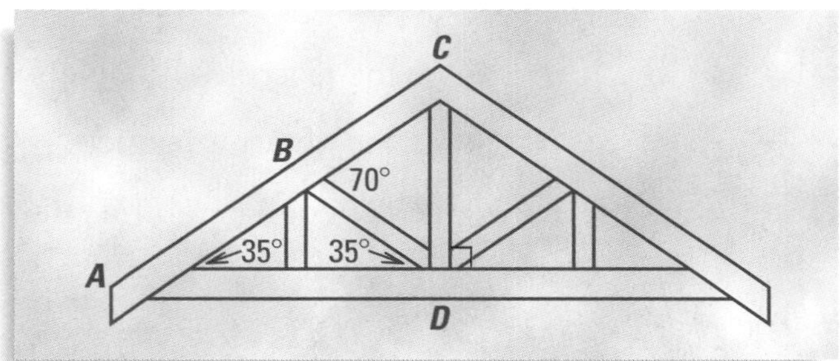

Solution

Triangle *BCD* is an acute triangle. Triangle *ACD* is a right triangle. Triangle *ABD* is an obtuse triangle.

EXAMPLE 5 Classifying by Sides and Angles

Classify the triangle shown at the right by its sides and angles.

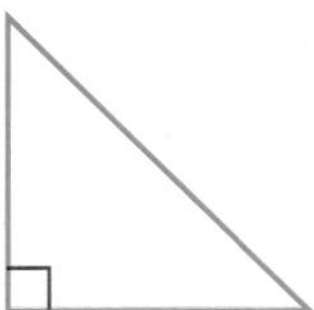

Solution

The triangle shown has a right angle, so it is a right triangle. Use a centimeter ruler to measure the sides. Two of the sides are 2 centimeters long, and the third side is about 2.8 centimeters long. Because two sides are the same length, this is an isosceles right triangle.

8.3 Exercises

Guided Practice

In Exercises 1 and 2, complete the statement.

1. Triangles can be classified by their __?__ or their __?__.

2. Every equilateral triangle is also a(n) __?__ triangle.

In Exercises 3–5, use a centimeter ruler to measure the sides. Then use as many words as possible to describe the triangle: *equilateral, isosceles, scalene, acute, right,* or *obtuse*.

3.
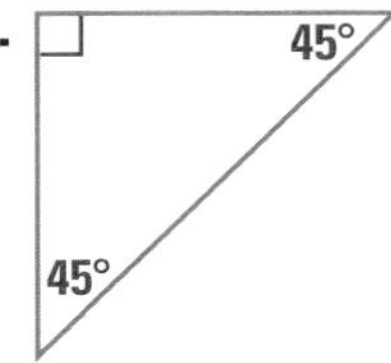

4.
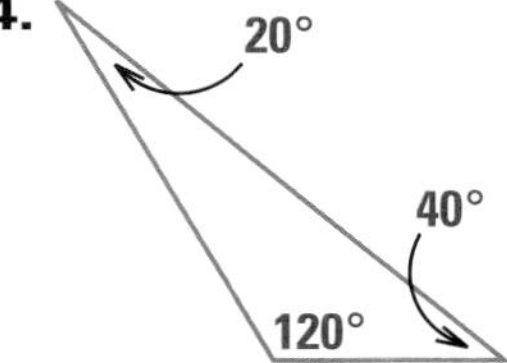

5.
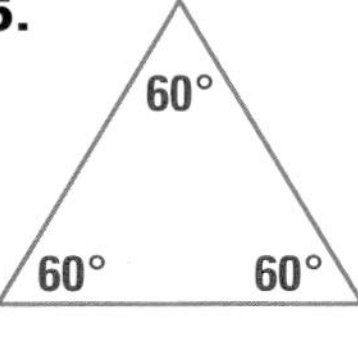

In Exercises 6–9, use the diagram at the right. Use a protractor to measure the angles if necessary.

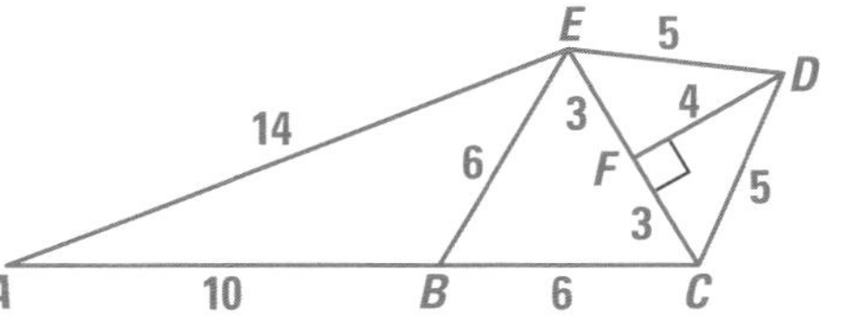

6. Name the right triangle(s).

7. Name the isosceles triangle(s).

8. Name the obtuse triangle(s).

9. Name the equilateral triangle(s).

Practice and Problem Solving

Student Help

▶ **More Practice** Extra practice to help you master skills is on page 580.

In Exercises 10–12, use a centimeter ruler to find the lengths of the sides of the triangle. Then use these lengths to classify the triangle.

10.
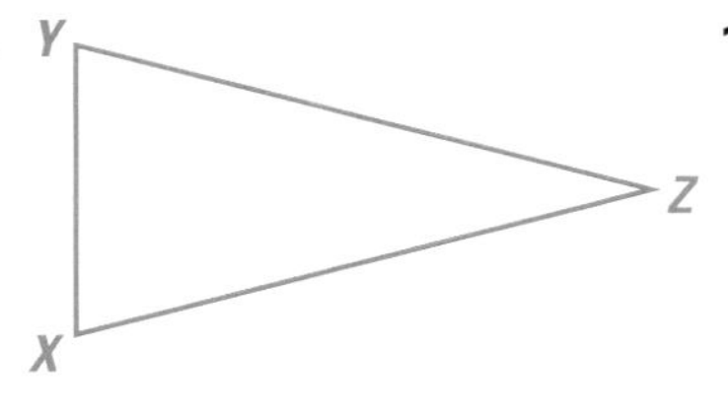

11.
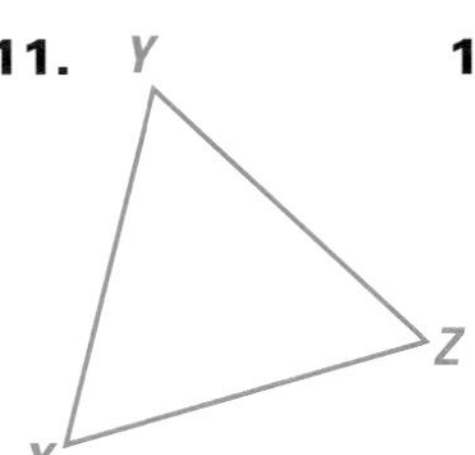

12.
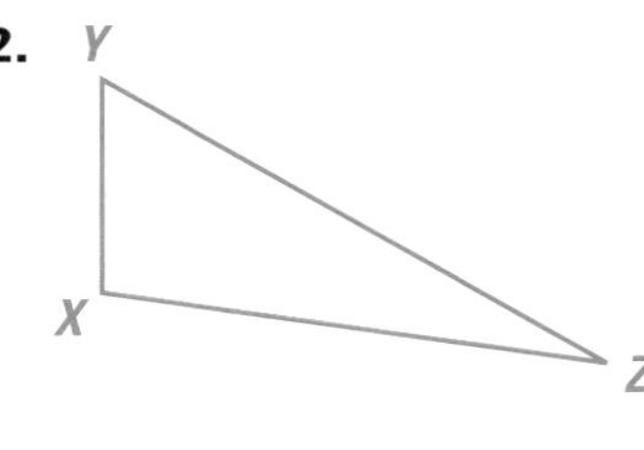

In Exercises 13–15, use a protractor to find the measures of the angles of the triangle. Then use these angle measures to classify the triangle.

13.
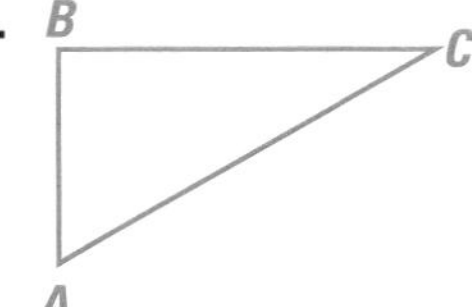

14.
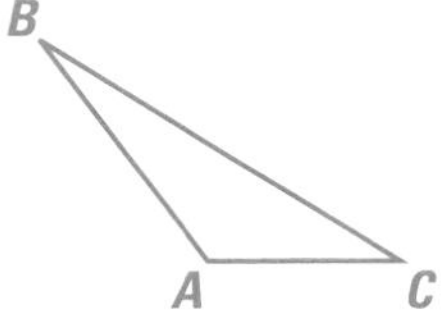

15.
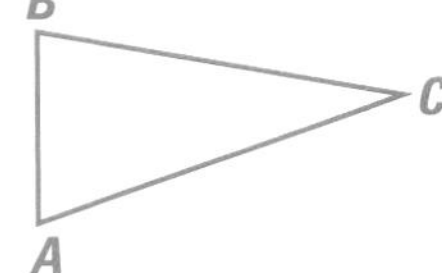

In Exercises 16–19, draw a triangle with the given description.

16. Acute and scalene

17. Acute and equilateral

18. Obtuse and isosceles

19. Right and scalene

Geodesic dome near Flaming Gorge National Recreation Area, Wyoming

20. **GEODESIC DOMES** A geodesic dome is a structure made using triangular braces. In the photo at the left, what type of triangles appear to be used in the structure of the roof?

ENGINEERING **In Exercises 21–23, refer to the bridge support at the right. Use a centimeter ruler and a protractor to measure sides and angles. Then use as many words as possible to describe the triangle: *equilateral, isosceles, scalene, acute, right,* or *obtuse*.**

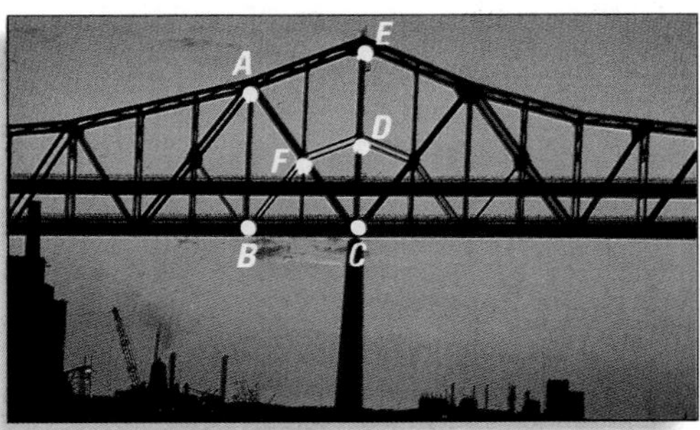

21. Triangle BCF

22. Triangle ABC

23. Triangle CDF

24. **QUILTING** The quilt pattern shown below is called the Pinwheel Star. The design is made by rotating the quarter block (shown enlarged at the right) four times and sewing the pieces together. Using a centimeter ruler and a protractor, measure the sides and angles so you can classify each numbered triangle. Organize the information in a table.

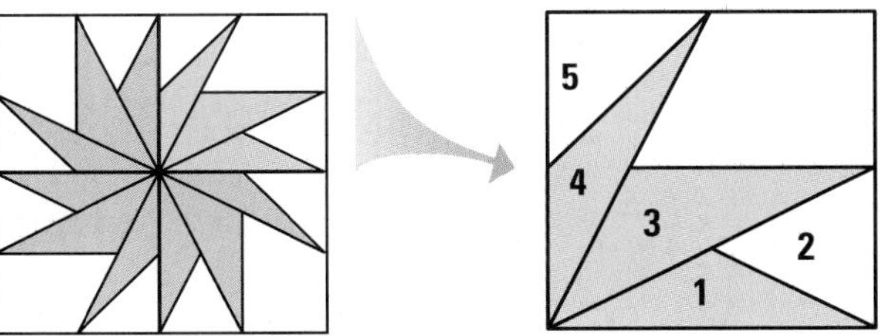

MATHEMATICAL REASONING **In Exercises 25–27, complete the statement using the words *sometimes, always,* or *never*. Explain.**

25. An isosceles triangle is __?__ a right triangle.

26. An equilateral triangle is __?__ an acute triangle.

27. A scalene triangle is __?__ an obtuse triangle.

28. Draw an equilateral triangle ABC. What are the different types of triangles that you can form by drawing a line segment from A to side $\overline{BC}$? Sketch your results.

29. **CHALLENGE** A *golden triangle* has two angles of equal measure that are each twice as large as the third angle. Find the measure of the angles of a golden triangle. Tell if a golden triangle is *acute*, *right*, or *obtuse*.

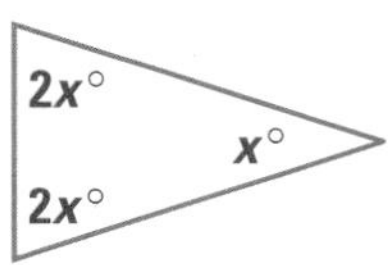

Multiple-Choice Practice

30. Which triangle is obtuse?

Ⓐ 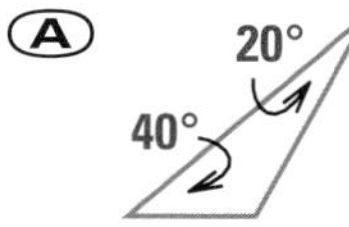

Ⓑ 

Ⓒ 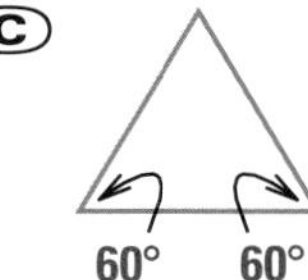

Ⓓ 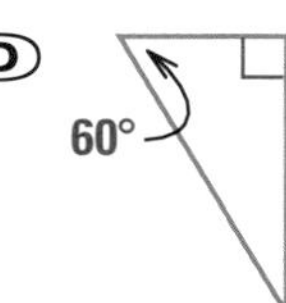

31. Which statement is false?

Ⓕ An isosceles triangle can never be a scalene triangle.

Ⓖ An acute triangle can also be a scalene triangle.

Ⓗ An obtuse triangle can also be an equilateral triangle.

Ⓙ A right triangle can also be an isosceles triangle.

Mixed Review

Tell whether the statement is *true* or *false*. Give an example to support your answer. *(4.3, 4.4)*

32. A negative number minus a negative number is negative.

33. A negative number plus a negative number is negative.

34. A positive number plus a negative number is positive.

35. A positive number minus a negative number is negative.

Find the probability that the spinner lands on blue. *(6.6)*

36.

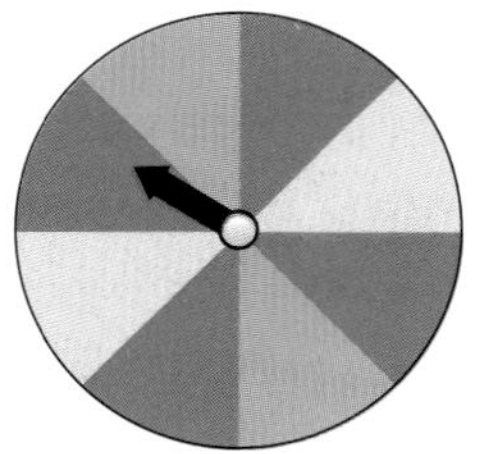

8 equal sections

37.

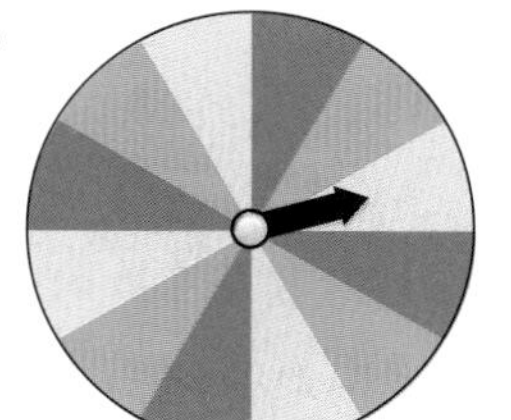

12 equal sections

38.

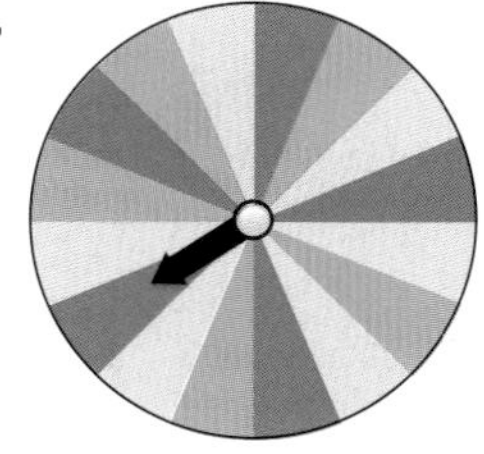

16 equal sections

Write the percent as a decimal and as a fraction in simplest form. *(7.1, 7.3)*

39. 20% **40.** 17% **41.** 34% **42.** 69%

43. 4.8% **44.** 3.7% **45.** $\frac{7}{8}\%$ **46.** $\frac{11}{5}\%$

47. 300% **48.** 120% **49.** 0.4% **50.** 1.4%

51. SHOPPING You pay $36 for a remote control toy car. The price was 75% of the regular price. What is the regular price? *(7.2)*

REASONING 8.4

DEVELOPING CONCEPTS
Finding Areas of Triangles

For use with Lesson 8.4

California Standards

- Express in symbolic form simple relationships arising from geometry. (AF 3.2)
- Use diagrams and models to explain mathematical reasoning. (MR 2.4)

MATERIALS

- Grid paper
- Scissors

SAMPLE 1 Finding the Area of a Triangle

You can use the area of a rectangle to find the area of a triangle. The triangle shown has been drawn on grid paper where each small square on the grid is 1 unit by 1 unit. The triangle has a base of 9 units and a height of 4 units. Find its area.

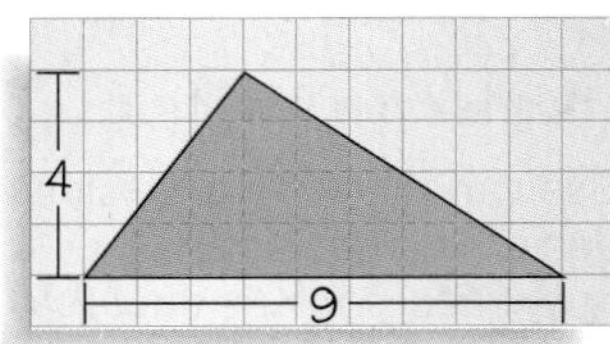

Here's How

1. Copy the given triangle. Then draw a rectangle that encloses the triangle.

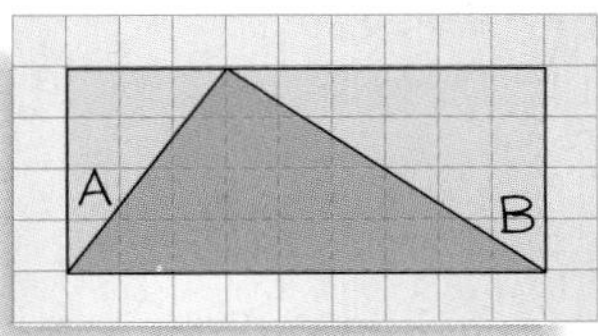

2. The rectangle is 9 units wide and 4 units high, so the area of the rectangle is 36 square units.

3. Cut out the rectangle. Then cut the original triangle out of the rectangle. The blue regions of the rectangle that are not part of the original triangle can be rearranged to form a triangle equal in area to the original, as shown. So the area of the original triangle is half the area of the rectangle, or 18 square units.

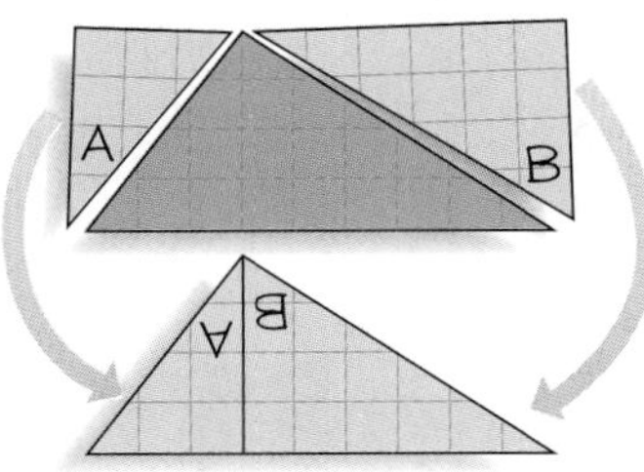

Student Help

SKILLS REVIEW
For help with areas of squares and rectangles, see page 562.

Try These

Each small square on the grid is 1 unit by 1 unit. Use the technique described above to find the area of the triangle.

1. 

2. 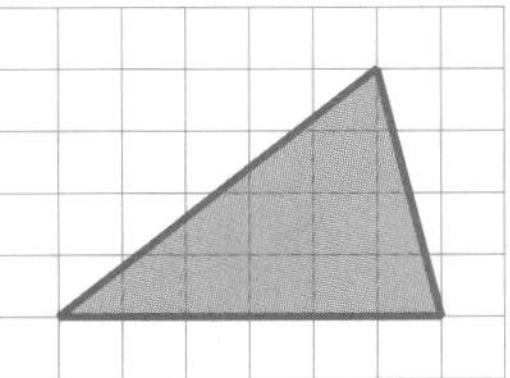

3. **MATHEMATICAL REASONING** Use the diagram to write a rule for finding the area of a triangle having a base of b units and a height of h units.

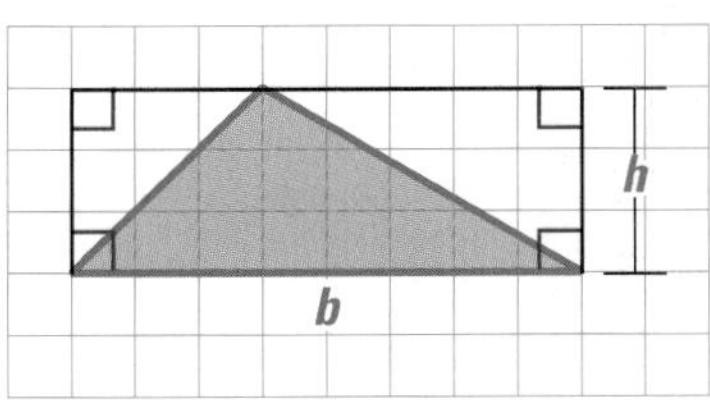

8.4 Area of a Triangle

California Standards

In this lesson you'll:

- Use variables in expressions describing geometric quantities, such as the area of a triangle. (AF 3.1)
- Express in symbolic form simple relationships arising from geometry. (AF 3.2)

Goal 1 AREA OF A TRIANGLE

Any side of a triangle can be labeled as the triangle's **base**. The triangle's **height** is the perpendicular distance from the base to the opposite vertex.

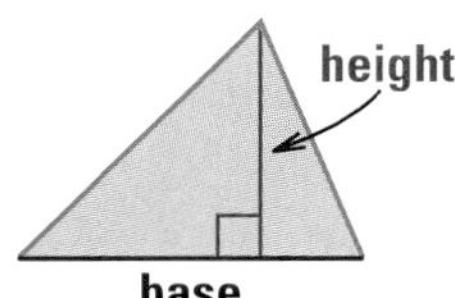

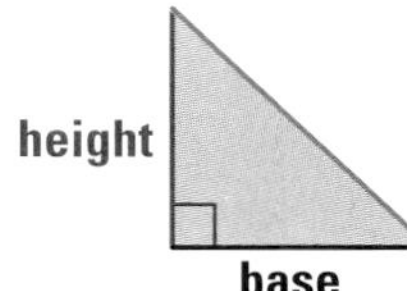

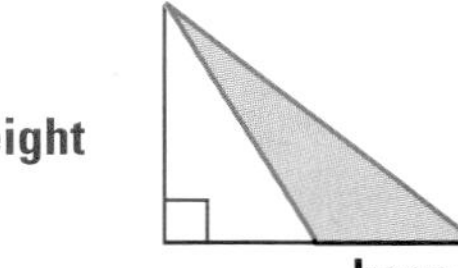

As you saw in Developing Concepts 8.4, page 371, you can use a formula to find the area of a triangle.

AREA OF A TRIANGLE

In Words The area of a triangle is one half the product of the base and the height of the triangle.

In Algebra $A = \frac{1}{2}bh$

In Arithmetic $A = \frac{1}{2} \cdot 12 \cdot 7 = 42$ square units

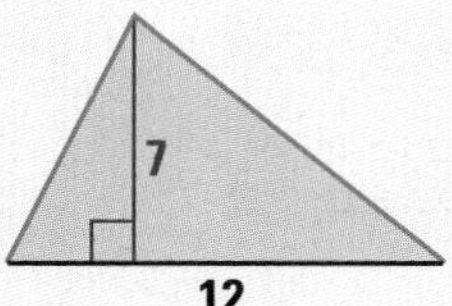

EXAMPLE 1 Finding the Area of a Triangle

Each small grid square is 1 unit by 1 unit. Find the area of the triangle.

a.

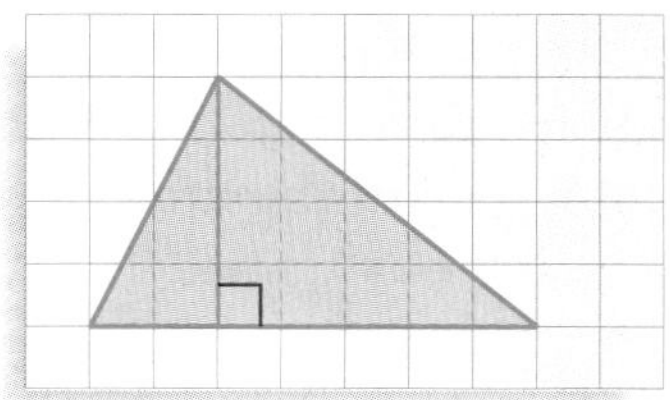

b.

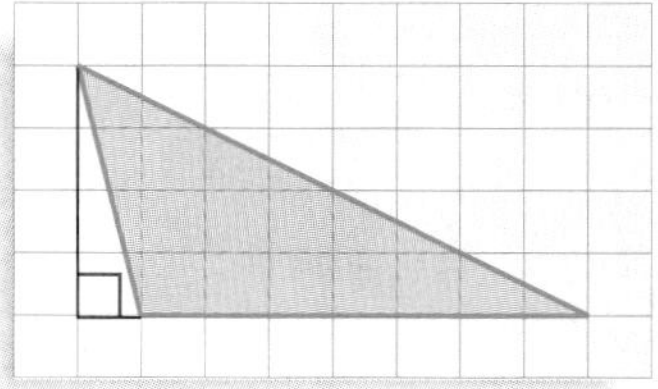

Solution

a. $A = \frac{1}{2}bh$

$= \frac{1}{2} \cdot 7 \cdot 4$

$= 14$ square units

b. $A = \frac{1}{2}bh$

$= \frac{1}{2} \cdot 7 \cdot 4$

$= 14$ square units

Notice that both triangles have the same area because they have the same base and height.

Student Help

STUDY TIP
With an obtuse triangle, it is convenient to use the side opposite the obtuse angle as the base. For example, use side $\overline{AB}$ as the base in triangle ABC below.

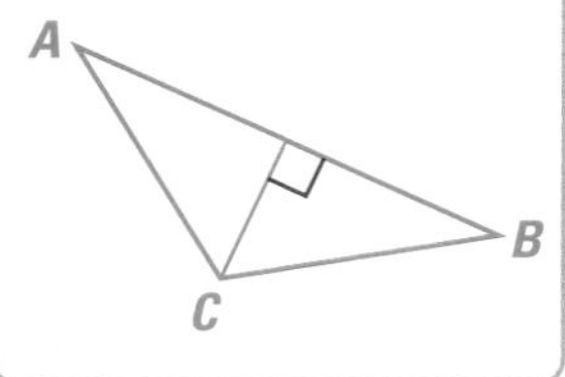

Goal 2 USING THE AREA OF A TRIANGLE

Student Help

▶ **MORE EXAMPLES**

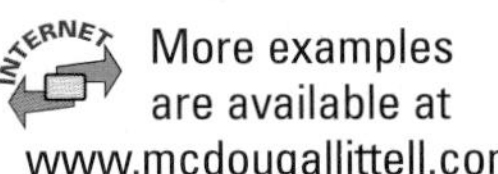

More examples are available at www.mcdougallittell.com

In real life there are many ways triangles are used. Sometimes you need to find the area of a triangle, for example, in order to buy the right amount of materials or to know how much paint you need.

EXAMPLE 2 Finding the Area of a Triangle

SAILS You are making sails for the sailboat shown below. How much material is in the two sails?

Solution

Each sail is a right triangle. Find the sum of the areas of the triangles.

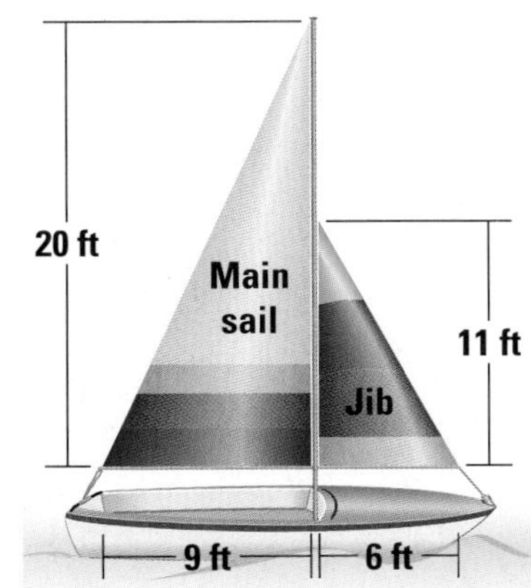

$$\text{Area of jib} = \frac{1}{2}bh$$

$$= \frac{1}{2} \cdot 6 \cdot 11$$

$$= 33 \text{ square feet}$$

$$\text{Area of main sail} = \frac{1}{2}bh$$

$$= \frac{1}{2} \cdot 9 \cdot 20$$

$$= 90 \text{ square feet}$$

Student Help

▶ **STUDY TIP**

The only time the height of a triangle can be the length of a side is when the triangle is a right triangle.

Sum of areas of triangles $= 33 + 90 = 123$ square feet

ANSWER ▶ The total amount of material in the two sails is 123 square feet.

EXAMPLE 3 Measuring a Triangle

CARPENTRY You are using the piece of wood at the right in making a bookstand. You use a tool called a square to measure the height. Find the area of the piece of wood.

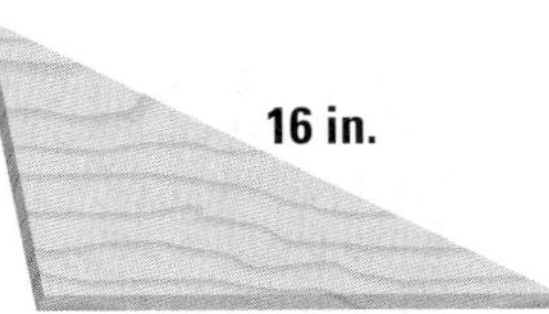

Solution

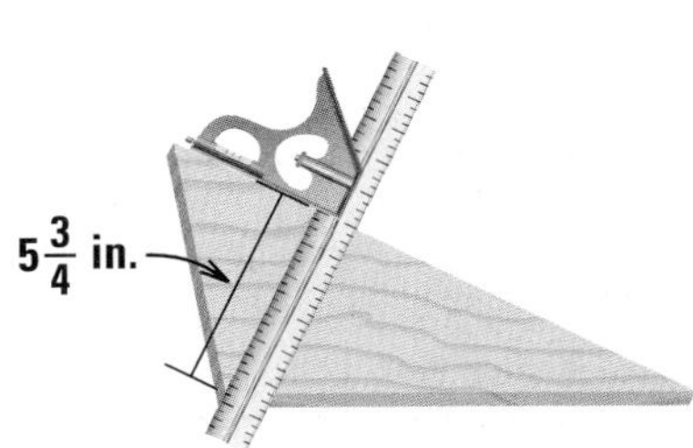

$$A = \frac{1}{2}bh$$

$$= \frac{1}{2} \cdot 16 \cdot 5\frac{3}{4}$$

$$= \frac{1}{2} \cdot 16 \cdot \frac{23}{4}$$

$$= 46 \text{ square inches}$$

ANSWER ▶ The area is 46 square inches.

8.4 Exercises

Guided Practice

Find the area of the triangle described.

1. Base = 8, height = 6
2. Base = 8, height = 3
3. Base = 6, height = 3
4. Base = 12, height = $2\frac{1}{2}$
5. Base = 9, height = $4\frac{1}{2}$
6. Base = 5, height = 5
7. Base = 4, height = 8.8
8. Base = 3.2, height = 1.5

9. ERROR ANALYSIS Your friend wants to find the area of the triangle below. Describe and correct your friend's error.

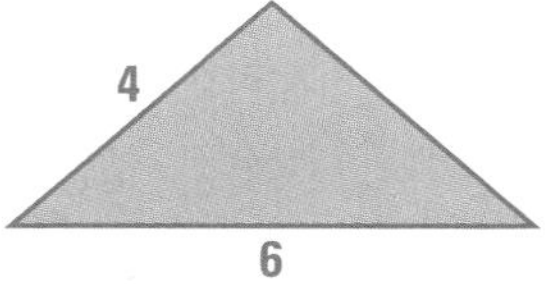

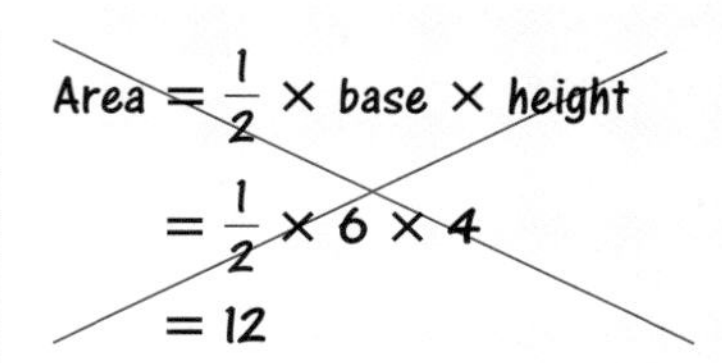

10. COOKING The dessert *baklava* is a pastry made with walnuts and honey that is sometimes cut into a triangle, as shown at the right. Find the area of the triangle.

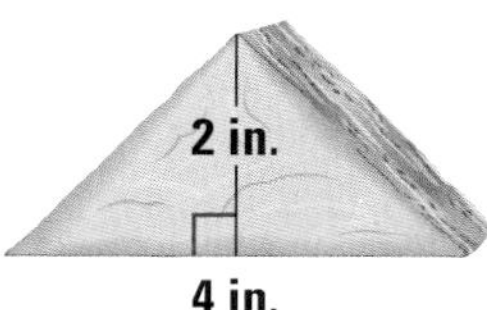

Practice and Problem Solving

Student Help

▶ **MORE PRACTICE** Extra practice to help you master skills is on page 580.

Find the area of the triangle.

11.

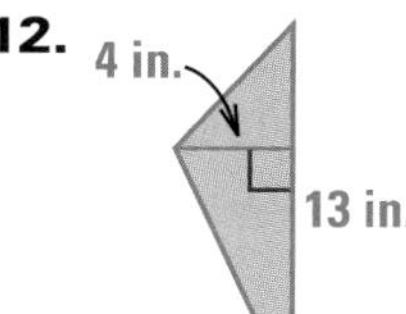

12.

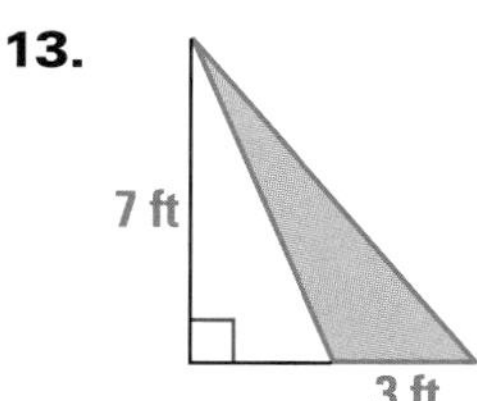

13. 7 ft

3 ft

Find the area of the polygon. All lengths are in feet.

Student Help

▶ **STUDY TIP** Recall that the formula for the area of a rectangle is $A = \ell w$.

14.

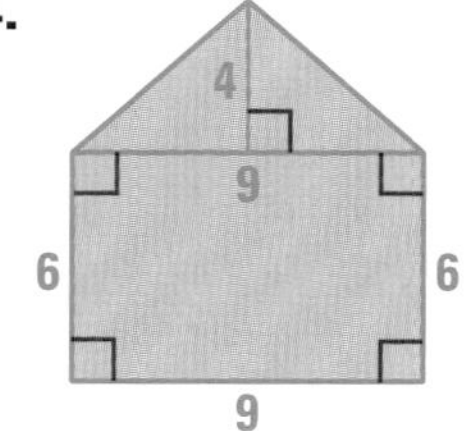

15.

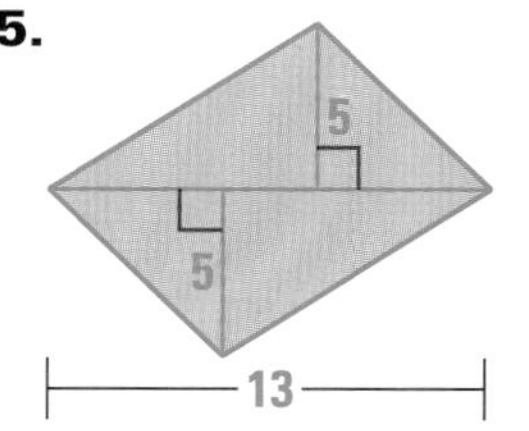

16.

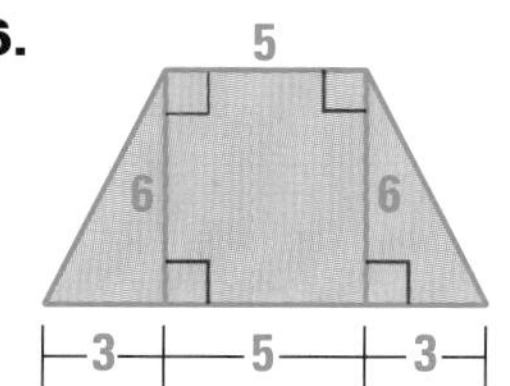

ENERGY A greenhouse is made of glass because glass allows solar radiation to enter but traps the heat that results.

Science Link **In Exercises 17 and 18, use the following information.** You are helping to build a greenhouse that has glass walls and a glass roof. The glass is cut into the two shapes shown below.

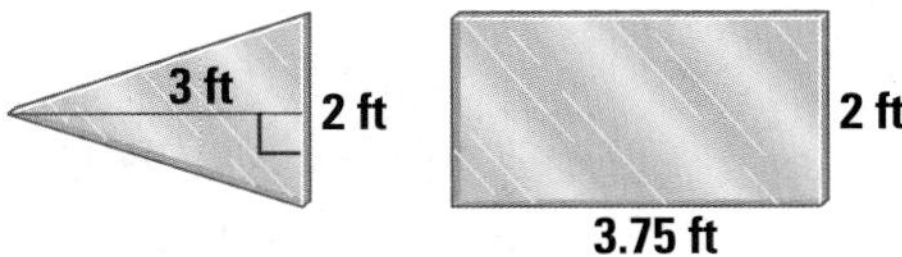

17. Find the area of each piece.

18. There are 27 triangular pieces and 62 rectangular pieces used for the walls and roof. Find the total area covered by these pieces.

19. **GEOGRAPHY** The diagram shows the approximate length and width of Nevada. Estimate the area of the state.

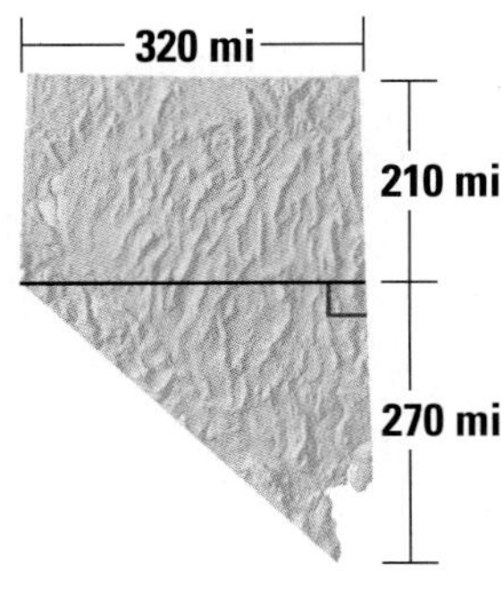

20. **MATHEMATICAL REASONING** Explain why triangles *ADE*, *BDE*, and *CDE* have the same area.

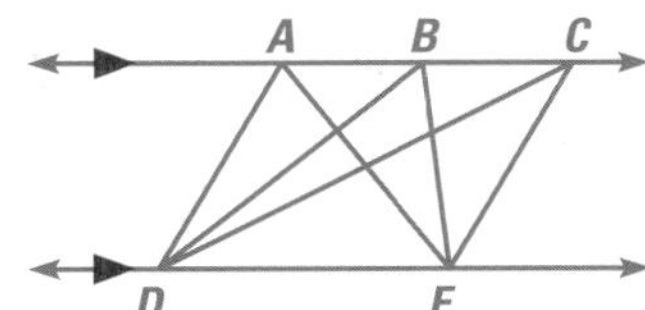

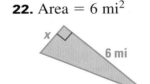

ALGEBRA **Find the value of *x*.**

21. Area = x ft^2

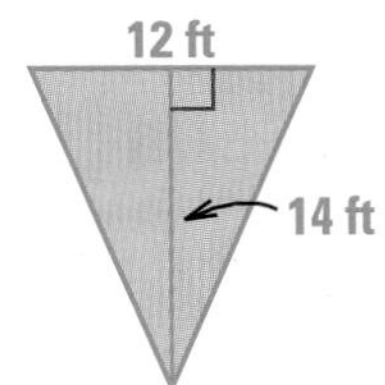

22. Area = 6 mi^2

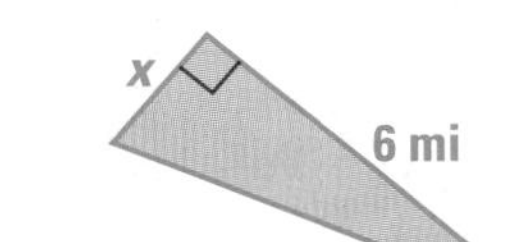

23. Area = 25 cm^2

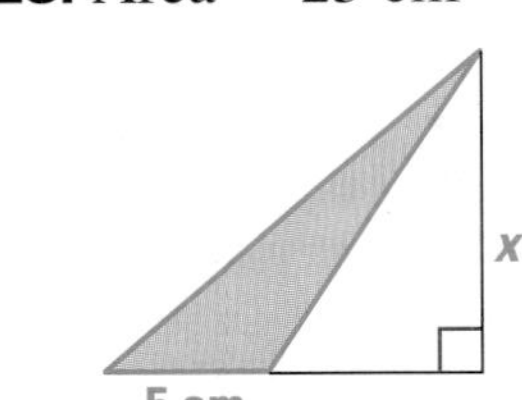

24. **CHALLENGE** If you double the base and height of a triangle, what happens to the area of the triangle? Use words, symbols, and diagrams to explain your reasoning.

Multiple-Choice Practice

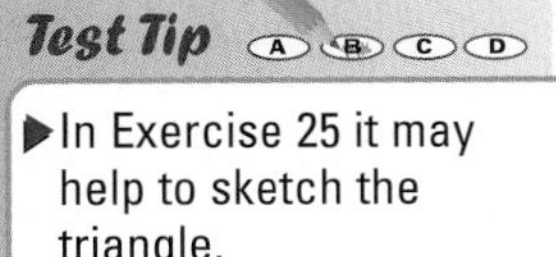

▶ In Exercise 25 it may help to sketch the triangle.

25. Find the area of a triangle with a base of 14 in. and a height of 5 in.

Ⓐ 140 in.^{2} Ⓑ 70 in.^{2} Ⓒ 35 in.^{2} Ⓓ 1.4 in.^{2}

26. The figure at the right is made up of a rectangle and two triangles with the same area. What is the area of the figure?

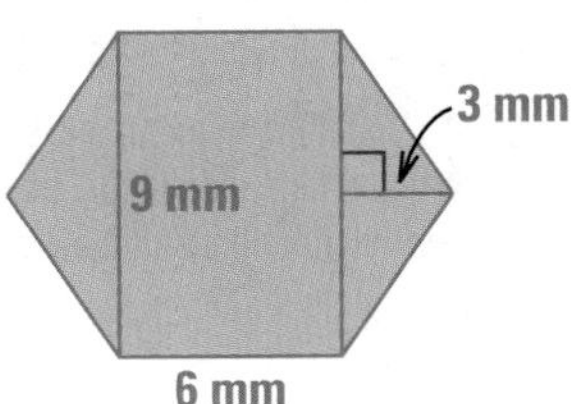

Ⓕ 54 mm^2 Ⓖ 81 mm^2

Ⓗ 98 mm^2 Ⓙ 108 mm^2

8.5 Parallelograms

In this lesson you'll:

- Identify and describe the properties of two-dimensional figures. (MG 2.0)
- Draw quadrilaterals from information given about them. (MG 2.3)

Goal 1 Using Properties of Parallelograms

A **quadrilateral** is a polygon with four sides. A **parallelogram** is a quadrilateral whose opposite sides are parallel.

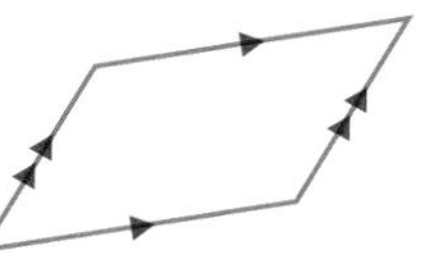

Properties of Parallelograms

In a parallelogram,

- opposite sides have the same length.
- opposite angles have the same measure.

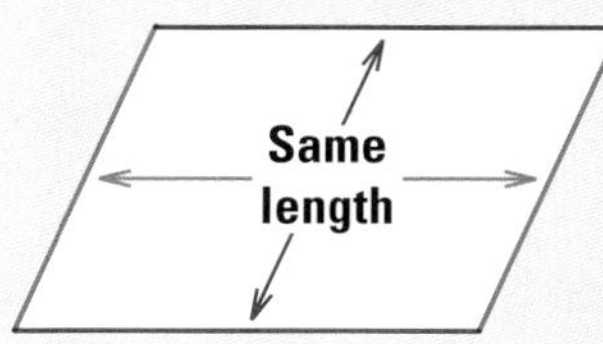

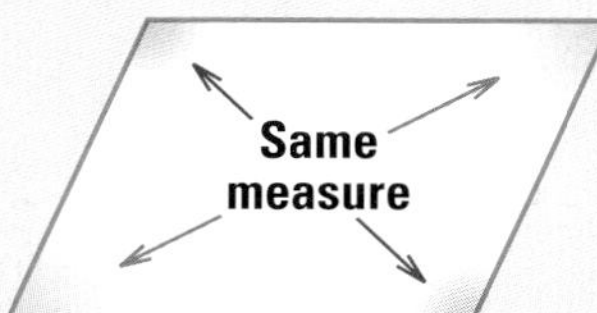

Student Help

Study Tip
In a later geometry course, you will prove these properties of parallelograms.

Example 1 Using Properties of Parallelograms

In parallelogram $ABCD$, you are given the measures of $\angle A$ and $\angle B$.

B 130° C 4 A 50° 6 D

a. Find the measures of $\angle C$ and $\angle D$.

b. Find the sum of the measures of the angles.

c. Find the lengths of sides AB and BC.

d. Find the perimeter of parallelogram $ABCD$.

Solution

a. Because $ABCD$ is a parallelogram, you know that opposite angles have the same measure.

$m\angle C = m\angle A = 50°$ $\qquad$ $m\angle D = m\angle B = 130°$

b. The sum of the four angles is $50° + 130° + 50° + 130° = 360°$.

c. Because $ABCD$ is a parallelogram, you know that opposite sides have the same length.

$AB = CD = 4$ $\qquad$ $BC = AD = 6$

d. The perimeter of parallelogram $ABCD$ is $4 + 6 + 4 + 6 = 20$.

Student Help

More Examples

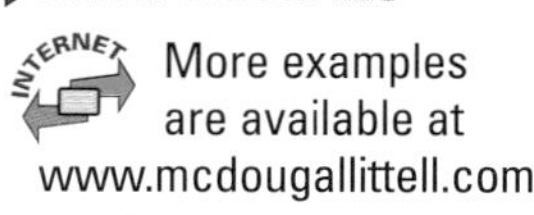

More examples are available at www.mcdougallittell.com

Goal 2 IDENTIFYING PARALLELOGRAMS

A **rectangle** is a parallelogram that has four right angles. A **square** is a rectangle with all sides the same length.

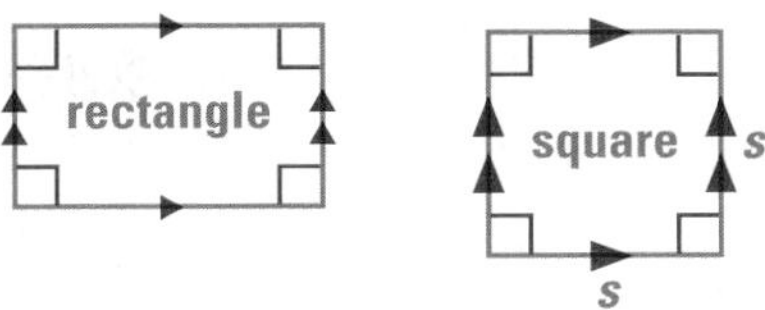

EXAMPLE 2 Classifying Quadrilaterals

Use as many words as possible to describe the figure: *square*, *rectangle*, *parallelogram*, or *quadrilateral*.

a.

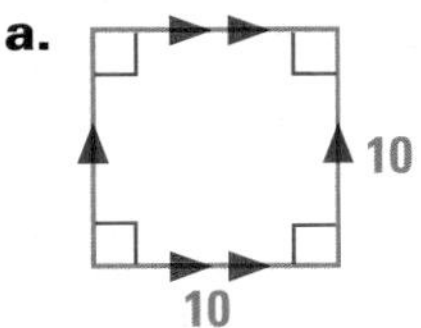

b.

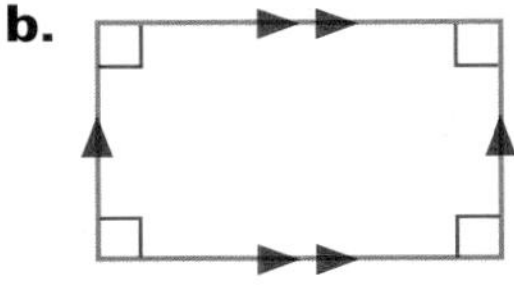

c.

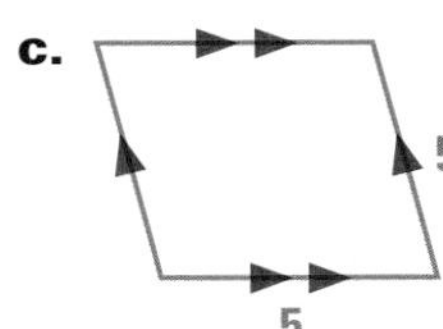

d.

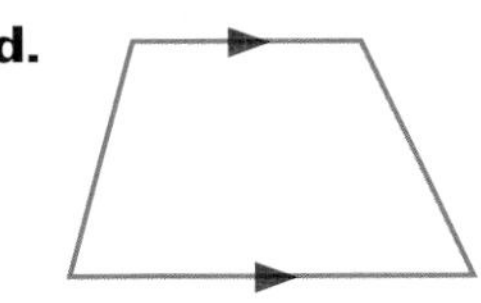

Solution

a. Square, rectangle, parallelogram, quadrilateral

b. Rectangle, parallelogram, quadrilateral

c. Parallelogram, quadrilateral

d. Quadrilateral

The Venn diagram at the right illustrates how four-sided figures are related. Any group (such as rectangles) that is part of a larger group (such as parallelograms) has all the properties of the larger group.

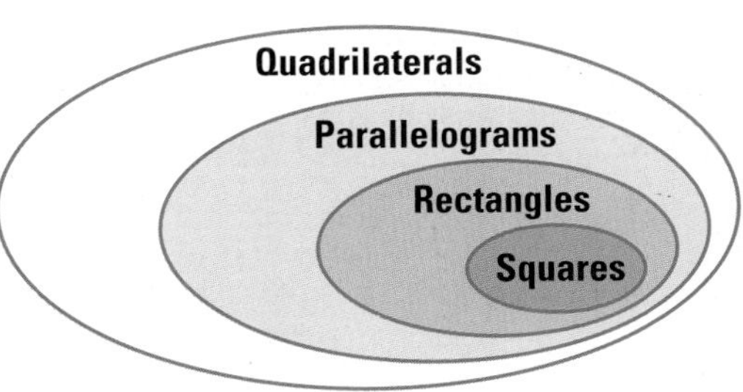

EXAMPLE 3 Drawing a Quadrilateral

To draw a parallelogram that has sides of the same length but is not a square, be sure that the figure has no right angles.

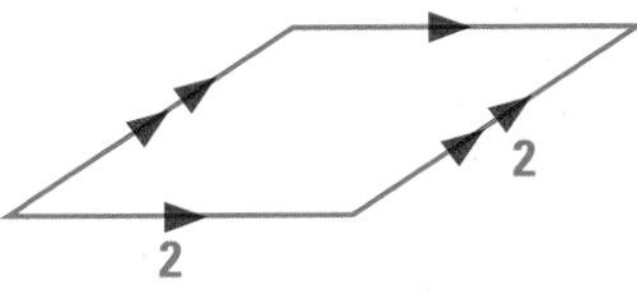

8.5 Exercises

Guided Practice

Find the indicated missing measures of the parallelogram.

1.

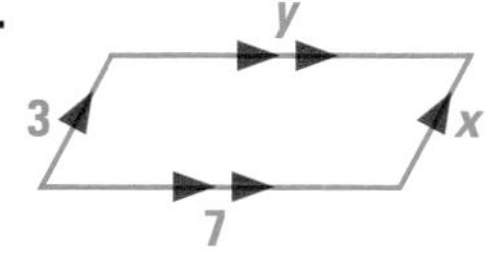

2.

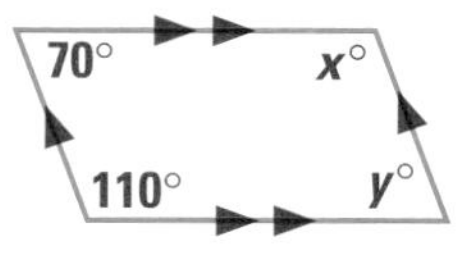

3.

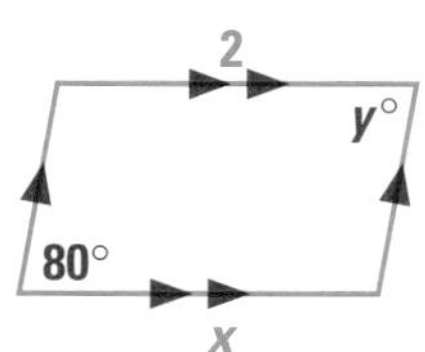

Match the figure with the sentence or sentences that describe it. You can use each sentence more than once.

4. Quadrilateral

5. Parallelogram

6. Rectangle

7. Square

A. It has four right angles.

B. It has four sides of equal length.

C. It has four sides.

D. It has opposite sides that are parallel.

In Exercises 8 and 9, use the figure shown.

8. Name one of each type of four-sided figure.

  a. Square **b.** Parallelogram

  c. Rectangle **d.** Quadrilateral

9. How many parallelograms does the figure contain?

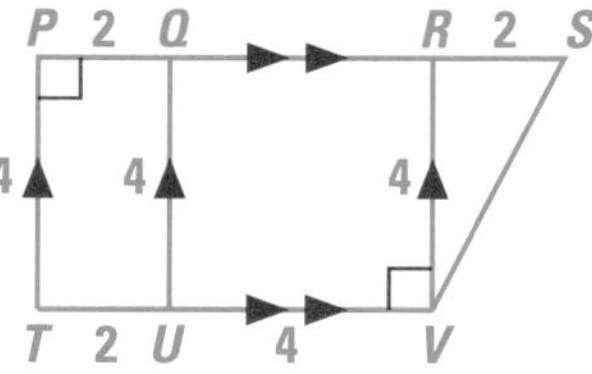

Practice and Problem Solving

Student Help

▶ **MORE PRACTICE**
Extra practice to help you master skills is on page 581.

In Exercises 10–15, find the indicated missing measures.

10.

x°, y°, 70°, 110°

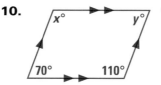

11.

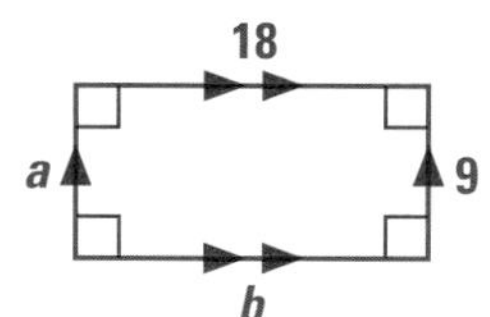

12.

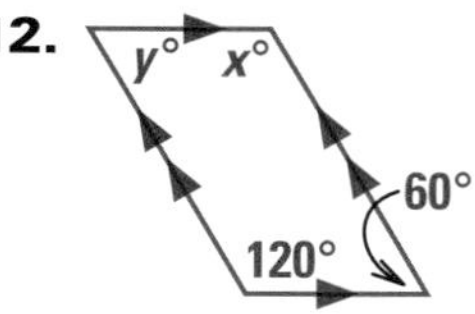

13. **14.**

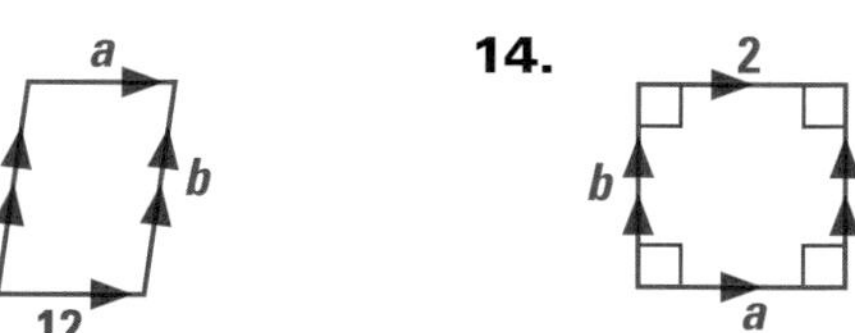

15.

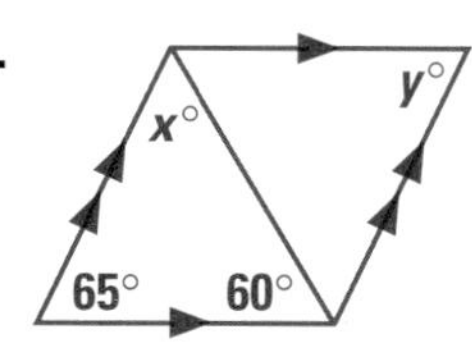

16. Jan says that the figure at the right is a parallelogram. Do you agree? Explain.

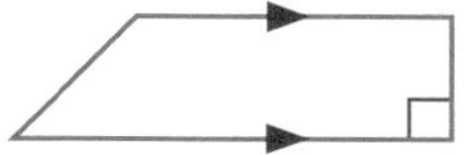

Link to History

BENJAMIN BANNEKER (1731–1806) was one of the surveyors appointed by President George Washington to plan Washington, D.C.

17. **History Link** Using the map at the right, identify four streets of Washington, D.C., that form a rectangle. Identify four streets that do *not* form a rectangle.

MATHEMATICAL REASONING In Exercises 18–21, decide whether the statement is *true* or *false*. If false, support your answer with a drawing.

18. All squares are parallelograms.

19. All rectangles are parallelograms.

20. All quadrilaterals are parallelograms.

21. All rectangles are squares.

Use as many words as possible to describe the figure: *square, rectangle, parallelogram,* or *quadrilateral*.

22. 

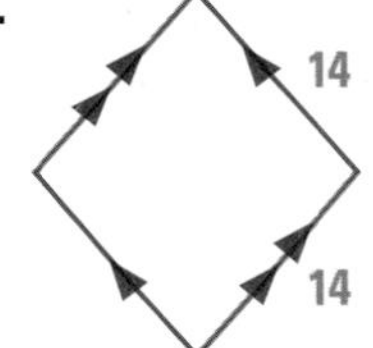

23.

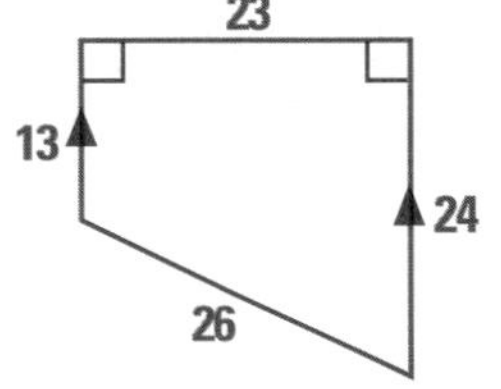

24.

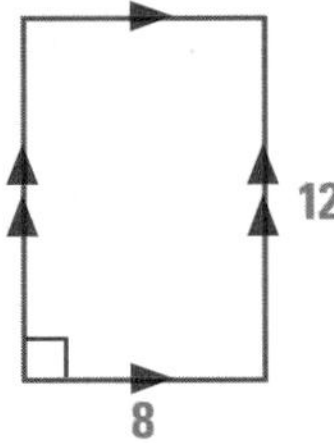

25. **MUSEUMS** The Louvre Museum in Paris is one of the largest art museums in the world. Visitors enter through a giant pyramid made of glass. Each side of the pyramid includes quadrilaterals and triangles. A model of one of the quadrilaterals is shown below. Is the quadrilateral a parallelogram? a rectangle? a square? Justify your answers.

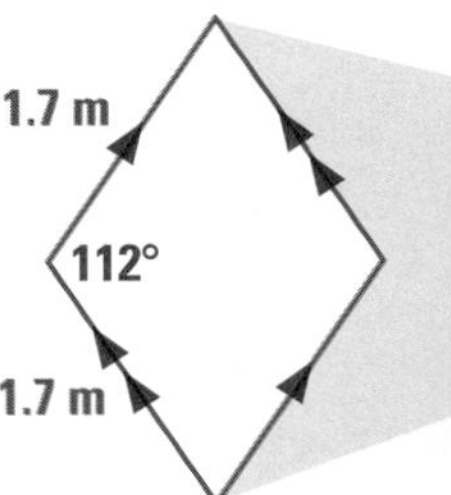

Draw the figure described.

26. A rectangle that is not a square

27. A quadrilateral that is not a parallelogram

28. A parallelogram that is neither a rectangle nor a square

29. CHALLENGE In parallelogram *ABDE*, find the value of *x*. Explain your reasoning.

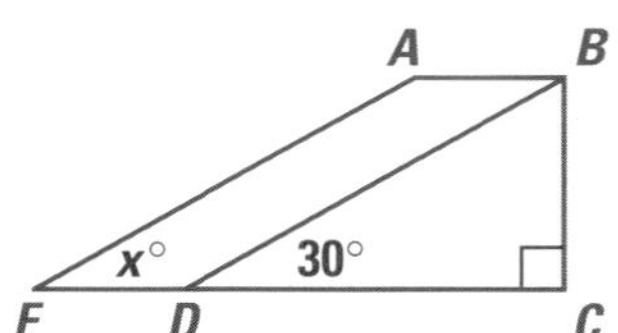

Multiple-Choice Practice

30. Which of the following statements is true?

Ⓐ All quadrilaterals have four right angles.

Ⓑ A parallelogram can have four right angles.

Ⓒ A quadrilateral can have three obtuse angles.

Ⓓ The sum of the angles of a parallelogram is 180°.

31. If $\angle A$ in parallelogram *ABCD* has a measure of 120°, what is the measure of the angle opposite $\angle A$?

Ⓕ 60° Ⓖ 90° Ⓗ 120° Ⓙ 180°

32. If side $\overline{AB}$ in parallelogram *ABCD* has a length of 5 inches, what is the length of the side opposite $\overline{AB}$?

Ⓐ 2 in. Ⓑ $2\frac{1}{2}$ in. Ⓒ 5 in. Ⓓ 10 in.

Mixed Review

WALKING **In Exercises 33–36, use the following information.** You are participating in a charity walk that is 15 miles long. It takes you 4 hours to walk 10 miles. 155 people take part in the event.

33. Write the unit rate for how fast you walked the first 10 miles. *(3.8)*

34. If you continue at this rate, how long will it take you to complete the charity walk? *(1.1)*

35. If you raise $4.75 for each mile that you walk, how much money will you raise by completing the charity walk? *(1.8)*

36. Identify any irrelevant information in the problem. *(1.1)*

Rewrite the improper fraction as a mixed number. *(2.7)*

37. $\frac{13}{4}$ **38.** $\frac{38}{9}$ **39.** $\frac{27}{24}$ **40.** $\frac{13}{8}$

41. SAVINGS You deposit $250 into a savings account. The annual interest rate is 5.5%. Find the simple interest you will earn in three months if you make no other deposits or withdrawals. *(7.6)*

Chapter 8 Mid-Chapter Test

Take this test as you would take a test in class. The answers to the exercises are given in the back of the book.

In Exercises 1–3, use the diagram. $m\angle 8$ is 55°.

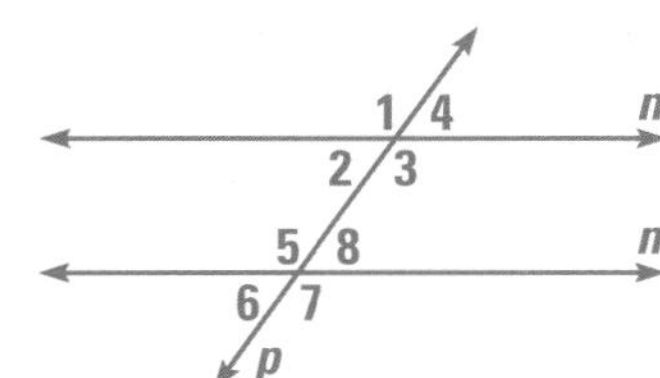

1. Name two pairs of adjacent angles.

2. Find the measure of $\angle 5$. Explain.

3. Name one angle that is congruent to $\angle 8$. Explain why they are congruent.

Use a centimeter ruler to measure the sides. Find the missing measure. Then use as many words as possible to describe the triangle: *equilateral, isosceles, scalene, acute, right,* or *obtuse*.

4.

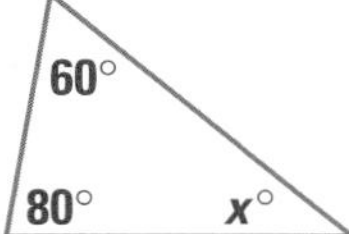

5.

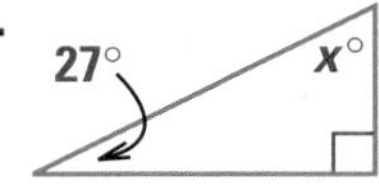

6.

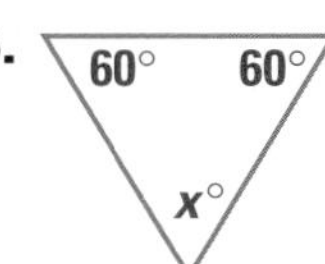

7.

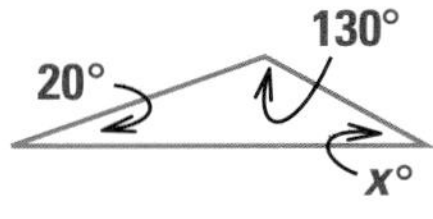

In Exercises 8–10, use the figure at the right.

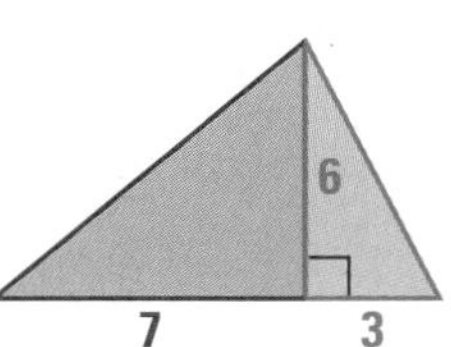

8. Find the area of the blue triangle.

9. Find the area of the red triangle.

10. Describe two ways to find the total area of both triangles.

Use as many words as possible to describe the figure: *square, rectangle, parallelogram,* or *quadrilateral*.

11.

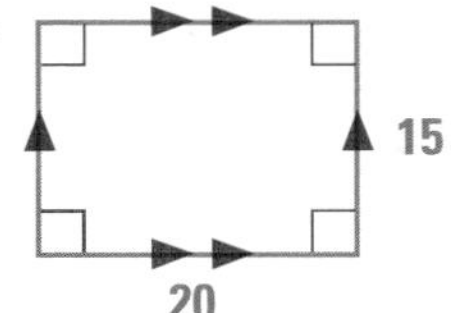

12

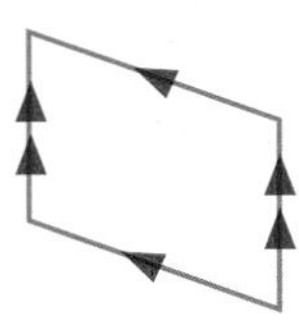

13.

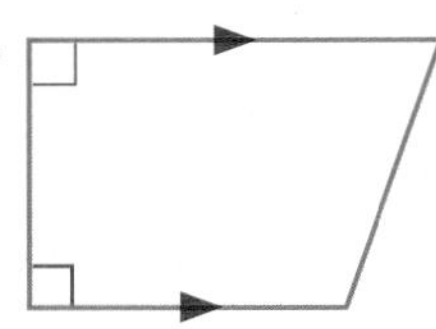

14.

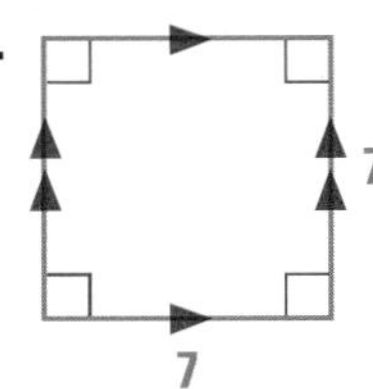

Assume that the figure at the right lies in a plane and that lines that look parallel are parallel.

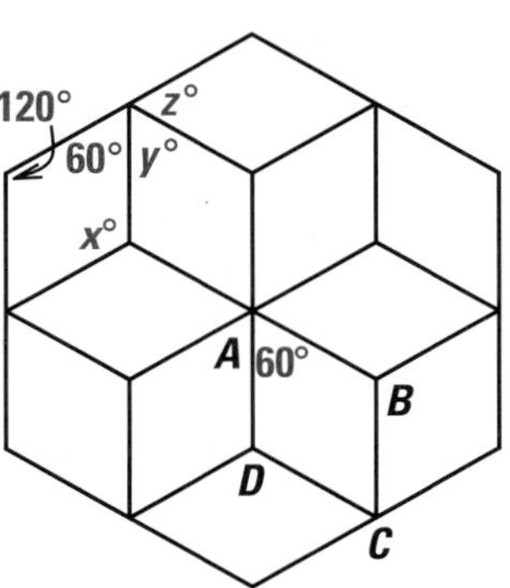

15. Use properties of parallelograms to find the value of x, of y, and of z.

16. In parallelogram $ABCD$, the length of $\overline{AB}$ is $\frac{1}{2}$ inch. Find the length of $\overline{CD}$.

8.6 Area of a Parallelogram

California Standards

In this lesson you'll:

- Use variables in expressions describing geometric quantities. (AF 3.1)
- Draw quadrilaterals from information given about them. (MG 2.3)

Goal 1 FINDING THE AREA OF A PARALLELOGRAM

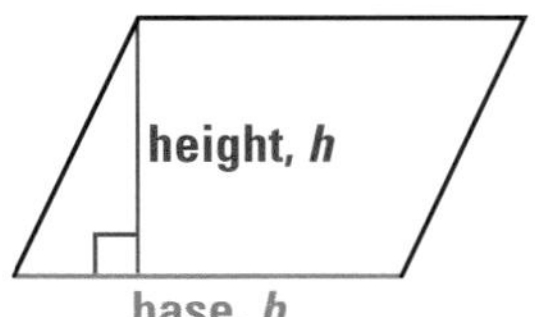

The diagram at the right shows the *base* and *height* of a parallelogram. Any side of a parallelogram can be the **base**. The **height** is the perpendicular distance between the base and the opposite side.

The formula for the area of a parallelogram follows from the formula for the area of a rectangle. The following diagram illustrates how the area of a parallelogram and the area of a rectangle are related.

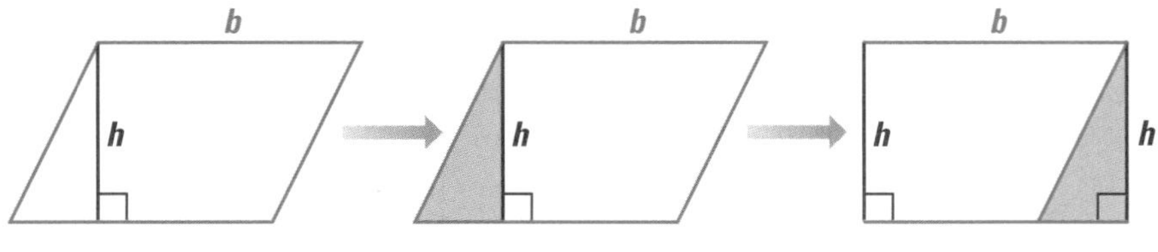

Start with parallelogram. **Cut off a right triangle.** **Form a rectangle.**

AREA OF A PARALLELOGRAM

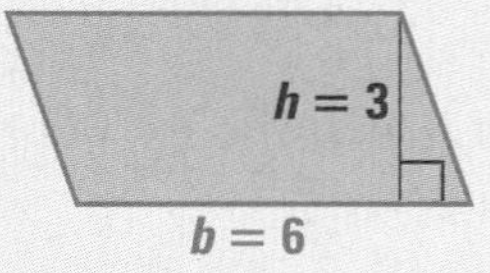

In Words The area of a parallelogram is the product of the base and the height.

In Algebra $A = bh$

In Arithmetic $A = 6 \cdot 3 = 18$ square units

EXAMPLE 1 Finding the Area of a Parallelogram

Find the area of the parallelogram.

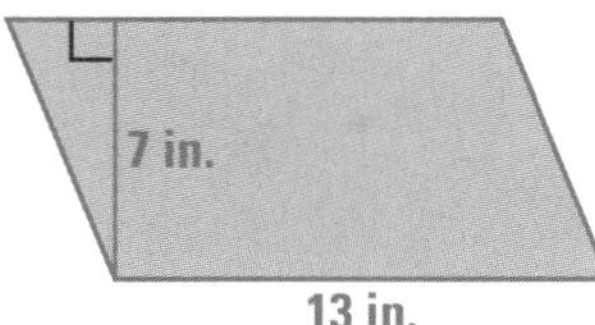

Solution

$A = bh$ Write area formula.

$= 13 \cdot 7$ Substitute 13 for *b* and 7 for *h*.

$= 91$ square inches Multiply.

ANSWER ▶ The area of the parallelogram is 91 square inches.

Goal 2 Solving Area Problems

Student Help

▶ **More Examples**

More examples are available at www.mcdougallittell.com

EXAMPLE 2 Estimating an Area

Use the map below to estimate the area of Tennessee.

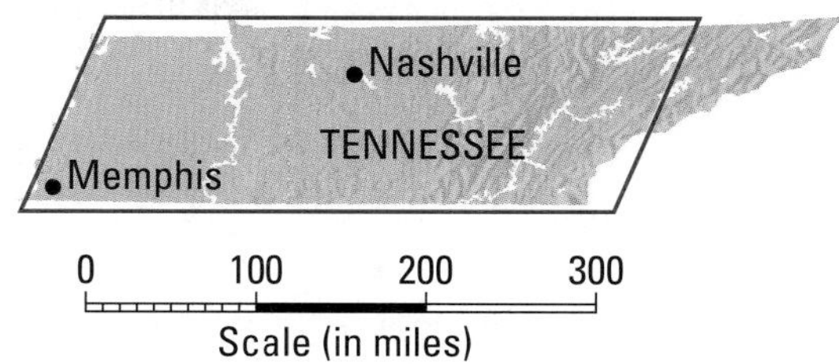

Solution

Begin by drawing a parallelogram that approximates the outline of the state. Then measure the base and height of the parallelogram. Use the map's scale to estimate the base and height in miles.

The base is about 350 miles, and the height is about 120 miles. Use these values in the formula for the area of a parallelogram.

$A = bh$ — Write area formula.

$= 350 \cdot 120$ — Substitute 350 for b and 120 for h.

$= 42{,}000$ square miles — Multiply.

ANSWER ▶ The area is about 42,000 square miles. (The actual area of Tennessee is 41,219 square miles.)

EXAMPLE 3 Comparing Two Areas

Draw a parallelogram. Then draw a straight line between two opposite corners to form two triangles. Do the two triangles that you drew have equal areas?

Solution

Draw a parallelogram as shown below.

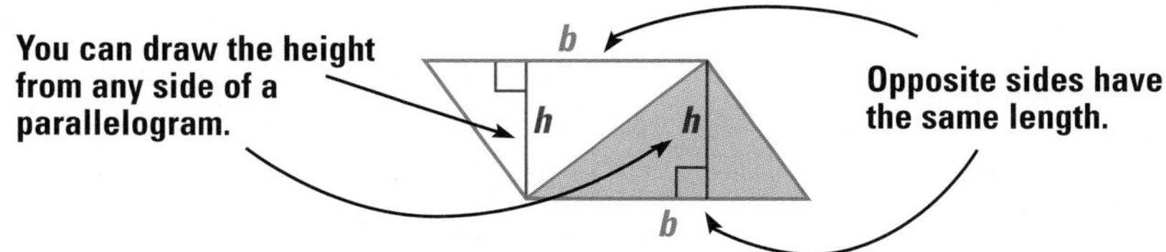

The area of each triangle is $A = \frac{1}{2}bh$, so the triangles do have equal areas. Notice that the area of the parallelogram is $A = \frac{1}{2}bh + \frac{1}{2}bh = bh$.

8.6 Exercises

Guided Practice

In Exercises 1–4, use the parallelogram at the right.

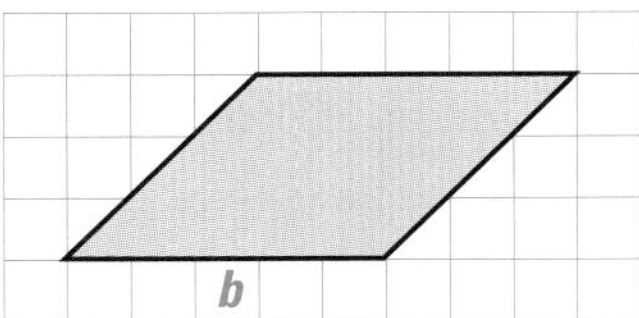

1. What is the length of the base b?

2. What is the height of the parallelogram?

3. Find the area of the parallelogram using the formula $A = bh$.

4. Does this parallelogram have the same area as a parallelogram with a base of 3 and a height of 5? Explain.

5. ERROR ANALYSIS Describe and correct the error.

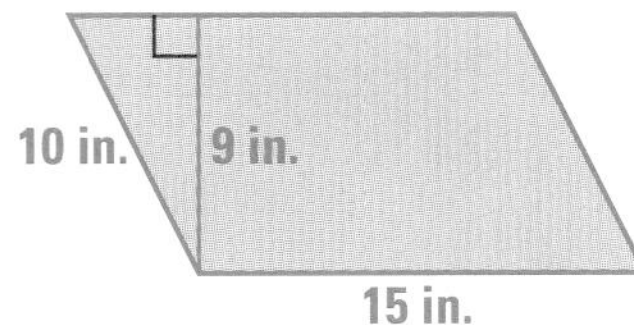

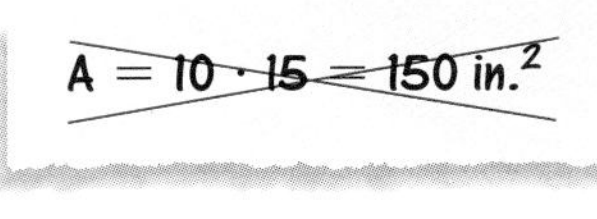

ALGEBRA **Find the indicated missing measure in the parallelogram.**

6. $A = 84 \text{ cm}^2$

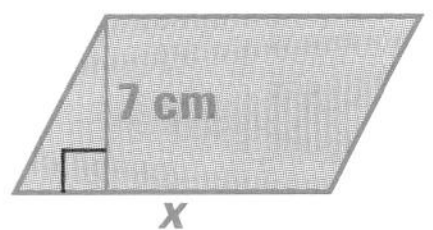

7. $A = 24 \text{ in.}^2$

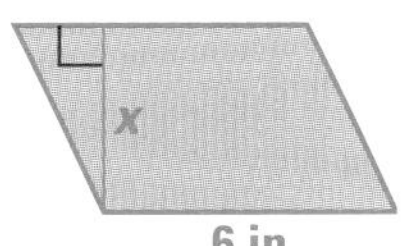

8. $A = 90 \text{ m}^2$

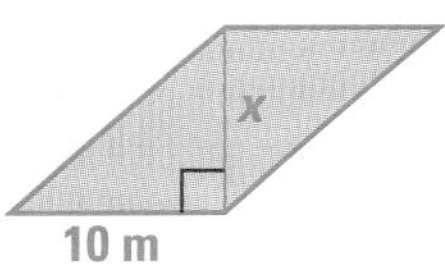

Practice and Problem Solving

Student Help

▶ **MORE PRACTICE**
Extra practice to help you master skills is on page 581.

In Exercises 9–11, find the area of the parallelogram.

9.

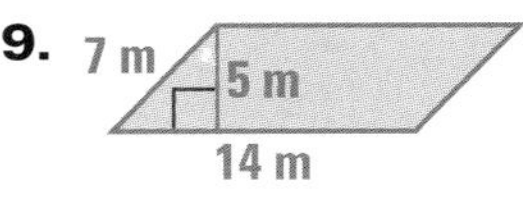

10.

8 ft
7 ft
7 ft

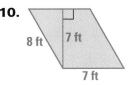

11.

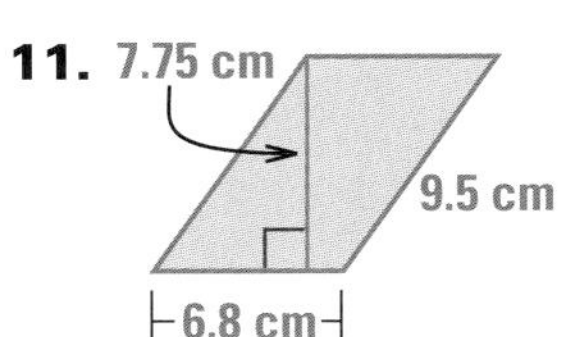

12. Find the area of each parallelogram. Use a table to organize your results. Describe the pattern.

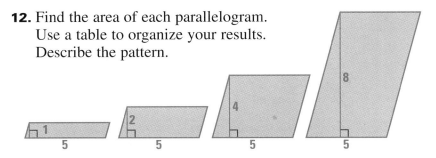

1
5
2
5
4
5
8
5

ALGEBRA Find the indicated missing measure in the parallelogram.

13. $A = 238 \text{ in.}^2$

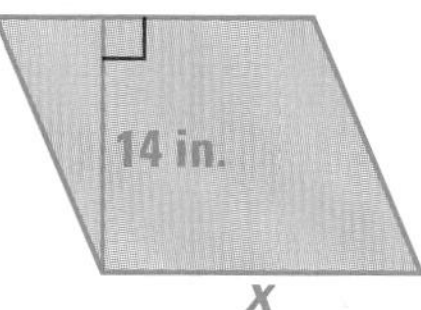

14. $A = 58.08 \text{ m}^2$

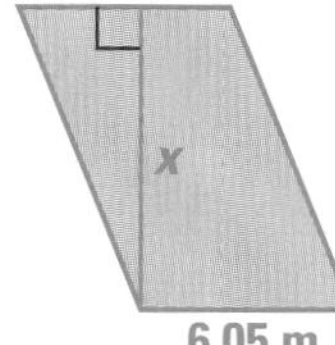

15. $A = 9\frac{5}{8} \text{ ft}^2$

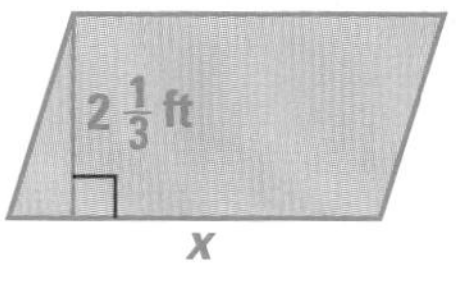

16. Copy the parallelogram. Divide it into two right triangles and a rectangle.

a. Find the area of each part. Then add the three areas to find the area of the parallelogram.

b. Compare the result from part (a) with what you get using the formula for the area of a parallelogram.

Link to Art

QUILTS Notice that the parallelograms in this quilt meet at corners. Where three parallelograms meet, each angle is 120°. Where six meet, each angle is 60°.

In Exercises 17–19, draw two different parallelograms that have the given area.

17. 12 square units

18. 30 square units

19. 36 square units

20. QUILTS The quilt at the left is made up of parallelograms. Each has a base of 2 inches and a height of $1\frac{3}{4}$ inches. What is the area of each parallelogram?

21. CHALLENGE Are the areas of the two parallelograms equal? Explain.

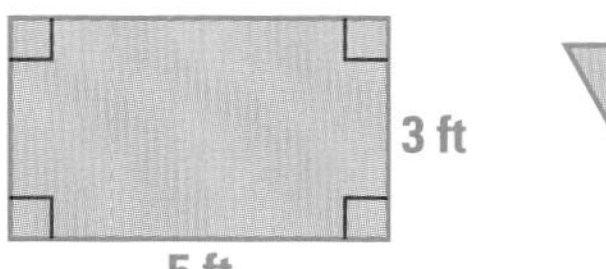

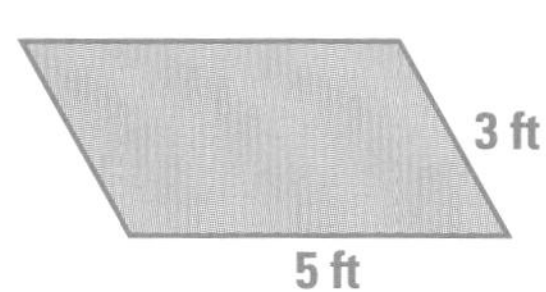

Multiple-Choice Practice

▶ In Exercise 22 it may help you to begin by identifying the base and the height.

22. Which expression can you use to find the area of the parallelogram?

Ⓐ 5×9 Ⓑ 4×9

Ⓒ 4×6 Ⓓ 3×5

5, 4, 3, 6

23. What is the area of the parallelogram?

Ⓕ 15 square units Ⓖ 39 square units

Ⓗ 60 square units Ⓙ 75 square units

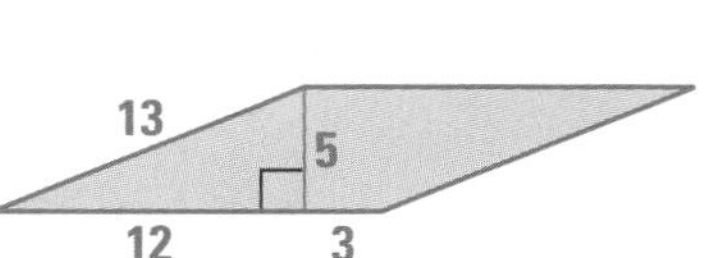

DEVELOPING CONCEPTS
Investigating Circumference

For use with Lesson 8.7

California Standards

- Investigate geometric patterns and describe them algebraically. (AF 3.0)
- Understand the concept of a constant such as π. (MG 1.1)
- Note the method of deriving the solution and demonstrate a conceptual understanding of the derivation by solving similar problems. (MR 3.2)

MATERIALS

- String
- Scissors
- Metric ruler
- Circular objects
- Calculator

A *circle* is the set of all points in a plane that are an equal distance from a given point called the *center*. The *diameter* is the distance across a circle through the center. The *circumference* is the distance around a circle.

SAMPLE 1 Comparing Circumference and Diameter

You can find a relationship between the circumference C and the diameter d of a circle. Use the circular cup shown.

Here's How

1. Find the diameter by laying a metric ruler across the circle so that the ruler's edge passes through the center of the circle. The diameter is about 5.3 centimeters.

2. To find the circumference, wrap a string around the cup. Then unwrap the string and measure the length of the string using a metric ruler. The length of the string is about 16 centimeters, so the circumference C is about 16 centimeters.

3. To find the relationship between the circumference and the diameter, find the ratio of the circumference to the diameter, $\frac{C}{d}$, to the nearest hundredth.

$$\frac{16}{5.3} \approx 3.02$$

The circumference is about three times the diameter.

Try These

1. Select four circular objects, such as a jar lid, a round waste basket, a CD, or a plate. Find the diameter and the circumference of each circular shape. Then find the ratio $\frac{C}{d}$ to the nearest hundredth. What do you notice about the ratios?

2. **MATHEMATICAL REASONING** If Circle 1 has five times the diameter of Circle 2, how does the circumference of Circle 1 compare with the circumference of Circle 2? Explain your reasoning.

Student Help

▶ **LOOK BACK**
For help with polygons, see page 31.

SAMPLE 2 Comparing Circumference and Diameter

You can use polygons with equal sides drawn inside and outside of a circle to approximate the ratio $\frac{C}{d}$.

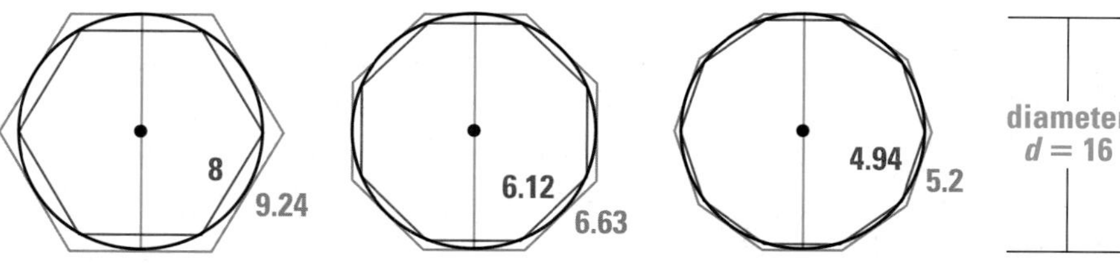

Here's How

1. Use the perimeter P of each polygon as an approximation of the circumference C of the circle. Then find the ratio of the perimeter P of the polygon to the diameter d of the circle.

Polygons Inside Circle		Polygons Outside Circle	
Perimeter (cm)	Ratio $\frac{P}{d}$	Perimeter (cm)	Ratio $\frac{P}{d}$
$8 \cdot 6 = 48$	$\frac{48}{16} = 3$	$9.24 \cdot 6 = 55.44$	$\frac{55.44}{16} \approx 3.47$
$6.12 \cdot 8 = 48.96$	$\frac{48.96}{16} = 3.06$	$6.63 \cdot 8 = 53.04$	$\frac{53.04}{16} \approx 3.32$
$4.94 \cdot 10 = 49.4$	$\frac{49.4}{16} \approx 3.09$	$5.2 \cdot 10 = 52$	$\frac{52}{16} = 3.25$

2. As the number of sides increases, the ratios get closer together. This suggests that the ratio $\frac{C}{d}$ is some number between 3.09 and 3.25. In fact, the ratio $\frac{C}{d}$ is the same for all circles and is denoted by the Greek letter π. A decimal approximation for π is 3.14.

Try These

Find the circumference given the diameter of a circle. Use $\pi \approx 3.14$.

3. $d = 10$ inches **4.** $d = 12$ centimeters **5.** $d = 9$ feet

6. **MATHEMATICAL REASONING** Write a formula for the circumference of a circle in terms of its diameter.

8.7 Circumference of a Circle

In this lesson you'll:

- Understand the concept of π and know the formula for the circumference of a circle. (MG 1.1)
- Know common estimates of π and use these values to estimate and calculate the circumference of a circle. (MG 1.2)
- Use variables in expressions describing geometric quantities. (AF 3.1)

Goal 1 Finding the Circumference of a Circle

A **circle** is the set of all points in a plane that are an equal distance from a given point, the **center**. The distance from a point on a circle to its center is the **radius** r. The distance across a circle through its center is the **diameter** d. The distance around a circle is called the **circumference** C.

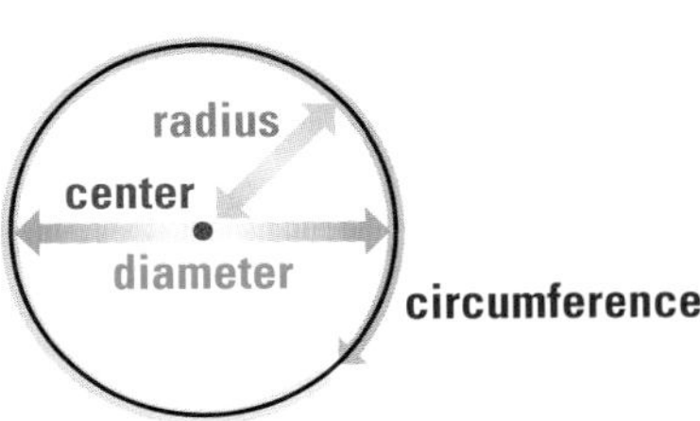

The ratio of any circle's circumference to its diameter is a number represented by the Greek letter pi, π.

Commonly used approximations for π are 3.14 and $\frac{22}{7}$. For exact measurements, use π.

Circumference of a Circle

In Words The circumference of a circle is the product of π and the diameter d.

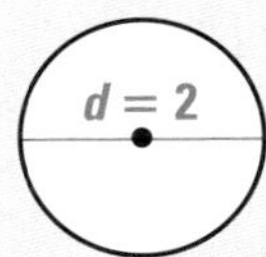

In Algebra $C = \pi d$

In Arithmetic $C = \pi(2) = 2\pi$ units — Exact circumference

$C \approx 3.14 \cdot 2 = 6.28$ units — Approximate circumference

EXAMPLE 1 Finding Circumference

Find the circumference of each circle.

a.

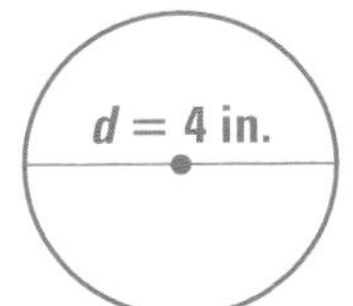

b.

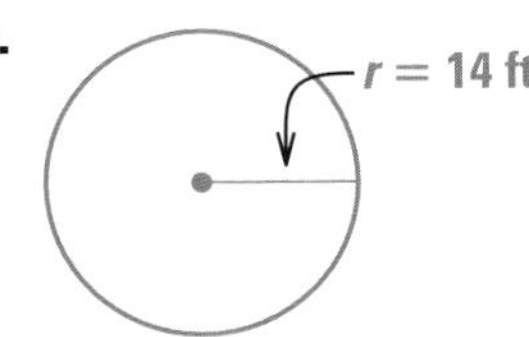

Solution

a. $C = \pi d$

$\approx 3.14 \cdot 4$

$= 12.56$ inches

b. First find the diameter:

$d = 2r = 2 \cdot 14 = 28$ feet

Then find the circumference.

$C = \pi d$

$\approx \frac{22}{7} \cdot 28$

$= 88$ feet

Student Help

Study Tip
The Greek letter π is a nonterminating, nonrepeating decimal whose first few digits are 3.14159. . . .

Goal 2 USING CIRCUMFERENCE TO SOLVE PROBLEMS

As you saw in Developing Concepts 8.7, page 386, the circumference of a circle is about three times the length of the diameter.

Link to Music

DRUMS Size, shape, and the tension of the drumhead determine the sound a drum makes. Generally speaking, the greater the circumference of the drumhead, the lower the sound.

EXAMPLE 2 Finding Circumference

DRUMS Find the circumference of the drum.

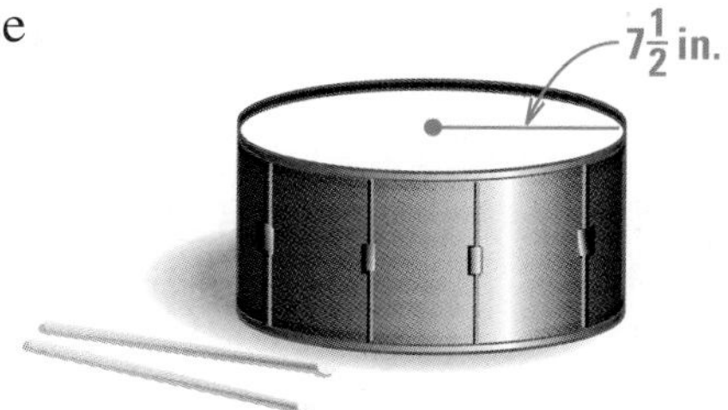

Solution

First find the diameter of the drum. The diameter is twice the radius.

$d = 2r$	The diameter is twice the radius.
$= 2 \cdot 7\frac{1}{2}$	Substitute $7\frac{1}{2}$ for r.
$= 15$ inches	Multiply.

Then use the diameter to find the circumference.

$C = \pi d$	Write the formula for circumference.
$\approx 3.14 \cdot 15$	Substitute 3.14 for π and 15 for d.
$= 47.1$ inches	Multiply.

ANSWER ▶ The circumference is about 47.1 inches.

EXAMPLE 3 Finding Diameter and Radius

BASKETBALL A basketball hoop has a circumference of about 56.5 inches. Find the diameter and the radius of the hoop.

Solution

You are given that $C \approx 56.5$ inches. To find d, use the formula for the circumference and solve for d.

$C = \pi d$	Write formula for circumference.
$56.5 \approx 3.14 \cdot d$	Substitute 56.5 for C and 3.14 for π.
$\frac{56.5}{3.14} \approx \frac{3.14 \cdot d}{3.14}$	Divide each side by 3.14.
$18.0 \approx d$	Use a calculator.

ANSWER ▶ The diameter is about 18 inches. The radius is about 9 inches.

8.7 Exercises

Guided Practice

In Exercises 1–3, measurements of one circle are given. Tell whether the measurement is the *radius*, the *diameter*, or the *circumference*.

1. 8 inches

2. 25.12 inches

3. 4 inches

4. Find the exact circumference of a circle with a diameter of 4.5 feet.

5. Find the approximate diameter and radius of a circle with a circumference of 22 centimeters.

Practice and Problem Solving

Student Help

▶**MORE PRACTICE** Extra practice to help you master skills is on page 581.

Find the circumference given the diameter. Use $\pi \approx 3.14$.

6. $d = 1.5$ ft

7. $d = 121$ mm

8. $d = 10.5$ in.

Find the circumference of the circle given the radius. Use $\pi \approx 3.14$.

9. 1 meter

10. 20 inches

11. 10.25 feet

In Exercises 12–14, match the object with its circumference.

A. $\frac{6}{25}$ feet

B. 75 feet

C. $3\frac{7}{10}$ feet

12. A pizza

13. A quarter

14. Base of a lighthouse

Use the given circumference of a circle to find the diameter.

15. 12 inches

16. 255 meters

17. 450 yards

18. 15.1 centimeters

19. 45.3 feet

20. 880 meters

21. 50 yards

22. 25.3 feet

23. 14.32 meters

ALGEBRA Find the dimension labeled *x*. Use $\pi \approx 3.14$.

24. $C = 94.2$ meters

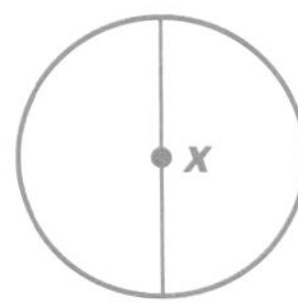

25. $C = 1$ inch

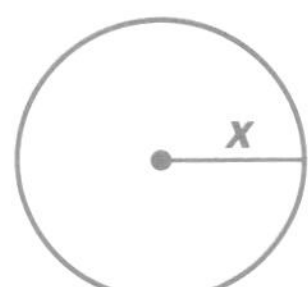

26. $C = 11.3$ meters

Student Help

▶ **HOMEWORK HELP**

Extra help with problem solving in Ex. 27 is available at www.mcdougallittell.com

27. **BICYCLE TIRE** A bicycle tire rim has a diameter of 24.5 inches, and the tire is 2.25 inches thick. Find the circumference of the outside of the tire.

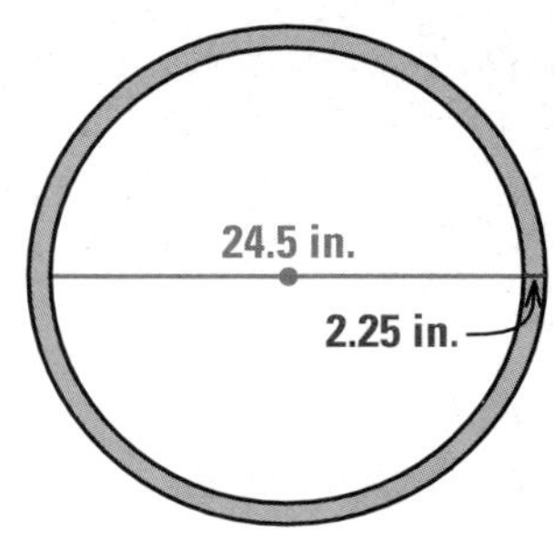

28. **AMUSEMENT PARK** You ride a Ferris wheel that has a circumference of 108 feet. Estimate the diameter of the Ferris wheel. (Use $\pi \approx 3.14$.)

GEOMETRY **Find the perimeter and the area of the rectangle.**

29.

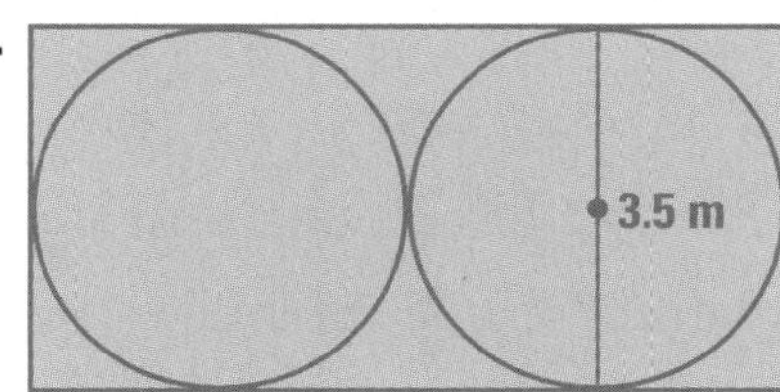

30.

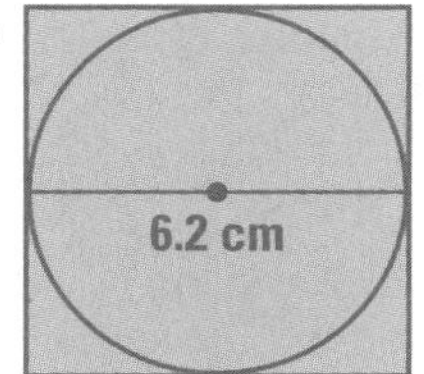

31. **MATHEMATICAL REASONING** Use the fact that the length of a diameter of a circle is twice the length of a radius ($d = 2r$). Rewrite the formula for the circumference of a circle in terms of the radius.

32. **MATHEMATICAL REASONING** How does the circumference of a circle change when its diameter is doubled? when its diameter is tripled? Give examples to support your answer.

33. **MATHEMATICAL REASONING** How does the circumference of a circle change when its radius is doubled? Explain your reasoning.

34. ***History Link*** The diagram shows the Rotunda of the Capitol Building in Washington, D.C. Around the edge of the Rotunda are 11 statues and a display case. Find the approximate circumference of the Rotunda.

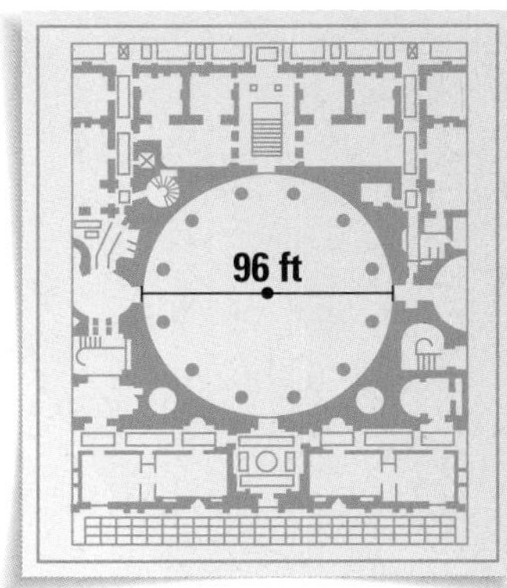

THE ROTUNDA The top of the Rotunda is the dome of the Capitol Building.

35. **CHALLENGE** About how far apart are the statues in Exercise 34? Is your estimate high or low? Explain.

Multiple-Choice Practice

36. Each tire on your bicycle has a diameter of 26 inches. About how far will you travel when the tires make one complete revolution?

(A) 163.36 in. (B) 81.64 in. (C) 40.84 in. (D) 26 in.

37. A circle has a circumference of about 226.08 centimeters. Which value best approximates the radius of the circle?

(F) 1017 cm (G) 226 cm (H) 72 cm (J) 36 cm

8.8 Area of a Circle

In this lesson you'll:

- Know the formula for the area of a circle. (MG 1.1)
- Know common estimates of π and use these values to estimate and calculate the area of a circle. (MG 1.2)
- Use variables in expressions describing geometric quantities. (AF 3.1)

Goal 1 The Area of a Circle

EXAMPLE 1 Estimating the Area of a Circle

A circle has a radius of 3. Estimate its area.

Solution

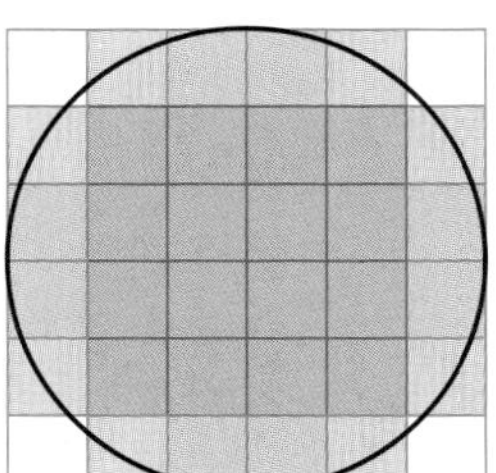

Draw a 6-by-6 grid. Then draw the circle on the grid. The grid has 36 small squares.

- **16** are entirely inside the circle.
- **8** are almost entirely inside the circle.
- **8** are about half inside the circle.

ANSWER ▶ You can estimate the area of the circle to be about

$$16 + 8 + 8\left(\frac{1}{2}\right) = 28 \text{ square units.}$$

Area of a Circle

In Words The area of a circle is the product of π and the square of radius r.

In Algebra $A = \pi r^2$

In Arithmetic $A = \pi \cdot 3^2 = 9\pi$ square units **Exact**

$A \approx 3.14 \cdot 3^2 = 28.26$ square units **Approximate**

$r = 3$

Notice that the actual area of the circle in Example 1 is $9\pi \approx 28.26$ square units, slightly greater than the estimate.

EXAMPLE 2 Finding the Area of a Circle

Find the area of the circle.

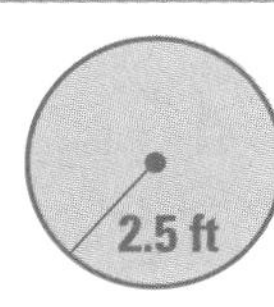

Solution

$A = \pi r^2$	Write formula for area of a circle.
$\approx 3.14 \cdot 2.5^2$	Substitute 3.14 for π and 2.5 for r.
$= 19.625 \text{ ft}^2$	Multiply.

ANSWER ▶ The area of the circle is about 19.6 square feet.

Goal 2 SOLVING AREA PROBLEMS

Link to Technology

COMPACT DISCS The 12 centimeter diameter of a CD was chosen as the standard because a disc that size could contain Beethoven's entire Ninth Symphony.

EXAMPLE 3 Finding the Area of a Circle

A compact disc has a diameter of 12.1 centimeters. Find the area of the compact disc.

Solution

The radius of the compact disc is one half the diameter, or 6.05 centimeters.

$A = \pi r^2$	Write formula for area of a circle.
$\approx 3.14 \cdot 6.05^2$	Substitute 3.14 for π and 6.05 for r.
$= 114.93185 \text{ cm}^2$	Multiply.

ANSWER ▶ The area of the disc is about 114.9 square centimeters.

EXAMPLE 4 Finding the Difference between Areas

You use a rotating sprinkler to water a circular portion of your rectangular yard. Find the area of the yard that is *not* watered.

Solution

Start by finding the area of the entire yard. The area of the yard *not* watered is the area of the entire yard minus the circular area that *is* watered.

First find the area of the entire yard.

$A = \ell w$	Write the formula for area of a rectangle.
$= 100 \cdot 40$	Substitute 100 for ℓ and 40 for w.
$= 4000 \text{ ft}^2$	Multiply.

Then find the area of the circular portion that is watered.

$A = \pi r^2$	Write formula for area of a circle.
$\approx 3.14 \cdot 15^2$	Substitute 3.14 for π and 15 for r.
$= 706.5 \text{ ft}^2$	Multiply.

Subtract to find the area that is not watered.

$4000 - 706.5 = 3293.5 \text{ ft}^2$

ANSWER ▶ An area of about 3300 square feet is not watered.

8.8 Exercises

Guided Practice

In Exercises 1–4, match the expression with the measurement.

A. πd **B.** πr^2 **C.** $2\ell + 2w$ **D.** bh

1. Circumference of a circle

2. Area of a parallelogram

3. Perimeter of a rectangle

4. Area of a circle

5. **DRUMS** A snare drum and a bass drum are shown at the right. The surface that is hit is called the drumhead. Find the exact area of each drumhead.

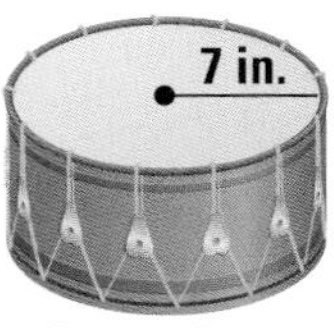

Snare drum

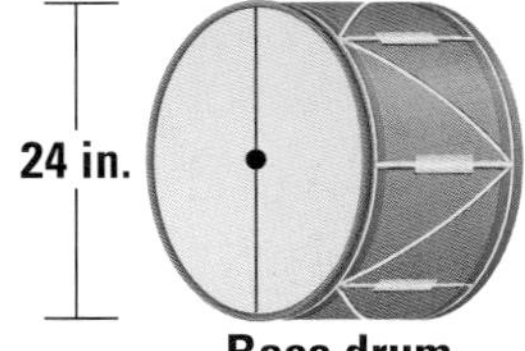

Bass drum

6. **PAINTING** You are painting a ceiling, part of which is covered by a round light fixture 2 feet in diameter. The ceiling is 12 feet by 8 feet. Find the area of the region you will paint.

Practice and Problem Solving

> **Student Help**
>
> ▶ **MORE PRACTICE**
> Extra practice to help you master skills is on page 581.

Find the area of the circle. Use $\pi \approx 3.14$.

7. $d = 30.5$ cm

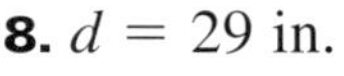

8. $d = 29$ in.

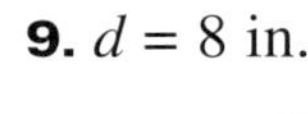

9. $d = 8$ in.

Find the area of the circle. Give both exact and approximate answers.

10. Radius = 5 feet

11. Diameter = 20 centimeters

12. Diameter = 19 inches

13. Radius = 14 miles

Use the formulas for the area of a circle and of a parallelogram to find the area of the shaded region. Use $\pi \approx \frac{22}{7}$.

14.

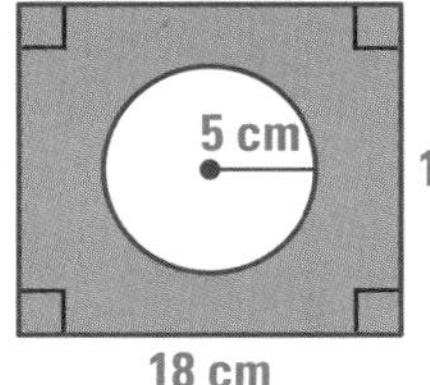

15.

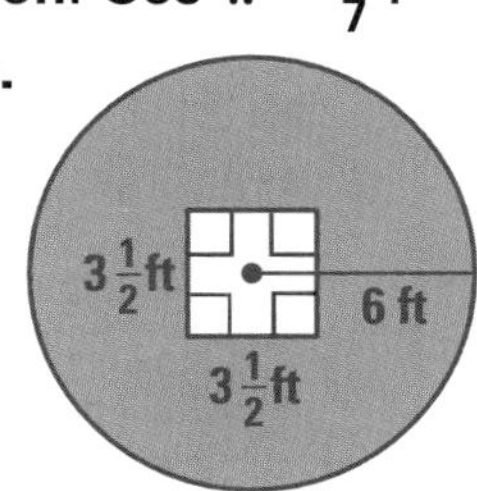

16.

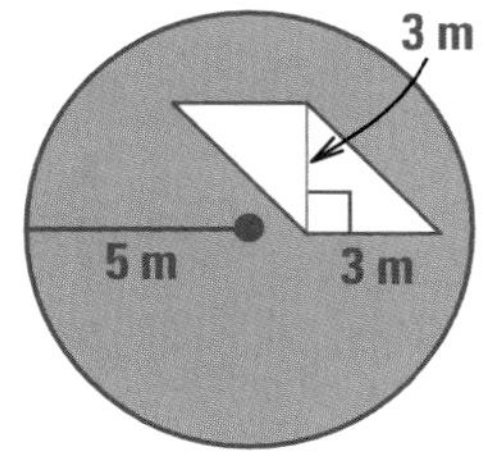

RADAR In Exercises 17 and 18, use the following information. An air traffic control radar screen is circular and has a radius of 12 inches.

17. Find the exact area of the radar screen.

18. On the screen, one inch represents 0.5 nautical miles. Find the approximate area of the region being monitored. Use $\pi \approx 3.14$.

MATHEMATICAL REASONING In Exercises 19–21, complete the statement using *less than, greater than,* or *equal to.* Explain your reasoning.

19. A circle with a radius of 3 meters has an area __?__ 27 square meters.

20. A circle with a diameter of 10 inches has an area __?__ 100 square inches.

21. A circle with a radius of 7 feet has an area that is __?__ the area of a circle with a diameter of 13 feet.

ARCHERY In Exercises 22–25, find the area of the target that represents the indicated score. The target has a radius of 2 feet. Each ring on the target is the same width.

22. 10 points

23. 5 or more points

24. 1 or 2 points

25. More than 2 points

26. ***Chapter Opener Link*** Look back at Exercise 1 on page 355. Find the area of the wall to be covered. Be sure to subtract the area of the door and the area of the window.

27. **CHALLENGE** The circle has a radius of 4 centimeters. The shaded region in the circle has an area of 10.05 square centimeters. What percent of the circle's area is shaded?

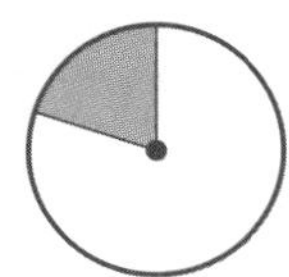

Multiple-Choice Practice

28. What is the approximate area of a circle with diameter 12 ft?

Ⓐ 18.84 ft^2 Ⓑ 37.68 ft^2 Ⓒ 75.36 ft^2 Ⓓ 113.04 ft^2

29. Find the exact area of the shaded region.

Ⓕ 5π cm^2 Ⓖ 15.7 cm^2

Ⓗ 75π cm^2 Ⓙ 235.5 cm^2

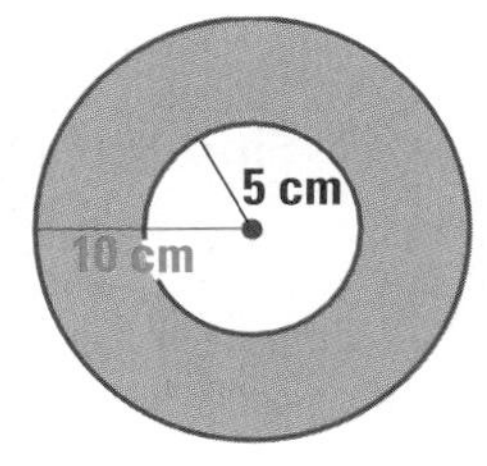

Chapter 8

Chapter Summary and Review

VOCABULARY

- **plane,** *p. 357*
- **parallel lines,** *p. 357*
- **vertical angles,** *p. 357*
- **congruent,** *p. 357*
- **complementary, supplementary angles,** *p. 358*
- **vertex,** *p. 358*
- **adjacent angles,** *p. 358*
- **right angle,** *p. 359*
- **perpendicular lines,** *p. 359*
- **acute, obtuse angles,** *p. 363*
- **equilateral, isosceles, scalene triangles,** *p. 366*
- **acute, right, obtuse triangles,** *p. 367*
- **base, height** *pp. 372, 382*
- **quadrilateral,** *p. 376*
- **parallelogram,** *p. 376*
- **rectangle,** *p. 377*
- **square,** *p. 377*
- **circle,** *p. 388* **center, radius, diameter,** *p. 388*
- **circumference,** *p. 388*

8.1 INTERSECTING LINES AND ANGLE MEASURES

Examples on pp. 357–359

EXAMPLE **In the diagram the measure of $\angle 5$ is 35° and the measure of $\angle 1$ is 35°. Find the measure of $\angle 2$.**

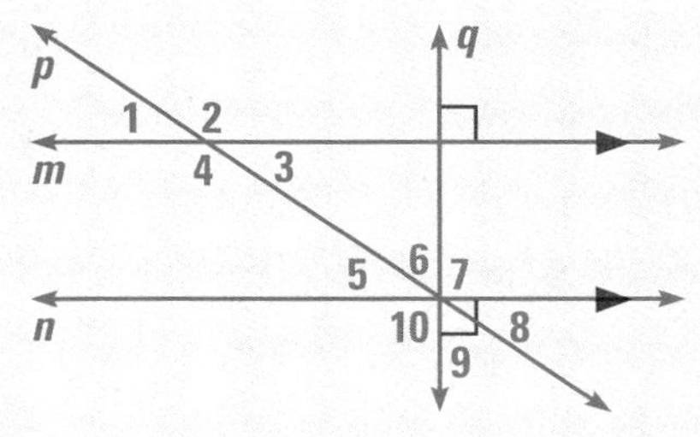

$\angle 1$ and $\angle 2$ are supplements, so the sum of their angles is 180°.

$35° + m\angle 2 = 180°$

$m\angle 2 = 145°$ The measure of $\angle 2$ is 145°.

1. Find the measures of $\angle 7$, $\angle 8$, and $\angle 9$ in the diagram above.

8.2 ANGLES OF A TRIANGLE

Examples on pp. 362–363

EXAMPLE To find the measure of $\angle A$ use the fact that the sum of the measures of the angles of a triangle is 180°.

Measure of $\angle A = 180° - 35° - 55° = 90°$

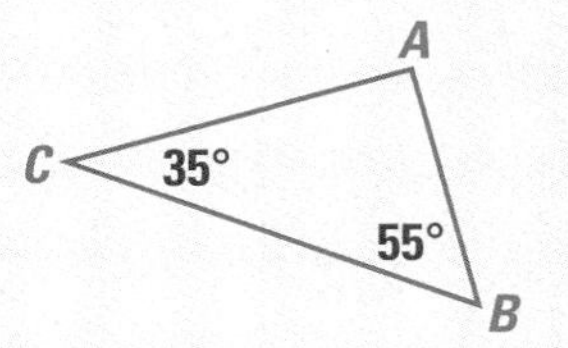

Find the value of *x*.

2.

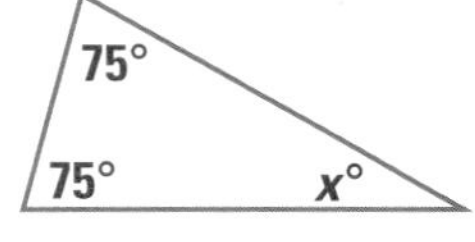

3.

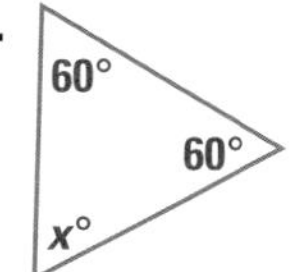

4.

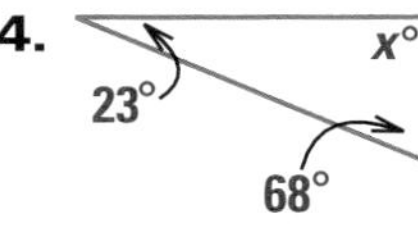

5.

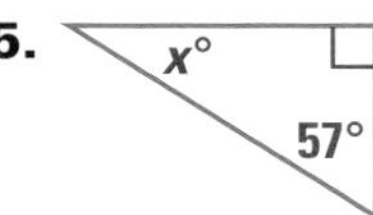

8.3 CLASSIFYING TRIANGLES

Examples on pp. 366–367

EXAMPLE **Classify the triangle by its angles. Use a centimeter ruler to measure its sides and classify it by its sides.**

a. 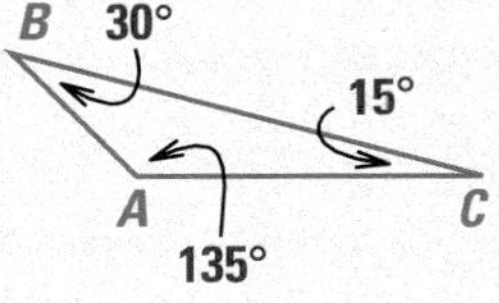

b. 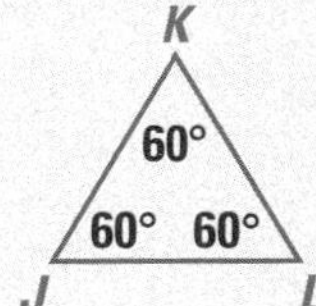

c. 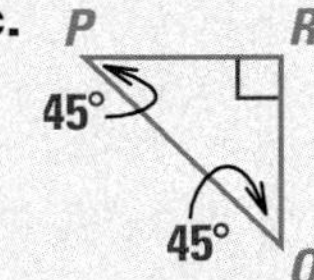

Solution

a. Obtuse, scalene **b.** Acute, equilateral **c.** Right, isosceles

Identify the triangle as *scalene, isosceles,* or *equilateral.*

6. 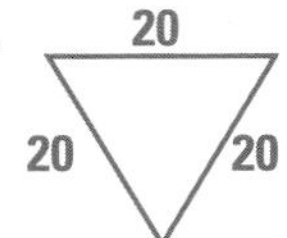

7. 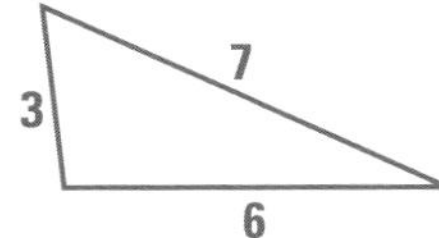

8. 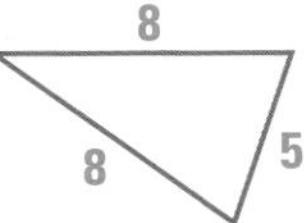

9. 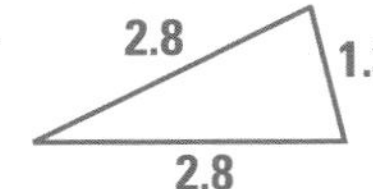

Identify the triangle as *obtuse, right,* or *acute.*

10. 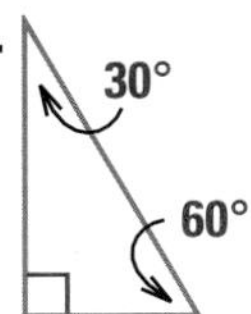

11. 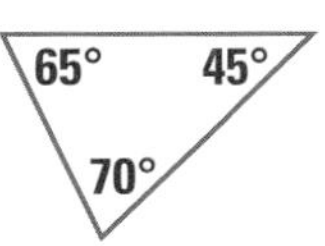

12. 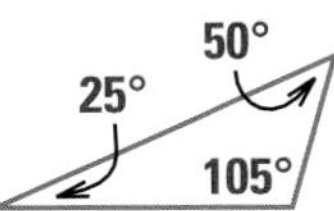

13. 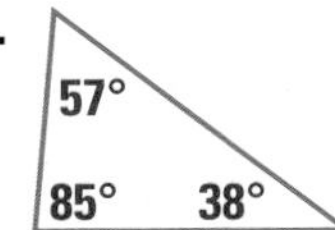

8.4 AREA OF A TRIANGLE

Examples on pp. 372–373

EXAMPLE $\text{Area} = \frac{1}{2} \cdot \text{Base} \cdot \text{Height}$

$= \frac{1}{2} \cdot 6 \cdot 3$

$= 9 \text{ m}^2$

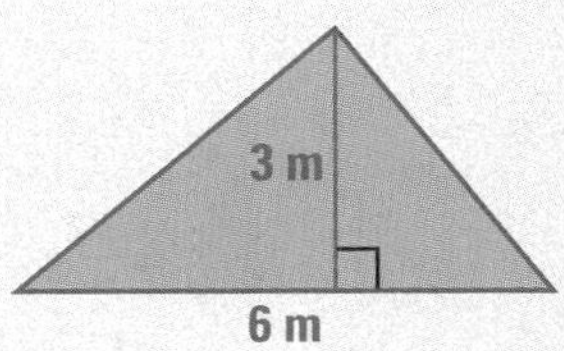

Find the area of the figure.

14. 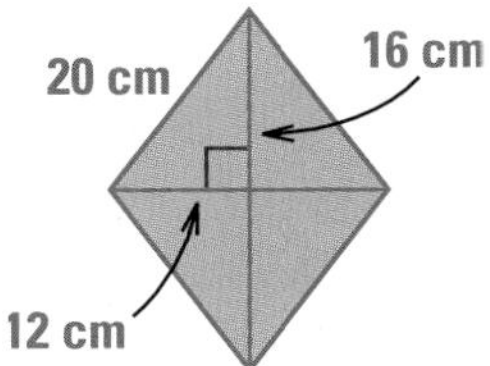

15. 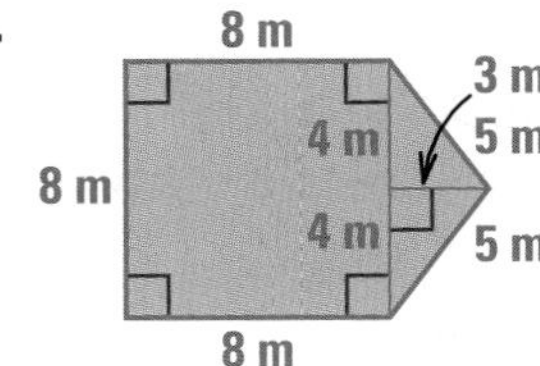

16. 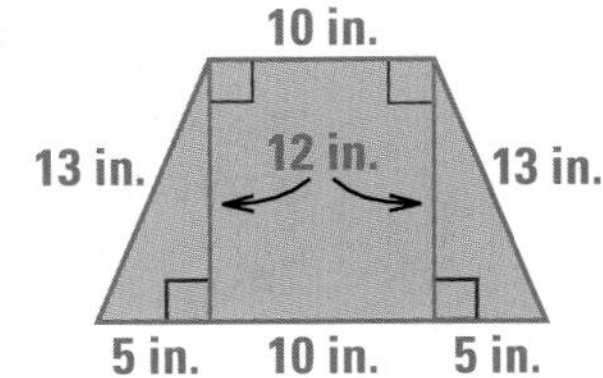

8.5 PARALLELOGRAMS

Examples on pp. 376–377

A parallelogram is a quadrilateral whose opposite sides are parallel. A rectangle is a parallelogram that has four right angles. A square is a rectangle with all sides the same length.

EXAMPLES

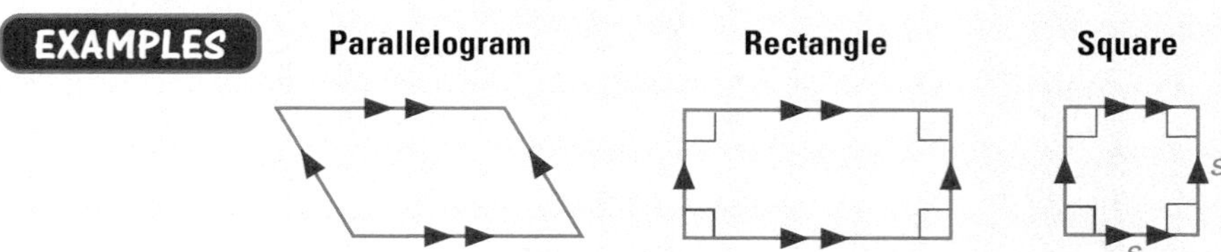

Use the figures shown. Name one of each polygon described.

17. Square

18. Parallelogram

19. Rectangle

20. Quadrilateral

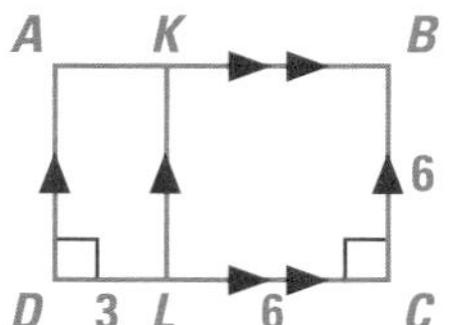

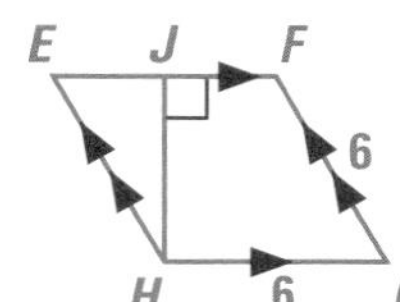

8.6 AREA OF A PARALLELOGRAM

Examples on pp. 382–383

To find the area of a parallelogram, multiply base by height.

EXAMPLE **Find the area of the parallelogram.**

$$\text{Area} = bh$$
$$= 9 \cdot 4$$
$$= 36 \text{ ft}^2$$

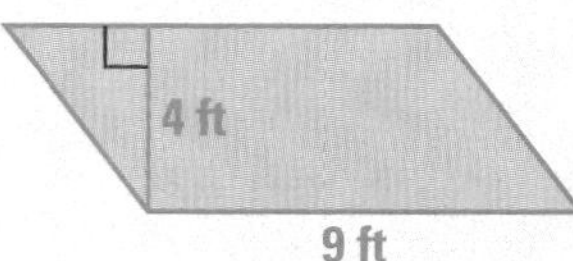

Find the area of the parallelogram.

21.

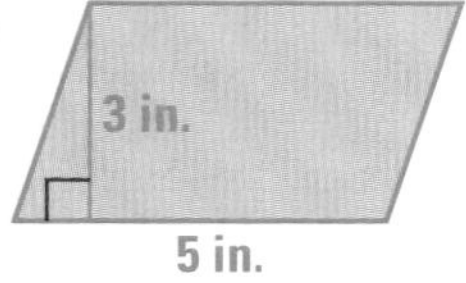

22.

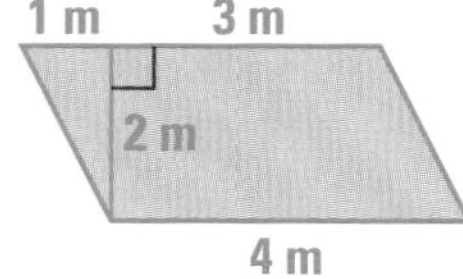

23.

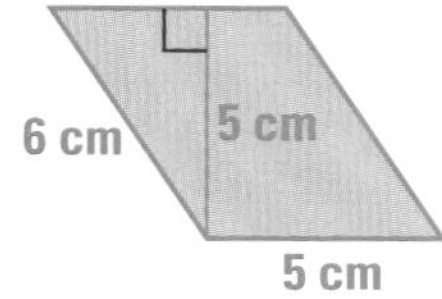

In Exercises 24 and 25, find the amount of blue material needed to make the kite composed of parallelograms.

24.

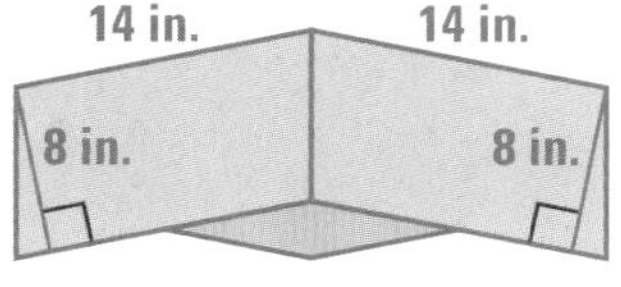

25.

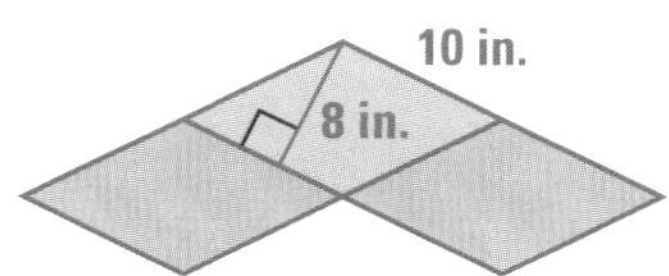

8.7 CIRCUMFERENCE OF A CIRCLE

Examples on pp. 388–389

To find the circumference of a circle, multiply π by the diameter d.

EXAMPLE **Find the circumference of the circle.**

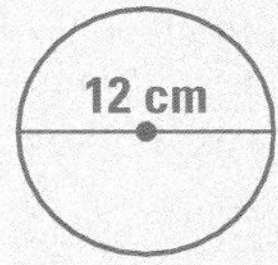

$$\text{Circumference} = \pi d$$
$$\approx 3.14 \cdot 12$$
$$= 37.68 \text{ cm}$$

The circumference is about 37.68 cm.

In Exercises 26–28, find the value of x for the given circle.

26. Circumference $= x$
Diameter $= 11$ ft

27. Circumference $= x$
Radius $= 14$ in.

28. Circumference $= 25.12$ m
Diameter $= x$

29. A carousel has a diameter of 35 feet. Write an expression to find how far you travel if you ride one full circle on the outer edge of the carousel.

8.8 AREA OF A CIRCLE

Examples on pp. 392–393

To find the area of a circle, multiply π by the square of the radius r.

EXAMPLE **Find the area of the circle.**

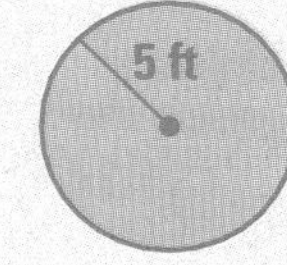

$$\text{Area} = \pi r^2$$
$$\approx 3.14 \cdot 5^2$$
$$= 78.5 \text{ ft}^2$$

The area is about 78.5 ft^2.

30. Find the area of a circle with a radius of 7 feet.

31. Find the area of a circle with a diameter of 24 meters.

Use the formulas for the area of a circle and of a parallelogram to find the area of the shaded region.

32.

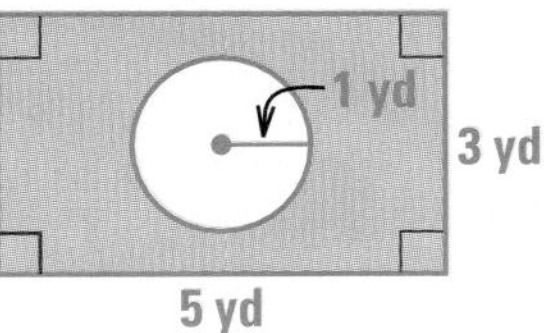

33.

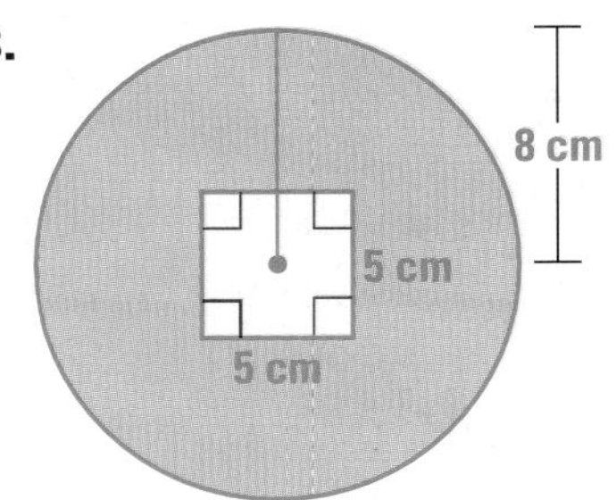

34.

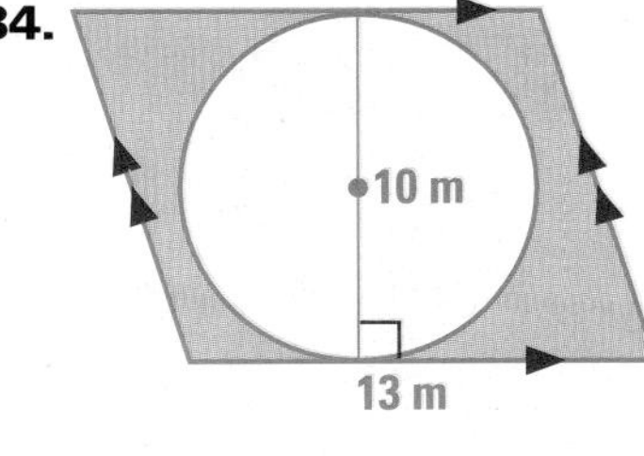

Chapter 8 Chapter Test

Use the figure at the right to complete the statement. The lines *m* and *n* are parallel.

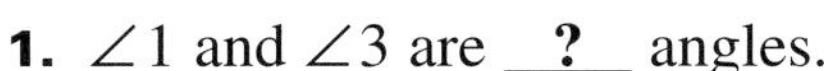

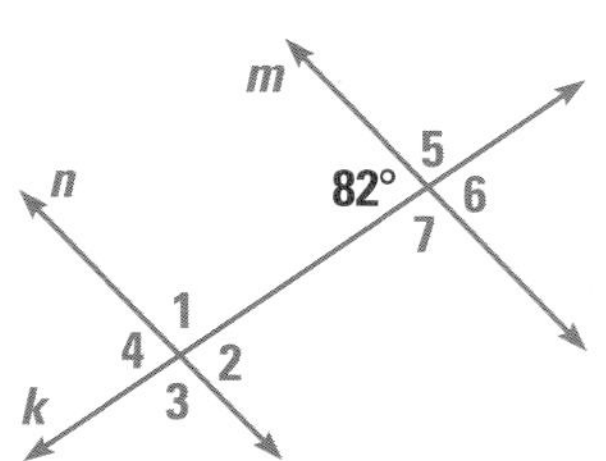

1. $\angle 1$ and $\angle 3$ are __?__ angles.

2. The measure of $\angle 6$ is __?__.

3. The measure of $\angle 7$ is __?__.

KITES **Each kite is made from triangles. Classify the triangles as *scalene, isosceles,* or *equilateral*. Then find *x*.**

4.

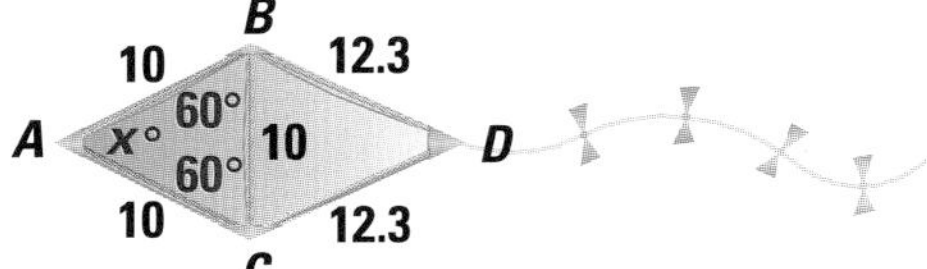

5.

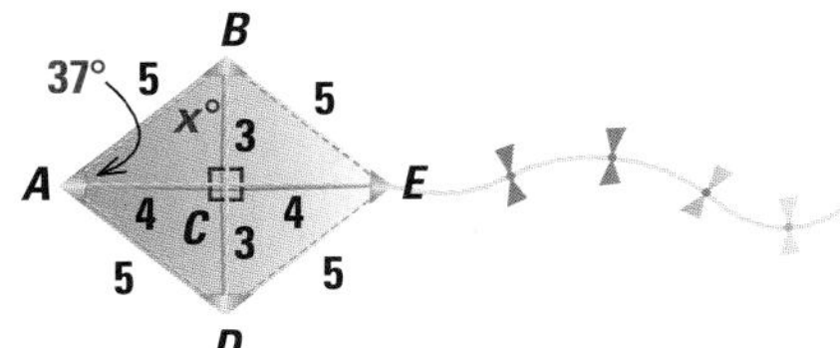

Find the area of the triangle.

6.

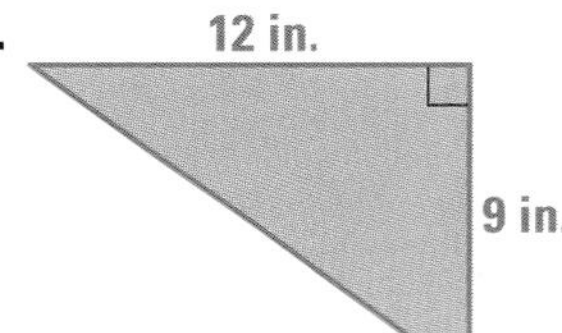

7.

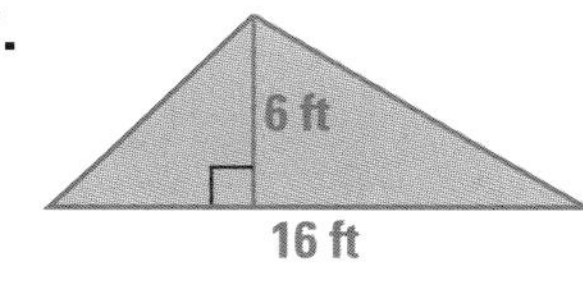

8.

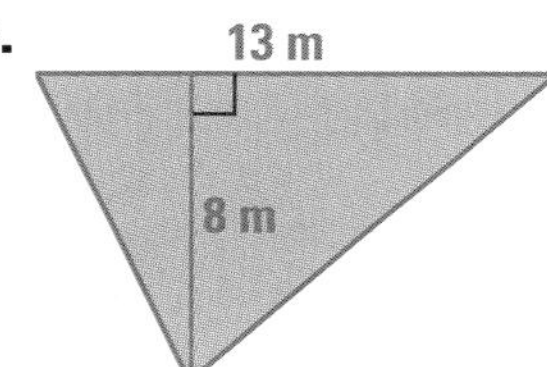

In Exercises 9–11, name the polygon in as many ways as you can. Then find the missing measures.

9.

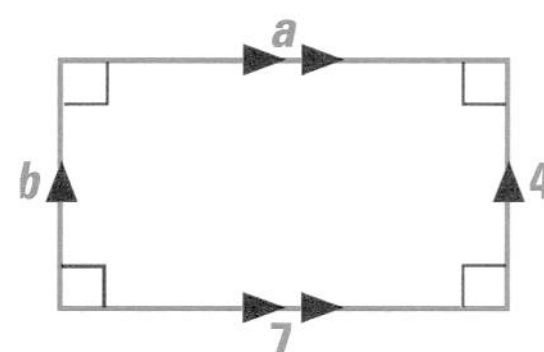

10.

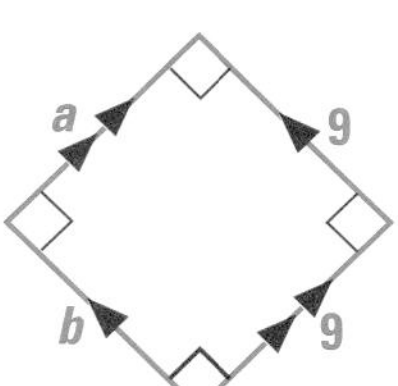

11.

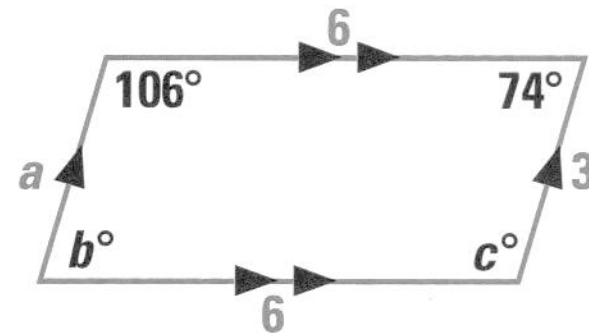

In Exercises 12–14, find the area of the figure.

12.

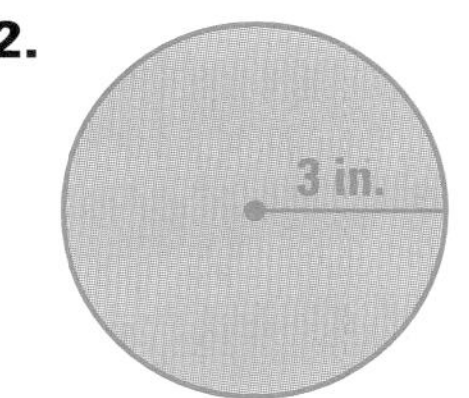

13.

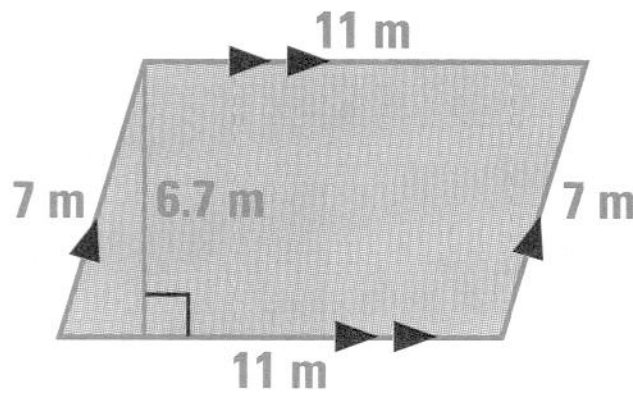

14.

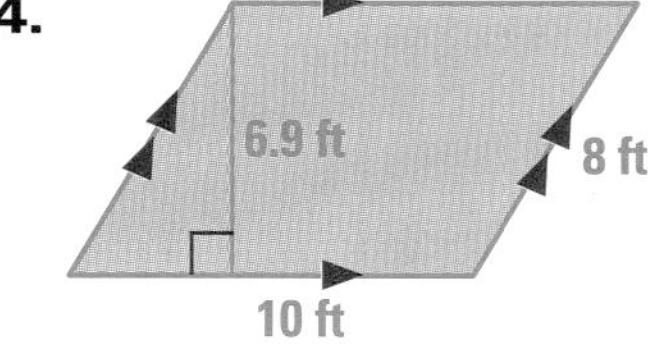

15. Find the circumference of the circle in Exercise 12.

Multiple-Choice Practice

Test Tip Avoid spending too much time on any one question.

In Exercises 1–3, use the figure below.

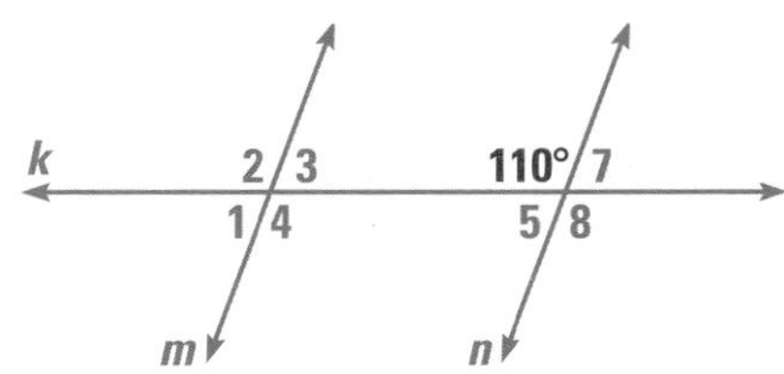

1. Which statement is false?

Ⓐ $\angle 2$ and $\angle 3$ are supplementary angles.

Ⓑ $\angle 5$ and $\angle 8$ are complementary angles.

Ⓒ $\angle 1$ and $\angle 3$ are vertical angles.

Ⓓ $\angle 2$ and $\angle 4$ are congruent.

2. What is the measure of $\angle 7$?

Ⓕ 20° Ⓖ 70°

Ⓗ 90° Ⓙ 110°

3. What is the measure of $\angle 8$?

Ⓐ 20° Ⓑ 70°

Ⓒ 90° Ⓓ 110°

4. Which of these statements cannot be true of an isosceles triangle?

Ⓕ An isosceles triangle may have an obtuse angle.

Ⓖ All sides are different lengths.

Ⓗ An isosceles triangle may have three acute angles.

Ⓙ Two of its sides are the same length.

5. Find the missing measure x in the parallelogram.

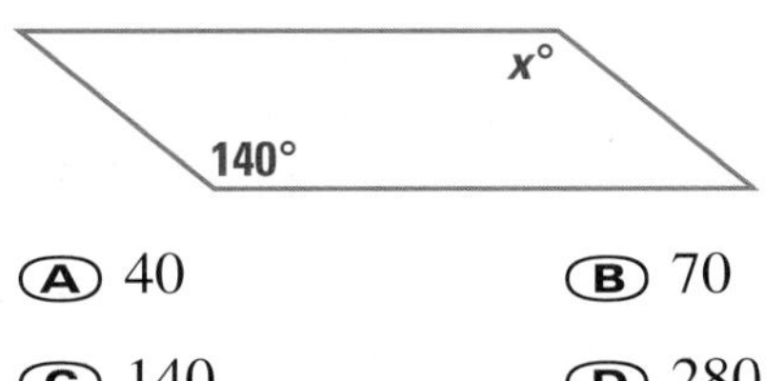

Ⓐ 40 Ⓑ 70

Ⓒ 140 Ⓓ 280

6. Find the area of a parallelogram with a base of 4 feet and a height of 3.2 feet.

Ⓕ 6.4 ft Ⓖ 6.4 ft^2

Ⓗ 12.8 ft Ⓙ 12.8 ft^2

7. A parallelogram has an area of 162 square meters and a height of 9 meters. What is the length of the base of the parallelogram?

Ⓐ 6 meters Ⓑ 18 meters

Ⓒ 22.5 meters Ⓓ 36 meters

8. You want to plant flowers around the outside of a circular garden that has a diameter of 4 feet. If the flowers have to be planted 6 inches apart, about how many flowers should you buy?

Ⓕ 50 Ⓖ 26

Ⓗ 25 Ⓙ 12

9. The area of the bottom of a pool with a radius of 9 feet is __?__.

Ⓐ 56.5 ft Ⓑ 254.3 ft

Ⓒ 254.3 ft^2 Ⓓ 1017.4 ft^2

Brain games

California Standards

- Express the solution clearly and logically by using the appropriate mathematical notation and terms and clear language. (MR 2.5)
- Make precise calculations and check the validity of the results from the context of the problem. (MR 2.7)

Area Scavenger Hunt

Materials

- **Index cards, each one listing one of these measurements: 50 cm², 100 cm², 150 cm², 300 cm², and 600 cm²**
- **Centimeter ruler**
- **Calculator (optional)**
- **Classroom objects**

Directions

Object of the Game

Play in pairs. Each round, players win points depending on how close an actual measurement is to the estimated area shown on a card. The winner is the player with the most points after all the cards have been played.

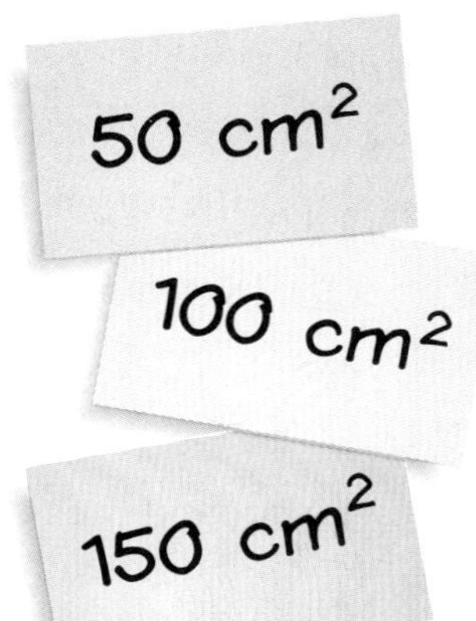

How to Play

STEP 1 Players shuffle the index cards and turn the top card up. Players have three minutes to choose an object they think has the area shown on the card. Measurement is allowed.

STEP 2 After three minutes, players name the objects and find their areas. The player who chose the object whose actual area is closer to the measurement on the card wins one point. Continue until all the cards are played.

Another Way to Play

Each player has one minute to choose three objects. Measure all the objects. Award one point to the player who chose the object whose area is closest to the area shown on a card. Award two points to the next closest, and so on. The player with the *fewest* points wins.

Brain Teaser

NIMBLE NUMBERS

Which number is the same whether it is doubled or squared?

The basic skills you'll review on this page will help prepare you for the next chapter.

Reviewing the Basics

EXAMPLE 1 Evaluating Powers

Evaluate the power. **a.** 2^2 **b.** 2^3

Solution

Write each power as a product, then multiply.

a. $2^2 = 2 \times 2 = 4$ **b.** $2^3 = 2 \times 2 \times 2 = 8$

Try These

Evaluate the power.

1. 3^2 **2.** 5^2 **3.** 4^3 **4.** 3^3

5. 11^2 **6.** 25^2 **7.** 10^3 **8.** 2^4

CALCULATOR **Evaluate the power. You may wish to use a calculator.**

9. 8.76^2 **10.** 96.5^2 **11.** 55.5^3 **12.** 6.1^4

EXAMPLE 2 Converting Units

Mark worked 8 hours. How many minutes did he work?

Solution

Use the conversion factor $\frac{60 \text{ minutes}}{1 \text{ hour}}$.

$$8 \text{ hours} = 8 \text{ hours} \times \frac{60 \text{ minutes}}{1 \text{ hour}}$$ Multiply by $\frac{60 \text{ minutes}}{1 \text{ hour}}$.

$$= \frac{8 \times 60}{1} \text{ minutes}$$ Multiply fractions.

$$= 480 \text{ minutes}$$ Simplify.

ANSWER ▶ He worked 480 minutes.

Try These

Convert.

13. 12 feet to inches

14. 14 yards to feet

15. 96 inches to feet

16. 4 cups to pints

17. 15 grams to milligrams

18. 25 meters to centimeters

19. 5000 meters to kilometers

20. 2000 grams to kilograms

Student Help

▶ **MORE EXAMPLES**

More examples and practice exercises available at www.mcdougallittell.com

Geometry in Space

Why is geometry in space important?

Geometry in space refers to the geometry of three-dimensional figures. Finding the volumes and surface areas of three-dimensional figures allows you to solve problems about the size of containers used for storage, the amount of paint needed to cover a surface, and so on.

Geometry is used in many careers, including volcanology (page 405) and industrial design (page 435). For example, volcanologists use volume formulas to estimate the amount of lava produced during a volcano's eruption.

Meeting the California Standards

The skills you'll learn in this chapter will help you meet state standards and prepare for standardized tests. In this chapter you'll:

- **Find the volumes of triangular prisms and cylinders; compare their volume formulas with those for rectangular solids.** LESSONS 9.1–9.4
- **Convert one unit of measure to another.** LESSONS 9.2, 9.4
- **Understand the measurement of plane and solid shapes and use this understanding to solve problems.** LESSON 9.5
- **Use common estimates of π to calculate the areas of circles.** LESSON 9.6
- **Express geometric relationships in symbolic form.** LESSON 9.6

Christina Neal (L) and Ed Wolfe (R) measure the temperature of lava flow. The lava shown here at the Kilauea Volcano in Hawaii is about 2100°F.

Career Link **VOLCANOLOGIST** A volcanologist uses geometry when:

- predicting where lava will flow.
- estimating the volume of lava that erupted from a volcano.

EXERCISES

The table shows estimated dimensions of three sections of lava flowing from a volcano in Mexico.

Estimated dimensions of lava flowing from Volcano Colima, January 8, 1999		
Location	**Length (in meters)**	**Average Width (in meters)**
Western Cordoban	2,800	150
Central Cordoban	3,100	150
Eastern Cordoban	2,500	150

1. Estimate the area covered by each section of lava by finding the area of a rectangle with the given length and width.

2. Estimate the total area covered by the three sections of lava.

In Lesson 9.2, you will learn how to estimate the volume of lava that erupted from the volcano.

Chapter 9 Getting Ready

PREVIEW — What's the chapter about?

- Identifying **prisms** and **circular cylinders**
- Finding the **volumes** of prisms and circular cylinders
- Finding the **surface areas** of prisms and circular cylinders

WORDS TO KNOW

- **polyhedron,** *p. 407*
- **faces, edges,** *p. 407*
- **prism,** *p. 407*
- **bases,** *pp. 407, 408*
- **height,** *pp. 407, 408*
- **right prism,** *p. 407*
- **circular cylinder,** *p. 408*
- **volume,** *p. 411*
- **surface area,** *pp. 430, 434*
- **circumference of a cylinder,** *p. 434*
- **lateral surface,** *p. 434*

PREPARE — Chapter Readiness Quiz

Take this quick quiz. If you are unsure of an answer, look back at the reference pages for help.

VOCABULARY CHECK *(refer to p. 388)*

In Exercises 1 and 2, use the circle at the right.

20 in.

1. Which number represents the radius?

Ⓐ 5 inches　Ⓑ 10 inches

Ⓒ 20 inches　Ⓓ 62.8 inches

2. Which number best approximates the circumference?

Ⓕ 5 inches　Ⓖ 10 inches

Ⓗ 20 inches　Ⓙ 62.8 inches

SKILL CHECK *(refer to pp. 372, 392)*

3. What is the approximate area of the shaded portion of the figure at the right?

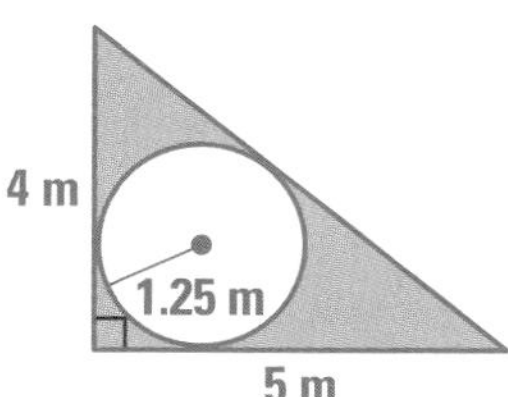

Ⓐ 1.8 m^2　Ⓑ 5.1 m^2

Ⓒ 5.3 m^2　Ⓓ 14.7 m^2

STUDY TIP — Check for Reasonable Answers

When doing homework or taking a test, always ask yourself if the answer to each problem makes sense. This will help you catch careless errors.

Always check the final answer to make sure it makes sense.

9.1 Prisms and Cylinders

In this lesson you'll:

- Understand solid shapes such as rectangular prisms, triangular prisms, and circular cylinders. (MG 1.0)

Goal 1 IDENTIFYING PRISMS

A **polyhedron** is a solid that is bounded by polygons, called **faces**, whose sides are called **edges** of the polyhedron. One type of polyhedron is a *prism*. A **prism** has two parallel **bases** that are polygons of the same size and shape. The **height of a prism** is the perpendicular distance between two bases. The shape of the bases determines the name of the prism.

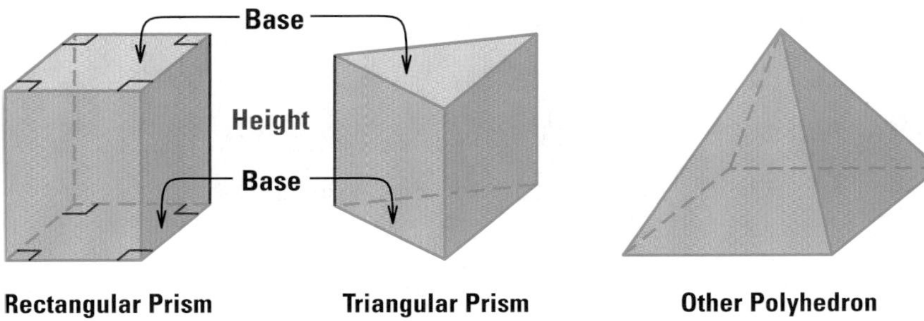

In a **right prism**, the edges connecting the bases are perpendicular to the bases. All of the prisms in this book are right prisms.

EXAMPLE 1 Identifying and Describing a Prism

Identify the prism. How many faces does it have? What is its height?

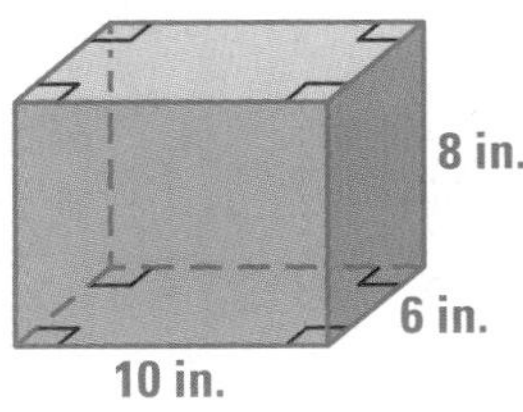

Solution

The bases are rectangles, so the prism is a rectangular prism. The prism has 6 faces. The height is 8 inches.

EXAMPLE 2 Identifying and Describing a Prism

Identify the prism. How many faces does it have? What is its height?

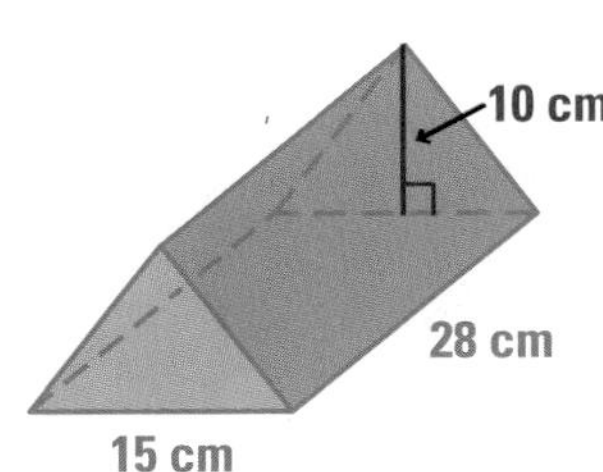

Solution

The bases are triangles, so the prism is a triangular prism. The prism has 5 faces. The height is 28 centimeters.

Goal 2 IDENTIFYING CYLINDERS

A **circular cylinder** has two parallel **bases** that are the same size circles. A circular cylinder is *not* a prism because the circular bases are *not* polygons. The **height of a cylinder** is the perpendicular distance between the bases.

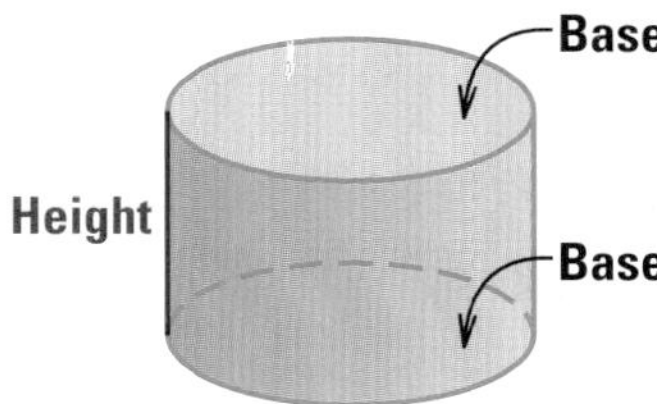

In a **right circular cylinder**, the line segment connecting the centers of the circular bases is perpendicular to the bases. All of the cylinders in this book are right circular cylinders.

Student Help

▶ MORE EXAMPLES

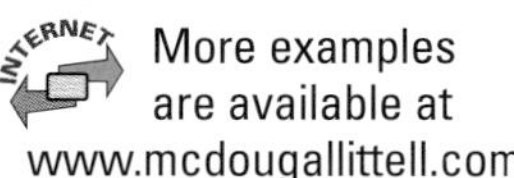

More examples are available at www.mcdougallittell.com

EXAMPLE 3 Identifying and Describing a Solid

Identify the solid at the right. What is its height?

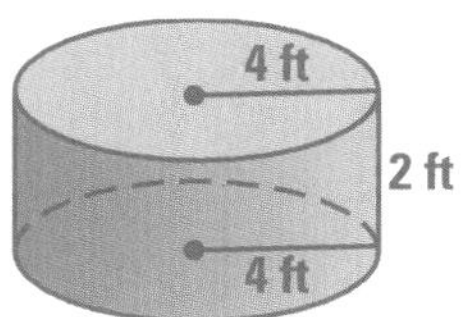

Solution

The bases are circles that are the same size, so the solid is a cylinder. The height is 2 feet.

Student Help

▶ READING TIP

The dimensions of a solid specify its size. For a rectangular prism, the dimensions are length, width, and height. For a cylinder, the dimensions are base radius or base diameter and height.

EXAMPLE 4 Identifying and Sketching a Solid

Identify the basic shape of the item as a *rectangular prism*, *triangular prism*, or *cylinder*. Then sketch the object and estimate its dimensions.

a. A can of corn

b. A box of cereal

Solution

a. A can of corn is a cylinder. Corn comes in many different sized cans. A typical size can is shown at the right. The diameter of a base is 3 inches, and the height is 5 inches.

b. A box of cereal is a rectangular prism. Cereal also comes in boxes of many different sizes. A typical size box is shown at the right. The length is 9 inches, the width is 2 inches, and the height is 10 inches.

9.1 Exercises

Guided Practice

In Exercises 1–3, tell whether the figure is a polyhedron. Explain your reasoning in words.

1.

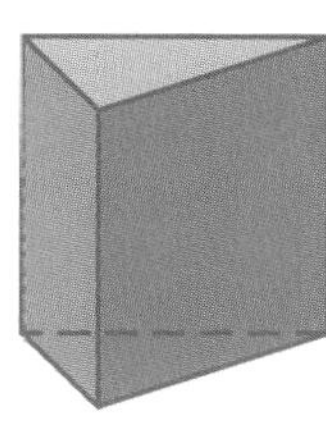

2.

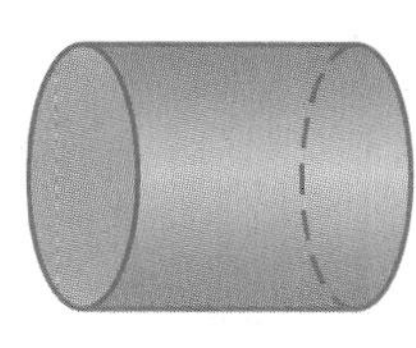

3.

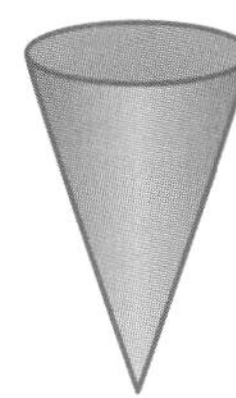

4. Identify the prism at the right. How many faces does it have? What is its height?

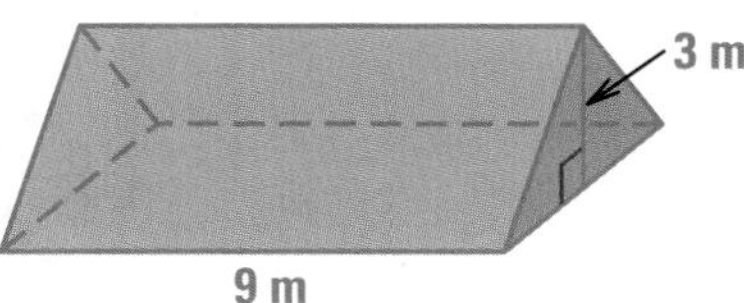

5. GEOMETRY Draw a rectangular prism using this method: lightly sketch two rectangles as in Step 1 below. Join corresponding vertices as in Step 2. Then darken the visible edges and make the hidden edges dashed as in Step 3.

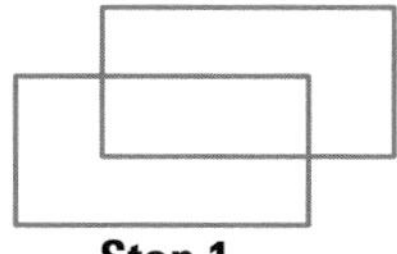

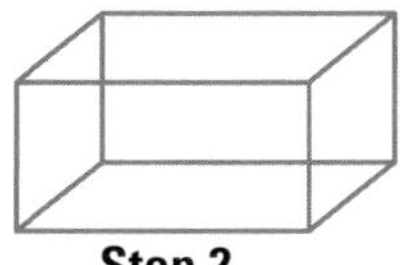

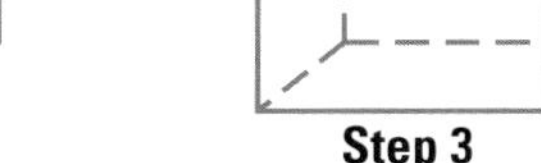

6. Use a similar method to the one in Exercise 5 to draw a triangular prism and a cylinder.

7. Name an actual object that has the shape of a cylinder. Sketch the object and estimate the diameter of a base and the height.

Practice and Problem Solving

> **Student Help**
>
> ▶ **MORE PRACTICE**
> Extra practice to help you master skills is on page 582.

Identify the solid as a *triangular prism*, a *rectangular prism*, or a *cylinder*. Then find its height. If the solid is a prism, find the number of faces.

8.

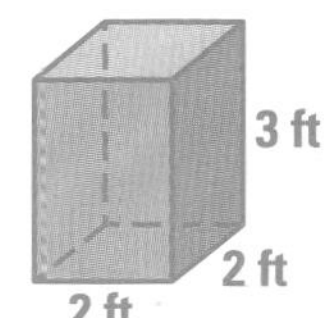

9.

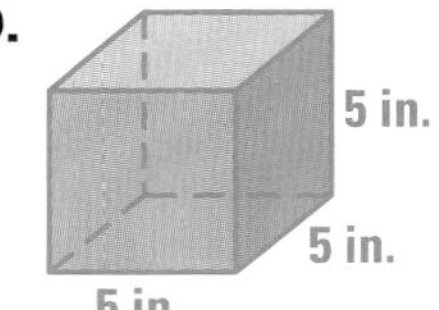

10.

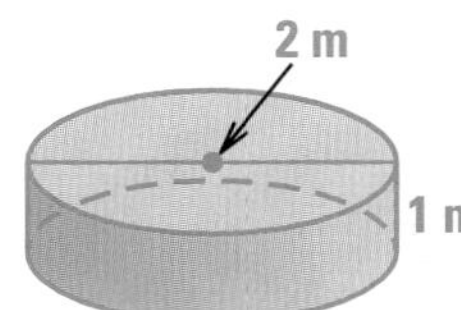

11.

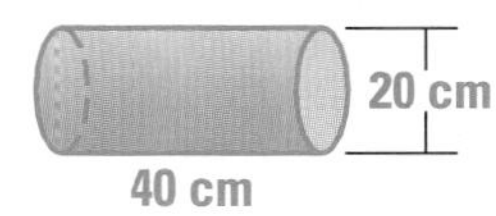

12.

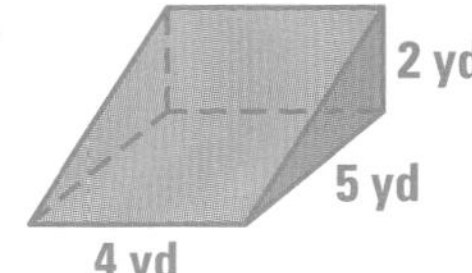

13.

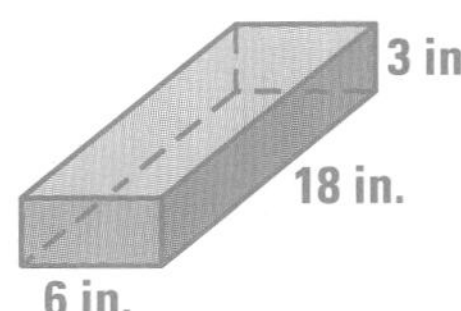

14. MATHEMATICAL REASONING A *cube* is a rectangular prism with six square faces that are all the same size. Are there other rectangular prisms whose faces are all the same shape and size? Explain.

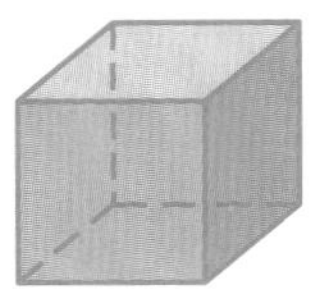

Identify the basic shape of the object a *rectangular prism*, a *triangular prism*, or a *cylinder*.

15. 

16. 

17. 

18. 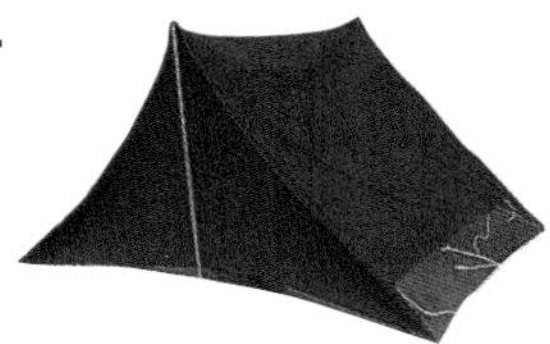

In Exercises 19–21, draw the prism or cylinder from its description.

19. A rectangular prism with a base of 5 inches by 3 inches and a height of 5 inches

20. A triangular prism with a base of 3, 4, and 5 centimeters and a height of 7 centimeters

21. A cylinder with a base radius of 10 centimeters and a height of 15 centimeters

22. CHALLENGE Which of the following could be folded along the dashed lines to form a cereal box? Explain your reasoning.

A. 

B. 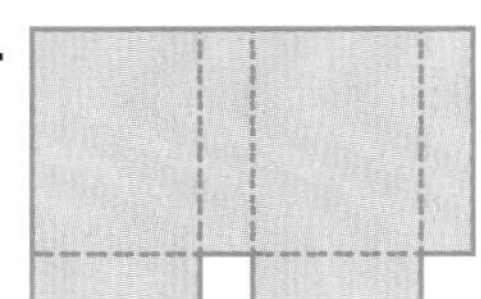

C. 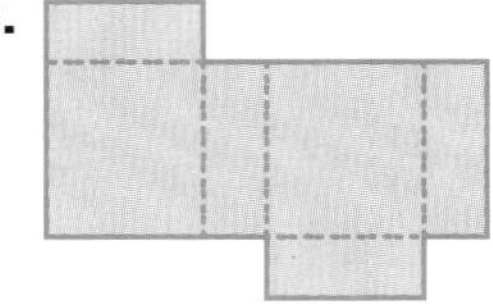

Multiple-Choice Practice

In Exercises 23 and 24, use the figure shown.

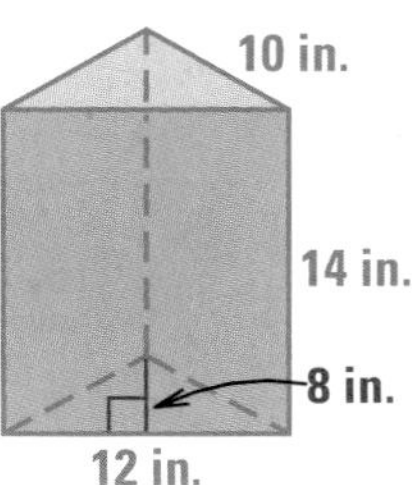

23. What is the name of the figure?

(A) Cylinder (B) Rectangular prism

(C) Cube (D) Triangular prism

24. What is the height of the figure?

(F) 8 in. (G) 10 in.

(H) 12 in. (J) 14 in.

Volume of a Rectangular Prism

In this lesson you'll:

- Know and use the formula for the volume of a rectangular prism. (MG 1.3)
- Convert one unit of measure to another. (AF 2.1)

Goal 1 Finding the Volume of a Rectangular Prism

When you measure objects, you need to know whether to use units for length, area, or volume.

MEASURES OF LENGTH	MEASURES OF AREA	MEASURES OF VOLUME
Feet (ft)	Square feet (ft^2)	Cubic feet (ft^3)
Meters (m)	Square meters (m^2)	Cubic meters (m^3)
Centimeters (cm)	Square centimeters (cm^2)	Cubic centimeters (cm^3)
1 cm	1 cm, 1 cm	1 cm, 1 cm, 1 cm

Volume of a Rectangular Prism

In Words As you learned in a previous course, the volume V of a rectangular prism is the product of the length ℓ, width w, and height h.

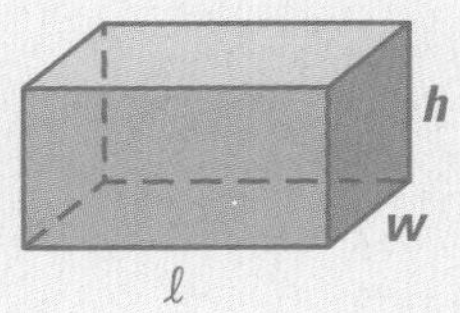

In Algebra $V = \ell wh$

EXAMPLE 1 Finding the Volume of a Prism

Find the volume of the videocassette box shown at the right.

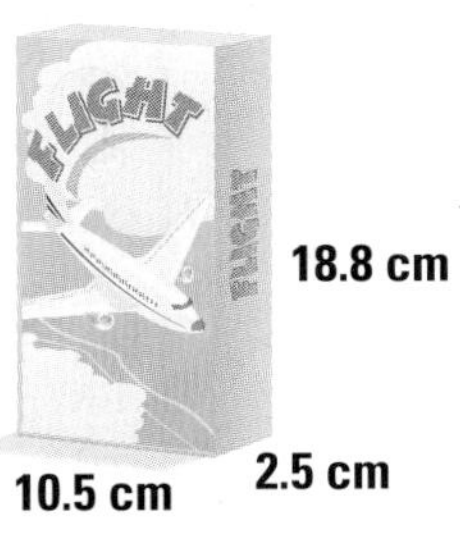

Solution

To find the volume of the box, use the formula for volume of a rectangular prism.

$V = \ell wh$ Write formula for volume.

$= (10.5)(2.5)(18.8)$ Substitute given values.

$= 493.5\ cm^3$ Multiply.

ANSWER ▶ The volume of the box is 493.5 cubic centimeters.

Link to Aviation

RUNWAY The longest runway is located at Edwards Air Force Base in Muroc, California. It is 7.13 miles long and can be used to land a space shuttle.

Goal 2 Converting Units of Measure

EXAMPLE 2 Finding a Volume

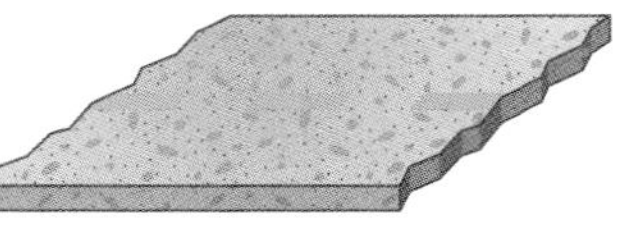

You are replacing a section of a concrete airport runway. The section can be modeled by a rectangular prism that measures $\frac{1}{2}$ mile long, 24 feet wide, and 18 inches deep. How many cubic yards of concrete do you need to replace this section of airport runway?

Solution

First, use the fact that 1 mi = 1760 yd and 36 in. = 3 ft = 1 yd to convert each measurement to yards.

$\frac{1}{2}\text{ mi} \times \frac{1760\text{ yd}}{1\text{ mi}} = 880\text{ yd}$ Convert from miles to yards.

$24\text{ ft} \times \frac{1\text{ yd}}{3\text{ ft}} = 8\text{ yd}$ Convert from feet to yards.

$18\text{ in.} \times \frac{1\text{ yd}}{36\text{ in.}} = \frac{1}{2}\text{ yd}$ Convert from inches to yards.

Second, use the formula for the volume of a rectangular prism.

$V = \ell wh$ Write formula for volume.

$= (\mathbf{880})(\mathbf{8})\left(\frac{1}{2}\right)$ Substitute given values.

$= 3520\text{ yd}^3$ Multiply.

ANSWER ▶ You need 3520 cubic yards of concrete.

Student Help

▶ **LOOK BACK** For help with converting units of measure, see page 144.

EXAMPLE 3 Finding the Height of a Prism

A rectangular prism has a volume of 5 cubic meters. The length and width of the prism are given. What is the height of the prism?

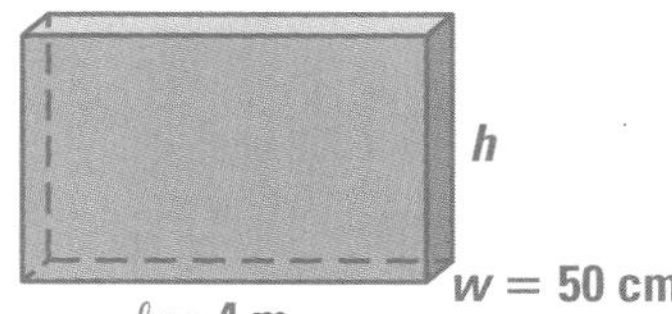

Solution

Use the fact that 100 cm = 1 m to write all measurements in meters. Then substitute known values in an equation for volume and solve the equation for height.

$V = \ell wh$ Write formula for volume.

$5 = (4)(0.5)(h)$ Substitute given values. Use 0.5 m for 50 cm.

$5 = 2h$ Simplify.

$2.5 = h$ Divide each side by 2.

ANSWER ▶ The height of the rectangular prism is 2.5 meters.

9.2 Exercises

Guided Practice

Match the description with the measurement.

A. 565 ft **B.** 105,625 ft^2 **C.** 2000 ft^3

1. Area of a baseball field

2. Volume of a swimming pool

3. Length of a city block

In Exercises 4 and 5, use the rectangular prism at the right.

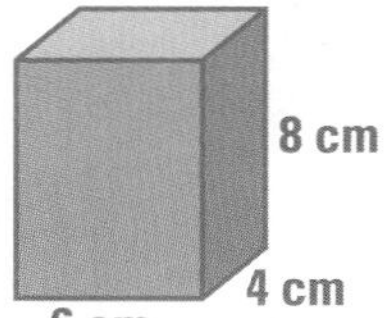

4. Identify the length, width, and height.

5. Find the volume of the prism.

6. ALGEBRA The volume of a rectangular prism is 1800 cubic millimeters. It has a length of 10 millimeters and a width of 15 millimeters. Find the height of the rectangular prism.

Practice and Problem Solving

> **Student Help**
>
> ▶ **MORE PRACTICE** Extra practice to help you master skills is on page 582.

7. Find the volume of the prism. What do you observe?

a.

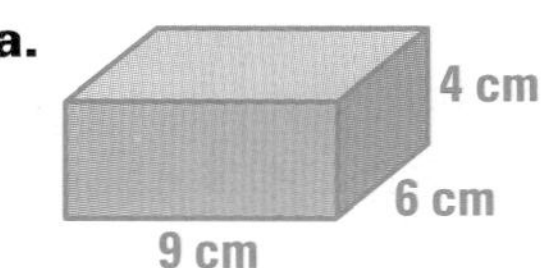

b.

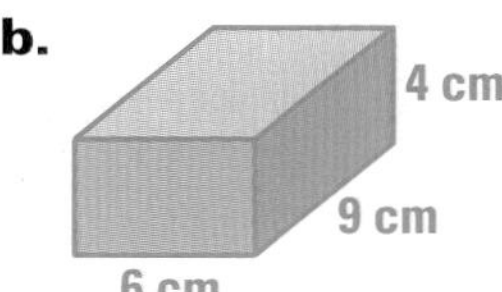

c.

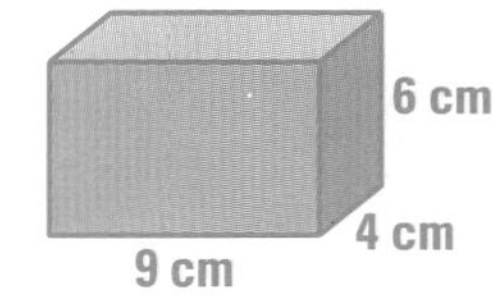

The object can be modeled by a rectangular prism. Find its approximate volume.

8. Sandbox

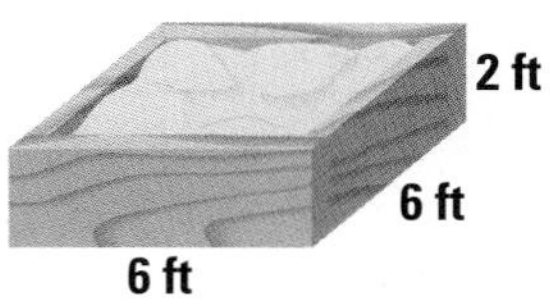

9. Cardboard box

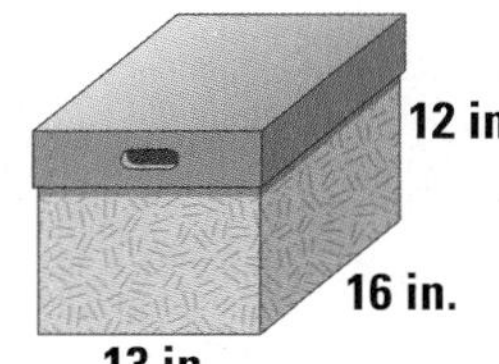

10. Suitcase

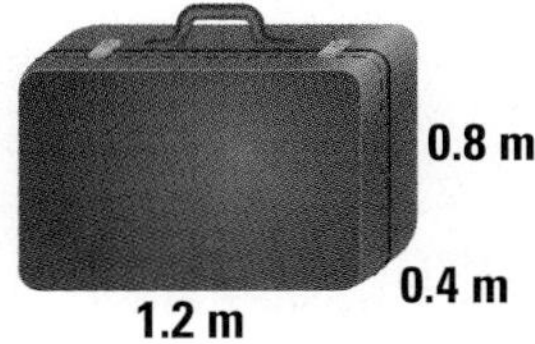

Draw a rectangular prism with the given dimensions. Find its volume.

11. 4 in. by 8 in. by 12 in.

12. 2.44 cm by 3.58 cm by 7.04 cm

Find the volume of the rectangular prism with the given dimensions.

13. 5 in. by $\frac{1}{2}$ ft by 2 yd

14. 10 cm by 160 mm by 1 m

15. 5000 mm by 2 m by 200 cm

16. 2 mi by 10,560 ft by 3520 yd

Link to Transportation

ICEBREAKER To break the ice, the bow of an icebreaker is pushed onto the top of the ice until the weight of the ship breaks the ice. At a slow, steady speed, large icebreakers can break ice that is about 8 feet thick.

ALGEBRA In Exercises 17 and 18, use the given volume to find x.

17. Volume = 390 in.^{3}

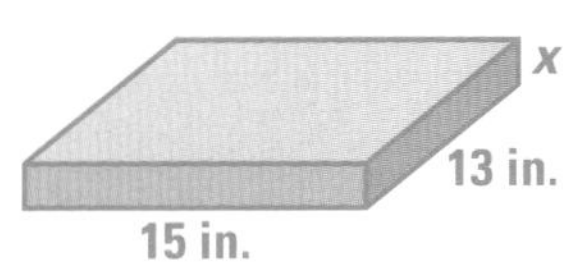

18. Volume = 1562.5 m^3

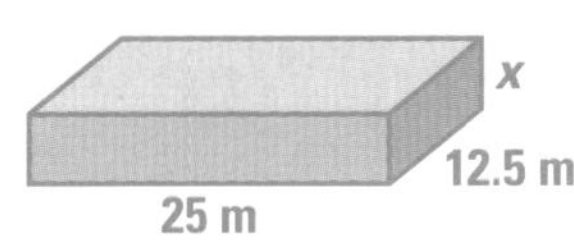

19. WRITING The volume of a rectangular prism is 280 cubic inches. What information is necessary to find the height? Explain.

20. *Chapter Opener Link* Look back at page 405. The average depth of the lava was about 15 meters. Estimate the total volume of the 3 sections of lava. Explain your reasoning.

21. ICEBREAKER An icebreaker is a ship designed to travel through ice-covered waters and break up ice. The ice on a section of river is approximately a rectangular prism that measures $\frac{1}{2}$ mile wide, 3 miles long, and 8 feet thick. Estimate the volume of the ice.

ANGELFISH **In Exercises 22–24, use the following information.** You are considering buying an aquarium for seven angelfish. The price tag gives the dimensions as 2 feet long, 1 foot wide, and 1.5 feet high.

22. Find the volume of the aquarium in cubic inches.

23. If 1 gallon is equal to 231 cubic inches, how many gallons does the aquarium contain? Use a calculator if you wish.

24. Each angelfish requires at least 3 gallons of water. Is this aquarium suitable for seven angelfish? Explain.

25. ALGEBRA The length of the side of a cube is x inches. Write an expression in terms of x that you can use to find the volume of the cube. Justify your reasoning.

26. CONSTRUCTION A cube of bricks has a volume of 33,750 cubic inches. A single brick measures 8 inches long, $3\frac{3}{4}$ inches wide, and $2\frac{1}{4}$ inches high. How many bricks are in a cube of bricks?

27. POPCORN The largest box of popcorn in the United States was filled at Pittsville Elementary School in Wisconsin. It measured 40 feet long by 28 feet wide and had a volume of 7470.4 cubic feet. What was the height of the popcorn box? Use estimation to check that your answer is reasonable.

Student Help

▶ **HOMEWORK HELP**
INTERNET Extra help with problem solving in Ex. 27 is available at www.mcdougallittell.com

28. CHALLENGE Two triangular prisms of the same shape and size make up the rectangular prism at the right. Find the volume of one of the triangular prisms.

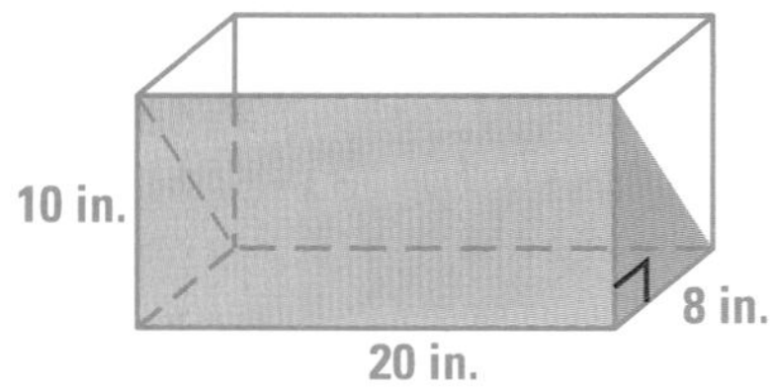

Multiple-Choice Practice

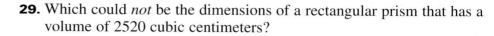

29. Which could *not* be the dimensions of a rectangular prism that has a volume of 2520 cubic centimeters?

Ⓐ 6 cm by 20 cm by 21 cm　　Ⓑ 7 cm by 15 cm by 27 cm

Ⓒ 8 cm by 9 cm by 35 cm　　Ⓓ 10 cm by 14 cm by 18 cm

Test Tip Ⓐ Ⓑ Ⓒ Ⓓ

▶In Exercise 30 remember that 1 foot is 12 inches, so 1 cubic foot is 12 • 12 • 12 cubic inches.

30. Which of the following is the same as 1 ft^3?

Ⓕ 12 $in.^3$　　Ⓖ 144 $in.^3$　　Ⓗ 1728 $in.^3$　　Ⓙ 1 m^3

31. Which rectangular prism has the greatest volume? (Assume all dimensions have the same units.)

Ⓐ
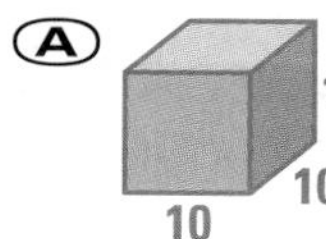

Ⓑ
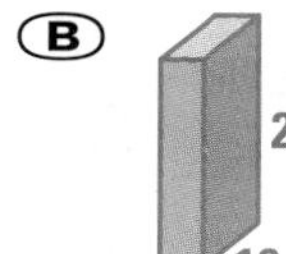

Ⓒ
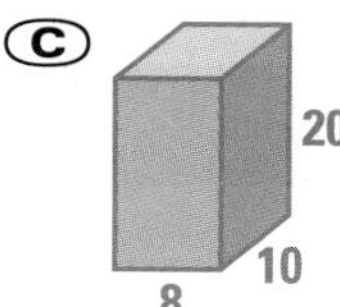

Ⓓ
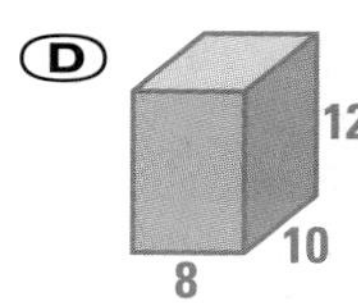

Mixed Review

32. BANNER You make a scale drawing of your planned banner for School Spirit Day. The letters on the drawing are each 3 inches tall. The drawing is 15 inches tall. The actual banner will be 5 feet tall. How tall should you make the letters on the banner? *(6.5)*

In Exercises 33–36, use a proportion to answer the question. *(7.4)*

33. 12 is 48% of what number?　　**34.** What percent of 105 is 63?

35. 30% of 80 is what number?　　**36.** 72 is 120% of what number?

37. Using the diagram below, identify all pairs of vertical angles. *(8.1)*

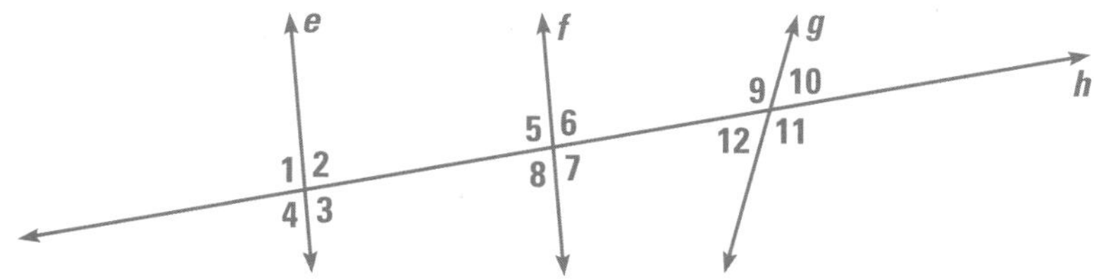

TRACK AND FIELD **Find the circumference and the area of the circle used for the track and field event.** *(8.7, 8.8)*

38. Shot-put circle

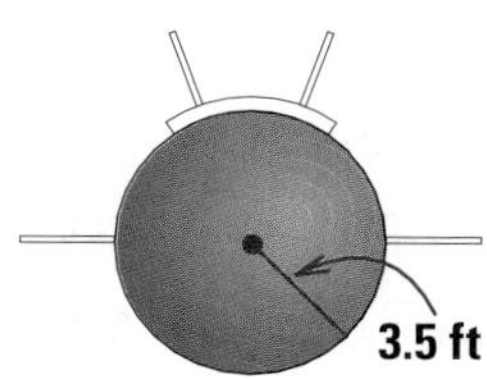

39. Discus circle

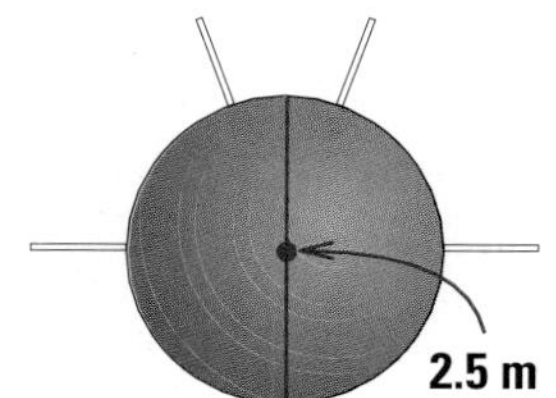

DEVELOPING CONCEPTS

Volume of a Triangular Prism

For use with Lesson 9.3

- Understand the measurement of plane and solid shapes. (MG 1.0)
- Express in symbolic form simple relationships arising from geometry. (AF 3.2)
- Determine when and how to break a problem into simpler parts. (MR 1.3)

MATERIALS

- Paper and pencil

The volume of a triangular prism is related to the volume of a rectangular prism.

SAMPLE 1 Finding the Volume of a Triangular Prism

Find the volume of the triangular prism shown.

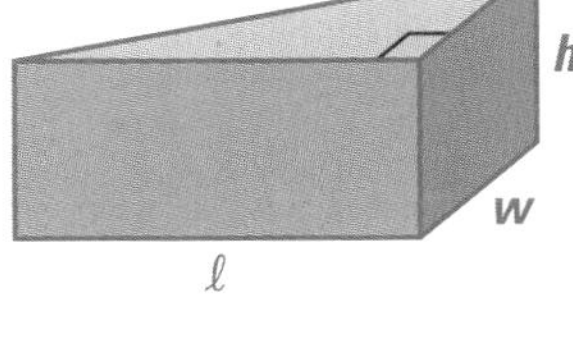

Here's How

1. Make a copy of the prism. Put the two prisms together so that the faces containing the longest sides of the bases are attached.
2. Find the volume of the rectangular prism you formed:

   $V = \ell wh$

3. The volume of one triangular prism equals half the volume of the rectangular prism:

   $V = \frac{1}{2}\ell wh$

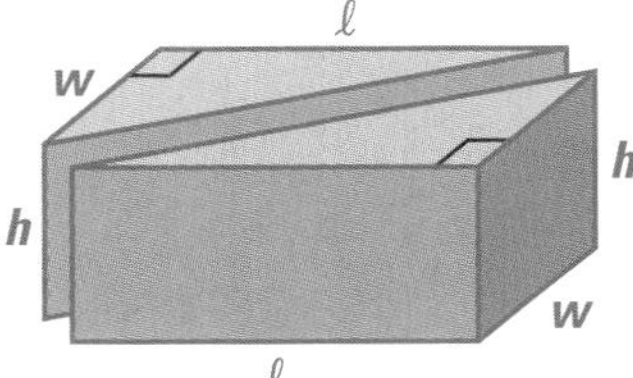

Try These

Find the volume of the triangular prism.

1.

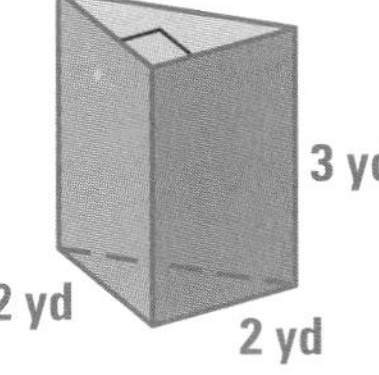

2.

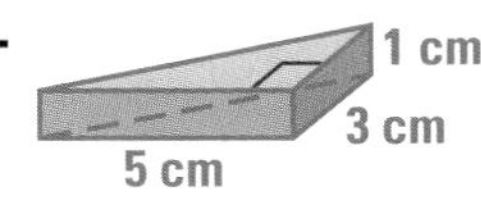

3.

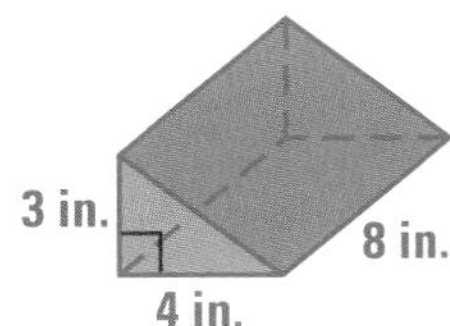

4. **MATHEMATICAL REASONING** In Step 2 of Sample 1, how do you know that the prism is rectangular? In other words, how do you know that the bases are rectangles when the right triangles are put together? Explain your reasoning.

5. **MATHEMATICAL REASONING** Express the base area B of the triangular prism in Sample 1 in terms of ℓ and w. Use this result to rewrite the formula $V = \frac{1}{2}\ell wh$ in terms of B and h.

In Sample 1 you explored a special case in which the triangular prism had bases that were right triangles. You will now consider the more general case in Sample 2.

SAMPLE 2 Finding the Volume of a Triangular Prism

Find the volume of the triangular prism shown.

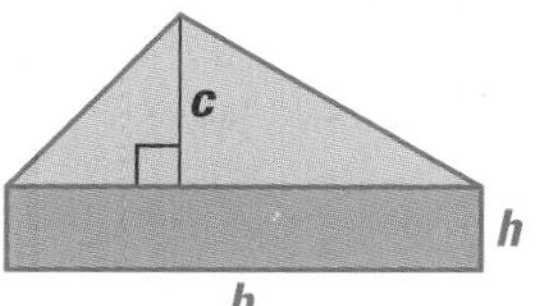

Here's How

1. Divide the prism into two prisms having bases that are right triangles.

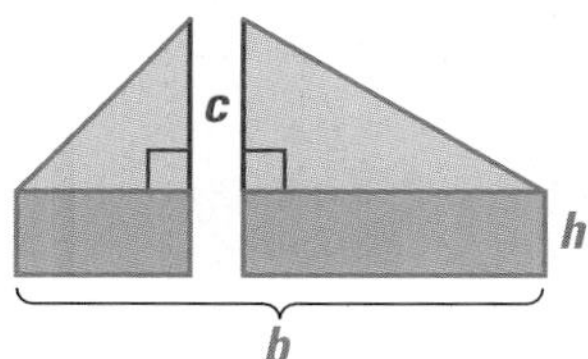

2. Following the method in Sample 1, make a copy of each smaller triangular prism. Arrange the triangular prisms to form a rectangular prism. Its volume is $V = bch$.

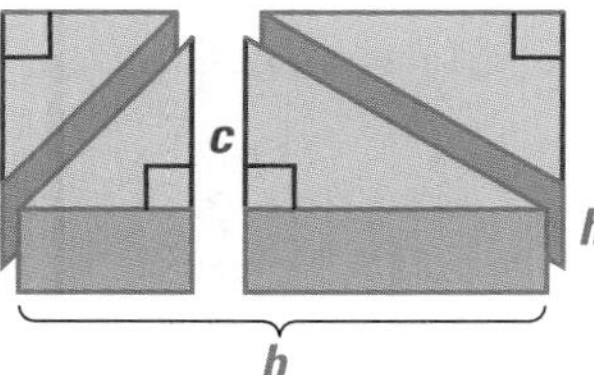

3. The volume of the original prism is half the volume of the rectangular prism, $V = \frac{1}{2}bch$.

The triangular prism in Sample 2 has a base area $B = \frac{1}{2}bc$. So the volume of a triangular prism with base area B and height h is $V = Bh$.

Try These

Find the volume of the triangular prism.

6.

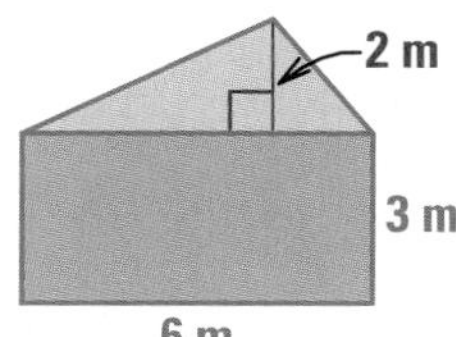

7.

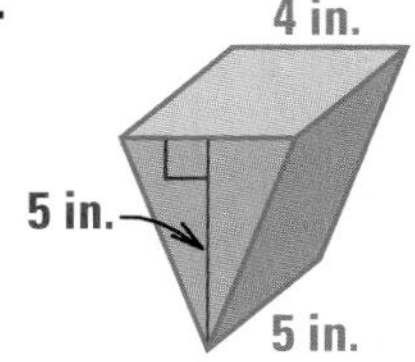

8.

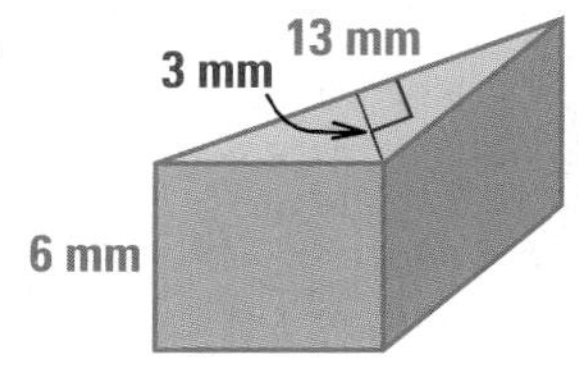

9. **MATHEMATICAL REASONING** Does the formula $V = Bh$ with base area B and height h also apply to rectangular prisms? Explain.

9.3 Volume of a Triangular Prism

In this lesson you'll:

- Know and use the formula for the volume of a triangular prism. (MG 1.3)
- Compare the formulas for the volume of triangular and rectangular prisms. (MG 1.3)

Student Help

LOOK BACK
For help with finding the area of a triangle, see page 372.

Goal 1 FINDING THE VOLUME OF A TRIANGULAR PRISM

As you saw in Developing Concepts 9.3, page 416, you can use the following formula to find the volume of a triangular prism.

VOLUME OF A TRIANGULAR PRISM

In Words The volume of a triangular prism is the product of the base area B and the height h.

In Algebra $V = Bh$

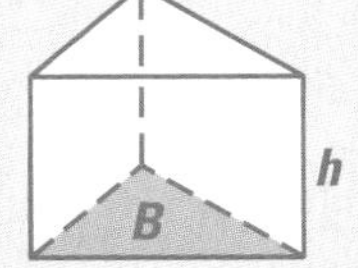

EXAMPLE 1 Finding the Volume of a Triangular Prism

Find the volume of the triangular prism.

a.

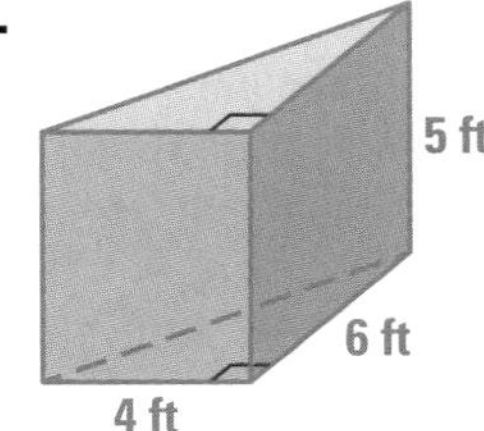

b.

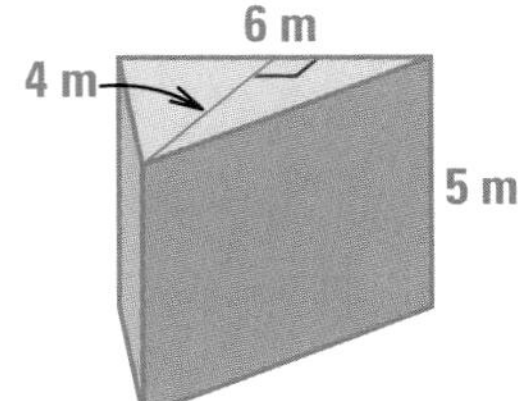

Solution

a. First find the base area B. Use the lengths of the sides that form a right angle in the formula for the area of a triangle.

$B = \frac{1}{2}(4)(6) = 12 \text{ ft}^2$ Use formula for area of a triangle.

Then use the base area to find the volume of the prism.

$V = Bh$ Write formula for volume of a triangular prism.

$= (12)(5) = 60 \text{ ft}^3$ Substitute 12 for B and 5 for h. Then multiply.

b. First find the base area B. Notice that the base and height of the prism's triangular bases are 6 meters and 4 meters, respectively.

$B = \frac{1}{2}(6)(4) = 12 \text{ m}^2$ Use formula for area of a triangle.

Then use the base area to find the volume of the prism.

$V = Bh$ Write formula for volume of a triangular prism.

$= (12)(5) = 60 \text{ m}^3$ Substitute 12 for B and 5 for h. Then multiply.

Student Help

STUDY TIP
Be careful not to confuse the base and height of a prism's triangular bases with the base area and height of the prism.

Link to **Archeology**

MAYAN PYRAMIDS
By reconstructing Mayan buildings, archeologists learn more about the Mayan architecture during the period it flourished from A.D. 250 to 900.

More about Mayan history is available at www.mcdougallittell.com

Goal 2 COMPARING VOLUME FORMULAS

EXAMPLE 2 Finding the Volume of a Rectangular Prism

A typical stone block used in the construction of Mayan pyramids was a rectangular prism. A block was 39 cm high, and its base area was 4320 cm^2. Find the volume of the rectangular prism.

Solution You know that the rectangular prism has a base area of 4320 cm^2 and that the area of a rectangle is the product of the length ℓ and the width w.

$V = \ell wh$ Write formula for volume of a rectangular prism.

$= \mathbf{4320(39)}$ Substitute 4320 for ℓw and 39 for h.

$= 168{,}480 \text{ cm}^3$ Multiply.

ANSWER ▶ The rectangular block has a volume of 168,480 cm^3.

You can write an alternate formula for the volume of a rectangular prism. It is the same formula as the volume of a triangular prism.

VOLUME OF A RECTANGULAR PRISM

In Words The volume of a rectangular prism is the product of the base area B and the height h.

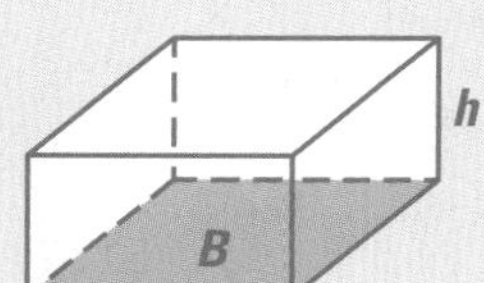

In Algebra $V = Bh$

EXAMPLE 3 Calculating and Comparing Volumes

Compare the volumes of both sections of the building. Find the total volume of the building.

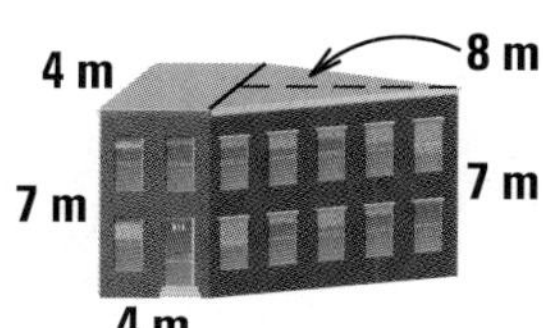

Solution

Divide the building into a triangular prism and a rectangular prism.

Base area of triangular prism: $B = \frac{1}{2}(4)(8) = 16 \text{ m}^2$

Base area of rectangular prism: $B = (4)(4) = 16 \text{ m}^2$

The triangular prism and the rectangular prism have the same base area and the same height. So, they must have the same volume.

$V = 16(7) = 112 \text{ m}^3$ Find total volume of either prism.

The building consists of two prisms. To find the total volume of the building, add the volumes of the prisms.

ANSWER ▶ The volume of the building is 224 m^3.

9.3 Exercises

Guided Practice

1. Complete the statement: You can calculate the volume of a triangular prism by finding the __?__ , then multiplying by the __?__.

In Exercises 2 and 3, find the volume of the triangular prism.

2.

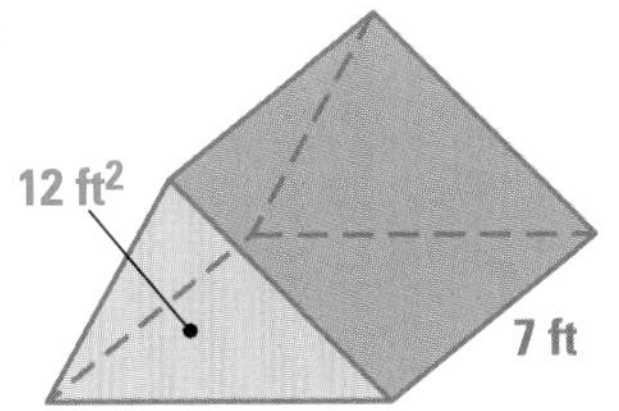

3.

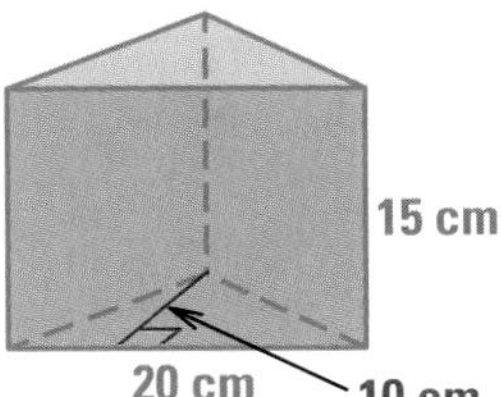

4. The base area of a triangular prism is 18 square inches. The height is 3 inches. Find the volume.

Practice and Problem Solving

Student Help

▶ **MORE PRACTICE**
Extra practice to help you master skills is on page 582.

Select all statements that are true for the given triangular prism.

A. The base area is 45 square meters.

B. The height of a base is 9 meters.

C. The height of the prism is 9 meters.

D. The volume of the prism is 360 cubic meters.

5.

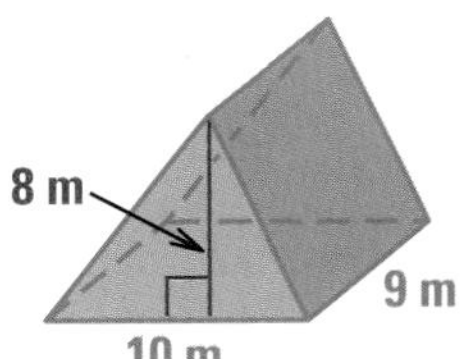

6.

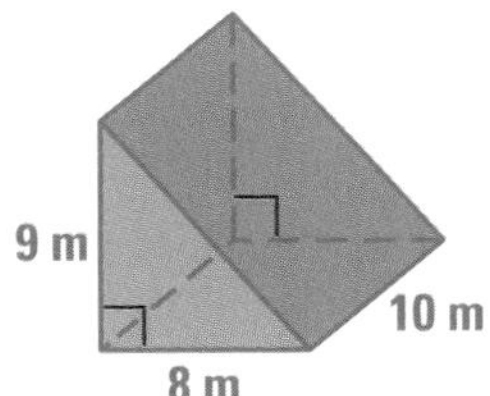

7.

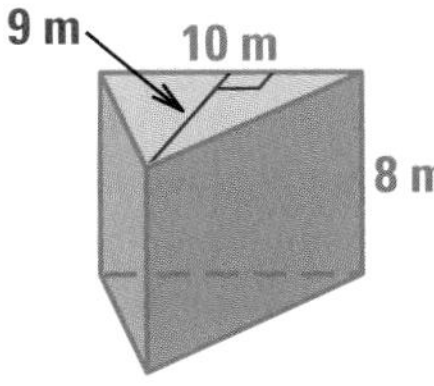

Find the volume of the triangular prism.

8.

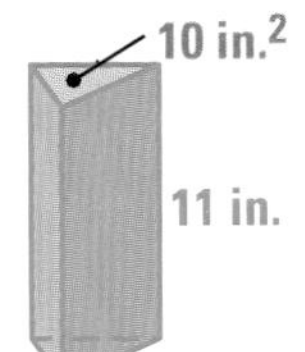

9.

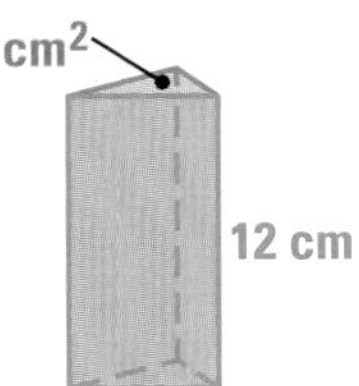

10.

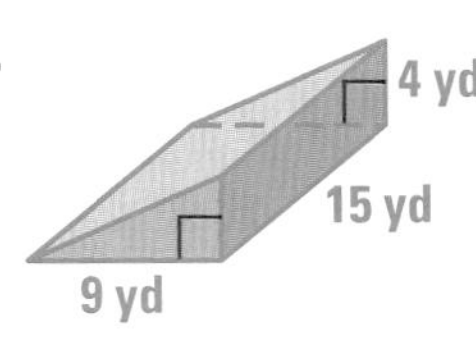

11.

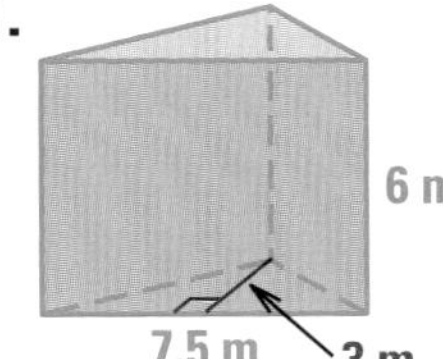

12.

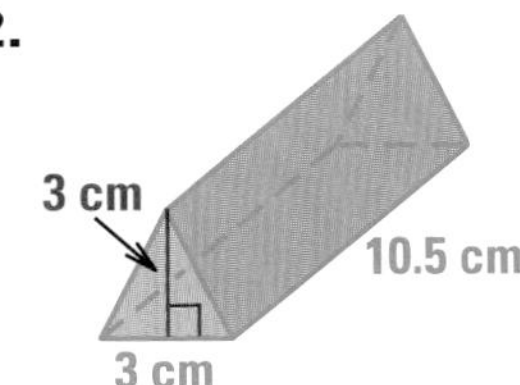

13.

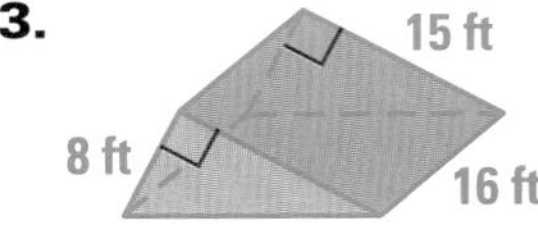

COMPARISON SHOPPING In Exercises 14 and 15, use the packages of cheddar cheese shown.

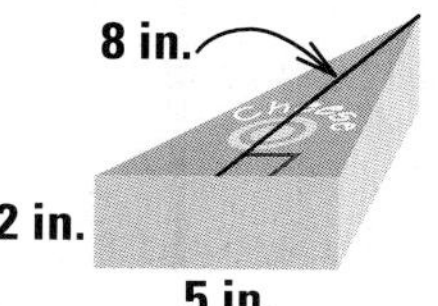

14. Find the volume of each package. Which has greater volume?

15. The price of the triangular package is \$4.39. The price of the rectangular package is \$3.59. Which package is the better buy? Use words and numbers to explain your reasoning.

In Exercises 16–18, use the building shown.

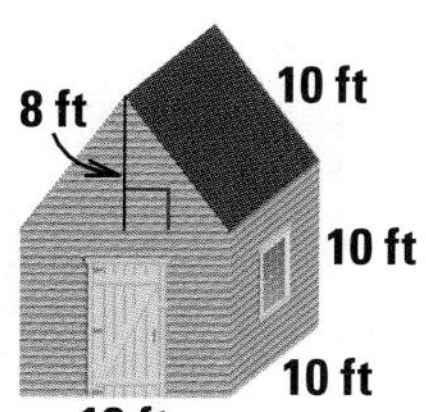

16. Describe the steps for finding the volume.

17. Identify which measurement is not needed to find the volume. Explain.

18. Calculate the volume of the building.

19. **ALGEBRA** A triangular prism has a volume of 1248 cubic meters. One of its triangular bases has a height of 8 meters and an area of 12 square meters. What is the height of the prism?

20. **History Link** The stones of the Great Pyramid are prisms with nonrectangular bases. To calculate the base area, you can divide it into a rectangle and a triangle. Find the volume of the stone.

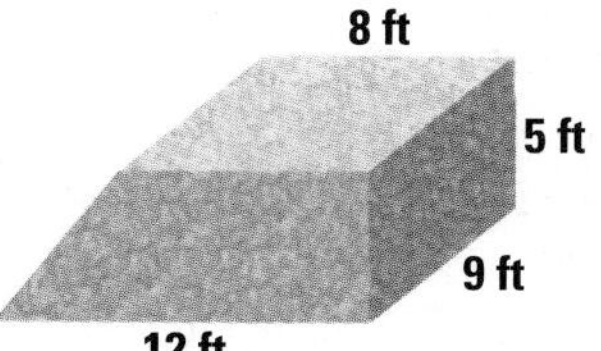

21. **CHALLENGE** The Landau building at the Massachusetts Institute of Technology is a triangular prism. One of its triangular bases has sides of 145 feet, 257 feet, and 290 feet. The building is 70 feet high. What additional information do you need to calculate the volume of the building? Explain your reasoning.

Multiple-Choice Practice

In Exercises 22 and 23, use the stereo speaker shown.

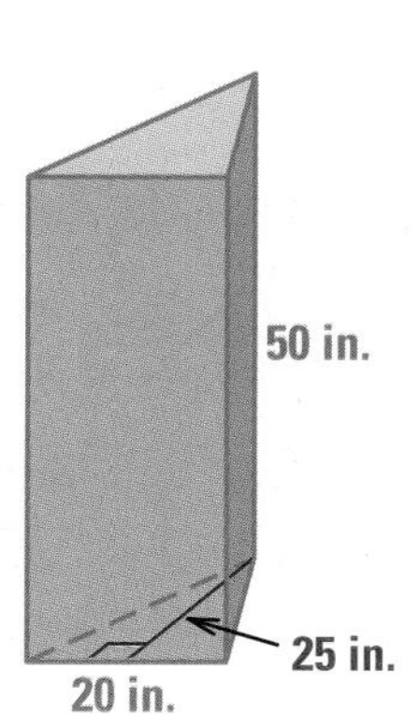

22. Which dimension is *not* needed to find the volume of the speaker?

Ⓐ 20 in. Ⓑ 25 in.

Ⓒ 50 in. Ⓓ All dimensions are necessary.

23. What is the volume of the stereo speaker?

Ⓕ 2,500 in.^3 Ⓖ 10,000 in.^3

Ⓗ 12,500 in.^3 Ⓙ 25,000 in.^3

Chapter 9 Mid-Chapter Test

Take this test as you would take a test in class. The answers to the exercises are given in the back of the book.

In Exercises 1–3, identify the solid as a *triangular prism*, a *rectangular prism*, or a *cylinder*. Then find its height. If the solid is a prism, find the number of faces.

1. 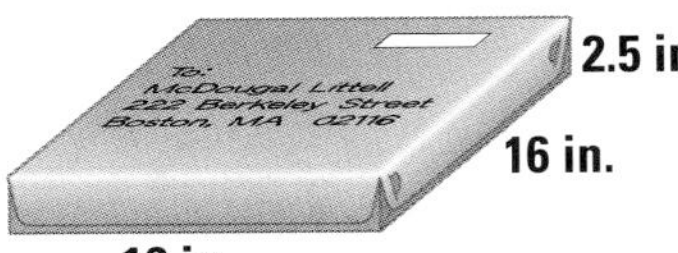

2. 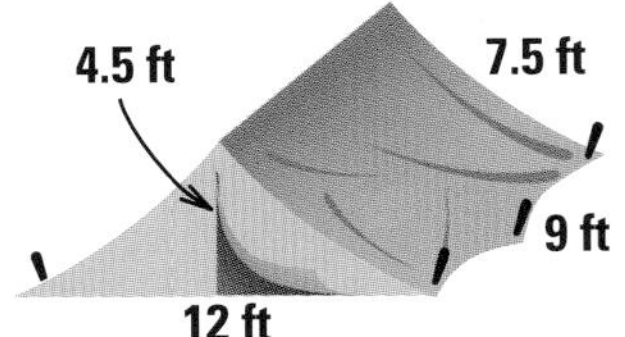

3. 

4. Sketch a triangular prism. How many faces does it have?

In Exercises 5–10, identify the prism. Then find the volume.

5. 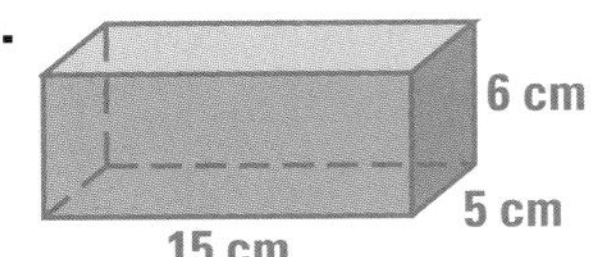

6. 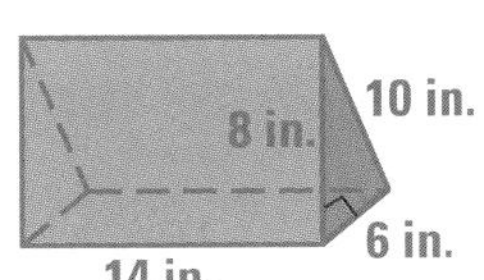

7. 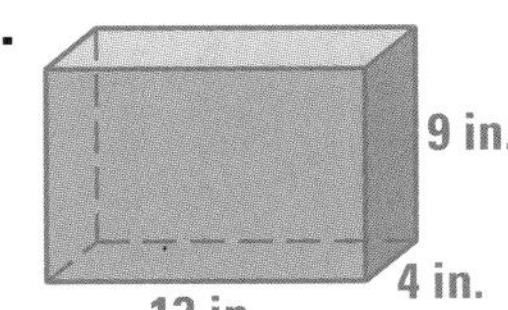

8. 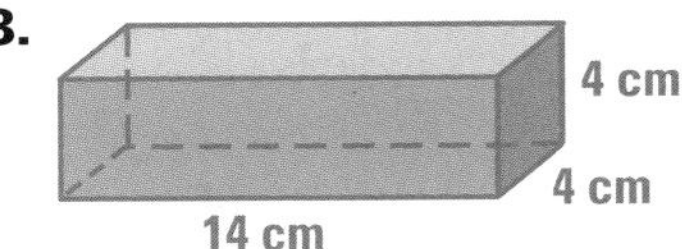

9. 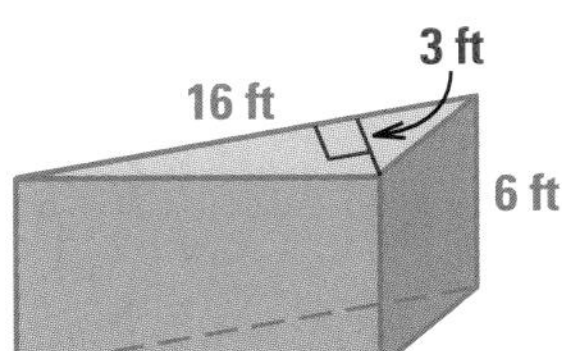

10. 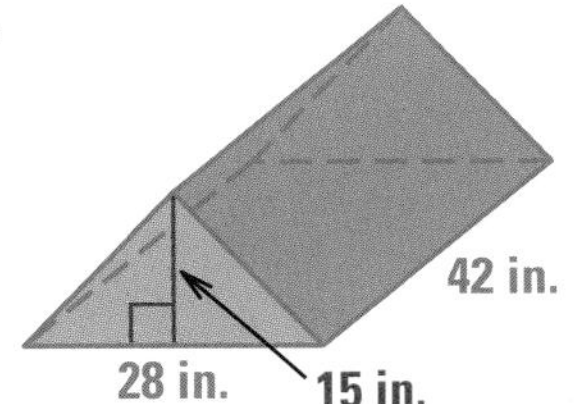

11. A rectangular prism has a volume of 12 cubic feet. The length is 3 feet and the height is 24 inches. Find the width of the prism.

12. The base area of a triangular prism is 54 square centimeters. The volume of the prism is 4320 cubic centimeters. Find the height of the prism.

BUILDING **In Exercises 13–15, use the building shown.**

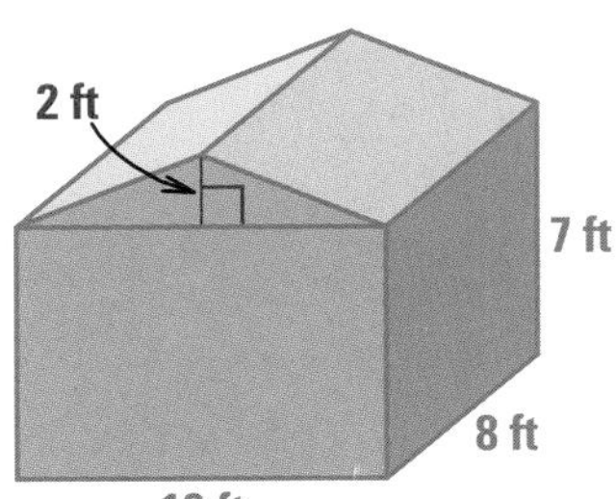

13. Find the volume of the portion of the building that is a triangular prism.

14. Find the volume of the portion of the building that is a rectangular prism.

15. Find the total volume of the building.

9.4 Volume of a Cylinder

In this lesson you'll:

- Know and use the formula for the volume of a cylinder. (MG 1.3)
- Convert one unit of measurement to another. (AF 2.1)

Student Help

STUDY TIP
A *unit cube* is a cube that has length, width, and height all equal to one unit.

Goal 1 FINDING THE VOLUME OF A CYLINDER

The faces of a unit cube are unit squares. Therefore, the base area of a prism is the number of unit cubes in one layer of cubes covering a base. The height is the number of layers that fill the figure.

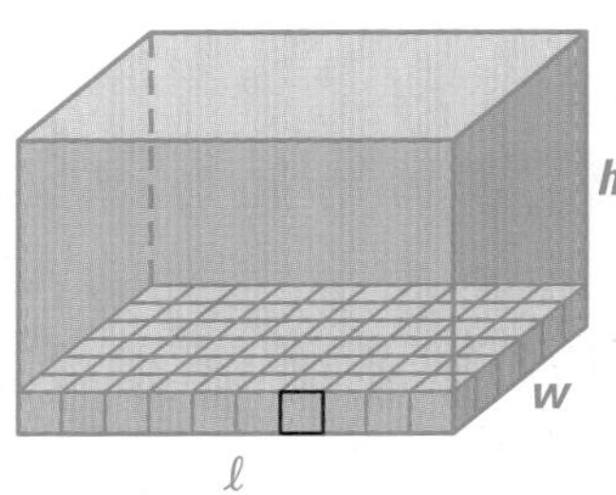

Area of base = ℓw

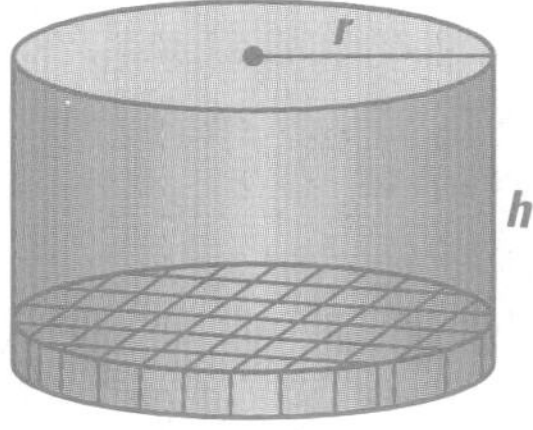

Area of base = πr^2

In Lesson 9.3, you learned that the volume of a rectangular prism can be found by multiplying the base area B times the height h. Likewise, the volume of a cylinder can be found by multiplying the base area πr^2 by the height h.

VOLUME OF A CYLINDER

In Words The volume V of a cylinder is the product of the base area πr^2 and the height h.

In Algebra $V = \pi r^2 h$

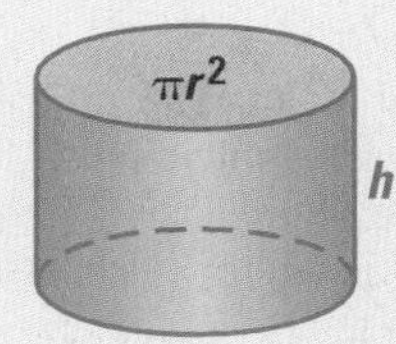

EXAMPLE 1 Finding the Volume of a Mug

The inside of the mug shown at the right has a radius of 4 centimeters and a height of 10 centimeters. Find the volume of the mug.

Solution

Volume = (Area of base)(Height)

$= \pi r^2 h$ Write formula for volume of cylinder.

$\approx (3.14)(4^2)(10)$ Substitute given values. Use 3.14 for π.

$= 502.4 \text{ cm}^3$ Multiply.

ANSWER ▶ The volume of the mug is about 502 cubic centimeters.

Goal 2 CONVERTING UNITS OF MEASURE

Volume is commonly measured in either cubic units or units of liquid volume. Cubic units are units such as cubic feet (ft^3) and cubic meters (m^3). Units of liquid volume are units such as gallons (gal) and liters (L). The table summarizes conversions between liquid volume and cubic units.

Liquid volume	Cubic units	
Gallon	231 in.^{3}	3785.41 cm^3
Liter	61.02 in.^{3}	1000 cm^3

Student Help

▶ MORE EXAMPLES

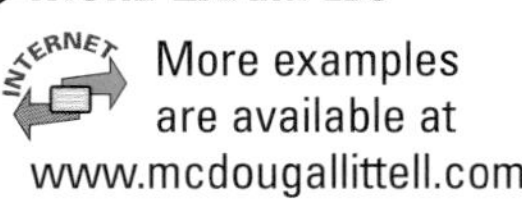

More examples are available at www.mcdougallittell.com

EXAMPLE 2 Finding the Volume of a Fountain

a. Find the volume of the fountain in cubic feet.

b. Find the volume of the fountain in gallons.

Solution

a. $V = \pi r^2 h$ — Write formula for volume of cylinder.

$\approx \mathbf{3.14} \cdot \mathbf{6^2} \cdot 2$ — Substitute given values. Use 3.14 for π.

$= 226.08 \text{ ft}^3$ — Multiply.

b. Use the fact that $1 \text{ ft}^3 \approx 7.48$ gal to find the volume in gallons.

$$226.08 \text{ ft}^3 \times \frac{7.48 \text{ gal}}{1 \text{ ft}^3} \approx 1691 \text{ gallons}$$

Student Help

▶ STUDY TIP

To find the number of gallons in 1 cubic foot, write a conversion factor using the information in the table above.

$$\frac{1 \text{ gal}}{231 \text{ in.}^3} \times \frac{1728 \text{ in.}^3}{1 \text{ ft}^3} \approx \frac{7.48 \text{ gal}}{1 \text{ ft}^3}$$

EXAMPLE 3 Using a Rate

A pump fills the fountain in Example 2 with water at a rate of 10 gallons per minute. How long does it take to fill the fountain?

Solution

You know that the volume of the fountain is 1691 gallons.

$$1691 \text{ gal} \times \frac{1 \text{ min}}{10 \text{ gal}} = 169.1 \text{ min}$$

ANSWER ▶ It takes 169.1 minutes to fill the fountain.

9.4 Exercises

Guided Practice

1. Which action could you take to measure the volume of a can of orange juice? Explain your reasoning in words.

A. Pour the juice into cup measures.

B. Peel the label off the can and find the area of the label.

In Exercises 2–4, use the cylinder shown.

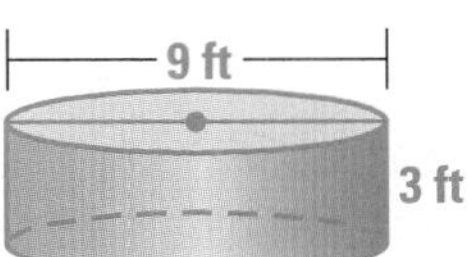

2. What is the base radius?

3. What is the base area?

4. What is the volume of the cylinder?

In Exercises 5–7, use the pool shown, which has the shape of a cylinder.

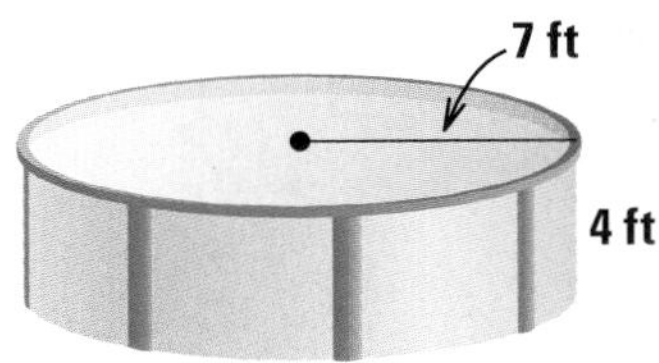

5. Find the volume of the pool in cubic feet.

6. Find the volume of the pool in gallons.

7. The pool drains at a rate of 12 gallons per minute. How long does it take to drain the pool? Explain your reasoning in words and numbers.

Practice and Problem Solving

Student Help

▶ **MORE PRACTICE** Extra practice to help you master skills is on page 583.

In Exercises 8–13, find the volume of the cylinder.

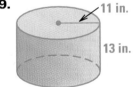

8. 6 mm; 14 mm

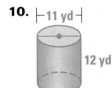

9. 11 in.; 13 in.

10. 11 yd; 12 yd

11. 16.6 cm; 5 cm

12. 6.2 ft; 17.8 ft

13. $14\frac{3}{4}$ yd; $4\frac{1}{2}$ yd

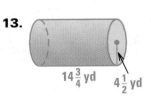

14. MATHEMATICAL REASONING A cylinder has a height of 1 unit and a base radius of 1 unit. What happens to its volume when the radius is doubled? tripled? quadrupled? Organize your data in a table. Describe the pattern.

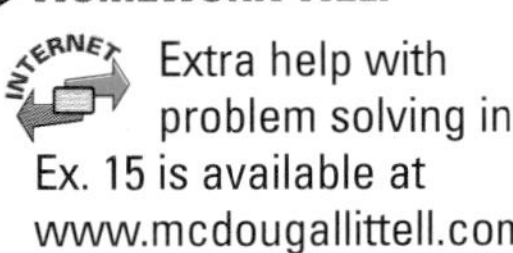

Student Help

▶ **HOMEWORK HELP**

Extra help with problem solving in Ex. 15 is available at www.mcdougallittell.com

15. PENCILS You want to manufacture cylindrical wooden pencils having a height of 18 centimeters (not including the eraser) and a diameter of 0.75 centimeter. Before the pencil is hollowed out to insert graphite, how much wood is needed to make one pencil?

16. ALGEBRA The volume of a cylinder is 42.39 cubic meters and the base radius is 1.5 meters. Find the height.

BUSINESS In Exercises 17–19, use the can shown, which a beverage company uses for packaging iced tea.

17. Find the volume of the can of iced tea in cubic inches.

18. If the company fills 86,400 iced tea cans in 24 hours (all shifts), how many gallons of iced tea are packaged in 24 hours?

19. How long does it take for the company to package 60,000 gallons of iced tea?

In Exercises 20 and 21, you will use approximation and displacement to find the volume of an object.

20. IRREGULAR OBJECTS Sometimes you can use approximation to find the volume of an irregular object. Suppose the shape of a rock resembles a rectangular prism. The approximate dimensions are 2.5 centimeters by 2 centimeters by 3 centimeters. Approximate the rock's volume.

21. *History Link* *Displacement* can be used to determine the volume of an object. To use displacement, find the volume of the water in a cylindrical container. Place the object in the container. Then find the new volume of the water in the container. The volume of the object is the difference between two volumes. Use the diagrams below to find the actual volume of the rock in Exercise 20.

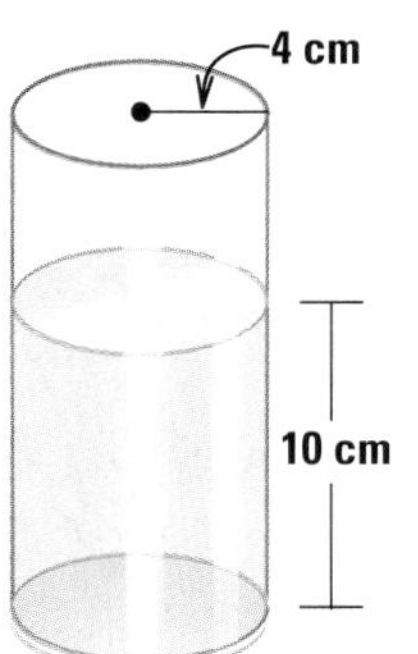

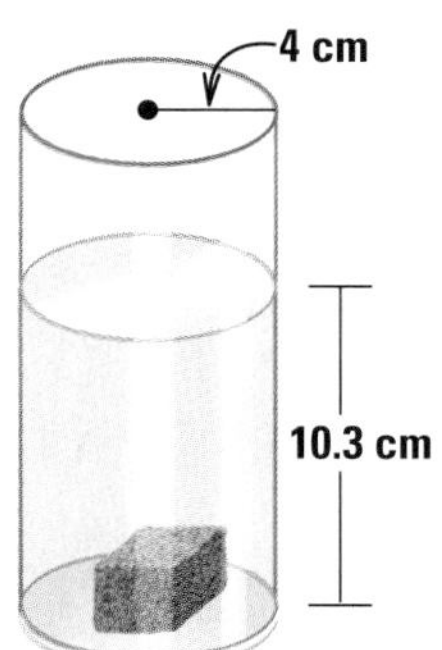

Link to History

DISPLACEMENT The Greek mathematician Archimedes described displacement as a means of measuring volume.

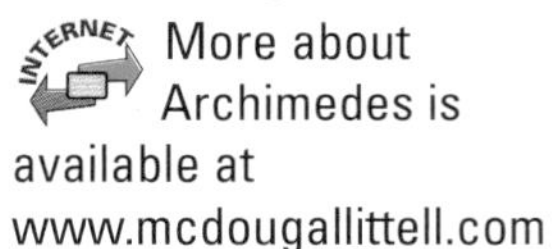

More about Archimedes is available at www.mcdougallittell.com

22. WRITING Use words and diagrams to describe the similarities and differences in the formulas for the volume of a rectangular prism, a triangular prism, and a cylinder.

23. CHALLENGE A cylindrical paint can is 8.1 inches high and has a base radius of 3.3 inches. An average coat of paint is 0.001 inch thick. Find the number of square feet that can be covered by the paint in the can.

Multiple-Choice Practice

Test Tip A B C D

▶ Remember that the height of a cylinder is the distance between the two bases.

In Exercises 24 and 25, use the cylinder below, which has a volume of about 2009.6 cubic centimeters.

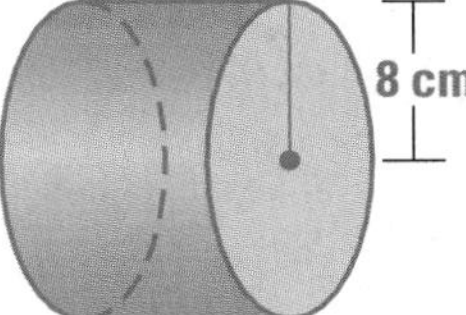

24. What is the base area? Use 3.14 for π.

Ⓐ 25.12 cm^2 Ⓑ 50.24 cm^2

Ⓒ 100.48 cm^2 Ⓓ 200.96 cm^2

25. What is the approximate height?

Ⓕ 6 cm Ⓖ 7 cm

Ⓗ 8 cm Ⓙ Not here

26. You are pouring water from a cylindrical can with a base diameter of 7 centimeters and a height of 10 centimeters into a cylindrical pan with a base diameter of 20 centimeters and a height of 14 centimeters. How many full cans can you pour into the pan?

Ⓐ 4 Ⓑ 7 Ⓒ 8 Ⓓ 11

Mixed Review

In Exercises 27–30, write the fraction as a decimal. Round to the nearest hundredth. *(2.8)*

27. $\frac{5}{9}$ **28.** $\frac{7}{12}$ **29.** $\frac{4}{15}$ **30.** $\frac{7}{11}$

In Exercises 31–33, find the average of the data set. *(4.6)*

31. $-38, 75, -16$ **32.** $11, -44, 69, -23$ **33.** $-5, -9, 57, -12, -6$

BAGEL SALES In Exercises 34–36, use the circle graph below, which shows the sales of 5 different types of bagels sold at a bakery in one day. *(7.5)*

34. Onion bagels account for 30% of the sales. How many degrees should this section of the graph contain?

35. Plain bagels account for 22% of the sales. How many degrees should this section of the graph contain?

36. Exactly 336 bagels, or 48%, were sesame, poppy seed, or pumpernickel. How many bagels of all types were sold?

DEVELOPING CONCEPTS

Surface Area

For use with Lesson 9.5

California Standards

- Understand the measurement of plane and solid shapes. (MG 1.0)
- Express in symbolic form simple relationships arising from geometry. (AF 3.2)
- Determine when and how to break a problem into simpler parts. (MR 1.3)

MATERIALS

- Paper and pencil

Imagine two-dimensional shapes being put together to make a solid. The *surface area* of the solid is the sum of the areas of the shapes that form it.

SAMPLE 1 Finding the Surface Area of a Prism

You can find the surface area of the box of cereal shown by dividing it into the rectangles that form it.

Here's How

Take the box of cereal and cut along 3 of the 4 folds on the top and bottom and 1 vertical fold so that the box lies flat. Then label the 6 rectangles as shown.

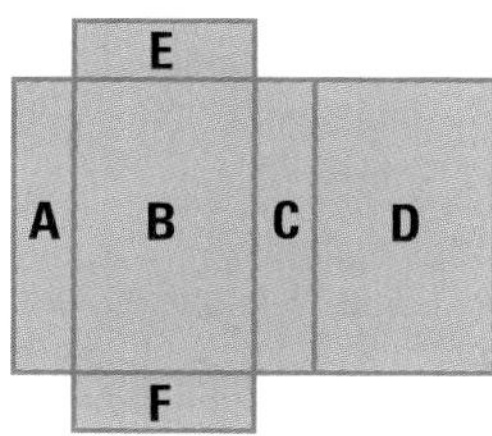

Use a ruler to find the dimensions of each rectangle. Record the dimensions in a table, then find the area of each piece.

Rectangle	A	B	C	D	E	F
Length (in.)	2	6	2	6	6	6
Width (in.)	10	10	10	10	2	2
Area (in.^{2})	20	60	20	60	12	12

The surface area of the box is the sum of the areas of the rectangles that form it:

$$20 + 60 + 20 + 60 + 12 + 12 = 184 \text{ in.}^2$$

Try These

In Exercises 1–3, use the rectangular prism shown.

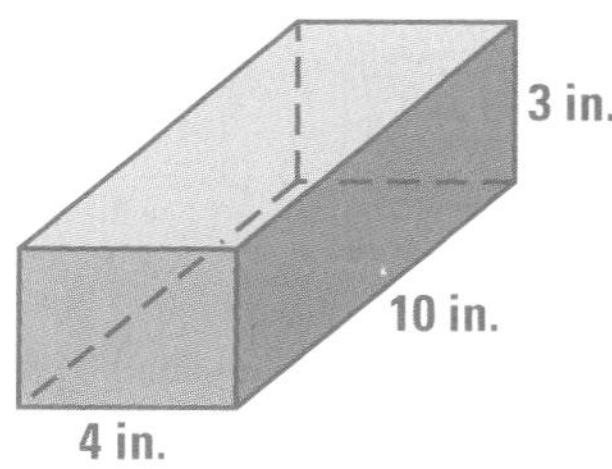

1. Sketch what the rectangular prism would look like if it were unfolded and laying flat. Label the dimensions of the rectangles formed.
2. Find the area of each rectangle.
3. Find the surface area of the rectangular prism.
4. **MATHEMATICAL REASONING** Write a formula for the surface area of a rectangular prism having length ℓ, width w, and height h.

The method of finding surface area in Sample 1 can be used for any solid.

SAMPLE 2 Finding the Surface Area of a Cylinder

You can find the surface area of the oats container shown by dividing it into the shapes that form it.

2.6 in.
OLD FASHIONED OATS
10 in.

Here's How

Take the oats container and cut almost all the way around the top and bottom circles. Then cut once vertically to make a rectangle when the container is flattened. Notice that the length of the rectangle is actually the circumference of either of the circles.

A 2.6 in.
$2\pi(2.6)$
C 10 in.
B 2.6 in.

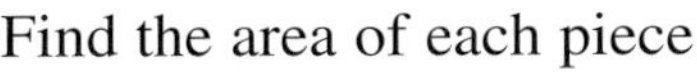

Find the area of each piece.

Circle A: $A = \pi r^2 \approx (3.14)(2.6)^2 \approx 21 \text{ in.}^2$

Circle B: $A = \pi r^2 \approx (3.14)(2.6)^2 \approx 21 \text{ in.}^2$

Rectangle C: $A = \ell w = (2\pi r)(h)$
$\approx 2(3.14)(2.6)(10) \approx 163 \text{ in.}^2$

The surface area of the cylinder is the sum of the areas:

$$21 + 21 + 163 = 205 \text{ in.}^2$$

Try These

Find the surface area of the cylinder.

5. 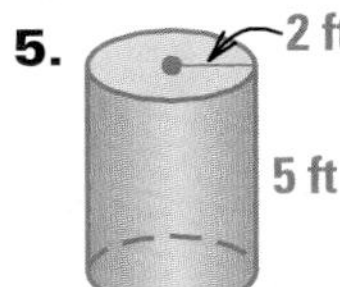

6. 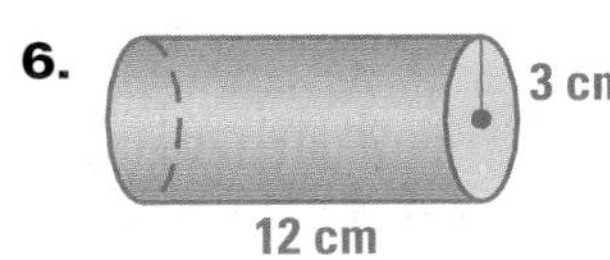

7. **MATHEMATICAL REASONING** Write a formula for the surface area of a cylinder having base radius r and height h.

8. **MATHEMATICAL REASONING** A company is deciding which package to use for a tea. Which package uses less materials? Explain.

A. 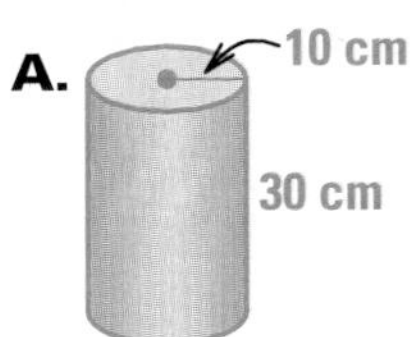

B. 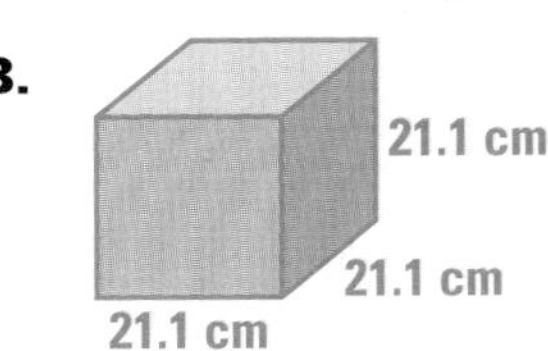

9.5 Surface Area of a Prism

In this lesson you'll:

- Understand the measurement of plane and solid shapes and use this understanding to solve problems. (MG 1.0)

Goal 1 Finding the Surface Area of a Prism

As you saw in Developing Concepts 9.5, page 428, the **surface area of a polyhedron** S is the sum of the areas of all of its faces.

EXAMPLE 1 Finding the Surface Area of a Prism

Find the surface area of the triangular prism.

Solution

To find the surface area, you need to find the area of each face. Then find the sum of all the areas.

Area of two triangular faces $= 2\left(\frac{1}{2} \cdot 3 \cdot 4\right) = 12 \text{ in.}^2$

Area of 3 in. by 6 in. rectangular face $= 3 \cdot 6 = 18 \text{ in.}^2$

Area of 4 in. by 6 in. rectangular face $= 4 \cdot 6 = 24 \text{ in.}^2$

Area of 5 in. by 6 in. rectangular face $= 5 \cdot 6 = 30 \text{ in.}^2$

Surface area of the triangular prism $= 12 + 18 + 24 + 30$

$= 84 \text{ in.}^2$

ANSWER ▶ The surface area of the prism is 84 square inches.

EXAMPLE 2 Finding the Surface Area of a Prism

Find the surface area of the rectangular prism.

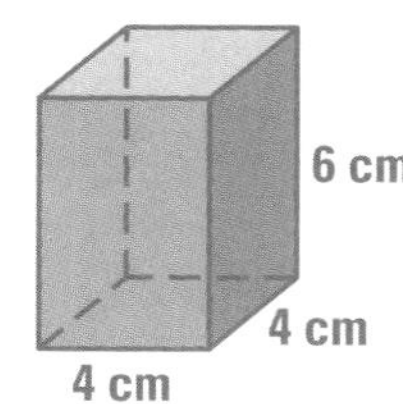

Solution

The two bases of the prism are squares. The four vertical faces are rectangles.

Area of two square bases $= 2(4 \cdot 4) = 32 \text{ cm}^2$

Area of four rectangular faces $= 4(4 \cdot 6) = 96 \text{ cm}^2$

Surface area of rectangular prism $= 32 + 96 = 128 \text{ cm}^2$

ANSWER ▶ The surface area of the rectangular prism is 128 square centimeters.

Student Help

▶ **More Examples**

INTERNET More examples are available at www.mcdougallittell.com

Goal 2 USING SURFACE AREA TO SOLVE PROBLEMS

EXAMPLE 3 Using Surface Area

You are making a set of wooden building blocks. The set has three sizes of blocks and there are 24 of each size. A small can of enamel paint will cover 10 square feet. If you want to paint each size of block a different color, how many cans of each color of paint will you need?

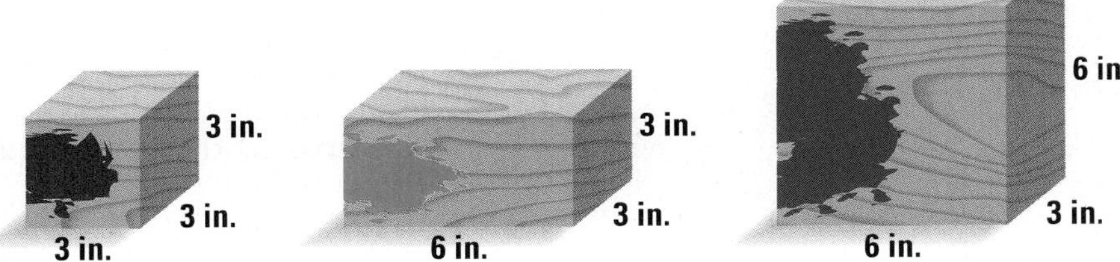

Solution

First, find the total surface area for each size of block. To do so, calculate the surface area of one of each size of block. Then multiply by 24, the number of blocks of each size.

RED BLOCKS: Each red block has six faces that are 3 inches by 3 inches.

Surface area of one block: $6 \times (3 \times 3) = 54 \text{ in.}^2$

Surface area of 24 blocks: $24 \times 54 = \mathbf{1296} \text{ in.}^2$

GREEN BLOCKS: Each green block has two faces that are 3 inches by 3 inches and four faces that are 3 inches by 6 inches.

Surface area of one block: $2 \times (3 \times 3) + 4 \times (3 \times 6) = 90 \text{ in.}^2$

Surface area of 24 blocks: $24 \times 90 = \mathbf{2160} \text{ in.}^2$

BLUE BLOCKS: Each blue block has two faces that are 6 inches by 6 inches and four faces that are 3 inches by 6 inches.

Surface area of one block: $2 \times (6 \times 6) + 4 \times (3 \times 6) = 144 \text{ in.}^2$

Surface area of 24 blocks: $24 \times 144 = \mathbf{3456} \text{ in.}^2$

Second, find the area that one can of paint will cover.

$1 \text{ ft}^2 = 144 \text{ in.}^2$, so $10 \text{ ft}^2 = 1440 \text{ in.}^2$

Finally, compare the area that one can of paint will cover, 1440 square inches, with the surface area of 24 blocks of each type.

RED BLOCKS	GREEN BLOCKS	BLUE BLOCKS
$\frac{1296}{1440} = 0.9$	$\frac{2160}{1440} = 1.5$	$\frac{3456}{1440} = 2.4$

You cannot buy part of a can of paint, so round to the next whole number.

ANSWER ▶ You will need one can of red paint, two cans of green paint, and three cans of blue paint.

Student Help

▶ **READING TIP**
Look for words such as *first, second,* and *finally* to follow the steps of a solution.

9.5 Exercises

Guided Practice

In Exercises 1 and 2, use the triangular prism shown.

1. Find the area of each face of the triangular prism.

2. Find the surface area of the triangular prism.

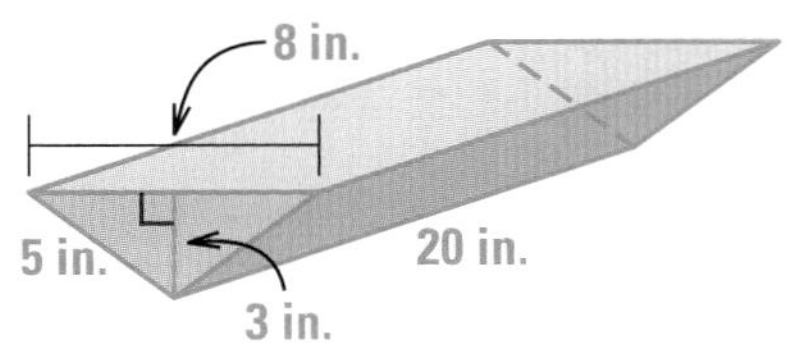

Find the surface area of the rectangular prism.

3. 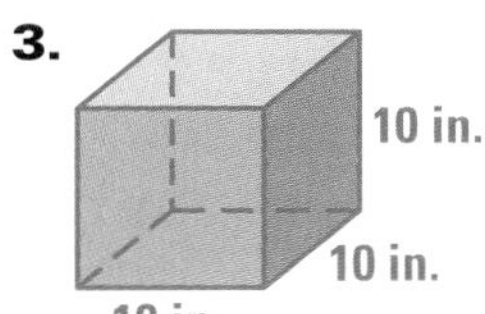

4. 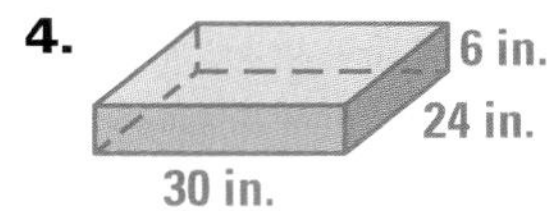

5. 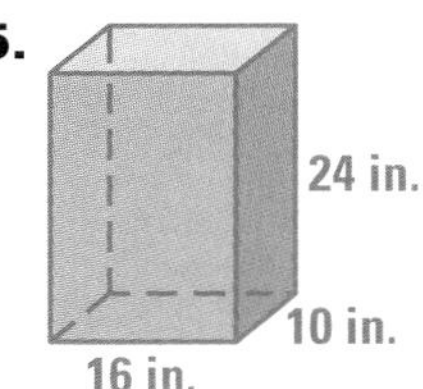

Practice and Problem Solving

Student Help

▶ **More Practice**
Extra practice to help you master skills is on page 583.

In Exercises 6–11, find the approximate surface area of the solid.

6. 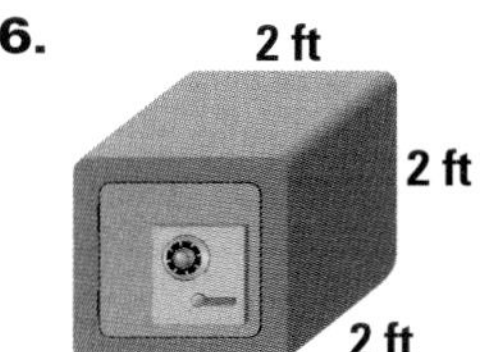

7. 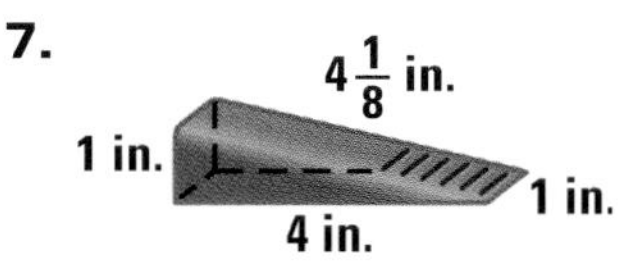

8. 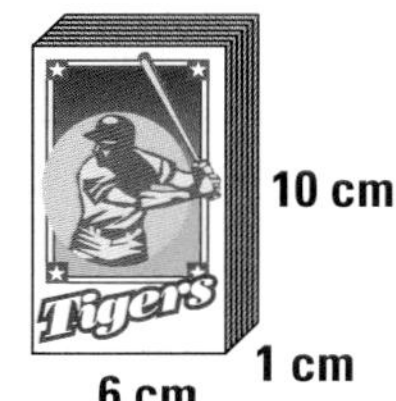

9. 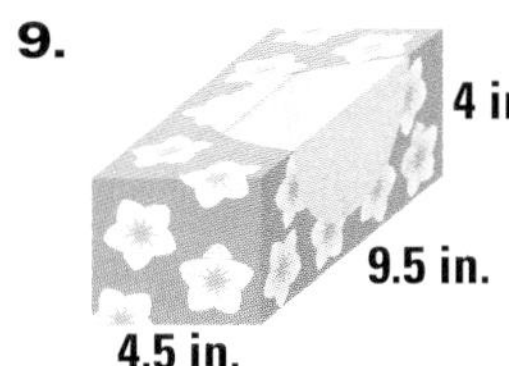

10. 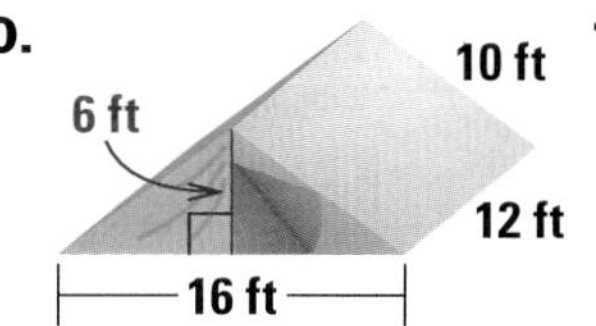

11. 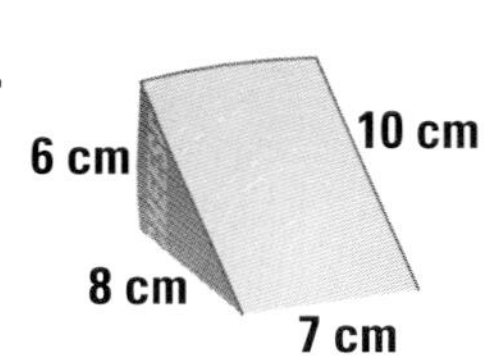

12. **MATHEMATICAL REASONING** Find the length of each edge of a cube that has a surface area of 864 square inches. Support your answer with a diagram of the cube and label the lengths of the edges with numbers or variables. Explain why you chose to approach the situation in the way that you did.

13. **MATHEMATICAL REASONING** A block of wood has the shape of a rectangular prism. You split the block into two triangular prisms with the same size and shape. Does the combined surface areas of the two triangular prisms equal the surface area of the original block? Explain why or why not.

In Exercises 14–16, find the surface area of the prism.

14.

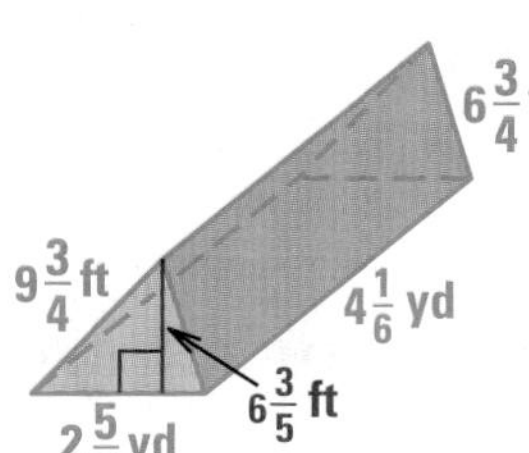

15.

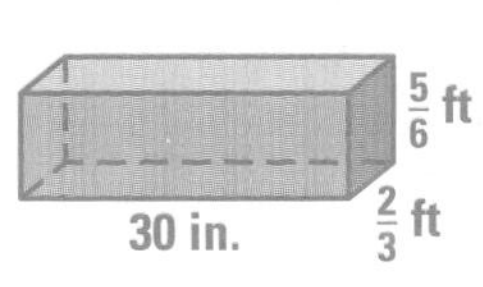

16.

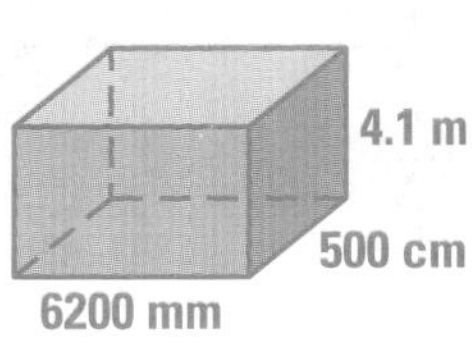

17. WALLPAPER You are wallpapering a living room. The room is 18 feet long, 9 feet high, and 16 feet wide. How much wallpaper is needed to cover the walls? (Ignore doors and windows.)

18. UPHOLSTERY You are covering a sofa cushion with fabric. Find the approximate amount of fabric you need.

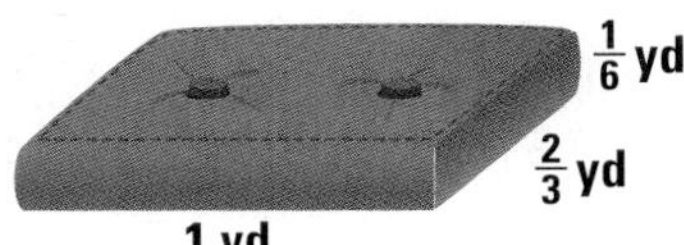

Link to Architecture

A-FRAME The design of A-frame houses allows snow to slide easily off the steep roof. The design is more popular in snowy regions.

ESTIMATION In Exercises 19 and 20, decide which is the best estimate of the surface area of the object. Explain your reasoning in words and numbers.

19. Sugar cube	**A.** 1.5 cm^2	**B.** 5.5 cm^2	**C.** 10.5 cm^2
20. Standard door	**A.** 8.5 ft^2	**B.** 43.5 ft^2	**C.** 105 ft^2

21. A-FRAME You are a contractor planning to install a new roof on an A-frame house. In order to estimate the cost, you need to know the surface area. Use a diagram and label the edges to find the surface area of the roof.

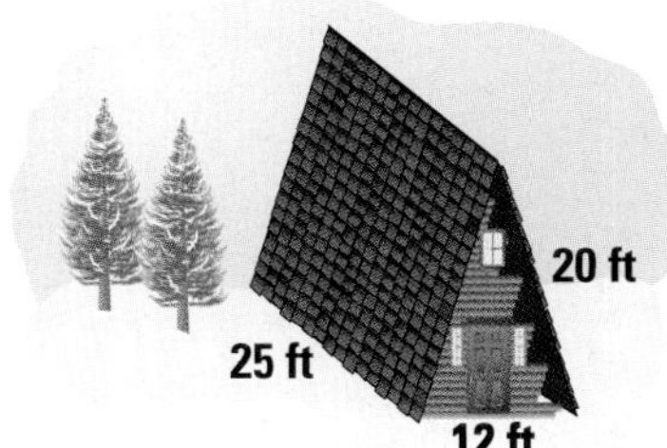

22. CHALLENGE What happens to the surface area of a cube if you double the length of each edge? Use a table and diagram to explain.

Multiple-Choice Practice

In Exercises 23 and 24, use the triangle shown.

23. The triangle is a base of a prism. What is the area of the triangle?

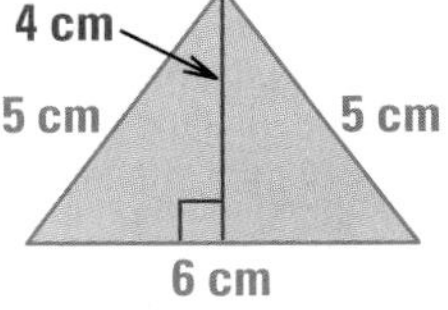

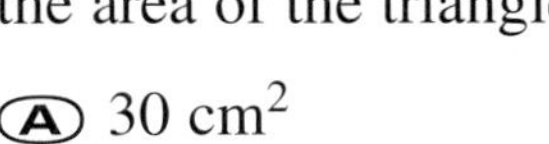

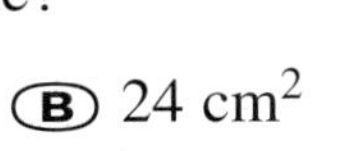

Ⓐ 30 cm^2 Ⓑ 24 cm^2

Ⓒ 15 cm^2 Ⓓ 12 cm^2

24. The triangle in Exercise 23 is the base of a triangular prism with a height of 6 cm. What is the surface area of the prism?

Ⓕ 120 cm^2 Ⓖ 126 cm^2 Ⓗ 132 cm^2 Ⓙ 138 cm^2

9.6 Surface Area of a Cylinder

California Standards

In this lesson you'll:

- Express in symbolic form simple relationships arising from geometry. (AF 3.2)
- Use common estimates of π to estimate and calculate the area of a circle. (MG 1.2)

Goal 1 Finding the Surface Area of a Cylinder

The **circumference of a cylinder** is the circumference of a base. The **lateral surface** is the surface that connects the two bases. The **surface area of a cylinder** is the sum of the areas of the two bases and the lateral surface area.

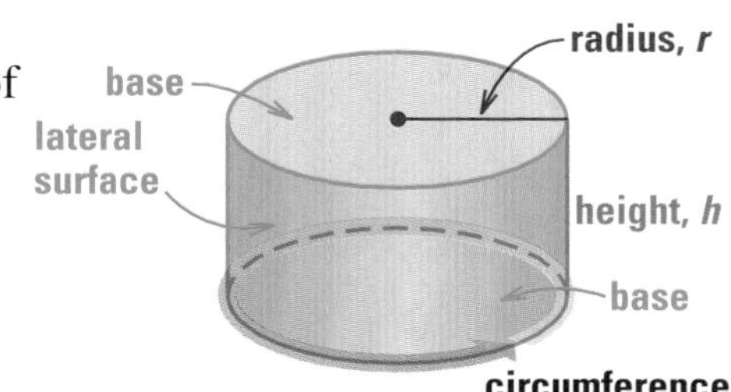

The diagrams below show that the lateral surface of a cylinder is a rectangle. The lateral surface area is equal to the base circumference $2\pi r$ times the cylinder's height h.

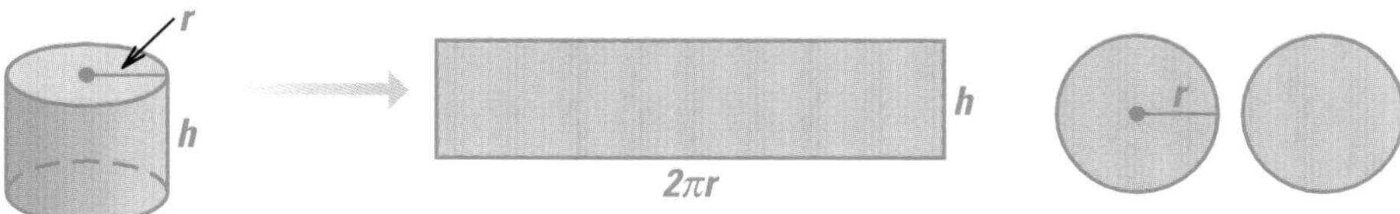

Surface Area of a Cylinder

In Words The surface area S of a right circular cylinder is the sum of the lateral surface area and the areas of the two bases.

In Algebra $S = 2\pi rh + 2\pi r^2$

lateral surface area (for $2\pi rh$); base areas (for $2\pi r^2$)

Example 1 Finding Surface Area

Find the surface area of the cylinder shown.

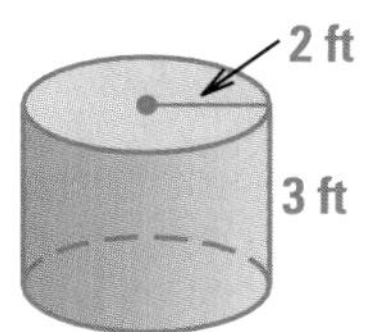

Solution

The cylinder has a base radius of 2 feet and a height of 3 feet. Use 3.14 for π.

$S = 2\pi rh + 2\pi r^2$ Write formula for surface area.

$\approx 2(3.14)(2)(3) + 2(3.14)(2^2)$ Substitute given values.

$= 37.68 + 25.12$ Multiply to find areas.

$= 62.8 \text{ ft}^2$ Add.

ANSWER ▶ The surface area is about 62.8 square feet.

Student Help

▶ **Study Tip**
For a cylinder with base radius r and base diameter d, the circumference can be expressed as πd or $2\pi r$ because $d = 2r$.

Goal 2 USING SURFACE AREA TO SOLVE PROBLEMS

Link to Careers

INDUSTRIAL DESIGNERS create the size and shape of different product packages.

INTERNET More about industrial designers is available at www.mcdougallittell.com

EXAMPLE 2 Finding Surface Area

You are designing two sizes of paint cans. You need to know the surface area to calculate how much metal you need. Approximate the surface area of each paint can.

a.

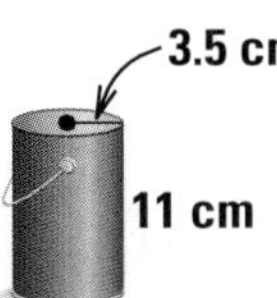

b.

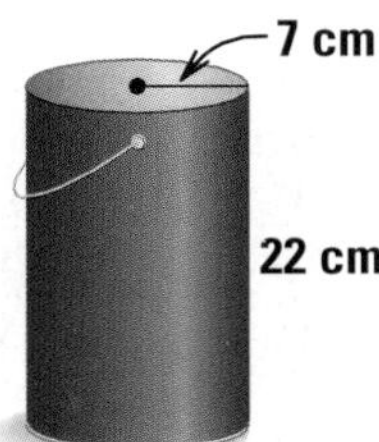

Solution

a. SMALL CAN: $r = 3.5$ cm and $h = 11$ cm. Use $\pi \approx 3.14$.

$S = 2\pi \boldsymbol{rh} + 2\pi \boldsymbol{r}^2$	Write formula.
$= (2 \cdot \pi \cdot \mathbf{3.5} \cdot \mathbf{11}) + (2 \cdot \pi \cdot \mathbf{3.5}^2)$	Substitute values.
$= 77\pi + 24.5\pi$	Multiply to find areas.
$= 101.5\pi$	Add.
$\approx 101.5(3.14) = 318.71 \text{ cm}^2$	Substitute 3.14 for π.

ANSWER ▶ The surface area of the small can is about 319 cm^2.

b. LARGE CAN: $r = 7$ cm and $h = 22$ cm. Use $\pi \approx \frac{22}{7}$.

$S = 2\pi \boldsymbol{rh} + 2\pi \boldsymbol{r}^2$	Write formula.
$= (2 \cdot \pi \cdot \mathbf{7} \cdot \mathbf{22}) + \left(2 \cdot \pi \cdot \mathbf{7}^2\right)$	Substitute values.
$= 308\pi + 98\pi$	Multiply to find areas.
$= 406\pi$	Add.
$\approx 406 \cdot \frac{22}{7} = 1276 \text{ cm}^2$	Substitute $\frac{22}{7}$ for π.

ANSWER ▶ The surface area of the large can is about 1276 cm^2.

EXAMPLE 3 Comparing Surface Areas

In Example 2, the dimensions of the large can are twice the dimensions of the small can. You can compare the surface areas of the cans by finding the ratio of the surface areas.

$$\frac{\text{Larger surface area}}{\text{Smaller surface area}} = \frac{406\pi}{101.5\pi} = \frac{406}{101.5} = \frac{4}{1}$$

The large can has 4 times the surface area of the small can.

9.6 Exercises

Guided Practice

1. Name the parts of the cylinder labeled a, b, c, d, and e. Write a definition of each part of the cylinder.

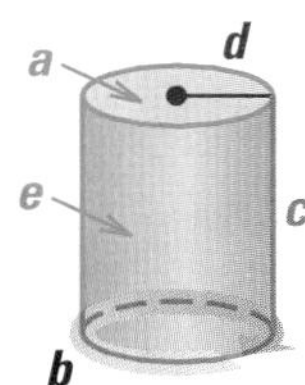

In Exercises 2–5, use the cylinder shown to match the description with its approximate measurement.

2. Area of one base **A.** 197.8 in.^{2}

3. Surface area **B.** 127.2 in.^{2}

4. Lateral surface area **C.** 325.0 in.^{2}

5. Area of two bases **D.** 63.6 in.^{2}

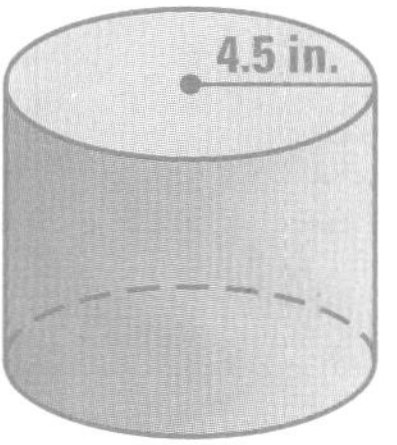

Practice and Problem Solving

Student Help

▶ MORE PRACTICE Extra practice to help you master skills is on page 583.

Match the object with its measurements. Find the surface area of the figure.

6. Pen **A.** $h = 190$ mm; $r = 4$ mm

7. AAA battery **B.** $h = 6\frac{3}{4}$ in.; $r = 1\frac{1}{4}$ in.

8. Juice can **C.** $h = 1$ mm; $d = 19$ mm

9. Penny **D.** $h = 4.2$ cm; $d = 1$ cm

Find the lateral surface area, base area, and total surface area of the cylinder with the given dimensions using the given value of π.

10. $h = 10$ cm; $d = 5$ cm; $\pi \approx 3.14$

11. $h = 3$ ft; $r = 4\frac{1}{3}$ ft; $\pi \approx 3.14$

12. $h = 7$ in.; $r = 3\frac{1}{2}$ in.; $\pi \approx \frac{22}{7}$

13. $h = 6$ m; $d = 14$ m; $\pi \approx \frac{22}{7}$

Student Help

▶ HOMEWORK HELP

Extra help with problem solving in Ex. 14 is available at www.mcdougallittell.com

14. Each of the containers below holds the same amount of liquid. Which do you think has less surface area? Check your guess by finding the surface area of each container. Use $\frac{22}{7}$ for π.

a.

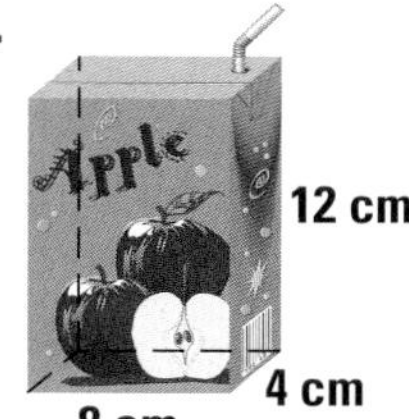

b.

Link to Science

JELLYFISH Cylindrical tanks are often used in aquariums to hold jellyfish. The cylindrical shape of the tank protects the jellyfish from becoming trapped in the corners.

More about jellyfish is available at www.mcdougallittell.com

Science Link **In Exercises 15–17, find the surface area of the cylindrical aquarium tanks. Use 3.14 for π.**

15. 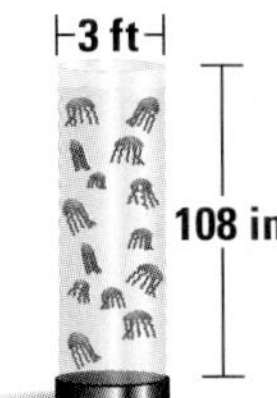

16. 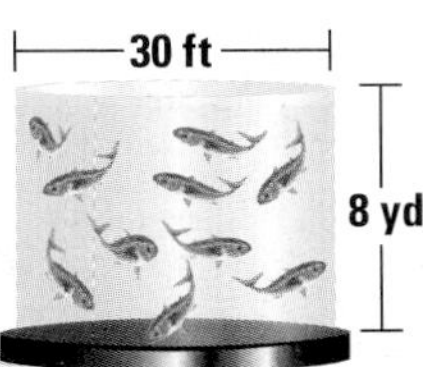

17. 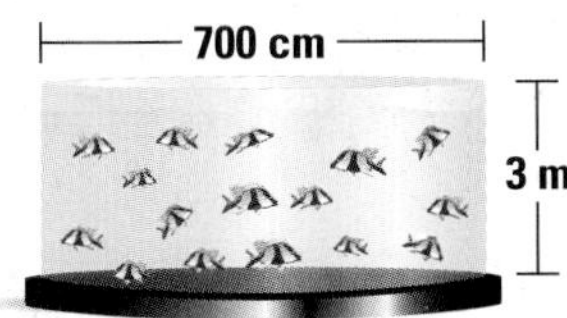

18. **CAMPING** Your sleeping bag fits in a cylindrical sack. When you unroll the bag, it is in the shape of a prism as shown. Do you think that the surface areas of the sack and the unrolled sleeping bag are the same? Find the surface areas to check your answer. Use 3.14 for π.

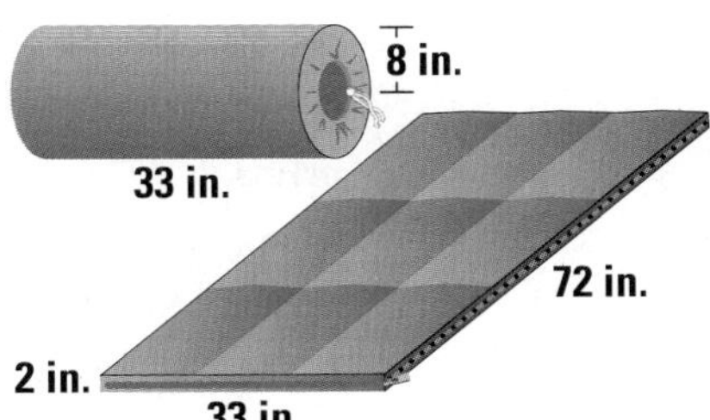

19. **MATHEMATICAL REASONING** The base radius of a cylinder is 7 inches and the height is 10 inches. Find the surface area. What is the surface area if the dimensions are doubled? tripled? quadrupled? Organize your results in a table and describe the pattern.

20. **STRUCTURES** You are planning to build the structure shown out of sheet metal. Calculate how much sheet metal is necessary to construct the structure. Do not include the floor. Use $\frac{22}{7}$ for π.

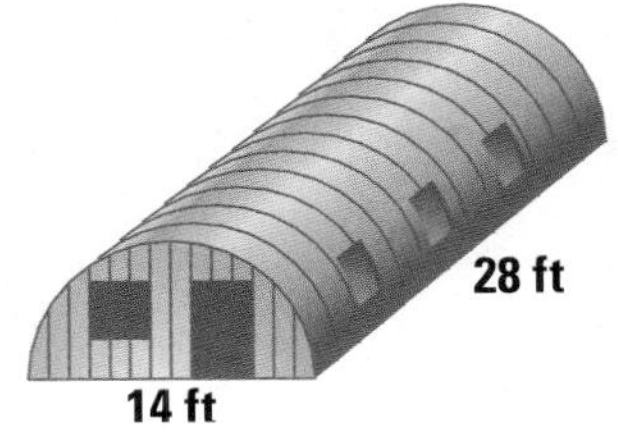

21. **CHALLENGE** A rectangle can be rolled to form the lateral surface of a cylinder. Can any parallelogram be rolled to form the lateral surface of a right cylinder? Explain your reasoning using words and diagrams.

Multiple-Choice Practice

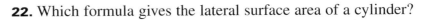

22. Which formula gives the lateral surface area of a cylinder?

Ⓐ $2\pi r^2$ Ⓑ $2\pi rh$ Ⓒ $2\pi dh$ Ⓓ $2\pi d$

23. Which formula gives one base area of a cylinder?

Ⓕ $2\pi rh$ Ⓖ $2\pi d$ Ⓗ πr^2 Ⓙ $2\pi r^2$

Test Tip Ⓐ Ⓑ Ⓒ Ⓓ

▶ Remember that the formula for the base area of a cylinder is the same as the formula for the area of a circle.

24. You are frosting the top and sides of a cylindrical cake that has a 9 inch base diameter. The cake is 6 inches tall. How much surface area do you need to cover?

Ⓐ 233 in.^{2} Ⓑ 297 in.^{2} Ⓒ 594 in.^{2} Ⓓ 848 in.^{2}

Chapter 9 Chapter Summary and Review

VOCABULARY

- **polyhedron,** *p. 407*
- **faces,** *p. 407*
- **edges,** *p. 407*
- **prism,** *p. 407*
- **bases,** *pp. 407, 408*
- **height of a prism,** *p. 407*
- **right prism,** *p. 407*
- **circular cylinder,** *p. 408*
- **height of a cylinder,** *p. 408*
- **right circular cylinder,** *p. 408*
- **volume,** *p. 411*
- **surface area of a polyhedron,** *p. 430*
- **circumference of a cylinder,** *p. 434*
- **lateral surface,** *p. 434*
- **surface area of a cylinder,**

9.1 PRISMS AND CYLINDERS

Examples on pp. 407–408

A prism has two parallel bases that are polygons of the same size and shape. The shape of the bases of a prism determines the name of a prism. A cylinder has two parallel, circular bases.

EXAMPLE **Identify the prism or cylinder.**

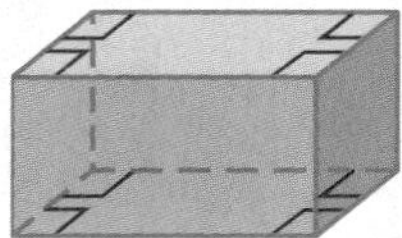
Rectangular prism

Triangular prism

Cylinder

In Exercises 1–3, match the description with the correct name below.

A. Triangular prism **B.** Rectangular prism **C.** Circular cylinder

1. A solid figure with faces that are rectangles and with two parallel bases that are the same size and shape
2. A solid figure with two circular, parallel bases of the same size
3. A solid figure with two parallel bases that are triangles of the same size and shape and other faces that are rectangles

In Exercises 4–7, identify the solid as a *triangular prism*, a *rectangular prism*, or a *cylinder*. Then find its height. If the solid is a prism, find the number of faces.

4.
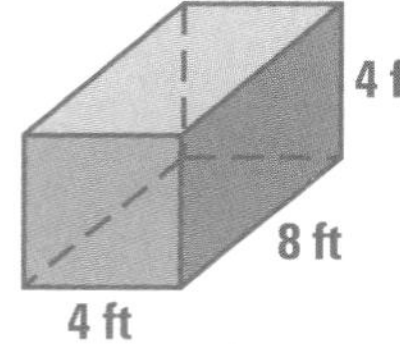

5.
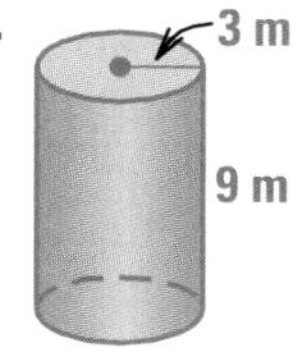

6.
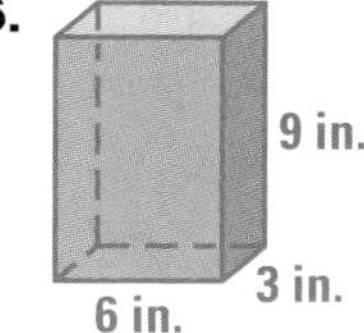

7.
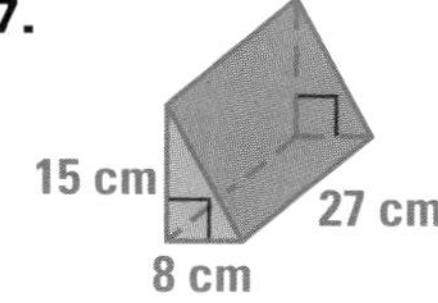

9.2 VOLUME OF A RECTANGULAR PRISM

Examples on pp. 411–412

To find the volume of a rectangular prism, multiply the length by the width by the height.

EXAMPLE **Find the volume in cubic feet of the rectangular prism.**

First, use the fact that 1 yd = 3 ft to convert yards to feet.

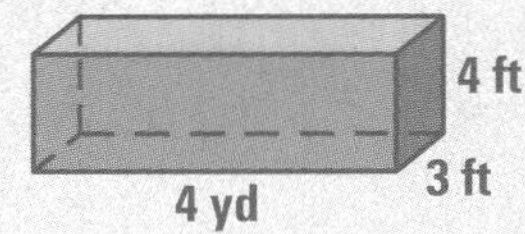

$$4 \not{yd} \times \frac{3 \text{ ft}}{1 \not{yd}} = 12 \text{ ft}$$

Then, use the formula for volume of a rectangular prism.

$$\text{Volume} = \ell \cdot w \cdot h = 12 \cdot 3 \cdot 4 = 144 \text{ ft}^3$$

Find the volume of the rectangular prism with the given dimensions.

8. 3 cm by 5 cm by 13 cm **9.** 8 ft by 2 in. by 3 yd **10.** 6,000 cm by 2 m by 300 mm

11. A rectangular prism has a volume of 378 cubic meters, a width of 7 meters, and a height of 6 meters. What is its length?

9.3 VOLUME OF A TRIANGULAR PRISM

Examples on pp. 418–419

To find the volume of a triangular prism, multiply the base area by the height.

EXAMPLE **Find the volume of the triangular prism.**

First, find the base area.

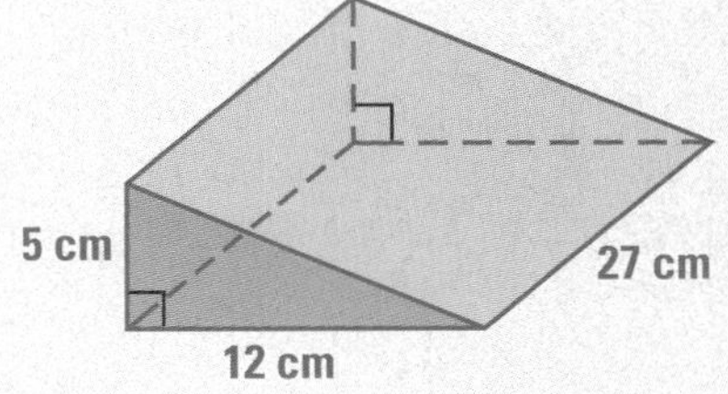

$$\text{Area} = \frac{1}{2} \cdot \text{Base} \cdot \text{Height}$$

$$= \frac{1}{2}(12)(5) = 30 \text{ cm}^2$$

Then, use the base area to find the volume.

$$\text{Volume} = \text{Base area} \cdot \text{Height} = 30(27) = 810 \text{ cm}^3$$

12. The base area of a triangular prism is 30 square centimeters. The height of the prism is 7 centimeters. Find the volume.

Find the volume of the triangular prism.

13.

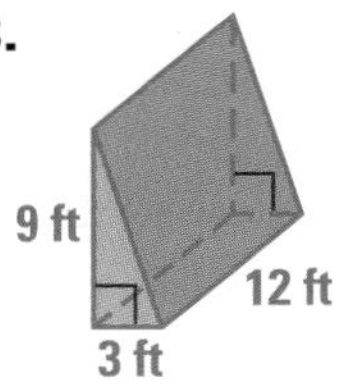

14.

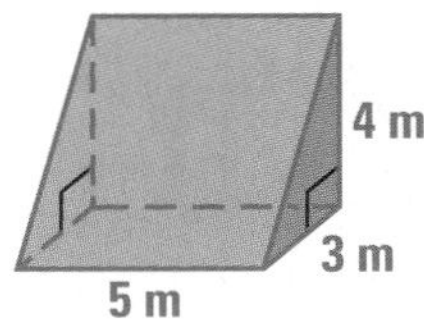

15.

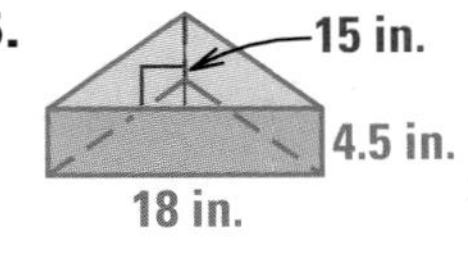

16.

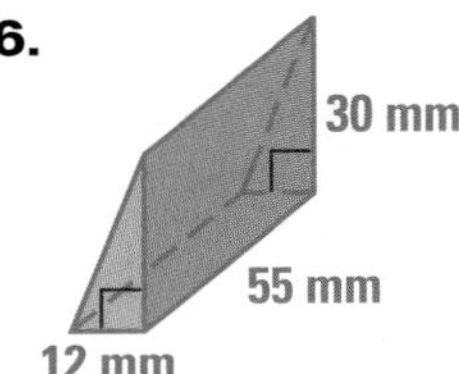

9.4 VOLUME OF A CYLINDER

Examples on pp. 423–424

To find the volume of a cylinder, multiply the base area times the height.

EXAMPLE **Find the volume of the cylinder in cubic feet and in gallons.**

$V = \text{Base area} \cdot \text{Height}$

$= \pi r^2 \cdot h$ **Write the formula.**

$\approx 3.14(2.5^2)(6)$ **Use 3.14 for π.**

$= 117.75 \text{ ft}^3$ **Multiply.**

Use the fact that $1 \text{ ft}^3 \approx 7.48$ gal to find the volume in gallons.

$$117.75 \cancel{\text{ft}^3} \times \frac{7.48 \text{ gal}}{1 \cancel{\text{ft}^3}} \approx 881 \text{ gallons}$$

17. **JUICE CONTAINERS** Which can holds more juice? Explain.

a.

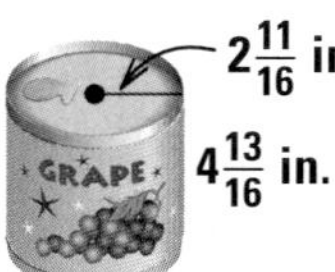

b.

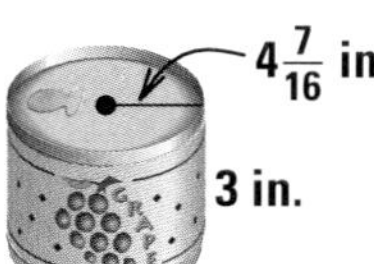

18. **ALGEBRA** The volume of a cylinder with a base diameter of 15 centimeters is about 402 cubic centimeters. Find the height.

19. Use the fact that $1 \text{ L} \approx 60.98 \text{ in.}^3$ to determine how many liters a 520 cubic inch cylinder holds.

9.5 SURFACE AREA OF A PRISM

Examples on pp. 430–431

To find the surface area of a prism, find the area of each face. Then find the sum of these areas.

EXAMPLE **Find the surface area of the triangular prism.**

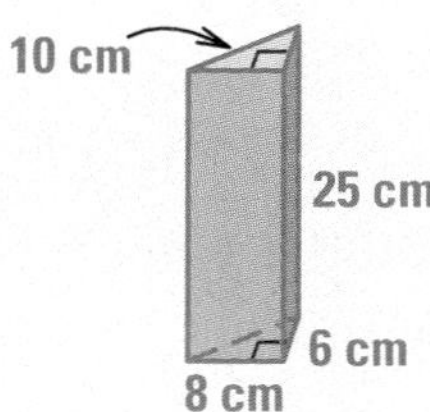

Area of 2 triangular bases $= 2\left(\frac{1}{2}\right)(8)(6) = 48 \text{ cm}^2$

Area of 8 cm by 25 cm face $= 8(25) = 200 \text{ cm}^2$

Area of 6 cm by 25 cm face $= 6(25) = 150 \text{ cm}^2$

Area of 10 cm by 25 cm face $= 10(25) = 250 \text{ cm}^2$

The surface area is the sum of all these areas.

Surface area $= 48 + 200 + 150 + 250 = 648 \text{ cm}^2$

In Exercises 20–22, find the surface area of the prism.

20. 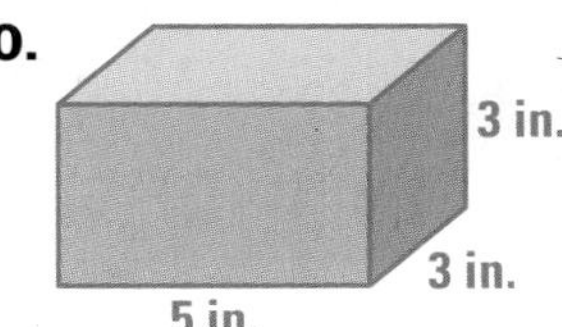

21. 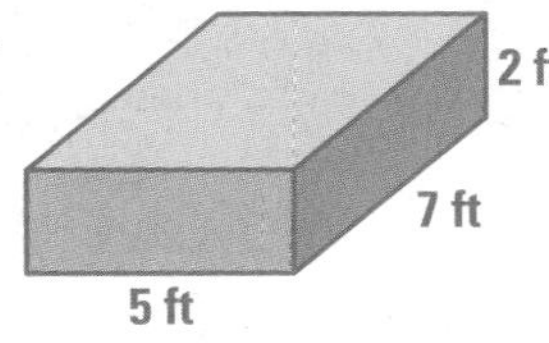

22. 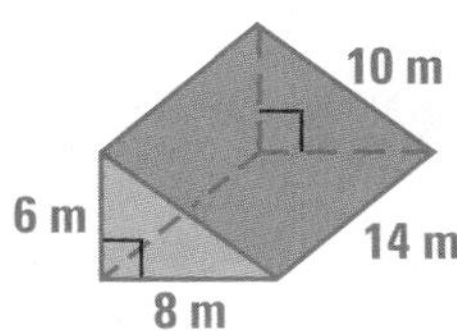

23. Sketch a triangular prism that is 12 feet high, and whose bases have sides of 9 feet, 12 feet, and 15 feet, with a right angle between the shorter sides. Then find the surface area of the prism.

24. **HOBBIES** You are building a glass trophy case that is in the shape of a rectangular prism. The case will have a length of 2.5 feet, a width of 1.5 feet, and a height of 2 feet. Sketch the case. Then find how many square feet of glass it will take to build the case.

9.6 SURFACE AREA OF A CYLINDER

Examples on pp. 434–435

To find the surface area of a cylinder, add the lateral surface area, $2\pi rh$, to the areas of the two bases, $2\pi r^2$.

EXAMPLE **Find the surface area of the cylinder.**

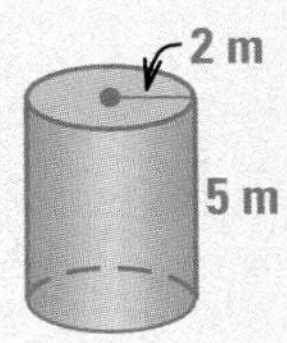

Surface area	$= 2\pi rh + 2\pi r^2$	Write formula.
	$\approx 2(3.14)(2)(5) + 2(3.14)(2^2)$	Substitute given values.
	$= 62.8 + 25.12$	Multiply to find areas.
	$= 87.92 \text{ cm}^2$	Add.

In Exercises 25–27, find the surface area of the cylinder.

25. 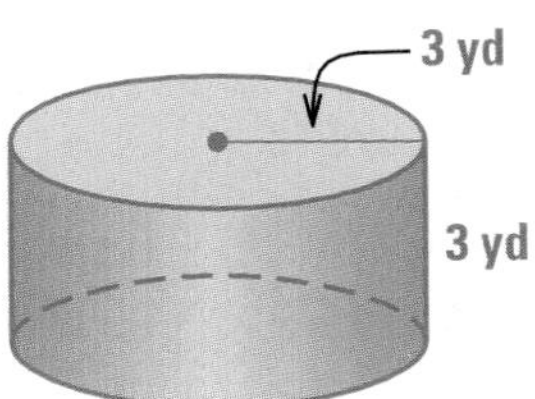

26. 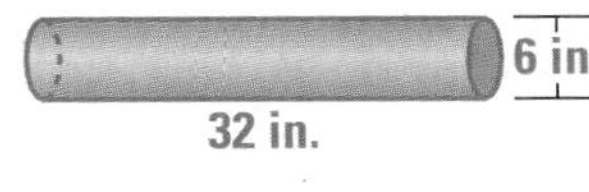

27. 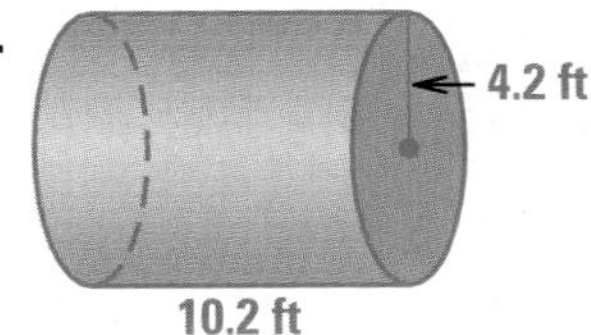

28. You plan to cover the entire surface area of a cylindrical dart board with cork. Find the surface area of the dart board if the radius is 7 inches and it is $\frac{3}{4}$ inch thick.

29. **MARKETING** A cylindrical container of salt is 6 inches high, and its base has a radius of 2 inches. How much paper is needed to completely cover the container?

30. **PAINTING** A cylindrical storage tank needs to be painted. The diameter of the tank is 24 feet. The height is 13.5 feet. If each gallon of paint covers 350 square feet, how many gallons are necessary to paint the top and lateral surface of the storage tank?

Chapter 9 Chapter Test

In Exercises 1–3, sketch an example of the solid.

1. Rectangular prism

2. Triangular prism

3. Cylinder

Find the volume and the surface area of the prism or cylinder.

4.

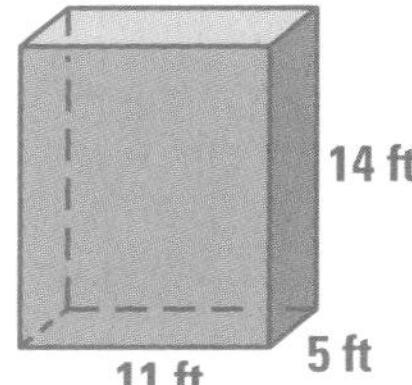

5.

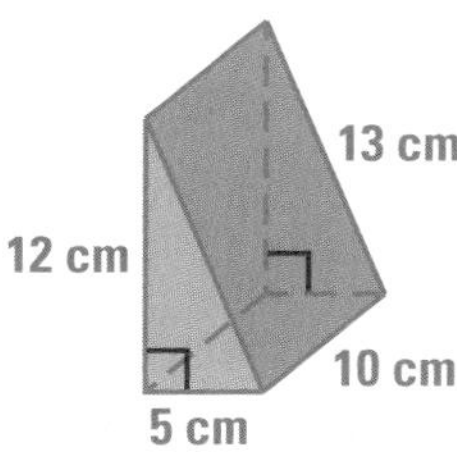

6.

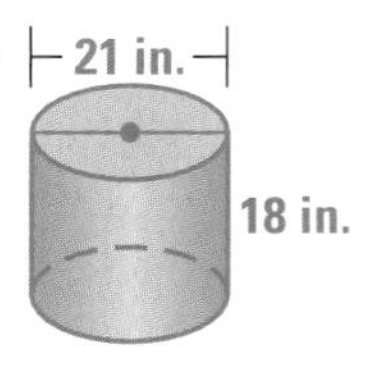

7.

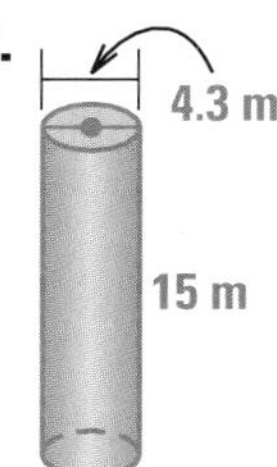

8. ENGINEERING You design a cylindrical container to hold an egg so the container can be dropped from the top of a building without breaking the egg. The base radius of the container is 12 centimeters and the height is 20 centimeters. Find the volume of the container.

ALGEBRA **In Exercises 9–11, find the height.**

9. Rectangular prism: volume = 1500 m^3, length = 20 m, width = 15 m

10. Cylinder: volume = 5266 yd^3, radius = 17 yd

11. Triangular prism: volume = 360 ft^3, base area = 20 ft^2

SHOPPING **In Exercises 12 and 13, use the two peach cans shown. The cost of Can A is $1.29, and the cost of Can B is $1.25.**

12. Which can is the better buy? Explain your reasoning.

13. Find the area of each label. What is this area called?

1.3 in.
3.5 in.
Peaches
A

1.7 in.
2.5 in.
Peaches
B

FISH TANK **In Exercises 14 and 15, you buy a fish tank that has a length of $\frac{1}{2}$ yard, a width of 12.5 inches, and a height of 1.25 feet.**

14. How much glass was used to make the bottom and sides of the tank?

15. How many gallons of water can the tank hold? (1 gal ≈ 231 $in.^3$)

In Exercises 16 and 17, use the diagram.

16. Find the total surface area of the room.

17. If you plan to paint the walls and ceiling, what is the surface area to be painted, excluding the window and door?

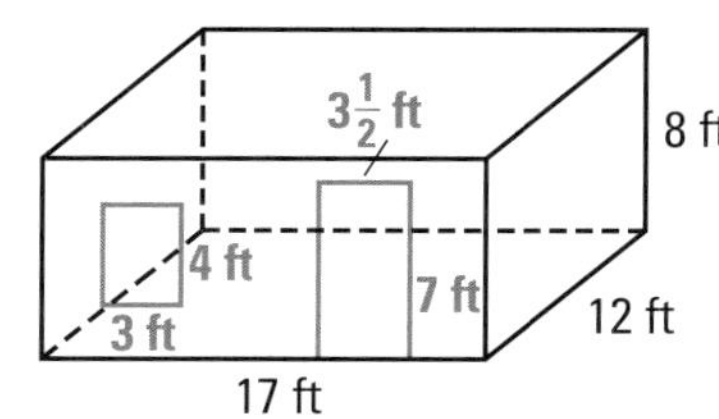

Multiple-Choice Practice

Do not become obsessed with how much time you have left during the test. Concentrate on the question in front of you.

In Exercises 1 and 2, use the figure shown.

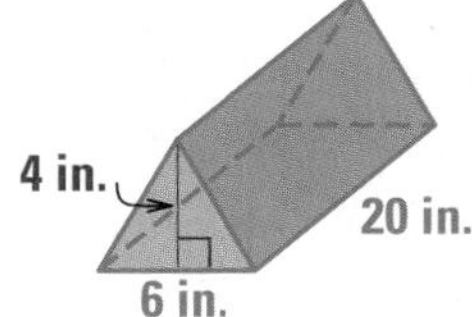

1. Which statement is *false*?

Ⓐ It has 5 faces.

Ⓑ It has rectangular bases.

Ⓒ It is a polyhedron.

Ⓓ It is a triangular prism.

2. What is the volume of the figure?

Ⓕ 240 in.^{3} Ⓖ 408 in.^{3}

Ⓗ 480 in.^{2} Ⓙ 480 in.^{3}

In Exercises 3 and 4, a cylinder has a radius of 5 centimeters and a height of 20 centimeters.

3. What is the surface area?

Ⓐ 707 cm^2 Ⓑ 785 cm

Ⓒ 785 cm^2 Ⓓ 1570 cm^3

4. What is the volume?

Ⓕ 628 cm^2 Ⓖ 628 cm^3

Ⓗ 785 cm^2 Ⓙ 1570 cm^3

5. What is the measure of the side labeled x when the volume is 3500 cubic meters?

Ⓐ $x = 8.75$ m

Ⓑ $x = 15$ m

Ⓒ $x = 17.5$ m

Ⓓ $x = 35$ m

6. A pond measures 55 inches long, 39 inches wide, and 28 inches deep. How much water will fill the pond? (1 gal $\approx$ 231 in.^{3})

Ⓕ 21 gallons Ⓖ 231 gallons

Ⓗ 260 gallons Ⓙ 693 gallons

7. Which size paper can be used to cover the gift box without overlap?

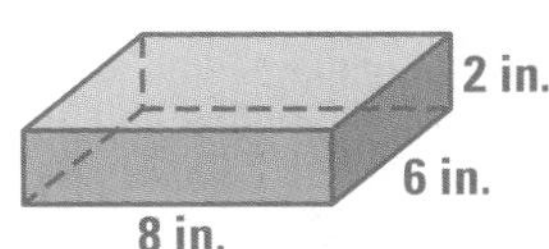

Ⓐ 16 inches by 20 inches

Ⓑ 8 inches by 19 inches

Ⓒ 10 inches by 15 inches

Ⓓ 6 inches by 30 inches

8. Which statement is *false*?

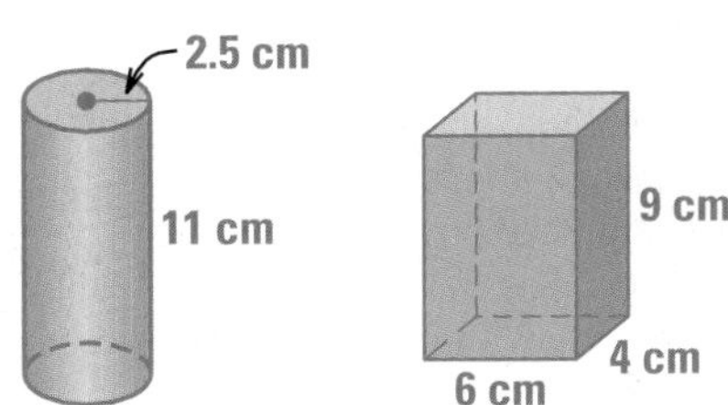

Ⓕ The surface area of the rectangular prism is greater than that of the cylinder.

Ⓖ The volume of the cylinder is greater than that of the rectangular prism.

Ⓗ The two containers hold about the same amount.

Ⓙ The cylinder uses more packaging than the rectangular prism.

Brain games

- Know and use the formulas for the volume of triangular prisms and cylinders. (MG 1.3)
- Estimate unknown quantities graphically and solve for them by using logical reasoning and arithmetic and algebraic techniques. (MR 2.3)

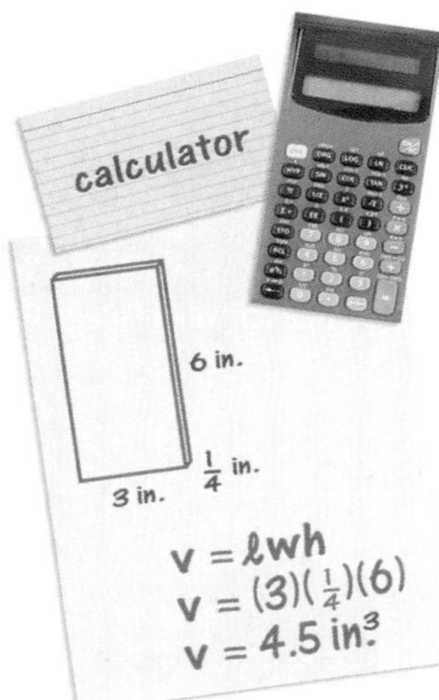

Perfect Picture

eraser

door stop

calculator

Materials

- **Ruler**
- **Paper and index cards**
- **Classroom objects such as an eraser and a door stop**

Directions

Object of the Game

Play this game in pairs or in small groups. Each round, players sketch an object and estimate the volume. The player who calculates the volume closest to the actual volume scores one point. The winner is the player with the most points.

How to Play

STEP 1 Gather 5 classroom objects of different shapes. Write the name of each object on an index card and then conceal the objects. Shuffle the cards and place them face down.

STEP 2 Turn over the top card. Each player sketches the object from memory on paper and estimates the dimensions. Players find the volume of the object from their sketch.

STEP 3 Players use a ruler to measure the object and then find the actual volume. The player whose sketch shows a volume that comes closest to that of the actual object scores one point.

Another Way to Play

Players use the rules above, but estimate the surface area.

Brain Teaser

Estimate the volume

Choose a classroom object whose volume can be found by taking the volume of two or more individual parts. Sketch the object, estimate its dimensions, and find the volume.

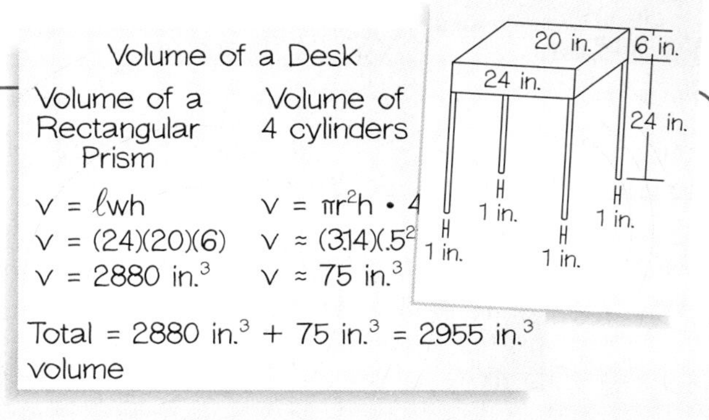

Volume of a Desk
Volume of a Rectangular Prism
Volume of 4 cylinders
V = ℓwh
V = (24)(20)(6)
V = 2880 in.³
V = πr²h • 4
V ≈ (3.14)(.5²
V ≈ 75 in.³
Total = 2880 in.³ + 75 in.³ = 2955 in.³ volume
20 in.
6 in.
24 in.
24 in.
1 in.
1 in.
1 in.
1 in.

Reviewing the Basics

The basic skills you'll review on this page will help prepare you for the next chapter.

EXAMPLE 1 Working with Decimals

Perform the indicated operation.

a. $4.56 + 8.096$ **b.** $20.5 \div 5$

Solution

a.
$$\begin{array}{r} 4.56 \\ +\ 8.096 \\ \hline 12.656 \end{array}$$

Line up the decimal places.

Add as you would with whole numbers.

b. $5\overline{)20.5}$ Line up the decimal point in the quotient with the decimal point in the dividend.

$$\begin{array}{r} 4.1 \\ 5\overline{)20.5} \end{array}$$

Divide as you would with whole numbers.

Try These

Perform the indicated operation.

1. $0.03 + 2.6$ **2.** $10.3 + 6.125$ **3.** $16.05 + 4.27$

4. $23.68 + 5.2$ **5.** $12 \div 5$ **6.** $80.5 \div 2$

7. $20.48 \div 8$ **8.** $32.5 \div 5$ **9.** $18.28 \div 4$

EXAMPLE 2 Finding the Mean (or Average)

Find the mean of the data: 20, 15, 42, 13, 16, 41, 10, 19.

Solution

To find the mean, add the numbers in the data set. Then divide by the number of items in the data set.

$$\text{Mean} = \frac{20 + 15 + 42 + 13 + 16 + 41 + 10 + 19}{8}$$

$$= \frac{176}{8} = 22$$

ANSWER ▶ The mean is 22.

Try These

Find the mean of the data. Round to the hundredths place.

10. 14, 7, 15, 13, 11, 20, 11 **11.** 17, 20, 16, 17, 18, 17, 14, 9

12. 6.5, 7.2, 8.1, 3.4, 9.1, 7.3, 12 **13.** 20.2, 11.3, 1.4, 25.7, 9.3, 8.6, 9.4

Student Help

▶ **MORE EXAMPLES**

INTERNET More examples and practice exercises available at www.mcdougallittell.com

Chapters 1-9 Cumulative Practice

Evaluate the expression. (1.7–1.9)

1. $10.03 - 4.567$ **2.** $10.3 \cdot 0.07$ **3.** $72.8 \div 11$ **4.** $8.45 + 0.005$

Find the GCF and LCM of the numbers. (2.2, 2.5)

5. 12, 32 **6.** 16, 25 **7.** 48, 72 **8.** 42, 52

Evaluate the expression. Simplify if possible. (3.1–3.5)

9. $\frac{1}{6} + \frac{5}{6}$ **10.** $\frac{4}{7} - \frac{2}{7}$ **11.** $\frac{3}{4} - \frac{1}{3}$ **12.** $\frac{7}{10} + \frac{11}{12}$

13. $\frac{7}{8} - \frac{2}{3} + \frac{1}{2}$ **14.** $6\frac{1}{4} - 3\frac{5}{6}$ **15.** $3\frac{3}{10} \times 5\frac{5}{6}$ **16.** $8\frac{3}{4} \div 3\frac{3}{8}$

Evaluate the expression. (4.3–4.6)

17. $-17 + (-11)$ **18.** $-6 - (-7)$ **19.** $17(-9)$ **20.** $-120 \div (-15)$

21. $225 \div (-5)$ **22.** $-27 + 16$ **23.** $-30 - (-12)$ **24.** $(-23)(-2)$

Write an equation for the sentence or situation. Then solve the equation. (5.2–5.7)

25. The sum of a number and -11 is 16.

26. After spending \$11.42, you have \$5.20 left. How much money did you have originally?

27. If you triple the number of servings of fruits and vegetables you eat each week, you will eat 33 servings per week. How many servings of fruits and vegetables do you eat each week?

28. The quotient of a number and 2.5 is -6.

29. The difference of three times a number and 17 is -11.

Rewrite the given ratio in two other ways. (6.1)

30. 9 : 13 **31.** 6 to 7 **32.** $\frac{11}{12}$

In Exercises 33–36, solve the proportion. (6.2)

33. $\frac{x}{6} = \frac{5}{30}$ **34.** $\frac{42}{y} = \frac{14}{5}$ **35.** $\frac{120}{18} = \frac{s}{15}$ **36.** $\frac{15}{22} = \frac{75}{t}$

37. Rectangles *ABCD* and *EFGH* are similar. Find the length of side *GH*. (6.4)

SURVEY In Exercises 38–40, use the circle graph, which shows the results of a survey of favorite vegetables among 150 students. (7.1, 7.2, 7.4, 7.5)

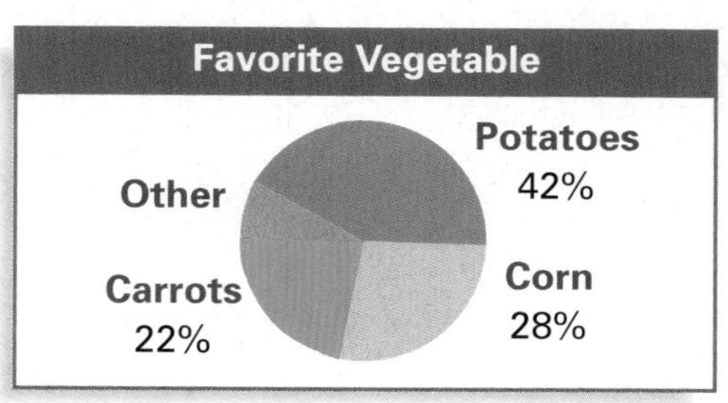

38. How many students chose carrots?

39. How many students had other favorites?

40. What is the angle measure of the Other section?

In Exercises 41 and 42, find the simple interest you pay for borrowing the given principal. (7.6)

41. $P = \$350$, $r = 21\%$, $t = 18$ months **42.** $P = \$1200$, $r = 7.5\%$, $t = 9$ months

43. A mattress set is on sale for 35% off. The sales tax is 7%. What is the total price of a mattress set that has an original price of $600? (7.7)

Use a centimeter ruler to measure the sides to the nearest tenth of a centimeter. Then use as many words as possible to describe the triangle: *equilateral, isosceles, scalene, acute, right,* or *obtuse*. (8.3)

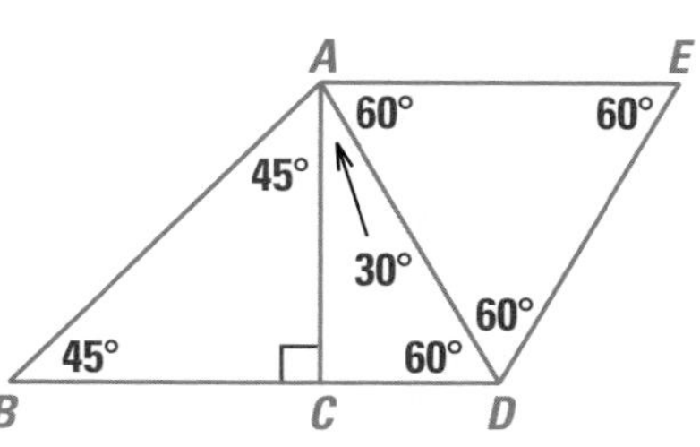

44. Triangle ACD **45.** Triangle ADE

46. Triangle BDA **47.** Triangle ABC

Find the unknown measurement. Use $\pi \approx 3.14$. (8.7, 8.8)

48. Circumference = ___?___ **49.** Area = ___?___ **50.** Circumference = 62.8 m

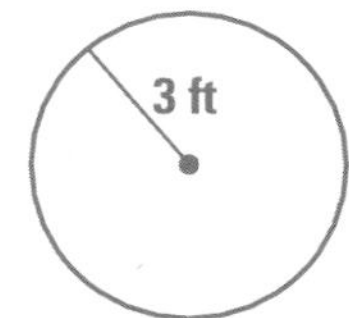

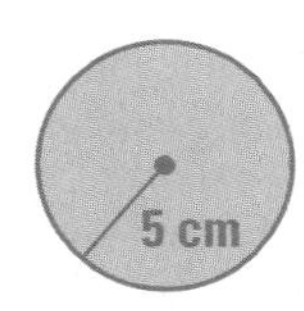

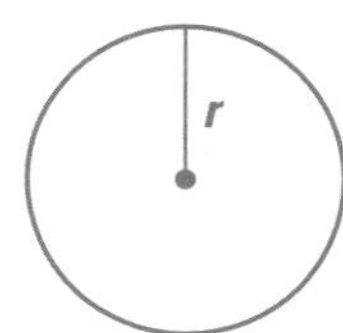

Identify the solid. Then find its volume and surface area. (9.1–9.6)

51.

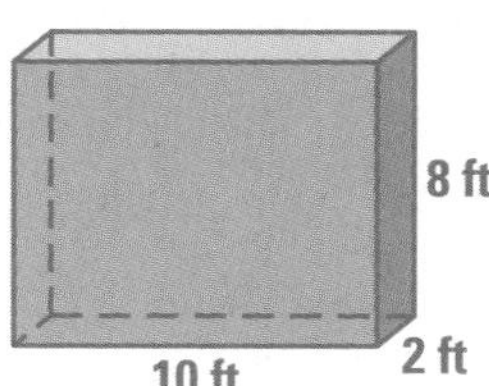

52.

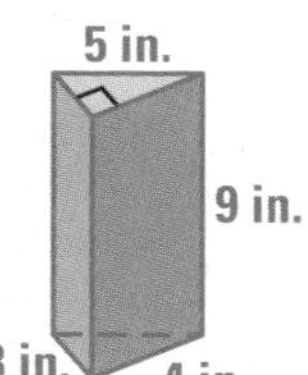

53.

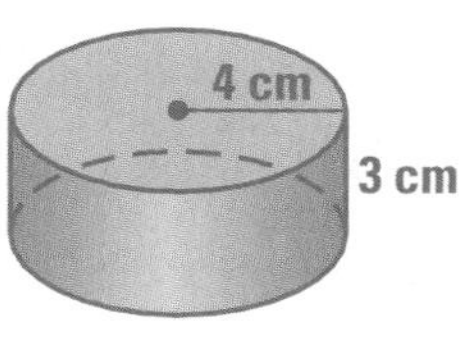

SILOS In Exercises 54–56, use the following information. Feed crops are stored in silos. A farmer is replacing a silo that has the shape of a rectangular prism with a silo that has the shape of a cylinder. (9.2, 9.4, 9.5, 9.6)

54. Which silo holds more feed?

55. Which silo requires more material for its construction?

56. Using the results of Exercises 54 and 55, write a sentence about the advantages of using cylindrical silos.

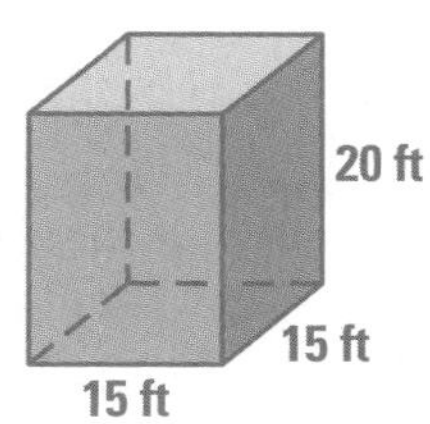

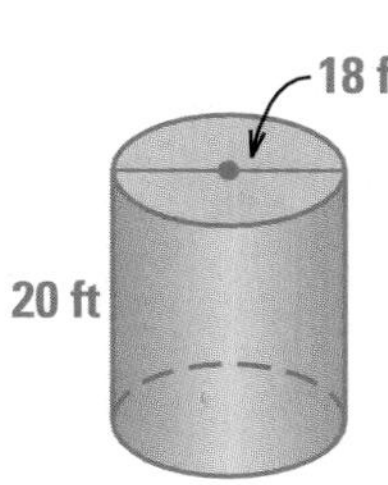

Chapters 7-9 Project

California Standards

- Interpret and use ratios in different contexts. (NS 1.2)
- Know and use the formulas for the volume of a cylinder and a rectangular solid. (MG 1.3)

Materials

- Calculator
- Paper
- Pencil
- Scissors

Comparing Surface Area and Volume

OBJECTIVE Compare the ratio of surface area to volume for various rectangular prisms.

INVESTIGATION

1. Each rectangular prism has a volume of 64 cubic inches. For each prism, find the value of x.

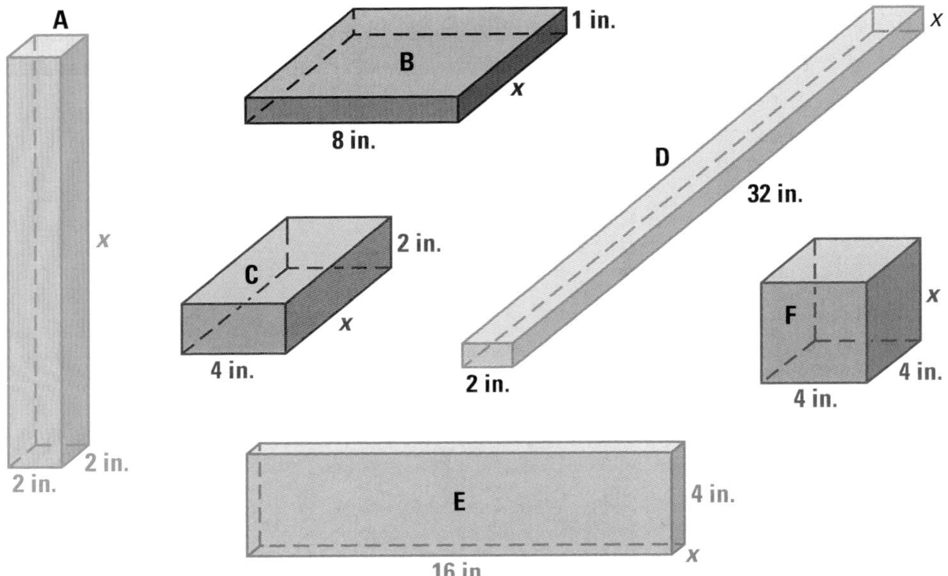

2. Find the surface area of each rectangular prism.

3. For each rectangular prism, find the ratio of the surface area to the volume. Write the ratio as a fraction or as a decimal. Copy and complete the table.

Prism	A	B	C	D	E	F
Surface area, S	?	?	?	?	?	?
Volume, V	64 in.^{3}	64 in.^{3}	64 in.^{3}	64 in.^{3}	64 in.^{3}	64 in.^{3}
$S:V$ ratio	?	?	?	?	?	?

4. Trace each figure above. Cut out your tracings and order them based on the ratio of surface area to volume. Which prism has the largest ratio? Which prism has the smallest ratio? What patterns do you notice as the ratio decreases?

Present Your Results

Write a report to present your results.

- Include your answers to Exercises 1–4.
- Describe the relationship between the dimensions of a rectangular prism and the ratio of surface area to volume. Support your description with examples.
- A rectangular prism is 1 inch by 1 inch by 64 inches. Draw the prism. Do you think the ratio of the surface area to the volume will be large or small? Explain your reasoning.

Volume = length × width × height

Surface area = sum of areas of faces

Extension

Materials
- Ruler
- 2 containers

Find two containers that hold the same product, but are different sizes. For example, you could use two soup cans of different sizes, or you could use a large cereal box and a small cereal box. The containers should be either prisms or cylinders. Note how much each costs.

5. Measure the two containers and calculate their volumes.

6. What percent of the larger volume is the smaller volume?

7. Compare the prices of the two items. What percent of the greater cost is the lesser cost?

8. Which is the better buy, the larger product or the smaller product? Explain your reasoning.

9. Which container has the larger ratio of surface area to volume? Show your work.

Data Analysis and Statistics

Why are data analysis and statistics important?

Researchers use data analysis and statistics to examine the characteristics of a portion of a population and make conclusions about the population as a whole. Understanding data analysis and statistics will help you as you study probability in the next chapter.

Data analysis and statistics are used in many careers, including automotive design (pages 451 and 462), meteorology (page 456), and dentistry (page 490). For example, automotive designers use data about people's physical characteristics to design cars that are comfortable to drive.

Meeting the California Standards

The skills you'll learn in this chapter will help you meet state standards and prepare for standardized tests. In this chapter you'll:

- **Understand the effects of additional data and outliers.** LESSON 10.1
- **Analyze data displays. Explain how the question affects the results and how the data display affects the conclusions.** LESSONS 10.2–10.6, 10.8
- **Evaluate claims based on statistical data.** LESSONS 10.5, 10.6, 10.8
- **Compare data from a population with data from samples.** LESSON 10.7
- **Compare ways of selecting a representative sample.** LESSON 10.7
- **Identify sampling errors.** LESSON 10.8

Career Link **AUTOMOTIVE DESIGNER** An automotive designer uses data analysis and statistics when:

- designing a car seat.
- interpreting the results of handling and crash tests.

EXERCISES

Automotive designers use statistics about leg lengths to decide how far back the driver's seat of a car should be able to move. The leg lengths (in inches) of 20 adults are listed at the right.

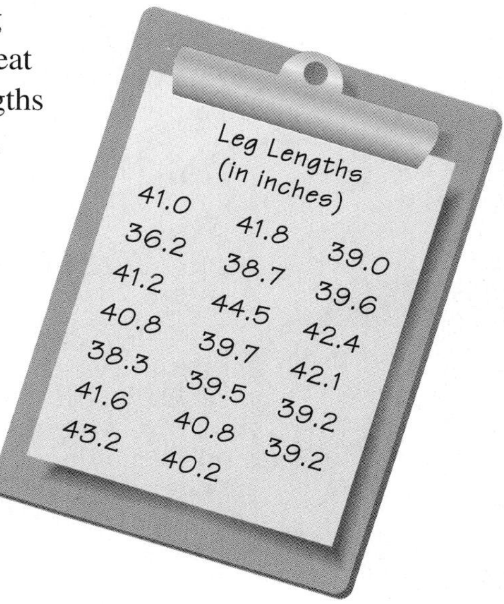

Leg Lengths
(in inches)
41.0 41.8 39.0
36.2 38.7 39.6
41.2 44.5 42.4
40.8 39.7 42.1
38.3 39.5 39.2
41.6 40.8 39.2
43.2 40.2

1. What is the longest leg length?

2. What is the shortest leg length?

3. What fraction of the people measured have leg lengths that are less than or equal to 41.7 inches?

In Lesson 10.3 you will learn how to make a data display that shows the range of leg lengths and divides the data into four groups.

Chapter 10 Getting Ready

PREVIEW What's the chapter about?

- Representing data with **measures of central tendency** and **graphs**
- Analyzing **samples** and interpreting **surveys**

WORDS TO KNOW

- **measure of central tendency,** *p. 453*
- **median,** *p. 453*
- **mode,** *p. 453*
- **histogram,** *p. 458*
- **box-and-whisker plot,** *p. 461*
- **range,** *p. 462*
- **coordinate plane,** *p. 468*
- **ordered pair,** *p. 468*
- **scatter plot,** *p. 469*
- **population,** *p. 483*
- **sample,** *p. 483*
- **biased sample,** *p. 484*

PREPARE Chapter Readiness Quiz

Take this quick quiz. If you are unsure of an answer, look back at the reference pages for help.

VOCABULARY CHECK *(refer to pp. 28, 148, 269, 285)*

1. What is another name for the average of a set of numbers?

(A) Scale (B) Mean (C) Rate (D) Proportion

SKILL CHECK *(refer to pp. 28, 333)*

2. What is the average of the numbers 20, 32, 35, 48, and 55?

(F) 35 (G) 36 (H) 37 (J) 38

3. A circle graph breaks a high school's student population into freshmen, sophomores, juniors, and seniors. Of the school's 1000 students, 300 are freshmen. What is the angle measure for the wedge of the circle graph representing freshmen?

(A) 30° (B) 54° (C) 108° (D) 300°

STUDY TIP Make Vocabulary Cards

For each new vocabulary term you learn, write the term's definition on an index card to help you remember it. Include an example or sketch that helps illustrate the term.

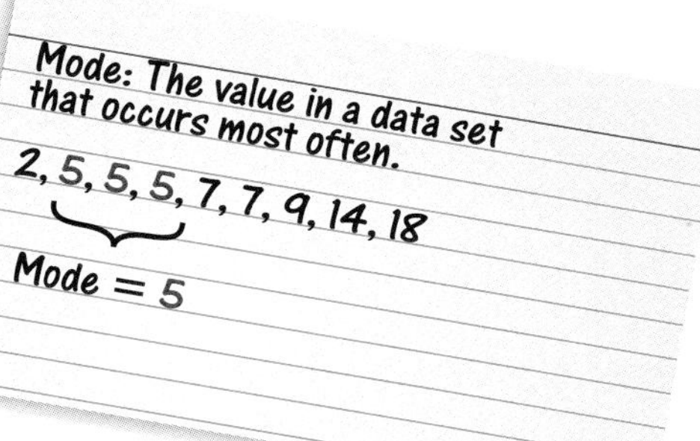

Mode: The value in a data set that occurs most often.
2, 5, 5, 5, 7, 7, 9, 14, 18
Mode = 5

10.1 Measures of Central Tendency

California Standards

In this lesson you'll:

- Compute the mean, median, and mode of data sets. (SDP 1.1)
- Understand how additional data added to data sets may affect measures of central tendency. (SDP 1.2)
- Understand how the inclusion or exclusion of outliers affects measures of central tendency. (SDP 1.3)
- Know why a specific measure of central tendency provides the most useful information in a given context. (SDP 1.4)

Goal 1 FINDING MEASURES OF CENTRAL TENDENCY

A **measure of central tendency** for a set of numerical data is a single number that represents a "typical" value for the set. Three important measures of central tendency are the *mean*, the *median*, and the *mode*.

- The mean, or average, of a data set is the sum of the values in the set divided by the number of values in the set.
- For a data set with an odd number of values, the **median** is the middle value when the values are written in numerical order. The median of a data set with an even number of values is the mean of the two middle values.

4, 4, **6**, 10, 19	4, 4, **6**, **10**, 19, 23
Median = **6**	Median $= \dfrac{\mathbf{6} + \mathbf{10}}{2} = 8$

- The **mode** of a data set is the value in the set that occurs most often. For example, the mode of each of the two data sets above is 4. The data set 2, 4, 6, 7, 9 has no mode because no value occurs more often than the others. The data set 3, 5, 5, 7, 7 has two modes: 5 and 7.

EXAMPLE 1 Finding the Mean, Median, and Mode(s)

AVIATION You ask 11 of your classmates how many times they have flown in an airplane. The results are shown below. Find the mean, median, and mode(s) of the data.

4, 0, 8, 2, 1, 7, 2, 4, 26, 2, 10

Solution

MEAN: To find the mean, divide the sum of the data values by the number of data values.

$$\text{Mean} = \frac{4 + 0 + 8 + 2 + 1 + 7 + 2 + 4 + 26 + 2 + 10}{11} = \frac{66}{11} = 6$$

MEDIAN: To find the median, write the data values in numerical order and identify the middle value. The median is 4.

Median

0, 1, 2, 2, 2, 4, 4, 7, 8, 10, 26

MODE: The mode is 2, the value that occurs most often in the data set.

Student Help

▶ **MORE EXAMPLES**

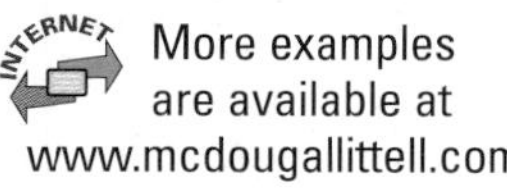

More examples are available at www.mcdougallittell.com

Goal 2 EFFECTS OF OUTLIERS AND ADDITIONAL DATA

An **outlier** is a value in a data set that is much greater than or much less than most other values in the set. An outlier usually has little effect on a data set's median or mode(s), but it can have a large effect on the mean.

EXAMPLE 2 Choosing Good Measures of Central Tendency

LAW You are writing a report about the length of jury trials. At a courthouse, you find and record the lengths of 20 recent trials.

Length of trial (in days)	1	2	3	4	5	7	9	183
Number of trials	7	3	5	1	1	1	1	1

a. Identify any outliers in the data set.

b. Find the mean, median, and mode(s). Which of these are good representations of a typical jury trial's length at this courthouse?

Solution

a. The value 183 is much greater than the other values in the data set, so it is an outlier.

b. Write the data set as a list of values in numerical order. You can see that the median is $\frac{2 + 3}{2} = 2.5$ days and the mode is **1** day.

1, 1, 1, 1, 1, 1, 1, 2, 2, **2**, **3**, 3, 3, 3, 3, 4, 5, 7, 9, 183

The sum of the values is 236 and the number of values is 20, so the mean is $\frac{236}{20} = 11.8$ days. The mean is greater than all but one value in the data set, so it is not a good representation of a typical trial's length. The median and mode are better representations.

Student Help

▶ **STUDY TIP**
In Example 2 suppose the outlier 183 is not included in the data set. The mode stays the same and the median changes only slightly, from 2.5 to 2. The mean changes significantly, from 11.8 to $\frac{53}{19} \approx 2.8$.

EXAMPLE 3 Adding New Values to a Data Set

You decide to add the lengths of 5 new trials to the data set in Example 2. The added trial lengths (in days) are 2, 3, 3, 3, and 5. How do these new values affect the data's mean, median, and mode?

Solution

The revised data set is given below with the new values shown in red.

1, 1, 1, 1, 1, 1, 1, 2, 2, 2, **2**, 3, 3, 3, 3, 3, **3**, **3**, **3**, 4, 5, **5**, 7, 9, 183

The median has increased from 2.5 days to 3 days. The mode has changed from 1 day to 3 days. The sum of the 25 values is 252, so the mean has decreased from 11.8 days to $\frac{252}{25} \approx 10.1$ days.

10.1 Exercises

Guided Practice

Match the measure of central tendency with its value using the data set 2, 5, 5, 5, 8, 10, 11, 13, 13, 28.

A. 5 **B.** 9 **C.** 10

1. Median **2.** Mean **3.** Mode

Find the mean, median, and mode(s) of the data.

4. 1, 1, 8, 9, 11

5. 17, 14, 14, 25, 51, 10, 25, 8, 25

6. 5, 13, 12, 20, 1, 6

7. 3, 20, 29, 17, 8, 3, 23, 17, 13, 7

BASEBALL **In Exercises 8 and 9, use the data set below. It gives the number of hits for each player on a professional baseball team during the 1999 season. The red numbers are hits for pitchers.**

0, 0, 0, 0, 0, 0, 0, 1, 2, 2, 4, 4, 4, 5, 7, 8, 9, 12, 16, 27, 41, 43, 44, 51, 58, 60, 66, 70, 80, 89, 156, 170, 170, 190, 206

8. Find the mean, median, and mode(s) of the data. Which measure do you think best represents a typical number of hits? Explain.

9. Suppose the numbers of hits for pitchers are not included in the data set. How does this affect the mean, median, and mode(s)?

Practice and Problem Solving

Student Help

▶MORE PRACTICE
Extra practice to help you master skills is on page 584.

Find the mean, median, and mode(s) of the data.

10. Price per pound for 8 types of fruit:

$3.65, $4.00, $3.25, $4.15, $3.00, $2.05, $3.25, $3.85

11. Lengths (in minutes) of 13 movies:

90, 102, 120, 180, 90, 85, 90, 137, 120, 151, 97, 93, 120

Science Link **In Exercises 12 and 13, use the table showing the longest recorded life spans (in years) for several animals.**

12. Find the mean, median, and mode(s) of the data.

13. Suppose the two highest and the two lowest life spans are removed from the data set. How does this affect the mean, median, and mode(s)?

Animal	Age	Animal	Age
Tortoise	152	Horse	62
Clam	100	Lobster	50
Whale	90	Cow	40
Cockatoo	70	Cat	34
Condor	70	Dog	29
Elephant	70	Rabbit	18
Ostrich	62	Mouse	6

Link to Careers

METEOROLOGIST
In 1997 meteorologists earned an average annual salary of about $57,000. Salaries for beginning meteorologists typically ranged from $20,000 to $43,000 depending on the person's level of education.

More about meteorologists at www.mcdougallittell.com

Identify the outlier in the data set. Find the mean, median, and mode(s) of the data set when the outlier is included and when it is not. Describe the outlier's effect on each measure of central tendency.

14. 2, 2, 3, 3, 4, 4, 4, 6, 68

15. 0, 72, 75, 75, 83, 83, 83, 91

16. 10.9, 12.4, 0.7, 11.6, 12.8, 11.6

17. 28, 20, 25, 28, 100, 25, 20

MUSIC **In Exercises 18 and 19, use the data set below. The values represent the lengths (in seconds) of the songs on a CD.**

227, 248, 228, 233, 241, 266, 231, 81, 279,
261, 305, 254, 305, 206, 302, 263, 282

18. Find the mean, median, and mode(s) of the data set. Which of these measures do you think are good representations of the length of a typical song on the CD? Explain.

19. Are there any outliers in the data set? If so, describe the effect of the outlier(s) on the mean, median, and mode(s).

SALARIES **In Exercises 20 and 21, use the table showing the salaries of employees at a TV station.**

20. Find the mean, median, and mode(s) of the salaries. Which do you think best represents the salary of a typical employee? Explain.

Job	Number employed	Annual salary
Owner	1	$200,000
Newscaster	5	$60,000
Meteorologist	1	$52,000
Reporter	5	$38,000
Set designer	2	$32,000
Camera operator	10	$27,000
Technician	10	$25,000

21. If the station hires a programming director at a salary of $125,000, how would the mean, median, and mode(s) of the salaries change?

CHALLENGE **Create a set of 5 data values with the given measures of central tendency.**

22. Mean: 6, median: 5, mode: 9

23. Mean: 7, median: 9, mode: 1

Multiple-Choice Practice

24. What is the median of the data set 10, 19, 14, 9, 10, 34?

Ⓐ 10 Ⓑ 12 Ⓒ 14 Ⓓ 16

25. What is (are) the mode(s) of the data set 8, 11, 2, 1, 11, 14, 2?

Ⓕ Only 2 Ⓖ Only 11 Ⓗ 2 and 11 Ⓙ No mode

26. What is the mean of the data set 35, 12, 20, 42, 26?

Ⓐ 26 Ⓑ 27 Ⓒ 28 Ⓓ 29

10.2 Histograms

California Standards

In this lesson you'll:

- Draw and analyze data displays. (SDP 2.3)

Goal 1 MAKING FREQUENCY TABLES

A **frequency table** can be used to group data values into intervals. The **frequency** for an interval is the number of values that lie in the interval.

EXAMPLE 1 Making a Frequency Table

GAS TAXES Below are the gasoline taxes for the 50 states as of 1999. The taxes are given in cents per gallon, rounded to the nearest cent. Make a frequency table of the data. ▶ Source: American Petroleum Institute

AL 18	**HI** 16	**MA** 22	**NM** 17	**SD** 22
AK 8	**ID** 25	**MI** 19	**NY** 30	**TN** 20
AZ 18	**IL** 19	**MN** 20	**NC** 21	**TX** 20
AR 20	**IN** 15	**MS** 18	**ND** 21	**UT** 25
CA 18	**IA** 20	**MO** 17	**OH** 22	**VT** 20
CO 22	**KS** 20	**MT** 28	**OK** 17	**VA** 18
CT 32	**KY** 15	**NE** 24	**OR** 24	**WA** 23
DE 23	**LA** 20	**NV** 23	**PA** 12	**WV** 21
FL 13	**ME** 19	**NH** 18	**RI** 28	**WI** 26
GA 8	**MD** 24	**NJ** 15	**SC** 16	**WY** 14

Solution

The frequency table is shown. You complete each column as follows.

INTERVAL: Choose intervals of equal size that cover all the data values, which range from 8 to 32. In the table the values are grouped into intervals of 3. The first interval is 0–2 and the last interval is 30–32.

TALLY: For each state, make a tally mark next to the interval containing the state's tax. For example, because Alabama's tax is 18 cents/gal, a mark is made next to the interval 18–20.

FREQUENCY: The frequency for each interval is the number of tally marks for the interval.

Interval	Tally	Frequency
0–2		0
3–5		0
6–8	II	2
9–11		0
12–14	III	3
15–17	~~IIII~~ III	8
18–20	~~IIII~~ ~~IIII~~ ~~IIII~~ II	17
21–23	~~IIII~~ ~~IIII~~	10
24–26	~~IIII~~ I	6
27–29	II	2
30–32	II	2

Student Help

▶ **STUDY TIP**
The "Tally" column of a frequency table gives a good visual indication of where most of the data lie. In Example 1 the "Tally" column shows that most state gas taxes are between 15 and 26 cents/gal.

Link to Transportation

GASOLINE In 1997 there were about 208 million motor vehicles in the United States. These vehicles used about 154 billion gallons of fuel that year.

Goal 2 DRAWING HISTOGRAMS

A **histogram** is a type of graph that displays data from a frequency table. A histogram is similar to a bar graph. In a histogram there is one bar for each interval of the frequency table that contains data values. The height of the bar indicates the frequency of values in that interval.

EXAMPLE 2 Drawing a Histogram

GAS TAXES Use the frequency table from Example 1 on page 457 to draw a histogram of the state gasoline taxes.

Solution

Follow these steps:

1. Draw a rectangle and divide the base into 11 equal intervals so there is one for each interval of the frequency table. Label each interval with the values it contains (0–2, 3–5, . . . , 30–32).
2. Make a scale on the rectangle's left side that starts at 0 and ends at a number at least as great as the largest frequency in the table. For the tax data, the scale should go from 0 to at least 17. At each number on the scale, draw a horizontal line across the rectangle. Make sure these lines are evenly spaced.
3. For each interval from Step 1 that contains data values, draw a bar whose base lies on the interval and whose height is the frequency for the interval. Use the horizontal lines from Step 2 to help you draw the bar heights correctly. The bars should all have the same width.
4. Add word labels, such as "Tax" and "Number of states," to the intervals and vertical scale. Also, give the histogram a title, such as "State Gasoline Taxes."

A completed histogram of the state gasoline taxes is shown below.

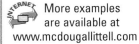

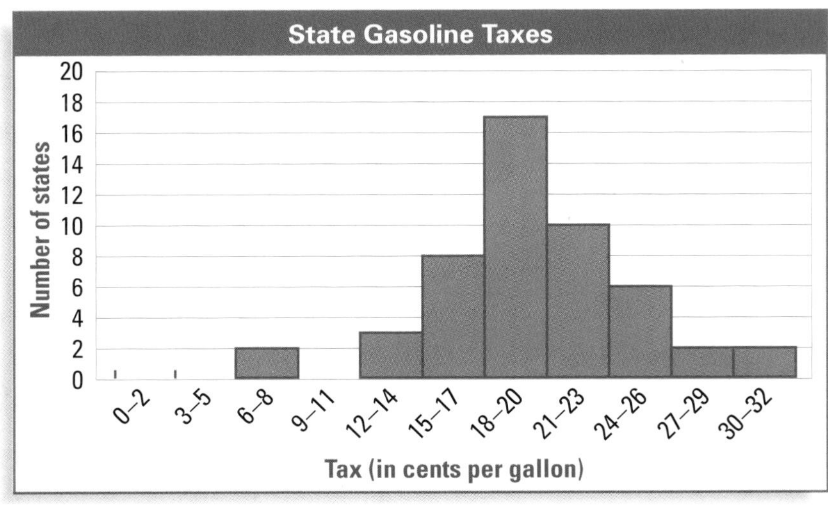

Student Help

▶ **MORE EXAMPLES**

INTERNET More examples are available at www.mcdougallittell.com

10.2 Exercises

Guided Practice

In Exercises 1 and 2, copy and complete the frequency table and draw a histogram using the given data set. The data represent test scores for two mathematics classes that were given the same test.

1. CLASS A: 90, 75, 84, 63, 100, 58, 70, 78, 61, 72, 55, 91, 67, 79, 52, 86, 90, 77, 63, 74

Interval	Tally	Frequency
51–60	?	?
61–70	?	?
71–80	?	?
81–90	?	?
91–100	?	?

2. CLASS B: 64, 80, 93, 81, 71, 97, 51, 75, 88, 83, 69, 81, 99, 72, 86, 93, 66, 57, 81, 92

Interval	Tally	Frequency
51–60	?	?
61–70	?	?
71–80	?	?
81–90	?	?
91–100	?	?

3. MATHEMATICAL REASONING In Exercises 1 and 2, which class performed better on the test? Explain.

Practice and Problem Solving

Student Help

▶MORE PRACTICE
Extra practice to help you master skills is on page 584.

BUSES In Exercises 4–6, use the histogram showing the distances traveled by 191 buses before their engines failed. ▶Source: *Technometrics*

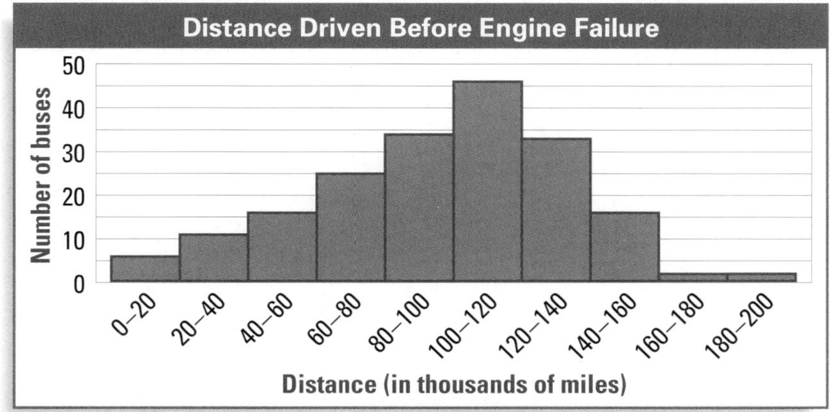

4. At what distance interval did the greatest number of buses experience engine failure?

5. About what *percent* of the buses experienced engine failure before traveling 100,000 miles?

6. Draw a histogram of the distance data using the intervals 0–40, 40–80, 80–120, 120–160, and 160–200.

HEALTH In Exercises 7–9, use the data set below. The data are the lengths of time (in minutes) that patients at a medical clinic had to wait before seeing a doctor. ▶ Source: *Statistics and Public Policy*

40, 30, 40, 55, 30, 60, 35, 55, 40, 35, 5, 10, 65, 35, 35,
30, 30, 60, 35, 25, 65, 30, 30, 45, 85, 25, 25, 10, 10, 15

7. Make a frequency table and a histogram of the data using the intervals 0–9, 10–19, . . . , 80–89.

8. Which interval from Exercise 7 represents the most common waiting times for patients at the clinic?

9. What is the probability that a patient at the clinic was able to see a doctor after waiting less than 30 minutes?

Link to History

U.S. CONGRESS When the United States Congress first met in 1789, the House of Representatives had only 65 members. Today it has 435 members.

More about the U.S. Congress available at www.mcdougallittell.com

History Link **In Exercises 10–12, use the data below giving each state's number of Democrats and Republicans in the U.S. House of Representatives for 1999. Make a frequency table and a histogram of the data set described. Use intervals of 3 for all tables and histograms.**

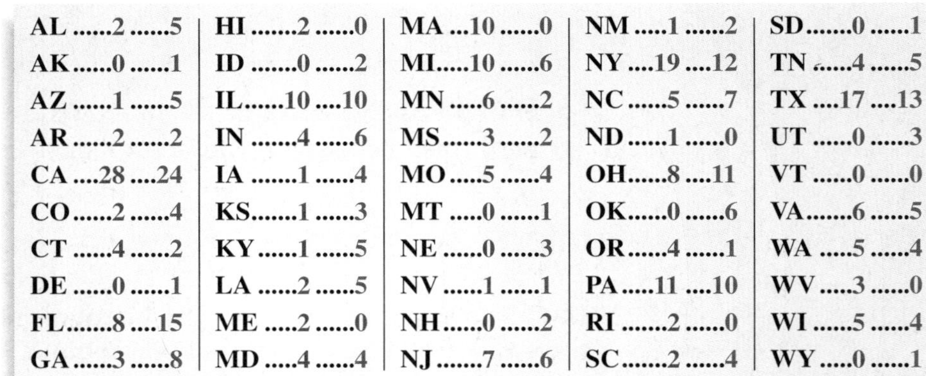

AL	2	5	HI	2	0	MA	10	0	NM	1	2	SD	0	1
AK	0	1	ID	0	2	MI	10	6	NY	19	12	TN	4	5
AZ	1	5	IL	10	10	MN	6	2	NC	5	7	TX	17	13
AR	2	2	IN	4	6	MS	3	2	ND	1	0	UT	0	3
CA	28	24	IA	1	4	MO	5	4	OH	8	11	VT	0	0
CO	2	4	KS	1	3	MT	0	1	OK	0	6	VA	6	5
CT	4	2	KY	1	5	NE	0	3	OR	4	1	WA	5	4
DE	0	1	LA	2	5	NV	1	1	PA	11	10	WV	3	0
FL	8	15	ME	2	0	NH	0	2	RI	2	0	WI	5	4
GA	3	8	MD	4	4	NJ	7	6	SC	2	4	WY	0	1

10. The numbers of Democratic representatives

11. The numbers of Republican representatives

12. **CHALLENGE** The states' *total* numbers of representatives (*Note:* Vermont had 1 Independent representative in 1999 who is not counted in the data above.)

Multiple-Choice Practice

In Exercises 13 and 14, use the histogram in Example 2 on page 458.

13. How many states have gasoline taxes that range from 15 cents/gal to 23 cents/gal?

Ⓐ 32 Ⓑ 33 Ⓒ 34 Ⓓ 35

14. What percent of states have gasoline taxes greater than 20 cents/gal?

Ⓕ 20 Ⓖ 37 Ⓗ 40 Ⓙ 74

10.3 Box-and-Whisker Plots

In this lesson you'll:

- Draw and analyze data displays. (SDP 2.3)
- Compute the range and the median of data sets. (SDP 1.1)

Goal 1 DRAWING BOX-AND-WHISKER PLOTS

A **box-and-whisker plot** is a display that divides a data set into four parts. The data set is first divided into lower and upper halves by the median. Each half is then subdivided into two parts by the *lower quartile* and the *upper quartile*. The **lower quartile** is the median of the lower half of the data. The **upper quartile** is the median of the upper half.

EXAMPLE 1 Drawing a Box-and-Whisker Plot

SCIENCE LINK The data below are distances (in centimeters) at which a bat first detected a nearby insect. ▶ Source: *Animal Behavior*

62, 23, 27, 56, 52, 34, 42, 40, 68, 45, 83

a. Find the median and the lower and upper quartiles of the data.

b. Draw a box-and-whisker plot of the data.

Solution

a. First write the data values in increasing order. You must find the median before finding the lower and upper quartiles.

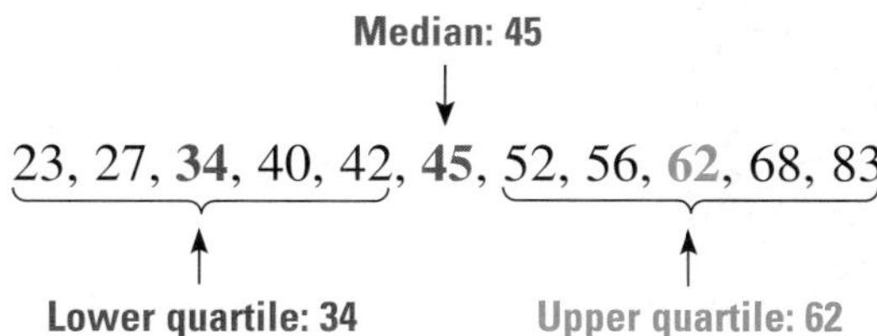

b. ***Draw*** a number line that includes the minimum data value, 23, and the maximum data value, 83.

Plot the minimum, the lower quartile, the median, the upper quartile, and the maximum below the number line.

Make a box extending from the lower quartile to the upper quartile.

Draw a vertical line through the box at the median.

Draw "whiskers" from the box to the minimum and maximum.

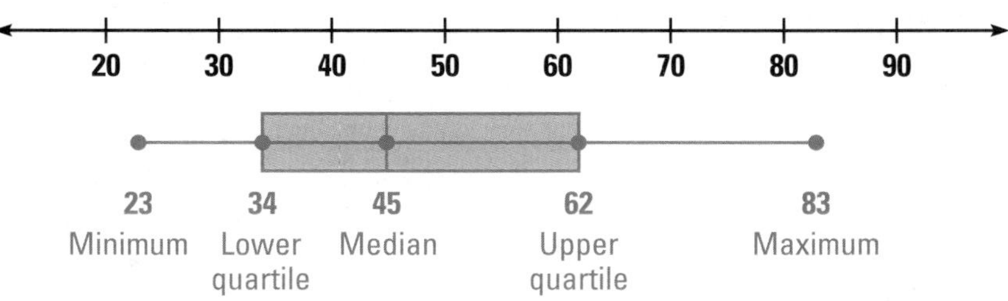

Student Help

▶ **STUDY TIP**
The box in a box-and-whisker plot represents (approximately) the middle 50% of the data values. Each whisker represents (approximately) either the lower or upper 25% of the values.

In Example 1 the median and quartiles are all values in the data set. This is not always the case. For instance, if the value 90 is added to the data set in Example 1, then the median and quartiles are *not* in the set, as shown.

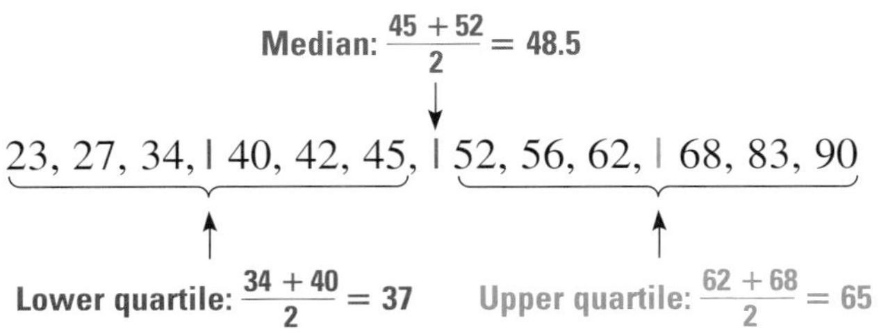

Median: $\frac{45 + 52}{2} = 48.5$
23, 27, 34, | 40, 42, 45, | 52, 56, 62, | 68, 83, 90
Lower quartile: $\frac{34 + 40}{2} = 37$
Upper quartile: $\frac{62 + 68}{2} = 65$

Goal 2 READING BOX-AND-WHISKER PLOTS

A box-and-whisker plot shows how "spread out" data are. The length of the entire plot represents the data's **range**, which is the difference of the maximum and minimum data values. The length of just the box represents the **interquartile range**—the difference of the upper and lower quartiles.

Link to Careers

AUTOMOTIVE DESIGNERS help conceive of and develop new automobiles. They have to consider such factors as appearance, performance, fuel economy, and price (the focus of Example 2).

INTERNET More about automotive design at www.mcdougallittell.com

EXAMPLE 2 Interpreting Box-and-Whisker Plots

VEHICLES The box-and-whisker plots show the base prices of minivans and sports-utility vehicles (SUVs) for 1999. ▶ Source: CarPrices.com

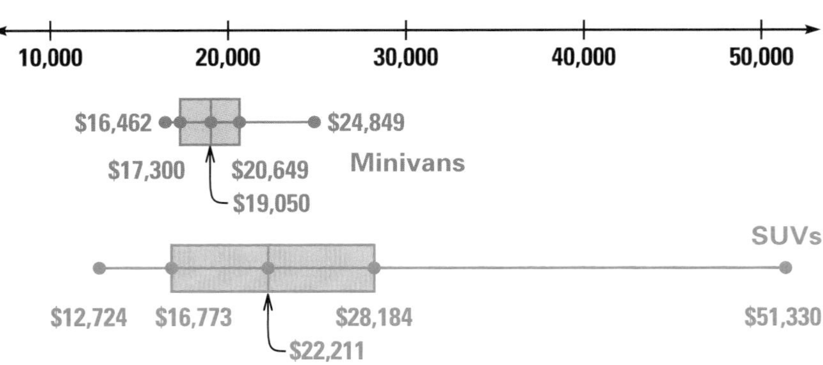

a. Find the range and interquartile range for each set of prices.

b. Compare the prices of minivans and SUVs.

Solution

a. For minivans, the range is $24,849 − $16,462 = $8387 and the interquartile range is $20,649 − $17,300 = $3349. For SUVs, the range is $51,330 − $12,724 = $38,606 and the interquartile range is $28,184 − $16,773 = $11,411.

b. SUV prices vary more than minivan prices, as shown by the much greater range and interquartile range of the SUV prices. Also, the higher median price of SUVs ($22,211 versus $19,050 for minivans) indicates that SUVs are generally more expensive.

10.3 Exercises

Guided Practice

In Exercises 1–6, use the box-and-whisker plot to find the quantity.

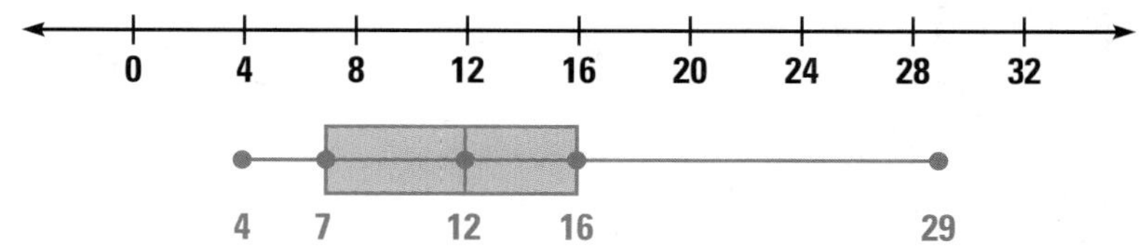

1. Median **2.** Lower quartile **3.** Upper quartile

4. Minimum data value **5.** Range **6.** Interquartile range

7. ERROR ANALYSIS A student tried to find the median and the lower and upper quartiles of a data set, as shown. Identify and correct any mistakes the student made.

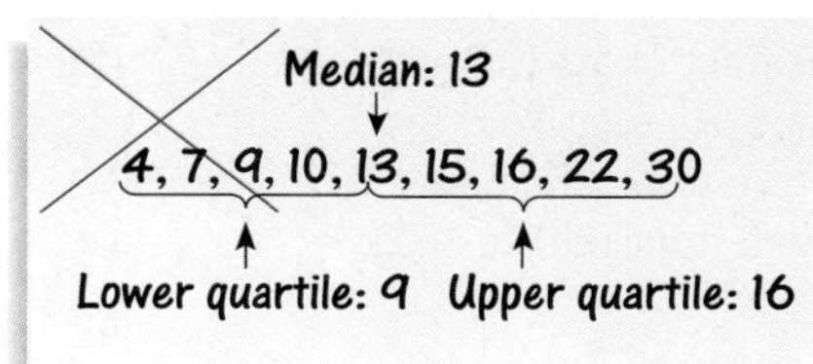

Practice and Problem Solving

Student Help

▶ **More Practice** Extra practice to help you master skills is on page 584.

In Exercises 8–11, match the data set with the box-and-whisker plot.

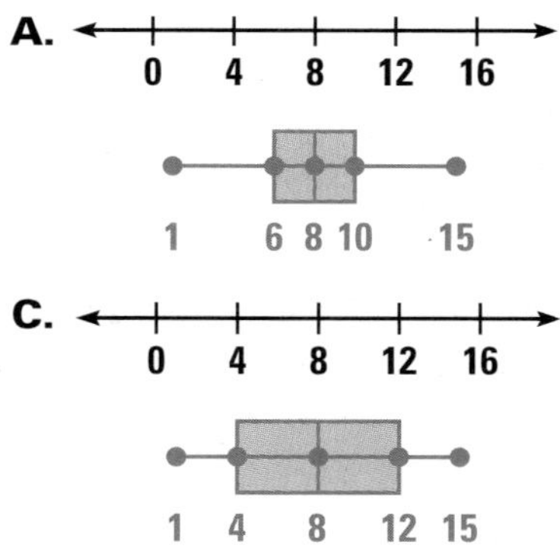

B. 0 4 8 12 16
1 7 9.5 13 15

D. 0 4 8 12 16
1 3 6 8 15

8. 6, 11, 3, 10, 15, 1, 4, 12, 6, 15

9. 10, 4, 6, 6, 1, 9, 15, 9, 13, 7

10. 3, 2, 15, 6, 8, 4, 7, 11, 6, 1

11. 1, 8, 11, 7, 5, 15, 11, 13, 8, 15

Find the median and the lower and upper quartiles of the data set. Then draw a box-and-whisker plot of the data.

12. 37, 31, 34, 10, 40, 36, 18, 32, 39, 32

13. 3, 9, 2, 25, 13, 10, 2, 18, 7, 9, 16, 12, 21

14. 36, 50, 3, 50, 6, 50, 11, 45, 15, 42, 18, 39, 18, 38, 30

15. 84, 66, 69, 41, 52, 70, 56, 33, 53, 90, 60, 37, 100, 70, 48, 67

Link to History

PRESIDENTS Theodore Roosevelt was the youngest person ever to be elected President of the United States. He was 42 at the time he took office and served from 1901 to 1909.

16. STRAWBERRIES In a study, 19 varieties of strawberries were frozen and thawed. The percentages of juice lost due to freezing are given below. Find the median and the lower and upper quartiles. Then draw a box-and-whisker plot. ▶Source: *Fruit Varieties Journal*

46, 51, 44, 50, 33, 46, 60, 41, 55, 46,
53, 53, 42, 44, 50, 54, 46, 41, 48

History Link **In Exercises 17–19, use the data below showing the ages of the first 42 Presidents of the United States at the time they took office.**

57, 61, 57, 57, 58, 57, 61, 54, 68, 51, 49, 64, 50, 48,
65, 52, 56, 46, 54, 49, 50, 47, 55, 55, 54, 42, 51, 56,
55, 51, 54, 51, 60, 62, 43, 55, 56, 61, 52, 69, 64, 46

17. Find the quantity.

a. Median **b.** Lower quartile **c.** Upper quartile

d. Range **e.** Interquartile range **f.** Mean

18. Draw a box-and-whisker plot of the data. In what interval do the middle 50% (approximately) of the Presidents' ages lie?

19. CHALLENGE In Lesson 10.1 you learned that an outlier is a value in a data set that is much greater than or much less than most other values in the set. An outlier can be defined more precisely as a value whose distance from the nearer quartile (upper or lower) is more than 1.5 times the interquartile range. According to this definition, are any of the Presidents' ages outliers? Explain.

20. ***Chapter Opener Link*** Draw a box-and-whisker plot of the leg length data on page 451.

BOSTON MARATHON **In Exercises 21 and 22, use the box-and-whisker plots below, which represent the men's and women's winning times (to the nearest minute) in the Boston Marathon from 1980 to 1999.**
▶Source: Boston Athletic Association

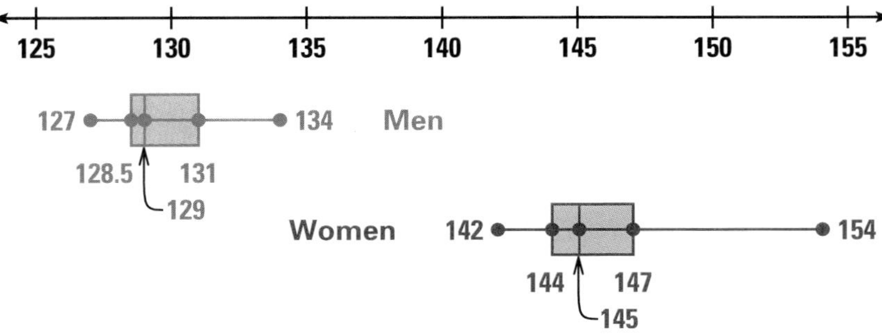

21. Find the range and interquartile range for each set of winning times.

22. WRITING Compare the men's and women's winning times. What has been a "typical" winning time for men? for women? Have the men's times or the women's times varied more? Explain.

Student Help

▶ HOMEWORK HELP

Extra help with problem solving in Ex. 23 is available at www.mcdougallittell.com

23. **Science Link** In 1878 Charles Darwin published the results of a study in which he compared the heights of cross- and self-fertilized corn plants. The heights (in inches) of the two groups of plants he grew are given below. Draw a box-and-whisker plot of each data set on the same number line. Describe what the plots show.

Cross-fertilized plants	Self-fertilized plants
23.5, 12, 21, 22, 19.125, 21.5, 22.125, 20.375, 18.25, 21.625, 23.25, 21, 22.125, 23, 12	17.375, 20.375, 20, 20, 18.375, 18.625, 18.625, 15.25, 16.5, 18, 16.25, 18, 12.75, 15.5, 18

▶ Source: *Effects of Cross- and Self-Fertilization in the Vegetable Kingdom*

Multiple-Choice Practice

In Exercises 24 and 25, use the box-and-whisker plot below.

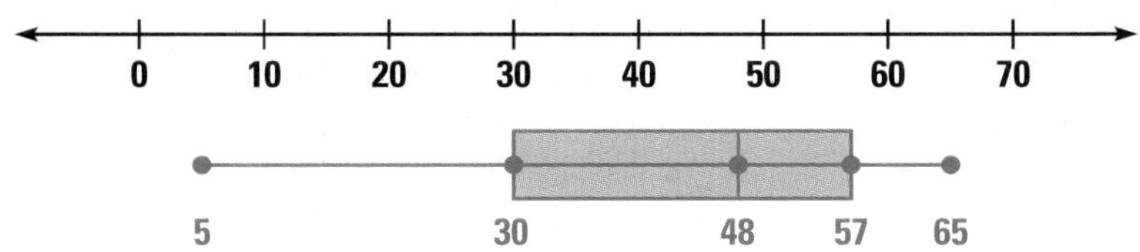

24. What is the median of the data?

Ⓐ 30 Ⓑ 35 Ⓒ 48 Ⓓ 57

25. What is the interquartile range of the data?

Ⓕ 8 Ⓖ 9 Ⓗ 18 Ⓙ 27

Mixed Review

Evaluate. Simplify if possible. *(3.1–3.3)*

26. $\frac{4}{9} + \frac{2}{9}$ **27.** $\frac{7}{8} - \frac{5}{12}$ **28.** $7\frac{1}{6} - 5\frac{1}{2}$ **29.** $1\frac{2}{5} + 4\frac{2}{3}$

Evaluate the expression. *(4.7)*

30. $-2 + 3 \times 5$ **31.** $(-4)(-6) + 5 \cdot 2^3$

32. $-7 + 9(-4) - 2$ **33.** $-48 \div (-5 + 8) - (-3)$

In Exercises 34–37, solve the proportion. *(6.2)*

34. $\frac{x}{30} = \frac{7}{6}$ **35.** $\frac{6}{15} = \frac{8}{m}$ **36.** $\frac{5}{60} = \frac{p}{12}$ **37.** $\frac{12}{r} = \frac{20}{9}$

38. **EXCHANGE RATES** You and your friend have just returned from a trip to Germany. At a bank your friend exchanges 152 deutsche marks (the German unit of money) for \$80. You want to exchange 247 deutsche marks for dollars. Write and solve a proportion to find the number of dollars you will receive. *(6.3)*

REASONING 10.4

DEVELOPING CONCEPTS
Scatter Plots

For use with Lesson 10.4

California Standards

- Draw and analyze data displays. (SDP 2.3)
- Use graphs to explain mathematical reasoning. (MR 2.4)

MATERIALS

- Measuring tape or meter stick
- Graph paper

You can graph an *ordered pair* of numbers, such as (2, 3), in a *coordinate plane* formed by two number lines called *axes* that intersect at a right angle. The graph of an ordered pair is a point in the plane. A collection of such points is called a *scatter plot*.

SAMPLE 1 Drawing a Scatter Plot

You can use a scatter plot to show the relationship between a person's height and lower-arm length.

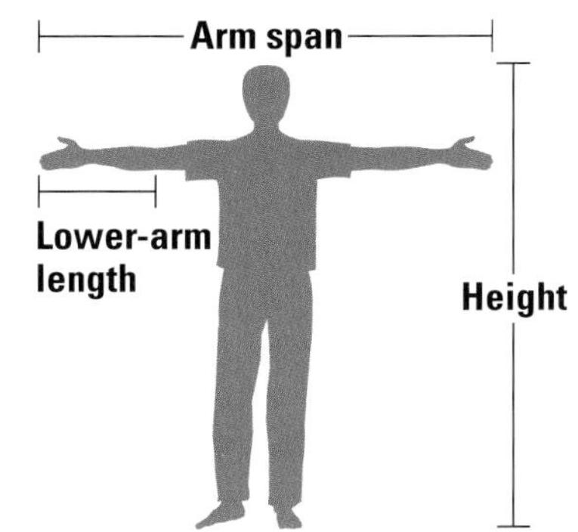

Here's How

1. Measure the heights and lower-arm lengths of several people to the nearest centimeter. Record the data in a table like the one shown below.

Person	Amy	Carl	Jose	Lisa	Matt	Sonya
Height (cm)	137	153	182	173	163	145
Lower-arm length (cm)	36	40	47	45	43	38

2. Write the data as ordered pairs (height, lower-arm length).

   (137, 36), (153, 40), (182, 47), (173, 45), (163, 43), (145, 38)

3. Draw a coordinate plane. Use the horizontal axis for height and the vertical axis for lower-arm length. Graph the ordered pairs from Step 2. For example, to graph (137, 36), first move right along the horizontal axis to 137 cm. Then move up until you are directly across from 36 cm on the vertical axis and plot a point.

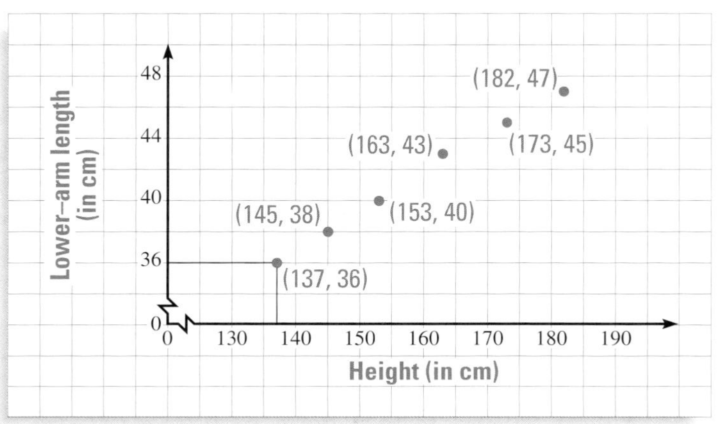

Student Help

STUDY TIP
In Sample 1, the horizontal and vertical axes have been broken after 0 (indicated by the symbol ⌇). This is because the numbers in the ordered pairs are much greater than 0.

If you can see a pattern in a scatter plot of real-life data, you can estimate values that are not in the original data set.

SAMPLE 2 Estimating a Value

You can use the scatter plot from Sample 1 to estimate the lower-arm length of a person 190 cm tall.

Here's How

The points in the scatter plot lie close to a line, as shown below. The line appears to pass through the point **(190, 49)**. So, you can estimate that the lower-arm length of a person 190 cm tall is about 49 cm.

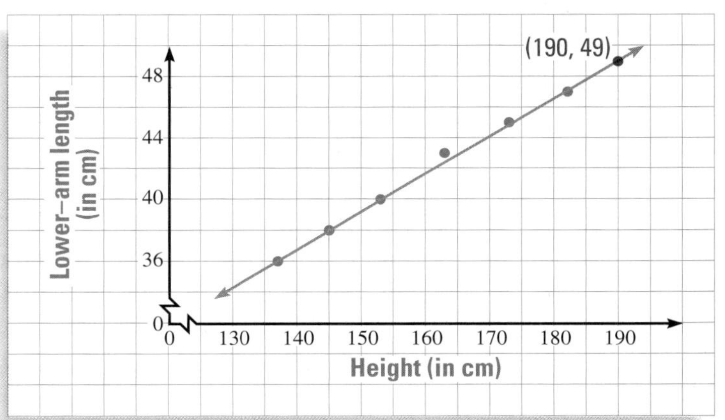

Try These

In Exercises 1–6, work in a group of at least five students.

1. Measure the height and arm span of each person in your group to the nearest centimeter. (See the diagram on the previous page for a definition of arm span.) Record your data in a table.
2. Write your data from Exercise 1 as ordered pairs (height, arm span).
3. Draw a scatter plot of the ordered pairs from Exercise 2.
4. Describe any pattern you see in your scatter plot from Exercise 3.
5. Estimate the arm span of a person 190 cm tall.
6. **MATHEMATICAL REASONING** Suppose Peter is 20 cm taller than Ben. How would you expect their arm spans to differ? Explain.

10.4 The Coordinate Plane and Scatter Plots

California Standards

In this lesson you'll:

- Draw and analyze data displays. (SDP 2.3)
- Graph ordered pairs and interpret the results. (AF 1.0)

Goal 1 GRAPHING ORDERED PAIRS

A **coordinate plane** is formed by two number lines that intersect at a right angle. The horizontal number line is the ***x*-axis**, and the vertical number line is the ***y*-axis**. The point where the *x*-axis and *y*-axis intersect is the **origin**. The axes divide the coordinate plane into four **quadrants**.

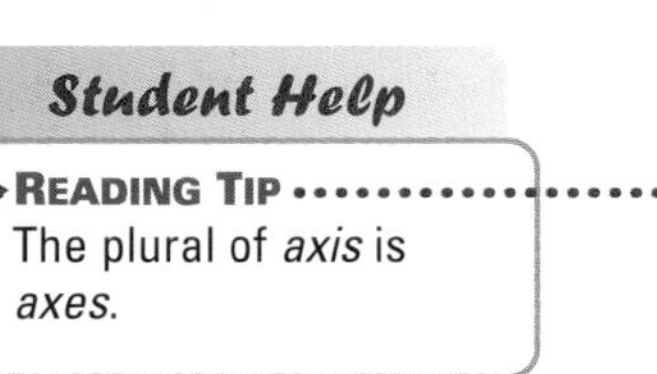

Student Help

READING TIP The plural of *axis* is *axes*.

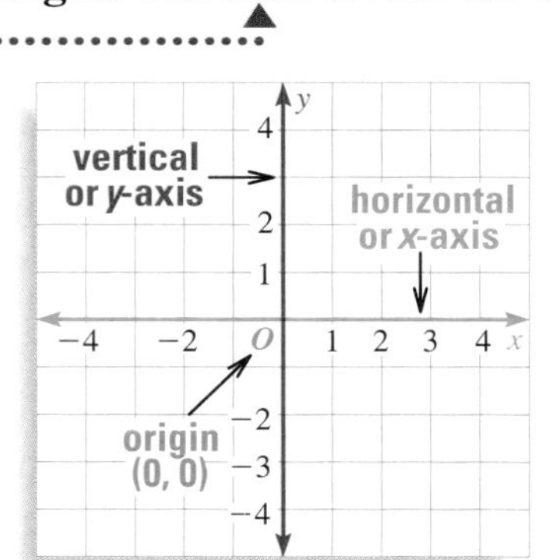

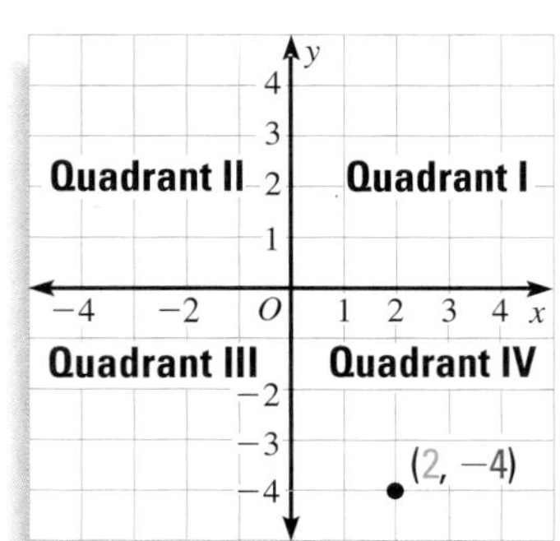

Each point in a coordinate plane corresponds to an **ordered pair** of numbers, such as (2, −4). The first number is the ***x*-coordinate**. The second number is the ***y*-coordinate**. The point corresponding to an ordered pair is the **graph** of the ordered pair. The graph of (2, −4) lies in Quadrant IV. Points on the *x*-axis or *y*-axis do not lie in any quadrant.

EXAMPLE 1 *Graphing Ordered Pairs*

Graph the ordered pair in a coordinate plane.

a. (3, 2) **b.** (−4, −5) **c.** (0, 3)

Solution

a. Starting at the origin, move right 3 units and up 2 units.

b. Starting at the origin, move left 4 units and down 5 units.

c. Starting at the origin, move up 3 units.

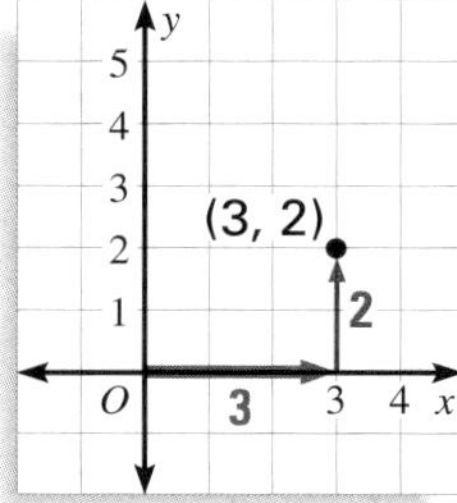

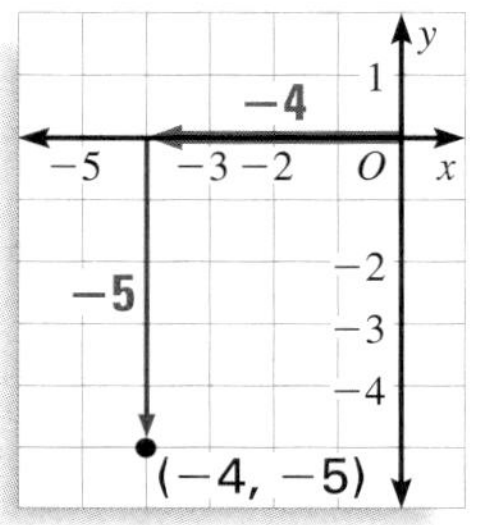

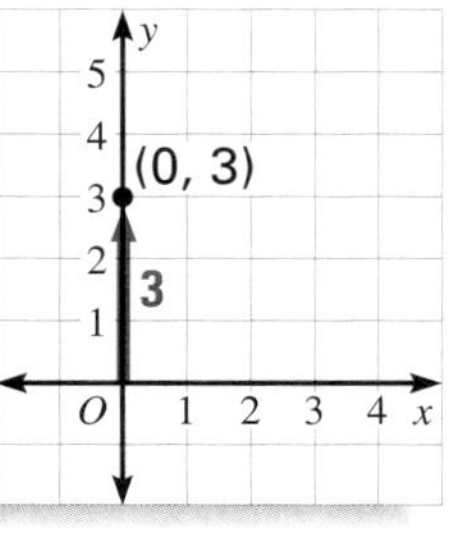

Goal 2 DRAWING SCATTER PLOTS

A **scatter plot** is a collection of points in a coordinate plane that represents a set of ordered pairs. In Developing Concepts 10.4, page 466, you saw how to use a pattern in a scatter plot of real-life data to estimate values that are not in the original data set.

Link to Science

CELSIUS SCALE
Anders Celsius, a Swedish astronomer, invented the Celsius scale in 1742. Originally, numbers on the scale *decreased* as the temperature became hotter, but this was later changed.

EXAMPLE 2 Drawing a Scatter Plot

SCIENCE LINK You have a thermometer with a Fahrenheit scale and a Celsius scale. To find the relationship between the two scales, you make a table of Fahrenheit temperatures (°F) and the corresponding Celsius temperatures (°C).

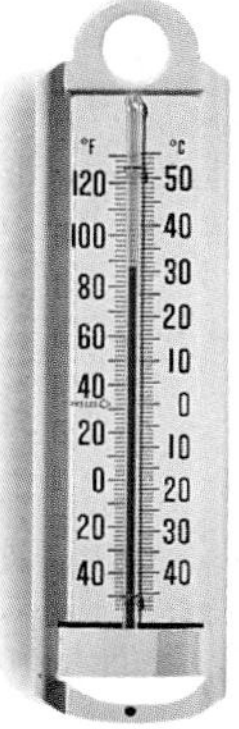

°F	−20	0	20	40	60	80	100
°C	−29	−18	−7	4	16	27	38

a. Draw a scatter plot of the data in the table. Describe the pattern that the scatter plot shows.

b. Estimate the Celsius temperature corresponding to 130°F.

Solution

a. First write the data in the table as a set of ordered pairs. Let x be Fahrenheit temperature and let y be Celsius temperature.

$$(-20, -29), (0, -18), (20, -7), (40, 4), (60, 16), (80, 27), (100, 38)$$

Draw a coordinate plane. Let 1 tick mark represent 10 degrees on both the x- and y-axes. Graph the ordered pairs in the plane.

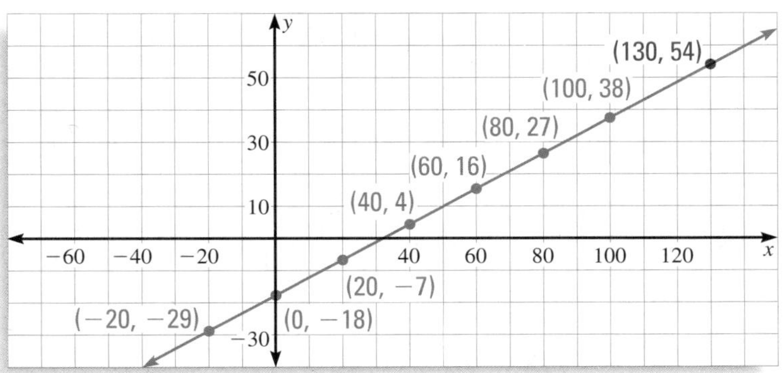

The points in the scatter plot appear to lie on a line. This suggests that there is a *linear* relationship between Fahrenheit temperature and Celsius temperature.

b. The line in the coordinate plane above appears to pass through the point **(130, 54)**. So, you can estimate that the Celsius temperature corresponding to 130°F is about 54°C.

Student Help

▶ **MORE EXAMPLES**

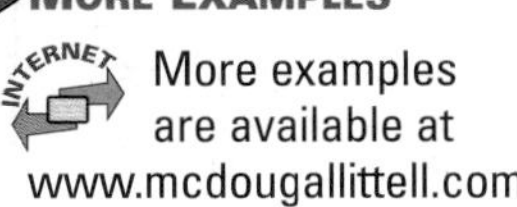

More examples are available at www.mcdougallittell.com

10.4 Exercises

Guided Practice

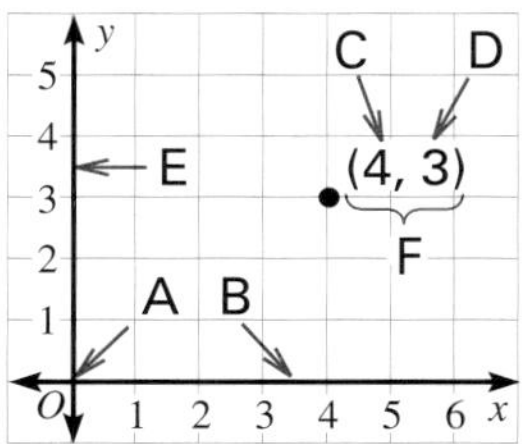

In Exercises 1–6, match the term with the letter in the coordinate plane.

1. x-coordinate
2. x-axis
3. y-coordinate
4. y-axis
5. Origin
6. Ordered pair

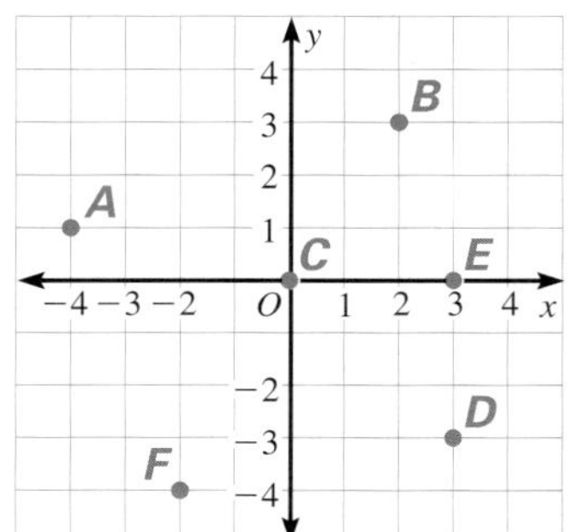

In Exercises 7–12, use the coordinate plane at the right to write the coordinates of the point. Identify the quadrant (if any) in which the point lies.

7. A
8. B
9. C
10. D
11. E
12. F

13. GEOGRAPHY A location's *latitude* is measured in degrees north (°N) or degrees south (°S) of the equator. The table shows the latitudes and average high temperatures for several cities in the Northern Hemisphere in January. Draw a scatter plot of the data. Use the x-axis for latitude and the y-axis for temperature. What is the trend in temperature as latitude increases?

Latitude (°N)	4	12	20	26	33	40	45	49	59	61
Temperature (°C)	19	33	19	23	13	6	−6	5	−24	−7

Practice and Problem Solving

Student Help

▶ MORE PRACTICE Extra practice to help you master skills is on page 584.

14. MATHEMATICAL REASONING What is true of all points whose x-coordinate is 0? whose y-coordinate is 0?

WRITING **Describe in words how to graph the ordered pair in a coordinate plane.**

15. (3, 4)
16. (2, −6)
17. (−4, 0)

Graph the ordered pairs in a coordinate plane and label the points.

18. (0, −3), (6, 4), (1, −1), (−5, −5), (−1, 2)

19. (4, 5), (−7, 1), (−2, 0), (5, −6), (−3, −1)

20. (−6, −2), (2, 0), (−4, 3), (8, 1), (0, 0)

Student Help

▶ **LOOK BACK**
For help with polygons, see pages 31 and 280.

GEOMETRY **Graph the ordered pairs in a coordinate plane and connect the points to form a polygon. Name the type of polygon.**

21. (5, 3), (−2, 0), (0, −4)

22. (−5, 2), (−3, −3), (2, −3), (4, 2), (0, 5)

23. (4, 4), (4, −4), (7, 1), (−6, 0)

Write the data in the table as a set of ordered pairs. Then draw a scatter plot of the data.

24.

x	0	1	2	3	4
y	0	2	4	6	8

25.

x	0	1	2	3	4
y	10	9	7	4	0

ATMOSPHERE **In Exercises 26–28, use the table below giving the air temperatures recorded by a weather balloon as it rises through Earth's atmosphere. The data are based on a ground temperature of 70°F.**

Altitude (mi)	1	2	3	4	5	6	7	8
Temperature (°F)	52	33	15	−4	−22	−41	−59	−78

26. Draw a scatter plot of the data. Use the x-axis for altitude and the y-axis for temperature. Describe any pattern you see.

27. An airplane flies not far from the weather balloon at an altitude of 4.5 miles. Use your scatter plot from Exercise 26 to estimate the temperature outside the airplane.

28. **CHALLENGE** By about how many degrees does the air temperature decrease for each mile of altitude? Use your answer to write an expression for temperature in terms of the altitude x. Evaluate your expression when $x = 4.5$ to check your answer to Exercise 27.

Link to Science

PIKEMINNOW can weigh up to 8 pounds and live as long as 20 years. They have dramatically reduced the salmon population in parts of the Pacific Northwest.

More about pikeminnow available at www.mcdougallittell.com

Science Link **In Exercises 29–31, use the table showing the relationship between a northern pikeminnow's length and the maximum length of the salmon it eats.** ▶ Source: *Transactions of the American Fisheries Society*

Length of pikeminnow (mm)	218	246	270	287	318	344	375	386	414	450	468
Maximum length of salmon eaten (mm)	82	85	94	127	141	157	165	216	219	238	249

29. Draw a scatter plot of the data. Use the x-axis for pikeminnow length and the y-axis for salmon length. Describe any pattern you see.

30. A pikeminnow is 550 millimeters long. Estimate the length of the largest salmon it eats.

31. A salmon is 300 millimeters long. Describe the sizes of the pikeminnow that might eat it.

Link to Science

ARCHAEOPTERYX lived about 150 million years ago in what is now southern Germany. A fossil of this animal is shown above.

Science Link **In Exercises 32–34, use the following information.** *Archaeopteryx* is an extinct animal that had feathers like a bird but teeth and a long, bony tail like a reptile. The table gives the lengths of the femur (a leg bone) and the humerus (an arm bone) for the five known fossils of *Archaeopteryx* that have both bones preserved. ▶Source: *Science*

Femur length (in mm)	38	56	59	64	74
Humerus length (in mm)	41	63	70	72	84

32. Draw a scatter plot of the data. Use the x-axis for femur length and the y-axis for humerus length.

33. Scientists are interested in the relationship between femur length and humerus length because it can help decide whether the five fossils belong to the same species or to different species. If they belong to the same species, a linear relationship between femur length and humerus length can be expected. Based on your scatter plot, is the conclusion that the fossils belong to the same species (*Archaeopteryx*) justified?

34. Suppose a partially preserved *Archaeopteryx* fossil is discovered. The length of the humerus is 50 millimeters, but the femur bones are missing. Use your scatter plot to estimate the femur length.

Multiple-Choice Practice

In Exercises 35 and 36, use the scatter plot at the right.

35. Which point is *not* shown in the scatter plot?

Ⓐ (2, 3) Ⓑ (3, 2)

Ⓒ (6, 2) Ⓓ (5, 5)

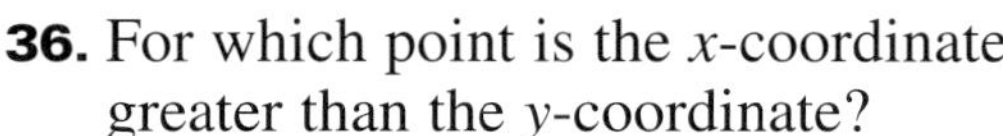

36. For which point is the x-coordinate greater than the y-coordinate?

Ⓕ A Ⓖ B Ⓗ C Ⓙ D

Test Tip ⒶⒷⒸⒹ

▶In Exercises 37 and 38, you may want to copy the diagram and graph the ordered pairs given in the answer choices before answering the questions.

In Exercises 37 and 38, use the diagram at the right.

37. Which point is inside the triangle but outside the circle?

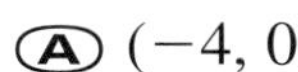

Ⓐ $(-4, 0)$ Ⓑ $(1, -1)$

Ⓒ $(2, 1)$ Ⓓ $(-1, -1)$

38. Which point is outside both the triangle and the circle?

Ⓕ $(-4, 0)$ Ⓖ $(1, -1)$ Ⓗ $(2, 1)$ Ⓙ $(-1, -1)$

Chapter 10 Mid-Chapter Test

Take this test as you would take a test in class. The answers to the exercises are given in the back of the book.

In Exercises 1 and 2, find the mean, median, and mode(s) of the data.

1. Prices of 10 types of sneakers:

$65, $70, $50, $90, $70, $55, $35, $40, $35, $70

2. Numbers of points scored by a football team in 13 games:

14, 22, 30, 21, 3, 10, 9, 19, 21, 14, 27, 24, 7

3. AGRICULTURE The data below give the number of farms (in thousands) for each state in 1997. Make a frequency table and a histogram of the data using the intervals 0–19, 20–39, 40–59, . . . , 200–219.

▶Source: *Statistical Abstract of the United States*

AL 45	CT 4	IL.........76	ME 7	MO 102	NM 14	OK.......73	SD........33	VA........47
AK.........1	DE 2	IN 62	MD 13	MT 24	NY 36	OR.......38	TN 80	WA 36
AZ 8	FL........40	IA 98	MA 6	NE 55	NC 57	PA........50	TX 205	WV......20
AR 43	GA 43	KS........64	MI........51	NV 3	ND 31	RI 1	UT 13	WI 79
CA 84	HI 5	KY.......88	MN 87	NH.........2	OH.......73	SC........22	VT 6	WY 9
CO.......25	ID 22	LA 27	MS.......43	NJ..........9				

SOAP **In Exercises 4 and 5, use the data below showing the number of hand washes possible for 14 kinds of bar soap.** ▶Source: *Consumer Reports*

90, 80, 80, 81, 100, 67, 90, 62, 52, 70, 71, 70, 41, 62

4. Find the quantity.

a. Median **b.** Lower quartile **c.** Upper quartile

d. Range **e.** Interquartile range **f.** Mean

5. Draw a box-and-whisker plot of the data.

HEIGHT **In Exercises 6 and 7, use the table below. It shows the results of a study that examined the relationship between the ages and heights of children in Kalama, Egypt.** ▶Source: Agency for International Development

Age (in months)	18	19	20	21	22	23	24	25	26	27	28	29
Average height (in cm)	76.1	77.0	78.1	78.2	78.8	79.7	79.9	81.1	81.2	81.8	82.8	83.5

6. Draw a scatter plot of the data in the table.

7. Estimate the average height of 32-month-old children in Kalama.

10.5 Using Appropriate Graphs

In this lesson you'll:

- Draw and analyze data displays. (SDP 2.3)
- Identify claims based on statistical data and evaluate the validity of the claims. (SDP 2.5)

Goal 1 Double Bar Graphs and Pictographs

In a **double bar graph**, pairs of bars are used to compare two data sets. A **pictograph** uses pictures or symbols to represent data.

EXAMPLE 1 Reading a Double Bar Graph

You can use the double bar graph below to compare the amounts of American and Italian cheese eaten by people in the United States.

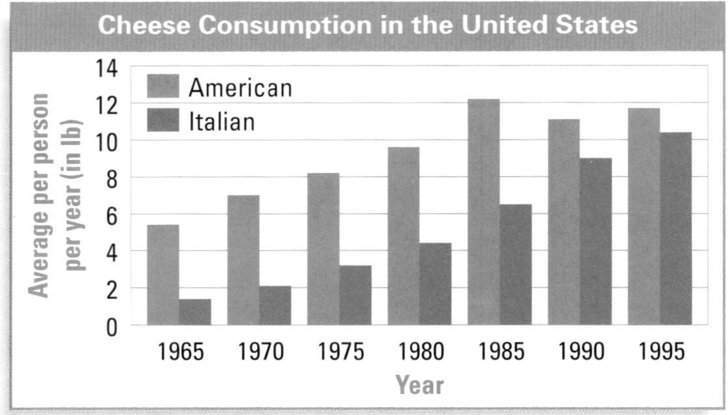

From 1965 to 1985, people ate much more American than Italian cheese. By 1995, consumption of the two cheeses was nearly equal.

Student Help

Skills Review
For help with double bar graphs, see page 565.

EXAMPLE 2 Using a Pictograph

Another way to display the cheese data is to use a pictograph. Each whole symbol in the pictograph below represents 2 lb of cheese.

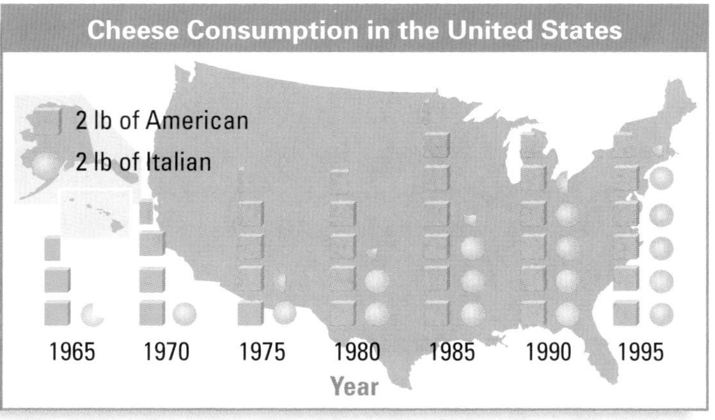

Goal 2 USING LINE GRAPHS

A **line graph** displays data using points joined by line segments. It can sometimes be used to show changes in one or more quantities over time.

EXAMPLE 3 Reading a Line Graph

The line graph shows the cheese data from Examples 1 and 2. Notice the large difference in the amounts of American and Italian cheese consumed during 1965–1985. This gap narrowed after 1985.

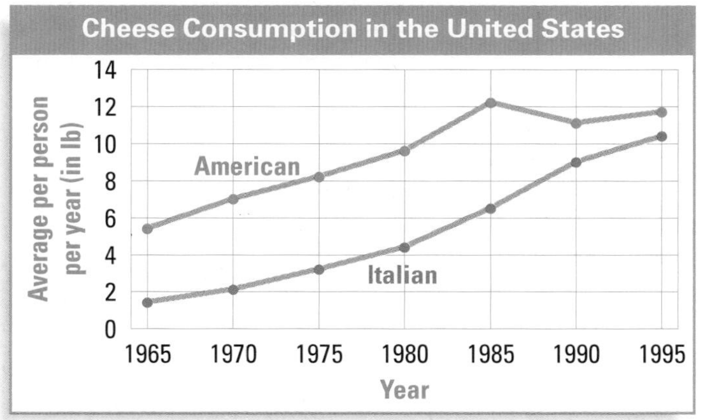

EXAMPLE 4 Using a Line Graph to Evaluate Claims

An article from 1995 claims that for 30 years whole milk consumption has been declining and that lowfat milk is now more popular than whole milk. The article includes the table below showing whole and lowfat milk consumption in quarts per person. By making a line graph of the data, you can visually confirm that the article's claims are true.

Year	1965	1970	1975	1980	1985	1990	1995
Whole	120	106	87	71	60	44	36
Lowfat	9	15	27	35	42	49	48

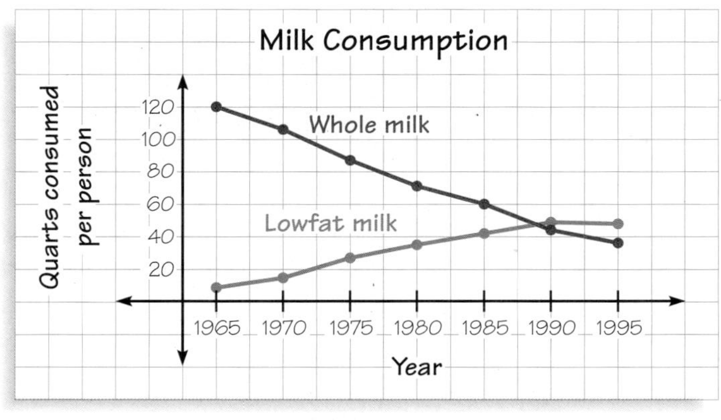

Student Help

▶ **MORE EXAMPLES**

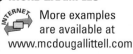

INTERNET More examples are available at www.mcdougallittell.com

10.5 Exercises

Guided Practice

HEALTH In Exercises 1 and 2, use the table. It shows the average number of visits a person made to a doctor in 1995 by age group. ▶ Source: U.S. National Center for Health Statistics

Age	Visits
0–4	6.5
5–17	3.4
18–24	3.9
25–44	5.2
45–64	7.1
65+	11.1

1. Draw a bar graph of the data.

2. MATHEMATICAL REASONING Explain why drawing a line graph of the data would not make sense.

INSECTS In Exercises 3–5, use the pictograph comparing the speeds of different insects.
▶ Source: *Reader's Digest Book of Facts*

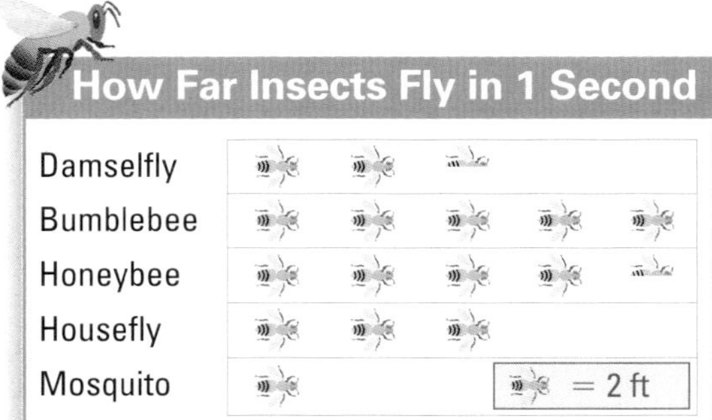

3. Estimate how many feet per second each insect can fly.

4. How many of the insects can fly at least 6 ft/sec?

5. In 3 seconds, how much farther can a bumblebee fly than a damselfly?

Practice and Problem Solving

Student Help
▶ **MORE PRACTICE** Extra practice to help you master skills is on page 585.

Draw a double bar graph and a line graph of the data in the table.

6.

Year	1960	1970	1980	1990	2000
Population of Town A	3500	5000	4000	7000	5500
Population of Town B	4500	6500	9500	13,500	18,500

7.

Age (in years)	0	1	2	3	4
Value of Car A (in $)	20,000	16,000	12,800	10,200	8200
Value of Car B (in $)	15,000	13,500	12,200	11,000	9800

MATHEMATICAL REASONING **Use the line graphs in Examples 3 and 4 on page 475 to predict the average amount of each food consumed per person in the year 2000. Justify your predictions.**

8. American cheese

9. Italian cheese

10. Whole milk

11. Lowfat milk

Link to Agriculture

PICKLES Each person in the United States eats an average of 9 pounds of pickles per year. Pickles are made from cucumbers, like those shown above.

12. **PICKLES** A survey asked a group of pickle eaters what types of pickles they buy. The percent of people who buy each type is shown in the table. Draw a pictograph of the data. ▶Source: *USA Today*

Type	Dill	Sweet	Garlic	Bread and butter	All others
Percent	83	45	24	48	10

13. **SPECIAL OLYMPICS** The table shows the approximate number of athletes (in thousands) who participated in the New Jersey Special Olympics for 1989–1996. Draw a line graph of the data.

Year	1989	1990	1991	1992	1993	1994	1995	1996
Number	5	5	7	7	9	10	10	12

SOCCER **In Exercises 14–16, use the table showing the numbers of male and female soccer participants in the United States for 1991–1996.** ▶Source: *Statistical Abstract of the United States*

14. Draw a double bar graph of the data.

15. Draw a line graph of the data.

16. **CHALLENGE** A reporter claims that the gap in male and female soccer participation has remained large during 1991–1996, but that female participation has increased more as a percentage of total participants. Do the table and your graphs support the reporter's claims? Explain.

Soccer Participants (in thousands)		
Year	**Male**	**Female**
1991	6657	3335
1992	7179	3439
1993	7467	3905
1994	8223	4284
1995	7691	4285
1996	8626	5251

Multiple-Choice Practice

17. Which graph does *not* represent the same data as the others?

(A)
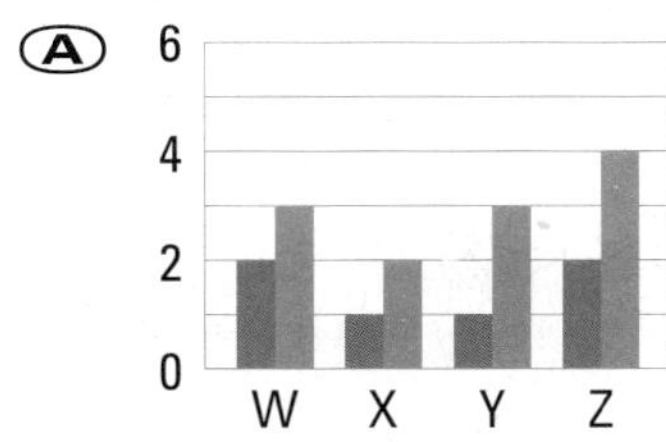

(B)
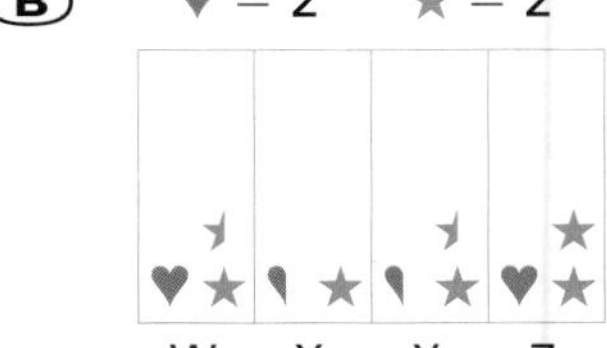

(C)
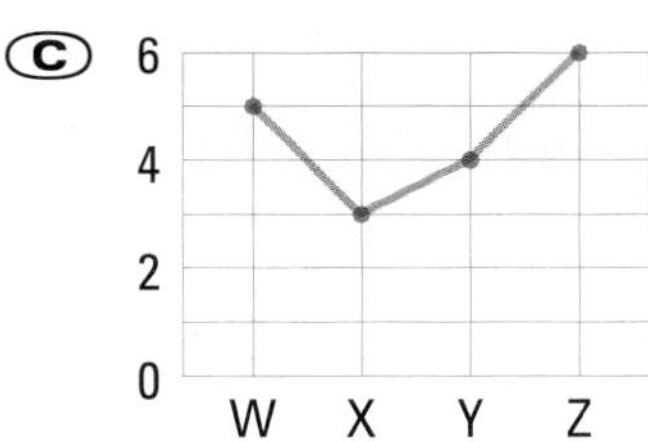

(D)
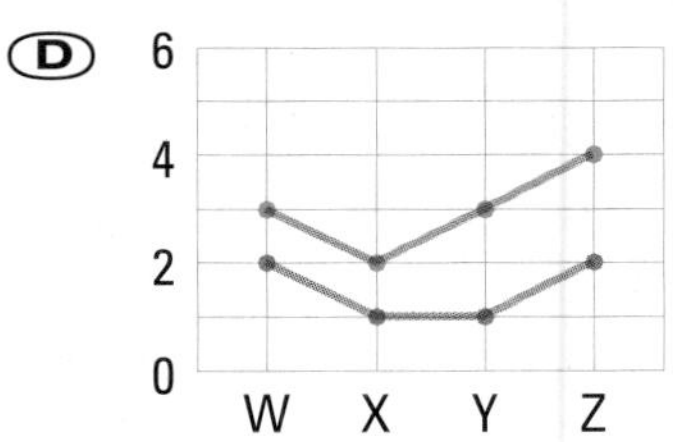

10.6 Interpreting Graphs

In this lesson you'll:

- Analyze data displays and explain why the way in which the results are displayed may influence the conclusions reached. (SDP 2.3)
- Identify claims based on statistical data and evaluate the validity of the claims. (SDP 2.5)

Goal 1 Analyzing Bar Graphs

Although two graphs of the same data may both be accurately drawn, they can emphasize different aspects of the data and give different impressions.

EXAMPLE 1 Comparing Bar Graphs

WEATHER The graphs show the number of tornadoes in the United States for various years. Because the left graph has a broken vertical scale, it emphasizes the *change* in the number of tornadoes from year to year. The right graph emphasizes the *total* number of tornadoes in each year.

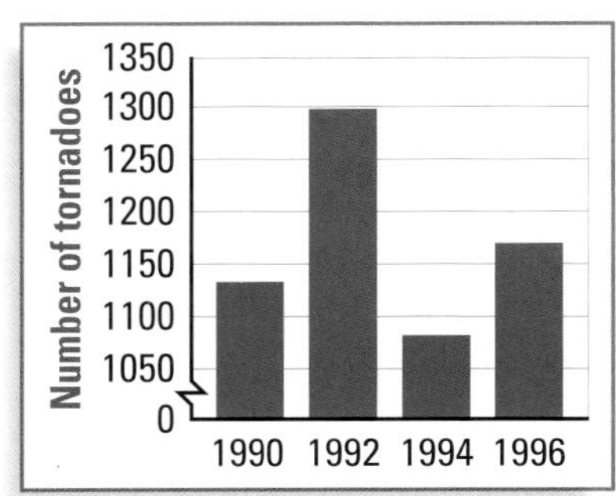

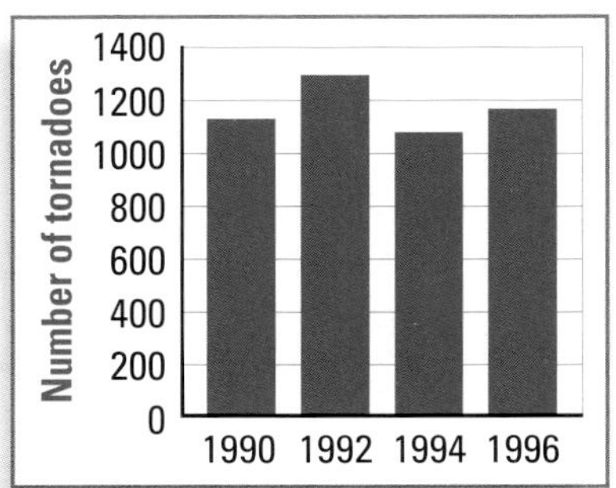

Student Help

STUDY TIP
If you look only at the bar heights in the left graph from Example 1, you might wrongly conclude that there were over 3 times as many tornadoes in 1992 as in 1994. You need to look at the vertical scale to see that this is not the case.

EXAMPLE 2 Interpreting a Bar Graph

CHOCOLATE You can use the bar graph below to compare the amounts of chocolate eaten per person in Switzerland and in the United States. Although the lengths of the bars may suggest that people in Switzerland eat more than 4 times as much chocolate as people in the United States, the scale shows that the Swiss eat only twice as much.

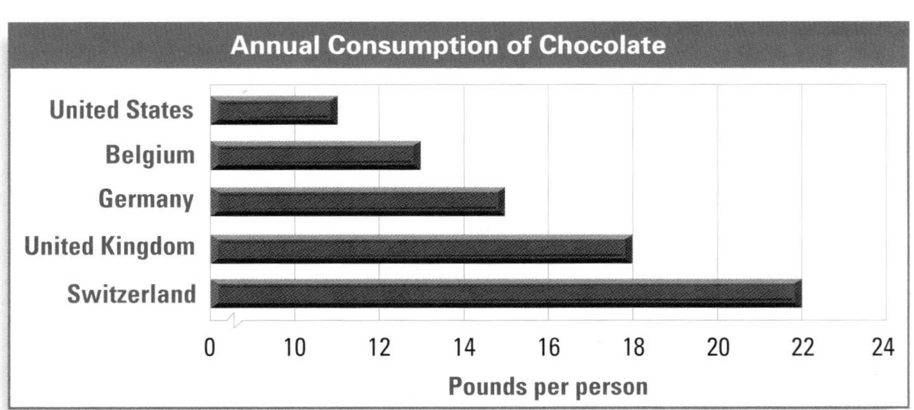

Goal 2 ANALYZING LINE GRAPHS

When the vertical scale of a line graph is broken, the graph may create a potentially misleading impression about the amount of change in a quantity. This is illustrated in the next example.

EXAMPLE 3 Interpreting Line Graphs

FLOWERS The line graphs show the wholesale values of domestic and imported cut flowers used by florist shops for 1991 through 1996. Compare the top two graphs with the bottom two graphs.

▶ Source: *Statistical Abstract of the United States*

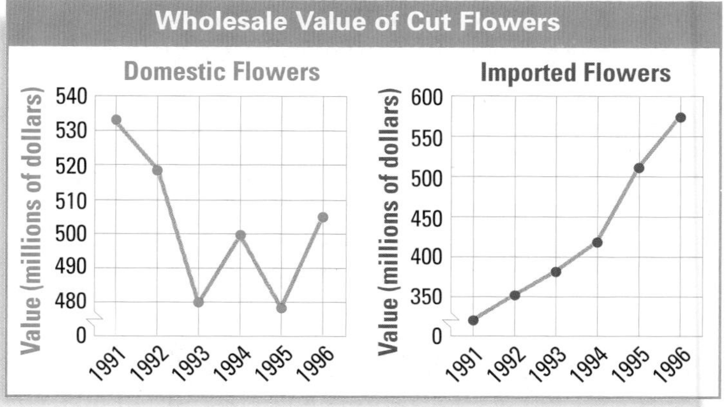

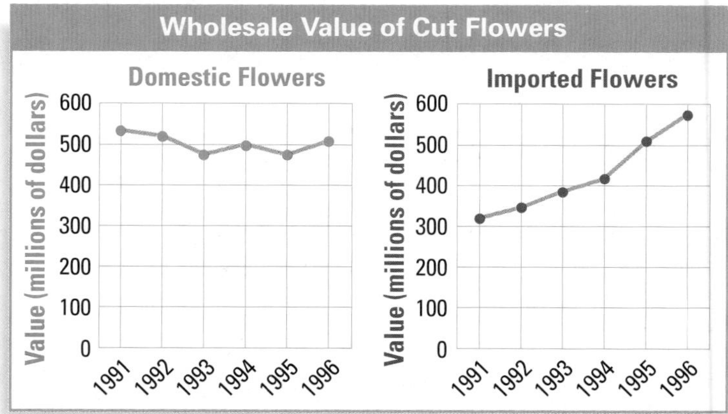

Solution

The top two graphs can be misinterpreted. The broken vertical scales and small dollar increments between tick marks may exaggerate the up-and-down swings in the domestic flowers' value and may make the value of imported flowers appear to increase more rapidly than it did.

The bottom two graphs display the data differently. They suggest that the value of domestic flowers was relatively constant during 1991–1996, and that the value of imported flowers increased noticeably but not drastically.

10.6 Exercises

Guided Practice

1. **MATHEMATICAL REASONING** Explain how a bar graph or a line graph can be misinterpreted. Draw examples of a bar graph and a line graph that are potentially misleading.

MUSIC In Exercises 2 and 3, use the line graph showing the average number of hours people in the United States spend listening to recorded music each year. ▶ Source: Veronis, Suhler & Associates

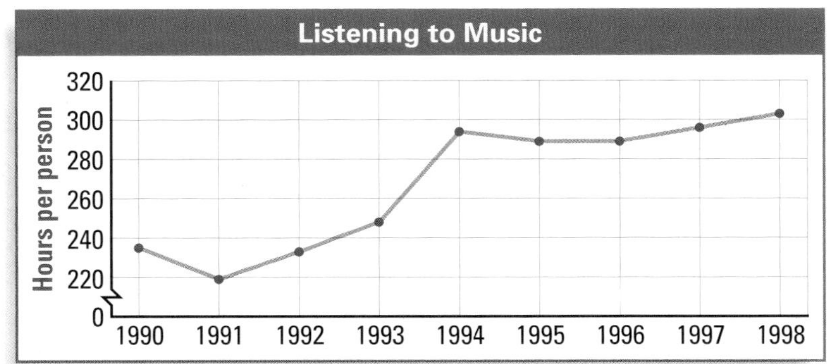

2. Without looking at the graph's vertical scale, compare the average times spent listening to recorded music in 1991 and in 1994.

3. Use the vertical scale to compare the listening times from Exercise 2. Explain how the graph can be misinterpreted.

Practice and Problem Solving

Student Help

▶ **MORE PRACTICE** Extra practice to help you master skills is on page 585.

SPORTS In Exercises 4–6, use the bar graph showing the number of people in the United States age 12 to 17 who participated in various sports in 1996. ▶ Source: National Sporting Goods Association

4. Use the lengths of the bars (not the scale) to compare the number of people who swam with the number who played volleyball.

5. Use the scale to answer Exercise 4. How can the graph be misinterpreted?

6. Draw a bar graph of the data that is *not* potentially misleading.

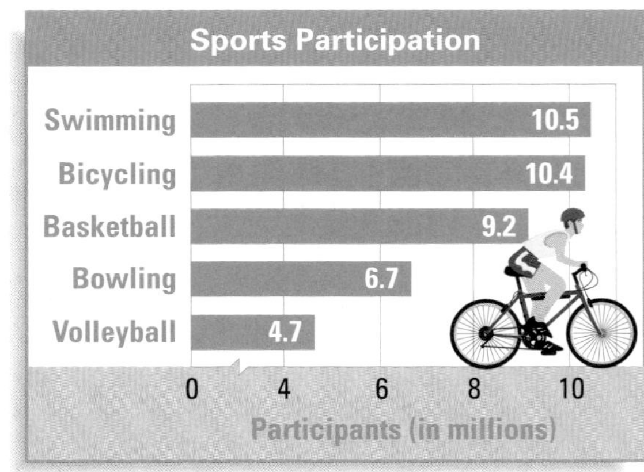

MOVIES In Exercises 7–9, use the line graphs showing the amount of money that people in the United States spent on movies for 1991 through 1997. ▶ Source: U.S. Census Bureau

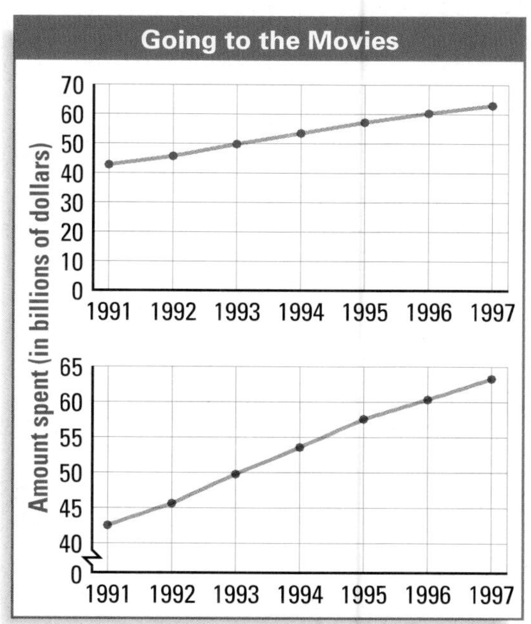

7. Which graph do you think represents the movie data more reasonably? Explain.

8. Suppose the bottom graph appeared in an article arguing that spending on movies rose dramatically during 1991–1997. How would you respond to the article's claim?

9. Draw a line graph of the data with a vertical scale from \$0 to \$400 billion in increments of \$50 billion. Why could this graph be misinterpreted even though its vertical scale is not broken?

POPULATION In Exercises 10 and 11, use the table showing the median age of people in the United States for various years. (Data for years after 1990 are based on U.S. Census Bureau projections.)

Year	1970	1980	1990	2000	2010	2020	2030
Median age	28.0	30.0	33.0	36.4	38.9	40.2	41.8

Student Help

▶ **HOMEWORK HELP**

INTERNET Extra help with problem solving in Exs. 10–11 is available at www.mcdougallittell.com

10. Suppose you want to emphasize the rise in the median age of the U.S. population in order to raise people's awareness of potentially higher health care and retirement costs in the future. Draw a bar graph and a line graph of the age data to get your point across.

11. Suppose you want to downplay the rise in the median age in order to calm people's fears about increasing health care and retirement costs. Draw a bar graph and a line graph to accomplish your goal.

12. CHALLENGE The numbers of plant species on the 15 largest Galápagos Islands are given below along with a box-and-whisker plot of the data. Explain why the box-and-whisker plot is misleading.

44, 51, 58, 58, 62, 70, 93, 97, 104, 108, 237, 280, 285, 347, 444

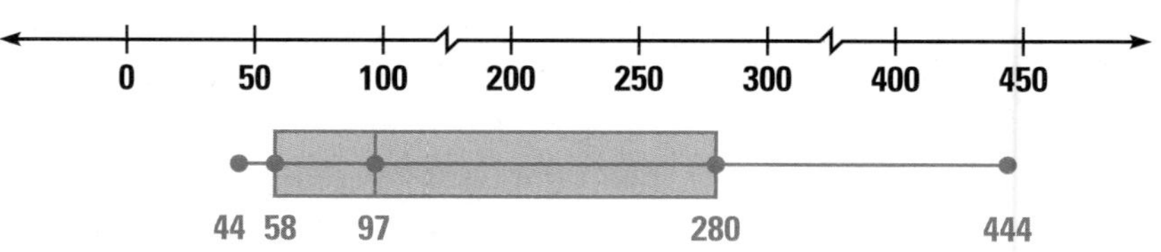

Multiple-Choice Practice

In Exercises 13 and 14, use the line graph shown.

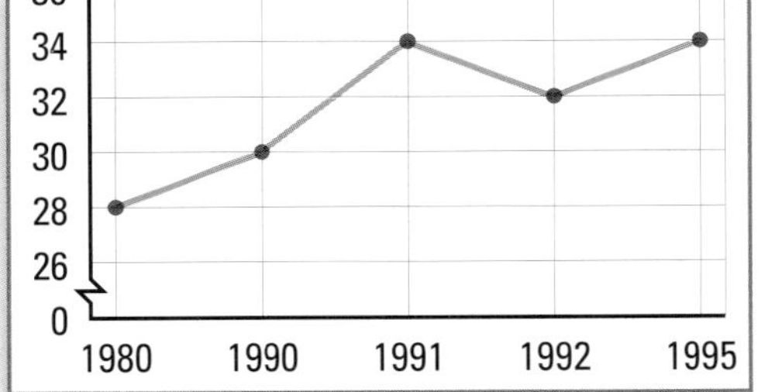

13. Which of the following is *not* a potentially misleading feature of the graph?

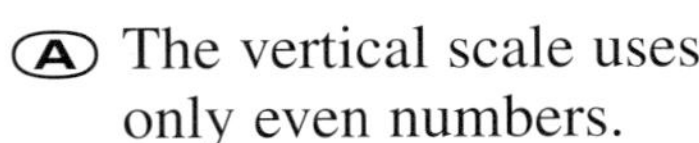

Ⓐ The vertical scale uses only even numbers.

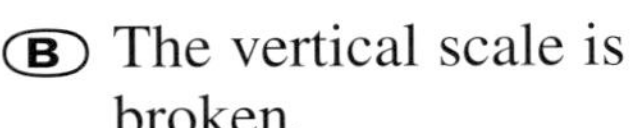

Ⓑ The vertical scale is broken.

Ⓒ The horizontal scale uses unequal time intervals.

Ⓓ The meaning of the vertical scale is unknown.

14. Which of the following conclusions can you make about the quantity modeled by the line graph?

Ⓕ The quantity increased steadily from one year to the next.

Ⓖ The quantity more than doubled between 1980 and 1991.

Ⓗ The minimum value of the quantity occurred in 1992.

Ⓙ The value of the quantity was the same in 1991 and 1995.

Mixed Review

Find the value of *x*. *(8.1, 8.2)*

15.

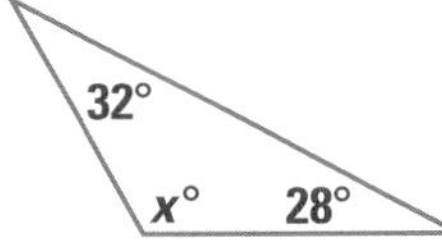

16.

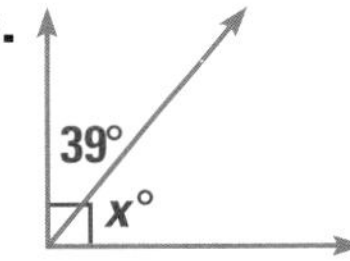

17.

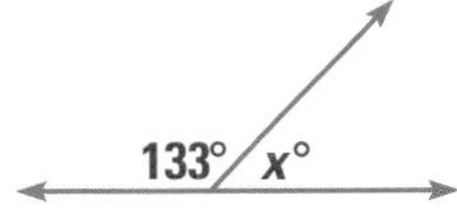

In Exercises 18–20, classify the triangle as *equilateral, isosceles,* or *scalene.* *(8.3)*

18.

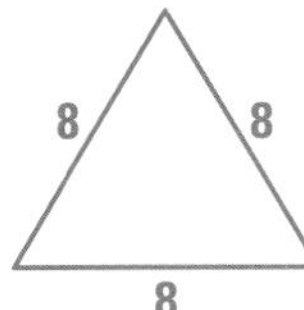

19.

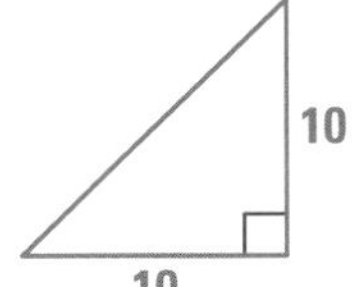

20.

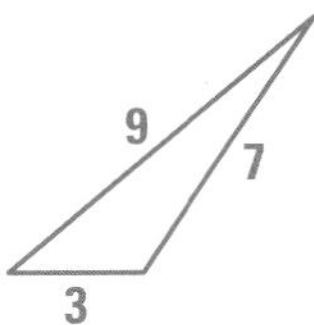

21. CAMERAS You decide to buy a new camera. The camera's original price is \$80, but it is discounted 30%. You also have to pay 7% sales tax on the discounted price. Find the total price you will pay for the camera. Break the problem into simpler parts and label the answer to each part. *(7.7)*

10.7 Samples and Populations

In this lesson you'll:

- Use data samples of a population and describe the characteristics and limitations of the samples. (SDP 2.0)
- Compare different samples of a population with the data from the entire population. (SDP 2.1)
- Identify different ways of selecting a sample and know which method makes a sample more representative. (SDP 2.2)

Goal 1 COMPARING SAMPLES OF A POPULATION

In statistics a **population** is the entire group of people or objects that you want information about. It is often difficult to gather data from every member of a population, so statisticians frequently use a *sample* instead. A **sample** is a subset of a population.

EXAMPLE 1 Comparing Two Samples

EDUCATION You are studying the amount of homework done by 8th graders in the United States. You survey twenty 8th graders from each of two schools. Below are their homework times (in hours per day).

Homework times for School A: 0, 0.5, 0.8, 0.9, 1.1, 1.2, 1.3, 1.4, 1.5, 1.5, 1.6, 1.7, 2.1, 2.1, 2.3, 2.6, 2.8, 3.1, 3.6, 3.9

Homework times for School B: 0.6, 1.1, 1.3, 1.4, 1.8, 1.8, 2.1, 2.3, 2.5, 2.6, 2.8, 2.9, 2.9, 3.1, 3.3, 3.4, 3.7, 3.9, 4.8, 5.7

a. Identify the population and the samples in your study.

b. Use data displays to compare the samples.

c. The mean amount of homework done by 8th graders in the United States is 2.3 hours per day. Compare this population mean with the means of your samples.

Solution

a. The population is all 8th graders in the United States. There are two samples: the 8th graders surveyed from School A and the 8th graders surveyed from School B.

b. One way to compare the samples is to draw two circle graphs.

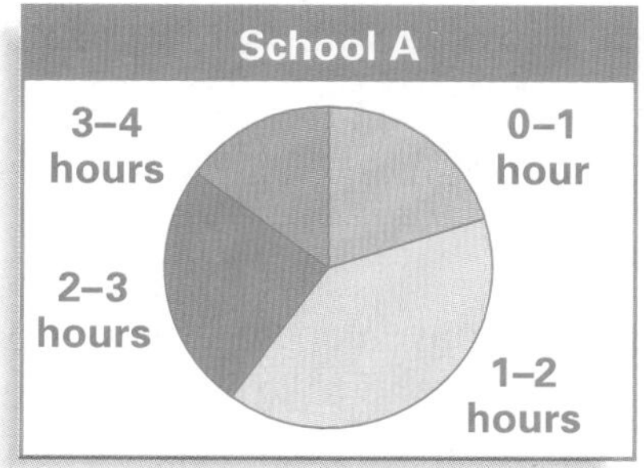

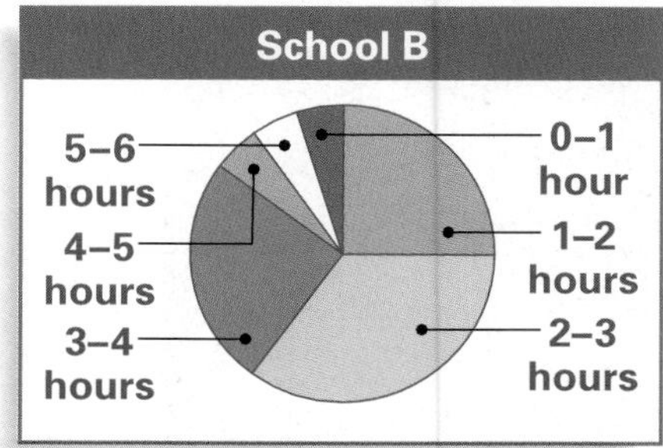

c. Use the definition of mean to find that the mean daily homework time is 1.8 hours for School A and 2.7 hours for School B. So compared with U.S. 8th graders in general, 8th graders at School A do less homework and 8th graders at School B do more homework.

Goal 2 Selecting a Sample from a Population

There are several ways to select a sample from a human population.

With *self-selected sampling*, you let people volunteer to be part of the sample.

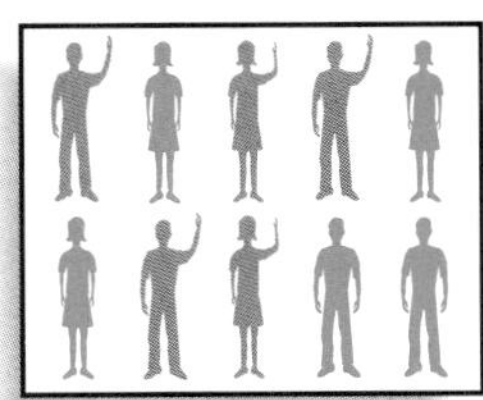

With *systematic sampling*, you use a pattern to select people, such as choosing every other person.

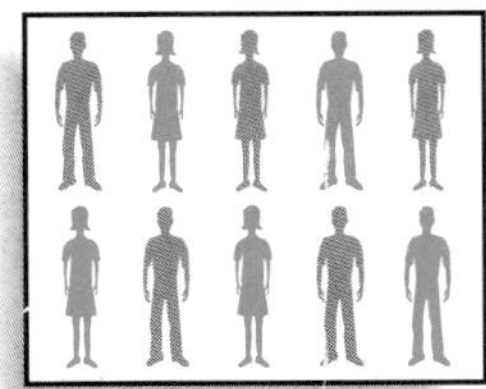

With *convenience sampling*, you choose easy-to-reach people, such as those in the first row.

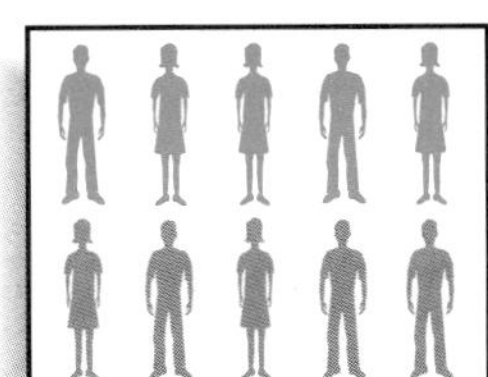

With *random sampling*, each person has an equally likely chance of being chosen.

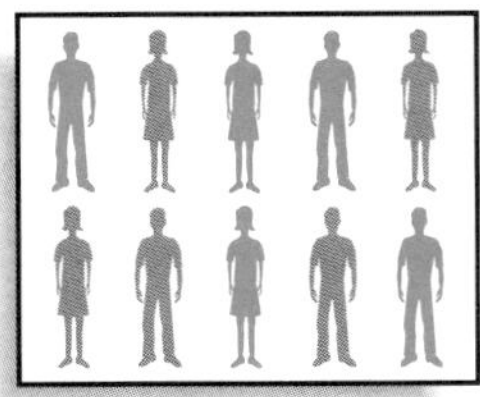

Of the sampling methods described above, random sampling is preferred because it is most likely to produce a sample that is representative of the population. A sample that is not representative is a **biased sample**.

EXAMPLE 2 Classifying Samples

FOOTBALL The owner of a football team wants to find out if people in the team's city will support higher taxes to build a new stadium. The owner considers several sampling methods. Identify the type of sample each method produces and tell whether the sample is biased.

a. Survey people at the current stadium as they enter to see a game.

b. Survey people who call in to a talk radio show.

c. Choose a person from each page of the city's phone book by pointing at a name on the page without looking.

Solution

a. This is a convenience sample. It is biased because football fans, who would tend to favor the new stadium, are overrepresented.

b. This is a self-selected sample. It is biased because callers likely have stronger-than-average opinions about the stadium issue.

c. This is a random sample (if you assume that everyone in the city is listed in the phone book). The sample is not biased.

Link to Football

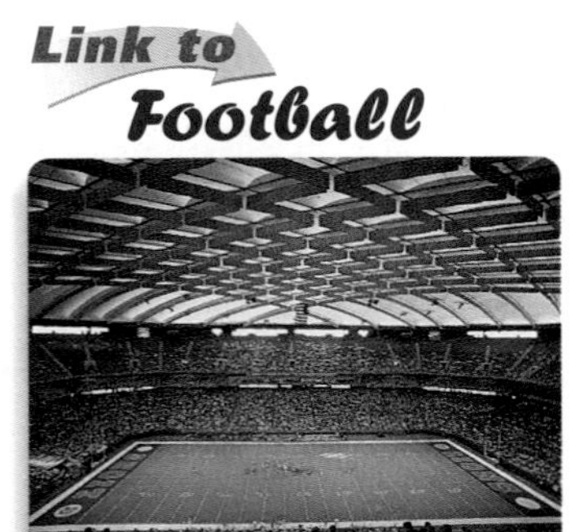

FOOTBALL STADIUMS
The largest stadium in professional football is located in Detroit, Michigan. It seats 80,311 people.

10.7 Exercises

Guided Practice

In Exercises 1–6, match the definition with the term.

A. Systematic sample **B.** Random sample **C.** Population

D. Convenience sample **E.** Self-selected sample **F.** Biased sample

1. A sample in which people volunteer to be a member
2. A sample from a population in which everyone has an equally likely chance of being selected
3. The entire group of people or objects that you want information about
4. A sample whose members are selected based on a pattern
5. A sample that is not representative of the population from which it is selected
6. A sample in which people who are easy to reach are selected

Practice and Problem Solving

Student Help

▶ MORE PRACTICE
Extra practice to help you master skills is on page 585.

BOOKS **In Exercises 7–10, use the following information.** The owner of a bookstore surveys 75 customers: 25 who shop at the store's Web site, 25 who shop from its catalog, and 25 who shop at the store itself. Customers are asked how many books they bought last year. The results are shown.

Customers who shop on-line: 1, 4, 5, 7, 8, 10, 12, 12, 13, 14, 15, 16, 17, 17, 18, 19, 21, 22, 24, 24, 24, 26, 28, 29, 29

Customers who shop from catalog: 1, 1, 2, 3, 3, 3, 4, 5, 6, 6, 7, 7, 9, 11, 12, 13, 14, 16, 17, 17, 18, 20, 21, 22, 23

Customers who shop in person: 3, 4, 4, 5, 6, 7, 7, 8, 9, 9, 10, 11, 12, 14, 15, 16, 16, 17, 19, 20, 20, 22, 24, 25, 27

7. Compare the samples by drawing a circle graph of each data set.
8. Find the mean for each sample. On average, which type of customer buys the most books?
9. In 1996 the United States population was about 265 million and the number of books bought in the U.S. was about 2.21 billion. What is the average number of books bought by a U.S. resident in 1996? Compare your answer with the means from Exercise 8.
10. MATHEMATICAL REASONING Is it appropriate to consider the population for the samples to be everyone in the United States? Use your results from Exercises 8 and 9 to help justify your answer.

NEWSPAPERS In Exercises 11–13, use the following information.

The layout and features of a newspaper have been redesigned. The editor-in-chief wants to know what the paper's readers think of the changes. She prints the request at the right in the paper's first redesigned issue.

> ?????????????????????????
> **What Do You Think?**
> Call 1-999-OPINION to give your opinion on the new design of this newspaper. Each call costs $1. The opinion poll lasts only until midnight on Friday, February 17.
> ?????????????????????????

11. Identify the population whose opinions the editor-in-chief wants to know. Also identify the sample for the request.

12. Explain why the sample may not be representative of the population.

13. WRITING Describe how a representative sample could be chosen.

Student Help

HOMEWORK HELP

Extra help with problem solving in Exs. 14–16 is available at www.mcdougallittell.com

In Exercises 14–16, identify the type of sample and describe the population. Then tell if the sample is biased. Explain your reasoning.

14. A news program asks viewers to phone in a vote for or against increasing funding for space exploration.

15. A reporter writing a story about Internet shopping e-mails her friends asking whether they purchased items on-line during the past year.

16. The names of all the students in an English class are put in a hat and mixed up. The teacher draws six names without looking and has those students give an oral report.

17. CHALLENGE A city librarian asks every fifth person who enters the library how many books he or she reads each year. Explain why the sample is biased if the population is the residents of the city but is not biased if the population is the users of the library.

Multiple-Choice Practice

In Exercises 18–20, use the following information.

You have to order 200 sweatshirts for your school store. You ask 25 of the 75 people who ride your bus what size of sweatshirt they wear. The results are shown in the table.

Size	Number
Small	4
Medium	9
Large	10
X-Large	2

18. Which method of sampling did you use?

Ⓐ Self-selected Ⓑ Systematic

Ⓒ Convenience Ⓓ Random

19. How many people are in the sample?

Ⓕ 25 Ⓖ 75 Ⓗ 200 Ⓙ Not known

20. How many people are in the population?

Ⓐ 25 Ⓑ 75 Ⓒ 200 Ⓓ Not known

10.8 Interpreting Surveys

California Standards

In this lesson you'll:

- Explain why the way in which a question is asked may influence the results obtained. (SDP 2.3)
- Identify data that represent sampling errors and explain why the sample might be biased. (SDP 2.4)
- Identify claims based on statistical data and evaluate the validity of the claims. (SDP 2.5)

Goal 1 Analyzing the Results of a Survey

When you conduct a survey, you should phrase the questions in such a way that the responses of the people surveyed accurately reflect their opinions or actions. If a survey uses biased questions, claims based on the survey results may not be valid.

EXAMPLE 1 A Survey with a Biased Question

INCOME TAXES In a survey of 60 randomly selected people, each person is asked the question below. The results of the survey are shown in the circle graph. Is the given claim valid? Explain.

QUESTION: Should income tax rates be raised even higher than they are now?

CLAIM: Most people oppose raising income tax rates.

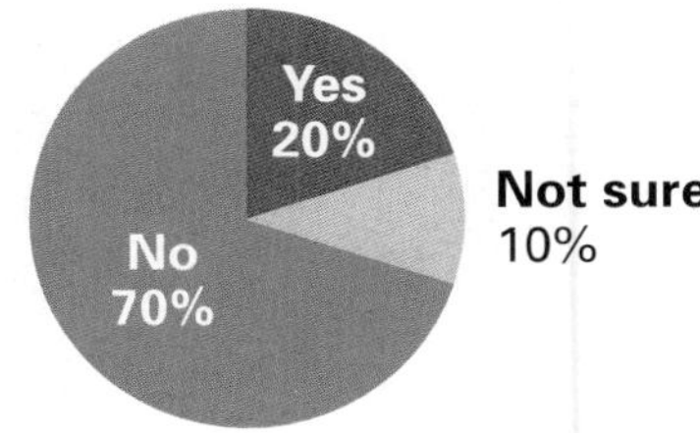

Solution

The claim may not be valid because the question is worded in a biased way. The phrase "even higher than they are now" implies that taxes are high enough already and encourages a response of "no."

EXAMPLE 2 A Survey with a Biased Question

INCOME TAXES Suppose the 60 people in Example 1 had been asked the question below instead. The results for this question might be as shown in the circle graph. Is the given claim valid? Explain.

QUESTION: Should income tax rates be raised so that education, health care, and the environment are not neglected?

CLAIM: Most people support raising income tax rates.

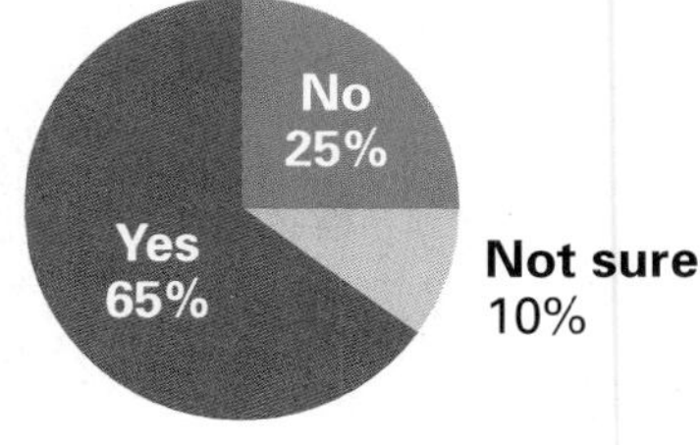

Solution

The claim may not be valid because the question is worded in a biased way. The question connects higher taxes with support for popular goals and encourages a response of "yes."

Student Help

STUDY TIP
In Examples 1 and 2, you can eliminate the pro-tax or anti-tax bias in the questions simply by asking, "Should income tax rates be raised?"

Goal 2 EVALUATING CLAIMS

In Examples 1 and 2, the survey results are flawed due to the way the survey questions are worded. Survey results may also be misleading because the survey uses a biased sample or is conducted inappropriately.

Student Help

▶ **MORE EXAMPLES**

INTERNET More examples are available at www.mcdougallittell.com

EXAMPLE 3 A Survey with a Biased Sample

MOVIES The owner of a movie theater wants to find out how often people go to the movies. He surveys 40 people standing in line at the theater. The survey results are shown. Is the given claim valid?

QUESTION: On average, how many times per month do you go to a movie?

CLAIM: Most people go to a movie at least twice per month.

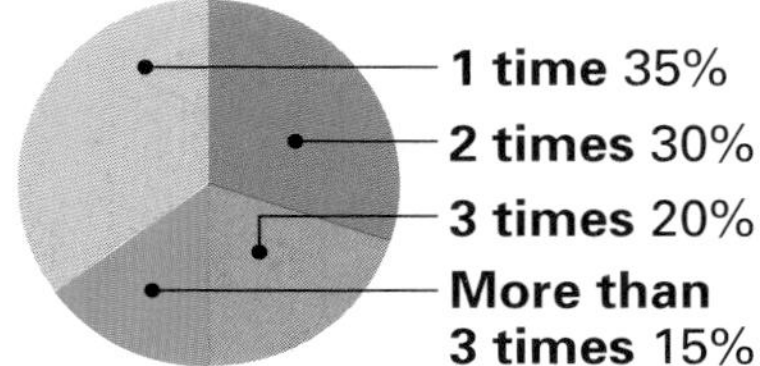

Solution

The claim may not be valid because the sample is biased. People standing in line for a movie are more likely to attend movies than people in general. A better sample could be obtained by choosing people at random from a telephone book, for example.

EXAMPLE 4 A Survey That Is Conducted Inappropriately

TV SURVEYS A television station is doing a special report on honesty. The news team stands on a busy street with a camera and asks passersby how well they keep their promises. The results of the survey are shown below. Is the given claim valid?

QUESTION: Have you broken a promise in the past year?

CLAIM: Most people keep their promises.

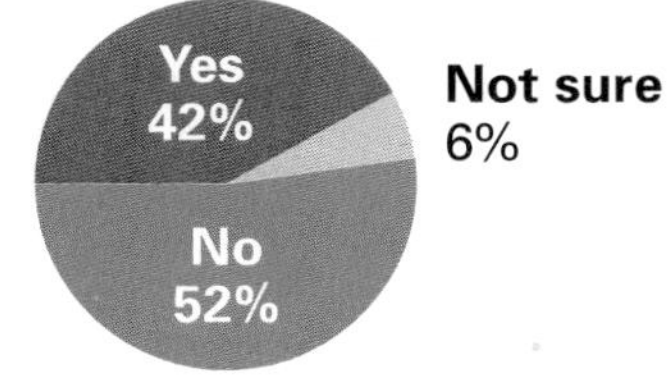

Solution

The claim may not be valid because it is likely that some people who *have* broken a promise were too embarrassed to admit it on camera. It might have been better to have people provide anonymous written responses to the survey question.

Finally, keep in mind that even if a survey avoids biased questions and samples and is conducted appropriately, it still provides only a temporary "snapshot" of people's opinions or actions. Because of this, researchers may repeat surveys periodically so the results do not become outdated.

10.8 Exercises

Guided Practice

1. WRITING Describe several ways in which claims based on survey results can be invalid.

2. Two similar survey questions are given below. Explain the sharp difference in the survey results and the claims based on the results.

QUESTION: Does the government spend too little, too much, or just the right amount on costly highway construction projects?

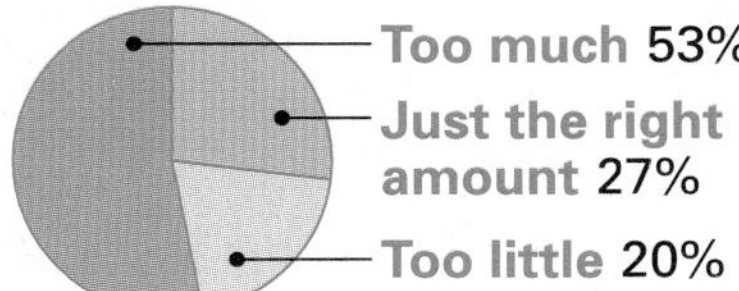

CLAIM: Most people think the government spends too much on highway construction projects.

QUESTION: Does the government spend too little, too much, or just the right amount on building and maintaining safe roads and bridges?

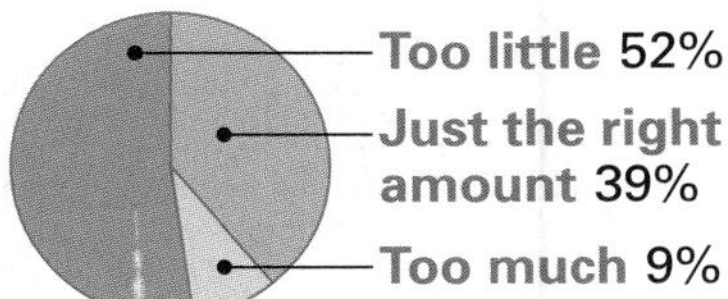

CLAIM: Most people think the government spends too little on building and maintaining roads and bridges.

Practice and Problem Solving

Student Help

MORE PRACTICE Extra practice to help you master skills is on page 585.

In Exercises 3–10, explain how the wording of the survey question could influence the results.

3. Do you think that playful, cuddly puppies are nicer than kittens?

4. Do you think that extreme violence on television affects young, impressionable children?

5. Which do you prefer in cold weather—the softness of leather gloves or the scratchy feel of wool mittens?

6. Do you prefer the loud, harsh beat of heavy-metal music or the rich, relaxing sounds of classical music?

7. Do you prefer the bitter taste of coffee or the refreshing taste of water?

8. Isn't it unfair for schools to force every student to take physical education classes?

9. Do you agree with experts' claims that video games are harmful?

10. Don't you think having three supermarkets in such a small town is ridiculous?

History Link **In Exercises 11–13, use the following information.**
In 1936 the magazine *Literary Digest* conducted a survey to predict the winner of the presidential election between Democratic candidate Franklin Roosevelt and Republican candidate Alfred Landon. The *Digest* mailed 10 million questionnaires to addresses selected from telephone books and automobile registration records. About 2.4 million responses were received. The results of the survey and the actual election are shown below.

Candidate	Survey results	Election results
Franklin Roosevelt	41%	61%
Alfred Landon	55%	37%
Others	4%	2%

11. Compare the survey results with the election results. How accurate was the *Literary Digest*'s survey at predicting the election winner?

12. In 1936 only relatively well-off Americans had telephones and automobiles. How does this fact help explain the difference between the survey results and the election results?

13. Describe a sampling method for the *Literary Digest* survey that might have produced a more accurate prediction of the election winner.

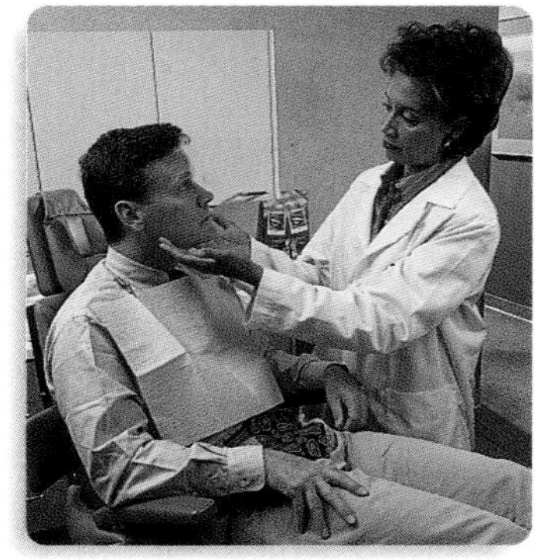

DENTISTS help prevent and treat diseases of the teeth and gums. In 1996 there were about 196,000 dentists in the United States.

More about dentists is available at www.mcdougallittell.com

DENTISTRY **In Exercises 14 and 15, use the following information.**
One hundred people are randomly stopped in a shopping mall and asked how many times per day they brush their teeth. The survey results and a claim based on these results are shown below.

QUESTION: On average, how many times per day do you brush your teeth?

CLAIM: Most people brush their teeth at least twice per day.

Never 1%
1 time 15%
2 times 43%
3 times 41%

14. Explain why the claim may not be valid.

15. Describe a method for surveying people about their tooth-brushing habits that might give more accurate results.

In Exercises 16 and 17, write a survey question that could be used to get the desired information. Describe how you would select a sample and what method you would use to conduct the survey.

16. A city's transportation department is trying to decide whether it should expand the number of hours during which subway service is offered.

17. A local television station wants to know what percent of viewers watch its newscast on weekday nights.

Multiple-Choice Practice

18. Which survey question would most accurately determine whether people prefer to watch basketball or soccer?

Ⓐ Do you prefer to watch a fast-paced, exciting game of basketball or a dull, low-scoring game of soccer?

Ⓑ Given that soccer is the most popular sport in the world, do you prefer to watch it over basketball?

Ⓒ Do you prefer to watch basketball or soccer?

Ⓓ Like most people in the United States, do you prefer to watch basketball over soccer?

19. You want to determine the average number of classes taken by students at a high school. Which method for gathering data is most likely to give you valid results?

Ⓕ Survey all the freshmen at the school.

Ⓖ Survey 50 students whose names are chosen at random by one of the school's computers.

Ⓗ Survey 20 students in an Honors English class.

Ⓙ Survey a group of friends sitting together at lunch in the school cafeteria.

Mixed Review

Find the product. *(1.8)*

20. 5.2×4 **21.** 8.3×0.2 **22.** 4.8×7.5

23. 2.25×9.68 **24.** 0.36×0.63 **25.** 5.237×1.809

Find the greatest common factor of the numbers. *(2.2)*

26. 2, 8 **27.** 6, 15 **28.** 36, 54

29. 27, 63 **30.** 20, 28, 36 **31.** 32, 64, 80

In Exercises 32–37, solve the equation and check the solution. *(5.3–5.7)*

32. $x + 8 = 6$ **33.** $m - 2 = -1$ **34.** $12k = 64$

35. $\frac{p}{5} = 11$ **36.** $4x - 3 = 17$ **37.** $\frac{w}{6} + 2 = -13$

38. **PIZZA** A pizzeria charges the following prices for cheese pizzas: \$7 for a 10 inch pizza, \$9 for a 12 inch pizza, and \$13 for a 14 inch pizza. (The pizza sizes are the diameters of the pizzas.) Find the area and cost per square inch of each pizza. Which size of pizza offers the best value? Explain. *(8.8)*

Chapter 10

Chapter Summary and Review

VOCABULARY

- **measure of central tendency,** *p. 453*
- **median,** *p. 453*
- **mode,** *p. 453*
- **outlier,** *p. 454*
- **frequency table,** *p. 457*
- **frequency,** *p. 457*
- **histogram,** *p. 458*
- **box-and-whisker plot,** *p. 461*
- **lower quartile,** *p. 461*
- **upper quartile,** *p. 461*
- **range,** *p. 462*
- **interquartile range,** *p. 462*
- **coordinate plane,** *p. 468*
- ***x*-axis,** *p. 468*
- ***y*-axis,** *p. 468*
- **origin,** *p. 468*
- **quadrant,** *p. 468*
- **ordered pair,** *p. 468*
- ***x*-coordinate,** *p. 468*
- ***y*-coordinate,** *p. 468*
- **graph of an ordered pair,** *p. 468*
- **scatter plot,** *p. 469*
- **double bar graph,** *p. 474*
- **pictograph,** *p. 474*
- **line graph,** *p. 475*
- **population,** *p. 483*
- **sample,** *p. 483*
- **biased sample,** *p. 484*

10.1 MEASURES OF CENTRAL TENDENCY

Examples on pp. 453–454

A measure of central tendency for a set of data values is a single number that represents a "typical" value for the set. Three important measures of central tendency are the mean, the median, and the mode.

EXAMPLE Below are the lengths (in minutes) of 10 telephone calls.

15, 17, 5, 1, 26, 1, 17, 38, 1, 9

The mean is the sum of the data values divided by the number of values.

$$\text{Mean} = \frac{15 + 17 + 5 + 1 + 26 + 1 + 17 + 38 + 1 + 9}{10} = \frac{130}{10} = 13$$

Because the number of data values is even, the median is the mean of the two middle values when the values are written in numerical order.

1, 1, 1, 5, **9**, **15**, 17, 17, 26, 38

$$\text{Median} = \frac{\mathbf{9 + 15}}{2} = \frac{24}{2} = 12$$

The mode is 1, the value that occurs most often in the data set.

1. **MUSIC** The prices charged by 8 different stores for a certain model of portable CD player are given below.

   \$95, \$79, \$100, \$60, \$79, \$97, \$105, \$65

   Find the mean, median, and mode(s) of the prices.

10.2 HISTOGRAMS

Examples on pp. 457–458

EXAMPLE Here are the scores of 18 students on a 20-question multiple choice quiz: 15, 19, 8, 16, 14, 12, 7, 19, 16, 13, 16, 4, 11, 7, 14, 20, 17, 9. A frequency table and a histogram of the scores are shown below.

Interval	Tally	Frequency
0–2		0
3–5	I	1
6–8	III	3
9–11	II	2
12–14	IIII	4
15–17	~~IIII~~	5
18–20	III	3

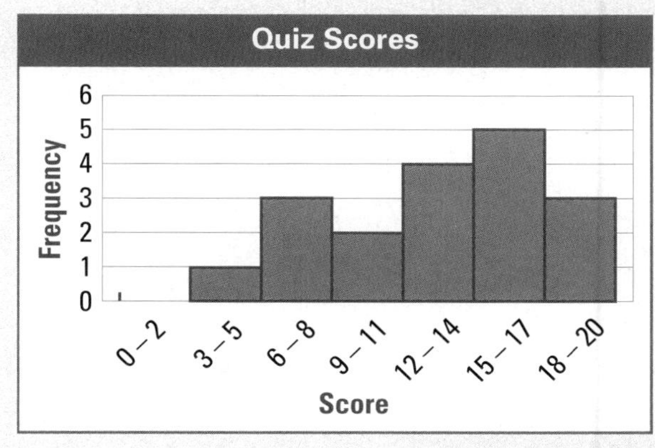

2. WEATHER The table shows the median monthly amounts of precipitation (in inches, rounded to the nearest inch) for Annette Island, Alaska. Make a frequency table and a histogram of the data.

Jan.	Feb.	Mar.	April	May	June	July	Aug.	Sept.	Oct.	Nov.	Dec.
10	8	7	7	6	4	4	6	9	15	11	11

10.3 BOX-AND-WHISKER PLOTS

Examples on pp. 461–462

EXAMPLE A company asks 14 employees how long it takes them to get to work. The times (to the nearest 5 minutes) are as follows:

5, 10, 10, 15, 20, 20, 20, 30, 35, 40, 45, 55, 55, 60

A box-and-whisker plot of the data is shown below.

Minimum value = 5

Lower quartile = 15

Median = 25

Upper quartile = 45

Maximum value = 60

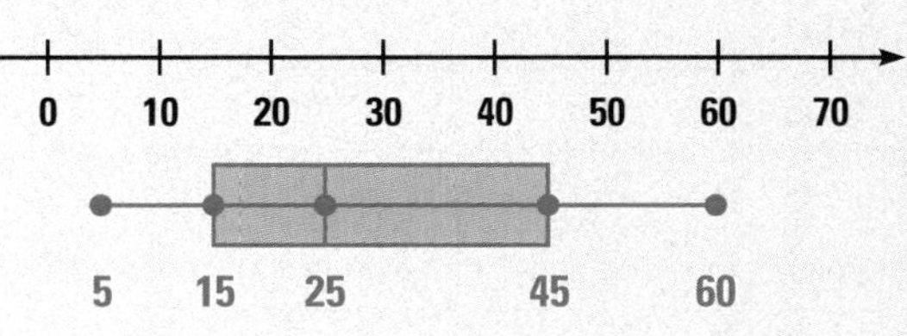

3. WEATHER Draw a box-and-whisker plot of the precipitation data from Exercise 2.

10.4 THE COORDINATE PLANE AND SCATTER PLOTS

Examples on pp. 468–469

EXAMPLE The table gives the total pressure on a diver for different depths. A scatter plot of the data is shown.

Depth (in ft)	Pressure (in lb/in.^{2})
0	15
20	24
40	33
60	41
80	50
100	59

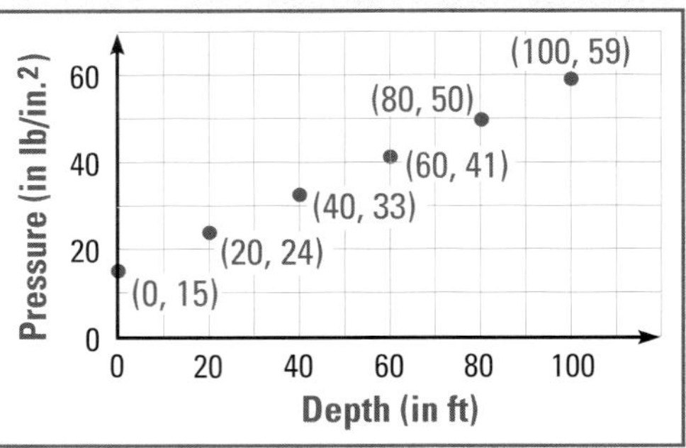

4. *Science Link* The pressures in the table above include both the atmospheric pressure and the water pressure on the diver. The table below gives just the water pressure for different depths. Draw a scatter plot of the data. Describe any pattern you see.

Depth (in ft)	0	20	40	60	80	100
Pressure (in lb/in.^{2})	0	9	18	27	36	45

10.5 USING APPROPRIATE GRAPHS

Examples on pp. 474–475

EXAMPLE The table gives the values (in billions of dollars) of corn and cotton exports for various years. A line graph of the data is shown.

Year	Corn value	Cotton value
1992	4.7	2.0
1993	4.2	1.5
1994	3.9	2.7
1995	7.3	3.7
1996	8.4	2.7
1997	5.2	2.7

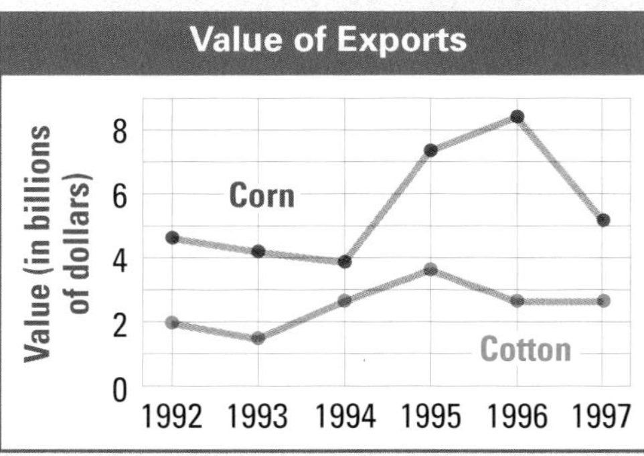

5. Draw a double bar graph of the corn and cotton data.

6. Draw a pictograph of the corn and cotton data.

10.6 INTERPRETING GRAPHS

Examples on pp. 478–479

EXAMPLE Because the bar graph's vertical scale is broken, the bar heights are not proportional to the quantities of freight, and the graph can be misinterpreted.

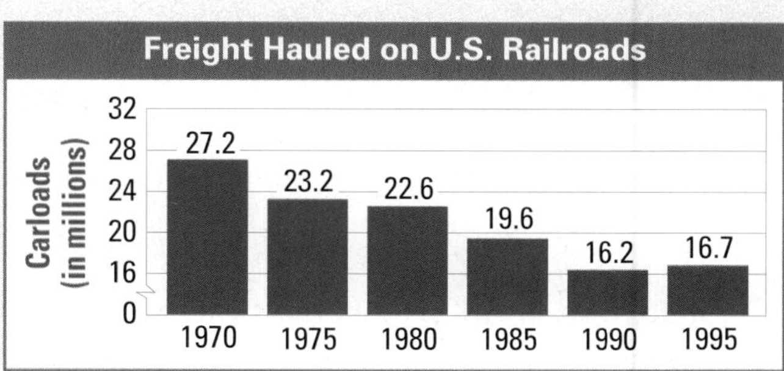

For instance, the bar heights imply that over 3 times as many train carloads of freight were hauled in 1970 as in 1990. However, the values on the scale and above the bars show that fewer than twice as many carloads were hauled in 1970.

7. Draw a bar graph of the freight data that is not potentially misleading.

10.7 SAMPLES AND POPULATIONS

Examples on pp. 483–484

To study a population, you can select a sample from it. Some types of samples are self-selected samples, systematic samples, convenience samples, and random samples. A random sample is most likely to be representative of the population. A biased sample is not representative.

EXAMPLE A pollster asks every third person getting off a subway train if he or she supports raising the toll for cars on a local highway. This is a systematic sample. It is biased because subway riders may not drive as often as people in general and so may be less affected by higher tolls.

8. A political Web site conducts an on-line poll asking the site's visitors to name the person they plan to vote for in a presidential election. Identify the type of sample and tell whether the sample is biased.

10.8 INTERPRETING SURVEYS

Examples on pp. 487–488

Survey results can be misleading if the survey questions are biased, if the sample for the survey is biased, or if the survey is conducted improperly.

EXAMPLE A survey question asks, "Do you prefer to live in the peaceful suburbs or the hectic city?" The survey results may overstate people's preference for the suburbs because the adjective "peaceful" has a positive meaning while the adjective "hectic" has a negative meaning.

9. Explain why this question is biased: "Are you afraid of flying even though air travel is the safest form of transportation?"

Chapter 10 Chapter Test

1. **CLAMS** Below are the widths (in centimeters) of 12 clams from Garrison Bay, Washington. Find the mean, median, and mode(s).

   38, 40, 29, 34, 8, 40, 47, 26, 43, 49, 14, 40

2. **TALLEST BUILDINGS** The heights (in meters) of the world's 20 tallest buildings are given below. Make a frequency table and a histogram of the heights using intervals of 25 meters.

   417, 305, 415, 344, 319, 300, 346, 421, 312, 310,
   452, 369, 322, 381, 348, 452, 325, 374, 442, 320

3. **APARTMENTS** Below are the monthly rents for 9 apartments that you are considering renting. Draw a box-and-whisker plot of the rents.

   \$510, \$745, \$800, \$450, \$670, \$725, \$490, \$625, \$580

4. **Science Link** The table shows the length of a certain spring when various weights are attached to it. Draw a scatter plot of the data.

Weight (lb)	0	2	4	6	8	10
Spring length (in.)	3	4	5	6	7	8

MAIL In Exercises 5 and 6, use the bar graph showing the average number of pieces of mail received by each person in the United States for various years. ▶Source: United States Postal Service

5. Draw a line graph of the data represented by the bar graph.

6. How might the bar graph be misinterpreted? Redraw the graph to avoid this problem.

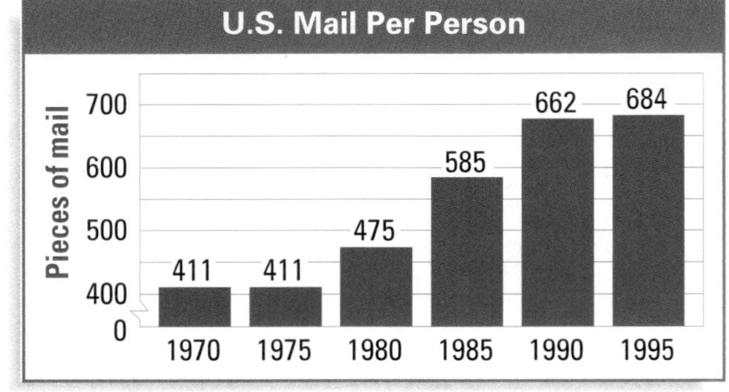

7. **LIGHT BULBS** A certain brand of light bulb has a mean lifetime of 750 hours. An engineer tests 6 of these bulbs from each of two plants that manufacture them. Below are the bulbs' lifetimes (in hours).

   Plant A: 725, 805, 780, 1000, 640, 910

   Plant B: 760, 695, 680, 735, 665, 875

   Identify the population and the samples in the engineer's test. Compare the means of the samples with the population mean.

8. **SEAT BELTS** To measure the success of a new law requiring seat belt use, police officers ask mall visitors, "Do you wear your seat belt regularly?" Because 85% of the people answer yes, the officers claim that the law has been successful. Why might this claim not be valid?

Multiple-Choice Practice

Test Tip Put an asterisk next to questions you skip so that you'll remember to come back to them later.

1. The lengths (in minutes) of a CD's songs are 4.8, 3.9, 4.2, 5.0, 4.4, 4.4, 5.5, 4.2, 3.1, 4.8, 4.2, and 5.5. Which statement is *false*?

Ⓐ The mode of the data is 4.4.

Ⓑ There are 12 songs on the CD.

Ⓒ The mean of the data is 4.5.

Ⓓ The median of the data is 4.4.

2. The histogram shows the scores of 20 students on a history quiz. How many students have a score of at least 7?

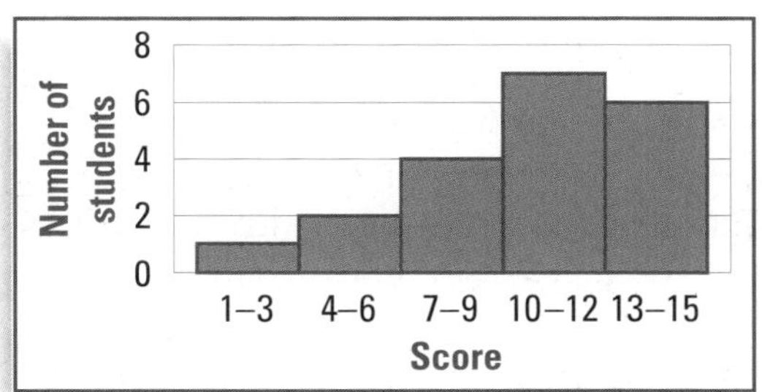

Ⓕ 3 Ⓖ 7

Ⓗ 13 Ⓙ 17

3. Which data set can be represented by the box-and-whisker plot?

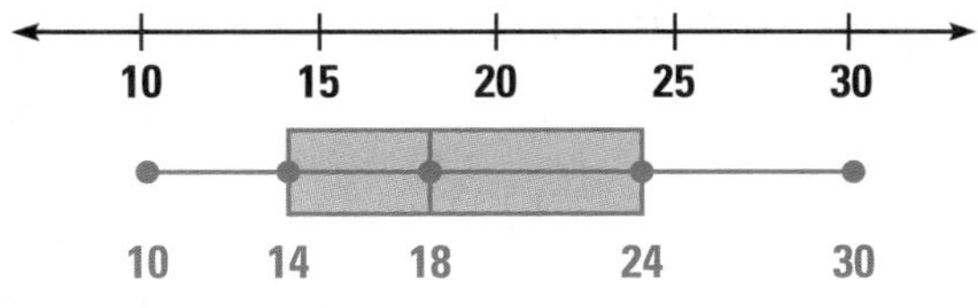

Ⓐ 10, 11, 14, 16, 18, 21, 24, 28, 30

Ⓑ 10, 11, 17, 18, 18, 22, 24, 27, 30

Ⓒ 10, 13, 14, 15, 18, 20, 21, 27, 30

Ⓓ 10, 12, 16, 17, 18, 20, 23, 25, 30

4. The scatter plot shows the temperature y when it is x hours after midnight. If the rate of increase stays the same, what will the temperature be at noon (when $x = 12$)?

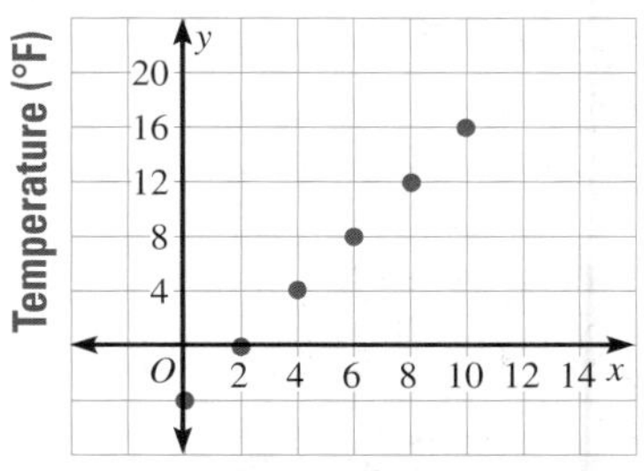

Ⓕ 20°F Ⓖ 31°F

Ⓗ 33°F Ⓙ 38°F

5. The bar graph shows your highest bowling score by year. Which statement is *false*?

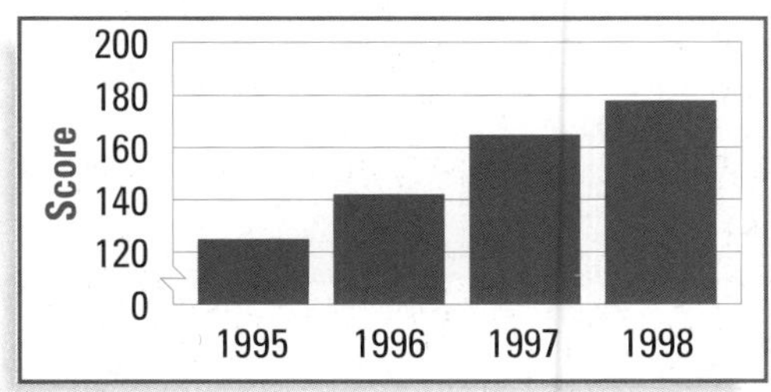

Ⓐ You could make a line graph of the data.

Ⓑ Your high score in 1997 was more than twice your high score in 1995.

Ⓒ Your score got higher each year.

Ⓓ The graph could be misinterpreted.

6. What type of sample is obtained if a store sends customers mail-in surveys to fill out?

Ⓕ Systematic Ⓖ Self-selected

Ⓗ Random Ⓙ Convenience

Brain games

California Standards

- Draw and analyze data displays. (SDP 2.3)
- Analyze problems by identifying relationships and observing patterns. (MR 1.1)

Plane 1 (Player B)

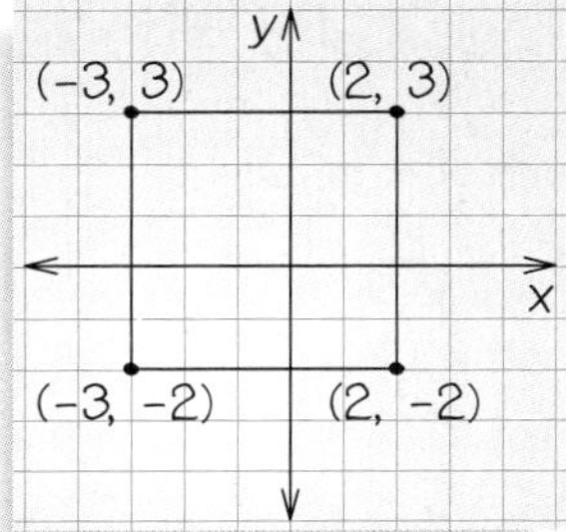

Plane 2 (Player A)

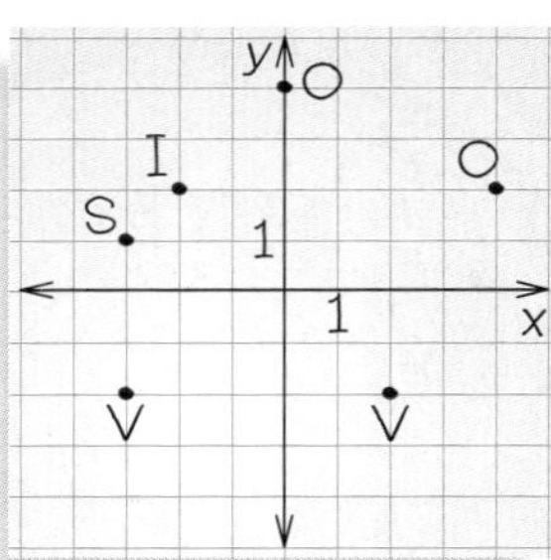

Figure Out the Figure

Materials

- **Graph paper**

Directions

Object of the Game

Play this game in pairs. In each round, each player tries to guess a vertex of a secret square drawn by the other player. The first player to correctly identify all four vertices of the other player's square wins the game.

How to Play

STEP 1 Each player makes two coordinate planes, labeled Plane 1 and Plane 2, and secretly draws a square on Plane 1. The vertices should have integer coordinates from −5 to 5.

STEP 2 Player A guesses a point he or she thinks is a vertex of Player B's square. Player B tells Player A whether the point is inside the square (I), outside the square (O), on a side of the square (S), or a vertex of the square (V). Player A then plots the point on Plane 2 and labels it with the appropriate letter (I, O, S, or V) to keep a record of the points already guessed.

STEP 3 The players switch roles, with Player B now trying to guess a vertex of Player A's square. Play continues until one player has guessed all four of the other player's vertices.

Another Way to Play

Play the game using rectangles or parallelograms.

Brain Teaser

Find the missing vertex

Three of the four vertices of a quadrilateral are (1, 2), (3, 5), and (6, 2).

The quadrilateral has two right angles.

The mean of the x-coordinates of the vertices is 4.

The basic skills you'll review on this page will help prepare you for the next chapter.

Reviewing the Basics

EXAMPLE 1 Performing Operations with Fractions

Evaluate. Simplify if possible.

a. $\frac{2}{5} + \frac{1}{4}$

b. $\frac{5}{8} \cdot \frac{2}{3}$

Solution

a. $\frac{2}{5} + \frac{1}{4} = \frac{2 \cdot 4}{5 \cdot 4} + \frac{1 \cdot 5}{4 \cdot 5} = \frac{8}{20} + \frac{5}{20} = \frac{8 + 5}{20} = \frac{13}{20}$

b. $\frac{5}{8} \cdot \frac{2}{3} = \frac{5 \cdot 2}{8 \cdot 3} = \frac{10}{24} = \frac{\cancel{2} \cdot 5}{\cancel{2} \cdot 12} = \frac{5}{12}$

Try These

Evaluate. Simplify if possible.

1. $\frac{6}{7} + \frac{5}{7}$ **2.** $\frac{4}{9} + \frac{1}{6}$ **3.** $\frac{5}{6} + \frac{9}{5}$ **4.** $2 + \frac{7}{8}$

5. $\frac{11}{13} - \frac{3}{13}$ **6.** $\frac{5}{8} - \frac{1}{3}$ **7.** $\frac{7}{12} - \frac{1}{9}$ **8.** $1 - \frac{3}{5}$

9. $\frac{3}{7} \cdot \frac{2}{3}$ **10.** $\frac{4}{11} \cdot \frac{1}{4}$ **11.** $\frac{9}{10} \cdot \frac{5}{3}$ **12.** $\frac{10}{7} \cdot \frac{49}{18}$

13. $\frac{2}{5} \div \frac{3}{13}$ **14.** $\frac{1}{9} \div \frac{1}{11}$ **15.** $\frac{3}{2} \div \frac{9}{4}$ **16.** $10 \div \frac{25}{3}$

EXAMPLE 2 Finding a Probability

Assume the spinner is divided into equal parts. The probability that the pointer lands on blue is:

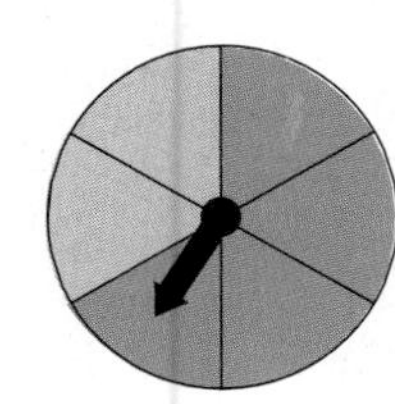

$$\text{Probability} = \frac{\text{Number of favorable outcomes}}{\text{Total number of outcomes}}$$

$$= \frac{4}{6} = \frac{\cancel{2} \cdot 2}{\cancel{2} \cdot 3} = \frac{2}{3}$$

Try These

Find the probability that the pointer lands on blue. Assume the spinner is divided into equal parts.

17.

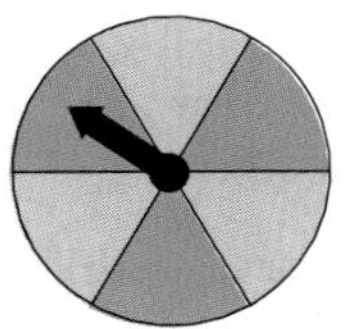

18.

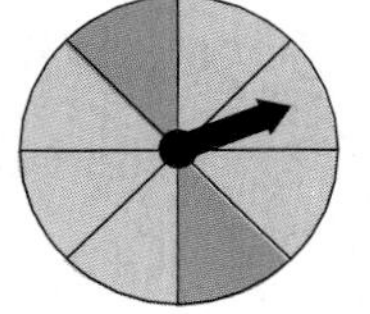

19.

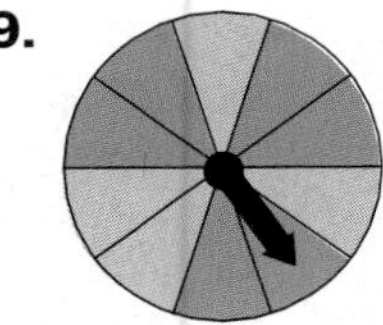

Student Help

▶ MORE EXAMPLES

INTERNET More examples and practice exercises available at www.mcdougallittell.com

Probability and Discrete Mathematics

Why are probability and discrete mathematics important?

One area of discrete mathematics involves techniques for counting possibilities. By counting possibilities, you can determine the probability of an event. You can use probability in everyday life to weigh options and assess risks.

Many people use probability and discrete mathematics in their careers, including animal behaviorists (page 501), botanists (page 526), and actuaries (page 532). For example, animal behaviorists use probability to determine whether a behavior is random.

Meeting the California Standards

The skills you'll learn in this chapter will help you meet state standards and prepare for standardized tests. In this chapter you'll:

- **Represent all possible outcomes for compound events and express the theoretical probability of each outcome.** LESSONS 11.1, 11.2, 11.4
- **Understand how to find the probability of an event not occurring, the probability of either of two disjoint events occurring, and the probability of one independent event following another.** LESSONS 11.1, 11.3–11.6
- **Understand how independent and dependent events differ.** LESSON 11.2
- **Use data to estimate the probability of future events.** LESSON 11.6

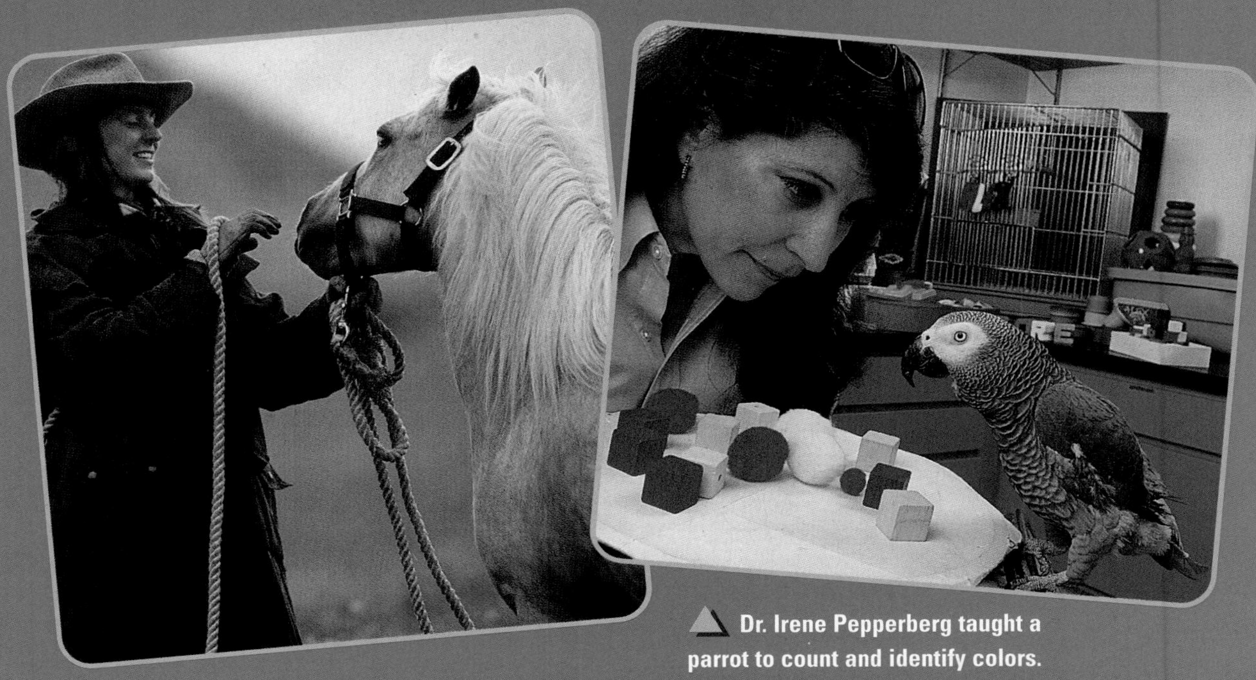

Dr. Irene Pepperberg taught a parrot to count and identify colors.

Career Link **ANIMAL BEHAVIORIST** An animal behaviorist uses probability and discrete mathematics when:

- predicting an animal's behavior.
- determining whether the results of an experiment are random.

EXERCISES

An animal behaviorist does an experiment in which a trained parrot is asked to identify colors. The behaviorist names a color and records whether the parrot chooses the correct object from among 5 differently colored objects. The table shows the results when the experiment is repeated 50 times.

Correct Answers	Wrong Answers
39	11

1. If the parrot chooses an object at random, what is the theoretical probability that the parrot chooses the correct object?

2. Use the data in the table to find the experimental probability that the parrot chooses the correct object.

3. Does the parrot's behavior seem random? Explain your reasoning.

In Lesson 11.3, you will learn how to find the probability that the parrot chooses the correct object two times in a row.

Chapter 11 Getting Ready

PREVIEW

What's the chapter about?

- **Organizing possible outcomes** of an event
- Identifying **disjoint**, **overlapping**, **independent**, and **dependent events**
- **Finding probabilities** of independent and disjoint events
- Using probability to **make predictions**

WORDS TO KNOW

- **tree diagram,** *p. 505*
- **disjoint events,** *p. 509*
- **overlapping events,** *p. 509*
- **independent events,** *p. 510*
- **dependent events,** *p. 510*

PREPARE

Chapter Readiness Quiz

Take this quick quiz. If you are unsure of an answer, look back at the reference pages for help.

VOCABULARY CHECK *(refer to p. 292)*

1. What do you call all the possible results of an experiment?

Ⓐ Events Ⓑ Probability

Ⓒ Outcomes Ⓓ Favorable outcomes

SKILL CHECK *(refer to p. 292)*

2. A jar contains 6 red marbles, 5 blue marbles, 4 yellow marbles, 3 green marbles, 2 orange marbles, and 1 purple marble. If a marble is randomly chosen, what is the probability that it will be red?

Ⓕ $\frac{1}{6}$ Ⓖ $\frac{6}{23}$ Ⓗ $\frac{2}{7}$ Ⓙ $\frac{2}{5}$

3. What is the probability that a letter chosen at random from the word *mathematics* will be a vowel?

Ⓐ $\frac{4}{11}$ Ⓑ $\frac{1}{2}$ Ⓒ $\frac{7}{11}$ Ⓓ 1

STUDY TIP

Make a Concept Map

As you study for a test, write down major concepts to be tested. Then write the vocabulary and ideas that fall under each major concept.

Organizing outcomes
- make a list
- draw a tree diagram
- make a table

Probability
- disjoint events
- overlapping events
- independent events
- dependent events

DEVELOPING CONCEPTS
Counting Possibilities

For use with Lesson 11.1

California Standards

- Represent all possible outcomes for a compound event in an organized way. (SDP 3.1)
- Use tables to explain mathematical reasoning. (MR 2.4)

MATERIALS

- Paper and pencil

SAMPLE 1 Using a Table to Count Possibilities

You work at a restaurant that serves tacos with three fillings: bean, beef, and chicken. Each taco can be ordered with a hard shell or a soft shell. You can use a table to show how many different tacos you serve.

Here's How

Organize the information in a table like the one below. Notice that each column of the table is a type of filling, and each row is a type of shell.

	Bean	Beef	Chicken
Hard			
Soft			

You can see from the table that it is possible for you to serve 6 different tacos.

Try These

1. The restaurant in Sample 1 adds nacho shells as a third option. Use a table to show how many different tacos you can serve now.

2. You are choosing uniforms for your new soccer team. You have five color choices for shorts and four color choices for shirts, as shown in the table at the right. How many different uniforms are possible?

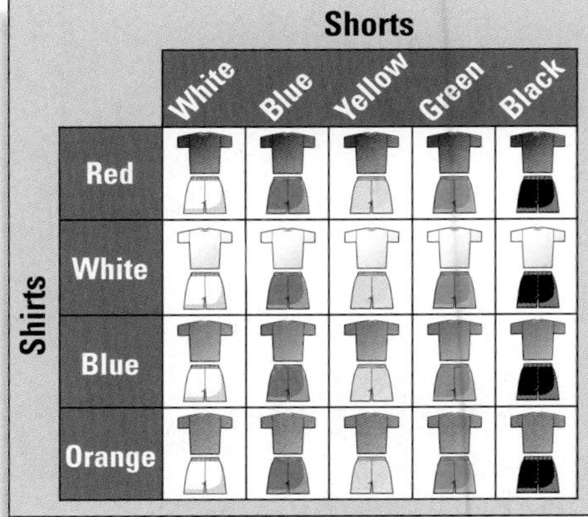

In Exercises 3 and 4, tell how many different uniforms are possible.

3. Shirts: 6 color choices; shorts: 5 color choices

4. Shorts: 7 color choices; shirts: 4 color choices

5. **MATHEMATICAL REASONING** How are the number of rows and the number of columns in a table of possibilities related to the number of possibilities?

Organizing Possible Outcomes

California Standards

In this lesson you'll:

- Represent all possible outcomes for a compound event in an organized way and express the theoretical probability of each outcome. (SDP 3.1)
- Represent probabilities as ratios, decimals, and percents. (SDP 3.3)

Goal 1 Listing All Possible Outcomes

In Lesson 6.6 you learned how to find the probability of an event in which all outcomes are equally likely, such as getting heads when tossing a coin.

$$\text{Probability} = \frac{\text{Number of favorable outcomes}}{\text{Total number of outcomes}}$$

You will now learn to apply this definition in more general situations than those considered in Chapter 6. You will consider *compound experiments* that occur in several stages. For example, you will learn to calculate the probability of getting exactly two heads when a coin is tossed three times.

Example 1 Listing All Possible Outcomes

Find the probability of the event when a coin is tossed three times.

a. Getting at least 2 heads **b.** Getting exactly 2 heads

Solution

Make a list of all the possible outcomes of tossing a coin three times. The following eight outcomes are equally likely.

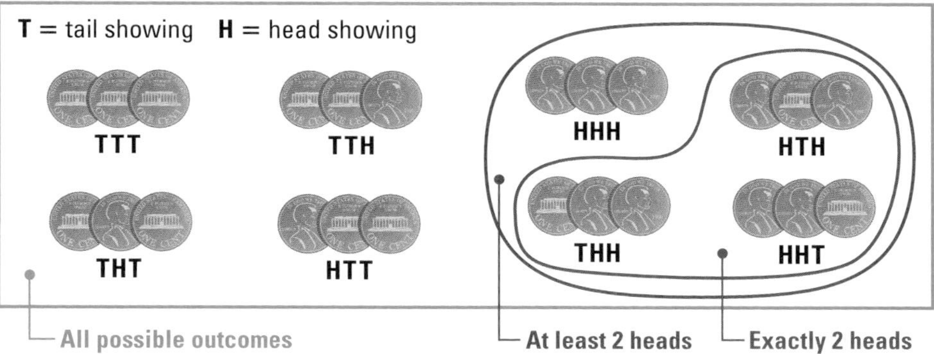

a. The event "getting at least 2 heads" can occur in four ways.

$$\text{Probability} = \frac{\text{Ways of getting at least 2 heads}}{\text{Total number of outcomes}} = \frac{4}{8} = \frac{1}{2}$$

You can also write this probability as 0.5 or 50%.

b. The event "getting exactly 2 heads" can occur in three ways.

$$\text{Probability} = \frac{\text{Ways of getting exactly 2 heads}}{\text{Total number of outcomes}} = \frac{3}{8}$$

You can also write this probability as 0.375 or 37.5%.

Student Help

Look Back
For help with fraction, decimal, and percent equivalents, see page 311.

Goal 2 USING A TREE DIAGRAM

In Developing Concepts 11.1, page 503, you organized possible outcomes in a table. A **tree diagram** is another way of showing all the possible outcomes of a process carried out in several stages. The outcomes are listed along the "branches" of the diagram.

Student Help

▶ **MORE EXAMPLES**

INTERNET More examples are available at www.mcdougallittell.com

EXAMPLE 2 Using a Tree Diagram

Use a tree diagram to find the probability of getting at least 2 heads when a coin is tossed three times.

Solution

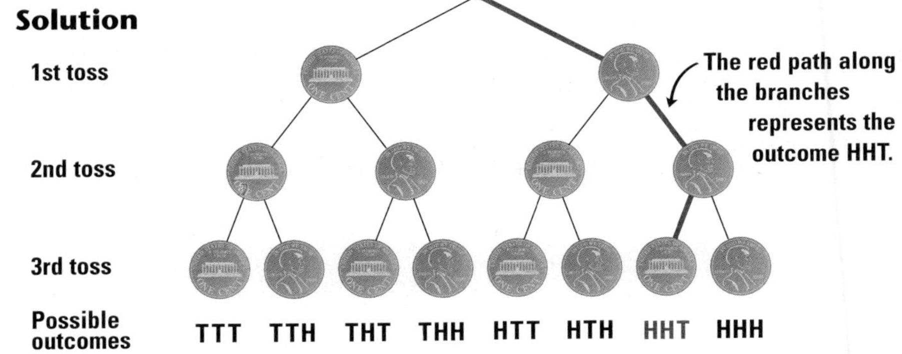

ANSWER ▶ Because 4 of the 8 outcomes have at least 2 heads, the probability is $\frac{4}{8}$, or $\frac{1}{2}$.

EXAMPLE 3 Using a Tree Diagram

TRAVEL You are taking a bus trip to and from New York City. Assume that there are equal numbers of window seats and aisle seats on each bus and that you are randomly assigned a seat. What is the probability that you will get a window seat on the bus to New York City and a window seat on the bus home?

Solution

Draw a tree diagram.

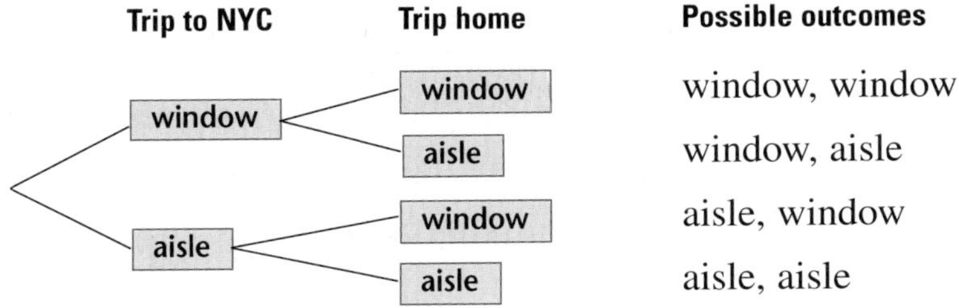

ANSWER ▶ From the tree diagram you can see that getting a window seat on both trips is 1 of the 4 outcomes. So, the probability is $\frac{1}{4}$.

11.1 Exercises

Guided Practice

1. Explain how to draw a tree diagram that shows the possible outcomes of tossing a coin twice.

Find the probability of the event when a coin is tossed three times.

2. Getting exactly 2 tails

3. Getting 3 heads

4. All 3 land with the same side up

5. Getting at least 2 tails

TRAVEL **In Exercises 6 and 7, use the following information.** You are planning a vacation to either New York City, Boston, or Philadelphia. You can travel by bus, train, or airplane.

6. Copy and complete the tree diagram.

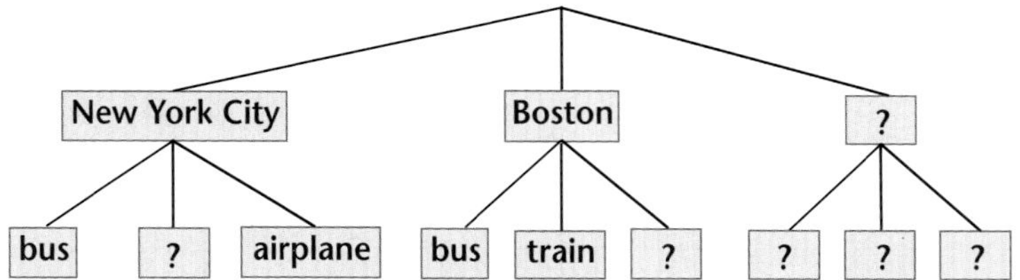

7. If you randomly choose a destination and a method of transportation, what is the probability that you take a train to Philadelphia?

Practice and Problem Solving

Student Help

▶ **MORE PRACTICE**
Extra practice to help you master skills is on page 586.

You have two bags, each containing the numbers 1, 2, 3, and 4 written on pieces of paper. Find the probability of the event when one piece of paper is drawn from each bag.

8. Both numbers are the same.

9. You draw a 1 and a 2.

10. At least one of the numbers is 1.

11. Both numbers are odd.

12. Exactly one number is 3.

13. You draw two 4's.

SANDWICH SHOP **In Exercises 14 and 15, use the following information.** You are ordering a ham and cheese sandwich. The server asks if you want it on wheat bread, white bread, or rye bread, and if you want Swiss cheese or cheddar cheese.

14. Make a list of the sandwich possibilities. How many different sandwiches are possible?

15. Since you have no preference, you tell the server to choose the bread and cheese at random. Write the probability that your sandwich is made on rye bread as a fraction, a decimal, and a percent.

Link to History

GAMES Games like *Rock, Paper, Scissors* date back to as far as 2000 B.C. In Japan *Rock, Paper, Scissors* is known as *Janken.* Janken is not only played by children, but also by adults to decide who goes first.

GAMES In Exercises 16–18, use the following information.
In the game *Rock, Paper, Scissors* two players display one of three hand symbols at the same time. As shown below, a rock symbol beats a scissors symbol, a scissors symbol beats a paper symbol, and a paper symbol beats a rock symbol. The game is a tie if both players display the same symbol.

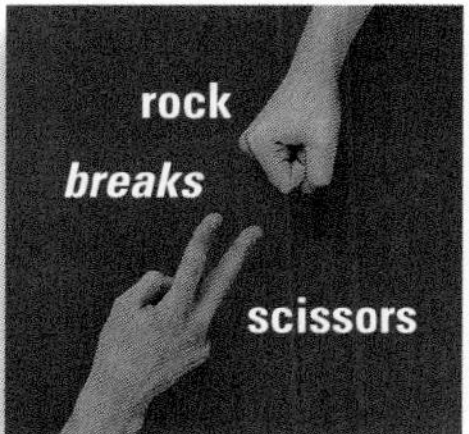

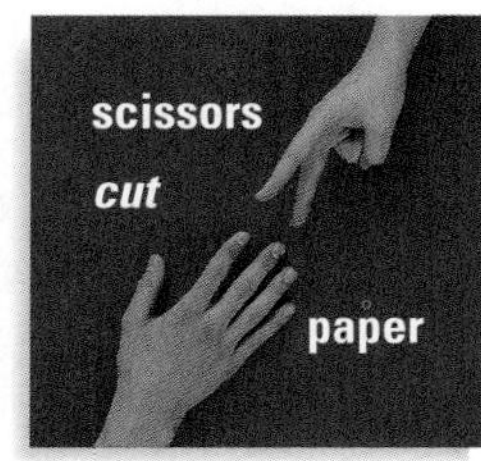

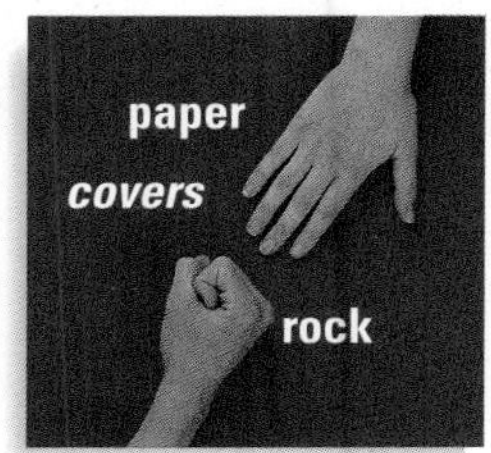

16. Make a list of the possible outcomes of *Rock, Paper, Scissors.*

17. What is the probability that the game is a tie? Write your answer as a fraction, a decimal, and a percent.

18. MATHEMATICAL REASONING If you played the game many times, what fraction of the times would you expect to win? Why?

CLOTHING In Exercises 19 and 20, use the following information.
You bought a new pair of jeans and a new pair of tan pants for school. You also bought a red shirt, a blue shirt, and a white shirt.

19. Copy and complete the tree diagram at the right to find all the possible outfits.

20. If you randomly select an outfit to wear, what is the probability that you wear your red shirt?

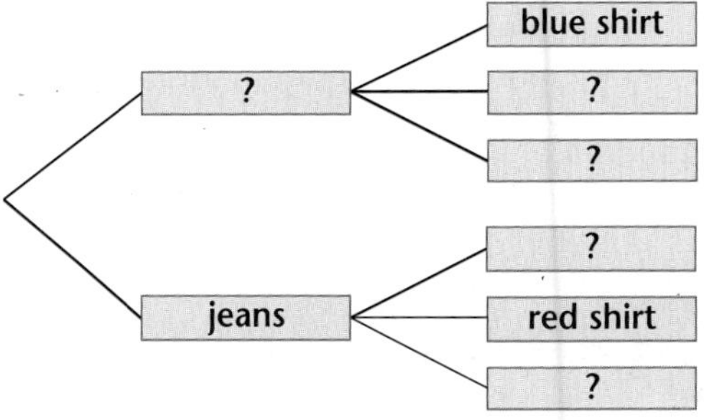

In Exercises 21–24, read the following information. Then draw a tree diagram to find the probability of the event.
A jar contains one red marble and two blue marbles. A second jar contains two white marbles and one blue marble. One marble is drawn from each jar.

21. Getting at least 1 blue marble

22. Getting 2 blue marbles

23. Getting 1 blue and 1 white marble

24. Getting 1 red and 1 blue marble

25. Each spinner at the right is divided into equal sections. You spin each spinner. Make a tree diagram of the possible outcomes.

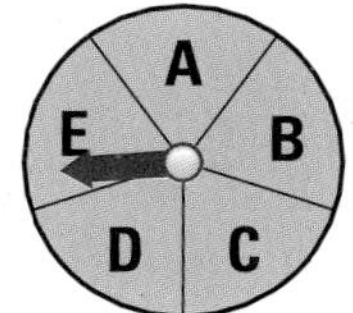

Use your tree diagram from Exercise 25 to find the probability of the event.

26. Spinning C and 1

27. Spinning E and an odd number

28. Spinning a vowel and 4

29. Spinning a consonant and 2

In Exercises 30 and 31, find the probability of the event when a coin is tossed four times.

30. Getting at least 3 heads

31. Getting 2 heads and 2 tails

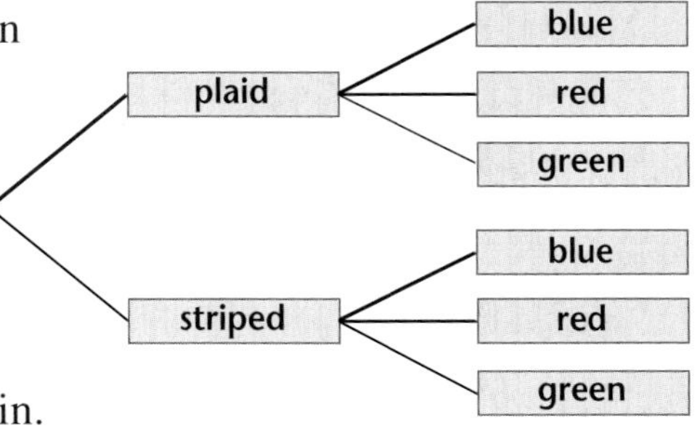

32. WRITING Write a problem that can be solved using the tree diagram at the right.

33. CHALLENGE You want to find the number of different initials a person could possibly have (first and last name only). How would you find an answer? Explain.

Student Help

▶ **HOMEWORK HELP**

Extra help with problem solving in Exs. 34–35 is available at www.mcdougallittell.com

In Exercises 34 and 35, use the following game rules.

Three chips are marked in the following way:

Chip 1:	**Chip 2:**	**Chip 3:**
red on one side, blue on the other	red on one side, white on the other	blue on one side, white on the other

You toss all three chips. If any two chips land with the same color facing up, Player A wins. If all three chips are different colors, Player B wins.

34. Draw a tree diagram of the possible outcomes.

35. MATHEMATICAL REASONING Would you choose to be Player A or Player B? Explain.

Multiple-Choice Practice

36. At a summer camp you can canoe, hike, play tennis, or make crafts each morning. In the afternoon you can swim, do archery, or play soccer. How many different ways can you spend your day?

Ⓐ 24 Ⓑ 12 Ⓒ 7 Ⓓ 4

37. You have two bags, each filled with blue, green, and red marbles. One marble from each bag is chosen. What additional information would you need in order to find the probability of choosing two blue marbles?

Ⓕ The number of blue marbles in each bag

Ⓖ The sizes of the marbles and the bags

Ⓗ The number of green marbles and blue marbles in each bag

Ⓙ The number of blue marbles and the total number of marbles in each bag

Disjoint Events and Independent Events

California Standards

In this lesson you'll:

- Represent all possible outcomes for compound events in an organized way. (SDP 3.1)
- Understand the difference between independent and dependent events. (SDP 3.5)

Goal 1 DISJOINT AND OVERLAPPING EVENTS

In Chapter 8, Venn diagrams were used to show relationships among types of triangles and types of four-sided figures. A Venn diagram is a drawing that uses geometric shapes to show relationships among sets. For example, there are four ways that two sets, A and B, can be related.

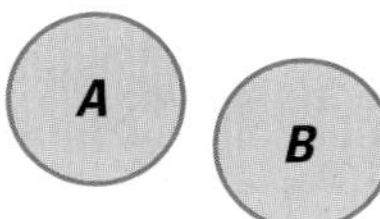

The sets have no elements in common.

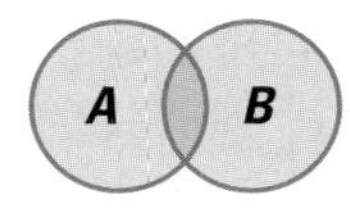

The sets have at least one element in common.

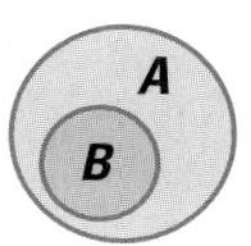

All elements in *B* are also in *A*.

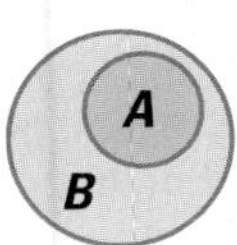

All elements in *A* are also in *B*.

Because events are sets of outcomes, Venn diagrams can be used to show how events are related. Two events are **disjoint** if they have no outcomes in common. Two events that have one or more outcomes in common are called **overlapping**.

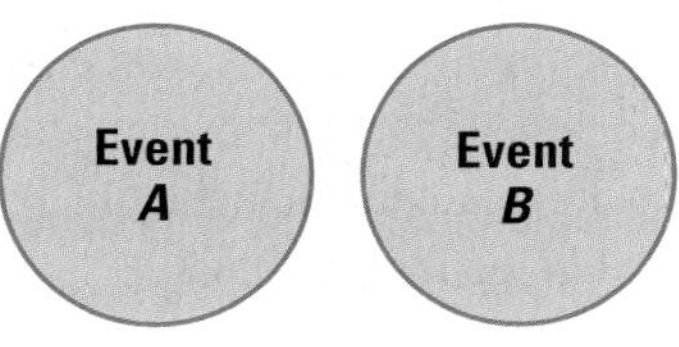

Disjoint events

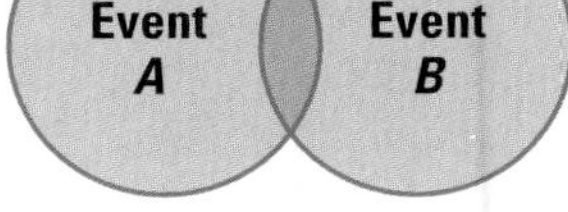

Overlapping events

EXAMPLE 1 Identifying Overlapping Events

You randomly choose a whole number from 1 through 10. Tell whether the events are *disjoint* or *overlapping*.

Event *A*: The number is less than 5.
Event *B*: The number is even.

Solution

A Venn diagram shows the relationship between the events.

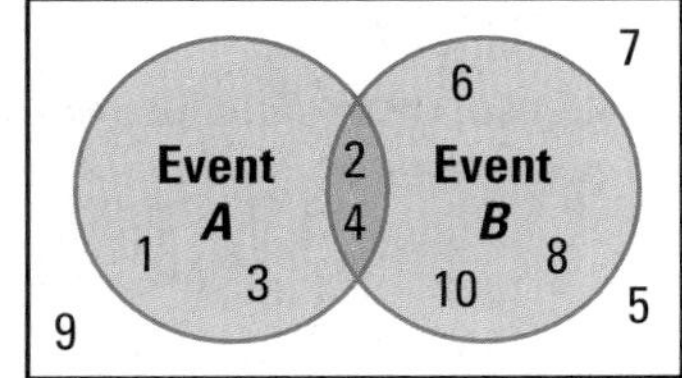

ANSWER ▶ The numbers 2 and 4 are both less than 5 and even. So, the events are overlapping.

Student Help

▶ **STUDY TIP**
In Example 1 the numbers 5, 7, and 9 are placed outside of the circles for events *A* and *B* because they are neither less than 5 nor even.

EXAMPLE 2 Identifying Disjoint Events

You randomly choose a whole number from 1 through 10. Tell whether the events are *disjoint* or *overlapping*.

Event *A*: The number is a perfect square.
Event *B*: The number is prime.

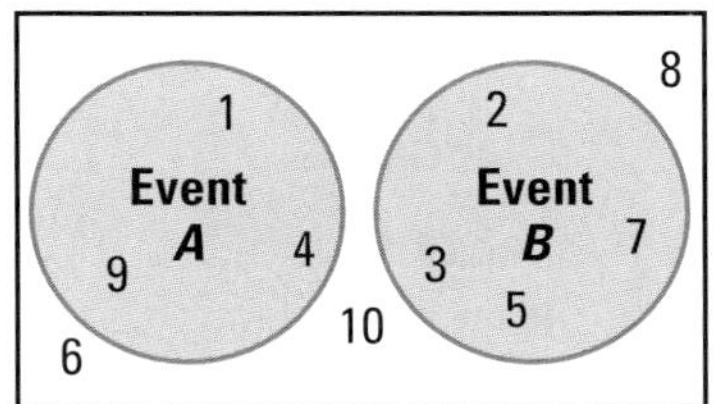

Solution

No number is both a perfect square and a prime number. So, the events are disjoint. The Venn diagram illustrates this fact.

Goal 2 INDEPENDENT AND DEPENDENT EVENTS

Student Help

▶**VOCABULARY TIP**
In common usage, being *independent* means being free of other people's control or influence. This may help you remember the mathematical meaning of independent events.

Two events are **independent** if the occurrence of one does *not* affect the likelihood that the other will occur. Two events are **dependent** if the occurrence of one *does* affect the likelihood that the other will occur.

EXAMPLE 3 Identifying Dependent Events

A jar contains 6 red marbles and 2 blue marbles. You randomly choose a marble from the jar. Without replacing the marble you took out, you randomly choose a second marble from the jar. Tell whether the events are *independent* or *dependent*.

Event *A*: The first marble is red. **Event *B*:** The second marble is blue.

Solution

Consider event B after event A has or has not occurred.

Before event *A*

Event *A*

After event *A*

- If event A has occurred, then the jar has 5 red marbles and 2 blue marbles. The probability of choosing a blue marble is $\frac{2}{7}$.
- If event A has not occurred, then the first marble chosen must have been blue. The jar now has 6 red marbles and 1 blue marble. The probability of choosing a blue marble is $\frac{1}{7}$.

ANSWER ▶ Because the occurrence of event A affects the likelihood of event B, the two events are dependent.

Student Help

▶ **MORE EXAMPLES**

INTERNET More examples are available at www.mcdougallittell.com

EXAMPLE 4 Identifying Events as Independent or Dependent

Tell whether the statement seems to describe *independent* or *dependent* events.

a. Each week you and your brother assign chores by writing the chores on pieces of paper and randomly drawing them out of a hat.

Event *A*: You draw "take the trash out" the first week of January.
Event *B*: You draw "take the trash out" the second week of January.

b. You have several covered textbooks in your locker that look identical. You pull the books out one at a time and put them in your backpack.

Event *A*: The first book you pull out is your history book.
Event *B*: The second book you pull out is your math book.

Solution

a. Each week your chances of getting "take the trash out" are the same, regardless of whether or not you took the trash out the week before. So, the events are independent.

b. Pulling your history book out first decreases the total number of books in your locker. This increases your chances of pulling out your math book next, so the events are dependent.

11.2 Exercises

Guided Practice

1. Describe the difference between disjoint and overlapping events.

2. Describe the difference between independent and dependent events.

Tell whether the Venn diagram represents *disjoint* or *overlapping* events.

3.

4.

A bag contains the whole numbers from 1 through 10 written on pieces of paper. You randomly select numbers one at a time, but do not replace them. Tell whether the events are *independent* or *dependent*. Explain your reasoning.

5. **Event *A*:** The first number you select is 1.
Event *B*: The second number you select is even.

6. **Event *A*:** The first number you select is 5.
Event *B*: The second number you select is a whole number.

Practice and Problem Solving

Student Help

▶ More Practice
Extra practice to help you master skills is on page 586.

Tell whether the Venn diagram represents *disjoint* or *overlapping* events.

7. Plays piano | Plays guitar

8. Allergic to cats | Not allergic to cats

You randomly choose a whole number from 1 through 10. Draw a Venn diagram of the given events. Then tell if they are *disjoint* or *overlapping*.

9. **Event *A*:** The number is odd.
Event *B*: It is greater than 3.

10. **Event *A*:** The number is even.
Event *B*: The number is prime.

You randomly choose a letter from the alphabet. Tell whether the events are *disjoint* or *overlapping*. (Assume that Y is a consonant.)

11. **Event *A*:** It is a vowel.
Event *B*: It is a consonant.

12. **Event *A*:** It is a consonant.
Event *B*: It is a letter in your name.

You randomly choose a location and check today's weather. Tell whether the events are *disjoint* or *overlapping*.

13. **Event *A*:** The sky is cloudy.
Event *B*: It is raining.

14. **Event *A*:** It is snowing.
Event *B*: The temperature is 80°F.

POPULATION **In Exercises 15–17, use the table below.**

15. Draw a Venn diagram for the sets "has an area less than 500,000 square kilometers" and "has a population greater than 100 million."

16. Are the sets in Exercise 15 disjoint or overlapping?

17. Australia has an area of about 7,740,000 square kilometers and a population of 18.3 million. Where does Australia belong in your Venn diagram?

Country	Area (in km^2)	Population (in millions)
China	9,600,000	1240
Japan	378,000	126
Morocco	447,000	27.5
Poland	323,000	38.6
United States	9,360,000	272

▶ Source: Infonation

Tell whether the events seem to be *independent* or *dependent*. Explain your reasoning.

18. **Event *A*:** You select the name Smith from the Chicago telephone book.
Event *B*: You select the name Smith from the Miami telephone book.

19. **Event *A*:** A coin is tossed and comes up heads.
Event *B*: The coin is tossed again and comes up tails.

20. **Event *A*:** Bill is elected class president.
Event *B*: Mary is elected class vice-president.

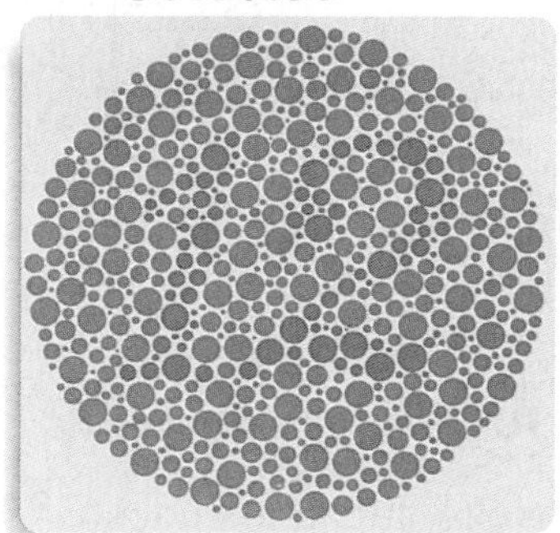

COLORBLINDNESS
A person who cannot distinguish red from green is not able to see the number 12 in the picture above.

More about colorblindness is available at www.mcdougallittell.com

Science Link **In Exercises 21–23, use the following information.** Colorblindness is the inability to distinguish colors. The table shows the results of a colorblindness survey given to 800 people chosen at random.

21. What does the survey suggest about the probability of being colorblind?

22. What does the survey suggest about the probability of being colorblind if you are female?

23. Are colorblindness and being female *independent* or *dependent* events? Explain your answer.

Survey of 800 people		
	Male	**Female**
Colorblind	32	2
Not colorblind	368	398
Total	400	400

CHALLENGE **In Exercises 24 and 25, use the following information.** You are playing a game based on a single roll of a number cube. If you roll 1, 2, 3, or 4, you win. If you roll 5 or 6, you lose.

24. Find the probability of each of the following events.

Event *A*: You win. **Event *B*:** You lose. **Event *C*:** The roll is even.

25. For each possible pair of events in Exercise 24, tell whether or not the events are independent. Explain your answer.

Multiple-Choice Practice

26. You roll a number cube. Which Venn diagram correctly represents the following events?

Event *A*: You roll an even number.
Event *B*: You roll a prime number.

Ⓐ 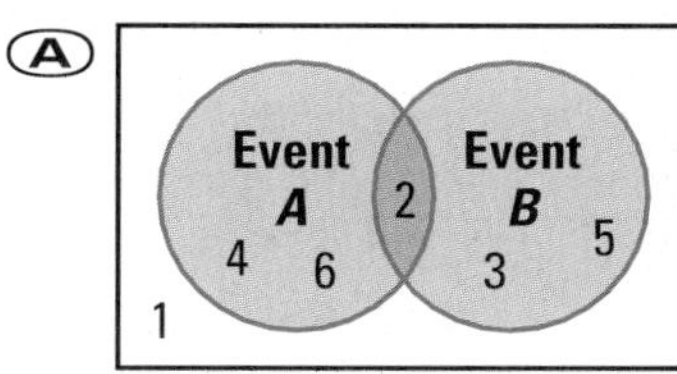

Ⓑ 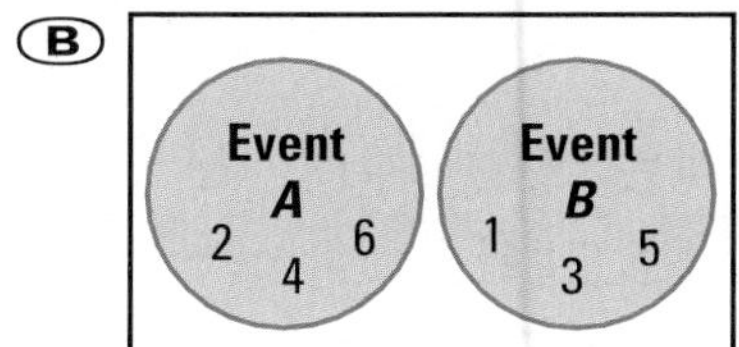

Ⓒ 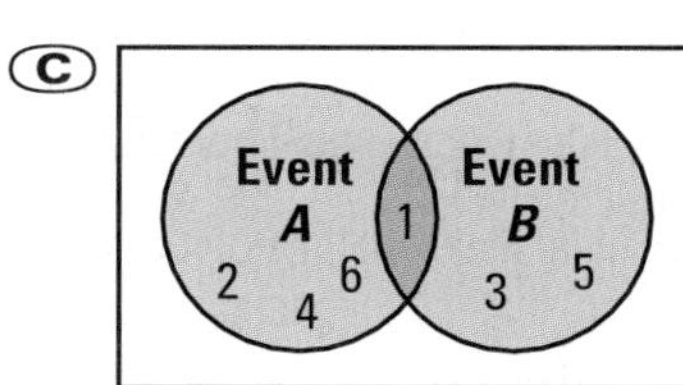

Ⓓ 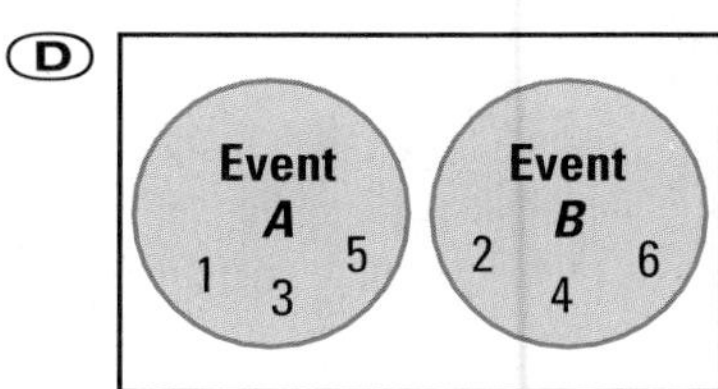

27. You roll two number cubes, one red and one green. What is true about the following events?

Event *A*: The red cube comes up even.
Event *B*: The green cube comes up odd.

Ⓕ They are dependent. Ⓖ They are overlapping.

Ⓗ They are independent. Ⓙ Not here

DEVELOPING CONCEPTS

Independent Events

For use with Lesson 11.3

California Standards

- Determine theoretical and experimental probabilities. (SDP 3.0)
- Understand how to find the probability that two independent events both occur. (SDP 3.4)
- Develop generalizations of the results obtained and the strategies used and apply them in new problem situations. (MR 3.3)

MATERIALS

- 2 paper bags
- Paper
- Scissors

You can conduct an experiment to find the experimental probability that two independent events both occur.

SAMPLE 1 Conducting an Experiment to Find a Probability

Your school is randomly choosing a representative to attend a student conference. Your school has approximately the same number of sixth, seventh, and eighth graders, so for each grade, the probability that the representative will be chosen from that grade is $\frac{1}{3}$. Each grade has approximately the same number of males as females, so the probability that the representative will be male is about $\frac{1}{2}$. Conduct an experiment to find the experimental probability that the representative chosen is a female in seventh grade.

Here's How

Write the possible genders and grade levels on pieces of paper. Put the pieces of paper in two bags as shown at the right. Randomly draw one piece of paper from each bag and record what is chosen. Then replace the pieces of paper. Repeat the experiment 10 times and record your results in a table like the one below.

Trial	1	2	3	4	5	6	7	8	9	10
M/F	M	F	**F**	M	M	F	M	M	F	**F**
Grade	6	8	**7**	8	6	8	7	8	6	**7**

From the table, you can see that the experimental probability that the representative is a female seventh grader is $\frac{2}{10}$, or $\frac{1}{5}$. Notice that the experimental probability $\frac{1}{5}$ is approximately equal to the product of the theoretical probability of being female, $\frac{1}{2}$, and the theoretical probability of being in seventh grade, $\frac{1}{3}$. As you will see in Sample 2, the probability that two independent events both occur is the product of the probabilities of the events.

SAMPLE 2 Using a Tree Diagram to Verify a Probability

Draw a tree diagram for the experiment in Sample 1. Use the tree diagram to verify that the probability that two independent events both occur is the product of the probabilities of the events.

Here's How

As shown in the tree diagram, the representative being female limits the favorable outcomes to just $\frac{1}{2}$ of the 6 possible outcomes. The representative being a seventh grader limits the favorable outcomes to $\frac{1}{3}$ of $\frac{1}{2}$ of the 6 possible outcomes. So, the probability that the representative is a female seventh grader is $\frac{1}{3} \cdot \frac{1}{2} = \frac{1}{6}$.

male — 6th grade, 7th grade, 8th grade

female — 6th grade, 7th grade, 8th grade

Try These

In Exercises 1–6, use the following information. In a hurry to get to school, you grab a bagel and a bottle of juice from the refrigerator without looking. There are 4 bagels in the refrigerator: a plain bagel, a raisin bagel, an onion bagel, and a sesame seed bagel. There are 3 bottles of juice in the refrigerator: orange juice, cranberry juice, and apple juice.

1. Use paper bags and pieces of paper to set up an experiment of randomly choosing a bagel and a bottle of juice.

2. Perform your experiment 10 times. Record your results in a table.

3. Combine your results with those of your classmates. What is the experimental probability of choosing a plain bagel and orange juice?

4. Compare your answer to Exercise 3 with the product of the theoretical probabilities of choosing a plain bagel and choosing orange juice.

5. Draw a tree diagram of the possible outcomes of the experiment.

6. **MATHEMATICAL REASONING** Explain how your tree diagram from Exercise 5 supports the rule that the probability that two independent events both occur is the product of the probabilities of the events.

Student Help

STUDY TIP
In general, the more times an experiment is repeated, the more accurate the experimental probability.

11.3 Probability of Independent Events

California Standards

In this lesson you'll:

- Understand that the probability of one event following another, in independent trials, is the product of the two probabilities. (SDP 3.4)

Goal 1 PROBABILITY OF TWO INDEPENDENT EVENTS

Your work in Developing Concepts 11.3, page 514, suggests the following.

PROBABILITY OF TWO INDEPENDENT EVENTS

In Words The probability that two independent events both occur is the product of the probabilities of the events.

In Algebra Let $P(A)$ represent the *probability of an event A*. If event A and event B are independent, then the probability that event A *and* event B will occur is:

$$P(A \text{ and } B) = P(A) \cdot P(B)$$

EXAMPLE 1 Finding a Probability

A dog is going to have puppies. The probability that a puppy is brown is $\frac{1}{4}$, the probability that it is tan is $\frac{1}{2}$, and the probability that it is black is $\frac{1}{4}$. The probability that a puppy is male is $\frac{1}{2}$. Assume that a puppy's color is independent of its gender. What is the probability that the first puppy born is brown and male?

Solution

Because the two events are independent,

$$P(\text{brown and male}) = P(\text{brown}) \cdot P(\text{male}) = \frac{1}{4} \cdot \frac{1}{2} = \frac{1}{8}.$$

ANSWER ▶ The probability that the first puppy is brown and male is $\frac{1}{8}$.

EXAMPLE 2 Approximating a Probability

Describe an experiment you could perform to approximate the probability in Example 1.

Solution

To approximate the probability in Example 1, you can use two bags with pieces of paper in them as shown at the left. Choose a piece of paper from the first bag and another piece of paper from the second bag. Record your results and repeat the experiment many times. You should get "brown" and "male" about one eighth of the time.

Goal 2 PROBABILITY OF MULTIPLE EVENTS

Just as with two independent events, the probability that three or more independent events all occur is the product of the probabilities of the events.

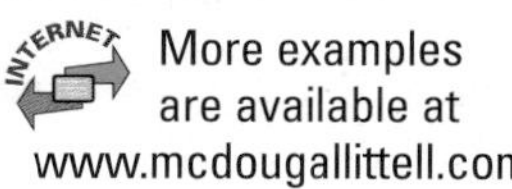

Student Help

MORE EXAMPLES

More examples are available at www.mcdougallittell.com

EXAMPLE 3 Finding a Probability

You roll four number cubes. What is the probability that you roll four even numbers?

Solution

Each number cube has six sides, which are numbered from 1 through 6. The probability that you roll an even number is $\frac{3}{6}$, or $\frac{1}{2}$.

Rolling an even number on each of the four number cubes are independent events. So, the probability that you roll *four* even numbers is the product of the events' probabilities.

$$P(\text{all 4 are even}) = \frac{1}{2} \cdot \frac{1}{2} \cdot \frac{1}{2} \cdot \frac{1}{2}$$

$$= \frac{1}{16}$$

ANSWER ▶ The probability that you roll four even numbers is $\frac{1}{16}$.

EXAMPLE 4 Finding a Probability

AREA CODES Area codes have the form *NXY* where *N* can be any digit from 2 through 9 and *X* and *Y* can be any digit from 0 through 9. You forget your friend's area code. If you randomly guess the three digits, what is the probability that you will be correct?

Solution

There are 8 possibilities for the first digit: 2, 3, 4, 5, 6, 7, 8, and 9. So, the probability of guessing the first digit correctly is $\frac{1}{8}$.

There are 10 possibilities for each of the second and third digits, so the probability of guessing each of these digits correctly is $\frac{1}{10}$.

The probability of guessing all three digits correctly is $\frac{1}{8} \cdot \frac{1}{10} \cdot \frac{1}{10} = \frac{1}{800}$.

11.3 Exercises

Guided Practice

1. Find the probability of landing on green on both spinners shown. Solve the problem by drawing a tree diagram. Then solve the problem without using a tree diagram.

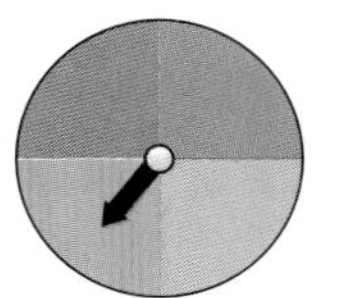
4 equal sections

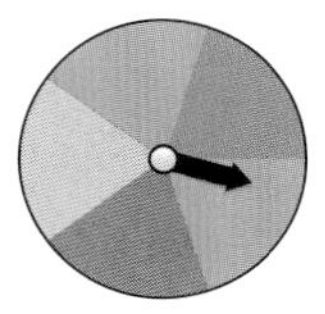
5 equal sections

You roll three number cubes. Find the probability of the event.

2. Getting three 6's

3. Getting three odd numbers

4. Getting three even numbers

5. Getting three prime numbers

Practice and Problem Solving

> *Student Help*
>
> ▶ **MORE PRACTICE**
> Extra practice to help you master skills is on page 586.

COUNTY FAIR **You and a friend go to a county fair and each spin the wheel shown below. (The wheel is divided into 10 equal sections.) Find the probability of the event.**

6. You win free admission.

7. You win $5 off admission.

8. You lose.

9. You and your friend both lose.

10. You win free admission and your friend loses.

11. You lose and your friend wins $5 off admission.

TELEPHONE NUMBERS **In Exercises 12 and 13, use the following information.** You forget the last two digits of a friend's phone number but remember that they are both even.

12. You randomly choose two even numbers to dial. Find the probability that you will dial the correct number.

13. Describe an experiment you could perform to approximate the probability in Exercise 12.

Chapter Opener Link **In Exercises 14 and 15, use the information on page 501. Assume that the parrot chooses objects at random.**

14. What is the theoretical probability that the parrot chooses the correct object two times in a row?

15. What is the theoretical probability that the parrot chooses an incorrect object two times in a row?

Student Help

▶LOOK BACK
For help with polygons, see page 31.

GEOMETRY In Exercises 16 and 17, one figure is randomly selected from each box shown at the right.

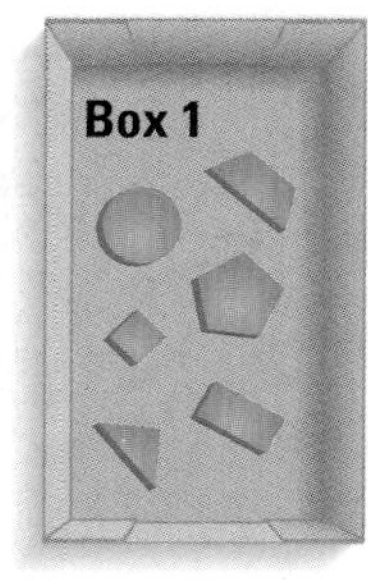

16. Find the probability that both selected figures are polygons.

17. Find the probability that both selected figures are quadrilaterals.

Link to History

TRAFFIC LIGHTS
Before the invention of the automatic traffic light in 1922, police officers directed traffic from booths located in the middle of the intersection. By 1926 New York City had as many as 98 automatic traffic lights.

18. TRAFFIC LIGHTS A road has two traffic lights that operate independently at consecutive intersections. You have a 40% chance of passing through the first intersection without stopping. You have a 70% chance of passing through the next intersection without stopping. What is the probability that you will be able to pass through both intersections without stopping?

19. WRITING Your friend tosses a coin and says, "I got three heads in a row! My next toss will surely be tails." Do you agree? Explain.

20. COMBINATION LOCK A combination lock has three dials with the numbers 0 through 9 printed on each dial. To open the lock you must turn each dial so that the correct number is showing. If you forget your combination and choose three numbers at random, what is the probability that you can open the lock in one try?

LICENSE PLATES In California, standard license plates have the form shown. Suppose you forget the license plate number of a friend who lives in California.

21. If you randomly guess the three letters, what is the probability that you are correct?

22. If you randomly guess the last three digits, what is the probability that you are correct?

23. If you randomly guess all four digits, what is the probability that you are correct?

Science Link **In Exercises 24–26, assume that the gender of a baby is independent of the gender of prior babies, and that having a boy and having a girl are equally likely outcomes.**

24. MATHEMATICAL REASONING Your friend thinks that having two babies of the same gender is as likely as having two babies of different genders. Do you agree or disagree? Explain.

25. Find the probability of having five baby boys in a row.

26. Describe an experiment you could perform to approximate the probability in Exercise 25.

CHALLENGE A jar contains two blue marbles and two red marbles. You randomly choose a marble. Without replacing the marble, you randomly choose a second marble. Consider the following events.

Event *A*: The first marble is red. **Event *B*:** The second marble is red.

27. Draw a tree diagram to find the probability that event A and event B both occur.

28. **MATHEMATICAL REASONING** Use your answer to Exercise 27 to explain why you cannot find the probability that event A and event B both occur by finding $\frac{1}{2} \cdot \frac{1}{2}$.

Multiple-Choice Practice

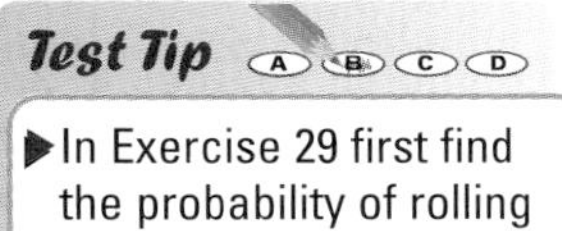

▶ In Exercise 29 first find the probability of rolling one 4.

29. You roll three number cubes. What is the probability of getting three 4's?

Ⓐ $\frac{3}{64}$ Ⓑ $\frac{1}{64}$ Ⓒ $\frac{3}{216}$ Ⓓ $\frac{1}{216}$

30. You spin the spinners shown. What is the probability of landing on red, the number 4, and the letter A?

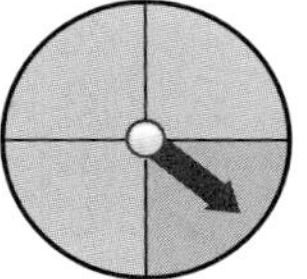

4 equal sections

1 2 3 4 5 6

6 equal sections

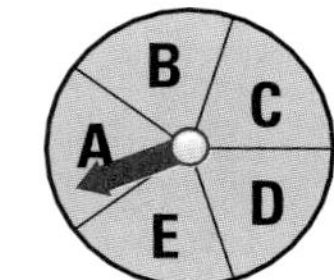

5 equal sections

Ⓕ $\frac{1}{120}$ Ⓖ $\frac{37}{180}$ Ⓗ $\frac{1}{3}$ Ⓙ $\frac{37}{60}$

Mixed Review

Find the area of the triangle. *(8.4)*

31.

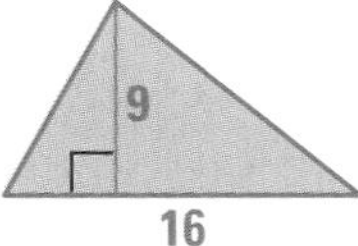

32.

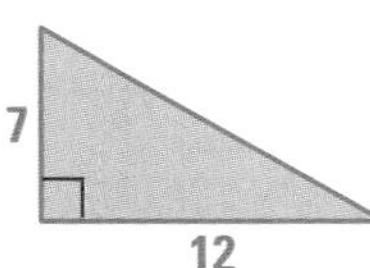

33.

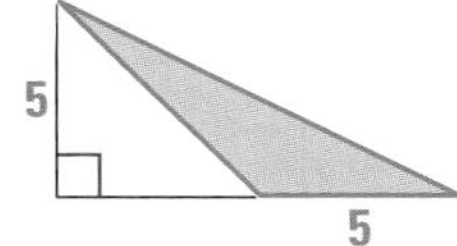

VIDEO GAMES In Exercises 34 and 35, use the following numbers of video games rented from a video store on 14 days. *(10.1, 10.2)*

49, 60, 78, 80, 85, 59, 60, 65, 63, 75, 88, 90, 59, 65

34. Find the mean, median, and mode(s) of the data.

35. Make a frequency table and a histogram of the data.

36. How could the bar graph at the right be misinterpreted? *(10.6)*

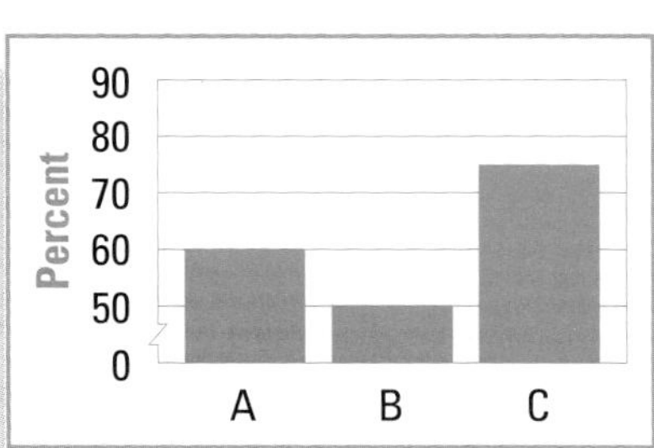

Chapter 11 Mid-Chapter Test

Take this test as you would take a test in class. The answers to the exercises are given in the back of the book.

In Exercises 1–3, you toss a coin four times.

1. Draw a tree diagram to find the number of possible outcomes.

2. Find the probability that you toss 4 tails.

3. Find the probability that you toss at least 2 heads.

Tell whether the Venn diagram represents *disjoint* or *overlapping* events.

4. 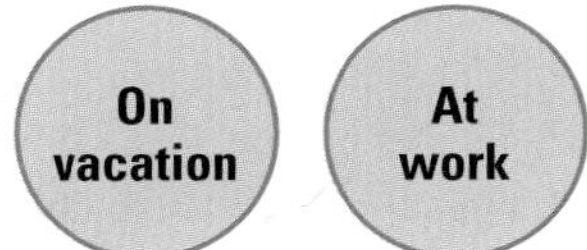

5. 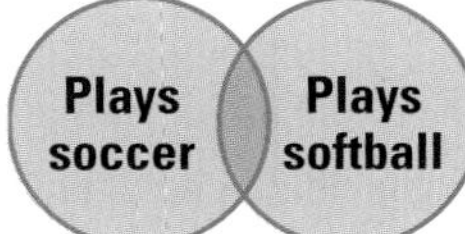

You randomly choose a whole number from 1 through 12. Tell whether the events are *disjoint* or *overlapping*.

6. **Event *A*:** The number is a multiple of 3.
Event *B*: The number is a multiple of 5.

7. **Event *A*:** The number is prime.
Event *B*: The number is greater than 8.

Tell whether the events seem to be *independent* or *dependent*. Explain your reasoning.

8. **Event *A*:** Without looking you reach into a barrel, pick out a red apple, and eat it.
Event *B*: You reach into the barrel again and pick out a green apple.

9. **Event *A*:** A tossed coin comes up heads.
Event *B*: A rolled number cube comes up 4.

LICENSE PLATES **In Exercises 10 and 11, use the fact that standard license plates in Taiwan have two letters followed by any four digits from 0 to 9.**

10. Assume that there are no restrictions on the letters used on a license plate in Taiwan. If you randomly guess the letters on a license plate in Taiwan, what is the probability that you are correct?

11. If you randomly guess the digits on a license plate in Taiwan, what is the probability that you are correct?

12. **LOCKER COMBINATION** The dial on your locker has numbers from 0 through 39 printed along the outer edge. To open the lock you must turn the dial to three numbers in the correct order. If you forget your combination and turn the dial to three numbers at random, what is the probability that you can open the lock in one try?

11.4 Probability of Disjoint Events

California Standards

In this lesson you'll:

- Understand that the probability of either of two disjoint events occurring is the sum of the individual probabilities. (SDP 3.4)
- Represent all possible outcomes for compound events in an organized way. (SDP 3.1)

Goal 1 THE PROBABILITY OF DISJOINT EVENTS

Suppose you randomly choose a whole number from 1 through 10. Event A is getting an odd number, and event B is getting an 8. The probability that event A occurs is $\frac{5}{10}$, or $\frac{1}{2}$. The probability that event B occurs is $\frac{1}{10}$. Now consider the probability that either event A *or* event B occurs. The favorable outcomes are 1, 3, 5, 7, 8, and 9, so the probability that either event occurs is $\frac{6}{10}$, or $\frac{3}{5}$. Notice that this is the sum of the individual probabilities for events A and B because the events have no outcomes in common.

PROBABILITY OF TWO DISJOINT EVENTS

In Words If two events are disjoint, then the probability that either event occurs is the sum of the probabilities of the events.

In Algebra If event A and event B are disjoint, then the probability that event A *or* event B occurs is:

$$P(A \text{ or } B) = P(A) + P(B)$$

Student Help

STUDY TIP
The following Venn diagram shows the relationship between events A and B discussed at the top of the page.

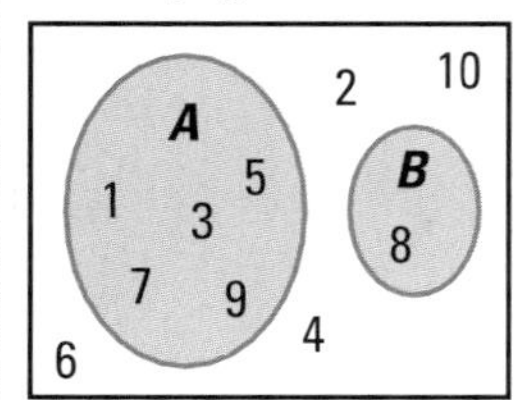

EXAMPLE 1 Finding a Probability

A jar contains 12 marbles: 5 red, 4 blue, and 3 white. You randomly choose one marble. Find the probability of the event.

a. Event *A*: The marble is red.

b. Event *B*: The marble is blue.

c. Event *A* or event *B*: The marble is red or blue.

Solution

a. There are 5 red marbles and a total of 12 marbles. So, the probability of choosing a red marble is $\mathbf{\frac{5}{12}}$.

b. There are 4 blue marbles. So, the probability of choosing a blue marble is $\mathbf{\frac{4}{12}}$.

c. Because the events are disjoint, the probability of choosing a red or a blue marble is the sum of the probabilities in parts (a) and (b):

$$P(A \text{ or } B) = \mathbf{P(A) + P(B)}$$

$$= \mathbf{\frac{5}{12}} + \mathbf{\frac{4}{12}} = \frac{9}{12} = \frac{3}{4}$$

Student Help

▶ **More Examples**

More examples are available at www.mcdougallittell.com

EXAMPLE 2 ***Finding a Probability***

SOCCER RAFFLE You are one of the 400 fans at a sold-out soccer game. At halftime one ticket number will be randomly chosen and the ticket holder will win a soccer ball. What is the probability that you will either win or not win the soccer ball?

Solution

$$P(\text{win or not win}) = P(\text{win}) + P(\text{not win})$$

$$= \frac{1}{400} + \frac{399}{400}$$

$$= \frac{400}{400} = 1, \text{ or } 100\%$$

The probability that you will either win or not win is 100%. This makes sense because the events are disjoint and cover all possibilities.

Goal 2 Organizing Events by Making a Table

If three or more events are disjoint, then the probability that any of the events occurs is the sum of the probabilities of the events.

EXAMPLE 3 ***Making a Table***

You roll two number cubes. What is the probability that the total (that is, the sum of the numbers rolled) is 6, 7, or 8?

Solution

Make a table to organize the possible outcomes. Write the possible numbers for one cube in the left column of the table, and write the possible numbers for the other cube in the top row of the table. The entries in the table show all the possible totals.

	1	2	3	4	5	6
1	2	3	4	5	6	7
2	3	4	5	6	7	8
3	4	5	6	7	8	9
4	5	6	7	8	9	10
5	6	7	8	9	10	11
6	7	8	9	10	11	12

There are 36 possible outcomes. The probability that the total is 6 is $\frac{5}{36}$. The probability that the total is 7 is $\frac{6}{36}$. The probability that the total is 8 is $\frac{5}{36}$. So, the probability that the total is 6, 7, or 8 is

$\frac{5}{36} + \frac{6}{36} + \frac{5}{36} = \frac{16}{36} = \frac{4}{9}$.

EXAMPLE 4 Using a Table

You roll two number cubes. What is the probability that the total is even?

Solution

Use the table shown in Example 3 on the previous page. The probability that the total is even is the sum of the probabilities that the total is 2, 4, 6, 8, 10, or 12.

$$\begin{aligned} P(\text{total is even}) &= P(2) + P(4) + P(6) + P(8) + P(10) + P(12) \\ &= \frac{1}{36} + \frac{3}{36} + \frac{5}{36} + \frac{5}{36} + \frac{3}{36} + \frac{1}{36} \\ &= \frac{18}{36} \\ &= \frac{1}{2} \end{aligned}$$

ANSWER ▶ The probability that the total is even is $\frac{1}{2}$, or 50%.

11.4 Exercises

Guided Practice

1. **WRITING** A number cube is rolled. Event A is getting an odd number. Event B is getting a 5. Explain why the probability that either event A or event B occurs is not the sum of the probability of event A and the probability of event B.

In Exercises 2–5, use the following information. A jar contains 15 marbles: 8 green, 4 blue, and 3 white. You randomly choose one marble.

2. What is the probability that the marble is blue?

3. What is the probability that the marble is white?

4. What is the probability that the marble is blue or white?

5. What is the probability that the marble is green or blue?

6. **RAFFLE** A total of 335 tickets are sold for a raffle. You bought 5 tickets. What is the probability that you either win or do not win the raffle?

You roll two number cubes. Find the probability of the event.

7. The total is 2 or 12.

8. The total is 7 or 10.

9. The total is at least 9.

10. The total is less than 6.

11. The total is odd.

12. The total is 2, 3, or 4.

Practice and Problem Solving

Student Help

▶ **MORE PRACTICE** Extra practice to help you master skills is on page 587.

You spin the spinner shown. Find the probability of the event.

12 equal sections

13. Getting 4 or 9

14. Getting 10 or a multiple of 3

15. Getting a multiple of 4 or a prime number

16. Getting a number less than 4 or greater than 9

MOTOR VEHICLES The table gives the number of motor vehicles registered in the United States in 1998. If a vehicle is randomly chosen, find the probability of the event.

Type	Number registered (in millions)
Auto	132
Truck	79
Bus	1
Total	**212**

▶ Source: *Highway Statistics 1998*

17. Choosing an auto or a truck

18. Choosing a bus or a truck

19. Choosing an auto or a bus

CARDS In Exercises 20–24, use the following information to find the probability of the given event. There are 52 cards in a standard deck of playing cards with 13 cards in each of 4 *suits.* You randomly choose a card from a standard deck.

Hearts	A ♥ ACE	2 ♥ TWO	3 ♥ THREE	4 ♥ FOUR	5 ♥ FIVE	6 ♥ SIX	7 ♥ SEVEN	8 ♥ EIGHT	9 ♥ NINE	10 ♥ TEN	JACK	QUEEN	KING
Clubs	A ♣ ACE	2 ♣ TWO	3 ♣ THREE	4 ♣ FOUR	5 ♣ FIVE	6 ♣ SIX	7 ♣ SEVEN	8 ♣ EIGHT	9 ♣ NINE	10 ♣ TEN	JACK	QUEEN	KING
Diamonds	A ♦ ACE	2 ♦ TWO	3 ♦ THREE	4 ♦ FOUR	5 ♦ FIVE	6 ♦ SIX	7 ♦ SEVEN	8 ♦ EIGHT	9 ♦ NINE	10 ♦ TEN	JACK	QUEEN	KING
Spades	A ♠ ACE	2 ♠ TWO	3 ♠ THREE	4 ♠ FOUR	5 ♠ FIVE	6 ♠ SIX	7 ♠ SEVEN	8 ♠ EIGHT	9 ♠ NINE	10 ♠ TEN	JACK	QUEEN	KING

20. Choosing a heart or a diamond

21. Choosing an ace or a 10

22. Choosing an ace or a face card (a jack, a queen, or a king)

23. Choosing an odd number or a king

24. **MATHEMATICAL REASONING** Why can't you find the probability of getting a face card or getting a spade by adding the probabilities of the events? Draw a Venn diagram to help explain your reasoning.

25. **BASKETBALL** In the 1998–1999 professional basketball season, Tim Duncan made 247 free throws out of 358 free-throw attempts. He missed 111 free throws. What is the probability that Duncan either made a free throw or missed a free throw that season?

▶Source: National Basketball Association

BOTANIST Some botanists specialize in genetics. By changing a plant's genes, scientists can create a new plant with certain desired traits.

More about botanists available at www.mcdougallittell.com

You roll two number cubes and multiply the numbers that show. Use the table to find the probability of the event.

	1	2	3	4	5	6
1	1	2	3	4	5	6
2	2	4	6	8	10	12
3	3	6	9	12	15	18
4	4	8	12	16	20	24
5	5	10	15	20	25	30
6	6	12	18	24	30	36

26. The product is 4 or 12.

27. The product is odd.

28. The product is less than 9.

29. The product is at least 12.

In Exercises 30–32, you spin the spinner at the right twice.

8 equal sections

30. Make a table showing the possible sums.

31. Find the probability of spinning a sum of 14, 15, or 16.

32. Find the probability of spinning a sum less than 10.

33. **Science Link** A *four-o'clock* is a plant that has red, pink, or white flowers. Each parent plant passes along a red (R) or a white (W) gene to its offspring. Use the table to find the probability that an offspring of two pink four-o'clocks (both with RW genes) will be pink or white.

Parents **Offspring**

MONEY **In Exercises 34 and 35, use the following information.**
You have a penny, a nickel, a dime, and a quarter in each of your two pockets. You draw one coin from each pocket. (Assume that you are equally likely to choose each kind of coin.)

34. Make a table of the total value of the coins you could choose.

35. What is the probability of choosing a total of more than $.15?

36. CHALLENGE What is the minimum number of times you must roll a number cube to have at least a 50% chance of getting a 6? Use words and numbers to explain your reasoning.

Multiple-Choice Practice

▶ Double-check your answer when a problem involves many pieces of information, as in Exercise 38.

37. Given the probabilities of two disjoint events A and B, what would you do to find the probability that either event A or event B occurs?

(A) Add (B) Subtract (C) Multiply (D) Divide

38. As you walk into a store you are given a coupon to scratch and reveal a discount. A salesperson says that 15% of the coupons give a 5% discount and 20% of the coupons give a 10% discount. What is the probability that you will get a 5% or 10% discount?

(F) 15% (G) 25% (H) 30% (J) Not here

Probability of an Event Not Occurring

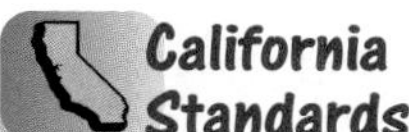

In this lesson you'll:

- Know that if P is the probability of an event, then $1 - P$ is the probability of the event not occurring. (SDP 3.3)

Goal 1 PROBABILITY OF AN EVENT NOT OCCURRING

As you saw in Example 2 of Lesson 11.4, the probability that an event will occur or will not occur is 1, or 100%. This suggests the following.

PROBABILITY OF AN EVENT NOT OCCURRING

In Words To find the probability that an event will not occur, subtract the probability that it will occur from 1.

In Algebra If $P(A)$ is the probability that event A will occur, then $P(\text{event } A \text{ does not occur}) = 1 - P(A)$.

EXAMPLE 1 Finding a Probability

LEFT-HANDEDNESS It is estimated that about 1 out of 10 people are left-handed. What is the probability that a person is not left-handed?

Solution

$P(\text{not left-handed}) = 1 - P(\text{left-handed})$

$\approx 1 - 0.1 = 0.9$ "1 out of 10" means $\frac{1}{10}$, or 0.1.

ANSWER ▶ The probability that a person is not left-handed is 0.9, or 90%.

EXAMPLE 2 Finding a Probability

LITERATURE In a survey of 1061 randomly chosen adults, each person was asked to name the author of *The Cat in the Hat*. A total of 764 people correctly answered "Dr. Seuss." Estimate the probability that a randomly chosen adult would not know the author of *The Cat in the Hat*. ▶ Source: The Gallup Organization

Solution

From the survey, the probability that an adult knows the author of *The Cat in the Hat* is:

$$P(\text{knows author}) = \frac{764}{1061} \approx 0.72 = 72\%$$

So, the probability that an adult would not know the author of *The Cat in the Hat* is:

$$P(\text{does not know author}) \approx 1 - 0.72 = 0.28 = 28\%$$

Goal 2 RE-EXPRESSING A PROBABILITY

Sometimes it is easier to find the probability that an event does not occur than to find the probability that it does occur.

EXAMPLE 3 Re-expressing a Probability

You roll two number cubes. What is the probability that the total is at least 6?

Solution

Make a table to organize the possible outcomes.

	1	2	3	4	5	6
1	2	3	4	5	6	7
2	3	4	5	6	7	8
3	4	5	6	7	8	9
4	5	6	7	8	9	10
5	6	7	8	9	10	11
6	7	8	9	10	11	12

Method 1 Use the fact that getting a total of at least 6 means getting a total of 6, 7, 8, 9, 10, 11, or 12.

$$P(\text{total} \geq 6) = P(6) + P(7) + P(8) + P(9) + P(10) + P(11) + P(12)$$

$$= \frac{5}{36} + \frac{6}{36} + \frac{5}{36} + \frac{4}{36} + \frac{3}{36} + \frac{2}{36} + \frac{1}{36}$$

$$= \frac{26}{36} = \frac{13}{18}$$

Method 2 Use the fact that getting a total of at least 6 means *not* getting a total of 2, 3, 4, or 5.

$$P(\text{total} \geq 6) = 1 - [P(2) + P(3) + P(4) + P(5)]$$

$$= 1 - \left[\frac{1}{36} + \frac{2}{36} + \frac{3}{36} + \frac{4}{36}\right]$$

$$= 1 - \frac{10}{36} = \frac{26}{36} = \frac{13}{18}$$

EXAMPLE 4 Re-expressing a Probability

You spin the spinner shown. What is the probability of landing on white?

Solution

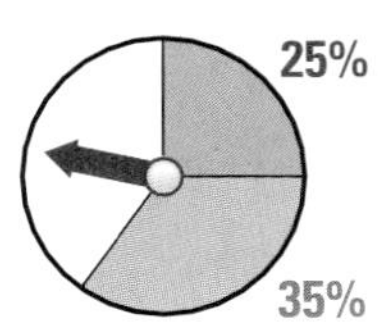

$$P(\text{white}) = 1 - [P(\text{red}) + P(\text{blue})]$$

$$= 1 - (0.25 + 0.35)$$

$$= 1 - 0.60 = 0.40$$

ANSWER ▶ There is a 40% probability of landing on white.

11.5 Exercises

Guided Practice

1. Complete the statement: The sum of the probability that an event occurs and the probability that it does not occur is equal to __?__.

In Exercises 2–7, you are given $P(A)$, the probability that event A occurs. Find $P(\text{not } A)$, the probability that event A does not occur.

2. $P(A) = \frac{1}{4}$ **3.** $P(A) = \frac{2}{5}$ **4.** $P(A) = 0.7$

5. $P(A) = 0.92$ **6.** $P(A) = 39\%$ **7.** $P(A) = 0.65\%$

8. **COMPUTERS** In 1999 about 66% of people in the United States had Internet access. What is the probability that a randomly chosen person in the United States did not have Internet access in 1999?
▶ Source: The Wirthlin Report

9. **WRITING** You roll two number cubes. Describe two ways to find the probability that the total is at least 4.

Practice and Problem Solving

Student Help

▶ **MORE PRACTICE**
Extra practice to help you master skills is on page 587.

In Exercises 10–18, you are given $P(A)$, the probability that event A occurs. Find $P(\text{not } A)$, the probability that event A does not occur.

10. $P(A) = \frac{1}{2}$ **11.** $P(A) = \frac{2}{3}$ **12.** $P(A) = \frac{5}{6}$

13. $P(A) = 0.8$ **14.** $P(A) = 0.35$ **15.** $P(A) = 0.86$

16. $P(A) = 56\%$ **17.** $P(A) = 23.5\%$ **18.** $P(A) = 71.4\%$

19. **LIGHT BULBS** A popular brand of 60 watt light bulb has a 92% chance of lasting 1000 hours or longer. Find the probability that the light bulb lasts less than 1000 hours.

20. **FORESTRY** In Illinois 57% of the trees are oak or hickory. If a tree in Illinois is randomly selected, what is the probability that it is neither oak nor hickory? ▶ Source: 1998 Forest Health Highlights

Student Help

▶ **HOMEWORK HELP**
INTERNET Extra help with problem solving in Exs. 21–23 is available at www.mcdougallittell.com

COLLEGE ADMISSION **Colleges try to predict what percent of students they accept will actually enroll. For each college, find the probability that an accepted student enrolls and the probability that an accepted student does not enroll.**

21. **College A:** 1750 students accepted, 700 students enroll

22. **College B:** 2000 students accepted, 1160 do not enroll

23. **College C:** 2700 students accepted, 1485 students enroll

COPERNICUS In 1543 astronomer Nicolaus Copernicus published a book on his theory that the planets revolve around the sun. Until then, it was widely believed that the sun and planets revolved around Earth.

24. ASTRONOMY SURVEY In a survey of 1016 randomly chosen adults, each person was asked whether Earth revolves around the sun or the sun revolves around Earth. A total of 213 people either said that the sun revolves around Earth or that they had no opinion. Estimate the probability that a randomly chosen adult would correctly answer that Earth revolves around the sun. ▶ Source: The Gallup Organization

You spin the spinner at the right twice.

7 equal sections

25. Make a table showing the possible sums of the two spins.

26. Find the probability of spinning a sum of at least 3.

27. Find the probability of spinning a sum of at least 4.

INTERNET USERS **In Exercises 28 and 29, use the table at the right.**

28. What is the probability that an Internet user chosen at random spends 2 or more hours on-line?

29. What is the probability that an Internet user chosen at random spends 20 hours or less on-line?

Internet Use in 1998	
Time spent on-line per week	Percent of Internet users
0–1 hour	1%
2–4 hours	9%
5–9 hours	24%
10–20 hours	34%
21–40 hours	21%
Over 40 hours	11%

▶ Source: Graphics, Visualization, and Usability Center

30. If you spin the spinner below, what is the probability of landing on red?

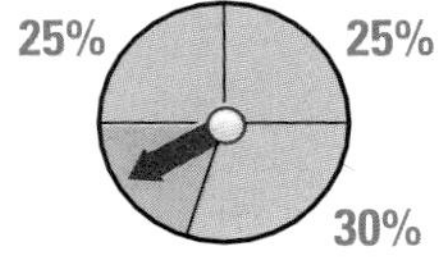

31. CHALLENGE Two friends are discussing their birthdays. Show two ways of finding the probability that they were born in different months. (Assume that a person is equally likely to be born in any month.)

Multiple-Choice Practice

32. You can win a prize by checking the bottle cap on a certain brand of juice. The probability that you win a prize is $\frac{1}{50}$. What is the probability that you do not win a prize?

Ⓐ $\frac{1}{50}$　Ⓑ $\frac{1}{2}$　Ⓒ $\frac{49}{50}$　Ⓓ 1

33. If you spin the spinner at the right, what is the probability of landing on red?

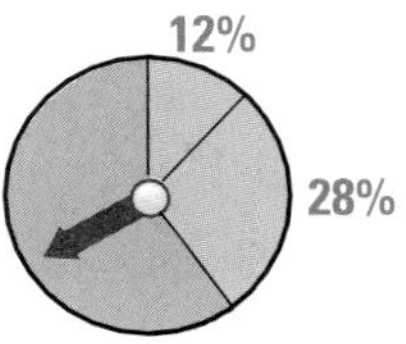

Ⓕ 12%　Ⓖ 28%

Ⓗ 40%　Ⓙ 60%

11.6 Making Predictions

In this lesson you'll:

- Determine theoretical probabilities and use them to make predictions about events. (SDP 3.0)
- Use data to estimate the probability of future events. (SDP 3.2)

Goal 1 Using Probabilities to Make Predictions

If you know $P(A)$, the theoretical probability of event A, you know the ratio of favorable outcomes to total outcomes. If you repeatedly perform an experiment involving these outcomes, some of the trials will result in *successes* that correspond to event A. The ratio of successes to trials should be approximately equal to $P(A)$:

$$\frac{\text{Number of successes}}{\text{Number of trials}} \approx P(A)$$

This suggests that you can estimate the number of successes as follows:

$$\text{Number of successes} \approx P(A) \cdot (\text{Number of trials})$$

EXAMPLE 1 Estimating the Number of Successes

Three coins will be tossed 200 times. Estimate how many times all three coins will be heads.

Solution

There are 8 possible outcomes of tossing three coins:

TTT, TTH, HTT, THT, HHH, HHT, THH, and HTH

To estimate the number of times 3 heads will occur out of 200 tosses, multiply the probability of getting 3 heads by 200:

$$\boxed{\text{Probability of getting 3 heads}} \cdot \boxed{\text{Number of tosses}} = \frac{1}{8} \cdot 200 = 25$$

ANSWER ▶ Getting 3 heads should occur about 25 times.

Student Help

▶ **LOOK BACK** For help with scatter plots, see page 469.

The scatter plot below shows the number of times three heads occurred when three coins were actually tossed. The blue line shows the estimated number of occurrences based on theoretical probability.

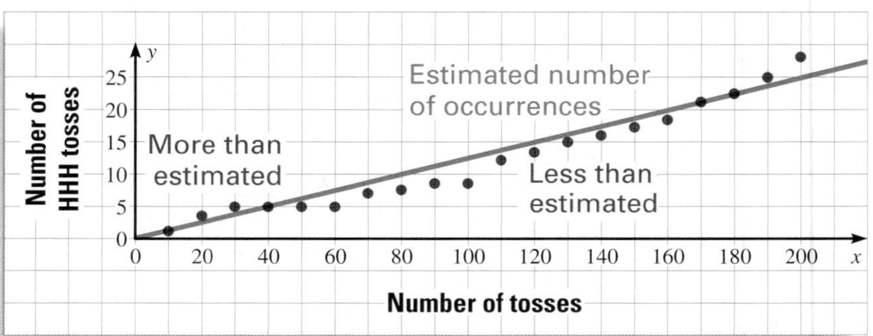

Link to Careers

ACTUARY Most actuaries work for insurance companies. Actuaries analyze data to make predictions about how much an insurance company will have to pay out in claims.

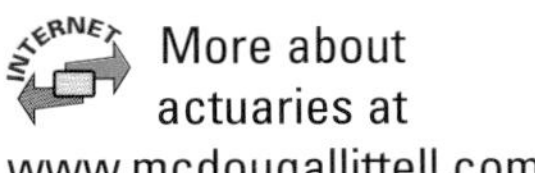
More about actuaries at www.mcdougallittell.com

Goal 2 USING DATA TO MAKE PREDICTIONS

EXAMPLE 2 Making Predictions

INSURANCE The table below gives information about motor vehicle accidents in the United States in 1998.

Motor Vehicle Accidents in 1998	
Number of registered motor vehicles (in millions)	215
Number of vehicles involved in an accident (in millions)	21.3
Cost of accidents (in billions of dollars)	192

▶ Source: National Safety Council

a. Your company insures 150,000 motor vehicles this year. Use the 1998 data to estimate how many vehicles insured by your company will be involved in an accident.

b. Use the 1998 data and your answer to part (a) to estimate how much your company will have to pay for motor vehicle accidents this year.

Solution

a. If you assume that the number of motor vehicles involved in an accident is related to the number of registered motor vehicles, the probability that a vehicle will have an accident during the year is:

$$\frac{21.3}{215} \approx 0.0991$$

You can multiply 150,000 by 0.0991 to estimate how many vehicles insured by your company will be involved in an accident:

$$150{,}000 \cdot 0.0991 \approx 14{,}900$$

ANSWER ▶ You can estimate that about 14,900 of the vehicles insured by your company will be involved in an accident this year.

b. In 1998 the average cost per vehicle in an accident was:

$$\frac{\$192 \text{ billion}}{21.3 \text{ million vehicles}} = \frac{\$192{,}000{,}000{,}000}{21{,}300{,}000 \text{ vehicles}} \approx \$9014 \text{ per vehicle}$$

In part (a) you estimated that 14,900 of the vehicles insured by your company will be involved in accidents this year, so the estimated total cost of the accidents is:

$$\$9014 \cdot 14{,}900 \approx \$134{,}000{,}000$$

ANSWER ▶ You can estimate that your company will have to pay about $134 million for accidents this year.

11.6 Exercises

Guided Practice

1. WRITING If you know the probability of an event, explain how you can estimate the number of times the event will occur in a given number of trials.

In Exercises 2 and 3, use the spinner at the right.

10 equal sections

2. Find the probability that the spinner will land on a prime number.

3. If you spin the spinner 150 times, how many times would you expect it to land on a prime number?

PET OWNERSHIP **In Exercises 4 and 5, use the following information.** In 2000, about 45.4 million of the 103 million households in the United States owned at least one pet. ▶ Source: Gale Group

4. Find the probability that a household in the United States owned at least one pet in 2000.

5. In 2000, Los Angeles had about 1.27 million households. Estimate the number of these households that owned at least one pet.

Practice and Problem Solving

Student Help

▶ MORE PRACTICE
Extra practice to help you master skills is on page 587.

In Exercises 6–11, you are given the theoretical probability of an event. Estimate the number of times the event will occur in the given number of trials.

6. Theoretical probability: $\frac{1}{5}$
Number of trials: 350

7. Theoretical probability: 0.75
Number of trials: 800

8. Theoretical probability: 0.45
Number of trials: 200

9. Theoretical probability: $\frac{5}{6}$
Number of trials: 1440

10. Theoretical probability: 0.02
Number of trials: 750

11. Theoretical probability: 0.9
Number of trials: 630

12. Two coins will be tossed 500 times. Estimate the number of times 2 tails will be tossed.

13. Two number cubes will be rolled 100 times. Estimate the number of times two 5's will be rolled.

14. There are 15 girls' names and 25 boys' names in a hat. A name will be chosen and then replaced 400 times. Estimate the number of times a girl's name will be chosen.

15. **QUALITY CONTROL** A quality control technician finds that 2 out of 150 CDs are defective. If 20,000 CDs are manufactured that day, estimate the total number of defective CDs.

16. **LANGUAGE** The letter E makes up about 13% of the total number of letters written in English. If you randomly select a newspaper article and count the first 1250 letters, how many would you expect to be E's?

Student Help

▶ **HOMEWORK HELP**
INTERNET Extra help with problem solving in Ex. 17 is available at www.mcdougallittell.com

17. **UNITED STATES MINT** It is estimated that each year $\frac{2}{3}$ of the pennies made by the United States Mint drop out of circulation (are no longer used for purchases) that same year. In 1998 about 10.3 trillion pennies were made by the United States Mint. Estimate how many of those pennies dropped out of circulation.

CONSUMERS IN CHINA **In Exercises 18–20, use the table giving the results of a 1997 survey of 3727 households in China. The table shows how many of these households owned each of several items.**

▶ Source: The Gallup Organization

Item	Telephone	Color TV	VCR	Refrigerator
Number of households	932	2087	447	1304

18. Out of a group of 100,000 households in China, estimate the number that would own a telephone.

19. Out of a group of 100,000 households in China, estimate the number that would own a VCR.

20. Out of a group of 100,000 households in China, estimate the number that would own a refrigerator.

BASEBALL **In Exercises 21–24, use the table showing batting statistics for three baseball players in the 1999 baseball season.**

▶ Source: Major League Baseball

Player	Number of hits	Times at bat
Scott Brosius	117	473
Derek Jeter	219	627
Shane Spencer	48	205

21. Find each player's batting average as a decimal rounded to the nearest thousandth.

Student Help

▶ **LOOK BACK**
For help with finding batting averages, see page 265.

22. Based on your answer to Exercise 21, rank the three players from worst hitter to best hitter.

23. Suppose that next season each player gets up to bat 150 times. Estimate how many hits each player will have.

24. **MATHEMATICAL REASONING** Given your rankings from Exercise 22, do your estimations in Exercise 23 make sense? Explain.

25. **CHALLENGE** Event A and event B are independent events. The probability that event A occurs is $\frac{3}{8}$, and the probability that event B occurs is $\frac{1}{6}$. Out of 500 trials, how many times would you expect event A *and* event B to occur?

Multiple-Choice Practice

26. If you toss a coin 60 times, about how many times would you expect to get heads?

Ⓐ 60 times Ⓑ 45 times

Ⓒ 30 times Ⓓ Not enough information

27. One school in Centerville has 300 students, and 6 of those students have red hair. If the town of Centerville has a total of 4500 students, how many students in the town would you estimate have red hair?

Ⓕ 900 students Ⓖ 150 students

Ⓗ 90 students Ⓙ 15 students

Mixed Review

RECYCLED PAPER In Exercises 28 and 29, use the following information. In 1998 the United States used 101.1 million tons of paper and paper board and recycled 45.3 million tons of paper and paper board. *(6.1, 6.3)*

28. Find the ratio of the amount of recycled paper and paper board to the total amount of paper and paper board used in 1998.

29. If the United States uses 120 million tons of paper and paper board this year, estimate how many millions of tons of paper and paper board will be recycled.

Find the volume of the prism or cylinder. *(9.2, 9.3, 9.4)*

30.
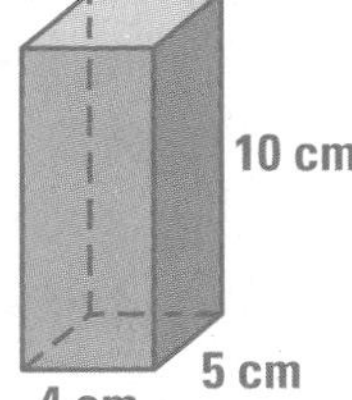

31.
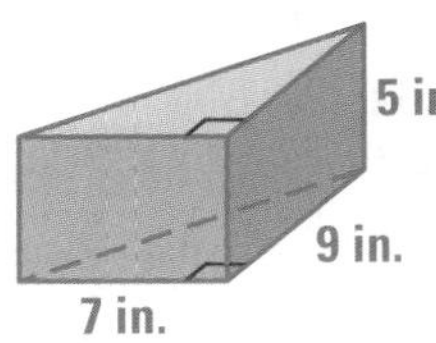

32.
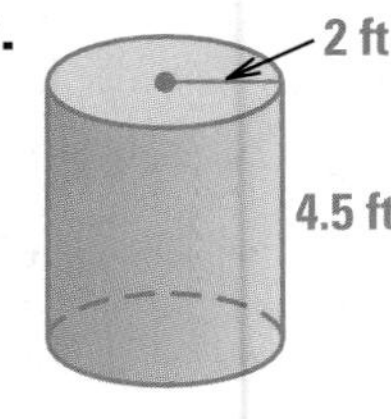

Graph the ordered pairs in a coordinate plane and label the points. *(10.4)*

33. $(0, -4), (5, 5), (-3, 1), (-2, -6), (4, 0)$

34. $(-1, -4), (0, 0), (8, -2), (3, 2), (1, 3)$

35. $(-5, 10), (20, 30), (-15, 15), (40, 30), (-10, -20)$

Chapter 11 Chapter Summary and Review

VOCABULARY

- **tree diagram,** *p. 505*
- **disjoint events,** *p. 509*
- **overlapping events,** *p. 509*
- **independent events,** *p. 510*
- **dependent events,** *p. 510*

11.1 ORGANIZING POSSIBLE OUTCOMES

Examples on pp. 504–505

EXAMPLE You are buying inline skating equipment. You can choose a white or a tan helmet, purple or black skates, and red, white, or black pads. You randomly choose a helmet, skates, and pads. What is the probability that you buy black pads?

Use a tree diagram to find the possible number of skating outfits.

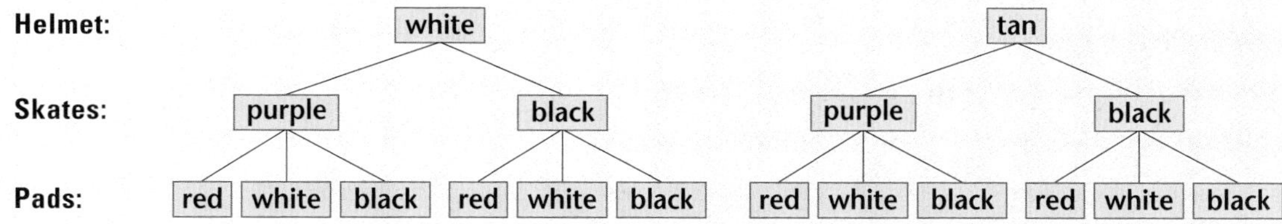

There are 12 possible outfits. Of the possible outfits, four have black pads.

$$\text{Probability} = \frac{\text{Outfits with black pads}}{\text{Total number of outfits}} = \frac{4}{12} = \frac{1}{3}$$

ANSWER ▶ The probability of buying black pads is $\frac{1}{3}$.

In Exercises 1 and 2, use the following information. A couple's choices for their child's first name are Yvonne, Pearl, Tasha, and Viola. Their choices for a middle name are Renee, Lynn, and Marie.

1. Make a list to find the number of ways the child can be named.

2. If a first and middle name are randomly chosen, what is the probability that the middle name is Renee?

3. You are attending a conference. You can choose from 2 morning events, 3 afternoon events, and 2 evening events. Draw a tree diagram to find the possible ways of scheduling a day at the conference.

4. Your two pockets each contain a \$1 bill, a \$5 bill, and a \$10 bill. If you randomly draw one bill from each pocket, what is the probability of drawing less than \$5? drawing more than \$10?

11.2 DISJOINT EVENTS AND INDEPENDENT EVENTS

Examples on pp. 509–511

EXAMPLE You randomly choose a whole number from 1 through 20. Tell whether the events are *disjoint* or *overlapping*.

Event *A*: The number is a multiple of 3.
Event *B*: The number is even.

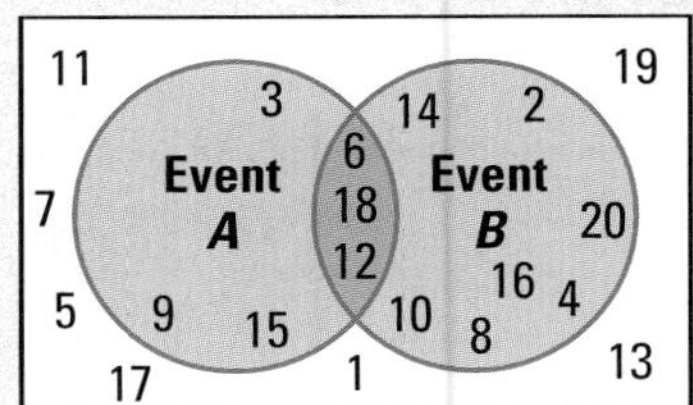

ANSWER ▶ The numbers 6, 12, and 18 are all multiples of 3 and are even. So, the events are overlapping. The Venn diagram illustrates this fact.

EXAMPLE Tell whether the statement describes *independent* or *dependent* events: You reach into a jar of coins and randomly choose a coin. Without replacing the first coin, you randomly choose a second coin.

ANSWER ▶ Choosing the first coin decreases the total number of coins in the jar for when you choose the second coin. So, the events are dependent.

5. A student in your middle school is randomly chosen. Tell whether the events are *disjoint* or *overlapping*.
Event *A*: The student is in sixth grade. **Event *B***: The student is in eighth grade.

6. Tell whether the statement seems to describe *independent* or *dependent* events: You pick a flower from a field, then pick another flower from another field.

11.3 PROBABILITY OF INDEPENDENT EVENTS

Examples on pp. 516–517

To find the probability that two or more independent events all occur, multiply the probabilities of the events.

EXAMPLE The probability of rolling a 4 is $\frac{1}{6}$.

The probability of landing on blue is $\frac{1}{4}$.

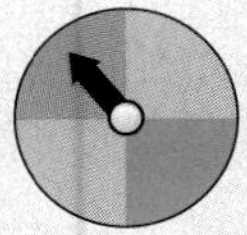
4 equal sections

The probability of rolling a 4 *and* landing on blue is $\frac{1}{6} \cdot \frac{1}{4} = \frac{1}{24}$.

7. You spin the spinner shown above twice. What is the probability of getting orange on the first spin and green on the second spin?

Your computer password consists of 3 letters followed by 4 digits. You remember only part of the password. If you randomly choose letters and digits to complete the password, find the probability that you are correct.

8. MLK ? 12 ? **9.** N ? A64 ? 7 **10.** ? ? M51 ? 5 **11.** B ? ? 39 ? ?

11.4 PROBABILITY OF DISJOINT EVENTS

Examples on pp. 522–524

If two or more events are disjoint, then the probability that any of the events occur is the sum of the probabilities of the events.

EXAMPLE You spin the spinner below twice. Use the table to find the probability that the sum is prime.

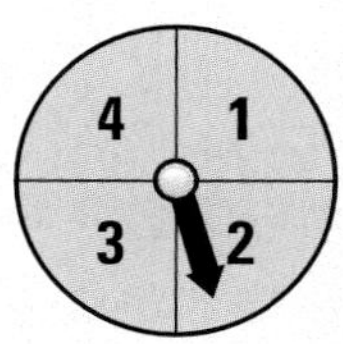

4 equal sections

	1	2	3	4
1	2	3	4	5
2	3	4	5	6
3	4	5	6	7
4	5	6	7	8

Because the possible prime sums are 2, 3, 5, and 7, the probability that the sum of the two spins is prime can be found as follows.

$$P(\text{sum is prime}) = P(2) + P(3) + P(5) + P(7)$$

$$= \frac{1}{16} + \frac{2}{16} + \frac{4}{16} + \frac{2}{16} = \frac{9}{16}$$

In Exercises 12 and 13, use the table above.

12. Find the probability that the sum is a multiple of 3 or a multiple of 4.

13. Can you find the probability that the sum is a multiple of 2 or a multiple of 3 by adding the probability of each event? Explain.

In Exercises 14 and 15, you spin the spinner shown above twice.

14. Make a table of the possible products of the two spins.

15. Find the probability that the product is odd.

11.5 PROBABILITY OF AN EVENT NOT OCCURRING

Examples on pp. 527–528

To find the probability that an event will not occur, subtract the probability that it will occur from 1.

EXAMPLE You toss three coins. Find the probability that at least one coin shows tails.

For the event not to occur, all three coins must show heads. Getting three heads is 1 of the 8 possible outcomes, so $P(\text{all heads}) = \frac{1}{8}$.

$$P(\text{at least one tail}) = 1 - P(\text{all heads}) = 1 - \frac{1}{8} = \frac{7}{8}$$

In Exercises 16–19, you are given $P(A)$, the probability that event A occurs. Find $P(\text{not } A)$, the probability that event A does not occur.

16. $P(A) = \frac{3}{5}$ **17.** $P(A) = 0.64$ **18.** $P(A) = 82\%$ **19.** $P(A) = \frac{11}{32}$

20. **SURVEYS** In a survey of 150 randomly chosen adults, each person was asked whether he or she uses grocery coupons. Of those surveyed, 102 answered yes and the rest answered no. Estimate the probability that a randomly chosen adult does not use grocery coupons.

11.6 MAKING PREDICTIONS

Examples on pp. 531–532

EXAMPLE A park contains an estimated 38,000 ponderosa pine trees. In a random sample of 400 trees in the park, it is found that 46 are infested with dwarf mistletoe, a parasitic plant that slowly kills trees. Estimate how many of the ponderosa pine trees in the park are infested with dwarf mistletoe.

First use the sample results to find the probability that a tree is infested:

$$P(\text{infested}) = \frac{46}{400} = 0.115$$

Now multiply the total number of trees by 0.115 to estimate the number of trees in the park that are infested:

$$38{,}000 \cdot 0.115 = 4370$$

ANSWER ▶ About 4370 of the trees in the park are infested with dwarf mistletoe.

21. Two coins will be tossed 500 times. Estimate how many times 1 head and 1 tail will be tossed.

FREE THROWS In Exercises 22 and 23, you are given a basketball player's season-to-date statistics. Estimate how many free throws the player would make out of 15 attempts in a basketball game.

22. The player has made 111 free throws in 186 attempts.

23. The player has made 180 free throws in 244 attempts.

POPULATION In Exercises 24 and 25, use the graph showing the population distribution by age in the United States.

24. A city has a population of 240,000. If the city has a typical population distribution, estimate how many residents are under the age of 20.

25. A state has a population of 6 million. If the state has a typical population distribution, estimate how many residents are at least 40 years old.

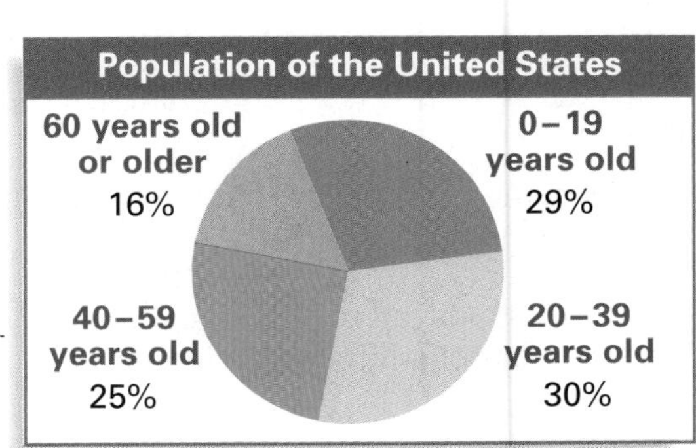

Chapter 11 Chapter Test

DINING In Exercises 1–3, use the following information. The specials at a seafood restaurant are salmon, whitefish, flounder, and scallops. The side dishes are a baked potato and rice pilaf. You have a choice of one special, one side dish, and either a soup or a salad.

1. Draw a tree diagram to find the possible meals you can order. How many different possibilities are there?

2. Find the probability that a randomly chosen meal includes soup.

3. Find the probability that a randomly chosen meal includes salmon and a baked potato.

4. You randomly choose a whole number from 1 through 20. Tell whether the events are *disjoint* or *overlapping*.

Event *A*: The number is at least 15. **Event *B*:** The number is less than 10.

5. Tell whether the events seem to be *independent* or *dependent*.

Event *A*: It rains in Washington, D.C. **Event *B*:** A new president is elected.

CHESS In Exercises 6–9, use the following information to find the probability of the given event. A chess set has each player's 16 playing pieces in separate bags. Each bag contains 1 king, 1 queen, 2 rooks, 2 bishops, 2 knights, and 8 pawns. You and a friend randomly select one piece from your respective bags.

6. You both choose pawns.

7. You choose a king or a rook.

8. You choose a queen and your friend chooses a knight.

9. Your friend chooses a bishop or a pawn.

In Exercises 10–13, you are given $P(A)$, the probability that event A occurs. Find $P(\text{not } A)$, the probability that event A does not occur.

10. $P(A) = \frac{5}{8}$

11. $P(A) = 0.54$

12. $P(A) = 83\%$

13. $P(A) = 1$

GRILLING In Exercises 14 and 15, use the graph showing the results of a survey of 600 randomly chosen adults.

14. Find the probability that a person surveyed never cooks on a grill.

15. Use the survey results to estimate how many of 150,000 adults grill only on special occasions.

Multiple-Choice Practice

If you become anxious, take a few deep breaths to relax.

1. You can have a hamburger on a white bun, a whole-grain bun, or pita bread. You can top it with either American, provolone, Swiss, or cheddar cheese. How many different hamburgers can you make?

Ⓐ 3 Ⓑ 4 Ⓒ 7 Ⓓ 12

2. You randomly choose a whole number from 10 through 20. Which events are disjoint?

Ⓕ **Event *A*:** The number is even.
Event *B*: The number is not prime.

Ⓖ **Event *A*:** The number is odd.
Event *B*: The number is not prime.

Ⓗ **Event *A*:** The number is less than 15.
Event *B*: The number is not prime.

Ⓙ **Event *A*:** The number is even.
Event *B*: The number is odd.

3. Which events seem to be independent?

Ⓐ You are tired. You go to bed early.

Ⓑ You choose one bracelet and then another from your jewelry box.

Ⓒ You toss a dime. You toss a penny.

Ⓓ It is raining. You carry an umbrella.

4. You are redecorating your bedroom. You can choose a white, blue, or green rug, a blue or white bedspread, and white or green curtains. If you randomly choose all three items, what is the probability that they will all be white?

Ⓕ $\frac{3}{7}$ Ⓖ $\frac{1}{3}$ Ⓗ $\frac{1}{6}$ Ⓙ $\frac{1}{12}$

5. You forget your friend's five-digit ZIP code, but remember that the first three digits are the same as your own ZIP code. If you randomly guess the last two digits, what is the probability that you are correct?

Ⓐ $\frac{1}{100}$ Ⓑ $\frac{1}{81}$

Ⓒ $\frac{1}{50}$ Ⓓ $\frac{1}{20}$

6. You and a friend are playing a board game. If you roll the number cube and get a 4 or a 1, you can send your friend back to Start. What is the probability that you roll a 4 or a 1?

Ⓕ $\frac{1}{36}$ Ⓖ $\frac{1}{6}$

Ⓗ $\frac{1}{3}$ Ⓙ $\frac{1}{2}$

7. You toss a coin 4 times. The probability that you will get 1, 2, or 3 heads is $\frac{7}{8}$. What is the probability that you will get 0 or 4 heads?

Ⓐ $\frac{1}{16}$ Ⓑ $\frac{1}{8}$

Ⓒ $\frac{2}{5}$ Ⓓ $\frac{7}{8}$

8. A number cube will be rolled 150 times. How many times do you expect the number rolled to be a 1 or a prime number?

Ⓕ 25 Ⓖ 50

Ⓗ 75 Ⓙ 100

Brain games

- Determine probabilities and use them to make predictions about events. (SDP 3.0)
- Develop generalizations of the results obtained and the strategies used and apply them in new problem situations. (MR 3.3)

Winning Totals

Materials

- 2 number cubes
- 2 different colored pencils

Directions

Object of the Game

Play in pairs. You and your opponent choose totals that are possible when two number cubes are rolled. The player whose totals are rolled the most (out of 50 rolls) wins the game.

How to Play

STEP 1 Make a table like the one shown below. It shows all the possible totals for a roll of two number cubes.

Total	2	3	4	5	6	7	8	9	10	11	12
Tally											

STEP 2 Each player uses a different colored pencil to shade totals in the table. Take turns shading totals until there is only one left. The player who goes second gets to shade the last total.

STEP 3 Roll two number cubes 50 times. Keep a tally in the table of the totals you roll. Add up all the tally marks for the totals you shaded. The player with the greatest number of tally marks wins the game.

Another Way to Play

Change the rules for choosing totals so that both players have an equal chance of winning.

Brain Teaser

What's in the BAG?

There are 20 colored cubes in a bag.
The probability of picking each color is:

red $= \frac{1}{2}$ blue $= \frac{1}{10}$ yellow $= \frac{2}{5}$

How many cubes of each color are in the bag?

Reviewing the Basics

The basic skills you'll review on this page will be useful in future courses and in real-life situations.

EXAMPLE 1 Solving Percent Problems

64 is 80% of what number?

Solution

Use the proportion $\frac{\text{Part of base}}{\text{Base}} = \frac{\text{Percent}}{100}$, or $\frac{a}{b} = \frac{p}{100}$.

$\frac{a}{b} = \frac{p}{100}$ Write proportion.

$\frac{64}{b} = \frac{80}{100}$ Substitute 64 for *a* and 80 for *p*.

$64 \cdot 100 = b \cdot 80$ Cross products property

$6400 = b \cdot 80$ Simplify.

$80 = b$ Divide each side by 80.

Try These

Use a proportion to answer the question.

1. 104 is 64% of what number?

2. 68 is what percent of 153?

3. What is 22.5% of 100?

4. 1.5 is what percent of 180?

EXAMPLE 2 Finding Measures of Central Tendency

Find the mean, median, and mode(s) of the data.

5, 7, 7, 10, 11, 12, 14, 14, 18, 21

Solution

$$\text{Mean} = \frac{5 + 7 + 7 + 10 + 11 + 12 + 14 + 14 + 18 + 21}{10} = \frac{119}{10} = 11.9$$

The number of data values is even, so the median is the mean of the two middle values. The two middle values are 11 and 12, so the median is 11.5.

The modes are 7 and 14, the numbers that occur most often.

Try These

Find the mean, median, and mode(s) of the data.

5. 1, 6, 7, 8, 9, 10, 11, 12

6. 11, 13, 15, 15, 18, 22, 24, 25, 91

7. 14, 15, 15, 16, 16, 22, 34, 34, 34, 35

Student Help

▶ MORE EXAMPLES

INTERNET More examples and practice exercises available at www.mcdougallittell.com

Chapters 1-11 Cumulative Practice

1. Find the least common denominator of $\frac{7}{5}, \frac{22}{15}, \frac{4}{3}$, and $\frac{43}{30}$. Then write the fractions in order from least to greatest. (2.6 and 2.7)

2. Convert the rates below to the same units. Use the fact that 1 yard = 0.9144 meters. Which rate is faster? (3.7 and 3.8)

A. 100 yards in 11.6 seconds

B. 100 meters in 12.4 seconds

In Exercises 3–6, evaluate the expression for the given values of the variables. (4.7)

3. $5(a - b)$ when $a = -2$ and $b = 4$

4. $\frac{(r + s)^2}{-3}$ when $r = -5$ and $s = 14$

5. $-4(x + y)$ when $x = 5$ and $y = -3$

6. $\frac{3 - m^2}{n}$ when $m = -5$ and $n = -11$

7. LONG DISTANCE You pay \$2.95 per month plus \$.05 per minute for long distance service. Your long distance bill was \$35.05 last month. Write a verbal model for the situation. Assign labels and write an equation to find how many minutes you talked. How many hours is this? (5.7)

TECHNOLOGY **In Exercises 8 and 9, use the following information.** A computer museum has a large scale model of a computer chip. The scale for the model is 1 m = 20 mm. The actual computer chip is a square with sides 36 millimeters long. (6.5)

8. How long is each side of the model?

9. What is the scale factor for the model?

In Exercises 10–13, use a proportion to answer the question. (7.2–7.4)

10. What is 35% of 140?

11. What percent is 126 of 315?

12. 75 is 48% of what number?

13. 170% of what number is 51?

In Exercises 14–17, use the following information. You buy a sweatshirt that is on sale for 30% off the original price of \$29. The sales tax is 7%. (7.7)

14. Find the amount of the discount.

15. Find the sale price.

16. Find the amount of the sales tax.

17. Find the total price.

Use a centimeter ruler to measure the sides to the nearest tenth of a centimeter. Then use as many words as possible to describe the triangle: *equilateral, isosceles, scalene, acute, right,* or *obtuse*. (8.3)

18.

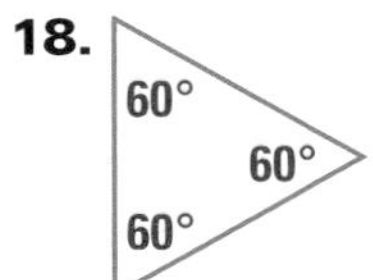

19.

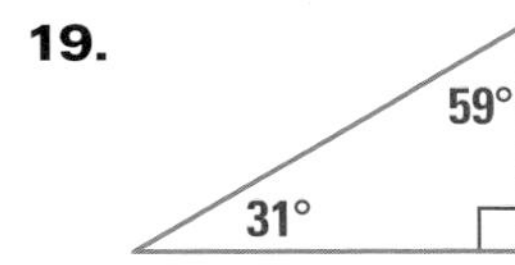

20.

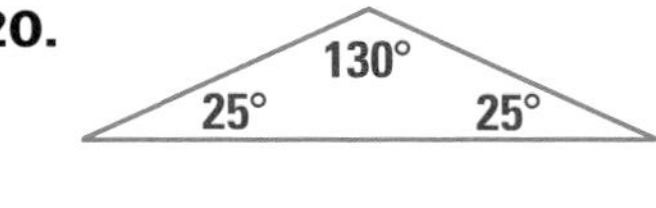

Find the volume and surface area of the prism or cylinder. (9.2–9.6)

21. 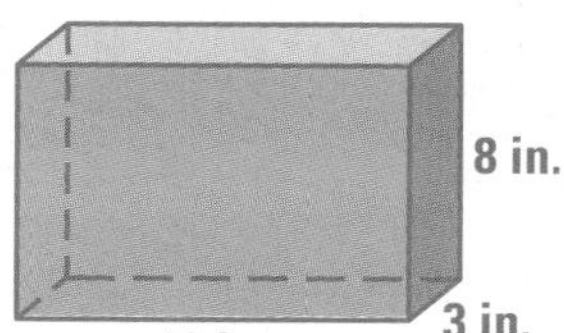

22. 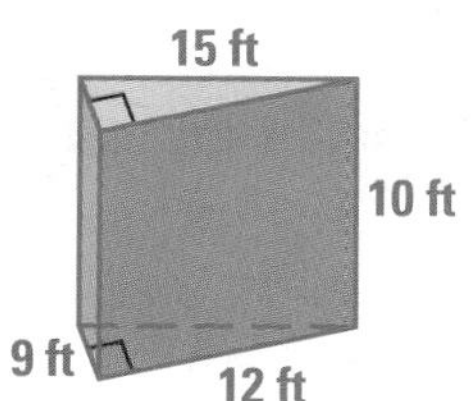

23. 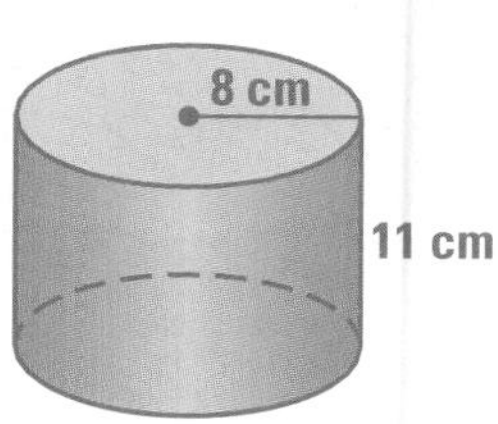

In Exercises 24 and 25, use the following scores from 10 bowling games.

131, 167, 155, 111, 132, 149, 131, 102, 148, 134

24. Find the mean, median, mode(s), and the range of the scores. (10.1)

25. Draw a box-and-whisker plot of the scores. (10.3)

26. Make a frequency table and a histogram for the data below. (10.2)

19, 32, 56, 21, 48, 11, 13, 24, 67, 45, 14,
60, 25, 22, 39, 20, 16, 18, 31, 27, 40

HOCKEY **In Exercises 27 and 28, use the table showing the number of points scored by a professional hockey team for several seasons.** (10.5)

Season	1994–95	1995–96	1996–97	1997–98	1998–99
Points	61	102	84	98	90

27. Make a line graph of the number of points scored.

28. What is another type of graph that would be appropriate for the data? Explain your reasoning.

29. PETS You are buying a Labrador retriever puppy. You can choose a male or a female. You can also choose a yellow lab, a chocolate lab, or a black lab. Draw a tree diagram of the gender and color possibilities. How many possibilities are there? (11.1)

In Exercises 30–33, you roll two number cubes. Find the probability of the event. (11.4 and 11.5)

30. The total is even.

31. The total is 7 or 11.

32. The total is greater than 4.

33. The total is greater than 1.

In Exercises 34–36, the spinner shown will be spun 120 times. (11.5 and 11.6)

34. Estimate the number of times the spinner will land on 8.

35. Estimate the number of times the spinner will land on a multiple of 3.

36. Estimate the number of times the spinner will land on a prime number.

12 equal sections

Chapter 10-11 Project

Conduct and Interpret a Survey

California Standards

- ▶ Compute the range, median, mean, and mode of a data set. (SP 1.1)
- ▶ Compare different samples of a population. (SP 2.1)
- ▶ Analyze data displays. (SP 2.3)

Materials

- pencil
- paper
- graph paper (optional)

OBJECTIVE **Conduct and interpret a survey.**

INVESTIGATION

Work with 1–3 classmates. Together you will survey at least 40 students and adults. Then you will analyze the data, comparing the student responses with the adult responses.

1. Choose three survey topics from the list.

About how much time do you spend each week

- *sleeping?*
- *getting ready for school or work?*
- *at school or work?*
- *doing homework or working at home?*
- *watching television?*
- *reading?*
- *working or playing outside?*
- *on the computer?*
- *exercising or playing a sport?*

2. Survey at least 20 students and 20 adults. Record your data.

3. Find the range, the mean, the median, and the mode of the data collected from the students.

4. Find the range, the mean, the median, and the mode of the data collected from the adults.

5. With your group, choose the most appropriate graph or plot for displaying the results of your survey. The graph or plot you choose should clearly show the comparison between student and adult responses.

PRESENT YOUR RESULTS

Prepare a report about the results of your survey. Include the following:

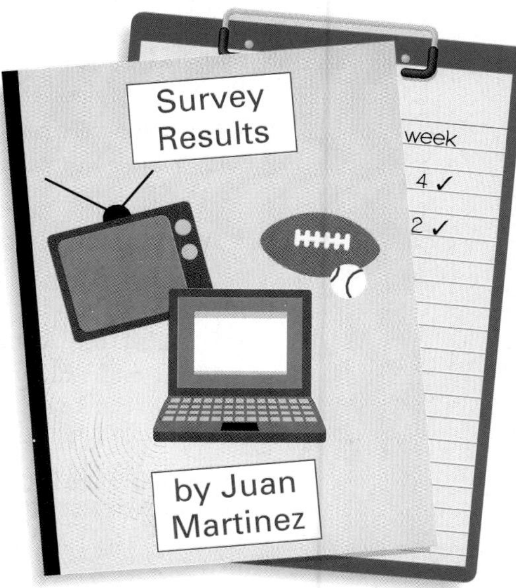

- A list of the survey questions.
- The data your group collected.
- Your calculations of the range, the mean, the median, and the mode.
- Your graph or plot.
- Justify your choice of graph or plot. Explain why you think your choice is the most appropriate method for displaying the data.
- Analyze the data. For example, compare the responses of the students with those of the adults. How were they similar? How were they different? Can you explain the differences?

EXTENSION

6. Repeat the survey with 20 different students. Use the same questions, but do not survey any of the students you surveyed the first time.

7. Find the range, the mean, the median, and the mode of the data. Make a graph.

8. Compare the results from the first group of students with the results from the second group of students. How are they alike? How are they different? Why?

9. Can you generalize your findings to all students in the nation? In your state? In your school? Justify your answers with an explanation of what, if anything, makes your sample similar to or different from the general population.

Contents of Student Resources

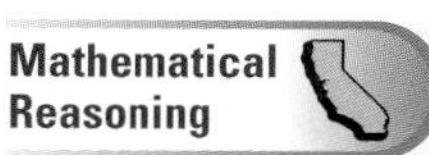

Problem Solving: Identifying and Extending Patterns   Grade 5, MR 1.1

EXAMPLE **Describe the pattern. List the next three numbers you expect to find in the sequence.**

3, 12, 48, 192, **?** , **?** , **?** , . . .

SOLUTION Follow the problem solving plan (see page 3) to find the pattern and use it to find the next three numbers.

UNDERSTAND THE PROBLEM You need to look for a relationship between the consecutive numbers in the sequence to help you see the pattern.

MAKE A PLAN Try comparing consecutive numbers by subtracting or dividing. See if you get the same result each time.

SOLVE THE PROBLEM Division shows that each number after the first is four times the previous number. To find the next three numbers, continue multiplying by four.

$4 \times 3 = 12$ $4 \times 12 = 48$ $4 \times 48 = 192$

$4 \times 192 = 768$ $4 \times 768 = 3072$ $4 \times 3072 = 12{,}288$

LOOK BACK Check your answer by dividing each number after the first by the preceding number. The result is always 4.

EXAMPLE **Describe the pattern. List the next four letters you expect to find in the sequence.**

A, Z, B, Y, **?** , **?** , **?** , **?** , . . .

SOLUTION The first and third letters are the first two letters of the alphabet in ascending order. Continue this pattern for the fifth and seventh letters.

The second and fourth letters are the last two letters of the alphabet in descending order. Continue this pattern for the sixth and eighth letters.

The next four letters in the sequence are: C, X, D, W.

Practice

Describe the pattern. List the next three numbers or letters you expect to find in the sequence.

1. 1, 3, 5, 7, **?** , **?** , **?** , . . .

2. 5, 15, 45, 135, **?** , **?** , **?** , . . .

3. 1, 2, 3, 5, 8, **?** , **?** , **?** , . . .

4. $\frac{1}{2}, \frac{1}{4}, \frac{1}{8}, \frac{1}{16},$ **?** , **?** , **?** , . . .

5. A, D, G, J, **?** , **?** , **?** , . . .

6. Z, X, V, T, **?** , **?** , **?** , . . .

7. A, N, B, O, **?** , **?** , **?** , . . .

8. B, C, E, F, H, **?** , **?** , **?** , . . .

PROBLEM SOLVING: USING A TABLE OR A GRAPH

A set of data is easier to understand when it is organized in a table or a graph.

EXAMPLE **Use the following information about public high schools in the United States. Make a table of the data. Then use the table to determine which type of school had the greatest increase in CD-ROM computers from 1992 to 1995 and from 1995 to 1997.**

- In 1992 there were 1,897 CD-ROM computers in elementary schools, 1,231 in middle schools, and 2,543 in high schools.
- In 1995 elementary schools had 22,305 CD-ROM computers, middle schools had 7,501 CD-ROM computers, and high schools had 10,354 CD-ROM computers.
- In 1997 there were 26,377 CD-ROM computers in elementary schools, 8,410 in middle schools, and 11,140 in high schools.

SOLUTION There are three different types of schools and three different years of data. You could use the different years as the column heads of a table and the types of schools as the row heads. This is shown in the table at the right.

Type of school	1992	1995	1997
Elementary schools			
Middle schools			
High schools			

Now, include the data to complete your table. Use the data to estimate the increases in CD-ROM computers for each type of school.

Type of school	1992	1995	1997
Elementary schools	1,897	22,305	26,377
Middle schools	1,231	7,501	8,410
High schools	2,543	10,354	11,140

ANSWER ▶ Elementary schools had the greatest increase in CD-ROM computers from 1992 to 1995 (an increase of about 20,000) and from 1995 to 1997 (an increase of about 4,000).

Practice

In Exercises 1–4, use the table, which shows the average daily high temperatures (in degrees Fahrenheit) for four months in three cities.

City	January	April	July	October
Acapulco, Mexico	87	87	89	89
Cairo, Egypt	65	83	96	86
Montreal, Canada	22	51	79	56

1. What was the average daily high temperature for Montreal in October?

2. Which city had the highest average daily temperature? In what month?

3. Which city had the lowest average daily temperature? In what month?

4. Which city had the most consistent temperatures for all four months?

In Exercises 5–8, use the following information about technology in public high schools in the United States.

- In 1997, 22,234 elementary schools had computers with modems, 7,417 middle schools had computers with modems, and 10,781 high schools had computers with modems.
- In 1997 the number of computer networks was 16,441 in elementary schools, 6,035 in middle schools, and 9,565 in high schools.
- In 1997 elementary schools had 6,001 satellite dishes, middle schools had 3,377 satellite dishes, and high schools had 6,769 satellite dishes.

5. Make a table of the data.

6. Which type of school had the most computers with modems?

7. Which type of school had the fewest satellite dishes?

8. Which type of school had over 10,000 more computer networks than satellite dishes?

EXAMPLE **One hundred adults were surveyed about the leisure activities in which they participate. Use the graph at the right to estimate the number of these adults who participate in each activity.** **(See page 564 for more about graphs.)**

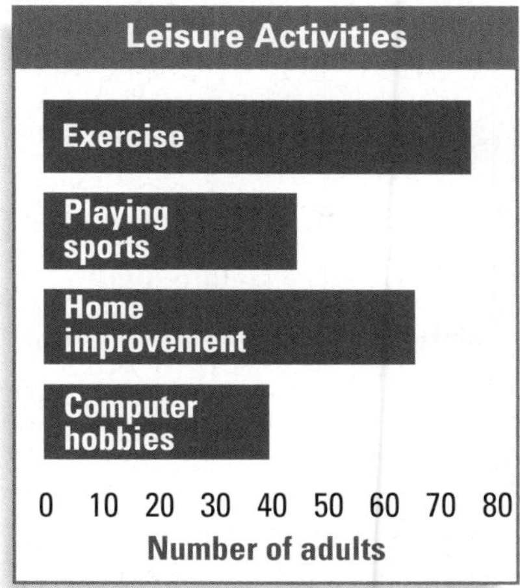

SOLUTION

The gap between grid lines represents 10 adults. Find the facts you need from the graph by estimating the lengths of the bars.

ANSWER ▶ About 76 adults exercise, and approximately 45 adults play sports. The graph also shows that approximately 66 adults work on home improvement activities and 40 adults have computer hobbies.

Practice

In Exercises 9–13, use the graph shown.

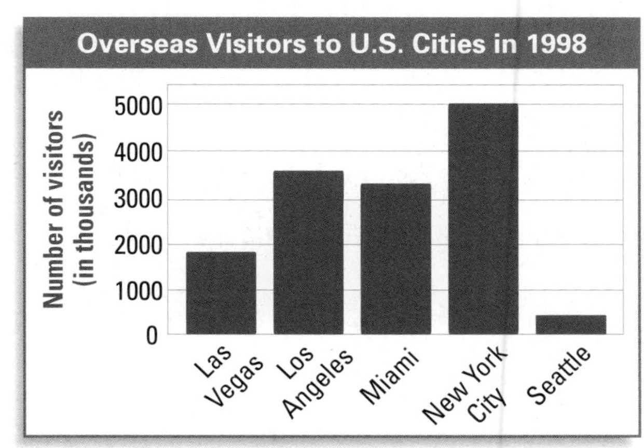

9. What does the gap between grid lines represent?

10. Which city had the greatest number of overseas visitors?

11. Which city had the fewest number of overseas visitors?

12. About how many fewer overseas visitors went to Las Vegas than Los Angeles?

13. Which city has about 10 times as many overseas visitors as Seattle?

PROBLEM SOLVING: BREAKING A PROBLEM INTO PARTS

Breaking a problem into simpler parts may make it easier to solve.

EXAMPLE **A bunch of bananas weighs 3 pounds and costs $1.68. Find the cost of a bunch that weighs 4 pounds.**

SOLUTION First you need to find the cost per pound.

$1.68 ÷ 3 pounds = $.56 per pound

Next, multiply the cost per pound by 4 pounds.

$.56 per pound × 4 pounds = $2.24

A bunch of bananas that weighs 4 pounds would cost $2.24.

EXAMPLE **Find the area of the shaded figure.** **(See page 562 for more about area.)**

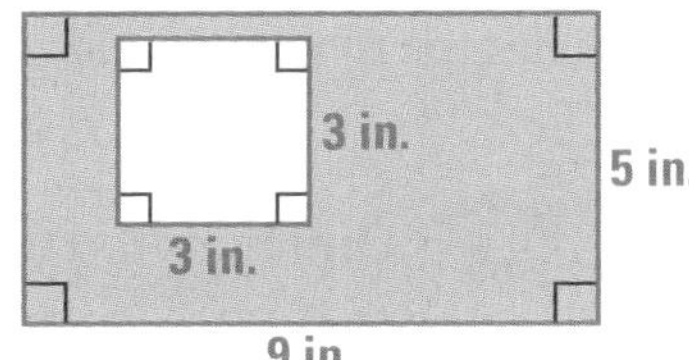

SOLUTION The area of the shaded figure is the difference of the areas of the rectangle and the square.

Square	**Rectangle**
Area = Length × Width	Area = Length × Width
= 3 × 3	= 9 × 5
= 9 square inches	= 45 square inches

ANSWER ▶ Area = 45 square inches − 9 square inches = 36 square inches

Practice

1. A square garden is enclosed by 64 meters of fencing. What is the area of the garden?
2. A plumber charges a basic service fee plus a labor charge for each hour of service. A 1 hour job costs $55, and a 2 hour job costs $70. Find the plumber's basic service fee.
3. Suppose you already saved $44 toward a bicycle that costs $140. If you can save $4 a week, how many weeks will it take you to save enough?
4. The perimeter of a rectangular yard is 140 feet, and the area of the yard is 1200 square feet. Find the length and the width of the yard.

Find the area of the shaded figure.

5.

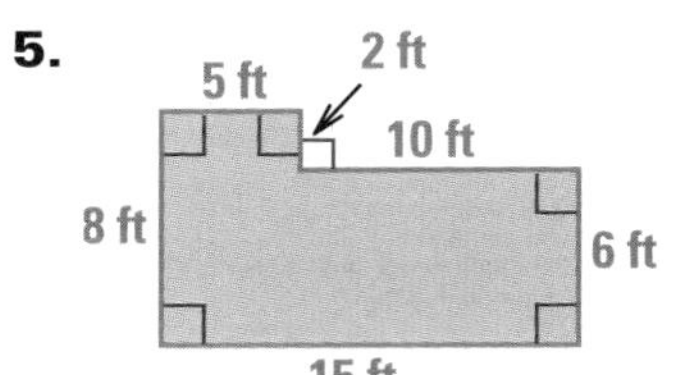

6.

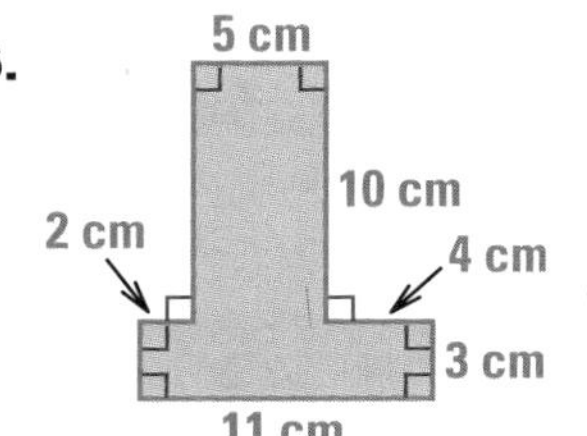

7.

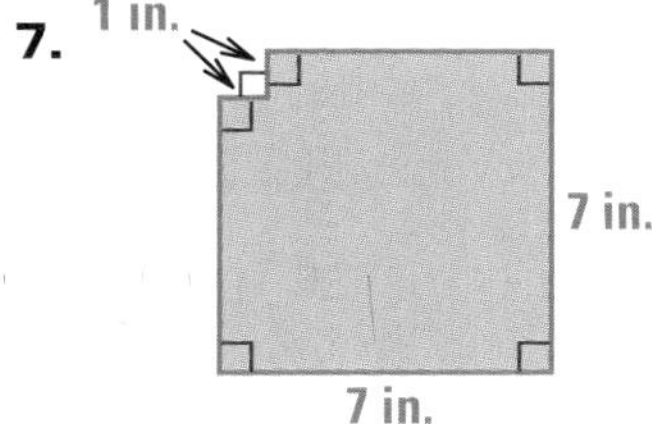

PROBLEM SOLVING: CHECKING REASONABLENESS

Check your answer to a problem by deciding if your answer is reasonable.

EXAMPLE **There are 75 students taking a bus trip to a museum. Each bus can hold 30 students. How many buses are needed?**

SOLUTION Sometimes the answer you get in a computation is not the answer to the problem. You calculate $75 \div 30 = 2.5$ buses. Since the number of buses must be a whole number, you need to round the calculated answer up.

ANSWER ▶ A total of 3 buses are needed.

EXAMPLE **A sweater costs $59.95 and is on sale for half off. Your friend says the sweater's sale price is $40. Is this answer reasonable?**

SOLUTION Use mental math. Since $59.95 is just a little less than $60, half of $59.95 should be just a little less than $30.

ANSWER ▶ The price your friend told you is too high.

EXAMPLE **Your science grade is based on 4 tests, which are 100 points each. To earn an "A," you need a total of 360 points. Your first three test scores are 89, 85, and 92. You estimate that you need to score 110 points on the next test to get an "A." Is this reasonable?**

SOLUTION Each test is 100 points. You cannot score 110 points on the test. Use estimation. The test scores 89, 85, and 92 cluster around 90.

Points earned so far: $3 \times 90 = 270$

Points needed to earn an "A": $360 - 270 = 90$

ANSWER ▶ Since the first two test scores are both less than 90, a more reasonable estimate would be about 95 points on the next test to get an "A."

Practice

1. Paperback books are on sale at a bookstore for $4 each. How many paperback books can you buy with $15?

Use mental math or estimation to choose the answer that is reasonable.

2. Three roommates split their monthly rent evenly. If the rent is $1020 per month, how much is each person's share?

A. $3060 **B.** $340 **C.** $1020

3. At a price of $1.28 each, how much will 8 cans of dog food cost?

A. $1.28 **B.** $.16 **C.** $10.24

4. A bakery sells rolls for $3.40 per dozen. How much will 6 dozen rolls cost?

A. $.57 **B.** $3.40 **C.** $20.40

USING A NUMBER LINE

Every point on a number line is associated with a number. Plotting the point that corresponds to a number is called *graphing the number*. Points that correspond to whole numbers are labeled with evenly spaced tick marks.

EXAMPLE **Order the following whole numbers from least to greatest: 10, 4, 36, 19, 1, and 21.**

SOLUTION Begin by graphing all six numbers on the same number line.

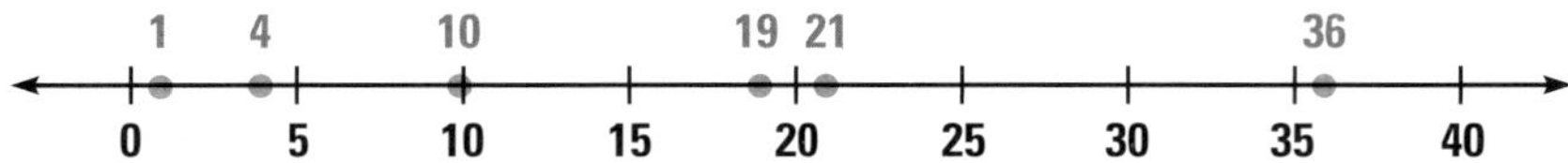

ANSWER ▶ From the relative positions of the graphed numbers, you can see that the correct order of the whole numbers from least to greatest is 1, 4, 10, 19, 21, and 36.

EXAMPLE **Use a number line to compare the numbers.**

a. 12 and 2 **b.** 20 and 32 **c.** 14 and 41

SOLUTION Begin by graphing the numbers on a number line.

a.

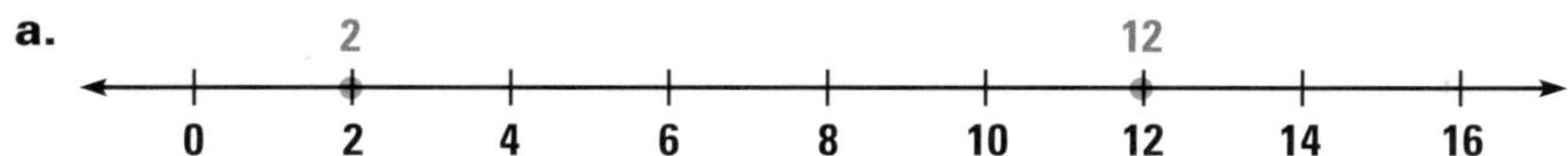

Remember: < means *is less than* and > means *is greater than*. Because 12 is to the right of 2, 12 is greater. You can write 12 > 2 or 2 < 12.

b.

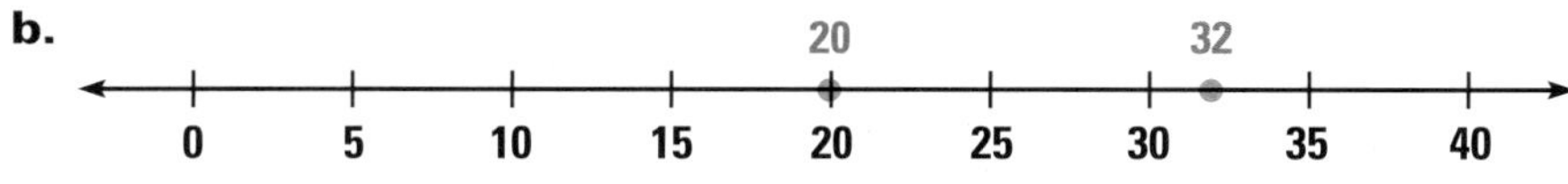

20 is less than 32, or 20 < 32.

c.

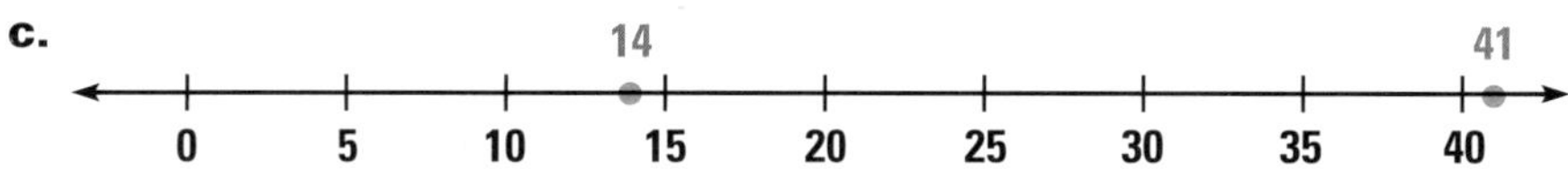

14 is less than 41, or 14 < 41.

Practice

Use a number line to order the numbers from least to greatest.

1. 3, 0, 8, 4, 16, and 1 **2.** 10, 5, 6, 12, 7, and 2 **3.** 18, 26, 13, 31, 7, and 15

4. 9, 29, 19, 5, 14, and 0 **5.** 12, 3, 7, 6, 17, and 21 **6.** 22, 25, 14, 9, 11, and 23

Use a number line to compare the numbers.

7. 30 and 13 **8.** 0 and 14 **9.** 8 and 10 **10.** 14 and 19

11. 2 and 7 **12.** 2 and 1 **13.** 19 and 8 **14.** 26 and 17

You can also use a number line to add and subtract numbers.

To add two whole numbers on a number line:

1. Start at 0. Move to the right to locate the first number.
2. Add the second number (the number after the "plus" sign). Because you are adding the numbers, you move that many more places to the right.
3. The sum of the two numbers is the final position on the number line.

EXAMPLE **Use a number line to find the sum of the two numbers.**

a. $5 + 2$

Start at 0. Move 5 units to the *right*. Then move 2 more units to the *right*.

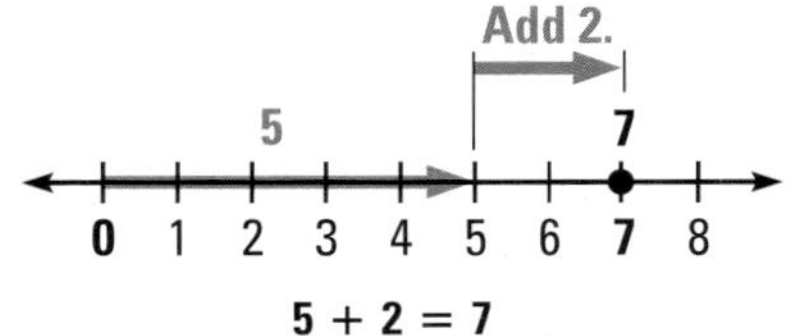

b. $9 + 3$

Start at 0. Move 9 units to the *right*. Then move 3 more units to the *right*.

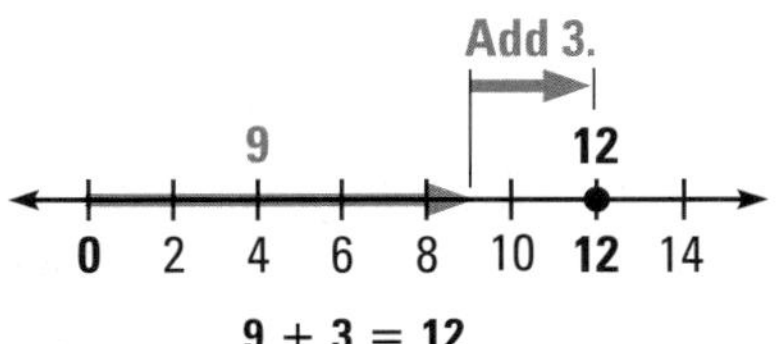

To subtract two whole numbers on a number line:

1. Start at 0. Move to the right to locate the first number.
2. Subtract the second number (the number after the "minus" sign). Because you are subtracting the numbers, you move that many places to the *left*.
3. The difference of the two numbers is the final position on the number line.

EXAMPLE **Use a number line to find the difference of the two numbers.**

a. $9 - 5$

Start at 0. Move 9 units to the *right*. Then move 5 units to the *left*.

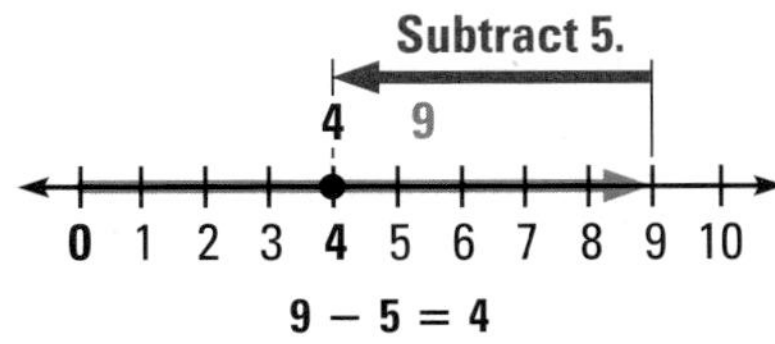

b. $16 - 12$

Start at 0. Move 16 units to the *right*. Then move 12 units to the *left*.

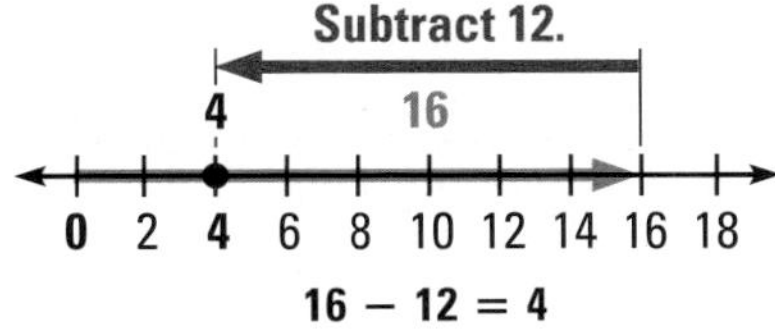

Practice

Use a number line to add or subtract the numbers.

15. $3 + 10$ **16.** $4 + 8$ **17.** $13 + 9$ **18.** $22 + 16$

19. $26 + 19$ **20.** $21 + 12$ **21.** $19 + 19$ **22.** $15 + 7$

23. $15 - 3$ **24.** $20 - 18$ **25.** $17 - 9$ **26.** $11 - 7$

27. $36 - 17$ **28.** $27 - 23$ **29.** $30 - 11$ **30.** $19 - 8$

Number Sense

OPERATIONS WITH WHOLE NUMBERS

GRADE 5, NS 1.1

Whole numbers are added and subtracted one place value at a time. Regrouping between place values is done as needed.

EXAMPLE **Find the sum 259 + 47.**

SOLUTION Line up the ones, tens, and hundreds in columns.

❶ Add the ones. Regroup 16 ones as 1 ten and 6 ones.

$$\begin{array}{r} \scriptstyle 1 \\ 259 \\ +\ \ 47 \\ \hline 6 \end{array}$$

❷ Add the tens. Regroup 10 tens as 1 hundred.

$$\begin{array}{r} \scriptstyle 11\ \\ 259 \\ +\ \ 47 \\ \hline 06 \end{array}$$

❸ Add the hundreds.

$$\begin{array}{r} \scriptstyle 11\ \\ 259 \\ +\ \ 47 \\ \hline 306 \end{array}$$

EXAMPLE **Find the difference 502 − 384.**

SOLUTION Line up the ones, tens, and hundreds in columns.

❶ Start with the ones. There are not enough ones to subtract 4.

$$\begin{array}{r} 502 \\ -\ 384 \\ \hline \end{array}$$

❷ There are no tens, so regroup 1 hundred as 9 tens and 10 ones.

$$\begin{array}{r} \scriptstyle 9\ \ \ \ \\ \scriptstyle 4\ \cancel{10}\ 12 \\ \cancel{5}\cancel{0}\cancel{2} \\ -\ 384 \\ \hline \end{array}$$

❸ Now you can subtract.

$$\begin{array}{r} \scriptstyle 9\ \ \ \ \\ \scriptstyle 4\ \cancel{10}\ 12 \\ \cancel{5}\cancel{0}\cancel{2} \\ -\ 384 \\ \hline 118 \end{array}$$

Because addition and subtraction are *inverse operations*, you can check your answer by adding: 384 + 118 = 502.

Practice

In Exercises 1–10, find the sum or difference.

1. $\begin{array}{r} 63 \\ +\ 51 \\ \hline \end{array}$ **2.** $\begin{array}{r} 78 \\ +\ 26 \\ \hline \end{array}$ **3.** $\begin{array}{r} 61 \\ +\ 27 \\ \hline \end{array}$ **4.** $\begin{array}{r} 309 \\ +\ 192 \\ \hline \end{array}$ **5.** $\begin{array}{r} 5611 \\ +\ \ 488 \\ \hline \end{array}$

6. $\begin{array}{r} 28 \\ -\ 13 \\ \hline \end{array}$ **7.** $\begin{array}{r} 71 \\ -\ 26 \\ \hline \end{array}$ **8.** $\begin{array}{r} 94 \\ -\ 58 \\ \hline \end{array}$ **9.** $\begin{array}{r} 903 \\ -\ 712 \\ \hline \end{array}$ **10.** $\begin{array}{r} 824 \\ -\ 532 \\ \hline \end{array}$

11. The distance between Oak Grove and Rockville is 132 miles. The distance between Rockville and Salem is 91 miles. If you drive through Rockville, how many miles is it between Oak Grove and Salem?

12. A cheetah can run about 70 miles per hour. A man can run about 28 miles per hour. How much faster is the cheetah than the man?

13. At 9:00 A.M., the temperature was 43° Fahrenheit. By noon, it had warmed up 14° more. What was the temperature at noon?

Whole numbers are multiplied by multiplying the entire first number by each place value of the second number, then adding the partial products.

EXAMPLE **Find the product 978 × 405.**

SOLUTION Line up the ones, tens, and hundreds in columns.

❶ Multiply by the ones digit.

$$\begin{array}{r} {\scriptstyle 34} \\ 978 \\ \times\ 405 \\ \hline \mathbf{4890} \end{array}$$

❷ Since 405 has no tens, multiply by the hundreds digit. Start the partial product in the hundreds place.

$$\begin{array}{r} {\scriptstyle 33} \\ 978 \\ \times\ 405 \\ \hline 4890 \\ \mathbf{3912} \end{array}$$

❸ Add the partial products.

$$\begin{array}{r} 978 \\ \times\ 405 \\ \hline 4890 \\ 3912 \\ \hline \mathbf{396{,}090} \end{array}$$

A division problem can be written several ways.

12 divided by 4 $\qquad 12 \div 4 \qquad 4\overline{)12} \qquad \frac{12}{4}$

The answer, called the *quotient*, is 3 because multiplication and division are *inverse operations* and $3 \times 4 = 12$.

EXAMPLE **Find the quotient.** **a.** $24 \div 8$ **b.** $7\overline{)35}$ **c.** $\frac{54}{6}$

SOLUTION

To find:	You think:	In words:	Answer:
a. $24 \div 8$	$8 \times$ **?** $= 24$	8 times what number equals 24?	3
b. $7\overline{)35}$	$7 \times$ **?** $= 35$	7 times what number equals 35?	5
c. $\frac{54}{6}$	$6 \times$ **?** $= 54$	6 times what number equals 54?	9

Practice

In Exercises 14–23, find the product or quotient.

14. 41×8 **15.** 42×17 **16.** 557×16 **17.** 245×83 **18.** 468×163

19. $63 \div 7$ **20.** $30 \div 6$ **21.** $9\overline{)81}$ **22.** $8\overline{)56}$ **23.** $\frac{18}{3}$

24. Every week, you put $9 into a savings account. How much money (not including interest) will you have in your savings account after 17 weeks?

25. A deck of 52 cards is dealt to 4 people. How many cards does each person receive?

26. Your father borrowed $5000 from the credit union to buy a used car. He has agreed to pay the credit union $134 each month for 48 months. What is the total amount he will have paid at the end of the 48 month period?

LONG DIVISION

GRADE 5, NS 2.2

SKILLS REVIEW

Long division is a process that can be used to find the quotient of two numbers.

EXAMPLE **Find 319 ÷ 7.**

SOLUTION

❶ Use the divisor and the dividend to decide where to write the first digit in the quotient.

$$\begin{array}{r} 4 \\ 7\overline{)319} \end{array}$$

divisor dividend

Estimate:

$$\begin{array}{r} 40 \\ 7\overline{)280} \end{array}$$

❷ Multiply 4 and 7. Subtract 28 from 31. Be sure the difference is less than the divisor. In this case 3 < 7.

$$\begin{array}{r} 4 \\ 7\overline{)319} \\ -\ 28 \\ \hline 3 \end{array}$$

❸ Bring down the next digit, 9. Divide 39 by 7. Multiply 5 and 7. Subtract 35 from 39.

$$\begin{array}{r} 45 \\ 7\overline{)319} \\ -\ 28 \\ \hline 39 \\ -\ 35 \\ \hline 4 \end{array}$$

45 ← **quotient**; 4 ← **remainder**

❹ Write the remainder next to the quotient.

$$\begin{array}{r} 45\ \text{R4} \\ 7\overline{)319} \\ -\ 28 \\ \hline 39 \\ -\ 35 \\ \hline 4 \end{array}$$

ANSWER ▶ The quotient is 45 with a remainder of 4.

EXAMPLE

The first digit is in the ones place.

$$\begin{array}{r} 8\ \text{R47} \\ 65\overline{)567} \\ -\ 520 \\ \hline 47 \end{array}$$

EXAMPLE

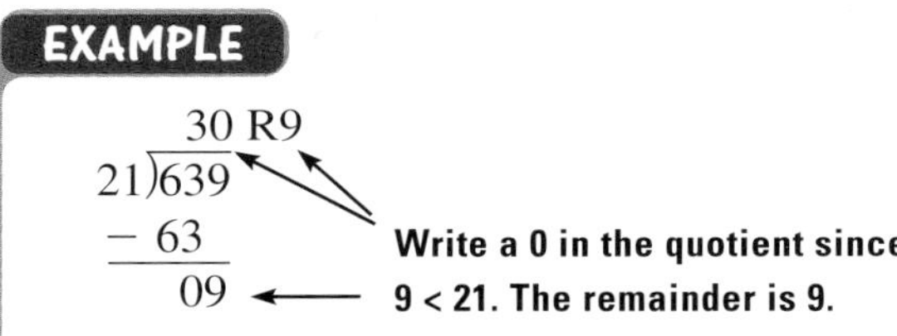

$$\begin{array}{r} 30\ \text{R9} \\ 21\overline{)639} \\ -\ 63 \\ \hline 09 \end{array}$$

Write a 0 in the quotient since 9 < 21. The remainder is 9.

To check a division problem, multiply the quotient by the divisor, then add the remainder. The result should equal the dividend.

Practice

Describe and correct the error.

1.

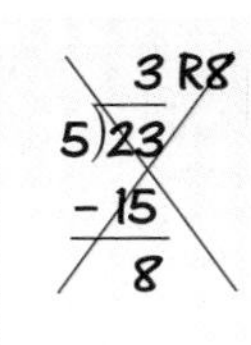

2.

$$\begin{array}{r} 15\ \text{R3} \\ 4\overline{)603} \\ -\ 4 \\ \hline 23 \\ -\ 20 \\ \hline 3 \end{array}$$

3.

$$\begin{array}{r} 5\ \text{R3} \\ 6\overline{)27} \\ -\ 30 \\ \hline 3 \end{array}$$

4.

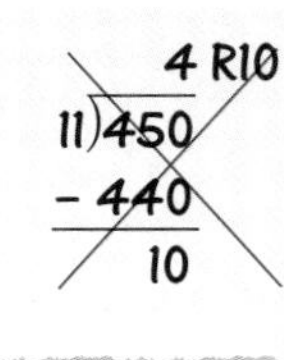

Divide.

5. $7\overline{)89}$ **6.** $4\overline{)205}$ **7.** $6\overline{)515}$ **8.** $4\overline{)339}$

9. $5\overline{)2314}$ **10.** $16\overline{)120}$ **11.** $28\overline{)540}$ **12.** $19\overline{)3621}$

13. $11\overline{)246}$ **14.** $21\overline{)2010}$ **15.** $5\overline{)4615}$ **16.** $17\overline{)5280}$

Divisibility Tests

A whole number is *divisible* by another whole number if the second number is a factor of the first. For example, $2 \times 5 = 10$, so 10 is divisible by 2 and 5.

You can write any whole number in expanded form and use the fact that any multiple of 10 or a power of 10 is divisible by 2 or 5.

EXAMPLE **Determine whether the number is divisible by 2.**

a. 54 **b.** 239

Solution

a. 54 can be written in expanded form as $50 + 4 = (5 \times 10) + 4$.

5×10 is a multiple of 10, so 50 is divisible by 2.

$4 \div 2 = 2$, so 4 is divisible by 2.

ANSWER ▶ Both terms of 54 written in expanded form are divisible by 2, so 54 is divisible by 2.

b. 239 can be written as $200 + 30 + 9 = (2 \times 100) + (3 \times 10) + 9$.

2×100 is a multiple of a power of 10, so 200 is divisible by 2.

3×10 is a multiple of 10, so 30 is divisible by 2.

$9 \div 2 = 4$ R1, so 9 is not divisible by 2.

ANSWER ▶ The units digit of 239 is not divisible by 2, so 239 is not divisible by 2.

EXAMPLE **Determine whether the number is divisible by 5.**

a. 63 **b.** 235

Solution

a. 63 can be written in expanded form as $60 + 3 = (6 \times 10) + 3$.

6×10 is a multiple of 10, so 60 is divisible by 5.

$3 \div 5 = 0$ R3, so 3 is not divisible by 5.

ANSWER ▶ The units digit of 63 is not divisible by 5, so 63 is not divisible by 5.

b. 235 can be written as $200 + 30 + 5 = (2 \times 100) + (3 \times 10) + 5$.

2×100 is a multiple of a power of 10, so 200 is divisible by 5.

3×10 is a multiple of 10, so 30 is divisible by 5.

$5 \div 5 = 1$, so 5 is divisible by 5.

ANSWER ▶ All three terms of 235 written in expanded form are divisible by 5, so 235 is divisible by 5.

Because any multiple of 10 or a power of 10 is divisible by both 2 and 5, you need to look only at the units digit of a number to determine whether the number is divisible by 2 or 5. Numbers whose units digit is even (0, 2, 4, 6, or 8) are divisible by 2. Numbers whose units digit is 0 or 5 are divisible by 5.

SKILLS REVIEW

EXAMPLE **Determine whether the number is divisible by 3.**

a. 52 **b.** 615

SOLUTION

a. The number 52 can be written as follows:

$$\begin{aligned} 52 &= (5 \times 10) + 2 \\ &= 5 \times (9 + 1) + 2 \\ &= (5 \times 9) + (5 \times 1) + 2 \\ &= (5 \times 9) + 5 + 2 \end{aligned}$$

ANSWER ▶ 9 is divisible by 3, so the term 5×9 is also divisible by 3. The sum of the remaining numbers, $5 + 2 = 7$, is not divisible by 3. So, the number 52 is not divisible by 3.

b. The number 615 can be written as follows:

$$\begin{aligned} 615 &= (6 \times 100) + (1 \times 10) + 5 \\ &= 6 \times (99 + 1) + 1 \times (9 + 1) + 5 \\ &= (6 \times 99) + (6 \times 1) + (1 \times 9) + (1 \times 1) + 5 \\ &= (6 \times 99) + (1 \times 9) + 6 + 1 + 5 \end{aligned}$$

ANSWER ▶ 99 and 9 are both divisible by 3, so the terms 6×99 and 1×9 are also divisible by 3. The sum of the remaining numbers, $6 + 1 + 5 = 12$, is divisible by 3. So, 615 is divisible by 3.

Notice in the example above that the remaining numbers in each case are the same as the digits in the original numbers.

Sum of the digits of 52: $5 + 2 = 7$. 52 is not divisible by 3.

Sum of the digits of 615: $6 + 1 + 5 = 12$. 615 is divisible by 3.

EXAMPLE **Is the number 693,495 divisible by 2, 3, and 5?**

SOLUTION The units digit of the number is not even, so it is not divisible by 2.

The sum of the digits is $6 + 9 + 3 + 4 + 9 + 5 = 36$, and 36 is divisible by 3. The number is divisible by 3.

The units digit of the number is 5. The number is divisible by 5.

Practice

1. In your own words, write the divisibility tests for 2, 3, and 5.

In Exercises 2–11, determine whether the number is divisible by 2, 3, and 5.

2. 27 **3.** 91 **4.** 438 **5.** 164 **6.** 940

7. 810 **8.** 2775 **9.** 3805 **10.** 27,854 **11.** 306,920

12. Find the units digit of 816 **?** so that the number is divisible by 2 and 5.

13. Find the units digit of 782 **?** so that the number is divisible by 2 and 3.

CONVERTING UNITS OF MEASUREMENT

To convert from one unit of measurement to another, multiply the given unit by an appropriate conversion fraction equal to 1.

EXAMPLE **Write a conversion fraction for 1 foot = 12 inches and use it to convert 5 feet to inches.**

SOLUTION

$1 \text{ foot} = 12 \text{ inches}$ Write original equation.

$\frac{1 \cancel{\text{foot}}}{1 \cancel{\text{foot}}} = \frac{12 \text{ inches}}{1 \text{ foot}}$ Divide each side by 1 foot.

$1 = \frac{12 \text{ inches}}{1 \text{ foot}}$ Fraction equal to 1

Because the fraction $\frac{12 \text{ inches}}{1 \text{ foot}}$ is equal to 1, you can multiply by this fraction without changing the given measurement.

$$5 \cancel{\text{feet}} \times \frac{12 \text{ inches}}{1 \cancel{\text{foot}}} = 5 \times 12 \text{ inches} = 60 \text{ inches}$$

ANSWER ▶ So, 5 feet is equal to 60 inches.

EXAMPLE **Write a conversion fraction for 1 yard = 36 inches and use it to convert 3 yards to inches.**

SOLUTION

$1 \text{ yard} = 36 \text{ inches}$ Write original equation.

$\frac{1 \cancel{\text{yard}}}{1 \cancel{\text{yard}}} = \frac{36 \text{ inches}}{1 \text{ yard}}$ Divide each side by 1 yard.

$1 = \frac{36 \text{ inches}}{1 \text{ yard}}$ Fraction equal to 1

Use the fraction to convert 3 yards to inches.

$$3 \cancel{\text{yards}} \times \frac{36 \text{ inches}}{1 \cancel{\text{yard}}} = 3 \times 36 \text{ inches} = 108 \text{ inches}$$

ANSWER ▶ So, 3 yards is equal to 108 inches.

Practice

1. a. Write a conversion fraction for converting inches to feet.

b. Use the conversion fraction from part (a) to find the number of feet in 96 inches.

2. a. Write a conversion fraction for converting inches to yards.

b. Use the conversion fraction from part (a) to find the number of yards in 216 inches.

3. Use the fact that 1 pound = 16 ounces to find the number of ounces in 8 pounds.

4. Use the fact that 1 mile = 1760 yards to find the number of yards in 4 miles.

SQUARES AND RECTANGLES

Measurement involves a comparison with a unit that is considered a standard.

When you measure objects you need to know whether to use units for length, area, or volume. Here you will consider *perimeters* and *areas* of *squares* and *rectangles*. Remember that a rectangle is a four-sided figure having opposite sides of equal length and four right angles. A square is a rectangle whose four sides all have the same length.

1
Unit length

Unit square

The *perimeter* of a figure is determined by the number of unit lengths that fit around the figure. Perimeter is measured in linear units such as inches, feet, or centimeters.

EXAMPLE **Find the perimeter.**

a. 

b. 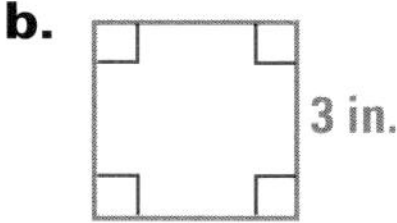

SOLUTION

a. Add the side lengths:
$8 + 5 + 8 + 5 = 26$ centimeters

b. Add the side lengths:
$3 + 3 + 3 + 3 = 12$ inches

The *area* of a figure is determined by the number of unit squares needed to cover the figure (where some squares might have to be cut to fit). Area is measured in square units such as square inches, square feet, or square centimeters.

EXAMPLE **Find the area of the rectangle shown.**

SOLUTION By definition, the area of the rectangle is the number of unit squares needed to cover the rectangle. By counting, you see that the rectangle is covered by 18 unit squares. So, the rectangle has an area of 18 square units.

Notice that the area of the rectangle in the example above is $6 \times 3 = 18$, the product of the length and width of the rectangle. In general, this is true for any rectangle.

Area of rectangle = Length × Width

Practice

Find the perimeter and the area of the figure.

1.  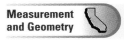

2. 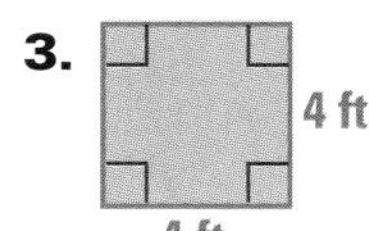

3.
4 ft
4 ft

4. 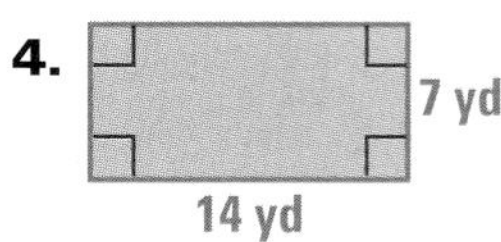

Sketch and label the figure described. Then find its perimeter and area.

5. A square with sides measuring 5 cm

6. A square with sides measuring 12 ft

7. A rectangle with a length of 9 cm and a width of 3 cm

8. A rectangle with a length of 5 in. and a width of 4 in.

Angles and Their Measures

A protractor is a geometric tool used to measure and draw angles. It has tick marks one degree (1°) apart along its outer edge. Protractors have two scales: the outer scale lists degree measures in a clockwise direction, and the inner scale lists degree measures in a counterclockwise direction.

EXAMPLE **Measure the angle shown.**

Solution

Place the protractor's center mark at the point where the two lines meet to form the angle.

Line up the protractor's 0° line with one side of the angle.

Read the measure of the protractor where the other side crosses it. The measure of the angle is 60°.

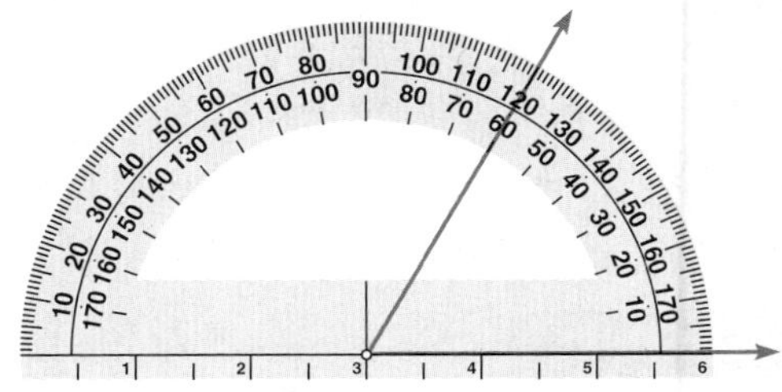

Read the inner scale since you are measuring counterclockwise.

EXAMPLE **Draw an angle whose measure is 120°.**

Solution

Draw a ray. Mark the endpoint.

Place the protractor's center mark at the endpoint of the ray.

Line up the protractor's 0° line with the ray.

Mark a point at 120°.

Draw another ray from the endpoint of the first ray through the marked point.

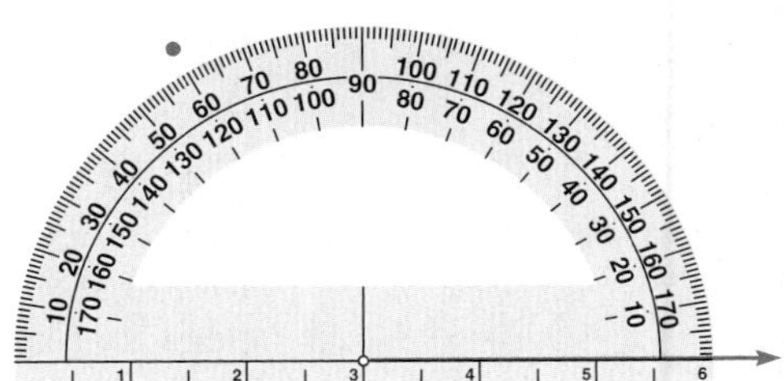

Practice

Use a protractor to measure the angle.

1. 

2. 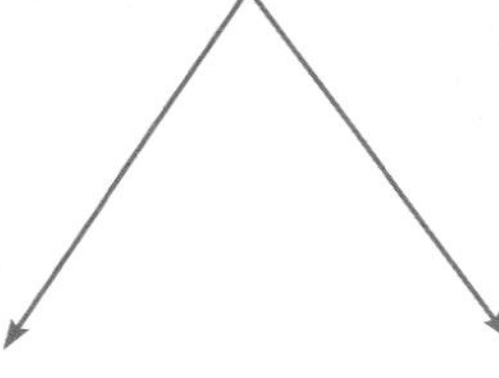

3. 

4. 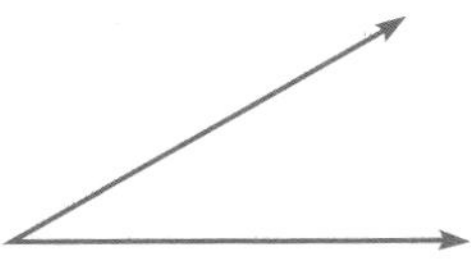

Use a protractor to draw an angle with the given measure.

5. 20° **6.** 55° **7.** 75° **8.** 165°

9. 35° **10.** 140° **11.** 80° **12.** 100°

READING AND DRAWING A BAR GRAPH

A *bar graph* is a type of graph in which the lengths of the bars are used to represent and compare data. There are several guidelines for drawing a bar graph.

- The numbers on the side of a bar graph are the scale. Choose a scale that is appropriate for the data. Label the scale to explain what the numbers represent.
- Use a ruler to draw evenly spaced grid lines.
- Draw the bars. Each bar should have the same width.
- Write a title for the graph.

EXAMPLE **One hundred adults in your city were surveyed. The table shows the number of adults who participate in lawn and garden activities. Draw a bar graph of the data.**

Number of Adults who Participate in Lawn and Garden Activities	
Lawn care	47
Flower gardening	37
Vegetable gardening	26
Herb gardening	9
Water gardening	4

SOLUTION

Choose and label a scale. The greatest number in the table is 47, so the scale should extend from 0 to 50. Use increments of 5.

Draw the bars. Use the scale to draw a bar of length 47 for *Lawn care*. Label the bar. Draw and label four more bars for the other categories.

Write a title.

Review all the information in your bar graph to check for errors.

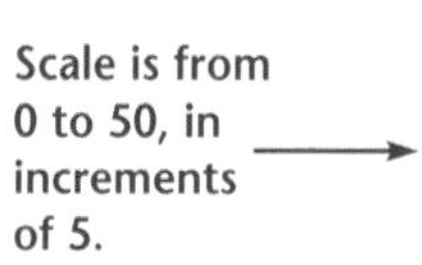

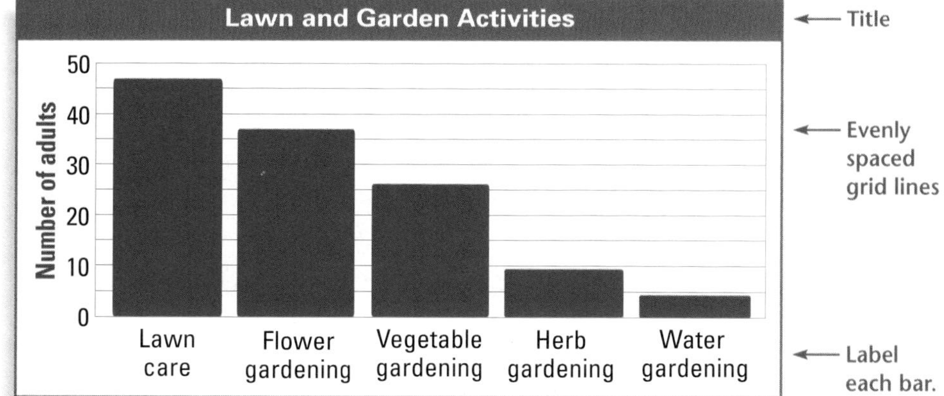

Practice

In Exercises 1 and 2, use the table, which shows the most popular vacation places for Americans in 1998.

Country	Mexico	Canada	United Kingdom	France	Germany
Number of visitors (in thousands)	18,338	14,880	3,645	2,399	1,892

1. What scale should you use? What increments would you use for the scale?

2. Draw a bar graph of the data.

READING AND DRAWING A DOUBLE BAR GRAPH

A *double bar graph* is a graph that uses pairs of bars (usually of different colors) to compare two data sets. A double bar graph shows how quantities in the same category compare with each other. A *legend* is used to identify the two sets.

EXAMPLE **The table at the right shows the number of adults who participated in lawn and garden activities for 1996 and 2000. Draw a double bar graph to determine the activity that had the most change.**

Number of Adults who Participate in Lawn and Garden Activities		
Activity	**1996**	**2000**
Lawn care	54	47
Flower gardening	39	37
Vegetable gardening	31	26
Herb gardening	7	9
Water gardening	0	4

SOLUTION

Choose and label a scale. The greatest number in the table is 54, so the scale should extend from 0 to 60. Use increments of 5.

Draw the bars. Use a different color for each year's data. In 1996, the number for *Lawn care* is 54. In 2000, the number for *Lawn care* is 47. Draw pairs of bars for these numbers. Use the table to complete the graph.

Write a title.

Write a legend to explain the bars.

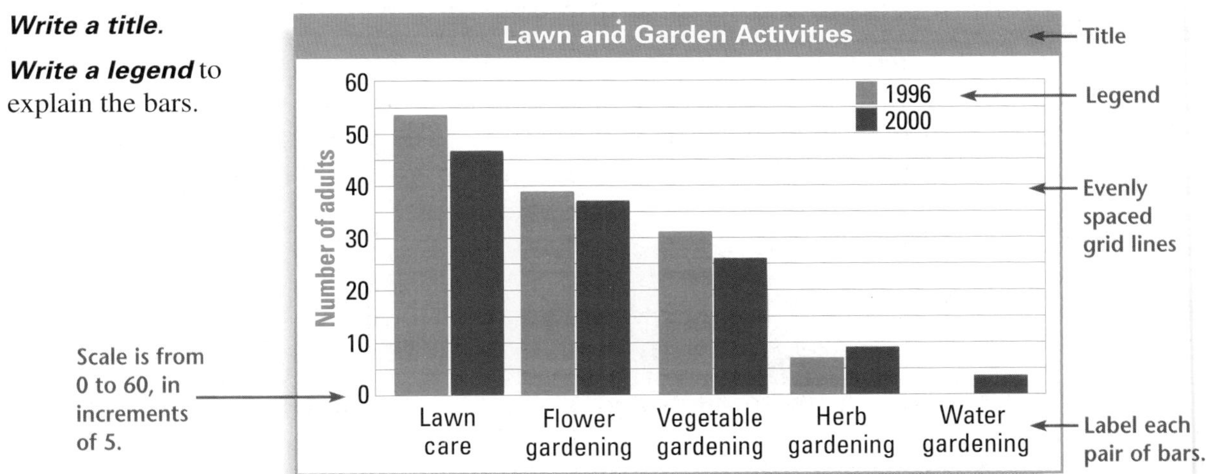

ANSWER ▶ You can see the change from 1996 to 2000 by looking at the difference in the heights of the bars for each category. The activity with the most change is lawn care, which decreased from 54 to 47.

Practice

1. Use the table at the right to draw a double bar graph.
2. Use your graph to determine which city has the least annual rainfall.
3. Which city has the greatest annual snowfall?
4. Which city has approximately the same annual rainfall and snowfall?

Average Annual Rain and Snow		
City	**Rain (in.)**	**Snow (in.)**
Boston, Massachusetts	43.81	41.8
Cheyenne, Wyoming	13.31	54.1
Miami, Florida	57.55	0

Extra Practice

EXTRA PRACTICE

Chapter 1

Use the problem solving plan to solve the problem. Identify any irrelevant information. (Lesson 1.1)

1. You take your dog for a 15 minute walk twice each day. Each walk covers about 1 mile. About how many miles per week do you walk your dog?
2. One cup of whole milk has 150 calories. One cup of skim milk has 80 calories. How many calories are in two glasses of whole milk?
3. A plumber charges \$25 for a service call plus \$40 per hour. What is the total charge for a service call that takes 3 hours?
4. Notebooks are on sale for \$2 each and pens are on sale for \$1 each. You use a \$10 bill to buy 2 notebooks and 3 pens. How much do you spend?

Evaluate the expression. Describe the result in words. (Lesson 1.2)

5. $12 + 37$ **6.** $113 + 8$ **7.** $85 - 62$ **8.** $215 - 180$

9. 11×12 **10.** $15 \cdot 20$ **11.** $340 \div 17$ **12.** $\frac{1000}{40}$

Evaluate the expression when $x = 8$, $y = 6$, and $z = 4$. (Lesson 1.2)

13. $x + y$ **14.** $x + 8$ **15.** $x - y$ **16.** $7 - z$

17. $3y$ **18.** $72 \div x$ **19.** $\frac{x}{z}$ **20.** $x + y + z$

Evaluate the expression. (Lesson 1.3)

21. $4 \times 3 + 7$ **22.** $15 - 2 \times 3$ **23.** $6 \times (7 - 5)$

24. $9 + 3 \times 4 - 2$ **25.** $30 \div 3 + 12 \times 2$ **26.** $(52 + 8) \div 6 + 4$

Use mental math to evaluate the expression. Justify each step. (Lesson 1.3)

27. $(9 \times 5) \times 4$ **28.** $4 + (16 + 71)$ **29.** $12 \times (5 \times 7)$ **30.** $(35 + 27) + 73$

31. $73 + (18 + 17)$ **32.** $(4 \times 17) \times 25$ **33.** $(93 + 71) + 107$ **34.** $5 \times (13 \times 20)$

Copy and complete the statement. (Lesson 1.4)

35. $9 = 3^{?}$ **36.** $25 = ?^2$ **37.** $36 = ?^2$ **38.** $1000 = 10^{?}$

39. $16 = 2^{?}$ **40.** $144 = ?^2$ **41.** $125 = ?^3$ **42.** $\frac{1}{100} = \frac{1}{10^{?}}$

Evaluate the expression. (Lesson 1.4)

43. $5 + 32$ **44.** $4 + 2 \times 5^2$ **45.** $50 - 4^2 \times 3$ **46.** $7 + 2^2 \div 4$

47. $10^2 \div (4 + 1)$ **48.** $(12 + 4) \div 4^2$ **49.** $5^2 - (9 - 7)^2$ **50.** $(6 - 3)^2 + 10$

Graph the numbers on a number line. (Lesson 1.5)

51. 0.5, 1.0, 1.5 **52.** 0.2, 0.8, 1.3 **53.** 0.7, 1.2, 2.0

54. 1.0, 1.6, 2.1 **55.** 0.2, 0.9, 1.1 **56.** 0.1, 0.6, 2.5

Order the numbers from least to greatest. (Lesson 1.5)

57. 1.24, 1.04, 1.2, 1.4, 1.52 **58.** 0.23, 0.209, 0.229, 0.21, 0.22

59. 2.32, 3.01, 2.15, 2.99, 2.89 **60.** 4.1, 4.01, 4.8, 4.25, 4.81

61. 0.202, 0.032, 0.302, 0.322, 0.03 **62.** 3.524, 3.442, 3.45, 3.502, 3.054

63. 6.77, 6.71, 6.107, 6.071, 6.70 **64.** 9.009, 9.10, 9.09, 9.901, 9.909

Round the number to the given place value. (Lesson 1.6)

65. 74 (tens) **66.** 2195 (thousands) **67.** 15,797 (hundreds)

68. 4.3052 (tenths) **69.** 43.653 (hundredths) **70.** 0.92173 (thousandths)

71. 4823 (thousands) **72.** 19 (tens) **73.** 2.339 (tenths)

74. 1.1257 (hundredths) **75.** 1.7562 (thousandths) **76.** 6618 (hundreds)

Round to the nearest dollar. (Lesson 1.6)

77. \$24.95 **78.** \$16.57 **79.** \$2.25 **80.** \$90.49

Use a vertical format to add. (Lesson 1.7)

81. 3.21 + 5.24 **82.** 21.93 + 6.47 **83.** 11.54 + 10.09 **84.** 15.85 + 7

85. 32.58 + 1.9 **86.** 3.907 + 28.26 **87.** 0.0008 + 78.4 **88.** 19.9 + 0.01

89. 22.73 + 5.8 **90.** 6.082 + 7.14 **91.** 23.7 + 19.005 **92.** 78.34 + 9

Use a vertical format to subtract. (Lesson 1.7)

93. 7.54 − 2.31 **94.** 9.68 − 7.46 **95.** 3.124 − 2.735 **96.** 49.5 − 27.23

97. 29.22 − 9.99 **98.** 7 − 5.32 **99.** 10 − 4.3 **100.** 3.701 − 2.003

101. 27.65 − 3.5 **102.** 54.2 − 30.05 **103.** 0.885 − 0.09 **104.** 12.304 − 9.6

Find the product. Use estimation to check your answer. (Lesson 1.8)

105. 1.3×4 **106.** 0.8×0.4 **107.** 6.44×3.9 **108.** 0.3×0.12

109. 0.07×0.04 **110.** 32.1×0.23 **111.** 5.32×1.2 **112.** 9.74×0.6

113. 0.35×2.4 **114.** 0.006×9.21 **115.** 3.12×2.05 **116.** 6.005×24.1

Divide using long division. Check your answer by multiplying. (Lesson 1.9)

117. $3.87 \div 3$ **118.** $19.26 \div 6$ **119.** $10.7 \div 5$ **120.** $18.8 \div 8$

121. $170.1 \div 7$ **122.** $174.3 \div 3$ **123.** $60.9 \div 3$ **124.** $50 \div 3.2$

125. $8 \div 0.4$ **126.** $12.6 \div 0.3$ **127.** $0.9 \div 0.3$ **128.** $28 \div 2.8$

129. $0.6 \div 0.02$ **130.** $16.8 \div 2.1$ **131.** $7 \div 0.04$ **132.** $119.4 \div 0.3$

EXTRA PRACTICE

Chapter 2

Tell whether the number is *prime* or *composite*. (Lesson 2.1)

1. 77 **2.** 151 **3.** 279 **4.** 115

5. 71 **6.** 83 **7.** 153 **8.** 61

9. 57 **10.** 29 **11.** 119 **12.** 220

Use a factor tree to write the prime factorization of the number. (Lesson 2.1)

13. 65 **14.** 152 **15.** 90 **16.** 102

17. 88 **18.** 133 **19.** 294 **20.** 124

21. 140 **22.** 450 **23.** 248 **24.** 300

Find the greatest common factor by listing all the factors of the numbers. (Lesson 2.2)

25. 24, 60 **26.** 42, 66 **27.** 51, 34 **28.** 36, 80

29. 9, 11, 17 **30.** 44, 28, 52 **31.** 18, 33, 51 **32.** 15, 35, 60

33. Three mathematics classes have 16, 28, and 20 students. The teachers want to divide the students of each class into equal-sized teams for a semester project. How many students should be on each team? How many teams will there be altogether? (Lesson 2.2)

Write the fraction given by the verbal phrase. Then identify the numerator and denominator. (Lesson 2.3)

34. One ninth **35.** Four fifteenths **36.** Seven tenths

37. Three twentieths **38.** Seven thirteenths **39.** Four elevenths

Draw an area model and a set model for the fraction. (Lesson 2.3)

40. $\frac{1}{5}$ **41.** $\frac{1}{9}$ **42.** $\frac{1}{8}$ **43.** $\frac{7}{8}$

44. $\frac{3}{10}$ **45.** $\frac{4}{9}$ **46.** $\frac{5}{7}$ **47.** $\frac{2}{7}$

Write three different fractions equivalent to the given fraction. Include the simplest form of the fraction. (Lesson 2.4)

48. $\frac{21}{49}$ **49.** $\frac{51}{85}$ **50.** $\frac{16}{72}$ **51.** $\frac{48}{64}$

52. $\frac{15}{60}$ **53.** $\frac{20}{48}$ **54.** $\frac{16}{40}$ **55.** $\frac{27}{72}$

Write the fraction in simplest form. (Lesson 2.4)

56. $\frac{24}{40}$ **57.** $\frac{60}{84}$ **58.** $\frac{66}{78}$ **59.** $\frac{64}{192}$

60. $\frac{35}{56}$ **61.** $\frac{18}{54}$ **62.** $\frac{30}{75}$ **63.** $\frac{120}{210}$

Use prime factorization to find the least common multiple of the numbers. (Lesson 2.5)

64. 8, 12 **65.** 5, 7 **66.** 10, 14 **67.** 6, 22

68. 15, 40 **69.** 25, 30 **70.** 5, 12 **71.** 10, 15

Find the least common denominator of the fractions. Then compare the fractions. (Lesson 2.6)

72. $\frac{3}{5}, \frac{4}{9}$ **73.** $\frac{5}{9}, \frac{4}{5}$ **74.** $\frac{3}{7}, \frac{2}{3}$ **75.** $\frac{3}{10}, \frac{1}{4}$

76. $\frac{5}{8}, \frac{7}{12}$ **77.** $\frac{5}{7}, \frac{7}{8}$ **78.** $\frac{3}{16}, \frac{2}{7}$ **79.** $\frac{7}{10}, \frac{3}{4}$

Write the fractions in order from least to greatest. (Lesson 2.6)

80. $\frac{1}{2}, \frac{1}{6}, \frac{1}{4}, \frac{1}{8}$ **81.** $\frac{7}{18}, \frac{11}{18}, \frac{15}{18}, \frac{5}{18}$ **82.** $\frac{3}{5}, \frac{2}{10}, \frac{1}{2}, \frac{11}{20}$ **83.** $\frac{1}{6}, \frac{5}{12}, \frac{4}{15}, \frac{1}{3}$

Rewrite the mixed number as an improper fraction. (Lesson 2.7)

84. $7\frac{1}{2}$ **85.** $2\frac{5}{6}$ **86.** $1\frac{14}{15}$ **87.** $3\frac{2}{11}$

Rewrite the improper fraction as a mixed number. (Lesson 2.7)

88. $\frac{23}{6}$ **89.** $\frac{17}{3}$ **90.** $\frac{29}{7}$ **91.** $\frac{39}{4}$

Plot the numbers on a number line. Then write them in order from least to greatest. (Lesson 2.7)

92. $2\frac{1}{5}, \frac{7}{5}, \frac{9}{5}, 1\frac{3}{5}$ **93.** $3\frac{1}{2}, \frac{5}{4}, 3\frac{3}{4}, \frac{9}{4}$ **94.** $4\frac{5}{8}, \frac{22}{4}, \frac{33}{8}, 4\frac{3}{4}$ **95.** $3\frac{2}{3}, \frac{15}{6}, \frac{10}{3}, \frac{7}{2}$

Write the fraction or mixed number as a decimal. Use bar notation if necessary. (Lesson 2.8)

96. $\frac{27}{5}$ **97.** $\frac{20}{9}$ **98.** $\frac{37}{10}$ **99.** $\frac{51}{8}$

100. $\frac{8}{3}$ **101.** $5\frac{5}{6}$ **102.** $10\frac{3}{5}$ **103.** $7\frac{3}{8}$

Write the fraction or mixed number as a decimal. Round to the nearest thousandth. (Lesson 2.8)

104. $\frac{1}{11}$ **105.** $\frac{8}{13}$ **106.** $\frac{1}{7}$ **107.** $\frac{4}{15}$

108. $\frac{17}{7}$ **109.** $\frac{15}{14}$ **110.** $2\frac{1}{12}$ **111.** $7\frac{5}{9}$

Write the decimal as a fraction in simplest form. (Lesson 2.8)

112. 0.1 **113.** 0.37 **114.** 0.29 **115.** 0.66

116. 1.125 **117.** 5.05 **118.** 12.75 **119.** 3.76

Chapter 3

Evaluate. Simplify if possible. (Lesson 3.1)

1. $\frac{2}{9} + \frac{3}{9}$ **2.** $\frac{11}{15} - \frac{6}{15}$ **3.** $\frac{5}{13} + \frac{3}{13}$ **4.** $\frac{17}{20} - \frac{13}{20}$

5. $\frac{3}{4} + \frac{5}{8}$ **6.** $\frac{7}{10} - \frac{3}{5}$ **7.** $\frac{3}{4} + \frac{5}{12}$ **8.** $\frac{13}{15} - \frac{2}{3}$

9. $\frac{5}{6} - \frac{2}{3}$ **10.** $\frac{5}{12} + \frac{1}{4}$ **11.** $\frac{2}{5} + \frac{3}{20}$ **12.** $\frac{7}{9} - \frac{1}{3}$

13. $\frac{1}{2} + \frac{3}{7}$ **14.** $\frac{7}{10} - \frac{1}{3}$ **15.** $\frac{5}{6} + \frac{5}{8}$ **16.** $\frac{7}{12} - \frac{2}{15}$

Evaluate. Simplify if possible. (Lesson 3.2)

17. $\frac{1}{12} + \frac{5}{6}$ **18.** $\frac{17}{3} + \frac{2}{5}$ **19.** $\frac{2}{3} + \frac{1}{7}$ **20.** $\frac{5}{12} + \frac{2}{5}$

21. $\frac{13}{15} - \frac{1}{2}$ **22.** $\frac{7}{20} + \frac{5}{12}$ **23.** $\frac{4}{13} + \frac{2}{3}$ **24.** $\frac{13}{16} - \frac{5}{12}$

25. $\frac{7}{10} + \frac{1}{2} - \frac{3}{5}$ **26.** $\frac{3}{4} + \frac{1}{2} - \frac{1}{3}$ **27.** $\frac{5}{6} - \frac{1}{3} + \frac{3}{4}$ **28.** $\frac{2}{9} + \frac{1}{3} + \frac{3}{4}$

29. $\frac{3}{8} + \frac{7}{12} - \frac{1}{3}$ **30.** $\frac{5}{6} + \frac{1}{3} - \frac{3}{4}$ **31.** $\frac{4}{5} - \frac{1}{2} + \frac{1}{10}$ **32.** $\frac{2}{3} + \frac{7}{9} - \frac{5}{6}$

Evaluate. Simplify if possible. (Lesson 3.3)

33. $7\frac{1}{3} + 1\frac{1}{3}$ **34.** $4\frac{5}{7} - 1\frac{3}{7}$ **35.** $3\frac{5}{6} - 1\frac{1}{6}$ **36.** $3\frac{2}{3} - 1\frac{1}{3}$

37. $1\frac{1}{7} + 5\frac{6}{7}$ **38.** $4\frac{1}{4} + 2\frac{3}{8}$ **39.** $5\frac{1}{2} + 1\frac{1}{4}$ **40.** $2\frac{2}{5} + 3\frac{1}{3}$

41. $7\frac{3}{4} + 2\frac{1}{3}$ **42.** $7\frac{1}{2} - 2\frac{1}{5}$ **43.** $8\frac{7}{9} + 4\frac{5}{6}$ **44.** $3\frac{5}{12} + 3\frac{5}{9}$

Regroup and subtract. Simplify if possible. (Lesson 3.3)

45. $5 - 2\frac{2}{5}$ **46.** $3 - 1\frac{7}{8}$ **47.** $4\frac{3}{8} - \frac{5}{8}$ **48.** $9\frac{1}{15} - \frac{4}{15}$

49. $8\frac{1}{4} - 3\frac{7}{8}$ **50.** $4\frac{2}{3} - 2\frac{5}{6}$ **51.** $7\frac{3}{10} - 5\frac{3}{5}$ **52.** $6\frac{2}{3} - 3\frac{3}{4}$

Multiply. Simplify if possible. (Lesson 3.4)

53. $\frac{3}{4} \times \frac{4}{7}$ **54.** $\frac{3}{4} \times \frac{3}{4}$ **55.** $\frac{1}{12} \times \frac{5}{6}$ **56.** $\frac{2}{7} \times \frac{3}{5}$

57. $4 \times \frac{1}{4}$ **58.** $8 \times \frac{3}{8}$ **59.** $\frac{7}{10} \times 12$ **60.** $11 \times 2\frac{1}{2}$

61. $2\frac{3}{4} \times \frac{1}{6}$ **62.** $\frac{2}{7} \times 8\frac{7}{8}$ **63.** $2\frac{2}{5} \times 1\frac{1}{2}$ **64.** $4\frac{2}{3} \times 3\frac{1}{4}$

Divide. Simplify if possible. (Lesson 3.5)

65. $\frac{3}{4} \div \frac{1}{2}$ **66.** $\frac{2}{5} \div \frac{1}{3}$ **67.** $\frac{1}{2} \div \frac{3}{7}$ **68.** $\frac{3}{8} \div \frac{2}{5}$

69. $3\frac{1}{2} \div 2$ **70.** $4 \div \frac{1}{6}$ **71.** $\frac{5}{9} \div 3$ **72.** $14 \div \frac{3}{14}$

73. $5\frac{1}{3} \div \frac{1}{3}$ **74.** $2\frac{2}{5} \div 1\frac{1}{6}$ **75.** $4\frac{1}{6} \div 2\frac{2}{9}$ **76.** $\frac{22}{25} \div 10\frac{1}{2}$

Use the distributive property to evaluate the expression. (Lesson 3.6)

77. $20(10 + 7)$ **78.** $24\left(\frac{1}{8} + 2\right)$ **79.** $5 \times 5 + 5 \times 7$ **80.** $19 \times 6 + 21 \times 6$

81. $\frac{3}{7} \times 25 + \frac{11}{7} \times 25$ **82.** $8\left(\frac{1}{16} \div \frac{1}{2}\right)$ **83.** $\left(\frac{1}{12} \div \frac{1}{6}\right)36$ **84.** $\left(1 \div \frac{2}{7}\right)14$

Use the distributive property to rewrite the expression. (Lesson 3.6)

85. $5(z + 13)$ **86.** $24(7 + n)$ **87.** $7(b + 11)$ **88.** $3(t + 9)$

89. $8(7 + b)$ **90.** $4(k + 16)$ **91.** $6(10 + y)$ **92.** $2(p + 35)$

Convert. (Lesson 3.7)

93. 12,000 centimeters to kilometers **94.** 28 kilograms to grams

95. 750 liters to kiloliters **96.** 8.5 meters to centimeters

97. 2 weeks to hours **98.** 120 inches to feet **99.** 48 pints to gallons

100. 1.5 miles to feet **101.** 8 pounds to ounces **102.** 180 inches to yards

Convert between systems. Round to the nearest hundredth. (Lesson 3.7)

103. A 250 meter path to feet (1 meter $\approx$ 3.28 feet)

104. A 20 foot ladder to meters (1 foot $\approx$ 0.3048 meter)

105. A 50 pound sack of flour to kilograms (1 pound $\approx$ 0.45 kilograms)

Find the unit rate. (Lesson 3.8)

106. An ice skater's heart beats 450 times during a 3 minute performance.

107. A car travels 576 miles on 18 gallons of gasoline.

108. A student taking a test answers 45 questions in 60 minutes.

109. A worker is paid $225 for 30 hours of work.

110. You type 205 words in 5 minutes.

111. You buy 12 pens for $4.80.

Tell which item is the better buy. (Lesson 3.8)

112. A. 8 ounces of crackers for $1.49 **B.** 12 ounces of crackers for $1.99

113. A. 64 ounces of juice for $1.99 **B.** 96 ounces of juice for $3.99

EXTRA PRACTICE

Chapter 4

Graph the numbers on a number line. Write the next two integers you expect to find in the pattern. (Lesson 4.1)

1. $-6, -4, -2, 0, 2$ **2.** $13, 10, 7, 4, 1$ **3.** $-4, 0, 4, 8, 12$ **4.** $-5, -4, -2, 1, 5$

Complete the statement using <, =, or >. (Lesson 4.1)

5. 7 ? -7 **6.** -10 ? -5 **7.** 20 ? -14 **8.** -12 ? -11

Order the integers from least to greatest. (Lesson 4.1)

9. $-5, 3, -7, 0, 12$ **10.** $-9, -3, -16, -1, 3$ **11.** $-18, 8, 7, -4, -2$

12. $-9, -13, 7, 12, 8$ **13.** $-17, -35, -8, -12, -41$ **14.** $-17, -22, -31, -11, -26$

15. On Tuesday, you deposit \$25 in your savings account. On Saturday, you withdraw \$10. Write an integer to represent each situation. (Lesson 4.1)

Use a number line to find the sum. (Lesson 4.2)

16. $7 + (-8)$ **17.** $12 + (-3)$ **18.** $-4 + 17$ **19.** $-20 + 8$

20. $0 + (-13)$ **21.** $-5 + (-1)$ **22.** $-7 + (-7)$ **23.** $10 + (-14)$

24. $-37 + 37$ **25.** $-15 + (-6)$ **26.** $-26 + 18$ **27.** $16 + 34$

Find the opposite of the number. (Lesson 4.2)

28. 71 **29.** -55 **30.** -91 **31.** 47 **32.** -65

33. The low temperatures for a week were 5°F, −1°F, 3°F, −7°F, −10°F, −8°F, and 4°F. Find the average low temperature for the week. (Lesson 4.2)

Find the absolute value of the number. (Lesson 4.3)

34. 41 **35.** -19 **36.** 31 **37.** -117 **38.** -53

Find the sum. (Lesson 4.3)

39. $-8 + (-9) + 12$ **40.** $-3 + (-11) + (-5)$ **41.** $23 + (-7) + 18$

42. $-30 + (-12) + (-5) + 2$ **43.** $21 + (-8) + 30 + (-7)$ **44.** $-11 + (-28) + (-6) + 80$

45. $14 + 27 + (-40) + 9$ **46.** $-6 + (-33) + 18 + 7$ **47.** $19 + (-42) + 25 + (-30)$

Use a number line to find the difference. (Lesson 4.4)

48. $3 - (-2)$ **49.** $5 - 8$ **50.** $-7 - 6$ **51.** $-4 - 8$

52. $6 - 9$ **53.** $-1 - (-8)$ **54.** $4 - (-3)$ **55.** $-10 - (-3)$

Find the difference without using a number line. (Lesson 4.4)

56. $7 - 15$ **57.** $18 - 25$ **58.** $-10 - 8$ **59.** $-1 - 22$

60. $-60 - (-5)$ **61.** $7 - 30$ **62.** $-8 - (-28)$ **63.** $16 - 15$

64. $16 - (-15)$ **65.** $200 - 325$ **66.** $-40 - 70$ **67.** $-10 - (-60)$

Without evaluating the expression, tell whether the product is *positive*, *negative*, or *zero*. Explain your reasoning. (Lesson 4.5)

68. $(-18)(5)$ **69.** $24(10)$ **70.** $3(-2)(0)(-6)$ **71.** $30(-5)(-17)$

Find the product. (Lesson 4.5)

72. $3(-5)$ **73.** $(-7)(-9)$ **74.** $(-4)(2)$ **75.** $(-6)(6)$

76. $15(-3)$ **77.** $8(-7)$ **78.** $(-10)(-19)$ **79.** $(-120)(-5)$

80. $3(-2)(3)$ **81.** $(-6)(2)(3)$ **82.** $5(-4)(-3)$ **83.** $(-4)(-8)(10)$

Find the quotient, if possible. (Lesson 4.6)

84. $-49 \div (-7)$ **85.** $52 \div (-4)$ **86.** $-144 \div 12$ **87.** $-99 \div (-11)$

88. $-21 \div 3$ **89.** $-120 \div (-12)$ **90.** $-48 \div 6$ **91.** $45 \div (-5)$

92. $\frac{350}{-7}$ **93.** $\frac{-16}{0}$ **94.** $\frac{0}{-15}$ **95.** $\frac{-44}{-2}$

96. The changes in your savings account over six weeks are −\$26, \$35, −\$10, \$25, \$40, and −\$10. Find the average change in your account. (Lesson 4.6)

Evaluate the expression. (Lesson 4.7)

97. $28 + (-5) - 6$ **98.** $12 + 3(-5)$ **99.** $16 - (3 + 8)$ **100.** $30 - 4(7)$

101. $5^2 - 3(4)$ **102.** $-6 + 3^2 - 2$ **103.** $10(-3) + 5$ **104.** $6(-8 + 2)$

105. $\frac{4 - 2^3}{-2}$ **106.** $\frac{20 + (-4)}{6 - 2}$ **107.** $\frac{(5 - 3)^2}{-2}$ **108.** $\frac{15 - 3 \cdot 0}{-2 + 7}$

Write a numerical expression for the verbal phrase. Then evaluate the expression. (Lesson 4.7)

109. Twice the quotient of 27 and −9

110. Four times the sum of 11, −5, 2, and −13

111. The product of −8 and the sum of 17 and −3

Graph the pair of numbers on a number line. (Lesson 4.8)

112. $-3.5, 1.2$ **113.** $-4\frac{1}{4}, -4.1$ **114.** $1\frac{5}{6}, 1\frac{3}{4}$ **115.** $-3\frac{1}{6}, 2\frac{1}{2}$

Complete the statement using <, =, or >. (Lesson 4.8)

116. $-\frac{3}{5}$? 0.75 **117.** -1.2 ? -2.8 **118.** $-8\frac{1}{6}$? $-8\frac{1}{4}$ **119.** $-\frac{32}{5}$? -6.2

Order the numbers from least to greatest. (Lesson 4.8)

120. $\frac{5}{8}, 0.6, \frac{1}{2}, -\frac{5}{6}, 0$ **121.** $1.2, 0, -\frac{7}{5}, -1\frac{1}{2}, 1\frac{3}{5}$ **122.** $-3, 3.25, -3\frac{1}{8}, 0, \frac{10}{3}$

123. $-4\frac{1}{4}, -4\frac{2}{5}, \frac{25}{6}, -4.35$ **124.** $2\frac{3}{8}, -\frac{17}{8}, 2.5, -2\frac{1}{4}, -2.1$ **125.** $-\frac{15}{4}, 3\frac{1}{2}, 0, -3.6, 3\frac{1}{4}$

EXTRA PRACTICE

EXTRA PRACTICE

Chapter 5

In Exercises 1–8, write a variable expression for the verbal phrase. (Lesson 5.1)

1. The sum of -40 and a number

2. The quotient of a number and 35

3. One less than a number

4. Fifteen divided by a number

5. The product of 51 and a number

6. A number plus 100

7. Twice the difference of a number and -5

8. Three times the sum of a number and -18

9. At an air temperature of 59°F, sound travels 1116 feet per second. Write a variable expression that gives the distance traveled by sound at this temperature in t seconds. Then evaluate the expression for $t = 1, 2, 3, 4$, and 5. Organize your results in a table. (Lesson 5.1)

10. You are buying movie tickets over the phone. The service fee is \$1.50 and each ticket costs \$8. Write a variable expression that gives the total cost of buying n tickets. Then evaluate the expression for $n = 1, 2, 3, 4, 5$, and 6. Organize your results in a table. (Lesson 5.1)

Check whether the given number is a solution of the equation. If it is not, find the solution. (Lesson 5.2)

11. $x - 8 = -16; -24$

12. $14 + n = 30; 16$

13. $70 - m = 8; 62$

14. $-5z = -25; -5$

15. $\frac{k}{2} = 36; 18$

16. $w - 3.5 = 2; 5.5$

17. $-3b = 63; 21$

18. $\frac{12}{r} = -2; -24$

Use mental math to solve the equation. Then check your solution. (Lesson 5.2)

19. $d - 45 = 50$

20. $\frac{x}{5} = 100$

21. $18 + n = 30$

22. $-4w = 84$

23. $30 - z = 15$

24. $k + 30 = 68$

25. $10v = 145$

26. $\frac{20}{t} = 5$

Write an algebraic equation for the sentence. Then solve the equation. (Lesson 5.2)

27. The sum of a number and 8 equals 40.

28. The quotient of a number and 9 equals 3.

29. The difference of a number and 40 equals 95.

30. Eleven times a number is 77.

Solve the equation. Then check your solution. (Lesson 5.3)

31. $c + 13 = 20$

32. $11 + n = 17$

33. $y + 9 = 33$

34. $15 = -12 + k$

35. $d + 11 = -20$

36. $m + 15 = 0$

37. $7 + r = -10$

38. $9 + p = 7$

39. $-20 = v + 31$

40. $a + \frac{1}{8} = \frac{1}{2}$

41. $-1 = \frac{3}{4} + m$

42. $3.5 = k + 0.2$

Write an algebraic equation for the sentence. Then solve the equation. (Lesson 5.3)

43. The sum of 18 and a number is 32.

44. A number added to 12 is 0.

45. Nine plus a number equals -4.

46. Thirty more than a number is 75.

Solve the equation. Then check your solution. (Lesson 5.4)

47. $k - 5 = 40$ **48.** $27 = w - 3$ **49.** $t - 7 = 3$ **50.** $q - 2 = -5$

51. $x - 4 = -11$ **52.** $k - \frac{1}{2} = \frac{3}{4}$ **53.** $9.3 = z + 4.1$ **54.** $a - 1.7 = 0$

Write an algebraic equation for the sentence. Then solve the equation. (Lesson 5.4)

55. Fourteen less than a number equals 8.

56. A number minus -3 equals 17.

57. The difference of a number and 9 is -6.

58. Twenty-one less than a number is 7.

Solve the equation. Then check your solution. (Lesson 5.5)

59. $-9t = 108$ **60.** $-15p = -75$ **61.** $0.4h = 63$ **62.** $-2y = \frac{1}{3}$

63. $0 = 8a$ **64.** $-14r = -42$ **65.** $1.5p = 7.5$ **66.** $-k = 22$

Write an algebraic equation for the sentence. Then solve the equation. (Lesson 5.5)

67. Forty-two is the product of 3 and a number.

68. A number times -17 equals 85.

69. A number multiplied by 14 is 49.

70. Seven is the product of 3 and a number.

Solve the equation. Then check your solution. (Lesson 5.6)

71. $\frac{m}{5} = 11$ **72.** $\frac{b}{16} = 0$ **73.** $\frac{v}{-4} = -7$ **74.** $\frac{c}{-12} = -8$

75. $\frac{a}{13} = -3$ **76.** $\frac{n}{12} = \frac{1}{6}$ **77.** $\frac{s}{-8} = 64$ **78.** $\frac{t}{3.6} = 2$

79. $\frac{w}{3} = \frac{4}{9}$ **80.** $\frac{b}{2.5} = 10$ **81.** $\frac{b}{1.4} = 5$ **82.** $\frac{h}{3.4} = 7.5$

Write an algebraic equation for the sentence. Then solve the equation. (Lesson 5.6)

83. The quotient of a number and 10 is 4.

84. A number divided by 4 equals 90.

85. The quotient of a number and -3 is -51.

86. A number divided by -12 is 108.

Solve the equation. Then check your solution. (Lesson 5.7)

87. $5t - 4 = 36$ **88.** $12 + 5m = -43$ **89.** $6w - 9 = 39$ **90.** $3t - 11 = -23$

91. $\frac{u}{9} + 7 = 13$ **92.** $\frac{d}{6} - 4 = -12$ **93.** $\frac{k}{-5} + 11 = 6$ **94.** $-3x + 5 = 11$

95. $2.5z - 7 = 4.5$ **96.** $14 - 2y = 0$ **97.** $3.4x - 2.2 = 25$ **98.** $16 - 5n = 4$

Write an algebraic equation for the sentence. Then solve the equation. (Lesson 5.7)

99. The difference of 3 times a number and 18 is 30.

100. Twelve plus the quotient of a number and 8 is 16.

Chapter 6

Write the ratio as a fraction in lowest terms. Include units (if any) in your answer. (Lesson 6.1)

1. $\frac{15 \text{ meters}}{3 \text{ meters}}$ **2.** $\frac{450 \text{ miles}}{9 \text{ hours}}$ **3.** $\frac{18 \text{ feet}}{9 \text{ yards}}$

4. 65 hours : 10 days **5.** 7 wins to 28 games **6.** 150 miles to 5 hours

Tell which of the two ratios is greater. (Lesson 6.1)

7. $\frac{18 \text{ hours}}{5 \text{ hours}}, \frac{9 \text{ hours}}{4 \text{ hours}}$ **8.** $\frac{280 \text{ feet}}{5 \text{ seconds}}, \frac{240 \text{ feet}}{6 \text{ seconds}}$ **9.** $\frac{54 \text{ wins}}{162 \text{ games}}, \frac{21 \text{ wins}}{54 \text{ games}}$

In Exercises 10–12, use the table showing the number of cans and bottles collected for a school recycling program. (Lesson 6.1)

Grade	Cans	Bottles
6	82	76
7	80	84
8	75	75

10. What is the ratio of cans to bottles collected by Grade 7?

11. What is the ratio of cans collected by Grade 8 to cans collected by Grade 7?

12. What is the ratio of cans and bottles collected by Grade 7 to cans and bottles collected by Grade 8?

Use cross products to tell whether the two ratios are equal. (Lesson 6.2)

13. $\frac{9}{15}$ and $\frac{3}{5}$ **14.** $\frac{5}{8}$ and $\frac{10}{24}$ **15.** $\frac{3}{11}$ and $\frac{9}{44}$ **16.** $\frac{25}{30}$ and $\frac{4}{6}$

In Exercises 17–24, solve the proportion. (Lesson 6.2)

17. $\frac{d}{12} = \frac{1}{3}$ **18.** $\frac{9}{15} = \frac{3}{x}$ **19.** $\frac{4}{5} = \frac{m}{40}$ **20.** $\frac{12}{k} = \frac{8}{10}$

21. $\frac{12}{x} = \frac{3}{16}$ **22.** $\frac{v}{14} = \frac{6}{21}$ **23.** $\frac{20}{30} = \frac{4}{n}$ **24.** $\frac{4}{3} = \frac{z}{7.8}$

25. A chef uses 7.5 pounds of chicken to make 10 quarts of soup. Use the proportion to find how much chicken is needed to make 4 quarts of soup. (Lesson 6.2)

$$\frac{\text{Pounds of chicken}}{\text{Quarts of soup}} = \frac{7.5}{10}$$

Use a proportion to solve the problem. (Lesson 6.3)

26. A faucet fills a 3 gallon bucket in 5 hours. How long will it take to fill a 24 gallon bucket?

27. A recipe that serves 12 people calls for 8 cups of grape juice. How much grape juice would you need for a recipe that serves 27 people?

28. You use a 3 centimeter-by-2 centimeter negative to print a photograph whose longer side measures 21 centimeters. How long is the shorter side?

29. You run 12 miles in 2 hours. At this rate, how far can you run in 3 hours?

30. An employee earns $30 for working 5 hours. At that rate, how much will the employee earn for working 8 hours?

31. In the figure below, the triangles are similar. Find the ratio of the length of a side of the smaller triangle to the length of the corresponding side of the larger triangle. **(Lesson 6.4)**

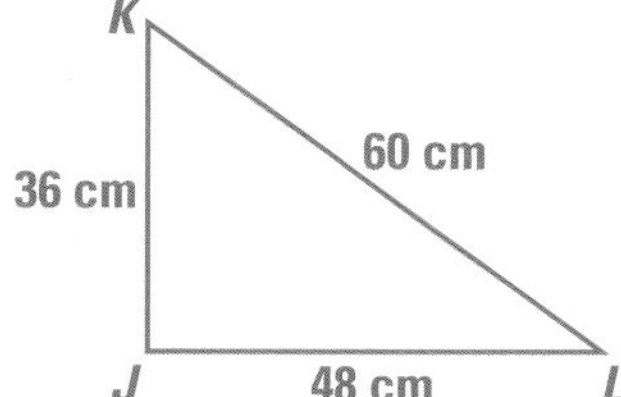

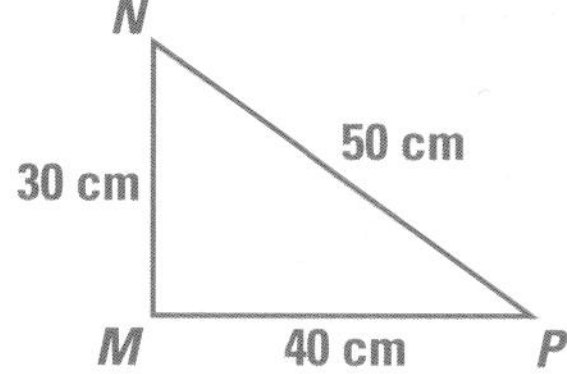

32. Two rectangles are similar. The smaller rectangle is 12 inches long and 5 inches wide. The larger rectangle is 30 inches long. How wide is the larger rectangle? **(Lesson 6.4)**

33. To estimate the height of a tree, Henry stands so that the end of his shadow meets the end of the tree's shadow. Henry is 5.5 feet tall and his shadow is 7 feet long. The tree's shadow is 56 feet long. Draw a diagram of the situation. Find the height of the tree. **(Lesson 6.4)**

In Exercises 34–37, find the scale factor for the given scale. (Lesson 6.5)

34. 1 in. = 3 ft **35.** 1 cm = 5 m **36.** 1 ft = 2.5 mi **37.** 1 cm = 250 km

38. The Wright brothers' first airplane had a wingspan of about 40 feet. You are building a model of the plane with a scale of 1 in. = 5 ft. What is the wingspan of the model in inches? **(Lesson 6.5)**

A map has a scale of 1 cm = 27.5 mi. Find the actual distance in miles. (Lesson 6.5)

39. 3 cm **40.** 14 cm **41.** 22 cm **42.** 3.25 cm **43.** 8.5 cm

In Exercises 44–48, match the event with its probability. (Lesson 6.6)

A. 1 **B.** $\frac{3}{4}$ **C.** $\frac{1}{2}$ **D.** $\frac{1}{3}$ **E.** 0

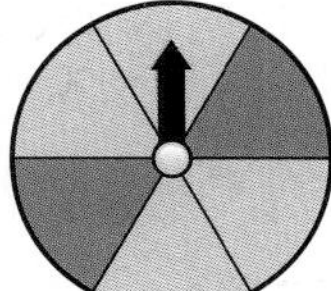

44. The pointer of the spinner at the right lands on blue when the spinner is spun once. Assume that the spinner is divided into equal parts.

45. You roll a number cube and get a positive number.

46. A tossed coin lands tails up.

47. The pointer of the spinner at the right lands on red.

48. You do not pick a blue marble when choosing a marble at random from a bag with 1 blue marble and 3 white marbles.

49. The table gives the probability that a randomly selected person has each of several hair colors. Of 100 randomly selected people, about how many would you expect to have each hair color? **(Lesson 6.6)**

Hair color	Brown	Black	Red	Blond
Probability	$\frac{7}{10}$	$\frac{1}{10}$	$\frac{1}{16}$	$\frac{1}{7}$

EXTRA PRACTICE

Chapter 7

Write the fraction as a percent. Round to the nearest tenth of a percent. (Lesson 7.1)

1. $\frac{1}{5}$ **2.** $\frac{3}{8}$ **3.** $\frac{8}{25}$ **4.** $\frac{9}{20}$ **5.** $\frac{7}{15}$

Write the decimal as a percent. (Lesson 7.1)

6. 0.38 **7.** 0.2 **8.** 0.01 **9.** 0.025 **10.** 0.019

Write the percent as a decimal and as a fraction in simplest form. (Lesson 7.1)

11. 60% **12.** 75% **13.** 95% **14.** 32% **15.** 9.6%

Find the percent of the number by multiplying by a fraction. (Lesson 7.2)

16. 10% of 50 **17.** 50% of 98 **18.** 40% of 90 **19.** 90% of 25

Find the percent of the number by multiplying by a decimal. Check that the answer is reasonable. (Lesson 7.2)

20. 4% of 75 **21.** 22% of 120 **22.** 43% of 70 **23.** 24% of 95

24. 68% of 90 **25.** 51% of 170 **26.** 76% of 120 **27.** 91% of 210

28. Of the 650 people that responded to a survey, 42% support a plan to build a new school. How many people support the plan? (Lesson 7.2)

Write the percent as a decimal and as a fraction in simplest form. (Lesson 7.3)

29. 240% **30.** $\frac{3}{5}\%$ **31.** 0.8% **32.** 175% **33.** $\frac{7}{12}\%$

Write the fraction or decimal as a percent. (Lesson 7.3)

34. $\frac{1}{250}$ **35.** 0.0002 **36.** 6.25 **37.** $\frac{7}{500}$ **38.** $\frac{33}{4}$

Find the percent of the number. (Lesson 7.3)

39. 250% of 10 **40.** $\frac{7}{10}\%$ of 20 **41.** 0.8% of 120 **42.** 130% of 150

43. $\frac{3}{4}\%$ of 50 **44.** 180% of 74 **45.** 0.05% of 160 **46.** $\frac{9}{10}\%$ of 220

In Exercises 47–50, use mental math to estimate the percent of the number. Explain your reasoning. (Lesson 7.3)

47. 151% of 20 **48.** 123% of 80 **49.** $\frac{1}{2}\%$ of 86 **50.** $\frac{1}{4}\%$ of 240

51. Estimate a 15% tip for a restaurant bill of $31.24. (Lesson 7.3)

In Exercises 52–57, use a proportion to answer the question. (Lesson 7.4)

52. What is 80% of 75?

53. What number is 35% of 80?

54. 36 is 40% of what number?

55. 14% of what number is 70?

56. What is 224% of 200?

57. What percent of 120 is 210?

58. You paid \$24 for a sweater that was on sale at 60% of the original price. What was the original price of the sweater? (Lesson 7.4)

Find the measure of the angle corresponding to the percent of a circle. (Lesson 7.5)

59. 60%

60. 45%

61. 74%

62. 32%

63. 8%

In Exercises 64 and 65, use the circle graph. It shows the chemical composition of Earth. (Lesson 7.5)

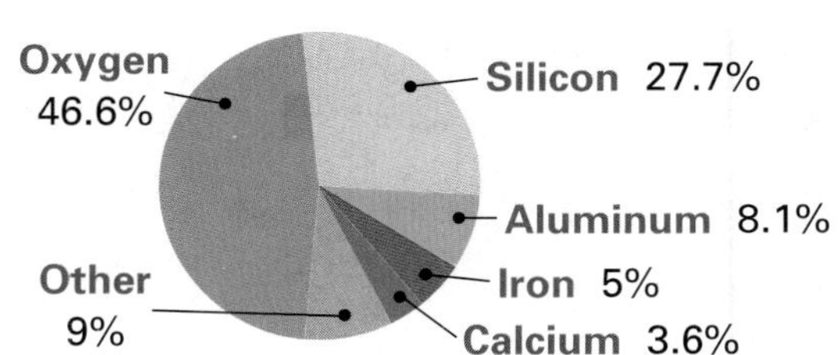

64. Find the angle measure of each part.

65. Show that the sum of the parts equals 100%. Show that the sum of the parts equals 1 when the percents are changed to fractions.

66. At a party, 50 guests were asked if they wanted fruit, cheese, both, or neither. The results were: fruit, 12; cheese, 5; both, 30; neither, 3. Make a circle graph of the data. (Lesson 7.5)

Find the interest you earn for depositing the given principal in an account earning simple interest. (Lesson 7.6)

67. $P = \$5000$, $r = 5\%$, $t = 2$ years

68. $P = \$1000$, $r = 3.5\%$, $t = 6$ months

69. $P = \$800$, $r = 4\%$, $t = 18$ months

70. $P = \$2500$, $r = 5.5\%$, $t = 3$ months

In Exercises 71–74, find the simple interest you pay for borrowing the given principal. (Lesson 7.6)

71. $P = \$1000$, $r = 16\%$, $t = 1$ year

72. $P = \$10{,}000$, $r = 18\%$, $t = 3$ years

73. $P = \$800$, $r = 12.5\%$, $t = 8$ months

74. $P = \$5000$, $r = 7.75\%$, $t = 6$ months

75. Your friend earns \$220 in simple interest in one year. If the annual interest rate on this account is 5.5%, how much was the original deposit? (Lesson 7.6)

Find the discount and sale price. (Lesson 7.7)

76. Original price: \$120
Discount percent: 25%

77. Original price: \$200
Discount percent: 40%

78. Original price: \$50.49
Discount percent: 20%

79. Original price: \$145.75
Discount percent: 35%

Find the sales tax and total price. (Lesson 7.7)

80. Price: \$27
Sales tax rate: 6%

81. Price: \$125
Sales tax rate: 5%

82. Price: \$74.35
Sales tax rate: 5.5%

EXTRA PRACTICE

Chapter 8

In Exercises 1–5, use the diagram. (Lesson 8.1)

1. Find the measure of each angle.

a. $\angle 1$ **b.** $\angle 2$ **c.** $\angle 3$

d. $\angle 4$ **e.** $\angle 5$ **f.** $\angle 6$

2. Name a pair of adjacent angles.

3. Name a pair of vertical angles.

4. Name two right angles. **5.** Name a pair of supplementary angles.

Find the value of *x*. (Lesson 8.2)

6.

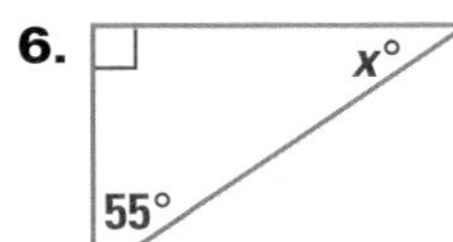

7.

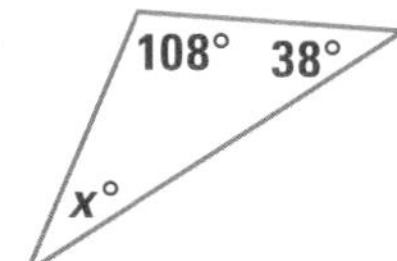

8.

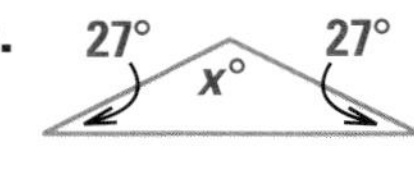

Determine whether a triangle can have the given angle measures. (Lesson 8.2)

9. 45°, 66°, 69° **10.** 52°, 43°, 87° **11.** 37°, 15°, 128°

12. 108°, 10°, 12° **13.** 112°, 57°, 10° **14.** 8°, 168°, 4°

Use a centimeter ruler to find the lengths of the sides of the triangle. Then use these lengths to classify the triangle. (Lesson 8.3)

15.

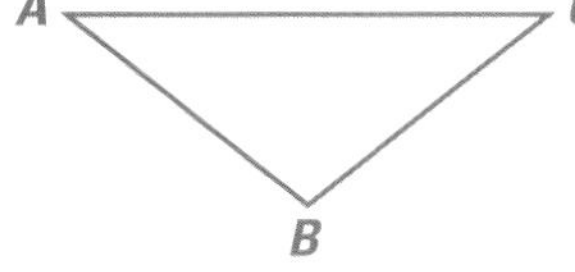

16.

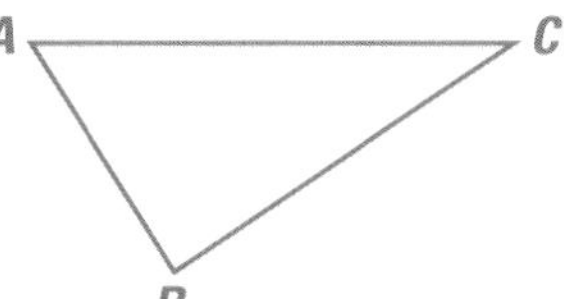

17.

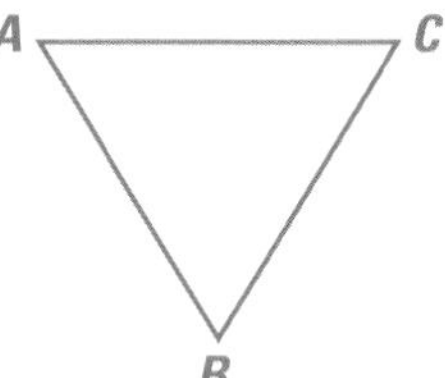

Use a protractor to find the measures of the angles of the triangle. Then use these angle measures to classify the triangle. (Lesson 8.3)

18.

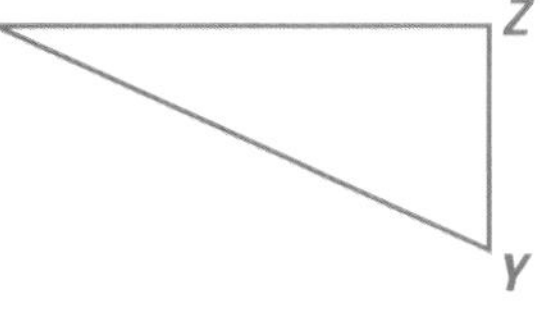

19.

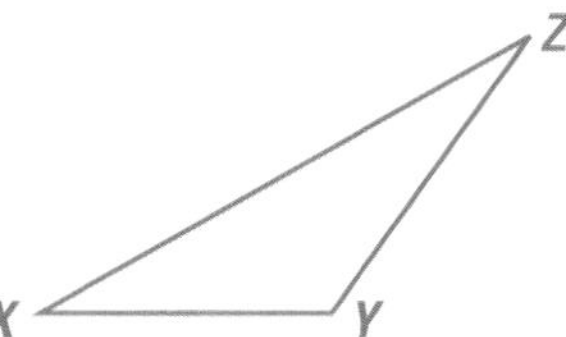

20.

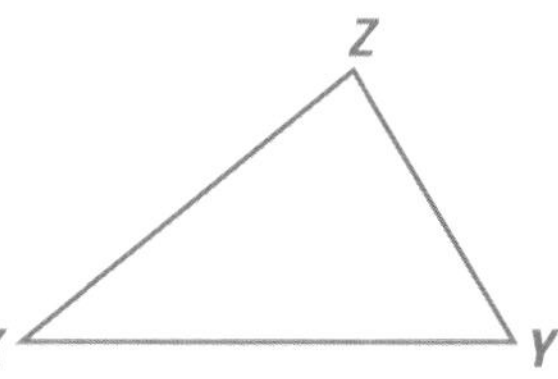

Find the area of the polygon. (Lesson 8.4)

21.

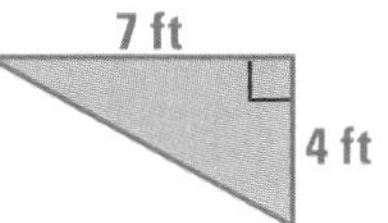

22.

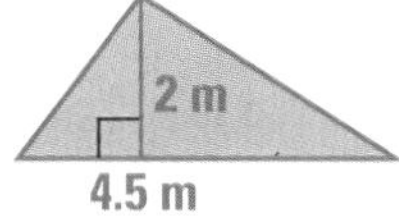

23.

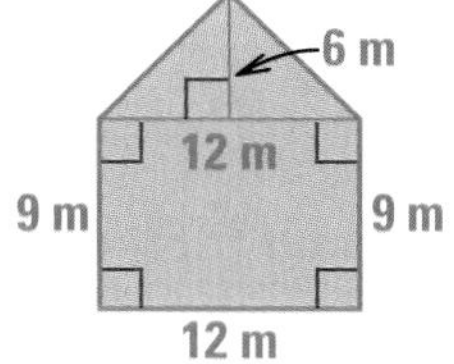

Use as many words as possible to describe the figure: *square, rectangle, parallelogram,* or *quadrilateral.* (Lesson 8.5)

24. 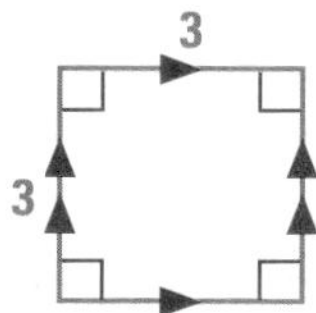

25. 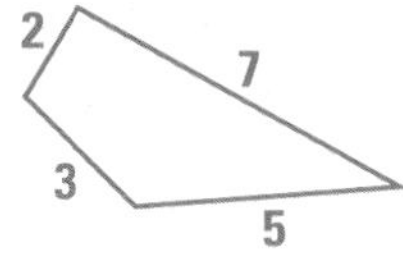

26. 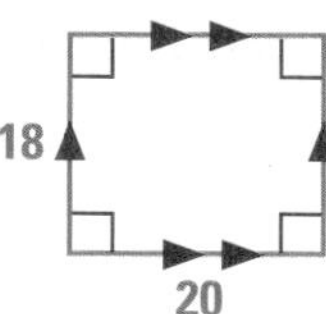

Find the indicated missing measures. (Lesson 8.5)

27. 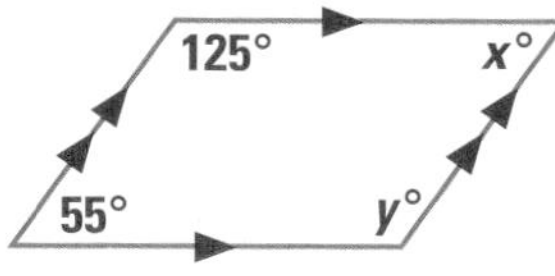

28. 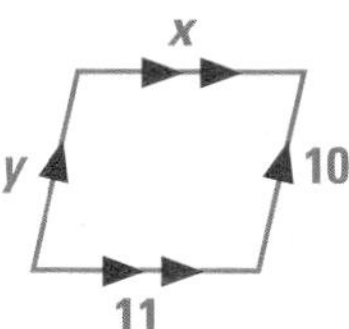

29. 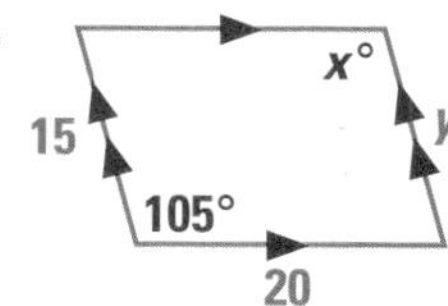

Find the area of the parallelogram. (Lesson 8.6)

30. 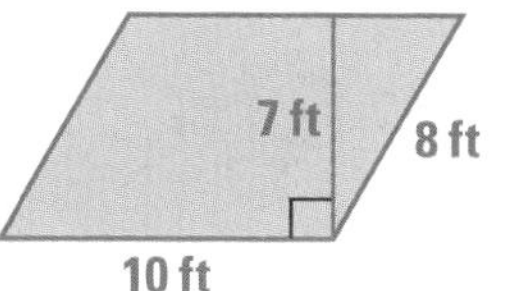

31. 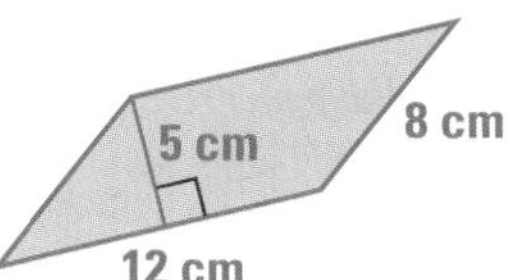

32. 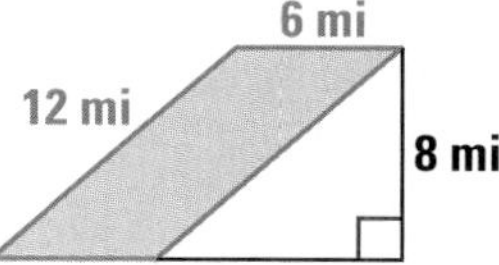

Find the indicated missing measure in the parallelogram. (Lesson 8.6)

33. $A = 600 \text{ mm}^2$

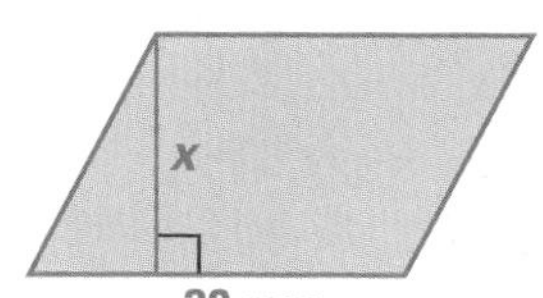

34. $A = 91 \text{ ft}^2$

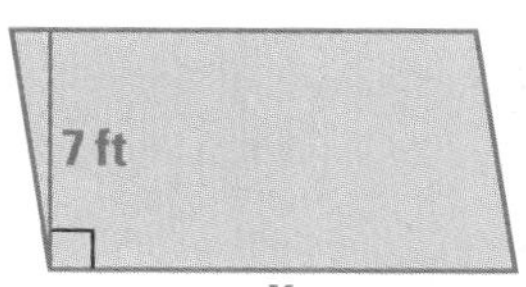

35. $A = 72 \text{ m}^2$

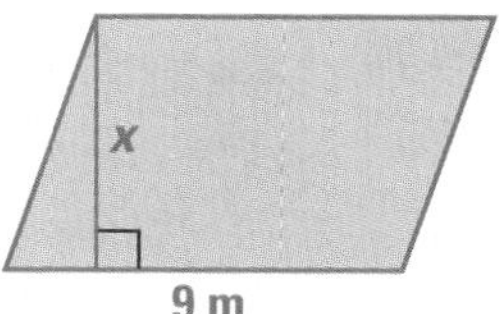

Find the circumference of the circle given the radius or the diameter. Use $\pi \approx 3.14$. (Lesson 8.7)

36. Radius = 10 feet

37. Radius = 18 centimeters

38. Diameter = 42 meters

Use the given circumference of a circle to find the diameter. (Lesson 8.7)

39. 35 centimeters

40. 16 inches

41. 215 feet

42. 42.5 meters

Find the area of the circle. Give both exact and approximate answers. (Lesson 8.8)

43. Radius = 5 inches

44. Diameter = 16 feet

45. Diameter = 9 meters

Use the formulas for the area of a circle and of a parallelogram to find the area of the shaded region. Use $\pi \approx \frac{22}{7}$. (Lesson 8.8)

46. 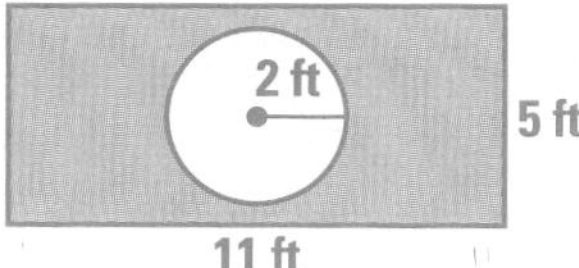

47. 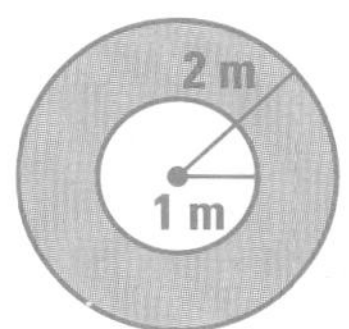

48. 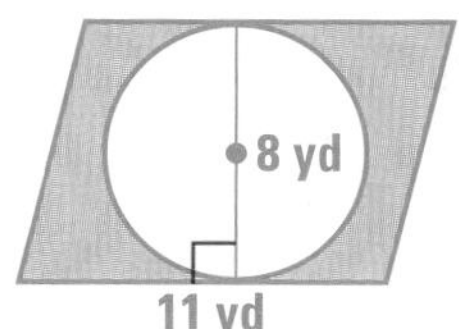

Chapter 9

Identify the solid as a *triangular prism*, a *rectangular prism*, or a *cylinder*. Then find its height. If the solid is a prism, find the number of faces. (Lesson 9.1)

1. 15 in., 20 in., 24 in.

2.

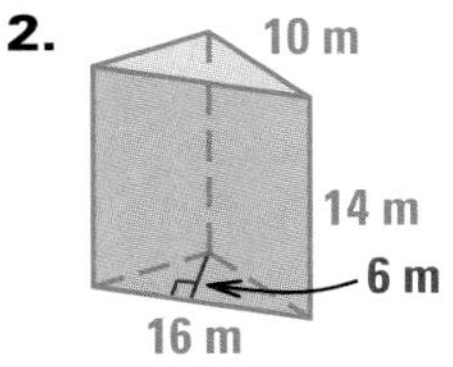

3.

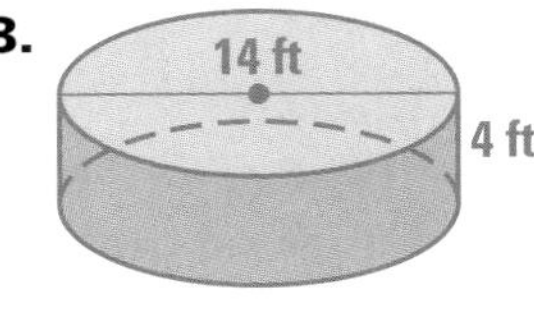

4. 3 cm, 5 cm, 4 cm

5.

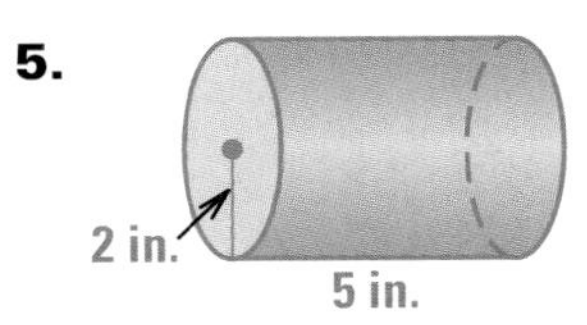

6.

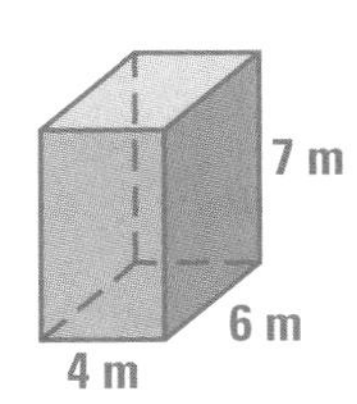

Draw a rectangular prism with the given dimensions. Find its volume. (Lesson 9.2)

7. 3 inches by 4 inches by 5 inches

8. 8 feet by 6 feet by 6 feet

9. 2.2 cm by 8.8 cm by 15 cm

10. 3 inches by 2 feet by 1 yard

Find the volume of the rectangular prism. (Lesson 9.2)

11. 7 in., 9 in., 20 in.

12.

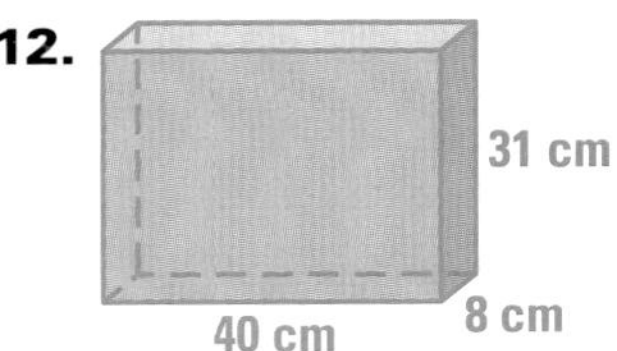

13.

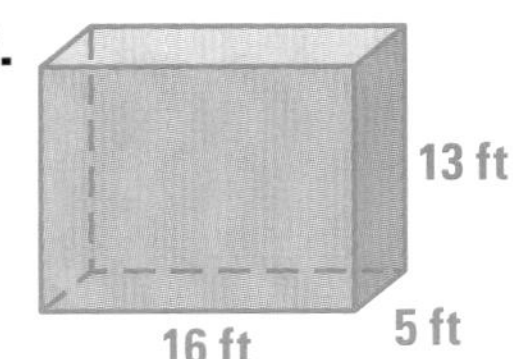

14. You are spreading peat moss over a flower bed. The layer of peat moss forms a rectangular prism that is 2 feet wide, 3 yards long, and 3 inches deep. Find the volume of the rectangular prism in cubic feet. (Lesson 9.2)

15. The volume of a rectangular prism is 300 cubic feet. The base of the prism is 5 feet long and 6 feet wide. Find the height of the prism. (Lesson 9.2)

Find the volume of the triangular prism. (Lesson 9.3)

16. 3 cm, 3 cm, 4 cm

17.

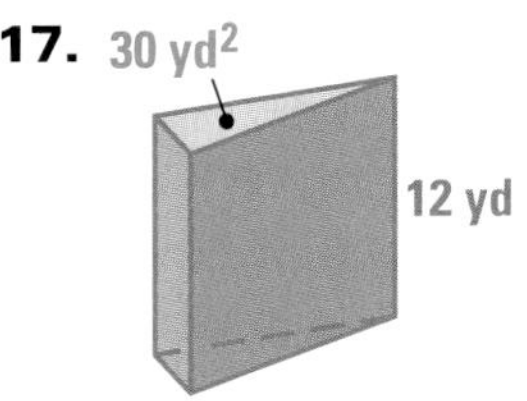

18.

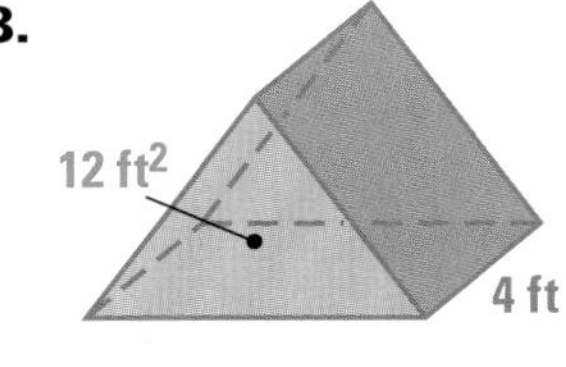

19. 42 m, 16 m, 28 m

20.

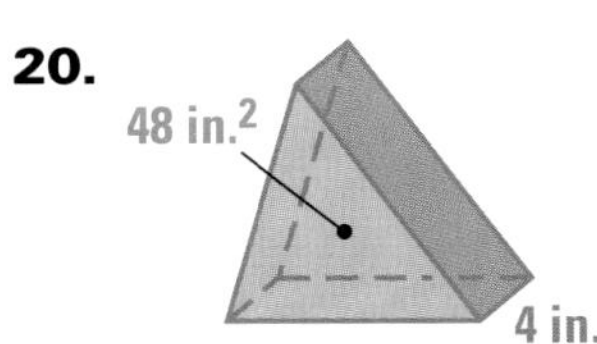

21.

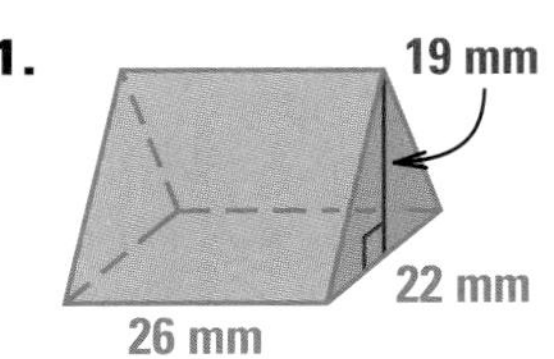

Find the volume of the cylinder. **(Lesson 9.4)**

22.

23. 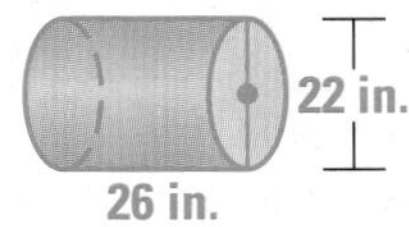

24. 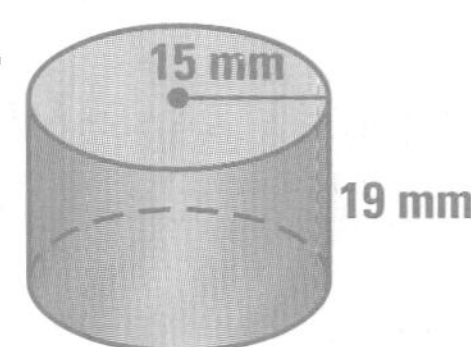

25. 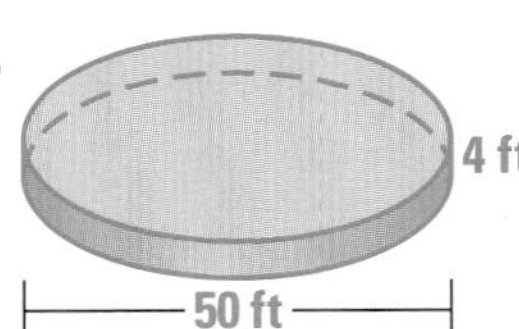

26. 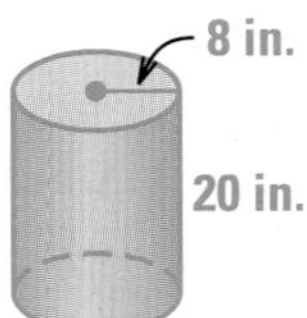

27. 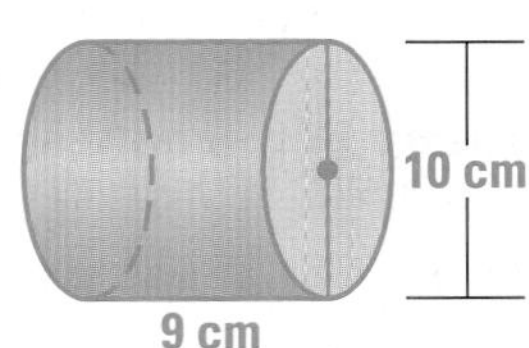

28. A cylinder has radius 3 feet and height 6 feet. Find the volume of the cylinder in cubic feet. Then use the fact that 1 $ft^3 \approx 7.48$ gal to find the volume of the cylinder in gallons. **(Lesson 9.4)**

Find the surface area of the prism. **(Lesson 9.5)**

29. 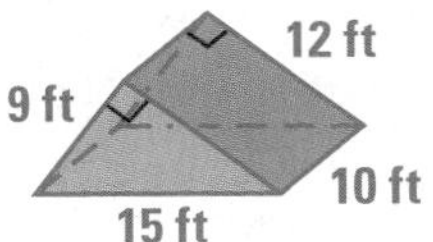

30. 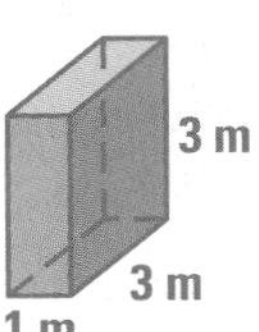

31. 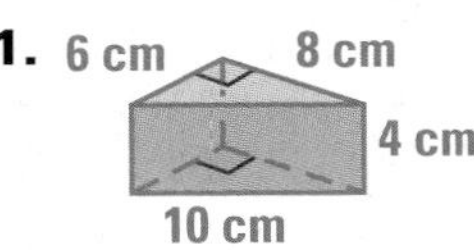

32. 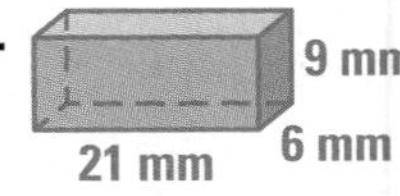

33. 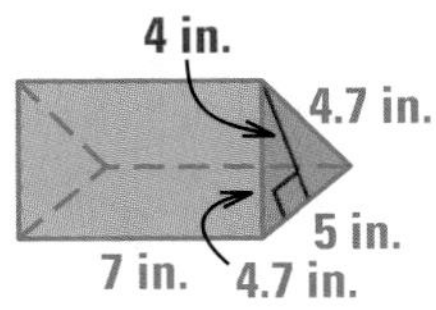

34. 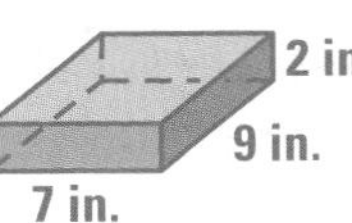

35. 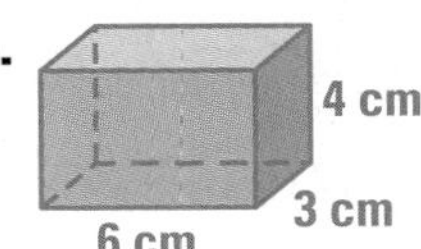

36. 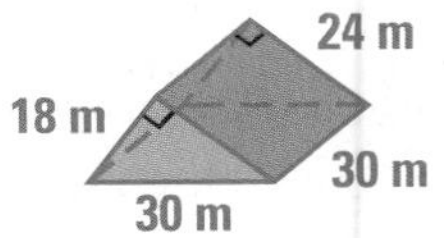

Find the surface area of the cylinder. Use 3.14 for π. **(Lesson 9.6)**

37. 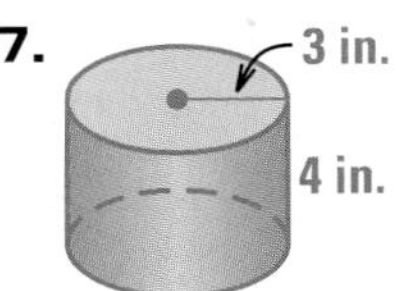

38. 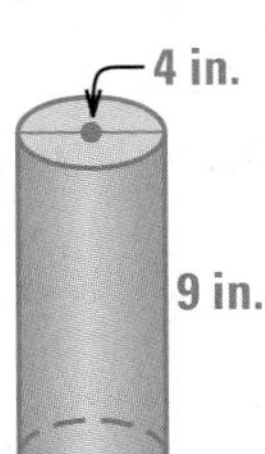

39. 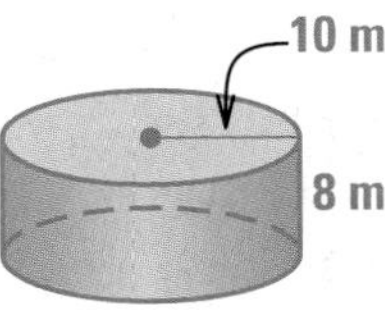

40. 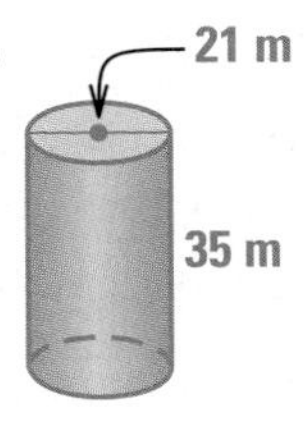

In Exercises 41–44, find the lateral surface area, base area, and total surface area of the cylinder with the given dimensions using the given value of π. **(Lesson 9.6)**

41. $h = 9$ ft, $r = 1\frac{3}{4}$ ft, $\pi \approx \frac{22}{7}$

42. $h = 6$ in., $d = 14$ in., $\pi \approx \frac{22}{7}$

43. $h = 20$ cm, $r = 5$ cm, $\pi \approx 3.14$

44. $h = 120$ m, $d = 60$ m, $\pi \approx 3.14$

45. A cylindrical cereal box is 4 inches in diameter and 7 inches high. Find the number of square inches of paper needed to cover the entire outer surface of the box. How many fewer square inches are needed if the bottom of the box is not covered? **(Lesson 9.6)**

Chapter 10

Find the mean, median, and mode(s) of the data. **(Lesson 10.1)**

1. Number of siblings of 9 students in a class: 4, 0, 1, 0, 2, 2, 1, 1, 3

2. Wind speed (in miles per hour) by month at Block Island, Rhode Island: 20, 20, 19, 17, 15, 14, 13, 12, 14, 17, 19, 20

Identify the outlier in the data set. Find the mean, median, and mode(s) of the data set when the outlier is included and when it is not. Describe the outlier's effect on each measure of central tendency. **(Lesson 10.1)**

3. 4, 5, 6, 6, 8, 8, 8, 12, 27

4. 0, 58, 60, 60, 64, 66, 68, 72

5. 15, 17, 14, 13, 16, 51, 15, 15

6. 1.5, 2.2, 1.0, 3.6, 3.8, 12.2, 1.6, 1.7

In Exercises 7–9, use the table showing the number of colleges in each state in 1995. **(Lesson 10.2)**

AL......82	CO....59	HI 17	KS.....54	MA..118	MT....26	NM ...35	OK....45	SD.....21	VA 89
AK........9	CT 42	ID......12	KY 61	MI...109	NE 35	NY ..311	OR....45	TN.....76	WA 64
AZ......45	DE 9	IL....169	LA 36	MN..107	NV 10	NC...121	PA ...217	TX ..179	WV.....28
AR......38	FL...114	IN......78	ME....33	MS 46	NH....30	ND 20	RI......12	UT.....17	WI......66
CA....348	GA...120	IA......59	MD....57	MO..101	NJ 61	OH..156	SC.....59	VT.....22	WY.......9

▶Source: U.S. National Center for Education Statistics

7. Make a frequency table of the data using intervals of 20.

8. Draw a histogram of the data using intervals of 20.

9. Which interval represents the most common numbers of colleges for states?

In Exercises 10 and 11, use the data below giving the average monthly temperatures (in degrees Fahrenheit) for January through December in two regions of the United States. **(Lesson 10.3)** ▶Source: *Old Farmer's Almanac*

Southwest Desert: 49, 57, 62, 69, 79, 75, 92, 89, 86, 57, 55, 55

Pacific Northwest: 32, 37, 48, 52, 59, 63, 66, 67, 64, 50, 43, 37

10. Draw a box-and-whisker plot for each set of temperatures.

11. Find the range and interquartile range for each set of temperatures.

Graph the ordered pairs in a coordinate plane. Label the points. **(Lesson 10.4)**

12. $(-3, 6)$, $(-1, 5)$, $(2, 3)$, $(4, 0)$, $(5, -2)$

13. $(-5, -3)$, $(4, 2)$, $(0, 6)$, $(3, -4)$, $(2, -4)$

14. The table shows a car's total braking distance at different speeds. Draw a scatter plot of the data. Use the x-axis for speed and the y-axis for distance. Describe any pattern you see. **(Lesson 10.4)**

Speed (in mi/h)	10	20	30	40	50	60	70
Distance (in ft)	20	45	78	125	188	272	381

In Exercises 15–17, use the table showing the percent of people of voting age who voted in United States presidential elections from 1964 to 1992. Percents are rounded to the nearest whole percent. (Lesson 10.5)

Year	1964	1968	1972	1976	1980	1984	1988	1992
Male	72	70	64	60	59	59	56	60
Female	67	66	62	59	59	61	58	62

▶ Source: U.S. Bureau of the Census

15. Draw a double bar graph of the data.

16. Draw a line graph of the data.

17. Use the line graph to describe the change in the gap in the percentages of males and females voting from 1964 to 1992.

In Exercises 18–20, use the bar graph showing the weights of different sizes of eggs. (Lesson 10.6)

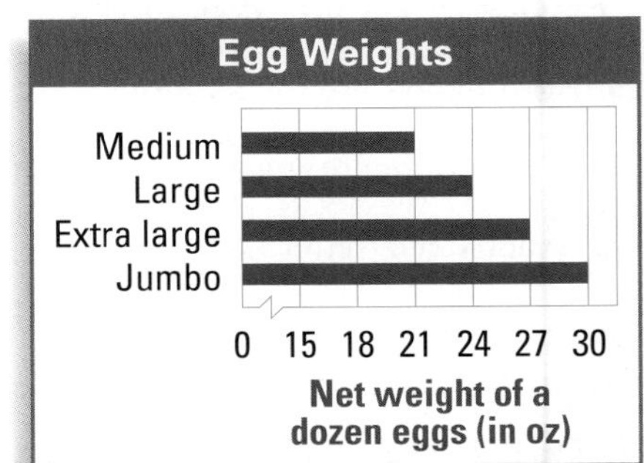

18. Use the lengths of the bars (not the scale) to compare the weight of a dozen jumbo eggs to the weight of a dozen medium eggs.

19. Use the scale to answer Exercise 18. How can the graph be misinterpreted?

20. Draw a bar graph of the data that is *not* potentially misleading.

In Exercises 21 and 22, use the following information. A local newspaper surveyed students who play a musical instrument. Each student was asked the age he or she began playing an instrument. The results are shown below. (Lesson 10.7)

Ages for School A: 13, 6, 10, 10, 8, 14, 9, 11, 12, 7, 10, 15, 12, 11, 11, 12, 18, 10, 11, 9, 10, 15, 14, 8, 13

Ages for School B: 15, 12, 5, 8, 7, 14, 9, 11, 8, 5, 9, 13, 8, 12, 11, 6, 12, 5, 6, 13, 10, 5, 3, 7, 5

21. Compare the samples by drawing a circle graph of each data set.

22. Find the mean for each sample. On average, in which school did the musicians begin playing at an earlier age?

In Exercises 23–25, explain how the wording of the survey question could influence the results. (Lesson 10.8)

23. Do you prefer the freedom of walking barefoot or the inconvenience of wearing shoes?

24. Do you think that the relaxing sound of a singing bird is better than the loud sound of a barking dog?

25. Do you support the ineffective policies of the town's mayor?

EXTRA PRACTICE

Chapter 11

In Exercises 1 and 2, use the following information. You keep your workout clothes in two drawers. One morning you have a white T-shirt, a blue T-shirt, and a green T-shirt in one drawer. You have a pair of blue shorts and a pair of gray shorts in the other drawer. Without looking, you randomly choose one article of clothing from each drawer. **(Lesson 11.1)**

1. Make a list of the possible workout outfits. How many different outfits are possible?

2. What is the probability that you pick the same color shirt and shorts?

In Exercises 3–8, use the following information. You have two bags. One bag contains the letters M, A, T, and H and the other contains the letters E, X, A, and M. You randomly draw one letter from each bag. Draw a tree diagram to find the probability of the event. **(Lesson 11.1)**

3. Both letters are the same.

4. You draw an M and an X.

5. Both letters are vowels.

6. At least one letter is a vowel.

7. Exactly one letter is A.

8. Both letters are A.

You randomly choose a whole number from 1 through 15. Tell whether the events are *disjoint* or *overlapping*. (Lesson 11.2)

9. **Event *A***: The number is a multiple of 3.
Event *B*: The number is even.

10. **Event *A***: The number is greater than 7.
Event *B*: The number is prime.

In Exercises 11 and 12, a jar contains 3 red marbles and 2 green marbles. Tell whether the events are *independent* or *dependent*. (Lesson 11.2)

11. You randomly choose a marble from the jar. Without replacing it, you randomly choose a second marble.
Event *A*: The first marble is red. **Event *B***: The second marble is red.

12. You randomly choose a marble from the jar. You note the color, replace the marble, then randomly choose a second marble.
Event *A*: The first marble is red. **Event *B***: The second marble is green.

In Exercises 13–16, use the following information. You have two bags. One bag contains the 26 letters of the alphabet written on pieces of paper. The other bag contains the whole numbers from 1 through 10 written on pieces of paper. You randomly draw one piece of paper from each bag. (Assume that Y is a consonant.) **(Lesson 11.3)**

13. What is the probability that you draw the letter A and the number 5?

14. What is the probability that you draw a vowel and an even number?

15. What is the probability that you draw a consonant and a number less than 4?

16. Suppose you add a third bag that contains the whole numbers from 1 through 10 written on pieces of paper. If you draw one piece of paper from each of the three bags, what is the probability that you draw a vowel and two odd numbers?

You spin the green spinner at the right once. Find the probability of the event. (Lesson 11.4)

8 equal sections

17. Getting 1 or 5

18. Getting a multiple of 4 or an odd number

19. Getting an even number or an odd number

20. Getting 7 or a factor of 6

You spin the blue spinner at the right twice. (Lesson 11.4)

5 equal sections

21. Make a table showing the possible sums of the two spins.

22. Find the probability of spinning a sum of 8 or 9.

23. Find the probability of spinning a sum that is less than 5.

24. Find the probability of spinning a sum that is even.

25. Find the probability of spinning a sum that is odd.

In Exercises 26–33, you are given *P*(*A*), the probability that event *A* occurs. Find *P*(not *A*), the probability that event *A* does not occur. (Lesson 11.5)

26. $\frac{3}{8}$ **27.** 0.2 **28.** $\frac{4}{15}$ **29.** 72%

30. 0.45 **31.** $\frac{2}{5}$ **32.** 0.63 **33.** 46%

34. In a survey of 150 randomly selected students, each student was asked whether he or she had no pets, one pet, two pets, or three or more pets. A total of 27 students said they had two pets and 26 said they had three or more. Estimate the probability that a randomly chosen student has at most one pet. (Lesson 11.5)

In Exercises 35–40, you are given the theoretical probability of an event. Estimate the number of times the event will occur in the given number of trials. (Lesson 11.6)

35. Theoretical probability: $\frac{3}{8}$
Number of trials: 1000

36. Theoretical probability: $\frac{1}{4}$
Number of trials: 600

37. Theoretical probability: 12.5%
Number of trials: 1400

38. Theoretical probability: 0.2
Number of trials: 450

39. Theoretical probability: 0.06
Number of trials: 900

40. Theoretical probability: 0.18
Number of trials: 200

41. Two coins will be tossed 1000 times. Estimate the number of times one head and one tail will be tossed. (Lesson 11.6)

42. A jar contains three white marbles, four red marbles, and one green marble. A marble will be chosen and replaced 500 times. Estimate the number of times a red marble will be chosen. (Lesson 11.6)

End-of-Course Test

Fractions and Decimals

NS 1.0, 1.1, 2.0, 2.4

Complete the statement using <, =, or >.

1. 0.074 **?** 0.47

2. $2\frac{16}{25}$ **?** 2.64

3. $-\frac{5}{9}$ **?** $-\frac{7}{12}$

Graph the numbers on a number line. Then order the numbers from least to greatest.

4. $\frac{3}{8}, \frac{1}{2}, \frac{3}{4}, \frac{5}{8}$

5. $-2.5, 1.25, -3, 0.75$

6. $-3\frac{1}{3}, -\frac{7}{3}, -1, -4$

Evaluate. Simplify if possible.

7. $1\frac{1}{6} - \frac{5}{6}$

8. $\frac{2}{9} + \frac{1}{6}$

9. $\frac{7}{12} - \frac{1}{3}$

10. $\frac{3}{4} + \frac{1}{8} - \frac{1}{3}$

11. $\frac{9}{10} \times \frac{5}{6}$

12. $1\frac{1}{4} \times 2\frac{1}{2}$

13. $3 \div \frac{1}{2}$

14. $\frac{5}{11} \div \frac{10}{33}$

Ratios and Rates

NS 1.0, 1.2; AF 2.2

15. Find the ratio of weekend days to other days in a week.

16. If you jog for 80 minutes, for how many hours did you jog?

17. A bus travels 399 miles in 9.5 hours. Find the average speed of the bus.

18. Team A has 7 wins and 3 losses. Team B has 9 wins and 4 losses. Which team has the best record of wins per game played? Explain.

Proportions and Percents

NS 1.0, 1.3, 1.4, 2.0; AF 1.1, 2.2

19. Find the value of N if $\frac{3}{35} = \frac{15}{N}$.

20. A copy machine can duplicate 18 pages in 45 seconds. At this rate, how many pages can be duplicated in 60 seconds?

21. 15% of what number is 30?

22. You deposit $500 in a savings account. The annual interest rate is 4.5%. How much simple interest will you earn in 2 years?

23. A camera store having a sale offers a 25% discount off the regular $275 price of a new camera. Find the dollar amount of the discount and the sale price of the camera.

24. A restaurant bill is $25.80, including tax. If you leave a 15% tip, find the total cost.

INTEGERS AND NUMBER PROPERTIES

NS 2.3, 2.4

In Exercises 25 and 26, explain each step.

25. $-8 + 12 + 8 = -8 + 8 + 12$
$= 0 + 12$
$= 12$

26. $12\left(\frac{1}{2} + \frac{2}{3}\right) = 12\left(\frac{1}{2}\right) + 12\left(\frac{2}{3}\right)$
$= 6 + 8$
$= 14$

Find the greatest common factor (GCF) of the numbers.

27. 45, 105 **28.** 27, 99 **29.** 44, 54 **30.** 42, 56, 112

Find the least common multiple (LCM) of the numbers.

31. 6, 14 **32.** 28, 21 **33.** 48, 32 **34.** 3, 6, 21

VARIABLE EQUATIONS

AF 1.1

Solve the equation.

35. $-9 = t + 6$ **36.** $x - 4.5 = 1.6$ **37.** $-16a = -6$

38. $\frac{y}{20} = 5$ **39.** $9 - 1.5c = 7$ **40.** $\frac{17}{25} = \frac{p}{100}$

GEOMETRY IN THE PLANE

NS 1.3; MG 1.1, 2.2

Find the indicated missing measures in the similar figures.

41.

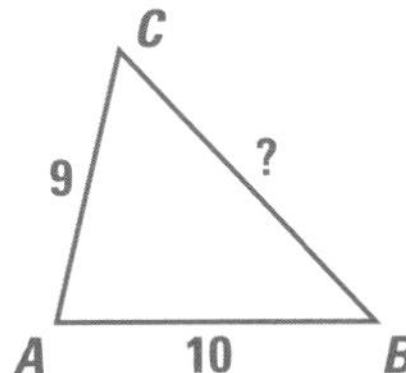

42.

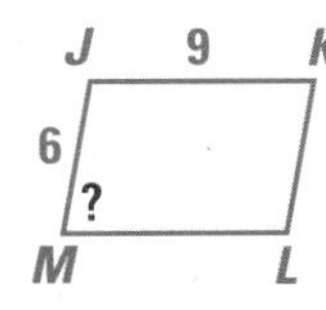

43. What is true about the ratio of the circumference of any circle and the diameter of the circle? Explain your answer.

44. A plate has a radius of 8 inches. Find its circumference and area. Give both exact and approximate answers.

Use the diagram to find the value of the variable.

45. a **46.** b

47. c **48.** d

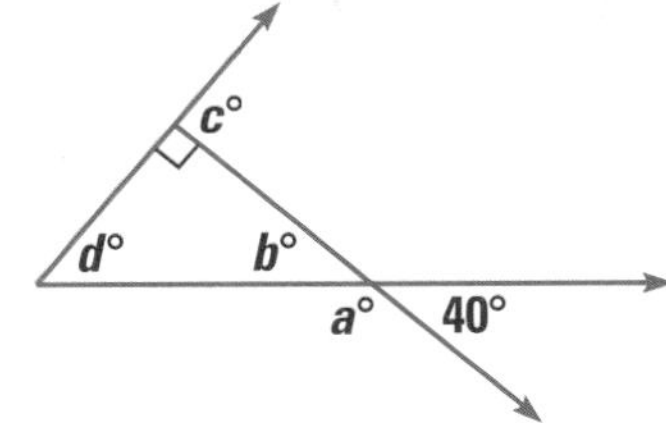

END-OF-COURSE TEST

SAMPLING AND DATA ANALYSIS

SDP 2.2–2.5

49. A library staff wants to find out if the people who use the library are satisfied with the services the library provides. They consider the sampling methods described below. Identify the type of sample each method produces. Tell whether the sample is biased, and why.

a. A survey of adults who come in the library one day

b. A mailing of questionnaires to residents of the city in which the library is located

50. Describe a sampling method for Exercise 49 which would produce a more representative sample than the methods described in Exercise 49.

51. A city planner uses the graph at the right to show that the unemployment rate in the city has decreased dramatically over the last four years. Is this conclusion reasonable? Explain your answer.

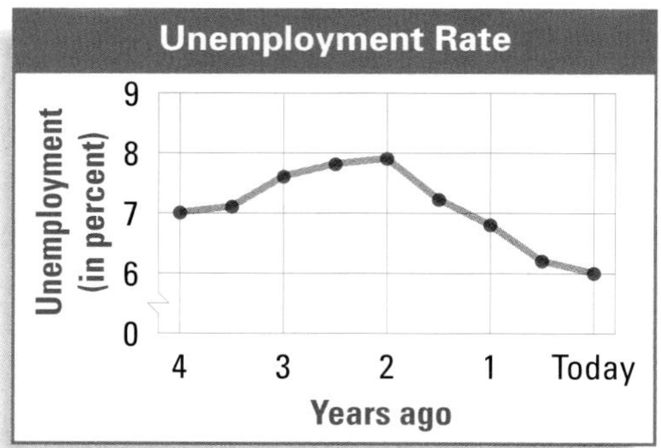

52. You want to find out if residents of your town support Smithers or Jones in the election for state governor. Explain how you could do an unbiased survey to find this out.

53. Explain how the wording of the following survey question could influence the results: Do you prefer to watch the crystal-clear, realistic picture on a new, digital television screen, or do you prefer to watch television on a standard television screen?

PROBABILITY

SDP 3.1, 3.3, 3.5

In Exercises 54–56, use the following information. The probability of Event A is 0.7. The probability of Event B is $\frac{3}{4}$.

54. Which event is more likely to occur, Event A or Event B?

55. What is the probability that Event A does *not* occur?

56. Event A and Event B are independent events. What is the probability that *both* Event A and Event B occur?

In Exercises 57 and 58, use the spinner at the right, which is divided into equal sections.

57. You spin the spinner twice. Make a tree diagram of the possible outcomes. Find the probability of each outcome.

58. Are the outcome on the first spin and the outcome on the second spin independent events or dependent events? Explain.

Table of Customary Measures

Time

60 seconds (sec)	=	1 minute (min)
3600 seconds 60 minutes	=	1 hour (h)
24 hours	=	1 day
7 days	=	1 week
365 days 12 months	=	1 year
366 days	=	1 leap year
10 years	=	1 decade
100 years	=	1 century

United States Customary

Length

12 inches (in.)	=	1 foot (ft)
36 in. 3 ft	=	1 yard (yd)
5280 ft 1760 yd	=	1 mile (mi)

Liquid Capacity

8 fluid ounces (fl oz)	=	1 cup (c)
2 c	=	1 pint (pt)
2 pt	=	1 quart (qt)
4 qt	=	1 gallon (gal)

Area

144 square inches (in.^2)	=	1 square foot (ft^2)
$9\ \text{ft}^2$	=	1 square yard (yd^2)
$43{,}560\ \text{ft}^2$	=	1 acre (A)
640 A	=	1 square mile (mi^2)

Weight

16 ounces (oz)	=	1 pound (lb)
2000 lb	=	1 ton (t)

Volume

1728 cubic inches (in.^3)	=	1 cubic foot (ft^3)
$27\ \text{ft}^3$	=	1 cubic yard (yd^3)

Temperature

Degrees Fahrenheit (°F)

32°F	=	freezing point of water
98.6°F	=	normal body temperature
212°F	=	boiling point of water

Converting Measurement within the United States Customary System

When you rewrite a measurement in another unit, you can use the relationships between the units to write a fraction that equals 1.

To change 45 miles per hour to feet per second:

$$\frac{45\ \text{mi}}{1\ \text{h}} = \frac{45\ \cancel{\text{mi}}}{1\ \cancel{\text{h}}} \times \frac{5280\ \text{ft}}{1\ \cancel{\text{mi}}} \times \frac{1\ \cancel{\text{h}}}{3600\ \text{s}}$$

$$= \frac{45 \times 5280 \times 1\ \text{ft}}{1 \times 1 \times 3600\ \text{s}}$$

$$= \frac{237{,}600\ \text{ft}}{3600\ \text{sec}}$$

$$= 66\ \text{ft/sec}$$

To change 120 ounces per square inch to pounds per square foot:

$$\frac{120\ \text{oz}}{1\ \text{in.}^2} = \frac{120\ \cancel{\text{oz}}}{1\ \cancel{\text{in.}^2}} \times \frac{144\ \cancel{\text{in.}^2}}{1\ \text{ft}^2} \times \frac{1\ \text{lb}}{16\ \cancel{\text{oz}}}$$

$$= \frac{120 \times 144 \times 1\ \text{lb}}{1 \times 1 \times 16\ \text{oz}}$$

$$= \frac{17{,}280\ \text{lb}}{16\ \text{ft}^2}$$

$$= 1080\ \text{lb/ft}^2$$

TABLES

Table of Metric Measures

Table of Units				
Prefix	**Power of 10**	**Length**	**Capacity**	**Mass**
kilo (k)	1000 units	kilometer	kiloliter	kilogram
hecto (h)	100 units	hectometer	hectoliter	hectogram
deka (da)	10 units	dekameter	dekaliter	dekagram
	1 unit	meter	liter	gram
deci (d)	0.1 unit	decimeter	deciliter	decigram
centi (c)	0.01 unit	centimeter	centiliter	centigram
milli (m)	0.001 unit	millimeter	milliliter	milligram

Metric

Length

10 millimeters (mm) = 1 centimeter (cm)
10 cm = 1 decimeter (dm)
100 cm, 1000 mm = 1 meter (m)
1000 m = 1 kilometer (km)

Liquid Capacity

10 deciliters (dL), 1000 mL = 1 L
1000 L = 1 kiloliter (kL)

Area

100 square millimeters (mm^2) = 1 square centimeter (cm^2)
10,000 cm^2 = 1 square meter (m^2)
10,000 m^2 = 1 hectare (ha)
1,000,000 m^2 = 1 square kilometer (km^2)

Mass

1000 milligrams (mg) = 1 gram (g)
1000 g = 1 kilogram (kg)
1000 kg = 1 metric ton (t)

Volume

1000 cubic millimeters (mm^3) = 1 cubic centimeter (cm^3)
1 cm^3 = 1 milliliter (mL)
1,000 cm^3 = 1 Liter (L)
1,000,000 cm^3 = 1 cubic meter (m^3)

Temperature

Degrees Celcius (°C)

0°C = freezing point of water
37°C = normal body temperature
100°C = boiling point of water

Converting Measurement within the Metric System

Use the relationships between units to convert measures with the metric system.

When you rewrite a measurement using a smaller unit, you multiply.

0.24 m = **?** cm

In the Table of Units, there are 2 steps from meters to centimeters, so multiply by 10^2, or 100.

$0.24 \text{ m} \times 100 = 24 \text{ cm}$

When you rewrite a measurement using a larger unit, you divide.

3500 mg = **?** kg

In the Table of Units, there are 6 steps from milligrams to kilograms, so divide by 10^6, or 1,000,000.

$3500 \text{ mg} \div 1{,}000{,}000 = 0.0035 \text{ kg}$

Table of Squares and Cubes

No.	Square	Cube
1	1	1
2	4	8
3	9	27
4	16	64
5	25	125
6	36	216
7	49	343
8	64	512
9	81	729
10	100	1,000
11	121	1,331
12	144	1,728
13	169	2,197
14	196	2,744
15	225	3,375
16	256	4,096
17	289	4,913
18	324	5,832
19	361	6,859
20	400	8,000
21	441	9,261
22	484	10,648
23	529	12,167
24	576	13,824
25	625	15,625
26	676	17,576
27	729	19,683
28	784	21,952
29	841	24,389
30	900	27,000
31	961	29,791
32	1,024	32,768
33	1,089	35,937
34	1,156	39,304
35	1,225	42,875
36	1,296	46,656
37	1,369	50,653
38	1,444	54,872
39	1,521	59,319
40	1,600	64,000
41	1,681	68,921
42	1,764	74,088
43	1,849	79,507
44	1,936	85,184
45	2,025	91,125
46	2,116	97,336
47	2,209	103,823
48	2,304	110,592
49	2,401	117,649
50	2,500	125,000
51	2,601	132,651
52	2,704	140,608
53	2,809	148,877
54	2,916	157,464
55	3,025	166,375
56	3,136	175,616
57	3,249	185,193
58	3,364	195,112
59	3,481	205,379
60	3,600	216,000
61	3,721	226,981
62	3,844	238,328
63	3,969	250,047
64	4,096	262,144
65	4,225	274,625
66	4,356	287,496
67	4,489	300,763
68	4,624	314,432
69	4,761	328,509
70	4,900	343,000
71	5,041	357,911
72	5,184	373,248
73	5,329	389,017
74	5,476	405,224
75	5,625	421,875
76	5,776	438,976
77	5,929	456,533
78	6,084	474,552
79	6,241	493,039
80	6,400	512,000
81	6,561	531,441
82	6,724	551,368
83	6,889	571,787
84	7,056	592,704
85	7,225	614,125
86	7,396	636,056
87	7,569	658,503
88	7,744	681,472
89	7,921	704,969
90	8,100	729,000
91	8,281	753,571
92	8,464	778,688
93	8,649	804,357
94	8,836	830,584
95	9,025	857,375
96	9,216	884,736
97	9,409	912,673
98	9,604	941,192
99	9,801	970,299
100	10,000	1,000,000
101	10,201	1,030,301
102	10,404	1,061,208
103	10,609	1,092,727
104	10,816	1,124,864
105	11,025	1,157,625
106	11,236	1,191,016
107	11,449	1,225,043
108	11,664	1,259,712
109	11,881	1,295,029
110	12,100	1,331,000
111	12,321	1,367,631
112	12,544	1,404,928
113	12,769	1,442,897
114	12,996	1,481,544
115	13,225	1,520,875
116	13,456	1,560,896
117	13,689	1,601,613
118	13,924	1,643,032
119	14,161	1,685,159
120	14,400	1,728,000
121	14,641	1,771,561
122	14,884	1,815,848
123	15,129	1,860,867
124	15,376	1,906,624
125	15,625	1,953,125
126	15,876	2,000,376
127	16,129	2,048,383
128	16,384	2,097,152
129	16,641	2,146,689
130	16,900	2,197,000
131	17,161	2,248,091
132	17,424	2,299,968
133	17,689	2,352,637
134	17,956	2,406,104
135	18,225	2,460,375
136	18,496	2,515,456
137	18,769	2,571,353
138	19,044	2,628,072
139	19,321	2,685,619
140	19,600	2,744,000
141	19,881	2,803,221
142	20,164	2,863,288
143	20,449	2,924,207
144	20,736	2,985,984
145	21,025	3,048,625
146	21,316	3,112,136
147	21,609	3,176,523
148	21,904	3,241,792
149	22,201	3,307,949
150	22,500	3,375,000

Table of Symbols

Symbol		Page	Symbol		Page
$a + b$	a plus b	7, 8	$^\circ$	degree(s)	168, 280
$a - b$	a minus b	7, 8	$\lvert a \rvert$	absolute value of a	177
$a \cdot b$, or ab	a times b	7, 8	$\stackrel{?}{=}$	is this statement true?	228
$a \div b$, or $\frac{a}{b}$	a divided by b	7, 8	$\frac{a}{b}$	ratio of a to b, or $a : b$	265
$=$	equal sign, is equal to	7, 221	$\overline{AB}$	side joining points A and B	280
( )	parentheses	12	AB	length of side $\overline{AB}$	280
[ ]	brackets	12	$\angle A$	angle A	280
a^n	nth power of a	17	$m\angle A$	measure of angle A	280
$<$	is less than	22	%	percent	311
$>$	is greater than	22	(parallel lines symbol)	parallel lines	357
$\approx$	is approximately equal to	28	$\cong$	is congruent to	357
$\ldots$	continues on	95	(right angle symbol)	right angle	282, 359
$1.\overline{54}$	the repeating decimal 1.5454. . .	95	(perpendicular lines symbol)	perpendicular lines	359
$\neq$	is not equal to	134	π	pi, an irrational number approximately equal to 3.14 or $\frac{22}{7}$	388
$\frac{1}{a}$	reciprocal of a, $a \neq 0$	134	(a, b)	ordered pair	468
5, or $+5$	positive 5	167	$P(A)$	the probability of A	516
-5	negative 5	167			

TABLES

Table of Formulas

Geometric Formulas	
Area of a square, p. 18	$A = s^2$ where s = side length
Area of a rectangle, p. 18	$A = \ell w$ where ℓ = length and w = width
Perimeter of a polygon, p. 31	P = Sum of the lengths of the sides
Perimeter of a rectangle, p. 39	$P = 2\ell + 2w$ where ℓ = length and w = width
Perimeter of a square, p. 39	$P = 4s$ where s = side length
Area of a triangle, p. 372	$A = \frac{1}{2}bh$ where b = base and h = height
Area of a parallelogram, p. 382	$A = bh$ where b = base and h = height
Circumference of a circle, p. 388	$C = \pi d$ where $\pi \approx 3.14$ and d = diameter
Area of a circle, p. 392	$A = \pi r^2$ where $\pi \approx 3.14$ and r = radius
Volume of a triangular prism, p. 418	$V = Bh$ where B = area of base and h = height
Volume of a rectangular prism, p. 419	$V = \ell wh$ where ℓ = length, w = width, and h = height
Volume of a cylinder, p. 423	$V = \pi r^2 h$ where $\pi \approx 3.14$, r = radius, and h = height
Surface area of a polyhedron, p. 430	S = Sum of the areas of the faces
Surface area of a cylinder, p. 434	S = Sum of the lateral surface area and the area of the two bases Lateral surface area = $2\pi rh$ Area of two bases = $2\pi r^2$
Other Formulas	
Distance traveled, p. 39	$d = rt$ where d = distance, r = rate, and t = time
Simple interest, p. 338	$I = Prt$ where I = interest, P = principal, r = rate, and t = time

Table of Properties

Basic Properties		
	Addition	**Multiplication**
Commutative, p. 13	$a + b = b + a$	$ab = ba$
Associative, p. 13	$(a + b) + c = a + (b + c)$	$(ab)c = a(bc)$
Inverse, pp. 134, 172	$a + (-a) = 0$	$\frac{a}{b} \times \frac{b}{a} = 1$
Distributive, p. 139	$a(b + c) = ab + ac$ or $(b + c)a = ba + ca$	

Properties of Equality	
Subtraction, p. 228	If $x + a = b$, then $x + a - a = b - a$.
Addition, p. 233	If $x - a = b$, then $x - a + a = b + a$.
Division, p. 239	If $ax = b$ and $a \neq 0$, then $\frac{ax}{a} = \frac{b}{a}$.
Multiplication, p. 243	If $\frac{x}{a} = b$ and $a \neq 0$, then $a \cdot \frac{x}{a} = a \cdot b$.

Properties of Fractions	
Addition, pp. 111, 112	$\frac{a}{c} + \frac{b}{c} = \frac{a + b}{c}$
	$\frac{a}{b} + \frac{c}{d} = \frac{ad + bc}{bd}$
Subtraction, pp. 111, 112	$\frac{a}{c} - \frac{b}{c} = \frac{a - b}{c}$
	$\frac{a}{b} - \frac{c}{d} = \frac{ad - bc}{bd}$
Multiplication, p. 126	$\frac{a}{b} \cdot \frac{c}{d} = \frac{ac}{bd}$
Division, p. 134	$\frac{a}{b} \div \frac{c}{d} = \frac{a}{b} \cdot \frac{d}{c}$

Properties of Proportions	
Cross products property, p. 269	If $\frac{a}{b} = \frac{c}{d}$, then $a \cdot d = b \cdot c$.

TABLES

Glossary

absolute value **(p. 177)** The absolute value of a number is its distance from 0 on a number line. The absolute value of a number a is written $|a|$. For example, the absolute value of -2, written $|-2|$, is 2.

acute angle **(p. 363)** An angle whose measure is between 0° and 90°.

acute triangle **(p. 367)** A triangle with 3 acute angles.

adjacent angles **(p. 358)** Two angles in the same plane that share a vertex and a common side, but do not overlap. In the diagram below, $\angle 1$ and $\angle 2$ are adjacent angles.

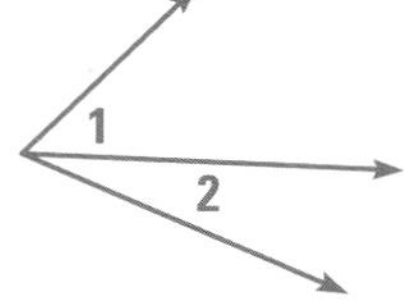

annual interest rate **(p. 338)** The percent of the principal earned (or paid) as interest for one year.

area **(pp. 18, 562)** A measure of how much surface is covered by a figure. Area is measured in square units.

associative property of addition **(p. 13)** Changing the grouping of terms will not change the sum. For all numbers a, b, and c, $(a + b) + c = a + (b + c)$.

associative property of multiplication **(p. 13)** Changing the grouping of factors will not change the product. For all numbers a, b, and c, $(ab)c = a(bc)$.

average **(p. 28)** The sum of the numbers in a set of data divided by the number of items in the set. It is also called the *mean*.

base of a circular cylinder **(p. 408)** *See* circular cylinder.

base of a parallelogram **(p. 382)** Any side of a parallelogram can be labeled as the base. *See also* parallelogram.

base of a power **(p. 17)** *See* power.

base of a prism **(p. 407)** *See* prism.

base of a triangle **(p. 372)** Any side of a triangle can be labeled as the base. *See also* height of a triangle.

biased sample **(p. 484)** A sample that is not representative of the population from which it is selected.

box-and-whisker plot **(p. 461)** A display that uses the median and the lower and upper quartiles to divide a data set into four parts.

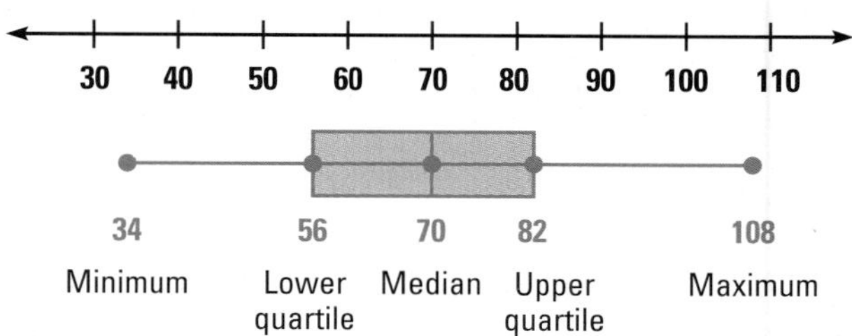

center of a circle **(p. 388)** The point inside a circle that is the same distance from all points on the circle.

circle **(p. 388)** The set of all points in a plane that are an equal distance from a given point, the center.

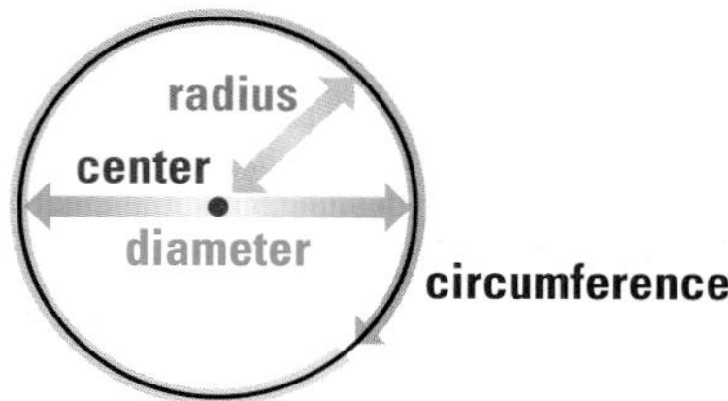

circle graph **(p. 333)** A graph that represents data as parts of a circle. The entire circle represents the whole.

circular cylinder **(p. 408)** A solid that has two parallel bases that are circles of the same size. The height of a cylinder is the perpendicular distance between the bases.

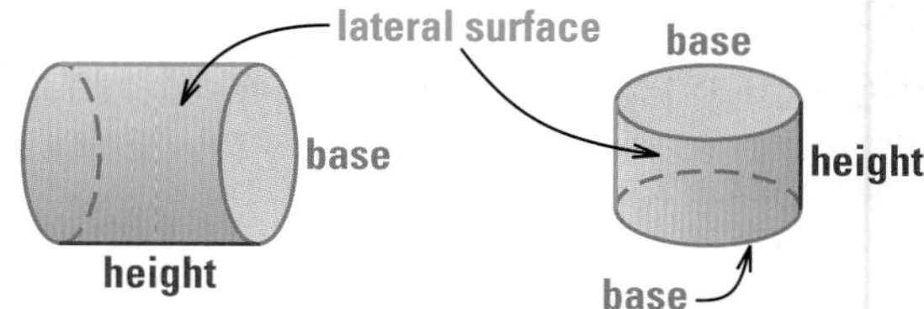

circumference of a circle **(p. 388)** The distance around a circle. Circumference is measured in linear units. *See also* circle.

circumference of a circular cylinder **(p. 434)** The circumference of a base of a cylinder.

common factor **(p. 65)** A whole number that is a factor of two or more nonzero whole numbers. For example, 1 and 5 are common factors of 10 and 25. *See also* factor.

GLOSSARY

common multiple (p. 79) A multiple shared by two or more numbers. For example, 10 and 20 are common multiples of 2 and 5. *See also* multiple.

commutative property of addition (p. 13) In a sum, you can add terms in any order. For all numbers a and b, $a + b = b + a$.

commutative property of multiplication (p. 13) In a product, you can multiply factors in any order. For all numbers a and b, $ab = ba$.

complementary angles (p. 358) Two angles whose measures have a sum of 90°.

composite number (p. 60) A whole number greater than 1 that has factors other than 1 and itself.

congruent angles (p. 357) Angles that have the same measure.

convenience sampling (p. 484) A sampling method in which easy-to-reach members of a population are chosen.

coordinate plane (p. 468) A coordinate system formed by a horizontal number line called the x-axis and a vertical number line called the y-axis.

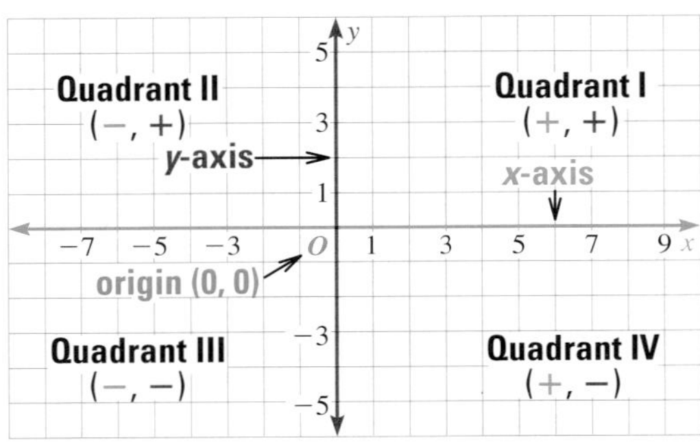

corresponding angles in similar polygons (p. 280) Two angles that have been paired up in two similar polygons. Corresponding angles have equal measure. *See also* similar polygons.

corresponding sides in similar polygons (p. 280) Two sides that have been paired up in two similar polygons. The ratios of the lengths of corresponding sides are equal. *See also* similar polygons.

cross multiplication (p. 269) The process of forming the cross products of a proportion.

cross products (p. 269) In the proportion $\frac{a}{b} = \frac{c}{d}$, the cross products are $a \cdot d$ and $b \cdot c$.

cube of a number (p. 17) The third power of a number.

data (p. 28) Numbers or facts that describe something.

decimal (p. 21) A number that is written using the base-ten place-value system.

denominator (p. 69) *See* fraction.

dependent events (p. 510) Two events are dependent if the occurrence of one affects the likelihood that the other will occur.

diameter of a circle (p. 388) The distance across a circle through its center.

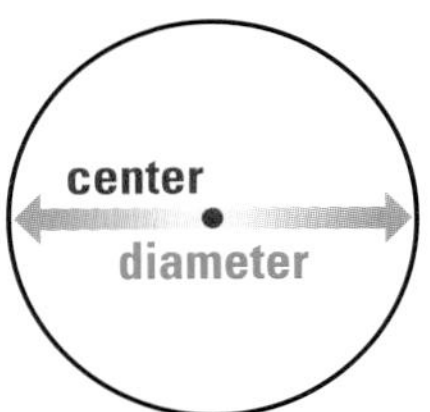

disjoint events (p. 509) Two events that have no outcomes in common.

distance traveled (p. 39) To find the distance traveled at a constant speed, multiply the speed by the time, or $d = rt$.

distributive property (pp. 139, 199) For all numbers a, b, and c, $a(b + c) = ab + ac$. For example, $3(5 + 2) = 3 \times 5 + 3 \times 2$. Also, $a(b - c) = ab - ac$. For example, $3(5 - 2) = 3 \times 5 - 3 \times 2$.

divisor (p. 60) A nonzero whole number that divides another nonzero whole number evenly. *See also* factor.

double bar graph (p. 474) A type of bar graph that uses pairs of bars to compare two data sets.

edge of a polyhedron (p. 407) A line segment where two faces meet. *See also* polyhedron.

equation (p. 221) A mathematical statement that uses an equal sign to separate two equal expressions.

equilateral triangle (p. 366) A triangle with three sides of the same length.

equivalent fractions (p. 73) Fractions that represent the same number.

evaluating a numerical expression (p. 7) Finding the value of an expression.

event (p. 292) A collection of outcomes.

experimental probability (p. 293) A probability based on repeated trials of an experiment. The experimental probability of an event is given by the ratio $\frac{\text{Number of successes}}{\text{Number of trials}}$.

exponent (p. 17) A number that indicates how many times a factor is repeated. In the power 10^3, the exponent 3 means that the base 10 is used as a factor 3 times: $10^3 = 10 \times 10 \times 10$.

face of a polyhedron **(p. 407)** A polygon that is part of the boundary of a polyhedron. *See also* polyhedron.

factor **(pp. 7, 59, 60)** When two nonzero whole numbers are multiplied together, each number is a factor of the product. Since $2 \times 3 = 6$, 2 and 3 are factors of 6. *See also* divisor.

factor tree **(p. 61)** A diagram that can be used to show the prime factorization of a number.

favorable outcome **(p. 292)** An outcome corresponding to a specified event. For example, if you roll a number cube, then there are 3 favorable outcomes for getting an odd number: 1, 3, and 5.

fraction **(p. 69)** A number of the form $\frac{a}{b}$ $(b \neq 0)$ where a and b are integers. Then a is called the numerator and b is called the denominator.

frequency **(p. 457)** The number of data values that lie in an interval of a frequency table.

frequency table **(p. 457)** A table that can be used to group the values in a data set into intervals.

graphing a number **(p. 21)** Plotting the point on a number line that corresponds to a number.

graph of an ordered pair **(p. 468)** The point in a coordinate plane whose coordinates are given by the ordered pair.

greatest common divisor, GCD **(p. 65)** The largest common divisor of two or more whole numbers. It is also called the *greatest common factor, GCF*.

greatest common factor, GCF **(p. 65)** The largest common factor of two or more whole numbers. It is also called the *greatest common divisor, GCD*. For example, the GCF of 10 and 25 is 5. *See also* common factor.

grouping symbols **(p. 12)** Symbols, such as parentheses ( ) and brackets [ ] , that are used to indicate operations that are performed first when evaluating an expression.

height of a cylinder **(p. 408)** The perpendicular distance between the two bases. *See also* circular cylinder.

height of a parallelogram **(p. 382)** The perpendicular distance between the base and the opposite side. *See also* parallelogram.

height of a prism **(p. 407)** The perpendicular distance between the two bases. *See also* prism.

height of a triangle **(p. 372)** The perpendicular distance between the base and the opposite vertex.

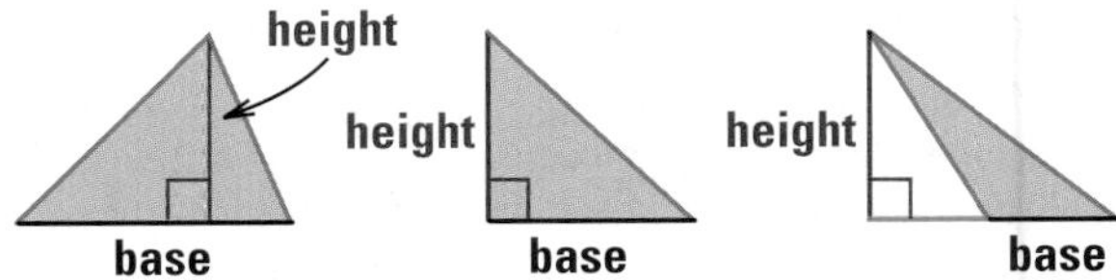

histogram **(p. 458)** A type of bar graph that displays data from a frequency table. There is one bar for each interval of the table. The height of the bar represents the frequency of data values in that interval.

improper fraction **(p. 90)** For positive fractions, a number that is greater than or equal to 1. For example, $\frac{7}{7}$ and $\frac{8}{7}$ are improper fractions.

independent events **(p. 510)** Two events are independent if the occurrence of one does not affect the likelihood that the other will occur.

integers **(p. 167)** The numbers . . ., $-4, -3, -2, -1, 0, 1, 2, 3, 4,$ . . ., consisting of the negative integers, zero, and the positive integers.

interest **(p. 338)** Money paid for the use of money.

interquartile range **(p. 462)** The difference of the upper and lower quartiles for a set of data values.

intersecting lines **(p. 357)** Two lines in a plane that meet at a common point.

inverse operations **(p. 250)** Operations that "undo" each other. For example, addition and subtraction are inverse operations, as are multiplication and division.

isosceles triangle **(p. 366)** A triangle with at least two sides of the same length.

lateral surface **(p. 434)** The surface of a cylinder that connects the two bases. *See also* circular cylinder.

least common denominator, LCD **(p. 84)** The least common multiple of the denominators of two or more fractions. For example, the LCD of $\frac{2}{9}$ and $\frac{1}{6}$ is 18.

least common multiple, LCM **(p. 79)** The smallest common multiple of two or more numbers. For example, the LCM of 2 and 3 is 6. *See also* common multiple.

line graph **(p. 475)** A type of graph that uses points connected by line segments.

lower quartile **(p. 461)** The median of the lower half of a set of data values. *See also* box-and-whisker plot.

mean **(pp. 28, 453)** The sum of the numbers in a set of data divided by the number of items in the set. It is also called the *average*.

measure of central tendency **(p. 453)** A single number that represents a "typical" value for a set of numerical data. The *mean*, *median*, and *mode* are common measures of central tendency.

median **(p. 453)** For a data set with an odd number of values, the median is the middle value when the values are written in numerical order. For a data set with an even number of values, the median is the mean of the two middle values.

mixed number **(p. 90)** A number that has a whole number part and a fraction part. For example, $3\frac{2}{5}$ is a mixed number.

mode **(p. 453)** The value in a data set that occurs most often.

multiple of a number **(p. 79)** The product of the number and any nonzero whole number. For example, 2, 4, and 6 are multiples of 2.

multiplicative inverses **(p. 134)** Two numbers whose product is 1. Multiplicative inverses are also called *reciprocals*.

negative integers **(p. 167)** The integers $-1, -2, -3, -4, \ldots$ which are to the left of 0 on a number line.

negative sign **(p. 167)** The symbol, $-$, used to represent negative numbers. For example, you read -3 as "negative three."

number line **(pp. 21, 167)** A line on which every point is associated with a real number.

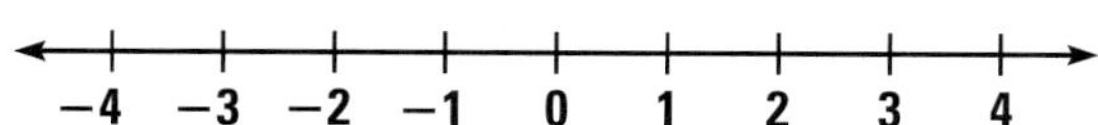

numerator **(p. 69)** *See* fraction.

numerical expression **(p. 7)** An expression that represents a particular number. It consists of numbers and arithmetic operations to be performed.

obtuse angle **(p. 363)** An angle whose measure is between 90° and 180°.

obtuse triangle **(p. 367)** A triangle with an obtuse angle.

opposites **(p. 171)** Two numbers that are the same distance from 0 on a number line but are on opposite sides of 0. For example, -3 and 3 are opposites.

ordered pair **(p. 468)** A pair of numbers, such as $(2, -4)$. It can be used to locate a point in a coordinate plane. The first number is the x-coordinate and the second number is the y-coordinate.

order of operations **(pp. 12, 18, 198)** A procedure for evaluating an expression involving more than one operation.

1. Evaluate expressions inside grouping symbols.
2. Evaluate powers.
3. Multiply and divide from left to right.
4. Add and subtract from left to right.

origin **(p. 468)** The point (0, 0) where the x-axis and y-axis intersect in a coordinate plane. *See also* coordinate plane.

outcome **(p. 292)** A possible result of an experiment. For example, the outcomes for tossing a coin are heads and tails.

outlier **(p. 454)** A value in a data set that is much greater than or much less than most other values in the set.

overlapping events **(p. 509)** Two events that have one or more outcomes in common.

parallel lines **(p. 357)** Lines in the same plane that do not intersect. (Identical lines are sometimes considered to be parallel.) In the diagram below, red arrowheads are used to indicate that the lines are parallel.

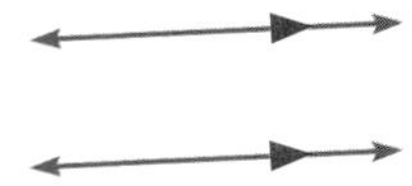

parallelogram **(p. 376)** A quadrilateral whose opposite sides are parallel.

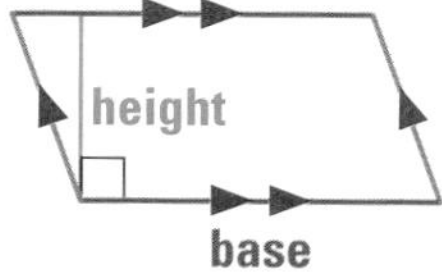

pentagon **(p. 31)** A polygon with 5 sides.

percent **(p. 311)** Per hundred; a ratio whose denominator is 100. For example, $21\% = \frac{21}{100}$.

perimeter **(pp. 31, 562)** The perimeter of a polygon is the sum of the lengths of its sides. Perimeter is measured in linear units.

perpendicular lines **(p. 359)** Lines that intersect to form a right angle.

pi (π) (p. 388) The number that is the ratio of the circumference of a circle to its diameter. Commonly used approximations for π are 3.14 and $\frac{22}{7}$.

pictograph (p. 474) A graph that uses pictures or symbols to represent data.

plane (p. 357) A flat surface that extends indefinitely in all directions.

polygon (p. 31) A closed plane figure bounded by line segments called the *sides* of the polygon. For example, a triangle and a rectangle are polygons.

polyhedron (p. 407) A solid that is bounded by polygons called the *faces* of the polyhedron. Adjacent faces meet at the *edges* of the polyhedron.

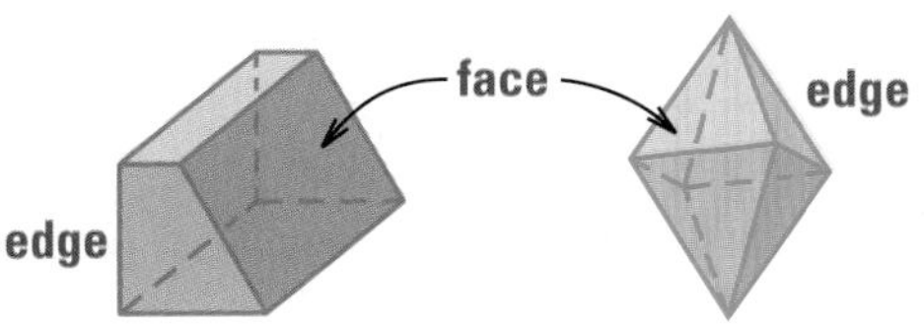

population (p. 483) In statistics, the entire group of people or objects about which you want information.

positive integers (p. 167) The integers 1, 2, 3, 4, . . . which are to the right of 0 on a number line.

power (p. 17) An expression such as x^4 that has an exponent. In the expression x^4, x is the base and 4 is the exponent.

prime factorization (p. 61) Writing a number as the product of prime numbers.

prime number (p. 60) A whole number greater than 1 whose only whole number factors are 1 and itself.

principal (p. 338) An amount of money borrowed, loaned, or saved.

prism (p. 407) A polyhedron with two parallel bases that are polygons of the same size and shape. The height of a prism is the perpendicular distance between the two bases.

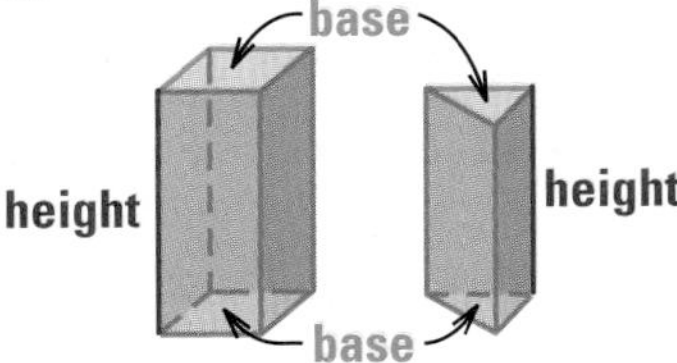

probability of an event (p. 292) A number from 0 to 1 that measures the likelihood that a particular event will occur.

proper fraction (p. 90) For positive fractions, a number between 0 and 1. For example, $\frac{7}{8}$ is a proper fraction.

proportion (p. 269) An equation that equates two ratios. A proportion has the form $\frac{a}{b} = \frac{c}{d}$.

proportional sides (p. 280) The sides of two polygons are proportional if each side of one polygon can be paired with a side of the other polygon so that the ratios of the lengths of the paired sides are equal.

quadrant (p. 468) One of the four regions into which a coordinate plane is divided by the x-axis and the y-axis. *See also* coordinate plane.

quadrilateral (pp. 280, 376) A polygon with 4 sides.

radius of a circle (p. 388) The distance between a point on a circle and its center. *See also* circle.

random sampling (p. 484) A sampling method in which each member of a population has an equally likely chance of being chosen.

range (in statistics) (p. 462) The difference of the maximum and minimum values in a data set.

rate of *a* per *b* (p. 148) If two quantities a and b have different units of measure, then the rate of a per b is $\frac{a}{b}$. For example, if you are paid $12 for 3 hours of work, then your hourly rate is $\frac{12 \text{ dollars}}{3 \text{ hours}}$, or $4 per hour.

ratio (p. 265) A comparison of a number a and a nonzero number b using division by b. The ratio of a to b can be written as $\frac{a}{b}$, as $a : b$, or as "a to b."

reciprocals (p. 134) Two numbers whose product is 1. For example, $\frac{5}{12}$ and $\frac{12}{5}$ are reciprocals. Reciprocals are also called *multiplicative inverses*.

rectangle (p. 377) A parallelogram that has 4 right angles.

relatively prime numbers (p. 67) Two whole numbers whose greatest common factor is 1. *See also* greatest common factor.

repeating decimal (p. 95) A fraction $\frac{a}{b}$ ($b \neq 0$) can be written in decimal form by using long division to divide a by b. If the division process does not stop, then it leads to a digit or a group of digits that repeats over and over. In this case the decimal form of the fraction is a repeating decimal.

right angle (pp. 282, 359) An angle whose measure is 90°.

right circular cylinder (p. 408) In a right circular cylinder, the line segment connecting the centers of the circular bases is perpendicular to the bases.

right prism (p. 407) In a right prism, the edges connecting the bases are perpendicular to the bases.

right triangle (p. 367) A triangle with a right angle.

sample (p. 483) A subset of a population.

scale (p. 285) In a scale drawing, the scale gives the relationship between the drawing's dimensions and the actual dimensions. For example, the scale 1 in. = 2 ft means that 1 in. in the drawing represents an actual distance of 2 ft.

scale drawing (p. 285) A drawing of an object such that the dimensions in the drawing are proportional to the actual dimensions of the object.

scale factor (p. 285) The ratio of the dimensions in a scale drawing to the corresponding actual dimensions.

scalene triangle (p. 366) A triangle whose 3 sides all have different lengths.

scatter plot (p. 469) A collection of points in a coordinate plane that represents a set of ordered pairs.

self-selected sample (p. 484) A sampling method in which members of a population volunteer to be part of the sample.

similar polygons (p. 280) Polygons whose angles and sides can be paired so that corresponding angles have equal measure and the ratios of the lengths of corresponding sides are equal.

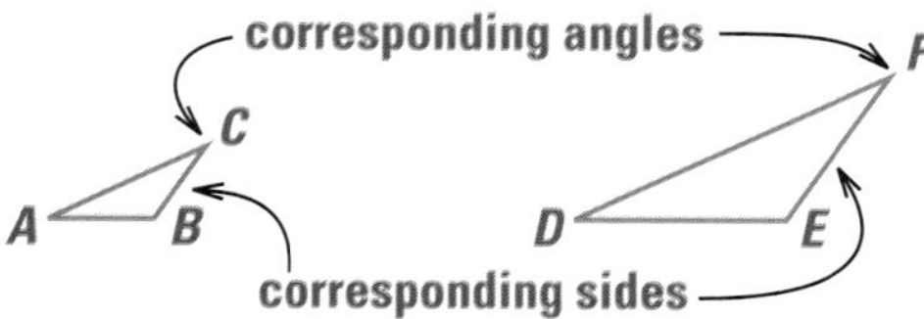

simple interest (p. 338) Interest that is calculated as the product of the principal, the annual interest rate, and the time in years. $I = Prt$

simplest form of a fraction (p. 73) A fraction is in simplest form if its numerator and denominator have a greatest common factor of 1.

solution of an equation in one variable (p. 221) A value of the variable that makes the equation true.

solving an equation (p. 221) Finding all the solutions of an equation.

square (p. 377) A rectangle with all sides the same length.

square of a number (p. 17) The second power of a number.

supplementary angles (p. 358) Two angles whose measures have a sum of 180°.

surface area of a cylinder (p. 434) The sum of the lateral surface area and the areas of the two bases.

surface area of a polyhedron (p. 430) The sum of the areas of the faces of a polyhedron.

systematic sampling (p. 484) A sampling method in which a pattern is used to select members of a population.

terminating decimal (p. 95) A fraction $\frac{a}{b}$ $(b \neq 0)$ can be written in decimal form by using long division to divide a by b. If the division process stops because a remainder is zero, then the decimal form of the fraction is a terminating decimal.

terms of a sum (p. 7) In a sum, the numbers or expressions that are added. In the sum 2 + 4, the terms are 2 and 4.

theoretical probability (p. 293) A probability that is found by mathematical reasoning. If the outcomes of an experiment are equally likely, then the theoretical probability of an event is given by the ratio $\frac{\text{Number of favorable outcomes}}{\text{Total number of outcomes}}$.

tree diagram (p. 505) A diagram that shows all the possible outcomes of a process carried out in several stages.

triangle (p. 31) A polygon with 3 sides.

unit rate (p. 148) A rate with a denominator of 1 unit. For example, a speed of $\frac{35 \text{ mi}}{1 \text{ h}}$, or 35 miles per hour, is a unit rate.

upper quartile (p. 461) The median of the upper half of a set of data values. *See also* box-and-whisker plot.

value of a variable (p. 8) A number represented by a variable.

variable (p. 8) A letter that represents one or more numbers.

variable expression (p. 8) An expression that contains one or more variables and operations to be performed.

Venn diagram (p. 509) A drawing that uses geometric shapes to show relationships among sets.

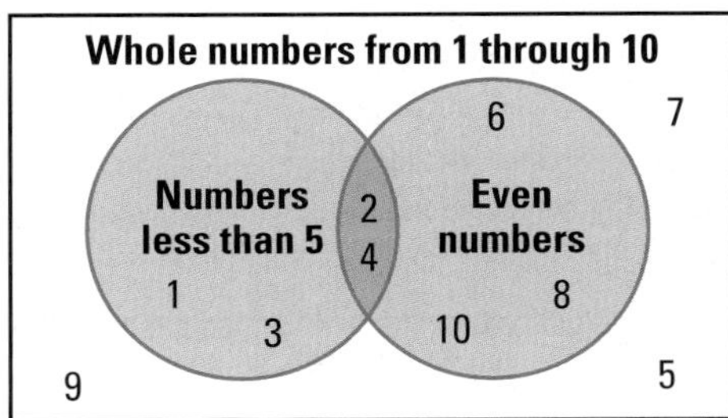

vertex of an angle (p. 358) A point where the sides of an angle meet.

vertical angles (p. 357) The angles opposite each other when two lines intersect. In the diagram below, $\angle 1$ and $\angle 3$ are vertical angles. $\angle 2$ and $\angle 4$ are vertical angles.

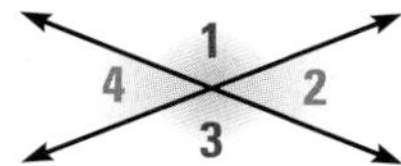

volume (p. 411) The volume of a solid is a measure of the amount of space the solid occupies. Volume is measured in cubic units.

***x*-axis** (p. 468) The horizontal axis in a coordinate plane. *See also* coordinate plane.

***x*-coordinate** (p. 468) The first number in the coordinates of a point. *See also* ordered pair.

***y*-axis** (p. 468) The vertical axis in a coordinate plane. *See also* coordinate plane.

***y*-coordinate** (p. 468) The second number in the coordinates of a point. *See also* ordered pair.

GLOSSARY

English-to-Spanish Glossary

absolute value (p. 177) **valor absoluto** El valor absoluto de un número es la distancia que hay entre ese número y 0 en una recta numérica. El valor absoluto de un número a se escribe $|a|$. Por ejemplo, el valor absoluto de -2, que se indica $|-2|$, es 2.

acute angle (p. 363) **ángulo agudo** Ángulo que mide entre 0° y 90°.

acute triangle (p. 367) **triángulo acutángulo** Triángulo que tiene 3 ángulos agudos.

adjacent angles (p. 358) **ángulos adyacentes** Dos ángulos del mismo plano que comparten un vértice y un lado común, pero sin superponerse. En el digrama abajo, $\angle 1$ y $\angle 2$ son ángulos adyacentes.

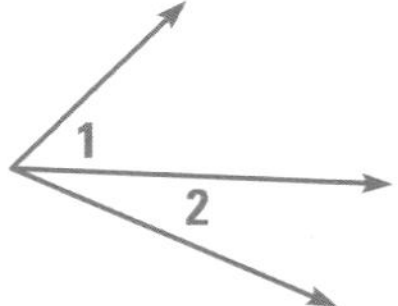

annual interest rate (p. 338) **tipo de interés anual** Porcentaje del capital ganado (o pagado) como intereses en un año.

area (pp. 18, 562) **área** Medida de la superficie que cubre una figura. El área se mide en unidades cuadradas.

associative property of addition (p. 13) **propiedad asociativa de la suma** Al cambiar la agrupación de los términos, no cambia la suma. Para todos los números a, b y c, $(a + b) + c = a + (b + c)$.

associative property of multiplication (p. 13) **propiedad asociativa de la multiplicación** Al cambiar la agrupación de los factores, no cambia el producto. Para todos los números a, b y c, $(ab)c = a(bc)$.

average (p. 28) **promedio** Suma de los números de un conjunto de datos dividida entre la cantidad de elementos del conjunto. Se llama también *media.*

base of a circular cylinder (p. 408) **base de un cilindro circular** *Ver* cilindro circular.

base of a parallelogram (p. 382) **base de un paralelogramo** Cualquier lado de un paralelogramo puede señalarse como la base. *Ver también* paralelogramo.

base of a power (p. 17) **base de una potencia** *Ver* potencia.

base of a prism (p. 407) **base de un prisma** *Ver* prisma.

base of a triangle (p. 372) **base de un triángulo** Cualquier lado de un triángulo puede señalarse como la base. *Ver también* altura de un triángulo.

biased sample (p. 484) **muestra sesgada** Muestra que no es representativa de la población de la cual fue elegida.

box-and-whisker plot (p. 461) **gráfica de frecuencias acumuladas** Representación que mediante la mediana y los cuartiles inferior y superior divide a un conjunto de datos en cuatro partes.

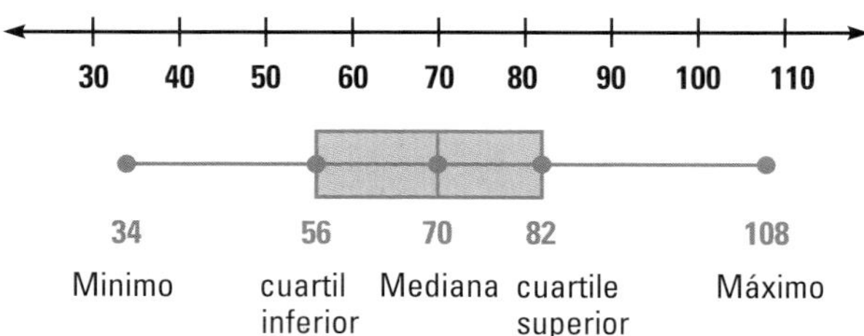

center of a circle (p. 388) **centro de un círculo** Punto del interior de un círculo que está a igual distancia de todos los puntos del círculo.

circle (p. 388) **círculo** Conjunto de todos los puntos de un plano que están a igual distancia de un punto dado llamado centro.

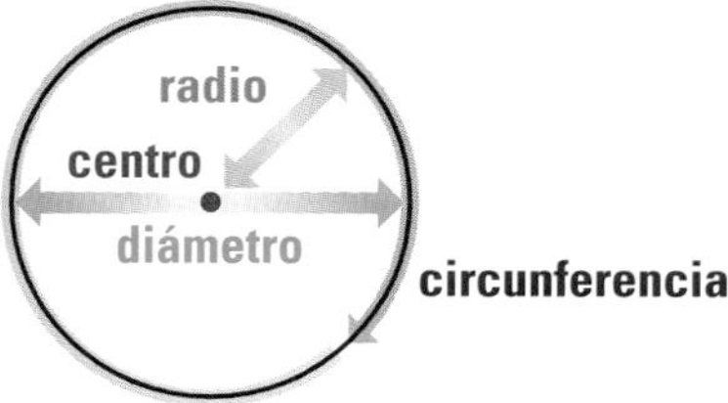

circle graph (p. 333) **gráfica circular** Gráfica que representa datos como partes de un círculo. Todo el círculo en sí representa el entero.

circular cylinder (p. 408) **cilindro circular** Sólido cuyos dos bases paralelas son círculos de igual tamaño. La altura de un cilindro es la distancia perpendicular que hay entre las bases.

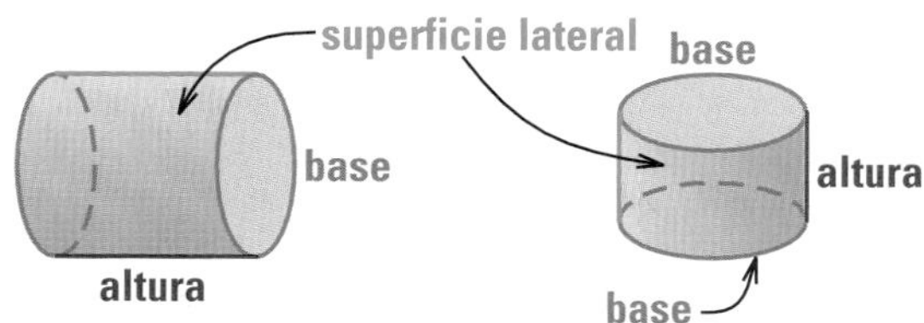

circumference of a circle (p. 388) **circunferencia de un círculo** Longitud del contorno de un círculo. La circunferencia se mide en unidades lineales. *Ver también* círculo.

circumference of a circular cylinder (p. 434) **circunferencia de un cilindro circular** Circunferencia de una base de un cilindro.

common factor (p. 65) **factor común** Número entero que es factor de dos o más números enteros distintos a cero. Por ejemplo, 1 y 5 son factores comunes de 10 y 25. *Ver también* factor.

common multiple (p. 79) **múltiplo común** Múltiplo compartido por dos o más números. Por ejemplo, 10 y 20 son múltiplos comunes de 2 y 5. *Ver también* múltiplo.

commutative property of addition (p. 13) **propiedad conmutativa de la suma** En una suma, no importa el orden de los términos. Para todos los números a y b, $a + b = b + a$.

commutative property of multiplication (p. 13) **propiedad conmutativa de la multiplicación** En un producto, no importa el orden de los factores. Para todos los números a y b, $ab = ba$.

complementary angles (p. 358) **ángulos complementarios** Dos ángulos cuyas medidas suman 90°.

composite number (p. 60) **número compuesto** Número entero mayor que 1 que tiene otros factores además de 1 y de él mismo.

congruent angles (p. 357) **ángulos congruentes** Ángulos que tienen igual medida.

convenience sampling (p. 484) **muestreo de conveniencia** Método de muestreo con el que se elige de entre una población a miembros a los que se tiene fácil acceso.

coordinate plane (p. 468) **plano de coordenadas** Sistema de coordenadas formado por una recta numérica horizontal llamada eje de las x y una recta numérica vertical denominada eje de las y.

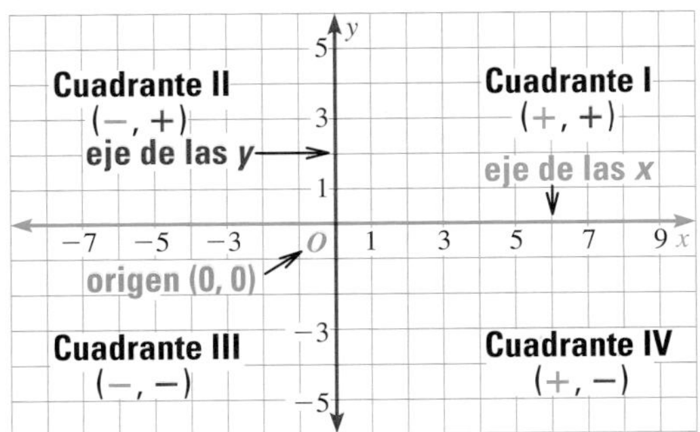

corresponding angles in similar polygons (p. 280) **ángulos correspondientes de polígonos semejantes** En dos polígonos semejantes, dos ángulos que se emparejan. Los ángulos correspondientes tienen igual medida. *Ver también* polígonos semejantes.

corresponding sides in similar polygons (p. 280) **lados correspondientes de polígonos semejantes** En dos polígonos semejantes, dos lados que se emparejan. Las razones de las longitudes de los lados correspondientes son iguales. *Ver también* polígonos semejantes.

cross multiplication (p. 269) **multiplicación en cruz** Proceso de formar los productos cruzados de una proporción.

cross products (p. 269) **productos cruzados** En la proporción $\frac{a}{b} = \frac{c}{d}$, los productos cruzados son $a \cdot d$ y $b \cdot c$.

cube of a number (p. 17) **cubo de un número** Tercera potencia de un número.

D

data (p. 28) **datos** Números o hechos que describen algo.

decimal (p. 21) **decimal** Número escrito según el sistema de valor relativo de base diez.

denominator (p. 69) **denominador** *Ver* fracción.

dependent events (p. 510) **sucesos dependientes** Dos sucesos son dependientes si la realización de uno afecta a la probabilidad de que ocurra el otro.

diameter of a circle (p. 388) **diámetro de un círculo** Distancia entre dos puntos de un círculo, pasando por el centro.

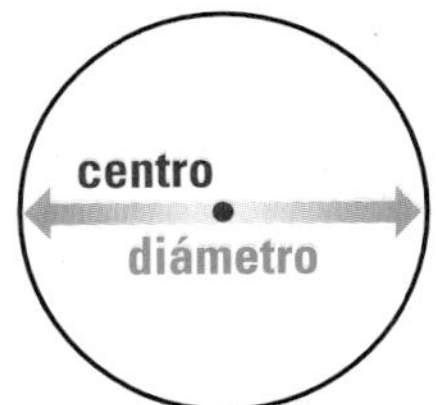

disjoint events (p. 509) **sucesos incompatibles** Dos sucesos que no tienen ningún resultado en común.

distance traveled (p. 39) **distancia recorrida** Para hallar la distancia recorrida a una velocidad constante se multiplica la velocidad por el tiempo, o $d = rt$.

distributive property (pp. 139, 199) **propiedad distributiva** Para todos los números a, b y c, $a(b + c) = ab + ac$. Por ejemplo, $3(5 + 2) = 3 \times 5 + 3 \times 2$. Además, $a(b - c) = ab - ac$. Por ejemplo, $3(5 - 2) = 3 \times 5 - 3 \times 2$.

divisor (p. 60) **divisor** Número entero distinto a cero que divide exactamente a otro número entero distinto a cero. *Ver también* factor.

double bar graph (p. 474) **gráfica de doble barra** Tipo de gráficas de barras que utiliza pares de barras para comparar dos conjuntos de datos.

edge of a polyhedron (p. 407) **arista de un poliedro** Segmento de recta donde se unen dos caras. *Ver también* poliedro.

equation (p. 221) **ecuación** Enunciado matemático cuyas dos expresiones iguales están separadas mediante un signo de igual.

equilateral triangle (p. 366) **triángulo equilátero** Triángulo de tres lados de igual longitud.

equivalent fractions (p. 73) **fracciones equivalentes** Fracciones que representan el mismo número.

evaluating a numerical expression (p. 7) **evaluar una expresión numérica** Hallar el valor de una expresión.

event (p. 292) **suceso** Conjunto de casos.

experimental probability (p. 293) **probabilidad experimental** Probabilidad basada en la realización de las pruebas de un experimento repetidas veces. La probabilidad experimental de un suceso viene dada por la razón $\frac{\text{Número de éxitos}}{\text{Número de pruebas}}$.

exponent (p. 17) **exponente** Número que indica las veces que se repite un factor. En la potencia 10^3, el exponente 3 indica que la base 10 se utiliza 3 veces como factor: $10^3 = 10 \times 10 \times 10$.

face of a polyhedron (p. 407) **cara de un poliedro** Polígono que forma parte del límite de un poliedro. *Ver también* poliedro.

factor (pp. 7, 59, 60) **factor** Al multiplicar dos números enteros distintos a cero, cada uno de ellos es factor del producto. Como $2 \times 3 = 6$, 2 y 3 son factores de 6. *Ver también* divisor.

factor tree (p. 61) **árbol de factorización** Diagrama que sirve para mostrar la descomposición de un número en sus factores primos.

favorable outcome (p. 292) **caso favorable** Resultado correspondiente a un suceso específico. Por ejemplo, al lanzar un dado hay 3 casos favorables a obtener un número impar: 1, 3 y 5.

fraction (p. 69) **fracción** Número de la forma $\frac{a}{b}$ $(b \neq 0)$, donde a y b son números enteros. Así, a se llama numerador y b denominador.

frequency (p. 457) **frecuencia** Número de valores de datos que se encuentran en un intervalo de una tabla de frecuencias.

frequency table (p. 457) **tabla de frecuencias** Tabla que sirve para agrupar en intervalos los valores de un conjunto de datos.

graphing a number (p. 21) **representar gráficamente un número** Marcar en una recta numérica el punto que corresponde a un número.

graph of an ordered pair (p. 468) **gráfica de un par ordenado** Punto situado en un plano de coordenadas cuyas coordenadas vienen dadas por el par ordenado.

greatest common divisor, GCD (p. 65) **máximo común divisor, MCD** Mayor divisor común de dos o más números enteros. Se llama también *máximo común factor, MCF.*

greatest common factor, GCF (p. 65) **máximo común factor, MCF** Mayor factor común de dos o más números enteros. Se llama también *máximo común divisor, MCD.* Por ejemplo, el MCF de 10 y 25 es 5. *Ver también* factor común.

grouping symbols (p. 12) **signos de agrupación** Signos como los paréntesis ( ) y los corchetes [ ] que indican las operaciones que se efectúan primero al evaluar una expresión.

height of a cylinder (p. 408) **altura de un cilindro** Distancia perpendicular entre las dos bases. *Ver también* cilindro circular.

height of a parallelogram (p. 382) **altura de un paralelogramo** Distancia perpendicular entre la base y el lado opuesto. *Ver también* paralelogramo.

height of a prism (p. 407) **altura de un prisma** Distancia perpendicular entre las dos bases. *Ver también* prisma.

height of a triangle (p. 372) **altura de un triángulo** Distancia perpendicular entre la base y el vértice opuesto.

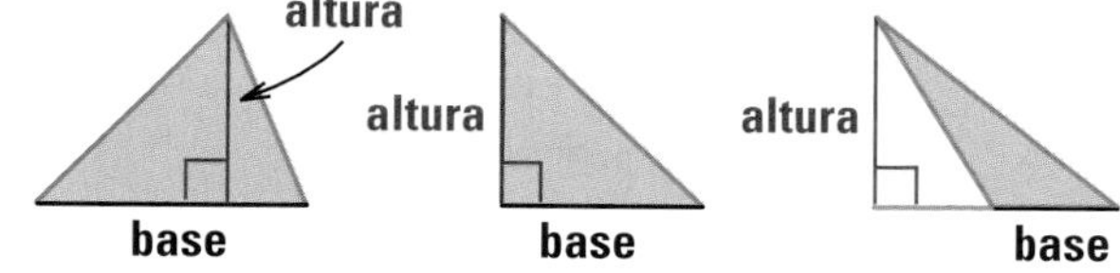

histogram (p. 458) **histograma** Tipo de gráficas de barras que presenta datos de una tabla de frecuencias. A cada intervalo de la tabla le corresponde una barra. La altura de la barra representa la frecuencia de los valores de datos de ese intervalo.

improper fraction (p. 90) **fracción impropia** Para fracciones positivas, un número mayor o igual a 1. Por ejemplo, $\frac{7}{7}$ y $\frac{8}{7}$ son fracciones impropias.

independent events (p. 510) **sucesos independientes** Dos sucesos son independientes si la realización de uno no afecta a la probabilidad de que ocurra el otro.

integers (p. 167) **números enteros** Los números ..., −4, −3, −2, −1, 0, 1, 2, 3, 4, ..., los cuales consisten en los números enteros negativos, los positivos y cero.

interest (p. 338) **interés** Dinero pagado a cambio del uso de otro.

interquartile range (p. 462) **recorrido intercuartílico** Diferencia entre los cuartiles superior e inferior de un conjunto de valores de datos.

intersecting lines (p. 357) **rectas secantes** Dos rectas de un plano que se cortan en un punto común.

inverse operations (p. 250) **operaciones inversas** Operaciones que "se anulan" mutuamente. Por ejemplo, la suma y la resta son operaciones inversas y también lo son la multiplicación y la división.

isosceles triangle (p. 366) **triángulo isósceles** Triángulo que tiene al menos dos lados de igual longitud.

lateral surface (p. 434) **superficie lateral** Superficie de un cilindro que une las dos bases. *Ver también* cilindro circular.

least common denominator, LCD (p. 84) **mínimo común denominador, mcd** Menor múltiplo común de los denominadores de dos o más fracciones. Por ejemplo, el mcd de $\frac{2}{9}$ y $\frac{1}{6}$ es 18.

least common multiple, LCM (p. 79) **mínimo común múltiplo, mcm** Menor múltiplo común de dos o más números. Por ejemplo, el mcm de 2 y 3 es 6. *Ver también* múltiplo común.

line graph (p. 475) **gráfica lineal** Tipo de gráficas en el que aparecen puntos unidos mediante segmentos de recta.

lower quartile (p. 461) **cuartil inferior** Mediana de la mitad inferior de un conjunto de valores de datos. *Ver también* diagrama de frecuencias acumuladas.

mean (pp. 28, 453) **media** Suma de los números de un conjunto de datos dividida entre la cantidad de elementos del conjunto. Se llama también *promedio.*

measure of central tendency (p. 453) **medida de tendencia central** Un solo número que representa un valor "típico" de un conjunto de datos numéricos. La *media, la mediana* y *la moda* son medidas de tendencia central comunes.

median (p. 453) **mediana** Para un conjunto de datos con un número impar de valores, la mediana es el valor central cuando los valores están escritos en orden numérico. Para un conjunto de datos con un número par de valores, la mediana es la media de los dos valores centrales.

mixed number (p. 90) **número mixto** Número formado por una parte entera y otra fraccionaria. Por ejemplo, $3\frac{2}{5}$ es un número mixto.

mode (p. 453) **moda** Valor que aparece más veces en un conjunto de datos.

multiple of a number (p. 79) **múltiplo de un número** Producto del número y cualquier número entero distinto a cero. Por ejemplo, 2, 4 y 6 son múltiplos de 2.

multiplicative inverses (p. 134) **inversos multiplicativos** Dos números cuyo producto es 1. Los inversos multiplicativos se llaman también *recíprocos.*

negative integers (p. 167) **números enteros negativos** Los números enteros −1, −2, −3, −4, ..., los cuales se encuentran a la izquierda del 0 en una recta numérica.

negative sign (p. 167) **signo negativo** El signo −, utilizado para representar números negativos. Por ejemplo, −3 se lee "menos tres".

number line (pp. 21, 167) **recta numérica** Línea donde cada punto está asociado a un número real.

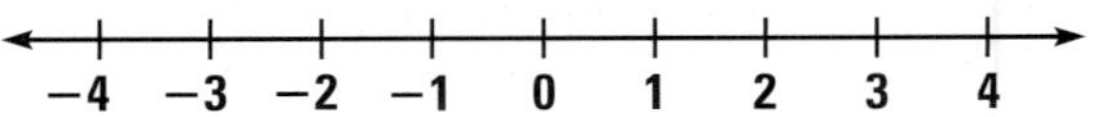

numerator (p. 69) **numerador** *Ver* fracción.

numerical expression (p. 7) **expresión numérica** Expresión que representa un número en particular. Contiene números y operaciones aritméticas que deben realizarse.

obtuse angle (p. 363) **ángulo obtuso** Ángulo que mide entre 90° y 180°.

obtuse triangle (p. 367) **triángulo obtusángulo** Triángulo que tiene un ángulo obtuso.

opposites (p. 171) **opuestos** Dos números situados a igual distancia de 0 en una recta numérica pero en lados opuestos del mismo. Por ejemplo, −3 y 3 son opuestos.

ordered pair (p. 468) **par ordenado** Par de números como (2, −4). Sirve para localizar un punto en un plano de coordenadas. El primer número es la coordenada *x* y el segundo la coordenada *y.*

order of operations (pp. 12, 18, 198) **orden de las operaciones** Proceso para evaluar una expresión relacionada con más de una operación.

1. Evaluar las expresiones de los signos de agrupación.
2. Evaluar las potencias.
3. Multiplicar y dividir de izquierda a derecha.
4. Sumar y restar de izquierda a derecha.

origin (p. 468) **origen** El punto (0, 0) donde el eje de las x y el de las y se cortan en un plano de coordenadas. *Ver también* plano de coordenadas.

outcome (p. 292) **caso** Resultado posible de un experimento. Por ejemplo, al lanzar al aire una moneda los casos son cara y cruz.

outlier (p. 454) **valor extremo** Valor de un conjunto de datos que es mucho mayor o mucho menor que la mayoría de los otros valores del conjunto.

overlapping events (p. 509) **sucesos compatibles** Dos sucesos que tienen en común al menos un caso.

parallel lines (p. 357) **rectas paralelas** Rectas del mismo plano que no se cortan. (A veces se consideran paralelas las rectas idénticas.) En el diagrama abajo, se utilizan flechas rojas para indicar que las rectas son paralelas.

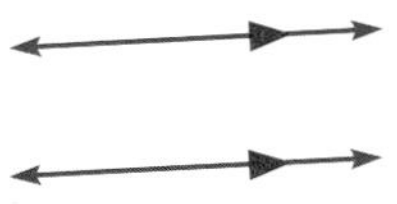

parallelogram (p. 376) **paralelogramo** Cuadrilátero cuyos lados opuestos son paralelos.

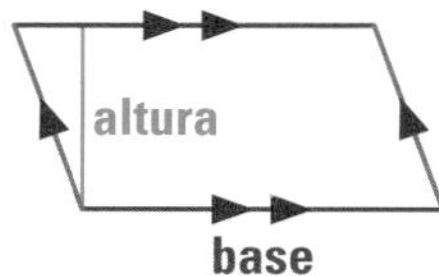

pentagon (p. 31) **pentágono** Polígono de 5 lados.

percent (p. 311) **porcentaje** Por ciento; razón cuyo denominador es 100. Por ejemplo, $21\% = \frac{21}{100}$.

perimeter (pp. 31, 562) **perímetro** El perímetro de un polígono es la suma de las longitudes de sus lados. El perímetro se mide en unidades lineales.

perpendicular lines (p. 359) **rectas perpendiculares** Rectas que se cortan formando un ángulo recto.

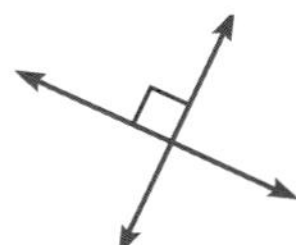

pi (π) (p. 388) **pi (π)** Número que es la razón de la circunferencia de un círculo a su diámetro. Algunas aproximaciones comunes de π son 3.14 y $\frac{22}{7}$.

pictograph (p. 474) **pictograma** Presentación gráfica que representa datos mediante dibujos o símbolos.

plane (p. 357) **plano** Superficie plana que se prolonga sin límites en todas las direcciones.

polygon (p. 31) **polígono** Figura plana cerrada limitada por segmentos de recta llamados *lados* del polígono. Por ejemplo, un triángulo y un rectángulo son polígonos.

polyhedron (p. 407) **poliedro** Sólido limitado por polígonos llamados *caras* del poliedro. Las caras adyacentes se unen en las *aristas* del poliedro.

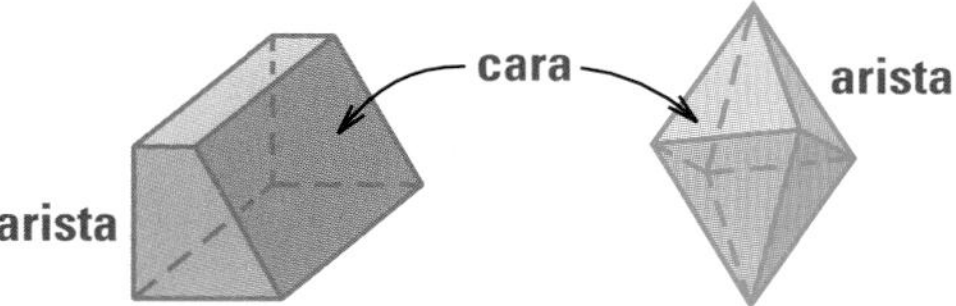

population (p. 483) **población** En estadística, el grupo total de personas u objetos sobre el que se desea obtener alguna información.

positive integers (p. 167) **números enteros positivos** Los números enteros 1, 2, 3, 4, ... los cuales se encuentran a la derecha del 0 en una recta numérica.

power (p. 17) **potencia** Expresión como x^4 que tiene un exponente. En la expresión x^4, x es la base y 4 el exponente.

prime factorization (p. 61) **descomposición en factores primos** Proceso de escribir un número como producto de números primos.

prime number (p. 60) **número primo** Número entero mayor que 1 y cuyos factores enteros son sólo el 1 y él mismo.

principal (p. 338) **capital** Cantidad de dinero tomada a préstamo, prestada o ahorrada.

prism (p. 407) **prisma** Poliedro con dos bases paralelas que son polígonos de igual tamaño y forma. La altura de un prisma es la distancia perpendicular entre las dos bases.

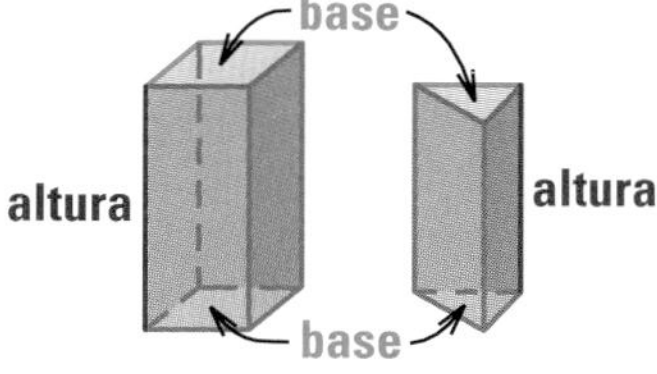

probability of an event (p. 292) **probabilidad de un suceso** Número comprendido entre 0 y 1 que mide las posibilidades de que ocurra cierto suceso.

proper fraction (p. 90) **fracción propia** Para fracciones positivas, un número comprendido entre 0 and 1. Por ejemplo, $\frac{7}{8}$ es una fracción propia.

proportion (p. 269) **proporción** Ecuación que indica la igualdad de dos razones. Una proporción tiene la forma $\frac{a}{b} = \frac{c}{d}$.

proportional sides (p. 280) **lados proporcionales** Los lados de dos polígonos son proporcionales cuando cada lado de un polígono se empareja con un lado del otro polígono, de manera que las razones de las longitudes de los lados emparejados sean iguales.

quadrant (p. 468) **cuadrante** Una de las cuatro regiones en que el eje de las x y el de las y dividen a un plano de coordenadas. *Ver también* plano de coordenadas.

quadrilateral (pp. 280, 376) **cuadrilátero** Polígono de 4 lados.

radius of a circle (p. 388) **radio de un círculo** Distancia entre un punto de un círculo y su centro. *Ver también* círculo.

random sampling (p. 484) **muestreo aleatorio** Método de muestreo en el que cada miembro de una población tiene la misma probabilidad de ser seleccionado.

range (in statistics) (p. 462) **recorrido (en estadística)** Diferencia entre los valores máximo y mínimo de un conjunto de datos.

rate of *a* per *b* (p. 148) **relación de *a* por *b*** Si dos cantidades a y b tienen distintas unidades de medida, entonces la relación de a por b es $\frac{a}{b}$. Por ejemplo, si te pagan \$12 por 3 horas de trabajo, entonces la relación es $\frac{12 \text{ dólares}}{3 \text{ horas}}$, ó \$4 por hora.

ratio (p. 265) **razón** Comparación de un número a y un numero b distinto a cero por medio de la división. La razón de a a b puede escribirse $\frac{a}{b}$, ó $a : b$ ó "a a b".

reciprocals (p. 134) **recíprocos** Dos números cuyo producto es 1. Por ejemplo, $\frac{5}{12}$ y $\frac{12}{5}$ son recíprocos. Los recíprocos se llaman también *inversos multiplicativos.*

rectangle (p. 377) **rectángulo** Paralelogramo que tiene 4 ángulos rectos.

relatively prime numbers (p. 67) **números primos relativos** Dos números enteros cuyo máximo común factor es 1. *Ver también* máximo común factor.

repeating decimal (p. 95) **decimal periódico** Para escribir en forma decimal una fracción $\frac{a}{b}$ $(b \neq 0)$, se divide a entre b mediante la división desarrollada. Cuando el proceso de división no concluye, entonces se llega a un dígito o a un grupo de dígitos que se repite indefinidamente. En ese caso, la fracción puede expresarse en forma de decimal periódico.

right angle (pp. 282, 359) **ángulo recto** Ángulo cuya medida es de 90°.

right circular cylinder (p. 408) **cilindro circular recto** En un cilindro circular recto, el segmento de recta que une los centros de las bases circulares es perpendicular a las bases.

right prism (p. 407) **prisma recto** En un prisma recto, las aristas que unen las bases son perpendiculares a ellas.

right triangle (p. 367) **triángulo rectángulo** Triángulo que tiene un ángulo recto.

sample (p. 483) **muestra** Subconjunto de una población.

scale (p. 285) **escala** En un dibujo a escala, la escala da la relación entre las dimensiones en el dibujo y las reales. Por ejemplo, la escala 1 pulg = 2 pies indica que 1 pulg en el dibujo representa una distancia real de 2 pies.

scale drawing (p. 285) **dibujo a escala** Dibujo de un objeto tal que las dimensiones en el dibujo son proporcionales a las reales del objeto.

scale factor (p. 285) **factor de escala** Razón entre las dimensiones en un dibujo a escala y las dimensiones reales correspondientes.

scalene triangle (p. 366) **triángulo escaleno** Triángulo que tiene sus 3 lados de distinta longitud.

scatter plot (p. 469) **diagrama de dispersión** Conjunto de puntos situados en un plano de coordenadas que representa un conjunto de pares ordenados.

self-selected sample (p. 484) **muestra autoseleccionada** Método de muestreo en el que miembros de una población se ofrecen voluntariamente para formar parte de la muestra.

similar polygons (p. 280) **polígonos semejantes** Polígonos cuyos ángulos y lados se emparejan de tal manera que los ángulos correspondientes tengan la misma medida y las razones de las longitudes de los lados correspondientes sean iguales.

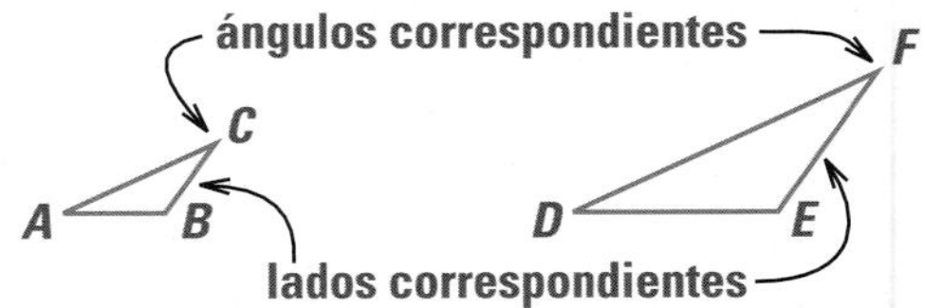

simple interest (p. 338) **interés simple** Interés calculado como el producto obtenido al multiplicar el capital, el tipo de interés anual y el tiempo en años. $I = Prt$

simplest form of a fraction (p. 73) **mínima expresión de una fracción** Una fracción está en su mínima expresión cuando su numerador y su denominador tienen un máximo común factor de 1.

solution of an equation in one variable (p. 221) **solución de una ecuación de una variable** Valor de la variable que satisface la ecuación.

solving an equation (p. 221) **resolver una ecuación** Hallar todas las soluciones de una ecuación.

square (p. 377) **cuadrado** Rectángulo que tiene todos los lados de igual longitud.

square of a number (p. 17) **cuadrado de un número** Segunda potencia de un número.

supplementary angles (p. 358) **ángulos suplementarios** Dos ángulos cuyas medidas suman 180°.

surface area of a cylinder (p. 434) **área superficial de un cilindro** Suma del área superficial lateral y las áreas de las dos bases.

surface area of a polyhedron (p. 430) **área superficial de un poliedro** Suma de las áreas de las caras de un poliedro.

systematic sampling (p. 484) **muestreo sistemático** Método de muestreo en el que se aplica un patrón para seleccionar miembros de una población.

terminating decimal (p. 95) **decimal exacto** Para escribir en forma decimal una fracción $\frac{a}{b}$ $(b \neq 0)$ se divide a entre b mediante la división desarrollada. Cuando el proceso de división concluye con un residuo de cero, la fracción puede expresarse en forma de decimal exacto.

terms of a sum (p. 7) **términos de una suma** Números ó expresiones que se suman. En la suma $2 + 4$, los términos son 2 y 4.

theoretical probability (p. 293) **probabilidad teórica** Probabilidad que se halla mediante el razonamiento matemático. Si los casos de un experimento son igualmente probables, entonces la probabilidad teórica del suceso viene dada por la razón $\frac{\text{Número de casos favorables}}{\text{Número total de casos}}$.

tree diagram (p. 505) **diagrama en árbol** Diagrama que muestra todos los casos posibles de un proceso realizado en varias etapas.

triangle (p. 31) **triángulo** Polígono de 3 lados.

unit rate (p. 148) **relación unitaria** Relación cuyo denominador es 1 unidad. Por ejemplo, una velocidad de $\frac{35 \text{ mi}}{1 \text{ h}}$, ó 35 millas por hora es una relación unitaria.

upper quartile (p. 461) **cuartil superior** Mediana de la mitad superior de un conjunto de valores de datos. *Ver también* gráfica de frecuencias acumuladas.

value of a variable (p. 8) **valor de una variable** Número representado por una variable.

variable (p. 8) **variable** Letra que representa uno o más números.

variable expression (p. 8) **expresión algebraica** Expresión que contiene una o más variables y operaciones que deben realizarse.

Venn diagram (p. 509) **diagrama de Venn** Dibujo que emplea figuras geométricas para mostrar las relaciones entre los conjuntos.

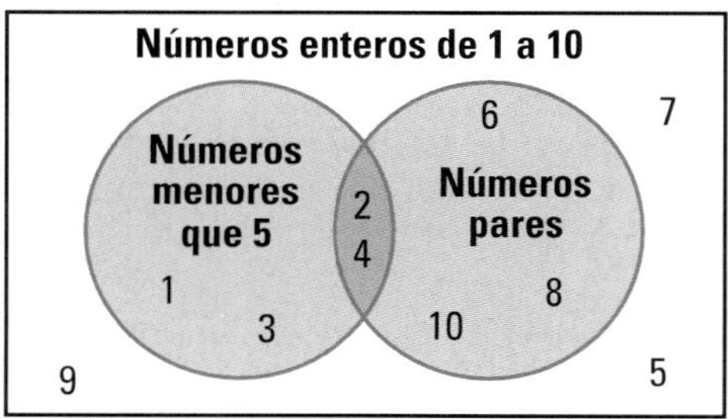

vertex of an angle (p. 358) **vértice de un ángulo** Punto donde se unen los lados de un ángulo.

vertical angles (p. 357) **ángulos opuestos por el vértice** Ángulos opuestos entre sí al cortarse dos rectas. En el diagrama abajo, tanto $\angle 1$ y $\angle 3$ como $\angle 2$ y $\angle 4$ son ángulos opuestos por el vértice.

volume (p. 411) **volumen** El volumen de un sólido es la medida del espacio que ocupa. El volumen se mide en unidades cúbicas.

x*-axis** (p. 468) **eje de las *x Eje horizontal de un plano de coordenadas. *Ver también* plano de coordenadas.

x*-coordinate** (p. 468) **coordenada *x Primer número de las coordenadas de un punto. *Ver también* par ordenado.

y*-axis** (p. 468) **eje de las *y Eje vertical de un plano de coordenadas. *Ver también* plano de coordenadas.

y*-coordinate** (p. 468) **coordenada *y Segundo número de las coordenadas de un punto. *Ver también* par ordenado.

Index

B

C

INDEX

D

E

F

G

H

I

L

M

S

Credits

Cover Photography

Ralph Mercer

Photography

i Ralph Mercer; **iii** RMIP/Richard Haynes; **1** David Young Wolff/Tony Stone Images (tl); John Feingersh/The Stock Market (tr); **11** Don Metzer/Tony Stone Images; **15** Doris De Witt/Tony Stone Images; **18** Michael Rosenfeld/Tony Stone Images; **20** CRDPHOTO/Corbis; **24** TEK IMAGE/SCIENCE PHOTO LIBRARY/Photo Researchers; **34** Gary M. Prior/Allsport; **39** Robert Tyrrell; **41** Corbis; **46** Leonard Lee Rue III/Animals Animals; **46** Spike Walker/Tony Stone Images; **54** Ken O'Donoghue (both); **57** Roger Ressmeyer/Corbis (tl); Paul Edmondson/Tony Stone Images (tr); **63** Bettmann/Corbis; **66** Carmen Redondo/Corbis; **68** Werner Forman/Art Resource; **74** RMIP/Richard Haynes; **76** Ed Eckstein/Corbis; **80** Bob Daemmrich Photography; **82** George Bernard/Animals Animals; **86** The Granger Collection, New York; **94** Gordon Gahan/National Geographic Image Collection; **96** Craig Aurness/Corbis; **98** Raffi Van Chromes; **106** Ken O'Donoghue; **109** Walter Hodges/Tony Stone Images (tl); Ron Chapple/FPG International (tr); **114** William Taufic/The Stock Market; **116** Lou Ellen Beckham-Davis/L.E.B.; **118** The Granger Collection, New York; **123** Bob Tringali/Sportschrome; **129** Stephen Studd/Tony Stone Images; **135** Jeff Greenberg/Unicorn Stock Photo; **137** David Muir/Masterfile; **142** Courtesy of the Massachusetts Turnpike Authority; **145** The Granger Collection, New York; **147** Jim Sugar Photography/Corbis; **149** Damian Strohmeyer/Allsport; **158** PhotoDisc, Inc. (bl); Ken O'Donoghue (cl, cr); **162** RMIP/Richard Haynes; **165** Wesley Bocxe/Photo Researchers, Inc. (tl); Emory Kristof/National Geographic Image Collection (tr); Kenneth Garrett/National Geographic Image Collection (bl); Reprinted, by permission, from *On the Edge of Splendor: Exploring Grand Canyon's Human Past*, by Douglas W. Schwatz, ©1989 by the School of American Research (cl); Denis Finnin/American Museum of Natural History (cr); Jim Sugar Photography/Corbis (br); **168** Noyosti/Science Photo Library/Photo Researchers, Inc; **170** Dr. Paul A. Zahl/Photo Researchers, Inc.; **173** Bob Daemmrich Photography; **174** Bob Daemmrich Photography; **180** Jeff Rotman/The Picture Cube; **183** Chuck Place/Place Stock Photo; **185** Mark E. Gibson; **190** Andy Sacks/Tony Stone Images; **192** David Noton/International Stock Photo; **194** James Blank/Stock Boston; **196** Mark Newman/Photo Researchers, Inc.; **201** The Granger Collection, New York; **205** U.S. Naval Historical Foundation Photo Service; **210** Dennis Netoff; **215** Jon Riley/Tony Stone Images (tl); Cotton Coulson/Woodfin Camp and Associates (tr); **218** Artville, LLC. (tl); Ken O'Donoghue (cl, cr); **220** Elliot Smith/International Stock Photo (tl); Spencer Swanger/Tom Stack & Associates (bl); **224** The Granger Collection, New York; **231** Peter Tenzer Studio Inc./International Stock Photo; **232** Bob Daemmrich Photography; **234** Clyde H. Smith/Peter Arnold, Inc. (both); **245** The Granger Collection, New York; **246** A. Ramey/PhotoEdit; **247** Courtesy of NASA Johnson Space Center; **263** Joe McDonald/Corbis (tr); Bobby Model/National Geographic Image Collection (tl); Damian Strohmeyer/Allsport (cr, br); **273** Monica Klum/National Geographic Image Collection; **274** Richard Passmore/Tony Stone Images; **275** Ken Sakamoto/Black Star; **276** Laurie Platt Winfrey, Inc.; **278** Darryl Torckler/Tony Stone Images; **284** Loek Polders/International Stock Photo (tl); Fujifotos/Image Works (cr); **288** Eric Grave/Photo Researchers, Inc.; **295** Mark Latti/Maine Dept. of Inland Fisheries; **306, 307** RMIP/Richard Haynes; **309** Flip Nicklin/Minden Pictures (tr); David M. Barron/A Prairie Gallery Illinois Natural History Survey (tl); **312** Philip James Corwin/Corbis; **315** David Woodfall/Tony Stone Images; **319** Eeland Bobbe/Tony Stone Images; **320** The Granger Collection, New York.; **326** Mike Vines/Tony Stone Images; **331** Jon Riley/Tony Stone Images; **337** M. Antman/Image Works; **341** Paul Hurd/AllStock/PictureQuest; **355** Stevens Peters/Tony Stone Images (both); **358** Corbis (all); **361** Michael S. Yamashita/Corbis; **365** Richard B. Levine; **367** Glenn Short/Gamma-Liaison; **369** Tom Prettyman/PhotoEdit (tl); Lincoln Russell/Stock Boston (tr); **375** Gottlieb/Monkmeyer Press; **379** U.S. Postal Service (tl); Bernard Soutrit/Woodfin Camp and Associates (bc); **385** Frank Pennington/Unicorn Stock Photo; **386** RMIP/Richard Haynes (both); **389** Gale Zucker/Stock Boston; **390** PhotoDisc, Inc. (all); **391** Robert C. Shafer/Uniphoto; **393** Steve Kahn/FPG International; **394** PhotoDisc, Inc. (cl, c); School Division, Houghton Mifflin Company (cr); **405** Courtesy of Christina Neal (tr); Krafft/Photo Researchers, Inc. (tl); **410** Bob Daemmrich Photography (br); PhotoDisc, Inc. (tr, tl); Artville, LLC. (bl); **412** Courtesy of NASA; **414** Kim Westerskov/Tony Stone Images; **419** Kenneth Garrett/National Geographic Image Collection; **423** School Division, Houghton Mifflin Company; **424** Mark E. Gibson; **426** The Granger Collection, New York; **433** Michael S. Yamashita/Corbis; **435** Bob Rowan, Progressive Image/Corbis; **437** Raymond Watt/Albuquerque Biological Park; **451** Michael Rosenfeld/Tony Stone Images (tl); Kevin Horan/Tony Stone Images (tr); **456** Andy Sacks/Tony Stone Images; **458** Joseph Sohm/Tony Stone Images; **460** Bettman/Corbis; **462** Hank Morgan/Photo Researchers, Inc.; **464** Underwood & Underwood/Corbis; **469** Jim Shippee/Unicorn Stock Photo (tl); The Granger Collection, New York (tr); **471** Brian Parker/Tom Stack & Associates; **472** James L. Amos/Photo Researchers, Inc.; **477** Charlie Westerman/Liaison Inc; **484** Dennis Cox/D.E. Cox Photo Library; **490** Don Mason/The Stock Market; **501** Caroline Wood/Tony Stone Images (tl); Steven Pumphrey (tr); **507** Brent Madison (tl); RMIP/Richard Haynes (cl, c, cr); **513** Michael Newman/PhotoEdit; **519** Bettman/Corbis; **526** Peter Beck/The Stock Market; **530** The Granger Collection, New York; **532** Jose L. Pelaez/The Stock Market; **546** Martha Granger/EDGE Productions.

Illustration

David Ballard **294**
Eliot Bergman **265; 266**
All others: School Division, Houghton Mifflin Company and McDougal Littell

Selected Answers

Pre-Course Practice

NUMBER SENSE (p. xx) **1.** 0, 3, 4, 9 **3.** 79, 84, 92, 101 **5.** 25, 35, 50, 60, 75 **7.** 1, 6, 12, 15, 20, 30 **9.** 124, 130, 135, 142, 149, 153 **11.** 48, 52, 58, 62, 68, 72, 78 **13.** 8 **15.** 1 **17.** 91 **19.** 77 **21.** 222 **23.** 1110 **25.** 9 **27.** 11 **29.** 14 **31.** 17 **33.** 25 **35.** 28 **37.** 47 **39.** 63 **41.** 6 **43.** 3 **45.** 8 **47.** 11 **49.** 14 **51.** 15 **53.** 41 **55.** 36 **57.** 66 **59.** 83 **61.** 137 **63.** 525 **65.** 867 **67.** 1712 **69.** 2796 **71.** 9454 **73.** 37 **75.** 12 **77.** 835 **79.** 667 **81.** 230 **83.** 117 **85.** 4313 **87.** 870 **89.** 378 **91.** 3721 **93.** 5863 **95.** 6930 **97.** 22,100 **99.** 267,741 **101.** 144,048 **103.** 1,588,301 **105.** 3 **107.** 2 **109.** 8 **111.** 9 **113.** 4 **115.** 6 **117.** 7 **119.** 13 **121.** 8 R1 **123.** 11 R3 **125.** 111 R5 **127.** 78 R2 **129.** 32 R11 **131.** 14 R13 **133.** 2870 R1 **135.** 491 R4 **137.** 125 R15 **139.** 27 R158

MEASUREMENT AND GEOMETRY (p. xxi) **141.** 36 inches **143.** 8 feet **145.** 336 hours **147.** 32 fluid ounces **149.** 500 centimeters **151.** 9000 milliliters **153.** 288 square inches **155.** 20,000,000 square meters **157.** 24 in.; 36 in.^{2} **159.** 120 cm; 900 cm^2 **161.** 72 ft; 288 ft^2 **163.** 12 in.; 9 in.^{2} **165.** 36 cm; 81 cm^2 **167.** 158 m; 1554 m^2 **169.** 150° **171.** 30°

STATISTICS, DATA ANALYSIS, & PROBABILITY (p. xxiii) **173.** 61 species **175.** 65 species

177.

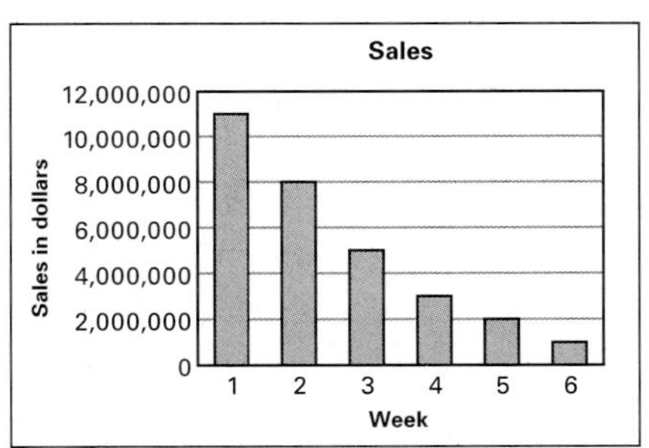

179. horror; romance

181.

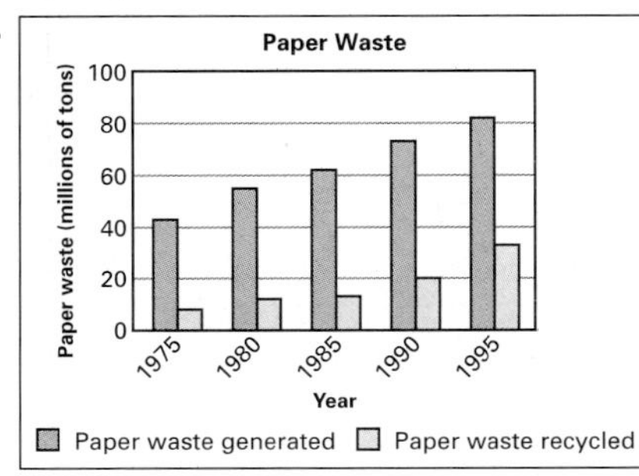

Chapter 1

GETTING READY (p. 2) **1.** B **2.** J **3.** B **4.** H **5.** B

1.1 GUIDED PRACTICE (p. 5) **1.** understand the problem: identify the question; make a plan: decide on a strategy; solve the problem: use the strategy to answer the question; look back: check that the answer is reasonable **3.** No; it took 50 minutes to walk the second mile, which is 15 minutes longer than the first mile.

1.1 PRACTICE AND PROBLEM SOLVING (pp. 5–6) **5.** \$108; you do not need to know that Jeff has a job walking dogs. **7.** 8 cards **9.** no irrelevant information; 2160 mm **11.** You do not need to know how much a bag of popcorn costs; 4 tickets

1.2 GUIDED PRACTICE (p. 9) **1.** D **3.** C **5.** 97; the sum of 35 and 62 is 97. **7.** 117; the difference of 125 and 8 is 117. **9.** 52; the product of 4 and 13 is 52. **11.** 7; the quotient of 56 and 8 is 7. **13.** $15 \div 3$; 5 **15.** $30 \cdot 7$; 210 **17.** $700 - 99$; 601 **19.** 5 **21.** 6 **23.** 40 **25.** 13

1.2 PRACTICE AND PROBLEM SOLVING (pp. 10–11) **27.** 72 is the dividend; 9 is the divisor. **29.** 92; the sum of 73 and 19 is 92. **31.** 782; the difference of 980 and 198 is 782. **33.** 108; the product of 9 and 12 is 108. **35.** 7; the quotient of 175 and 25 is 7. **37.** $54 \div 3$ or $\frac{54}{3}$; 18 **39.** $67 - 19$; 48 **41.** $14 + 16$; 30 **43.** 18×2 or $18 \cdot 2$ or $18(2)$; 36 **45.** $a + b$ **47.** $m \cdot n$ **49.** $x \cdot y$ **51.** 60 **53.** 7 **59.** 99 **61.** 9 **63.** 270 **65.** 150 beats/min **67.** decrease **69.** false; $(862 + 958 + 343) - (976 + 468)$ **71.** true; $976 + 958 + 862 + 468 + 343 - 3000$

1.3 GUIDED PRACTICE (p. 14) **1.** C **3.** D **5.** 4 **7.** $7 - (2 + 3) = 2$

1.3 PRACTICE AND PROBLEM SOLVING (pp. 14–16) **9.** 21 **11.** 8 **13.** 4 **15.** 18 **17.** 16 **19.** $25 - 4 \times 5$; 5 **21.** 52; answers may vary.
23. *Sample answer:*
step 1: $(54 + 267) = 321$
step 2: $(7 \times 8) = 56$
step 3: $168 \times 321 = 53{,}928$
step 4: $13 \times 56 = 728$
step 5: $53{,}928 - 728 = 53{,}200$
25. 33 **27.** 12 **29.** 90

31. $(43 + 29) + 57$	$= (29 + 43) + 57$	Commutative Property of Addition
	$= 29 + (43 + 57)$	Associative Property of Addition
	$= 29 + 100$	Add 43 and 57.
	$= 129$	Add 100 and 29.

33a. 3 **33b.** 7 **33a.–b.** No; regrouping does not produce the same answer. **35.** 4, 9, 2 **37.** $+, \times, -$ **39.** $(43 \times 4) + (60 \times 2)$ or $43 \times 4 + 60 \times 2$ **41.** 292; 408 **43.** $888 **45.** $173 above **49.** 2 **51.** 27 **53.** 7

1.4 Guided Practice (p. 19)

1. 2 **3.** 2^6 **5.** 32 **7.** 125 **9.** 2,097,152 **11.** no; 9

1.4 Practice and Problem Solving (pp. 19–20)

13. $36 = 6^2$ **15.** $27 = 3^3$ **17.** $81 = 9^2$ **19.** $\frac{1}{1000} = \frac{1}{10^3}$ **21.** 4 to the 4th power; 256 **23.** 9 to the 3rd power or 9 cubed; 729 **25.** 1 **27.** 162 **29.** 15 **31.** 42 **33.** 0 **35.** 1,953,125 **37.** 6,250,000 **39.** 1,048,576 **41.** 1,679,616 **43.** 27 **45.** 7 **47.** 17 **49.** 13 **51.** 60 **53.** 22 **55.** 911 **57.** 16 **61.** $1^8, 8^2, 5^3$ **63.** 200 ft^2 **65.** $200 - 144 = 56$ ft^2

1.5 Guided Practice (p. 23)

1. D **3.** B **5.** $A = 1.6$
$B = 2.1$
$C = 1.1$
$D = 0.2$
$E = 0.8$

7. 0.07, 0.10, 0.17, 0.7, 1.7 **9.** =
11. A = 0.4
B = 0.6
C = 0.15
D = 0.8
E = 0.7

13. B, D, E

1.5 Practice and Problem Solving (pp. 23–24)

15. 1.305 **17.** 1.35

19.
0.1 0.9 1.2
0 1 2

21.
0.7 1.7 2.2
0 1 2 3

23. 0.08, 0.09, 0.8, 0.89 **25.** 12.001, 12.04, 12.5, 12.608, 12.8 **27.** 5.1, 5.104, 5.13, 5.14, 5.143 **29.** 4.081, 4.118, 4.18, 4.218, 4.281 **31.** < **33.** < **35.** > **37** > **39.** = **41.** < **43.** Nebraska **45.** 1013.3, 1014.2, 1014.8, 1015.4, 1016.6, 1016.7, 1017.7, 1023.7 **47.** 9.84, 9.92, 9.96, 9.99, 10.25 **49.** 0.923, 7.45, 30.6, 114.0 **55.** 858 h **57.** 70 **59.** 26

61. $(27 + 98) + 73$	$= 73 + (27 + 98)$	Commutative property of addition
	$= (73 + 27) + 98$	Associative property of addition
	$= 100 + 98$	Add 73 and 27.
	$= 198$	Add 100 and 98.

63. 64 people; 4^3

Mid-Chapter Test (p. 26)

1. 19 **2.** 60 **3.** 24 **4.** 47 **5.** 125 **6.** 8

7. $4 \times (17 \times 25)$	$= (17 \times 25) \times 4$	Commutative property of multiplication
	$= 17 \times (25 \times 4)$	Associative property of multiplication
	$= 17 \times 100$	Multiply 25 and 4.
	$= 1700$	Multiply 17 and 100.

8. $60 \div (15 + 3)$; You can ride the roller coaster 3 times. Height of hill is irrelevant. **9.** 64 **10.** 15 **11.** 125 **12.** 32 **13.** B **14.** D **15.** A **16.** C **17.** strawberry **18.** kiwi **19.** peach, citrus, banana, kiwi, cranberry, strawberry

20. *Sample answer:* 0.66, 0.68, and 0.70 **21.**

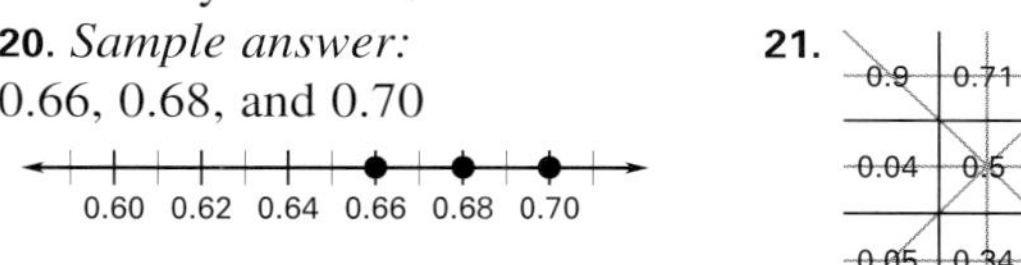

1.6 Guided Practice (p. 29)

1. is approximately equal to **3.** 500 **5.** 453 **7.** 453.07 **9.** mean **11.** 12 **13.** 38.75

1.6 Practice and Problem Solving (pp. 29–30)

15. 6.3 **17.** 270 **19.** 412,000 **21.** 20 **23.** true **25.** false; 5.4 **27.** 99 **29.** $32 **31.** $612 **33.** $89 **35.** $17.99 **37.** 19.8 **39.** 72.9 **41.** 12.5 cm, 26.8 cm, 48.4 cm, 67.1 cm **43.** about 2247 people per square mile; using the compatible numbers 160,000 (for the population) and 80 (for the area) gives a quotient of 2000, so 2247 is reasonable.

1.7 Guided Practice (p. 33)

1. 5.58 **3.** 15.848 **5.** 5.7 ft **7.** incorrect; $\begin{array}{r} 3.00 \\ -2.85 \\ \hline 0.15 \end{array}$ **9.** $10.15

1.7 Practice and Problem Solving (pp. 33–35)

11. 9.36 **13.** 16.75 **15.** 6, 8, 4, **17.** 4, 2, 9 **19.** The decimal places were not properly lined up in vertical format. $\begin{array}{r} 16.0 \\ +\ 0.4 \\ \hline 16.4 \end{array}$

21. 5.82 cm **23.** 229.5; bronze medal

25.

22.18

14.26 7.92

8.92 5.34 2.58

4.52 4.4 0.94 1.64

27. 0.43 **29.** 2.542 **31.** 4.348 **33.** 1.194 **35.** No; you should have received $9.20 in change. **37.** 1.71% **39.** 68.07%; 90.25%; some of the respondents may be shorter than 5 ft 2 in. and some may be taller than 5 ft 11 in. These heights are not accounted for in the table. **41.** 205°C **43.** 1064.43°C **45.** 5.4 gallons

1.8 Guided Practice (p. 40) **1.** 3 **3.** 6 **5.** 11.5128 **7.** 13.05 **9.** 8.8479

1.8 Practice and Problem Solving (pp. 40–41) **11.** C **13.** B **15.** 10.25 **17.** 16.1001 **19.** 400, 1000, 1600, 1800, 1900, 1980; the product gets closer to 2000. **21.** 2.4625 **23.** 0.6176 **25.** 6.62625 **27.** 0.299268 **29.** 8.4 mm; 3.77 mm^2 **31.** 3.664 cm, 0.80064 cm^2 **33.** 4.10 **35.** 4.77 **37.** 4.02 **39.** $736.40 **41.** $253.60 **43.** 208.3 mi **45.** 1026.8 mi **47.** 35,046.44 mi **49.** 4279.44 m **53.** dividend, 40; divisor, 10 **55.** 62 **57.** 18 **59.** 4.8 **61.** 57.8 **63.** 5.8 **65.** 10.25 **67.** 2.5

1.9 Guided Practice (p. 45) **1.** Use long division as you would with whole numbers. Line up the decimal place in the quotient with the decimal place in the dividend. **3.** 3.25 **5.** 1.15 **7.** Multiplying by 1000 would move the decimal 3 places to the right; Students might change 1000 to 100 or they might change the word "two" to "three." **9.** 22 **11.** 220 **13.** 5.8 **15.** 4.78 **17.** 24.84 **19.** 56.49 **21.** The quotient should be 8.03 instead of 8.3; 2 divided by 7 equals 0. **23.** The quotient should be 0.309 instead of 0.3109; 3 times 5 is 15, not 10. **25.** $9.86 **27.** $1.54 **29.** 1996 **31.** always; *Sample answers:* $8 \div 0.2 = 40$, $3 \div 0.6 = 5$ **33.** 0.4 **35.** 300 **37.** 1.2 **39.** 40.4 **41.** 1200 **43.** about 0.79 mi/min **45.** 4.5 m **47.** 203.34

49. *Sample answer:* You read a novel for about 10.5 hours over 3 days last week. What is the average number of hours you read each day? **51.** about 1.64 in.

Chapter Summary and Review (pp. 48–51) **1.** 4 **3.** 50 **5.** 5 **7.** 42

9.

$125 + 67 + 875 = 67 + 125 + 875$	Commutative property of addition
$= 67 + 1000$	Add 125 and 875.
$= 1067$	Add 67 and 1000.

11. 16 **13.** 90 ft^2 **15.** 10.54, 10.82, 10.94, 10.97 **17.** 2.943 **19.** $3, $3, $4, $4, $2 **21.** yes; $.11 more **23.** 78 **25.** 1.786 **27.** 0.17 **29.** 19,100 **31.** 0.175 lb

Reviewing the Basics (p. 55) **1.** 2, 4, 6, 8, 10, 12, 14, 16, 18, 20, 22, 24 **3.** 7, 14, 21, 28, 35, 42, 49, 56, 63, 70, 77, 84 **5.** 10, 20, 30, 40, 50, 60, 70, 80, 90, 100, 110, 120 **7.** 13, 26, 39, 52, 65, 78, 91, 104, 117, 130, 143, 156 **9.** 11, 22, 33, 44, 55, 66, 77, 88, 99, 110, 121, 132 **11.** 25, 50, 75, 100, 125, 150, 175, 200, 225, 250, 275, 300 **13.** 2 R 2 **15.** 2 R 5 **17.** 4 R 5 **19.** 7 R 7 **21.** 26 R 5

Chapter 2

2.1 Getting Ready (p. 58) **1.** B **2.** F **3.** C **4.** F

2.1 Guided Practice (p. 62) **1.** composite **3.** 1 **5.** 1, 2, 3, 4, 6, 9, 12, 18, 36 **7.** 21; 2, 3, 3, 7; $2 \times 3^2 \times 7$

2.1 Practice and Problem Solving (pp. 62–64) **9.** 1, 2, 3, 5, 6, 10, 15, 30 **11.** 1, 2, 17, 34 **13.** 1, 2, 3, 4, 6, 8, 9, 12, 18, 24, 36, 72 **15.** 1, 2, 4, 5, 10, 20, 25, 50, 100

17.

5; prime	12; composite	19; prime
6; composite	13; prime	20; composite
7; prime	14; composite	21; composite
8; composite	15; composite	22; composite
9; composite	16; composite	23; prime
10; composite	17; prime	24; composite
11; prime	18; composite	25; composite

19. prime **21.** prime **23.** composite **25.** composite **27.** prime **29.** prime **31.** prime **33.** composite **35.** 26; composite **37.** 80; composite **39.** 41; prime **41.** 47; prime **43.** 65; composite **45.** 83; prime **47.** *Sample answer:* 79

49. 2^5 **51.** $2^3 \times 3 \times 5$

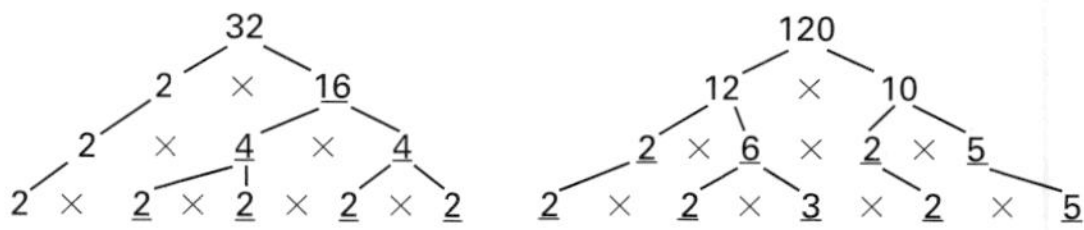

53. $2^4 \times 3$

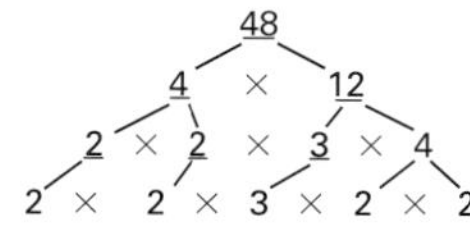

55. 2×3^2 **57.** 2^6 **59.** 2×7^2 **61.** $2 \times 3 \times 5^2$ **63.** $3^2 \times 11$ **65.** $3 \times 5 \times 23$

67.

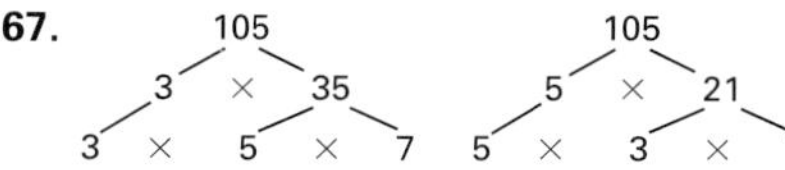

Both factor trees give the answer $3 \times 5 \times 7$.

69. $2^8 \times 3 \times 5^3 \times 7$ **71.** $2 \times 3 \times 5 \times 7^2 \times 11$ **73.** $2^4 \times 3^2 \times 5^4$ **75.** $2^7 \times 3 \times 79$ **77.** $2 \times 29 \times 53$ **79.** 39 **85.** 39, 78 **87.** 101, 104 **89.** 27 **91.** 66.3 **93.** 12.4 m, 9.61 m^2 **95.** 112.8 in., 653.63 $in.^2$

2.2 Guided Practice (p. 67) **1.** common factor **3.** 1 **5.** 1, 2, 3, 6 **11.** 6 ft

2.2 Practice and Problem Solving (pp. 67–68) **13.** 1 **15.** 1, 3 **17.** 1, 2, 3, 6, 9, 18 **19.** 1, 2 **21.** 1, 2, 5, 10, 25, 50 **23.** 1, 23 **25.** 1 **27.** 12 **29.** 1 **31.** 4 **33.** 12 and 35, 31 and 35 **35a.** 16 **35b.** 16 **35c.** *Sample answer:* prime factorization; because it is quicker. **39.** 2 ft **41.** The last month on the Haab calendar would have 1 week.

2.3 Guided Practice (p. 71) **1.** $\frac{1}{4}$; 1 is the numerator, 4 is the denominator. **3.** $\frac{5}{12}$; 5 is the numerator, 12 is the denominator. **5.** No; the shaded area does not represent $\frac{4}{6}$ because there are not 6 equal parts. **7.** C

9.

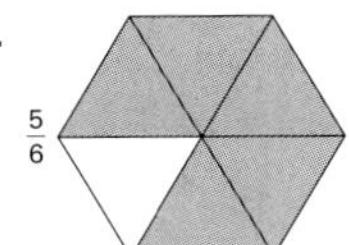

2.3 Practice and Problem Solving (pp. 71–72) **11.** $\frac{1}{3}$; 1 is the numerator, 3 is the denominator. **13.** $\frac{7}{8}$; 7 is the numerator, 8 is the denominator. **15.** $\frac{5}{7}$; 5 is the numerator, 7 is the denominator. **17.** Yes; $\frac{3}{6}$ **19.** Yes; $\frac{2}{10}$ **21.** No; not equal parts of the whole.

23.

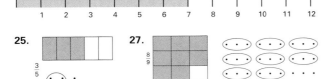

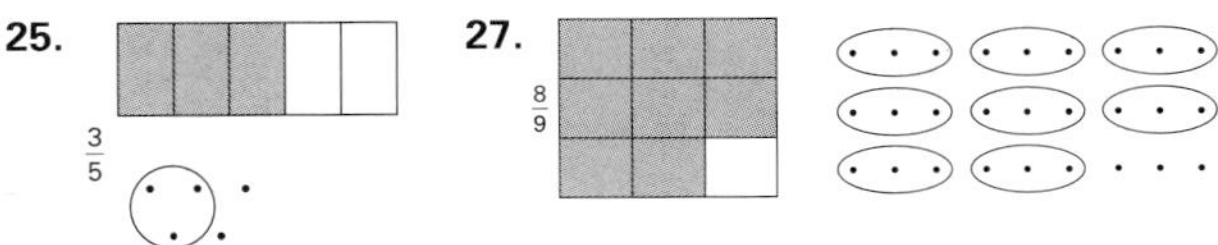

25. $\frac{3}{5}$ **27.** $\frac{8}{9}$

29. *Sample answer:* $\frac{3}{4}$ is larger since $\frac{3}{4}$ = 15 dots out of 20 dots and $\frac{3}{5}$ = 12 dots out of 20 dots. **31.** The number of feet in a mile.

2.4 Guided Practice (p. 75) **1.** *Sample answer:* $\frac{3}{5}$, $\frac{12}{20}$ **3.** Yes; the numerator and denominator have a greatest common factor of 1. **5.** No; the numerator and denominator can be divided by the factor 5. **7a.** yes **7b.** yes **7c.** yes **7d.** no **7e.** yes

2.4 Practice and Problem Solving (pp. 75–77) **11.** *Sample answer:*

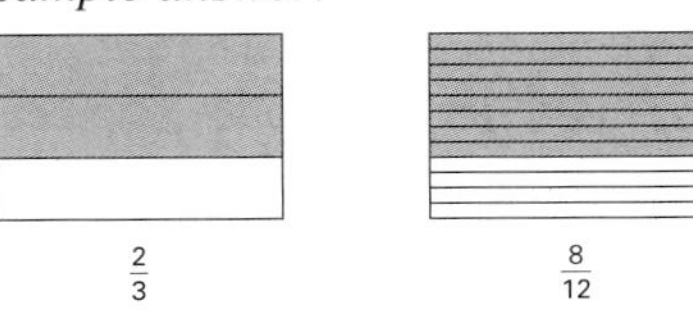

13. $\frac{36}{42}$ **15.** No; in simplest form one is $\frac{1}{2}$ and the other is $\frac{2}{3}$. **17.** Yes; $\frac{5}{8}$ is the simplest form for both. **19.** *Sample answers:* $\frac{1}{4}$ and $\frac{4}{16}$; they represent the same quantity. **21.** *Sample answers:* $\frac{8}{9}$ and $\frac{24}{27}$; they represent the same quantity. **23.** *Sample answers:* $\frac{1}{6}$ and $\frac{4}{24}$; they represent the same quantity. **25.** *Sample answers:* $\frac{1}{5}$ and $\frac{5}{25}$; they represent the same quantity. **27.** *Sample answers:* $\frac{1}{2}$ and $\frac{15}{30}$; they represent the same quantity. **29.** *Sample answers:* $\frac{2}{61}$ and $\frac{10}{305}$; they represent the same quantity. **31.** $\frac{2}{3}$ **33.** $\frac{1}{10}$ **35.** 1 **37.** $\frac{1}{2}$ **39.** $\frac{3}{4}$ **41.** $\frac{7}{11}$ **43.** $\frac{1}{6}$ **45.** $\frac{11}{18}$ **47.** $\frac{160}{240}$ or $\frac{2}{3}$ **49.** $\frac{14}{65}$ **51.** $\frac{19}{130}$ **53.** $\frac{221}{500}$ **61.** The number of divisions can be calculated as 2^X where X = the number of folds. **63.** 3 **65.** 12

Mid-Chapter Test (p. 78) **1.** 1, 2, 3, 6, 9, 18, 27, 54 **2.** 1, 83 **3.** 1, 2, 3, 4, 5, 6, 8, 10, 12, 15, 20, 24, 30, 40, 60, 120 **4.** 1, 2, 3, 5, 6, 7, 10, 14, 15, 21, 30, 35, 42, 70, 105, 210 **5.** prime **6.** composite **7.** composite **8.** prime

9.

Shells/Row	1	2	3	4	6	8	12	24
No. Rows	24	12	8	6	4	3	2	1

10. $2^3 \times 3^2 \times 5$ **11.** $3^3 \times 5^2$ **12.** $2 \times 3 \times 5 \times 7^2$ **13.** $2^5 \times 37$ **14.** 1, 19 **15.** 1, 3, 9 **16.** 1 **17.** 1, 2, 4, 8 **18.** 3 **19.** 1 **20.** 36 **21.** 2 **22.** $\frac{7}{8}$ **23.** $\frac{8}{12}$ or $\frac{2}{3}$ **24.** $\frac{3}{5}$ or $\frac{9}{15}$ **25.** $\frac{2}{3}$ **26.** The 4 parts are not equal in size. **27.** $\frac{1}{6}$ **28.** It is in simplest form. **29.** $\frac{5}{8}$ **30.** $\frac{5}{8}$ **31.** $\frac{3}{5}$

2.5 Guided Practice (p. 81) **1.** multiples of 8: 8, 16, 24, 32, 40, 48, 56, 64, 72, 80, 88, 96
multiples of 10: 10, 20, 30, 40, 50, 60, 70, 80, 90
common multiples: 40, 80
LCM = 40

3. multiples of 4: 4, 8, 12, 16, 20, 24, 28, 32, 36, 40, 44, 48, 52, 56, 60, 64, 68, 72, 76, 80, 84, 88, 92, 96
multiples of 6: 6, 12, 18, 24, 30, 36, 42, 48, 54, 60, 66, 72, 78, 84, 90, 96
common multiples: 12, 24, 36, 48, 60, 72, 84, 96
LCM = 12

5. multiples of 9: 9, 18, 27, 36, 45, 54, 63, 72, 81, 90, 99
multiples of 11: 11, 22, 33, 44, 55, 66, 77, 88, 99
common multiple: 99
LCM = 99

7. multiples of 12: 12, 24, 36, 48, 60, 72, 84, 96
multiples of 16: 16, 32, 48, 64, 80, 96
common multiples: 48, 96
LCM = 48
9. multiples of 16: 16, 32, 48, 64, 80, 96
multiples of 20: 20, 40, 60, 80
common multiple: 80
LCM = 80
11. multiples of 13: 13, 26, 39, 52, 65, 78, 91
multiples of 39: 39, 78
common multiples: 39, 78
LCM = 39
13a. $2 \times 2, 2 \times 5$ **13b.** $(2) \times 2, (2) \times 5; 2 \times 2 \times 5$
13c. 20

2.5 Practice and Problem Solving (pp. 81–82)

15. multiples of 3: 3, 6, 9, 12, 15, 18, 21, 24
multiples of 7: 7, 14, 21, 28, 35, 42, 49, 56
common multiple: 21
LCM = 21
17. multiples of 5: 5, 10, 15, 20, 25, 30, 35, 40
multiples of 10: 10, 20, 30, 40, 50, 60, 70, 80
common multiples: 10, 20, 30, 40
LCM = 10
19. multiples of 12: 12, 24, 36, 48, 60, 72, 84, 96
multiples of 14: 14, 28, 42, 56, 70, 84, 98, 112
common multiple: 84
LCM = 84
21. multiples of 4: 4, 8, 12, 16, 20, 24, 28, 32
multiples of 6: 6, 12, 18, 24, 30, 36, 42, 48
multiples of 8: 8, 16, 24, 32, 40, 48, 56, 64
common multiple: 24
LCM = 24
23. 72 **25.** 230 **27.** 200 **29.** 180 **31.** 10, 15; 30
33. 16, 24; 48 **35.** yes **37.** 30,000 mi
39a. GCF: 6
LCM: 12
The products are equal.
39b. *Sample answer:* 3 and 4
GCF: 1
LCM: 12
The products are equal.
39c. From parts (a) and (b) we might conjecture that the product of the GCF and LCM of any two nonzero whole numbers is equal to the product of the numbers.

2.6 Guided Practice (p. 85)

1. $\frac{5}{20}, \frac{8}{20}; \frac{5}{20} < \frac{8}{20}$
3. $\frac{5}{7} < \frac{5}{6}$ **5.** $12; \frac{1}{3} < \frac{3}{4}$ **7.** $25; \frac{4}{5} = \frac{20}{25}$ **9.** $12; \frac{5}{6} > \frac{1}{4}$
11. $\frac{6}{21}, \frac{6}{20}, \frac{6}{17}$ **13.** $\frac{3}{80}, \frac{19}{60}, \frac{13}{40}$

2.6 Practice and Problem Solving (pp. 85–87)

15. $\frac{25}{30}, \frac{24}{30}; \frac{25}{30} > \frac{24}{30}$ **17.** $\frac{6}{7} > \frac{3}{7}$ **19.** $\frac{7}{10} < \frac{9}{10}$
21. $\frac{3}{5} > \frac{3}{8}$ **23.** $\frac{7}{10} < \frac{7}{9}$ **25.** $\frac{3}{5} < \frac{5}{6}$ **27.** $\frac{17}{20} > \frac{11}{15}$
29. $12, \frac{1}{3} < \frac{5}{12}$ **31.** $8, \frac{3}{8} < \frac{1}{2}$ **33.** $48, \frac{2}{3} < \frac{11}{16}$
35. $72, \frac{4}{9} > \frac{3}{8}$ **37.** *Sample answer:* $\frac{1}{4}$ **39.** *Sample answer:* $\frac{24}{25}$
41. $\frac{3}{10}, \frac{2}{5}, \frac{5}{10}, \frac{4}{5}$

43. $\frac{1}{10}, \frac{1}{2}, \frac{6}{10}, \frac{4}{5}$

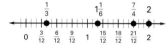

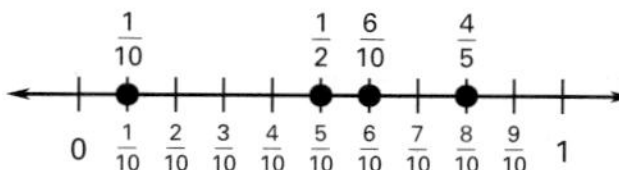

45. Abraham Lincoln, Stephen Douglas, John Breckinridge, John Bell **47.** $\frac{1}{7}$; it is the smallest number in the set and therefore closest to 0. **49.** $\frac{3}{5} > \frac{1}{2}, \frac{3}{6} = \frac{1}{2}; \frac{3}{5}$ **51.** $\frac{5}{9} > \frac{1}{2}, \frac{6}{13} < \frac{1}{2}; \frac{5}{9}$ **53.** *Sample answer:* $\frac{4}{8}$ **55.** *Sample answer:* $\frac{5}{8}$ **61.** 90 **63.** 7
65. 8 **67.** 8.3, 8.32, 8.35, 8.45, 8.53 **69.** 2.01, 2.015, 2.05, 2.105, 2.15 **71.** $2 \times 5 \times 13$ **73.** $5^2 \times 29$

2.7 Guided Practice (p. 92)

1. $\frac{5}{2}$ **3.** $\frac{38}{5}$ **5.** $\frac{163}{8}$
7. $5\frac{2}{3}$ **9.** $3\frac{1}{7}$
11. $\frac{1}{3}, 1\frac{1}{6}, \frac{7}{4}, 2$

13. $8\frac{2}{3} = \frac{24}{3} + \frac{2}{3} = \frac{26}{3}$, not $\frac{10}{3}$

2.7 Practice and Problem Solving (pp. 93–94)

15. proper fraction **17.** mixed number **19.** $3\frac{3}{4}, \frac{15}{4}$
21. never **23.** $\frac{11}{2}$ **25.** $\frac{25}{3}$ **27.** $\frac{13}{6}$ **29.** $\frac{34}{7}$ **31.** $\frac{155}{12}$
33. $\frac{75}{4}$ **35.** $3\frac{1}{2}$ **37.** $1\frac{5}{6}$ **39.** $6\frac{3}{4}$ **41.** $3\frac{1}{9}$ **43.** $3\frac{2}{15}$
45. $9\frac{11}{18}$
47. $\frac{1}{2}, \frac{5}{4}, 1\frac{3}{4}, \frac{9}{4}$

49. $\frac{1}{4}, 1\frac{3}{4}, \frac{16}{8}, \frac{19}{8}$

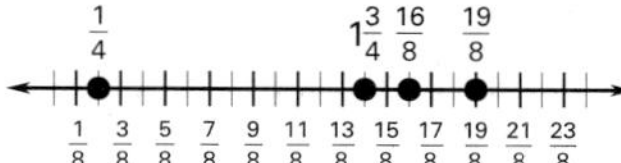

SELECTED ANSWERS

51. $\frac{1}{2}, \frac{2}{3}, \frac{5}{6}, 1\frac{1}{3}$

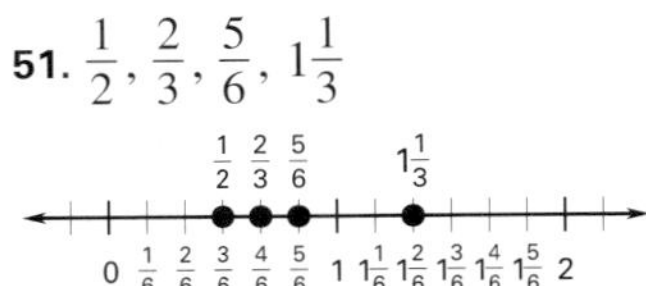

53. $16\frac{1}{4}, 16\frac{3}{16}, 16\frac{1}{8}, 15\frac{15}{16}, 15\frac{7}{8}$; $16\frac{1}{4}, 16\frac{3}{16}, 16\frac{1}{8}$

55. 17; $2\frac{5}{6} = \frac{17}{6}$ so writing the improper fraction shows the number of pie servings in the numerator.

57.

2.8 Guided Practice (p. 97) **1.** Divide the numerator by the denominator. **3.** 0.1 **5.** 0.7 **7.** 1.6 **9.** 0.9 **11.** 70 **13.** 49

19. $0.47, \frac{5}{8}, 1\frac{5}{8}, 2\frac{5}{6}$

2.8 Practice and Problem Solving (pp. 97–99)
21. $0.\overline{3}$ **23.** $0.\overline{15}$ **25.** 0.274747474 **27.** 0.143643643 **29.** 0.625 **31.** 14.5 **33.** $1.\overline{8}$ **35.** 1.6 **37.** 0.786 **39.** 0.294 **41.** 3.571 **43.** 3.417 **45.** $\frac{4}{5}$ **47.** $\frac{12}{25}$ **49.** $\frac{11}{40}$ **51.** $\frac{51}{5}$ **53.** $\frac{151}{50}$ **55.** $\frac{11}{4}$ **57.** $\frac{32}{68}$; 0.47 **59.** 0.11 **61.** \$.01, $\frac{1}{100}$ **63.** \$.25, $\frac{25}{100}$ **65.** Maria; $3\frac{3}{4}$ is the greatest of the 3 distances. **67.** $\frac{5}{4}, 2\frac{2}{3}$, 2.85, 2.9, 3.3, $\frac{7}{2}$

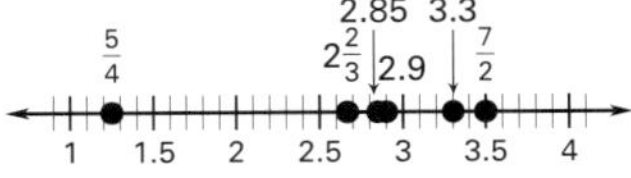

69. $\frac{21}{10}, \frac{13}{5}$, 3.1, $3\frac{4}{5}$, 4.1

71. the one that rose $2\frac{7}{8}$ points **73.** no **75.** yes

Chapter Summary and Review (pp. 100–103)
1. prime **3.** $2 \times 3 \times 5^3$ **5.** 1 **7.** 32 **9.** $\frac{3}{4}$; 3, 4 **11.** $\frac{7}{12}$; 7, 12 **13.** $\frac{5}{12}$

15.

17. $\frac{130}{140}$ **19.** $\frac{6}{7}$ **21.** $\frac{1}{7}$ **23.** 4, 8, 12, 16, 20, 24, 28, 32; 8, 16, 24, 32, 40, 48, 56, 64; 8, 16, 24, 32; 8 **25.** 3, 6, 9, 12, 15, 18, 21, 24; 4, 8, 12, 16, 20, 24, 28, 32; 12, 24; 88; none; 66 **27.** 60 **29.** 176 **31.** 20; $>$ **33.** 16; $<$

35. 20; $<$ **37.** 20; $>$ **39.** $\frac{17}{2}$ **41.** $\frac{23}{3}$ **43.** $6\frac{4}{5}$ **45.** $1\frac{8}{9}$

47.

$\frac{7}{9}, 1\frac{1}{7}, \frac{7}{3}, \frac{18}{6}, \frac{13}{4}, 3\frac{1}{2}$

49. $\frac{2}{25}$ **51.** $3\frac{4}{5}$

Reviewing the Basics (p. 107) **1.** 9 **3.** 1.5 **5.** 5 **7.** 3 **9.** $1\frac{1}{2}$ **11.** $\frac{1}{4}$ **13.** $\frac{3}{4}$

Chapter 3

Getting Ready (p. 110) **1.** B **2.** H **3.** B **4.** F

3.1 Guided Practice (p. 113)

1. A good answer should include all of these points.
- To add or subtract fractions with different denominators, first rewrite the fractions with a common denominator.
- Add or subtract the numerators. For example, to add $\frac{3}{4} + \frac{1}{3}$, first rewrite the fractions with 12 as the common denominator: $\frac{9}{12} + \frac{4}{12}$, then add the numerators: $\frac{13}{12}$ or $1\frac{1}{12}$. The same strategy is used to subtract $\frac{3}{4} - \frac{1}{3}$: $\frac{9}{12} - \frac{4}{12} = \frac{5}{12}$.

3. $\frac{5}{6}$

5. *Sample answer:* 48; you can always find a common denominator by multiplying the two denominators, even though this may not produce the least common denominator.

7. Denominators cannot be added. Therefore, $\frac{12}{18} + \frac{3}{18} = \frac{15}{18}\left(\text{not } \frac{15}{36}\right)$.

3.1 Practice and Problem Solving (pp. 113–114) **9.** $\frac{2}{3}$ **11.** $\frac{1}{5}$ **13.** $\frac{3}{4}$ **15.** $\frac{11}{20}$ **17.** $\frac{13}{15}$ **19.** $\frac{7}{18}$ **21.** $1\frac{17}{44}$ **23.** $\frac{1}{2}$ **25.** $\frac{2}{11}$ **27.** $\frac{1}{3}$ **29.** $\frac{19}{20}$ **31.** $\frac{1}{2}$ **33.** always; *Sample answer:* $\frac{3}{4} - \frac{1}{2} = \frac{1}{4}$ **35.** always; *Sample answers:* $\frac{1}{3} + \frac{1}{4} = \frac{4}{12} + \frac{3}{12}$, $\frac{1}{4} + \frac{1}{6} = \frac{6}{24} + \frac{4}{24}$ **37.** $\frac{4}{5}$

3.2 Guided Practice (p. 117) **1.** 42; 42 is the least common denominator because it is the lowest common multiple of 14 and 21. **3.** $\frac{1}{2}$ **5.** $1\frac{11}{12}$ **7.** $1\frac{1}{120}$ **9.** add; $\frac{13}{16}$ cup

3.2 Practice and Problem Solving (pp. 117–118)
11. 42 **13.** 36 **15.** $\frac{5}{9}$ **17.** $\frac{1}{20}$ **19.** $1\frac{19}{30}$ **21.** $\frac{19}{20}$ **23.** $\frac{23}{36}$ **25.** $\frac{107}{110}$ **27.** $\frac{31}{42}$ **29.** $\frac{1}{10}$ **33.** $\frac{17}{24}$ **35.** no **37.** yes

3.3 GUIDED PRACTICE (p. 121) **1.** Add or subtract fractions; add or subtract whole numbers; simplify if necessary. *Sample answers:* $2\frac{1}{3} + 4\frac{1}{3} =$

$\left(2 + \frac{1}{3}\right) + \left(4 + \frac{1}{3}\right)$	Write the mixed numbers as sums.
$= (2 + 4) + \left(\frac{1}{3} + \frac{1}{3}\right)$	Use properties to reorder.
$= 6 + \frac{2}{3}$	Add fractions and add whole numbers.
$= 6\frac{2}{3}$	Write as mixed number.

$6\frac{9}{10} - 2\frac{7}{10} = \left(6 + \frac{9}{10}\right) - \left(2 + \frac{7}{10}\right)$	Write the mixed numbers as sums.
$= (6 - 2) + \left(\frac{9}{10} - \frac{7}{10}\right)$	Use properties to reorder.
$= 4 + \frac{2}{10}$	Subtract fractions and subtract whole numbers.
$= 4\frac{2}{10}$	Write as mixed number.
$= 4\frac{1}{5}$	Simplify.

3. $9\frac{3}{4}$ **5.** $2\frac{2}{9}$ **7.** $2\frac{17}{24}$ **9.** $9\frac{13}{18}$ **11.** 11 **13.** 13 **15.** $2\frac{2}{3}$ **17.** $10\frac{3}{5}$ **19.** $\frac{11}{12}$ **21.** $2\frac{13}{15}$

3.3 PRACTICE AND PROBLEM SOLVING (pp. 121–123)
23. $5\frac{4}{5}$ **25.** $2\frac{2}{11}$ **27.** $17\frac{1}{4}$ **29.** $16\frac{2}{3}$ **35.** $12\frac{4}{5}$ **37.** $4\frac{1}{3}$ **39.** $8\frac{23}{24}$ **41.** $3\frac{1}{6}$ **43.** $1\frac{1}{2}$ in., $4\frac{1}{2}$ in. **45.** finding a common denominator **47.** both

49. $2\frac{2}{5} - 1\frac{3}{5} =$ The area model illustrates this difference.
$1\frac{7}{5} - 1\frac{3}{5} =$ Regroup $2\frac{2}{5}$ as $1\frac{7}{5}$.
$\frac{4}{5}$ Subtract.

51. $2\frac{5}{12}$ **53.** $2\frac{1}{2}$ **55.** $1\frac{4}{5}$ **57.** $3\frac{1}{4}$ **59.** $3\frac{23}{30}$ **61.** $4\frac{7}{9}$ **63.** $1\frac{1}{2}$ yd^2 **65.** $\frac{4}{5}$ mi; subtract the distance traveled from the total length of the trail to obtain the remaining distance.

67.

$11\frac{2}{3} + 26\frac{1}{2} + 8\frac{1}{6} + 24\frac{1}{12} =$	Find the perimeter.
$11\frac{8}{12} + 26\frac{6}{12} + 8\frac{2}{12} + 24\frac{1}{12} =$	Rewrite fractions with a common denominator.
$69\frac{17}{12} =$	Add fractions and add whole numbers.
$70\frac{5}{12}$	Simplify.
$75 - 70\frac{5}{12} =$	Find difference between total fence and perimeter.
$74\frac{12}{12} - 70\frac{5}{12} =$	Regroup.
$4\frac{7}{12}$	Subtract fractions and subtract whole numbers.

$4\frac{7}{12}$ ft of fence will be left over.

69.

$25\frac{1}{3} + 40\frac{3}{4} + 25\frac{1}{3} + 50\frac{1}{4} =$	Find the perimeter.
$140\frac{20}{12} =$	Add.
$141\frac{2}{3}$	Simplify.
$180 - 141\frac{2}{3} =$	Find difference between total fence and perimeter.
$38\frac{1}{3}$	Subtract.

$38\frac{1}{3}$ ft of fence will be left over.

3.4 GUIDED PRACTICE (p. 128) **1.** $\frac{2}{5} \times \frac{3}{4}$; $\frac{3}{10}$ **3.** $\frac{2}{9}$ **5.** $\frac{4}{21}$ **7.** $\frac{3}{4}$ **9.** 2 **11.** To multiply fractions, multiply their numerators and multiply their denominators; $\frac{c}{d} \times \frac{e}{f} = \frac{ce}{df}$.

3.4 PRACTICE AND PROBLEM SOLVING (pp. 128–130)
13. $\frac{2}{15}$ **15.** $\frac{1}{21}$ **17.** $\frac{5}{52}$ **19.** $\frac{1}{2}$ **21.** $\frac{9}{85}$ **23.** $\frac{10}{19}$ **25.** $4\frac{2}{3}$ **27.** $3\frac{1}{2}$ **29.** $8\frac{2}{3}$ **31.** $16\frac{32}{63}$ **33.** $7\frac{1}{3}$ ft^2 **35.** $\frac{1}{100}$ mi^2 **37.** $4\frac{3}{8}$ yd^2 **39.** $1\frac{8}{9}$ **41.** $6\frac{1}{2}$ **43.** $8\frac{13}{60}$ **45.** $472\frac{1}{3}$ ft **47.** always **49.** never **51.** $64\frac{1}{5}$ lb **57.** 11 **59.** 5

MID-CHAPTER TEST (p. 131) **1.** 1 **2.** $\frac{2}{3}$ **3.** 2 **4.** $\frac{2}{7}$ **5.** $\frac{9}{50}$ **6.** $\frac{39}{100}$ **7.** $\frac{9}{100}$ **8.** $6\frac{3}{5}$ **9.** $4\frac{4}{9}$ **10.** $3\frac{1}{16}$ **11.** $9\frac{11}{24}$ **12.** $2\frac{9}{10}$ **13.** $\frac{19}{24}$ **14.** $2\frac{11}{12}$ **15.** $5\frac{29}{35}$ **16.** $\frac{1}{6}$ **17.** $\frac{9}{40}$ **18.** $\frac{20}{63}$ **19.** $\frac{12}{77}$ **20.** $3\frac{1}{8}$ **21.** $7\frac{12}{25}$ **22.** $11\frac{1}{9}$ **23.** $14\frac{14}{45}$ **24.** $1\frac{4}{5}$ yd^2 **25.** $\frac{7}{20}$ mi^2 **26.** 30 ft^2 **27.** 13 cups

3.5 GUIDED PRACTICE (p. 136) **1.** $\frac{5}{7}$ **3.** $\frac{3}{7}$ should be multiplied by the reciprocal of $\frac{1}{5}$, which is $\frac{5}{1}$; $\frac{3}{7} \times \frac{5}{1} = \frac{15}{7}$ or $2\frac{1}{7}$.

5.

$1\frac{3}{4} \div 2\frac{5}{8} = \frac{7}{4} \div \frac{21}{8}$	Rewrite as improper fractions.
$= \frac{7}{4} \times \frac{8}{21}$	Multiply by the reciprocal.
$= \frac{56}{84}$	Multiply fractions.
$= \frac{2}{3}$	Simplify.

7. yes; 10 strips; *Sample answer:* When $7\frac{1}{2}$ is divided by $\frac{3}{4}$, the answer is 10 whole strips.

3.5 PRACTICE AND PROBLEM SOLVING (pp. 136–138) **9.** $\frac{9}{7}$ **11.** $\frac{6}{11}$ **17.** $2\frac{1}{4}$ **19.** $1\frac{1}{3}$ **21.** $1\frac{11}{15}$ **23.** $4\frac{1}{2}$ **25.** 18 **27.** $\frac{21}{25}$ **29.** $\frac{5}{6}$ **31.** $\frac{5}{6}$ **33.** $1\frac{3}{4}$ **35.** Always; a mixed number is greater than 1. Therefore, the reciprocal is less than 1. **37.** Sometimes; if the whole number is greater than the mixed number, then the quotient will be less than 1, but if it is less than the mixed number, the quotient will be greater than 1. **39.** $1\frac{2}{3}$ times longer

41. 8 houses; the 6 acres of land is divided into eight $\frac{3}{4}$ acre lots; $\frac{6}{1} \div \frac{3}{4} = 8$ **43.** $3\frac{1}{9}$ **45.** $3\frac{11}{24}$ in. **47.** 21 min

3.6 GUIDED PRACTICE (p. 141) **1.** $\times$, $\times$, $\times$ **3.** The two 3s should not be added, just distributed: $3(10) + 3(15) = 3(10 + 15) = 3(25) = 75$

3.6 PRACTICE AND PROBLEM SOLVING (pp. 141–143) Exs. 7–12 can all be solved using either order of operations or distributive property. **7.** 55 **9.** 71 **11.** $3\frac{1}{5}$ **13.** 22, 22; the 2 expressions are equivalent because of the distributive property. **15.** $3t + 12$ **17.** $24 + 6c$ **19.** $x + 24$ **21.** $46 + 2c$ **23.** $93 + 3y$ **25.** B; 50 **27.** A; 54 **29.** 100.5 **31.** 25.3 **33.** 24.8 **35.** \$60.90 **37.** \$485 **39.** Exercise 38 illustrates the distributive property because $5(75 + 5) = 5(75) + 5(5)$. **41.** If you estimate that each package weighs nearly 20 lb, you can carry only 2 packages; $3(12 + 3 + 4) =$ 57 lb, which is 7 lb more than you can carry; obtaining an approximate answer is faster, but the exact answer is more accurate. **47.** 72: 1, 2, 3, 4, 6, 8, 9, 12, 18, 24, 36, 72; 98: 1, 2, 7, 14, 49, 98; GCF: 2 **49.** 45: 1, 3, 5, 9, 15, 45; 72: 1, 2, 3, 4, 6, 8, 9, 12, 18, 24, 36, 72; GCF: 9 **51.** 35: 1, 5, 7, 35; 210: 1, 2, 3, 5, 6, 7, 10, 14, 15, 21, 30, 35, 42, 70, 105, 210; GCF: 35 **53.** 120: 1, 2, 3, 4, 5, 6, 8, 10, 12, 15, 20, 24, 30, 40, 60, 120; 64: 1, 2, 4, 8, 16, 32, 64; GCF: 8 **55.** $\frac{7}{12}$ **57.** $\frac{4}{11}$ **59.** $\frac{2}{5}$ **61.** $\frac{12}{37}$ **63.** $1\frac{1}{4}$, 1.5, $\frac{10}{3}$, $3\frac{1}{2}$, 4.3

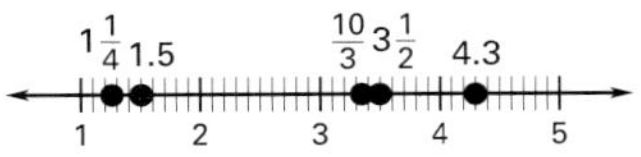

3.7 GUIDED PRACTICE (p. 146) **1.** 36 in./1 yd **3.** 1 kg/1000 g **5.** 3 gallons **7.** 3300 ft **9.** 112 oz **11.** 8000 mL **13.** 864 in. **15.** \$1.97/m

3.7 PRACTICE AND PROBLEM SOLVING (pp. 146–147) **17.** $\frac{45}{1}$ mg should be multiplied by $\frac{1\text{ g}}{1000\text{ mg}}$, not $\frac{1000\text{ mg}}{1\text{ g}}$, $\frac{45}{1} \times \frac{1}{1000} = 0.045$ g **19.** 5 ft **21.** 12 wk **23.** 48 oz **25.** 4620 ft **27.** 2 gal **29.** 105 min **31.** 34,000 mg **33.** 10,500 g **35.** 0.875 kL **37.** 22.1 lb **39.** Convert yards to feet, then feet to inches: $\frac{100}{1}\text{ yd} \times \frac{3\text{ ft}}{1\text{ yd}} \times \frac{12\text{ in.}}{1\text{ ft}} = 3600$ in.; then divide the amount of ribbon in inches by the amount needed per album to find out how many albums can be trimmed: $\frac{3600}{72} = 50$ albums. **41.** Mount Shasta = 14,163.04 ft, Mount Hood = 11,240.56 ft, Mount Rainier = 14,409.04 ft, Lassen Peak = 10,456.64 ft, Mount Jefferson = 10,496 ft, Mount Saint Helens = 8360.72 ft

3.8 GUIDED PRACTICE (p. 150) **1a.** 0.8 min/question **1b.** 1.25 questions/min **3.** 50 mi/h

3.8 PRACTICE AND PROBLEM SOLVING (pp. 150–151) **5.** 3.5 in./h **7.** 650 mi/h **13.** 51.2 h/yr

15.

Name	Distance	Time	Rate
Susan	6 mi	2 h	3 mi/h
Ricardo	5 mi	3 h	$1\frac{2}{3}$ mi/h

Susan hiked at a rate of 3 mi/h and Ricardo hiked at a rate of $1\frac{2}{3}$ mi/h; the relevant information includes the distance traveled and the time it took to travel it; the time they each started and the locations to which they hiked are irrelevant.

17.

	Distance	Time	Rate of Spread
Mid-Atlantic	25 km	1,000,000 yr	0.000025 km/yr or 2.5 cm/yr
East Pacific Rise	15 cm	1 yr	15 cm/yr

The East Pacific Rise has a faster rate of spread; calculate and compare the rates of spread in cm/year: the Mid-Atlantic Ridge spread 2.5 cm/yr versus 15 cm/yr for the East Pacific Rise.

CHAPTER SUMMARY AND REVIEW (pp. 152–154) **1.** $\frac{3}{11}$ **3.** $\frac{14}{15}$ **5.** $\frac{11}{14}$ **7.** 1 **9.** $7\frac{1}{24}$ **11.** $5\frac{3}{4}$ **13.** $\frac{1}{8}$ **15.** $4\frac{1}{2}$ **17.** $\frac{15}{16}$ **19.** $1\frac{3}{5}$ **21.** 400 **23.** 26.4 **25.** $5\left(1\frac{1}{4} + 1 + 1\frac{1}{3}\right) = 17\frac{11}{12}$ cups **27.** 48 oz **29.** No. You bought about 61 meters. **31.** 26 mi/gal **33.** B

CUMULATIVE PRACTICE (p. 160) **1.** 3 **3.** 16 **5.** 4.04, 4.45, 5.05, 5.40 **7.** 15 **9.** 7.85 **11.** 8.5 ft **13.** False. 1 and 18 are also factors of 18. **15.** True **17.** False. The greatest common factor of 125 and 25 is 25. **19.** Not a good model since the middle column width is unknown and not the same as the other two columns. **21.** yes; $\frac{3}{5}$ **23.** ; 12 **25.** $\frac{35}{72}$ **27.** $\frac{11}{12}$ **29.** 60 **31.** 120 **33.** B **35.** A **37.** 0.417 **39.** 0.222 **41.** 1 **43.** $1\frac{23}{35}$ **45.** $6\frac{1}{2}$ **47** $2\frac{1}{6}$ **49.** $\frac{2}{5}$ **51.** $\frac{24}{35}$ **53.** $10\frac{5}{8}$ **55.** $1\frac{141}{184}$ **57.** $6x + 42$; 84 **59.** $12x + 60$; 144 **61.** 3 lb **63.** 6000 mL **65.** 1968.5 in. **67.** 27.5 mi/gal **69.** Lorenzo's. More miles per gallon.

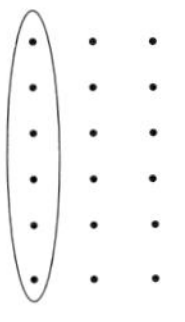

Chapter 4

GETTING READY (p. 166) **1.** C **2.** H **3.** B **4.** F

4.1 GUIDED PRACTICE (p. 169) **1.** right **3.** 0 **9.** $<$ **11.** $>$ **13.** $-4, -3, 1, 3, 6$ **15.** $-6, -5, -3, -1, 0$

4.1 PRACTICE AND PROBLEM SOLVING (pp. 169–170)
17. The numbers increase in increments of 2; 4, 6.

−6 −4 −2 0 2 4 6

19. The numbers increase in increments of 1, 2, 3, 4, 5, 6 and so on; 7, 13.

−10 −8 −6 −4 −2 0 2 4 6 8 10

21. $>$ **23.** $<$ **25.** $>$ **27.** $<$ **29.** $-10, -6, -2, 2, 8$ **31.** $-57, -36, -15, -3, 28$ **33.** false **35.** $-12°$ **37.** $-\$45$

39.

small carving | twig figure | basket | belt buckle

−1500 −1000 −500 0 500 1000 1500

41. 1800 ft, 3300 ft, 6000 ft, 15,500 ft

4.2 GUIDED PRACTICE (p. 173) **1.** 8; 0 **3.** The error was made by moving 3 units to the right rather than moving 3 units to the left of 0; -7

5. -1

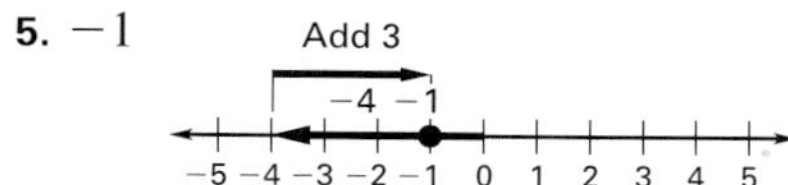

7. -7

Subtract 6
−7 −1
−7 −6 −5 −4 −3 −2 −1 0 1 2 3

4.2 PRACTICE AND PROBLEM SOLVING (pp. 174–175)
9. $-5 + 4 = -1$

15. 4

Subtract 3
4 7
−3 −2 −1 0 1 2 3 4 5 6 7

17. -1

Add 1
−2 −1
−7 −6 −5 −4 −3 −2 −1 0 1 2 3

19. -14

Subtract 5
−14 −9
−14 −12 −10 −8 −6 −4 −2 0

21. 7

Add 13
−6 7
−10 −8 −6 −4 −2 0 2 4 6 8 10

23. -5 **25.** 100 **27.** 0 **29.** -2 **31.** 13 **33.** -16

35. -3 **37.** 0 **39.** -273 ft **41.** The sum of a positive integer and a negative integer can be positive when the positive integer is larger than the opposite of the negative integer. *Sample answer:* $100 + (-97) = 3$
The sum of a positive integer and a negative integer can be negative when the opposite of the negative integer is larger than the positive integer. *Sample answer:* $-90 + 5 = -85$
The sum of a positive integer and a negative integer can be 0 when the negative integer is the opposite of the positive integer. *Sample answer:* $-7 + 7 = 0$
43. The average score per hole is 1, so the player tends to be above par. **47.** 81 in.^{2}

49. $\frac{1}{2}, \frac{9}{16}, \frac{3}{4}, \frac{7}{8}$

$\frac{1}{2}$ $\frac{9}{16}$ $\frac{3}{4}$ $\frac{7}{8}$
0 $\frac{2}{16}$ $\frac{4}{16}$ $\frac{6}{16}$ $\frac{8}{16}$ $\frac{10}{16}$ $\frac{12}{16}$ $\frac{14}{16}$ 1

51. $\frac{3}{4}$ **53.** $\frac{5}{18}$ **55.** $4\frac{4}{21}$ **57.** 18

4.3 GUIDED PRACTICE (p. 179) **1.** 8 **3.** 1 **5.** 0; $|a| > |b|$ **7.** negative; $|a| > |b|$ **9.** 0 **11.** 11 **13.** 0 **15.** 7 **17.** $-6 + (-8) = -14$

4.3 PRACTICE AND PROBLEM SOLVING (pp. 179–180)
19. 9 **21.** $\frac{1}{2}$ **25.** negative; -16 **27.** positive; 2 **29.** negative; -5 **31.** 0; 0 **33.** negative; -4 **35.** *Sample answer:* $10 + (-1) = 9$ **37.** *Sample answer:* $3 + (-18) = -15$ **39.** *Sample answer:* $3 + (-28) = -25$ **41.** *Sample answer:* $1044 + (-3050) = -2006$ **43.** -1 **45.** 8 **47.** 0 **49.** 51 **51.** 35 ft below sea level **53.** more; $40 + (-25) + (-20) + 10 + (-35) + 20 + 25 = 15$, so you had \$15 more at the end of the month.

4.4 GUIDED PRACTICE (p. 183)
1. -2

Subtract 3
−2 1
−5 −4 −3 −2 −1 0 1 2 3 4 5

3. 6

Add 7
−1 6
−3 −2 −1 0 1 2 3 4 5 6 7

5. $-8 + (-6)$; negative **7.** $-6 + (-6)$; negative **9.** $0 + 5$; positive **11.** 0 **13.** -18 **15.** 12

4.4 PRACTICE AND PROBLEM SOLVING (pp. 184–185)
17. -6

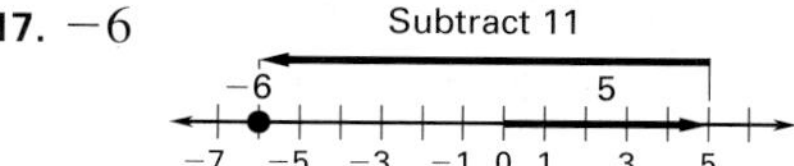

19. 11

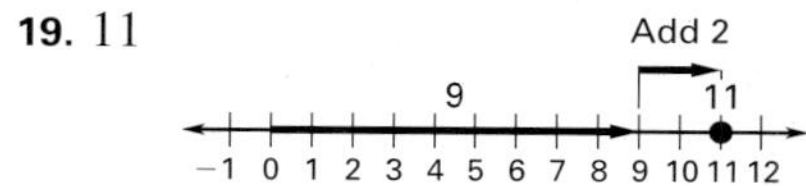

21. 9

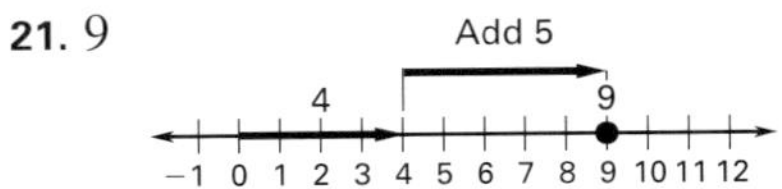

23. −80

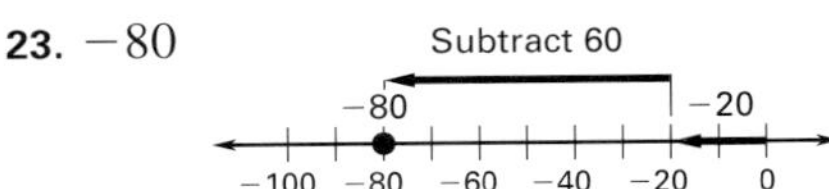

25. 25

Add 10
15
25
−5 0 5 10 15 20 25 30 35

27. −15 **29.** 9 **31.** 2 **33.** −30 **39.** 6, 13 **41.** 9, 2 **43.** −10, −3 **45.** −4, −11 **47.** Positive; if x is negative, then $0 - x$ is equal to $0 + |x|$, which is positive. **49.** −2810; −19; −4 **51.** −115 ft

57. *Sample answer:*

90
9 × 10
3 × 3 × 2 × 5

Prime factorization: $2 \times 3^2 \times 5$

59. *Sample answer:*

165
5 × 33
5 × 3 × 11

Prime factorization: $3 \times 5 \times 11$

61. $\frac{29}{30}$ **63.** $4\frac{2}{3}$

MID-CHAPTER TEST (p. 186) **1.** B **2.** C **3.** E **4.** D **5.** A **6.** < **7.** > **8.** < **9.** > **10.** > **11.** < **12.** < **13.** > **14.** −10, −5, −1, 2, 4 **15.** −15, −13, −12, −11, 10 **16.** 2 **17.** −4 **18.** −10 **19.** −10 **20.** −2 **21.** −7 **22.** −5 **23.** 10 **24.** 5 **25.** −11 **26.** −19 **27.** 1 **28.** $-7 + 4 - 2 = -5$ **29.** $-3 - 5 + 1 = -7$ **30.** 4; −3; 0; −2; 1 second less

4.5 GUIDED PRACTICE (p. 190) **1.** positive **3.** 30 **5.** −36 **7.** 21 **9.** 28 **11.** 40

4.5 PRACTICE AND PROBLEM SOLVING (pp. 191–192) **13.** Positive; when you multiply 2 positive integers, the result is positive. **15.** Positive; when you multiply 2 positive integers, the result is positive. **17.** Negative; when you multiply a positive and a negative integer, the result is negative. **19.** 56 **21.** −9 **23.** −250 **25.** −51 **27.** −200 **29.** 72 **31.** −30 **33.** −4 **35.** −36 **37.** Positive; both numbers are negative, so their product would be positive. **39.** Negative; a is negative and d is positive, so their product would be negative. **41.** $-1 \times (-7) \times 9$; 63 **43.** $1 \times 4 \times (-1) \times (-8)$; 32 **45.** *Sample answers:* -6×2, $4 \times (-3)$ **47.** *Sample answers:* 5×7; $-5 \times (-7)$ **49.** *Sample answers:* 8×4; $-2 \times (-16)$ **51.** *Sample answers:* -6×14; -12×7 **53.** on **55.** −18 ft **57.** The flag equals 1 when n is the square of a positive integer: 1, 4, 9, 16, and so on.

4.6 GUIDED PRACTICE (p. 195) **1.** False; because one number is positive and the other negative, the quotient will be negative (−1). **3.** 8 **5.** 2 **7.** −5 **9.** You cannot divide by zero, so $-\frac{12}{0}$ is undefined. **11.** −1.5 in.

4.6 PRACTICE AND PROBLEM SOLVING (pp. 195–197) **13.** negative **15.** positive **17.** −3 **19.** −3 **21.** −25 **23.** 44 **25.** 19 **27.** undefined **29.** $-28 \div (-14) = 2$ **31.** $18 \div (-9) = -2$ **33.** 2, −2 **35.** 3, −3 **37.** −3° **39.** −\$1 **41.** −4470 ft **43.** You need to know how many holes were played. **49.** 48 **51.** $\frac{3}{5}$

4.7 GUIDED PRACTICE (p. 200) **1.** $48 \div (-6)$ **3.** $(-8)(-5)$ **5.** 2 **7.** 22 **9.** −3 **11.** $3(6 + (-4) + (-7))$; $3(6) + 3(-4) + 3(-7) = -15$

4.7 PRACTICE AND PROBLEM SOLVING (pp. 200–201) **13.** $(-2)^5 = -32$ **15.** 53 **17.** 24 **19.** 20 **21.** −28 **23.** 9 **25.** 7 **27.** −13 **29.** −33 **31.** −6 **33.** 3 **35.** $\frac{1}{2}[(-12)^2 \div (-8)]$; −9 **37.** $-700 + 100 - 5(100)$; −1100 ft **39.** $-73\frac{1}{3}$

4.8 GUIDED PRACTICE (p. 204) **5.** It is easy to compare decimals one place value at a time to see which is greater.

7. $-\frac{27}{4} < -6$

$-\frac{27}{4}$ −6
−7 −6.5 −6 −5.5 −5

9. $-\frac{5}{6} < -0.8$

$-\frac{5}{6}$ −0.8
−1 −0.5 0

11. −5, 5.6, $\frac{107}{18}$

4.8 PRACTICE AND PROBLEM SOLVING (pp. 204–205) **13.** 0.88 **15.** 1.33 **17.** −2.14 **19.** −0.11

21.

−2 4
−4 −2 0 2 4

23.

$-\frac{3}{4}$ $-\frac{3}{5}$
−1 −0.5 0 0.5 1

25.

−4 $-\frac{11}{3}$
−4 −3.5 −3 −2.5 −2

27.

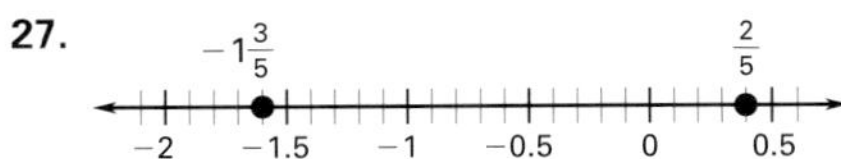

29. $>$ **31.** $<$ **33.** $>$ **35.** $<$ **37.** $=$ **39.** $-2.5, -\frac{9}{4}, -\frac{1}{2}, 2, 5.5$ **41.** $-6.8, -2.3, -2\frac{1}{5}, \frac{3}{8}, \frac{7}{4}$ **43.** $-2\frac{1}{11}, -\frac{1}{8}, -0.1, 2.7, \frac{26}{9}$ **45.** Tuesday; $-2\frac{5}{8} = -2.625$, which is a greater fall than -2.25. **47.** Marianas

CHAPTER SUMMARY AND REVIEW (pp. 206–209) **1.** $-7, -6, -2, 1, 6$ **3.** $-54, -48, -45, -34$ **5.** -17 **7.** 0 **9.** \$75 **11.** -14 **13.** 1 **15.** -1 **17.** -50 **19.** 16 **21.** 52 ft **23.** 72 **25.** -3 **27.** 54 **29.** -44 **31.** $-\$6$ **33.** -5 **35.** -8 **37.** 15 **39.** -40 **41.** -16 **43.** -8 **45.** $-2\frac{1}{8}, -2.03, -2, 0.15, \frac{1}{6}$ **47.** $-4.2, -\frac{13}{4}, -3, 3\frac{5}{8}, 4.15$

REVIEWING THE BASICS (p. 213) **1.** $55 \div 11$ **3.** 4×14 **5.** $6 - (9)(4)$ **7.** 9 **9.** -16 **11.** -3 **13.** 4.8

Chapter 5

GETTING READY (p. 216) **1.** B **2.** F **3.** B **4.** H **5.** C

5.1 GUIDED PRACTICE (p. 219) **1.** subtraction **3.** $5a$ **5.** $x + 1$ **7.** $9 - n$ **9.** *Sample answer:* the sum of a number and 3.2 **11.** *Sample answer:* eight divided by a number **13.** *Sample answer:* the quotient of a number and 20 **15.** $T - 12$, $100 - T$

5.1 PRACTICE AND PROBLEM SOLVING (pp. 219–220) **17.** $n + 8$ **19.** $\frac{x}{12}$ **21.** $-4n$ **23.** $2(y + (-7))$

25. add; "increased by" indicates addition.

27. subtract; "younger than" indicates subtraction.

29. *Sample answers:* nine times a number; the product of 9 and a number **31.** *Sample answers:* the quotient of 100 and a number; 100 divided by a number

33.

x	1	2	3	4	5	6
$7 + 4x$	11	15	19	23	27	31

35.

x	1	2	3	4	5	6
$33 - 2x$	31	29	27	25	23	21

37.

x	1	2	3	4	5	6
$\frac{3x}{4}$	0.75	1.5	2.25	3	3.75	4.5

39. $5 + 3n$ **41.** up to five times

5.2 GUIDED PRACTICE (p. 223) **1.** *Sample answer:* Solving an equation is finding a value of the variable that makes the equation a true statement. For example, to solve $x + 6 = 11$, you find the value of x that makes the equation true. The required value is 5 since $5 + 6 = 11$.
3. no, -19 **5.** D **7.** B
9. Labels: Number of CDs = 4 (number of CDs)
Cost for each CD = C (dollars per CD)
Total Cost = 60 (dollars)

$4C = 60$; \$15

5.2 PRACTICE AND PROBLEM SOLVING (pp. 223–225) **11.** no, 8 **13.** yes **15.** no, 3 **17.** yes **19.** no, 7 **21.** 6 **23.** 23 **25.** 4 **27.** 35 **29.** 35 **31.** 14 **33.** C **35.** A **37.** $\frac{x}{18} = 2$; 36 **39.** $x - 5 = 10$; 15 **41.** $35 = 5y$; 7 **43.** division; $\frac{x}{4} = 1.50$, \$6.00
45. *Sample answer:* subtraction; $60 - n = 8$, \$52
47. *Sample answer:* By the commutative Prop. of Addition, $x + 3 = 3 + x$. Subtraction is not commutative, so $x - 3 \neq 3 - x$. **53.** 0.49 million **55.** $3 \cdot 5 \cdot 7$ **57.** $3^2 \cdot 5^2$ **59.** $2 \cdot 101$ **61.** $2 \cdot 3^2 \cdot 17$ **63.** $6\frac{1}{2}$ **65.** $\frac{15}{28}$ **67.** 0 **69.** 18

5.3 GUIDED PRACTICE (p. 230) **1.** *Sample answer:* Write the original equation, subtract 12 from each side of the equation, simplify. **7.** 3 **9.** $y + 5 = -10$; -15

5.3 PRACTICE AND PROBLEM SOLVING (pp. 230–232) **11.** yes **13.** no, -6 **15.** yes **17.** -5 **19.** 8 **21.** -13 **23.** -9 **25.** -39 **27.** 2 **29.** 0.9 **31.** $\frac{1}{2}$
33. $15 + y = -15$; -30 **35.** $26 = n + 17$; 9
37. Subtraction in right-hand side is wrong.
Correct: $x + 5 = -3$
$\quad - 5 \quad -5$
$\quad x = -8$

39. *Sample answers:* $x + 2 = 6$, $x + 5 = 9$
41. *Sample answers:* $p + 2 = 11$, $30 = p + 21$
43. Labels: Original temperature = -4 (°F)
Increase = T (°F)
New temperature = 45 (°F)
$-4 + T = 45$, 49°F
45. Labels: Amount Saved = 172 (dollars)
Amount left to save = x (dollars)
Cost of clarinet = 224 (dollars)
$172 + x = 224$, \$52
47. *Sample answer:* A student cut a 70-in. long piece of string into two pieces. One piece is 12 in. long. What is the length of the other piece? The other piece is 58 in. long.
49. *Sample answer:*

[Melting point of ice] + [Temperature increase] = [Boiling point of water]

Labels: Melting point of ice = 32 (°F)
Temperature increase = t (°F)
Boiling point of water = 212 (°F)
$32 + t = 212$; 180°F
51. 6 packages, *Sample answer:* The sum of the cost of one package of streamers and n packages of balloons is \$20. $5.60 + 2.25n = 20.00$, $n = 6.4$; the largest integer less than 6.4 is 6.

5.4 GUIDED PRACTICE (p. 235) **1.** add; adding 3 to both sides isolates t; 17 **3.** add; adding 12 to both sides of the equation isolates s; -2 **5.** C **7.** A

9. *Sample answer:*

High-tide water level − Drop in water level = Low-tide water level

Labels: High-tide water level = y (feet)
Drop in water level = $14\frac{3}{4}$ (feet)
Low-tide water level = $12\frac{1}{2}$ (feet)

$y - 14\frac{3}{4} = 12\frac{1}{2}$; $27\frac{1}{4}$ feet

5.4 PRACTICE AND PROBLEM SOLVING (pp. 235–237)

11. *Sample answer:* You must add 6 to both sides of the equation, not 6 on one side and −6 on the other side.

$$\begin{array}{rl} x - 6 &= -5 \\ +6 & \;\;+6 \\ \hline x &= 1 \end{array}$$

13. 26 **15.** 65 **17.** 4 **19.** −3 **21.** 4.03 **23.** $3\frac{1}{2}$ **25.** $26 = y + 40$; −14 **27.** *Sample answer:* Yes; the equation on the right can be rewritten as $y - 13 = 10$, which is identical to the equation on the left. **29.** *Sample answer:* Yes; add 5 to both sides of the equation on the right and add 4 to both sides of the equation on the left. Both equations are now $m = 9$. **31.** *Sample answer:* No; the equations state that the difference of a number and 8 has two different values, so the equations do not have the same solution.

33. *Sample answers:* $x + 3 = -6$, $x - 5 = -14$

35. *Sample answers:* $n + 2 = 14$, $n - 34 = -22$

37. Labels: Original temperature = x (°F)
Amount the temperature dropped = 100 (°F)
New temperature = −56 (°F)

$x - 100 = -56$; 44°F

39. *Sample answer:*

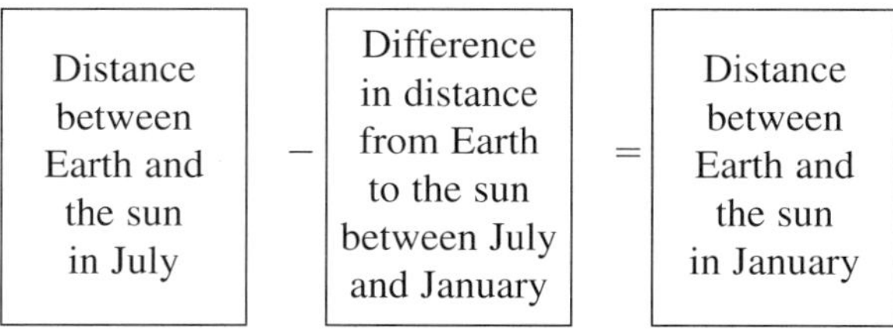

Distance between Earth and the sun in July
−
Difference in distance from Earth to the sun between July and January
=
Distance between Earth and the sun in January

41. The tilt of Earth's axis causes the Northern Hemisphere to receive more direct solar energy in July than at any other time of year.

43. *Sample answer:*

Sale price + Sales tax = Total price

Labels: Sale price = 27 (dollars)
Sales tax = x (dollars)
Total price = 28.35 (dollars)

$27 + x = 28.35$; $1.35

51. $\frac{1}{2}$ **53.** $\frac{1}{5}$ **55.** $-2 + (-7)$; −9

MID-CHAPTER TEST (p. 238) **1.** $9 + n$ **2.** $11x$ **3.** $\frac{y}{3}$ **4.** $n - 5$ **5.** 11, 14, 17, 20, 23, 26 **6.** 95, 90, 85, 80, 75, 70 **7.** 120, 60, 40, 30, 24, 20 **8.** 2, 8, 14, 20, 26, 32 **9.** 18 **10.** 49 **11.** 13 **12.** 11 **13.** 9 **14.** 9 **15.** 28 **16.** 96 **17.** $44 + n = 98$; 54 **18.** $y + 12 = 180$; 168 **19.** $125 - n = 65$; 60 **20.** $\frac{54}{x} = 3$; 18 **21.** −17 **22.** 68 **23.** 54 **24.** 3.5 **25.** −24 **26.** 44 **27.** 61 **28.** 56 **29.** 48 **30.** $-\frac{2}{3}$ **31.** 6.5 **32.** $1\frac{1}{2}$ **33.** C; 123 **34.** B; 57 **35.** A; 168

5.5 GUIDED PRACTICE (p. 241) **1.** *Sample answer:* The quotient $\frac{-48}{3.2}$ is a negative number; $x = \frac{-48}{3.2} = -15$ **3.** B **5.** A

5.5 PRACTICE AND PROBLEM SOLVING (pp. 241–242)

7. negative **9.** positive **11.** no; −4 **13.** no; 7.24 **15.** 2 **17.** 0 **19.** $\frac{3}{4}$ or 0.75 **21.** −3 **23.** 3.1 **25.** $\frac{1}{6}$ **27.** $-22 = -8p$; 2.75 **29.** $18p = 45$; 2.5 **31.** $9x = 135$; 15 in. **33.** $3x = 2\frac{2}{5}$; $\frac{4}{5}$ m **35.** $100 = \left(\frac{1}{5}\right)T$, $T = 500$. Reasonable. **37.** $4p = 22.10$, $5.525; no, the smallest coinage possible is $.01.

5.6 GUIDED PRACTICE (p. 245) **1.** multiply **3.** 75 **5.** −44

7. Labels: Average speed = 45 (miles/hour)
Distance traveled = d (miles)
Time you traveled = 62 (hours)

$45 = \frac{d}{62}$, 2790 miles

5.6 PRACTICE AND PROBLEM SOLVING (pp. 246–247)

9. positive **11.** negative **13.** yes **15.** 120 **17.** 120 **19.** −78 **21.** 24.6 **23.** 9.2 **25.** 2 **27.** $\frac{n}{9} = \frac{2}{3}$; 6 **29.** *Sample answers:* $6x = 30$, $\frac{x}{2} = 2.5$ **31.** *Sample answers:* $10x = 25$; $\frac{x}{5} = 0.5$ **33.** C; about 32.8 gal

35. B; about 0.4 gal

37. Labels: Weight of food per person per day = 3.8 (pounds per person per day)
Crew size = 6 (persons)
Total weight of Food = W (pounds)
Number of days = 8 (days)

$3.8 \cdot 6 = \frac{W}{8}$, 182.4 pounds

39. $51.33 **43.** 100 **45.** 320 **47.** $\frac{7}{10}$ **49.** $\frac{1}{6}$

51. *Sample answer:*

Opponent's final score + Valley's lead = Valley's final score

Labels: Opponent's final score = s (points)
Valley's lead = 19 (points)
Valley's final score = 96 (points)

$s + 19 = 96$; 77 points

SELECTED ANSWERS

5.7 GUIDED PRACTICE (p. 252)
1. Write original equation. subtract 6 from each side; simplify; multiply each side by 2; simplify. **3.** yes **5.** no, 16 **7.** yes

9. Labels:

Cost of shoes = 0.75	(dollar)
Cost per game = 2.25	(dollars/game)
Number of games = n	(games)
Total cost of bowling = 12	(dollars)

$0.75 + 2.25n = 12$; 5 games

5.7 PRACTICE AND PROBLEM SOLVING (pp. 252–253)
11. Add 16 to each side of the equation. **13.** 6 **15.** -64 **17.** -3 **19.** 0 **21.** -10 **23.** 1.2 **25.** $-2x + 5 = -7$, 6 **27.** $5y + 9 = -6$, -3 **29.** $a = -6$, $b = 2$, $c = -1$, $d = 8$; *Sample answer:* Start with the equation $b = 2$, the only equation in which there is one variable. Substitute the value of b in the equation $\frac{a}{3} + b = 0$. Now this equation has only one variable, a. The solution is a equals -6. Substitute the values of a and b in the equation $4c - b = a$. Now this equation has only one variable, c. The solution is c equals -1. Substitute the values of b and c in the equation $\frac{d}{8} - b = c$. The solution is d equals 8. **31.** *Sample answer:* The 250 tons fall over a large area of 49.3 million square miles in 24 hours. So the amount of material falling on a small area at any one moment is very small.

CHAPTER SUMMARY AND REVIEW (pp. 254–257)
1. $(-13) \cdot n$ **3.** $\frac{18}{x}$ **5.** $15 + 0.5 \cdot x$ **7.** 8 **9.** 53 **11.** $25 - x = 9$, \$16 **13.** -26 **15.** $\frac{5}{4}$ **17.** 0 **19.** 5.6 **21.** 15.5 **23.** 50 **25.** 62.5 **27.** 45.5 **29.** *Sample answer:*

Erosion in 1 yr	$\cdot$	No. of years	=	Total Erosion

Labels:

Rate of erosion = 18	(cm/year)
Number of years = x	(years)
Total erosion = 72 cm	(cm)

$18x = 72$; 4 years

31. 12 **33.** 30

REVIEWING THE BASICS (p. 261) **1.** $\frac{1}{2}$ **3.** $\frac{1}{4}$ **5.** $\frac{2}{3}$ **7.** $\frac{5}{2}$ **9.** $<$ **11.** $>$ **13.** $<$

Chapter 6

GETTING READY (p. 264) **1.** A **2.** J **3.** C

6.1 GUIDED PRACTICE (p. 267) **1.** $\frac{1}{2}$, 1 : 2, 1 to 2 **3.** The student failed to use common units; $\frac{3}{5}$ **5.** $\frac{4 \text{ in.}}{20 \text{ in.}}$

6.1 PRACTICE AND PROBLEM SOLVING (pp. 267–268)
7. 9 : 10, 9 to 10 **9.** $\frac{3}{2}$ **11.** $\frac{1}{3}$ **13.** $\frac{1 \text{ win}}{4 \text{ games}}$ **15.** $\frac{4 \text{ trees}}{3 \text{ trees}}$ **17.** $\frac{6 \text{ feet}}{3 \text{ yards}}$ **19.** $\frac{1}{2}$ **21.** $\frac{1 \text{ hand}}{5 \text{ fingers}}$ **23.** $\frac{1}{4}$ **25.** $\frac{2}{1}$ **27.** $\frac{60 \text{ pictures}}{1 \text{ sec}}$; $\frac{120 \text{ pictures}}{1 \text{ sec}}$

6.2 GUIDED PRACTICE (p. 271) **1.** $\frac{5}{x} = \frac{2}{3}$ **3.** $\frac{5}{2} = \frac{x}{3}$ **5.** equal **7.** unequal **9.** $x = 3$ **11.** $n = 35$

6.2 PRACTICE AND PROBLEM SOLVING (pp. 272–273)
13. $\frac{7}{x} = \frac{14}{20}$ **15.** $\frac{35}{25} = \frac{p}{5}$ **17.** The student did not use cross products property to find the variable. $9 = x$ **19.** unequal **21.** equal **23.** unequal **25.** equal **27.** $x = 3$ **29.** $x = 5$ **31.** $a = 30$ **33.** $r = 0.375$ **35.** $v = 28$ **37.** $w = 4$ **39.** 24 counselors **41.** about 857 meters **43.** $x = 6$ **45.** $n = 4$ **47.** $x = 18$ **49.** false; *Sample answer:* Let $a = 1$, $b = 2$, $c = 3$ and $d = 6$. $\frac{a}{b} = \frac{c}{d}, \frac{1}{2} = \frac{3}{6}; \frac{a}{d} \neq \frac{b}{c}, \frac{1}{6} \neq \frac{2}{3}$

6.3 GUIDED PRACTICE (p. 276) **1.** 330 min $\left(5\frac{1}{2}\text{ hours}\right)$ **3.** 24 cm

6.3 PRACTICE AND PROBLEM SOLVING (pp. 276–278)
7. \$1800 **9.** \$125 **11.** about 1.6 in. **13a.** about 22,015,000 **13b.** The nation's population grew at a greater rate than Maryland's population as more states joined. **19.** 0.450 L **21.** 1440 min **23.** 0.3 m^2 **25.** -9 **27.** -45 **29.** 8 **31.** 11 **33.** -21 **35.** 2.2

MID-CHAPTER TEST (p. 279) **1.** 3 : 5, 3 to 5 **2.** $\frac{17}{2}$, 17 : 2 **3.** $\frac{2}{17}$, 2 : 17 **4.** $\frac{1}{9}$, 1 to 9 **5.** $\frac{5}{7}$ **6.** $\frac{2}{3}$ mi/h **7.** $\frac{19 \text{ people}}{4 \text{ pies}}$ **8.** $\frac{1}{4}$ **9.** $\frac{30 \text{ books}}{8 \text{ books}}$ **10.** $\frac{\$5}{2 \text{ gallons}}$ **11.** $\frac{1 \text{ day}}{1 \text{ hour}}$ **12.** $\frac{5}{28}$ **13.** $\frac{5}{7}$ **14.** $\frac{1}{3}$ **15.** $\frac{x}{3} = \frac{6}{18}$ **16.** $\frac{11}{t} = \frac{1}{5}$ **17.** $\frac{28}{42} = \frac{10}{p}$ **18.** $\frac{a}{u} = \frac{b}{v}$ **19.** equal **20.** unequal **21.** unequal **22.** equal **23.** 16 **24.** 9 **25.** $\frac{14}{3}$ **26.** 12.9 **27.** about 153 steps **28.** about 429 tons of rock, about 0.023 oz

6.4 GUIDED PRACTICE (p. 283) **1.** No; *Sample answer:* Any quadrilateral that has corresponding angles of equal measure and equal ratios of the lengths of corresponding sides with those of quadrilateral *PQRS* is also similar to *PQRS*. **3.** 60° **5.** $\frac{8}{5}$

6.4 PRACTICE AND PROBLEM SOLVING (pp. 283–284) **7.** pentagon; The sides are $\overline{XT}$, $\overline{TU}$, $\overline{UV}$, $\overline{VW}$, and $\overline{WX}$. The lengths of the sides are $XT = 16$, $TU = 12$, $UV = 16$, $VW = 12$, and $WX = 12$. The angle measures are $m\angle X = 150°$, $m\angle T = 90°$, $m\angle U = 90°$, $m\angle V = 150°$, and $m\angle W = 60°$. **9.** $\frac{4}{5}$ **11.** All equilateral triangles are similar. *Sample answer:* Each angle in an equilateral triangle has measure 60°. So, corresponding angles have equal measure. An equilateral triangle has sides of equal length. So, the ratios of corresponding side lengths of two equilateral triangles are equal. **13.** All rectangles are not similar. *Sample answer:* For example, one rectangle could have two sides of length 10 and two sides of length 1; and another could have all sides equal in length. In this case, the ratios of corresponding side lengths are not equal. **15.** $m\angle H = 135°$; $m\angle Y = 45°$; $WZ = 30$; $FG = 56$ **17.** obelisk shadow = 110.6 ft

6.5 GUIDED PRACTICE (p. 287) **5.** 91 miles

6.5 PRACTICE AND PROBLEM SOLVING (pp. 287–289) **7.** $\frac{1}{108}$ **9.** $\frac{1}{1700}$ **11.** $\frac{1}{2640}$ **13.** $\frac{1}{120}$ **15.** 18 ft **17a.** 5 cm **17b.** $\frac{2000}{1}$ **19.** 325 mi **21.** 156 mi **23.** 13 mi **25.** 30 m **31.** $(7 + 5) \times (9 - 3) = 72$ **33.** 125 **35.** $\frac{2}{5}$ **37.** $\frac{1}{3}$ **39.** $50 + 90 = 140$ **41.** $2x + 14$ **43.** $3u + 3v$

6.6 PRACTICE AND PROBLEM SOLVING (pp. 294–295) **11.** $\frac{12}{77}$ **13.** $\frac{2}{13}$ (about 0.15); *Sample answer:* reasonable since $\frac{8}{52} \approx \frac{8}{50} = \frac{16}{100}$. **15.** 13 or 14 **17.** 0.36

CHAPTER SUMMARY AND REVIEW (pp. 296–299) **1.** $\frac{5}{9}$ **3.** 15 ft/sec **5.** $\frac{39}{2}$, 39 : 2, 39 to 2 **7.** 3 **9.** 120 **11.** about 21.6 million gallons **13.** 8 **15.** width: 28 in., length: 40 in. **17.** 0.3 **19.** 0.05

REVIEWING THE BASICS (p. 303) **1.** 0.5 **3.** 0.875 **5.** $0.58\overline{3}$ **7.** $1.\overline{1}$ **9.** $1.\overline{8}$ **11.** 3.75 **13.** 5 **15.** 4.05 **17.** 118.8 **19.** 1.53 **21.** 14.792 **23.** 12.1725

CUMULATIVE PRACTICE (pp. 304–305) **1.** 17 **3.** 2 **5.** 128 **7.** 3.02, 3.12, 3.19, 3.2, 3.22 **9.** $\frac{3}{8}$, $\frac{4}{9}$, $\frac{3}{5}$, $\frac{3}{4}$ **11.** $\frac{5}{9}$, 1.75, $\frac{9}{5}$, 2.65, $\frac{8}{3}$, $\frac{7}{2}$ **13.** 6.9 **15.** 7.512 **17.** $3 \cdot 5^2$ **19.** $3^3 \cdot 7$ **21.** 8, 168 **23.** 6, 504 **25.** $\frac{4}{15}$ **27.** $\frac{5}{6}$ **29.** $1\frac{7}{8}$ **31.** $\frac{3}{14}$ **33.** $1\frac{7}{9}$ **35.** 60 **37.** 70 **39.** −13 **41.** 5 **43.** −32 **45.** −15 **47.** $35{,}000 - 1200t$ **49.** −19 **51.** 9 **53.** −64 **55.** −7 **57.** $5\frac{1}{6}$ cm **59.** 5 **61.** 84 **63.** 1500 kilowatt-hours **65.** 80 ft **67.** 1 in. = 20 ft **69.** 0.25 **71.** 0.55

Chapter 7

GETTING READY (p. 310) **1.** B **2.** H **3.** C **4.** H

7.1 GUIDED PRACTICE (p. 313) **1.** 0.65, $\frac{13}{20}$, 65% **3.** First write the decimal as a fraction with denominator 100. Then write the fraction as a percent. **5.** 0.15; 15% **7.** 0.67; $\frac{67}{100}$ **9.** 84%

7.1 PRACTICE AND PROBLEM SOLVING (pp. 313–315) **11.** $\frac{35}{100}$; 35% **13.** $\frac{82}{100}$; 82% **15.** false, 2% **17.** true **19.** false, 1% **21.** 10% **23.** 16.7% **25.** 66.7% **27.** 87.5% **29.** 13.3% **31.** 56% **33.** 24% **35.** 49% **37.** 60% **39.** 2% **41.** 9.5% **43.** 8.8% **45.** 0.43; $\frac{43}{100}$ **47.** 0.05; $\frac{1}{20}$ **49.** 0.18; $\frac{9}{50}$ **51.** 0.45; $\frac{9}{20}$ **53.** 0.043; $\frac{43}{1000}$ **55.** 0.045; $\frac{9}{200}$ **57.** 44% **59.** 20% **61.** 70% **63.** $\frac{14}{25}$ does not belong because it equals 56%, but the rest are equivalent to 68%. **65.** 2.4 because the rest are equivalent to 24%. **71.** 0.781, $\frac{781}{1000}$; 0.209, $\frac{209}{1000}$; 0.01, $\frac{1}{100}$ **73.** 50.7%; 36.2%; 8.7%; 2.9%; 1.4% **75.** *Sample Answer:* rounding

7.2 GUIDED PRACTICE (p. 319) **1.** $\frac{1}{4}$ **3.** $\frac{3}{20}$ **5.** $\frac{9}{20}$ **7.** $\frac{1}{10}$ **9.** 25 **11.** 160 **13.** 9.6 **15.** 28.8 **17.** 37.8 **19.** 79.2 **21.** *Sample answer:* $\frac{100}{150} = \frac{2}{3} \approx 67\%$, so it is reasonable.

7.2 PRACTICE AND PROBLEM SOLVING (pp. 320–321) **23.** 32 **25.** 40 **27.** 12 **29.** $243\frac{3}{4}$ **31.** 98 **33.** 68 **35.** 12 **37.** 24 **39.** 2.4 **41.** 7% is 0.07; $0.07 \times 160 = 11.2$. The answer seems reasonable because 7% is about $\frac{1}{10}$ and $\frac{1}{10} \times 160 = 16$. **43.** 316.22 million cubic miles **45.** 231,919; 17,409,691 **51.** 0 **53.** > **55.** > **57.** $n \div (-4) = 5$; −20 **59.** 35 **61.** 27

7.3 GUIDED PRACTICE (p. 325) **5–7.** *Estimates may vary.* **5.** 390; (300% of 120) + (25% of 120) = 360 + 30 = 390 **7.** 180; (100% of 150) + (20% of 150) = 150 + 30 = 180

7.3 PRACTICE AND PROBLEM SOLVING (pp. 325–326) **11.** 0.00375; $\frac{3}{800}$ **13.** 1.35; $1\frac{7}{20}$ **15.** 4.5; $4\frac{1}{2}$ **17.** about 0.00762; $\frac{4}{525}$ **19.** 133.3% **21.** 650% **23.** 250% **25.** 0.75% **27.** > **29.** 55 **31.** 0.0072 **33.** 0.42 **35.** 0.056 **37.** 0.0035 **39–49.** *Estimates may vary.* **39.** 24; (100% of 16) + (50% of 16) = 16 + 8 = 24 **41.** 90; (100% of 75) + (20% of 75) = 75 + 15 = 90 **43.** 500; 400% of 125 = 500 **45.** 1% is 0.42, so $\frac{1}{2}$% is 0.21 **47.** \$3; \$4 **49.** \$9; \$12 **51.** 165, 240, 325, 420; 525, 640 **53.** *Estimates may vary:* about 510

MID-CHAPTER TEST (p. 327) **1.** $\frac{75}{100}$ or $\frac{3}{4}$; 75% **2.** $\frac{22}{100}$ or $\frac{11}{50}$; 22% **3.** $\frac{57}{100}$; 57% **4.** 12.4% **5.** 3.7% **6.** 6.7% **7.** 28.9% **8.** 60% **9.** 7.2% **10.** 35% **11.** 24.6% **12.** 1,902,030 **13.** 850,300 **14.** 1,168,080 **15.** 768,180 **16.** 0.8 **17.** 132 **18.** 261% **19.** 750% **20.** 0.4% **21.** 0.7% **22.** $<$ **23.** $=$ **24.** $<$ **25.** $=$ **26.** $24.75

7.4 GUIDED PRACTICE (p. 330) **1.** $\frac{17}{20} = \frac{p}{100}$; 85 **3.** The proportion should be $\frac{36}{150} = \frac{p}{100}$; 24%.

7.4 PRACTICE AND PROBLEM SOLVING (pp. 331–332) **5.** 18 **7.** 25% **9.** 12 **11.** 300 **13.** 7.2 h **15.** 201 **17.** 52,854,600 dogs; 46.0% cats; 12,602,800 birds; 3.1% horses; the percents add up to 100% because the 4 types of animals are the common companion animals in the U.S. The numbers do not add up because of rounding. **19.** 63 beats per minute **25.** 11.5 **27.** 13.38 **29.** 9 in. in large triangle, 8 in. in small one **31.** $\frac{4}{5}$ = 80%; the rest are equal to 45%.

7.5 GUIDED PRACTICE (p. 335) **1.** D, B, C, A **3.** 50° **5.** 144° **7.** 187.2° **9.** 40° should be 30°.

7.5 PRACTICE AND PROBLEM SOLVING (pp. 335–337) **11.** 180° **13.** 324° **15.** 43.2° **17.** 129.6° **19.** 35%; 144° **21.** 10%, 36°; 20%; 162° **23.** 56.5% + 21.9% + 10.9% + 8.5% + 2.2% = 100%; 203.4° + 78.84° + 39.24° + 30.6° + 7.92° = 360° **25.** 78 **27.** 57.6° **29.** Sum of degrees should be 360°. Sum of percents should be 100%.

31.

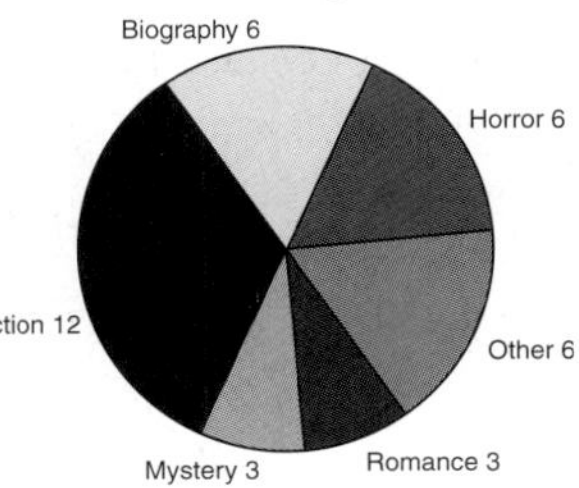

33. Yes, because the numbers shown add up to 200.

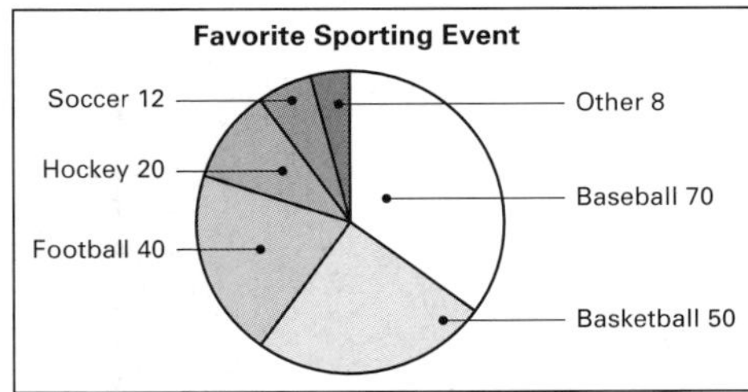

7.6 GUIDED PRACTICE (p. 340) **5.** 2.5% **7.** $\frac{1}{6}$ **9.** $\frac{7}{12}$ **11.** $3.13; $12.50

7.6 PRACTICE AND PROBLEM SOLVING (pp. 340–341) **13.** $\frac{1}{2}$ **15.** $\frac{3}{4}$ **17.** $12.50 **19.** $9000 **21.** $135 **23.** $800 **25.** $3.20 **27.** $12 **29.** $13.83 **31.** Yes, at 2% you would get $5 per year, so in slightly less than 2 yr, you would get slightly less than $10.

7.7 GUIDED PRACTICE (p. 344) **1.** $80 **3.** $60 **5.** $1.40 **7.** $3.47 **9.** $105 **11.** $18.35

7.7 PRACTICE AND PROBLEM SOLVING (pp. 344–345) **13.** The sale price is $15.75 − $7.09, or $8.66. **15.** $12.10; $48.40 **17.** $53.64; $303.95 **19.** $58.87; $176.62 **21.** $1.41; $19.06 **23.** $3.53; $52.24 **25.** $8.06; $127.43 **27.** Store A **29a.** $25.70 (without tip) **b.** about $3.86 **33.** same

CHAPTER SUMMARY AND REVIEW (pp. 346–349) **1.** 42.5% **3.** 4.4% **5.** 0.4; $\frac{2}{5}$ **7.** 0.72; $\frac{18}{25}$ **9.** 8 **11.** 13.6 **13.** 7.2 **15.** 0.12 **17.** 231 **19.** 300 **21.** 0.4 **23.** 120; (100% of 80) + (50% of 80) = 80 + 40 = 120 **25.** 60% **27.** 8 **29.** $100 **31.** $16\frac{2}{3}$%, 45°, $12\frac{1}{2}$%, 120°, $37\frac{1}{2}$% **33.** 5th, 10; 6th, 10; 7th, 5; 8th, 5

35.

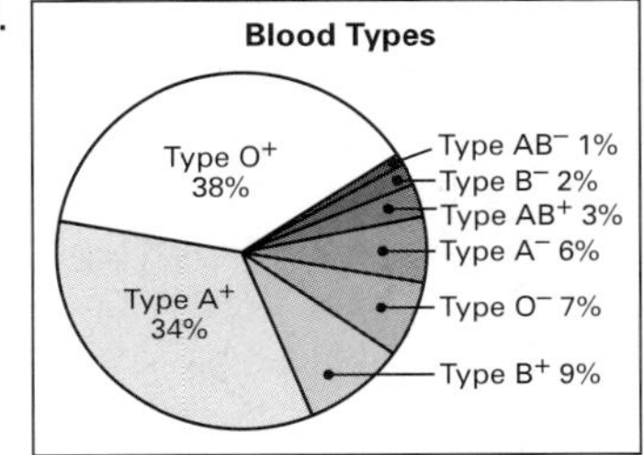

37. the first bank **39.** $6.60 **41.** $905.10

REVIEWING THE BASICS (p. 353) **1.** 11 **3.** 16 **5.** 18 **7.** perimeter, 26 units; area, 32 square units

Chapter 8

GETTING READY (p. 356) **1.** D **2.** J

8.1 GUIDED PRACTICE (p. 359) **1.** 1 and 3, 2 and 4, 5 and 7, and 6 and 8 **3a.** false **3b.** false **3c.** true **3d.** true

8.1 PRACTICE AND PROBLEM SOLVING (pp. 360–361) **5.** 60° **7.** 90° **9.** never **11.** sometimes **13.** never **15.** $m\angle 1 = 45°$, $m\angle 2 = 90°$ **17.** 50° **23.** 128 **25.** West 6th Street **27.** 45° **29.** 125° **31.** Yes, two angles have the same measure if each is supplementary to the same angle.

8.2 GUIDED PRACTICE (p. 364) **1.** 180° **3.** 45° **5.** 130° **7.** 35° **9.** $m\angle 1 = 87°$, $m\angle 2 = 93°$, $m\angle 3 = 87°$

8.2 PRACTICE AND PROBLEM SOLVING (pp. 364–365) **11.** 60° **13.** 30° **19.** No, the sum is 190°. **21.** Yes, the sum is 180°. **23.** No, the sum is only 160°. **25.** Yes, the sum is 180°. **27.** $m\angle 1 = 59°$, $m\angle 2 = 93°$, $m\angle 3 = 87°$ **29.** always **31.** never **33.** 90°

8.3 GUIDED PRACTICE (p. 368) **1.** sides or angles **3.** right, isosceles **5.** acute, equilateral, isosceles **7.** *CDE*, *BCE* **9.** *BCE*

8.3 PRACTICE AND PROBLEM SOLVING (pp. 368–370)
11. equilateral **13.** right **15.** acute **21.** isosceles, acute **23.** isosceles, acute **25.** Sometimes; an isosceles triangle can be acute, right, or obtuse. **27.** Sometimes; a scalene triangle can be acute, right, or obtuse. **33.** true; *Sample answer:* $-5 + (-4) = -9$ **35.** false; *Sample answer:* $4 - (-5) = 9$ **37.** $\frac{1}{3}$ **39.** 0.2; $\frac{1}{5}$ **41.** 0.34; $\frac{17}{50}$ **43.** 0.048; $\frac{6}{125}$ **45.** 0.00875; $\frac{7}{800}$ **47.** 3; $\frac{3}{1}$ **49.** 0.004; $\frac{1}{250}$ **51.** $48

8.4 GUIDED PRACTICE (p. 374) **1.** 24 **3.** 9 **5.** $20\frac{1}{4}$ **7.** 17.6 **9.** The value 4 is a side length, not the height.

8.4 PRACTICE AND PROBLEM SOLVING (pp. 374–375)
11. 15 cm^2 **13.** $10\frac{1}{2}$ ft^2 **15.** 65 ft^2 **17.** 3 ft^2, $7\frac{1}{2}$ ft^2 **19.** 110,400 mi^2 **21.** 84 ft^2 **23.** 10 cm

8.5 GUIDED PRACTICE (p. 378) **1.** $x = 3$; $y = 7$ **3.** $x = 2$; $y = 80$ **9.** 3

8.5 PRACTICE AND PROBLEM SOLVING (pp. 378–380)
11. $a = 9, b = 18$ **13.** $a = 12, b = 18$ **15.** $x = 55$, $y = 65$ **17.** *Sample answers:* L St., G St., 10th St., 4th St.; K St., G St., 4th St., Massachusetts Ave. **19.** true **21.** false **23.** quadrilateral **25.** parallelogram; opposite sides are parallel, with no right angles **33.** $2\frac{1}{2}$ mi/h **35.** $71.25 **37.** $3\frac{1}{4}$ **39.** $1\frac{1}{8}$ **41.** $3.44

MID-CHAPTER TEST (p. 381) **1.** *Sample answer:* $\angle 1$ and $\angle 2$, $\angle 5$ and $\angle 8$ **2.** $m\angle 5 = 180° - 55° = 125°$; because $\angle 8$ and $\angle 5$ are supplementary. **3.** *Sample answer:* $\angle 6$ because $\angle 8$ and $\angle 6$ are vertical angles **4.** 40°; acute, scalene **5.** 63°; right, scalene **6.** 60°; equilateral, acute, isosceles **7.** 30°; obtuse, scalene **8.** 9 **9.** 21
10. Add $\frac{1}{2} \times 7 \times 6$ and $\frac{1}{2} \times 3 \times 6$; or find the product $\frac{1}{2} \times 10 \times 6$. **11.** rectangle, parallelogram, quadrilateral **12.** parallelogram, quadrilateral **13.** quadrilateral **14.** square, rectangle, parallelogram, quadrilateral **15.** $x = 120, y = 60, z = 60$ **16.** $\frac{1}{2}$ in.

8.6 GUIDED PRACTICE (p. 384) **1.** 5 **3.** 15 **5.** The height is 9 in., so the area is $9 \times 15 = 135$ $in.^2$. **7.** 4 in.

8.6 PRACTICE AND PROBLEM SOLVING (pp. 384–385)
9. 70 m^2 **11.** 52.7 cm^2 **13.** 17 in. **15.** $4\frac{1}{8}$ ft

8.7 GUIDED PRACTICE (p. 390) **1.** diameter **3.** radius **5.** diameter: 7 cm; radius: $3\frac{1}{2}$ cm

8.7 PRACTICE AND PROBLEM SOLVING (pp. 390–391)
7. 379.94 mm **9.** 6.3 m **11.** 64.4 ft **15–23.** Answers are rounded to the nearest tenth. **15.** 3.8 in. **17.** 143.3 yd **19.** 14.4 ft **21.** 15.9 yd **23.** 4.6 m **25.** about 0.16 in. **27.** about 91 in. **29.** perimeter: 21 m; area: 24.5 m^2 **31.** $C = 2\pi r$ **33.** It doubles. If the circumference is $2\pi r$ and the radius is doubled, the new circumference is $2\pi(2r) = 4\pi r$, which is twice the original circumference.

8.8 GUIDED PRACTICE (p. 394) **5.** 49π $in.^2$; 144π $in.^2$

8.8 PRACTICE AND PROBLEM SOLVING (pp. 394–395)
7. 730.2 cm^2 **9.** 50.2 $in.^2$ **11.** 100π cm^2; 314 cm^2 **13.** 196π mi^2; 615.4 mi^2 **15.** 100.9 ft^2 **17.** 144π $in.^2$ **19.** $>$; since $\pi > 3$, $9\pi > 27$. **21.** $>$; A diameter of 13 ft gives a radius of $6\frac{1}{2}$, which is less than 7, so the area of the circle with a 13-ft diameter will be less than one with a radius of 7 ft. **23.** 651.1 $in.^2$ or 4.52 ft^2 **25.** 1157.5 $in.^2$ or 8.04 ft^2

CHAPTER SUMMARY AND REVIEW (pp. 396–399)
1. $m\angle 7 = 90°$, $m\angle 8 = 35°$, $m\angle 9 = 55°$ **3.** 60 **5.** 33 **7.** scalene **9.** isosceles **11.** acute **13.** acute **15.** 76 m^2 **17.** *BCLK* **19.** *Sample answer: ABCD* **21.** 15 $in.^2$ **23.** 25 cm^2 **25.** 80 $in.^2$ **27.** 87.9 in. **29.** $35\pi \approx 110$ ft **31.** 452.2 m^2 **33.** 176 cm^2

REVIEWING THE BASICS (p. 403) **1.** 9 **3.** 64 **5.** 121 **7.** 1000 **9.** 76.7376 **11.** 170,953.875 **13.** 144 in. **15.** 8 ft **17.** 1500 mg **19.** 5 km

Chapter 9

GETTING READY (p. 406) **1.** B **2.** J **3.** B

9.1 GUIDED PRACTICE (p. 409) **1.** Yes, this triangular prism is a polyhedron because its faces are polygons. **3.** No, this cone is not a polyhedron because not all of its faces are polygons.
7. *Sample answer:* can of beans

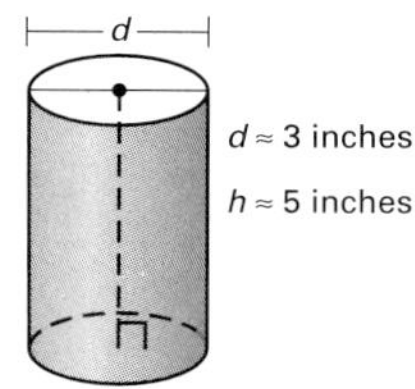

9.1 PRACTICE AND PROBLEM SOLVING (pp. 409–410)
9. rectangular prism (cube), 5 in., 6 faces **11.** cylinder, 40 cm **13.** rectangular prism, 3 in., 6 faces **15.** triangular prism **17.** cylinder
19.
5 in.
5 in.
3 in.
21.

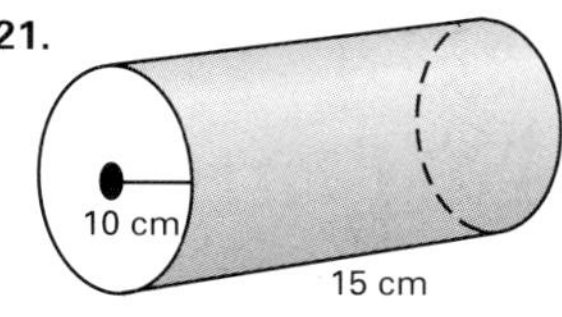

9.2 GUIDED PRACTICE (p. 413) **5.** 192 cm^3

9.2 PRACTICE AND PROBLEM SOLVING (pp. 413–415)
7a. 216 cm^3 **7b.** 216 cm^3 **7c.** 216 cm^3; The volume is the same regardless of which side the prism is standing on. **9.** 2496 $in.^3$

SELECTED ANSWERS

11. 384 in.^{3}

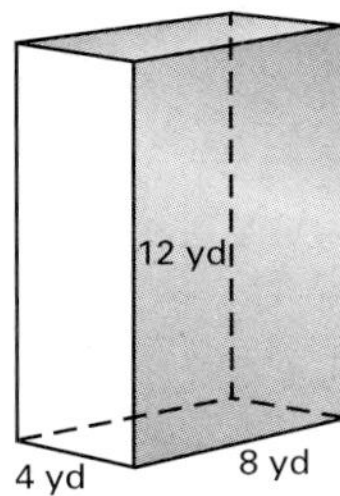

13. 2160 in.^{3} **15.** 20 m^3 **17.** 2 in. **19.** You would need to know the length and width in order to calculate the height by substituting the volume, length, and width into the equation $V = lwh$ and solving for h. **21.** 0.0022727 mi^3 **23.** about 22.4 gal **25.** $V = x^3$ because volume equals length (x) times width (x) times height (x). **27.** 6.67 ft **33.** 25 **35.** 24 **37.** 1, 3; 2, 4; 5, 7; 6, 8; 9, 11; 10, 12 **39.** 7.85 m, 4.9 m^2

9.3 GUIDED PRACTICE (p. 420) **1.** area of the base, height of the prism **3.** 1500 cm^3

9.3 PRACTICE AND PROBLEM SOLVING (pp. 420–421)
5. C, D **7.** A, B, D **9.** 96 cm^3 **11.** 67.5 m^3 **13.** 960 ft^3 **15.** $\frac{3.59}{15} \approx \$.24/\text{ in.}^3$, $\frac{4.39}{40} \approx \$.11/\text{ in.}^3$; triangular prism package is better buy **17.** 10 ft from top edge of roof to bottom edge of roof **19.** 104 m

MID-CHAPTER TEST (p. 422) **1.** rectangular prism, 2.5 in., 6 faces **2.** triangular prism, 9 ft, 5 faces **3.** cylinder, 3.9 in.
4. 5 faces

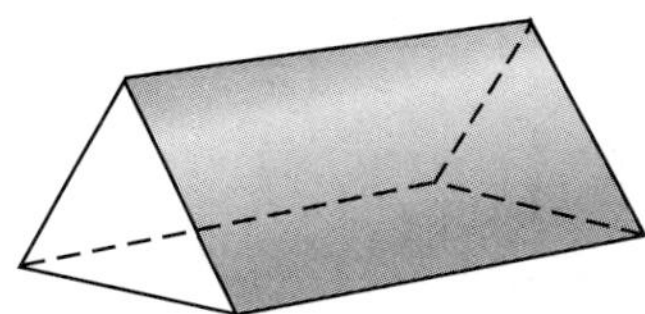

5. rectangular prism; 450 cm^3 **6.** triangular prism; 336 in.^{3} **7.** rectangular prism; 468 in.^{3} **8.** rectangular prism; 224 cm^3 **9.** triangular prism, 144 ft^3 **10.** triangular prism, 8820 in.^{3} **11.** 2 ft **12.** 80 cm **13.** 80 ft^3 **14.** 560 ft^3 **15.** 640 ft^3

9.4 GUIDED PRACTICE (p. 425) **1.** A; method B finds the area of a rectangle, not the volume of the cylinder. **3.** about 63.6 ft^2 **5.** about 615 ft^3
7. $4603.49 \text{ gal} \times \frac{1 \text{ min}}{12 \text{ gal}} \approx 384 \text{ min}$

9.4 PRACTICE AND PROBLEM SOLVING (pp. 425–427)
9. 4939.22 in.^{3} **11.** 1081.573 cm^3 **13.** 937.87875 yd^3 **15.** 7.948125 cm^3 **17.** 35.33 in.^{3} **19.** 4.54 days **21.** 15.07 cm^3 **27.** 0.56 **29.** 0.27 **31.** 7 **33.** 5 **35.** 79.2°

9.5 GUIDED PRACTICE (p. 432) **1.** Each of the 2 triangular faces has an area of 12 in.^{2}; each of the two 5 by 20 rectangles has an area of 100 in.^{2}; the 8 by 20 rectangle has an area of 160 in.^{2}. **3.** 600 in.^{2} **5.** 1568 in.^{2}

9.5 PRACTICE AND PROBLEM SOLVING (pp. 432–433)
7. $13\frac{1}{8}$ in.^{2} **9.** 197.5 in.^{2} **11.** 216 cm^2 **13.** No; the cut edges of the 2 triangular prisms are now included in the surface area but were not part of the surface of the original rectangular prism. **15.** 1240 in.^{2} **17.** 612 ft^2 **19.** B; a sugar cube is roughly 1 cm per side, so it would have 6 sides that each have a surface area of about 1 cm^2, for a total of 6 cm^2.
21. 1000 ft^2

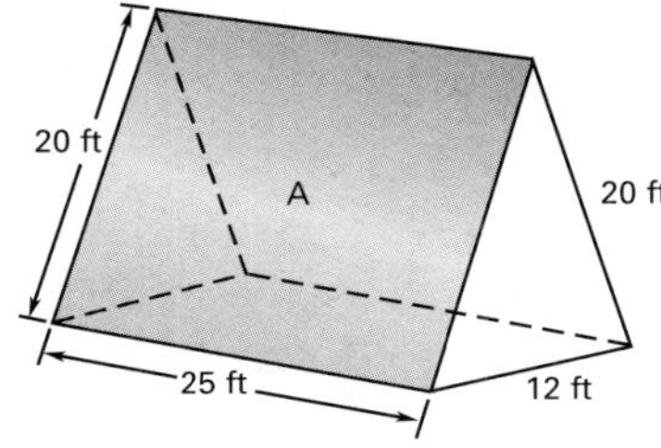

9.6 GUIDED PRACTICE (p. 436) **1a.** base: the circular surface of a cylinder **1b.** circumference: the distance around a base **1c.** height: the distance between the two circular bases **1d.** radius: half the diameter of one of the bases **1e.** lateral surface: the area of the surface between the two circular bases

9.6 PRACTICE AND PROBLEM SOLVING (pp. 436–437)
7. D; 14.758 cm^2 **9.** C; 626.43 mm^2 **11.** 81.64 ft^2, 58.96 ft^2, 199.56 ft^2 **13.** 264 m^2, 154 m^2, 572 m^2 **15.** 98.9 ft^2 **17.** 142.87 m^2
19.

Dimensions	Single	Doubled	Tripled	Quadrupled
Surface area	747 in.^{2}	2989 in.^{2}	6726 in.^{2}	11,957 in.^{2}

When the dimensions double, the surface area is multiplied by 2^2; when the dimensions triple, the surface area is multiplied by 3^2; when the dimensions quadruple, the surface area is multiplied by 4^2.

CHAPTER SUMMARY AND REVIEW (p. 438–441)
5. cylinder; 9 m **7.** triangular prism; 27 cm; 5 faces **9.** 20,736 in.^{2} **11.** 9 m **13.** 162 ft^3 **15.** 607.5 in.^{3} **17.** b; larger volume **19.** about 8.53 L **21.** 118 ft^2
23. 540 ft^2

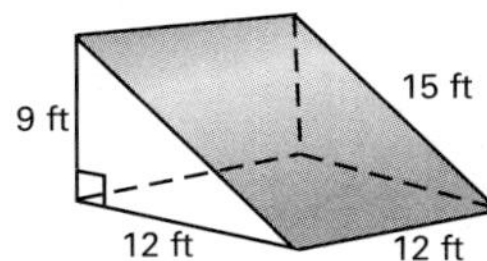

25. 113.04 yd^2 **27.** 379.8 ft^2 **29.** 100.48 in.^{2}

REVIEWING THE BASICS (p. 445) **1.** 2.63 **3.** 20.32 **5.** 2.4 **7.** 2.56 **9.** 4.57 **11.** 16 **13.** 12.27

CUMULATIVE PRACTICE (pp. 446–447) **1.** 5.463 **3.** 6.61818 **5.** GCF = 4, LCM = 96 **7.** GCF = 24; LCM = 144 **9.** 1 **11.** $\frac{5}{12}$ **13.** $\frac{17}{24}$ **15.** $19\frac{1}{4}$ **17.** -28 **19.** -153 **21.** -45 **23.** -18 **25.** $n + (-11) = 16$; 27

SELECTED ANSWERS

27. $n \times 3 = 33$; 11 **29.** $3n - 17 = -11$; 2 **31.** $\frac{6}{7}$, 6 : 7 **33.** 1 **35.** 100 **37.** 42 **39.** 12 **41.** $110.25 **43.** $417.30 **45.** AD = 2.6 cm, DE = 2.6 cm, EA = 2.6 cm; equilateral, isosceles acute **47.** AB = 3.3 cm, BC = 2.3 cm, CA = 2.3 cm; isosceles, right **49.** 78.5 cm^2 **51.** rectangular prism; 160 ft^3; 232 ft^2 **53.** cylinder; 150.7 cm^3; 175.8 cm^2 **55.** the rectangular prism-shaped silo

Chapter 10

GETTING READY (p. 452) **1.** B **2.** J **3.** C

10.1 GUIDED PRACTICE (p. 455) **5.** 21, 17, 25 **7.** 14, 15, 3 and 17 **9.** The mean increases to about 70.0, the median increases to 54.5, and there are now three modes, 2, 4, and 170.

10.1 PRACTICE AND PROBLEM SOLVING (pp. 455–456) **11.** ≈113.5, 102, 90 and 120 **13.** Mean is lowered to 57.7, median is the same at 62, mode is the same at 70. **15.** 0; ≈70.3, 79, 83; ≈80.3, 83, 83; the outlier lowers the mean by about 10, lowers the median by 4, and does not affect the mode. **17.** 100; ≈35.1, 25, modes 20, 25, and 28; ≈24.3, 25, no mode; the outlier raises the mean by about 10.8, it does not affect the median, and without the outlier there is no mode because each data value occurs twice. **19.** Yes, the outlier is 81. It lowers the mean and median but does not affect the mode. **21.** The mean would be increased, but the median and modes would remain the same.

10.2 GUIDED PRACTICE (p. 459)

1.

Interval	Tally	Frequency
51–60	|||	3
61–70	~~||||~~	5
71–80	~~||||~~ |	6
81–90	||||	4
91–100	||	2

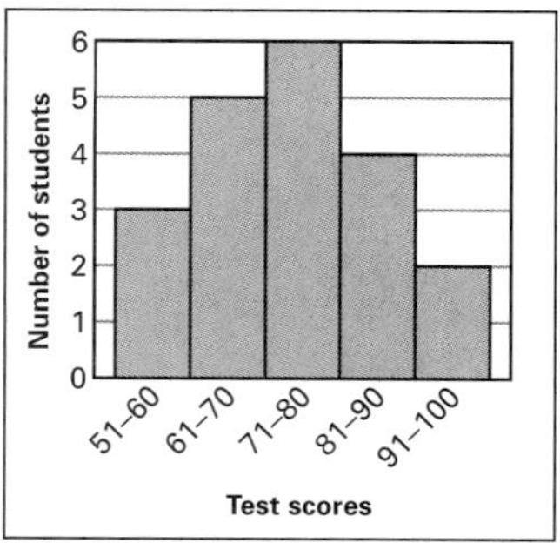

3. Class B has fewer students that scored below 70% and more students in the 80% to 100% range, so overall Class B did better.

10.2 PRACTICE AND PROBLEM SOLVING (pp. 459–460)
5. about 48%

7.

Interval	Tally	Frequency
0–9	|	1
10–19	||||	4
20–29	|||	3
30–39	~~||||~~ ~~||||~~ |	11
40–49	||||	4
50–59	||	2
60–69	||||	4
70–79		0
80–89	|	1

9. $\frac{4}{15}$ or about 27%

11.

Interval	Tally	Frequency
0–2	~~||||~~ ~~||||~~ ~~||||~~ ~~||||~~ |	21
3–5	~~||||~~ ~~||||~~ ~~||||~~ |	16
6–8	~~||||~~ |	6
9–11	|||	3
12–14	||	2
15–17	|	1
18–20		0
21–23		0
24–26	|	1

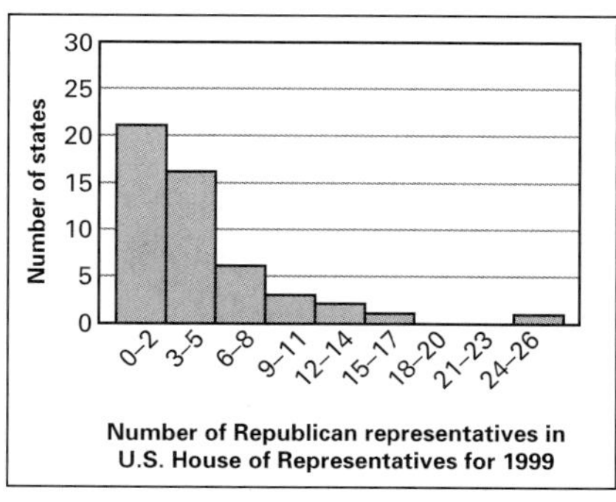

10.3 GUIDED PRACTICE (p. 463) **1.** 12 **3.** 16 **5.** 25 **7.** Don't include median when finding quartiles; lower quartile: 8; upper quartile: 19

10.3 PRACTICE AND PROBLEM SOLVING (pp. 463–465)

13.

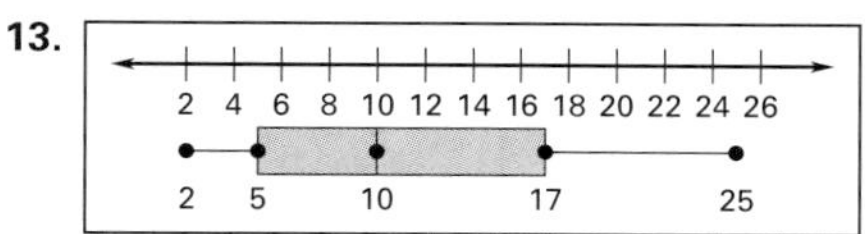

15.

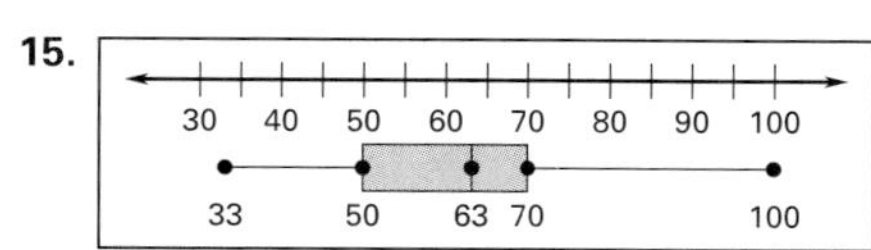

17.a. 55 **b.** 51 **c.** 58 **d.** 27 **e.** 7 **f.** ≈54.8
21. Men: 7 min, 2.5 min; Women: 12 min, 3 min

SELECTED ANSWERS

23.

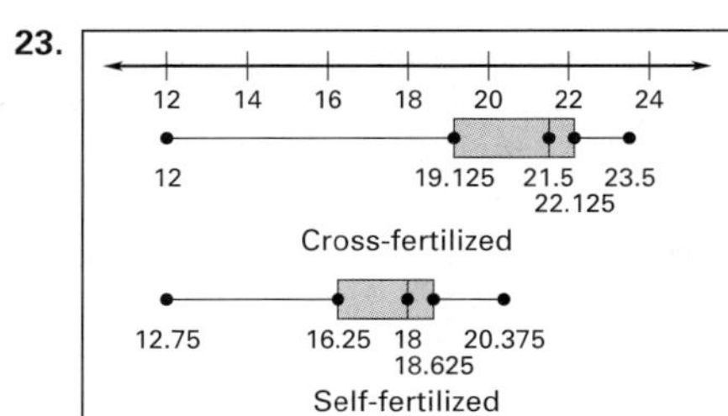

The box-and-whisker plots show that in general the cross-fertilized corn plants grew taller than the self-fertilized corn plants.

27. $\frac{11}{24}$ **29.** $6\frac{1}{15}$ **31.** 64 **33.** -13 **35.** 20 **37.** 5.4

10.4 GUIDED PRACTICE (p. 470) **7.** $(-4, 1)$; II **9.** $(0, 0)$; none **11.** $(3, 0)$; none

13. As the latitude increases, the temperature decreases.

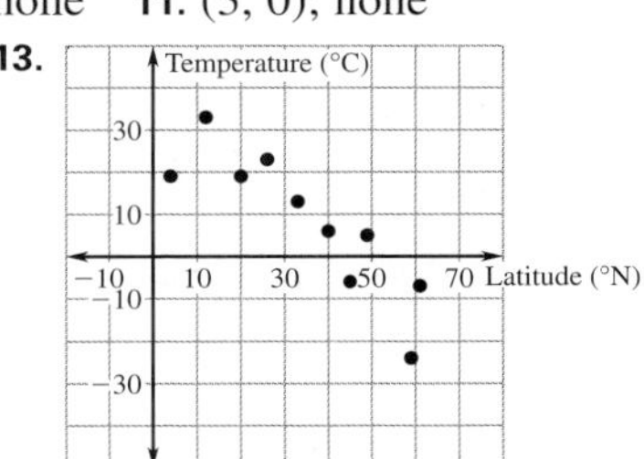

10.4 PRACTICE AND PROBLEM SOLVING (pp. 470–472)

15. From the origin, move right 3 units and up 4 units.

17. From the origin, move left 4 units.

19.

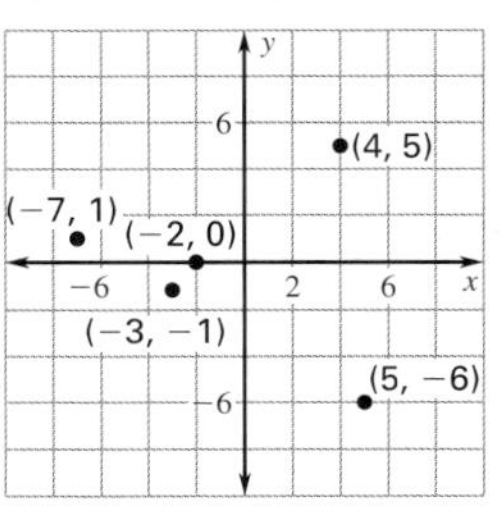

21. triangle

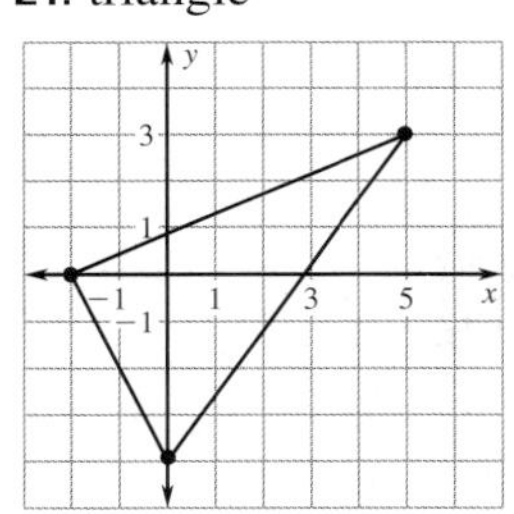

23. quadrilateral

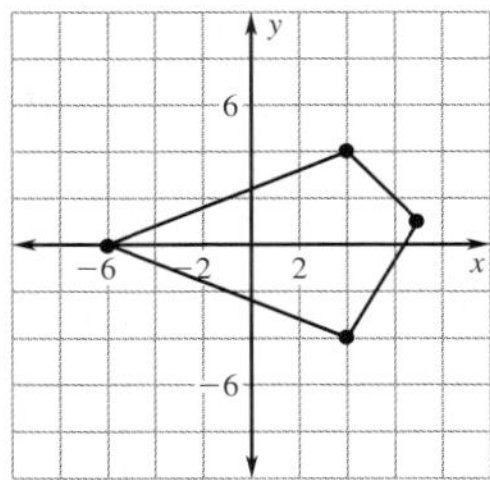

25. $(0, 10)$, $(1, 9)$, $(2, 7)$, $(3, 4)$, $(4, 0)$

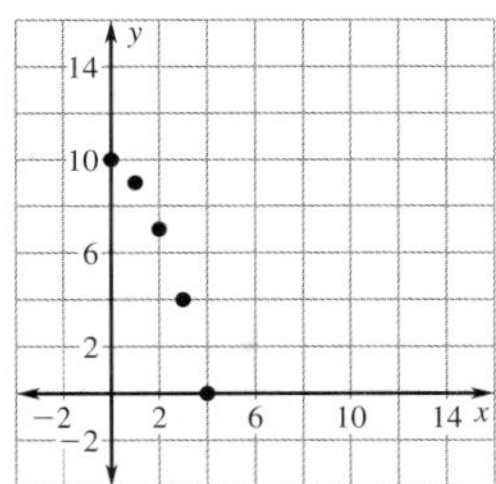

27. about -13°F

29. The points almost lie on a line.

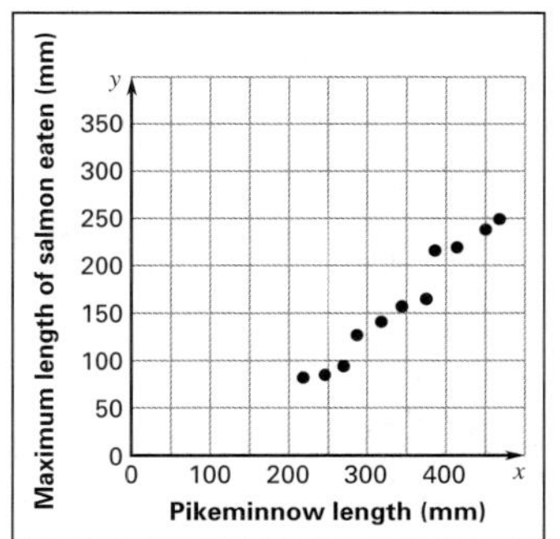

31. *Sample answer:* about 550 mm to 600 mm

33. *Sample answer:* Yes, the points appear to be linear.

MID-CHAPTER TEST (p. 473) **1.** \$58, \$60, \$70

2. 17, 19, 14 and 21

3.

Interval	Tally	Frequency
0–19	𝍸 𝍸 𝍸 |	16
20–39	𝍸 𝍸 |	11
40–59	𝍸 𝍸	10
60–79	𝍸 |	6
80–99	𝍸	5
100–119	|	1
120–139		0
140–159		0
160–179		0
180–199		0
200–219	|	1

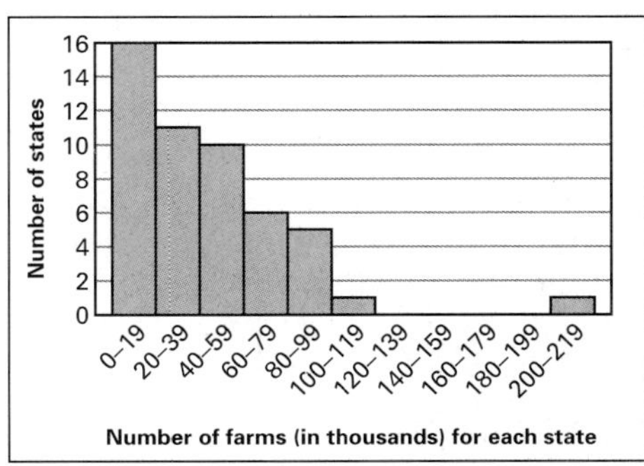

4.a. 70.5 **b.** 62 **c.** 81 **d.** 59 **e.** 19 **f.** 72.6

5.

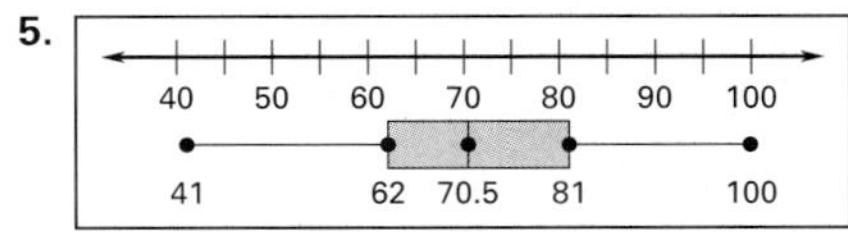

SELECTED ANSWERS

6.

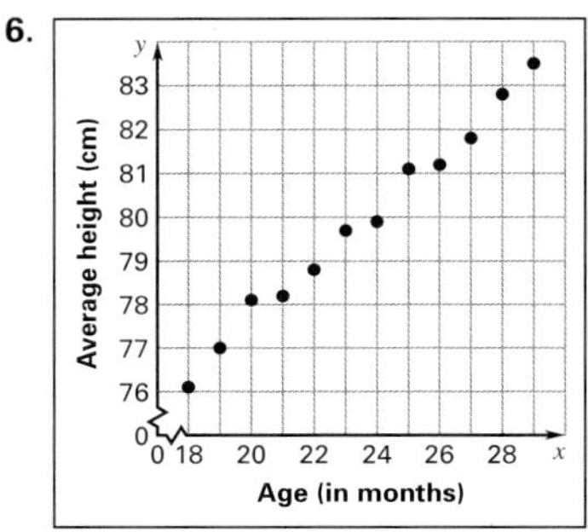

7. *Sample answer:* about 85 cm

10.5 Guided Practice (p. 476)

1.

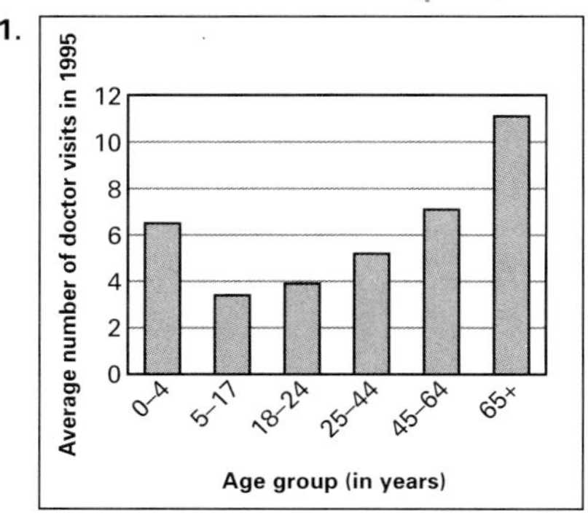

3. Damselfly = 5 ft/sec; Bumblebee = 10 ft/sec; Honeybee = 9 ft /sec; Housefly = 6 ft/sec; Mosquito = 2 ft/sec **5.** 15 ft

10.5 Practice and Problem Solving (pp. 476–477)

7.

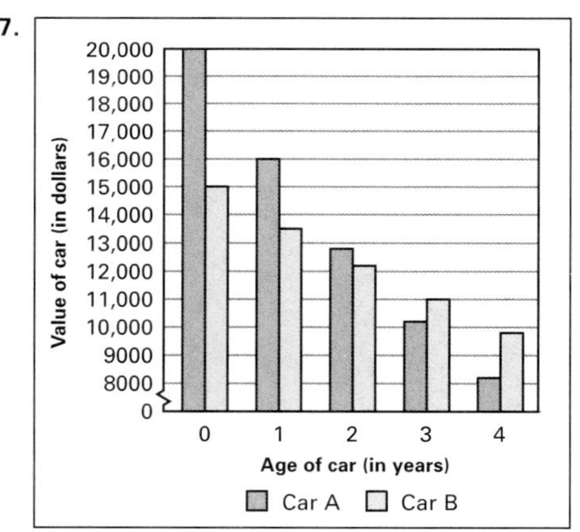

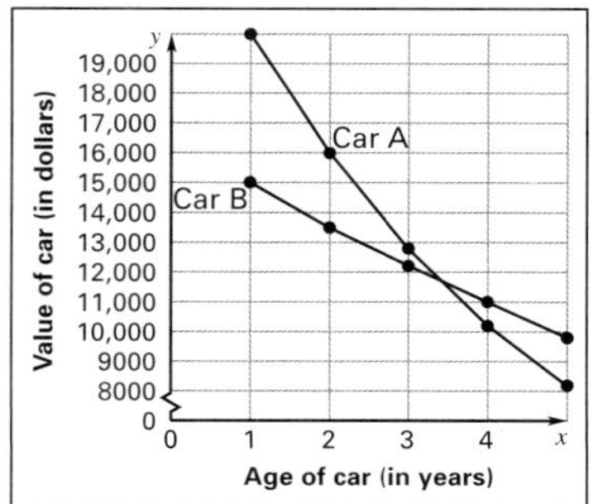

9. *Sample answer:* About 12 or 13 lb; the amount consumed increased by about 1 to 2 pounds in most of the 5-year intervals. **11.** *Sample answer:* About 55 qt; the amount consumed increased by about 5 to 10 quarts in most of the 5-year intervals.

13.

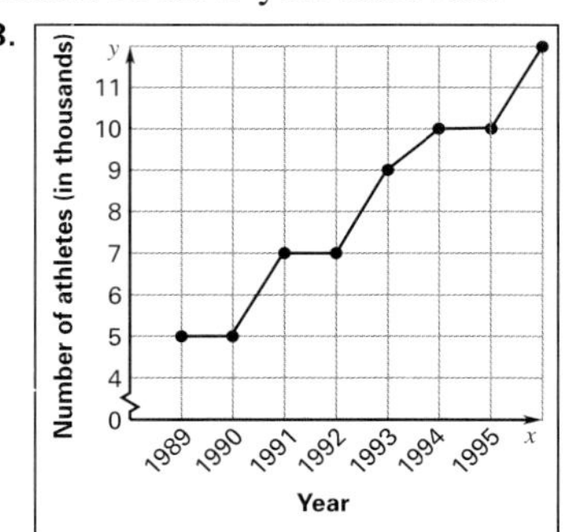

15.

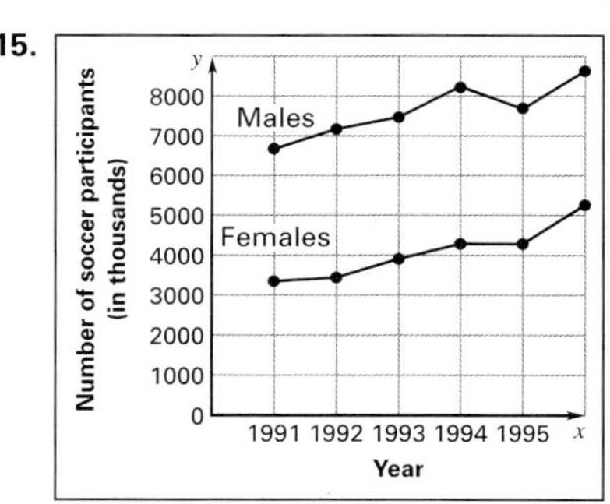

10.6 Guided Practice (p. 480)

1. *Sample answer:* When the vertical axis of a bar graph or line graph is broken, the graph is distorted and can be misleading.

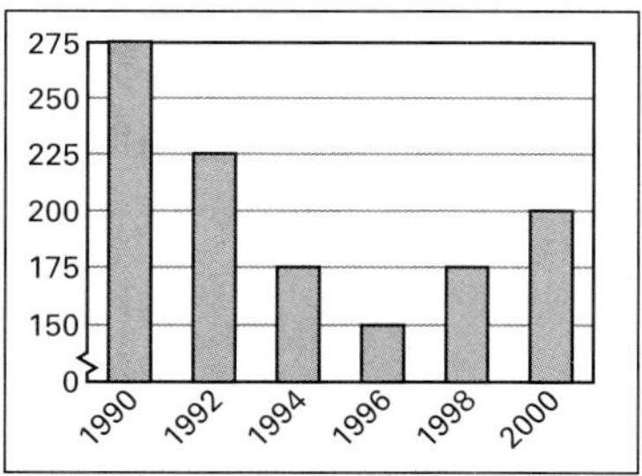

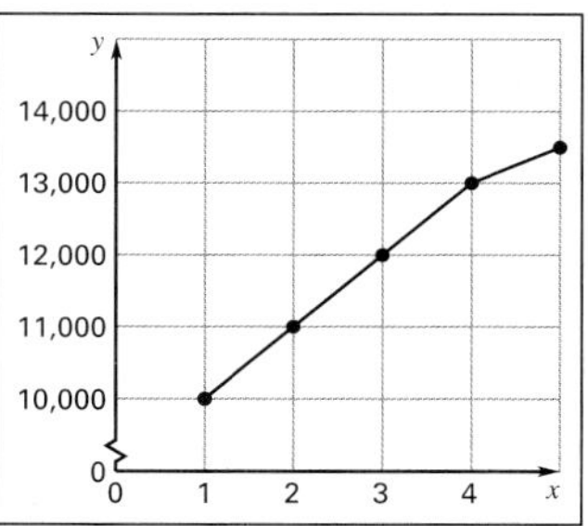

3. *Sample answer:* The average time in 1996 is 70 hours longer than in 1991, which is about 30% longer, or 1.3 times as long. The graph is misleading since the vertical axis is broken and it makes the gap between the total number of hours seem bigger than it is.

10.6 PRACTICE AND PROBLEM SOLVING (pp. 480–482)
5. *Sample answer:* About 10.5 million people swam compared to about 4.7 million people who played volleyball. There were about 2.2 times as many swimmers as volleyball players (not 3 times as many). The graph is misleading because the horizontal scale is broken. **7.** *Sample answer:* The graph at the top is more reasonable (not misleading) since the vertical scale starts at zero and does not skip values.
9. *Sample answer:* This could be misleading because it would make it appear that there is almost no increase in spending in the six-year period.

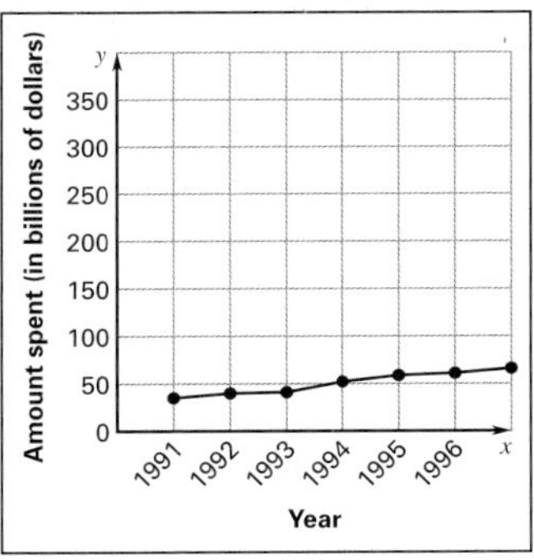

11. *Sample answer:*

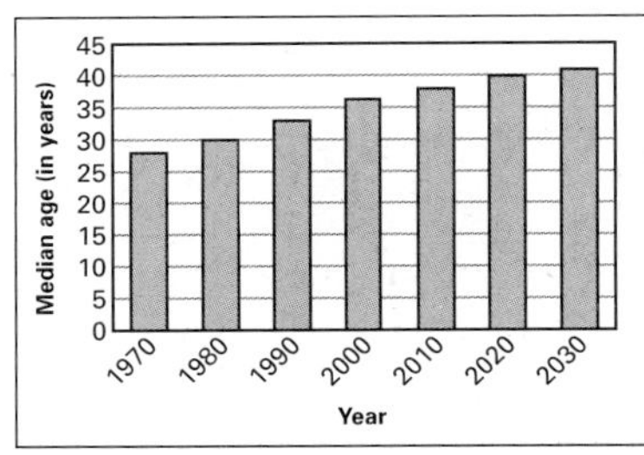

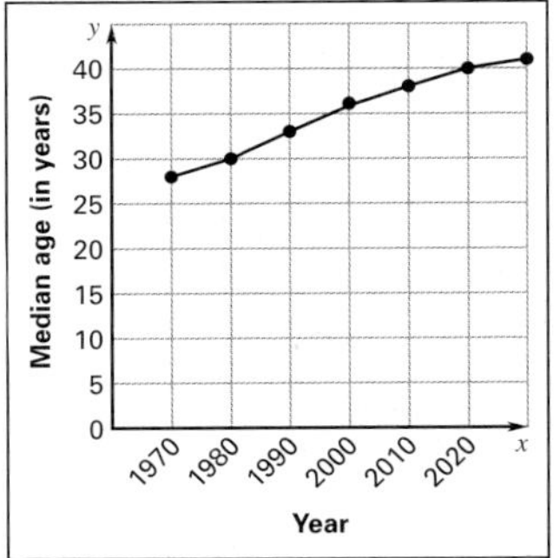

15. 120 **17.** 47 **19.** isosceles **21.** discounted price: $56; total price including tax: $59.92

10.7 PRACTICE AND PROBLEM SOLVING (pp. 485–486)
7. *Sample answer:*

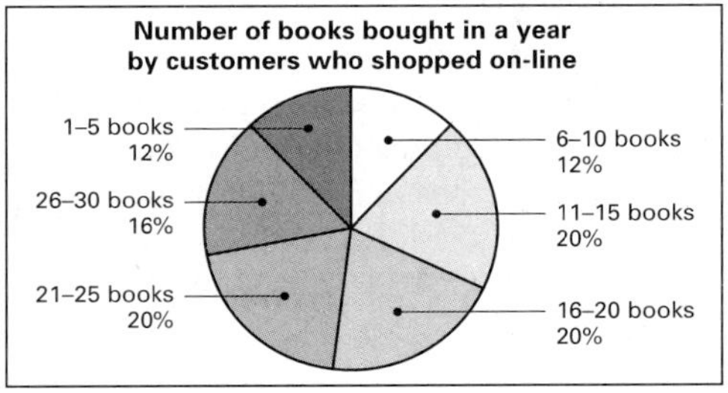

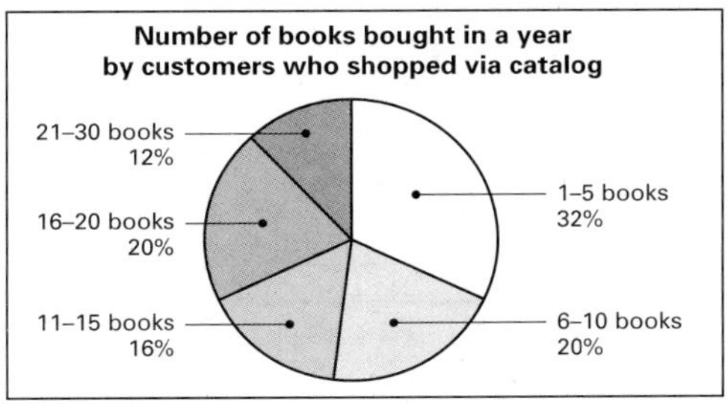

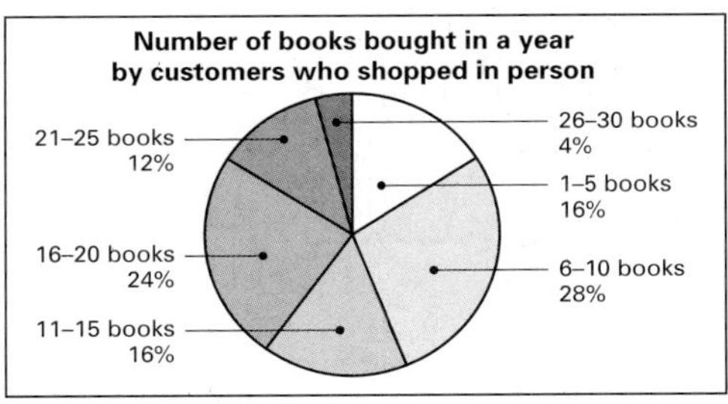

9. About 8.3 books; this average is lower than all of the means found in Exercise 8. **11.** *Sample answer:* The population is all people who read the newspaper, and the sample is all people who call and respond to the poll. **13.** *Sample answer:* Assuming only readers would be polled, contact every n^{th} customer. **15.** Convenience; the sample includes only people who use e-mail and are her friends, who may not be representative of the general population.

10.8 GUIDED PRACTICE (p. 489) **1.** *Sample answer:* If the question is biased, or the sample is biased, or the method used to gather data is inappropriate for the situation, the results of a survey can be invalid.

10.8 PRACTICE AND PROBLEM SOLVING (pp. 489–491)
3. *Sample answer:* The words "playful, cuddly" imply that the puppies are more playful and cuddly than kittens. **5.** *Sample answer:* The words "softness" and "scratchy" imply that leather is more comfortable than wool. **7.** *Sample answer:* The words "bitter" and "refreshing" would influence someone to choose water. **9.** *Sample answer:* The word "experts" influences a person to agree with the claims. **11.** *Sample answer:* The survey was inaccurate and predicted the wrong answer.

13. *Sample answer:* The *Literary Digest* could have used a random sampling method from postal addresses. **15.** *Sample answer:* The questions could be answered anonymously in a written form. **17.** *Sample answer:* "Do you watch a newscast on weekday nights, and if so, which one?" The sample could be chosen by selecting names and phone numbers from a phone book covering the area that is serviced by the local television station. **21.** 1.66 **23.** 21.78 **25.** 9.473733 **27.** 3 **29.** 9 **31.** 16 **33.** 1 **35.** 55 **37.** −90

CHAPTER SUMMARY AND REVIEW (pp. 492–495) **1.** \$85, \$87, \$79

3.

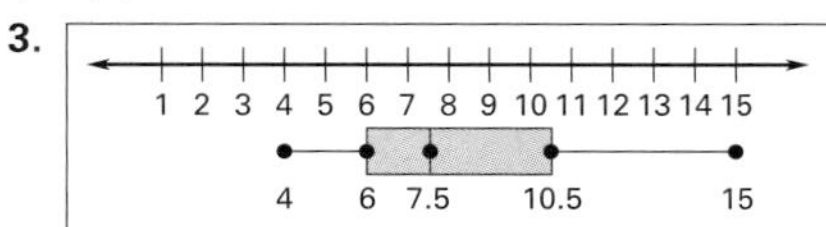

5.

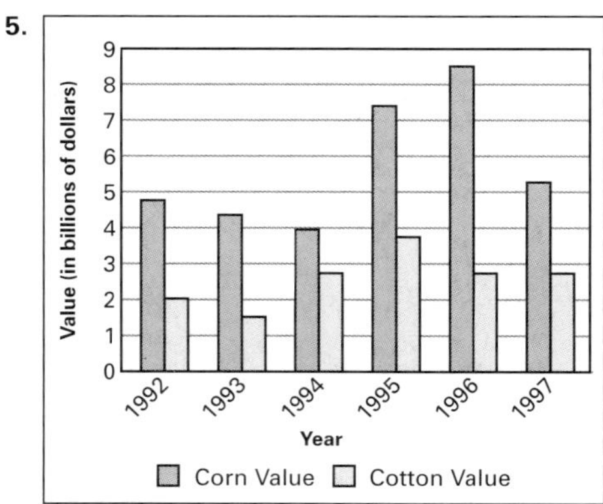

7.

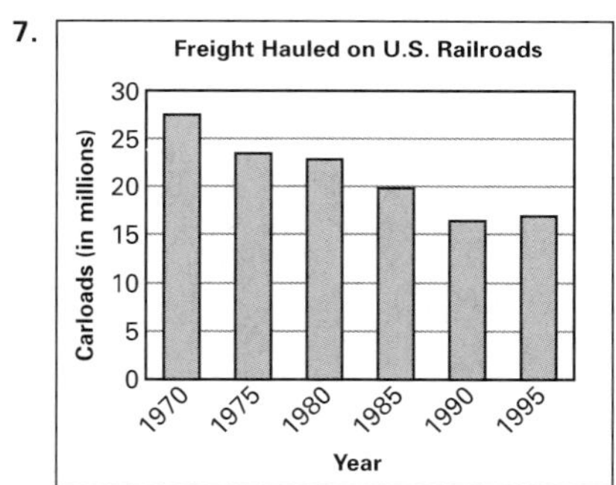

9. *Sample answer:* The claim that air travel is the safest form of transportation could influence people to say they are not afraid of flying.

REVIEWING THE BASICS (p. 499) **1.** $\frac{11}{7}$ **3.** $\frac{79}{30}$ **5.** $\frac{8}{13}$ **7.** $\frac{17}{36}$ **9.** $\frac{2}{7}$ **11.** $\frac{3}{2}$ **13.** $\frac{26}{15}$ **15.** $\frac{2}{3}$ **17.** $\frac{1}{2}$ **19.** $\frac{3}{5}$

Chapter 11

GETTING READY (p. 502) **1.** C **2.** H **3.** A

11.1 GUIDED PRACTICE (p. 506) **1.** *Sample answer:* From the chance that the first toss is heads (*H*), draw a branch to each of the second toss possibilities (*H*), (*T*). From the chance that the first toss is tails (*T*), draw a branch to each of the second toss possibilities (*H*), (*T*). **3.** $\frac{1}{8}$ **5.** $\frac{1}{2}$ **7.** $\frac{1}{9}$

11.1 PRACTICE AND PROBLEM SOLVING (pp. 506–508) **9.** $\frac{1}{8}$ **11.** $\frac{1}{4}$ **13.** $\frac{1}{16}$ **15.** $\frac{1}{3}$, about 0.33, about 33% **17.** $\frac{1}{3}$, about 0.33, about 33%

19.

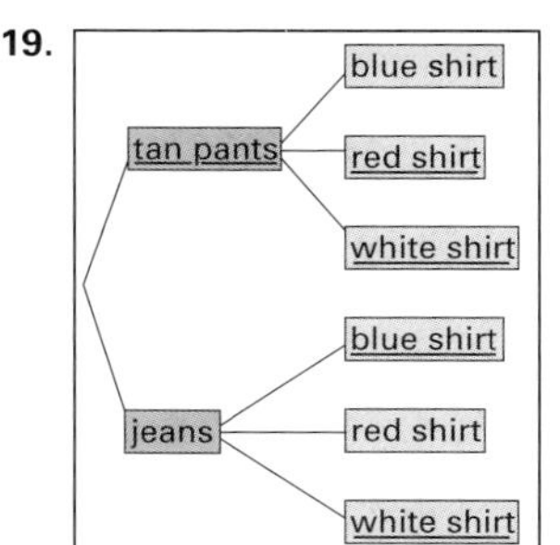

21. $\frac{7}{9}$ **23.** $\frac{4}{9}$

25.

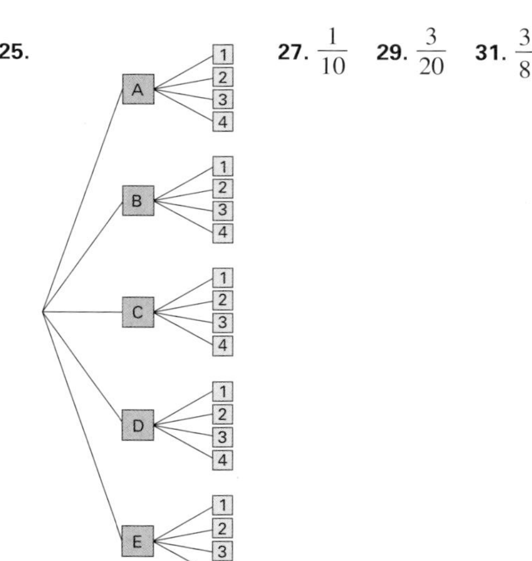

27. $\frac{1}{10}$ **29.** $\frac{3}{20}$ **31.** $\frac{3}{8}$

11.2 GUIDED PRACTICE (p. 511) **1.** Disjoint events are two events that have no outcomes in common. Overlapping events are two events that have one or more outcomes in common. **3.** disjoint events **5.** dependent; Selecting a number and not replacing it affects the probability of the next event occurring.

11.2 Practice and Problem Solving (pp. 512–513)

7. overlapping events
9. overlapping events

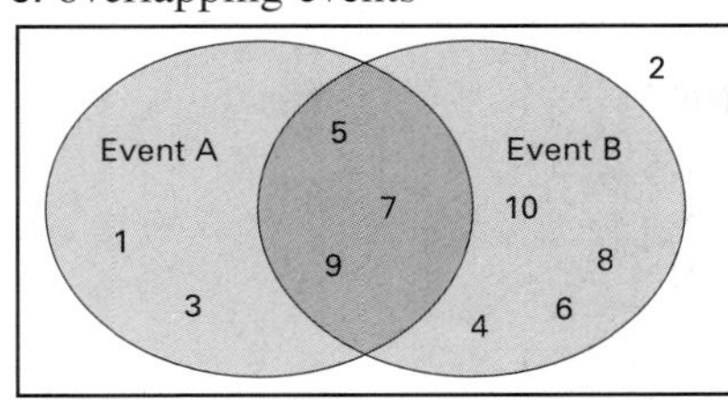

11. disjoint events **13.** overlapping events
15.

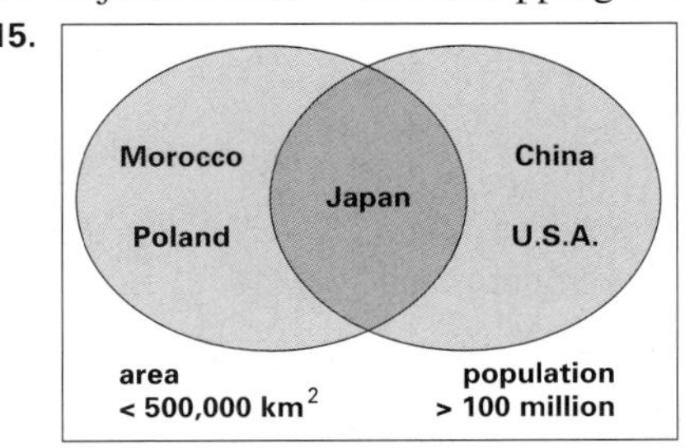

17. outside the two ovals **19.** independent; The outcome of the first toss does not affect the outcome of the second toss. **21.** 4.25%
23. dependent; The probability of being colorblind is less if you are a female.

11.3 Guided Practice (p. 518)

1. $\frac{1}{10}$

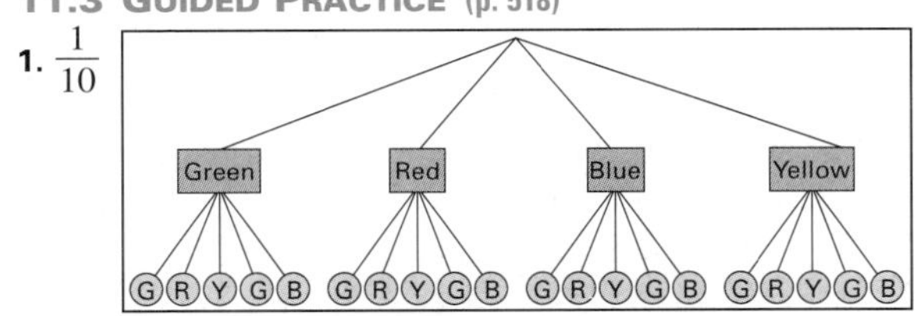

3. $\frac{1}{8}$ **5.** $\frac{1}{8}$

11.3 Practice and Problem Solving (pp. 518–520)

7. $\frac{2}{5}$ **9.** $\frac{1}{4}$ **11.** $\frac{1}{5}$ **13.** *Sample answer:* Write 0, 2, 4, 6, and 8 on similarly sized paper sheets. Place the sheets in a bag and randomly select one from the bag. Replace it and select a second time at random. **15.** $\frac{16}{25}$ **17.** $\frac{3}{16}$
19. no; The outcome of the toss is independent of previous events; so, the chance is $\frac{1}{2}$. **21.** $\frac{1}{15,625}$
23. $\frac{1}{9000}$ **25.** $\frac{1}{32}$ **31.** 72 **33.** 12.5

35.

Rentals	Frequency
40–49	1
50–59	2
60–69	5
70–79	2
80–89	3
90–99	1

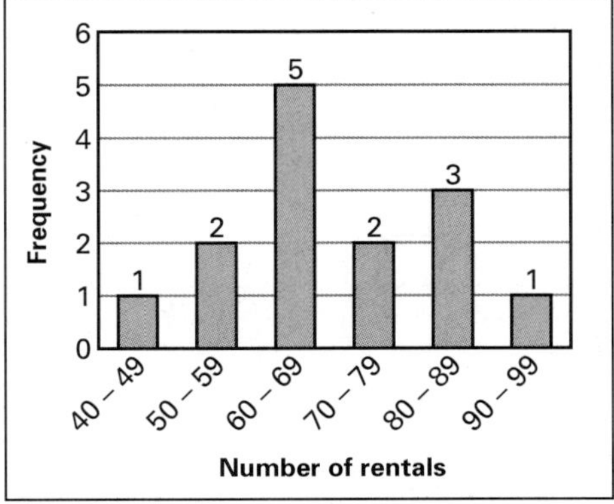

Mid-Chapter Test (p. 521)

1. 16

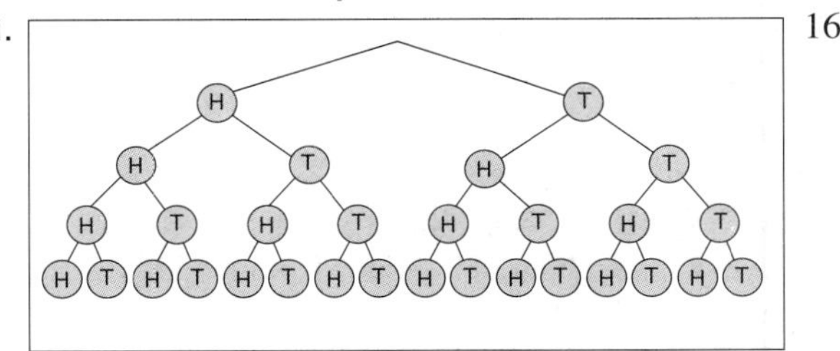

2. $\frac{1}{16}$ **3.** $\frac{11}{16}$ **4.** disjoint events **5.** overlapping events
6. disjoint events **7.** overlapping events **8.** dependent events **9.** independent events **10.** $\frac{1}{676}$ **11.** $\frac{1}{10,000}$
12. $\frac{1}{64,000}$

11.4 Guided Practice (p. 524) **1.** *Sample answer:* You cannot add the two probabilities of event *A* (getting an odd number) and event *B* (getting a 5) because the two events are not disjoint. (Event *B* is an overlapping event of Event *A*.) **3.** $\frac{1}{5}$ **5.** $\frac{4}{5}$ **7.** $\frac{1}{18}$ **9.** $\frac{5}{18}$ **11.** $\frac{1}{2}$

11.4 Practice and Problem Solving (pp. 525–526)

13. $\frac{1}{6}$ **15.** $\frac{2}{3}$ **17.** $\frac{211}{212}$ **19.** $\frac{133}{212}$ **21.** $\frac{2}{13}$ **23.** $\frac{5}{13}$ (unless you consider an ace to be an odd number, then it is $\frac{6}{13}$)
25. 100% **27.** $\frac{1}{4}$ **29.** $\frac{17}{36}$ **31.** $\frac{3}{32}$ **33.** $\frac{3}{4}$ **35.** $\frac{1}{2}$

11.5 GUIDED PRACTICE (p. 529) **1.** 1 or 100% **3.** $\frac{3}{5}$ **5.** 0.08 **7.** 99.35% **9.** Adding $P(4)$, $P(5)$, $P(6)$, $P(7)$, $P(8)$, $P(9)$, $P(10)$, $P(11)$, and $P(12)$ or subtracting $P(1)$, $P(2)$, and $P(3)$ from 1. The latter method is preferred because it requires less work.

11.5 PRACTICE AND PROBLEM SOLVING (pp. 529–530)
11. $\frac{1}{3}$ **13.** 0.2 **15.** 0.14 **17.** 76.5% **19.** 8% **21.** 40%, 60% **23.** 55%, 45%

25.

	1	2	3	4	5	6	7
1	2	3	4	5	6	7	8
2	3	4	5	6	7	8	9
3	4	5	6	7	8	9	10
4	5	6	7	8	9	10	11
5	6	7	8	9	10	11	12
6	7	8	9	10	11	12	13
7	8	9	10	11	12	13	14

27. $\frac{46}{49}$ **29.** 68%

11.6 GUIDED PRACTICE (p. 533) **1.** To predict the number of times an event will occur in a given number of trials, you multiply the probability of the event by the number of trials. **3.** 60 **5.** about 0.56 million

11.6 PRACTICE AND PROBLEM SOLVING (pp. 533–535)
7. 600 **9.** 1200 **11.** 567 **13.** about 3 **15.** about 267 **17.** about 6.9 trillion **19.** about 12,000 **21.** 0.247, 0.349, 0.234 **23.** about 37, about 52, about 35 **29.** about 53.8 million tons **31.** 157.5 in.^{3}

33.

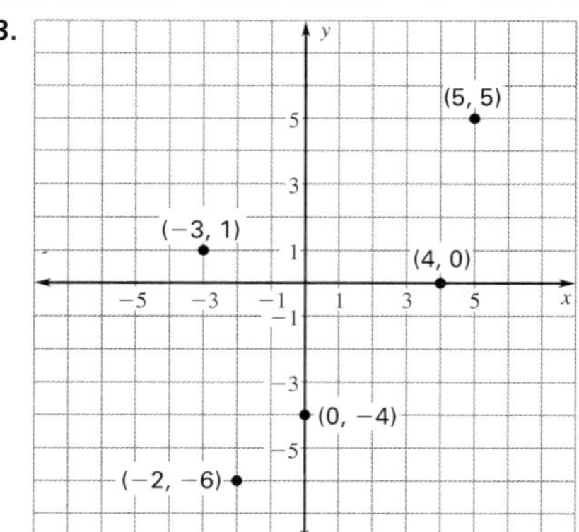

CHAPTER SUMMARY AND REVIEW (pp. 536–539)
1. Yvonne Renee, Yvonne Lynn, Yvonne Marie; Pearl Renee, Pearl Lynn, Pearl Marie; Tasha Renee, Tasha Lynn, Tasha Marie; Viola Renee, Viola Lynn, Viola Marie

3.

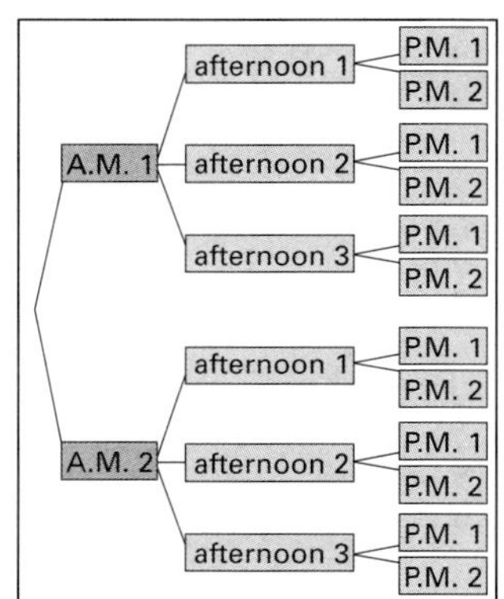

5. disjoint **7.** $\frac{1}{8}$ **9.** $\frac{1}{260}$ **11.** $\frac{1}{67{,}600}$ **13.** no; Multiples of 2 and multiples of 3 appearing are not disjoint events because 6 is a multiple of both 2 and 3. **15.** $\frac{1}{4}$ **17.** 0.36 **19.** $\frac{21}{32}$ **21.** 250 **23.** about 11 **25.** 2,460,000

REVIEWING THE BASICS (p. 543) **1.** 162.5 **3.** 22.5 **5.** 8, 8.5, none **7.** 23.5, 19, 34

CUMULATIVE PRACTICE (pp. 544–545)
1. 30; $\frac{4}{3}$, $\frac{7}{5}$, $\frac{43}{30}$, $\frac{22}{15}$ **3.** −30 **5.** −8

7. [Total Bill] = [Monthly Charge] + [Rate] · [Time]

Labels: Total Bill = 35.05 dollars
Monthly charge = 2.95 dollars
Rate = 0.05 dollars per minute
Time = t minutes
$35.05 = 2.95 + 0.05t$, 642 min, 10.7 h

9. 50 : 1 **11.** 40% **13.** 30 **15.** \$20.30 **17.** \$21.72 **19.** scalene, right **21.** 288 in.^{3}, 312 in.^{2} **23.** about 2211 cm^3, about 955 cm^2

25. Q1 median Q3
102 131 133 149 167

27.

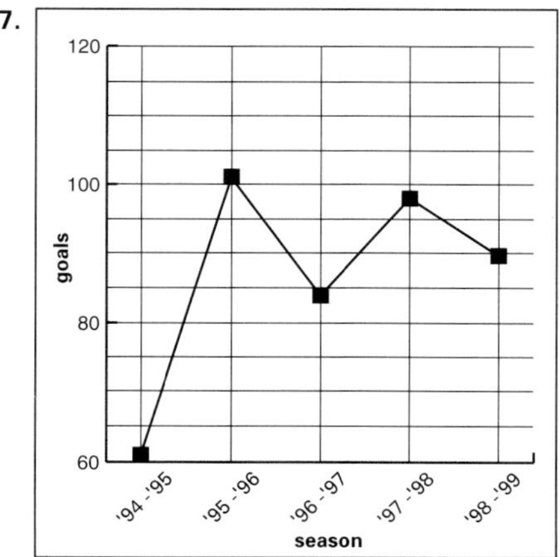

SELECTED ANSWERS

29. 6

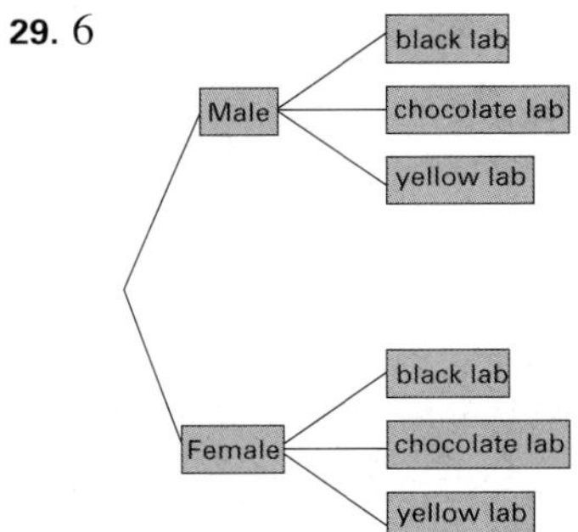

31. $\frac{2}{9}$ **33.** 1 **35.** 40

Selected answers for the Skills Review Handbook begin on page SA27.

Extra Practice

CHAPTER 1 (pp. 566–567) **1.** 14 mi; you take your dog for a 15 min walk. **3.** \$145 **5.** 49; 37 added to 12 is 49. **7.** 23; 62 subtracted from 85 is 23. **9.** 132; 11 multiplied by 12 is 132. **11.** 20; 340 divided by 17 is 20. **13.** 14 **15.** 2 **17.** 18 **19.** 2 **21.** 19 **23.** 12 **25.** 34 **27.** 180; associative property of multiplication **29.** 420; associative property of multiplication **31.** 108; commutative and associative properties of addition **33.** 271; commutative and associative properties of addition **35.** 2 **37.** 6 **39.** 4 **41.** 5 **43.** 37 **45.** 2 **47.** 20 **49.** 21

51. **53.**

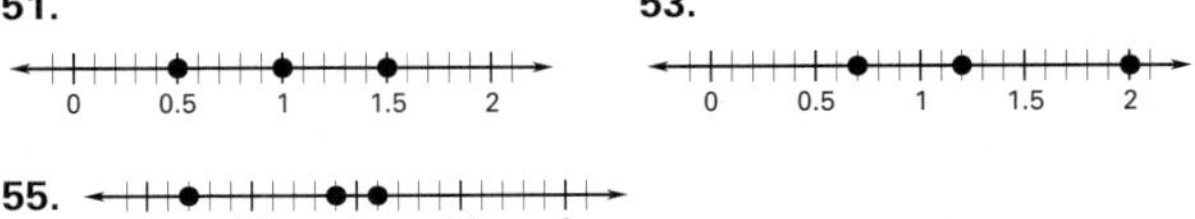

55.

57. 1.04, 1.2, 1.24, 1.4, 1.52 **59.** 2.15, 2.32, 2.89, 2.99, 3.01 **61.** 0.03, 0.032, 0.202, 0.302, 0.322 **63.** 6.071, 6.107, 6.70, 6.71, 6.77 **65.** 70 **67.** 15,800 **69.** 43.65 **71.** 5000 **73.** 2.3 **75.** 1.756 **77.** \$25 **79.** \$2 **81.** 8.45 **83.** 21.63 **85.** 34.48 **87.** 78.4008 **89.** 28.53 **91.** 42.705 **93.** 5.23 **95.** 0.389 **97.** 19.23 **99.** 5.7 **101.** 24.15 **103.** 0.795 **105.** 5.2 **107.** 25.116 **109.** 0.0028 **111.** 6.384 **113.** 0.84 **115.** 6.396 **117.** 1.29 **119.** 2.14 **121.** 24.3 **123.** 20.3 **125.** 20 **127.** 3 **129.** 30 **131.** 175

CHAPTER 2 (pp. 568–569) **1.** composite **3.** composite **5.** prime **7.** composite **9.** composite **11.** composite **13.** 5×13 **15.** $2 \times 3^2 \times 5$ **17.** $2^3 \times 11$ **19.** $2 \times 3 \times 7^2$ **21.** $2^2 \times 5 \times 7$ **23.** $2^3 \times 31$ **25.** 12 **27.** 17 **29.** 1 **31.** 3 **33.** 2 students and 32 teams or 4 students and 16 teams **35.** $\frac{4}{15}$; 4; 15 **37.** $\frac{3}{20}$; 3; 20 **39.** $\frac{4}{11}$; 4; 11

41. *Sample answer:* **43.** *Sample answer:*

45. *Sample answer:* **47.** *Sample answer:*

49. *Sample answer:* $\frac{3}{5}, \frac{6}{10}, \frac{9}{15}$ **51.** *Sample answer:* $\frac{3}{4}, \frac{6}{8}, \frac{9}{12}$ **53.** *Sample answer:* $\frac{5}{12}, \frac{10}{24}, \frac{15}{36}$ **55.** *Sample answer:* $\frac{3}{8}, \frac{6}{16}, \frac{9}{24}$ **57.** $\frac{5}{7}$ **59.** $\frac{1}{3}$ **61.** $\frac{1}{3}$ **63.** $\frac{4}{7}$ **65.** 35 **67.** 66 **69.** 150 **71.** 30 **73.** 45; $\frac{5}{9} < \frac{4}{5}$ **75.** 20; $\frac{3}{10} > \frac{1}{4}$ **77.** 56; $\frac{5}{7} < \frac{7}{8}$ **79.** 20; $\frac{7}{10} < \frac{3}{4}$ **81.** $\frac{5}{18}, \frac{7}{18}, \frac{11}{18}, \frac{15}{18}$ **83.** $\frac{1}{6}, \frac{4}{15}, \frac{1}{3}, \frac{5}{12}$ **85.** $\frac{17}{6}$ **87.** $\frac{35}{11}$ **89.** $5\frac{2}{3}$ **91.** $9\frac{3}{4}$

93. $\frac{5}{4}, \frac{9}{4}, 3\frac{1}{2}, 3\frac{3}{4}$

95. $\frac{15}{6}, \frac{10}{3}, \frac{7}{2}, 3\frac{2}{3}$

97. $2.\overline{2}$ **99.** 6.375 **101.** $5.8\overline{3}$ **103.** 7.375 **105.** 0.615 **107.** 0.267 **109.** 1.071 **111.** 7.556 **113.** $\frac{37}{100}$ **115.** $\frac{33}{50}$ **117.** $5\frac{1}{20}$ **119.** $3\frac{19}{25}$

CHAPTER 3 (pp. 570–571) **1.** $\frac{5}{9}$ **3.** $\frac{8}{13}$ **5.** $1\frac{3}{8}$ **7.** $1\frac{1}{6}$ **9.** $\frac{1}{6}$ **11.** $\frac{11}{20}$ **13.** $\frac{13}{14}$ **15.** $1\frac{11}{24}$ **17.** $\frac{11}{12}$ **19.** $\frac{17}{21}$ **21.** $\frac{11}{30}$ **23.** $\frac{38}{39}$ **25.** $\frac{3}{5}$ **27.** $1\frac{1}{4}$ **29.** $\frac{5}{8}$ **31.** $\frac{2}{5}$ **33.** $8\frac{2}{3}$ **35.** $2\frac{2}{3}$ **37.** 7 **39.** $6\frac{3}{4}$ **41.** $10\frac{1}{12}$ **43.** $13\frac{11}{18}$ **45.** $2\frac{3}{5}$ **47.** $3\frac{3}{4}$ **49.** $4\frac{3}{8}$ **51.** $1\frac{7}{10}$ **53.** $\frac{3}{7}$ **55.** $\frac{5}{72}$ **57.** 1 **59.** $8\frac{2}{5}$ **61.** $\frac{11}{24}$ **63.** $3\frac{3}{5}$ **65.** $1\frac{1}{2}$ **67.** $1\frac{1}{6}$ **69.** $1\frac{3}{4}$ **71.** $\frac{5}{27}$ **73.** 16 **75.** $1\frac{7}{8}$ **77.** 340 **79.** 60 **81.** 50 **83.** 18 **85.** $5z + 65$ **87.** $7b + 77$ **89.** $56 + 8b$ **91.** $60 + 6y$ **93.** 0.12 km **95.** 0.75 kL **97.** 336 h **99.** 6 gal **101.** 128 oz **103.** 820 ft **105.** 22.5 kg **107.** 32 mi/gal **109.** \$7.50/h **111.** \$.40/pen **113.** A

CHAPTER 4 (pp. 572–573)

1. 4, 6 **3.** 16, 20

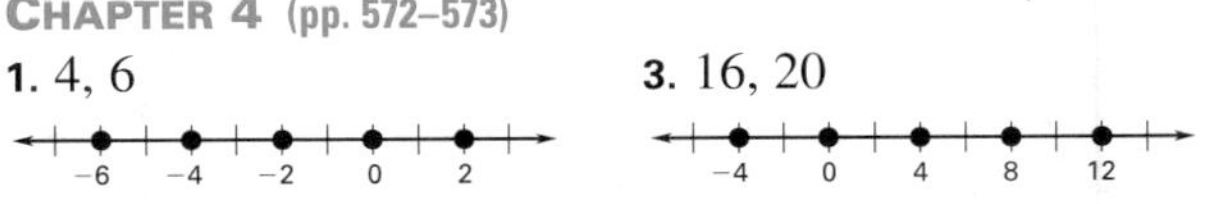

5. > **7.** > **9.** −7, −5, 0, 3, 12 **11.** −18, −4, −2, 7, 8 **13.** −41, −35, −17, −12, −8 **15.** 25; −10 **17.** 9 **19.** −12 **21.** −6 **23.** −4 **25.** −21 **27.** 50 **29.** 55 **31.** −47 **33.** −2°F **35.** 19 **37.** 117 **39.** −5 **41.** 34 **43.** 36 **45.** 10 **47.** −28 **49.** −3 **51.** −12 **53.** 7 **55.** −7 **57.** −7 **59.** −23 **61.** −23 **63.** 1 **65.** −125

67. 50 **69.** Positive; there are no negative factors. **71.** Positive; there are two negative factors. **73.** 63 **75.** -36 **77.** -56 **79.** 600 **81.** -36 **83.** 320 **85.** -13 **87.** 9 **89.** 10 **91.** -9 **93.** undefined **95.** 22 **97.** 17 **99.** 5 **101.** 13 **103.** -25 **105.** 2 **107.** -2

109. $2\left(\frac{27}{-9}\right)$; -6 **111.** $-8[17 + (-3)]$; -112

113.

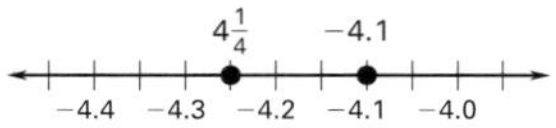

115.

117. > **119.** < **121.** $-1\frac{1}{2}, -\frac{7}{5}, 0, 1.2, 1\frac{3}{5}$

123. $-4\frac{2}{5}, -4.35, -4\frac{1}{4}, \frac{25}{6}$ **125.** $-\frac{15}{4}, -3.6, 0, 3\frac{1}{4}, 3\frac{1}{2}$

Chapter 5 (pp. 574–575) **1.** $-40 + x$ **3.** $x - 1$ **5.** $51x$ **7.** $2[x - (-5)]$

9. $1116t$;

time (seconds)	1	2	3	4	5
Distance (feet)	1116	2232	3348	4464	5580

11. no; -8 **13.** yes **15.** no; 72 **17.** no; -21 **19.** 95 **21.** 12 **23.** 15 **25.** 14.5 **27.** $x + 8 = 40$; 32 **29.** $x - 40 = 95$; 135 **31.** 7 **33.** 24 **35.** -31 **37.** -17 **39.** -51 **41.** $-1\frac{3}{4}$ **43.** $18 + x = 32$; 14 **45.** $9 + x = -4$; -13 **47.** 45 **49.** 10 **51.** -7 **53.** 5.2 **55.** $x - 14 = 8$; 22 **57.** $x - 9 = -6$; 3 **59.** -12 **61.** 157.5 **63.** 0 **65.** 5 **67.** $42 = 3x$; 14 **69.** $x(14) = 49$; 3.5 **71.** 55 **73.** 28 **75.** -39 **77.** -512 **79.** $1\frac{1}{3}$ **81.** 7 **83.** $\frac{x}{10} = 4$; 40 **85.** $\frac{x}{-3} = -51$; 153 **87.** 8 **89.** 8 **91.** 54 **93.** 25 **95.** 4.6 **97.** 8 **99.** $3x - 18 = 30$; 16

Chapter 6 (pp. 576–577) **1.** 5 **3.** $\frac{2}{3}$ **5.** $\frac{1}{4}$ win/game **7.** $\frac{18 \text{ h}}{5 \text{ h}}$ **9.** $\frac{21 \text{ wins}}{54 \text{ games}}$ **11.** 15 cans : 16 cans **13.** yes **15.** no **17.** 4 **19.** 32 **21.** 64 **23.** 6 **25.** 3 lb **27.** 18 c **29.** 18 mi **31.** $\frac{5}{6}$

33. 44 ft

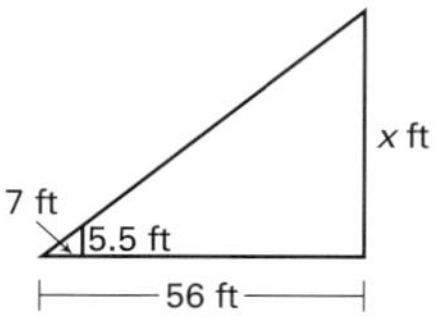

35. 1 : 500 **37.** 1 : 25,000,000 **39.** 82.5 mi **41.** 605 mi **43.** 233.75 mi **49.** 70 brown, 10 black, 6 red, 14 blond

Chapter 7 (pp. 578–579) **1.** 20% **3.** 32% **5.** 46.7% **7.** 20% **9.** 2.5% **11.** 0.6; $\frac{3}{5}$ **13.** 0.95; $\frac{19}{20}$ **15.** 0.096; $\frac{12}{125}$ **17.** 49 **19.** $22\frac{1}{2}$ **21.** 26.4 **23.** 22.8 **25.** 86.7 **27.** 191.1 **29.** 2.4; $2\frac{2}{5}$ **31.** 0.008; $\frac{1}{125}$ **33.** $0.0058\overline{3}$; $\frac{7}{1200}$ **35.** 0.02% **37.** 1.4% **39.** 25 **41.** 0.96 **43.** 0.375 **45.** 0.08 **47.** *Sample answer:* 150% of 20 = 30 **49.** *Sample answer:* $\frac{1}{2}$% of 86 = 0.43 **51.** *Sample answer:* \$4.50 **53.** 28 **55.** 500 **57.** 175% **59.** 216° **61.** 266.4° **63.** 28.8° **65.** 46.6% + 27.7% + 8.1% + 5% + 3.6% + 9% = 100%; $\frac{233}{500} + \frac{277}{1000} + \frac{81}{1000} + \frac{1}{20} + \frac{9}{250} + \frac{9}{100} = 1$ **67.** \$500 **69.** \$48 **71.** \$160 **73.** \$66.67 **75.** \$4000 **77.** \$80; \$120 **79.** \$51.01; \$94.74 **81.** \$6.25; \$131.25

Chapter 8 (pp. 580–581) **1a.** 65° **1b.** 115° **1c.** 65° **1d.** 90° **1e.** 90° **1f.** 90° **3.** *Sample answer:* $\angle 1$ and $\angle 3$ **5.** *Sample answer:* $\angle 1$ and $\angle 2$ **7.** 34 **9.** yes **11.** yes **13.** no **15.** 3.3 cm, 2.1 cm, 2.1 cm; isosceles **17.** 2.4 cm, 2.4 cm, 2.4 cm; equilateral **19.** 125°, 25°, 30°; obtuse **21.** 14 ft^2 **23.** 144 m^2 **25.** quadrilateral **27.** $x = 55$; $y = 125$ **29.** $x° = 105$; $y = 15$ **31.** 60 cm^2 **33.** 20 mm **35.** 8 m **37.** 113.04 cm **39.** 11.15 cm **41.** 68.47 ft **43.** 25π in.^2; 79 in.^2 **45.** 20.25π m^2; 64 m^2 **47.** $9\frac{3}{7}$ m^2

Chapter 9 (pp. 582–583) **1.** rectangular prism; 15 in.; 6 **3.** cylinder; 4 ft **5.** cylinder; 5 in.

7. 60 in.^3

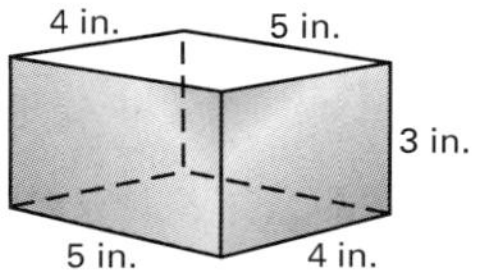

9. 290.4 cm^3

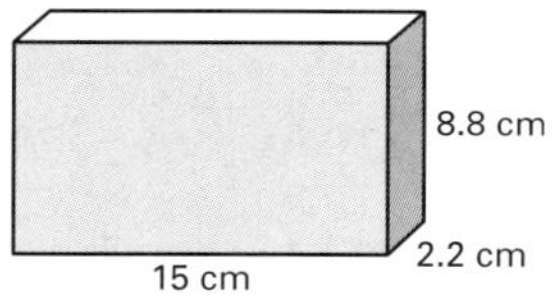

11. 1260 in.^3 **13.** 1040 ft^3 **15.** 10 ft **17.** 360 yd^3 **19.** 9408 m^3 **21.** 5434 mm^3 **23.** 9878.4 in.^3 **25.** 7850 ft^3 **27.** 706.5 cm^3 **29.** 468 ft^2 **31.** 144 cm^2 **33.** 120.8 in.^2 **35.** 108 cm^2 **37.** 131.9 in.^2 **39.** 1130.4 m^2 **41.** 99 ft^2; $9\frac{5}{8}$ ft^2; $118\frac{1}{4}$ ft^2 **43.** 628 cm^2; 78.5 cm^2; 785 cm^2 **45.** 113.0 in.^2; 12.6 in.^2

Chapter 10 (pp. 584–585) **1.** $1\frac{5}{9}$; 1; 1 **3.** 27; $9\frac{1}{3}$, 8, 8; $7\frac{1}{8}$, 7, 8; the outlier increases the mean, increases the median, and does not affect the mode. **5.** 51; 19.5, 15, 15; 15, 15, 15; the outlier increases the mean, does not affect the median, and does not affect the mode.

7.

Interval	Tally	Frequency
0–19	𝍸 |||	8
20–39	𝍸 𝍸		11
40–59	𝍸 𝍸	10
60–79	𝍸		6
80–99	||	2
100–119	𝍸	5
120–139	||	2
140–159			1
160–179	||	2
180–199		0
200–219			1
220–239		0
240–259		0
260–279		0
280–299		0
300–319			1
320–339		0
340–359			1

9. 20–39 **11.** 43, 26.5; 35, 23.5

13.

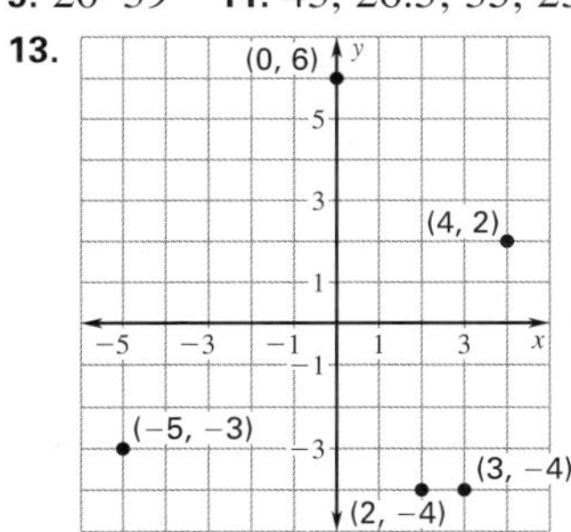

15.

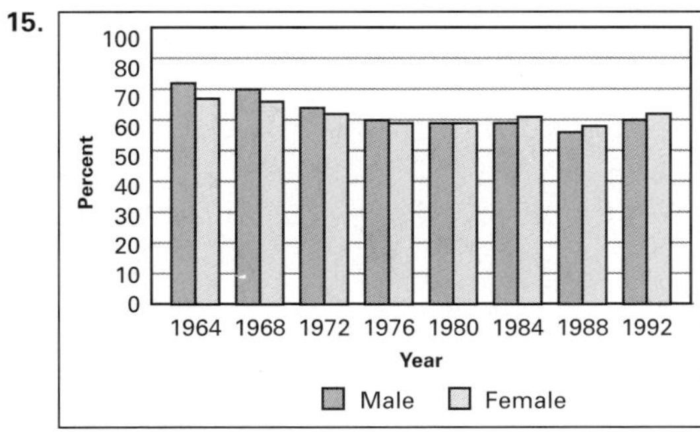

17. Before 1980 the male voting percent was greater than the female voting percent, but after 1980 the female voting percent was greater than the male voting percent. **19.** The weight of a dozen jumbo eggs is about one and one-half times the weight of a dozen medium eggs; the graph can be misinterpreted because the broken horizontal scale exaggerates the difference in the weights.

23. *Sample answer:* Using the word "freedom" with walking barefoot versus "inconvenience" with wearing shoes favors walking barefoot. **25.** *Sample answer:* Calling the mayor's policies "ineffective" favors a negative response.

CHAPTER 11 (pp. 586–587) **1.** white T-shirt and blue shorts, white T-shirt and gray shorts, blue T-shirt and blue shorts, blue T-shirt and gray shorts, green T-shirt and blue shorts, green T-shirt and gray shorts; 6 **3.** $\frac{1}{8}$ **5.** $\frac{1}{8}$ **7.** $\frac{3}{8}$ **9.** overlapping **11.** dependent **13.** $\frac{1}{260}$ **15.** $\frac{63}{260}$ **17.** $\frac{1}{4}$ **19.** 1

21.

	1	2	3	4	5
1	2	3	4	5	6
2	3	4	5	6	7
3	4	5	6	7	8
4	5	6	7	8	9
5	6	7	8	9	10

23. $\frac{6}{25}$ **25.** $\frac{12}{25}$ **27.** 0.8 **29.** 28% **31.** $\frac{3}{5}$ **33.** 54% **35.** 375 **37.** 175 **39.** 54 **41.** 500

Skills Review Handbook

INDENTIFYING AND EXTENDING PATTERNS (p. 549)
1. Each number after the first is 2 more than the previous number; 9, 11, 13
3. Each number after the first two numbers is the sum of the previous two numbers; 13, 21, 34
5. Each letter after the first is 3 letters later in the alphabet; M, P, S
7. The first and third letters are the first two letters of the alphabet in ascending order. Continue this pattern for the fifth and seventh letters. The second and fourth letters are letters of the alphabet in ascending order starting with N. Continue this pattern for the sixth letter; C, P, D

USING A TABLE OR A GRAPH (pp. 550–551)
1. 56°F **3.** Montreal, Canada; January

5.

Type of school	Computers with modems	Computer networks	Satellite dishes
Elementary schools	22,234	16,441	6001
Middle schools	7417	6035	3377
High schools	10,781	9565	6769

7. middle schools **9.** 1,000,000 visitors **11.** Seattle **13.** New York City

BREAKING A PROBLEM INTO PARTS (p. 552)
1. 256 m^2 **3.** 24 weeks **5.** 100 ft^2 **7.** 48 $in.^2$

SELECTED ANSWERS

Checking Reasonableness (p. 553)

1. 3 paperback books **3.** C

Using a Number Line (pp. 554–555)

1. 0, 1, 3, 4, 8, 16 **3.** 7, 13, 15, 18, 26, 31
5. 3, 6, 7, 12, 17, 21 **7.** $30 > 13$ **9.** $8 < 10$
11. $2 < 7$ **13.** $19 > 8$ **15.** 13 **17.** 22 **19.** 45
21. 38 **23.** 12 **25.** 8 **27.** 19 **29.** 19

Operations with Whole Numbers (pp. 556–557)

1. 114 **3.** 88 **5.** 6099 **7.** 45 **9.** 191 **11.** 223 mi
13. 57°F **15.** 714 **17.** 20,335 **19.** 9 **21.** 9 **23.** 6
25. 13 cards

Long Division (p. 558)

1. 8 is not less than 5 so the first digit in the quotient is too small; 4 R3

3. 30 is not less than 27 so the first digit in the quotient is too big; 4 R3

5. 12 R5 **7.** 85 R5 **9.** 462 R4 **11.** 19 R8 **13.** 22 R4
15. 923

Divisibility Tests (pp. 559–560)

1. Sample answer: A number is divisible by 2 if its units digit is divisible by 2. A number is divisible by 3 if the sum of its digits is divisible by 3. A number is divisible by 5 if its units digit is 0 or 5.
3. 91 is not divisible by 2, 3, or 5.
5. 164 is divisible by 2, but not by 3 or 5.
7. 810 is divisible by 2, 3, and 5.
9. 3805 is divisible by 5, but not by 2 or 3.
11. 306,920 is divisible by 2 and 5, but not by 3.
13. 4

Converting Units of Measurement (p. 561)

1. a. $\frac{1 \text{ foot}}{12 \text{ inches}}$ **b.** 8 feet **3.** 128 oz

Squares and Rectangles (p. 562)

1. 16 in.; 15 in.^{2} **3.** 16 ft; 16 ft^2 **5.** 20 cm; 25 cm^2

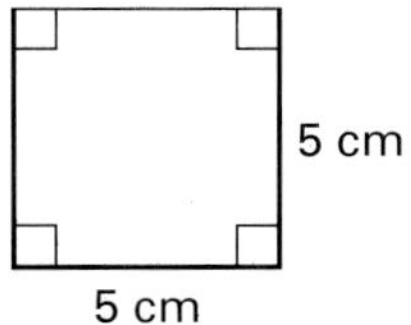

7. 24 cm; 27 cm^2

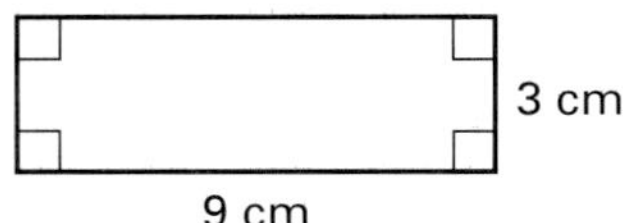

Angles and Their Measures (p. 563)

1. 160° **3.** 90°

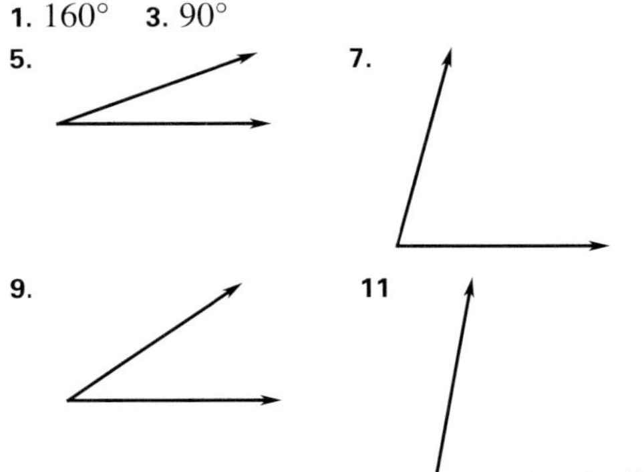

Reading and Drawing a Bar Graph (p. 564)

1. *Sample answer:* 0–20,000; 5000

Reading and Drawing a Double Bar Graph (p. 565)

1.

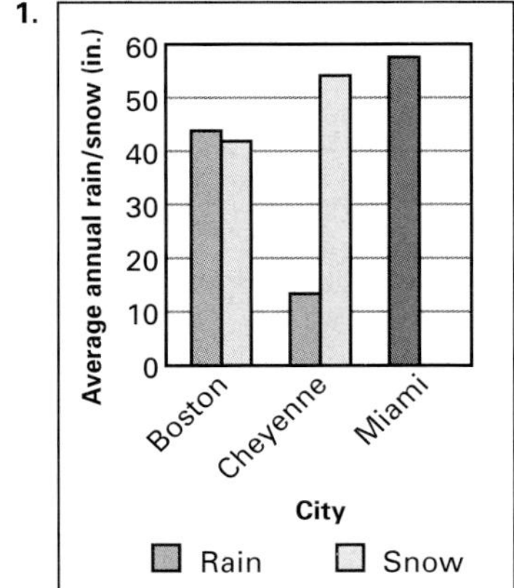

3. Cheyenne, Wyoming